Welcome to

McGraw-Hill Education
SAT

*C*ongratulations! You've chosen the SAT guide from America's leading educational publisher. You probably know us from many of the textbooks you used in school. Now we're ready to help you take the next step—and get into the college or university of your choice.

This book gives you everything you need to succeed on the test. You'll get in-depth instruction and review of every topic tested, tips and strategies for every question type, and practice exams to boost your test-taking confidence. To get started, go to the following pages where you'll find:

- **How to Use This Book:** Step-by-step instructions to help you get the most out of your test-prep program.

- **Your SAT Action Plan:** Learn how to make the best use of your preparation time.

- **SAT Format Table:** This handy chart shows the test structure at a glance: question types, time limits, and number of questions per section.

- **The 40 Top Strategies for Test Day:** Use this list to check your knowledge, or as a last-minute refresher before the exam.

- **The 5 Top SAT Calculator Tips:** Learn some smart ways that your calculator can help you.

- **Getting the Most from the Free Online Practice Tests:** Log on to the companion website for more test-taking practice.

ABOUT McGRAW-HILL EDUCATION

This book has been created by McGraw-Hill Education. McGraw-Hill Education is a leading global provider of instructional, assessment, and reference materials in both print and digital form. McGraw-Hill Education has offices in 33 countries and publishes in more than 65 languages. With a broad range of products and services—from traditional textbooks to the latest in online and multimedia learning—we engage, stimulate, and empower students and professionals of all ages, helping them meet the increasing challenges of the 21st century knowledge economy.

Learn more. Do more.

How to Use This Book

This book is designed for students who want an effective program for the most dramatic SAT score improvements. It is based on the College Hill Method™, the elite training system used by the tutors of College Hill Coaching since 1990. It focuses on what works best in SAT prep: mindful training in the reasoning skills at the core of the SAT, and not just test-taking tricks or mindless drills.

This book provides all the material you need to score well on the SAT. It will teach you the knowledge that is required for this exam, including information about each type of question on the test. It also provides ample practice for you to refine the skills you are learning and then test yourself with full-length practice tests. For best results as you work your way through the book and the accompanying online tests, use this four-step program that follows:

1 Learn About the SAT

Don't skip Chapter 1. In it you'll meet the SAT and learn exactly what academic skills it tests. You'll also find valuable test-taking strategies and information about how the test is scored.

2 Take a Realistic Practice SAT

Take the SAT diagnostic test in Chapter 2 of this book. Take the test strictly timed, in one sitting, and proctored if possible. Then use the answer key to evaluate your results so you can learn your strengths and weaknesses.

3 Study What You Need to Learn with the Lessons and Exercises

If you miss a question on your practice SAT, read its answer explanation at the end of the test. If it refers to a lesson in Chapters 4–10, make that lesson part of your weekly review.

▸ First read each **Lesson** carefully, underlining important ideas or writing notes in the margins.

▸ Check your understanding of the concepts and skills in these lessons by working through the questions and answers in each Exercise Set.

▸ When you're done, read all of the explanations in the **Answer Key**, even for questions that you got right. Why? Because very often, there are many ways to get a question right, and some may be much more efficient than the one you used!

4 Repeat the Cycle Until You've Surpassed Your SAT Score Goal

Take the practice tests in this book and on the companion website, trying each time to simulate actual testing conditions. Then correct your test with the detailed answer key, and review the relevant lessons in Chapters 4–10 that will help you to improve your skills for the next test.

Your SAT Action Plan

To make the best use of your SAT preparation time, you'll need a personalized action plan that's based on your needs and the time you have available. This book has been designed for flexibility; you can work through it from cover to cover or you can move around from one chapter to another in the order you want based on your own priorities and needs. However, before you jump in, maximize the effectiveness of your preparation time by spending a few minutes to develop a realistic action plan. Use the tools provided in these pages to help you focus on the areas where you are weakest, plan your study program, and gain the discipline you need to pace yourself and achieve your goals.

The College Hill SAT Study Plan

Each time you take a practice SAT in this book or online, take a few minutes to review your performance and make a plan for improving your scores on the next test.

Questions About Your Performance

1 **What were your test conditions?** Did you take your practice SAT as you would take a real SAT? Were you sitting at a desk and at a neutral site? Did you time yourself strictly? Did you take the test all at one sitting? If your conditions were not realistic, make sure that they are more realistic next time. Also, note any conditions that may have affected your performance, like "broken clock," "noisy radiator," "freezing room," or "phone interruption." Learning to deal with distractions and with the length and time limits of the SAT is very important to peak performance.

2 **What was your pre-test routine?** What you do just before the test can be very important to your performance. Having a raging argument with someone, for instance, probably won't help. To perform your best, get at least 8 hours of sleep the night before, get 30 minutes of exercise prior to the SAT, and have a good breakfast. Write down anything significant that you did just prior to the test, like "ran 4 miles," "had oatmeal and orange juice," "was yelled at by Dad," or "did 15 minutes of yoga."

3 **Did you attack the questions you need to attack?** The score conversion tables at the end of each practice test (for instance, those on pages 68–69), show you how many questions you need to answer correctly on each section to make your score goals. After each test, ask yourself, "How many more points do I need, and how can I get them?" Try to find patterns among the questions you missed, so you know which sections in this book to review before the next test.

4 **Did you rush to complete any section?** Rushing is never a good strategy on the SAT. You must learn to work briskly, but attentively. After you complete a practice SAT, ask yourself: did I make any careless errors because I was rushing?

5 Study Plan. This is the real key to improving your SAT score. Go to the answer explanations and carefully read the explanations for the questions you missed. Then notice the types of questions you missed, and make a plan to review the corresponding lessons in this book. For instance, you might write down in your notebook that you need to "Learn about dangling participles," or "Review how to simplify polynomials."

Your Weekly SAT Study Schedule

A complete SAT preparation program usually requires between 8 and 12 weeks, depending on your skill and comfort level with the test. Be diligent, but don't overwhelm yourself. Your schoolwork should take priority over SAT prep—colleges care a lot about those grades, and for good reason! But if you make a manageable plan to work for at least 30 minutes every weeknight on your SAT review, you will see great results in just a matter of weeks.

Remember that it is more productive to do some work every day rather than a lot of work just one day a week.

Your daily SAT work should include learning 5–10 new vocabulary words and roots from Chapter 3 and, if you are taking the Essay component, reading and analyzing at least one Op-Ed from the *New York Times*. (Chapter 6 will explain how to do this.) Analytical reading is more important than ever on the SAT, so practice it every day! Also, set aside 20–30 minutes each day to work through the lessons and worksheets in this book.

How to Stick to Your Study Plan

▶ Twenty minutes of cardiovascular exercise is a great warm-up before you start your homework. Exercise doesn't help just your muscles; it also helps your brain. When your brain is well oxygenated, it works more efficiently, so you do your work better and faster. If you don't already have an exercise routine, try to build up to a good 20- to 45-minute aerobic workout—running, rowing, swimming, biking—every day. Your routine will also help you enormously on test day; exercising on the morning of the SAT will help you to relax, focus, and perform!

▶ If you get nervous when you think about the SAT, try learning "mindfulness" exercises, like deep breathing, meditation, or yoga. Such exercises will also help enormously on test day.

▶ Prepare your space. Many students waste a lot of study time because they don't prepare their work space properly. Find a quiet, clean place where you can stay focused for a good stretch of time, away from the TV and troublesome siblings. Sit in an upright chair at a table or desk with good lighting. Also, make sure that all the tools you will need are within easy reach: a dictionary, note cards, calculator, and pencils with erasers. Turn off your cell phone and close the door!

▶ Sit up straight when you work. Don't work on your bed, on the floor, or in a reclining chair. When your body tilts, your brain goes into "sleep mode" and has to work harder to focus.

▶ Whenever you feel fatigued from studying, take a 10-minute break. Get a quick snack or listen to a couple of your favorite songs. But stay focused. Don't get sucked into returning twenty text messages.

40 Top Strategies for Test Day

Here are 40 key reminders for success on test day. Take a quick glance through this list on the morning of the test to make sure you can put all of your preparation to use and get your best score.

General Strategies

1 Take control. Not every student will ace the SAT, but any student can *take charge of it*. Go into the test with confidence and the game plan that you've put together.

2 Lay everything out the night before. You'll sleep easier the night before the SAT knowing that you're ready to go. Lay out three #2 pencils *with good erasers*, your calculator *with fresh batteries*, your admission ticket, your photo ID, and a snack.

3 Have a good breakfast. Your brain can't work well without fuel. Have a good breakfast including fruit, complex carbohydrates, and protein. You'll be glad you ate a good breakfast when you're entering hour 3 of the SAT!

4 Know where you're going. If you're taking the SAT at an unfamiliar school, acquaint yourself with it before test day. Take a trip there in a few days before the test so you don't worry about getting lost on test day.

5 Dress properly. Dress in light layers so you'll be comfortable whether the testing room is sweltering or frigid. An uncomfortable body makes for a distracted brain.

6 Get a good two nights' sleep. A rested brain is a smarter brain. The nights before the SAT are for sleeping, not for all-nighters. Get a good eight hours each of the two nights before your SAT.

7 Get some exercise. The SAT is given in the morning, when most of us are a bit foggy, so get a leg up on the competition by waking your brain with exercise. Twenty minutes of cardio will keep you alert.

8 Bring a snack. Your brain burns calories when it's thinking hard. Bring a granola bar, banana, or energy bar to the SAT to refuel during the break.

9 Know what to attack. As you begin each section of your SAT, know how many points you need to make your score goal on that section, and focus on hitting that goal. Even if you have to guess on all the rest of the questions for that section, you won't feel discouraged if you've hit your goal.

10 Take a "two-pass" approach. If you've built a smart game plan and practiced with it, you should have enough time to tackle all of your "must answer" questions, then take one more pass through them, checking for common mistakes. Once all of your "must answer" questions have been double-checked, you can approach the hardest questions carefully.

11 Shut out distractions. If you have a game plan and have practiced it, you should feel confident enough to shut out everyone else during the test. Don't speed up just because the girl next to you is racing through her test. Ignore her: she's probably rushing because she's nervous. Stick to your game plan. Also, if you are easily distracted by noises around you like tapping pencils, sniffling testers, or clanking radiators, bring a pair of wax earplugs.

12 Watch the clock—but not too much. If you have taken enough practice SATs, you should go into the test with confidence in your ability to pace yourself through each section. But, for insurance, you might want to bring a silent stopwatch (not a cell phone timer) and check it occasionally to make sure you're on pace.

13 Work briskly, but not carelessly. Don't get bogged down on tough questions: if you get stuck on a question, just make a guess, circle the question in your test booklet (in case you have time to come back to it later), and move on. Remember, rushing is never a good strategy. Optimize your score by working briskly enough to attack all of the questions you need to, but not so quickly that you make careless errors.

14 Don't worry about answer patterns. Some SAT takers refuse to make certain patterns on their answer sheet. For instance, they won't mark (C)—even if it's clearly the best answer—if they already have three (C)s in a row. Bad idea: pick what you think is the best answer, regardless of any answer patterns.

Reading Test

15 Don't psych yourself out on the reading sections. On the Reading Test, don't psych yourself out with negative self-talk. Instead, take a positive attitude, remind yourself of the key strategies from Chapter 5, and tell yourself that you're going to learn something interesting.

16 Focus on the 3 key questions. The key to good reading comprehension is answering three key questions discussed in Chapter 5: What is the purpose? What is the main idea? And what is the overall structure of the passage?

17 Get your own answer first. On the Reading Test, don't jump to the choices too quickly. Instead, read each question carefully and think of your own answer first, then find the choice that best matches it. This will help you avoid the "traps."

18 Deal with your "space outs." Many students "space out" on the Reading Test because they get overwhelmed or disoriented when reading about topics like paleontology or primitivism. If it happens to you, don't panic and don't rush. Just continue from where you left off.

19 Be selective on the reading questions. Unlike the other SAT sections, the reading questions don't get progressively harder. If you get to a tough reading question, make a guess and move on; the next one might be easier.

20 Don't fall for the traps. Always read critical reading questions very carefully. Many choices are "traps:" they make true statements about the passage, but they are not "correct" because they do not answer the question asked. You won't fall for them if you get your own answer first.

21 Know how to attack the "paired passages." On the "paired" passages (Passage 1 vs. Passage 2), it is generally best to read Passage 1 and then go right to the questions that pertain to Passage 1 before moving on to Passage 2. If you try to read the passages back-to-back, it may be harder to recall and distinguish the key information from the two passages. Don't let them run together.

Writing and Language Test

22 Know the key grammar rules. Go into the SAT writing with a solid understanding of the key grammar rules. If you can't explain parallelism, dangling participles, or pronoun case errors, make sure you study Chapter 4 carefully!

23 Trust your ear (at least at first). If you've read a lot of good prose in your life, you have probably developed a good ear for the rules of grammar and usage grammar. On the easy and medium writing questions, then, your ear will be your best guide: bad phrases will "sound" wrong. On harder questions, however, your skill in analyzing sentences will come into play.

24 Know how to analyze the tricky sentences. Chapter 4 provides lots of exercises to help you to recognize the most relevant grammar mistakes and to analyze sentences like a pro. You'll need to know how to do things like "trim" sentences to catch the trickiest errors.

25 Don't fear perfection. On SAT Writing and Language Test questions, the NO CHANGE choice should be correct roughly 1/4 of the time over the long term. Bottom line: don't shy away from NO CHANGE but choose it only after careful analysis.

26 Make sure it's a real mistake. On SAT Writing and Language Test questions, a word or phrase isn't necessarily wrong just because you might say it differently. For instance, if the word *since* is underlined, don't assume it's incorrect just because you prefer to say *because*—the words are interchangeable. Make sure that you know how to fix the mistake—and that it's a *real* grammatical or semantic mistake—before choosing it.

27 Keep the overall purpose and tone in mind. Many Writing and Language Test questions require you to understand the overall purpose and tone of particular paragraphs or the passage as a whole. Don't lose the overall picture by focusing too narrowly on the details.

28 Read it again to check. Before choosing an answer on a Writing and Language Test question, always re-read the entire sentence, including the correction, to make sure the sentence flows smoothly and logically. If the whole *sentence* doesn't sound better, it's wrong.

Math Test

29 Mark up the test. The best SAT takers do lots of scratch work, particularly on the math section. Don't be afraid to write on your test booklet. The SAT doesn't award points for neatness! Write down what you know and show your steps. Mark up diagrams, write equations, and show your work so that you can check it when you come back later.

30 Look for patterns and use them. One important skill the SAT Math Test is "pattern finding." Always pay special attention to simple patterns or repetitions in a problem, because exploiting them is usually the key to the solution.

31 Keep it simple. If you're doing lots of calculations to solve an SAT math problem, you might be overlooking a key fact that simplifies the problem. Always look for the easy way.

32 Know the basic formulas. Many formulas you will need for the SAT Math Test are given to you in the "Reference Information" at the beginning of each Math Test section. Even so, get fluent in them so you can easily recognize when to use them. Also, use flash cards to review the key formulas from algebra, geometry, trigonometry, and statistics from Chapters 7–10.

33 Check your work. There are many ways to make careless mistakes on the SAT math. Give yourself time to go back and check over your arithmetic and algebra, and make sure everything's okay.

34 Consider different approaches. If you're stuck on a math question, try working backwards from the choices, or plugging in numbers for the unknowns.

35 Watch out for key words. Pay special attention to words like *integer, even, odd*, and *consecutive* when they show up, because students commonly overlook them. And make sure you don't confuse *area* with *perimeter*!

36 Don't overuse your calculator. Your calculator can be handy on the the Math with Calculator section, but don't overuse it. If you're doing a lot of calculator work for a problem, you're probably making it too hard. Keep it simple.

37 Re-read the question. Before finalizing your answer, re-read the question to be sure you've answered the right question. If it asks for $5x$, don't give the value for x!

Essay

38 Be ready for the essay. If you are taking the Essay component of the SAT, you will need to go in to the test with a clear understanding of what SAT essay readers are looking for: an essay that shows good reading comprehenison, thorough rhetorical analysis, logical organization, and strong writing skills.

39 Put aside 20 minutes. When the essay section starts, take at least 20 minutes to read the target essay carefully, analyze it, and plan your response, as discussed in Chapter 6. You should still have plenty of time to write a solid essay, and it will flow much more easily.

40 Write at least 5 paragraphs. According to The College Board, a good SAT essay "is well organized and clearly focused, demonstrating clear coherence and smooth progression of ideas." This means that you must use paragraphs effectively. Think of your paragraphs as the "stepping stones" of your essay. Three or four stepping stones don't make for much of a journey, do they?

The 5 Top SAT Calculator Tips

1. Don't Overuse the Calculator

Even though a calculator is permitted on one of the SAT Math sections, don't let your calculator think for you. The SAT Math Test is more of a reasoning test than a calculation test. If you find yourself depending on your calculator for every question, you need to wean yourself off of it and start working on your thinking skills!

Of course, smart calculator use is occasionally helpful, as the following examples show.

2. Know How to MATH▶FRAC

Let's say you're solving an SAT math problem about probabilities and you get 34/85 as an answer, but the choices are

A. 4/17
B. 2/7
C. 2/5
D. 3/7
E. 7/17

Did you mess up? No—you just have to simplify. Here, a TI-83 or similar calculator with ▶FRAC might save you time. Type "34/85" and enter, then press the MATH button and then ▶FRAC. Like magic, it will convert the fraction to lowest terms: 2/5. Sweet!

On "grid in" questions, it's also a good idea to MATH▶FRAC any decimal answer you get to make sure that it gives a fraction that can fit into the grid. If not, you've probably done something wrong!

3. Know How to Get a Remainder

Consider this math question: The tables at a wedding reception are set up to accommodate 212 people. There are 24 tables, some seating 8 people and the rest seating 9 people. How many 9-seat tables are there?

Without getting into the details, the answer is simply the remainder when 212 is divided by 24. You could do this by long division, but you can probably do it faster with a calculator:

Enter the division problem and enter:	$212 \div 24 = 8.833333\ldots$
Subtract the integer part:	$ANS - 8 = 0.833333\ldots$
Multiply by the original divisor:	$ANS \times 24 = 20$

So the answer is 20! Memorize this handy procedure to streamline "remainder" problems.

4. Beware of "Killer Program" Gimmicks

Don't believe your friends who tell you they have a killer "SAT-busting" calculator program. They don't. These are usually gimmicks that waste time rather than save it. Again, if you're depending on your calculator to do anything but check basic calculations, you're thinking about the SAT in the wrong way.

5. Get Fresh Batteries

Even if you don't use your calculator much, you won't be happy if it dies halfway through the SAT. Put in a set of fresh batteries the night before!

McGRAW-HILL EDUCATION

SAT
2021

McGRAW-HILL EDUCATION

SAT 2021

CHRISTOPHER BLACK, MA

MARK ANESTIS, MA

and the TUTORS of
COLLEGE HILL COACHING™

New York | Chicago | San Francisco | Athens | London | Madrid | Mexico City
Milan | New Delhi | Singapore | Sydney | Toronto

1 2 3 4 5 6 7 8 9   LHS   25 24 23 22 21 20   (Elite)
1 2 3 4 5 6 7 8 9   LHS   25 24 23 22 21 20   (book alone)

ISBN   978-1-260-46418-4   (Elite)
MHID   1-260-46418-0

e-ISBN   978-1-260-46419-1   (e-book Elite)
e-MHID   1-260-46419-9

ISBN   978-1-260-46416-0   (book alone)
MHID   1-260-46416-4

e-ISBN   978-1-260-46417-7   (e-book alone)
e-MHID   1-260-46417-2

SAT is a registered trademark of the College Board, which was not involved in the production of, and does not endorse, this product.

College Hill Coaching® is a trademark under the control of Christopher F. Black. Visit the College Hill Coaching website at www.collegehillcoaching.com.

McGraw Hill books are available at special quantity discounts to use as premiums and sales promotions or for use in corporate training programs. To contact a representative, please visit the Contact Us pages at www.mhprofessional.com.

ACKNOWLEDGMENTS

We would like to acknowledge the help of those who have contributed to this project: Elizabeth, Sarah, and Anna Black for their patience and support; Stephanie Anestis for her invaluable efforts in reading and editing the text and for her incredible love and support; and Robert, Janice, Michael, and Matthew Anestis, who also gave their insight on the work in progress. We appreciate the hard work of those at McGraw-Hill Education who made this project work and the thoughtful help of our agent, Grace Freedson. Finally, we would like to thank all the students of College Hill Coaching who have contributed to the growth of these materials over the years.

CONTENTS

CHAPTER 1 **FAQs about the SAT** 1

What does the SAT Test? / 2
What is the Format of the SAT? / 2
How is the SAT Scored? / 2
What will Colleges do with my SAT Scores? / 3
What Control do I have over my SAT Scores? / 3
How Should I Prepare for the SAT? / 4
How can I get the most out of my SAT Study Sessions? / 5
When should I take the SATs and Subject Tests? / 6
What should I do the Week before my SAT? / 6

CHAPTER 2 **Diagnostic SAT** 7

Reading Test / 16
Writing and Language Test / 35
Math Test – No Calculator / 48
Math Test – Calculator / 54
Essay (optional) / 66

CHAPTER 3 **SAT Vocabulary: The Language of Ideas** 89

The Language of Ideas and Learning / 92
The Language of Argument, Reasoning, and Persuasion / 94
The Language of Dissent, Criticism, and Rebellion / 104
The Language of Power and Submission / 108
The Language of Language and Literature / 115

The Language of Judgment / 118
The Language of Extremism and Exaggeration / 121
The Language of Care and Restraint / 122
The Language of Freedom / 125
The Language of Change and Force / 126
The Language of Dullness and Stasis / 128
The Language of Truth, Truthfulness, and Beauty / 129
The Language of Deceit, Error, and Confusion / 130
The Language of Creativity and Productivity / 133
The Language of Mystery, Surprise, Adventure, and Discovery / 135
The Language of Harm, Deficit, and Decline / 137
The Language of Kindness, Favor, and Benefit / 139
The Language of Wisdom, Strength, and Skill / 143
The Language of Capital and Wealth / 145
The Language of Passion, Emotion, and Sensation / 147
The Power Roots and Affixes for the SAT / 150

CHAPTER 4   The SAT Reading Test   157

The Core Analytical Reading Skills / 159
The Three Key Questions / 161
The Three Secondary Questions / 170
Advanced SAT Reading Techniques / 180

CHAPTER 5   The SAT Writing and Language Test   195

Writing and Language Question Types / 197
Parsing Sentences / 199
Trimming Sentences / 200
Verb Agreement / 202
Developing and Coordinating Ideas / 204
Transitions and References / 207
Parallelism / 210
Coordinating Modifiers / 213
Using Modifiers Logically / 216
Making Comparisons / 219
Pronoun Agreement / 221
Pronoun Case / 223
Verb Tense and Aspect / 225
Diction and Redundancy / 229
Idiomatic Expression / 233
The Active and Passive Voices / 235
Verb Mood / 236
Punctuation / 239

CHAPTER 6   **The SAT Essay**   **251**

Understand the Analytical Task / 253
Read the Passage Using the "Three-Pass Approach" / 258
Construct Your Thesis and Outline / 266
Write the Essay / 269
Sample Essay / 273

CHAPTER 7   **The SAT Math Test: The Heart of Algebra**   **275**

Word Problems / 277
The Order of Operations and Laws of Arithmetic / 278
Simplifying Expressions / 285
Conversions / 287
Constructing and Interpreting Linear Equations / 292
Solving Equations with the Laws of Equality / 294
Analyzing Linear Graphs / 295
Absolute Values / 303
The Laws of Inequality / 304
Graphing Inequalities / 305
Linear Systems / 310
Solving Systems with Algebra / 312

CHAPTER 8   **The SAT Math Test: Problem Solving
                     and Data Analysis**   **319**

Averages / 321
Medians and Modes / 322
Data Spread / 323
Direct and Inverse Variations / 324
Rate Problems / 331
Ratios / 333
Percentages / 339
Percent Change / 340
Proportions and Scaling / 341
Tables and Venn Diagrams / 346
Conditional Probabilities from Tables / 347
Analyzing Relations with Tables / 348
Scatterplots / 353
Nonlinear Relationships / 354
Drawing Inferences from Graphs / 355
Pie Graphs / 356

CHAPTER 9   **The SAT Math: Passport to Advanced Math**   **361**

Functions / 363
Representing Functions / 365
Compositions and Transformations / 366
Analyzing and Factoring Quadratics / 373
Solving Quadratic Equations / 375
Analyzing Graphs of Quadratic Equations / 377
Higher Order Equations / 383
Higher Order Systems / 384
The Laws of Exponentials / 389
The Laws of Radicals / 391
Solving Exponential and Radical Equations / 392
Rational Expressions / 397
Simplifying Rational Expressions / 399
Solving Rational Equations / 400

CHAPTER 10   **The SAT Math Test: Additional Topics**   **407**

Angles and Parallel Lines / 409
Triangles / 411
Working in the *xy*-Plane / 413
The Pythagorean Theorem / 415
Circles / 421
Radians, Chords, Arcs, and Sectors / 423
Areas and Volumes / 426
Similarity / 428
Basic Trigonometry / 435
The Pythagorean Identity / 437
The Cofunction Identities / 438
Imaginary and Complex Numbers / 441

CHAPTER 11   **Practice Test 1**   **447**

                   Practice Test 2   **527**

                   Practice Test 3   **605**

                   Practice Test 4   **681**

100 EXTRA CHALLENGING SAT QUESTIONS
EVERY TOP-SCORER SHOULD KNOW   **757**

ANSWERS   **815**

CHAPTER 1

FAQs ABOUT THE SAT

1. What does the SAT test?   2

2. What is the format of the SAT?   2

3. How is the SAT scored?   2

4. What will colleges do with my SAT scores?   3

5. What control do I have over my SAT scores?   3

6. How should I prepare for the SAT?   4

7. How can I get the most out of my SAT study sessions?   5

8. When should I take the SATs and Subject Tests?   6

9. What should I do the week before my SAT?   6

1 WHAT DOES THE SAT TEST?

The SAT assesses a broad range of reasoning skills in the liberal arts. It does not test specific subject knowledge, but rather the broadly applicable skills of analytical reading, analytical writing, and mathematical problem solving. Here is a more comprehensive list of SAT skills, broken down by test:

SAT Reading

- Interpreting, analyzing, and drawing inferences from college-level texts across the liberal arts and sciences such as arguments, narratives, and personal or expository essays
- Interpreting and drawing inferences from data in the form of graphs, tables, and diagrams that accompany reading passages

SAT Writing and Language

- Analyzing sentences and paragraphs in terms of their grammatical correctness and semantic coherence

- Analyzing essays in terms of their overall development, tone, and effectiveness

SAT Math

- Solving algebraic problems involving equations, inequalities, systems, formulas, and functions
- Solving data-analysis problems involving concepts such as ratios, proportions, percentages, units, and numerical relationships
- Solving problems in advanced mathematics involving concepts such as quadratics, polynomials, angles, polygons, areas, volumes, exponentials, complex numbers, and trigonometry

SAT Essay (Optional)

- Writing an effective essay that analyzes and critiques a given argumentative passage

2 WHAT IS THE FORMAT OF THE SAT?

The SAT is a 3-hour test (3 hours 50 minutes with Essay) consisting of four mandatory sections and an optional Essay. It consists of four or five sections: Reading, Writing and Language, Math without calculator, Math with calculator, and an optional Essay.

1. Reading Test	52 questions	65 minutes
2. Writing and Language Test	44 questions	35 minutes
3. Mathematics Test (No calculator)	20 questions	25 minutes
4. Mathematics Test (Calculator)	38 questions	55 minutes
5. Essay (optional)	1 question	50 minutes

3 HOW IS THE SAT SCORED?

The SAT composite score (400–1600) is the sum of the Reading and Writing score (200–800) and the Math score (200–800). The Essay is scored on a scale of 6–24 broken down into three sub-scores: reading (2–8), analysis (2–8),

and writing (2–8). In addition, the College Board provides 14 additional "Insight Scores" as shown in the table that follows.

SAT Insight Scores

	Composite Score (400–1600)			Optional
Sections (200–800)	Math	Reading and Writing		
Test Scores (10–40)	Math	Writing and Language	Reading	Essay (6–24)
Cross-Test Scores (10–40)	Analysis in History/Social Studies			
	Analysis in Science			
Subscores (1–15)	Heart of Algebra	Relevant Words in Context		Reading (2–8)
	Problem Solving and Data Analysis	Command of Evidence		Analysis (2–8)
	Passport to Advanced Math	Expression of Ideas		Writing (2–8)
		Standard English Conventions		

4 | WHAT WILL COLLEGES DO WITH MY SAT SCORES?

Your SAT scores show colleges your readiness to do college-level work. Students with high SAT scores are more likely to succeed with college-level math, writing, and reading assignments. SAT scores correlate strongly with post-college success, particularly in professions like medicine, law, the humanities, the sciences, and engineering. Students with high SAT scores are more likely to graduate from college and to have successful careers after college.

But let's face it: one reason colleges want you to send them SAT scores is that high scores make *them* look good. The higher the average SAT score of their applicants, the better their rankings and prestige. This is why most colleges cherry-pick your top subscores if you submit multiple SAT results. (It's also why some colleges have adopted "SAT-optional" policies: only the high-scoring students are likely to submit them, and so the college's average scores automatically increase, thereby improving its national rankings.) In addition to your SAT scores, most colleges are interested in your grades, your curriculum, your recommendations, your leadership skills, your extracurricular activities, and your essay. But standardized test scores are becoming more important as colleges become more selective. High SAT scores provide you with an admission advantage, even if the college does not require them. Some large or specialized schools will weigh test scores heavily. If you have any questions about how heavily a certain college weighs your SAT scores, call the admissions office and ask.

The majority of colleges "superscore" your SAT, which means that they cherry-pick your top SAT Reading and Writing score and your top SAT Math score from all of the SATs you submit. So, for instance, if you submit your March SAT scores of 520R 610M (1130 composite) and your June SAT scores of 550R 580M (1130 composite), the college will consider your SAT score to be 550R 610M (1160 composite). Nice of them, huh?

5 | WHAT CONTROL DO I HAVE OVER MY SAT SCORES?

No college will see any of your SAT or Subject Test scores until you choose to release them to that particular school. Most colleges also allow you to use Score Choice to select which particular SAT and SAT Subject Test scores are submitted to the colleges among all that you've taken. Some colleges, however, may request that you submit all scores of all SATs you've taken. Typically, colleges do this to give you the maximum possible SAT "superscore."

So don't worry about taking the SAT two or three times, if you need to. In fact, most colleges encourage students to take multiple tests, since one data point isn't as trustworthy as multiple data points. But don't go overboard. If you take it more than four times, a college might think you're test-obsessed.

6 HOW SHOULD I PREPARE FOR THE SAT?

"Start where you are. Use what you have. Do what you can."
—Arthur Ashe

Step 1: Make a testing schedule

First, decide when you will take your first SAT. Sit down with your guidance counselor early in your junior year and work out a full testing schedule for the year, taking into account the SAT, SAT Subject Tests, AP tests, and possibly the ACT. Once you have decided on your schedule, commit yourself to beginning your SAT preparation at least 3 months prior to your first SAT. Commit to setting aside 30–40 minutes per night for review work and practice, and to taking at least two or three full-scale practice tests on the weekends.

Step 2: Take a diagnostic SAT or two

When you're ready to begin your SAT preparation (ideally 3 months before your SAT), you'll first need to assess your readiness. Chapter 2 contains a full-scale practice SAT. It requires 3 hours (or 3 hours and 50 minutes if you include the essay). Take it on a Saturday morning, if possible, at roughly the time you will start the real SAT (around 8:00 a.m.), and make sure that you have a quiet place, a stopwatch, a calculator, and a few #2 pencils. This will give you a solid idea of what the experience of taking the new SAT is like.

Step 3: Use the lessons in this book

The detailed answer keys after each practice test will give you plenty of feedback about the topics that you may need to review in order to prepare for your SAT. If you set aside about 30 minutes per night to work through the chapters, review the lessons, and complete the exercises in this book, you can make substantial progress and see big SAT score improvements in just a few weeks. But to get the full benefit of this book, you should start at least three months before your SAT.

Step 4: Take practice tests regularly and diagnose your performance

Practice is the key to success. This book includes several "heavyweight" practice SATs in Chapter 11 (that is, tests that are slightly harder than the real SAT). Use them. Take one every week or two to assess your progress as you work through the specific skills review in Chapters 3–10.

Step 5: Register at the College Board and Khan Academy and take advantage of their online materials

The College Board and Khan Academy provide free online SAT practice materials, such as 8 full-scale practice SATs that can be scored automatically with a handy smartphone app, and a "10 SAT Questions Per Day" service that sends you a daily e-mail with a link to online practice to keep your skills sharp.

Register on Khan Academy as an SAT student to take advantage of these free review materials, and check in regularly for new updates and additions.

Step 6: Read often and deeply

Engaging big ideas and honing your analytical reading skills are keys to success in college and on the SAT. Make a point of working your way though these books and checking these periodicals regularly.

Online/Periodical

The New York Times (Op-Ed, Science Times, Front Page)
BBC News (Views, Analysis, Background)
The Atlantic (Feature Articles)
Slate (Voices, Innovation)
Scientific American (Feature Articles)
The Economist (Debate, Science & Technology)
TED Talks (Innovation, Culture, Politics, Inspiration)
The New Yorker (Talk of the Town, Feature Articles)
ProPublica (Feature Articles)
Edge (Essays)
Radiolab (Weekly Podcast)

Books

To Kill a Mockingbird, Harper Lee
Macbeth, William Shakespeare
Frankenstein, Mary Shelley
The Color Purple, Alice Walker
Pride and Prejudice, Jane Austen
Jane Eyre, Charlotte Bronte
Heart of Darkness, Joseph Conrad
Narrative of the Life of Frederick Douglass, Frederick Douglass
The Great Gatsby, F. Scott Fitzgerald
Walden, Henry David Thoreau
The American Language, H. L. Mencken
Notes of a Native Son, James Baldwin
The Stranger, Albert Camus
Night, Elie Wiesel
Animal Farm, George Orwell
Things Fall Apart, Chinua Achebe
The Language Instinct, Steven Pinker
The Mismeasure of Man, Stephen J. Gould
The Republic, Plato
A People's History of the United States, Howard Zinn
Guns, Germs, and Steel, Jared Diamond
A Short History of Nearly Everything, Bill Bryson

Step 7: Take strong math courses

Challenge yourself with strong math courses that introduce you to the ideas, skills, and methods or advanced mathematics, such as trigonometry, analysis of polynomials, statistical reasoning, plane geometry, and even complex numbers. These advanced topics have become a greater focus for both the SAT and ACT.

Step 8: Take strong writing courses

Take courses from teachers who emphasize strong writing skills, particularly by giving challenging writing assignments and providing timely and detailed feedback. Reading and writing skills are at the core of both the SAT and the ACT, so working with strong reading and writing teachers is invaluable.

7 HOW CAN I GET THE MOST OUT OF MY SAT STUDY SESSIONS?

1. **Create a schedule, a study log, and a place to study.** Stick to a firm schedule of 30–40 minutes a day for SAT preparation. Write it down in your daily planner and commit to it like you would to a daily class. Also, keep a log of notes for each study session, including key strategies, important formulas, vocabulary words, and advice for your next test. Then make an effective study space: a well-lit desk with a straight-back chair, plenty of pencils, a timer for practice tests, flashcards, your study log, and even a stash of brain-healthy snacks.

2. **Eliminate distractions.** Turn off all alerts on your phone and laptop, and tell everyone in the house that this is your study time. Make sure everyone is in on the plan. Even kick the dog out of the room.

3. **Stick to focused 30- to 40-minute sessions.** Set a very clear agenda for each study session, such as "Master six new roots and complete the first half of Algebra Practice 4 in Chapter 7" or "Read and annotate one complete New York Times Op-Ed and read Lesson 2 in Chapter 9." Then find your study spot, shut out all distractions, and set to work. Try not to go beyond 40 minutes for each session: stay focused and engaged, and keep it brisk.

4. **Do 30-second checks.** Once you've completed your session, take out your study log. Give yourself 30 seconds to write down the most important idea(s) that helped you through that study session. Reread your notes just before you begin your next session.

5. **Learn it like you have to teach it.** Now step away from your log and imagine you have to run into a class of eighth graders and teach them what you just learned. How would you communicate these ideas clearly? What examples would you use to illustrate them? What tough questions might the students ask, and how would you answer them? How can you explain the concepts and strategies in different ways? How can you help the students manage potential difficulties they might have in a testing environment?

6. **Sleep on it.** A good night's sleep is essential to a good study program. You need at least eight hours of sleep per night. To make your sleep as effective as possible, try to fall asleep while thinking about a challenging problem or strategy you're trying to perfect. As you sleep, your brain will continue to work on the problem by a process called consolidation. When you awake, you'll have a better grasp on the problem or skill whether you realize it or not.

7. **Make creative mnemonics.** Whenever you're challenged by a tough vocabulary word, grammar rule, or mathematical concept, try to visualize the new idea or word as a crazy, colorful picture or story. The memory tricks are called mnemonics, and the best ones use patterns, rhymes, or vivid and bizarre visual images. For instance, if you struggle to remember what a "polemic" is, just turn the word into a picture based on its sound, for instance a "pole" with a "mike" (microphone) on the end of it. Then incorporate the meaning into the picture. Since a polemic is a "strong verbal attack, usually regarding a political or philosophical issue," picture someone having a vehement political argument with someone else and hitting him over the head with the "pole-mike." The crazier the picture, the better. Also, feel free to scribble notes as you study, complete with helpful drawings. Write silly songs, create acronyms—be creative.

8. **Consider different angles.** Remember that many math problems can be solved in different ways: algebraically, geometrically, with tables, through guess-and-check, by testing the choices, etc. Try to find elegant, simple solutions. If you struggled with a problem, even if you got it right, come back to it later and try to find the more elegant solution. Also, consider experimenting with pre-test rituals until you find one that helps you the most.

9. **Maintain constructive inner dialogue.** Constantly ask yourself, What do I need to do to get better? Do I need to focus more on my relaxation exercises? Should I try to improve my reading speed? Should I ask different questions as I read? Should I refresh myself on my trigonometry? Having a clear set of positive goals that you reinforce with inner dialogue helps you to succeed. Banish the negative self-talk. Don't sabotage your work by saying, "This is impossible," or "I stink at this."

10. **Make a plan to work through the struggles.** Before you take each practice test, have a clear agenda. Remind yourself of the key ideas and strategies for the week. But remember that there will always be challenges. Just meet them head on and don't let them get you down.

8 WHEN SHOULD I TAKE THE SATS AND SUBJECT TESTS?

Most competitive colleges require either SAT or ACT scores from all of their applicants, although some schools allow you to choose whether or not to submit standardized test scores with your application. Many competitive colleges also require two or three Subject Test scores. The Subject Tests are hour-long tests in specific subjects like mathematics, physics, chemistry, foreign languages, U.S. history, world history, and literature.

If you want to be able to apply to any competitive college in the country, plan to take the SAT at least twice, as well as two to four SAT Subject Tests, by the end of spring semester of junior year, and retake any of those tests, if necessary, in the fall of your senior year. This way, you will have a full testing profile by the end of your junior year, and you'll have a much clearer picture of where you stand before you start your college applications. Also, if you plan well, you will have some choices about which scores to submit.

Even if your favorite colleges don't require standardized tests, you may be able to submit them anyway to boost your application. The Subject Tests, specifically, can provide a strong counterbalance to any weaknesses in your grades.

Take your Subject Test when the subject material is fresh in your mind. For most students, this is in June, just as you are preparing to take your final exams. However, if you are taking AP exams in May, you might prefer to take the SAT Subject Tests in May, also. Learn which SAT Subject Tests your colleges require, and try to complete them by June of your junior year. You can take up to three SAT Subject Tests on any test date.

9 WHAT SHOULD I DO THE WEEK BEFORE MY SAT?

1. **Get plenty of sleep.** Don't underestimate the power of a good night's sleep. During sleep, not only do you restore balance and energy to your body, but you also consolidate what you've learned that day, and even become more efficient at tasks you've been practicing.
2. **Eat healthy.** Don't skip meals because you're studying. Eat regular, well-balanced meals.
3. **Exercise.** Stick to your regular exercise program the weeks before the SAT. A strong body helps make a strong mind.
4. **Visualize success.** In the days before your SAT, envision yourself in the test room, relaxed and confident, working through even the toughest parts of the test without stress or panic.
5. **Don't cram, but stay sharp.** In the days before the SAT, resist the urge to cram. Your best results will come if you focus on getting plenty of sleep and staying positive and relaxed. If you're feeling anxious, take out your flashcards for a few minutes at a time, or review your old tests just to remind yourself of basic strategies, but don't cram.
6. **Keep perspective.** Remember that you can take the SAT multiple times, and that colleges will almost certainly "superscore" the results, so don't get down about any single set of test results. Also, keep in mind that colleges don't base their acceptance decisions on SAT scores alone.
7. **Lay everything out.** The night before your SAT, lay out your admission ticket, your photo ID, your #2 pencils, your calculator (with fresh batteries), your snack, and directions to the test site (if necessary). Having these all ready will let you sleep better.

CHAPTER 2

DIAGNOSTIC SAT

1. Reading Test

   65 MINUTES   52 QUESTIONS   16

2. Writing and Language Test

   35 MINUTES   44 QUESTIONS   35

3. Math Test – No Calculator

   25 MINUTES   20 QUESTIONS   48

4. Math Test – Calculator

   55 MINUTES   38 QUESTIONS   54

5. Essay (optional)

   50 MINUTES   1 QUESTION   66

ANSWER SHEET for SAT DIAGNOSTIC

Use a No. 2 pencil and fill in the entire circle darkly and completely.
If you change your response, erase as completely as possible.

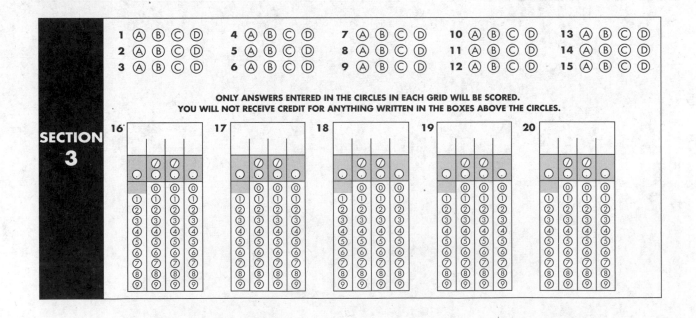

SECTION
4

1 Ⓐ Ⓑ Ⓒ Ⓓ   7 Ⓐ Ⓑ Ⓒ Ⓓ   13 Ⓐ Ⓑ Ⓒ Ⓓ   19 Ⓐ Ⓑ Ⓒ Ⓓ   25 Ⓐ Ⓑ Ⓒ Ⓓ
2 Ⓐ Ⓑ Ⓒ Ⓓ   8 Ⓐ Ⓑ Ⓒ Ⓓ   14 Ⓐ Ⓑ Ⓒ Ⓓ   20 Ⓐ Ⓑ Ⓒ Ⓓ   26 Ⓐ Ⓑ Ⓒ Ⓓ
3 Ⓐ Ⓑ Ⓒ Ⓓ   9 Ⓐ Ⓑ Ⓒ Ⓓ   15 Ⓐ Ⓑ Ⓒ Ⓓ   21 Ⓐ Ⓑ Ⓒ Ⓓ   27 Ⓐ Ⓑ Ⓒ Ⓓ
4 Ⓐ Ⓑ Ⓒ Ⓓ   10 Ⓐ Ⓑ Ⓒ Ⓓ   16 Ⓐ Ⓑ Ⓒ Ⓓ   22 Ⓐ Ⓑ Ⓒ Ⓓ   28 Ⓐ Ⓑ Ⓒ Ⓓ
5 Ⓐ Ⓑ Ⓒ Ⓓ   11 Ⓐ Ⓑ Ⓒ Ⓓ   17 Ⓐ Ⓑ Ⓒ Ⓓ   23 Ⓐ Ⓑ Ⓒ Ⓓ   29 Ⓐ Ⓑ Ⓒ Ⓓ
6 Ⓐ Ⓑ Ⓒ Ⓓ   12 Ⓐ Ⓑ Ⓒ Ⓓ   18 Ⓐ Ⓑ Ⓒ Ⓓ   24 Ⓐ Ⓑ Ⓒ Ⓓ   30 Ⓐ Ⓑ Ⓒ Ⓓ

ONLY ANSWERS ENTERED IN THE CIRCLES IN EACH GRID WILL BE SCORED.
YOU WILL NOT RECEIVE CREDIT FOR ANYTHING WRITTEN IN THE BOXES ABOVE THE CIRCLES.

31   32   33   34

35   36   37   38

SECTION 5: ESSAY

PLANNING PAGE   You may plan your essay in the unlined planning space below, but use only the lined pages following this one to write your essay. Any work on this planning page will not be scored.

BEGIN YOUR ESSAY HERE

DO NOT WRITE OUTSIDE OF THE BOX.

Cut Here

DO NOT WRITE OUTSIDE OF THE BOX.

3

DO NOT WRITE OUTSIDE OF THE BOX.

Cut Here

Test begins on the next page.

1   1

Reading Test

65 MINUTES, 52 QUESTIONS

Turn to Section 1 of your answer sheet to answer the questions in this section.

Each passage or pair of passages below is followed by a number of questions. After reading each passage or pair, choose the best answer to each question based on what is stated or implied in the passage or passages and in any accompanying graphics.

Questions 1–10 are based on the following passage and supplementary material.

This passage is adapted from Kevin Drum, *"America's Real Criminal Element: Lead"* ©2013 Mother Jones.

Experts often suggest that crime resembles an epidemic. But what kind? Economics
Line professor Karl Smith has a good rule of thumb for categorizing epidemics: If it spreads along
5   lines of communication, he says, the cause is information. Think Bieber Fever.[1] If it travels along major transportation routes, the cause is microbial. Think influenza. If it spreads out like a fan, the cause is an insect. Think malaria. But
10 if it's everywhere, all at once—as both the rise of crime in the '60s and '70s and the fall of crime in the '90s seemed to be—the cause is a molecule.

A molecule? That sounds crazy. What molecule could be responsible for a steep and
15 sudden decline in violent crime?

Well, here's one possibility: $Pb(CH_2CH_3)_4$.

In 1994, Rick Nevin was a consultant working for the US Department of Housing and Urban Development on the costs and benefits of
20 removing lead paint from old houses. A growing body of research had linked lead exposure in small children with a whole raft of complications later in life, including lower IQ, hyperactivity, behavioral problems, and learning disabilities.
25 A recent study had also suggested a link between childhood lead exposure and juvenile

delinquency later on. Maybe reducing lead exposure had an effect on violent crime too?

That tip took Nevin in a different direction. The
30 biggest source of lead in the postwar era, it turns out, wasn't paint, but leaded gasoline. If you chart the rise and fall of atmospheric lead caused by the rise and fall of leaded gasoline consumption, you get an upside-down U. Lead emissions from
35 tailpipes rose steadily from the early '40s through the early '70s, nearly quadrupling over that period. Then, as unleaded gasoline began to replace leaded gasoline, emissions plummeted.

Intriguingly, violent crime rates followed the
40 same upside-down U pattern (see the graph). The only thing different was the time period. Crime rates rose dramatically in the '60s through the '80s, and then began dropping steadily starting in the early '90s. The two curves looked eerily
45 identical, but were offset by about 20 years.

So Nevin dug up detailed data on lead emissions and crime rates to see if the similarity of the curves was as good as it seemed. It turned out to be even better. In a 2000 paper he concluded
50 that if you add a lag time of 23 years, lead emissions from automobiles explain 90 percent of the variation in violent crime in America. Toddlers who ingested high levels of lead in the '40s and '50s really were more likely to become violent
55 criminals in the '60s, '70s, and '80s.

---

[1] Enthusiasm for the music and person of Justin Bieber.

CONTINUE →

1   1

And with that we have our molecule: tetra-ethyl lead, the gasoline additive invented by General Motors in the 1920s to prevent knocking and pinging in high-performance engines. As
60 auto sales boomed after World War II, and drivers in powerful new cars increasingly asked service station attendants to "fill 'er up with ethyl," they were unwittingly creating a crime wave two decades later.

65   It was an exciting conjecture, and it prompted an immediate wave of . . . nothing. Nevin's paper was almost completely ignored, and in one sense it's easy to see why—Nevin is an economist, not a criminologist, and his paper
70 was published in *Environmental Research*, not a journal with a big readership in the criminology community. What's more, a single correlation between two curves isn't all that impressive, econometrically speaking. Sales of vinyl LPs rose
75 in the postwar period too, and then declined in the '80s and '90s. No matter how good the fit, if you only have a single correlation it might just be

a coincidence. You need to do something more to establish causality.
80   So in 2007, Nevin collected lead data and crime data for Australia, Canada, Great Britain, Finland, France, Italy, New Zealand and West Germany. Every time, the two curves fit each other astonishingly well.

85   The gasoline lead hypothesis helps explain some things we might not have realized even needed explaining. For example, murder rates have always been higher in big cities than in towns and small cities. Nevin suggests that,
90 because big cities have lots of cars in a small area, they also had high densities of atmospheric lead during the postwar era. But as lead levels in gasoline decreased, the differences between big and small cities largely went away. And guess
95 what? The difference in murder rates went away too. Today, homicide rates are similar in cities of all sizes. It may be that violent crime isn't an inevitable consequence of being a big city after all.

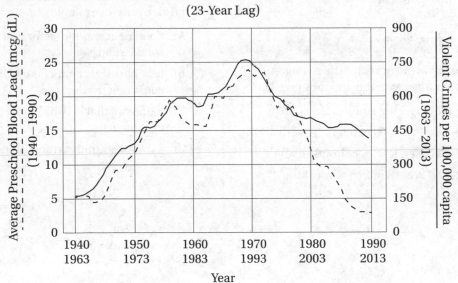

PRESCHOOL BLOOD LEAD LEVELS VS. VIOLENT CRIME RATES IN THE U.S.
(23-Year Lag)

Source: Rick Nevin, *Lead Poisoning and The Bell Curve*, 2012

CONTINUE ➡

1

In the first paragraph, Karl Smith's work is presented primarily as

A) a controversial sociological hypothesis.

B) a warning about potentially dangerous economic trends.

C) a useful model for conceptualizing a variety of phenomena.

D) a potential medical solution to a persistent social problem.

2

The author suggests that promising research in the social sciences is sometimes ignored because it

A) is not presented by authorities with the proper credentials.

B) is not supported by controlled scientific experiments.

C) relies on complex mathematical calculations that are not easily understood.

D) uses historical data that are not necessarily valid in the modern era.

3

Which of the following provides the strongest evidence for the answer to the previous question?

A) Lines 25–27 ("A recent study . . . later on")

B) Lines 49–52 ("In a 2000 paper . . . America")

C) Lines 68–72 ("Nevin is . . . community")

D) Lines 72–74 ("What's more . . . speaking")

4

According to the graph for which of the following time periods was the percent increase in per capita violent crime the greatest?

A) 1940–1970

B) 1963–1993

C) 1970–1990

D) 1993–2013

5

According to the graph, which decade of violent crime statistics provides the LEAST support to Rick Nevin's hypothesis?

A) 1963–1973

B) 1980–1990

C) 1983–1993

D) 2003–2013

6

The author mentions "sales of vinyl LPs" (line 74) primarily as an example of

A) another economic factor that may explain a social trend.

B) how harmful chemicals can be spread via consumer products.

C) a statistic that may be more coincidental than explanatory.

D) a counterintuitive trend in consumer behavior.

CONTINUE

1   **1**

7

The "complications" in line 22 are

A) obstacles to gathering relevant data.

B) controversies about theoretical models.

C) challenges to the implementation of social policies.

D) psychological problems.

8

The author regards the "drivers" in line 60 as

A) inadvertent abettors.

B) unintentional heroes.

C) greedy consumers.

D) devious conspirators.

9

In line 49, "even better" most nearly means

A) less controversial.

B) more correlative.

C) easier to calculate.

D) more aesthetically engaging.

10

The final paragraph (lines 85–98) serves primarily to

A) suggest topics for future research.

B) concede a theoretical drawback.

C) propose a novel alternative.

D) describe a supportive implication.

CONTINUE ➡

1   1

Questions 11–21 are based on the following passages.

Passage 1 is adapted from an essay written by John Aldridge in 1951. ©1951 by John Aldridge. Passage 2 is adapted from Brom Weber, *"Ernest Hemingway's Genteel Bullfight,"* published in The American Novel and the Nineteen Twenties. ©1971 by Hodder Education.

Passage 1

By the time we were old enough to read Hemingway, he had become legendary. Like
Line Lord Byron a century earlier, he had learned to play himself, his own best hero, with superb
5   conviction. He was Hemingway of the rugged outdoor grin and the hairy chest posing beside a lion he had just shot. He was Tarzan Hemingway, crouching in the African bush with elephant gun at ready. He was War Correspondent Hemingway
10   writing a play in the Hotel Florida in Madrid while thirty fascist shells crashed through the roof. Later, he was Task Force Hemingway swathed in ammunition belts and defending his post singlehandedly against fierce German
15   attacks.

But even without the legend, the chest-beating, wisecracking pose that was later to seem so incredibly absurd, his impact upon us was tremendous. The feeling he gave us was one
20   of immense expansiveness, freedom and, at the same time, absolute stability and control. We could follow him, imitate his cold detachment, through all the doubts and fears of adolescence and come out pure and untouched. The words
25   he put down seemed to us to have been carved from the living stone of life. They conveyed exactly the taste, smell and feel of experience as it was, as it might possibly be. And so we began unconsciously to translate our own sensations
30   into their terms and to impose on everything we did and felt the particular emotions they aroused in us.

The Hemingway time was a good time to be young. We had much then that the war later
35   forced out of us, something far greater than Hemingway's strong formative influence.

Later writers who lost or got rid of Hemingway have been able to find nothing to put in his place. They have rejected his time as untrue
40   for them only to fail at finding themselves in their own time. Others, in their embarrassment at the hold he once had over them, have not profited by the lessons he had to teach, and still others were never touched by him at all. These last are
45   perhaps the real unfortunates, for they have been denied access to a powerful tradition.

Passage 2

One wonders why Hemingway's greatest works now seem unable to evoke the same sense of a tottering world that in the 1920s established
50   Ernest Hemingway's reputation. These novels should be speaking to us. Our social structure is as shaken, our philosophical despair as great, our everyday experience as unsatisfying. We have had more war than Hemingway ever dreamed
55   of. Our violence—physical, emotional, and intellectual—is not inferior to that of the 1920s. Yet Hemingway's great novels no longer seem to penetrate deeply the surface of existence. One begins to doubt that they ever did so significantly
60   in the 1920s.

Hemingway's novels indulged the dominant genteel tradition in American culture while seeming to repudiate it. They yielded to the functionalist, technological aesthetic of the
65   culture instead of resisting in the manner of Frank Lloyd Wright. Hemingway, in effect, became a dupe of his culture rather than its moral-aesthetic conscience. As a consequence, the import of his work has diminished. There is some evidence
70   from his stylistic evolution that Hemingway himself must have felt as much, for Hemingway's famous stylistic economy frequently seems to conceal another kind of writer, with much richer rhetorical resources to hand. So, *Death in the*
75   *Afternoon* (1932), Hemingway's bullfighting opus and his first book after *A Farewell to Arms* (1929), reveals great uneasiness over his earlier accomplishment. In it, he defends his literary method with a doctrine of ambiguity: "If a writer
80   of prose knows enough about what he is writing

CONTINUE

1   1

about he may omit things that he knows and the reader, if the writer is writing truly enough, will have a feeling of those things as strongly as though the writer had stated them."

85   Hemingway made much the same theoretical point in another way in *Death in the Afternoon* apparently believing that a formal reduction of aesthetic complexity was the only kind of design that had value.

90   Perhaps the greatest irony of *Death in the Afternoon* is its unmistakably baroque prose, which Hemingway himself embarrassedly admitted was "flowery." Reviewers, unable to challenge Hemingway's expertise in the art of
95   bullfighting, noted that its style was "awkward, tortuous, [and] belligerently clumsy."

      Death in the Afternoon is an extraordinarily self-indulgent, unruly, clownish, garrulous, and satiric book, with scrambled chronologies,
100   willful digressions, mock-scholarly apparatuses, fictional interludes, and scathing allusions. Its inflated style can hardly penetrate the façade, let alone deflate humanity.

11

On which topic do the authors of the two passages most strongly disagree?

A) The economy of Hemingway's writing

B) The incisiveness of Hemingway's prose

C) The sincerity of Hemingway's portrayals

D) The extent of Hemingway's reputation

12

Which pair of sentences provides the strongest evidence for the answer to the previous question?

A) Lines 5–7 ("He was . . . just shot") and lines 85–89 ("Hemingway . . . had value")

B) Lines 37–39 ("Later writers . . . his place") and lines 55–56 ("Our violence . . . the 1920s")

C) Lines 24–26 ("The words . . . stone of life") and lines 57–58 ("Yet . . . existence")

D) Lines 34–36 ("We had much . . . influence") and lines 90–93 ("Perhaps the greatest . . . was 'flowery'")

13

Which of the following best describes how each passage characterizes Hemingway?

A) Passage 1 portrays him as a tortured poet, but Passage 2 portrays him as a crass amateur.

B) Passage 1 portrays him as a master of refinement, but Passage 2 portrays him as a literary revolutionary.

C) Passage 1 portrays him as a hero, but Passage 2 portrays him as a cultural conformist.

D) Passage 1 portrays him as an absurd warmonger, but Passage 2 portrays him as an undisciplined artist.

14

Which statement about Hemingway is supported by both passages?

A) He was an artistic pioneer, although he was underappreciated in his time.

B) He was a consistent practitioner of spare and evocative prose.

C) His characters serve as archetypes for masculine adventure.

D) His wartime narratives do not fully capture the horrors of war.

CONTINUE ➡

15

In line 26, the phrase "living stone" most nearly means

A) salient experience.

B) inevitable regret.

C) stubborn resistance.

D) durable memorial.

16

Lines 28–32 ("And so we . . . aroused in us") suggests that many of Hemingway's readers were inclined to

A) emulate his adventures.

B) resent his glorification of war.

C) imitate his literary style.

D) identify with his language.

17

The "lessons" mentioned in line 43 most likely include stories of

A) transformative romantic love.

B) confidence in the face of danger.

C) indulgent self-examination.

D) corporate or political ambition.

18

In line 49, the word "tottering" is intended to evoke a sense of

A) infantile frailty.

B) economic instability.

C) artistic immaturity.

D) societal upheaval.

19

The author of Passage 1 would most likely regard the statement in lines 66–68 ("Hemingway, in effect . . . conscience"), with

A) journalistic detachment.

B) grudging acquiescence.

C) vehement disagreement.

D) good-natured amusement.

1

1

20

Which statement provides the best evidence for the answer to the previous question?

A) Lines 2–5 ("Like Lord . . . superb conviction")

B) Lines 28–32 ("And so . . . aroused in us")

C) Lines 34–36 ("We had much . . . formative influence")

D) Lines 39–41 ("They have rejected . . . own time")

21

The author of Passage 2 suggests that, in comparison to Hemingway, Frank Lloyd Wright was relatively

A) minimalist.

B) iconoclastic.

C) volatile.

D) traditional.

Questions 22–32 are based on the following passage.

This passage is from S. K. Mukherjee, *"The Mysteries of the Strong Nuclear Force."* ©2015 College Hill Coaching.

As any good contractor will tell you, a sound structure requires stable materials. But atoms,
Line the building blocks of everything we know and love—bunnies, brownies, and best friends—
5 don't appear to be models of stability. Why are some atoms, like sodium, so hyperactive while others, like helium, are so aloof? Why do the electrons that inhabit atoms jump around so strangely, from one bizarrely shaped orbital to
10 another? And why do protons, the bits that give atoms their heft and personality, stick together at all?

We are told that every atom has a tiny nucleus containing positively charged protons
15 and uncharged neutrons, swarmed by a cloud of speedy electrons. We are also told that like charges, such as protons, repel each other with a force that shoots up to infinity as they get closer. Even worse, you can't get much closer
20 than two protons in the nucleus of an atom. So what's keeping atomic nuclei from flying apart? Obviously, some other force must be at work inside the atom, something that we can't detect at our human scale. Physicists call this the
25 "strong nuclear force." But where does it come from?

In order for this force to account for the binding of protons in the nucleus, it must have certain interesting features. First, it can't have any
30 sizeable effect beyond the radius of the atom itself, or it would play havoc with the nuclei of adjacent atoms, destroying matter as we know it. Second, it must perfectly balance the repulsive force of electricity at an "equilibrium point" of about

35 0.7×10^{-15} meters, the average distance between bound protons, in order to create a stable nucleus. Third, it must *repel* at even shorter distances, or else neutrons (which don't have any electrostatic repulsion to balance the strong nuclear force)
40 would collapse into each other. The graph shows the behavior of such a force relative to the repulsive electrostatic force.

In 1935, Japanese physicist Hideki Yukawa proposed that the nuclear force was conveyed by
45 a then-undiscovered heavy subatomic particle he called the pi meson (or "pion"), which (unlike the photon, which conveys the electrostatic force) decays very quickly and therefore conveys a powerful force only over a very short distance.
50 Professor Yukawa's theory, however, was dealt a mortal blow by a series of experiments conducted at Los Alamos National Laboratory in the early 1990s that demonstrated that pions carry force only over distances greater than the
55 distance between bound protons. The pion was a plumber's wrench trying to do a tweezer's job.

Current atomic theory suggests that the strong nuclear force is most likely conveyed by massless particles called "gluons" according
60 to the theory of quantum chromodynamics, or QCD for short. According to QCD, protons and neutrons are composed of smaller particles called quarks, which are held together by the aptly named gluons. This quark-binding force has
65 a "residue" that extends beyond the protons and neutrons themselves to provide just enough force to bind the protons and neutrons together.

If you're hoping that QCD ties up atomic behavior with a tidy little bow, you may be just
70 a bit disappointed. As a quantum theory, it conceives of space and time as tiny chunks that occasionally misbehave, rather than smooth predictable quantities, and its mathematical formulas are perhaps as hard to penetrate as the
75 nucleus itself.

CONTINUE ➔

1   **1**

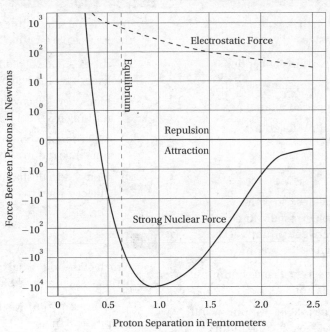

ELECTROSTATIC AND STRONG NUCLEAR FORCES BETWEEN PROTONS

22

The primary purpose of the first paragraph
(lines 1–12) is to

A) describe a popular misconception.

B) introduce a physical theory.

C) suggest a scientific conundrum.

D) present a personal account.

23

In line 7, "aloof" most nearly means

A) impenetrable.

B) formal.

C) retracted.

D) nonreactive.

24

The question in lines 10–12 ("And why . . . at all?")
indicates

A) a minor curiosity to scientists exploring deeper
   questions.

B) a socially significant puzzle that is
   unfortunately ignored in scientific circles.

C) a humorous irony in an otherwise serious field
   of investigation.

D) a central conundrum at the heart of an
   important scientific field.

25

Which sentence provides the best evidence for the
answer to the previous question?

A) Lines 2–5 ("But atoms . . . stability")

B) Lines 19–20 ("Even worse . . . an atom")

C) Lines 55–56 ("The pion . . . tweezer's job")

D) Lines 68–70 ("If you're . . . disappointed")

CONTINUE ➤

26

In lines 13–16, the repetition of the phrase "We are" serves primarily to emphasize

A) the predominance of certain conceptions.

B) the personal nature of scientific research.

C) the effectiveness of a particular analogy.

D) the deficiencies in public education.

27

Which of the following best describes the relationship between the electrostatic force and the strong nuclear force between protons at the equilibrium point as shown in the graph?

A) The strong nuclear force is at its maximum, but the electrostatic force is not.

B) The strong nuclear force is at its minimum, but the electrostatic force is near its maximum.

C) The sum of the two forces is zero.

D) The strong nuclear force is zero and the electrostatic force is greater than 100 Newtons.

28

According to the graph, the electrostatic repulsion between two protons separated by 1.5 femtometers is closest to

A) 2 Newtons.

B) 20 Newtons.

C) 100 Newtons.

D) 1,000 Newtons.

29

The "mortal blow" (line 51) to Hideki Yukawa's theory was the fact that

A) the existence of pions was not confirmed by experimental evidence.

B) pions were discovered to be massless, thereby refuting his theory that they were heavy.

C) experiments showed pions to be ineffective in the range required by atomic theory.

D) pions had a destabilizing effect on atomic nuclei, rather than a stabilizing one.

30

Which of the following best describes the structure of the passage as a whole?

A) a series of intuitive illustrations of a complex physical theory

B) a description of a technical puzzle and the attempts to solve it

C) an account of an experimental finding and its surprising implications

D) a historical overview of a heated scientific controversy

1 | | **1**

31

The author's writing style is particularly notable for its use of all of the following EXCEPT

A) rhetorical questions.

B) illustrative metaphors.

C) technical specifications.

D) appeals to common intuition.

32

In line 68, "ties up" most nearly means

A) constrains restrictively.

B) resolves neatly.

C) obstructs completely.

D) fastens securely.

CONTINUE →

Questions 33–42 are based on the following passage.

This passage is adapted from Jean-Jaques Rousseau, *"Discourse on Inequality and Social Contract."* Originally published in 1762.

Just as, before putting up a large building, the architect surveys and sounds the site to see if it will bear the weight, the wise legislator does not begin by laying down laws good in themselves,
5 but by investigating the fitness of the people, for which they are destined, to receive them. Plato refused to legislate for the Arcadians and the Cyrenæans,[1] because he knew that both peoples were rich and could not tolerate equality. Also,
10 good laws and bad men were found together in Crete, because Minos had inflicted discipline on a people already burdened with vice.

A thousand nations that have achieved earthly greatness could never have endured good
15 laws. Even those nations that could have endured good laws could have done so only for a very brief period of their long history. Most peoples, like most men, are docile only in youth. As they grow old they become incorrigible. Once customs have
20 become established and prejudices inveterate, it is dangerous and useless to attempt their reformation. The people, like the foolish and cowardly patients who rave at sight of the doctor, can no longer bear that any one should lay hands on its
25 faults to remedy them.

There are indeed times in the history of States when, just as some kinds of illness turn men's heads and make them forget the past, periods of violence and revolution do to peoples
30 what these crises do to individuals. Horror of the past takes the place of forgetfulness, and the state, set on fire by civil wars, is born again, so to speak, from its ashes, and takes on anew, fresh from the jaws of death, the vigor of youth. Such
35 was Sparta at the time of Lycurgus.

But such events are rare exceptions, the cause of which is always to be found in the particular constitution of the state concerned. Such renewals cannot even happen twice to the same nation,
40 for it can make itself free as long as it remains barbarous, but not when the civic impulse has lost its vigor. Then disturbances may destroy it, but revolutions cannot mend it: it needs a master, and not a liberator. Free peoples, be mindful of this
45 maxim: "Liberty may be gained, but can never be recovered."

There is for nations, as for men, a threshold of maturity before which they should not be made subject to laws. But the maturity of a
50 people is not always easily recognizable, and, if it is anticipated, the work is spoiled. One people is amenable to discipline from the beginning; another, not after ten centuries. Russia will never be really civilized, because it was civilized too
55 soon. Peter the Great had a genius for imitation, but he lacked true genius, which is creative and makes all from nothing. He did some good things, but most of what he did was out of place. He saw that his nation was barbarous, but did not see
60 that it was not ripe for civilization: he wanted to civilize it when it needed only hardening. His first wish was to make Germans or Englishmen, when he ought to have been making Russians; and he prevented his subjects from ever becoming what
65 they might have been by persuading them that they were what they are not. In this fashion too a French teacher turns out his pupil to be an infant prodigy, and for the rest of his life to be nothing whatsoever. The empire of Russia will aspire to
70 conquer Europe, but will itself be conquered. The Tartars,[2] its subjects or neighbors, will become its masters and ours, by a revolution that I regard as inevitable.

[1] the peoples of two regions of ancient Greece
[2] a Mongol-Turkic tribe of Eurasia

1   **1**

33

This passage is primarily concerned with

A) restoring the reputation of some widely maligned leaders of the past.

B) comparing the merits of various ancient systems of government.

C) examining the social conditions that foster effective legal systems.

D) establishing the philosophical basis for universal democracy.

34

In line 2, the word "sounds" most nearly means

A) resonates.

B) enunciates.

C) probes.

D) appears.

35

In the first paragraph, the author discusses the activities of an architect in order to make the point that

A) the success of a nation's civil code depends on the nature of its people.

B) good laws must be based on sound philosophical principles.

C) nations that lack good laws cannot support a professional class.

D) effective government requires experts to design civic infrastructure.

36

The author suggests that long-established societies are characterized primarily by

A) stubborn resistance to political change.

B) an honorable respect for good laws.

C) periodic but predictable social renewal.

D) a tendency toward imperialist expansion.

37

Which sentence provides the best evidence for the answer to the previous question?

A) Lines 9–12 ("Also, good laws . . . vice")

B) Lines 19–21 ("Once customs . . . reformation")

C) Lines 30–34 ("Horror . . . vigor of youth")

D) Lines 71–73 ("The Tartars . . . as inevitable")

CONTINUE ➤

1   **1**

38

In lines 17–18, the distinction between "peoples" and "men" is essentially one between

A) barbarism and civilization.

B) societies and individuals.

C) youth and maturity.

D) rebellion and obedience.

39

The author mentions "Sparta at the time of Lycurgus" (line 35) primarily as an example of a place where

A) the citizens were paralyzed with fear in the face of invasion.

B) the society was rejuvenated through conflict.

C) the people lost sight of their own sacred traditions.

D) the leaders had become foolish and cowardly.

40

In lines 37–38, the phrase "particular constitution of the state" refers most specifically to

A) the documented rules by which a nation defines its governmental institutions.

B) the social composition and cultural habits of a population.

C) the enumeration of popular rights in a democratic society.

D) a manifesto about the philosophical motivations for political change.

CONTINUE →

1   **1**

41

In line 52, the phrase "amenable to discipline" most nearly means

A) ready to be governed by the rule of law.

B) susceptible to exploitation by neighboring countries.

C) prepared to accept an oppressive ruler.

D) trained for offensive or defensive military activity.

42

The author suggests that Peter the Great's main flaw was

A) military ruthlessness.

B) undue reverence for custom.

C) excessive political guile.

D) irresolution in exerting control.

CONTINUE ➤

1   1

**Questions 43–52 are based on the
following passage.**

This passage is adapted from Bertrand Russell, *A
History of Western Philosophy*. ©1945 by Bertrand
Russell, renewed by Edith Russell. Reprinted with
permission of Simon & Schuster.

To understand the views of Aristotle, as of most
Greeks, on physics, it is necessary to apprehend
his imaginative background. Every philosopher,
in addition to the formal system that he offers to
the world, has another much simpler system of
which he may be quite unaware. If he is aware of
it, he probably realizes that it won't quite do; he
therefore conceals it, and sets forth something more
sophisticated, which he believes because it is like
his crude system, but which he asks others to accept
because he thinks he has made it such as cannot
be disproved. The sophistication comes in by way
of refutation of refutations, but this alone will never
give a positive result. It shows, at best, that a theory
may be true, not that it must be. The positive result,
however little the philosopher may realize it, is
due to his imaginative preconceptions, or to what
Santayana calls "animal faith."

In relation to physics, Aristotle's imaginative
background was very different from that of a
modern student. Nowadays, students begin with
mechanics, which, by its very name, suggests
machines. They are accustomed to automobiles
and airplanes; they do not, even in the dimmest
recesses of their subconscious imagination,
think that an automobile contains some sort of
horse inside, or that an airplane flies because
its wings are those of a bird possessing magical
powers. Animals have lost their importance in
our imaginative pictures of the world, in which
humans stand comparatively alone as masters of
a mainly lifeless and largely subservient material
environment.

To the ancient Greek, attempting to give
a scientific account of motion, the purely
mechanical view hardly suggested itself,
except in the case of a few men of genius such
as Democritus and Archimedes. Two sets of
phenomena seemed important: the movements
of animals, and the movements of the heavenly
bodies. To the modern man of science, the body
of an animal is a very elaborate machine, with
an enormously complex physical and chemical
structure. Every new discovery consists in
diminishing the apparent gulf between animals
and machines. To the Greek, it seemed more
natural to assimilate apparently lifeless motions
to those of animals. A child still distinguishes live
animals from other things by the fact that animals
can move themselves. To many Greeks, and
especially to Aristotle, this peculiarity suggested
itself as the basis of a general theory of physics.

But how about the heavenly bodies? They
differ from animals by the regularity of their
movements, but this may be only due to their
superior perfection. Every Greek philosopher,
whatever he may have come to think in adult life,
had been taught in childhood to regard the sun
and moon as gods. Anaxagoras was prosecuted
for impiety because he thought that they were
not alive. It was natural that a philosopher who
could no longer regard the heavenly bodies
themselves as divine should think of them as
moved by the will of a Divine Being who had a
Hellenic love of order and geometric simplicity.
Thus the ultimate source of all movement is
Will: on earth the capricious Will of human
beings, but in heaven the unchanging Will of the
Supreme Artificer.

CONTINUE ▶

1   **1**

43

The passage as a whole primarily serves to

A) contrast the ideas of several ancient Greek philosophers.

B) examine the means by which philosophical ideas become popular.

C) describe the conceptions that inform a particular mindset.

D) discuss the debt that modern physics owes to ancient thinkers.

44

The statement that "animals have lost their importance" (line 29) means that

A) humans no longer treat other species with appropriate respect.

B) animistic beliefs no longer inform our physical theories.

C) scientists no longer regard animal behavior as a productive topic of study.

D) humans do not use animals for transportation to the extent that they once did.

45

The "simpler system" in line 5 is a

A) method for translating complex writings of ancient thinkers.

B) streamlined system for reaching logically valid conclusions.

C) formal theory based on a very small number of assumptions.

D) relatively unrefined way of thinking.

46

Which of the following statements about ancient Greek philosophers is best supported by the passage?

A) Their astronomical theories were closely associated with their religious ideas.

B) Their ideas about mechanics inspired many important technological innovations.

C) They regarded human intellect as a divine gift, rather than a cultivated skill.

D) They valued imagination and creativity even more than reason and logic.

47

Which sentence provides the best evidence for the answer to the previous question?

A) Lines 3–6 ("Every philosopher . . . quite unaware")

B) Lines 41–46 ("To the modern . . . animals and machines")

C) Lines 46–48 ("To the Greek . . . of animals")

D) Lines 61–65 ("It was natural . . . simplicity")

48

In line 47, "assimilate" most nearly means

A) incorporate.

B) comprehend.

C) embrace.

D) liken.

CONTINUE ➡

1   **1**

49

The passage suggests that the "men of genius" (line 37) are noteworthy for their

A) creative metaphors for the laws of motion.

B) ability to integrate many different fields of study.

C) effectiveness in articulating their ideas to others.

D) willingness to disregard conventional wisdom.

50

Which of the following would best bridge the "gulf" in line 45?

A) creating a system of gestures to help humans better communicate with dolphins

B) writing a computer program that analyzes and categorizes mockingbird calls

C) discovering the mechanical laws that describe bumblebee flight

D) teaching modern students more about ancient Greek philosophy

51

The passage suggests that the "views of Aristotle" (line 1) are characterized primarily by their

A) logical rigor.

B) animistic tendencies.

C) reliance on refutation.

D) unwavering skepticism.

52

Which sentence provides the best evidence for the answer to the previous question?

A) Lines 3–6 ("Every philosopher . . . quite unaware")

B) Lines 12–14 ("The sophistication . . . positive result")

C) Lines 19–21 ("In relation . . . modern student")

D) Lines 46–48 ("To the Greek . . . animals")

STOP

If you finish before time is called, you may check your work on this section only.
Do not turn to any other section of the test.

2　　　　　　　　　　　　　　　　　　　　　**2**

Writing and Language Test
35 MINUTES, 44 QUESTIONS

Turn to Section 2 of your answer sheet to answer the questions in this section.

DIRECTIONS

Each passage below is accompanied by a number of questions. For some questions, you will consider how the passage might be revised to improve the expression of ideas. For other questions, you will consider how the passage might be edited to correct errors in sentence structure, usage, or punctuation. A passage or a question may be accompanied by one or more graphics (such as a table or graph) that you will consider as you make revising and editing decisions.

Some questions will direct you to an underlined portion of a passage. Other questions will direct you to a location in a passage or ask you to think about the passage as a whole.

After reading each passage, choose the answer to each question that most effectively improves the quality of writing in the passage or that makes the passage conform to the conventions of Standard Written English. Many questions include a "NO CHANGE" option. Choose that option if you think the best choice is to leave the relevant portion of the passage as it is.

CONTINUE ➡

2   **2**

Questions 1–11 are based on the following passage and supplementary material.

Physician Assistants

As the American population grows, ages, and gains better access to affordable health insurance, the demand for primary medical services **1** are expected to skyrocket. As a result, the United States Department of Health and Human Services projects a shortage of about 20,000 primary care physicians by 2020. Therefore, an important challenge facing the healthcare industry is how to address this shortfall without sacrificing quality of care. One possible solution is to **2** elevate more medical school graduates to choose primary care as their field instead of **3** their choosing the more lucrative specialties like surgery and dermatology.

1

A) NO CHANGE
B) is
C) has been
D) would be

2

A) NO CHANGE
B) interest
C) incentivize
D) expect

3

A) NO CHANGE
B) to choose the more lucrative specialties
C) the more lucrative specialties
D) the more lucrative specialties they might choose

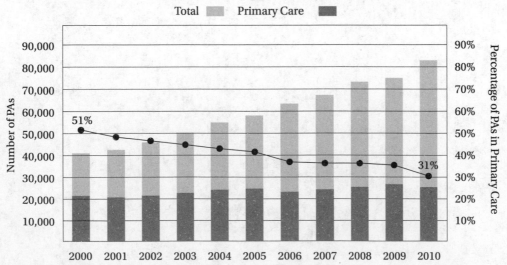

PAs (PHYSICIAN ASSISTANTS) IN THE U.S.

Total █ Primary Care █

Source: American Academy of PAs, *American Medical News*, September 27, 2011

2   **2**

[1] Another option is to incorporate more medical professionals like physician assistants (PAs) and nurse practitioners (NPs) into primary care teams. [2] They can talk with patients about treatment options, prescribe medications, and even **4** perform technical procedures like bone marrow aspirations. [3] Many healthcare providers are moving toward this "team-based" model, **5** where physicians can better focus on their specialties while relying on trained professionals to provide other necessary services. [4] Team-based medicine allows medical practitioners to best utilize their particular skills, **6** still sharing the successes and struggles of the team. [5] If organized around the principles of professionalism, trust, communication, and accountability, these teams may be able to provide better care to patients at less cost. **7**

For all the promise of team-based primary medicine, it cannot work without an adequate supply of well-trained health professionals. Although the total number of PAs in the United States more than doubled between 2000 and 2010, **8** the number of PAs going into primary care has decreased by 20% over that same time period. In the years ahead, we must encourage more of these new PAs to choose careers in primary care.

4

A) NO CHANGE
B) performing technical procedures
C) technical procedures
D) to perform technical procedures

5

A) NO CHANGE
B) whereby
C) by this
D) when

6

A) NO CHANGE
B) while at the same time
C) while
D) although

7

The author is considering inserting the following sentence into this paragraph.

> Although they receive less training than physicians do, these professionals have advanced degrees and can provide direct treatment to patients.

Where should it be placed?

A) Immediately after sentence 1
B) Immediately after sentence 3
C) Immediately after sentence 4
D) Immediately after sentence 5

8

Which choice is best supported by the data in the graph?

A) NO CHANGE
B) the number of PAs going into primary care has increased by only 50%
C) more PAs have gone into dermatology than into primary care
D) the fraction of those PAs going into primary care has declined from over one-half to under one-third

CONTINUE ➡

2   **2**

Undergraduate students considering a career in medicine have many more options 9 than they did just a generation ago. Graduate PA and NP programs, which take about three years, are becoming increasingly attractive, especially 10 being that MD programs, including residency, lasting seven to ten years and often leave students saddled with tens of thousands of dollars in debt.

Anyone thinking about pursuing a PA or NP degree should keep in mind that these programs aren't cheap, either, and that most states impose strict limits on the kinds of treatment 11 they can provide.

9

A) NO CHANGE
B) than
C) than it was
D) to choose from than

10

A) NO CHANGE
B) when MD programs, including residence, are lasting
C) being that MD programs last, including residency,
D) because MD programs, including residency, can last

11

A) NO CHANGE
B) he or she
C) these professions
D) these professionals

2

2

Questions 12–22 are based on the following passage.

Maria Montessori

What is education? Is it a program of institutionally approved performances, or a collection of self-directed experiences? Such questions absorbed Maria Montessori throughout her life. Born in 1870 in **12** Chiaravalle Italy, Montessori showed a strong independent will even as a child. As a teenager, she told her parents that she wanted to study engineering, **13** a position that was widely thought unladylike. By the age of 20, she had changed her mind and decided to pursue an even less traditional path: medicine. Despite suffering ridicule and isolation, **14** Montessori's medical studies at the University of Rome were completed and she became one of the first female physicians in Italy.

Although Montessori's practice focused on psychiatry, her interests gravitated toward education. In 1900, she was appointed co-director of the *Scuola Magistrale Ortofrenica*, a training institute for special education teachers. Montessori believed that, in order for so-called "deficient" children to thrive, they needed respect and stimulation rather than **15** the regimentation they were receiving in institutions.

12

A) NO CHANGE

B) Chiaravalle, Italy. Montessori showed a strong independent will, even

C) Chiaravalle, Italy, Montessori showed a strong, independent will, even

D) Chiaravalle, Italy; Montessori showed a strong, independent will even

13

A) NO CHANGE

B) despite its reputation for being unladylike

C) although widely considered unladylike

D) which was unladylike in reputation

14

A) NO CHANGE

B) Montessori completed her medical studies at the University of Rome by becoming

C) Montessori's medical studies were completed, at the University of Rome, and thus she became

D) Montessori completed her medical studies at the University of Rome and became

15

A) NO CHANGE

B) receiving regimentation in institutions

C) the regimented institutions they were receiving

D) the regimentation of the institutions they were receiving

2 **2**

In 1907 Maria opened the Casa dei Bambini, or "Children's House," a daycare center for impoverished children in which she could test her theory that **16** children's minds each learn according to they're own schedule. She personalized a curriculum for each child rather than providing a standardized course of study. While learning important academic and life skills, many formerly aggressive and unmanageable children became more emotionally balanced and self-directed. Word of her success with the Casa dei Bambini soon began to **17** distribute internationally, and her methods for child-centered education became widely adopted across Europe.

18 In the 25 years after their founding, Montessori schools were regarded as a remedy to the educational problems associated with rapid urban population

16

A) NO CHANGE

B) each child's mind learns according to its own schedule

C) childrens' minds learn according to its own schedule

D) children's minds each learn according to their own schedule

17

A) NO CHANGE

B) increase

C) spread

D) exhibit

18

Which choice provides the most effective introduction to this paragraph?

A) Montessori dedicated herself to travelling the world and preaching the benefits of child-centered education.

B) Montessori's first school enrolled 50 students from poor working families.

C) Montessori did not have a particularly nurturing relationship with her own son, Mario, who was raised by another family.

D) As the Montessori method was gaining a foothold, Europe was undergoing dramatic social and political change.

2

2

growth throughout Europe. **19** So as fascism began to proliferate in the 1930s throughout Spain, Italy, and Germany, child-centered education came to be seen as a threat to the power of the state. In 1933, the totalitarian regimes in Italy and Germany closed all Montessori schools and declared **20** them subversive and that they were undermining their power.

Even outside of Europe, **21** the response to Montessori's ideas were divided. Many eminent scholars, inventors, and politicians—among them Alexander Graham Bell, Helen Keller, Thomas Edison, Mahatma Gandhi, and Woodrow Wilson— greeted her ideas with enthusiasm. But her theories were challenged by William H. Kirkpatrick, a leading educational reformer and professor at Teachers College, Columbia University. His 1914 book, *The Montessori System Examined*, declared Montessori's psychological theories wildly out-of-date. **22**

It was not until 1958 that a new generation of Montessorians revived and updated her methods in the United States. In 1958, the first American Montessori school, the Whitby School, was founded in Greenwich, Connecticut, where it thrives today.

19

A) NO CHANGE
B) When
C) However, as
D) Furthermore, as

20

A) NO CHANGE
B) that they were subversive in undermining their power
C) them subversive in undermining power
D) them subversive

21

A) NO CHANGE
B) the response to Montessori's ideas was
C) Montessori's ideas had a response that was
D) Montessori's ideas response was

22

At this point, the paragraph would benefit most from a discussion of

A) how Kirkpatrick's book was received among American educators
B) why totalitarian governments regarded Montessori's methods as a threat
C) those American educators whose influence was comparable to Montessori's
D) how other reform movements of the era contrasted with Montessori's

CONTINUE →

2   2

Questions 23–33 are based on the following passage.

Platonic Forms

When we look at the moon, we see a spherical object. But do "spheres" really exist? This may seem to be a silly question, because it's not hard to understand the definition of a sphere: "the set of all points in space that are a fixed distance (called the radius) from a fixed point (called the center)." We see examples of "spherical" objects all the time, don't we?

[23] First, nothing that we can observe in our physical world [24] complies perfectly to this mathematical definition of a sphere. The moon, a beach ball, and even water droplets are all "bumpy," at least at the atomic level. So can we say that the concept of "sphere" is real [25] if there is no such thing as a real sphere?

Pondering this question as so many ancient Greek philosophers did, [26] the argument Plato made was that the sphere is an "ideal form," inaccessible to our physical senses yet [27] the mind can apprehend it

23

A) NO CHANGE
B) So
C) While
D) In fact,

24

A) NO CHANGE
B) overlaps
C) corresponds
D) concurs

25

A) NO CHANGE
B) where no such thing exists
C) as if nothing is
D) if there were nothing

26

A) NO CHANGE
B) it was Plato who argued
C) Plato had argued
D) Plato argued

27

A) NO CHANGE
B) it can be apprehended by the mind
C) apprehensible to the mind
D) it is apprehensible to the mind

2　　　　　　　　　　　　**2**

through pure reason. He also reasoned that, since our senses can be fooled, logic provides a much more reliable path to the truth. Therefore, a Platonic idealist believes that these abstract forms are **28** as effective, if not more so, than sensory experience at revealing the nature of reality. **29**

Modern scientists and philosophers are unlikely to be Platonic idealists. Today, we can understand the origin of abstract concepts **30** and not having to believe that they come from a higher, physically inaccessible reality. We simply need to understand **31** the process by which our brains make inferences.

Take an abstract idea like "orangeness." Most of us would say that orangeness "exists" because we see examples of it every day, such as carrots, traffic cones, and pumpkins. But what if, by some magic, we could remove all orange-colored objects from the universe? In other words, what if, as with "sphereness," no real examples of "orangeness" **32** would exist? Would "orangeness" still exist?

28

A) NO CHANGE
B) as effective as, if not more effective than,
C) as effective, if not more effective, than
D) equally as effective, if not more effective than,

29

At this point, the author is considering adding the following true statement:

> The sphere is just one of many ideal forms, like lines and tetrahedrons, that are studied in geometry.

Should the author make this addition here?

A) Yes, because it indicates a particular application of ideal forms.
B) Yes, because explains a claim made in the previous sentence.
C) No, because it detracts from this paragraph's discussion of philosophy.
D) No, because it undermines the Platonists' point of view.

30

A) NO CHANGE
B) in not having to believe
C) and not be believing
D) without having to believe

31

A) NO CHANGE
B) our brain's process by which they
C) the process by which our brain's
D) the process by which our brain

32

A) NO CHANGE
B) would have existed
C) existed
D) had an existence

CONTINUE ▶

In an important sense, the answer is yes. We can demonstrate the existence of "orangeness" without appealing to any higher reality. We could measure the wavelength of red light (about 650 nm), and yellow light (about 570 nm) and make the reasonable inference, because wavelengths fall on a continuum, that a color exists with an intermediate wavelength, of 610 nm, even if we have never directly measured such light.

Our brains do not contain sophisticated instruments for measuring wavelengths of light, but they do make similar inferences constantly. **33** For instance, when you drive, you unconsciously make inferences about quantities like the speeds of surrounding cars and qualities like dangerous driving conditions. Our brains are continually making inferences based on the limited information from our senses, and these inferences are the substance of abstract thought.

33

Which of the following changes would best improve this sentence's cohesiveness with the rest of the paragraph?

A) Change "For instance" to "Nevertheless."

B) Change both instances of "you" to "we."

C) Change "you unconsciously make changes" to "changes are unconsciously made"

D) Delete the phrase "like dangerous driving conditions."

2   **2**

Questions 34–44 are based on the following passage and supplementary material.

The Eureka Effect

You've probably had the experience. After racking your brain for hours to solve a problem, you finally put it aside and move on to other things. Then, much later, seemingly out of [34] nowhere, perhaps while showering or driving—the answer suddenly strikes you. Psychologists call this the "Eureka effect," from the ancient Greek word meaning "I have found it," [35] which Archimides is said to have shouted as he ran naked from his bathtub through the streets of Syracuse upon suddenly solving a vexing physics problem.

Does this feeling arise from our emotional centers or our cognitive centers? In other words, is it simply an emotional response to finding a solution, or does it [36] foretell a fundamentally different way of thinking? Psychologists have tried to answer this question by looking inside subjects' brains as they solve problems, using electroencephalograms (EEGs) and other tools.

34

A) NO CHANGE
B) nowhere—perhaps
C) nowhere: perhaps
D) nowhere; perhaps

35

A) NO CHANGE
B) what Archmides is said to shout
C) that Archimedes shouted, it is said
D) which Archimedes it is said had shouted

36

A) NO CHANGE
B) indicate
C) provide
D) generate

CONTINUE ➡

2   2

In one **37** experiment, subjects performed a word association task, scientists measured the activity in the region of the brain called the right hemisphere anterior superior temporal gyrus (RH aSTG). This region is known to be active in tasks, such as finding a theme in a story, **38** that requires integrating and bringing together information from many distant parts of the brain, but is not particularly active in emotional responses.

The subjects were asked to perform a challenging verbal association task, press a button as soon as **39** solving it, and report whether or not they felt the "Aha!" feeling. If they did, the response was classified as an "insight" solution. If they did not, it was classified as a "non-insight" solution.

40 What was interesting, experimenters found that the insight solutions were accompanied by an elevated level of "gamma band" activity in the RH aSTG, supporting the theory that the feeling **41** had corresponded

37

A) NO CHANGE
B) experiment by which subjects
C) experiment where subjects
D) experiment, in which subjects

38

A) NO CHANGE
B) that require integrating and bringing together
C) that require integrating
D) that requires integrating

39

A) NO CHANGE
B) it was being solved
C) they solved it
D) it's solution

40

A) NO CHANGE
B) The interesting thing was that
C) It was interesting that
D) Interestingly,

41

A) NO CHANGE
B) corresponds
C) is corresponding
D) will correspond

2   **2**

to a cognitive process rather than purely an

emotional one. **42**

    Interpreting **43** <u>this data is</u> not a very simple

matter, however. Many questions remain to be

answered. For instance, does the increased gamma-

band activity represent a transition of cognitive

processing from an unconscious state to a conscious

one? **44** <u>If that is true, a question would be what are</u>

<u>the unconscious processes that are working? Also, in</u>

<u>what way do those processes become conscious all of a</u>

<u>sudden?</u>

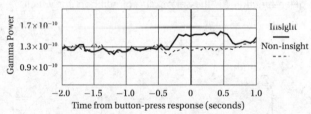

GAMMA-BAND INTENSITY IN RIGHT ANTERIOR TEMPORAL REGION
DURING VERBAL ASSOCIATION TASK

Source: Adapted from Beeman, Bowden et al., "Neural Activity
When People Solve Problems with Insight," *PLOS*, 2004

42

At this point in the passage, the author wants to
mention specific evidence indicated by the graph.
Which statement is most justified by the data in
this graph?

A) The gamma power in the RH aSTG for the
insight solution is more than double that for
the non-insight solution.

B) This increase in activity seems to begin about
0.3 seconds prior to the button-press response,
and to lasts about 1 second.

C) The gamma activity for the insight solution
appears to be roughly equivalent to that for
the non-insight solution until the instant the
button is pushed.

D) This increase in activity seems to begin about
0.3 seconds after the button-press response,
and to last about 0.5 second.

43

A) NO CHANGE

B) this data are

C) these data are

D) these data is

44

Which of the following best combines the last two
sentences into one?

A) If so, what are the unconscious processes that
are working, suddenly becoming conscious?

B) If so, what unconscious processes are at work,
and how do they suddenly become conscious?

C) If so, what would be the unconscious processes
working, and how would they suddenly
become conscious?

D) If so, what are both the unconscious process
at work, and how do they suddenly become
conscious?

STOP

**If you finish before time is called, you may check your work on this section only.
Do not turn to any other section of the test.**

3 **3**

Math Test – No Calculator
25 MINUTES, 20 QUESTIONS

Turn to Section 3 of your answer sheet to answer the questions in this section.

DIRECTIONS

For questions 1–15, solve each problem, choose the best answer from the choices provided, and fill in the corresponding circle on your answer sheet. **For questions 16–20,** solve the problem and enter your answer in the grid on the answer sheet. Please refer to the directions before question 16 on how to enter you answers in the grid. You may use any available space in your test booklet for scratch work.

NOTES

1. The use of a calculator is NOT permitted.

2. All variables and expressions used represent real numbers unless otherwise indicated.

3. Figures provided in this test are drawn to scale unless otherwise indicated.

4. All figures lie in a plane unless otherwise indicated.

5. Unless otherwise indicated, the domain of a given function f is the set of all real numbers for which $f(x)$ is a real number.

REFERENCE

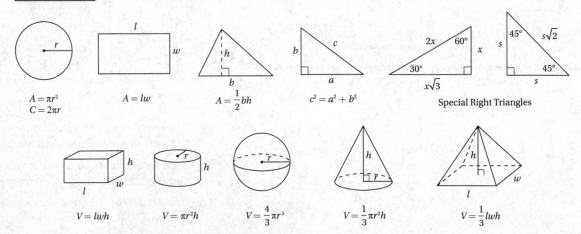

$A = \pi r^2$
$C = 2\pi r$

$A = lw$

$A = \dfrac{1}{2}bh$

$c^2 = a^2 + b^2$

Special Right Triangles

$V = lwh$

$V = \pi r^2 h$

$V = \dfrac{4}{3}\pi r^3$

$V = \dfrac{1}{3}\pi r^2 h$

$V = \dfrac{1}{3}lwh$

The number of degrees of arc in a circle is 360.
The number of radians of arc in a circle is 2π.
The sum of the measures in degrees of the angles of a triangle is 180.

CONTINUE ➔

3 **3**

1

If $6x + 9 = 30$, what is the value of $2x + 3$?

A) 5

B) 10

C) 15

D) 20

2

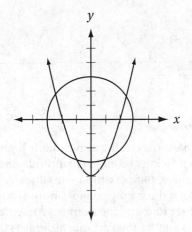

$$x^2 + y^2 = 9$$
$$y = x^2 - 4$$

A system of two equations and their graphs in the xy-plane are shown above. How many solutions does the system have?

A) One

B) Two

C) Three

D) Four

3

A total of 300 tickets were sold for a performance of a school play. The ticket prices were \$5 for each adult and \$3 for each child, and the total revenue from tickets was \$1,400. Solving which of the following systems of equations would yield the number of adult tickets sold, a, and the number of children's tickets sold, c ?

A) $a + c = 1,400$
   $5a + 3c = 300$

B) $a + c = 300$
   $5a + 3c = 1,400$

C) $a + c = 300$
   $3a + 5c = 1,400$

D) $a + c = 300$
   $3a + 5c = 1,400 \times 2$

4

Which of the following expressions is equivalent to $2(x - 4)^2 - 5x$?

A) $2x^2 - 21x + 32$

B) $2x^2 - 21x - 32$

C) $2x^2 - 13x + 32$

D) $2x^2 - 16x - 21$

5

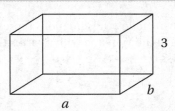

Note: Figure not drawn to scale

A rectangular solid above has dimensions 3, a, and b, where a and b are integers. Which of the following CANNOT be the areas of three different faces of this solid?

A) 15, 18, and 30

B) 18, 24, and 48

C) 12, 15, and 24

D) 15, 24, and 40

CONTINUE ➤

3 **3**

6

The cost in dollars, C, to manufacture n necklaces is given by the equation $C(n) = an + b$, where a and b are positive constants. In this equation, what does a represent?

A) the fixed costs, in dollars, independent of any necklaces being manufactured

B) the total cost, in dollars, to produce n necklaces, not including fixed costs

C) the total cost, in dollars, to produce one necklace, including fixed costs

D) the cost, in dollars, to produce one necklace, not including any fixed costs

7

Line l intersects the graph of the function $f(x) = 2x^2 - 4x + 1$ at two points where $x = -1$ and $x = 2$, respectively. What is the slope of line l ?

A) -2

B) $-\dfrac{2}{3}$

C) $\dfrac{3}{2}$

D) 2

8

Which of the following equations represents a parabola in the xy-plane with a vertex that lies on the x-axis?

A) $y = (x - 3)^2 + 2$

B) $y = 2(x - 3)^2$

C) $y = 2x^2 - 3$

D) $y = 3x^2 + 2$

9

If the function $m(x)$ satisfies the equation $\dfrac{m(x)}{x+3} - \dfrac{x+1}{x-1} = 1$ for all values of x greater than 1, then $m(x) =$

A) $\dfrac{2(x+3)}{x-1}$

B) $\dfrac{2(x^2 + 3x + 3)}{x-1}$

C) $\dfrac{2(x+6)}{x-1}$

D) $\dfrac{2x(x+3)}{x-1}$

10

In the mesosphere, the atmospheric layer between 50 km and 80 km in altitude, the average atmospheric temperature varies linearly with altitude. If the average temperature at 50 km altitude is 10°C and the average temperature at 80 km is −80°C, then at what altitude is the average temperature −50°C?

A) 60 km

B) 65 km

C) 70 km

D) 75 km

11

The graph of the equation $y = 2x^2 - 16x + 14$ intersects the y-axis at point A and the x-axis at points B and C. What is the area of triangle ABC ?

A) 42

B) 48

C) 54

D) 56

CONTINUE

3   **3**

12

What is the total number of x- and y-intercepts in the graph of the equation $y = (x + 2)^2(x - 3)^2$?

A) Two

B) Three

C) Four

D) Five

13

If the complex number A satisfies the equation

$A(2 - i) = 2 + i$, where $i = \sqrt{-1}$, what is the value

of A ?

A) $5 - i$

B) $5 + i$

C) $\dfrac{3}{5} + \dfrac{4}{5}i$

D) $\dfrac{3}{4} + \dfrac{5}{4}i$

14

If $k > 2$, which of the following could be the graph of $y + x = k(x - 1)$ in the xy-plane?

A)

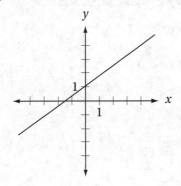

B)

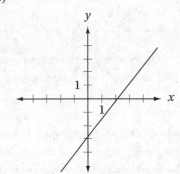

C)

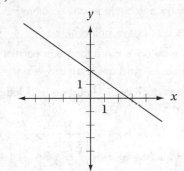

D)

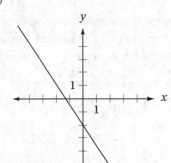

15

The function $g(x) = ax^3 + bx^2 + cx + d$ has zeroes at $x = -2$, $x = 3$, and $x = 6$. If $g(0) < 0$, which of the following must also be negative?

A) $g(-3)$

B) $g(-1)$

C) $g(4)$

D) $g(5)$

CONTINUE ➡

DIRECTIONS

For questions 16–20, solve the problem and enter your answer in the grid, as described below, on the answer sheet.

1. Although not required, it is suggested that you write your answer in the boxes at the top of the columns to help you fill in the circles accurately. You will receive credit only if the circles are filled in correctly.

2. Mark no more than one circle in any column.

3. No question has a negative answer.

4. Some problems may have more than one correct answer. In such cases, grid only one answer.

5. **Mixed numbers** such as $3\frac{1}{2}$ must be gridded as 3.5 or $\frac{7}{2}$.

   (If $3\frac{1}{2}$ is entered into the grid as [3 1 / 2], it will be interpreted as $\frac{31}{2}$, not $3\frac{1}{2}$).

6. **Decimal answers:** If you obtain a decimal answer with more digits than the grid can accommodate, it may be either rounded or truncated, but it must fill the entire grid.

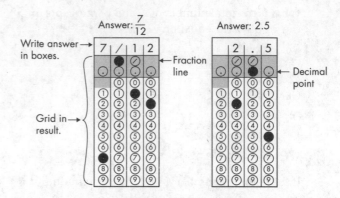

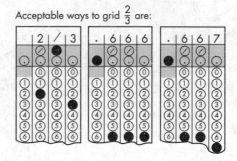

CONTINUE ▶

3   **3**

If $\dfrac{2}{3}x + \dfrac{1}{2}y = 5$, what is the value of $4x + 3y$?

If $\dfrac{5}{x} - \dfrac{2}{5} = 1$, what is the value of x?

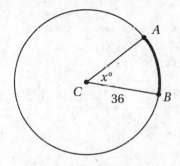

Note: Figure not drawn to scale.

In the circle above, arc AB has a measure of 7π. What is the value of x?

$$\frac{1}{2}x = \frac{1}{3}y + \frac{1}{10}$$
$$6x - 4y = k$$

For what value of k will the system of equations above have at least one solution?

If x represents the radian measure of an angle, where $0 \le x \le \dfrac{\pi}{2}$, and $\sin x = \dfrac{5}{13}$, then what is the value of $\tan\left(\dfrac{\pi}{2} - x\right)$?

STOP

If you finish before time is called, you may check your work on this section only. Do not turn to any other section of the test.

4 **4**

Math Test – Calculator
55 MINUTES, 38 QUESTIONS

Turn to Section 4 of your answer sheet to answer the questions in this section.

DIRECTIONS

For questions 1–30, solve each problem, choose the best answer from the choices provided, and fill in the corresponding circle on your answer sheet. **For questions 31–38,** solve the problem and enter your answer in the grid on the answer sheet. Please refer to the directions before question 31 on how to enter your answers in the grid. You may use any available space in your test booklet for scratch work.

NOTES

1. The use of a calculator **is permitted.**

2. All variables and expressions used represent real numbers unless otherwise indicated.

3. Figures provided in this test are drawn to scale unless otherwise indicated.

4. All figures lie in a plane unless otherwise indicated.

5. Unless otherwise indicated, the domain of a given function f is the set of all real numbers for which $f(x)$ is a real number.

REFERENCE

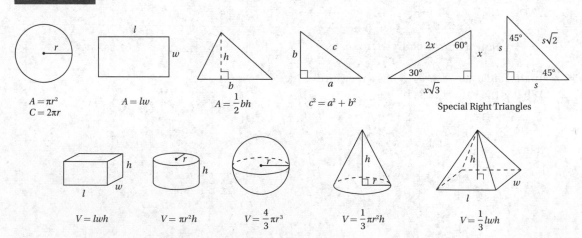

$A = \pi r^2$
$C = 2\pi r$

$A = lw$

$A = \frac{1}{2}bh$

$c^2 = a^2 + b^2$

Special Right Triangles

$V = lwh$

$V = \pi r^2 h$

$V = \frac{4}{3}\pi r^3$

$V = \frac{1}{3}\pi r^2 h$

$V = \frac{1}{3}lwh$

The number of degrees of arc in a circle is 360.
The number of radians of arc in a circle is 2π.
The sum of the measures in degrees of the angles of a triangle is 180.

CONTINUE ➡

4   4

1

$$a - b = 10$$
$$a - 2b = 8$$

Based on the system of equations above, what is the value of b ?

A) −2

B) −1

C)   1

D)   2

2

The average (arithmetic mean) of three numbers is 50. If two of the numbers have a sum of 85, what is the third number?

A) 75

B) 70

C) 65

D) 55

3

What number is the same percent of 225 as 9 is of 25?

A) 27

B) 54

C) 64

D) 81

4

RESULTS OF FAVORABILITY POLL

	Favorable	Unfavorable	No Opinion	Total
Men	26		12	
Women			13	89
Total	59			162

The table above shows the partial results of a favorability poll for a local politician. If the data shown are correct, how many of the women who were polled viewed the politician unfavorably?

A) 33

B) 43

C) 61

D) It cannot be determined by the information given.

5

If $2^{2n-2} = 32$, what is the value of n ?

A) 2.0

B) 2.5

C) 3.0

D) 3.5

6

A bag of Nellie's Nut Mix contains x ounces of walnuts, 15 ounces of peanuts, and 20 ounces of pecans. Which of the following expresses the fraction of the mix, by weight, that is walnuts?

A) $\dfrac{x}{35}$

B) $\dfrac{x}{35 - x}$

C) $\dfrac{x}{35 + x}$

D) $\dfrac{35 - x}{35 + x}$

CONTINUE

7

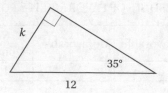

In the triangle above, what is the value of k?
($\sin 35° = 0.574$, $\cos 35° = 0.819$, $\tan 35° = 0.700$)

A) 6.00

B) 6.88

C) 8.40

D) 9.83

8

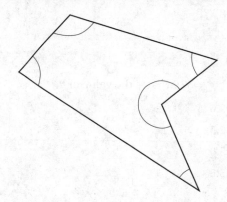

The figure above shows a polygon with five sides. What is the average (arithmetic mean) of the measures, in degrees, of the five angles shown?

A) 108°

B) 110°

C) 112°

D) 114°

Questions 9 and 10 are based on the graph below.

ANNUAL REVENUE PER STORE

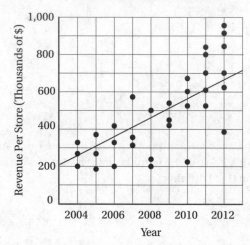

9

The scatterplot above shows the annual revenue for each of the individual retail stores operated by a clothing company for each year from 2004 through 2012. Based on the line of best fit to the data shown, which of the following is closest to the average annual increase in revenue per store?

A) $5,000

B) $50,000

C) $100,000

D) $500,000

4   **4**

10

Which of the following statements is most directly justified by the data shown in the scatterplot above?

A) The average revenue per store increased by over 100% from 2005 to 2009.

B) The total number of retail stores increased by 50% from 2005 to 2012.

C) The total revenue from all stores in 2012 was more than three times the total revenue from all stores in 2004.

D) The total revenue from all stores in 2008 was over $1 million.

11

Which of the following statements expresses the fact that the product of two numbers, a and b, is 6 greater than their sum?

A) $ab + 6 > a + b$

B) $ab = a + b + 6$

C) $ab + 6 = a + b$

D) $ab > a + b + 6$

12

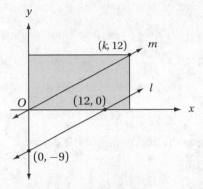

Note: Figure not drawn to scale.

In the figure above, if $m \parallel l$, what is the area, in square units, of the shaded rectangle?

A) 156

B) 168

C) 180

D) 192

13

The Glenville Giants have played a total of 120 games and have a win-to-loss ratio of 2 to 3. How many more games have they lost than won?

A) 24

B) 30

C) 40

D) 48

CONTINUE ➡

4 **4**

14

A culture of bacteria initially contained p cells, where $p > 100$. After one hour, this population decreased by $\dfrac{1}{3}$. In the second and third hours, however, the population increased by 40% and 50%, respectively. At the end of those first three hours, what was the population of the culture?

A) $1.3p$

B) $1.4p$

C) $1.5p$

D) $1.6p$

15

If $(6^{-2})(m^{-2}) = \dfrac{1}{16}$, what is the value of m^2?

A) $\dfrac{1}{9}$

B) $\dfrac{4}{9}$

C) $\dfrac{9}{16}$

D) $\dfrac{9}{4}$

16

A jar contains only red, white, and blue marbles. It contains twice as many red marbles as white marbles and three times as many white marbles as blue marbles. If a marble is chosen at random, what is the probability that it is <u>not</u> red?

A) $\dfrac{1}{5}$

B) $\dfrac{2}{5}$

C) $\dfrac{3}{5}$

D) $\dfrac{4}{5}$

17

$$y = -3(x - 2)^2 + 2$$

In the xy-plane, line l passes through the point $(-1, 3)$ and the vertex of the parabola with equation above. What is the slope of line l?

A) $-\dfrac{2}{3}$

B) $-\dfrac{1}{2}$

C) $-\dfrac{1}{3}$

D) $\dfrac{1}{3}$

18

A certain function takes an input value and transforms it into an output value according to the following three-step procedure:

Step 1: Multiply the input value by 6.

Step 2: Add x to this result.

Step 3: Divide this result by 4.

If an input of 7 to this function yields an output of 15, what is the value of x?

A) 12

B) 16

C) 18

D) 24

CONTINUE ➡

4   4

19

The variables x and y are believed to correlate according to the equation $y = ax^2 + bx + c$, where a, b, and c are constants. Which of the following scatterplots would provide the strongest evidence in support of the hypothesis that $a < 0$?

A)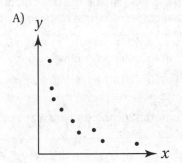

B)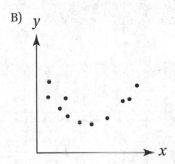

C)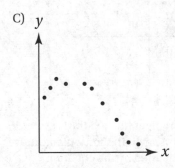

D)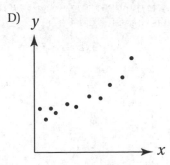

20

On a number line, the coordinates of points P and R are p and r, respectively, and $p < r$. If the point with coordinate x is closer to p than to r, then which of the following statements must be true?

A) $x < \dfrac{p-r}{2}$

B) $x < \dfrac{p+r}{2}$

C) $|x - p| < r$

D) $|x + p| < r - p$

21

Let function $f(x)$ be defined by the equation $f(x) = \dfrac{1}{2-x}$. If m is a positive integer, then $f\left(\dfrac{1}{m}\right) =$

A) $\dfrac{m}{2m-1}$

B) $\dfrac{m}{m^2 - 1}$

C) $\dfrac{1}{2-m}$

D) $2 - m$

22

The value of y varies with x according to the equation $y = a(x-2)(x+1)$, where $a < 0$. As the value of x increases from 0 to 5, which of the following best describes the behavior of y ?

A) It increases and then decreases.

B) It decreases and then increases.

C) It increases only.

D) It decreases only.

CONTINUE ➡

4 **4**

23

If the expression $\dfrac{n^2-9}{n^2+3}$ is equivalent to the

expression $1-\dfrac{k}{n^2+3}$ for all values of n, what is the

value of k?

A)   −12

B)   −6

C)   6

D)   12

24

An online trading company charges a 3% commission for all stock purchases. If a trader purchases 200 shares of a stock through this company and is charged $3,399 including commission, what is the cost per share for this stock?

A) $16.45

B) $16.48

C) $16.50

D) $16.52

25

For nonzero numbers w and y, if w is 50% greater than y, then what is the ratio of w^{-2} to y^{-2}?

A) 4 to 9

B) 2 to 3

C) 9 to 4

D) 4 to 1

26

Every athlete in a group of 60 female varsity athletes at Greenwich High School either runs track, plays soccer, or does both. If one-third of the athletes in this group who play on the soccer team also run on the track team, and one-half of the athletes in this group who run on the track team also play on the soccer team, which of the following statements must be true?

A) This group contains 40 soccer players.

B) This group contains 20 athletes who play soccer but do not run track.

C) This group contains 20 athletes who play both track and soccer.

D) The number of soccer players in this group is 15 greater than the number of track team members in this group.

27

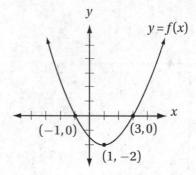

A portion of the graph of the quadratic function $y = f(x)$ is shown in the xy-plane above. The function g is defined by the equation $g(x) = f(x) + b$. If the equation $g(x) = 0$ has exactly one solution, what is the value of b?

A) −2

B) −1

C)   1

D)   2

CONTINUE ▶

4   **4**

28

If $\cos x = a$, where $\dfrac{\pi}{2} < x < \pi$, and $\cos y = -a$,

then which of the following could be the value of y?

A) $x + 2\pi$

B) $x + \pi$

C) $x + \dfrac{\pi}{2}$

D) $-x + 2\pi$

Questions 29 and 30 refer to the following table.

OPINION POLL ON PROPOSAL 81A

Age of Voter	Approve	Disapprove	No Opinion	Total
18 to 39	918	204	502	1,624
40 to 64	1,040	502	102	1,644
65 and older	604	420	115	1,139
Total	2,562	1,126	719	4,407

29

Of those surveyed who expressed an opinion on Proposal 81A, approximately what percentage are under 40 years of age?

A) 30%

B) 38%

C) 68%

D) 72%

30

If the data in the table above are assumed to be representative of the general voting population, which of the following statements is most directly justified by these data?

A) The approval rate for Proposal 81a generally decreases with the age of the voter.

B) The disapproval rate for Proposal 81a generally increases with the age of the voter.

C) Those who express an opinion on Proposal 81a are more likely to be over 64 than they are to be under 40.

D) In all three age categories, voters are more than twice as likely to approve of Proposal 81a than to have no opinion about it.

CONTINUE ➡

4   **4**

DIRECTIONS

For questions 31–38, solve the problem and enter your answer in the grid, as described below, on the answer sheet.

1. Although not required, it is suggested that you write your answer in the boxes at the top of the columns to help you fill in the circles accurately. You will receive credit only if the circles are filled in correctly.

2. Mark no more than one circle in any column.

3. No question has a negative answer.

4. Some problems may have more than one correct answer. In such cases, grid only one answer.

5. **Mixed numbers** such as $3\frac{1}{2}$ must be gridded as

   3.5 or $\frac{7}{2}$.

   (If $3\frac{1}{2}$ is entered into the grid as 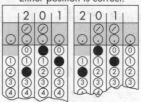, it will be

   interpreted as $\frac{31}{2}$, not $3\frac{1}{2}$.)

6. **Decimal answers:** If you obtain a decimal answer with more digits than the grid can accommodate, it may be either rounded or truncated, but it must fill the entire grid.

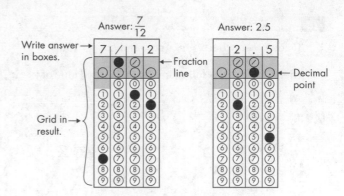

Answer: $\frac{7}{12}$ Answer: 2.5

Write answer in boxes.   Fraction line   Decimal point

Grid in result.

Answer: 201
Either position is correct.

Acceptable ways to grid $\frac{2}{3}$ are:

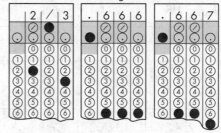

CONTINUE

4   **4**

31

If y varies inversely as x, and $y = 0.5$ when $x = 10$, then for what value of x does $y = 25$?

32

If $x^2 + 12x = 13$, and $x < 0$, what is the value of x^2 ?

33

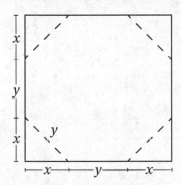

Four triangles are to be cut and removed from a square piece of sheet metal to create an octagonal sign with eight equal sides, as shown in the figure above. If the total area of the removed material is 196 square centimeters, what is the perimeter, in centimeters, of the octagon?

34

If m and n are integers such that $m^2 + n^2 = 40$ and $m < 0 < n$, what is the value of $(m + n)^2$?

35

If $(\cos x)(\sin x) = 0.2$, what is the value of $(\cos x + \sin x)^2$?

36

MONTHLY SALES (FEBRUARY)

Item	Price Per Item	Number Sold
Model AT350	$120	20
Model U32	$98	80
Model GY53	$140	62
Model CDP3	$162	38
Model AP14	$110	40

The table above shows information about the February sales for five different cell phone models at a local store. What was the median price, to the nearest dollar, of the 240 phones sold in February?

CONTINUE ➤

4 **4**

Questions 37 and 38 refer to the following information.

Performance Banner Company creates promotional banners that include company logos. The Zypz Running Shoe Company would like a 4-foot high and 20-foot long rectangular banner that includes its logo, which has a height-to-length ratio of 5:8.

37

If the logo were scaled so that its height matched the height of the banner and then were placed in the center of the banner, then what would be the width, in feet, of each margin on either side of the logo?

38

Performance Banner Company charges its customers $1.20 per square foot for the banner material, $2.50 per square foot of any printed logo, and $32 in fixed costs per banner. The Zypz Running Shoe Company is considering two options for the banner: one with a single logo, and another with two logos. If these logos are all to be the same size as described in Part 1, what percent of the banner costs would the company save by choosing the single-logo option instead of the two-logo option? (Ignore the % symbol when entering into the grid. For example, enter 27% as 27.)

STOP

**If you finish before time is called, you may check your work on this section only.
Do not turn to any other section of the test.**

No test material on this page.

| 5   **5 |**

Essay
50 MINUTES, 1 QUESTION

DIRECTIONS

As you read the passage below, consider how Steven Pinker uses

- evidence, such as facts or examples, to support his claims
- reasoning to develop ideas and connect claims and evidence
- stylistic or persuasive elements, such as word choice or appeals to emotion, to add power to the ideas expressed

Adapted from Steven Pinker, "Mind Over Mass Media." ©2010 by *The New York Times*.
Originally published June 10, 2010.

1   New forms of media have always caused moral panics: the printing press, newspapers, paperbacks and television were all once denounced as threats to their consumers' brainpower and moral fiber.

2   So too with electronic technologies. PowerPoint, we're told, is reducing discourse to bullet points. Search engines lower our intelligence, encouraging us to skim on the surface of knowledge rather than dive to its depths. Twitter is shrinking our attention spans.

3   But such panics often fail reality checks. When comic books were accused of turning juveniles into delinquents in the 1950s, crime was falling to record lows, just as the denunciations of video games in the 1990s coincided with the great American crime decline. The decades of television, transistor radios and rock videos were also decades in which I.Q. scores rose continuously.

4   For a reality check today, take the state of science, which demands high levels of brainwork and is measured by clear benchmarks of discovery. Today, scientists are never far from their e-mail and cannot lecture without PowerPoint. If electronic media were hazardous to intelligence, the quality of science would be plummeting. Yet discoveries are multiplying like fruit flies, and progress is dizzying. Other activities in the life of the mind, like philosophy, history and cultural criticism, are likewise flourishing.

5   Critics of new media sometimes use science itself to press their case, citing research that shows how "experience can change the brain." But cognitive neuroscientists roll their eyes at such talk. Yes, every time we learn a fact or skill the wiring of the brain changes; it's not as if the information is stored in the pancreas. But the existence of neural plasticity does not mean the brain is a blob of clay pounded into shape by experience.

6   Experience does not revamp the basic information-processing capacities of the brain. Speed-reading programs have long claimed to do just that, but the verdict was rendered by Woody Allen after he read War and Peace in one sitting: "It was about Russia." Genuine multitasking, too, has been exposed as a myth, not just by laboratory studies but by the familiar sight of an SUV undulating between lanes as the driver cuts deals on his cellphone.

CONTINUE

5 **5**

7   Moreover, the evidence indicates that the effects of experience are highly specific to the experiences themselves. If you train people to do one thing, they get better at doing that thing, but almost nothing else. Music doesn't make you better at math; conjugating Latin doesn't make you more logical; brain-training games don't make you smarter. Accomplished people don't bulk up their brains with intellectual calisthenics; they immerse themselves in their fields. Novelists read lots of novels; scientists read lots of science.

8   The effects of consuming electronic media are also likely to be far more limited than the panic implies. Media critics write as if the brain takes on the qualities of whatever it consumes, the informational equivalent of "you are what you eat." As with primitive peoples who believe that eating fierce animals will make them fierce, they assume that watching quick cuts in rock videos turns your mental life into quick cuts or that reading bullet points and Twitter postings turns your thoughts into bullet points and Twitter postings.

9   Yes, the constant arrival of information packets can be distracting or addictive, especially to people with attention deficit disorder. But distraction is not a new phenomenon. The solution is not to bemoan technology but to develop strategies of self-control, as we do with every other temptation in life. Turn off e-mail or Twitter when you work, put away your BlackBerry at dinner time, ask your spouse to call you to bed at a designated hour.

10   And to encourage intellectual depth, don't rail at PowerPoint or Google. It's not as if habits of deep reflection, thorough research and rigorous reasoning ever came naturally to people. They must be acquired in special institutions, which we call universities, and maintained with constant upkeep, which we call analysis, criticism and debate. They are not granted by propping a heavy encyclopedia on your lap, nor are they taken away by efficient access to information on the Internet.

11   The new media have caught on for a reason. Knowledge is increasing exponentially; human brainpower and waking hours are not. Fortunately, the Internet and information technologies are helping us manage, search, and retrieve our collective intellectual output at different scales, from Twitter and previews to e-books and online encyclopedias. Far from making us stupid, these technologies are the only things that will keep us smart.

Write an essay in which you explain how Steven Pinker builds an argument to persuade his audience that new media are not destroying our moral and intellectual abilities. In your essay, analyze how Pinker uses one or more of the features listed in the box above (or features of your own choice) to strengthen the logic and persuasiveness of his argument. Be sure that your analysis focuses on the most relevant features of the passage.

Your essay should NOT explain whether you agree with Pinker's claims, but rather explain how Pinker builds an argument to persuade his audience.

CONTINUE ➡

DIAGNOSTIC SAT ANSWER KEY

Section 1: Reading	Section 2: Writing and Language	Section 3: Math (No Calculator)	Section 4: Math (Calculator)
1. C	1. B	1. B	1. D
2. A	2. C	2. D	2. C
3. C	3. C	3. B	3. D
4. B	4. A	4. A	4. B
5. D	5. B	5. C	5. D
6. C	6. C	6. D	6. C
7. D	7. A	7. A	7. B
8. A	8. D	8. B	8. A
9. B	9. A	9. D	9. B
10. D	10. D	10. C	10. C
11. B	11. D	11. A	11. B
12. C	12. C	12. B	12. D
13. C	13. B	13. C	13. A
14. D	14. D	14. B	14. B
15. A	15. A	15. B	15. B
16. D	16. B	-------	16. B
17. B	17. C	16. 30	17. C
18. D	18. D	17. 25/7 or 3.57	18. C
19. C	19. C	18. 35	19. C
20. B	20. D	19. 1.2	20. B
21. B	21. B	20. 2.4	21. A
22. C	22. A		22. A
23. D	23. D		23. D
24. D	24. C		24. C
25. A	25. A		25. A
26. A	26. D		26. D
27. C	27. C		27. D
28. C	28. B		28. B
29. C	29. C		29. A
30. B	30. D		30. B
31. A	31. A		-------
32. B	32. C		31. 1/5 or 0.2
33. C	33. B		32. 169
34. C	34. B		33. 112
35. A	35. A		34. 16
36. A	36. B		35. 1.4
37. B	37. D		36. 115
38. B	38. C		37. 6.8
39. B	39. C		38. 25
40. B	40. D		
41. A	41. B		
42. D	42. B		
43. C	43. D		
44. B	44. B		
45. D			
46. A			
47. D			
48. D			
49. D			
50. C			
51. B			
52. D			

Total Reading Points (Section 1)	Total Writing and Language Points (Section 2)	Total Math Points (Section 3)	Total Math Points (Section 4)

SCORE CONVERSION TABLE

Scoring Your Test

1. Use the answer key to mark your responses on each section.

2. Total the number of correct responses for each section:

    1. Reading Test   Number correct: _____ **(Reading Raw Score)**

    2. Writing and Language Test   Number correct: _____ **(Writing and Language Raw Score)**

    3. Mathematics Test – No Calculator Number correct: _____

    4. Mathematics Test – Calculator   Number correct: _____

3. Add the raw scores for sections 3 and 4. This is your **Math Raw Score**: _____

4. Use the Table 1 to calculate your **Scaled Test (10–40)** and **Section Scores (200–800)**.

    Math Section Score (200–800):   _____

    Reading Test Score (10–40):   _____

    Writing and Language Test Score (10–40):   _____

5. Add the **Reading Test Scaled Score** and the **Writing and Language Test Scaled Score** and multiply this sum by 10 to get your **Reading and Writing Test Section Score (20–80)**.

    Sum of Reading + Writing and Language Scores: _____ × 10 =

    Reading and Writing Section Score: _____

Table 1: Scaled Section and Test Scores (10–40)

Raw Score	Math Section Score	Reading Test Score	Writing/ Language Test Score	Raw Score	Math Section Score	Reading Test Score	Writing/ Language Test Score
58	800			29	520	27	28
57	790			28	520	26	28
56	780			27	510	26	27
55	760			26	500	25	26
54	750			25	490	25	26
53	740			24	480	24	25
52	730	40		23	480	24	25
51	710	40		22	470	23	24
50	700	39		21	460	23	23
49	690	38		20	450	22	23
48	680	38		19	440	22	22
47	670	37		18	430	21	21
46	670	37		17	420	21	21
45	660	36		16	410	20	20
44	650	35	40	15	390	20	19
43	640	35	39	14	380	19	19
42	630	34	38	13	370	19	18
41	620	33	37	12	360	18	17
40	610	33	36	11	340	17	16
39	600	32	35	10	330	17	16
38	600	32	34	9	320	16	15
37	590	31	34	8	310	15	14
36	580	31	33	7	290	15	13
35	570	30	32	6	280	14	13
34	560	30	32	5	260	13	12
33	560	29	31	4	240	12	11
32	550	29	30	3	230	11	10
31	540	28	30	2	210	10	10
30	530	28	29	1	200	10	10

DIAGNOSTIC SAT DETAILED ANSWER KEY

Section 1: Reading

1. C   Specific Purpose

Let's translate this question into a "stand-alone" question: "How is Smith's work presented in the first paragraph?" The passage states (line 3) that *Karl Smith has a good rule of thumb for* **categorizing** *epidemics*, then goes on to describe various types of epidemics in an effort to help visualize the types of spread. In other words, he is proposing a model for *conceptualizing phenomena*. (Note that the word *phenomena* refers simply to common occurrences. It has a neutral tone, not a positive one.)

2. A   Inference

The passage states in lines 67–72 that *Nevin's paper was almost completely ignored* because *Nevin was an economist, not a criminologist, and his paper was published in* Environmental Research, *not a journal with a big readership in the criminology community*. In other words, Nevin's paper was ignored because it *was not presented by authorities with the proper credentials*.

3. C   Textual Evidence

As the explanation to question 2 indicates, the evidence for this answer is lines 67–72, which includes the statement in (C).

4. B   Inference from Data

According to the graph, the percent increase in violent crimes per 10,000 capita increased by 400% from 1963–1993. Notice that the graph only gives crime data for 1963–2013.

5. D   Inference from Data

Nevin's hypothesis is phrased in the form of a question in lines 27–28: *Maybe reducing lead exposure had an effect on violent crime too?* Therefore, the portion of the graph that would *least* support his hypothesis is the portion that shows the *least* correlation between lead exposure and crime. The biggest gap in the two graphs (and hence the portion that provides the least support for his thesis) corresponds to the set of violent crime statistics from 2003 to 2013.

6. C   Specific Purpose

The *sales of vinyl LPs* are mentioned to describe a statistic that also happens to correlate with preschool blood lead levels, thereby making the point that *a single correlation between two curves isn't all that impressive, econometrically speaking . . . No matter how good the fit, if you only have a single correlation it might just be coincidence.* Hence, it is a statistic that may be more coincidental than explanatory.

7. D   Interpretation

The sentence in lines 21–24 indicates that *lead exposure in small children [had been linked] with a whole raft of complications later in life, including lower IQ, hyperactivity, behavioral problems, and learning disabilities.* These *complications* are *psychological problems* for those exposed to lead at a young age.

8. A   Interpretation

When the passage states that the drivers *were unwittingly creating a crime wave two decades later* (lines 63–64), it indicates that they were *inadvertent abettors*.

9. B   Word in Context

The phrase *even better* (line 49) refers to the finding mentioned in the previous sentence that *the similarity of the curves was as good as it seemed*, suggesting that the data showed an even stronger correlation than Nevin had hoped.

10. D   Specific Purpose

The final paragraph discusses the fact that the *gasoline lead hypothesis* explains many additional phenomena, such as the difference between the murder rates in large cities (where there are lots of cars) and small cities (where there are fewer cars and therefore less lead exhaust exposure). These implications further support the hypothesis.

11. B   Cross-Textual Inference

The author of Passage 1 indicates that Hemingway was a legendary figure whose work *seemed . . . to have been carved from the living stone of life* (lines 25–26) and therefore had a great impact on the author and his friends. Passage 2, however, suggests that Hemingway's works don't have the impact they once did, saying that they *now seem unable to evoke the same sense of a tottering world that in the 1920s established Ernest Hemingway's reputation* (lines 48–50) and *no longer seem to penetrate deeply the surface of existence* (lines 57–58). Therefore, the two passages disagree most strongly on the *incisiveness* (deep analytical quality) of Hemingway's work.

12. C   Textual Evidence

As the answer to the previous question indicates, the best evidence for this answer is found in lines 24–26 and lines 56–58.

13. C   Cross-Textual Interpretation

The author of Passage 1 regards Hemingway as a *legend* (line 16) whose *impact upon us was tremendous* (lines 18–19), but the author of Passage 2 calls Hemingway a *dupe of his culture rather than its moral-aesthetic conscience* (lines 66–67).

14. D   Cross-Textual Inference

The author of Passage 1 indicates that, although Hemingway's work had a strong formative impact on him, it ultimately could not capture the true horrors of war that he and his friends were later to encounter:

The Hemingway time was a good time to be young. We had much then that the war later forced out of us, something far greater than Hemingway's strong formative influence (lines 33–36).

Likewise, the author of Passage 2 indicates that Hemingway's work did not fully capture the horrors of war: *We have had more war than Hemingway ever dreamed of* (lines 53–54) . . . *yet Hemingway's great novels no longer seem to penetrate deeply the surface of existence* (lines 56–58).

15. A   Word in Context, Purpose

In saying that *the words he put down seemed to us to have been carved from the living stone of life* (lines 24–26), the author of Passage 1 means that Hemingway's words represent living truths that have the weight and permanence of stone carvings. In other words, his words represent the *salient* (prominent and important) *experience* of life.

16. D   Interpretation

In saying that *we began unconsciously to translate our own sensations into their terms and to impose on everything we did and felt the particular emotions they aroused in us* (lines 28–32) the author is saying that he and his friends *identified* with Hemingway's language.

17. B   Inference

According to Passage 1, the *lessons that [Hemingway] had to teach* (line 43) included the example he set as a war correspondent *writing a play in the Hotel Florida in Madrid while thirty fascist shells crashed through the roof* (lines 10–12) and as a soldier *defending his post single-handedly against fierce German attacks* (lines 13–15), both of which exemplify *confidence in the face of danger*.

18. D   Specific Purpose

The phrase *a tottering world* (line 49) is used to describe the Europe of the 1920s that Ernest Hemingway depicts in his novels. The author compares this world to one whose *social structure is . . . shaken* (lines 51–52) and which had *more war than Hemingway ever dreamed of* (line 54). In other words, a world filled with *societal upheaval*.

19. C   Cross-Textual Inference

The author of Passage 1 clearly views Hemingway as a personal and literary hero. Hence, a withering accusation such as the one in Passage 2 that *Hemingway, in effect, became a dupe of his culture rather than its moral-aesthetic conscience* (lines 66–67) would almost certainly be met with *vehement disagreement*.

Tip: Questions about how the author of one passage might *most likely* respond to some statement in another passage require us to focus on the *thesis and tone* of that author. Before attempting to answer such questions, remind yourself of the central theses of the passages.

20. B   Textual Evidence

The best evidence for this answer comes from lines 28–32, where the author of Passage 1 says that *we began to unconsciously translate our own sensations into their terms and to impose on everything we did and felt the particular emotions they aroused in us*. In other words, Hemingway was in fact a kind of *moral-aesthetic conscience* for the author of Passage 1 and his friends.

21. B   Interpretation

Passage 2 states that Hemingway's novels *yielded to the functionalist, technological aesthetic of the culture instead of resisting in the manner of Frank Lloyd Wright* (lines 63–66). In other words, Frank Lloyd Wright was more *iconoclastic* (culturally rebellious) than Hemingway.

22. C   Specific Purpose

The first paragraph establishes the idea that *atoms, the building blocks of everything we know and love . . . don't appear to be models of stability*, a fact that represents a *scientific conundrum* (riddle), because instability is not a quality that we expect of *building blocks*.

23. D   Word in Context

By asking *[w]hy are some atoms, like sodium, so hyperactive while others, like helium, are so aloof?* the author is drawing a direct contrast between chemical reactivity and relative *nonreactivity*.

24. D   Inference

This question, about why protons stick together in atomic nuclei, is the guiding question for the passage as a whole. The next paragraph analyzes this question in more detail, explaining why this well-known fact is actually so puzzling. The remainder of the passages discusses attempts to resolve this puzzle, which remains at the heart of quantum physics.

25. A — **Textual Evidence**

The evidence that this question represents a *central conundrum* is found in lines 1–5, where the author makes the uncontroversial claim that *a sound structure requires stable materials*, but then makes the paradoxical claim that *atoms, the building blocks of everything we know and love . . . don't appear to be models of stability.*

26. A — **Specific Purpose**

The two sentences in lines 13–19 (*We are told . . . electrons. We are also told . . . closer*) indicate that we, the educated public, have been taught two seemingly contradictory facts about atoms. In other words, these are *predominant conceptions.*

27. C — **Inference from Data**

In the graph, the equilibrium point is indicated by a dashed vertical line labeled *Equilibrium*. If we notice where this line intersects the two curves, we can see that the corresponding electrostatic force is precisely opposite to the corresponding strong nuclear force. That is, the equilibrium point is where the two forces "cancel out" and have a sum of 0.

28. C — **Inference from Data**

Tip: When a question asks about a graph or table, it helps to circle the words or phrases in the question that correspond to the words or phrases in the graph or table. In this case, circle the key phrases *electrostatic repulsion* and *separated by 1.5 femtometers* in both the question and the graph.

Now, if we go to the graph and find the vertical line that corresponds to a *separation of 1.5 femtometers*, we can see that it intersects the curve for *electrostatic force* at the horizontal line representing 10^2, or 100, Newtons.

29. C — **Interpretation**

In the fourth paragraph, we are told that Hideki Yukawa *proposed that the nuclear force was conveyed by a then-undiscovered heavy subatomic particle he called the pi meson (or "pion"), which (unlike the photon) decays very quickly and therefore conveys a powerful force only over a very short distance* (lines 44–49). However, his theory *was dealt a mortal blow by a series of experiments . . . that demonstrated that pions carry force only over distances greater than the distance between bound protons* (lines 50–55). In other words, pions are *ineffective in the range required by atomic theory,* so they cannot be the carriers of the strong nuclear force.

30. B — **General Structure**

The first paragraph of this passage introduces the *scientific conundrum* of how protons adhere in atomic nuclei. The second paragraph analyzes this strange situation.

The third paragraph describes a force, the strong nuclear force, that could solve the conundrum. The fourth paragraph describes a particular theory, now refuted, about what might convey this strong nuclear force. The fifth and sixth paragraphs indicate that the problem has yet to be satisfactorily resolved. Thus, the passage as a whole is *a description of a technical puzzle and the attempts to solve it.*

31. A — **Literary Devices**

A **rhetorical question** is a question intended to convey a point of view, rather than suggest a point of inquiry. Although the first and second paragraphs include five questions, they are all inquisitive, not rhetorical.

The passage includes **illustrative metaphors** in lines 15–16 (*a cloud of speedy electrons*) and lines 55–56 (*a plumber's wrench trying to do a tweezer's job*), **technical specifications** in lines 29–40 (*First, it can't have . . . each other*), and **appeals to common intuition** in lines 1–2 (*a sound structure . . . materials*) and lines 13–16 (*We are . . . electrons*).

32. B — **Word in Context**

The hope that *QCD ties up atomic behavior with a tidy little bow* is the hope that the QCD theory *resolves* the problem in a tidy way.

33. C — **General Purpose**

The passage as a whole develops the thesis that *the wise legislator does not begin by laying down laws good in themselves, but by investigating the fitness of the people, for which they are destined, to receive them* (lines 3–6). In other words, the passage is concerned with *examining the social conditions that foster effective legal systems.*

34. C — **Word in Context**

In saying that *the architect sounds the site to see if it will bear the weight,* the author means that the architect *probes* the proposed location for a building to make sure that it is safe to build upon.

35. A — **Specific Purpose**

The analogy of the architect in the first paragraph illustrates the thesis of the passage that *the wise legislator does not begin by laying down laws good in themselves, but by investigating the fitness of the people, for which they are destined, to receive them* (lines 3–6). That is, that a *nation's civil code depends on the nature of its people.* Choice (B) is incorrect because the analogy is not about the *foundational principles* of laws, but rather the *fitness of the people* for whom they are intended.

36. A — **Inference**

The author states that as a nation grows older, its citizens *become incorrigible* (unable to be improved). *Once customs have become established and prejudices inveterate* (deep-seated), *it is dangerous and useless to attempt their reformation* (lines 19–21). That is, the people become stubbornly resistant to political change.

---

37. B   Textual Evidence

As the explanation to the previous question indicates, the relevant evidence is found in lines 20–21.

---

38. B   Interpretation

When the author says that *[m]ost peoples, like most men, are docile only in youth* (lines 17–18), he is saying that societies (the *peoples*) as well as individuals (*men*) become less manageable as they age.

---

39. B   Specific Purpose

The author refers to *Sparta at the time of Lycurgus* (line 35) as an example of a *state, set on fire by civil wars, [which] is born again* (lines 31–32). That is, a *society rejuvenated by conflict*. Choice (A) may seem tempting, because the beginning of the paragraph mentions the fact that *periods of violence* (lines 28–29) can make people *forget the past*, but the paragraph explains that this forgetting has the effect of renewal, not paralysis.

---

40. B   Interpretation

Although the word *constitution* can be used to mean *the documented rules by which a nation defines its governmental institutions* (as in the *Constitution of the United States of America*), the phrase *the constitution of the state*, as it is used in this passage, clearly refers to the *composition* of the state, that is, the people who constitute the nation.

---

41. A   Interpretation

In saying that *[o]ne people is amenable to discipline from the beginning; another, not even after ten centuries* (lines 51–53), the author means that some nations are *ready to be governed by the rule of law* as soon as they are founded, but others require much more time.

---

42. D   Inference

The passage states that *Peter the Great . . . lacked true genius [because he] did not see that [his nation] was not ripe for civilization: he wanted to civilize it when it needed only hardening* (lines 55–61). In other words, he did not give his nation the *hardening* it needed: his flaw was his *irresolution* (hesitancy due to a lack of conviction) *in exerting control*.

---

43. C   General Purpose

The first sentence of the passage establishes its central purpose: *to understand the views of Aristotle*, and asserts that to do this *it is necessary to apprehend his imaginative background* (lines 1–3). In other words, the purpose of this passage is to *describe the conceptions that inform a particular mindset.*

---

44. B   Interpretation

When the author states that *Animals have lost their importance in our imaginative pictures of the world* (lines 29–30), he is reinforcing his point that modern students *are accustomed to automobiles and airplanes; they do not, even in the dimmest recesses of their subconscious imagination, think that an automobile contains some sort of horse inside, or that an airplane flies because its wings are those of a bird possessing magical powers* (lines 23–29). In other words, *animistic beliefs no longer inform our physical theories.*

---

45. D   Interpretation

When the author states that *[e]very philosopher, in addition to the formal system that he offers to the world, has another much simpler system of which he may be quite unaware* (lines 3–6), the *simpler system* refers to the *imaginative background* (line 3) that informs a scientist's formal theories. However, if a scientist is aware of this simpler system, *he probably realizes that it won't do* (line 7). Therefore, this system is a *relatively unrefined way of thinking.*

---

46. A   Inference

In lines 61–65, the author states that *It was natural that a philosopher who could no longer regard the heavenly bodies themselves as divine should think of them as moved by the will of a Divine Being who had a Hellenic love of order and geometric simplicity*. In other words, the astronomical theories of some ancient Greek philosophers were closely associated with their religious ideas.

---

47. D   Textual Evidence

As the explanation to the previous question indicates, the evidence for this answer is in lines 61–65.

---

48. D   Word in Context

When the author states that, to the Greek, *it seemed more natural to assimilate apparently lifeless motions to those of animals* (lines 46–47), he means that the ancient Greeks found it easy to *liken* the motion of machines to the motion of animals.

---

49. D   Inference

The passage states that *To the ancient Greek, attempting to give a scientific account of motion, the purely mechanical view hardly suggested itself, except in the case of a few men of genius such as Democritus and Archimedes*. In other words, most Greeks were not inclined toward the mechanical view, except for the men of genius, who had more accurate *metaphors for the laws of motion, and therefore were "willing to disregard conventional wisdom."*

50. C   **Inference**

As it is discussed in the passage, the *apparent gulf between animals and machines* (lines 44–45) is the ever-shrinking gap between the animistic and the mechanistic view of animal physiology. To the modern scientist, each piece of evidence that demonstrates how *the body of an animal is a very elaborate machine, with an enormously complex physical and chemical structure* (lines 41–43) serves to bridge this gulf. One example of such evidence might be *the mechanical laws that describe bumblebee flight.*

51. B   **Inference**

The first paragraph discusses the fact that *the views of Aristotle* (line 1) are *due to his imaginative preconceptions, or to what Santayana calls "animal faith"* (lines 17–18), which the author goes on to explain include *animistic tendencies,* that is, tendencies toward seeing living spirits in all physical phenomena.

52. D   **Textual Evidence**

Lines 45–47 also reinforce the author's point that Aristotle, like other ancient Greeks, was inclined toward an animistic view of the world: *To the Greek, it seemed more natural to assimilate apparently lifeless motions to those of animals.*

Section 2: Writing and Language

1. B   **Subject-Verb Agreement**

The subject of this verb is *demand,* which is singular. Therefore, *are* must be changed to *is.*

2. C   **Diction**

This question asks you to choose the word that best fits the semantic context of the sentence, that is, the word that helps the sentence to convey a logical idea in the context of the paragraph.

This previous sentence states that *an important challenge facing the healthcare industry is how to address this shortfall without sacrificing quality of care.* Among our options, the only one that suggests a *possible solution* to this problem is *to incentivize more medical school graduates to choose primary care.*

Although it may seem that *interest* is a reasonable choice, notice that its use would violate idiom in this sentence: the correct idiom is not *interest someone to do something,* but rather *interest someone in doing something.*

3. C   **Logical Comparisons**

This portion of the sentence is part of a parallel construction in the form *A instead of B.* In such constructions, the

words or phrases in *A* and *B* must have the same grammatical form and describe logically comparable (or contrastable) things. Since in this case *A* is *primary care* (a noun phrase indicating a medical specialty), the most logical choice for *B* is *the more lucrative specialties* (a noun phrase indicating medical specialties). The original phrasing is incorrect because *their choosing* does not indicate a medical specialty, (B) is incorrect because *to choose* does not indicate a medical specialty, and choice (D) is incorrect because it is redundant.

4. A   **Parallelism**

Words or phrases in a list should have the same grammatical form. In the original phrasing, the three items in the list are all present tense verbs: *talk … prescribe … perform.*

5. B   **Diction**

Because a *"team-based" model* is not a location, the use of the pronoun *where* is incorrect. Likewise, choice (D) *when* is incorrect because a *"team-based" model* is not a time. Choice (C) is incorrect because it produces a comma splice. The correct answer is (B) *whereby,* which means *by which.*

6. C   **Diction**

The adverb *still* means *even now* or *nevertheless,* neither of which fit the logical context of this sentence. Only choice (C) *while,* meaning *at the same time,* fits logically. Choice (B) *while at the same time* is redundant, and choice (D) *although* implies a contrast, which is illogical.

7. A   **Coordination of Ideas, Cross-References**

The subject of the inserted sentence is *these professionals.* The pronoun *these* requires an antecedent, which is best provided if the sentence is placed after sentence 1, which specifies *medical professionals like physician assistants (PAs) and nurse practitioners (NPs).*

8. D   **Data Analysis**

The descending line in the graph shows clearly that the percentage of PAs in primary care has declined from 51% in 2000 (over one-half) to 31% in 2010 (under one-third).

9. A   **Logical Comparisons, Pronoun-Antecedent Agreement**

This sentence is correct as written. The pronoun *they* agrees in number and kind with its antecedent *students,* and the comparison is logical. Choice (D) is redundant.

10. D   **Idiom, Pronoun-Antecedent Agreement**

Using the phrase *being that* to mean *because* is colloquial and nonstandard for written American English, therefore choices (A) and (C) are incorrect. Choice (B) is incorrect because *when* should only be used to refer to a time.

11. D   **Pronoun-Antecedent Agreement, Cross-References**

The definite pronoun *they* must refer to some plural noun, but the only possible plural antecedent in this sentence is *programs*, which would be illogical. Choice (D) clarifies the reference.

12. C   **Punctuation**

The four choices differ only in their punctuation. Any reference to a city-and-country or city-and-state must separate the two with commas: e.g. *London, England* or *Providence, Rhode Island.* Therefore the original punctuation in (A) is incorrect. Choice (B) is incorrect because it produces a sentence fragment. Choice (D) is incorrect because it misuses the semicolon: the two phrases on either side of the semicolon should be independent clauses.

13. B   **Logic, Dangling Participles**

Since *engineering* is a class of profession and not a *position*, the original phrasing is illogical. Choice (C) is incorrect because it is a dangling participial phrase: the past participle *considered* does not share a subject with the main clause. Choice (D) is incorrect because the phrase *in reputation* is not idiomatic.

14. D   **Dangling Participles**

The sentence begins with the participial phrase *suffering ridicule and isolation.* Any participial phrase must have the same subject as the main clause. In the original phrasing, the subject of the main clause is *Montessori's medical studies,* but this cannot be the subject of *suffering ridicule and isolation.* Therefore, choices (A) and (C) are both incorrect. Choices (B) and (D) both correct this problem by changing the subject of the main clause to *Montessori,* but (B) is incorrect because the phrase *by becoming* is illogical.

15. A   **Parallelism**

This sentence contains the parallel construction *A rather than B.* The original phrasing provides parallel phrasing: *respect and stimulation* shares the same grammatical form and semantic category as *the regimentation.* Choice (D) provides a parallel phrasing but illogically implies that the students *were receiving* institutions.

16. B   **Diction, Agreement**

The original phrasing is incorrect because *they're* is a contraction of *they are,* which is illogical in this context. Choice (C) is incorrect because *childrens'* is not a word at all. *Children* is the plural form of *child,* and the possessive form of *children* is *children's.* Choice (D) is incorrect because *their* disagrees in number with the antecedent *each.*

17. C   **Diction**

This sentence discusses how word of Montessori's success with her school began to *spread* of its own merit

and accord. Choices (A) and (D) are incorrect because both *distribute* and *exhibit* imply intentional action. Choice (B) is illogical: *word* of someone's success cannot *increase.*

18. D   **Logical Cohesiveness**

To understand which sentence most effectively introduces this paragraph, we must first understand what the paragraph is about. As a whole, the paragraph discusses how *Montessori schools were regarded as a remedy to the educational programs associated with rapid urban population growth in Europe . . .* but then *came to be seen as a threat to the power of the state.* Choice (D) encapsulates this idea the best.

19. C   **Logical Transitions**

Choice (C) provides the most logical transition between ideas in the paragraph: the shift from a positive view of Montessori's work to a negative view requires a contrasting transition like *however.*

20. D   **Redundancy**

The original phrasing is redundant: being *subversive* is the same as *undermining power.* The most concise correct phrasing is that in (D).

21. B   **Subject-Verb Agreement**

In the original phrasing, the subject *response* (singular) disagrees with the verb *were* (plural) *divided.* Choice (B) provides the most effective correction.

22. A   **Logical Cohesiveness**

The remarkable thing about this paragraph is its introduction of dissenting views on Montessori's work from within the field of education, rather than merely from political opponents. Any additional discussion in this paragraph should elaborate on the nature of that dissent in the educational community. Only choice (A) extends the discussion in a relevant way.

23. D   **Redundancy**

This sentence is asserting a claim that directly contrasts the point of view presented in the previous paragraph. Choice (D) *In fact,* introduces just such an assertion. Choice (A) *First* is incorrect because this claim is not part of an enumerated list. Choice (B) *So* is incorrect, because this sentence is not asserting a logical consequence of the previous claim. Choice (C) *While* is incorrect because it produces a sentence fragment.

24. C   **Diction, Idiom**

The original phrasing is incorrect because the phrase *complies [to]* is not idiomatic. The same is true of (B) *overlaps [to]* and (D) *concurs [to].* Choice (C) *corresponds [to],* however, is idiomatic and logical.

25. A   **Coordination of Ideas**

This phrase is correct as written. It is expressing a condition, and so the use of the conjunction *if* is correct.

26. D   **Dangling Participles**

The participle *pondering* and the main clause must share the same subject, or else the participle "dangles." Who was *pondering*? Plato. Therefore *Plato* must be the subject of the main clause. Choice (C) is incorrect, however, because there is no need for the past participle form *had argued*.

27. C   **Parallelism**

The sentence contains the parallel construction *A yet B*. The phrasing *inaccessible . . . yet apprehensible* provides a parallel form, since both *inaccessible* and *apprehensible* are adjectives.

28. B   **Modifier Usage**

The phrase between the commas is an interrupting modifier. Any sentence should remain grammatically complete even when any interrupting modifier is removed. Notice that if we did this with the original sentence, it would read *as effective . . . than sensory experience*, which is clearly unidiomatic. (The correct comparative idiom is *as effective as*.) The only choice that corrects this problem is (B).

29. C   **Logical Cohesiveness**

The information the author is proposing does not fit with the discussion about the philosophy of Platonic idealism.

30. D   **Modifier Form**

In the original phrasing, the conjunction *and* is incorrect because it does not conjoin comparable words or phrases; therefore, choices (A) and (C) are incorrect. In choice (B) the prepositional phrase *in not having to believe* is illogical. Choice (D) is correct because the prepositional phrase *without having to believe* logically modifies the verb *understand*.

31. A   **Possessives**

This sentence is correct as written. Choice (B) is incorrect because the pronoun *they* has no clear antecedent. Choice (C) misuses the possessive *brain's*, and choice (D) yields the subject-verb disagreement *brain make*.

32. C   **Verb Mood**

This clause is part of a counterfactual hypothesis. As we discuss in Chapter 4, Lesson 30, a present counterfactual hypothesis takes the form of the present subjunctive mood, which is usually the same form as the simple past tense: *existed*.

33. B   **Pronoun Consistency**

Since the previous sentence refers to *our brains*, pronoun consistency requires that this sentence continue to use the first-person plural pronoun *we*.

34. B   **Coordination of Clauses**

The interrupting modifier (*perhaps while showering or driving*) must be "bracketed" on either end by commas, em dashes, or parentheses. Since it clearly ends with an em dash, it must start with an em dash as well.

35. A   **Pronoun Form**

This sentence is correct as written. Choice (B) uses the wrong pronoun form *what* and incorrectly implies that Archimedes is shouting in the present. Choice (C) uses the wrong pronoun form *that* and misplaces the modifying clause *it is said*. Choice (D) misuses the past perfect form *had shouted*.

36. B   **Diction**

The sentence discusses the relationship between the *feeling* of the Eureka effect and *a fundamentally different way of thinking*. In the context of the discussion, the only choice that indicates a logical relationship is (B): this feeling *indicates* a different way of thinking.

37. D   **Coordination of Clauses**

The original phrasing is incorrect because it includes a comma splice. Choice (B) is incorrect because the prepositional phrase *by which* is illogical. In choice (C), the use of the pronoun *where* is incorrect because an experiment is not a place.

38. C   **Subject-Verb Agreement, Redundancy**

The verb *requires* (singular) disagrees with the subject *tasks* (plural), therefore choices (A) and (D) are incorrect. Choice (B) is redundant.

39. C   **Subject-Verb Agreement**

The modifying phrase *as soon as solving it* is vague and awkward. Choice (C) clarifies the modifier by indicating that the *subjects* are solving the task.

40. D   **Awkwardness, Logical Transitions**

The underlined phrase is a sentence modifier, that is, a phrase that modifies the statement in the main clause *experimenters found*. Choices (A), (B), and (C) are needlessly awkward and wordy, but choice (D) provides a concise and clear modifier.

41. B   **Verb Tense**

This clause is describing a general fact (*the theory that . . .*), not an event. To express general facts, we use the simple present tense: *corresponds*.

42. B   **Data Analysis**

According to the graph, the line indicating the Insight condition separates from the line representing the Non-insight condition approximately 0.3 seconds prior to the button being pushed, and remains elevated until about 0.7 seconds after the button is pushed, for a duration of approximately 1 second.

43. D   **Pronoun-Antecedent Agreement,**
Subject-Verb Agreement

The verb *is* agrees with the subject *interpreting* (both are singular), but the pronoun *this* disagrees with its antecedent *data* (*this* is singular, but *data* is plural).

44. B   **Coordinating Clauses**

The correct choice should combine the two questions into a single sentence. Choice (A) misstates the second question. Choice (C) inappropriately uses the subjunctive mood. Choice (D) misuses the parallel construction *both A and B.*

Section 3: Math (No Calculator)

1. B   **Algebra (solving equations) EASY**

$$6x + 9 = 30$$

To solve in one step, just divide
both sides by 3: $2x + 3 = 10$
Most students waste time solving for x,
which will work, but takes longer: $6x + 9 = 30$
Subtract 9: $6x = 21$
Divide by 6: $x = 3.5$
Evaluate $2x + 3$ by
substituting $x = 3.5$: $2x + 3 = 2(3.5) + 3 = 7 + 3 = 10$

2. D   **Advanced Mathematics (nonlinear systems)**
EASY

The solutions to the system correspond to the points of intersection of the two graphs. The figure shows four such intersection points.

3. B   **Algebra (algebraic expressions) EASY**

Let a = # of adult tickets sold, and c = # of child tickets sold. If 300 tickets were sold altogether: $c + a = 300$

The revenue for a adult tickets sold at $5 each is $5a$, and the revenue for c child tickets sold at $3 each is $3c$. Since the total revenue is $1,400: $5a + 3c = 1,400$

4. A   Advanced Mathematics (polynomials) EASY

$$2(x - 4)^2 - 5x$$

Factor: $2[(x - 4)(x - 4)]\quad 5x$
FOIL: $2[x^2 - 4x - 4x + 16] - 5x$

Simplify: $2[x^2 - 8x + 16] - 5x$
Distribute: $2x^2 - 16x + 32 - 5x$
Combine like terms: $2x^2 - 21x + 32$

5. C   Special Topics (three-dimensional geometry)
MEDIUM

On the drawing, we should first mark the areas of the three faces. The front and back faces both have an area of $3a$. The left and right faces both have an area of $3b$. The top and bottom faces both have an area of ab. We should now try to find integer values for a and b so that these areas match those given in the choices.

(A) 15, 18, and 30   This is possible if $a = 5$ and $b = 6$.
(B) 18, 24, and 48   This is possible if $a = 6$ and $b = 8$.
(C) 12, 15, and 24   This cannot work for any integer
values of a and b.
(D) 15, 24, and 40   This is possible if $a = 5$ and $b = 8$.

6. D   **Algebra (linear equations) MEDIUM**

$$C(n) = an + b$$

Since this expression is linear in n (the input variable, which represents the number of necklaces produced), the constant a represents the slope of this line, which in turn represents the "unit rate of increase," in other words, the increase in total cost for each individual necklace produced.

The constant b represents the "y-intercept" of this line, which in this case means the costs when $n = 0$ (that is, the fixed costs before any necklaces are produced).

7. A   **Algebra (lines) MEDIUM**

To find the slope of line l, we can find two points on l and then use the slope formula.

$$f(x) = 2x^2 - 4x + 1$$

Plug in −1 for x: $f(-1) = 2(-1)^2 - 4(-1) + 1$
Simplify: $f(-1) = 2(1) + 4 + 1 = 2 + 4 + 1 = 7$
Therefore line l intersects the function at $(-1, 7)$.
Plug in 2 for x: $f(2) = 2(2)^2 - 4(2) + 1$
Simplify: $f(2) = 2(4) - (8) + 1 = 8 - 8 + 1 = 1$
Therefore line l intersects the function at $(2, 1)$. Now we find the slope of the line containing these two points.

$$\text{slope} = \frac{y_2 - y_1}{x_2 - x_1} = \frac{7 - 1}{-1 - 2} = \frac{6}{-3} = -2$$

8. B   Advanced Mathematics (parabolas) MEDIUM

The general equation of a parabola in the xy-plane is $y = a(x - h)^2 + k$, in which (h, k) is the vertex. Now let's express each choice in precisely this form.

(A) $y = (x - 3)^2 + 2$ $y = 1(x - 3)^2 + 2$ $a = 1, h = 3, k = 2$
(B) $y = 2(x - 3)^2$ $y = 2(x - 3)^2 + 0$ $a = 2, h = 3, k = 0$
(C) $y = 2x^2 - 3$ $y = 2(x - 0)^2 - 3$ $a = 2, h = 0, k = -3$
(D) $y = 3x^2 + 2$ $y = 3(x - 0)^2 + 2$ $a = 3, h = 0, k = 2$
If this vertex is on the x-axis, then $k = 0$. The only equation in which $k = 0$ is (B).

9. D　Advanced Mathematics (rational equations) MEDIUM

$$\frac{m(x)}{x+3} - \frac{x+1}{x-1} = 1$$

Add $\frac{x+1}{x-1}$:

$$\frac{m(x)}{x+3} = \frac{x+1}{x-1} + 1$$

Express right side in terms of a common denominator:

$$\frac{m(x)}{x+3} = \frac{x+1}{x-1} + \frac{x-1}{x-1}$$

Combine terms on right into one fraction:

$$\frac{m(x)}{x+3} = \frac{x+1+x-1}{x-1}$$

Combine terms:

$$\frac{m(x)}{x+3} = \frac{2x}{x-1}$$

Multiple by $x+3$:

$$m(x) = \frac{2x(x+3)}{x-1}$$

10. C　Algebra (linear relationships) MEDIUM

We are told that the temperature varies linearly with altitude, so if y represents the temperature (in °C) and x represents altitude (in km), these variables are related by the equation $y = mx + b$, where m (the slope) and b (the y-intercept) are constants.

We are given two points on this line: (50 km, 10°) and (80 km, −80°). We can use these points to find the slope, m:

$$\text{slope} = \frac{y_2 - y_1}{x_2 - x_1} = \frac{10 - (-80)}{50 - (80)} = \frac{90}{-30} = -3$$

Recall that the slope of a linear relationship is the "unit rate of change." In other words, the slope of −3 means that the temperature declines by 3° for every 1 km of additional altitude. Since we want the altitude at which the temperature is −50°, we want the value of x such that $(x, -50°)$ is on this line. To find x, we can simply use the slope formula again, using either of the other two points: Slope formula using (50, 10) and $(x, -50)$:

$$\text{slope} = \frac{y_2 - y_1}{x_2 - x_1} = \frac{10 - (-50)}{50 - x} = \frac{60}{50 - x} = -3$$

Multiply by $50 - x$:　　　　$60 = -3(50 - x)$
Distribute:　　　　　　　　$60 = -150 + 3x$
Add 150:　　　　　　　　　$210 = 3x$
Divide by 3:　　　　　　　　$70 = x$

11. A　Advanced Mathematics (triangles/quadratics) MEDIUM-HARD

Any point that intersects the y-axis has an x-value of 0. So, to find point A, plug in 0 for x and solve for y:

$$y = 2x^2 - 16x + 14$$

Plug in 0 for x:　　$y = 2(0)^2 - 16(0) + 14 = 14$

Any point that intersects the x-axis has a y-value of 0. So, to find points B and C, plug in 0 for y and solve for x:

$$y = 2x^2 - 16x + 14$$

Substitute 0 for y:　　$0 = 2x^2 - 16x + 14$
Divide by 2:　　　　　　$0 = x^2 - 8x + 7$

Factor:　　　　　　　　$0 = (x - 7)(x - 1)$
Use the Zero Product Property:　　$x = 7$ and $x = 1$

If we connect these three points, we get a triangle with a height of 14 (from $y = 0$ to $y = 14$) and a base of 6 (from $x = 1$ to $x = 7$).

Use the triangle area formula $A = \frac{1}{2}bh$:

$$A = \frac{1}{2}bh = \frac{1}{2}(14)(6) = 42$$

12. B　Advanced Mathematics (polynomials) MEDIUM-HARD

Given equation:　　　　　　　$y = (x + 2)^2(x - 3)^2$
To find the y-intercept, set $x = 0$:　　$y = (0 + 2)^2(0 - 3)^2$
Simplify:　$y = (2)^2(-3)^2 = (4)(9) = 36$

Therefore the y-intercept is at (0, 36).

To find the x-intercepts, set $y = 0$:　　$0 = (x + 2)^2(x - 3)^2$

By the Zero Product Property, the only solutions to this equation are $x = -2$ and $x = 3$, so there are two x-intercepts and a total of three x- and y-intercepts.

13. C　Special Topics (complex numbers) HARD

$$A(2 - i) = 2 + i$$

Divide by $(2 - i)$:　　$A = \frac{2 + i}{2 - i}$

Multiply numerator and denominator by the conjugate $(2 + i)$:

$$A = \frac{(2 + i)(2 + i)}{(2 - i)(2 + i)}$$

FOIL:

$$A = \frac{4 + 2i + 2i + i^2}{4 - i^2}$$

Combine terms:

$$A = \frac{4 + 4i + i^2}{4 - i^2}$$

Substitute $i^2 = -1$:

$$A = \frac{4 + 4i + (-1)}{4 - (-1)}$$

Simplify:

$$A = \frac{4 + 4i - 1}{4 + 1}$$

Combine terms:

$$A = \frac{3 + 4i}{5}$$

Distribute to express in standard $a + bi$ form:

$$A = \frac{3}{5} + \frac{4}{5}i$$

14. B　Algebra (graphs of linear equations) HARD

Given equation:　　　$y + x = k(x - 1)$
Subtract x:　　　　　$y = k(x - 1) - x$
Distribute:　　　　　　$y = kx - k - x$
Collect like terms:　　$y = (k - 1)x - k$

The slope of this line is $k - 1$ and its y-intercept is $-k$. If $k > 2$, then $k - 1 > 1$, and $-k < -2$. In other words, the slope of the line is greater than 1 and the y-intercept is less than −2. The only graph with these features is the one in choice (B).

15. B   **Advanced Mathematics (analyzing polynomial functions) HARD**

Because this polynomial has a degree of 3 (which is the highest power of any of its terms), it cannot have more than 3 zeros. These three zeros are given as −2, 3, and 6. We also know that $g(0)$, the y-intercept of the graph, is negative. This gives us enough information to make a rough sketch of the graph.

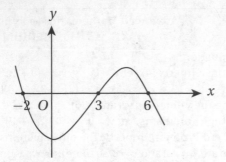

This shows that the only values of x for which the function is negative are $-2 < x < 3$ and $x > 6$. Therefore the only negative value among the choices is (B) $g(-1)$.

---

16. 30   **Algebra (linear equations) EASY**

$$\frac{2}{3}x + \frac{1}{2}y = 5$$

Multiply by 6 (the common denominator):

$$6\left(\frac{2}{3}x + \frac{1}{2}y = 5\right)$$

Distribute:

$$\frac{12}{3}x + \frac{6}{2}y = 30$$

Simplify:

$$4x + 3y = 30$$

---

17. 25/7 or 3.57   **Advanced Mathematics (rational equations) EASY**

$$\frac{5}{x} - \frac{2}{5} = 1$$

Add $\frac{2}{5}$:

$$\frac{5}{x} = 1 + \frac{2}{5}$$

Simplify:

$$\frac{5}{x} = \frac{7}{5}$$

Cross multiply:

$$25 = 7x$$

Divide by 7:

$$\frac{25}{7} = x$$

---

18. 35   **Special Topics (radians and arcs) MEDIUM-HARD**

Since an arc is simply a portion of a circumference, let's first calculate the circumference of the circle:

$$C = 2\pi r = 2\pi(36) = 72\pi$$

Because arc AB has a measure of 7π, it is $\frac{7\pi}{72\pi} = \frac{7}{72}$ of the entire circumference. Since $x°$ is the measure of the central angle that corresponds to this arc, it must be the same fraction of the whole:

$$\frac{x°}{360°} = \frac{7}{72}$$

Cross multiply:

$$72x = 7(360)$$

Divide by 72:

$$x = 7(5)$$

Simplify:

$$x = 35$$

---

19. 1.2   **Algebra (linear systems) MEDIUM-HARD**

First, we should simplify the first equation:

$$\frac{1}{2}x = \frac{1}{3}y + \frac{1}{10}$$

Subtract $\frac{1}{3}y$:

$$\frac{1}{2}x - \frac{1}{3}y = \frac{1}{10}$$

Multiply by 12:

$$6x - 4y = 1.2$$

This equation represents a line with slope of $\frac{6}{4} = \frac{3}{2}$. The second equation, $6x - 4y = k$, also represents a line with slope $\frac{6}{4} = \frac{3}{2}$. In order for this system of equations to have at least one solution, these two lines must have an intersection. How can two lines with the same slope intersect? They must be identical lines, and therefore intersect in all of their points. If this is the case, then k must equal 1.2.

---

20. 2.4   **Special Topics (trigonometry) HARD**

Since x represents the radian measure of an acute angle, and $\sin x = \frac{5}{13}$, we can use the definition of sine $\left(= \frac{O}{H}\right)$ to draw a right triangle:

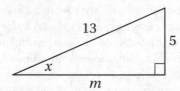

We might notice that this is a 5-12-13 special right triangle, or simply use the Pythagorean Theorem to show that $m = 12$. We can also show that the other acute angle in the triangle must be complementary to x (that is, together they form a right angle), and so must have a measure of $\frac{\pi}{2} - x$.

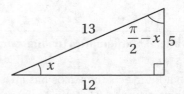

To find $\tan\left(\frac{\pi}{2} - x\right)$, we simply have to use the angle with measure $\frac{\pi}{2} - x$ as our new reference angle, and use TOA:

$$\tan\left(\frac{\pi}{2} - x\right) = \frac{12}{5} = 2.4$$

Section 4: Math (Calculator)

1. D   Algebra (systems) EASY

When faced with a system of equations, notice whether the two equations can be combined in a simple way—either by subtracting or adding the corresponding sides—to get the expression the question is asking for.

$$a - b = 10$$
$$a - 2b = 8$$

Subtract corresponding sides: $b = 2$

---

2. C   Data Analysis (central tendency) EASY

The average of three numbers is 50: $50 = \dfrac{a+b+c}{3}$

Multiply by 3: $150 = a + b + c$
Two of the numbers have a sum of 85: $85 = a + b$
Substitute into the previous equation: $150 = 85 + c$
Subtract 85 to find c: $65 = c$

---

3. D   Problem Solving/Data Analysis
(proportions) EASY

Set up a proportion: $\dfrac{9}{25} = \dfrac{x}{225}$

Cross multiply: $2{,}025 = 25x$
Divide by 25: $81 = x$

---

4. B   Data Analysis (tables) EASY

Let's fill in the table with the information we're given and work our way to the value the question asks us to find. First, use the information in the FAVORABLE column to determine how many women viewed the politician favorably:

$$26 + w = 59$$
Subtract 26: $w = 33$
Next, go to the WOMEN row: $33 + x + 13 = 89$
Combine terms: $46 + x = 89$
Subtract 46: $x = 43$

---

5. D   Algebra (exponentials) EASY

$$2^{2n-2} = 32$$

When dealing with exponential equations, it helps to see if we can express the two sides of the equation in terms of the same base. Since $32 = 2^5$, we can express both sides in base 2:

$$2^{2n-2} = 2^5$$

If $x^a = x^b$ and $x > 1$, then $a = b$ (if the bases are equal, the exponents are equal): $2n - 2 = 5$
Add 2: $2n = 7$

Divide by 2: $n = \dfrac{7}{2} = 3.5$

---

6. C   Algebra (representing quantities) EASY

The question asks us to find the "part-to-whole" ratio of walnuts: walnut fraction $= \dfrac{\text{ounces of walnuts}}{\text{ounces of nuts}}$.

Since the walnuts weigh x ounces, and the total weight of all the nuts is $x + 15 + 20 = x + 35$ ounces,

$$\text{walnut fraction} = \dfrac{x}{x+35}$$

---

7. B   Advanced Mathematics (triangle
trigonometry) EASY

Remember the definitions of the basic trigonometric functions: SOH CAH TOA. Since the "side of interest" (k) is the OPPOSITE side to the given angle (35°), and since we know the length of the HYPOTENUSE (12), we should use SOH.

$$\sin x = \dfrac{\text{opp}}{\text{hyp}}$$

Plug in the values: $\sin 35° = \dfrac{k}{12}$

Substitute $\sin 35° = 0.574$: $0.574 = \dfrac{k}{12}$

Multiply by 12: $(12)(0.574) = 6.88 = k$

---

8. A   Special Topics (polygons) EASY

The sum of the measures if the interior angles of any polygon is $(n - 2)180°$, where n is the number of sides in the polygon. Since this is a 5-sided polygon, the sum of its interior angles is $(5 - 2)(180°) = 3(180°) = 540°$. Therefore the average of these measures is $540°/5 = 108°$.

---

9. B   Data Analysis (scatterplot) MEDIUM

We want to find the slope of the line of best fit because it represents the average annual increase in revenue per store. Although the question asks about the years 2004 and 2012, we can choose ANY two points on this line to find its slope. We should choose points on the line of best fit that are easy to calculate with, such as (2005, $300,000) and (2011, $600,000).

$$\text{slope} = \dfrac{\text{rise}}{\text{run}} = \dfrac{y_2 - y_1}{x_2 - x_1} = \dfrac{600{,}000 - 300{,}000}{2011 - 2005}$$

$$= \dfrac{300{,}000}{6} = 50{,}000$$

---

10. C   Data Analysis (scatterplot) MEDIUM-HARD

When faced with a question like this, we must analyze each statement individually.

(A) *The average revenue per store increased by over 100% from 2005 to 2009.* True or false? In 2005, according to the line of best fit, the average revenue per store was approximately $300,000. In 2009, the average revenue per store was approximately $500,000. This is a percent increase of

$$\dfrac{500{,}000 - 300{,}000}{300{,}000} \times 100\% = \dfrac{2}{3} \times 100\% = 67\%$$

FALSE

(B) *The total number of retail stores increased by 50% from 2005 to 2012.* True or false? According to the scatterplot, in 2005 there were 3 stores corresponding to the three dots above 2005. In 2012 there were 6 stores corresponding to the 6 dots above 2012. This is a percent increase of

$$\frac{6-3}{3} \times 100\% = 100\%$$

FALSE

(C) *The total revenue for all stores in 2012 is more than three times the total revenue from all stores in 2004.* True or false? In 2004, there were 3 stores with an average revenue per store of approximately $250,000. Therefore the total revenue in 2004 was approximately $3 \times \$250,000 = \$750,000$. In 2012, there were 6 stores with an average revenue per store of approximately $650,000. Therefore the total revenue in 2012 was approximately $6 \times \$650,000 = \$3,900,000$. Since $3,900,000 is more than three time $750,000, this statement is TRUE.

---

11. B   **Algebra (translating quantitative information) MEDIUM**

This question tests your ability to translate words into algebraic expressions. Systematically translate the sentence phrase by phrase.

The product of two numbers, a and b is 6 greater than their sum.
Translation: $ab = 6 + a + b$
Use commutative law of equality
on right side: $ab = a + b + 6$

---

12. D Special Topics (coordinate geometry) MEDIUM

First, find the slope of l using the points $(0, -9)$ and $(12, 0)$:

$$\text{slope} = \frac{y_2 - y_1}{x_2 - x_1} = \frac{0 - (-9)}{12 - 0} = \frac{9}{12} = \frac{3}{4}$$

Since the two lines are parallel, line m must also have a slope of $\frac{3}{4}$. Now we can solve for k using the slope equation and the two points on line m, $(0, 0)$ and $(k, 12)$:

$$\text{slope} = \frac{y_2 - y_1}{x_2 - x_1} = \frac{12 - (0)}{k - 0} = \frac{12}{k} = \frac{3}{4}$$

Cross multiply: $4(12) = 3(k)$
Simplify: $48 = 3k$
Divide by 3: $16 = k$

Notice that the coordinates of the point $(16, 12)$ correspond to the *width* and the *length* of the rectangle, respectively. Therefore, the area of the rectangle is $16 \times 12 = 192$ square units.

---

13. A   **Problem Solving/Data Analysis (ratios) MEDIUM**

If the Giants' win-loss is 2:3, then they won $2n$ games and lost $3n$ games, where n is some unknown integer. (For instance, perhaps they won 2 games and lost 3, in which case $n = 1$, or perhaps they won 20 games and lost 30, in which case $n = 10$, etc.) This means that the total number of games they played is $2n + 3n = 5n$. Since they won 120 games,

$$5n = 120$$
Divide by 5: $n = 24$

Therefore they won $2n = (2)(24) = 48$ games and lost $3n = (3)(24) = 72$ games, and so they lost $72 - 48 = 24$ more games than they won.

---

14. B   Advanced Mathematics (exponential growth) MEDIUM

We might begin by plugging in a number for p. Let's say $p = 120$ cells to start. We are told that after one hour the population decreased by $\frac{1}{3}$. Since $\frac{1}{3}$ of 120 is 40, the population decreased by 40 and the population was then $120 - 40 = 80$ cells. In the second hour, the population *increased* by 40%. Increasing a number by 40% is equivalent to it by 1.40 (because it becomes 140% of what it was), so the population was then $80(1.40) = 112$ cells. In the third hour, the population *increased* by 50%, so it became $112(1.50) = 168$ cells.

Substituting $p = 120$ into each of the answer choices yields (A) $1.3p = 1.3(120) = 156$, (B) $1.4p = 1.4(120) = 168$, (C) $1.5p = 1.5(120) = 180$, and (D) $1.6p = 1.6(120) = 192$. Therefore the answer is (B).

Alternately, you can solve this problem algebraically: $p(2/3)(1.40)(1.50) = 1.40p$.

---

15. B   **Advanced Mathematics (exponentials) MEDIUM**

For this one, we'll need the Laws of Exponentials from

Chapter 9, Lesson 9. $(6^{-2})(m^{-2}) = \frac{1}{16}$

Translate by using Exponential Law #3: $\frac{1}{6^2} \times \frac{1}{m^2} = \frac{1}{16}$

Multiply by m^2: $\frac{1}{6^2} = \frac{1}{16}m^2$

Multiply by 16: $\frac{16}{6^2} = m^2$

Simplify: $\frac{16}{6^2} = \frac{16}{36} = \frac{4}{9} = m^2$

---

16. B   **Data Analysis (probability) MEDIUM**

Let $R =$ the number of red marbles, $W =$ the number of white marbles, and $B =$ the number of blue marbles. If the jar contains twice as many red marbles as white marbles, then $R = 2W$. If the jar contains three times as many white marbles as blue marbles, then $W = 3B$. We can substitute numbers to these equations to solve the problem. Let's say $B = 10$. This means there are $3(10) = 30$ white marbles and $2(30) = 60$ red marbles. The total number of marbles is therefore $10 + 30 + 60 = 100$, and the number of non-red marbles is therefore $10 + 30 = 40$ marbles, so the probability that the marble is *not* red is $\dfrac{40}{100} = \dfrac{2}{5}$.

---

17. C   **Advanced Mathematics (parabolas)**
                                    MEDIUM

The vertex of a parabola with the equation $y = A(x - h)^2 + k$ is (h, k). For this parabola, $h = 2$ and $k = 2$. So, the vertex is $(2, 2)$. The slope of the line that passes through $(1, -3)$ and $(2, 2)$ is

$$\text{slope} = \frac{y_2 - y_1}{x_2 - x_1} = \frac{3 - 2}{-1 - 2} = \frac{1}{-3} = -\frac{1}{3}$$

---

18. C   **Advanced Mathematics (functions)**
                                    MEDIUM-HARD

Let the input number be 7.
Step 1: Multiply the input value by 6:   42
Step 2: Add x to that result: $42 + x$

Step 3: Divide this result by 4: $\dfrac{42 + x}{4}$

This must yield an output of 15: $15 = \dfrac{42 + x}{4}$

Multiply by 4: $60 = 42 + x$
Subtract 42: $18 = x$

---

19. C   Data Analysis (graphing data) MEDIUM-HARD

The graph of the quadratic $y = ax^2 + bx + c$ is a parabola. If $a < 0$, the parabola is "open-down" like a frowny-face. The only graph with this feature is (C).

---

20. B   **Algebra (expressing relationships)**
                                    MEDIUM-HARD

Draw a number line, and to show that $p < r$, place p to the left of r on the number line. The points that are closer to p than to r are all the points to the left of their midpoint. The midpoint is the average of the endpoints: $\dfrac{p + r}{2}$, so if the point with coordinate x is closer to p than to r, then

$$x < \frac{p + r}{2}.$$

---

21. A   **Algebra (simplifying expressions)**
                                    MEDIUM-HARD

$$f(x) = \frac{1}{2 - x}$$

Substitute $\dfrac{1}{m}$ for x: $f\left(\dfrac{1}{m}\right) = \dfrac{1}{2 - \left(\dfrac{1}{m}\right)}$

Simplify the denominator:

$$f\left(\frac{1}{m}\right) = \frac{1}{2 - \left(\dfrac{1}{m}\right)} = \frac{1}{\dfrac{2m}{m} - \dfrac{1}{m}} = \frac{1}{\dfrac{2m - 1}{m}}$$

Divide by multiplying by the reciprocal:

$$1 \div \frac{2m - 1}{m} = 1 \times \frac{m}{2m - 1} = \frac{m}{2m - 1}$$

---

22. A   **Advanced Mathematics (quadratics)**
                                    MEDIUM-HARD

The graph of $y = a(x - 2)(x + 1)$ is a quadratic with zeros (x-intercepts) at $x = 2$ and $x = -1$. The axis of symmetry of this parabola is halfway between the zeros, at $x = (2 + -1)/2 = 1/2$. Since $a < 0$, the parabola is "open down," and so we have a general picture like this:

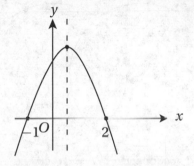

If you trace the curve from $x = 0$ to $x = 5$, that is, from the y-intercept and then to the right, you can see that the graph goes up a bit (until $x = 1/2$), and then goes down again.

Alternately, you can pick a negative value for a (like -2) and graph the equation on your calculator.

---

23. D   **Advanced Mathematics (rational equations)**
                                    HARD

Given equation: $\dfrac{n^2 - 9}{n^2 + 3} = 1 - \dfrac{k}{n^2 + 3}$

Add $\dfrac{k}{n^2 + 3}$: $\dfrac{n^2 - 9}{n^2 + 3} + \dfrac{k}{n^2 + 3} = 1$

Combine the fractions into one: $\dfrac{n^2 - 9 + k}{n^2 + 3} = 1$

Multiply by $n^2 + 3$: $n^2 - 9 + k = n^2 + 3$
Subtract n^2: $-9 + k = 3$
Add 9: $k = 12$

---

24. C Problem Solving (percentages) MEDIUM-HARD

Let $p =$ the price per share of the stock. The cost of 200 of these shares (before commission) is therefore $200p$. With a 3% commission, the cost becomes $(1.03)(200p)$

$$(1.03)(200p) = \$3,399$$

Divide by 1.03: $200p = \$3,300$
Divide by 200: $p = \$16.50$ per share

---

25. A **Algebra (expressing quantities)**
MEDIUM-HARD

It may be easiest to choose number for w and y. Assume $y = 4$. If w is 50% greater than y, then $w = 1.5(4) = 6$. Therefore $w^{-2} = 6^{-2} = 1/36$, and $y^{-2} = 4^{-2} = 1/16$. Therefore the ratio of w^{-2} to y^{-2} is

$$\frac{\frac{1}{36}}{\frac{1}{16}} = \frac{1}{36} \times \frac{16}{1} = \frac{16}{36} = \frac{8}{18} = \frac{4}{9}$$

---

26. D **Data Analysis (set relations) HARD**

Let's let $s =$ the total number of athletes in the group who play soccer, and $t =$ the number of athletes in the group who run track. We can set up a Venn diagram to show the relationship between these two overlapping sets.

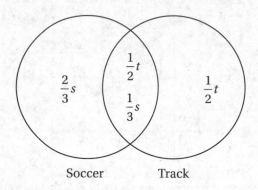

Soccer   Track

Since one-third of the soccer players also run track, we must put $\frac{1}{3}s$ in the overlapping region between soccer and track, and therefore the number who play only soccer is $\frac{2}{3}s$. Likewise, since one-half of the athletes who run track also play soccer, we must put $\frac{1}{2}t$ in the overlapping region, and therefore the number of athletes who only run track is $\frac{1}{2}t$.

Sincer there are 60 athletes in total: $\frac{2}{3}s + \frac{1}{2}t + \frac{1}{2}t = 60$

Simplify: $\frac{2}{3}s + t = 60$

Multiply by 3 to simplify: $2s + 3t = 180$
The number of soccer players who run track must equal the number of track athletes who play soccer: $\frac{1}{3}s = \frac{1}{2}t$

Multiply by 6 (the common denominator): $2s = 3t$
Substitute $2s = 3t$ into the previous equation: $3t + 3t = 180$

Simplify: $6t = 180$
Divide by 6: $t = 30$
Substitute $t = 30$ into the other equation to solve for s: $2s = 3(30)$
Simplify: $2s = 90$
Divide by 2: $s = 45$

Now we can use these values to complete the Venn diagram:

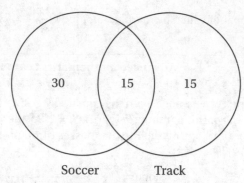

Soccer   Track

From this diagram, we can see that the only true statement among the choices is (D).

---

27. D **Advanced Mathematics (transformations)**
HARD

The graph of $y = g(x) = f(x) + b$ is the graph of f vertically shifted up by b units. If $g(x) = 0$ has exactly one solution, the graph of $y = g(x)$ can touch the x-axis at only one point: the vertex. Since the vertex of f has a y-coordinate of -2, this can only happen if f is shifted up 2 units, so $b = 2$.

---

28. B **Special Topics (trigonometry) HARD**

The statement $\frac{\pi}{2} < x < \pi$ indicates that x is an angle in quadrant II, where the cosine is negative. Let's draw this situation on the unit circle so we can visualize it. (We don't want to confuse the *angles* called x and y in the problem with the x-coordinates and y-coordinates in the xy-plane. For this reason, let's label the terminal rays for the angles "angle x" and "angle y.") Recall that the cosine of any angle is the x-coordinate of the point on the unit circle that corresponds to that angle. If $\cos x = a$, then a is the x-coordinate of the point on the unit circle that corresponds to "angle x," as shown in the diagram.

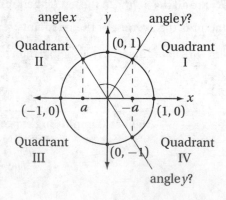

Now notice that, since a is a negative number, $-a$ (that, is, the *opposite* of a), is a *positive* number. More specifically, it is the reflection of the point labeled a over the x-axis, as shown in the diagram. Now, if $\cos y = -a$, then "angle y" corresponds to a point on the unit circle with an x-coordinate of $-a$. There are two possible locations for this point on the circle, and both are shown in the diagram above. Notice that one of these angles is the reflection of "angle x" over the y-axis. This is the supplement of "angle x," that is, $\pi - x$. The other is the reflection of "angle x" over the origin, that is, $x + \pi$. Therefore, the correct answer is (B).

Alternately, we could use the calculator to solve this problem by process of elimination. We can choose a value of "angle x" between $\pi/2$ and π. (In radian mode this is an angle between 1.57 and 3.14, and in degree mode it is an angle between 90° and 180°.) Let's pick "angle x" to be 2 radians (about 115°). According to the calculator, $\cos(2) = -.416$. Therefore, $\cos y$ must equal .416. Now we can substitute $x = 2$ into all of the choices and see which angle has a cosine of .416.

(A) $\cos(2 + 2\pi) = -.416$

(B) $\cos(2 + \pi) = .416$

(C) $\cos(2 + \pi/2) = -.909$

(D) $\cos(-2 + 2\pi) = -.416$

Therefore the correct answer is (B).

---

29. A Data Analysis (table) HARD

Since the question asks about those "who expressed an opinion on Proposal 81a," we must *ignore* those who are listed as having No Opinion.

The number at the bottom right of the table indicated that there were 4,407 total people surveyed. But 719 of those had No Opinion, so $4,407 - 719 = 3,688$ *did* have an opinion. What percentage of *those* are under 40? The answer is in the first row of the table (18 to 39): 917 of these Approve and 204 of these Disapprove. Therefore $917 + 204 = 1,121$ of those showing an opinion are under 40 years of age.

Therefore the percentage of those showing an opinion who are under 40 is $\left(\dfrac{1,121}{3,688}\right)100 = 30.4\%$

---

30. B Data Analysis (table) HARD

(A) The approval rate for Proposal 81a generally decreases with the age of the voter.

Age 18 to 39:   918 out of 1,624 approve (56%)
Age 40 to 64:   1,040 out of 1,644 approve (64%)
Age 65 and older: 604 out of 1,139 approve (53%)

The approval rate increases and then decreases with age, so (A) is not correct.

(B) The disapproval rate for Proposal 81a generally increases with the age of the voter:

Age 18 to 39:   204 out of 1,624 disapprove (13%)
Age 40 to 64:   502 out of 1,644 disapprove (31%)

Age 65 and older: 420 out of 1,139 disapprove (37%)

The disapproval rate INCREASES as age increases, therefore (B) is correct.

---

31. 1/5 or 0.2 Data Analysis (variation) MEDIUM

If y varies inversely as x: $\qquad y = \dfrac{k}{x}$

Substitute $\frac{1}{2} = y$ and $10 = x$: $\qquad \dfrac{1}{2} = \dfrac{k}{10}$

Cross multiply: $\qquad 10 = 2k$
Divide by 2: $\qquad 5 = k$

Therefore the general equation is: $\qquad y = \dfrac{5}{x}$

Substitute $25 = y$: $\qquad 25 = \dfrac{5}{x}$

Multiply by x: $\qquad 25x = 5$

Divide by 25: $\qquad x = \dfrac{5}{25} = \dfrac{1}{5}$

---

32. 169 Advance Mathematics (quadratics) MEDIUM

$$x^2 + 12x = 13$$
Subtract 13: $\qquad x^2 + 12x - 13 = 0$
Factor: $\qquad (x + 13)(x - 1) = 0$
Use the Zero Product Property: $\qquad x = -13$ or $x = 1$
If $x < 0$, x must be -13. Therefore $x^2 = (-13)^2 = 169$.

Alternately, if you have QUADFORM (a quadratic formula program) programmed into your calculator, select PROGRAM, QUADFORM, and input $a = 1$, $b - 12$ and $c = -13$ to find the zeros (-13 and 1).

---

33. 112 Special Topics (polygons) MEDIUM-HARD

Notice that the "cutouts" can be reassembled to form two squares with side x and diagonal y, leaving an octagon with perimeter $8y$.

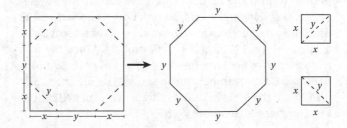

Since each of the cutout triangles is a
right triangle: $\qquad x^2 + x^2 = y^2$
Simplify: $\qquad 2x^2 = y^2$
If the total area of the "cutouts"
is 196 square centimeters: $\qquad 2x^2 = 196$
Substitute $2x^2 = y^2$: $\qquad y^2 = 196$
Take square root: $\qquad y = 14$
Therefore the perimeter of the octagon is $8 \times 14 = 112$.

34. **16**   Algebra (solving equations) HARD

Because $m^2 + n^2 = 40$, where m and n are both integers, we must look for two perfect squares that have a sum of 40. The perfect squares are 1, 4, 9, 16, 25, 36, 49, 64, 81, 100 . . . and the only two of these with a sum of 40 are 4 and 36. So either $m^2 = 4$ and $n^2 = 36$ or $m^2 = 36$ and $n^2 = 4$.

CASE 1:	$m^2 = 4$ and $n^2 = 36$
Take square root:	$m = \pm 2$ and $n = \pm 6$
Since $m < 0 < n$:	$m = -2$ and $n = 6$
Evaluate $(m + n)^2$:	$(m + n)^2 = (-2 + 6)^2 = 4^2 = 16$
CASE 2:	$m^2 = 36$ and $n^2 = 4$
Take square root:	$m = \pm 6$ and $n = \pm 2$
Since $m < 0 < n$:	$m = -6$ and $n = 2$
Evaluate $(m + n)^2$:	$(m + n)^2 = (-6 + 2)^2 = (-4)^2 = 16$

35. **1.4**   Advanced Mathematics (trigonometry) MEDIUM-HARD

Recall the Pythagorean Trigonometric Identity, which is true for all x: $\sin^2 x + \cos^2 x = 1$
Expression to be evaluated: $(\sin x + \cos x)^2$
FOIL: $(\sin x + \cos x)(\sin x + \cos x) = \sin^2 x + 2(\sin x)(\cos x) + \cos^2 x$
Rearrange with Commutative and Associative Laws of Addition: $2(\sin x)(\cos x) + (\sin^2 x + \cos^2 x)$
Substitute $\sin^2 x + \cos^2 x = 1$: $2(\sin x)(\cos x) + 1$
Substitute $(\sin x)(\cos x) = 0.2$: $2(0.2) + 1 = 1.4$

36. **115**   Data Analysis (central tendency) MEDIUM

Begin by putting the data in order from least expensive to most expensive:

80 phones sold for $98
40 phones sold for $110
20 phones sold for $120
62 phones sold for $140
38 phones sold for $162

We don't have to actually write out the prices of all 240 phones to find the median price. We can divide any set of 240 numbers, in ascending order, into two sets of 120 numbers. The median is in the middle of these, so it is the average of the 120th and 121st numbers. Since the first two categories account for $40 + 80 = 120$ of these numbers, the 120th number in the set is $110, and the 121st number in the set is in the next higher category, $120. The median price is therefore $(\$110 + \$120)/2 = \$115$.

37. **6.8**   Problem Solving (extended thinking) HARD

If the height of the logo is to match the height of the banner, it must have a height of 4 feet. Let x be the corresponding length of the logo.
Since the logo has a height-to-length ratio of 5:8: $\dfrac{5}{8} = \dfrac{4}{x}$
Cross multiply: $5x = 32$
Divide by 5: $x = 6.4$

Since the banner is 20 feet long, there are $20 - 6.4 = 13.6$ feet in total for the side margins. If the logo is centered, then each margin is half this length, $13.6 \div 2 = 6.8$ feet.

38. **25**   Problem Solving (extended thinking) HARD

The banner has dimensions of 20 feet by 4 feet, so its area is $20 \times 4 = 80$ square feet. If the company charges $1.20 per square foot for the banner material, this cost is $80 \times \$1.20 = \$96$. Based on the logo dimensions we determined in the previous problem, the area of the logo is $4 \times 6.4 = 25.6$ square feet. If the company charges $2.50 per square foot for the logo, the cost per printed logo is $25.6 \times \$2.50 = \$64$.

If the company charges a fixed cost of $32 per banner, then the total cost of a banner with ONE logo would be $\$96 + \$64 + \$32 = \$192$. The total cost of a banner with TWO logos would be $\$96 + \$64 + \$64 + \$32 = \$256$.

We can calculate the percent savings with the "percent change" formula, since we are considering a "change" from the more expensive banner to the less expensive banner.

$$\frac{192 - 256}{256} \times 100\% = \frac{-64}{256} \times 100\% = -25\%$$

Therefore the percent savings is 25(%).

Section 5: Essay

Sample Response

In his essay, "Mind Over Mass Media," Steven Pinker examines the "moral panics" (1) about the supposed moral and cognitive declines caused by new forms of media. He uses vivid imagery to illustrate the misconceptions about how new media affect the brain. His central claim, that "such panics often fail reality checks" (3), is supported with historical examples, logical analysis, and touches of humor. He provides scientific context for his claims, and analyzes the misconceptions that cultural critics have about the relationship between modern media and the human brain. He occasionally argues by assertion rather than providing evidence, and might be accused of oversimplifying the opposing viewpoint.

Pinker puts this debate in historical context by giving examples of similar moral panics from past dec des, and uses inductive reasoning to show that the new arguments fail for the same reason that the old ones did. He says that new forms of media "have always caused moral panics" (1) but that these panics have not been based in reality. He says that "comic books were accused of turning juveniles into delinquents in the 1950s" (3) and that similarly "television, transistor radios and rock videos" (3) were supposed to be rotting young minds, but that really "IQs rose continuously" (3) during those periods.

Pinker uses strong action verbs to illustrate theories about how the brain works, clarifying these concepts for the reader and also enhancing his ethos as an expert. He says new media opponents are afraid that these technologies make us "skim on the surface of knowledge rather than dive into its depths" (2) and cause the quality of scientific thinking to "plummet" (4). But in fact, Pinker says, scientific discoveries are "multiplying" and progress is "dizzying." When he describes how the brain processes information, he uses verbs like "pounded" (5) and "revamp" (6). These lively action verbs help the reader to see the different sides of the argument, and they show that Pinker understands the issues very well, enhancing Pinker's ethos as a writer.

Pinker attempts to counter moral outrage with an appeal to the value of "intellectual depth" (10), and provides practical advice for achieving that goal. This is helpful to readers who want to do more than understand the brain, but also want to make people smarter. He tells us that intellectual skills are developed "in special institutions, which we call universities, and maintained with constant upkeep" (10).

Some readers might object that Pinker sometimes makes claims without evidence, such as "music doesn't make you better at math" (7). They might also accuse him of creating a "straw man" by oversimplifying the claims of his opponents, like when he says "yes, every time we learn a fact or skill the wiring of our brain changes; it's not as if the information is stored in the pancreas" (5). Nevertheless, Pinker addresses the attacks on modern media, and gives an effective counterargument.

Scoring

Reading—4 out of 4

This essay demonstrates a strong comprehension of Pinker's central claims, using summary, paraphrase, and quotations. It summarizes Pinker's central thesis, modes of argument, and tone (*his central claim, that "such panics often fail reality checks," is supported with historical examples, logical analysis, and touches of humor*). The quotations are carefully chosen to illustrate the central ideas of Pinker's argument, and are accompanied by relevant and accurate commentary.

Analysis—4 out of 4

This essay provides a thoughtful and critical analysis of Pinker's argument and style, demonstrating a strong understanding of the analytical task. The essay identifies Pinker's primary modes of expression (*historical examples, logical analysis, and touches of humor*), examines his mode of reasoning (*inductive reasoning*), and even identifies possible gaps in his argument (*assertions without evidence . . . "straw man"*) without taking a side for or against Pinker's thesis. It also provides substantial textual evidence for its claims, and demonstrates a strong understanding of Pinker's rhetorical task.

Writing—4 out of 4

This essay shows mastery of language, organization, and sentence structure. It remains focused on a clear central claim, and develops its secondary claims in well-organized paragraphs. It demonstrates effective variation in sentence structure and generally appropriate word choice. Largely free from grammatical error, this essay demonstrates strong command of language and proficiency in writing.

CHAPTER 3

SAT VOCABULARY: THE LANGUAGE OF IDEAS

1. The Language of Ideas and Learning   92

2. The Language of Argument, Reasoning, and Persuasion   94

3. The Language of Dissent, Criticism, and Rebellion   104

4. The Language of Power and Submission   108

5. The Language of Language and Literature   115

6. The Language of Judgment   118

7. The Language of Extremism and Exaggeration   121

8. The Language of Care and Restraint   122

9. The Language of Freedom   125

10. The Language of Change and Force   126

11. The Language of Dullness and Stasis   128

12. The Language of Truth, Truthfulness, and Beauty   129

13. The Language of Deceit, Error, and Confusion   130

14. The Language of Creativity and Productivity   133

15. The Language of Mystery, Surprise, Adventure, and Discovery   135

16. The Language of Harm, Deficit, and Decline   137

17. The Language of Kindness, Favor, and Benefit   139

18. The Language of Wisdom, Strength, and Skill   143

19. The Language of Capital and Wealth   145

20. The Language of Passion, Emotion, and Sensation   147

The Power Roots and Affixes for the SAT   150

The SAT Reading Test: Vocabulary

Why is vocabulary important on the SAT Reading, Writing, and Essay tests?

Although the SAT no longer includes strictly vocabulary-focused questions—such as antonym, analogy, or sentence completion questions—vocabulary-building is still an essential component of improving your SAT Reading, SAT Writing, and SAT Essay scores. The new SAT assesses your *effective* vocabulary by asking you to comprehend, analyze, and write about extended college-level passages that may include vocabulary from the humanities, like *iconoclast, aesthetic,* and *colloquial*; vocabulary from the physical and human sciences, like *catalyst, catharsis,* and *anomaly*; and vocabulary from rhetoric, like *apologist, polemic,* and *advocate*.

According to the College Board, numerous SAT Reading and Writing questions will assess

> *whether students are able to interpret the meanings of relevant words and phrases in context and/or analyze how word choice influences meaning, shapes mood and tone, reflects point of view, or lends precision or interest.*

Sound intimidating? It's not. Here's how to build an effective vocabulary for the SAT:

- Spend one hour per week making 30 flashcards of new words and/or roots from this chapter, using the formats described below.
- Spend 10 minutes per night, at least three nights per week reviewing the flashcards.

Vocabulary Flashcards

> Although some people appreciate obedience in others, I find OB-_SEQUI-_ _OUS_ behavior revolting.

Front: Since the SAT tests your vocabulary in context, **write each new word in a meaningful sentence** on the front of the card. Also, **capitalize** the new word and **underline the important roots and affixes**.

> Excessively obedient or servile
> (to + follow + (adj))
> *servile, sycophantic, deferential, fawning, ingratiating*
>
> O

Back: On the back, **write the definition** of the word, as well as the **meanings of the roots and affixes** below it. Also **include the synonyms** from the synonym entry for each word, and the **first letter of the word** in the lower right-hand corner. (This is for the **crossword method** of vocabulary review described below.)

Root Flashcards

> mag, maj, max
> *magnus* (L)

Front: Write the **different forms of the root or prefix** as it commonly appears in English words. You may also want to include the original Latin or Greek word.

> great
> *magnificent* (impressively elaborate)
> *magnanimous, maxim, majesty, magnitude*

Back: Write the **definition of the root or affix** on the back of the flashcard, followed by the **anchor word** (that is, the word with the clearest and most meaningful connection to the root or affix). Below that, write the **root family**, that is, those words (especially the SAT "challenge" words) that also contain the root.

Daily Flashcard Study Methods

Sentence Method: Your friend reads you the word, and you give its definition and use it in a sentence different from the one on the front of the card. Try to come up with a different sentence each time.

Root Method: Your friend reads you the word, and you identify and define its roots and affixes and give examples of other words that share the root or affixes.

Crossword Method: Your friend reads you the definition and first letter of the word, and you give the word.

Mnemonic Method: For obscure words, teach your friend a clever mnemonic trick—like a crazy picture or sound association—for remembering its meaning.

1 THE LANGUAGE OF IDEAS AND LEARNING

☐ **abstract** (adj)   *ab-* away + *tractus* pulled

existing as an idea but not as a tangible experience : *For over a thousand years, mathematicians regarded subtracting a large number from a small one as impossible because the concept of negative numbers was too abstract.*
Form: abstraction = something that exists only as an idea
Root family: [tract] ***retraction*** (a pulling back), ***protract*** (to extend in time), ***tractor*** (vehicle that pulls farm instruments), ***detract*** (reduce the value of someone or something), ***tractable*** (manageable)

☐ **anthropology** (n)   *anthro* human + *-ology* study

the study and comparison of human cultures : *The Amazon basin has long been a focus of anthropological research because of its many isolated indigenous tribes.*
Root family: [anthro] ***misanthrope*** (one who distrusts all people), ***philanthropy*** (generosity to charitable causes), ***anthropomorphic*** (having human form), ***anthropocentric*** (pertaining to the belief that humans are the center of the universe)
Don't confuse with: ***archaeology*** (the study of ancient civilizations), ***paleontology*** (the study of fossils)

☐ **comprehensive** (adj)   *com-* together + *prehendere* to grasp

thorough and complete; covering all relevant subjects : *My doctor gave me a comprehensive physical examination.*
Synonyms: ***exhaustive, encyclopedic***
Root family: [prehens] ***reprehensible*** (morally objectionable), ***apprehensive*** (fearful)
Don't confuse with: ***comprehensible*** (understandable)
Mnemonic: To avoid confusing ***comprehensive*** with ***comprehensible***, focus on the roots and, especially, the suffixes. Recall that *–ible* or *–able* means "able to be"; for instance, ***defensible*** means "able to be defended." Therefore, ***comprehensible*** means "able to be grasped by the mind (*prehendere* = to grasp), while ***comprehensive*** means "encompassing (or grasping) everything relevant."

☐ **construe** (v)   *con-* together + *struere* to build

to interpret in a particular way : *Some opinion polls are unreliable because their biased phrasing encourages people to construe issues to conform to the ideology of the pollster.*
Form: misconstrue = to interpret incorrectly
Root family: [con-, co-, com-, col-] ***conjecture*** (guess), ***consensus*** (general agreement), ***conspire*** (to plot together), ***coalesce*** (to come together), ***coherent*** (forming a united whole), ***compliant*** (willing to obey), ***confluence*** (a place at which two things merge)
Root family: [stru, stroy, stry] ***destroy*** (put an end to by attacking), ***instruct*** (to teach), ***industry*** (manufacturing activity), ***obstruct*** (impede)
Don't confuse with: ***construct*** (to build)

☐ **discerning** (adj)   *dis-* apart + *cernere* to separate

showing a keen ability to distinguish subtle elements : *Elena has a very discerning palate for olives and can even tell in what region of Italy they were grown.*
Forms: discern = to recognize and distinguish, ***discernment*** = keen judgment, ***discernible*** = perceivable
Synonyms: ***discriminating, judicious, astute, percipient, perspicacious***
Root family: [dis-] ***disparate*** (very different; variegated), ***discrepancy*** (a lack of compatibility between facts or claims), ***disseminate*** (to cast widely), ***disperse*** (to spread or scatter), ***diffuse*** (spread over a wide area)
Root family: [cern, cert, cret, cre] ***ascertain*** (find something out for certain), ***certain*** (known for sure), ***certify*** (formally attest or confirm), ***discretion*** (behavior to avoid offense or revealing private information; freedom to make decisions)

☐ **discriminating** (adj)   *dis-* apart + *crimen* judicial decision

showing good taste or judgment : *Our interior designer has a discriminating eye for bold fabrics.*
Forms: indiscriminate = done without careful judgment
Synonyms: ***discerning, judicious, astute, percipient, perspicacious***
Root family: [dis-] ***disparate*** (very different; variegated), ***discrepancy*** (a lack of compatibility between facts or claims), ***disseminate*** (to cast widely), ***disperse*** (to spread or scatter), ***disputatious*** (argumentative), ***dispel*** (to drive away; to eliminate), ***diffuse*** (spread over a wide area)

CHAPTER 3 / SAT VOCABULARY: THE LANGUAGE OF IDEAS

Root family: [crim] *criminal* (one who commits a crime), *recrimination* (counteraccusation), *crime* (illegal act)

Usage: The word *discrimination* generally has a negative connotation because of its association with unfair practices like racial or sexual discrimination and because of its connection, via the Latin root *crimen* (judicial decision) with words like *crime* and *criminal*. *Discriminating*, however, has a generally positive connotation because it is associated with an expert's judicious ability to distinguish good things from bad.

☐ **disseminate** (v)   *dis-* widely + *semen* seed

to cast (something, usually information) widely, as seed is scattered : *The rumor was disseminated almost instantaneously over the Internet.*

Form: *dissemination* = the process or act of spreading information widely

Synonyms: *promulgate, propagate, circulate*

Root family: [dis-] *disconcerting* (unsettling), *disparate* (very different; variegated), *discrepancy* (a lack of compatibility between facts or claims), *disperse* (to spread or scatter), *dispel* (to drive away; to eliminate), *diffuse* (spread over a wide area)

Root family: [semin] *seminary* (a college to prepare clergy), *seminal* (serving as a primary influence on later works), *seminar* (a discussion-based class)

Don't confuse *dissemination* with *disinformation* (incorrect or misleading information)

Mnemonic: Picture a farmer casting *seed widely* (*dis* = widely + *semen* = seed).

☐ **erudite** (adj)   *e-* not + *rudis* untrained, unwrought

having or showing great learning or knowledge : *Professor Jacoby could be engagingly erudite without seeming pompous.*

Form: *erudition* = an expression of great learning or knowledge; the quality of having great learning or knowledge

Root family: [rud] *rudiment* (a most basic element or undeveloped first form of something), *rudimentary* (basic or undeveloped), *rude* (ill-mannered)

Synonyms: *scholarly, cerebral, learned*

Don't confuse with: *eradicate* (to destroy completely)

☐ **indoctrinate** (v)   *in-* in + *docere* to teach

to teach someone to accept a set of beliefs uncritically : *The parents were concerned that the guest speaker was going to indoctrinate their children.*

Forms: *doctrine* = a set of beliefs held by a political, philosophical, or religious group

Synonyms: *proselytize, inculcate, propagandize*

Root family: [in-] *inundate* (to flood), *incisive* (showing keen judgment), *ingratiate* (to curry favor), *inherent* (existing as an inseparable element), *infiltrate* (to gain access secretly)

Root family: [doc, dox] *doctrinaire* (seeking to impose rigid doctrine), *orthodox* (conforming strictly to traditional teachings), *docile* (compliant and easy to instruct), *paradox* (a self-contradictory statement or situation)

☐ **insular** (adj)   *insula* island

isolated from cultural and intellectual influences outside one's own experience : *The farming village was too insular for Madeleine, who wanted to experience the outside world.*

Form: *insularity* = the quality of being culturally isolated

Root family: [insula] *insulation* (the state of being protected from loss of heat, electrical conduction, or unpleasant effects, or the materials or situations that provide such protection), *isolate* (to set apart from others), *island* (land mass surrounded by water), *peninsula* (land mass surrounded on three sides by water)

Mnemonic: An *insular* community is *insulated* from outside influences.

☐ **orthodox** (adj)   *orthos* right, straight + *docere* to teach

conforming strictly to traditional teachings : *Doctor Altbaum is respectfully skeptical of treatments that have not been tested via orthodox trials.*

Forms: *orthodoxy* = authorized theory or practice, *unorthodox* = straying from conventional teachings

Root family: [ortho] *orthogonal* (at right angles), *orthopedics* (the branch of medicine dealing with correcting bone and muscle deformities), *orthodontics* (the treatment of the misalignment of teeth)

Root family: [doc, dox] *doctrinaire* (seeking to impose rigid doctrine), *indoctrinate* (to teach someone to accept a set of beliefs uncritically), *docile* (compliant and easy to instruct)

☐ *pedantic* (adj)   *pedante* schoolmaster (< *pais* child)

inclined to show off one's learning or knowledge; acting like a know-it-all : *Jennifer's pedantic displays in class earned her the scorn of her classmates.*
Forms: *pedant* = a know-it-all; *pedantry* = the quality or practice of being a know-it-all
Root family: [ped] *pediatrician* (a children's doctor), *pedagogy* (the art of teaching)
Mnemonic: The word *pedant* derives from *pedagogue* (schoolmaster, or literally "leader of children"), so a *pedant* is anyone who acts like a know-it-all schoolmaster. Or, for a wacky visual mnemonic, picture a gigantic *pet ant* that comes to school and raises his hand all the time because he knows all the answers.
Don't confuse words that derive from *ped* (foot)—like *pedestrian*, *podiatrist*, and *pedal*—with words that derive from *pais* (child)—like *pediatrician*, *pedagogy*, and *pedant*.

☐ *peruse* (v)   *per-* thoroughly + *use* use

to read thoroughly and carefully : *Pitifully few of the congressmen perused the bill before signing it.*
Form: *perusal* = the act of reading thoroughly
Root family: [per-] *perfect* (as good as can be), *perpetuate* (to help to continue for an extended period of time), *perfunctory* (carried out with a minimum of effort), *perturb* (to make uncomfortable or anxious)
Don't confuse with: *carouse* (drink alcohol abundantly, merrily, and boisterously), *pursue* (to follow in order to catch or attack)
Mnemonic: It's common to mistake *perusal* with *cursory (casual) reading* when in fact it means *careful reading*. Remember that it derives from *per* which means "thoroughly," so to *peruse* means to "use thoroughly."

☐ *postulate* (v)

[POS chew late] assume the existence or truth of something as a basis for reasoning : *Copernicus postulated that the simplest explanation for planetary motion was probably the best explanation.*
Form: *postulate* (n) [POS chew let] = an assumption made for the purpose of reasoning
Synonyms: *posit, presume, hypothesize*
Don't confuse with: *pustule* (a small pimple)

☐ *provincial* (adj)

unsophisticated or narrow-minded; particular to the narrow views of an isolated community : *Glen's comments reflected his provincial political views rather than an understanding of the national interest.*
Form: *provincialism* = narrow-mindedness or lack of sophistication
Synonyms: *parochial*
Don't confuse with: *providential* (opportune; involving benevolent divine intervention)
Mnemonic: A *province* is a small region within an empire, so someone who has never been beyond his or her *province* is *provincial*.

☐ *revelation* (n)

a fact revealed in a surprising way : *The biography provided many interesting revelations.*
Form: *revelatory* = revealing something previously unknown
Synonym: *epiphany*
Don't confuse with: *revelry* (noisy festivities)

2   THE LANGUAGE OF ARGUMENT, REASONING, AND PERSUASION

☐ *advocate* (v)   *ad-* for + *vocare* to call, to give voice

[AD vo kate] to provide public support for a person, cause, or policy : *Gina is a tireless advocate for human rights and freedom.*
Form: *advocate* (n) [AD voh kit] = one who advocates
Root family: [ad-] *allude* (to hint at indirectly), *aspire* (to strive for a lofty goal), *adhere* (stick fast (to)), *acquiesce* (to comply reluctantly), *annul* (to declare invalid)
Root family: [voc, vok] *evocative* (bringing strong images or feelings to mind), *revoke* (to take back), *provocative* (causing anger or annoyance), *equivocate* (to speak ambiguously and noncommittally)
Mnemonic: To *advocate* is to *give voice to* (*vocare* = to call) someone or something.
Don't confuse with: *abdicate* = to step down from a position of power

☐ **apologist** (n)   *apo-* away + *logos* word, study

one who argues for a particular, often controversial, position : *We were surprised to discover that a few of the history professors seemed to be apologists for fascism.*
Forms: apology = an argument for a particular position, **apologetics** = the study or practice of arguing for a particular position
Synonym: polemicist
Root family: [apo-] **apostasy** (the renunciation of a religious belief), **apocryphal** (having doubtful authenticity)
Root family: [log] **eulogy** (a praising speech), **epilogue** (afterword), **anthology** (a collection of literary works)
Don't confuse with: apologizer (one who expresses regret); **apologizers** regret their positions, but **apologists** do not.

☐ **appease** (v)   *pais* peace

to yield to demands in order to conciliate : *We must not appease belligerent dictators.*
Form: appeasement = the act of conciliating
Synonyms: propitiate, pacify, mollify, placate
Root family: [pac, peas] **pacify** (to calm), **pact** (a peace agreement)
Usage: See usage note at **pacify** in section 4.

☐ **bolster** (v)

to strengthen or support : *The case was bolstered by the testimony of three eyewitnesses.*
Synonyms: fortify, augment, buttress
Don't confuse with: booster (one who promotes something), **holster** (a handgun holder)

☐ **buttress** (n) or (v)

[1] (n) a projecting support for a building, usually of stone or brick; any strong support : *Each buttress on the cathedral was over forty feet long.*
Synonym: bulwark
[2] (v) to provide with support or justification : *The prince's claim to the throne was buttressed by papal decree.*
Synonyms: fortify, augment, bolster

☐ **cajole** (v)

to persuade through flattery or coaxing : *Theo could not be cajoled into accepting the position.*
Form: cajolery = flattery designed to persuade
Synonyms: wheedle, coax, inveigle

☐ **circumlocutory** (adj)   *circum* around + *loqui* to talk

inclined to speak evasively; speaking as if to avoid the subject : *We expected the candidate to give a circumlocutory and politically correct answer to the question, but were surprised to hear her give a direct and candid response.*
Form: circumlocution = evasive speech
Synonym: periphrastic (*peri-* around + **phrasis** speech)
Root family: [circum] **circumspect** (cautious), **circuitous** (roundabout)
Root family: [loqu, locu] **loquacious** (talkative), **colloquial** (conversational), **eloquent** (well-spoken), **obloquy** (verbal abuse)

☐ **circumscribe** (v)   *circum* around + *scribere* to write or draw

to define the limits of something, often an issue or problem : *Although the Reimann Hypothesis has yet to be proven, many mathematicians believe that the problem is so well circumscribed that it soon will be.*
Synonym: encompass
Root family: [circum] **circumspect** (wary, cautious)
Root family: [scrib, script] **inscribe** (to write on or carve into something indelibly), **description** (a spoken or written representation of a person, event, or object)
Don't confuse with: circumstance (general situation or condition), **circumspect** (cautious)

☐ **cohesive** (adj)   *co-* together + *haerere* to stick

forming a united whole : *A good jazz band must be cohesive, because its members must communicate instantaneously with subtle musical and gestural cues.*
Form: cohesion = the act of forming a united whole
Synonym: coherent

Root family: [con-, co-, com-, col-] *consensus* (general agreement), *conspire* (to plot together), *coalesce* (to come together), *compliant* (willing to obey), *confluence* (a place at which two things merge)

Root family: [her, hes] *adhesive* (glue-like substance), *coherent* (clear and rational), *inherent* (existing as an inseparable attribute), *adherent* (a faithful believer in a particular practice or philosophy)

Don't confuse with: *adhesive* (a glue-like substance)

Usage: See usage note at *coherent* in section 5.

☐ *conjecture* (n)   *con-* together + *ject* thrown

a guess based on incomplete information : *Our controversial conjecture on the nature of the newly discovered planet turned out to be correct.*

Form: *conjectural* = based on conjecture

Synonyms: *speculation, postulation*

Root family: [con-, co-, com-, col-] *conformist* (one who conscientiously complies with the standards of a group), *conventional* (according to common practice), *consensus* (general agreement), *conspire* (to plot together), *coalesce* (to come together), *coherent* (forming a united whole), *confluence* (a place at which two things merge)

Root family: [ject] *objective* (based on fact), *subjective* (based on opinion), *reject* (to throw back), *eject* (to throw outward)

Mnemonic: A conjecture is an idea that is "thrown together" (*con* (together) + *ject* (throw)) from incomplete evidence, rather than determined definitively.

☐ *consensus* (n)   *con-* together + *sentire* to feel

[1] general agreement : *The senators were happy to finally reach consensus on the bill.*

Synonyms: *concord, unanimity*

[2] the generally held opinion on a matter : *The consensus was that David was the better player.*

Root family: [sens, sent] *sentient* (having the ability to feel), *sensation* (the experience of feeling), *dissent* (disagreement with conventional views)

Don't confuse with: *census* (an official survey of a population), *concession* (something granted due to a demand)

☐ *contentious* (adj)

causing or likely to provoke an argument : *Carl's accusation was as contentious as it was false.*

Forms: *contend (with)* = struggle to surmount, *contend (for)* = struggle to win (something), *contention* = disagreement; an assertion made in an argument, *contentiousness* = argumentativeness

Synonyms: *belligerent, bellicose, pugnacious, truculent*

Don't confuse with: *content* (adj) (satisfied)

☐ *credulous* (adj)   *credere* to believe

willing to believe : *None of Dave's friends were credulous when he said he was going to start his own business.*

Forms: *incredulous* = unwilling to believe, *credulity* = willingness to believe, *incredulity* = skepticism

Synonyms: *gullible, ingenuous*

Root family: [cred] *credence* (acceptance as true; believability), *credit* (good faith, particularly with regard to financial loans), *credible* (believable)

☐ *criteria* (n, pl)   *kritikos* judge

principles or standards by which something is judged or decided : *The candidate did not meet our criteria for a management position.*

Form: *criterion* (n, sing) = a single standard or principle by which something is judged or decided

Root family: [crit] *critic* (one who judges the merit of something; one who expresses a negative opinion), *critique* (a detailed evaluation), *diacritic* (a symbol above or below a letter indicating its pronunciation)

Usage: Remember that *criteria* is the plural of *criterion*.

☐ *cursory* (adj)   *currere* to run

hasty and superficial : *Marco was only able to take a cursory glance at the report before making his presentation.*

Synonyms: *perfunctory, desultory*

Root family: [cur] *cursive* (written so that adjacent characters are connected), *courier* (messenger), *curriculum* (a course of study), *incur* (to become subject to something because of one's own actions), *precursor* (a forerunner; a substance from which something else is formed)

Don't confuse with: *cursive* (written such that letters run together), *curse* (a solemn utterance intended to bring harm; a swear)

Mnemonic: If you perform a *cursory* reading, you just *run* through it quickly and hastily (*currere* = to run).

☐ **debunk** (v)

to expose the falseness of a belief : *Harry Houdini debunked all of the mediums who claimed to be able to talk to his dead mother.*

Form: *debunker* = one who debunks; *bunk* = nonsense

Synonyms: *refute*, *invalidate*

Don't confuse *debunker* with *bunker* (reinforced underground shelter; sand hazard on a golf course).

☐ **delineate** (v)   *de-* completely + *lineare* to create with lines

to describe or portray precisely : *The committee delineated the rules by which future officers would be chosen.*

Forms: *delineation* = the process or act of describing something precisely

Root family: [line] *collinear* (on the same line), *alignment* (the process of arranging in a line), *lineage* (family tree)

Don't confuse with: *lineage* (family tree)

Usage: Because of their common root *lineare* (to create with lines), *delineate* is often confused with *outline*. But while *outline* means to sketch briefly, *delineate* means nearly the opposite: to describe *precisely and in detail.*

☐ **dispel** (v)   *dis-* away + *pellere* to force

to drive away; to eliminate a rumor, misconception, or bad feeling : *Even the trip to the fair did not dispel Jerome's sadness.*

Synonyms: *banish*, *allay*, *quell*

Root family: [dis-] *disconcerting* (unsettling), *disdain* (feeling that something is unworthy), *discredit* (harm the reputation of something or someone), *disparate* (very different; variegated), *discrepancy* (a lack of compatibility between facts or claims), *disseminate* (to cast widely), *disperse* (to spread or scatter)

Root family: [pul, pel] *expel* (to force out), *repel* (to drive back), *propel* (to exert a forward push), *compel* (to force someone to do something)

Don't confuse with: *disperse* (to scatter)

☐ **disputatious** (adj)   *dis-* apart + *putare* to reckon

[1] (of a person) fond of having heated arguments : *Ron was ostracized from the group because of his disputatious attitude.*

[2] (of a situation) likely to cause an argument : *The meetings became more disputatious over time, forcing the group to disband.*

☐ **elucidate** (v)   *lux* light

to make clear; to shed light on : *The mysterious disappearance was elucidated by the discovery of the ransom note.*

Root family [luc, lum] *lucid* (clear), *illuminate* (to shed light on), *luminary* (a person who inspires others), *translucent* (allowing light through, but not transparently)

Synonym: *explicate*

Don't confuse with: *elusive* (hard to catch)

Mnemonic: When you *elucidate* something you make it more *lucid*.

☐ **enticement** (n)

something that attracts or tempts, particularly because it offers pleasure or advantage : *The school offered an iPod as an enticement to the student who sells the most candy bars.*

Form: *entice* = to attract or tempt

Synonyms: *lure*, *bait*

☐ **enumerate** (v)   *e-* out + *numerus* number

to list one by one : *We calmly enumerated our complaints to the committee.*

Form: *enumeration* = the process of listing one by one

Synonym: *itemize*

Root family: [numer] *denumerable* (countable), *innumerable* (uncountably infinite), *numerous* (plentiful)

Don't confuse with: *remunerate* (to pay for services rendered)

☐ *equivocate* (v)   *equi-* same + *vocare* to call

to speak ambiguously so as to avoid commitment : *Sheila complained about her boyfriend's tendency to equivocate when the conversation turned to marriage.*
Forms: *equivocation* = the use of noncommittal language, *equivocal* = noncommittal, *unequivocal* = clear and unambiguous
Synonyms: *dither, waver, waffle*
Root family: [voc, vok] *advocate* (to provide vocal support (for)), *provoke* (to cause a strong negative response), *revoke* (to officially take back), *evocative* (having the effect of drawing out emotions or ideas), *invoke* (to bring to bear)
Mnemonic: Politicians frequently *equivocate* about issues, that is, give "equal voice" (*equi-vocare*) to both sides so as not to offend any potential voters.

☐ *exhortation* (n)   *ex-* out + *hortari* to encourage

a strong plea, usually through an urgent speech : *The mayor's exhortation that we conserve water seems to have fallen on deaf ears.*
Forms: *exhort* = to encourage vehemently
Root family: [ex-] *extol* (to praise highly), *extemporaneous* (without planning), *exuberant* (filled with liveliness and energy)
Don't confuse with: *extortion* (the practice of obtaining something by threat), *excitation* (application of energy or stimulation), *exertion* (great effort)
Mnemonic: In *Horton Hears a Who*, the tiny Whos living on a speck of dust *ask Horton* to save them. They are *exhortin'* when they *ask Horton*.

☐ *exonerate* (v)   *ex-* out, from + *onus* burden

to absolve someone of blame or fault : *The testimony of the eyewitnesses exonerated the defendant.*
Synonyms: *absolve, acquit, exculpate, vindicate*
Root family: [onus, oner] *onus* (burden), *onerous* (burdensome)
Don't confuse with: *exaggerate* (to overstate), *exasperate* (to irritate (someone))
Mnemonic: To *exonerate* is to take the *burden* (of guilt) *from* someone (*ex-* = from + *onus* = burden).

☐ *fallacious* (adj)   *fallere* to deceive, to be untrue

based on a mistaken belief or unsound reasoning : *The argument presented by the defense is fallacious because it is founded on an invalid assumption.*
Form: *fallacy* = a mistaken belief or example of unsound reasoning
Synonyms: *specious, spurious*
Root family: [fall, fals] *fallible* (capable of making errors), *fault* (an unsatisfactory feature), *fail* (to be unsuccessful)
Don't confuse with: *ferocious* (savagely cruel), *felicitous* (well-chosen for the circumstances)

☐ *harangue* (n)

a lengthy and bombastic speech : *The dictator's harangues were designed to inspire fear as much as patriotism.*
Synonyms: *tirade, rant, diatribe*
Don't confuse with: *harass* (to intimidate; to bother in an aggressive and annoying way), *heresy* (an anti-orthodox act or belief)
Usage: See usage note at *tirade* in this section.
Mnemonic: Imagine a vivid scene, from your own experience, when one person was really chewing someone else out. Then imagine that the person yelling is also throwing *meringue* pies at him (or her), to add injury to insult.

☐ *incongruous* (adj)   *in-* not + *con* together + *ruere* to fall

not consistent with expectations or surroundings : *An incongruous football-shaped telephone sat amid the otherwise tasteful and expensive auction items.*
Form: *incongruity* = something out of place or out of keeping
Synonyms: *dissonant, jarring, anomalous, discordant, anachronistic*
Root family: [in-, im-] *insipid* (flavorless), *insuperable* (impossible to overcome), *inert* (lacking vigor), *interminable* (unending), *innocuous* (harmless), *indefatigable* (untiring)
Don't confuse with: *not congruent* (not having the same shape and size)

☐ *induce* (v)   *in-* in + *ducere* to lead

[1] to bring about : *The doctor had to induce vomiting after Helen accidentally swallowed drain cleaner.*
Synonyms: *instigate*
[2] to persuade to do something : *The clever advertisements induced many customers to come see what the store had to offer.*
Synonyms: *wheedle, cajole, coax*

[3] to derive by inductive (from specific instances to general principles) reasoning : *From my experiences in the hotel, I have induced that the people of Jamaica are unusually friendly.*

Form: *induction* = the process of drawing general conclusions from specific instances

Root family: [in-] *inundate* (to flood), *infer* (to conclude from evidence), *incisive* (showing keen judgment), *ingratiate* (to curry favor), *inherent* (existing as an inseparable element), *invoke* (to bring to bear), *indoctrinate* (to teach doctrine), *infiltrate* (to gain access secretly)

Don't confuse with: *induct* (to admit someone into an organization in a formal ceremony)

☐ *inexorable* (adj)

[1] (of an eventuality) unpreventable : *We cannot stop the inexorable march of time.*

Synonyms: *relentless, inevitable, irrevocable, unremitting*

[2] (of a person) impossible to persuade : *She was inexorable in her belief in the defendant's innocence.*

Form: *inexorability* = inevitability

Synonyms: *obdurate, staunch, obstinate, recalcitrant, intransigent*

☐ *infer* (v)　　*in-* into + *ferre* to bring, to bear

to conclude from evidence : *The fossil record allows us to infer the existence of reptiles during this era.*

Form: *inference* = a conclusion drawn by reasoning from evidence; the process of reaching such a conclusion

Root family: [in-] *inundate* (to flood), *incisive* (showing keen judgment), *ingratiate* (to curry favor), *inherent* (existing as an inseparable element), *invoke* (to bring to bear), *indoctrinate* (to teach doctrine), *induce* (to bring about), *infiltrate* (to gain access secretly)

Root family: [fer] *fertile* (productive), *defer* (to put off until later; to submit to the authority of another), *coniferous* (cone-bearing), *aquifer* (rock formation that carries groundwater)

Usage: Don't use *infer* when you mean *imply* (suggest). Although a fingerprint at a crime scene might *imply* guilt, only a person can *infer* that guilt.

☐ *insinuate* (v)

to suggest or hint at something, usually something morally dubious : *The lawyers released the racy photographs in order to insinuate that the defendant was not as morally upright as he claimed to be.*

Form: *insinuation* = a sly hint

Don't confuse with: *instigate* (to initiate an event or action)

☐ *intransigent* (adj)

stubbornly unwilling to compromise or agree with someone : *The peace talks reached an impasse when the rebels became intransigent with their demands.*

Form: *intransigence* = reluctance to compromise or agree

Synonyms: *obdurate, staunch, obstinate, recalcitrant*

Don't confuse with: *intransitive* ((of a verb) not taking a direct grammatical object)

Usage: See usage note at *tenacious* in section 4.

☐ *irresolute* (adj)　　*ir-* not + *re-* (intensive) + *solvere* to loosen

hesitant; showing a lack of certainty or determination : *This irresolute and inept congress seems unable to put aside its petty bickering and do what is best for the country.*

Form: *resolute* = determined and unwavering; *resolve* = determination to do something; *resolution* = determination

Synonyms: *wavering, equivocating, dithering, ambivalent*

Root family: [solv, solu] *absolve* (to free from blame), *dissolve*

Don't confuse with: *low resolution*

Mnemonic: The words *solve, solution, resolve,* and *resolution* derive from the Latin *solvere* (to loosen, to break into parts). To *solve* a problem almost always involves analyzing it first, that is, breaking it into parts. Similarly, it's easier to make a saltwater *solution* if you break the salt into smaller pieces, and the *resolution* of your television or computer screen depends on how many pieces, or pixels, it is broken into. Because people have historically liked to institutionalize *solutions* to big problems, the term *resolution* came to mean not just the action of solving a problem (*the pact provided a temporary resolution to the conflict*), but also the formal decision that resulted from it (*the legislature passed a resolution declaring its commitment to balancing the budget*), and then the commitment required to stick to that decision (*she maintained her resolution to abstain from chocolate*).

☐ *litigious* (adj)

unreasonably prone to suing as a means of settling disputes : *I try to appease my customers whenever they are angry, because I know how litigious our society is.*
Forms: *litigiousness* = tendency to settle dispute with lawsuits, *litigate* = to settle a dispute with a lawsuit, *litigant* = someone involved in a lawsuit
Don't confuse *litigate* **with** *mitigate* (to make a situation less severe).
Mnemonic: After someone *lit* my *gate* on fire, I decided to *litigate*.

☐ *obstinate* (adj)

stubbornly refusing to change one's position : *He obstinately refused to accept the plea bargain.*
Form: *obstinacy* = strong reluctance to change
Synonyms: *obdurate, staunch, intransigent, recalcitrant*
Don't confuse with: *obstreperous* (noisy and difficult to control)
Usage: See usage note at *tenacious* in section 4.
Mnemonic: Imagine *Nate* the *obstetrician* stubbornly refusing to deliver a baby.

☐ *partisan* (adj)

prejudiced in favor of a particular party, typically a political one : *I don't watch cable news because it is so partisan.*
Forms: *nonpartisan* = unbiased, *bipartisan* = (of a legislative action) partaken by members of two different parties
Don't confuse with: *partition* (a process of dividing into parts; a physical barrier between areas)
Usage: See usage note at *objective* in section 18.

☐ *placate* (v)   *placare* to please

to pacify with conciliatory gestures : *The angry customer could only be placated by the offer of a full refund and a sincere apology.*
Forms: *implacable* = unable to be appeased
Synonyms: *propitiate, conciliate, appease, mollify*
Root family: [plac, plais] *complacent* (self-satisfied), *implacable* (unable to be pleased), *placid* (peaceful), *placebo* (a sugar pill used as a control in a medical experiment), *pleasant*
Don't confuse with: *placid* (peaceful)
Usage: See usage note at *pacify* in section 4.

☐ *precedent* (n)   *pre-* before + *cedere* to go

a previous occurrence that is used as an example, particularly in a legal context : *There are few precedents for truly interactive textbooks.*
Form: *precedence* = the condition of being more important, *unprecedented* = unheard of before a recent or hypothetical occurrence
Root family: [pre-] *premeditated* (planned in advance), *precocious* (having exceptional ability at an early age)
Root family: [ced, ces] *concession* (something surrendered), *recede* (move back from a previous position), *secede* (withdraw from a formal union or alliance), *proceed* (go forth)
Don't confuse with: *president* (head of a republican state; head of an organization)

☐ *prevalent* (adj)   *pre-* before + *valere* to have power

abundant and widespread in a particular area : *Be careful—poison ivy is prevalent in this forest.*
Form: *prevail* = to be victorious; to be the most powerful, *prevalence* = widespread abundance
Synonyms: *prolific, profuse, copious*
Root family: [pre-] *precedent* (a previous example), *premeditated* (planned in advance), *precocious* (having exceptional ability at an early age)
Root family: [val] *ambivalent* (having mixed feelings), *valence* (the power of an atom to make bonds with other atoms), *valor* (courage and nobility in the face of danger)
Don't confuse with: *relevant* (connected and appropriate to the matter at hand)

☐ *propensity* (n)   *pro-* forward + *pendere* to hang

a natural inclination to behave a certain way : *Warner has a propensity for needless exaggeration.*
Root family: [pro-] *protracted* (lasting longer than expected), *prophecy* (prediction), *promote* (further the progress of something; raise in rank), *progeny* (offspring), *reciprocate* (to respond in kind)

Root family: [pond, pend, pens] *pendant* (a piece of jewelry hanging from a necklace), *impending* (about to happen; imminent), *dependent* (requiring something or someone for support), *appendix* (a table or other supporting matter at the end of a book; a vestigial sac on the large intestine), *ponderous* (heavy)
Don't confuse with: *preposterousness* (absurdity)
Mnemonic: If you have a *propensity* for something, you are *propelled* toward it with great *intensity*.

☐ *provocative* (adj)   *pro-* forward + *vocare* to call.

[1] intended to cause a strong negative emotional response : *Daniel's protest was designed to be provocative, rather than informative.*
Form: *provocation* = action intended to annoy or anger
Synonyms: *vexing*, *galling*, *incendiary*, *inflammatory*
[2] intended to arouse sexual desire : *The school dress code imposes severe restrictions on provocative clothing.*
Synonyms: *alluring*, *seductive*
Root family: [pro-] *protracted* (lasting longer than expected), *prophecy* (prediction), *promote* (further the progress of something; raise in rank), *progeny* (offspring), *reciprocate* (to respond in kind)
Root family: [voc, vok] *revoke* (to take back), *evocative* (bringing strong images or emotions to mind), *advocate* (to give public support), *avocation* (hobby), *equivocate* (to speak ambiguously), *vocation* (calling; chosen career)
Don't confuse with: *evocative* (bringing strong images or emotions to mind)
Usage: *Provocative* and *evocative* have very similar meanings, but *provocative* is usually reserved to describe something that elicits emotions that are not desired or appropriate, while *evocative* describes something that elicits emotions to enrich an experience.

☐ *pugnacious* (adj)   *pugnare* to fight

quarrelsome; prone to fighting : *Senator McGinley was a pugnacious defender of his causes, but a sweet and gentle man outside of chambers.*
Form: *pugnacity* = belligerence; tendency to pick fights
Synonyms: *belligerent*, *bellicose*, *contentious*, *truculent*
Root family: [pug] *impugn* (to attack as invalid or dishonest), *pugilist* (prize fighter), *repugnant* (extremely distasteful)
Mnemonic: Imagine a combative little *pug* dog.

☐ *qualify* (v)   *qualis* of what kind

[1] to moderate a statement to make it less extreme : *I should qualify my statement so that I don't seem to be advocating total anarchy.*
[2] to meet a necessary condition (for) : *Carlos qualified for the state tennis tournament.*
Form: *qualification* — a moderation of a previous statement; an accomplishment or quality that makes a person suitable for a position or activity
Synonyms: *temper*, *moderate*
Don't confuse *qualify* (a statement) with *qualify* (for a position or privilege).

☐ *rebut* (v)

to respond to an accusation by asserting or proving it false; refute : *The candidate spent as much time rebutting her opponent's accusations as she did describing her own positions.*
Form: *rebuttal* = an act of refutation
Synonyms: *repudiate*, *discredit*
Don't confuse with: *rebuff* (to reject ungraciously)

☐ *recalcitrant* (adj)   *re-* back + *calcitrare* to kick with the heel

stubbornly uncooperative : *The entire kindergarten class was finger-painting, save for one recalcitrant toddler.*
Synonyms: *obdurate*, *staunch*, *obstinate*, *intransigent*, *steadfast*
Root family: [re-] *reprehensible* (deserving of condemnation), *recluse* (a person who lives a solitary lifestyle), *refute* (to prove something false), *revoke* (to take back), *renounce* (to give up or put aside publicly), *reciprocate* (to respond in kind), *resigned* (accepting of an undesirable situation), *regress* (to return to a less developed state)
Don't confuse with: *calcified* ((as of a fossil) hardened into stone, particularly one consisting of calcium compounds)
Usage: See usage note at *tenacious* in section 4.
Mnemonic: What do the words *calcium*, *calculator*, *chalk*, and *recalcitrant* have in common? They all derive from the Latin root *calx*, which means "limestone," a mineral composed primarily of calcium carbonate, or "heel," perhaps because the heel is likewise very hard. From this root came *calculus*, which means "small pebble," and *calcitrare*, which means "to kick back

with the heel." *Calculate* derives from the practice of accounting with pebbles, and *recalcitrant* derives from the tendency of mules to kick back with their heels rather than obey.

☐   *refute* (v)   *re-* back + *futare* to beat

to prove something false : *Just because a claim has yet be refuted does not mean that it is true.*
Forms: *refutation* = the process of proving something wrong, *irrefutable* = proven beyond a shadow of a doubt
Synonyms: *debunk*, *invalidate*
Root family: [re-] *revoke* (to take back), *renounce* (to give up or put aside publicly), *reciprocate* (to respond in kind), *resigned* (accepting of an undesirable situation), *regress* (to return to a less developed state), *relegate* (to place in a lower rank)
Don't confuse with: *refuse* (to decline (something))

☐   *resolute* (adj)

unwaveringly purposeful and dutiful : *Despite the threat of violence, the marchers were resolute about making their voices heard.*
Form: *resolve* (n) = unwavering commitment to a principle, *resolution* = statement of determination, *irresolute* = hesitant
Synonym: *steadfast*
Don't confuse with: *high-resolution* ((of an optical device or image) exceedingly clear down to very fine details)
Usage: See usage note at *tenacious* in section 4.

☐   *rhetoric* (n)

[1] the art of persuasion through language : *He was an expert orator, skilled in rhetoric.*
Forms: *rhetorical* = intended for persuasive effect, *rhetorician* = one who is adept at the language of persuasion
Synonyms: *argumentation*, *forensics*, *oratory*, *disputation*
Usage: A *rhetorical question* (such as *Who would ever buy such a lousy car?*) is not merely a question that is not answered, but one whose answer is *assumed* by the speaker or writer, because that question is being used to persuade and not to inquire. That is, the question is being used for rhetorical effect.
[2] language that is persuasive but insincere or meaningless : *His speech was dismissed as mere rhetoric.*
Synonyms: *bombast*, *grandiloquence*

☐   *specious* (adj)

seemingly plausible, but actually incorrect : *Beck's specious theories are informed more by hysteria than by reason.*
Synonyms: *spurious*, *fallacious*
Don't confuse with: *species* (a classification of similar organisms that can interbreed)
Mnemonic: A *specious* claim is one that should make you su-*spicious*.

☐   *speculation* (n)   *specere* to look

a guess based on meager evidence : *The theory was based more on speculation than on fact.*
Forms: *speculate* = to form a theory without firm evidence, *speculative* = based on flimsy evidence
Synonyms: *conjecture*, *surmise*, *postulation*
Root family: [spec] *introspective* (meditative), *circumspect* (cautious), *inspect* (to examine closely)
Don't confuse with: *inspection* (close examination)

☐   *steadfast* (adj)

dutifully firm and unwavering : *The steadfast soldier held his post for days without sleeping.*
Form: *steadfastness* = resolute refusal to waver
Synonym: *resolute*
Usage: See usage note at *tenacious* in section 4.

☐   *strident* (adj)

annoyingly loud and harsh, particularly when presenting a point of view : *The political operatives were instructed to take very strident tones at the town hall meeting, to make it seem as if their views were widely held.*
Form: *stridency* = harshness in presenting one's views
Synonyms: *vociferous*
Don't confuse with: *stride* (to walk briskly), *trident* (a three-pronged pitchfork)
Mnemonic: Imagine a protester *striding* with a *trident* and shouting *strident* slogans during a protest march.

☐ **subjective** (adj)   *sub* under + *ject* thrown

based on personal feelings or opinions : *Movie reviews are highly subjective.*
Root family: [ject] **objective** (based on fact), **conjecture** (guess), **reject** (to throw back), **eject** (to throw outward)
Mnemonic: In late Middle English, **subjective** originally meant "submissive, as a royal *subject* to a king or queen," but evolved to mean "pertaining to the points of view that were brought by the subjects to the monarch."
Usage: In modern usage **subjective** is the opposite of **objective** (based on fact rather than opinion).

☐ **substantiate** (v)

provide evidence for : *The scientists could not substantiate their hypothesis, because they could not replicate the results of their experiment.*
Form: substantive = significant because it is based in reality
Synonyms: vindicate, corroborate, authenticate
Don't confuse with: substandard (less than the norm in quality)

☐ **tenuous** (adj)   *tenuare* to make thin, to stretch

flimsy; very weak or slight (esp. pertaining to a link, argument, or relationship) : *The link between lowering taxes and stimulating business is more tenuous than most people think.*
Root family: [ten] **extend** (to stretch forward), **pretend** (to act as if something is so when it is not), **pretentious** (affecting an exaggerated importance), **contend** (with) (to struggle to defeat), **attenuate** (to reduce the force or effectiveness of something)
Don't confuse with: tense (taut)
Mnemonic: A **tenuous** connection is a real **stretch** (**tendere** = to stretch).

☐ **tirade** (v)

a long, angry, and critical speech : *His tirades against communism are well known.*
Synonyms: harangue, rant, diatribe
Don't confuse with: torrent (a strong and sudden stream)
Usage: Tirade, harangue, rant, and **diatribe** are similar, but offer different shades of meaning. **Tirade** is the most general of these, describing any long, critical speech; a **harangue** is particularly bombastic, usually inflaming the passions of listeners, and is the primary tool of the demagogue; a **rant** is primarily an instrument of catharsis, allowing the speaker to blow off steam, but not necessarily persuade or do harm; a **diatribe** is more tiresome—while a **harangue** can arouse passion, and a **rant** can be entertaining to watch, a **diatribe** is neither inspiring, informative, nor entertaining.

☐ **viable** (adj)   *vivere* to live

capable of working successfully : *We did not want to invest in a company that had not yet shown that it was viable.*
Synonyms: feasible
Root family: [viv, vita] **convivial** (lively and friendly), **revive** (bring back to life), **vivid** (inducing clear images in the mind), **bon vivant** (a person who enjoys a lively and social lifestyle), **vivacious** (full of lively energy)
Don't confuse with: enviable (worthy of envy), **verifiable** (able to be proven true or accurate)

☐ **vindicate** (v)   *vin* force + *dictum* declaration

to clear of blame or suspicion : *Victor was vindicated when another suspect confessed to the crime.*
Form: vindication = the process of clearing someone of blame or suspicion
Synonyms: exonerate, exculpate
Root family: [dict] **vindictive** (vengeful), **dictatorial** (tyrannical), **dictum** (formal declaration), **benediction** (blessing), **malediction** (curse)
Don't confuse with: vindictive (vengeful)
Mnemonic: The words **vindictive** and **vindicate** are easy to confuse because they both derive from the Latin **vindex** (from **vin**, "force" and **dictum**, "declaration"), which means "avenger." But they describe different aspects of vengeance: to **vindicate** means "to avenge by proving innocent," while **vindictive** means "consumed with vengeance."

☐ **zealot** (n)

a fanatic; one who is uncompromising and vehement in pursuing ideals : *The party zealots had taken over the meeting, so compromise had become impossible.*
Forms: zeal = feeling of deep passion for an ideal, **zealous** = passionate for one's ideals
Don't confuse zealous (passionate) with **jealous** (envious)

3   THE LANGUAGE OF DISSENT, CRITICISM, AND REBELLION

☐ *adversary* (n)   *ad-* to + *vertere* to turn

a committed enemy or opponent : *The lawsuit turned former friends into adversaries.*
Forms: *adversarial* = inclined to picking fights, pugnacious, *adverse* = unfavorable, harmful
Synonyms: *rival*, *contender*, *antagonist*
Root family: [ad-] *allude* (to hint at indirectly), *aspire* (to strive for a lofty goal), *adhere* (stick fast (to)), *advocate* (to provide vocal support for), *acquiesce* (to comply reluctantly), *annul* (to declare invalid)
Root family: [vers, vert] *diverse* (various), *diversion* (entertainment), *adverse* (harmful), *subvert* (undermine), *averse* (opposed), *versatile* (adaptable to different functions)

☐ *antipathy* (adj)   *anti-* against + *pathos* feeling

deep-seated dislike : *Despite the long-standing antipathy between their families, Romeo and Juliet believed their love would triumph.*
Synonyms: *aversion*, *animus*, *antagonism*, *enmity*, *loathing*, *abhorrence*
Root family: [path] *sympathy* (feeling of sorrow for the misfortunes of another), *pathology* (the science of the causes and course of diseases), *apathetic* (lacking concern), *empathy* (the ability to share the feelings of others)
Don't confuse with: *apathy* (lack of concern)

☐ *audacious* (adj)

willing to take bold risks : *Desperate to score points, the audacious quarterback called a trick play against the coach's wishes.*
Form: *audacity* = boldness
Synonyms: *impudent*, *impertinent*, *insolent*, *intrepid*
Don't confuse with: *mendacious* (lying)

☐ *averse* (adj)   *ab-* away + *vertere* to turn

having a strong dislike : *Although many considered Will a daredevil, he was actually scrupulous in his planning and highly averse to senseless risk.*
Form: *aversion* = strong dislike
Synonyms: *antipathetic*
Root family: [ab-] *abhor* (to regard with hate and disgust), *abstruse* (very difficult to understand), *absolve* (to free from guilt or blame), *abstemious* (self-disciplined and restrictive with regard to consumption)
Root family: [vers, vert] *adversary* (enemy), *diverse* (various), *diversion* (entertainment), *subvert* (undermine), *adverse* (harmful), *versatile* (adaptable to different functions)
Don't confuse with: *adverse* (harmful)

☐ *belligerent* (adj)   *bellum* war

hostile and aggressive : *We might take your suggestions more seriously if you were not so belligerent when you presented them.*
Form: *belligerence* = hostility and aggression
Synonyms: *pugnacious*, *bellicose*, *contentious*, *truculent*
Root family: [bell] *rebellion* (act of violent resistance), *bellicose* (war-mongering), *antebellum* (characteristic of the culture in the southern United States prior to the Civil War)

☐ *berate* (v)

to scold angrily : *The coach berated us for not keeping in shape during the off-season.*
Synonyms: *reproach*, *censure*, *rebuke*, *admonish*, *chastise*, *upbraid*, *reprove*
Don't confuse with: *irate* (very angry)
Usage: See usage note at *rebuke* in this section.

☐ *cantankerous* (adj)

grouchy and argumentative : *Mrs. Grieves was a cantankerous old woman who would scream at us from her porch for not wearing shoes.*
Synonyms: *irascible*, *curmudgeonly*, *churlish*, *peevish*, *fractious*, *ornery*

☐ *circumspect* (adj)   *circum* around + *specere* to look

wary; cautious : *Ken's unpleasant experiences with telemarketers made him circumspect about answering the phone.*
Form: *circumspection* = caution, wariness
Synonyms: *wary, vigilant, leery, skeptical*
Root family: [circum] *circumscribe* (to define the limits of something), *circuitous* (roundabout), *circumlocution* (evasive speech)
Root family: [spec] *speculation* (guess based on insufficient evidence), *introspective* (meditative), *inspect* (to examine closely)
Don't confuse with: *circumscribe* (to define the limits of something)
Mnemonic: Those who are *circumspect* are always "looking around" (*circum* = around + *specere* = to look) to make sure they are not in danger.

☐ *clamor* (n)   *clamare* to cry out

an uproar, usually from a crowd showing disapproval : *The guards were awakened by a clamor at the gate.*
Form: *clamor* (v) = to raise an outcry, usually in a group
Root family: [clam, claim] *acclaim* (to praise publicly), *proclaim* (announce publicly and officially)
Don't confuse with: *clamber* (to climb awkwardly)

☐ *condescend* (v)   *con-* together + *de-* down + *scandere* to climb

to act superior to someone else : *Teachers should give clear instructions and not condescend to their students.*
Forms: *condescending* = acting superior or arrogant, *condescension* = looking down on others
Synonyms: *patronize, deign*
Root family: [con-, co-, com-, col-] *conventional* (according to common practice), *conjecture* (guess), *convoluted* (complicated), *coalesce* (to come together), *coherent* (forming a united whole), *confluence* (a place at which two things merge)
Root family: [de-] *deplore* (to express strong disapproval), *denounce* (declare as bad), *debase* (reduce in value), *denigrate* (criticize unfairly), *deference* (submission to the authority of another)
Root family: [scend, scal] *transcend* (to rise above something), *ascend* (to climb), *escalate* (to increase in intensity or magnitude), *echelon* (level or rank)

☐ *encroach* (v)

to intrude on a territory or domain : *The teachers were beginning to worry that the school board was encroaching on their right to teach as they see fit.*
Form: *encroachment* = intrusion on a territory or domain
Synonyms: *trespass, impinge*
Don't confuse with: *reproach* (to reprimand)

☐ *estranged* (adj)   *extra* outside of

no longer emotionally close to someone; alienated : *After being estranged for many years, the couple finally reconciled.*
Form: *estrangement* = the state of being alienated
Synonym: *alienated*
Root family: [extra] *extraneous* (irrelevant to the subject at hand), *extravagant* (excessive, particularly in spending), *extraterrestrial* (from beyond Earth)

☐ *evade* (v)   *e-* out of + *vadere* to go

to escape or avoid, usually through clever means : *The fighter pilot was able to evade the missile with his deft maneuvers.*
Forms: *evasion* = the act of escaping or avoiding, *evasive* = with the intention of cleverly avoiding something
Synonyms: *elude, avoid, skirt*
Root family: [vad, vas] *invade* (to intrude on a region and occupy it), *pervasive* (widespread)
Don't confuse with: *invade* (to intrude on a region and occupy it)

☐ *flout* (v)

openly disregard (a rule or convention) : *It was shocking how openly Gino flouted school rules.*
Synonyms: *defy, contravene, breach*
Don't confuse with: *flaunt* (to show off)
Mnemonic: Imagine a *flautist* (flute-player) playing loudly in the middle of the library, obviously *flouting* the rule of silence.

☐ **heresy** (n)

a belief or act that contradicts religious orthodoxy : *The Republican senator's vote for the tax increase was regarded as an unforgiveable heresy.*
Forms: heretic = a person guilty of heresy, **heretical** = having the qualities of heresy
Synonyms: blasphemy, apostasy, heterodoxy, dissension, iconoclasm
Don't confuse with: harangue (a bombastic speech)
Mnemonic: The first person in beauty school to sport a Mohawk was guilty of **hair-esy.**

☐ **iconoclast** (n)   *eikon* likeness + *klan* to break

(literally a "breaker of icons") one who attacks cherished beliefs : *The Cubist movement consisted of bold iconoclasts shattering the definition of art and reassembling its pieces in disarray.*
Synonyms: heretic, skeptic, infidel, renegade
Root family: [clas] **pyroclastic** relating to the breaking of rocks by volcanic eruptions)
Don't confuse with: idiosyncrasy (a quirky mannerism)
Mnemonic: Imagine an **iconoclast** as someone making religious **icons crash** to the floor.

☐ **indignant** (adj)   *in-* not + *dignus* worthy

angered by unjust treatment : *Perry became indignant at the suggestion that he was cheating.*
Form: indignation = anger at unjust treatment
Synonyms: aggrieved, affronted, disgruntled
Root family: [in-, im-] **insipid** (flavorless), **insuperable** (impossible to overcome), **inert** (lacking vigor), **interminable** (unending), **innocuous** (harmless), **indefatigable** (untiring), **ineffable** (inexpressible in words), **inscrutable** (beyond understanding), **impassive** (unemotional), **incongruous** (not consistent with expectations)
Root family: [dign, dain] **dignity** (state of being worthy of respect), **dignify** (to make worthy), **disdain** (contempt), **deign** (to do something that one considers beneath one's dignity)
Don't confuse with: indigenous (native), **indignity** (a circumstance or treatment that makes one feel humiliated)

☐ **instigate** (v)

bring about or initiate (an action or event) : *The regime instigated a brutal crackdown on intellectuals.*
Form: instigator = one who brings about an action or event
Synonyms: goad (to provoke or annoy someone into action), **incite**
Don't confuse with: investigate (to examine in order to determine the truth of a situation)
Usage: Although **instigate** is nearly synonymous with **cause**, it has a more negative and intentional connotation than does **cause**. A crime is **instigated** by its perpetrators, but a beautiful cirrus cloud is **caused** by ice crystals forming in the upper atmosphere.

☐ **insurgent** (n)   *in-* into + *surgere* to rise

a rebel : *We were attacked by armed insurgents.*
Form: insurgency = campaign of rebellion
Synonyms: rebel, insurrectionist, subversive, incendiary
Root family: [in-] **inundate** (to flood), **infer** (to conclude from evidence), **incisive** (showing keen judgment), **ingratiate** (to curry favor), **inherent** (existing as an inseparable element), **invoke** (to bring to bear), **indoctrinate** (to teach doctrine), **induce** (to bring about), **infiltrate** (to gain access secretly)
Root family: [surg] **resurgence** (a revival of activity or popularity), **resurrection** (the act of rising again)

☐ **malign** (v)   *malignus* tending to evil

to speak harmful untruths about : *I am disgusted by political commercials that merely malign the candidate's opponent, rather than offering constructive information.*
Synonyms: disparage, denigrate, revile, vilify, slander
Root family: [mal] **malignant** (disposed to causing harm or suffering), **malicious** (full of spite), **malevolence** (evil intent)
Don't confuse with: malignant (disposed to causing harm or suffering)

☐ **maverick** (n)

a person who thinks independently : *Lowell Weicker was a maverick Republican senator who later ran as an independent and was elected governor of Connecticut.*
Synonyms: nonconformist, individualist, eccentric, dissident

☐ *misanthrope* (n)   *mis* bad + *anthropos* mankind

one who dislikes and avoids humans : *Ebenezer Scrooge was a miserly and miserable misanthrope until he learned the value of friends and family.*

Form: *misanthropic* = characterized by a hatred of mankind

Synonym: *cynic* (one who believes that all people are fundamentally selfish and dishonorable)

Root family: [anthro] ***anthropology*** (the study of human cultures), ***philanthropy*** (generosity to charitable causes), ***anthropomorphic*** (having human form), ***anthropocentric*** (pertaining to the belief that humans are the center of the universe)

Don't confuse with: *malapropism* (a mistaken use of a word for a similar-sounding one, as in, *He is a vast suppository (rather than repository) of information.*)

☐ *rancor* (n)   *rancidus* stinking

deep-seated resentment : *The rancor endured from their acrimonious divorce.*

Form: *rancorous* = characterized by deep-seated resentment

Synonyms: *malice, animosity, antipathy, enmity, acrimony, vitriol*

Root family: [ranc] ***rancid*** (stinking due to staleness or rot)

Don't confuse *rancorous* with *raucous* (annoyingly noisy)

☐ *rebuke* (v)

to express sharp and stern disapproval for someone's actions : *His wife rebuked him for staying out too late.*

Synonyms: *reproach, censure, reprove, admonish, chastise, upbraid, berate*

Don't confuse with: *rebut*

Usage: There are many ways to express disapproval. To ***admonish*** is to go easy on the wrongdoer, emphasizing advice over scolding; to ***reprove*** or ***reproach*** is to criticize with a little more force, chiefly to encourage someone to stop whatever he or she is doing wrong. To ***censure*** is to scold formally and in public. To ***rebuke*** is to scold harshly and sternly, often with a tone of sharp revulsion or condescension; to ***berate*** is scold in particular harsh and unreasonable terms, with the intention of belittling.

☐ *renounce* (v)   *re-* back + *nuntiare* to announce

to give up or put aside publicly : *He renounced his membership in the club when he heard that it would not allow women as members.*

Form: *renunciation* = an act of renouncing

Synonym: *relinquish*

Root family: [re-] ***refute*** (to prove something false), ***revoke*** (to take back), ***reciprocate*** (to respond in kind), ***resigned*** (accepting of an undesirable situation), ***regress*** (to return to a less developed state), ***relegate*** (to place in a lower rank)

Root family: [nunc, nounc] ***announce*** (declare publicly), ***denounce*** (to rebuke publicly), ***enunciate*** (to pronounce clearly)

☐ *reprehensible* (adj)   *re-* back + *prehendere* to grasp

deserving of condemnation : *David's reprehensible behavior during practice earned him a benching for the next two games.*

Synonyms: *deplorable, despicable, repugnant*

Root family: [re-] ***recluse*** (a person who lives a solitary lifestyle), ***refute*** (to prove something false), ***recalcitrant*** (stubbornly uncooperative), ***revoke*** (to take back), ***renounce*** (to give up or put aside publicly), ***regress*** (to return to a less developed state), ***relegate*** (to place in a lower rank)

Root family: [prehens] ***comprehensive*** (thorough and complete), ***apprehensive*** (fearful)

Don't confuse with: *apprehensive* (fearful), ***comprehensible*** (understandable)

Mnemonic: A ***reprehensible*** act is one that any good person would want to ***take back*** (***re-*** back + ***prehendere*** to grasp).

☐ *reprove* (v)

to reprimand : *The teacher reproved Jonah for insulting Caroline in front of the class.*

Form: *reproof* = a reprimand

Synonyms: *reproach, censure, rebuke, admonish, chastise, upbraid, berate*

Don't confuse with: *disprove* (to prove false), ***prove again***

Usage: See usage note at ***rebuke*** in this section.

☐ **revoke** (v)   *re-* back + *vocare* to call

to take back a formal decree, decision, or permission : *Glen's hunting license was revoked soon after the shotgun accident.*
Forms: *irrevocable* = unable to be taken back
Root family: [re-] *recluse* (a person who lives a solitary lifestyle), *refute* (to prove something false), *renounce* (to give up or put aside publicly), *reciprocate* (to respond in kind), *regress* (to return to a less developed state), *relegate* (to place in a lower rank)
Root family: [voc, vok] *evocative*, *advocate*, *provocative*, *equivocate*
Synonyms: *rescind*, *annul*, *countermand*, *repeal*

☐ **subvert** (v)   *sub-* under + *vertere* to turn

to undermine the authority or power of another : *The opposition planned to subvert the Democrats and thwart the lawmaking process.*
Forms: *subversion* = an act that serves to undermine the authority or power of another, ***subversive*** = having the effect or intension of undermining the authority or power of another
Synonyms: *destabilize*, *sabotage*
Root family: [sub-] *submissive* (meekly obedient), *surreptitious* (secret), *subjugate* (to dominate), *subterfuge* (trickery)
Root family: [vers, vert] *adversary* (enemy), *diverse* (various), *diversion* (entertainment), *adverse* (harmful), *averse* (opposed), *versatile* (adaptable to different functions)

☐ **supplant** (v)

to replace in importance or relevance : *The old economic system was supplanted by a more sustainable one.*
Synonyms: *supersede*, *override*

☐ **vilify** (v)   *vilis* worthless

to denounce someone bitterly : *After her callous remarks about the poor, Michelle was vilified in the press.*
Form: *vilification* = the act or process of denouncing bitterly
Synonyms: *disparage*, *denigrate*, *revile*, *malign*, *slander*
Root family: [vil] *vile* (profoundly unpleasant), *revile* (to criticize angrily)
Don't confuse with: *verify* (to demonstrate something to be true)
Mnemonic: To *vilify* is to treat someone like a *villain*. (Actually, *vilify* and *villain* have different roots, but it's a pretty good way to remember the word.)

☐ **vindictive** (adj)   *vin* force + *dictum* declaration

showing a deep desire for revenge : *The vindictive tone of the letter showed that Tom harbored deep resentments.*
Form: *vindictiveness* = desire for revenge
Synonyms: *vengeful*, *spiteful*, *rancorous*
Root family: [dict] *vindicate* (to clear of blame), *dictatorial* (tyrannical), *dictum* (an authoritative pronouncement), *benediction* (blessing), *malediction* (curse)
Don't confuse with: *vindicate* (to clear of blame), *verdict* (official ruling of a court)

4   THE LANGUAGE OF POWER AND SUBMISSION

☐ **acquiesce** (v)   *ad-* to + *quiescere* to rest

to accept an unpleasant situation or comply to a demand reluctantly : *Since the rest of the family wanted to drive to the beach, I stopped my protests and acquiesced.*
Form: *acquiescent* = being inclined to acquiesce
Root family: [ad-] *allude* (to hint at indirectly), *aspire* (to strive for a lofty goal), *adhere* (stick fast (to)), *advocate* (to provide vocal support for)
Root family: [quies, quiet] *quietude* (a state of calmness), *quiescence* (a state of dormancy), *disquiet* (anxiety)
Don't confuse with: *acquaintance* (a passing knowledge; a person one knows only slightly), *aquatic* (pertaining to water and particularly the creatures that live in it)
Mnemonic: When someone keeps badgering you noisily over and over to do something, you can make *a* (more) *quiet scene* by just *acquiescing*.

☐ **capitulate** (v)   *capit* head

to surrender; to stop resisting : *The corporation finally capitulated to the labor union's demands.*
Form: capitulation = the act of surrendering
Synonym: concede
Root family: [cap, capit] **capital** (city that serves as administrative seat), **decapitate** (remove the head), **captain** (a person in command of a team, ship, or similar organization)
Don't confuse with: recapitulate (or **recap**) (summarize and restate)

☐ **coerce** (v)   *co-* together + *arcere* to restrain

to force someone to do something by use of threats : *I will not be coerced into betraying my friends.*
Form: coercion = the act of forcing someone against his or her will
Root family: [con-, co-, com-, col-] **conformist** (one who conscientiously complies with the standards of a group, **conventional** (according to common practice), **consensus** (general agreement), **conspire** (to plot together), **coalesce** (to come together)
Root family: [erc] **exercise** (physical activity)
Don't confuse with: co-opt (to divert something to a role other than it was intended for), **commerce** (the activity of buying and selling)

☐ **concession** (n)   *con-* together + *cedere* to yield, to go

[1] the act of admitting reluctantly that something is true : *I will make the concession that you have a point.*
[2] something surrendered, as land or a right : *The territory was gained as a concession from a neighboring country after the war.*
Form: concede = to yield
Root family: [con-, co-, com-, col-] **conformist** (one who conscientiously complies with the standards of a group, **conventional** (according to common practice), **consensus** (general agreement), **conspire** (to plot together), **coalesce** (to come together), **compliant** (willing to obey), **confluence** (a place at which two things merge)
Root family: [ced, ces] **precedent** (a previous occurrence used as an example), **recede** (move back from a previous position), **secede** (withdraw from a formal union or alliance), **proceed** (go forth)
Don't confuse with: consensus
Don't confuse with: concession stand. Most people associate the word **concession** with **concession stands,** such as those that sell food at sporting events and assume that **concession** means food. However, in this context, the term **concession** refers to the fact that the owner of the venue (a company or town, perhaps), **conceded** to another party the right to sell food on its property. That is, the stadium owner granted a **concession** for someone else to run a **stand.**

☐ **contrite** (adj)   *con-* together + *tritus* rubbed

remorseful; full of regret : *Harold felt contrite after insulting Jacqueline and bought her flowers to make amends.*
Form: contrition = an expression or feeling of remorse
Synonyms: penitent, chastened, rueful
Root family: [con-, co-, com-, col-] **conformist** (one who conscientiously complies with the standards of a group, **conventional** (according to common practice), **consensus** (general agreement), **compliant** (willing to obey)
Root family: [trit] **attrition** (a wearing down via sustained attack), **trite** (worn out; overused)
Don't confuse with: content (adj) (satisfied), **trite** (worn out: overused)
Don't confuse contrition with **attrition** (a wearing down via sustained attack).
Mnemonic: The word **contrite** comes from the Latin word **contritus** which means "ground to pieces," from **con-** (together) + **terere** (to rub). This may be because the feeling of guilt—of **contrition**—feels like a grinding in the stomach.

☐ **deference** (n)   *de-* down + *ferre* to bring

respect for or submission to the authority or opinion of another : *The villagers showed their deference by removing their hats as the duke's coach passed them.*
Forms: deferential = showing humility and respect, **defer** (to) = to submit to the authority or opinion of another
Synonyms: capitulation, submissiveness, acquiescence
Root family: [de-] **decadent** (excessively self-indulgent), **derivative** (imitative of someone else's work), **deplore** (to express strong disapproval), **denounce** (declare as bad), **detract** (reduce the value of something), **debase** (reduce in value), **denigrate** (criticize unfairly), **condescend** (to act superior to someone else)
Don't confuse with: difference (a point or way in which things are not the same), **deferment** (postponement)

Mnemonic: To *defer* can also mean "to postpone (a decision)." It is easy to confuse the two meanings of *defer*, particularly when you are thinking about applying to college. To keep the two straight, pay attention to the preposition that follows: if you are *deferred from* a college, the decision about your acceptance has been *postponed* to a later date; however, when you *defer to* another person, you are submitting to his or her authority or opinion.

☐ **demagogue** (n)   *demos* people + *agogos* leading

a leader who persuades followers through emotional populist appeal rather than rational argument : *The nation had grown tired of its demagogues and elected a well-educated technocrat as its new leader.*
Form: *demagoguery* = speechmaking by a political leader that appeals to popular prejudices
Root family: [dem] *democracy* (government elected by and representative of the people), *demographics* (the study of human populations), *epidemic* (a widespread occurrence of a disease)
Root family: [agog] *pedagogy* (the art of teaching), *synagogue* (a Jewish house of worship)

☐ **despot** (n)   *potentia* power

a (usually cruel) ruler with absolute power : *The colonists regarded King George as a despot.*
Forms: *despotism* = the cruel exercise of absolute power, *despotic* = having the qualities of a despot
Root family: [poten] *potentate* (powerful ruler), *impotence* (ineffectiveness), *potency* (strength), *omnipotent* (all-powerful)
Don't confuse with: *depot* (a railroad or bus station, or a large storage area)

☐ **dictatorial** (adj)   *dicere* to declare

characteristic of a ruler with total power; tyrannical : *Kevin was voted out of office because the other members objected to his dictatorial style.*
Form: *dictate* (v) = to lay down authoritatively
Synonyms: *autocratic, peremptory, overweening, overbearing, imperious*
Root family: [dict] *vindictive* (vengeful), *malediction* (curse), *dictum* (command), *benediction* (blessing)

☐ **diffident** (adj)   *dis-* away + *fidere* to trust

lacking in self-confidence; shy and modest : *Kate had to overcome her natural diffidence in order to audition for the musical.*
Form: *diffidence* = lack of self-confidence
Root family: [dis-] *disconcerting* (unsettling), *dispassionate* (not influenced by strong emotions), *disparate* (very different; variegated), *discrepancy* (a lack of compatibility between facts or claims), *disseminate* (to cast widely)
Root family: [fid] *fidelity* (faithfulness), *confidence* (faith in oneself), *perfidious* (untrustworthy), *infidel* (nonbeliever)
Don't confuse with: *indifferent* (lacking concern), *different*, *deferent* (respectful of the authority of others)
Mnemonic: To avoid confusing it with words like *different* and *deferent*, focus on the root *fidere* (to trust): one who is *diffident* lacks *confidence*.

☐ **domineering** (adj)   *dominus* lord, master

arrogantly overbearing : *Some admired Dave's confidence, but others considered him arrogant and domineering.*
Form: *domineer* = to act in a domineering manner
Synonyms: *imperious, overbearing, dictatorial, despotic*
Root family: [domit, domin] *dominate* (to have power over), *dominion* (sovereignty; control), *domain* (an area controlled by a ruler; a specific sphere of knowledge), *predominant* (acting as the most important or dominant element), *indomitable* (unconquerable)

☐ **eminent** (adj)

famous and respected in a particular domain : *George is an eminent pediatric oncologist.*
Forms: *eminence* = fame; recognized superiority, *preeminent* = well known as being superior
Don't confuse with: *imminent* (about to happen : *The black clouds indicated that the storm was imminent*), *emanate* (to spread out from : *His confidence emanated from him like warmth from a fire*), *immanent* (inherent : *The rights of all humanity are immanent in the Constitution*)
Mnemonic: *Eminem* was one of the first *eminent* white hip hop-artists.

☐ **enthralling** (adj)   *thrall* slave

fascinating; captivating : *The circus provided an enthralling array of exotic acts.*
Forms: *enthrall* = to captivate, *enthrallment* = state of captivation
Synonyms: *enchanting, beguiling, mesmerizing*

Don't confuse with: *appalling* (shocking)

Mnemonic: *Thrall* was an old Norse word meaning "slave," so to *enthrall* someone was to acquire great power over someone, as a master over a slave.

Usage: *Enthralling*, *enchanting*, *beguiling*, and *mesmerizing* offer different shades of meaning to "captivating." *Enthralling* derives from the Norse word for "slave," so it suggests a captivation almost against one's will; *enchanting* describes captivation as if by spell or charm (see *incantation*); *beguiling* likewise suggests the power of charm, but perhaps with deceitful motives; *mesmerizing* connotes a hypnotic power, since it derives from 18th century Austrian physician Franz Anton Mesmer whose theories led to the development of hypnosis.

☐ **exploitative** (adj)

intended to take selfish advantage of a situation or person : *A free market system should allow new companies to exploit the changing demands of consumers.*

Form: *exploit* (v) [ex PLOIT] = to make full use of, often in a selfish way

Don't confuse with: *exploit* (n) [EX ploit] (a bold feat)

☐ **hierarchy** (n)   *hieros* sacred + *arkhes* ruler

a power structure in which members are ranked by status : *Helen has spent many years working her way up the hierarchy of her law firm.*

Form: *hierarchical* = pertaining to or characteristic of a hierarchy

Synonym: *pecking order*

Root family: [hiero] *hieroglyphics* (stylized and symbolic writing as found in ancient Egypt), *hieratic* (pertaining to priests)

Root family: [arch] *monarchy* (government ruled by a king or queen), *autarchy* (government ruled by an individual with absolute power), *matriarchy* (social order in which the female line of descent is predominant), *anarchist*

☐ **imperious** (adj)   *imperare* to command

bossy and domineering : *Glenda became resentful of her manager's imperious demands.*

Synonyms: *peremptory*, *overweening*, *overbearing*, *dictatorial*, *tyrannical*

Root family: [imper, emper] *imperialist* (one who believes in the value of expanding an empire), *empire* (domain of a particularly ruler), *imperial* (royal)

Don't confuse with: *impious* (lacking reverence), *impervious* (unable to be affected), *imperial* (royal)

☐ **impervious** (adj)   *im-* not + *per-* through

not able to be influenced (by) : *Jonah was seemingly impervious to the swarming gnats.*

Synonym: *insusceptible* *(to)*

Root family: [per-] *perspicacious* (showing keen insight), *permeable* (allowing liquids or gases to pass through), *pervasive* (widespread in a certain area)

Don't confuse with: *imperious* (domineering)

Mnemonic: A good raincoat is *impervious* to rain because it does *not* let water *through* (*im-* not + *per* through).

☐ **indelible** (adj)   *in-* not + *delere* to destroy, to eliminate

forming an enduring impression; unforgettable : *The ink created an indelible stain on my tie.*

Synonyms: *ineradicable*, *ingrained*, *enduring*

Root family: [in-, im-] *interminable* (unending), *indefatigable* (untiring), *ineffable* (inexpressible in words), *inscrutable* (beyond understanding)

Root family: [delet] *delete* (to remove completely), *deleterious* (harmful)

Don't confuse with: *inedible* (repulsive to eat)

☐ **insolent** (adj)

rude and disrespectful : *Craig grew from an insolent adolescent into a well-mannered young adult.*

Form: *insolence* = rudeness and disrespectfulness

Synonyms: *impertinent*, *impudent*

Don't confuse with: *indolent* (lazy)

Mnemonic: Picture the *insole* of your shoe making really rude and disrespectful remarks to you about your foot odor.

□ ***insubordination*** (n)   *in-* not + *sub-* under + *ordinare* to rank

an act of defying authority; disobedience : *The captain was irate about the act of insubordination by his first mate.*
Forms: ***subordinate*** = lower in rank, ***subordination*** = the act of placing something in a position of lesser importance
Synonyms: ***mutiny, recalcitrance***
Root family: [in-, im-] ***insipid*** (flavorless), ***insuperable*** (impossible to overcome), ***inert*** (lacking vigor), ***interminable*** (unending), ***innocuous*** (harmless), ***ineffable*** (inexpressible in words), ***inscrutable*** (beyond understanding)
Root family: [sub-] ***submissive*** (meekly obedient), ***subvert*** (to undermine the authority of another), ***surreptitious*** (secret), ***subjugate*** (to dominate)
Root family: [ord] ***ordinal*** (relating to a ranking or order), ***ordain*** (to decree from a high authority)
Don't confuse *subordination* with *subornation* (the act of bribing someone to perform a criminal act, especially perjury)

□ ***mandate*** (n)   *manus* hand + *dare* to give

an official order or commission to do something : *We objected to our teacher's mandate that we all write our essays according to her rigid formula.*
Form: ***mandatory*** = required, usually by official order
Root family: [man] ***manipulate*** (to control skillfully), ***maneuver*** (a skillful movement), ***manual*** (done by hand rather than automatically)
Root family: [dar, don, dos, dot, dow] ***donation*** (charitable gift), ***endow*** (to donate funds to establish a position or project), ***antidote*** (a medicine to counteract a poison), ***dose*** (a recommended quantity of medicine), ***anecdote*** (a humorous or instructive story), ***dowry*** (property or money given to a husband by a bride's family), ***pardon*** (to forgive), ***rendition*** (the act of sending a foreign criminal to another country for interrogation)
Don't confuse with: ***mendacious*** (lying)

□ ***obtrusive*** (adj)   *ob-* toward + *trudere* to push

[1] (of things) prominent in an annoying way : *Although cell phones themselves have become less physically obtrusive over time, their users have become far more obnoxious.*
Synonyms: ***conspicuous, intrusive***
[2] (of people) obnoxiously intrusive : *Donna's questions seemed solicitous at first, but soon became obtrusive.*
Form: ***unobtrusive*** = not tending to get in the way
Synonyms: ***officious, meddlesome***
Root family: [trus, trud] ***extrude*** (to thrust out), ***abstruse*** (very difficult to understand), ***intruder*** (one who pushes in where he or she is unwelcome)

□ ***pacify*** (v)   *pax* peace

to quell the agitation of something; to make peaceful : *The lullaby seemed to pacify the crying baby.*
Form: ***pacifist*** = one who advocates for peace rather than war
Synonyms: ***propitiate, appease, mollify, placate***
Root family: [pac, peas] ***appease*** (to pacify), ***pact*** (a peace agreement)
Usage: The words ***pacify, placate, appease, propitiate, mollify***, and ***conciliate*** all share the meaning of "making someone feel better," but they offer different shades of meaning. To ***pacify*** is to calm someone down, like a crying child, but to ***placate*** is to pacify and gain favor at the same time. To ***appease*** is to calm someone down by complying (perhaps reluctantly) with his or her demands, but to ***propitiate*** is to make a deliberate show of pleasing someone (as a god or superior). To ***mollify*** is to soothe, as a mother soothes an anxious child, but to ***conciliate*** is to win over someone who may not trust you.

□ ***pervasive*** (adj)   *per-* through + *vadere* to go

widespread : *Bigotry is still pervasive in this region, and fear of outsiders is preventing its economic development.*
Form: ***pervade*** = to be present throughout a region or area
Root family: [per-] ***perspicacious*** (showing keen insight), ***permeable*** (allowing liquids or gases to pass through), ***impervious*** (not able to be influenced)
Root family: [vad] ***invade*** (to intrude on a region and occupy it), ***evade*** (to escape or avoid)
Don't confuse with: ***perverse*** (showing a stubborn desire to do something unacceptable)

□ ***potent*** (adj)   *potentia* power

particularly powerful, influential, or effective : *Oprah's endorsement is a potent marketing tool.*
Forms: ***impotent*** = weak and ineffective, ***potency*** = strength
Synonyms: ***formidable, efficacious, redoubtable***

Root family: [poten] *despot* (cruel ruler), *potentate* (powerful ruler), *omnipotent* (all-powerful)
Don't confuse with: *potable* (drinkable)

☐ *predominant* (adj)   *dominat* ruled, governed

acting as the main element or the most powerful influence : *After their demoralizing defeat, the predominant mood among the players was gloom.*
Form: *predominance* = the state of being the controlling influence
Synonyms: *paramount, foremost*
Root family: [domit, domin] *dominate* (to have power over), *dominion* (sovereignty; control), *domain* (an area controlled by a ruler; a specific sphere of knowledge), *domineering* (overbearing), *indomitable* (unconquerable)
Don't confuse with: *preeminent* (highly distinguished)

☐ *propagate* (v)

[1] to spread and promote : *The followers of Plato propagated the concept of "ideal forms" that transcended ordinary sensory experience.*
[2] to breed, as organisms : *The poison ivy propagated throughout the garden.*
Form: *propagation* = the process of spreading or breeding
Synonyms: *disseminate, promulgate*
Don't confuse with: *propaganda* (biased and misleading information used to promote a particular political cause), *prognosticate* (to foretell an event)

☐ *recluse* (n)   *re-* back + *claudere* to close

a person who lives a solitary lifestyle : *Scout and Jem Finch were fascinated by Boo Radley, a mysterious recluse who lived near them.*
Form: *reclusive* = solitary
Synonym: *hermit*
Root family: [re-] *revoke* (to take back), *renounce* (to give up or put aside publicly), *reciprocate* (to respond in kind), *resigned* (accepting of an undesirable situation), *regress* (to return to a less developed state)
Root family: [clud, clus, claus, clois] *claustrophobia* (fear of being in enclosed spaces), *cloister* (seclude as in a monastery), *exclusive* (highly restricted), *preclude* (render impossible), *secluded* (isolated)
Don't confuse *reclusive* with *exclusive* (highly restricted)

☐ *relinquish* (v)   *re-* (intensive) + *linquere* to abandon

to voluntarily give up : *Simmons relinquished his position in order to start his own company.*
Synonym: *renounce*
Root family: [linqu, lict] *delinquent* (failing in one's duties), *relic* (a surviving object of historical value), *derelict* (shamefully negligent in one's duties)
Don't confuse with: *distinguish* (to recognize as different)

☐ *ruthless* (adj)

without mercy : *The piranhas attacked with ruthless abandon.*
Synonyms: *callous, inhumane*

☐ *sanction* (n)   *sanctus* holy

[1] official approval : *The king gave his sanction to the agreement among the nobles.*
Form: *sanction* (v) = to give official approval to
[2] a penalty, usually one imposed by one government upon another : *The United Nations voted to impose sanctions on the rogue nation until its government freed its dissidents.*
Form: *sanction* (v) = to impose a penalty
Root family: *sanctimonious* (acting morally superior), *sanctify* (to make holy), *sanctity* (sacredness), *sanctuary* (place of refuge)
Mnemonic: *Sanction* is an unusual word because its two meanings are nearly opposite. It derives from *sanctus* (holy) and originally referred to any decree by a church representative, such as the Pope, which officially condemned or approved something. In modern usage, the positive sense (official approval) is usually intended when the words is applied in a domestic context, but in the negative sense (an official penalty) when applied to foreign affairs.

☐ *sequester* (v)

to isolate from outside influences : *Andrew Wiles sequestered himself for months at a time to work on proving Fermat's theorem.*
Synonyms: *cloister, seclude, segregate*
Don't confuse with: *semester* (one half of an academic year)
Mnemonic: Picture a *sequined quester* (that is, someone like Frodo Baggins or Don Quixote who is on a quest, wearing a sequined cape) who is being *sequestered* in a dungeon by an evil nemesis.

☐ *servile* (adj)   *servus* slave

[1] excessively willing to serve others : *The new intern is helpful without being servile.*
Form: *servility* = the quality or habit of being servile
Synonyms: *obsequious, sycophantic, deferential, fawning, ingratiating*
[2] pertaining to or akin to slave labor : *She accepted even the most servile task with good nature.*

☐ *subjugate* (v)   *sub-* under + *jugum* yoke (< *jungere* to join)

to bring under one's domination : *The West Indians were subjugated by the early European settlers.*
Form: *subjugation* = the act or process of dominating
Synonyms: *vanquish, subdue*
Root family: [sub-] *submissive* (meekly obedient), *subvert* (to undermine the authority of another), *surreptitious* (secret)
Root family: [junc, join] *conjunction* (a part of speech, such as *and*, *but*, or *or*, used to join clauses or terms in a list), *disjoint* (separate and nonoverlapping), *juncture* (a place where things join)
Don't confuse with: *subjunctive* (relating to the mood of verbs indicating something imagined, wished, possible, or counter to fact), *conjugate* (to give different forms of a verb)
Mnemonic: Imagine a lowly royal *subject* trapped under the *gate* outside the royal palace and being held there by the royal guards. He is clearly a victim of *subjugation*.

☐ *tenacious* (adj)   *tenere* to hold

holding fast to a position or claim; stubbornly persistent : *Reynolds is a tenacious debater and will rarely yield a single point to an opponent.*
Form: *tenacity* = stubborn persistence
Synonyms: *dogged, unflagging, obdurate, staunch, indefatigable, obstinate, intransigent*
Root family: [ten, tain] *retain* (to hold back), *abstain* (to refrain), *attention* (the process of focusing mental energy), *sustain* (to keep something going), *untenable* (not able to be defended or maintained)
Don't confuse *tenacity* **with** *temerity* (boldness).
Usage: You can be stubborn in many ways. If you are *tenacious*, you "hold fast" to a position (*tenax* = holding tight) like a pit bull holding on to a bone. When you refuse to change your mind even in the face of substantial evidence, you are being *obstinate*. If you refuse to compromise with or accommodate another person or position, you are *intransigent*. When you "kick back" at someone who is trying to guide you or change your mind, you are being *recalcitrant* (*recalcitrare* = to kick back at something). If your stubbornness is an attempt to fulfill a duty or commitment, you are more noble than pigheaded, so you are *steadfast* or *resolute*.

☐ *tractable* (adj)   *tractare* to pull, to handle

easily managed or influenced : *The children proved to be more tractable after they had been given their afternoon snack.*
Form: *intractable* = difficult to manage
Root family: [tract] *abstract* (lacking concrete existence), *protract* (to extend in time), *tractor* (vehicle that pulls farm instruments), *detract* (reduce the value of someone or something)
Don't confuse with: *trackable* (able to be followed)
Mnemonic: Something *tractable* is *pull-able* (*tractare* = to pull), which means it's easy to manage, handle, or control.

☐ *unremitting* (adj)   *un-* not + *re-* back + *mittere* to send

incessant; never decreasing in intensity : *The unremitting winds threatened to tear the roof off the house.*
Form: *remit* = [1] to cease from inflicting something, [2] to send payment, [3] to refer to an authority
Synonyms: *relentless, inexorable, unabating, interminable*
Root family: [re-] *recluse* (a person who lives a solitary lifestyle), *refute* (to prove something false), *revoke* (to take back), *renounce* (to give up or put aside publicly), *reciprocate* (to respond in kind), *resigned* (accepting of an undesirable situation), *regress* (to return to a less developed state), *relegate* (to place in a lower rank)
Root family: [miss, mit] *submissive* (meekly obedient), *dismiss* (send away), *intermittent*

☐ **usurper** (n)

one who forcibly takes a position of power : *Henry was the usurper of his uncle's throne.*
Forms: usurp = to take power by force, **usurpation** = act of usurping
Don't confuse usurpation with usury (the practice of charging excessively high interest rates for loans)

5 THE LANGUAGE OF LANGUAGE AND LITERATURE

☐ **allude** (v)   *ad-* to + *ludere* to play

to hint at indirectly : *Many of the* Harry Potter *novels allude to events that occurred in previous books.*
Form: allusion = an indirect reference
Root family: [ad-] **aspire** (to strive for a lofty goal), **adhere** (stick fast (to)), **advocate** (to provide vocal support for), **acquiesce** (to comply reluctantly), **annul** (to declare invalid)
Root family: [lud, lus] **collusion** (a secret understanding that has a harmful purpose), **delude** (to make someone believe something that is not true), **illusion** (something that gives a false impression of reality), **ludicrous** (foolish and ridiculous)
Don't confuse with: elude (to avoid a pursuer skillfully)
Don't confuse allusion with illusion (a false idea or perception)

☐ **analogy** (n)

a correspondence between two things based on structural similarity : *To explain the behavior of a magnetic field, our physics professor used the analogy of a field of wheat.*
Forms: analogous = similar in terms of general structure, **analog** = something that is regarded as structurally similar to another thing
Don't confuse with: apology (argument for a particular position)

☐ **anecdote** (n)

a short amusing or informative story : *My grandfather told many funny anecdotes about life on a submarine.*
Form: anecdotal = pertaining to or deriving from an anecdote
Don't confuse with: antidote (a medicine taken to counteract a poison)

☐ **anthology** (n)   *anthos* flower + *logia* collection

a published collection of writings : *Several of the poems in the anthology were chosen for national awards.*
Synonym: chrestomathy (an instructive collection of passages)
Don't confuse with: anthropology (the study of human cultures)

☐ **bombastic** (adj)

(pertaining to speech) pompous and blustery, with little meaning : *Some cable news shows have replaced reputable journalists with bombastic blowhards.*
Form: bombast = pompous, blustery speech
Synonyms: pompous, turgid, orotund

☐ **coherent** (adj)   *co-* together + *haerere* to stick

[1] clear, rational and consistent : *David could not construct a coherent sentence, so we couldn't understand his point.*
[2] forming a united whole : *The several tribes joined to form a coherent fighting force.*
Forms: coherence = the quality of being clear and rational; the quality of forming a whole, **incoherent** = unclear or irrational; lacking coherence
Synonym: cohesive
Root family: [con-, co-, com-, col-] **conformist** (one who conscientiously complies with the standards of a group, **conventional** (according to common practice), **consensus** (general agreement), **conspire** (to plot together), **coalesce** (to come together), **confluence** (a place at which two things merge)
Root family: [her, hes] **adhesive** (glue-like substance), **cohesive** (forming a united whole), **inherent** (existing as an inseparable attribute), **adherent** (a faithful believer in a particular practice or philosophy)
Usage: Coherent and **cohesive** derive from the same roots and are synonyms as long as they are used to mean "forming a whole." However, **coherent** is more commonly used to mean "clear, rational and consistent," whereas **cohesive** is the preferred adjective for describing things that form a whole.

☐ *colloquial* (adj)   *co-* together + *loqui* to talk

pertaining to informal, conversational speech : *The teacher said that my essay was well reasoned, but that I should avoid colloquial terms like "totally" in a formal paper.*
Forms: *colloquy* = casual conversation, *colloquialism* = a word or phrase commonly heard in casual, but not formal, conversation
Synonym: *vernacular*
Root family: [loqu, locu] *loquacious* (talkative), *eloquent* (well-spoken), *circumlocutory* (inclined to speak evasively), *obloquy* (verbal abuse)
Mnemonic: A fancy word for casual conversation is *colloquy* (*co-* together + *loqui* to talk), so *colloquial* language is the language you use when talking to friends, but not when giving a formal speech or writing a formal essay.

☐ *derivative* (adj)   *de-* down + *rivus* stream

imitative of someone else's work and therefore unoriginal : *The judges suggested that Daria's version of the song was too derivative and suggested that she try to make it more original.*
Root family: [de-] *decadent* (excessively self-indulgent), *deplore* (to express strong disapproval), *denounce* (declare as bad), *detract* (reduce the value of something), *debase* (reduce in value), *denigrate* (criticize unfairly), *deference* (submission to the authority of another), *condescend* (to act superior to someone else)
Root family: [riv] *river* (a large stream), *arrival* (coming)

☐ *eclectic* (adj)   *ex-* out + *legere* to choose

deriving from a variety of sources : *Ted has very eclectic tastes in music, ranging from country to jazz to reggae.*
Root family: [lect] *elect* (to choose by voting), *select* (to choose carefully), *delectable* (very tasty)
Don't confuse with: *electric* (powered by electricity), *ecstatic* (extremely happy)

☐ *eloquent* (adj)   *loqui* to talk

articulate and well spoken : *The jury was clearly persuaded by the attorney's eloquent summary.*
Form: *eloquence* = fluency in speaking or writing
Root family: [loqu, locu] *loquacious* (talkative), *colloquial* (conversational), *circumlocutory* (inclined to speak evasively), *obloquy* (verbal abuse)
Don't confuse with: *elegant* (graceful and stylish)
Mnemonic: Avoid confusing *eloquent* and *elegant* by focusing on the root *loqu*, meaning "talk." A dress can be *elegant*, but it certainly can't be *eloquent* because it can't talk.

☐ *epilogue* (n)   *epi-* upon, in addition + *logos* words

a section at the end of a novel or play that explains the conclusion : *The epilogue explained that the protagonist never remarried.*
Root family: [epi-] *epigram* (a pithy saying), *epidemic* (a widespread disease)
Root family: [log] *eulogy* (a praising speech, usually for a deceased person)
Don't confuse with: *monologue* (a long speech in a play)

☐ *evocative* (adj)   *e-* out + *vocare* to call

tending to draw out strong feelings, ideas, or sensations : *Gabriel Garcia Marquez's magical novels are as evocative as they are disorienting.*
Forms: *evoke* = to draw out an idea, emotion, or sensation; to elicit, *evocation* = the process of bringing a feeling or idea into the conscious mind
Root family: [e-, ex-] *extol* (to praise highly), *extemporaneous* (without planning), *exuberant* (filled with liveliness and energy), *elusive* (difficult to catch or achieve), *exorbitant* (excessive)
Root family: [voc, vok] *advocate* (to speak out for), *revoke* (to take back), *provocative* (causing anger or annoyance), *equivocate* (to speak ambiguously and noncommittally)
Don't confuse with: *provocative* (causing anger or annoyance)

☐ *irony* (n)

a situation that directly contradicts expectations : *Rose considered it a delicious irony that her accountant friend Teri miscalculated the waiter's tip so egregiously.*
Form: *ironic* = contradicting expectations, often humorously
Don't confuse with: *iron* (a strong, hard, magnetic metal). Although *irony* can be used as an adjective to mean "like iron," it is best to avoid this usage because of the confusion with the adjective, which has an entirely different origin.

Usage: It is common to confuse *irony* with *interesting coincidence*, but they are not the same thing. Dying on one's birthday may well be an interesting coincidence, but it is certainly not *ironic*, because death is no less expected on one's birthday than on any other day. *Dramatic irony* is a literary device in which the audience is aware of an important fact that is unknown to one or more of the characters in a play.

☐ *laconic* (adj)   *Laconia* Sparta

inclined to use very few words : *Harold was so laconic at parties that few knew that he was an articulate and celebrated writer.*
Synonyms: *taciturn, reticent*
Mnemonic: *Sparta*, the martial city-state of ancient Greece, was known for its disciplined warrior culture. Hence, *spartan* has come to mean "disciplined, austere, or strict." From the Latin word for Sparta, *Laconia*, we get *laconic*, meaning "inclined to use very few words," because Spartans, unlike the Athenians, who were educated in philosophy, poetry, and oration, were not considered particularly well spoken.

☐ *lament* (v)

to mourn or express deep regret : *Our friends lamented the loss of our old playground.*
Forms: *lamentable* = regrettable, *lamentation* = a passionate expression of mourning
Synonyms: *rue, deplore*

☐ *loquacious* (adj)   *loqui* to talk

talkative; tending to chatter : *Although Anita is well liked, she is a bit too loquacious to be a good listener.*
Form: *loquacity* = the quality of being loquacious
Synonyms: *garrulous, voluble*
Root family: *colloquial* (conversational), *eloquent* (well-spoken), *circumlocutory* (inclined to speak evasively)

☐ *melodrama* (n)   *melos* music + drama

sensational drama designed to appeal to the emotions : *I prefer realistic crime dramas to melodramas like soap operas.*
Form: *melodramatic* = excessively dramatic
Root family: [melo] *melodious* (tuneful)

☐ *platitude* (n)

an overused proverb : *My father bored us with his platitudes about hard work and sacrifice.*
Synonym: *banality, bromide, inanity, cliché*
Don't confuse with: *platypus* (a semiaquatic egg-laying mammal)
Mnemonic: Imagine a *platypus* with an *attitude* spouting inane *platitudes* like "Don't put all your eggs in one basket!"

☐ *poignant* (adj)   *pungere* to prick

emotionally moving; keenly distressing : *The climax of the movie was so poignant that virtually the entire audience was reduced to tears.*
Form: *poignancy* = the quality of being emotionally moving
Synonyms: *moving, affecting, plaintive*
Root family: [punc, pung, poign] *punctilious* (scrupulously attentive to rules), *punctual* (on time), *compunction* (sharp feeling of guilt), *puncture* (to pierce), *pungent* (sharp tasting or smelling)
Don't confuse with: *pugnacious*
Mnemonic: *Poignant* derive from *pungere* (to prick) because sharp emotions often elicit a sharp physical sensation, like a poke in the stomach.

☐ *satiric* (adj)

employing humor, irony, or ridicule to poke fun at something : *The skit was a satiric jab at the gridlocked congress.*
Forms: *satire* = humor, irony, or ridicule used to poke fun at something, *satirize* = to poke fun at something with satire, *satirical* = satiric
**Don't confuse *satire* with *satyr* (in Greek mythology, a lustful, drunken god with a horse's ears and tail)

☐ *verbose* (adj)   *verbum* word

excessively wordy : *Sadly, many academics cannot distinguish intelligent prose from that which is merely verbose.*
Synonyms: *prolix, discursive*
Root family: [verb] *verbatim* (word for word), *proverb* (a pithy, well-known saying)

6   THE LANGUAGE OF JUDGMENT

☐   *ambivalent* (adj)   *ambi-* both + *valere* to be strong

having mixed feelings about something : *She was surprisingly ambivalent about attending her own birthday party.*
Form: *ambivalence* = lack of conviction on an issue
Root family: [ambi-] *ambiguous* (vague), *ambidextrous* (able to use both hands skillfully)
Root family: [val] *prevalent* (widespread and abundant), *valor* (bravery)
Don't confuse with: *ambiguous* (vague; having multiple meanings)

☐   *arbitrary* (adj)   *arbiter* judge

based on personal whim, rather than reason : *His coworkers resented his imperious and arbitrary decision-making style.*
Root family: [arbit] *arbitration* (the process of submitting a dispute to a judge), *arbiter* (a judge with absolute power)
Usage: The word *arbitrary* is sometimes misused as a synonym for *random*, as in *The shells were scattered on the beach in an arbitrary pattern.* This is a misuse of the term, because *arbitrary* derives from *arbiter*, meaning "judge," so it should only be used to describe a decision or the result of a decision.

☐   *arbitrate* (v)   *arbiter* judge

to serve as a neutral third-party judge in a dispute : *My mother arbitrated a resolution to the fight between my sister and me.*
Forms: *arbitration* = the process of resolving a dispute via a neutral third party, *arbiter* = one who serves as a judge in a dispute
Synonyms: *adjudicate*, *mediate*
Don't confuse with: *arbitrary* (based on whim rather than reason)
Mnemonic: Picture a judge *arbitrating* on an *Arby's tray*.

☐   *carping* (adj)

constantly finding fault, particularly about trivial matters : *April's constant carping about the movie forced me to walk out of the theater.*
Synonyms: *caviling*, *grousing*, *griping*
Don't confuse with: *carp* (n) (a freshwater fish)
Mnemonic: Imagine an annoying patron at a restaurant *carping* about the *carp* she's been served: *It's too dry! It smells fishy!*

☐   *censor* (v)   *censere* to assess

to edit out or repress objectionable material : *The prisoners' outgoing letters were being censored by the prison officials.*
Form: *censorious* = severely critical of others
Synonyms: *expurgate*, *bowdlerize*
Root family: [cens] *census* (the official tally of a population), *censure* (to express formal disapproval)
Don't confuse with: *censure* (to express formal disapproval)

☐   *censure* (v)   *censere* to assess

to express formal disapproval of someone's behavior : *The senator was censured for her misconduct, but was permitted to stay in office.*
Synonyms: *chastise*, *rebuke*, *upbraid*, *reprove*, *reproach*
Don't confuse with: *censor* (to edit out objectionable material)
Usage: See usage note at *rebuke* in section 3.

☐   *clemency* (n)   *clemens* mildness

leniency, particularly in judicial sentencing : *The judge showed clemency because the convict showed great remorse for his actions.*
Synonyms: *mercy*, *compassion*
Root family: [clemen] *inclement* (stormy)

☐   *conformist* (n)   *con-* together + *form*

one who conscientiously complies with the standards of a group : *I'd rather be an individualist than a conformist.*
Forms: *conformity* = compliance with the standards of a group, *nonconformist* = an individualist
Synonym: *traditionalist*
Root family: [con-, co-, com-, col-] *conventional* (according to common practice), *conjecture* (guess), *convoluted* (complicated), *consensus* (general agreement), *conspire* (to plot together), *coalesce* (to come together), *coherent* (forming a united whole), *compliant* (willing to obey), *confluence* (a place at which two things merge)
Root family: [form] *reformist* (supporting gradual change rather than revolution), *formality* (rigid observance of conventional rules), *deformation* (change of form; distortion)

□ *contempt* (n)

sharp disgust for something deemed unworthy : *Her contempt for Mr. Jones was so deep that she would not even acknowledge his presence.*
Forms: *contemptible* = worthy of contempt, *contemptuous* = filled with contempt
Synonyms: *scorn, disdain, derision, disparagement*
Usage: See usage note at *disdain* in this section.

□ *cynic* (n)

one who believes that humans are essentially selfish : *Warren was such a cynic that he mistrusted every word of praise from his teachers.*
Forms: *cynical* = distrustful of the goodwill of others, *cynicism* = belief that everyone is essentially selfish
Don't confuse with: *skeptic* (one who doubts)

□ *demeaning* (adj)

causing a loss of respect or dignity : *The student protest did not elevate the debate, but instead reduced it to a demeaning travesty of intellectual discourse.*
Synonyms: *degrading, abject*
Don't confuse with: *demeanor* (general bearing or behavior)

□ *denounce* (v)   *de-* down + *nuntiare* declare

publicly declare as bad or evil : *She was denounced for making a racist slur.*
Forms: *denunciation* = the act of denouncing
Synonyms: *censure, revile, malign*
Root family: [de-] *decadent* (excessively self-indulgent), *derivative* (imitative of someone else's work), *deplore* (to express strong disapproval), *detract* (reduce the value of something), *debase* (reduce in value), *denigrate* (criticize unfairly), *deference* (submission to the authority of another), *condescend* (to act superior to someone else)
Root family: [nunc, nounc] *renounce* (to give up or put aside publicly), *announce* (make a formal declaration), *enunciate* (state clearly), *pronounce* (sound a word in a particular way)
Don't confuse with: *renounce* (to disavow)

□ *depraved* (adj)

immoral or wicked : *The murderer showed depraved indifference to human life.*
Form: *depravity* = moral corruption
Synonyms: *corrupt, degenerate, debased, nefarious, iniquitous*
Don't confuse with: *deprived* (denied of the benefit of something, particularly basic amenities and cultural advantages)

□ *derision* (n)

mockery; contemptuous ridicule : *The derision Phil received in the locker room scarred him for life.*
Forms: *derisive* = filled with derision, *deride* = express contempt for; ridicule
Synonyms: *scorn, disdain, contempt, disparagement*
Usage: See usage note at *disdain* in this section.

□ *disdain* (n)   *dis-* not + *dignus* worthy

feeling that something or someone is unworthy : *I could feel only disdain for Glen's self-serving apology.*
Synonyms: *scorn, contempt, derision, disparagement*
Root family: [dis-] *disconcerting* (unsettling), *discredit* (harm the reputation of something or someone), *discernment* (the ability to make fine distinctions), *dispassionate* (not influenced by strong emotions), *disparate* (very different; variegated), *discrepancy* (a lack of compatibility between facts or claims), *disseminate* (to cast widely), *disperse* (to spread or scatter), *disputatious* (argumentative), *dispel* (to drive away; to eliminate), *diffident* (lacking in self-confidence), *diffuse* (spread over a wide area)
Root family: [dign] *dignify* (to make worthy), *indignant* (angry about unjust treatment), *deign* (to do something that one considers beneath one's dignity)
Usage: *Disdain, contempt, derision, disparagement*, and *denigration* are similar, but offer different shades of meaning. *Disdain* includes a feeling of social superiority; *contempt* includes a particularly acute disgust; *derision* suggests not just a contemptuous feeling but also an outright verbal attack; *disparagement* suggests a long-term campaign to bring someone or something down; and *denigration* involves unjustly harsh criticism.

☐ *dogmatic* (adj)

proclaiming an inflexible adherence to religious or political principles : *Some reporters spend too much time spouting dogmatic opinions rather than providing objective analysis.*
Forms: *dogma* = rigid doctrines of a religion or philosophy, *dogmatist* = a dogmatic person
Synonyms: *peremptory*, *imperious*, *doctrinaire*
Don't confuse with: *pragmatic* (concerned with practical, rather than idealistic, considerations)
Mnemonic: Imagine a robot dog (*dog-a-matic*) barking out political beliefs.

☐ *extol* (v)   *ex-* out + *tol* ring out

to praise enthusiastically : *She extolled the technical beauty of Chopin's etudes.*
Synonyms: *acclaim*, *exalt*, *eulogize*
Don't confuse with: *exhort* (to strongly encourage someone to do something)

☐ *futile* (adj)   *futilis* leaky (< *fundere* to pour)

doomed to fail; pointless : *All attempts to defeat me are futile!*
Form: *futility* = pointlessness
Root family: [fus, fund, found] *confuse* (to cause to become perplexed), *confound* (to fail to distinguish different elements), *diffuse* (spread over a wide area), *fusion* (the process of joining two things into a single entity), *profuse* (abundant), *transfusion* (a transfer, usually of blood, from one person or animal to another), *refuse* (to reject)
Don't confuse with: *utile* (advantageous)

☐ *inane* (adj)

silly, stupid : *I find most reality shows to be an inane waste of time.*
Forms: *inanity* = a silly act, *inaneness* = the quality of being inane
Synonyms: *fatuous*, *asinine*, *vapid*, *puerile*
Don't confuse with: *insane* (mentally ill)

☐ *irreverent* (adj)   *ir-* not + *re-* (intensive) + *vereri* to respect

showing no respect for things that are ordinarily given respect : *The comedy troupe performed an irreverent sketch that thoroughly insulted the Vice President.*
Form: *reverent* = very respectful
Synonyms: *impudent*, *flippant*, *insolent*
Root family: [ir-, in-, im-] *insipid* (flavorless), *insuperable* (impossible to overcome), *inert* (lacking vigor), *interminable* (unending), *innocuous* (harmless), *ineffable* (inexpressible in words), *inscrutable* (beyond understanding), *impassive* (unemotional), *incongruous* (not consistent with expectations)
Root family: [rever] *reverend* (a title for a member of the clergy), *reverential* (highly respectful)
Don't confuse with: *irrelevant* (not appropriate to the matter at hand)

☐ *mundane* (adj)   *mundus* world

dull and uninteresting : *She wanted to escape her mundane existence.*
Synonyms: *humdrum*, *monotonous*, *prosaic*

☐ *punitive* (adj)   *punire* to punish

intended to punish : *The court imposed punitive damages to discourage such reckless behavior in the future.*
Form: *impunity* = exemption from punishment
Synonyms: *retributive*, *disciplinary*
Root family: [puni, peni] *punish* (to impose a penalty for an offense), *penitence* (remorse for an offense), *penitentiary* (prison), *penalty* (punishment), *penal* (related to prison or punishment)
Don't confuse with: *putative* (generally considered to be)
Don't confuse *impunity* **with** *immunity* (the ability to resist infection) or *impugn* (to attack as invalid)
Mnemonic: *Punitive* damages are those imposed on someone in court as a *punishment* to discourage behavior.

☐ *repudiate* (v)

to refuse association with : *I repudiate those governments that deny people equal protection under the law.*
Form: *repudiation* = the act of repudiating something
Synonyms: *renounce*, *abjure*
Don't confuse with: *reputed* (generally believed), *reputation* (the generally held value judgments about a person)

☐ *skeptical* (adj)

inclined to doubt; not easily convinced : *I was skeptical of Dawn's claim that she could talk to the dead.*
Forms: *skeptic* = a skeptical person, *skepticism* = quality of being skeptical
Don't confuse with: *cynical* (distrustful of others), *septic* (infected with bacteria)
Usage: Students commonly confuse *skeptical* with *cynical*, but they are very different words. *Skeptical* describes a questioning attitude toward *claims*, while *cynical* describes a negative attitude toward *people*.

7   THE LANGUAGE OF EXTREMISM AND EXAGGERATION

☐ *embellish* (v)   *bellus* beautiful

to make a story more interesting by fabricating or exaggerating entertaining details; to decorate; *Paul always embellishes his stories with false intrigue.*
Form: *embellishment* = a decorative detail; a detail added to a story to make it more entertaining
Synonyms: *festoon, gild, embroider*

☐ *eradicate* (v)   *e-* out + *radix* root

to eliminate completely : *By the 1960s, the Polk vaccine had virtually eradicated polio in North America.*
Form: *eradicable* = capable of being completely destroyed
Root family: [radic] *radical* (affecting fundamental change), *radish* (a pungent edible root)
Synonyms: *annihilate, abolish*

☐ *hyperbole* (n)   *hyper* above, beyond

exaggeration for persuasive effect: *The author's claim that there was a "literacy crisis" in America was dismissed as hyperbole.*
Form: *hyperbolic* = exaggerated
Root family: [hyper] *hyperactive* (excessively active), *hyperventilate* (to breathe too quickly)
Don't confuse with: *hyperbola* (a two-part geometric curve).
Mnemonic: It's interesting to note that three of the "conic sections" you may have studied in math class—the *ellipse*, the *hyperbola*, and the *parabola*—correspond to three literary terms:
- *ellipsis* (*elleipein* to leave out) = the omission of language from a quotation or of words that are implied in a sentence, or the symbol (...) indicating such an omission
- *hyperbole* (*huperbole* excess) = exaggerated comments
- *parable* (*parabola* comparison) = a story used to illustrate a moral lesson

The names of the curves are derived from their "eccentricities": a conic with an eccentricity less than 1 is "deficient," hence the name "ellipse"; a conic with an eccentricity greater than 1 is "excessive," hence the name "hyperbola"; and a conic with an eccentricity of exactly 1 is "comparable," hence the name "parabola."

☐ *indulgent* (adj)

excessively generous or lenient : *Her mother was strict, but her grandmother was indulgent.*
Forms: *indulge (in)* = allow oneself to enjoy the pleasure of, *indulgence* = an act of indulging
Don't confuse with: *indolent* (lazy)

☐ *superfluous* (adj)   *super* above + *fluere* to flow

unnecessary, excessive : *After a week of celebrations, the anniversary ball seemed superfluous.*
Form: *superfluity* = an excessive amount
Root family: [super] *insuperable* (impossible to overcome), *superlative* (of the highest degree or quality), *superficial* (on the surface only), *supercilious* (haughty and pompous)
Root family: [flu] *fluent* (able to flow freely; easily conversant in a language or field), *affluent* (wealthy), *confluence* (a place where two things flow together)

☐ *unstinting* (adj)

without reservations; given liberally : *She was unstinting in her support for animal rights.*
Form: *stint* = to give only sparingly
Synonyms: *unsparing, magnanimous, munificent, profuse*
Mnemonic: The verbs *stint*, *stump* and *stunt* (to retard the progress of, as in *Smoking stunts your growth*.) derive from the same Germanic root. So one who is *unstinting* does not have a stunted sense of generosity.

8   THE LANGUAGE OF CARE AND RESTRAINT

☐ *ameliorate* (v)

to make a situation better : *The recent highway improvements have done much to ameliorate many of commuters' biggest concerns.*
Synonym: *mitigate*
Don't confuse with: *emancipate* (to free from bondage)
Usage: See usage note at *mitigate* in section 17.
Mnemonic: Imagine *Eeyore* from *Winnie the Pooh* who finally gets a cake after he thinks everyone has forgotten his birthday. The cake is *a meal Eeyore ate* which *ameliorated* his depression.

☐ *assuage* (v)

to make something unpleasant less intense : *The news story was intended to sensationalize the epidemic rather than assuage people's fears about it.*
Synonyms: *mitigate, palliate, attenuate, allay, ameliorate*
Don't confuse with: *dissuade* (to persuade someone not to do something)
Usage: See usage note at *mitigate* in section 17.

☐ *curtail* (v)   *curtus* short

to cut back; to impose a restriction on an activity : *The library committee decided to curtail its expenses until it balanced its budget.*
Synonyms: *pare, retrench, curb*
Root family: [curt] *curt* (rudely abrupt)
Mnemonic: If you *cut* off the *tail* of a beaver, it will really *curtail* its abilities.

☐ *equanimity* (n)   *equa* same + *anima* spirit, mind

evenness of temper : *During the lockdown drill, our teacher's equanimity helped assuage the fears of several students.*
Synonyms: *composure, imperturbability, sangfroid, equability*
Root family: [equa, equi-] *equilateral* (having equal sides), *equilibrium* (a state of balance between opposing forces or trends)
Root family: [anim] *magnanimous* (generous), *pusillanimous* (cowardly)
Don't confuse with: *equity* (fairness)

☐ *fastidious* (adj)

showing great attention to details, particularly in matters of cleanliness : *Julia is fastidious about her food, making sure that the vegetables never touch the meat on her plate.*
Forms: *fastidiousness* = the quality of being fastidious
Synonyms: *scrupulous, meticulous, punctilious*
Usage: See usage note at *scrupulous* in this section.

☐ *impassive* (adj)   *in-* not + *passivus* suffered

unemotional; calm : *Despite all the turmoil, Randall was able to remain impassive.*
Form: *impassivity* = a state of calmness and restraint from emotion
Synonyms: *stoic, dispassionate, forbearing, phlegmatic, stolid*
Root family: [in-, im-] *insipid* (flavorless), *insuperable* (impossible to overcome), *inert* (lacking vigor), *interminable* (unending), *indefatigable* (untiring), *inscrutable* (beyond understanding), *incongruous* (not consistent with expectations)
Don't confuse with: *impassioned* (passionate), *impasse* (deadlock; point beyond which passage is impossible)
Mnemonic/Usage: Strangely, *impassive* and *passive* are closer to being synonyms than antonyms. As they are most commonly used, both suggest a *lack* of activity or emotion. To make things even more confusing, the similar-sounding words *passionate* and *impassioned*, while also seeming to be opposites of each other, actually both mean "full of emotion," essentially the *opposite* of *impassive* or *passive*. If this distinction is vexing for you, remember that a *sieve* lets things pass through, so the *–sive* words, *passive* and *impassive*, describe someone who lets things pass easily, without getting too emotional about them.

☐ *meticulous* (adj)

showing finicky attention to details and precision : *A meticulous baker, she often measures her ingredients twice before combining any of them.*
Form: *meticulousness* = attention to details and precision
Synonyms: *scrupulous, fastidious, punctilious*
Usage: See usage note at *scrupulous* in this section.

☐ *nonchalant* (adj)

calm and unconcerned, often inappropriately so : *My lab partner took a nonchalant approach to the experiment and almost caused a dangerous explosion.*
Form: *nonchalance* = lack of concern or enthusiasm
Synonyms: *blithe, blasé, dispassionate, apathetic, indifferent, insouciant*
Usage: A *nonchalant* person is usually putting on airs, but a *blithe* person is innocently unself-conscious. One who is *blasé* has usually become *jaded* to the point of *indifference*. One who is *dispassionate* is adopting a neutral attitude in order to render an objective judgment. One who is *apathetic* typically has neither airs, innocence, nor *judicious* motive.

☐ *parsimony* (n)   *parcere* to be sparing

extreme reluctance to spend money, use unnecessary language, or expend resources : *Mastering the art of haiku requires mastering the art of parsimony.*
Form: *parsimonious* (adj) = extremely reluctant to spend money, use unnecessary language, or expend resources

☐ *placid* (adj)   *placere* to please

[1] (of a person or animal) calm and unexcitable : *I chose to ride the most placid horse.*
[2] (of a place) calm and peaceful : *The chateau was a placid retreat from the city.*
Forms: *placidity* (n) = calmness; peacefulness
Root family: [plac] *placate, implacable* (unable to be pleased), *complacent*
Don't confuse with: *passive* (permitting things to happen without resistance or involvement), *platitude* (a trite proverb)

☐ *refurbish* (v)

to renovate; to restore to good condition : *David studied for weeks to refurbish his conversational Italian before traveling to Rome.*
Don't confuse with: *refurnish* (to restock with furniture)

☐ *rejuvenate* (v)   *juvenis* young

to restore the vitality of : *She felt rejuvenated after her trip to the mountains.*
Synonym: *revitalize*
Root family: [juven] *juvenile* (immature)

☐ *reticent* (adj)   *re-* (intensive) + *tacere* to be silent

unwilling to speak or express one's feelings : *When the conversation turned to her college years, Sheila became uncharacteristically reticent.*
Forms: *reticence* = unwillingness to speak or reveal one's feelings or thoughts
Root family: [tice, tace] *tacit* (unspoken, but understood, as a *tacit agreement*), *taciturn* (quiet and reserved)
Usage: Do not confuse *reticent* with *reluctant*. For instance, *He was reticent to talk about his experiences* is redundant. The correct phrasing is *He was reluctant to talk about his experiences* or *He was reticent about his experiences.*

☐ *scrupulous* (adj)

[1] diligent and attentive to details : *George is a scrupulous researcher.*
Synonyms: *meticulous, fastidious*
[2] concerned with moral correctness : *He is too scrupulous to consider cheating on his taxes.*
Forms: *scruples* = concerns about moral rectitude, *unscrupulous* = lacking in moral character
Don't confuse with: *scrutinize* (to examine closely)
Usage: *Scrupulous, meticulous, fastidious,* and *punctilious* are nearly synonymous, but each offers a different shade of meaning. *Scrupulous* suggests an exactitude combined with high moral standards; *meticulous* suggests a finicky precision, often but

not necessarily about trivial things; *fastidious* suggests a precision born of a compulsive neatness; and *punctilious* suggests an extreme attention to rules, such as etiquette.

Mnemonic: Think of the most precise and detailed-oriented person you know (or the most moral person you know) *pulling* on a *screw*.

☐ *sedate* (adj)   *sedere* to sit

calm, to the point of being dull : *Small-town life was too sedate for Maia.*

Forms: *sedate* (v) = to calm or put to sleep with drugs, *sedative* = a drug used to sedate

Root family: [sed, sid] *sedentary*, *dissident* (one who opposes official policy), *assiduous* (hardworking), *insidious* (subtly dangerous), *preside* (to sit in a position of authority), *reside* (to live in a particular location), *sediment* (material that settles to the bottom of a liquid or body of water, particularly a river)

Don't confuse with: *sedition* (incitement to rebellion)

☐ *stoic* (adj)

enduring hardship without complaint : *William remained stoic throughout the funeral.*

Form: *stoicism* = the belief that emotions are the enemy of reason

Synonyms: *dispassionate*, *forbearing*, *phlegmatic*, *stolid*, *impassive*

Don't confuse *stoicism* with *solecism* (an error in grammar or usage, particularly a tactless one) or *solipsism* (the belief that nothing exists except for oneself)

Mnemonic: Stoicism was a Hellenic school of philosophy founded by Zeno of Citium (and which met at the "painted porch"—Stoa Poikile—from which the school got its name) who taught that emotions were incompatible with reasoning and so cultivated a systematic detachment.

☐ *succinct* (adj)   *cingere* to cinch, as with a belt

expressed clearly and concisely : *The documentary was prefaced with a succinct description of the 15-year study it chronicled.*

Form: *succinctness* = the quality of being brief and to the point

Root family: [cinc] *cinch* (to gird with a belt), *precinct* (an administrative district)

Mnemonic: The connection between *succinct* and *precinct* comes in the idea of "cinching" or "encircling" (*cingere* = to cinch or encircle). When you make something more *succinct*, you make it "smaller and tighter" much as cinching a girdle around your waist would make you smaller and tighter. A *precinct* is a well-defined (or well "encircled") district.

☐ *temperance* (n)   *temperare* to restrain

self-control with regard to consumption : *After years of gluttonous behavior, he has learned remarkable temperance.*

Forms: *temper* = to moderate or act as a moderating force, *temperate* = showing moderation, *intemperate* = lacking self-control

Root family: [temper] *temperature* (degree of heat), *temperament* (disposition or degree of personal restraint)

Don't confuse the *tempe-* words that derive from *temperare* (to restrain) with the *tempo-* words that derive from *tempus* (time), like *extemporaneous*, *temporize* (to delay making a decision), and *contemporary* ((adj) modern; (n) one who lives during the same time period as another).

Mnemonic: The Temperance Movement in the 19th century was designed to curb excessive consumption of alcohol and ultimately led to the Prohibition Era.

To avoid confusing the cognate words *temperance*, *temperament*, and *temperature*, notice how they are all related to the root word *temperare* (to restrain): *temperance* is essentially one's "ability to restrain oneself"; *temperament* refers to much the same thing but has been generalized to encompass emotional dispositions in general; *temperature* was originally a synonym of *temperament* but lent its sense of "degree of emotional heat" to the scientific term for "degree of physical heat."

☐ *vigilant* (adj)   *vigil* awake

watchful for danger or difficulties : *We must remain vigilant against tyranny.*

Form: *vigilance* = watchfulness

Synonyms: *circumspect*, *wary*, *leery*

Root family: [vigil] *vigilante* (one who takes the law into his or her own hands); *vigil* (a prayerful period in the night)

Forms: *dispute* = a heated argument, *disputant* = a person involved in a heated argument, *disputation* = the art of debate

Root family: [dis-] *disconcerting* (unsettling), *disdain* (feeling that something is unworthy), *discredit* (harm the reputation of something or someone), *diffident* (lacking in self-confidence)

Root family: [put] *compute* (to calculate), *reputation* (social standing), *impute* (to attribute)

9 THE LANGUAGE OF FREEDOM

☐ **anarchist** (n)   *an-* without + *arkhos* ruler

one who believes in freedom from government : *The anarchists wanted to protest the summit but had difficulty organizing themselves.*
Forms: *anarchy* = absence of governmental rule, ***anarchism*** = the belief in freedom from government, ***anarchic*** = lacking systematic government
Root family: [arch] ***monarchy*** (government ruled by a king or queen), ***autarchy*** (government ruled by an individual with absolute power), ***matriarchy*** (social order in which the female line of descent is predominant), ***hierarchy*** (a ranked system of organization)
Don't confuse *anarchic* (lacking government) with ***archaic*** (old and outdated)
Usage: Don't use ***anarchy*** to mean ***chaos*** unless it refers to chaos that results directly from a rejection of authority.

☐ **capricious** (adj)

prone to unpredictable behavior : *Her decisions seemed more capricious than reasoned.*
Forms: *capriciousness* = unpredictability of mood or behavior, ***caprice*** = a sudden and unaccountable change of behavior
Synonyms: *fickle, volatile, whimsical, arbitrary*
Don't confuse with: *capris* (close-fitting calf-length pants), ***capiche*** ((from Italian *capisci*) slang for "do you understand?")

☐ **emancipate** (v)

to free from bondage : *The prisoners of war were finally emancipated by the liberating army.*
Form: *emancipation* = the act of freeing those in bondage, ***emancipator*** = one who sets prisoners free
Synonyms: *unfetter, liberate*
Don't confuse with: *emaciate* (to make abnormally thin and weak)

☐ **extemporaneous** (adj)   *ex-* out of + *tempor* time

improvised; performed without preparation : *The senator's extemporaneous speech was surprisingly coherent and very well received.*
Form: *extemporize* (v) = to improvise
Root family: [tempor] ***temporize*** (to delay making a decision), ***contemporary*** ((adj) modern; (n) one who lives during the same time period as another)
Don't confuse with: *temporize* (to delay making a decision), ***contemporaneous*** (occurring or existing at the same time)
Mnemonic: If you must make a speech but you are ***out of time*** (*ex tempor*) to plan it, you must ***extemporize***.

☐ **extricate** (v)   *ex-* out + *tricae* perplexities

to free from a constraint or difficult situation : *We found it difficult to extricate ourselves from our duties.*
Synonyms: *disentangle, extract*
Root family: [tric] ***intricate*** (complex), ***trick***
Don't confuse with: *explicate* (to analyze and develop (an idea) in detail)

☐ **impetuous** (adj)   *im-* toward + *petere* to drive

done without careful thought or planning; spontaneous : *David's jocular and impetuous nature made him the most popular player in the locker room, but it often caused problems on the field.*
Form: *impetuousness* = tendency to be impetuous
Synonyms: *whimsical, impulsive, capricious*
Root family: [im-] ***impugn*** (to call into question), ***impetus*** (energizing force), ***impute*** (to attribute something to someone)
Root family: [pet] ***impetus*** (driving force), ***perpetuate*** (to help continue for an extended period), ***petulant*** (childishly ill-tempered)
Don't confuse with: *impetus* (driving force), ***petulant*** (childishly ill-tempered)

☐ **mercurial** (adj)

inclined to unpredictable mood swings : *He was a brilliant but mercurial composer, susceptible to manic bouts of productivity and debilitating depression.*
Synonyms: *volatile, capricious, temperamental*
Mnemonic: A ***mercurial*** personality runs hot and cold, up and down, like the ***mercury*** in a thermometer.

☐ *unfettered* (adj)   *feter* foot (< *ped* foot)

freed from harsh restraints : *Shawn finally felt unfettered from her oppressive relationship.*
Forms: *fetter* = (n) chain or manacle used to restrain a prisoner; (v) to restrain the feet with manacles, *unfetter* = to free from restraint
Synonyms: *liberated, uninhibited, rampant, unbridled, emancipated*
Mnemonic: Someone who is *fettered* has his *feet tied* up in chains.

10 THE LANGUAGE OF CHANGE AND FORCE

☐ *catalyst* (n)   *kata-* down, fall + *luein* loosen

something that stimulates and expedites a process, often a chemical one : *Coach Johnson's speech was the catalyst that turned our football season around.*
Form: *catalyze* = to cause (a process) to accelerate, *catalytic* = acting as or relating to a catalyst, *catalysis* = the acceleration of a process via a catalyst
Root family: [cata] *cataclysm* (a violent natural event), *catastrophe* (disaster), *catapult* (a machine for heaving heavy objects), *cataract* (a waterfall), *category* (a class under which many elements "fall")
Don't confuse with: *cataclysm* (a violent natural event)
Mnemonic: The word *catalyst* (*kata-* down + *luein* loosen) may have come from the idea of a single event, like a shifting stone, causing snow or rocks to cascade into an avalanche.

☐ *disperse* (v)   *dis-* apart + *spargere* to scatter or sprinkle

to spread or scatter over a wide area : *The crowd soon dispersed after it was announced that the band had left the stadium.*
Form: *dispersion* = scattering over a wide area
Root family: [dis-] *discernment* (the ability to make fine distinctions), *disparate* (very different; variegated), *discrepancy* (a lack of compatibility between facts or claims), *disseminate* (to cast widely), *dispel* (to drive away; to eliminate), *diffuse* (spread over a wide area)
Root family: [spers] *aspersion* (a derogatory remark), *interspersed* (distributed at intervals)
Don't confuse with: *dispense* (supply, distribute, or provide), *diverse* (showing great variety)

☐ *ephemeral* (adj)

lasting a very short time : *Designers try to capture the most ephemeral trends.*
Forms: *ephemera* (plural of *ephemeron*) = things that last only a short time : *The trappings of fame are mere ephemera.*
Synonyms: *fleeting, transient, evanescent*
Don't confuse with: *ethereal* (delicate and sublime, as an ether)

☐ *impetus* (n)   *im-* toward + *petere* to strive after

the force that makes something move or energizes a process : *The coach's speech provided the impetus for the team to redouble its efforts in the second half.*
Root family: [im-] *impugn* (to call into question), *impute* (to attribute something to someone)
Root family: [pet] *impetuous* (spontaneous and without planning), *perpetuate* (to help continue for an extended period), *petulant* (childishly ill-tempered)
Don't confuse with: *impious* (not devoutly religious), *impish* (mischievous)
Mnemonic: Imagine an *imp* (a mischievous child) poking you (*impaling* you?) in the back and giving you the *impetus* to run faster.

☐ *intermittent* (adj)   *inter-* between + *mittere* to send

occurring at irregular intervals; not continuous : *The sound of intermittent gunfire revealed that the peace accord was a fragile one.*
Forms: *intermit* (v) = to postpone, *intermittence* = the quality of being intermittent
Root family: [inter-] *intervene* (to come between to alter events), *international* (pertaining to one or more countries)
Root family: [miss, mit] *submissive* (meekly obedient), *dismiss* (send away), *unremitting* (not letting up)
Don't confuse with: *interminable* (unending)

☐ **mutable** (adj)   *mutare* to change

changeable : *Her moods are as mutable as the weather.*
Forms: *immutable* = unchangeable, ***mutability*** = changeability
Synonyms: *protean, fickle, mercurial*
Root family: [mut] ***commute*** (to travel to and from work; to reduce a criminal sentence; to rearrange numbers that are being added or multiplied), ***mutation*** (a change in the structure of a gene, or the result of that change), ***permutation*** (rearrangement)
Don't confuse with: *mute* (to silence)
Mnemonic: Something that is ***malleable*** can be shaped by a ***mallet***, like clay or a soft metal can.

☐ **ossify** (adj)   *os* bone + *-ify* to make

to turn into bone; to become stagnant or rigid : *Julia could feel her creative impulses ossify as she became inured to the bureaucratic regulations of her job.*
Synonym: *stagnate*
Don't confuse with: *oscillate* (swing back and forth)
Mnemonic: The Latin *os*, meaning "bone," can be found in a few medical terms you might be familiar with, like ***osteoarthritis*** (degeneration of the bone that causes pain in joints) or ***osteoporosis*** (the gradual weakening of the bones from loss of tissue due to hormonal changes). Therefore, to ***ossify*** is to "make into bone."

☐ **precipitous** (adj)   *praecipitare* to throw headlong

[1] dangerously high or steep : *It was a precipitous drop to the lake.*
[2] (of a decline) sudden and dramatic : *The merger led to a precipitous decline in the company's stock value.*
[3] (also *precipitate* [pre sip eh TET]) hasty : *The announcement of the layoffs, unfortunately, was precipitous (or precipitate).*
Form: *precipice* = steep rock face or cliff
Don't confuse with: *precipitation* (rain, snow, sleet, or hail)
Mnemonic: The nouns ***precipitation*** (rain, snow, sleet, or hail), ***precipice*** (high cliff), and ***precipitousness*** (hastiness) all derive from the Latin ***praecipitare***, (to throw headlong), from ***prae-*** (before) + ***caput*** (head). Notice how they all pertain to the action of "throwing down" in different ways.
Usage: See usage note at ***expedite*** in section 14.

☐ **synthesis** (n)   *syn-* together + *tithenai* to place

the act of combining elements into a whole, as ideas into a system, or simpler elements into a compound : *The concert was a synthesis of modern dance, jazz, and slam poetry*
Forms: *synthesize* = to create something by combining elements, ***synthetic*** = formed by human agency via assembling chemical components
Root family: [thes, thet, them] ***thesis*** (a theory proposed as a premise), ***antithesis*** (a theory presented to oppose a given thesis), ***prosthesis*** (an artificial body part), ***epithet*** (an adjective or descriptive phrase referring to a defining quality of a person or thing, such as *lionhearted* in *Richard the Lionhearted*), ***anathema*** (something that is vehemently disliked)

☐ **transient** (adj)   *trans* to a different place + *ire* to go

lasting a short period of time : *Selena's sense of satisfaction was transient.*
Forms: *transience* = impermanence, ***transitory*** = transient, ***transient*** (n) = a homeless person
Synonyms: *fleeting, ephemeral, evanescent*
Root family: [trans-] ***transcend*** (to rise above), ***transportation*** (means of carrying from place to place), ***translation*** (the act or result of expressing something in a different language)
Don't confuse with: *intransigent* (stubbornly unwilling to change one's views)

☐ **volatile** (adj)   *volare* to fly

prone to unpredictable, rapid, and undesirable changes or displays of emotion; explosive : *The convergence of the opposing protest marches created a volatile and dangerous situation.*
Synonyms: *incendiary, inflammatory*
Root family: [vol] ***volley*** (an exchange of tennis shots; a series of utterances; a flurry of projectiles)
Don't confuse with: *versatile*
Mnemonic: In chemistry, a ***volatile*** liquid (such as gasoline) is one that evaporates very quickly and, often, one whose vapors are flammable or explosive. The vapors "fly" (***volare*** = to fly) from the liquid, just as ***volatile*** situations tend to "fly" out of control.

11 THE LANGUAGE OF DULLNESS AND STASIS

☐ **banal** (adj)

lacking in originality; dull and boring : *Ironically, even the most exciting car chases have become banal cinematic devices.*
Form: banality = an overused saying or device
Synonyms: trite, hackneyed, vapid, platitudinous
Mnemonic: Today's romantic comedies are so **banal** that we should **ban all** of them.

☐ **conventional** (adj)   *con-* together + *venire* to come

according to common practice : *It's not a conventional love story.*
Forms: convene = come together in a group; **convention** = standard way of doing something; **unconventional** = demonstrating original thinking
Root family: [con-, co-, com-, col-] **conformist** (one who conscientiously complies with the standards of a group, **conjecture** (guess), **convoluted** (complicated), **consensus** (general agreement), **conspire** (to plot together), **coalesce** (to come together), **coherent** (forming a united whole), **compliant** (willing to obey), **confluence** (a place at which two things merge)
Root family: [ven, vene, vent] **intervene** (to come between to alter events), **venture** (daring undertaking), **revenue** (income), **circumvent** (to avoid by finding a way around)

☐ **homogeneous** (adj)   *homo* same + *gen* kind

consisting of parts or members all of the same kind : *The club was a homogeneous band of like-minded thinkers.*
Root family: [gen] **indigenous** (native), **progenitor** (the first in a family tree), **heterogeneous** (diverse in character or content), **disingenuous** (not sincere or candid)
Don't confuse with: homogenous (having a common biological lineage or structure)

☐ **indigenous** (adj)   *indi-* into + *gignere* to be born

native; occurring naturally in a particular place : *There are over twenty different tribes indigenous to this river valley.*
Synonyms: native, aboriginal
Root family: [gen] **progeny** (offspring), **disingenuous** (not candid or sincere), **progenitor** (the first in a family tree), **heterogeneous** (diverse in character or content), **homogeneous** (consisting of parts or members all of the same kind)
Don't confuse with: ingenious (brilliant), **indignant** (showing anger at unfair treatment)
Mnemonic: The phrase **indigenous** people refers to a tribe **born into** (**indi-** into + **gignere** to be born) a particular area.

☐ **insipid** (adj)   *in-* not + *sapere* to taste

lacking vigor or interest, flavorless : *His latest album drones with insipid songs.*
Root family: [in-, im-] **insuperable** (impossible to overcome), **inert** (lacking vigor), **interminable** (unending), **innocuous** (harmless), **indefatigable** (untiring), **ineffable** (inexpressible in words), **inscrutable** (beyond understanding), **impassive** (unemotional), **incongruous** (not consistent with expectations)
Root family: [sap, sav] **sapid** (flavorful), **savor** (taste and enjoy thoroughly), **savory** (having a flavorful spiciness or saltiness)
Mnemonic: It would be **insane** to **sip** such an **insipid** soup.
Don't confuse with: insidious (subtly harmful or dangerous)

☐ **languish** (v)

to lack energy; to grow weak : *My favorite baseball team has been languishing in last place for two weeks now.*
Forms: languor = a state of weakness or stillness, **languid** = lacking in energy; weak
Synonyms: atrophy, wither
Don't confuse with: language (a symbolic means of communication), **anguish** (great distress)
Mnemonic: When your favorite team is **languishing**, it can cause you **long anguish**.

☐ **prosaic** (adj)   *prosa* straightforward discourse

[1] commonplace : *The envoy's duties in Paris were less romantic and more prosaic than she had hoped.*
[2] lacking poetic beauty : *The band's arrangements are powerful, but their lyrics are prosaic.*
Synonyms: workaday, tedious, pedestrian, mundane
Mnemonic: Your writing might become **prosaic** and less creative if you take too much **Prozac** (the antidepressant drug).
Don't confuse with: mosaic (a picture produced by arranging colorful tiles or pieces of glass).

☐ **protracted** (adj)   *pro-* forward + *tractus* pulled

lasting longer than desired or expected : *The interview turned into a protracted debate about bigotry.*
Form: *protract* = to prolong
Root family: [pro-] *prophecy* (prediction), ***promote*** (further the progress of something; raise in rank) ***progeny*** (offspring), ***reciprocate*** (to respond in kind)
Root family: [tract] *tractable* (manageable), ***abstract*** (lacking a concrete existence), ***detract*** (to reduce the value of something)

☐ **stagnant** (adj)   *stare* to stand

[1] (of a pool of water or the air in a confined space) unmoving and hence having an unpleasant smell : *The stagnant air of the gym made us feel sick.*
[2] sluggish : *The economy has been stagnant for years.*
Forms: *stagnate* = to become stagnant, ***stagnation*** = the state of being or becoming stagnant
Root family: [stan, stat, stag, stas, stab] *stasis* (a period of inactivity), ***constant*** (unchanging), ***stable*** (resistant to movement or failure), ***apostasy*** (heresy)

12 THE LANGUAGE OF TRUTH, TRUTHFULNESS, AND BEAUTY

☐ **aesthetic** (adj)   *aistheta* perceptible things

concerned with the appreciation of beauty or art : *The painting gave aesthetic pleasure.*
Forms: *aesthete* = one who has or pretends to have special aesthetic sense, ***aesthetics*** = the principles or study of beauty and art
Root family: [esthe] *anesthetic* (a substance that reduces sensitivity to pain), ***synesthesia*** (stimulation of one sense modality by another, such as seeing colors while hearing music)
Don't confuse with: *ascetic* (a person who practices strict religious self-discipline), ***prosthetic*** (pertaining to an artificial limb or other body part)

☐ **candid** (adj)   *candidus* white

honest and straightforward : *The president gave a very candid interview just one month after leaving office.*
Form: *candor* = honesty and forthrightness
Synonyms: *frank*, *ingenuous*
Mnemonic: *Candid* derives from the Latin ***candidus***, which means "white," because white has long been associated with purity and honesty. The related word, ***candidate***, derives from the fact that, in ancient Rome, candidates for office wore white togas. In naming his title character ***Candide***, Voltaire was emphasizing his pure, ingenuous nature.

☐ **fallible** (adj)   *fallere* to deceive

capable of making mistakes or errors : *I was crestfallen to discover that my father was fallible.*
Forms: *infallible* = incapable of making errors
Root family: [fall, fals] *fallacy* (a mistaken belief), ***fault*** (an unsatisfactory feature), ***fail*** (to be unsuccessful)

☐ **incontrovertible** (adj)   *in-* not + *contra-* against + *vertere* to turn

unable to be disputed; beyond controversy : *The proof of the theorem was incontrovertible.*
Forms: *controvertible* = able to be disputed, ***controversy*** = dispute
Synonyms: *irrefutable*, *indubitable*, *unassailable*, *airtight*
Root family: [in-, im-] *insipid* (flavorless), ***insuperable*** (impossible to overcome), ***inert*** (lacking vigor), ***interminable*** (unending), ***innocuous*** (harmless), ***incongruous*** (not consistent with expectations)
Don't confuse *controvertible* with ***convertible*** (able to be changed in form or function)

☐ **introspective** (adj)   *intro-* into + *specere* to look at

inclined to look inward; meditative : *Unlike most artists, Warhol eschewed the introspective lifestyle and in fact reveled in his life of celebrity.*
Form: *introspection* = the act of self-examination
Synonyms: *reflective*, *meditative*, *pensive*
Root family: [spec] *speculation* (guess based on insufficient evidence), ***circumspect*** (cautious), ***inspect*** (to examine closely)
Don't confuse with: *retrospective* (looking back in time)

☐ *rectify* (v)   *rectus* right

to make correct; to put right : *The journalist rectified her error by publishing a retraction.*
Synonyms: *amend*, *emend*, *redress*, *remedy*
Root family: [rect] *correct* (right), *rectangle* (quadrilateral with four right angles), *direct* (by the shortest path)

☐ *sublime* (adj)   *sub-* just beneath + *limen* threshold

supremely excellent or beautiful : *The pâté was a sublime complement to the homemade bread.*
Root family: [sub-] *submissive* (meekly obedient), *subvert* (to undermine the authority of another), *surreptitious* (secret), *subjugate* (to dominate)
Root family: [lim] *limit* (the point beyond which something may not pass), *eliminate* (completely remove), *subliminal* (below the threshold of perception), *sublimate* (to alter a crude impulse so as to make it more culturally or socially acceptable)
Don't confuse with *subliminal*. Although both words derive from the Latin roots meaning "below the threshold," *subliminal* means "below the threshold of perception," while *sublime* means "near the threshold of heaven."
Don't confuse with *sublimate*. To *sublimate* a lowly impulse, such as hatred or sexual desire, means to literally "raise it up" (since the *limen*, or threshold, of a doorway includes the top part, then bringing something *sub limen*, just below the threshold, involves raising it up), that is, to channel the energy that would otherwise be dedicated to that impulse into a more culturally and socially acceptable behavior. In chemistry, a substance *sublimates* when it transforms from a solid directly to a gas, without passing through the liquid phase.

13 THE LANGUAGE OF DECEIT, ERROR, AND CONFUSION

☐ *anachronism* (n)   *ana-* backward or mixed up + *chronos* time

something out of place in time, especially something that is outdated : *The modern-sounding dialogue was conspicuously anachronistic for a movie set in the 1920s.*
Root family: [ana-] *anagram* (a rearrangement of the letters in a word or phrase to make another word or phrase)
Root family: [chron] *synchronize* (to make to happen simultaneously or at the same pace), *chronological* (in proper time order)
Don't confuse with: *anarchic* (lacking government)
Mnemonic: Since *Anna Karenina* is set in the 19th century, *Anna's chronograph* (wristwatch) would be very *anachronistic*.

☐ *belie* (v)

[1] to fail to give a true impression of something : *David's bluster belies his lack of self-confidence.*
[2] to betray; to show to be untrue : *The evidence belies the defendant's claim.*
Mnemonic: To *belie* something is to *be* a *lie* about something (meaning [1]) or to show it to *be* a *lie* (meaning [2]).

☐ *chicanery* (n)

devious trickery or evasion : *Unlike most politicians, she discusses tax policies openly, rather than using chicanery to hide her true motives and affiliations.*
Synonyms: *ruse*, *machination*
Don't confuse with: *chimera* (something unrealistic or hopelessly wishful)
Mnemonic: Imagine a *chick* doing magic in a *cannery*.

☐ *circuitous* (adj)   *circum* around + *ire* to go

indirect; roundabout : *We took a circuitous route to the cabin because the main highway was closed.*
Synonyms: *meandering*, *tortuous*, *serpentine*
Root family: [circum] *circumscribe* (to define the limits of something), *circumspect* (wary), *circumlocution* (evasive speech)

☐ *confound* (v)   *con-* together + *fundere* to pour

[1] to cause someone to become confused : *She was confounded by the puzzle for many weeks.*
Synonyms: *befuddle*, *baffle*
[2] to confuse two elements as being one : *We should not confound patriotism and loyalty to the government.*
Root family: [con-, co-, com-, col-] *consensus* (general agreement), *conspire* (to plot together), *coalesce* (to come together), *coherent* (forming a united whole), *confluence* (a place at which two things merge)

Root family: [fus, fund, found] **confuse** (to cause to become perplexed), **effusive** (freely expressive), **fusion** (the process of joining two things into a single entity), **profuse** (abundant), **transfusion** (a transfer, usually of blood, from one person or animal to another), **refuse** (to reject), **diffuse** (spread out over a large area)
Don't confuse with: **compound** (to make something worse : *Don't compound the problem.*)

☐ **convoluted** (adj)   *con-* together + *volutus* rolled

(1) (of an argument or story) complicated and difficult to follow : *The account the witness provided was so convoluted that the jury could not follow it.*
(2) intricately folded : *The human cortex is a convoluted shell of interconnected neurons.*
Form: convolution = a deep fold, esp. one of many; something complex and difficult to understand
Synonyms: tortuous, byzantine
Root family: [con-, co-, com-, col-] **conformist** (one who conscientiously complies with the standards of a group, **coherent** (forming a united whole), **compliant** (willing to obey), **confluence** (a place at which two things merge)
Root family: [vol] **revolution** (one complete rotation; a complete political overthrow), **involved** ("rolled up in"), **voluble** (fluently talkative)

☐ **digress** (v)   *di-* away + *gradi* to walk

stray from the topic in speaking or writing : *Powell digressed for several pages to describe the history of the village he was visiting.*
Forms: digression = an act of digressing, **digressive** = prone to digression; having the characteristics of a digression
Root family: [grad, gress] **progress** (forward movement), **regressive** (moving backward), **egress** (exit)
Don't confuse with: **regress** (to return to a less developed state)

☐ **disingenuous** (adj)   *dis-* away + *in-* in + *gignere* to be born

not candid or sincere; deceitful : *The senator's disingenuous comments were just another example of political posturing.*
Form: ingénue = a naive and innocent person, **ingenuous** = innocent and naive
Synonyms: duplicitous, mendacious
Root family: [dis-] **disconcerting** (unsettling), **disdain** (feeling that something is unworthy), **discredit** (harm the reputation of something or someone), **dispel** (to drive away; to eliminate)
Root family: [in] **inundate** (to flood), **infer** (to conclude from evidence), **incisive** (showing keen judgment), **ingratiate** (to curry favor), **innate** (inborn)
Root family: [gen] **indigenous** (native), **progenitor** (the first in a family tree), **heterogeneous** (diverse in character or content), **homogeneous** (consisting of parts or members all of the same kind)
Don't confuse ingenuous (innocent and naive) with **ingenious** (brilliant) or **not genuine**.
Mnemonic: An **ingénue** is someone who is as innocent and naive as a baby (**in** + **genuus** born), so to be **ingenuous** means to be innocent and naive. Therefore, to be **disingenuous** is to be the opposite: deceitful and full of guile.

☐ **dubious** (adj)   *dubium* doubt

[1] questionable : *That is a dubious claim, bordering on the absurd.*
Synonyms: controvertible, suspect
[2] doubting : *I'm dubious that our team will be able to come back and win.*
Forms: dubiousness = doubtfulness
Synonyms: vacillating
Root family: [dub] **indubitable** (without a doubt), **doubt**

☐ **duplicity** (n)   *duplicitas* twofold

deceitfulness; double-dealing : *He considered a career as a spy but wondered whether he had the skill or moral flexibility to engage in such duplicity.*
Form: duplicitous = deceitful
Synonyms: chicanery, subterfuge, treachery, perfidy
Root family: [dupl, duo] **duplicate** (to make a copy), **duplex** (a two-floor apartment building), **dual** (twofold)
Don't confuse with: **duplication** (the process of making a copy)

☐ **guile** (n)

cunning or slyness in attaining a goal : *David Rohde was able to use guile and patience to escape his Taliban captors.*
Form: guileless = innocent; incapable of deceit
Synonyms: cunning, artfulness, wiles
Don't confuse with: **guise** (outward appearance)

☐ **inept** (adj)   *in-* not + *aptus* well suited

unskilled; clumsy : *Todd's awkward joke was a sincere but inept attempt to lighten the mood.*
Form: ineptitude = clumsiness; lack of skill
Synonyms: feckless, maladroit, bumbling, ineffectual
Root family: [in-, im-] **insipid** (flavorless), **insuperable** (impossible to overcome), **inert** (lacking vigor), **interminable** (unending), **incongruous** (not consistent with expectations)
Root family: [apt, ept] **aptitude** (natural skill), **adapt** (to make to fit a new situation or use), **adept** (skillful)
Don't confuse with: inapt (inappropriate or unsuitable to the situation)

☐ **machination** (n)   *machina* contrivance

a plot or scheme : *Dawn's artful machinations succeeded in gaining her the title of class president.*
Root family: [mech, mach] **machine** (apparatus), **mechanical** (pertaining to the workings of a machine)
Mnemonic: In *Austin Powers: International Man of Mystery*, Dr. Evil's **machinations** involve building a doomsday **machine**, "Project Vulcan," in order to hold the world's **nations** hostage.
Usage: A **deus ex machina** ("god in the machine") is an unexpected and highly implausible plot twist in a novel or play that magically saves a seemingly hopeless situation.

☐ **perjure** (v)   *per-* (negative) + *jurare* to swear

to lie under oath : *Martha Stewart's conviction for conspiracy to commit perjury landed her six months in prison.*
Form: perjury = the act of lying under oath
Root family: [jur] **jurisprudence** (the study of law), **abjure** (to swear off; renounce), **adjure** (to command solemnly), **conjure** (to create, as if by magic), **jurisdiction** (the power to make official decisions)
Root family: [dict] **vindictive** (vengeful), **dictatorial** (tyrannical), **malediction** (curse), **benediction** (blessing)
Don't confuse with: modicum (a small amount)

☐ **spurious** (adj)

false or fake; not what it seems to be (esp. as applied to claims or theories) : *The stories about Jordan's career as a spy were spurious, generated by his friends' wild imaginations.*
Synonyms: specious, fallacious
Don't confuse with: furious (very angry), **spurned** (jilted, rejected)
Mnemonic: Imagine a **spurious** cowboy in fake tinfoil **spurs**.

☐ **subterfuge** (n)   *sub-* beneath + *fugere* to flee

a trick or expedient used to escape a consequence or achieve a goal : *Max's subterfuge involved three alibis and a full-scale replica of himself.*
Synonyms: ruse, chicanery
Root family: [sub-] **submissive** (meekly obedient), **subvert** (to undermine the authority of another), **subjugate** (to dominate)
Root family: [fug] **fugitive** (one who is fleeing arrest), **refugee** (one fleeing strife or persecution), **refuge** (safe haven), **centrifugal** (moving away from the center)
Mnemonic: Imagine the Joker using a **sub to** flee (**fugere** = to flee) from Batman.

☐ **surreptitious** (adj)   *sub-* under, secretly + *rapere* to seize

kept secret because it is objectionable : *Charlotte was upset when she heard about her husband's surreptitious affair.*
Synonyms: clandestine, furtive, stealthy
Root family: [sub-] **submissive** (meekly obedient), **subvert** (to undermine the authority of another), **subjugate** (to dominate)
Root family: [rap, rav] **rapacious** (extremely greedy), **ravenous** (extremely hungry), **ravage** (to bring destruction to)
Don't confuse with: superfluous (unnecessary)

☐ **treacherous** (adj)

[1] characterized by or guilty of betrayal : *Benedict Arnold's treacherous actions are etched in our national history.*
Form: treachery = abject betrayal
Synonyms: traitorous, duplicitous, perfidious
[2] hazardous : *The ocean currents here are very treacherous.*
Synonyms: perilous, precarious
Don't confuse with: tortuous (full of twists and turns), **lecherous** (showing excessive sexual desire), **trenchant** (cutting and incisive)

☐ **unscrupulous** (adj)

dishonest; showing no moral principles : *The broker's unscrupulous dealings only came to light after he had stolen several million dollars of his client's money.*
Form: scrupulous = very concerned with avoiding sin or rule-breaking
Synonyms: reprobate, unethical, corrupt, venal
Usage: Although **scrupulous** is primarily used to mean "attentive to rules and details," whether or not those rules are moral ones, **unscrupulous** refers exclusively to a lack of moral principles.

☐ **vex** (v)

to make to feel annoyed or frustrated : *I am constantly vexed by my inability to remember the names of all of your friends.*
Form: vexation = state of confusion or frustration
Synonyms: nettle, exasperate, pique, gall
Don't confuse with: hex (a spell or curse)

14 THE LANGUAGE OF CREATIVITY AND PRODUCTIVITY

☐ **assiduous** (adj)

showing great care and perseverance : *He was assiduous in his research, checking every reference and tracing its history.*
Synonyms: diligent, industrious, sedulous
Don't confuse with: deciduous ((of tree) shedding its leaves annually), **arduous** ((of a task) requiring strenuous effort)
Mnemonic: Imagine a hardworking scientist mixing **acid** in two (**duo**) beakers.

☐ **efficacy** (n)   *facere* to do, to make

the ability to produce the intended result : *The efficacy of the new medicine could hardly be denied.*
Forms: efficacious = effective, **inefficacious** = ineffective
Root family: [fic, fac, fec, -ify] **facile** (simplistic), **munificent** (generous), **diversify** (to make more varied), **ossify** (to turn into bone), **proficient** (competent or skilled)
Don't confuse with: efficiency (quality of achieving substantial results with a minimum of energy)
Usage: A process or instrument that works **efficaciously** performs its task particularly well. One that works **efficiently**, on the other hand, performs its task at least adequately, but with minimal expense or input.

☐ **expedite** (v)   *ex-* out + *ped* foot

(of a process) to make happen more quickly or efficiently : *We could expedite deliveries by streamlining our method of dispatching the trucks.*
Form: expeditious = done with speed and efficiency
Synonyms: precipitate, facilitate
Root family: [e-, ex-] **extol** (to praise highly), **extemporaneous** (without planning), **exuberant** (filled with liveliness and energy), **elusive** (difficult to catch or achieve), **exorbitant** (excessive), **evocative** (drawing out strong emotions, ideas, or feelings)
Root family: [ped] **pedestrian** (ordinary), **impede** (to hinder or obstruct)
Mnemonic: It is interesting to note that **impede** and **expedite** both derive from **ped**, the Latin root for "foot." **Impede**, literally "bind the feet," means to hinder or delay, whereas **expedite**, literally "free the feet," means to make happen more quickly.
Usage: Although **expedite**, **precipitate**, and **facilitate** are similar, they differ in certain important aspects. To **expedite** a process is to make it happen faster and more efficiently, whereas to **facilitate** a process is to make it *easier* on the person or people involved. The verb **precipitate** applies more to an *event* than a *process*; it is to make the event happen more quickly, although it would likely have happened on its own.
Don't confuse with: expedition. The words **expedite** and **expedition** derive from the same roots but have very different meanings. To **expedite** is to "free the feet," but to go on an **expedition** is to "go out on foot."
Don't confuse expeditious (done with speed and efficiency) with **expedient** (convenient and practical, but perhaps improper or immoral).

☐ **facilitate** (v)   *facilis* easy (< *facere* to do or make)

to make easier : *A team of clinicians was assembled to facilitate the development of the new vaccine.*
Forms: facile = simplistic, **facilitator** = one who makes a process easier, **facility** = a natural ability; ease

Root family: [fac, fec, fic] *benefactor* (one who provides a benefit), *munificent* (generous)
Don't confuse *facility* with *felicity* (intense happiness).
Don't confuse *facile* with *vassal* (a feudal landowner) or *docile* (submissive).
Usage: See usage note at *expedite* in this section.

☐ *flourish* (v)   *florere* to flower

to grow vigorously; prosper : *The arts and letters flourished during the Harlem Renaissance.*
Don't confuse with: *florid* (characterized by flowery language), *flourish* (n) (an extravagant action, usually done to attract attention : *The dance number concluded with a flourish of backflips*)
Mnemonic: The noun *flourish* and the verb *flourish* both derive from *florere* (to flower) but have distinct meanings. A *flourish* is a "flowery or extravagant display to attract attention," whereas to *flourish* means to "blossom like a flower." *Florid* also derives from *florere* but means "characterized by flowery language."

☐ *lineage* (n)   *lineare* to create with lines

descent from an ancestor : *In most medieval European societies, one's social status was decided by family lineage.*
Synonyms: *pedigree*, *ancestry*, *genealogy*
Root family: [line] *collinear* (on the same line), *alignment* (the process of arranging in a line), *delineate* (to describe precisely)
Don't confuse with: *delineate* (to describe precisely)

☐ *prodigious* (adj)   *prodigus* lavish

great in size or degree : *The team consumed prodigious amounts of pizza after the game.*
Forms: *prodigiously* = abundantly
Synonyms: *copious*
Root family: [prodigi] *prodigy* (a young person with exceptional talent), *prodigal* (tending to spend money recklessly)

☐ *profuse* (adj)   *pro-* forward + *fusus* poured

very abundantly offered or available : *Even the profuse offerings of cards and flowers did not assuage his grief.*
Form: *profusion* = an abundance
Synonyms: *prolific*, *prevalent*, *copious*
Root family: [pro-] *protracted* (lasting longer than expected), *prophecy* (prediction), *promote* (further the progress of something; raise in rank), *progeny* (offspring), *reciprocate* (to respond in kind)
Root family: [fus, fund, found] *confuse* (to cause to become perplexed), *confound* (to fail to distinguish different elements), *diffuse* (spread over a wide area), *fusion* (the process of joining two things into a single entity), *effusive* (freely expressive), *transfusion* (a transfer, usually of blood, from one person or animal to another), *refuse* (to reject)
Don't confuse with: *refuse* (to indicate unwillingness to accept something)

☐ *progeny* (n)   *pro-* forward + *gignere* to create

the collective descendants of one ancestor : *The family trust was established to ensure the well-being of the billionaire's progeny.*
Form: *progenitor* = the primary ancestor of a collection of descendants
Synonyms: *offspring*, *brood*, *scions*
Root family: [pro-] *protracted* (lasting longer than expected), *prophecy* (prediction), *promote* (further the progress of something; raise in rank), *reciprocate* (to respond in kind)
Root family: [gen] *indigenous* (native), *homogeneous* (uniform), *heterogeneous* (diverse in character)
Don't confuse *progenitor* with *prognosticator* (one who foretells or attempts to foretell future events).
Mnemonic: Think of someone named *Jenny* you know, and then imagine a *profuse* number of them in the lower branches of a family tree (*progeny* = *pro*fuse *Jennys*).

☐ *proliferate* (v)

to increase rapidly in numbers or extent : *Bootlegging proliferated during the era of Prohibition to satisfy the demand for alcohol.*
Form: *proliferation* = a rapid increase in numbers or extent
Synonyms: *burgeon*, *mushroom*

☐ *prolific* (adj)

[1] highly productive : *Johann Strauss was a prolific composer of waltzes.*
Synonyms: *fertile fecund*
[2] plentiful : *The mountain laurel is prolific along the side of the highway.*

Forms: *proliferate* = to multiply or reproduce rapidly
Synonyms: *copious*, *profuse*, *prevalent*
Don't confuse with: *prophetic* (accurately predictive of the future)

☐ ***vigor*** (n)

good health and physical strength : *The therapy helped him regain the vigor of his youth.*
Forms: *invigorating* = giving energy or strength, ***vigorous*** = full of energy and strength
Synonyms: *robustness*, *hardiness*, *virility*
Don't confuse with: *rigor* (thoroughness or strictness)
Don't confuse with: *erudite* (scholarly)

15 THE LANGUAGE OF MYSTERY, SURPRISE, ADVENTURE, AND DISCOVERY

☐ ***ambiguous*** (adj)   *ambi-* both + *agere* to do

having more than one meaning or interpretation : *In her poem, the meaning of the cloak is intentionally ambiguous.*
Form: *ambiguity* = quality of having more than one interpretation
Synonym: *equivocal*
Root family: [ambi-, amphi-] ***ambidextrous*** (able to use both hands skillfully), ***ambivalent*** (having mixed feelings), ***amphibian*** (an animal that lives partially in water and partially on land), ***amphitheater*** (an outdoor theater with seats surrounding (on *both* sides of) the stage)
Don't confuse with: *ambivalent* (having mixed feelings)

☐ ***anomaly*** (n)

something that deviates from the norm or expectation : *Astronomers scan the night sky looking for anomalies such as radiation bursts or unusual planetary motions.*
Form: *anomalous* = out of the norm
Synonyms: *incongruity*, *aberration*
Don't confuse with: *animosity* (strong hostility)
Don't confuse *anomalous* with *anonymous* (unnamed).

☐ ***diversion*** (n)   *di-* away + *vertere* to turn

[1] an entertaining activity to distract one from everyday concerns : *In the mountains, our diversions include hiking, fishing, and reading.*
Form: *diverting* = entertaining
[2] an action intended to distract someone : *I will create a diversion while you sneak into the house.*
Form: *divert* = to cause something, such as traffic or a river, to change course; to distract someone's attention from something
Root family: [di-, dis-] ***discredit*** (harm the reputation of something or someone), ***dispassionate*** (not influenced by strong emotions), ***disparate*** (very different; variegated), ***discrepancy*** (a lack of compatibility between facts or claims), ***disseminate*** (to cast widely), ***disperse*** (to spread or scatter), ***disputatious*** (argumentative), ***diffident*** (lacking in self-confidence), ***diffuse*** (spread over a wide area)
Root family: [vers, vert] ***adversary*** (enemy), ***diverse*** (various), ***adverse*** (harmful), ***subvert*** (undermine), ***averse*** (opposed), ***versatile*** (adaptable to different functions)
Don't confuse with: *diverse* (various)

☐ ***divulge*** (v)   *di-* widely + *vulgare* to make public

to make widely known, particularly information that was previously kept private : *I cannot divulge the information that was discussed in our private meeting.*
Form: *divulgence* = the act of making something widely known
Root family: [dis-, di-] ***disparate*** (very different; variegated), ***discrepancy*** (a lack of compatibility between facts or claims), ***disperse*** (to spread or scatter), ***diffuse*** (spread over a wide area)
Root family: [vulg] ***vulgar*** (crude and unrefined)
Don't confuse *divulgence* with *indulgence* (an act of being excessively generous or lenient)

☐ *elusive* (adj)   *e-* out + *ludere* to play

difficult to catch, find, understand, or achieve : *The snow leopard is one of nature's most beautiful yet elusive creatures, rarely seen by human eyes.*
Form: *elude* = to evade capture or understanding
Synonyms: *evasive, impalpable, intangible*
Root family: [e-, ex-] *extol* (to praise highly), *extemporaneous* (without planning), *exuberant* (filled with liveliness and energy)
Root family: [lud, lus] *collusion* (a secret understanding that has a harmful purpose), *delude* (to make someone believe something that is not true), *illusion* (something that gives a false impression of reality), *ludicrous* (foolish and ridiculous), *allusion* (to hint at indirectly)
Don't confuse with: *illusory* (giving a false impression), *allusive* (providing or pertaining to an indirect hint)

☐ *empirical* (adj)

pertaining to or based on observation or experience : *Although string theory provides elegant mathematical solutions to many vexing problems in physics, it lacks any empirical evidence.*
Form: *empiricism* = the belief that all knowledge is derived from sensory experience
Mnemonic: Imagine an *empire* in which everyone, especially the *emperor*, is a scientist, with telescopes on every rooftop and chemistry labs in every basement, where they constantly gather *empirical* data.

☐ *enigma* (n)

someone or something that is difficult to understand : *King Lear's motivation remains an enigma.*
Form: *enigmatic* = difficult to understand
Synonyms: *conundrum, quandary, riddle*

☐ *idiosyncrasy* (n)   *idios* unique + *syn* with + *krasis* mixture

a mannerism or quirk peculiar to an individual : *One of the stranger idiosyncrasies of professional athletes is their tendency to refer to themselves in the second or third person during interviews.*
Form: *idiosyncratic* = quirky
Synonyms: *quirk, peculiarity, eccentricity, mannerism, foible*
Root family: [idio] *idiom* (a common phrase that has a nonliteral meaning, such as "at the end of your rope"), *idiot* (stupid person)
Don't confuse with: *ideology* (a system of ideals central to the political power of a group), *iconoclast* (one who attacks cherished beliefs), *idiotic* (stupid)

☐ *inscrutable* (adj)   *in-* not + *scrutari* to search

beyond understanding : *I find quantum physics to be almost as inscrutable as the motivations of my girlfriend.*
Synonyms: *enigmatic, abstruse*
Root family: [in-, im-] *insipid* (flavorless), *insuperable* (impossible to overcome), *inert* (lacking vigor), *interminable* (unending), *innocuous* (harmless), *indefatigable* (untiring), *ineffable* (inexpressible in words), *impassive* (unemotional), *incongruous* (not consistent with expectations)
Root family: [scrut] *scrutinize* (to examine closely)
Don't confuse with: *unscrupulous* (showing no moral principles)
Mnemonic: Something that is *inscrutable* is *un-scrutinize-able*, that is, it's impossible to examine closely because it is beyond our understanding.

☐ *intrepid* (adj)   *in-* not + *trepidus* alarmed

fearless and adventurous : *The intrepid explorers set out for the summit.*
Root family: [in-, im-] *insipid* (flavorless), *insuperable* (impossible to overcome), *inert* (lacking vigor), *interminable* (unending), *innocuous* (harmless), *indefatigable* (untiring), *ineffable* (inexpressible in words), *inscrutable* (beyond understanding), *impassive* (unemotional), *incongruous* (not consistent with expectations)
Root family: [trepid] *trepidation* (fear)
Synonyms: *undaunted, stouthearted*
Don't confuse with: *insipid* (flavorless; uninteresting)
Mnemonic: The aircraft carrier *Intrepid*, now a museum moored off of Manhattan, is an impressive ship that represents the fearlessness of the U.S. Navy.

☐ **nebulous** (adj)   *nebula* mist

vague; hazy; having the form of a cloud : *The ghost appeared first as a nebulous near-human form.*
Synonyms: *amorphous, obscure*

☐ **paradox** (n)   *para-* distinct from, beside + *doxa* teaching

a logically self-contradictory statement or state of affairs : *It seemed to be a paradox that light could behave both as a wave and as a particle.*
Root family: [para-] *paralegal* (a lawyer's assistant), *parallel* (next to and aligned with), *paramedic* (a first aid professional)
Root family: [doc, dox] *doctrinaire* (seeking to impose rigid doctrine), *orthodox* (conforming strictly to traditional teachings), *docile* (compliant and easy to instruct)
Don't confuse with: *paradigm* (a worldview; a typical model or example)

16 THE LANGUAGE OF HARM, DEFICIT, AND DECLINE

☐ **adverse** (adj)   *ad-* to + *vertere* to turn

harmful to success or progress : *The short holiday season has had an adverse effect on sales.*
Form: *adversity* = misfortune or difficulties, usually over an extended period
Synonyms: *inauspicious, detrimental, deleterious*
Root family: [ad-] *adhere* (stick fast (to)), *advocate* (to provide vocal support for), *annul* (to declare invalid)
Root family: [vers, vert] *adversary* (enemy), *diverse* (various), *diversion* (entertainment), *subvert* (undermine), *averse* (opposed), *versatile* (adaptable to different functions)
Don't confuse with: *averse* (opposed)

☐ **archaic** (adj)   *archaios* old

old and outdated : *My cell phone, which didn't even have Internet access, seemed archaic compared to Kris's tiny smartphone.*
Synonyms: *outmoded, outdated, anachronistic, obsolete*
Root family: [arch] *archaeology* (the study of ancient civilizations and their artifacts), *archetype* (a very typical example)
Don't confuse with: *anarchic* (having no hierarchical government)

☐ **bane** (n)

a cause of great and persistent distress : *The bane of the traveling salesman is the time spent away from family and friends.*
Form: *baneful* = causing great distress
Synonyms: *scourge, blight, affliction*
Mnemonic: For farmers, **ban**ning the *rain* would be a great *bane* for their livelihood.

☐ **dearth** (n)

an utter lack of something : *I am disappointed by the dearth of good jazz clubs in this city.*
Synonym: *paucity*
Don't confuse with: *death, dirge* (a funereal song), *mirth* (good-natured amusement)
Mnemonic: The words *dearth* and *dear* (expensive) derive from the same root. If there is a *dearth* of something desired, then it is likely to be very *dear*.

☐ **debilitating** (adj)

causing someone or something to become weak : *What seemed like a slight ankle sprain soon turned into a debilitating injury.*
Forms: *debilitate* = to make weak or infirm, *debility* = a weakness or infirmity
Synonyms: *incapacitating, enervating*
Don't confuse with: *rehabilitate* (to restore to health)

☐ **deleterious** (adj)   *delere* to destroy, to eliminate

very harmful : *Prolonged and hopeless poverty has a very deleterious effect on children.*
Synonyms: *detrimental, injurious, adverse*
Root family: [delet] *delete* (to remove completely), *indelible* (forming an enduring impression)
Mnemonic: Imagine how *deleterious* it would be to your grade if you accidentally *deleted* the research paper that you had spent over a month researching and writing.

☐ **enervate** (v)   *e-* out of + *nervus* sinew, strength

to drain of energy or strength : *The arduous hike enervated the boys, who decided to rest for the night.*
Forms: *enervation* = the process of draining something of strength; weakness, *enervated* = weakened
Synonyms: *debilitate, enfeeble*
Don't confuse with: *energize* (to fill with energy), *enumerate* (to list numerically), *innervate (to supply an organ or body part with nerves)*
Mnemonic: To avoid confusing *enervate* with *energize*, focus on the roots *e-* (out) and *nervus* (sinew, strength or muscle): to *enervate* is to weaken, as if by removing the muscle fibers from one's body. Gross? Yes, but vivid enough to remember.

☐ **exacerbate** (v)   *ex-* (making) + *acerbus* bitter

to make a situation worse : *The lawsuit only exacerbated the animosity between the neighbors.*
Synonyms: *aggravate, compound, inflame*
Root family: [acer, acu] *acrid* (pungent), *acerbic* (having a bitter taste), *acrimonious* (defined by bitter feelings), *acute* (keen, as pain or ability)
Don't confuse with: *exaggerate* (to overstate)

☐ **insidious** (v)   *in-* on + *sedere* to sit

having a harmful effect, but in a subtle way : *Many viral diseases are insidious, remaining dormant for months or even years before symptoms are expressed.*
Synonyms: *stealthy, surreptitious, treacherous*
Root family: [in-] *inundate* (to flood), *infer* (to conclude from evidence), *incisive* (showing keen judgment), *ingratiate* (to curry favor), *inherent* (existing as an inseparable element), *invoke* (to bring to bear), *indoctrinate* (to teach doctrine), *induce* (to bring about), *infiltrate* (to gain access secretly)
Root family: [sed, sid] *sedentary* (inactive), *dissident* (one who opposes official policy), *assiduous* (hard working), *sedate* (calm), *preside* (to sit in a position of authority), *reside* (to live in a particular location), *sediment* (material that settles to the bottom of a liquid or body of water, particularly a river)
Don't confuse with: *invidious* (causing resentment)
Mnemonic: An *insidious* disease lurks *inside us* until it decides to pounce.

☐ **malevolence** (n)   *male* evil + *volent* wishing

evil intent : *The villain eyed his victim with malevolence.*
Form: *malevolent* = with evil intent
Synonyms: *maliciousness, rancor*
Root family: [mal] *malignant* (disposed to causing harm or suffering), *malicious* (full of spite), *malign* (to speak about someone in a spiteful manner)
Root family: [vole] *benevolent* (kindly), *volition* (free will), *voluntary* (performed by choice)

☐ **obsolete** (adj)

outdated; no longer in production : *Mr. King still types all of his manuscripts on an obsolete Corona typewriter.*
Forms: *obsolesce* = to become obsolete, *obsolescence* = the state of being obsolete
Synonyms: *outmoded, outdated, anachronistic, archaic*

☐ **regress** (v)   *re-* back + *gressus* walking

to return to a less developed state : *As he got angrier, Gary seemed to regress into childhood, and began kicking his feet and pouting like a toddler.*
Form: *regression* = the process of moving toward a less developed state, *regressive* = moving backward or toward a less developed state
Root family: [re-] *reprehensible* (deserving of condemnation), *refute* (to prove something false), *revoke* (to take back), *renounce* (to give up or put aside publicly), *relegate* (to place in a lower rank)
Root family: [grad, gress] *progress* (forward movement), *egress* (exit), *digress* (to stray from the topic)

☐ **vestige** (n)

[VEST idge] a trace of something that no longer exists : *The archaeologists wondered whether this small clay shard was a vestige of a once-great civilization.*

Form: *vestigial* = remaining as a trace of something long since gone
Synonyms: *remnant*, *relic*, *residue*
Don't confuse with: *vestment* (clothing), *prestige* [press TEEGE] (widespread respect)

☐ *virulent* (adj)   *virus* poison

bitterly hostile; extremely harmful : *The speech was an incoherent and virulent diatribe against the dangers of socialism.*
Form: *virulence* = ability to cause extreme harm; poisonousness
Synonyms: *toxic*, *pernicious*
Root family: [viru] *virus* (a nucleic acid molecule that acts as an infective agent)
Don't confuse with: *violent* (involving physical force to hurt or damage)

17 THE LANGUAGE OF KINDNESS, FAVOR, AND BENEFIT

☐ *affable* (adj)

friendly and good-natured : *Gena is so affable that she will surely make new friends at camp.*
Form: *affability* = friendliness and good nature
Synonyms: *amiable*, *genial*, *gregarious*
Don't confuse with: *ineffable* (unable to be described in words)
Mnemonic: An *affable* person is *able* to *laugh* easily (*affable* = *laugh-able*) which makes him or her very easy to like. But be careful not to confuse *affable* with *laughable* (ridiculous to the point of being amusing).

☐ *alleviate* (v)   *ad-* to + *levare* to lift

to make something, such as suffering, less severe : *She regretted that she could not alleviate her friend's pain.*
Synonyms: *mitigate*, *palliate*, *attenuate*, *allay*, *assuage*
Root family: [ad-] *allude* (to hint at indirectly), *aspire* (to strive for a lofty goal), *adhere* (stick fast (to)), *advocate* (to provide vocal support for), *acquiesce* (to comply reluctantly)
Root family: [lev] *levity* (good-natured humor), *elevate* (to lift), *relevant* (raised to an important level), *relieve* (to lift a burden from another)
Don't confuse with: *abbreviate* (to make shorter)

☐ *altruistic* (adj)   *alter* other

selfless; putting the concerns of others before one's own : *Only the most altruistic doctors can tolerate the hardships of running disease clinics in poor communities.*
Form: *altruism* = the belief in or practice of putting the concern of others before one's own
Root family: [alter] *altercation* (a noisy fight), *alter* (to change or cause to change), *alternate* (to occur in turn repeatedly, *adulterate* (to render (something) inferior, usually by adding something to it), *alter ego* (alternative personality)
Mnemonic: An *altruistic* person puts others (*alter* = other) before himself or herself, and is *always true* to the idea of charity.

☐ *amicable* (adj)   *amicus* friend

showing goodwill and a spirit of friendliness : *I hope we can reach an amicable settlement.*
Root family: [ami] *amiable* (friendly), *inimical* (antagonistic), *enmity* (hostility or active opposition)
Don't confuse with: *applicable* (relevant or appropriate)
Usage: Although *amicable* and *amiable* derive from the same roots, *amicable* is more commonly used to describe friendly *situations*, while *amiable* is more commonly used to describe friendly *people*.

☐ *auspicious* (adj)   *avis* bird + *specere* to look

conducive to success; favorable to a positive outcome : *The rainstorm did not provide an auspicious start to the wedding ceremony.*
Form: *inauspicious* = not favorable
Synonyms: *propitious*, *opportune*, *felicitous*
Root family: [spic, spec] *introspective* (reflective), *speculation* (guess based on insufficient evidence), *circumspect* (cautious), *inspect* (to examine closely)

Don't confuse with: *suspicious* (showing cautious distrust), *vicious* (cruel)
Mnemonic: *Auspicious* derives from the Latin *avis* (bird) and *specere* (to look) because in mid-16th-century Europe it was believed that observing particular birds in flight was a favorable sign in divination. From this meaning of "favorable omen," we also get the word *auspice*, which means "patronage or support," as in *The study was conducted under the auspices of the Labor Board.*

☐ **benefactor** (n)   *bene* good + *facere* to do or make

one who gives money to benefit a person or cause : *The letter acknowledged the many benefactors who had helped the Arts Society stay afloat in trying economic times.*
Synonyms: *patron, sponsor*
Root family: [ben, bon] *beneficiary* (one who receives a benefit), *benevolent* (kindly), *benign* (harmless)
Root family: [fac, fec, fic] *facile* (simplistic), *munificent* (generous)
Don't confuse with: *beneficiary* (one who receives a benefit)

☐ **beneficiary** (n)   *bene* good + *facere* to do or make

one who receives a benefit : *Wayne was the beneficiary of his friend's generosity.*
Synonym: *legatee*
Root family: [ben, bon] *benefactor* (one who provides a benefit), *benevolent* (kindly), *benign* (harmless)
Root family: [fac, fec, fic] *facile* (simplistic), *munificent* (generous)
Don't confuse with: *benefactor* (one who provides a benefit)

☐ **benevolent** (adj)   *bene* good + *velle* to wish

kindly; well meaning : *She was a benevolent queen, attentive to the needs of all of her subjects.*
Form: *benevolence* = kindness
Synonyms: *altruistic, philanthropic, magnanimous*
Root family: [ben, bon] *beneficiary* (one who receives a benefit), *benefactor* (one who provides a benefit)
Root family: [vol] *malevolent* (having evil intent), *volition* (free will), *voluntary* (performed by choice)
Mnemonic: English words containing *vol* can be confusing because they can derive from three different Latin roots: *velle* ((to wish) (from which we get *malevolent* (having evil intent) and *benevolent*), *volare* ((to fly) from which we get *volatile* and *volley* (to throw at a target)), or *volvere* ((to roll) from which we get *convoluted* and *revolution* (a complete turn)).

☐ **benign** (adj)   *bene* good + *genus* born

gentle; causing no harm : *Rather than rousing indignation, Senator Paulson's concession speech was benign and gracious.*
Synonyms: *innocuous, anodyne*
Root family: [ben, bon] *beneficiary* (one who receives a benefit), *benevolent* (kindly), *benefactor* (one who provides a benefit)
Don't confuse with: *benighted* (in a woeful state of ignorance, literally "in the darkness of night")

☐ **complement** (v) or (n)   *com-* (intensive) + *plere* to fill

[1] (v) to add to something to make it complete or perfect : *The savory sautéed spinach complemented the rich and dense portobello mushroom to make the perfect side dish.*
[2] (n) something that completes a whole : *Calculus is an important complement to the study of physics.*
Forms: *complementary* = acting to form a complete or perfect whole
Root family: [ple] *deplete* (to use the supply of), *replete* (filled to the fullest extent)
Don't confuse with: *compliment* (to say something kind about someone else)

☐ **conciliatory** (adj)   *concilium* council

likely to appease or to bring people together in goodwill : *The student exchange was intended as a conciliatory gesture between the formerly antagonistic countries.*
Forms: *conciliate* = to appease or to gain goodwill, *conciliation* = the act of appeasing or gaining goodwill
Synonyms: *appeasing, mollifying, placatory, propitiatory*
Root family: [concilium] *council* (an advisory or legislative body)
Usage: See usage note at *pacify* in section 4.
Mnemonic: The verb *conciliate* derives from the Latin *concilium*, which means "an assembly or council." If you know anything about how modern city councils work, you know that a lot of compromise and appeasement—a lot of *conciliation*—is often needed to get people from different backgrounds, temperaments, and political parties to work together.

☐ *decorum* (n)   *decorus* showing good taste

dignified and tasteful behavior : *Please show some decorum while we are touring the palace.*
Forms: *decorous* = in keeping with good taste and propriety, ***indecorum*** = lack of decorum, ***indecorous*** = lacking in decorum
Synonyms: *propriety, etiquette, protocol*
Root family: [deco, dec] ***decoration*** (ornamentation), ***decent*** (conforming to standards of appropriate behavior), ***decor*** (the furnishing and decoration of a home)
Don't confuse with: *decor* (the furnishing and decoration of a home). To avoid confusing these, you might remember that the *um* in decorum is like the *um* in *human*; only *humans* can show *decorum*, while only homes have *decor*.

☐ *empathy* (n)   *pathos* feeling

the ability to understand and share the feelings of another : *Dawn has a great empathy for fellow cancer survivors.*
Forms: *empathize* = to understand and share the feelings of others, ***empathetic*** = able to empathize
Root family: [path] ***sympathy*** (feeling of sorrow for the misfortunes of another), ***pathology*** (the science of the causes and course of diseases), ***apathetic*** (lacking concern), ***antipathy*** (animosity)

☐ *eulogy* (n)   *eu* good + *logos* word

a praising speech, particularly for one who is deceased : *Glen's eulogy was touching yet humorous.*
Form: *eulogize* = to recite or write a eulogy
Synonyms: *accolade, paean, encomium*
Root family: [eu] ***euthanasia*** (mercy killing), ***euphonious*** (pleasant sounding), ***euphoria*** (extreme happiness), ***euphemism*** (a mild term or phrase intended to replace a harsher one)
Don't confuse *eulogize* with ***euthanize*** (to put a person or animal to death humanely)

☐ *euphemism* (n)   *eu* good + *pheme* speaking

a mild term or phrase intended to replace a harsh, embarrassing, or unpleasant one : *Senators are adept at inserting euphemisms like "patriot" into the names of their bills to divert the public's attention from the true nature of the laws.*
Form: *euphemistic* = pertaining to the use of euphemisms; having the qualities of euphemism
Root family: [eu] ***euthanasia*** (mercy killing), ***euphonious*** (pleasant sounding), ***euphoria*** (extreme happiness), ***eulogy*** (a praising speech, usually for the deceased)
Root family: [phem] ***blasphemy*** (speaking profanely about holy things), ***dysphemism*** (a deliberately derogatory or unpleasant term or phrase), ***prophecy*** (significant prediction of the future)
Don't confuse with: *euphoria* (extreme happiness)

☐ *innocuous* (adj)   *in-* not + *nocuus* harmful

not harmful or offensive : *The interviewer asked only innocuous questions rather than probing into more interesting topics.*
Synonyms: *benign, anodyne*
Root family: [in-, im-] ***insipid*** (flavorless), ***insuperable*** (impossible to overcome), ***inert*** (lacking vigor), ***interminable*** (unending), ***indefatigable*** (untiring), ***ineffable*** (inexpressible in words), ***inscrutable*** (beyond understanding), ***impassive*** (unemotional), ***incongruous*** (not consistent with expectations)
Root family: [nocu, noxi] ***innocent*** (not guilty), ***noxious*** (harmful), ***obnoxious*** (rudely unpleasant)

☐ *mitigate* (v)

to make less serious or severe : *The effects of hurricanes can be mitigated by the presence of a thriving barrier island system.*
Forms: *mitigating* = serving to make less serious or severe, ***unmitigated*** = without redeeming qualities
Synonyms: *palliate, attenuate, allay, assuage*
Don't confuse with: *litigate* (to file and execute a lawsuit), ***migrate*** (to move from one habitat to another, usually according to the season)
Usage: While ***pacify, placate, appease, propitiate,*** and ***conciliate*** all describe things done to *people*, words like ***palliate, mollify,*** and ***assuage*** generally apply to *feelings*, and words like ***mitigate*** and ***ameliorate*** can pertain to *situations* as well as *feelings*.
Mnemonic: Judges or juries often consider ***mitigating*** circumstances before sentencing someone who has been convicted of a crime. Assaulting someone who is perceived as a threat is not as serious as assaulting someone without provocation, so the threatening could be a ***mitigating*** circumstance that reduces the sentence for assault.

☐ *mollify* (v)   *mollis* soft

to appease someone's anger or anxiety : *The tax bill was taken off of the agenda to mollify the angry citizens.*
Form: *mollification* = the process of appeasing anger or anxiety
Synonyms: *propitiate, conciliate, placate, appease*
Root family: [moll] *emollient* (an agent that softens skin), *mollusk* (an invertebrate with a soft unsegmented body, usually protected by a shell)
Don't confuse with: *mortify* (to make to feel embarrassed or humiliated)
Usage: See usage note at *pacify* in section 4.
Mnemonic: Imagine someone you know named *Molly* trying to settle down an angry friend.

☐ *obliging* (adj)   *ob-* toward + *ligare* to bind

eager to help : *The bellhops were very obliging to those who were good tippers.*
Root family: [lig] *ligament* (a band of connective tissue), *obligatory* (mandatory; necessary to do), *religion* (belief in a supernatural power which obligates one to perform rituals)
Don't confuse with: *obligatory* (mandatory; necessary to do)
Mnemonic: When you feel *obliged* to do something for something, you feel *bound* to do it (*ob-* to + *ligare* to bind). It is *obligatory* (mandatory; necessary to do). If you always feel *bound* to your responsibility to help others, you are *obliging*.

☐ *propriety* (n)   *proprius* one's own

conformity to standards of proper behavior : *As representatives of our school, we must conduct ourselves with the utmost propriety.*
Form: *impropriety* = improper behavior
Root family: [prop] *appropriate* (adj) (proper of suitable to the circumstances); (v) (to take something that doesn't belong to you for your own use, typically without the owner's permission : *The Spanish appropriated many of the discoveries of the Mayans as their own*), *proprietor* (the legal owner of a business)
Don't confuse with: *proprietor* (the legal owner of a business)
Mnemonic: Although *proprietor* and *propriety* are easily confused, they derive from different aspects of the root word *proprius* (one's own). A *proprietor* is the legal owner of a small business, but *propriety* is the respect with which one treats *one's own* family and tribe.

☐ *reciprocate* (v)   *re-* back + *pro-* forward

to respond to an action or gesture by doing something in kind : *If you act kindly to strangers, they are likely to reciprocate.*
Forms: *reciprocal* = done in return, *reciprocity* = the practice of acting with mutual benefit
Root family: [re-] *recluse* (a person who lives a solitary lifestyle), *refute* (to prove something false), *revoke* (to take back), *renounce* (to give up or put aside publicly), *regress* (to return to a less developed state)
Root family: [pro-] *protracted* (lasting longer than expected), *prophecy* (prediction), *promote* (further the progress of something; raise in rank), *progeny* (offspring)

☐ *refinement* (n)   *finire* to finish

[1] elegance in taste and manners : *Jerrod has all the refinement one would expect of a world traveler.*
[2] the process of bringing to a purer state : *Crude oil must undergo refinement before it can be used as fuel.*
Forms: *refined* = cultured and well-mannered, *refine* = to make more cultured, *unrefined* = uncultured or unimproved
Don't confuse *refine* **with** *define* (to set forth the meaning of something).

☐ *solicitous* (adj)   *citus* set in motion

showing interest or concern : *Lisa's office mates became solicitous when they heard that her daughter was ill.*
Forms: *solicitude* = care or concern for someone or something, *solicit* = to ask (someone) for something
Root family: [cit] *excite* (to elicit energetic feelings in someone; to energize something), *incite* (to encourage violence or illicit behavior), *resuscitate* (to bring back to life)
Usage: Many Americans assume that *solicitous* has a negative connotation because *solicitations* (requests for money or other donations) can be annoying. However, *solicitude* is not badgering but sincere concern. This meaning is conveyed more accurately in the British definition of *solicitor* as "an attorney who assists a client," rather than the American definition of "one who requests donations."
Don't confuse with: *solicitor* (one who requests donations for charity; (in the U.K.) an attorney)

☐ **symbiosis** (n)   *sym-* together + *bio* life

a mutually beneficial relationship between different species : *One example of symbiosis is the relationship between the clownfish and the sea anemone, whereby the clownfish receives protection from its enemies and the anemone receives food.*
Form: symbiotic = characterized by symbiosis
Root family: [sym] **sympathy** (compassion), **symmetry** (a geometric correspondence among similar parts)
Root family: [bio] **biology** (the study of living things), **biodegradable** (able to decompose into nutrients for living things)
Don't confuse with: symbolic (pertaining to the use of symbols)

☐ **tactful** (adj)   *tactus* sense of touch

showing sensitivity to the needs of others with difficult private issues : *Jerry Springer rarely shows any desire to be tactful about his guests' embarrassing personal problems.*
Forms: tact = sensitivity to the needs of others with difficult private issues, **tactless** = utterly without tact
Synonyms: politic, discreet, judicious, decorous
Root family: [tang, tact, ting, tig, tag, teg] **tactile** (pertaining to the sense of touch), **tangential** (barely related to the topic), **tangible** (touchable), **contact** (to touch, or get in touch with), **contagious** (spreadable, as a disease, via close contact), **contiguous** (physically touching or bordering, as *the contiguous 48 states*), **integrity** (the quality of wholeness or wholesomeness; moral uprightness)
Don't confuse with: tacky (showing poor taste)

☐ **utility** (n)   *utilis* useful

the state of being useful : *When searching for a new car, the Kearns were clearly more interested in utility than beauty.*
Form: utilitarian = designed to be useful rather than attractive; pragmatic, **utile** = advantageous, **utilize** = to use effectively
Don't confuse with: futility (pointlessness)

18 THE LANGUAGE OF WISDOM, STRENGTH, AND SKILL

☐ **adroit** (adj)   *a droit* as to the right (Fr < L *dexter* right)

skillful : *He was such an adroit salesman that he could sell ice cubes to polar bears.*
Form: adroitness = skillfulness
Synonyms: adept, dexterous, deft, proficient
Root family: [dext, droit] **dexterity** (skill), **ambidextrous** (having skill in using either hand)
Mnemonic: French speakers will recognize the word **adroit** from the French phrase **a droit**, "to the right." This continues a trend in Romance languages to associate right-handedness with skill and the left-handedness with awkwardness or deceit. For instance, the French word **gauche**, "left," in English means "socially inept." Similarly, the Latin word **dexter**, "on the right," is the root of **dexterity** (skill) and **ambidextrous** (skilled in using both hands), and the Latin word **sinister**, "left," has come to mean "malevolent" in English.

☐ **astute** (adj)

having or showing keen insight : *The announcers made many astute comments about the game.*
Synonyms: sagacious, prudent, shrewd, canny, incisive
Don't confuse with: acute (keen, as pain or ability)
Usage: Although **astute, sagacious, prudent, judicious, shrewd, canny,** and **incisive** are similar, they offer different shades of meaning. **Astute** comes from the Latin **astutus** (craft), so an **astute** person is likely to have acquired keen insight through careful study; a **sagacious** person, however, is likely to have acquired this insight from the benefit of age and trial; a **prudent** person is both wise and conservative; a **judicious** person is a keen overall adjudicator, whether he or she has acquired that ability through study, age, or trial; a **shrewd** or **canny** person is insightful and even a bit cunning, particularly in pursuit of a goal like power, compromise, or money; an **incisive** commentator has the power to "cut" (**cis** = cut) to the heart of the matter.

☐ **discernment** (n)   *dis-* apart + *cernere* to distinguish

the ability to make sound judgments and fine distinctions : *Becoming a master oenologist requires not only discernment but also constant study of wines and how they are produced.*
Forms: discern = to perceive something as being distinct from other things, **discerning** = having a keen ability to make fine distinctions

Synonyms: *perspicacity*, *percipience*
Root family: [dis-] *disparate* (very different; variegated), *discrepancy* (a lack of compatibility between facts or claims), *disseminate* (to cast widely), *disperse* (to spread or scatter), *dispel* (to drive away; to eliminate), *diffuse* (spread over a wide area)
Root family: [cern, cert] *ascertain* (find something out for certain), *certain* (known for sure), *certify* (formally attest or confirm)

☐ *discretion* (n)   *discretus* separate

sensitivity in dealing with others, particularly in not causing offense : *The teacher showed admirable discretion in not revealing the students' grades out loud.*
Forms: *discreet* = careful in not causing offense, *discretionary* = subject to a particular judgment, *indiscreet* = not careful to avoid offense
Synonyms: *tact*, *tactfulness*
Don't confuse *discreet* with *discrete* (individually distinct : *The program is broken down into 12 discrete steps.*)

☐ *ethics* (n)   *ethos* customs, behavior

[1] a set of moral principles : *His ethics were dubious.*
[2] the study of moral principles : *David failed his course in medical ethics.*
Forms: *ethicist* = one who studies ethics (*ethologists* study animal behavior), *ethic* = moral principles relating to a specific group or field (*puritan ethic*), *ethical* = morally correct; pertaining to ethics

☐ *exacting* (adj)   *ex-* (intensive) + *agere* to perform

making great demands on one's skills : *Rock climbing is a very exacting task.*
Form: *exact* (v) = to demand and obtain, usually as a payment : *Caesar exacted a tax on all Roman citizens.*
Root family: [agi, age, act] *agent* (someone or something that produces a desired effect), *agenda* (list of items to be accomplished at a meeting), *agile* (able to move quickly and skillfully), *exigent* (pressing; placing demands on someone or something), *inactive* (not active)
Usage: *Exacting* does not mean *exact* (adj). Both words derive from *exigere* (to drive out), but the adjective *exact* derives from a more recent Latin word, *exactus* (precise).

☐ *exemplar* (n)   *exemplum* sample (< *ex-* out + *emere* to take)

someone or something serving as an ideal example of something : *William "Boss" Tweed stands as the exemplar of American political corruption and greed.*
Form: *exemplary* = serving as an excellent example
Synonyms: *apotheosis*, *nonpareil*, *paragon*
Root family: [e-, ex-] *extol* (to praise highly), *extemporaneous* (without planning), *exuberant* (filled with liveliness and energy), *elusive* (difficult to catch or achieve)
Root family: [emp, empt, sumpt] *consumption* (the process of eating or using resources), *presumptuous* (failing to observe appropriate limits of behavior), *preempt* (take action to prevent another event from happening), *peremptory* (insisting on immediate attention), *sumptuous* (splendid and abundant)

☐ *lithe* (adj)

limber and graceful : *The dancers resembled nothing so much as rippling water as their lithe bodies undulated rhythmically.*
Synonyms: *agile*, *supple*, *limber*, *lissome*
Don't confuse with: *loathe* (to hate), *blithe* (carefree), *lathe* (a rotating machine for shaping wood)
Mnemonic: *Lithe* dancers can *lightly writhe*, like weightless strips of silk waving in the breeze.

☐ *objective* (adj)

focused on fact rather than opinion : *A good journalist must try to remain objective even when covering emotionally poignant stories.*
Form: *objectivity* = the state of being objective
Synonyms: *impartial*, *dispassionate*, *disinterested*, *nonpartisan*
Usage: Although *objective*, *impartial*, *dispassionate*, *disinterested*, and *nonpartisan* are similar, they offer different shades of meaning. A scientist or journalist should be *objective*, that is, focused on facts (*objects*), to the exclusion of opinions, in the pursuit of gathering and analyzing information; a good judge should be *impartial*, that is, lacking any bias for or against any of the disputants (legal *parties*); a wise judge is also *dispassionate*, that is, actively discounting his or her feelings (*passions*) in favor of the facts; a *disinterested* judge avoids considerations of personal advantage (*interest*); and a fair-minded politician is *nonpartisan*, that is, inclined to elevate pragmatic concerns over political ideology (the *party* line).
Usage: In modern usage *objective* is the opposite of *subjective* (based on opinion rather than fact).

☐ *pragmatic* (adj)   *pragma* deed

concerned with practical rather than idealistic considerations : *Her choice of car was more pragmatic than aesthetic.*
Forms: *pragmatism* = belief that practical qualities are more important than idealistic ones, ***pragmatist*** = a pragmatic person
Don't confuse with: *dogmatic*
Usage: *Pragmatic* and ***practical*** have very similar meanings and origins, but while a pair of shoes might be ***practical*** (suitable to and effective for general purposes), only people can be ***pragmatic***. ***Pragmatic*** can describe a frame of mind or a method, but not a thing.

☐ *proficient* (adj)   *pro-* for + *facere* to do or make

competent or skilled in a particular task : *He is a proficient drummer, if not an exceptionally talented one.*
Form: *proficiency* = skill in a particular task
Synonyms: *adept, adroit, deft, dexterous*
Root family: [pro-] ***protracted*** (lasting longer than expected), ***prophecy*** (prediction), ***promote*** (further the progress of something; raise in rank), ***progeny*** (offspring), ***reciprocate*** (to respond in kind)
Root family: [fic, fac, fec, -ify] ***facile*** (simplistic), ***munificent*** (generous), ***diversify*** (to make more varied), ***ossify*** (to turn into bone), ***efficacy*** (ability to produce the intended result)

☐ *sagacious* (adj)

having or showing good judgment and discernment : *We needed the sagacious mind of Uncle Ted to help us resolve our differences.*
Forms: *sagacity* = wisdom and discernment, ***sage*** = a wise person
Synonyms: *astute, prudent, judicious, shrewd, canny, incisive*
Usage: See usage note at ***astute*** in this section.

☐ *valor* (n)   *valere* to be strong

courage and nobility in the face of danger : *His valor on the battlefield earned him the Congressional Medal of Honor.*
Form: *valiant* = courageous
Root family: [val] ***prevalent*** (widespread and abundant), ***ambivalent*** (having mixed feelings), ***valence*** (the power of an atom to make bonds with other atoms)
Don't confuse with: *pallor* an unhealthy pale appearance

19   THE LANGUAGE OF CAPITAL AND WEALTH

☐ *avarice* (n)

extreme greed : *David was repulsed by the avarice that thrived on Wall Street in the 1990s.*
Form: *avaricious* = extremely greedy
Synonyms: *cupidity, rapacity, covetousness*
Don't confuse *avaricious* with *vicious* (deliberately cruel or violent), ***auspicious*** (favorable), or ***avatar*** (a worldly incarnation of a god; a moving icon representing a person in cyberspace)
Mnemonic: Someone who is ***avaricious*** wants to ***have all riches***.

☐ *bourgeois* (adj)   *burgus* castle, fortified town

pertaining to or characteristic of the conventional and materialistic life of the middle class : *He rebelled against the stultifying bourgeois lifestyle and yearned for the life of a bohemian.*
Form: *bourgeoisie* = the middle class
Synonyms: *conventional*
Root family: [burg] ***burg*** (city or town), ***borough*** (an administrative district, as or within a town or city), ***burglar*** (one who breaks into homes to rob them (< *burgier* to pillage a town))

☐ *decadent* (adj)   *de-* down + *cadere* to fall

excessively self-indulgent : *I decided that since I had adhered strictly to my diet for two months, I could be decadent at the wedding.*
Form: *decadence* = excessive self-indulgence
Root family: [de-] ***denounce*** (declare as bad), ***detract*** (reduce the value of something), ***debase*** (reduce in value), ***denigrate*** (criticize unfairly), ***deference*** (submission to the authority of another), ***condescend*** (to act superior to someone else)

Root family: [cide, cade, cas, cay] *accident* (an unintentional, unexpected, and unfortunate incident), *cadence* (the rising and falling inflection of the voice), *coincide* (to occur at the same time), *cascade* (small waterfall), *recidivism* (falling back into a life of crime)

☐ *exorbitant* (adj)   *ex-* out + *orbita* track, course

excessive ; exceeding the bounds of propriety or reason : *She charged an exorbitant fee for only a few hours' work.*
Synonym: *prohibitive*
Root family: [e-, ex-] *extol* (to praise highly), *extemporaneous* (without planning), *exuberant* (filled with liveliness and energy), *elusive* (difficult to catch or achieve)
Root family: [orb] *orbit* (elliptical path of a satellite)

☐ *frugal* (adj)

reluctant to spend money or expend resources : *He was too frugal to even pay for a cab ride home.*
Form: *frugality* = thriftiness; reluctance to expend resources
Synonyms: *miserly, stingy*

☐ *indigent* (adj) or (n)

[1] (adj) poor; needy : *We've donated the proceeds to a charity that provides food and shelter to the indigent of our city.*
Synonyms: *impecunious, destitute, insolvent, penurious*
[2] (n) a poor and homeless person : *Fewer indigents can be found on the streets since the city opened the new shelter and soup kitchen.*
Form: *indigence* = poverty
Don't confuse with: *indigenous* (native)
Mnemonic: During the Depression, homeless wanderers may have been disparaged as hobos or *indigents*, but many of them might have just considered themselves *inde*pendent *gent*lemen.

☐ *lavish* (adj) or (v)

[1] (adj) extravagant or elaborate : *It was a lavish affair, elegant to the last detail.*
[2] (v) to give in extravagant quantities : *His aunts lavished little Stephen with attention.*
Don't confuse with: *slavish* (like or characteristic of a slave)

☐ *lucrative* (adj)   *lucrum* profit

highly profitable : *He abandoned his lucrative banking job for a more fulfilling career in teaching.*
Synonyms: *remunerative, gainful*
Root family: [lucr] *lucre* (profit, usually that which is ill-gotten)

☐ *mercenary* (adj) or (n)   *merces* payment

[1] (adj) primarily concerned with making money : *When our CEO left for a higher-paying job after only six months, he was rightly castigated for being mercenary.*
Synonyms: *acquisitive, venal, avaricious, covetous*
[2] (n) a soldier who fights for money rather than patriotism; a person concerned primarily with making money rather than with personal integrity : *The general preferred to work with dedicated soldiers rather than mercenaries.*
Synonym: *soldier of fortune*
Root family: [merc] *merchant* (s trader or store owner), *mercantilism* (belief in the benefits of profitable trading), *commerce* (the activity of buying and selling), *merchandise* (goods that are bought and sold)

☐ *opulent* (adj)

ostentatiously rich or lavish : *Jay Gatsby threw opulent parties at his elegant mansion.*
Form: *opulence* = lavishness
Synonyms: *grandiose, ritzy, splendid*
Don't confuse with: *opalescent* (exhibiting a milky iridescence, as an opal)

☐ *ostentatious* (adj)   *ostens* presented for display

intended to attract attention; characterized by vulgar and pretentious display : *We decorated our house tastefully, avoiding the ostentatious Christmas displays that were so common in town.*

Form: *ostentation* = pretentious and vulgar display
Synonyms: *pretentious, flamboyant, gaudy, ornate, garish*
Root family: [osten] *ostensible* (appearing to be true, but not necessarily so)
Don't confuse with: *austere*

☐   *prodigal* (adj)   *prodigus* lavish

tending to spend resources wastefully : *A prodigal manager can squander a year's worth of careful savings in just a few weeks.*
Form: *prodigality* = wastefulness
Synonyms: *profligate, spendthrift, improvident*
Root family: [prodigi] *prodigy* (a young person with exceptional talent), *prodigious* (great in size or degree)
Mnemonic: The Biblical story of the *prodigal* son is about a son who squanders all of his inheritance and later comes to regret it.

☐   *remuneration* (n)   *munero* to share, to give a gift

payment for services : *We were unhappy with the remuneration we received for the hard work we put into the project.*
Forms: *remunerate* = to pay someone for services, *remunerative* = pertaining to payment for services
Synonyms: *recompense, reimbursement, compensation*
Root family: [muni, muner] *immunity* (resistance to an infection or toxin), *munificent* (generous)
Don't confuse with: *enumeration* (listing in numerical order)
Mnemonic: *Remuneration* is received *money* for your *action.*

☐   *squander* (v)

to waste recklessly, particularly money or opportunity : *We must not squander this opportunity to get our financial house in order.*
Don't confuse with: *wander* (roam)

20   THE LANGUAGE OF PASSION, EMOTION, AND SENSATION

☐   *abash* (v)

to cause to feel embarrassed or ashamed : *I was abashed at the sight of her photograph.*
Form: *abashed* = embarrassed, *unabashed* = confidently unashamed
Don't confuse with: *bash* ((v) hit forcefully; (n) a lively party)
Mnemonic: *Abash* means to make *bashful.*

☐   *alacrity* (n)

cheerful eagerness : *Howard accepted our invitation to brunch with alacrity.*
Synonyms: *ardor, fervor, dispatch*
Don't confuse with: *anachronism* (something out of place in time), *clarity* (clearness)

☐   *apathy* (n)   *a-* without + *pathos* suffering, emotion

lack of interest or concern : *Although Glen was happy and excited about the trip, Philip's glum apathy tempered everyone's mood.*
Form: *apathetic* = lacking interest or concern
Synonyms: *indifference, dispassion, languor*
Root family: [a-, an-] *amorphous* (lacking definite shape), *anarchy* (lack of hierarchical government)
Root family: [path, pati, pass] *sympathy* (feeling of sorrow for the misfortunes of another), *pathology* (the science of the causes and course of diseases), *empathy* (the ability to share the feelings of others), *antipathy* (hostility)
Don't confuse with: *antipathy* (hostility)

☐   *apprehensive* (adj)   *prehendere* to grasp, to seize

anxious that something bad might happen : *Kyra was apprehensive about entering the abandoned house.*
Form: *apprehension* = fear that something bad might happen; the taking of a criminal suspect into custody
Synonyms: *fretful, disquieted*
Root family: [prehens] *comprehensive* (thorough and complete), *reprehensible* (morally objectionable)
Don't confuse with: *comprehensive* (thorough and complete)

Mnemonic: The word **apprehend**, deriving as it does from the Latin **prehendere**, meaning "to grasp or seize," means "to arrest" (*apprehend a criminal*) or "to perceive or understand superficially" (*apprehend danger*). **Apprehensive**, however, does not derive from either of those meanings, but rather the idea of being "seized" with fear.

☐ **ardor** (n)   *ardere* to burn

enthusiasm; passion : *He has maintained the same ardor for campaigning as he had when he first ran for office.*
Form: **ardent** = passionate
Root family: [ard, ars] **arsonist** (one who illegally sets fires)
Don't confuse with: **arbor** (a shady alcove covered by trees or climbing plants), **barter** (exchange of goods or services for payment instead of money)
Mnemonic: **Ardor** is a **burning** passion (**ardere** = to burn).

☐ **callous** (adj)

emotionally insensitive to the suffering of others : *He showed callous disregard of the pain that we were going through.*
Form: **callousness** = disregard for the suffering of others
Synonyms: **ruthless, inhumane, sadistic**
Don't confuse with: **callowness** (immaturity)

☐ **catharsis** (n)

the process of purging unwanted or unhealthy emotions : *After a frustrating day at the office, kickboxing class offers a welcome catharsis.*
Form: **cathartic** = providing an elimination of unwanted emotions
Synonyms: **purgation, venting**
Don't confuse with: **catheter** (a tube inserted into the body to remove fluid), **catechism** (a summary of questions and answers summarizing the principles of the Christian religion)

☐ **complacent** (adj)   *com-* (intensive) + *placent* pleasing

smugly and uncritically satisfied with one's situation : *A nation should not be complacent about its security.*
Form: **complacency** = smug self-satisfaction
Root family: [plac] **placate** (to appease), **implacable** (unable to be pleased), **placid** (peaceful)
Don't confuse with: **complaisant** (willing to please)
Mnemonic: One who is **complacent** is satisfied with his or her **place** in the world, but one who is **complaisant** wants to **please** (**plais**).

☐ **ebullient** (adj)   *e-* out + *bullire* to boil

full of cheerful energy : *Jennifer was ebullient about her acceptance to Brown.*
Form: **ebullience** = cheerful energy
Don't confuse with: **emollient** (a skin softening agent)
Mnemonic: Someone who is **ebullient** lets the joy **bubble out** (**e-** out + **bullire** to boil).

☐ **effusive** (adj)   *e-* out + *fusus* poured

freely expressive, particularly of emotions; pouring out : *Julie was effusive in her greeting, hugging each of us like a mother bear.*
Forms: **effusion** = an outpouring, usually of emotion
Root family: [fus, fund, found] **confuse** (to cause to become perplexed), **confound** (to fail to distinguish different elements), **diffuse** (spread out over a large area), **fusion** (the process of joining two things into a single entity), **profuse** (abundant), **transfusion** (a transfer, usually of blood, from one person or animal to another), **refuse** (to reject)
Don't confuse with: **elusive** (difficult to find, catch, or achieve)

☐ **fervent** (adj)   *fervere* to be hot

displaying a passionate intensity : *The protest rally was punctuated by several fervent speeches.*
Form: **fervor** = intense and passionate feeling
Synonyms: **vehement, zealous, fervid**
Root family: [ferv] **effervescent** (bubbly), **fervid** (passionate), **fever** (elevated body temperature due to infection; state of nervous excitement)
Don't confuse with: **fever** (elevated body temperature due to infection; state of nervous excitement)
Mnemonic/Usage: Although **fervent** doesn't mean exactly the same thing as **feverish**, both words derive from the same Latin root and both share the meaning of "intense feeling." In the case of **fervent**, the feeling is primarily emotional, but in **feverish**, the feeling is primarily physical.

☐ *forlorn* (adj)

pitifully sad and lonely : *The city was filled with forlorn souls with unfulfilled dreams.*
Synonyms: *despondent, disconsolate, abject, melancholy*
Don't confuse with: *foregone* (predetermined)

☐ *grudging* (adj)   *grouchier* to grumble

given reluctantly or resentfully : *Although his opponents hate to compete against him, they give him grudging respect.*
Root family: [grudg, grouch] ***grouchy*** (irritable and bad-tempered), ***begrudge*** (to envy someone's enjoyment of something)
Don't confuse with: *dredging* (cleaning a riverbed by scooping)

☐ *indifferent* (adj)

having no particular concern or interest : *The king was indifferent to the suffering of his own people.*
Form: *indifference* = lack of concern or interest
Synonyms: *insouciant, nonchalant, dispassionate, apathetic*
Don't confuse with: *not different*
Mnemonic: People tend to be ***indifferent*** about those things that they think make ***no difference*** *in the world.*
Usage: See usage note at ***nonchalant*** in section 8.

☐ *inhibited* (adj)

reluctant to act or restrained from acting in a natural way, usually because of self-consciousness : *Faith felt inhibited in front of her classmates, but was very much a free spirit with her friends.*
Forms: *inhibit* = to restrain or hinder, ***inhibition*** = self-conscious reluctance to behave naturally, ***uninhibited*** = free-spirited
Synonyms: *reticent, diffident*
Don't confuse with: *inhabited* (occupied as a living space by a person, animal, or group)

☐ *palpable* (adj)   *palpare* to touch gently

perceivable by touch; so intense as to seem touchable : *The tension in the room was palpable.*
Form: *palpate* = to touch gently, especially to diagnose a medical condition
Mnemonic: When you go the doctor with stomach pains, the doctor ***palpates*** your stomach with his or her ***palm*** to feel the ***pain***.

☐ *qualitative* (adj)

pertaining to the quality of something rather than a measurable quantity : *There has been a qualitative change in the mood of the workers ever since the new contract was signed.*

☐ *resigned* (adj)   *re-* back + *signare* to sign officially

reluctantly accepting of an undesirable situation : *We were resigned to the fact that Ms. Davis, our favorite teacher, would be absent for several weeks.*
Form: *resignation* = reluctant acceptance of an undesirable situation
Synonyms: *forbearing, stoical, acquiescent, compliant*
Root family: [re-] ***recluse*** (a person who lives a solitary lifestyle), ***renounce*** (to give up or put aside publicly), ***regress*** (to return to a less developed state), ***relegate*** (to place in a lower rank)
Root family: [sign] ***consign*** (to deliver into another's custody), ***designate*** (to appoint officially), ***signature*** (a person's name written as an official identification mark), ***significant*** (noteworthy), ***assign*** (to allocate officially)

☐ *vehement* (adj)   *vehere* to carry

showing intense feeling : *The lawyer's accusation was met with a vehement denial.*
Form: *vehemence* = intense feeling
Synonym: *ardent*
Root family: [veh, vect] ***vehicle*** (a mechanical transportation device; a means of expression), ***vector*** (a quantity with magnitude and direction; a means of transmitting disease), ***convection*** (the circulation of air by heating and cooling)
Don't confuse with: *violent* (physically forceful)
Mnemonic: *Vehement* sounds like ***vehicle*** because they both derive from the Latin verb ***vehere***, "to carry": someone who is ***vehement*** is getting "carried away."

THE POWER ROOTS AND AFFIXES FOR THE SAT

a-, an-	without	***asymmetric***, *apathy, amoral, amorphous, anarchy*
ab-	away	***absent***, *absolve, abstemious, abhor, abstruse, abstract*
-able, -ible	(adj) able to be	***paintable***, *indomitable, malleable, insuperable, tractable, interminable*
acer, acr	bitter, sharp	***acrid***, *exacerbate, acrimonious, acerbic*
act, agi, age	to act, to perform	***action***, *exacting, agent, agenda, exigent, agile*
acu	sharp	***acute***, *acumen, acuity, acupuncture*
ad-	to, toward, for	***advance***, *advocate, aspire, allude, acquiesce, adhere*
agog	leading, teaching	***demagogue***, *pedagogy, synagogue*
agon	struggle	***agony***, *antagonistic, protagonist, agonize*
-al	(adj) like, pertaining to	***personal***, *ephemeral, comical, conventional*
	(n) the act of	***denial***, *refusal, perusal*
altr, alter, ulter	other	***alter ego***, *altruism, altercation, alternate, adulterate*
ambi-, amphi-	both	***ambidextrous***, *ambivalent, ambiguous, amphibian*
ami, amic	friend	***amiable***, *amicable, inimical, amity, enemy*
ana-	backward, mixed up	***anagram***, *anachronism, anabolism, analect*
-ance, -ence	(n) act, quality, being	***tolerance***, *reticence, temperance, nonchalance, ambivalence*
anima	life, spirit, mind	***animate***, *unanimous, magnanimous, equanimity, inanimate, pusillanimous*
ante-	before	***ante***, *antecedent, antebellum, antedeluvian, antedate, anterior*
anthro	humankind	***anthropology***, *misanthrope, philanthropist, anthropomorphism*
anti-	against	***anticlimactic***, *antipathy, antagonistic, antidote, antithesis*
apo-	away, from, not	***apology***, *apostrophe, apocryphal, apostasy, apogee, apologetics*
apt, ept	well-suited	***aptitude***, *inept, apt, adapt, adept*
arbit	judge	***arbitration***, *arbitrary, arbiter*
arch	ancient	***archaeology***, *archive, archaic, archaeopteryx*
	chief, most important	***archrival***, *architect, archipelago, archetype*
	govern, rule	***anarchy***, *monarch, hierarchy, oligarchy*
-ation	(n) act of, result of	***imitation***, *saturation, cultivation, recitation, conflagration*
audi	to hear	***auditory***, *audition, audience, auditorium, audio, audit*
auto-	self	***automatic***, *autobiography, autocracy, autotroph*
bellum, belli	war, fighting	***belligerent***, *antebellum, bellicose, rebellious*
bene, bon	good	***beneficiary***, *benign, benediction, benefactor, bon mot*
bi-	two, twice	***bisect***, *biannually, bifurcate, binomial*
bio-	life	***biology***, *biography, biome, bioluminescence, symbiosis*
cad, cid, cas	to fall	***decay***, *decadent, casualty, recidivist, cascade*
cant, chant	to sing, to recite	***incantation***, *recant, cantata, enchant, chant*
cap, capit	head	***decapitate***, *capitulation, capital, recap, chapter*
carn	flesh	***carnivore***, *carnival, reincarnation, incarnate*
cata	down, fall, precipitate	***catalyst***, *cataract, cataclysm, catastrophe, catapult*
ced, ces	to go	***proceed***, *precedent, concession, recede, secede*
cern, cert	to set apart	***discern***, *discernment, ascertain, certain, certify*
chron	time	***chronological***, *synchronize, anachronism, chronograph*

cinc	to cinch, as with a belt	***succinct***, *cinch, precinct*
circum	around	***circumference***, *circuitous, circumscribe, circumlocution, circumspect*
cis, schis	to cut, to split	***scissors***, *incision, precise, concise, schism, schizophrenia*
clam, claim	to cry out	***clamor***, *proclaim, acclaim, exclaim*
clus, clud	to close	***conclude***, *recluse, preclude, claustrophobia, cloistered*
co-, com-, con-	together, with (intensive)	***cooperate***, *conform, convention, consensus, confluence, conspire* ***consummate***, *condone, conflagration, complacent*
cogn, conn	to know	***recognize***, *connoisseur, reconnoiter, cognizant, incognito, cognoscenti*
contra-	against	***contradiction***, *incontrovertible, contrary, contraband, contravene*
cor, cour	heart	***cardiac***, *cordial, concord, discord, courage*
cred	to trust	***incredible***, *discredit, credence, incredulous, credible, credit*
crim	judgment, offense	***crime***, *discriminating, criminal, incriminate, recrimination*
crit	judge	***critic***, *criteria, critique, diacritic, hypocritical*
crypt, cryph	hidden	***cryptic***, *apocryphal, encryption, decrypt, cryptogram*
culpa	blame	***culprit***, *exculpate, culpable, mea culpa*
cur, cour	to run	***course***, *discursive, cursory, incur, precursor, courier*
de-	down, from, away	***descend***, *indefatigable, denigrate, detract, decadent, condescend*
deca-, deci-	ten; one-tenth	***decade***, *decathlon; decimeter, decimal, decibel*
delet, deli	to destroy, to eliminate	***delete***, *deleterious, indelible*
dem	people	***democracy***, *demographics, epidemic, demagogue*
dext, droit	right-handed, skilled	***dexterity***, *ambidextrous, adroit*
di-	apart, away	***diverge***, *digress, diversion, diffident, diffuse*
dia-	through	***diagonal***, *diameter, diaphanous, diatribe*
dic, dict	to declare	***dictate***, *vindictive, dictum, malediction, dictatorial*
dign, dain	worthy	***dignity***, *indignation, disdain, deign*
dis-	apart, away	***disband***, *discrepancy, discernment, disparate, disseminate, discriminate*
	against, not	***discredit***, *disquiet, disconcerting, disinterested, disdain*
doc, dox, doct	to teach	***indoctrinate***, *orthodox, docile, doctrinaire, paradox*
domin, domit	to dominate	***dominate***, *indomitable, domineering, predominant, domain, dominion*
duc	to lead, to carry	***conduction***, *induce, conduct, ductile, produce*
dupl, duo	twofold	***duplicate***, *duo, duplicity, duplex, dual, duality*
e-, ex-	out	***emit***, *evanescent, extemporaneous, emigrate, exonerate, extol*
-en	(v) to make	***harden***, *frighten, dampen*
	(adj) made of	***golden***, *woolen, wooden*
en-	cause to be, in	***endanger***, *entangle, enrage, envelop*
epi-	upon, in addition	***epidemic***, *epidermis, epicenter, epilogue*
equi, equa	the same	***equal***, *equanimity, equilateral, equilibrium, equivocate*
esthe	perceive, discern	***anesthetic***, *aesthetic, synesthesia, aesthete*
eu-	good	***eulogy***, *euphemism, euphonious, euphoria, eugenics*
extra-	beyond, outside	***extraneous***, *extraterrestrial, estranged, extravagant, extracurricular*
fac, fec, fic	to make, to do	***factory***, *efficacy, facilitate, facile, benefactor, munificent*
fer, pher	to bear, to carry	***fertile***, *infer, deference, coniferous, aquifer, pheromone*
ferv	to boil, to bubble	***effervescent***, *fervent, fervid, fever*

fide	faith, trust	*fidelity*, infidel, perfidious, diffident
flu	to flow	*fluid*, superfluous, influx, affluent, fluctuate, confluence
fore-	before	*foreshadow*, foremost, forewarn, foreground
fort, forc	strong	*force*, fortify, forte, enforce, effort, reinforcement
fract, frag	broken up	*fracture*, refractory, fractious, refraction, fragile, fragment
fug	to flee	*refugee*, fugitive, centrifuge, refuge, subterfuge
-ful	(adj) full of	*suspenseful*, tactful, mirthful, wrongful, deceitful
funct, fung	to perform	*function*, perfunctory, defunct, dysfunctional, fungible
fus, found	to pour	*effusive*, diffuse, profuse, confound, confuse, refuse
gen	race, kind	*homogeneous*, progenitor, heterogeneous, indigenous
	to create, to be born	*generate*, genetic, disingenuous, progeny, congenital
geo-	earth	*geography*, geology, geometry
grad, gress	to walk	*progress*, digress, regress, egress
grand	great	*grandeur*, grandiose, grandiloquent, aggrandize
graph	write, draw, study	*geography*, biography, orthography, cartography, demographics
grat	pleasing, thankful	*gratitude*, gratuitous, gratuity, ingrate, ingratiate
greg	flock	*congregation*, gregarious, aggregate
her, hes	to stick	*adhesive*, adherent, cohesive, inherent, coherent
-hood	(n) state of being	*childhood*, statehood, adulthood
hyper	over, above	*hyperactive*, hyperbole, hyperventilate, hyperextend
hypo	under	*hyposensitive*, hypoglycemic, hypochondria, hypothesis, hypothalamus
idio	unique	*idiosyncrasy*, idiom, idiot
-ify	to make	*solidify*, ossify, vilify, fortify, diversify, edify, petrify
imper, emper	to command	*imperial*, imperious, empire, imperative
in-, ir-, il-, im-	not	*irrelevant*, inert, intractable, insuperable, inscrutable, incongruous
	in, into, toward	*intrude*, inundate, infer, incisive, insurgent, impetuous, indoctrinate
inter-	between, among	*international*, intervene, interloper, intermittent
intro-	into	*introspective*, introduction, introverted
ir	anger	*irritated*, irascible, irate, ire
-ism	(n) belief, quality of	*realism*, fatalism, pragmatism, polytheism, narcissism
-ist	(n) one who is or does	*pacifist*, conformist, narcissist, pragmatist
-ity	(n) quality, instance of	*curiosity*, futility, adversity, celebrity, passivity
-ive	(adj) quality	*offensive*, obtrusive, corrective, ruminative, evocative, elective
-ize	(v) to make	*polarize*, satirize, fraternize, lionize, scrutinize, civilize, sanitize
ject	throw	*eject*, conjecture, objective, subjective, reject
jud	judge	*judiciary*, judicious, adjudicate, prejudice
jur, jus	to give an oath	*perjury*, abjure, conjure
	right, law	*justice*, jurisdiction, injury, jurisprudence, injustice
lect, leg, lig	to choose	*select*, elect, eclectic, eligible, collect, recollect
leg	lawful	*legal*, relegate, delegate, privilege, allege, legacy
-less	(adj) without	*painless*, listless, relentless, ruthless, dauntless
lev	to raise	*levitation*, alleviate, levity, elevate, relieve
lig	to bind	*ligament*, obliging, ligature, obligatory
linqu, lict	to abandon	*relinquish*, delinquent, relic, derelict, reliquary

line	to create with lines	***linear**, lineage, delineate, collinear, align*
locu, loqu	to talk	***eloquent**, colloquial, circumlocution, grandiloquent, loquacious*
-logy, -logue	study, discourse	***geology**, apologist, eulogy, chronology, anthology, epilogue*
luc, lum	light	***illuminate**, lucid, elucidate, luminous, translucent*
lud, lus	to be playful	***ludicrous**, allude, collude, illusion, delude*
mag, maj, max	great	***magnificent**, magnanimous, maxim, majesty, magnitude*
mal	bad, badly	***malicious**, malevolent, malady, malediction, malign, maladjusted, malodorous*
med, mod	middle	***median**, medium, modicum, mediocre, mediation*
-ment	act of, state of being	***resentment**, enticement, discernment, refinement, bereavement*
merc	payment	***commerce**, mercenary, commercial, mercantilism, merchandise*
meta-	change, beyond	***metaphysics**, metamorphose, metabolism*
mis-	wrong	***mistake**, misapprehension, misprint, misfit, mislead*
mit, miss	to send	***mission**, intermittent, unremitting, submit, emit, permit*
moll	soft	***mollusk**, mollify, emollient*
mono-	one	***monotone**, monolith, monotonous, monologue, monopoly*
morph	shape	***metamorphosis**, amorphous, polymorphic, morphology*
multi-	many	***multiply**, multinational, multicolor*
muni, muner	to share	***community**, munificent, immunity, remuneration, commune*
mut	to change	***mutation**, commute, immutable*
nat, nas, nai	born	***prenatal**, innate, natural, nascent, renaissance*
-ness	(n) quality of, state of	***soreness**, callousness, boldness, fondness*
noc, nox	harmful	***noxious**, innocuous, obnoxious, innocent*
nom, nomen, nym	name	***nominate**, ignominious, pseudonym, anonymous, nomenclature*
non-	not	***nonfiction**, nonprofit, nonsense*
null, nihil	nothing	***nil**, nihilism, annul, annihilate*
nunc, nounc	to declare	***announce**, denounce, renounce, enunciate, pronounce*
omni-	all	***omnivore**, omnipresent, omniscient, omnipotent*
onus, oner	burden	***onus**, exonerate, onerous*
ortho	right, straight, strict	***orthodontist**, orthodox, orthogonal, orthopedics*
-ous	(adj) full of	***gracious**, voracious, garrulous, superfluous, gratuitous, homogeneous*
pac, peas	peace	***pacify**, appease, pact, pacifist*
palp	to touch	***palpate**, palpable, palpitate*
pan-	everything, all	***panorama**, pandemic, pantheon, panoply, panacea*
para-	beside, distinct from	***parallel**, paradox, paradigm, paralegal, paramedic*
path, pass	to suffer	***passion**, sympathy, empathy, apathetic, antipathy, dispassionate, patient*
patr	father	***patriarch**, patronize, compatriot, patronage*
pecc	to sin	***impeccable**, peccadillo, peccant*
ped	child	***pediatrician**, pedagogy, pedantic*
ped, pod	foot	***pedestrian**, podiatrist, impede, expedite*
pel, pul	to drive, to force	***repel**, compulsion, impulsive, repulsive, dispel*
per-	through, throughout	***permeable**, impervious, permit, permeate, pervasive*
	thoroughly	***perfect**, peruse, perturb, perpetuate, perfunctory*

peri-	around	**perimeter**, *peripheral, peripatetic, perihelion*
pet	to drive	**impetus**, *impetuous, perpetuate, petulant*
phem, **phes**	way of speaking	**euphemism**, *dysphemism, blasphemy, prophesy*
pher, **phor**	to carry, to convey	**euphoria**, *metaphor, peripheral, semaphore*
phila	attraction, interest	**bibliophile**, *philanthropy, philosophy, hydrophilic*
phon	voice, sound	**phonetic**, *microphone, phonics, symphony, cacophony*
phren, **fren**	mind, delirium	**frenzy**, *frenetic, phrenology, schizophrenia, frantic*
plac	to please	**placate**, *placid, implacable, complacent*
plaud, **plaus**	to clap, show approval	**applaud**, *plausible, plaudits, explode*
ple	to fill	**complete**, *complement, deplete, replete, supplement, compliant*
plic, **ply**	to fold	**complicated**, *complicit, explication, implication*
pol	city, citizen	**metropolis**, *cosmopolitan, policy, politics, police, polite*
pond, **pend**	weight, hanging	**pendant**, *ponderous, impending, propensity, pendulum, dependent*
pos	to place	**position**, *juxtapose, posit, disposition, appose, oppose*
post-	after	**postscript**, *postdoctoral, posthumous*
poten	strength, power	**potent**, *impotent, despot, potentate, omnipotent, potency*
pre-	before	**precede**, *premonition, precedent, prescience, premeditated, precocious*
prehens	to grasp	**comprehend**, *apprehensive, reprehensible, prehensile, comprehensive*
pro-	forward	**propel**, *protracted, reciprocate, provocative, prophecy, progeny, profuse*
prodig	lavish	**prodigious**, *prodigal, prodigy*
proper, **propr**	one's own	**property**, *propriety, expropriation, proprietor, appropriate*
pug, **pugn**	to fight	**pugnacious**, *impugn, pugilist, repugnant*
punct, **pung**	point, sharp	**punctual**, *punctilious, poignant, punctuation, punctilio*
	to prick	**puncture**, *compunction*
puni, **peni**	to punish	**punish**, *penitent, punitive, penitentiary, punishment*
quies, **quiet**	to rest	**quiet**, *quietude, acquiesce, quiescence, disquiet*
radic	root	**radical**, *eradicate, radish*
rap, **rav**, **rept**	to seize	**enrapt**, *rapture, surreptitious, rapacious, ravenous, ravage*
re-	back	**return**, *reciprocate, revoke, recluse, refute, renounce*
	again	**repaint**, *reconsider, replenish, resurgence*
rect	right, straight	**correct**, *rectify, direct, rectangle*
rud	untrained	**rude**, *erudite, rudiment, rudimentary*
rupt	broken	**rupture**, *erupt, interrupt, corrupt*
sacer, **secr**	to make holy	**sacred**, *sacrifice, sacrilege, sacrosanct, consecrate*
sanct	holy	**sanctify**, *sanction, sanctuary, sacrosanct, sanctimonious*
sang	blood	**sanguinary**, *consanguineous, sanguine, sangfroid*
sap, **sav**, **sip**	to taste	**savory**, *insipid, savor, sapid*
sat	full	**satisfy**, *saturate, insatiable, sated*
scend, **scal**	to climb	**descend**, *condescend, scale, ascend, transcend, escalate, echelon*
scien	to know	**science**, *conscience, omniscience, prescient, conscious*
scrib, **script**	to write or draw	**script**, *circumscribe, prescribe, proscribe, inscription*
sed	to sit, to settle	**sediment**, *sedentary, sedate, assiduous, insidious*
semi-	half	**semicircle**, *semiannual, semiconductor, semi*

semin	seed	*seminal*, *seminary*, *disseminate*, *seminar*
sent, sens	to feel	*sense*, *sentient*, *sensation*, *consensus*, *dissent*
sequ, secu	to follow	*sequel*, *sequence*, *obsequious*, *inconsequential*, *consecutive*, *consequence*
-ship	(n) quality of, ability	*friendship*, *hardship*, *workmanship*, *kinship*
solv, solu	to loosen	*dissolve*, *absolve*, *irresolute*, *resolve*, *solution*
-some	(adj) causing, tending	*fearsome*, *worrisome*, *bothersome*
son	sound	*sonic*, *dissonance*, *assonance*, *consonant*, *resonate*
spect, spic	to look	*inspect*, *introspective*, *circumspect*, *conspicuous*, *speculation*
spir	to breathe	*respiration*, *aspire*, *conspire*, *expire*
spers	to scatter or sprinkle	*disperse*, *aspersion*, *interspersed*
stat, stag, stan	to stand, to stay	*stationary*, *stagnate*, *static*, *constant*, *apostasy*
strait, strict	to bind, to confine	*strict*, *constrict*, *stringent*, *straitened*, *strangle*, *restriction*, *distress*
stru, stroy, stry	to build	*construct*, *construe*, *destroy*, *industry*, *obstruct*
sub-	under	*submarine*, *surreptitious*, *subjugate*, *subvert*, *subdued*, *somber*
sum	highest	*summit*, *consummate*, *summa cum laude*, *summary*
super-	over, above	*superior*, *superlative*, *superfluous*, *supercilious*, *insuperable*
surg, surr	to rise	*surge*, *insurgent*, *resurrection*, *resurgence*
sym-, syn-	together, same	*synthesize*, *synchronize*, *symbiosis*, *sympathy*, *idiosyncrasy*, *synonym*
tace, taci	to be silent	*tacit*, *reticent*, *taciturn*
tang, tact, tag	to touch	*tangible*, *tangential*, *tactile*, *integral*, *tactful*
tele-	from a distance	*teleport*, *telephone*, *telekinesis*, *telecast*, *telemetry*
temper	to restrain	*temperate*, *temperance*, *temper*, *temperature*
tempo	time	*tempo*, *extemporaneous*, *contemporary*, *temporary*
ten	to stretch, to make thin	*extend*, *tense*, *tenuous*, *attenuate*, *pretentious*
ten, tain	to hold	*retain*, *tenacious*, *obtain*, *retention*, *untenable*, *detention*
term	to end	*terminate*, *interminable*, *indeterminate*, *exterminate*, *terminal*
terr	earth	*terrestrial*, *disinter*, *extraterrestrial*, *subterranean*, *terrain*
thes, thet, them	to construct	*synthesis*, *prosthesis*, *epithet*, *anathema*
-tion, -sion	(n) action	*discussion*, *incantation*, *revelation*, *convention*
	(n) quality, state	*discretion*, *consternation*, *trepidation*
tract	to pull	*tractor*, *extract*, *abstract*, *tractable*, *protracted*, *retract*, *detractor*
trans-	to a different place	*transport*, *transient*, *transplant*, *transcribe*
	across, through	*transparent*, *translucent*, *transcend*, *transaction*
trit	rubbed, worn	*trite*, *attrition*, *contrite*, *detritus*
troph	nourishment	*autotroph*, *atrophy*, *eutrophic*, *allotrophic*
trunc, trench	to cut	*truncate*, *trenchant*, *truncheon*, *trunks*
trus, trud	to push	*intrude*, *abstruse*, *extrude*, *obtrusive*, *intrusive*
turb	to disturb	*disturb*, *perturb*, *turbulence*
un-	not	*unspoken*, *unassuming*, *unfettered*, *unstinting*, *unabridged*
umbra	shade	*umbrella*, *somber*, *adumbrate*, *umbrage*, *penumbra*
unda, ound	wave	*undulate*, *inundate*, *abundance*, *abound*, *redundant*
under-	beneath	*underground*, *undernourished*, *undermine*, *underestimate*
uni-	one	*unified*, *universe*, *uniformity*, *united*, *unilateral*, *unanimity*
vac, void	empty, void	*vacuum*, *vacuous*, *evacuate*, *devoid*, *avoid*

vad, **vas**	to go	***evade***, *pervasive, invade*
vag	wandering	***vagrant***, *vague, vagabond, vagary*
val, **vail**	to be strong	***valid***, *ambivalent, prevalent, valor*
van, **vain**	gone, empty	***vanish***, *vain, evanescent*
vehe, **vect**	to carry	***vehicle***, *vehement, vector, convect*
vene, **vent**	to come	***convention***, *intervention, conventional, circumvent, prevent*
ver	true	***verify***, *verisimilitude, verities, aver*
verb	word	***verbal***, *verbatim, verbose, proverb, verbiage*
vert, **vers**	to turn	***convert***, *diversion, diverse, aversion, versatility, adversary, vertex*
vid, **vis**	to see	***invisible***, *revision, individual, video*
vigil	awake	***vigilant***, *vigil, invigilate, vigilante*
vil	worthless	***vile***, *vilify, reviled*
vinc, **vanq**, **vict**	to conquer	***victory***, *vanquish, invincible, convince, conviction, evict*
viva, **vita**	to live	***revive***, *viable, convivial, vivid, vivacious*
voc, **vok**	to call, to give voice to	***vocal***, *advocate, revoke, vociferous, provocative, equivocate, evocative*
vol	(> *volvere*) to roll	***revolve***, *revolution, convoluted, evolve, volume, voluble*
	(> *velle*) to wish	***volunteer***, *volition, benevolent, malevolent*
	(> *volare*) to fly	***volatile***, *volley*
vor	to devour	***carnivore***, *omnivore, voracious, herbivore*

CHAPTER 4

THE SAT READING TEST

1. The Core Analytical Reading Skills   159

2. The Three Key Questions   161

3. The Three Secondary Questions   170

4. Advanced SAT Reading Techniques   180

The SAT Reading Test

What is the SAT Reading test?

The SAT includes a 65-minute Reading test designed to assess your

> *proficiency in reading and comprehending a broad range of high-quality, appropriately challenging literary and informational texts in the content areas of U.S. and world literature, history/social studies, and science.*

The SAT Reading test consists of four passages, each 500–750 words long. (For an example of the Reading test, look at Section 1 of the Diagnostic Test in Chapter 2.) You are to read the passages and answer multiple-choice questions about

- the purpose and main idea of the passage
- the meaning and purpose of particular words and phrases in context
- the inferences that can be justifiably drawn from the passage
- the tone and attitude conveyed by the author

Additionally, some passages with a common theme are paired and accompanied by questions about

- points of agreement or disagreement between the paired passages
- differences in tone or emphasis between the paired passages

Also, some of the passages will be accompanied by tables or graphs and questions about

- how to interpret the data represented in the table or graph
- how to incorporate these data appropriately into the passage

How is it used?

Colleges use your SAT Reading test score as a measure of your ability to perform demanding college-level reading tasks. The SAT Reading test score represents one-half of your Evidence-Based Reading and Writing score. The other half of this score comes from the Writing and Language test.

Sound intimidating? It's not.

There are only four rules of analytical reading to learn in order to ace the SAT Reading test, and the 12 lessons in this chapter will give you the knowledge and practice you need to master all of them.

The Core Analytical Reading Skills

Lesson 1: Learn to read analytically

Which is correct?

A. *The SAT Reading test is primarily a test of your multiple-choice test-taking skill.*
B. *The SAT Reading test is primarily a test of your analytical reading skill.*
C. *The SAT Reading test is primarily a test of your literary reading skill.*

Although basic test-taking skills are helpful, they won't get you very far. Acing the SAT Reading test requires solid **analytical reading skills**, that is, the ability to **extract the key information** from any passage and **to identify its evidence**. Specifically, you should be able to read any SAT passage on any topic and determine its

- purpose
- central idea
- structure
- functional elements
- tone

It's important to remember that the SAT Reading test is *not* **a literary skills test**. You may spend a lot of time in English class learning to

- explore connections between a text and its cultural context

- evaluate the emotional effect of a literary piece
- explore abstract ideas that are implicit in a work, such as "the concept of utopia"
- find examples of symbolism, foreshadowing, and other subtle and figurative literary elements

But these literary skills, while important for your enjoyment and edification, are not tested by the SAT Reading test.

Although it is helpful to know a few important **test-taking skills**, just knowing these tricks won't get you very far. The SAT Reading test is essentially a test of **analytical reading skill**, *not* **literary reading skills**.

According to the College Board, the SAT Reading test is **evidence-based**. That is, it specifically assesses your ability to justify your responses with **literal evidence** from the passage and **quantitative evidence** from associated tables or graphs. Therefore, be ready to supply the **evidence** for any answers you give.

Lesson 2: Get your mind right

Which is correct?

A. *The SAT Reading passages are chosen to be as difficult and boring as possible.*

B. *The SAT Reading passages are chosen because they represent the kinds of prose students are most likely to encounter in a college liberal arts curriculum.*

The answer, despite popular belief, is B. The SAT Reading passages are not chosen by sadists. They are selected to represent the kind of reading you will do in college. Don't begin the SAT Reading Test with the attitude, "Oh no, not another tedious and pointless SAT reading passage!" This will only sabotage your performance by creating a negative self-fulfilling prophecy.

How well you do on the SAT Reading test depends very much on the mindset you bring to the test.

If you expect a passage to be tedious and pointless, it will be, because you will miss its interesting key points. If instead you expect to learn something new and interesting, you will remain more focused and engaged and attack the questions much more confidently and accurately.

Keep an open mind and—we promise—you'll learn something new from every SAT you take.

How do you avoid "spacing out?"

Many students occasionally "space out" on high-pressure reading tests like the SAT: their eyes scan over the words, but the words don't go in the brain. The best way to avoid space-outs is to **master the skills of active reading**. When your brain is active and engaged, it can't "space out." The heart of active reading is focusing on the **analytical questions** that we will discuss in the upcoming lessons.

The Three Key Questions

Lesson 3: Ask, "What is the purpose of this passage?"

To comprehend a passage analytically, you must first categorize it in terms of which three categories?

A. *Fiction, nonfiction, or poetry*
B. *Exposition, rhetoric, or narrative*
C. *History, science, or humanities*

The correct answer is B. Don't worry so much about whether the passage is fiction or nonfiction, or if the topic is unfamiliar to you. You need a plan of attack for any passage the SAT throws your way. Strong analytical reading begins with asking, **"What is the overall purpose of this passage?"** Any well-written piece of prose has one of three possible purposes corresponding to the following categories:

- **Expository prose** presents **objective information** and is organized around a **guiding question**, such as "What happened in the Battle of Bull Run?" or "What is polarized light, and what is it used for?" Examples of expository prose include news articles and science textbooks.

- **Rhetorical prose** presents **an author's personal point of view** and is organized around a **thesis**, such as "We have an exaggerated perception of gang violence," or "Hiking is good for the soul." Examples of rhetorical prose include Op-Ed essays, blog posts, and some magazine articles.

- **Narrative prose** presents **a fictional or nonfictional story** and is organized around a **protagonist and a transformative struggle**, such as "Jean Valjean struggles to redeem himself," or "King Lear struggles to establish a legacy." Examples of narrative prose include memoirs, short stories, biographies, and novels.

As you read any SAT Reading passage, first ask, **"What is its overall purpose: to present objective information** (expository), **to present a point of view** (rhetorical), **or to tell a story** (narrative)**?"**

You can often determine overall purpose from the introduction or the first paragraph. For instance, if a passage is described as a *discussion* or *description*, it's likely to be expository. If it is described as a *speech* or an *essay*, it's probably rhetorical. If it is described as an excerpt from a *memoir* or *novel*, then it's probably narrative.

But **be careful**. Authors often combine different modes of prose. For instance, an essay arguing for tougher gun laws (rhetorical purpose) might tell a heart-wrenching story (narrative element) to make the point. Similarly, a short story (narrative purpose) might include a lengthy description (expository element) of the town in which it is set.

Always confirm your theory about purpose by carefully reading the final paragraph. If the final paragraph focuses on describing an interesting fact, the passage is probably expository. If it focuses on a proposal, evaluation, or suggestion, the passage is probably rhetorical. If it describes a person's resolution of a problem, the passage is probably a narrative. **Most passages confirm their overall purpose in the final paragraph.**

Lesson 4: Ask, "What is the central idea of this passage?"

What is the best way to determine the central idea of a passage?

    A. *Read the first paragraph, which always summarizes the main idea.*
    B. *Read the topic sentence of the final paragraph.*
    C. *It depends on the passage type and structure.*

The correct answer is C. Although the first and last paragraphs often contain key information, sometimes the first paragraph or two simply provide background information or summarize a misconception to be refuted. Sometimes a passage doesn't get around to the central idea until the third or fourth paragraph.

> **Once you have determined the general purpose of the passage, focus immediately on finding the central idea.** The purpose and central idea are intimately linked.
>
> - The central idea of any **expository essay** is a **guiding question**, such as "What is the carbon cycle?"
> - The central idea of any **rhetorical essay** is a **thesis**, such as "Perseverance is more important to success than skill is."
> - The central idea of any **narrative** is the **protagonist's transformative struggle**, such as "The narrator discovers how to be an artist."
>
> **The central idea is often, but not always, revealed at the beginning of the passage and reinforced at the end of the passage.** Sometimes your first guess about the main idea, based on the first paragraph, may be wrong and need to be revised.

Consider this excerpt and the question that follows:

Without some appreciation of common large numbers, it's impossible to react with the proper skepticism to terrifying reports that more than a million American kids are kidnapped each year, or with the proper sobriety to a warhead carrying a megaton of explosive power—the equivalent of a million tons (or two billion pounds) of TNT.

And if you don't have some feeling for probabilities, automobile accidents might seem a relatively minor problem of local travel, whereas being killed by terrorists might seem to be a major risk when going overseas. As often observed, however, the 45,000 people killed annually on American roads are approximately equal in number to all American dead in the Vietnam War. On the other hand, the seventeen Americans killed by terrorists in 1985 were among the 28 million of us who traveled abroad that year—that's one chance in 1.6 million of becoming a victim . . .

The primary purpose of this passage is to

    A) warn against the dangers associated with daily living in the United States

    B) compare the costs of war-related activities to the costs of domestic activities

    C) discuss common misunderstandings about statistical data

    D) propose solutions to some problems in American domestic and foreign policy

Most students get this question wrong, because they focus too much on **specific details** and not enough on **overall purpose** and **logical structure**.

So what is the central idea in this passage? If you look at some of the passage details, such as the references to car accidents and kidnapping, you might be reminded of *the dangers associated with daily living* or the *cost of domestic activities* or even *domestic policy problems.* If you notice the references to warheads, the Vietnam War, and terrorism, you might be reminded of *war-related activities* or *American foreign policy problems.* For these reasons, choices A, B, and D might all seem like good answers.

But they are all wrong.

Consider choice A. Is kidnapping mentioned in order to *warn against danger*? No: the author says that the *proper* response to the *terrifying reports that more than a million American kids are kidnapped each year* is not fear and caution, but *skepticism.* In fact, his point is that if we had *some appreciation of common large numbers,* we would see that this statistic is preposterous.

How about choice B? The statement that *the 45,000 people killed annually on American roads are approximately equal in number to all American dead in the Vietnam War* seems to be comparing *the costs of war-related activities to the costs of domestic activities.* But is this the *primary purpose of the passage*? No, this statistic is mentioned only to make a broader point: that it is irrational to fear terrorism more than daily driving, and that this irrationality is due, in least in part, to our lack of *feeling about probabilities.*

Now look at choice D. Does the passage *propose any solutions* to the problems of kidnapping, terrorism, nuclear weapons, car accidents, or war? Certainly not in these first two paragraphs. More important, these paragraphs suggest a very different overall purpose.

The point of these first two paragraphs is that *[w]ithout some appreciation of common large numbers* and a *feeling for probabilities*, we will overreact to some dangers and underreact to others. In other words, there is some danger inherent in our *common misunderstandings about statistical data.* Therefore, the best answer is choice C.

How to attack purpose questions

Many SAT Reading questions ask about the **purpose** of particular words, phrases, or references. Here are some examples:

> The author uses the word "debacle" (line 3) in order to emphasize her belief that . . .

> The quotation in lines 42–51 primarily serves to . . .

To attack these questions, first remind yourself of the **overall purpose and central idea** of the passage, and remember that **every portion of the passage must help convey the central idea of the passage.**

Consider this question about the "innumeracy" passage that is the source of the earlier quote:

> The author mentions the work of Drs. Kronlund and Phillips (lines 53–58) primarily in order to
>
> A) warn against the risks of certain medical procedures
>
> B) highlight a promising medical breakthrough
>
> C) demonstrate the fallibility of medical experts
>
> D) dispute a common medical theory

Even without reading lines 53–58, you can see which choices don't fit with the overall purpose and central idea that we identified in the previous question. Since the primary purpose of this passage is to "discuss common misunderstandings about statistical data," the reference to *the work of Drs. Kronlund and Phillips* must serve this primary purpose in some way. Choices B and D are not strongly connected to the understanding of statistical data. Choices A and C, however, are plausible answers because *warning against risks* often involves understanding the data that show the likelihood of those risks, and *the fallibility of medical experts* might include their inability to understand and interpret statistics (which is precisely the main theme of the essay).

Exercise 1

This passage is adapted from John Allen Paulos,
Innumeracy ©1988 Hill and Wang, a division
of Farrar, Straus and Giroux, LLC. Paulos is a
mathematician discussing the role of mathematics in
American culture.

Line   Without some appreciation of common large
numbers, it's impossible to react with the proper
skepticism to terrifying reports that more than a
million American kids are kidnapped each year,
5 or with the proper sobriety to a warhead carrying
a megaton of explosive power—the equivalent of
a million tons (or two billion pounds) of TNT.
    And if you don't have some feeling for
probabilities, automobile accidents might
10 seem a relatively minor problem of local travel,
whereas being killed by terrorists might seem
to be a major risk when going overseas. As often
observed, however, the 45,000 people killed
annually on American roads are approximately
15 equal in number to all American dead in the
Vietnam War. On the other hand, the seventeen
Americans killed by terrorists in 1985 were
among the 28 million of us who traveled abroad
that year—that's one chance in 1.6 million of
20 becoming a victim. Compare that with these
annual rates in the United States: one chance in
68,000 of choking to death; one chance in 75,000
of dying in a bicycle crash; one chance in 20,000
of drowning; and one chance in only 5,300 of
25 dying in a car crash.
    Confronted with these large numbers and
with the correspondingly small probabilities
associated with them, the innumerate will
inevitably respond with the non sequitur, "Yes, but
30 what if you're that one," and then nod knowingly,
as if they've demolished your argument with
penetrating insight. This tendency to personalize
is a characteristic of many who suffer from
innumeracy. Equally typical is a tendency to
35 equate the risk from some obscure and exotic
malady with the chances of suffering from heart
and circulatory disease, from which about 12,000
Americans die each week.
    There's a joke I like that's marginally
40 relevant. An old married couple in their nineties
contact a divorce lawyer, who pleads with them
to stay together. "Why get divorced now after
seventy years of marriage?" The little old lady
finally pipes up in a creaky voice: "We wanted to
45 wait until the children were dead."

    A feeling for what quantities or time spans
are appropriate in various contexts is essential
to getting the joke. Slipping between millions
and billions or between billions and trillions
50 should in this sense be equally funny, but it isn't,
because we too often lack an intuitive grasp for
these numbers.
    A recent study by Drs. Kronlund and Phillips
of the University of Washington showed that
55 most doctors' assessments of the risks of various
operations, procedures, and medications (even
in their own specialties) were way off the mark,
often by several orders of magnitude. I once
had a conversation with a doctor who, within
60 approximately 20 minutes, stated that a certain
procedure he was contemplating (a) had a one-
chance-in-a-million risk associated with it;
(b) was 99 percent safe; and (c) usually went
quite well. Given the fact that so many doctors
65 seem to believe that there must be at least eleven
people in the waiting room if they're to avoid
being idle, I'm not surprised at this new evidence
of their innumeracy.

1

The primary purpose of this passage is to

A) warn against the dangers associated with daily
living in the United States

B) compare the costs of war-related activities to
the costs of domestic activities

C) discuss common misunderstandings about
statistical data

D) propose solutions to some problems in
American domestic and foreign policy

2

The author regards the "reports" (line 3) with an
attitude of

A) journalistic objectivity

B) informed incredulity

C) intense alarm

D) lighthearted humor

3

The activities listed in lines 21–25 serve primarily as examples of

A) underappreciated dangers

B) intolerable risks

C) medical priorities

D) policy failures

4

The passage includes all of the following EXCEPT

A) ad hominem

B) verifiable statistics

C) amusing illustration

D) social assessment

5

In line 32, the author's use of the word "penetrating" is an example of

A) subtle euphemism

B) deliberate hyperbole

C) sincere acclamation

D) ironic sarcasm

6

In line 32, "personalize" most nearly means

A) customize decoratively

B) describe insultingly

C) represent humanely

D) interpret out of context

7

The passage suggests that the "exotic malady" (lines 35–36) is an example of

A) a delusion that is slowly being dispelled

B) a risk that is wildly overestimated

C) a peril that is rapidly growing

D) a disease that defies conventional treatment

8

Which choice provides the best evidence for the answer to the previous question?

A) Lines 1–7 ("Without some . . . of TNT")

B) Lines 12–16 ("As often . . . War")

C) Lines 39–40 ("There's a joke . . . relevant")

D) Lines 58–64 ("I once . . . quite well")

9

The author mentions the work of Drs. Kronlund and Phillips (lines 53–58) primarily in order to

A) warn against the risks of certain medical procedures

B) highlight a promising medical breakthrough

C) demonstrate the fallibility of medical experts

D) dispute a common medical theory

Lesson 5: Ask, "What is the structure of this passage?"

Here is a sample SAT Reading passage, with some notes about its **functional structure**.

This passage is adapted from Cleveland Hickman, Larry Roberts, and Allan Larson, Integrated Principles of Zoology. *©2001 The McGraw-Hill Companies.*

Line

In ancient times, people commonly believed that new life could arise not only by parental reproduction, but also, on occasion, by spontaneous generation from nonliving material.
5   For example, frogs appeared to arise from damp earth, mice from putrefied matter, insects from dew, and maggots from decaying meat. Warmth, moisture, sunlight, and even starlight often were mentioned as factors that encouraged
10   spontaneous generation of living organisms.

> **Misconception** about the origin of life: spontaneous generation.

One of the early efforts to synthesize organisms in the laboratory can be seen in a recipe for making mice given by the Belgian plant nutritionist Jean Baptiste van Helmont (1648):
15   . . . press a piece of underwear soiled with sweat together with some wheat in an open jar, after about 21 days the odor changes and the ferment. . . . changes the wheat into mice . . . not small mice, not even miniature adults or aborted
20   mice, but adult mice emerge!

> **Example** of this misconception: recipe for synthesizing adult mice from soiled underwear.

In 1861, Louis Pasteur demonstrated that, in fact, living organisms cannot so easily arise spontaneously from nonliving matter. In his experiments, Pasteur introduced fermentable
25   material into a flask with a long S-shaped neck that was open to the air. The flask and its contents were boiled to kill any microorganisms, then cooled and left undisturbed. No fermentation could occur because new microorganisms
30   could not enter through the neck. But when the neck was removed, microorganisms in the air could enter the fermentable material and proliferate. Thus, Pasteur showed that life came from previously existing organisms and their
35   reproductive elements, such as eggs and spores or, in the case of van Helmont's "recipe," adult mice that crept into the jar. Announcing his results to the French Academy, Pasteur proclaimed, "Never will the doctrine of spontaneous generation arise
40   from this mortal blow."

> **Refutation** of theory of spontaneous generation by a clever experiment.

But Pasteur, for all his brilliance, wasn't entirely correct. The first "life," if we can call it that, appears to have assembled over the course of millions of years of random collisions of
45 nonliving molecules in the chemical-rich cauldron of early Earth, until, by chance, very basic self-replicating units formed. These first self-replicating units, which arose almost 4 billion years ago, are most likely the ancestors we share
50 with every living thing on earth today. But with no scientist to witness it, how can we know that the dawn of life happened that way? The evidence is embedded in the complex molecules common to all living things—DNA, RNA, proteins, lipids,
55 hormones—which can be painstakingly traced back to simpler chemicals that most likely preceded them in the family tree. Even more profoundly, astrophysicists can now trace the building blocks of life—carbon, nitrogen, and
60 oxygen—to a spectacular birth inside ancient exploding stars!

Implication of rare biogenesis over millions of years: it seems to have happened only once, so all life is related.

To read analytically, you must pay attention to the functional structure of the passage. In other words, think about how **each paragraph** serves the central idea.

Notice that, in the passage above, the notes indicate that the first paragraph *describes a misconception*, the second *provides an example of that misconception*, the third *provides a refutation of that misconception*, and the fourth *describes an implication of the corrected theory*. All of these paragraphs serve the central purpose of *describing the history and implications of a biological theory*.

The **structure** of a passage depends very much on its **purpose.**

Expository essays can be structured in many possible ways in order to answer the guiding question. They may include background information, illustrations of concepts, examples of general claims, relevant data, anecdotes, or discussions of implications. Of course, any of these elements may be omitted, supplemented, or rearranged.

Narratives have a fairly consistent structure: (1) the struggle is introduced, (2) the struggle is developed, and (3) the struggle is resolved, transforming the protagonist. The details may differ dramatically from narrative to narrative, but the overall structure probably will not.

Rhetorical essays can also be structured in many possible ways. A **rhetorical argument** is likely to describe a position, then refute it with a counterargument. A **rhetorical narrative** tells a story in order to highlight a particular point of view. Rhetorical essay can include paragraphs dedicated to logical analysis of a claim, explanation, illustration, discussion of implications, modification of a claim, and so on.

Exercise 2

This passage is adapted from Cleveland Hickman, Larry Roberts, and Allan Larson, Integrated Principles of Zoology. *©2001 The McGraw-Hill Companies.*

Line   In ancient times, people commonly
believed that new life could arise not only by
parental reproduction, but also, on occasion, by
spontaneous generation from nonliving material.
5 For example, frogs appeared to arise from damp
earth, mice from putrefied matter, insects from
dew, and maggots from decaying meat. Warmth,
moisture, sunlight, and even starlight often
were mentioned as factors that encouraged
10 spontaneous generation of living organisms.
     One of the early efforts to synthesize
organisms in the laboratory can be seen in a
recipe for making mice given by the Belgian plant
nutritionist Jean Baptiste van Helmont (1648):
15   . . . press a piece of underwear soiled with
sweat together with some wheat in an open jar,
after about 21 days the odor changes and the
ferment. . . . changes the wheat into mice . . . not
small mice, not even miniature adults or aborted
20 mice, but adult mice emerge!
     In 1861, Louis Pasteur demonstrated that,
in fact, living organisms cannot so easily arise
spontaneously from nonliving matter. In his
experiments, Pasteur introduced fermentable
25 material into a flask with a long S-shaped neck
that was open to the air. The flask and its contents
were boiled to kill any microorganisms, then
cooled and left undisturbed. No fermentation
could occur because new microorganisms
30 could not enter through the neck. But when
the neck was removed, microorganisms in the
air could enter the fermentable material and
proliferate. Thus, Pasteur showed that life came
from previously existing organisms and their
35 reproductive elements, such as eggs and spores or,
in the case of van Helmont's "recipe," adult mice
that crept into the jar. Announcing his results to
the French Academy, Pasteur proclaimed, "Never
will the doctrine of spontaneous generation arise
40 from this mortal blow."

But Pasteur, for all his brilliance, wasn't
entirely correct. The first "life," if we can call it
that, appears to have assembled over the course
of millions of years of random collisions of
45 nonliving molecules in the chemical-rich
cauldron of early Earth, until, by chance, very
basic self-replicating units formed. These first
self-replicating units, which arose almost 4 billion
years ago, are most likely the ancestors we share
50 with every living thing on earth today. But with
no scientist to witness it, how can we know that
the dawn of life happened that way? The evidence
is embedded in the complex molecules common
to all living things—DNA, RNA, proteins, lipids,
55 hormones—which can be painstakingly traced
back to simpler chemicals that most likely
preceded them in the family tree. Even more
profoundly, astrophysicists can now trace the
building blocks of life—carbon, nitrogen, and
60 oxygen—to a spectacular birth inside ancient
exploding stars!

1

The author regards the examples listed in lines 5–7 as

A) scientific frauds

B) astonishing discoveries

C) faulty conclusions

D) quaint traditions

2

Which choice provides the best evidence for the answer to the previous question?

A) Lines 1–4 ("In ancient . . . material")

B) Lines 7–10 ("Warmth . . . organisms")

C) Lines 21–23 ("In 1861 . . . matter")

D) Lines 30–33 ("But when . . . proliferate")

3

Louis Pasteur would most likely fault the "recipe" described in lines 15–20 for its lack of

A) scientific controls

B) quantitative precision

C) fermentable material

D) airborne microorganisms

4

In line 40, "mortal" most nearly means

A) human

B) earthly

C) bitter

D) fatal

5

The final paragraph suggests that Pasteur was mistaken about

A) the chemical composition of living cells

B) the possibility of life arising from nonliving matter

C) when the earliest forms of life arose on Earth

D) the existence of a common ancestor to all living things

6

In line 47, "basic" most nearly means

A) innate

B) quintessential

C) easily understood

D) rudimentary

7

In the final paragraph, the author characterizes the early earth primarily as

A) idyllic

B) mysterious

C) perilous

D) chaotic

8

Which best describes the content and organization of the passage as a whole?

A) the account of a discovery followed by a discussion of its practical applications

B) the description of a common belief followed by a presentation of the evidence refuting it

C) the illustration of a complex theory followed by a consideration of its inadequacies

D) the story of the struggles of a scientist followed by an appreciation of his legacy

The Three Secondary Questions

Lesson 6: Ask, "How does the author use language?"

Good writers choose their words carefully. Each word should serve a purpose in conveying an idea or tone to the reader. Often, SAT Reading questions ask you to determine the meaning or tone of particular words or phrases based on context.

How to attack word-in-context questions

Word-in-context questions test your "verbal inference" skills, that is, your ability to determine the meanings of words by how they are used in context. Here's an example:

> In line 24, the word "decline" most nearly means . . .

The word *decline* isn't really a **challenging** word. Instead, it's an **ambiguous** word. That is, it has a variety of possible meanings. It can mean "politely refuse," "diminish in strength," or "move downward." Its meaning depends on its context.

To attack a word-in-context question, reread the sentence in which the word is used, recalling the purpose of that paragraph and the specific meaning of that sentence. Then think of a word or phrase you could replace the word with without altering the meaning of the sentence, and then find its best match among the choices.

Check your answer by rereading the sentence with the replacement word or phrase. Make sure the resulting sentence sounds okay, that is, it conveys the proper meaning and tone, and it follows Standard English idiom.

Consider question 4 in Exercise 2:

4. In line 40, "mortal" most nearly means

    A) human

    B) earthly

    C) bitter

    D) fatal

We can use the word *mortal* in many different ways. In *Socrates is merely mortal*, it means "human." In *The coffin contained our dog's mortal remains*, it means "earthly."

In *They were mortal enemies*, it means "bitter." In *The infection turned out to be a mortal one*, it means "fatal." So answering this question requires knowing more than the definition of *mortal*; it requires understanding the context of this particular sentence. When Pasteur said, *"Never will the doctrine of spontaneous generation arise from this mortal blow,"* he meant that the doctrine is as dead as an opponent who has been struck with a sword. Therefore, in this context, *mortal* means "fatal," and the correct answer is D.

How to attack tone questions

The SAT Reading question will sometimes ask about the **tone or attitude** conveyed by the passage as a whole or in particular words or phrases. Here are some examples:

> The author's attitude toward the "critics" (line 22) can best be described as

> The tone of lines 13–16 ("It was not until. . . . emergency") is one of

When attacking tone questions, make sure to first recall the *overall* tone of the passage, and think about how the specified portion fits the overall tone. For instance, imagine that a question asks about the tone of a discussion about "voodoo practices." In an expository essay about Caribbean anthropology, this discussion may have an "objective" tone. In a rhetorical essay about the dangers of superstitious behavior, it may have a "disdainful" tone. In a narrative about a woman's fond recollections of her grandmother's rituals, it may have an "affectionate" tone. **Don't assume that the author's attitude toward a topic matches your own.**

Before choosing an answer that suggests a very strong tone, like "alarmism," "glorification," or "disgust," **make sure that you can justify your choice with literal evidence from the passage**.

When answering tone or attitude questions, **pay attention to the voice of the speaker**. Does the line in question represent the opinion of the author, or the opinion of someone else? Does it represent a point of view the author agrees with, or disagrees with?

Consider question 7 in Exercise 2:

7. In the final paragraph, the author characterizes the early Earth primarily as

   A) idyllic

   B) mysterious

   C) perilous

   D) chaotic

The passage is Exercise 2 is an **expository essay**, and therefore has an **objective overall purpose**. This means that the **author's point of view** is not at issue here. However, the author may still use language to convey tone. In the final paragraph, early Earth is described as a *chemical-rich cauldron* in which, *by chance*, the first self-replicating chemical units were formed. Although this is obviously not a portrayal of an *idyllic* ("blissful") scene, a *chemical-rich cauldron* could certainly be *mysterious*, *perilous*, or *chaotic*. So which tone does the author primarily mean to convey?

To answer this question, as with so many SAT Reading questions, we must step back and look at the bigger picture. The point of this paragraph is that the earliest life most likely arose from the hot, seething, bubbling mixture of gas and liquid that pervaded the earth billions of years ago. In other words, the author describes a *chaotic* world. He is not portraying early Earth as *mysterious*, because he is claiming to understand important aspects of that ancient environment. He is also not portraying the early Earth as *perilous*, because no creatures yet existed to suffer its dangers.

Exercise 3

Hominid Family Tree

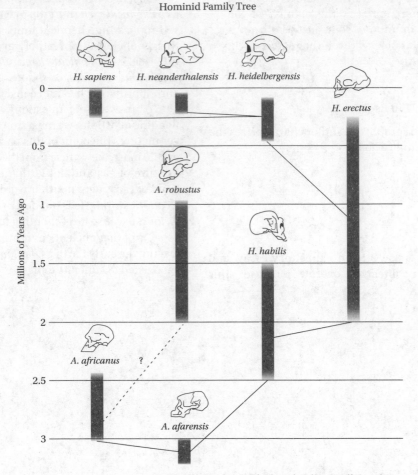

©2015 Christopher F. Black and College Hill Coaching.

This passage is adapted from John R. Skoyles and Dorion Sagan, Up from Dragons. *©2002 The McGraw-Hill Companies. Here, the authors discuss the evolution of human intelligence.*

Line   We are a bright species. We have gone into
space and walked on the moon. Yet you would
never have guessed that if you traveled back
to between 100,000 and 40,000 years ago.
5   At that time our *Homo sapiens* ancestors
and Neanderthals (*Homo neanderthalensis*)
coexisted. Neanderthals were like us but
physically stronger, with large bones and teeth,
protruding brows and face, and hardly a chin.
10   Perhaps what we lacked in brawn we made up for
in brains. But for most of our history, our species
was not bright enough to act very differently from
the Neanderthals, let alone be more successful
than they were. Only around 40,000 to 32,000
15   years ago, in Western Asia and Europe, did

Neanderthal people disappear, to be replaced by
our species.
        Why did we coexist with Neanderthals for
60,000 years—a far longer case of hominids living
20   side by side than any other in human history? And
why did we eventually win out? Brains alone
cannot provide the answer, as Neanderthals may
in fact have had the larger ones. Perhaps they
lacked the long vocal chamber needed for speech.
25   Equal certainty exists among those who study the
base of their skulls that they did and that they did
not. If they did lack one, then this could be the
explanation, but maybe not, since even without a
voice box, gestures can communicate, as can be
30   seen among the deaf. Indeed, hunters find
advantages in using sign language (speech
sounds would warn off potential prey), and
not just while hunting but in everyday life.
Anthropologists find that hunter-gatherers use
35   sophisticated sign languages to complement
their speech. Sign language might even have

other advantages—evidence even suggests that it is easier to learn than speech: deaf children start to pick up signs earlier than hearing ones learn
40 to speak. So "spoken speech" is not in all ways superior to "signed speech." It is not something that can explain our replacement of the Neanderthals.

The reason we—anatomically modern humans—won out lies, we suspect, not in being
45 brighter or better able to speak but in our very physical frailty and our resulting need to exploit our minds. Neanderthals, stronger than us, did not need to take this route. They could survive with their physical strength rather than tapping
50 the potential of their brains. An analogy is with countries: the richest ones, such as Switzerland, Finland, Singapore, and Japan, are not blessed with, but rather lack, natural resources. Without them, they have been forced to use their brains
55 to innovate, providing products and services ranging from cell phones to diplomacy.

1

The authors use the phrase "equal certainty" (line 25) to make the point that

A) the reason for the Neanderthals' extinction is now well known

B) Neanderthals may not have coexisted with modern humans after all

C) scientists disagree about the vocal ability of Neanderthals

D) the ability to communicate is necessary to the survival of a hunting species

2

The authors of this passage would most likely agree with which of the following statements?

A) anthropological research should adopt higher standards of evidence

B) physical weakness is not necessarily a disadvantage in the fight for survival

C) Neanderthals lacked the vocal ability to develop sophisticated language

D) modern humans could not have achieved as much without the help of the Neanderthals

3

Which choice provides the best evidence for the answer to the previous question?

A) Lines 25–27 ("Equal certainty . . . did not")

B) Lines 30–34 ("Indeed, hunters . . . everyday life")

C) Lines 41–42 ("It is not . . . the Neanderthals")

D) Lines 43–47 ("The reason . . . our minds")

4

The term *Cro-Magnon* refers to the earliest members of the species *H. sapiens*. Which of following statements is most justified by the diagram in Figure 1?

A) The *Cro-Magnon* are direct descendants of *H. neanderthalensis*.

B) The *Cro-Magnon* and *H. heidelbergensis* both share *A. afarensis* as a common ancestor.

C) Competition with the *Cro-Magnon* led to the extinction of *H. erectus*.

D) The *Cro-Magnon* and *A. robustus* both descended from *H. habilis*.

5

If the fossil record indicated in the accompanying diagram is assumed to be accurate and complete, what is the longest period of time that any single hominid species lived on the earth?

A) 1,000,000 years

B) 1,250,000 years

C) 1,750,000 years

D) 2,000,000 years

6

Which of the following best describes how the diagram supports the main argument of this passage?

A) It shows that hominid species have existed for over 2,000,000 years.

B) It shows that *H. neanderthalensis* had a long vocal chamber.

C) It shows that *H. sapiens* and *H. neanderthalensis* both existed in the period between 100,000 and 40,000 years ago.

D) It shows that *H. sapiens* and *H. neanderthalensis* had a common ancestor.

7

The authors mention that "hunter-gatherers use sophisticated sign language" (lines 34–35) primarily in order to

A) refute a common misconception about hunter-gatherers

B) specify the mechanism by which modern humans came to replace Neanderthals

C) bolster their claim about the larger brain size of Neanderthals

D) suggest that long vocal chambers might not provide a decisive evolutionary advantage

8

In line 49, "tapping" most nearly means

A) exploiting

B) exhausting

C) nominating

D) monitoring

9

The authors mention "cell phones" and "diplomacy" (line 56) primarily as examples of

A) universally admired commercial products

B) effective means of global communication

C) goods and services based on intellectual resources

D) activities that require little physical strength

Lesson 7: Ask, "How does the author use evidence?"

Always be ready to justify your answer to any SAT Reading question, and to answer **literal evidence** questions and **quantitative evidence** questions.

How to attack literal evidence questions

Literal evidence questions are of the form

> Which choice provides the best evidence for the answer to the previous question?

Every literal evidence question asks you to find a specific line in the passage that directly supports the point in the previous question. Make sure that the evidence you cite in the passage is **clear**, **direct evidence**, and does not require any broad inferences or dramatic leap of logic.

Consider questions 1 and 2 in Exercise 2:

1. The author regards the examples listed in lines 5–7 as

   A) scientific frauds

   B) astonishing discoveries

   C) faulty conclusions

   D) quaint traditions

2. Which choice provides the best evidence for the answer to the previous question?

   A) Lines 1–4 ("In ancient . . . material")

   B) Lines 7–10 ("Warmth . . . organisms")

   C) Lines 21–23 ("In 1861 . . . matter")

   D) Lines 30–33 ("But when . . . proliferate")

Lines 5–7 list the following examples: *frogs appeared to arise from damp earth, mice from putrefied matter, insects from dew, and maggots from decaying meat.* In line 1, the author indicates that these are things that *people commonly believed* in ancient times. But the passage then goes on to explain that these beliefs are mistaken, and that life in fact does not arise that way. Therefore, the answer to question 1 is C: *faulty conclusions.*

What literal evidence best shows that the author regards these statements as *faulty conclusions*? In lines 21–23, the author states *that in fact, living organisms cannot so easily arise from nonliving matter.* Notice that this is a **clear, direct statement** that the author regards the beliefs listed in lines 5–7 as *faulty conclusions.* Therefore, the correct answer to question 2 is C. Choice A is incorrect because lines 1–4 simply state that ancient people believed these things, not that the author disagrees. Choice B is incorrect because lines 7–10 just give details about these beliefs, but no indication that the author doesn't share them. Choice D is incorrect because lines 30–33 just give a detail about Pasteur's experiment, and no direct indication that the author disagrees with the list of beliefs.

Consider questions 2 and 3 in Exercise 3:

2. The authors of this passage would most likely agree with which of the following statements?

   A) anthropological research should adopt higher standards of evidence

   B) physical weakness is not necessarily a disadvantage in the fight for survival

   C) Neanderthals lacked the vocal ability to develop sophisticated language

   D) modern humans could not have achieved as much without the help of the Neanderthals

3. Which choice provides the best evidence for the answer to the previous question?

   A) Lines 25–27 ("Equal certainty . . . did not")

   B) Lines 30–34 ("Indeed, hunters . . . everyday life")

   C) Lines 41–42 ("It is not . . . the Neanderthals")

   D) Lines 43–47 ("The reason . . . our minds")

The answer to question 2 is B: *physical weakness is not necessarily a disadvantage in the fight for survival.* How do we know? Because this is a direct implication of the main thesis that humans came to dominate the Neanderthals by taking advantage of their intellectual abilities rather than relying on their physical strength.

Where is the best literal evidence for this? In lines 43–47, where the authors state their main thesis: *The reason we—anatomically modern humans—won out lies, we suspect, not in being brighter or better able to speak but in our very physical frailty and our resulting need to exploit our minds.* Therefore, the correct answer to question 3 is choice D. Choice A is incorrect because this sentence merely states that scientists disagree about the length of the Neanderthal vocal chamber. Choice B is incorrect because this sentence merely states that hunters sometimes find it helpful to communicate silently. Choice C is incorrect because this sentence merely states that the ability to speak cannot explain our dominance over the Neanderthals.

How to attack quantitative evidence questions

Quantitative evidence questions ask about the content of graphs, tables, or diagrams that may be associated with the passage. Here are some examples:

> Which claim about the United States prison population is best supported by the graph in Figure 1?

> Which of the following best describes how Figure 1 supports the main argument of this passage?

As with literal evidence questions, quantitative evidence questions require you to identify the **clear and direct** evidence contained in the graph, table, or diagram.

When interpreting data, remember that **correlation does not imply causation**: the mere fact that quantity B goes up at the same time that (or soon after) quantity A goes up does **not** mean that A *causes* B.

Consider questions 4, 5, and 6 in Exercise 3:

4. The term *Cro-Magnon* refers to the earliest members of the species *H. sapiens*. Which of the following statements is most justified by the diagram in Figure 1?

   A) The *Cro-Magnon* are direct descendants of H. neanderthalensis.

   B) The *Cro-Magnon* and *H. heidelbergensis* both share *A. afarensis* as a common ancestor.

   C) Competition with the *Cro-Magnon* led to the extinction of *H. erectus*.

   D) The *Cro-Magnon* and *A. robustus* both descended from *H. habilis*.

5. If the fossil record indicated in the diagram in Figure 1 is assumed to be accurate and complete, what is the longest period of time that any single hominid species lived on the earth?

   A) 1,000,000 years

   B) 1,250,000 years

   C) 1,750,000 years

   D) 2,000,000 years

6. Which of the following best describes how Figure 1 supports the main argument of this passage?

   A) It shows that hominid species have existed for over 2,000,000 years.

   B) It shows that *H. neanderthalensis* had a long vocal chamber.

   C) It shows that *H. sapiens* and *H. neanderthalensis* both existed between 100,000 and 40,000 years ago.

   D) It shows that *H. sapiens* and *H. neanderthalensis* had a common ancestor.

The figure shows a "family tree" of hominid species going back approximately 3 million years. The vertical bars represent the approximate time periods in which each species lived (according to the fossil record), and lines between species indicate the most likely lines of heritage. The dotted line in the lower left portion of the diagram indicates some uncertainty about whether or not *A. robustus* descended from *A. africanus*.

The correct answer to question 4 is B. The undotted lines in the diagram indicate that *H. sapiens* (which includes the *Cro-Magnon*) descended from *H. heidelbergensis*, which descended from *H. erectus*, which descended from *H. habilis*, which descended from *A. afarensis*. Therefore, the *Cro-Magnon* and *H. heidelbergensis* both share *A. afarensis* as a common ancestor. Choice A is incorrect because the diagram shows no line of descent from *H. neanderthalensis* to *H. sapiens*. Choice C is incorrect because the diagram contains no information about the reasons for extinction. Choice D is incorrect because there is no line of descent from *H. habilis* to *A. robustus*.

The correct answer to question 5 is C. The longest vertical bar for any hominid species is that for *H. erectus,* which begins at about the 2-million-year mark and ends at about the 250,000-year mark. Subtracting these two values gives us a time span of about 1,750,000 years.

The correct answer to question 6 is C. Although statements A and D are both valid conclusions based on the information in the diagram, neither of these facts supports the main argument of the passage, which is found in lines 43–47: *The reason we—anatomically modern humans—won out [in our competition with the Neanderthals] lies, we suspect, not in being brighter or better able to speak but in our very physical frailty and our resulting need to exploit our minds.* Therefore, the argument rests on the fact that *H. sapiens* coexisted with *H. neanderthalensis.* The diagram clearly shows that both species lived in the period between approximately 100,000 years ago and 40,000 years ago, and so could have been in direct competition. It also shows that *H. neanderthalensis* appears to have gone extinct, because its vertical bar does not reach all the way up to the 0 mark.

Lesson 8: Ask, "How does the author use rhetorical devices?"

The SAT Reading test may ask you about the **rhetorical effect** of particular sections of the passage. These questions test your ability to recognize particular **rhetorical and literary devices** that the author may use to persuade the reader.

---

16 Basic Stylistic and Rhetorical Devices

An **ad hominem** is an attack "on the person" rather than an attack on his or her ideas or reasoning. For example, *Her political opinions can't be trusted because she is just an actress* is not an argument, but merely an ad hominem.

An **allusion** is an implicit reference to something. For example, the statement *He's gone down the rabbit hole* is an allusion to the bizarre and fanciful episodes in the story *Alice in Wonderland.*

An **analogy** is an illustrative comparison between things that have a similar function or structure. For example, the levels of processing in a computer provide an analogy for understanding levels of processing in the human brain.

An **anecdote** is an illustrative story. For example, a story about a friend whose headache went away after he stood on his head for ten minutes is anecdotal evidence, not scientific evidence, for the health benefits of inversion.

An **aphorism** is a widely accepted truth. For example, the aphorism *If it ain't broke, don't fix it* can provide a concise argument against spending a lot of money on a new program. Aphorisms are also called **maxims**, **adages**, or **proverbs**.

An **appeal to authority** is a suggestion that the reader should agree with an idea because a respected authority happens to believe it. For example: *The world's greatest scientist, Sir Isaac Newton, believed that iron could be turned into gold, so who are we to question the idea?*

An **appeal to emotion** is an attempt to persuade the reader through an emotionally charged anecdote or allusion. For example, a story about an infuriating experience with an insurance salesman may be an effective way to argue against aggressive sales tactics.

Characterization is the use of imagery, diction, or description to convey a particular attitude toward a person, thing, or idea. For example, referring to a proposal as a *scheme* characterizes it as being deceitful.

A **euphemism** is a term that makes something seem more positive than it is. For example, salespersons or political canvassers often use the term *courtesy call* as a euphemism for an unwanted disruption.

Hyperbole is deliberate exaggeration for persuasive effect. For example, saying that *Molly's comma usage is a catastrophe* is almost certainly hyperbole.

Irony is a deliberate reversal of expectations in order to surprise a reader. For example, Christopher Hitchens justified his attitude toward free will by using irony: *I believe in free will, because I have no other choice.*

A **metaphor** is an application of a word or phrase to something it doesn't literally apply to. For example, calling a refusal a *slap in the face* uses metaphor to emphasize its harshness.

Rhetorical **parallelism** is the use of repeated grammatical form to emphasize a point. For example, John F. Kennedy used parallelism in his inaugural address when he said *we shall pay any price, bear any burden, meet any hardship, support any friend, oppose any foe to assure the survival and the success of liberty.*

Personification is the attribution of personal qualities to something that is not a person. For example, we are using rhetorical personification when we say that an idea is *on its last legs* or *gave its last gasp.*

A **simile** is a comparison using *like* or *as*. For instance, Irena Dunn used rhetorical simile when she said *A woman without a man is like a fish without a bicycle.*

An **understatement** suggests that some situation is less signicant than it obviously is. For example, in *Monty Python and the Holy Grail*, the Black Knight looks at his severed arm and says, "'Tis but a scratch!"

Consider questions 4 and 5 from Exercise 1:

4. The passage includes all of the following EXCEPT

   A) ad hominem

   B) verifiable statistics

   C) amusing illustration

   D) social assessment

5. In line 32, the author's use of the word "penetrating" is an example of

   A) subtle euphemism

   B) deliberate hyperbole

   C) sincere acclamation

   D) ironic sarcasm

The correct answer to question 4 is A: *ad hominem*. Although the passage criticizes widespread innumeracy, at no point does the author attack anyone personally. Choice B is incorrect because the author uses verifiable statistics liberally in the first, second, third, and sixth paragraphs. Choice C is incorrect because the joke described in the fourth paragraph is an *amusing illustration*. Choice D is incorrect because the passage makes a *social assessment* in lines 32–34 when he states that *[t]his tendency to personalize is a characteristic of many who suffer from innumeracy,* and again in lines 52–53 when he states that *we too often lack an intuitive grasp for these numbers.*

The correct answer to question 5 is D: *ironic sarcasm.* The author states that *the innumerate will inevitably respond with the non sequitur, "Yes, but what if you're that one," and then nod knowingly, as if they've demolished your argument with penetrating insight* (lines 29–32). In other words, the *penetrating insight* is really not *penetrating* at all: it is a *non sequitur* (a statement that does not follow logically from the premises). The author is using the word *penetrating* ironically and sarcastically. Choice A is incorrect, because the author is not using the word *penetrating* to make the insight seem more positive than it is. In fact, he is criticizing, not euphemizing. Choice B is incorrect because the author is not using exaggeration for rhetorical effect. Choice C is incorrect because *penetrating* is not intended as an *acclamation* (word of praise).

Advanced SAT Reading Techniques

Lesson 9: Master the "preemptive attack" strategies

Which is the best way to attack SAT Reading *passages*?

A. *Read the **questions** first, then go back to the passage and look for the answers to those particular questions.*

B. *Read the **passage** first, with the key questions in mind, then attack the questions with the passage summary in mind.*

Which is the best way to attack SAT Reading *questions*?

C. *Read the question, check any line references, then read all of the choices, crossing out the "unreasonable" answers, then choose the most reasonable choice that remains.*

D. *Read the question, check any line references, then answer it in your own mind before looking at any of the choices, then choose the answer that best matches yours.*

These two questions have been roundly debated in the SAT prep industry for decades. I've seen hundreds of students use all of these strategies, and in my experience, the most reliable attack strategy is the **"preemptive attack" strategy**.

The "preemptive attack" strategy for SAT Reading

- **Attack the passage before it attacks you.** Some test takers try to outsmart the SAT Reading Test by reading the questions first before reading the passage, so they have a "head start." The problem with this strategy is that **it forces you to read inefficiently and incompletely by wasting time on details, thereby putting you at a disadvantage on "main purpose" or "main idea" questions.** If, instead, you read with your attention on **purpose**, **central idea**, and **structure**, you will be more prepared for any reading question the SAT may throw at you.

- **Attack the question before it traps you.** That is, formulate your own answer to each reading question before looking at the answer choices. Some test takers think they are saving time by reading the answer choices immediately after reading each question. The problem with this strategy is that **those who read the answer choices too soon tend to fall for the "traps."**

The "traps" are the wrong answer choices that are included to catch careless readers. They sound plausible because they include words or ideas that remind you of the content of the passage, but they do not answer the question correctly. If, instead, you formulate a reliable answer in mind before reading the choices, you will avoid the traps.

Consider question 9 from Exercise 3:

9. The authors mention "cell phones" and "diplomacy" (line 56) primarily as examples of

A) universally admired commercial products

B) effective means of global communication

C) goods and services based on intellectual resources

D) activities that require little physical strength

This question can easily trip you up if you do not use the preemptive attack strategy. If you try to answer it without understanding the "big picture," you will focus on the sentences in the vicinity of line 56. This paragraph mentions that these are *products and services* (line 55) coming from *Switzerland, Finland, Singapore, and Japan* (lines 51–52), so choice A: *universally coveted commercial products* may seem reasonable. It is also obvious that *cell phones* and *diplomacy* are *effective means of global communication*, so choice B also may seem reasonable. The paragraph also mentions using *physical strength rather than tapping the potential of their brains* (lines 49–50), so choice D may seem reasonable, as well.

But all of those choices are traps.

Instead, attack this question "preemptively." First, read the passage and summarize it in terms of the three key questions: it is a **rhetorical essay** arguing for the **thesis** that *the reason [Homo sapiens won out over the Neanderthals] lies, we suspect, not in being brighter or better able to speak but in our very frailty and our resulting need to exploit our minds.* Then translate question 9 into an open-ended question: *the authors mention "cell phones" and "diplomacy" primarily as examples of* what? If these examples serve the purpose of the essay (which of course they do), then they are examples of how countries also *exploit their minds* rather than relying on natural resources. Therefore the correct answer is C: *goods and services based on intellectual resources*. Notice that choices A, B, and D don't fit at all with the purpose of the paragraph.

Exercise 4

This passage is adapted from Reginald V. Kaplan, "Elements of Explanation." ©2016 College Hill Coaching.

Line   The march of human intellectual progress over the last 2,500 years has been, in brief, a journey from teleological to mechanistic explanations. We have moved, slowly and
5 tortuously, from beliefs about the "purpose" of phenomena like lightning and earthquakes to debates about which theories, equations, and mechanisms best represent them. We've deepened our understandings by strengthening our mode
10 of explanation. But we can't pat ourselves on the back just yet. We are all—even the most scientific among us—still plagued by faulty intuitions.

We are all born teleologists. From the Latin "telos" or "goal," teleology is the act of explaining
15 phenomena in terms of their presumed purposes or desires, rather than their causes: we have brains so we can think, the sun shines so we can be warm, rain falls so we can have fresh water. Such explanations come so easily to us that we
20 find it hard to appreciate how misguided and unhelpful they are. They fail because they can't predict the future as accurately as mechanistic explanations can: the laws of chemistry predict reactions, the laws of fluid dynamics predict
25 tomorrow's weather, and the laws of physics predict when and where our interplanetary probes will land.

Teleological explanations seem intuitive because our consciousness is a constant stream
30 of urge followed by action: we are thirsty so we get some water, we are frightened so we run away, we want to make a friend so we say hello. These urge-action connections are so constant inside of our brains that we fool ourselves into thinking
35 that they apply outside of our brains as well. We program ourselves to mistake urges for causes.

Teleological explanations fail when we try to describe phenomena that are outside of our skulls: rocks do not fall because they want to
40 return to the earth, tornadoes don't form because the sky gods are angry. We know now that rocks and clouds lack the mental machinery required for desire or anger. The real explanations for these phenomena are found in the mechanisms of
45 physics and meteorology.

Still, when a friend asks you why you're not going to a party, you're not going to describe the mechanisms by which your brain processed the information, weighing rational and emotional
50 inputs in various cortical and limbic centers, and produced a decision-response. You're just going to say you don't want to go. In personal conversations, teleological explanations are fine, if crude.
55 Even the most clear-minded scientist slides into teleology from time to time when describing natural phenomena to laypeople. When, in a recent documentary, evolutionary biologist Neil Shubin stated that "to combat the dry air on land,
60 reptiles evolved a new kind of skin" he wasn't disavowing the theory of natural selection and embracing the belief that an animal can evolve a feature just to satisfy a need. He was merely trying to explain something complex in terms we
65 could understand.

The superior accuracy of mechanistic explanations comes at a price. They are not only more complex, but also more unsettling. If I skipped the party because of electro-chemical
70 reactions governed by the laws of physics and chemistry, where is my free will?

We will only continue our progress toward deeper understanding if we see our self-centered intuitions as obstacles rather than guides to
75 our pursuit. If we are to cure diseases, eradicate social scourges, and create a better world, we must embrace the disciplined, if counterintuitive, methods of scientific mechanism.

1

The first paragraph characterizes the "march of human intellectual progress" as

A) halting

B) inspirational

C) misguided

D) controversial

2

The first paragraph is notable primarily for its use of

A) euphemism

B) understatement

C) metaphor

D) anecdote

3

In line 3, "mechanistic" most nearly means

A) unemotional

B) automatic

C) complex

D) scientific

4

To the author, the examples in lines 16–18 ("we have brains . . . fresh water") primarily represent

A) scientific theories

B) beneficial circumstances

C) unsound beliefs

D) unintuitive phenomena

5

The author faults teleological explanations primarily for their

A) imprecision

B) intuitiveness

C) conciseness

D) impenetrability

6

Which choice provides the best evidence for the answer to the previous question?

A) Lines 4–8 ("We have moved . . . represent them")

B) Lines 19–21 ("Such explanations . . . they are")

C) Lines 21–27 ("They fail . . . will land")

D) Lines 28–32 ("Teleological explanations . . . say hello")

7

According to the author, Neil Shubin's error was that he

A) failed to appreciate the education level of his audience

B) confused purpose with cause in a scientific explanation

C) used a complex metaphor to describe a simple concept

D) did not properly define technical terms

8

The main function of the seventh paragraph (lines 66–71) is to

A) concede a drawback

B) propose an alternative

C) address an injustice

D) correct a misunderstanding

9

The tone of the final paragraph (lines 72–78) is best described as

A) beseeching

B) jocular

C) sardonic

D) journalistic

Lesson 10: Play "devil's advocate"

Strong analytical readers use the strategy of "devil's advocate," that is, they **read not just to understand the passage, but to criticize it**. Even if you are absorbed by the discussion, agree with the argument, or identify with the narrative, you will understand and appreciate it more deeply if you take a critical stance.

If the passage is **expository**, ask

How could the descriptions or explanations in this passage be clearer or more effective?

Does the author leave any relevant questions unanswered?

Is the passage logically and effectively organized?

If the passage is **rhetorical**, ask

Did the author address alternate points of view on this subject?

What kind of evidence would weaken this argument or point of view?

What could the author do to make this essay more persuasive?

If the passage is a **narrative**, ask

Is the conflict or struggle indicated clearly?
Are the characterizations effective?
Is the dialogue realistic, given the time, place, and circumstance?

The passage in Exercise 4 is a rhetorical essay, but since the topic is unfamiliar to most readers, it also contains a healthy dose of exposition. Its **rhetorical thesis** is that mechanistic explanations are more reliable, if less intuitive, than teleological explanations. The **expository guiding question** is *What are the two "modes of explanation," and what are they good for?*

So think about the critical questions for expository and rhetorical essays, and apply them to the passage in Exercise 4. How do you think the author did? Were the explanations clear? Was the analysis thorough? Was the passage organized logically? Did the author address alternate points of view? Is there evidence that could weaken its thesis? Could it have been more persuasive?

Consider questions 8 and 9 from Exercise 4:

8. The main function of the seventh paragraph (lines 66–71) is to

   A) concede a drawback

   B) propose an alternative

   C) address an injustice

   D) correct a misunderstanding

9. The tone of the final paragraph (lines 72–78) is best described as

   A) beseeching

   B) jocular

   C) sardonic

   D) journalistic

If you are reading with the "devil's advocate" questions in mind, you should notice that the seventh paragraph plays a special role. It is **acknowledging an alternate point of view**, which is that mechanistic explanations of our own decisions seem to deny the possibility of free will. Therefore, the correct answer to question 8 is A: *concede a drawback.*

Understanding the rhetorical function of the seventh paragraph makes it easier to understand the tone of the final paragraph. Since the author has **conceded a drawback** to his thesis, he must work harder to demonstrate its validity. Therefore, he uses *beseeching* language, like *only . . . if*, and *must*. Therefore, the answer to question 9 is A.

When you keep the critical questions in mind, you sharpen your reading skills by bringing higher-order reasoning to bear. You also hone the analytical skills you need to attack the SAT Essay, which asks you to write a critical analysis of a rhetorical essay.

Lesson 11: Mark up the passage

A great way to maintain your focus on an SAT Reading passage is to mark it up by underlining and annotating. But do it thoughtfully and carefully. Here are some tips for using underlining and annotating as **analytical tools**.

- **Read the entire paragraph** before underlining or annotating. You can't be sure of the overall idea and purpose until you read the entire paragraph.
- **Don't overdo it.** Underlining and annotation should be tools for comprehension, not just ways of keeping track of what you've read. Try to limit yourself to one underlined sentence or one brief note per paragraph.

- **Focus on purpose and central idea.** If you want to underline, underline only the topic sentence. If you want to annotate, note only the purpose and main idea.
- **Circle key abstractions.** Abstractions like *empiricism* and *modernism* are harder to understand than concrete objects or experiences like *hummingbirds* and *football games*. So circle the key abstractions, if only to slow down and think about them. For instance, in Exercise 4, you might circle words like *progress*, *teleological*, and *mechanistic*. If you don't stop and think about these abstractions, you can't understand the passage.

Lesson 12: Learn how to attack the paired passages

The SAT Reading Test will include one set of **paired passages** on a common topic followed by questions in which you will be asked to compare or contrast the perspectives, content, or tone of the passages, such as the following:

- Which of the following best describes the relationship between the two passages?
- On which of the following points would the authors of the two passages most likely disagree?
- On which of the following points would the authors of the two passages most likely agree?
- Which point is made explicitly in Passage 1, but only implicitly in Passage 2?
- The author of Passage 1 would most likely respond to the question in lines 84–85 of Passage 2 by claiming that
- The two passages differ in tone in that, in contrast to Passage 1, Passage 2 is more

Attacking the paired passages

Step 1. Read Passage 1 as you would any other SAT Reading passage, focusing on the three key questions and annotating each paragraph.

Step 2. Once you have finished reading, analyzing, and summarizing Passage 1, go directly to the questions, find any that pertain exclusively to Passage 1, and answer those first.

Step 3. Now read, annotate, and summarize Passage 2, focusing not only on the three key questions, but also on four additional questions:

- Do the passages emphasize different topics? If so, what are they?
- What are the important points of agreement between the two passages?
- What are the important points of disagreement between the two passages?
- How do the two passages differ in tone and attitude?

Exercise 5

Passage 1 is adapted from Teresa Audesirk, Gerald Audesirk, and Bruce E. Byers, Biology: Life on Earth. ©2006 Pearson Education, Inc. Passage 2 is adapted from Sheryl Kmetz, "The Stuff of Life." ©2013 College Hill Coaching.

Passage 1

Line   The study of life on Earth ultimately involves the study of the molecules of which living organisms are composed. How does photosynthesis convert the energy of sunlight into the energy
5   of sugar molecules? What is the structure of the cell membrane, and how does it function in controlling the movement of materials into and out of the cell? How do muscles contract? How do the nerve cells in your brain communicate with
10   one another? What causes cancer? To understand the answers to these questions, you must first learn about energy and matter, the properties of atoms, and how atoms interact with one another to form molecules.

Passage 2

15   The idea that photosynthesis is essential to life has long been fundamental to our understanding of Earth's biosystems. If the sun were to go out, we assumed, life would soon follow. Yet in the 1970s, scientists discovered organisms thriving
20   in deep-sea hydrothermal vents far from any solar energy. These organisms rely on bacteria that harvest energy not from light but from the chemical bonds in sulfides and other molecules in a process called chemosynthesis. Other more
25   complex organisms then incorporate the living bacteria into their tissues. Such relationships mirror the myriad complex relationships we see in the photosynthetic food chain, in which bacteria are incorporated into organisms to
30   provide benefits such as breaking down or synthesizing chemicals that the organisms' own tissues cannot.

1

Which question posed in Passage 1 most directly concerns the author of Passage 2?

A) Lines 3–5 ("How does photosynthesis . . . molecules?")

B) Lines 5–8 ("What is the structure . . . the cell?")

C) Lines 8–10 ("How do the nerve . . . one another?")

D) Line 10 ("What causes cancer?")

2

Both passages are primarily concerned with

A) the complexity of structures in living tissue

B) the origin and evolution of life on Earth

C) the chemical processes that sustain life

D) the symbiotic relationship among species

3

The questions in lines 3–10 represent

A) points of scientific controversy

B) sources of frustration to biologists

C) areas of productive inquiry

D) inspirations for recent innovations

4

The "bacteria" mentioned in line 29 are best regarded as

A) insidious infections

B) exotic parasites

C) symbiotic partners

D) rudimentary progenitors

5

The author of Passage 2 would most likely suggest that the discussion of "life on Earth" (line 1) in Passage 1 also include mention of

A) atypical sources of energy

B) long extinct life forms

C) parasitic relationships among species

D) the human role in preserving biodiversity

6

Which of the following is most representative of the "complex relationships" mentioned in line 27?

A) a species of deciduous tree competing with another species for exposure to sunlight

B) a fungus living within a grass plant that renders the grass more drought resistant

C) a human white blood cell destroying invasive bacteria in an infection

D) a mother bear protecting her cub by charging an intruder

7

In line 18, the phrase "we assumed" suggests that biologists

A) accepted a proposition uncritically

B) adopted a significant social role

C) acquired a new research technique

D) overstepped the boundaries of their expertise

Exercise 6

This passage is from Wassily Kandinsky, Concerning the Spiritual in Art. ©1997 Dover Publications. Reprinted by permission of Dover Publications. In this essay, Kandinsky (1866–1944), a Russian abstract painter, discusses the relationship between Primitivism, a movement to revive the art of ancient peoples, and Materialism, a movement that denies the existence or value of the spiritual realm.

Line Every work of art is the child of its age and, in many cases, the mother of our emotions. It follows that each period of culture produces an art of its own which can never be repeated. Efforts
5 to revive the art-principles of the past will at best produce an art that is stillborn. It is impossible for us to live and feel as did the ancient Greeks. In the same way those who strive to follow the Greek methods in sculpture achieve only a similarity
10 of form, the work remaining soulless for all time. Such imitation is mere aping. Externally the monkey completely resembles the human being; he will sit holding a book in front of his nose, and turn over the pages with a thoughtful aspect, but
15 his actions have for him no real meaning.

There is, however, in art another kind of external similarity that is founded on a fundamental truth. When there is a similarity of inner tendency in the whole moral and spiritual
20 atmosphere, a similarity of ideals, at first closely pursued but later lost to sight, a similarity in the inner feeling of any one period to that of another, the logical result will be a revival of the external forms which served to express those
25 inner feelings in an earlier age. An example of this today is our sympathy, our spiritual relationship, with the Primitives. Like ourselves, these artists sought to express in their work only internal truths, renouncing in consequence all
30 considerations of external form.

This all-important spark of inner life today is at present only a spark. Our minds, which are even now only just awakening after years of materialism, are infected with the despair
35 of unbelief, of lack of purpose and ideal. The nightmare of materialism, which has turned the life of the universe into an evil, useless game, is not yet past. It holds the awakening soul still in its grip. Only a feeble light glimmers like a
40 tiny star in a vast gulf of darkness. This feeble light is but a presentiment, and the soul, when it sees it, trembles in doubt whether the light is not a dream, and the gulf of darkness reality. This doubt and the still-harsh tyranny of the
45 materialistic philosophy divide our soul sharply

from that of the Primitives. Our soul rings cracked when we seem to play upon it, as does a costly vase, long buried in the earth, which is found to have a flaw when it is dug up once more.
50 For this reason, the Primitive phase, through which we are now passing, with its temporary similarity of form, can only be of short duration.

1

The passage is primarily concerned with

A) the obstacles to a particular undertaking

B) the motivation for a specialized practice

C) the origins of a philosophical debate

D) a contrast between ancient and modern techniques

2

In the first sentence, the contrast between "child" and the "mother" is primarily one of

A) immaturity versus maturity

B) creation versus creator

C) disobedience versus supervision

D) joy versus anxiety

3

In line 14, "aspect" most nearly means

A) particular feature

B) individual perspective

C) degree of feeling

D) facial expression

4

Which of the following best exemplifies the "truth" mentioned in line 18?

A) Many great artists find it difficult to achieve renown in their own lifetimes.

B) Painters and musicians from all cultures tend to eschew materialist conventions.

C) Sculptures celebrating the virtue of liberty share common features across eras.

D) It is impossible to faithfully reproduce cave paintings created in prehistoric times.

5

According to the passage, materialism affects artists primarily by

A) awakening them with a glimmer of inspiration

B) establishing their connection to an earlier time

C) denying them access to meaningful and spiritual activity

D) mocking their attempts to make a living from art

6

Which choice provides the best evidence for the answer to the previous question?

A) Lines 27–30 ("Like ourselves . . . external form")

B) Lines 31–32 ("This all-important . . . a spark")

C) Lines 38–39 ("It holds . . . grip")

D) Lines 46–49 ("Our soul rings . . . once more")

7

The author uses the phrase "trembles in doubt" (line 42) in order to emphasize his belief that

A) philosophers are unsure about the meaning of materialism

B) true artists question whether the era of materialism is truly past

C) highly creative people have only a tenuous grip on reality

D) artists are particularly susceptible to feelings of fear and obsession

8

In line 48, the "costly vase" represents

A) a materialistic aspiration

B) a finely crafted piece of art

C) a cynical attempt at forgery

D) an irretrievable frame of mind

CHAPTER 4 ANSWER KEY

Exercise 1

1. **C**   The thesis of the passage is that *[w]ithout some appreciation of common large numbers and a feeling for probabilities, we will overreact to some dangers and underreact to others.* In other words, there is some danger inherent in our *common misunderstandings about statistical data.*

2. **B**   The author regards these "reports" with *informed incredulity* because he has good reason to believe they are not accurate. He expresses this fact when he suggests that we should regard them with *skepticism* (lines 2–3). (There are only about 74 million kids in the U.S., so if 1 million kids were kidnapped every year, then about 6 kids would be kidnapped from the average American elementary school *every year.*)

3. **A**   The list of activities in lines 21–25 are dangerous events that are more probable than terrorism. Therefore, they are *underappreciated dangers.*

4. **A**   *Ad hominem* is personal attack. Although the passage criticizes widespread innumeracy, at no point does the author attack anyone personally. Choice B is incorrect because the author uses verifiable statistics liberally in the first, second, third, and sixth paragraphs. Choice C is incorrect because the joke described in the fourth paragraph is an *amusing illustration*. Choice D is incorrect because the passage makes a *social assessment* in lines 32–34 when he states that *[t]his tendency to personalize is a characteristic of many who suffer from innumeracy*, and again in lines 51–52 when he states that *we too often lack an intuitive grasp for these numbers.*

5. **D**   The author states that *the innumerate will inevitably respond with the non sequitur, "Yes, but what if you're that one," and then nod knowingly, as if they've demolished your argument with penetrating insight* (lines 28–32). In other words, the *penetrating insight* is really not *penetrating* at all: it is a *non sequitur* (a statement that does not follow logically from the premises). The author is using the word *penetrating* ironically and sarcastically. Choice A is incorrect, because the author is not using the word *penetrating* to make the insight seem more positive than it is. In fact, he is criticizing, not euphemizing. Choice B is incorrect because the author is not using exaggeration for rhetorical effect. Choice C is incorrect because *penetrating* is not intended as an *acclamation* (word of praise).

6. **D**   When the author uses the phrase *this tendency to personalize*, he is referring to the *non sequitur* in the previous sentence: *"Yes, but what if you're that one,"* which is an attempt to individualize the horror of terrorism out of the context in which its probability is calculated.

7. **B**   The third paragraph (lines 26–38) discusses the tendency of people to overestimate the chances of certain horrific event precisely because they are exotic and attention-grabbing. The *exotic malady* is mentioned as one such *risk that is wildly overestimated.*

8. **A**   The first sentence of the passage provides direct evidence that the author believes that people commonly overestimate particular risks, such as *reports that more than a million American kids are kidnapped each year.*

9. **C**   The final paragraph mentions Drs. Kronlund and Phillips because their study *showed that most doctors' assessments of the risks of various operations, procedures, and medications were way off the mark*. In other words, they were *fallible* (capable of error) with regard to their own specialties.

Exercise 2

1. **C**   Lines 5–7 list the following examples: *frogs appeared to arise from damp earth, mice from putrefied matter, insects from dew, and maggots from decaying meat.* In line 1, the author indicates that these are things that *people commonly believed* in ancient times. But the passage then goes on to explain that these beliefs were mistaken, and that life in fact does not arise that way.

2. **C**   In lines 21–23, the author states that *in fact, living organisms cannot so easily arise from nonliving matter.* Notice that this is a clear, direct statement that the author regards the beliefs listed in lines 5–7 as *faulty conclusions*. Therefore, the correct answer to question 2 is C. Choice A is incorrect because lines 1–4 simply state that ancient people believed these things, not that the author disagrees. Choice B is incorrect because lines 7–10 just give details about these beliefs, but no indication that the author doesn't share them. Choice D is incorrect because lines 30–33 just give a detail about Pasteur's experiment, and no direct indication that the author disagrees with the list of beliefs.

3. **A**   Lines 21–40 describe Pasteur's experiment, in which he demonstrates that *living organisms*

cannot so easily arise spontaneously from nonliving matter, and that the mice in van Helmont's demonstration likely *crept into the jar.* In other words, van Helmont's recipe lacked scientific controls to keep living things out.

4. **D** When Pasteur said, *"Never will the doctrine of spontaneous generation arise from this mortal blow,"* he meant that the doctrine is as dead as an opponent who has been struck with a sword. Therefore, in this context, *mortal* means "fatal."

5. **B** The final paragraph describes how Pasteur *wasn't entirely correct* about the possibility of life arising from nonliving matter by describing the most likely scenario by which *basic self-replicating units,* the precursors of life, could have arisen from nonliving molecules in the *chemical-rich cauldron of early Earth.*

6. **D** The phrase *very basic self-replicating units* refers to the most *rudimentary* chemical building blocks of life.

7. **D** The point of this paragraph is that the earliest life most likely arose from the *chemical-rich cauldron of early Earth.* In other words, the author describes a *chaotic* world. He is not portraying early earth as *mysterious,* because he is claiming to understand important aspects of that ancient environment. He is also not portraying the early earth as *perilous,* because no creatures yet existed to suffer its dangers.

8. **B** The passage begins by describing the *common belief* that *new life could arise . . . by spontaneous generation from nonliving material* then presents evidence, in the form of Pasteur's experiment, that refutes that belief.

Exercise 3

1. **C** In saying that *[e]qual certainty exists among those [scientists] who study the base of their skulls that [Neanderthals] did [lack the long vocal chamber needed for speech] and that they did not,* the author is saying that there is considerable disagreement about the vocal abilities of Neanderthals.

2. **B** The main thesis of this passage is that humans came to dominate the Neanderthals by taking advantage of their intellectual abilities rather than relying on their physical strength. This directly implies that *physical weakness is not necessarily a disadvantage in the fight for survival.*

3. **D** In lines 43–47, the authors state their main thesis: *The reason we—anatomically modern humans—won out lies, we suspect, not in being brighter or better able to speak but in our very physical frailty and our resulting need to exploit our minds.* Choice A is incorrect because this sentence

merely states that scientists disagree about the length of the Neanderthal vocal chamber. Choice B is incorrect because this sentence merely states that hunters sometimes find it helpful to communicate silently. Choice C is incorrect because this sentence merely states that the ability to speak cannot explain our dominance over the Neanderthals.

4. **B** The solid lines in the diagram indicate that *H. sapiens* (which includes the *Cro-Magnon*) descended from *H. heidelbergensis,* which descended from *H. erectus,* which descended from *H. habilis,* which descended from *A. afarensis.* Therefore, the *Cro-Magnon* and *H. heidelbergensis* both share *A. afarensis* as a common ancestor. Choice A is incorrect because the diagram shows no line of descent from *H. neanderthalensis* to *H. sapiens.* Choice C is incorrect because the diagram contains no information about the reasons for extinction. Choice D is incorrect because there is no line of descent from *H. habilis* to *A. robustus.*

5. **C** In the diagram, the longest vertical bar for any hominid species is that for *H. erectus,* which begins at about the 2-million-year mark and ends at about the 250,000-year mark. Subtracting these two values gives us a time span of about 1,750,000 years.

6. **C** Although statements A and D are both valid conclusions based on the information in the diagram, neither of these facts supports the main thesis of the passage, which is found in lines 43–47: *The reason we—anatomically modern humans—won out [in our competition with the Neanderthals] lies, we suspect, not in being brighter or better able to speak but in our very physical frailty and our resulting need to exploit our minds.* Therefore, the argument rests on the fact that *H. sapiens* coexisted with *H. neanderthalensis.* The diagram clearly shows that both species lived in the period between approximately 100,000 years ago and 40,000 years ago, and so could have been in direct competition. It also shows that *H. neanderthalensis* appears to have gone extinct, because its vertical bar does not reach all the way up to the 0 mark.

7. **D** The author mentions that *hunter-gatherers use sophisticated sign language* to provide evidence that speech is not necessary for success in hunting, and that therefore *long vocal chambers might not provide a decisive evolutionary advantage.*

8. **A** In saying that Neanderthals *could survive with their physical strength rather than tapping the potential of their brains,* the authors are saying that, unlike *Homo sapiens,* the Neanderthals did not need to *exploit* (take advantage of) their intelligence.

9. **C** These are examples of how countries *exploit their minds* rather than relying on natural

resources to compete with other nations economically. Therefore, the correct answer is C: *goods and services based on intellectual resources*. Notice that choices A, B, and D don't fit at all with the overall purpose of the paragraph.

Exercise 4

1. **A** The first paragraph states that the we have moved *slowly and tortuously* toward *strengthening our mode of explanation*. In other words, that the *march of human intellectual progress* has not been steady and direct, and that indeed we are still *plagued by faulty intuitions*. In other words, this progress has been *halting* (slow and hesitant).

2. **C** The first paragraph describes human intellectual progress with the metaphor of a *march*. It does not employ any *euphemism* (a word or phrase used to make something unpleasant sound less so), *understatement* (phrasing that makes something seem less intense than it is), or *anecdote* (illustrative story).

3. **D** The main idea of the passage is that *mechanistic* explanations are those *theories, equations, and mechanisms[that] best represent* physical phenomena. These are the *scientific* modes of explanation.

4. **C** The statements listed in line 16–18 are examples of *explaining phenomena in terms of their presumed purposes or desires, rather than their causes*. The passage as a whole explains how such *teleological* explanations are in fact *misguided and unhelpful* (lines 20–21). Therefore, these are *unsound beliefs*.

5. **A** The problem with teleological explanations, according to the author, is that they *can't predict the future as accurately as mechanistic explanations can* (lines 21–23). Therefore, they are *imprecise* in this regard.

6. **C** The author explains the *imprecision* of teleological explanations in lines 21–27, where he states that they *can't predict the future as accurately as mechanistic explanations can*.

7. **B** Neil Shubin is mentioned as an example of a *clear-minded scientist [who] slides into teleology from time to time when describing natural phenomena to laypeople* (lines 55–57). That is, he is *confusing purpose with cause in a scientific explanation*.

8. **A** The purpose of this paragraph is to acknowledge the *drawback* that mechanistic explanations of our own decisions seem to deny the possibility of free will, which is something that most people consider precious.

9. **A** Since the author has conceded a drawback to his thesis in his previous paragraph, this paragraph uses *beseeching* language, like *only . . . if*, and *must* to make a plea to the reader to reject teleological explanations.

Exercise 5

1. **A** Passage 2 is primarily concerned with the chemical reactions that harness energy to sustain life, specifically *photosynthesis* (line 15) and *chemosynthesis* (line 24). Therefore the question *How does photosynthesis convert the energy of sunlight into the energy of sugar molecules?* is most directly relevant to Passage 2.

2. **C** Passage 1 focuses on *the study of the molecules of which living things are composed* (lines 1–3) and how those molecules convert energy, make muscles contract, help nerve cells communicate, and so on. Passage 2 focuses on the chemical reactions that harness energy to sustain life. Therefore, both passages are primarily concerned with *the chemical processes that sustain life*.

3. **C** This list of questions represent some of the questions that guide *the study of the molecules of which living organisms are composed* (lines 1–3), therefore they are *areas of productive inquiry*. Passage 1 does not discuss any scientific controversies, innovations, or sources of frustration.

4. **C** The bacteria mentioned in line 29 are *incorporated into organisms to provide benefits*. This is a *symbiotic* relationship, in which both organisms benefit. These bacteria are not *infections* or *parasites*, because they are not doing harm, and they are not *progenitors*, because they are not the original ancestors of a species or kind.

5. **A** Since Passage 2 is focused on the recent discovery of a new way by which living organisms on Earth can harvest energy, namely chemosynthesis, its author would likely suggest that the study of life on earth include research into *atypical sources of energy*.

6. **B** The *complex relationships* mentioned in line 27 are those *in which bacteria are incorporated into organisms to provide benefits*. The choice that best resembles such a relationship is *a fungus living within a grass plant that renders the grass more drought resistant*.

7. **A** The phrase *we assumed* in line 18 refers to the belief among biologists that solar energy is required to sustain life on Earth. In other words, they accepted this proposition *uncritically*, and, it turns out, erroneously.

Exercise 6

1. **A** This rhetorical essay focus on the author's thesis that *the Primitive phase . . . can only be of short duration* (lines 50–52). The first paragraph explains how an attempt *to revive the art-principles of the past will at best produce an art that is stillborn* (lines 5–6), the second paragraph gives

a glimmer of hope to the Primitivists by stating that our *spiritual relationship with the Primitives* (lines 26–27) may lead to a *revival of the external forms* (lines 23–24). The last paragraph describes the obstacle that materialism places in the way of the Primitivist movement. Therefore, as a whole, the passage is concerned with *the obstacles to a particular undertaking.*

2. **B** The statement *every work of art is the child of its age and, in many cases, the mother of our emotions* means that art derives from the culture in which its created, and in turn forms our emotional response to that culture. Therefore the metaphor is one of *creation versus creator.*

3. **D** The phrase *thoughtful aspect* is used to describe the face of a monkey that is acting as if it is reading but really is not. That is, he has a *thoughtful facial expression*, but is not really thinking.

4. **C** The *fundamental truth* described in the second paragraph is that *when there is a similarity . . . in the spiritual atmosphere, a similarity of ideals . . . the logical result will be a revival of the external forms which served to express those feelings.* In other words, the art forms will be similar if the cultural feelings are similar. This suggests that *sculptures celebrating the virtue of liberty share common features across eras.*

5. **C** The passage states that *[o]ur minds . . . are infected with the despair of unbelief, of lack of purpose and ideal* (lines 32–35) because of the *nightmare of materialism* (line 36). Therefore the effect of materialism is to *deny [artists] access to meaningful and spiritual activity.*

6. **C** The best evidence for this answer comes in lines 38–39, where the author states that *[materialism] holds the awakening soul still in it its grip.*

7. **B** The last paragraph uses the metaphor of a *feeble light* to represent the awakening soul of the artist, and the *darkness* to represent the *nightmare of materialism,* so when the author states that the soul *trembles in doubt whether the light is not a dream,* he is saying that artists are wondering whether their artistic ideals can survive the era of materialism.

8. **D** The *costly vase* is compared to the beleaguered artist's soul, which *is found to have a flaw when it is dug up once more.* In other words, the principles and ideals of primitive art cannot be completely recovered, and so the primitive *frame of mind* is *irretrievable.*

CHAPTER 5

THE SAT WRITING AND LANGUAGE TEST

1.	Writing and Language Question Types	197
2.	Parsing Sentences	199
3.	Trimming Sentences	200
4.	Verb Agreement	202
5.	Developing and Coordinating Ideas	204
6.	Transitions and References	207
7.	Parallelism	210
8.	Coordinating Modifiers	213
9.	Using Modifiers Logically	216
10.	Making Comparisons	219
11.	Pronoun Agreement	221
12.	Pronoun Case	223
13.	Verb Tense and Aspect	225
14.	Diction and Redundancy	229
15.	Idiomatic Expression	233
16.	The Active and Passive Voices	235
17.	Verb Mood	236
18.	Punctuation	239

What is the SAT Writing and Language Test?

The second section of the SAT is the Writing and Language Test, a 35-minute, 44-question multiple-choice test that is, according to the College Board, designed to assess your

> *proficiency in revising and editing of a range of texts in a variety of content areas, both academic and career-related, for expression of ideas and for conformity to the conventions of Standard Written English grammar, usage, and punctuation.*

The Writing and Language Test consists of four passages, each 400–450 words long, in four categories: careers, social studies, humanities, and science. (For an example of the Writing and Language Test, look at Section 2 of the Diagnostic SAT in Chapter 2.) You are asked to analyze underlined portions of each passage and determine whether they need to be revised according to the standards of

- clear expression
- verb, modifier, and pronoun agreement
- standard idiomatic expression
- logical diction
- verb tense, mood, and voice
- logical transitions
- coordination and development of ideas
- stylistic consistency
- punctuation

How is the Writing and Language Test used?

Colleges use your SAT Writing and Language Test score as a measure of your ability to write clearly and effectively according to the rules of Standard Written English. Good writing and editing skills are essential to success in the liberal arts and sciences, so most colleges expect you to develop proficiency in those areas.

The Writing and Language Test is scored on a scale from 10 to 40. It is added to your Reading Test score and the sum of these scores is multiplied by 10 to give your Reading and Writing score, which ranges from 200 to 800.

Sound intimidating? It's not.

If you just take the time to master the 18 lessons and complete the 15 exercise sets in this chapter, you will be ready for anything the SAT Writing and Language Test can throw at you.

Lesson 1: Writing and Language Question Types

Writing and Language Test Questions

Questions on the SAT Writing and Language Test ask you to consider the **clarity, grammar, coherence**, or **style** of an underlined portion of a passage, and make any necessary changes to improve it. They focus more on the **clear expression of ideas** than on obscure grammar rules.

Clarity Questions

Clarity questions ask whether a phrasing conveys an idea clearly and precisely. You must use your reading skills and language sense to understand what the writer is trying to say—even if the phrasing is awkward and unclear—and to clarify the writer's idea when necessary.

In fact, nothing that we observe in our physical world—not the moon, not a beach ball, not even a water droplet— **24** complies perfectly with the mathematical definition of a sphere.

24

A)   NO CHANGE

B)   overlaps perfectly with

C)   corresponds perfectly to

D)   concurs perfectly on

This sentence is trying to express the relationship between the real world and the abstract world of mathematical definitions, but *complies* doesn't quite fit because it means *acts in accordance with a wish, command, or regulation*, and a mathematical definition is none of those. Also, *overlaps* doesn't work, because it means *extends over so as to cover partly*, and this idea does not apply to the relationship between the real world and an abstraction. Finally, *concurs* doesn't work because it means *is of the same opinion*, but mathematical definitions don't have opinions. The best choice is C because it makes sense to say that a situation does or does not *correspond to* a definition.

Grammar and Usage Questions

Grammar and usage questions ask whether a word or phrase obeys the rules of Standard Written English. They require you to understand the rules of verb and pronoun agreement, punctuation, mood, voice, syntax, coordination, and idiom. If that sounds scary—or if you haven't received much instruction in these rules—don't worry. We will cover all of them in the lessons to follow.

As the American population grows, ages, and gains better access to affordable health care insurance, the demand for primary medical services are expected to skyrocket.

1

A)   NO CHANGE

B)   is

C)   has been

D)   would be

In the original phrasing, the verb *are* does not **agree in number** (Lesson 4) with the singular subject *demand*. All of the other choices correspond to a singular subject, but only choice B works in this context. Choice C is incorrect because the **present perfect** (Lesson 13) form, *has been*, implies that a previous event extends a consequence to the present, but the sentence is about an *ongoing* and *future* state of affairs. Choice D is incorrect because the **subjunctive mood** (Lesson 17), *would be*, implies a hypothetical or counterfactual statement, but this sentence is making a factual claim.

Coherence and Development Questions

Coherence and development questions ask you to pay attention to the logical flow of the passage from phrase to phrase, sentence to sentence, and paragraph to paragraph, as well as how the ideas in a passage relate to the main idea.

Pay attention when the sentences or paragraphs in a passage are **numbered**. This numbering means you will be asked about the logical flow and coherence of the passage, for example whether the sentences in a paragraph should be **rearranged**, where a given sentence should be **inserted**, or whether a given sentence should be **deleted**.

18 Montessori dedicated herself to traveling the world and preaching the benefits of child-centered education. In the 25 years after their founding, Montessori schools were regarded as a remedy to the educational problems associated with rapid urban population growth throughout Europe. However, as fascism began to proliferate in the 1930s throughout Spain, Italy, and Germany, child-centered education came to be seen as a threat to the power of the state. In 1933, the totalitarian regimes in Italy and Germany closed all Montessori schools and declared them subversive.

18

Which choice provides the most effective introduction to the paragraph?

A) NO CHANGE

B) Montessori's first school enrolled 50 students from poor working class families.

C) Montessori did not have a particularly nurturing relationship with her own son, Mario, who was raised by another family.

D) As the Montessori method was gaining a foothold, Europe was undergoing dramatic social and political change.

Choice A is a poor introduction because it indicates a fact that is not developed in the rest of the paragraph. The only appropriate option is choice D, since the paragraph is about how the growth of fascism in Europe affected Montessori schools. Choice B is incorrect because the paragraph is not about the first Montessori school. Choice C is incorrect because the paragraph is not about Montessori's personal family relationships.

Style Questions

Style questions ask whether a word, phrase, or sentence is consistent in style and pattern with other elements of the passage.

Don't be surprised when you don't hit your goal on the first try. You need to fail to succeed. And although you should ask for help when you need it, don't whine about your failures and setbacks. **22** If one cannot learn to process failure with dignity, any ultimate victory is less honorable.

22

Which choice best maintains the stylistic pattern of the previous sentences?

A) NO CHANGE

B) You can't have a pity party and a victory party at the same time.

C) Self-pity is not conducive to success in either the short or long term.

D) The honor of one's victory is measured by the dignity with which it is met.

The question asks you to focus on **style** more than **content**. The style of the first two sentences is **imperative, informal**, and **aphoristic**. That is, they directly command the reader with simple, pithy instructions. Choice A, however, is **indirect, formal**, and **abstract**. It uses the **formal third person** pronoun *one*, which breaks from the use of the **second person** *you* in the rest of the paragraph. Choice C breaks the pattern of addressing the reader directly, and a word like *conducive* is overly formal. Choice D also is too abstract and formal to fit the pattern. The best choice is therefore B, which maintains the tone and style of a snappy dictum with a second-person subject.

Lesson 2: Parsing Sentences

What Is Parsing?

Good writers know how sentences work. They can take every sentence apart and examine how its essential components—**clauses**, **verbs**, **subjects**, **objects**, **punctuation**, **conjunctions**, and **modifiers**—work together to convey one or more clear ideas. This task is called **parsing**.

To ace the SAT Writing and Language Test, and to become a better writer, you must learn how to parse your sentences into their clauses. A **clause** is any phrase that conveys a complete idea. It must contain a **subject**, a **verb**, and any necessary **verb complements**, like objects or predicate adjectives.

Sentences and Their Clauses

Every sentence consists of one or more clauses. Let's look at two sentences—one simple and one complicated—and parse them into their clauses.

Sentence 1: *Go!* This is the simplest sentence in the English language. It consists of just a single verb, *go*, and an implied subject, *you*. That's all we need to convey an idea. In this case, the idea is a command to leave.

Independent clauses are phrases that **can stand on their own as sentences** because they contain a **subject**, a **verb**, and any necessary **verb complements**, and convey a complete thought.

Dependent clauses are phrases that include a **subject**, a **verb**, and any necessary **verb complements**, but **cannot stand on their own as sentences** because they include elements that depend on **other** clauses.

For instance, in the sentence

Although we were tired, we kept going.

the phrase before the comma is a **dependent clause**, and the phrase after the comma is an **independent clause**. The first clause depends on the second one because it includes the word *although*.

Sentence 2: *Generally regarded as the most daunting course in the undergraduate science curriculum,* Introduction to Organic Chemistry *not only provides a necessary foundation in the principles of physical chemistry, but also introduces students to important experimental methods at the heart of modern medical research.*

This sentence is more complicated, because it conveys *three* ideas: two main ideas and one secondary idea.

Main idea 1:	Introduction to Organic Chemistry *provides a necessary foundation in the principles of physical chemistry.*
Main idea 2:	Introduction to Organic Chemistry *introduces students to important experimental methods at the heart of modern medical research.*
Secondary idea:	[Introduction to Organic Chemistry is] generally regarded as the most daunting course in the undergraduate science curriculum.

These three ideas are **coordinated** within the sentence to clarify the relationships among them. The two main ideas are conveyed in independent clauses—that is, they could stand alone as **independent sentences**—while the secondary idea is conveyed in a **dependent clause** (which can't stand on its own as a sentence). The phrase *not only...but also* shows that the two main ideas express supporting facts.

Lesson 3: Trimming Sentences

The Law of Trimming

Every sentence must convey a clear and coherent idea even after it has been "trimmed."

Trimming means eliminating modifiers and modifying phrases from a sentence to see its **core**—the **subject**, **verb**, and any necessary **verb complements** of each clause. Once you've trimmed a sentence, it's much easier to pinpoint any problems in grammar, logic, or clarity.

Trimming involves three steps:

1. Eliminate any nonessential **prepositional phrases**.
2. Eliminate introductory, interrupting, or concluding **modifying phrases**.
3. Eliminate any remaining **nonessential modifiers** like adjectives and adverbs.

Prepositional Phrases

A **preposition** is any word—such as *up, to, around, from, into, by, on, for, of, as,* or *with*—that can be used to complete sentences like these:

> *The squirrel ran _____ the tree.*
> *Democracy is government _____ the people.*
> *I went to the party _____ a brain surgeon.*

A **prepositional phrase** consists of a preposition plus the **noun phrase** that follows it, such as

> *...from sea to shining sea...*
> *...in the beginning...*
> *...for the money...*

Modifying Phrases

Modifying phrases, which include **participial phrases** (Lesson 8), **appositive phrases** (Lesson 8), **adjectival** phrases, and **adverbial phrases**, are typically separated from the main clause by commas or dashes.

> *As luck would have it, we were saved at the last minute.*
> *We were saved—as luck would have it—at the last minute.*
> *We were saved at the last minute, as luck would have it.*

Nonessential Modifiers

Nonessential modifiers are **adjectives** or **adverbs** that are not essential to conveying the central idea of the clause.

> *I have a terrible headache.*
> *She ran quickly from the house.*

Essential Modifiers

One type of *essential* modifier is the **predicate adjective**, which is tied to the subject by a **linking verb**. Predicate adjectives should not be trimmed because they are essential to conveying the core idea of the clause.

> *The sky is blue.*

Prepositional phrases are also sometimes essential.

> *The cake is in the oven.*

Trimming sentences helps you to eliminate clutter so you can better analyze the essential parts of the sentence.

Untrimmed sentence:	*In one experiment in which subjects performed a word association task, scientists measured the activity in the region of the brain called the aSTG.*
Core:	*Scientists measured the activity.*

Exercise Set 1: Sentence Cores

1

The team of advisors, arriving slightly ahead of schedule, <u>were</u> met at the airport by the Deputy Prime Minister.

A) NO CHANGE

B) were being

C) was

D) being

2

Today, juggling the demands of family and work often <u>seem</u> too difficult for many young professionals.

A) NO CHANGE

B) seems

C) will seem

D) would seem

3

The fact that even well-intentioned institutions can so easily become dysfunctional <u>have forced</u> many observers to become cynical about social change.

A) NO CHANGE

B) would force

C) has forced

D) are forcing

4

The Immigrant Defense Project, based in New York City, <u>provide</u> expert legal advice and advocacy for immigrants and their loved ones.

A) NO CHANGE

B) have provided

C) provides

D) have been providing

5

The intensity of these workouts, which include both agility circuits and weight training, <u>are a problem</u> for many who are not already in good shape.

A) NO CHANGE

B) are problems

C) are problematic

D) is a problem

6

The anthology focuses on the works of modern poets, <u>but includes</u> some older works as well.

A) NO CHANGE

B) includes

C) but include

D) include

7

The theory of quantum electrodynamics, although maddeningly counterintuitive, <u>makes</u> astonishingly accurate predictions about the behavior of subatomic particles.

A) NO CHANGE

B) making

C) would make

D) make

8

Surprisingly absent from the game <u>were the crowds</u> traditional routine of taunting the opposing players.

A) NO CHANGE

B) was the crowds

C) were the crowd's

D) was the crowd's

9

An education at an inexpensive public university can be <u>as good, if not better, than</u> an elite private college.

A) NO CHANGE

B) as good as, if not better than, one at

C) as good as, if not better than,

D) as good, if not better, than one at

Lesson 4: Verb Agreement

Subject-Verb Agreement

> After you've trimmed the sentence, ask: **does every verb agree with its subject?** For instance, in the sentence *My favorite team are losing*, the verb disagrees with its subject in **number**: since *team* is a singular subject, *are* should be changed to *is*. Subject-verb agreement problems often show up when sentences have **tricky subjects** or **inverted syntax**.

Tricky Subjects

> The phenomena studied by climate scientists **32** is of interest to the entire planet.
>
> **32**
>
> A) NO CHANGE
> B) has been
> C) are
> D) being

The correct answer is C because the subject, *phenomena*, is the plural of *phenomenon*. Some Latin-derived words have tricky plurals, for instance *bacterium/bacteria*, *continuum/continua*, *criterion/criteria*, *curriculum/curricula*, *datum/data*, and *medium/media*.

> Neither of the books **15** are appropriate for a fourth-grade class.
>
> **15**
>
> A) NO CHANGE
> B) is
> C) have been
> D) being

The correct answer is B because the subject is not *books*, but *neither*, which is singular. Notice that the phrase *of the books* is a prepositional phrase, so it can be trimmed.

Inverted Syntax

> Some sentences have an **inverted** syntax: the subject comes *after* the verb, making it a bit tricky to see whether they agree. It often helps to "un-invert" these sentences by **removing any "dummy subjects" and rearranging the remaining phrases**.

> Behind every Portiello sculpture **12** lies countless hours of work.
>
> **12**
>
> A) NO CHANGE
> B) lie
> C) laid
> D) lain

The correct answer is B, because the subject of the sentence is *hours*, which is plural. This one is hard to catch because the sentence is inverted. You can "un-invert" the sentence by just swapping the phrases on either side of the verb: *Countless hours of work lie behind every Portiello sculpture*. Notice that *sculpture* cannot be the subject of the verb because it is the **object** of the prepositional phrase *behind every Portiello sculpture*.

> Last year, there **19** was nearly fifty applications submitted for every seat in the first-year class.
>
> **19**
>
> A) NO CHANGE
> B) would be
> C) were
> D) has been

The correct answer is C, because the subject of the sentence is the plural *applications*. Again, this sentence is inverted, and the "un-inverted" version is *Last year, nearly fifty applications were submitted for every seat in the first-year class*. Notice that every word in the original sentence is accounted for, except for *there*, which is a **dummy subject**.

Exercise Set 2: Verb Agreement

1

Just as dusk was settling on the pond, the flock of geese <u>scattered</u> by a shotgun blast.

A) NO CHANGE

B) were scattered

C) was scattered

D) was scattering

2

In every teaspoon of topsoil <u>is</u> over two million microorganisms, forming a highly complex ecosystem.

A) NO CHANGE

B) was

C) are

D) being

3

How important <u>should</u> strength conditioning to a marathon training regimen?

A) NO CHANGE

B) are

C) is

D) would

4

This technology, <u>developed</u> by the American military for field communications, has become essential to many private industries as well.

A) NO CHANGE

B) was developed

C) was being developed

D) having developed

5

The committee agreed that the new principal should both inspire students and <u>should maintain</u> a rigorous academic culture.

A) NO CHANGE

B) should also maintain

C) also maintain

D) maintain

6

The labor coalition, which consists of representatives from all of the skilled worker unions, <u>have expressed concern in</u> the new hiring policies.

A) NO CHANGE

B) has expressed concern about

C) have expressed concern with

D) has expressed concern with

7

The explosiveness of political revelations in the book <u>explain why it is selling at such a feverish pace</u>.

A) NO CHANGE

B) explains why it is selling at such a feverish pace

C) explain the feverish pace of it's sales

D) explains why its selling at such a feverish pace

8

<u>S. J. Perelman's absurdist and florid writing style</u> is regarded as one of America's greatest humorists.

A) NO CHANGE

B) The absurdist and florid writing style of S. J. Perelman

C) S. J. Perelman, whose writing is characterized by an absurdist and florid style,

D) S. J. Perelman and his absurdist and florid writing style

9

Grizzlies rarely attack humans, but they will protect their territory from anyone they <u>would have regarded</u> as a threat.

A) NO CHANGE

B) regarded

C) had regarded

D) regard

Lesson 5: Developing and Coordinating Ideas

Paragraph Cohesiveness

Every good paragraph must be **focused, logical, and consistent**. It should focus on a single main idea, develop any necessary aspects of that idea, and avoid irrelevancies. Many SAT Writing and Language questions ask you to address problems with **cohesiveness**.

One natural gas extraction technique, hydraulic fracturing or "fracking," continues to spark debate. Opponents suggest that the high-pressure fluid used to fracture deep rock formations may release carcinogens such as radon into groundwater supplies and that fracking can induce earthquakes. Supporters, on the other hand, counter that this activity is taking place well below even the deepest aquifers and is sealed off from public water supplies. **30** <u>Earthquakes, also known as seismic tremors, are notoriously difficult to predict.</u>

30

Which choice best develops the main idea of the paragraph?

A) NO CHANGE

B) Seismologists have been studying such human-induced seismic activity for may years.

C) Most of these supporters have financial ties to the industry.

D) Further, any seismic activity fracking induces is minuscule, since the rock fractures it creates are tiny.

The correct answer is D. The first sentence of the paragraph establishes that the central idea is the debate sparked by fracking. The second sentence specifies two objections to fracking made by its opponents. The third sentence specifies a counterpoint to this first objection, but not to the second one. If the paragraph is to continue developing its main idea, therefore, it should specify a counterpoint to the second objection, as in choice D. The other choices are incorrect because they depart from the central purpose of the paragraph, which is to describe the substantive points on both sides of the fracking debate.

Coordinating Style

Pay attention to the **consistency of style** within and between paragraphs. Although individual sentences should vary in content, length, and structure as needed, they should nevertheless maintain a consistent style, unless a shift in style serves a clear purpose.

When you make a decision, you can never be fully aware of the millions of little chemical and electrical reactions in your brain that have nudged you toward that choice. But even if somehow you could be, you could never say that you *chose* any of those reactions. They are beyond your control. **18** <u>So how can we ever really say that we "make" our own decisions?</u> What you call your free will may not be so free after all.

18

Which change to this sentence best maintains the stylistic cohesiveness of the paragraph?

A) Change "So" to "But."

B) Omit "really."

C) Change "we" to "you" and "our" to "your."

D) Omit "that."

This question asks you to focus on **style** rather than logic. (Of course, the logic has to work, too.) Choice C is best because the rest of the paragraph is written in the **second person** (*you* and *your*). Using first person plural pronouns (*we* and *our*) in this sentence doesn't violate any rule of grammar or logic, but it does disrupt the style of the paragraph as a whole.

Coordinating Ideas within Sentences

A sentence with multiple ideas must use proper phrasing to indicate the **importance** and **logical relationship** of those ideas. The main idea should be expressed in the **main independent clause**, and secondary ideas are usually conveyed with **dependent clauses** or with **modifiers** or **modifying phrases**. The logical relationships among ideas are usually conveyed with **logical conjunctions or adverbs** such as *because, therefore,* and *however.*

28 We are not the customers; we are the product in this transaction, even when we subscribe to a newspaper or website. We are an audience being sold to advertisers, and our attention must be maintained and manipulated regardless of our needs and wants.

28

A) NO CHANGE

B) In this transaction, we are the product and not the customers, even when we subscribe to a newspaper or website.

C) We are the product in this transaction, even when we subscribe to a newspaper or website, not the customers.

D) Even when we subscribe to a newspaper or website, we are not the customers in this transaction, but the product.

In choices A, B, and C, the reference to *this transaction* is not clear, because in each case this phrase precedes the referent clause, *we subscribe to a newspaper or website*. (The *transaction* is the act of subscribing, a fact that is clear only if the reference to subscribing comes before the reference to the transaction.) Only choice D arranges the clauses to make this reference clear. Also, the sequencing of the clauses in choice D emphasizes the ironic relationship between them: it should surprise us to know that we are not the customers *even when* we are paying for a service. Lastly, the concluding phrase in choice D, *but the product*, sets up the following sentence, which explains how we are *the product*.

Coordinating with Punctuation

When coordinating ideas within a sentence, you often have to decide whether and how to use **commas, semicolons,** and **colons**. Here are three rules to remember:

- When combining independent clauses with a **comma**, you must also use a **logical conjunction**. Leaving out this conjunction is a mistake called a **comma splice**. For instance, you can't write *We had a great time, T.J. played his guitar*, but you can write *We had a great time, but T.J. played his guitar*.

- You can join two independent clauses with a **semicolon**, but only if the clauses support, but don't explain, each another. For instance: *We were having a great time; T.J. played his guitar.*

- You can join two independent clauses with a **colon**, but only if the second clause **explains** the first. For instance: *We had a great time: T.J. played his guitar.* (This means that we had a great time *because* T.J. played his guitar.)

31 Despite being a best-selling author, Brian Greene is a professor of physics, he is also a cofounder of the World Science Festival in New York City, an event that draws nearly half a million people each year.

31

A) NO CHANGE

B) As a physics professor and best-selling author, Brian Greene is the cofounder of the World Science Festival in New York City, which

C) The World Science Festival in New York City, being cofounded by physics professor and best-selling author Brian Greene,

D) Cofounded by best-selling author and physics professor Brian Greene, the World Science Festival in New York City

This sentence coordinates four separate but related ideas. Choice A has two main problems: it contains a comma splice, and it is logically incoherent because it implies that being an author contrasts with being a physics professor. Choice B is incorrect because the introductory modifier, *As a physics professor and best-selling author*, does not logically modify the main clause. Choice C is incorrect because the interrupting modifier, which is phrased as an explanation, doesn't logically modify the main clause. The only choice that logically coordinates all three ideas is choice D.

Exercise Set 3: Coordinating Ideas

1

Director H. K. Schaffer's third movie has received widespread critical acclaim. This movie is entitled *The Return,* and she is the daughter of legendary playwright George Schaffer.

A) NO CHANGE

B) *The Return*, the third movie directed by H. K. Schaffer, daughter of legendary playwright George Schaffer, has received widespread critical acclaim.

C) The daughter of legendary playwright George Schaffer, director H. K. Schaffer's third movie, *The Return*, has received widespread critical acclaim.

D) H. K. Schaffer's third movie is *The Return*: as the daughter of legendary playwright George Schaffer, her movie has received widespread critical acclaim.

2

Neuroscientists have made an important discovery concerning the prefrontal cortex of the brain. They discovered that this governs impulse control in humans. This discovery can help us to understand the causes of criminal behavior.

A) NO CHANGE

B) have discovered that impulse control in humans is governed by the prefrontal cortex of the brain, which can help us

C) have discovered that the prefrontal cortex of the brain governs impulse control in humans, which in turn can help us

D) have discovered that impulse control in humans is governed by the prefrontal cortex of the brain. This finding can help us

3

Electric cars may not be as environmentally friendly as we think, because the electricity they use is often produced in coal-burning power plants, this can produce large quantities of greenhouse gas.

A) NO CHANGE

B) the burning of which

C) which

D) which, when it burns,

4

Regular exercise not only strengthens your muscles, it also strengthens your brain by keeping it well oxygenated.

A) NO CHANGE

B) muscles; by keeping it well oxygenated it also strengthens your brain

C) muscles, but also it oxygenates your brain to make it strong

D) muscles, but also strengthens your brain by keeping it well oxygenated

5

Widely regarded as one of the most influential economic treatises of the 20th century, John Maynard Keynes's *The General Theory of Employment, Interest, and Money* forever changed the way social scientists view recessions.

A) NO CHANGE

B) John Maynard Keynes, with his book *The General Theory of Employment, Interest, and Money*

C) *The General Theory of Employment, Interest, and Money* was written by John Maynard Keynes, which

D) John Maynard Keynes, through his book *The General Theory of Employment, Interest, and Money*, which

Lesson 6: Transitions and References

Paragraph Transitions

When starting a new paragraph, pay attention to its logical relationship to the previous paragraph, and make sure you include any language necessary to clarify the **transition** from the previous paragraph to the new one. Such transitions serve as guideposts to help readers follow your train of thought.

- **To extend an idea:** *indeed, further, furthermore, also, moreover, in fact, additionally*

- **To illustrate or clarify an idea:** *for instance, for example, such as, especially, in particular, to illustrate, namely, specifically, in other words, that is, actually*

- **To show a contrast:** *however, although, despite, nevertheless, but, on the other hand*

- **To make a comparison:** *similarly, likewise, alternatively, also, too*

- **To show consequence:** *as a result, so, thus, subsequently, therefore, hence, accordingly, for this reason*

- **To show explanation or reason:** *because, since, how, why, as, thus*

...Therefore, an important challenge facing the health care industry is how to address the shortfall in primary caregivers without sacrificing quality of care. One possible solution is to incentivize more medical school graduates to choose primary care as their field instead of the more lucrative specialties like surgery and dermatology.

 It is possible to incorporate more medical professionals like physician assistants (PAs) into primary care teams. They can talk to patients about treatment options, prescribe medications, and even perform technical procedures like bone marrow aspirations.

17

Which choice provides the best transition between paragraphs?

A) NO CHANGE

B) Nevertheless, it is possible

C) Another option is

D) Similarly, we must

The first paragraph indicates a challenge that is *facing the health care industry* and also presents *one possible solution* to this problem. The sentence that starts the next paragraph, however, doesn't indicate any clear connection to the previous paragraph. Choice B is illogical, because *Nevertheless* implies that the previous paragraph indicates an obstacle to incorporating PAs into primary care teams, but it does not. Choice D is also illogical, because the two proposed solutions are not similar. Choice C, therefore, is the most logical choice.

References

> When a sentence uses a **pronoun**—such as *this, such,* or *that*—to refer to an idea or event from a previous clause or sentence, make sure that this reference is **clear and precise**. If it is not, you may need to replace the pronoun with a more precise **noun or noun phrase** in order to clarify the idea.

The opponents of fracking are correct to ask questions about the safety and sustainability of this practice. Could it poison the local water supply with carcinogens? Can we spare the vast amount of injection water it requires, especially in times of drought? Could it be causing potentially dangerous seismic activity? **13** But this is not enough—it must also be followed by careful, scientific, and impartial investigation, not just more fear-peddling.

13

     A)   NO CHANGE

     B)   this questioning

     C)   these practices

     D)   such a concept

In the original phrasing, the pronoun *this* is ambiguous. What does *this* refer to? *seismic activity? drought? fracking?* No, the developmental pattern of the paragraph as a whole indicates that the *questioning* is what must be followed by careful investigation. Therefore, the only logical choice is B.

Anyone thinking about pursuing a PA (physician assistant) or NP (nurse practitioner) degree should keep in mind that these programs aren't cheap, and that most states impose strict limits on the kinds of treatment **11** they can provide.

11

     A)   NO CHANGE

     B)   he or she

     C)   these professions

     D)   these professionals

The phrases *physician assistant* and *nurse practitioner* cannot serve as the antecedents of the pronoun *they*, because, first, they are parenthetical, and second, they are not actually nouns: they are adjectives modifying the noun *degree*. Therefore, the pronoun reference must be specified. Choice B is incorrect because *he or she* is no more specific than the original. To choose between C and D, we must ask ourselves, are physician assistants and nurse practitioners examples of *professions* or *professionals*? They are individual caregivers, so they are *professionals*. The *professions* they represent are *medicine* or *nursing*. The correct answer is D.

Exercise Set 4: Transitions and References

1

Even though the ancient Greeks were likely to see themselves as victims of fate, they were also inclined to regard humans as a privileged species. <u>Coincidentally</u>, in Sophocles's *Antigone*, the chorus proclaims that "many wonders there be, but naught more wondrous than man."

A) NO CHANGE

B) For example,

C) Furthermore,

D) Nevertheless,

2

As satisfying as it may be to punish wrongdoers, the real impetus behind tough sentencing laws is the belief that long prison terms deter crime. <u>Even worse</u>, the loss of autonomy and dignity that many prisoners experience often exacerbates any psychological issues that made them susceptible to crime in the first place.

A) NO CHANGE

B) However,

C) In other words,

D) As a result,

3

As societies become more complex and diverse, many people become more fearful and anxious, and thus are inclined to become more reactionary in their political views. <u>Consequently</u>, extremists in the media—talk radio hosts, cable news pundits, and radical bloggers—have access to a deep pool of resentment that they can exploit for financial gain.

A) NO CHANGE

B) Nevertheless,

C) Likewise,

D) For instance,

Lesson 7: Parallelism

The Law of Parallelism

When a sentence contains a **list**, **contrast**, or **comparison**, it must follow the **Law of Parallelism**: the items being listed, contrasted, or compared should have the **same grammatical form**.

In the 70s and 80s, American high school math teachers taught almost exclusively by lecture; today, **25** interactive and cooperative methods are more likely to be used.

25

A) NO CHANGE

B) interactive and cooperative methods are more likely to be used by those teachers

C) they are more likely to use interactive and cooperative methods

D) they would be more likely to use interactive and cooperative methods

The two clauses share a common topic, but they are not in the same grammatical form. The first is in the **active voice** (Lesson 16) but the second is in the **passive voice**. The Law of Parallelism demands that we phrase the second clause in the active voice as well, as in choice C. Choice D is incorrect because, although it is phrased in the active voice, it uses the **subjunctive mood** (Lesson 17), *would be*, which violates both the parallelism and the logic of the sentence.

Ms. Kelly always tries to provide **23** clear instructions that show respect and are fair to all of her students.

23

A) NO CHANGE

B) clear instructions, showing respect and being

C) clear instructions that also are respectful and are

D) instructions that are clear, respectful, and

Choice D provides the most concise and parallel list: *clear, respectful,* and *fair* are all simple adjectives. Also, all of these adjectives work **idiomatically** (Lesson 15) with the prepositional phrase *to all of her students*.

Standard Parallel Constructions

In Standard Written English, many contrasts or comparisons are made with **standard parallel constructions**. When using any of these constructions, you must follow two rules:

• Use the standard phrasing **precisely**.

• Make sure the words or phrases in the *A* and *B* slots are **parallel**.

...rather A than B...   *...neither A nor B...*
...prefer A to B...   *...both A and B...*
...less A than B...   *...not A but B...*
...A more than B...   *...A is like B...*
...either A or B...   *...not so much A as B...*
...the more A, the more B...

It often seems that politicians would rather give snappy sound bites **13** instead of working to solve our problems.

13

A) NO CHANGE

B) than work

C) rather than working

D) but not work

Although this sentence sounds okay to most people, it doesn't conform to Standard Written English. It uses the standard parallel construction *rather A than B*, but neither choice A nor choice D uses the correct phrasing, since they both omit the word *than*. Only choice B plays by the rules of idiom and parallelism: *rather (give snappy sound bites) than (work to solve our problems)*.

Analyzing Parallel Constructions

Sometimes tackling parallelism problems can be tough. Here's a step-by-step approach to make it easier:

1. **Underline** any phrase that shows a list, contrast, or comparison.
2. **Put parentheses** around each item being listed, contrasted, or compared.
3. Make sure that anything **outside** the parentheses uses **standard idiomatic phrasing**.
4. Make sure the items **inside** the parentheses have **parallel form**.

The film festival was not so much a celebration of independent artists; instead it was garish, not to mention a series of commercials for overproduced blockbusters.

27

A) NO CHANGE

B) artists but rather a garish

C) artists as a garish

D) artists, instead it was a garish

The phrase *not so much* indicates a contrast between two things: someone's expectations of a film festival and the reality. Let's isolate this portion that makes the contrast and put parentheses around the items being contrasted:

> *not so much (a celebration of independent artists); instead it was (garish, not to mention a series of commercials for overproduced blockbusters)*

Does the part *outside* the parentheses use standard idiomatic phrasing? No. On the previous page, we saw that the proper phrasing is *not so much A as B*. Let's fix that:

> *not so much (a celebration of independent artists) as (garish, not to mention a series of commercials for overproduced blockbusters)*

Now, are the items parallel? No. The first item is a noun phrase starting with a **determiner** (a word such as *the, a, an, some, any,* or *many*), but the second item starts with an adjective. Let's fix that:

> *not so much (a celebration of independent artists) as (a garish series of commercials for overproduced blockbusters)*

Therefore, the correct answer is C.

Gerunds vs. Infinitives

Some **nouns** look like verbs. For instance, an **infinitive**— the basic *to* form of a verb such as *to eat, to think,* or *to be*—serves as the subject of the sentence *To know her is to love her.* Likewise, a **gerund**—a noun formed by adding *-ing* to a verb like *eating, thinking,* and *being*—serves as the subject of the sentence *Being healthy is better than being thin.*

When constructing a list, contrast, or comparison, you can often choose between an **infinitive form** (for example, *I like to hunt, swim, and fish*) and a **gerund form** (for example, *I like hunting, swimming, and fishing*). Often, the two forms are interchangeable, but sometimes one is clearly preferable to the other.

When using an **infinitive** or **gerund** in a sentence, always ask: **would the alternative form sound better?** There are few clear-cut rules for choosing between infinitives and gerunds, and most are based on convention or idiom, so once you've taken care of all grammatical considerations, trust your ear.

The real purpose of this meeting is **27** for brainstorming ideas about opening new markets for our European product line.

27

A) NO CHANGE

B) to brainstorm

C) the brainstorming of

D) brainstorm

The core of this sentence is *the purpose is*, so what follows this phrase must be a noun phrase that defines the *purpose*. The prepositional phrase *for brainstorming* cannot serve as a noun phrase, because prepositional phrases are modifiers, not nouns. The only two choices that could serve as noun phrases are B and C. However, choice C is not **idiomatic** (Lesson 15), and therefore the correct answer is B. As a rule of thumb, **infinitives** serve concisely to express **purpose**, as in *I went to the store to buy milk.*

Exercise Set 5: Parallel Structure

1

The new party platform focuses on <u>tax code reform</u>, improving the schools, and repairing relations with the labor unions.

A)   NO CHANGE

B)   reformation of the tax code

C)   reforming the tax code

D)   tax code reformation

2

Good study habits are not so much about working <u>hard, but rather about how wisely you use your time</u>.

A)   NO CHANGE

B)   hard, but using your time wisely

C)   hard as how wisely you use your time

D)   hard as about using your time wisely

3

The food here is not only very fresh, but <u>the price is also very reasonable</u>.

A)   NO CHANGE

B)   also very reasonably priced

C)   it is also very reasonably priced

D)   also very reasonably priced as well

4

The financial crisis was exacerbated by two important factors: the skittishness of investors and <u>the fecklessness of regulators</u>.

A)   NO CHANGE

B)   the feckless regulators

C)   how feckless the regulators were

D)   the regulators' fecklessness

5

I can't decide whether <u>I should give Maria the tickets or</u> Caitlyn.

A)   NO CHANGE

B)   to give Maria the tickets or

C)   Maria should get the tickets or

D)   to give the tickets to Maria or to

6

I prefer Liszt's technical <u>virtuosity, as opposed to</u> Chopin's romantic beauty.

A)   NO CHANGE

B)   virtuosity, rather than

C)   virtuosity to

D)   virtuosity, to

7

The festival draws tourists from all over who come not so much for the music <u>but rather because of</u> the free-wheeling, Bohemian atmosphere.

A)   NO CHANGE

B)   as for

C)   but for

D)   as because of

Lesson 8: Coordinating Modifiers

Dangling Participles

> When a sentence begins with a **participial phrase**, the **subject** of that participial phrase must match the subject of the main clause. If these subjects don't match, then this phrase is called a **dangling participle**.

- **Participles** are words, such as *broken* and *thinking*, that derive from verbs but cannot, by themselves, serve as verbs in a sentence.

- **Present participles** are words that end in *-ing*, such as *swimming*, that serve either as **components of verb phrases** (as in, *I am swimming*) or as **adjectives** (as in, *The swimming children could not hear the ice cream truck*).

  [**Note:** Although **present participles** and **gerunds** (Lesson 7) look identical, don't confuse them. Gerunds are *-ing* words that serve as **nouns**, as in *I love swimming*.]

- **Past participles** are words, such as *toasted* or *broken*, that either end in *-ed* or take an irregular past participle form, and that also serve either as **components of verb phrases** (as in, *I have toasted the bagels* or *The glass has broken*) or as **adjectives** (as in, *I love toasted bagels* or *Be careful of the broken glass*).

- **Consequential (or "perfect") participles** combine *having* with a past participle, as in *Having broken the curse, Fiona could finally become her true self.* Consequential participles indicate that some previous action or status **extends a consequence** to the subject of the participial phrase. In this case, the breaking of the curse affects what Fiona can do.

- A **participial phrase** is a modifying phrase that includes a participle (as in, *Having finished our project, we celebrated with a nice dinner*).

Widely considered one of the most challenging pieces for piano, Franz Liszt stretched the boundaries of musical technique with his *Etude no. 5*.

7

A) NO CHANGE

B) the boundaries of musical technique were stretched by Franz Liszt's *Etude no. 5*

C) Franz Liszt's *Etude no. 5* stretched the boundaries of musical technique

D) the boundaries of musical technique were stretch by Franz Liszt with his *Etude no. 5*

The sentence begins with a participial phrase based on the past participle *considered*. What is its subject? That is, what is *widely considered one of the most challenging pieces for piano*? Clearly, it is *Etude no. 5*. Since the subject of the main clause must match the subject of the participial phrase, the correct answer is C.

Pondering this question as so many ancient Greek philosophers did, **20** the argument Plato made was that the sphere is an "ideal form," inaccessible to our physical senses.

20

A) NO CHANGE

B) it was Plato who argued

C) Plato argues

D) Plato argued

The sentence begins with a participial phrase based on the present participle *pondering*. What is its subject? That is, who was *pondering this question as so many ancient Greek philosophers did*? Clearly, it is *Plato*. The subject of the main clause must therefore also be *Plato*. This eliminates A and B. Since this sentence is stating a historical fact about a long-dead philosopher, it must use the past tense, so the correct answer is D.

Misplaced Modifiers

> Modifying phrases must obey the **Law of Proximity: Every modifying phrase should be placed as close as possible to the word it modifies without disrupting the sentence.**

---

31 In an emergency, I am amazed by how composed Marco can be.

31

A) NO CHANGE

B) I am amazed, in an emergency, by how composed Marco can be.

C) I am amazed by how composed Marco can be in an emergency.

D) I am, in an emergency, amazed by how composed Marco can be.

All of these sentences are identical except for the placement of the prepositional phrase *in an emergency*. Where should it go? The Law of Proximity says it should be as close as possible to the word that it modifies. So what word does it modify? A good way to answer that is to ask: what *question* does it answer? It answers the question, *when is Marco* composed? Therefore, it is an adverbial phrase modifying the adjective *composed*. Therefore, choice C is best, because it places the prepositional phrase after *composed*. Notice that choices A, B, and D imply that *in an emergency* modifies the main verb of the sentence, which implies that *I am amazed* in an emergency, not that Marco is *composed* in an emergency.

---

40 A splendid example of synthetic cubism, Picasso painted *Three Musicians* in the summer of 1924.

40

A) NO CHANGE

B) Picasso painted *Three Musicians*, a splendid example of synthetic cubism,

C) Picasso, who painted *Three Musicians*, a splendid example of synthetic cubism

D) Picasso painted *Three Musicians*, a splendid example of synthetic cubism, it was

---

This sentence starts with a modifying phrase known as an **appositive**. An **appositive** is a **noun or noun phrase that acts like an adjective** and modifies the noun or noun phrase that it is adjacent to. For instance, in the phrase *baseball game*, the word *baseball* is an appositive, modifying the noun *game*. Even though *baseball* is a noun, it is acting like an adjective. Appositives are always adjacent to the nouns they modify. Since the appositive phrase *a splendid example of synthetic cubism* describes the painting, and not Picasso himself, choice A is incorrect. Choice C is incorrect because it does not contain an independent clause, and choice D is incorrect because it commits a comma splice. Therefore, the correct answer is B.

Exercise Set 6: Coordinating Modifiers

1

Although emotionally drained, <u>Martha's creative instinct compelled her</u> to keep writing.

A) NO CHANGE

B) it was her creative instinct that compelled Martha

C) Martha was compelled by her creative instinct

D) her creative instinct compelled Martha

2

<u>Even with a sprained ankle, the coach forced Adam</u> to go back into the game.

A) NO CHANGE

B) Even though Adam had a sprained angle, the coach forced him

C) The coach, even with a sprained ankle, forced Adam

D) Adam was forced by the coach, even with a sprained ankle,

3

Lacking any real sailing skills, <u>David's primary concern was</u> keeping the boat upright.

A) NO CHANGE

B) David had the primary concern of

C) it was David's primary concern to

D) David was primarily concerned with

4

<u>We found the long-lost manuscript searching through a box of old letters in the attic.</u>

A) NO CHANGE

B) Searching through a box of old letters in the attic, we found the long-lost manuscript.

C) We found the long-lost manuscript in the attic searching through a box of old letters.

D) In the attic, we found the long-lost manuscript searching through a box of old letters.

5

<u>To get a good jump out of the blocks, sprinters say that proper hip positioning is essential.</u>

A) NO CHANGE

B) For getting a good jump out of the blocks, sprinters say that proper hip positioning is essential.

C) Sprinters say it is essential for getting a good jump out of the blocks for hip positioning to be proper.

D) Sprinters say that proper hip positioning is essential to getting a good jump out of the blocks.

6

Although unhappy with the angry tone of the debate, <u>the senator's plan was</u> to remain calm and rational and to stick to her central policy issues.

A) NO CHANGE

B) the senator planned

C) it was the senator's plan

D) the plan was for the senator

7

After searching for months for the perfect rug, <u>we finally found one</u> at a garage sale.

A) NO CHANGE

B) then we finally found one

C) one finally appeared

D) one was finally found by us

Lesson 9: Using Modifiers Logically

Illogical Modifiers

> The modifiers in a sentence must never convey **contradictory** or **redundant** ideas.

---

21 Whenever I use Grand Central Station, my train usually never comes on time.

21

A) NO CHANGE

B) My train usually never comes on time whenever I use Grand Central Station.

C) My train usually always doesn't come on time whenever I use Grand Central Station.

D) When I use Grand Central Station, my train rarely comes on time.

The original sentence contains three words that modify the main verb: the conjunction *whenever* and the adverbs *usually* and *never*. But they are contradictory. Is my train late *whenever* I use Grand Central Station? Is it *usually* late? Is it *never* on time? Choice B just swaps the location of the modifying phrase, so it doesn't solve the problem. In choice C, *usually* contradicts both *always* and *whenever*. Choice D is best because it contains no contradictory modifiers.

Although the twins were reared by different adoptive parents in different countries, many of their idiosyncrasies **27** and peculiarities are absolutely identical.

27

A) NO CHANGE

B) are absolutely identical

C) and peculiarities are identical

D) are identical

Choices A and C are redundant because *idiosyncrasies* and *peculiarities* are synonyms. Choice B is incorrect because *identical* is an **absolute modifier**, which means that it is redundant to modify it further with adverbs such as *so, very, more, most, extremely,* or *absolutely.* (One pair of things cannot be *more identical* than another pair.) Therefore, the correct answer is D.

Adjectives vs. Adverbs

> Never use an **adjective** to do the job of an **adverb**.
>
> - **Adverbs** (such as *quickly* and *gently*) modify **verbs, adjectives,** or **other adverbs**, and **usually end in -ly.** Some common adverbs that don't end in -ly are *always, away, ever, never, there, here, so, too, yet,* and *very.*
> - **Adjectives** (such as *fast* and *gentle*) modify **nouns,** and usually **don't** end in -ly, but some do, such as *lovely, lonely, motherly, fatherly, neighborly, friendly, costly, sickly, beastly, lively, womanly, likely,* and *scholarly.*

I was impressed by how poised Ricardo was and **36** how cogent his argument was presented.

36

A) NO CHANGE

B) how cogently he presented his argument

C) his argument was presented cogently

D) he presented his argument cogently

The Law of Parallelism (Lesson 7) requires the underlined phrase to begin with *how* or a similar **interrogative pronoun** (Lesson 11). However, we can't use the adjective *cogent* to modify the verb *was presented*; we must use the adverb *cogently.* The only parallel option that doesn't misuse a modifier is choice B.

The movers carried the dishes **16** gentler than they did the lamp, which they had broken by accident.

16

A) NO CHANGE

B) gentler than

C) more gently than they did

D) more gently than

The underlined modifier describes the verb *carried*, so it must be a comparative adverb *more gently* rather than the comparative adjective *gentler.* Choice D is incorrect because the phrase *than the lamp* makes an **illogical comparison** (Lesson 10) between a verb and a noun. The correct answer, therefore, is C.

Ambiguous Modifiers

> Some words can serve as **either** adjectives or adverbs, depending on the context.
>
> | **Adjective** | **Adverb** |
> |---|---|
> | I drove that <u>very</u> car. | It is <u>very</u> hot. |
> | The cat is not <u>well</u>. | She performed <u>well</u>. |
> | She is a <u>fast</u> reader. | Don't go so <u>fast</u>. |
> | It was a <u>straight</u> shot. | I can't shoot <u>straight</u>. |
> | It was a <u>just</u> decision. | She <u>just</u> arrived. |
> | We had a <u>late</u> lunch. | She arrived <u>late</u>. |
> | You have set a <u>low</u> bar. | Don't sink so <u>low</u>. |
> | I have <u>high</u> standards. | I can't jump very <u>high</u>. |
> | That test was <u>hard</u>. | Don't push so <u>hard</u>. |

> You are not expected to come into the office if you are **21** <u>feeling sickly; please stay home until you are well</u>.
>
> **21**
>
> A) NO CHANGE
>
> B) feeling sick; please stay home until you are good
>
> C) feeling sickly; please stay home until you are good
>
> D) feeling sick; please stay home until you are well

The word *sickly*, although it may look like an adverb because it ends in -*ly*, is an adjective meaning *feeble and often sick*. It is not appropriate to use *sickly* to describe someone who just doesn't feel well occasionally. Since the sentence is clearly referring to a temporary illness, the correct phrase is *feeling sick*. Also, the opposite of *sick* is *well*, not *good*. Therefore, the correct answer is D.

Binary and Nonbinary Comparisons

> **Comparative** adjectives (such as *faster, more beautiful, cheaper,* or *more interesting*) are used to make **binary** comparisons, that is, comparisons between only two things. **Superlative** adjectives (such as *fastest, most beautiful, cheapest,* or *most interesting*) are used only to compare **more than two things**.

> I don't know which is **33** <u>most troubling</u>: his apathy or his incompetence.
>
> **33**
>
> A) NO CHANGE
>
> B) most troubling;
>
> C) more troubling:
>
> D) more troubling;

Since the sentence is considering only two qualities, his *apathy* and his *incompetence*, the comparison is binary, and so it requires the comparative adjective, *more troubling*. To choose between C and D, you need to know the rules of **colons** and **semicolons** (Lesson 5 and Lesson 18). Except in very rare situations, when you use a semicolon, both phrases it separates must be **independent clauses**. However, the phrase that follows the underlined portion is not an independent clause but a **specifier**, specifying the pronoun *which*. Therefore, it should be preceded by a colon, as in choice C.

Comparative Forms

> Comparative adjectives that are **participial** always take *more*: *more grueling, more tired, more shocked*. Those with **more than two syllables** usually take *more*: *more beautiful, more painstaking, more confrontational*. But adjectives with **one or two syllables** usually take the -*er* suffix: *faster, kinder, gentler*.

> Incorporating the partnership turned out to be **11** <u>much more simple</u> than our lawyers had thought it would be.
>
> **11**
>
> A) NO CHANGE
>
> B) much more simply
>
> C) much simpler
>
> D) simpler by much

Since the adjective *simple* is not participial and doesn't have more than two syllables, its standard comparative form is *simpler*. Also, since it modifies the gerundive noun *incorporating*, it must take the comparative adjective form, *simpler*, rather than the comparative adverb form, *more simply*. Therefore, the correct answer is C.

Exercise Set 7: Using Modifiers Logically

1

In the second debate, she was able to emphasize her points much stronger than she did in the first one.

A)   NO CHANGE

B)   her much stronger points

C)   her points much more strongly

D)   much more her strong points

2

Although we love to hike as a family, we never usually get to spend extended time in the wilderness.

A)   NO CHANGE

B)   almost never

C)   usually never

D)   hardly never

3

Once the storm winds subsided and their vehicles could be dispatched, the response teams coordinated their efforts much more effective than they had during the last hurricane.

A)   NO CHANGE

B)   much more effectively than

C)   much more effectively than they had during

D)   much more effective than

4

The joy on the children's faces proved that the party was an unqualified success.

A)   NO CHANGE

B)   successfully unqualified

C)   a disqualified success

D)   unqualified in its success

5

Good trainers know that, although challenge is a key to success, pushing athletes harder doesn't always lead to better outcomes.

A)   NO CHANGE

B)   more hardly doesn't always

C)   more hard always doesn't

D)   harder always doesn't

6

Our chemistry teacher never told us about the test until three minutes before she gave it.

A)   NO CHANGE

B)   didn't tell

C)   never had told

D)   hardly ever told

7

Even the drastic spending cutbacks won't hardly address the growing budget deficit.

A)   NO CHANGE

B)   hardly wouldn't

C)   wouldn't hardly

D)   will hardly

Lesson 10: Making Comparisons

Logical Comparisons

> All comparisons must be **logical** in two ways: they must compare **only things in the same category**, and they must **not be self-contradictory**.

Anna has earned the respect of her fellow teammates by working **14** harder than anyone on the team.

14

A) NO CHANGE

B) more hardly than anyone

C) more hardly than anyone else

D) harder than anyone else

Recall from Lesson 9 that *hard* can serve as either an adjective or an adverb, depending on the context. Here, *harder* works as a comparative adverb, modifying the verb *work*. However, the comparison is **illogical** because Anna herself is on the team, and she cannot work *harder* than she herself can. Therefore, she must be excluded from the comparison, and the correct answer is D.

The turnout for this year's art festival was even better than it was for **14** last year's.

14

A) NO CHANGE

B) last year

C) that of last year's festival

D) last year's festival's turnout

This sentence contrasts two things: *the turnout for last year's festival* and *the turnout for this year's festival*. The correct answer is A, because this phrasing makes a clear and logical contrast even though the noun phrase *art festival* is omitted. This is okay because it is implied by **parallel inference**: *The turnout for this year's art festival was even better than it was for last year's (art festival)*. Choice B makes an illogical comparison (a *turnout* cannot be compared to a *year*), and choices C and D are redundant because they both repeat the reference to the *turnout*, which is already accomplished by the pronoun *it*.

Quantitative Comparisons

> In general, we use *less*, *much*, and *amount* to refer to **continuous or uncountable quantities**, as in *less traffic, much more money*, and *a large amount of food*. In contrast, we use *fewer*, *many*, and *number* to refer to **countable quantities**, as is in *fewer cars, many more dollars*, and *a large number of pizzas*.
>
> If you want to refer to a quantity that is both **countable *and* continuous**, you can go either way, depending on which aspect of the quantity you want to emphasize. For instance, units like *miles* are countable yet can take continuous values, so it is not technically incorrect to say either *This car gets fewer miles per gallon* or *This car gets less miles per gallon*. But both phrases are awkward. You can avoid this awkwardness altogether by saying something like *This car is less fuel-efficient*.

In an attempt to decrease the **41** amount of violent incidents at the festival, authorities will be selling less licenses to vendors of alcoholic beverages.

41

A) NO CHANGE

B) amount of violence at the festival, authorities will be selling fewer

C) number of violent incidents at the festival, authorities will be selling less

D) amount of violent incidents at the festival, authorities will be selling fewer

Choice A is incorrect because *amount* should not be used with a countable and noncontinuous quantity such as *incidents*, and *less* should not be used with a countable and noncontinuous quantity such as *licenses*. Choice B corrects both problems because *violence* is uncountable but *licenses* are countable, so *amount of violence* and *fewer licenses* are both logical phrases. Choice C is incorrect because *less licenses* is illogical, and choice D is incorrect because *amount of violent incidents* is illogical.

Exercise Set 8: Logical Comparisons

1

Ignoring online trolls, **especially the persistent ones**, is often more difficult than <u>attacking them outright</u>.

A) NO CHANGE

B) to outright attack them

C) to attack them outright

D) it is attacking them outright

2

Many critics agree that Kyrchek's latest film is better than <u>anything she has done</u>.

A) NO CHANGE

B) everything she has done

C) anything else she has done

D) any of the work she did

3

The motors of all-electric cars are much quieter than <u>combustion engine cars</u>.

A) NO CHANGE

B) combustion engines

C) cars with combustion engines

D) those of combustion engines

4

The Surrealists were as <u>inscrutable, if not more so, than</u> the Dadaists.

A) NO CHANGE

B) inscrutable as, if not more inscrutable than,

C) inscrutable as, if not more so, than

D) inscrutable, if not more inscrutable, than

5

Mathematics lessons given by the Japanese teachers, unlike <u>teachers in American classrooms</u>, were focused on solving a single complex problem rather than many simpler but similar problems.

A) NO CHANGE

B) American teachers

C) those given by American teachers

D) American classrooms

6

To contemporary readers, Modernist poetry is much less accessible than even <u>Victorian or Elizabethan poetry.</u>

A) NO CHANGE

B) Victorian or Elizabethan poets

C) those of Victorian or Elizabethan poets

D) that of Victorian or Elizabethan poetry

7

As transparency in banking increases, <u>less customers will</u> voluntarily pay unreasonable account fees.

A) NO CHANGE

B) fewer customers would

C) fewer customer will

D) less customers would

Lesson 11: Pronoun Agreement

Pronoun-Antecedent Agreement

> Every **definite pronoun**, such as *it*, *him*, *herself*, and *their*, must **agree in number with its antecedent**.

> Our team of financial advisors safeguards the identity and confidentiality **10** of their clients.
>
> **10**
>
> A) NO CHANGE
> B) of each and every client of theirs
> C) of its clients
> D) of every one of their clients

The pronoun *their* disagrees in number with its antecedent, *team*. (This may seem strange to those of you from the UK or Commonwealth countries, where collective nouns like *team* are treated as plurals. In American English, such collectives are singular.) The only choice with a singular pronoun is C.

Interrogative Pronouns

> **Interrogative pronouns** are the pronouns we use to ask questions such as *who? what? where? when? why?* and *how?* When used as **definite pronouns**, they must agree in **category** with their antecedents: *who* refers to a **person**; *what* refers to a **thing**, **action**, or **concept**; *where* refers to a **place**; *when* refers to a **time**; *why* refers to a **reason**; and *how* refers to an **explanation.**

> The filibuster is a strategy **18** where senators can extend debate in order to delay or prevent a vote.
>
> **18**
>
> A) NO CHANGE
> B) when
> C) that
> D) whereby

A *strategy* is a plan of action, not a place. Therefore, the pronoun *where* disagrees with its antecedent in kind. Likewise, a strategy is not a time, so choice B is wrong also. Choice C creates an illogical sentence fragment. The correct answer is D because *whereby* means *by which*. (Unlike *where*, *whereby* does not necessarily refer to a place.)

Ambiguous Pronouns

> Every **definite pronoun** should have an **unambiguous antecedent**. Avoid using pronouns that could refer to more than one antecedent.

> **19** The coach told Mike that he would have to miss the next game due to the infraction.
>
> **19**
>
> A) NO CHANGE
> B) Mike was told by the coach that he would have to miss the next game due to the infraction.
> C) The coach told Mike that, due to the infraction, Mike would have to miss the next game.
> D) The coach told Mike that, due to the infraction, he would have to miss the next game.

In the original phrasing, the pronoun *he* is ambiguous: would Mike have to miss the game, or would the coach? Choice B only changes the voice from active to passive, so it does not solve the problem. Choice D moves the modifying phrase but does not correct the ambiguous antecedent problem. Choice C avoids the problem by not using a pronoun at all.

Shifting Pronouns

> Once you choose a pronoun to refer to a particular antecedent, **stick with it**.

> My wife and I enjoy going to all of our alumni events because **19** you meet so many interesting people there.
>
> **19**
>
> A) NO CHANGE
> B) the many people that you meet there are so interesting
> C) we meet so many interesting people there
> D) of meeting so many interesting people there

Choices A and B contain **pronoun shifts**: the first person plural pronouns (*my wife and I, our*) shift to the second person (*you*), even though these pronouns refer to the same antecedent. Choice D is unclear and awkward because the gerund *meeting* is not linked to the subject.

Exercise Set 9: Pronoun Agreement

1

There are many times during a match <u>where you can lose points</u> if you fail to focus on the fundamentals.

A) NO CHANGE

B) where one's points can be lost

C) when you can lose points

D) when one's points can be lost

2

Although <u>one should never</u> read so quickly that you can't absorb the material, increasing your reading speed slightly can actually help to increase your focus and retention.

A) NO CHANGE

B) you should never

C) one could never

D) you shouldn't even

3

Learning new vocabulary words requires much more than memorizing <u>their definitions</u>.

A) NO CHANGE

B) it's definition

C) they're definitions

D) its definition

4

The mission of the Arts Council is to encourage young students to appreciate the fine and the performing arts. <u>Their</u> programs have been adopted by schools citywide.

A) NO CHANGE

B) It's

C) Its

D) They're

5

Our study shows that the new training program has helped players to avoid injuries, and to recover more quickly <u>when they do</u>.

A) NO CHANGE

B) if they do

C) when their injured

D) if they do get injured

6

The bonobo, *Pan paniscus*, may be the most peaceful primate species, but <u>it is</u> not beyond occasional outbreaks of violence.

A) NO CHANGE

B) its

C) they are

D) their

7

The nitrogen cycle is the process <u>when</u> nitrogen becomes converted into different chemical forms as it is processed by marine and terrestrial ecosystems.

A) NO CHANGE

B) where

C) by which

D) so that

Lesson 12: Pronoun Case

The Subjective and Objective Cases

A pronoun must take the **subjective** case—*I*, *he*, *she*, *we*, or *they*—when it acts as or is being equated with **the subject of a verb**. A pronoun must take the **objective case**—*me*, *him*, *her*, *us*, or *them*—when it is acting as **the object of a verb or a prepositional phrase**.

As the waiter was talking to Jenna and me, we could see the enormous tattoo on his neck.

12

A) NO CHANGE

B) Jenna and I, we

C) Jenna and I, both of us

D) Jenna and me both

To determine the proper case of a pronoun, you must ask, *is it the **subject** of a verb, or the **object** of a verb or prepositional phrase*? Since the phrase *Jenna and me* is the object of the prepositional phrase *to Jenna and me*, this pronoun is correctly in the objective case. Since the pronoun *we* serves as the subject of the verb *could see*, it is correctly in the subjective case. Therefore, the correct answer is A.

I am honored that the team has selected **7** Alex and myself as captains.

7

A) NO CHANGE

B) Alex and I as

C) Alex and myself for

D) Alex and me as

The original sentence uses a **reflexive** pronoun where an **objective** pronoun is required. Since the phrase *Alex and myself* is the object of the verb *has selected*, it should take the objective form, *Alex and me*, as in choice D.

But wait—isn't the reflexive *myself* required because the subject of the sentence is *I*? No, because *I* is the subject of the *first* clause, *I am honored*, but the underlined phrase is part of the *second* clause, *the team has selected Alex and me*. Since the subject and object are not one and the same in the second clause, the reflexive case is incorrect.

The Reflexive Case

Reflexive pronouns—*myself, himself, herself, oneself, ourselves,* or *themselves*— serve in two situations:

*   as the **object of a verb or preposition when it is identical to the subject of the same verb**.

    I did it all by myself. She cut herself.

*   as an **emphatic adjective**.

    Joan had dinner with Oprah herself.

    I myself would never have been invited.

After Ronaldo's written request was rebuffed by the board, **22** he took his case to Elena.

22

Which choice best emphasizes the fact that Elena has a special status?

A) NO CHANGE

B) he himself took his case to Elena

C) he took his case by himself to Elena

D) he took his case to Elena herself

The only choice that *emphasizes Elena's status* is D. In choice B, the reflexive pronoun emphasizes Ronaldo's *initiative*. In choice C, it emphasizes Ronaldo's *solitude*.

The Possessive Case

Possessive pronouns—*your, whose, their, its*—do not use apostrophes. Their homophones with apostrophes—*you're, who's, they're, it's*—are **contractions**.

29 Its hard to know when you're dog is becoming dehydrated unless you check it regularly.

29

A) NO CHANGE

B) It's hard to know when your

C) Its hard to know when your

D) It's hard to know when you're

The correct answer is B. Only the contractions should get the apostrophes. Notice that the only contraction in the underlined phrase is *It's = It is.*

Exercise Set 10: Pronoun Case

1

The challenge problems were much easier for Alexa and Jill than they were for <u>Julian and I</u>.

A) NO CHANGE

B) myself and Julian

C) Julian and me

D) mine and Julian's

2

Since our flight leaves on Saturday, it might be difficult for <u>him and me</u> to stay for the entire conference.

A) NO CHANGE

B) him and I

C) he and I

D) he and myself

3

There really is no point in <u>us</u> delaying this decision any longer.

A) NO CHANGE

B) ourselves

C) we

D) our

4

If we are going to resolve this matter, <u>you and me</u> are going to have to make some compromises.

A) NO CHANGE

B) you and myself

C) you and I

D) I and yourself

5

Although we haven't seen each other in years, Justine and <u>myself</u> have always been closest friends.

A) NO CHANGE

B) me

C) I

D) mine

6

<u>Us Giants fans</u> have suffered through our share of disappointing defeats.

A) NO CHANGE

B) Us Giant's fans

C) We Giants fan's

D) We Giants fans

7

The owner of the restaurant offered my wife and <u>me</u> a complimentary bottle of wine.

A) NO CHANGE

B) myself

C) I

D) mine

Lesson 13: Verb Tense and Aspect

Coordinating Tenses

The **tense** of any verb must coordinate logically with that of **any other verbs in the sentence**, as well as with the **developmental pattern of the passage as a whole**. Multiple verbs in the same sentence **do not always have to have the same tense**, but they do have to **work together to convey a clear and logical set of ideas**.

Although Frances Perkins was not the first government official to advocate for workplace safety, she **12** has been the first who implemented substantial labor reform through legislation such as the Fair Labor Standards Act of 1938.

12

A) NO CHANGE

B) is the first to have implemented

C) was the first having implemented

D) was the first to implement

Since both clauses refer to events that happened many decades ago, they should both use past tense verbs. Choices A and B are incorrect because they both use present tense verbs. Choice D is best because it uses the correct tense and the infinitive *to implement* is parallel to the infinitive *to advocate* in the first clause.

When Marie Curie shared the 1903 Nobel Prize in Physics with two other scientists—her husband Pierre Curie and Henri Becquerel— she **40** has been the first woman to win the prize.

40

A) NO CHANGE

B) would be

C) was

D) is

The two clauses in this sentence are linked by the conjunction *when*, indicating that they are indicating simultaneous events or states of being. Since the first verb, *shared*, is in the past tense, the second one should be as well. Therefore, the correct answer is C.

Historical vs. Timeless Facts

In standard English, **historical** facts take the **past tense**, but **timeless** facts or beliefs take the **present tense**.

The ancient Greek philosopher Zeno **19** taught that change is an illusion.

19

A) NO CHANGE

B) teaches that change is an illusion

C) teaches that change was an illusion

D) taught that change would be an illusion

The fact that Zeno taught is a *historical* fact and should take the past tense, but the belief that *"change is an illusion"* may or may not be tied to a previous era. If you want to imply that this belief is no longer accepted, you may put it in the past tense: *The ancient Greek philosopher Zeno taught that change was an illusion*. But if you want to imply that it is still widely believed, you may use the present tense: *The ancient Greek philosopher Zeno taught that change is an illusion*. The only grammatically correct option, then, is choice A.

Currency of Art and Ideas

Facts about the content of currently available works of art or literature have **currency**, and therefore take the **present tense**.

In Act V of *King Lear*, Cordelia and Lear **10** were captured by Edmund, who had promised to show them no mercy.

10

A) NO CHANGE

B) were captured by Edmund, who has

C) are captured by Edmund, who had

D) are captured by Edmund, who has

Since *King Lear* is a widely available work of literature, its action is conventionally described in the present tense. Only choice D places both verbs correctly in the present tense.

Verb Aspects

The **aspect** of a verb indicates **how its action or status applies to the subject or situation**. For instance, here are examples of a **present tense** verb with five different aspects:

I eat.   = I am in the habit of eating. (**habitual** aspect)

I am eating.   = I am in the process of eating. (**progressive** aspect)

I have to eat.   = I feel compelled to eat. (**compulsive** aspect)

I have eaten.   = My present status is a consequence of previous eating. (**consequential** aspect)

I have been eating. = My present status is a consequence of previous eating, and I am still eating. (**consequential** and **progressive** aspects)

Ever since it reached its peak in 1991, violent crime **10** declined precipitously, not just in the United States but around the globe.

10

A) NO CHANGE
B) have declined
C) has declined
D) would decline

This sentence indicates that a current status is a **consequence** of a previous situation, and therefore the present consequential form in choice C, *has declined*, is correct. Choice A is incorrect because the phrase *ever since* indicates that the decline is not in isolated event in the past. Choice B is incorrect because the verb does not agree in number with the subject, *crime*. Choice D is incorrect because this statement is not counterfactual or hypothetical, and therefore the **subjunctive mood** (Lesson 17) is inappropriate.

The Consequential Aspect

Many people—English teachers included—are confused about what the **consequential aspect** means. Verbs in the consequential aspect—such as *have eaten, had eaten,* and *will have eaten*—are often said to represent the "**perfect tenses.**" This is a double misnomer: "**perfect**" does not describe the function of the verb, and an aspect is not a **tense**. The term **consequential aspect** is more accurate, because it indicates that the verb indicates **status-as-consequence**.

Consider the sentence *I have lived in New York.* This indicates that my **current status is a consequence** of the fact that I lived (and might still live) in New York. Some people claim that the consequential aspect implies **ongoing** status. Wrong: I can say this even if I currently live in Connecticut. Some people claim it implies an **indefinite time period**. Wrong again: I can say this even if I know that I lived there precisely from August of 1989 to September of 1990. Some claim it implies **completion of action or status**. Wrong: I can say this even if I still live in Manhattan, as in *I have lived in New York for over 25 years now.*

Your English (or French or Spanish or Latin) teachers may still insist on referring to the "perfect tenses." Just remember that they are **really** talking about verbs in the **consequential aspect**, and that this aspect indicates **status-as-consequence**.

Unlike its competitors, which have enjoyed a long period of profitability, PinkCorp **31** had its share of financial troubles.

31

A) NO CHANGE
B) has had
C) would have
D) would have had

Since the first verb, *have enjoyed*, is in the present tense, this sentence is comparing the *current* fortunes of PinkCorp with the *current* fortunes of its competitors. Therefore, choice A is incorrect because it is in the past tense. Choices C and D are incorrect because the sentence is indicating facts, not hypothetical or counterfactual situations, and therefore the **subjunctive mood** (Lesson 17) is incorrect. Choice B is correct because it uses the **present consequential** form to show that PinkCorp's previous troubles affect its current status.

Irregular Verb Forms

> Verbs in the **consequential aspect** always use the **past participle** (Lesson 8) form of the verb, as in *had taken, has taken,* and *will have taken.* Some of these past participles take **irregular forms**.

Verb	Past tense	Past participle
to arise	arose	arisen
to beat	beat	beaten
to begin	began	begun
to blow	blew	blown
to break	broke	broken
to come	came	come
to do	did	done
to draw	drew	drawn
to drink	drank	drunk*
to drive	drove	driven
to fly	flew	flown
to go	went	gone
to know	knew	known
to lay (put)	laid	laid
to lie (down)	lay	lain
to ride	rode	ridden
to run	ran	run
to shrink	shrank	shrunk*
to sink	sank	sunk*
to speak	spoke	spoken
to spring	sprang	sprung
to swim	swam	swum
to take	took	taken
to tear	tore	torn
to write	wrote	written

*When these participles are used as **adjectives**, they can also take the *-en* suffix, as in *drunken sailor, shrunken heads,* and *sunken ship.* However, these alternative forms are **not** used in verb phrases. For instance, we would never say *baby Leonard has drunken his milk.* Instead, we would say *baby Leonard has drunk his milk.*

Douglas did not get the CEO position, even though he **10** has ran one of the largest divisions within the company for nearly ten years.

10

A) NO CHANGE

B) runs

C) is running

D) has run

Choice A is incorrect because the present consequential form requires the past participle, but *ran* is the past tense form of *to run,* not the past participle. Choices B and C are incorrect because neither the simple present tense *runs* nor the present progressive *is running* works logically with the modifier *for nearly ten years.*

Present vs. Consequential Participles

> A **present participle phrase** indicates that the participial verb and the main verb have the **same tense.** If you want to indicate that the participial verb **precedes and extends a consequence to** the main verb, use the **consequential participle.** The consequential participle combines *having* with the past participle, as in *having spoken.*

---

36 Taking the honors-level introductory physics course, Jess felt more than prepared to take AP physics level 2.

36

A) NO CHANGE

B) Having took

C) Having taken

D) She took

This sentence is trying to indicate not only how Jess feels about taking AP physics 2, but *why* she feels that way. However, the **present participle** *taking* implies that Jess took introductory physics and AP physics at the **same time.** Of course, this is illogical: she felt good about taking AP physics because she had *already taken* introductory physics. Therefore, the consequential participle *having taken* is required, as in choice C. Choice B is incorrect because *took* is the past tense form, not the past participle form. Choice D is incorrect because it creates a comma splice and does not indicate any logical relationship between the clauses.

Exercise Set 11: Verb Tense and Aspect

1

Developing the first hydrogen cell engine, the team should hope to reveal it at the technology expo this December.

A) NO CHANGE

B) Having developed the first hydrogen cell engine, the team would hope

C) Developing the first hydrogen cell engine, the team hopes

D) Having developed the first hydrogen cell engine, the team hopes

2

Without spending so much as an hour on research, Dale already wrote the first draft of her term paper.

A) NO CHANGE

B) having spent so much as an hour on research, Dale has already written

C) spending so much as an hour on research, Dale has written

D) having spent so much as an hour on research, Dale has already wrote

3

As soon as Hannah arrived home from vacation, she had immediately started to plan her next trip.

A) NO CHANGE

B) had arrived home from vacation, she

C) had arrived home from vacation, she had

D) arrived home from vacation, she

4

Having taken the wrong path, the hikers feared that they might not be able to reach base camp by nightfall.

A) NO CHANGE

B) Taking the wrong path, the hikers feared

C) Having taken the wrong path, the hikers had feared

D) Taking the wrong path, the hikers had feared

5

Although *Pinocchio* seems like a quaint children's story, its characters would represent some of the central archetypes from Greek, Roman, Judeo-Christian, and even Babylonian mythological traditions.

A) NO CHANGE

B) represented

C) represent

D) had represented

6

Elayna is well qualified for this position because she has performed very well as a team leader on many similar projects.

A) NO CHANGE

B) had performed

C) would perform

D) was performing

7

Hundreds of recreational divers come each year to explore the site where the galleon had sank over three hundred years ago.

A) NO CHANGE

B) sank

C) has sunk

D) has sank

8

At his death in 2010, J. D. Salinger was regarded as one of the premier writers of the 20th century, he had only published one full-length novel, *The Catcher in the Rye*.

A) NO CHANGE

B) although he would have published only

C) despite having published only

D) although he would publish only

Lesson 14: Diction and Redundancy

Redundancy

> **The Law of Parsimony:** All else being equal, **the shorter the better**.
>
> When considering whether to add a word or phrase to a sentence, always ask: does this actually **add relevant meaning** to the sentence? If not, leave it out.

Michael stole the ball and **31** sped quickly down the court with only seconds remaining left to go in the game.

31

A) NO CHANGE

B) sped quickly down the court with only seconds remaining

C) sped down the court with only seconds left

D) sped down the court with only seconds remaining to go

The original sentence is triply redundant. The verb *to speed* means *to run quickly*, so the phrase *sped quickly* is redundant. Also, the phrase *remaining left to go* is doubly redundant, since the phrases *seconds remaining in the game, seconds left in the game,* and *seconds to go in the game* all mean the same thing. The only option without redundancy is C.

In 1922, the totalitarian governments of Italy and Germany closed all Montessori schools and declared **20** them subversive in that they might undermine the regimes.

20

A) NO CHANGE

B) that they were subversive in undermining the regimes

C) them subversive in undermining the regimes

D) them subversive

The adjective *subversive* means *seeking to undermine the established power structure*. Therefore, the phrases in choices A, B, and C are redundant, so the best choice is D.

Logical Diction

> **Logical diction** questions ask you to choose the word to best convey a particular idea. When tackling **logical diction** questions, look at **any phrase in which the word is embedded**, and make sure that it **clearly and logically conveys the idea** that the sentence intends.

Word of Montessori's success with the Casa dei Bambini soon began to **17** distribute internationally, and her methods for child-centered education became widely adopted across Europe.

17

A) NO CHANGE

B) increase

C) spread

D) exhibit

The subject of the verb *distribute* is *Word of Montessori's success*, which is a type of information. But information cannot logically *distribute* anything, so choice A is incorrect. Choice B is incorrect because information cannot *increase*. Choice D is incorrect because information cannot *exhibit*. The only choice that conveys a clear and logical idea is choice C, *spread*, which helps convey the fact that news of Montessori's success became widely known.

Common Mix-Ups

Some diction errors are "**sound-alike**" errors, in which words are confused with similar-sounding words. Below is a list of common mix-ups. Make flashcards for the pairs that confuse you.

accept (v) = to agree to take
  I accept the offer.
except (prep) = not including
  I like all except that one.

adapt (v) = to make suitable to a purpose
  I adapted the motor to fit the boat.
adopt (v) = to choose as one's own
  They adopted a child.
adept (adj) = highly skilled
  She's an adept speaker.

affect (v) = to influence
  It affected me deeply.
effect (n) = result or consequence
  It had a good effect.

allude (v) = to make an indirect reference
  He alluded to their secret.
elude (v) = to escape from; to avoid
  They eluded capture.

allusion (n) = an indirect reference
  Her speech included an allusion to Othello.
illusion (n) = misconception or misperception
  I love optical illusions.

ambivalent (adj) = having conflicting feelings
  I feel ambivalent about going to the party.
ambiguous (adj) = having more than one meaning
  That phrase is ambiguous.

cite (v) = to credit as a source of information
  The author cited many sources.
cite (v) = to commend for meritorious action
  She was cited for bravery.
site (n) = location of a particular activity or structure
  That is the site of the battle of Antietam.
sight (v) = to see at a specific location
  She was sighted in the crowd.

compliment (n) = a praising personal comment
  Compliments are always appreciated.
complement (n) = something that makes a whole
  Brie is a fine complement to this wine.

council (n) = an advisory committee
  I'm a member of the executive council.
counsel (v) = to give advice
  She counseled me wisely.

discrete (adj) = distinct
  The machine has hundreds of discrete parts.
discreet (adj) = prudently secretive
  Please be discreet about our meeting.

elicit (v) = to bring out or to call forth
  The joke elicited uncomfortable laughter.
illicit (adj) = unlawful
  Don't engage in illicit activities.

eminent (adj) = prominent and distinguished
  She is an eminent historian.
imminent (adj) = about to happen
  I sense imminent laughter.

flaunt (v) = to show (something) off
  If you've got it, flaunt it.
flout (v) = to show disregard for
  Don't flout the rules.

gambit (n) = a risky opening move
  He made a bold strategic gambit.
gamut (n) = the complete range
  Her emotions ran the gamut.

imply (v) = to suggest or hint at
  A handshake implies an agreement.
infer (v) = to draw a conclusion from evidence
  Please don't infer hostile intent.

phase (n) = stage in a process
  This is the third phase of the project.
faze (n) = to disturb (someone's) composure
  She was not fazed by the interruption.

precede (v) = to come before
  Thunder is always preceded by lightning.
proceed (v) = to go on, usually after a pause
  Please proceed with the task.

principal (n) = head of a school
  Our principal spoke at the assembly.
principal (n) = the initial investment in an account
  Many investments risk a loss of principal.
principle (n) = guiding rule or value
  I reject that proposal on principle.

reticent (adj) = reserved or reluctant to talk freely
  He has been reticent in our therapy sessions.
reluctant (adj) = disinclined to do something
  I'm reluctant to reveal personal information.

Exercise Set 12: Diction and Redundancy

1

Even the strongest pesticides could not <u>abolish</u> the beetles.

A) NO CHANGE

B) delete

C) retract

D) eradicate

2

Although statistics cannot prove theories, <u>but they can invalidate</u> them by ruling out the correlations they imply.

A) NO CHANGE

B) they can refute

C) but they can debunk

D) they can smear

3

Well-trained wine experts can <u>separate out</u> the tastes of dozens of different grapes, regions, and vintages.

A) NO CHANGE

B) certify

C) acknowledge

D) discern

4

It's almost impossible to achieve <u>a consensus of unified opinion</u> on those matters on which the group members have widely different priorities and values.

A) NO CHANGE

B) a unified consensus of opinion

C) a consensus in opinion

D) consensus

5

Often, the town council will debate an issue for weeks before <u>appointing</u> a formal decision.

A) NO CHANGE

B) compelling

C) making

D) predetermining

6

Although loved by audiences worldwide, the film was soundly <u>disparaged</u> by many critics.

A) NO CHANGE

B) confronted

C) impaired

D) repudiated

7

<u>At the present moment in time, we</u> cannot process your request because we have lost the connection to our server.

A) NO CHANGE

B) At this moment in time, we

C) Currently, we

D) We

8

After the neighbors filed a noise complaint, the workers had to <u>hamper</u> their work by 6:00 every evening or risk municipal fines.

A) NO CHANGE

B) subside

C) curtail

D) lower

9

Once she found a supportive group of friends who appreciated her talents and idiosyncrasies, Daryl's self-esteem began to <u>proliferate</u>.

A) NO CHANGE

B) blossom

C) multiply

D) enlarge

10

Taxpayers are unlikely to fund an expensive public project unless it is designed to solve <u>an imminent problem that is likely to occur in the future</u>.

A) NO CHANGE

B) a problem that is imminently likely to occur in the future

C) a problem that is imminently likely

D) an imminent problem

11

Originally built as an engine for a small tractor, the motor had to be <u>evolved</u> in order to meet the needs of the portable generator.

A) NO CHANGE

B) correlated

C) amended

D) adapted

12

The sounds, themes, and images in advertisements are carefully chosen to subtly <u>intimidate</u> consumers to buy things they may not need.

A) NO CHANGE

B) propel

C) induce

D) oppress

13

The negotiations became very <u>apprehensive when</u> the topic shifted to company ownership.

A) NO CHANGE

B) neurotic

C) tense

D) worried

14

Although he is usually <u>reticent to talk about</u> his personal life, he is more than happy to talk about the merits of the various *Star Wars* films.

A) NO CHANGE

B) reticent about

C) disinclined to talk with regard to

D) unwilling about

15

Many of the government ministers have been in exile since they were <u>impeded</u> in the 2016 military coup.

A) NO CHANGE

B) scuttled

C) ousted

D) snubbed

16

Corporations that value cooperation over competition tend to see <u>less incidents of elicit</u> behavior such as embezzlement.

A) NO CHANGE

B) fewer incidents of illicit

C) fewer incidence of illicit

D) less incidents of illicit

Lesson 15: Idiomatic Expression

Idioms

An **idiom** is a common phrase that **has a rigid wording and (usually) a nonliteral meaning**. Examples include *a piece of cake, push through, on fire, see the light, go in on, drop by,* and *under fire*. When using idioms, be sure that you **understand their meanings and phrase them precisely**.

To catch idiom errors on the SAT, **pay attention to prepositions, and trust your ear**: when a preposition is underlined, ask: **would another preposition sound better here, or is a preposition necessary at all?** Don't think too hard: idioms often have nonliteral meanings, so they sometimes defy logic.

Games and other group challenges are a means **39** through fostering team spirit to the campers.

39

A) NO CHANGE

B) of fostering team spirit among

C) for fostering team spirit for

D) of fostering team spirit with

Always pay special attention when an underlined phrase contains a **preposition** (Lesson 3). Notice whether the choices include alternative prepositions, and (if so) **trust your ear** to choose among them. Which sounds more natural: *a means through fostering, a means for fostering,* or *a means of fostering*? Hopefully, your ear tells you that the last choice is the most idiomatic. In order to choose between B and D, you have to check another idiomatic phrase. Which sounds more natural: *team spirit among the campers,* or *team spirit to the campers*? The first one is more idiomatic, so the correct answer is B.

Prepositional Idioms

Most **idiom errors** are **wrong preposition errors**. Prepositions play an essential role in many idiomatic phrases, and it's easy to mix them up. A wrong preposition can make a phrase **unidiomatic**, or it can turn it into a **completely different idiom**.

agree with = share the opinion of (a person)
agree to = accept (a proposal or offer)
agree on = arrive at (a mutual decision)
agree about = have similar sentiments about (a situation)

angry with = annoyed at (a person)
angry about = annoyed about (a situation)

concerned with = involved with (an activity or issue)
concerned about = worried about (a situation)

take in = apprehend (an idea or perception)
take on = undertake (a challenge); oppose (a person)
take after = resemble (a parent or mentor)

wait for = stay until (an event)
wait on = serve (someone) at a restaurant

The first amendment to the Constitution is concerned primarily **39** about the Enlightenment values of free thought and free expression.

39

A) NO CHANGE

B) for

C) with

D) DELETE the underlined word

Although it is idiomatic to say *the first amendment is about* something, it is **not** idiomatic to say *the first amendment is concerned about* something, because the idiomatic phrase *concerned about* means *worried about*, and a constitutional amendment cannot worry. On the other hand, *concerned with* means *involved with as a matter of interest*, which fits the context of this sentence perfectly. Therefore, the correct answer is C.

Exercise Set 13: Standard Idiom

1

After exchanging dozens of texts over several weeks, we all finally agreed <u>with</u> a plan to go hiking in the Adirondacks.

A) NO CHANGE

B) to

C) on

D) for

2

The new color scheme for the living room is not very different <u>than</u> the old one.

A) NO CHANGE

B) to

C) compared to

D) from

3

The lawyers will be reviewing employee contracts in the next few days to be sure that they comply <u>in</u> the recently updated regulations.

A) NO CHANGE

B) about

C) with

D) to

4

I prefer the soft, diffuse light of the new LED bulbs <u>more than</u> the light of the old compact fluorescent bulbs.

A) NO CHANGE

B) over

C) to

D) in comparison to

5

Although the terms of the plea deal seemed very generous, the defendant did not agree <u>to</u> the offer because it included an admission of guilt.

A) NO CHANGE

B) about

C) with

D) on

6

Several agents were dispatched to Philadelphia <u>for the purpose of investigating</u> the new leads.

A) NO CHANGE

B) for investigating

C) to investigate about

D) to investigate

7

The professor has sole authority to determine <u>about which activities qualify for</u> field credit.

A) NO CHANGE

B) which activities qualify for

C) about which activities qualify in

D) which activities that qualify for

8

The teens were at the school board meeting to voice their arguments <u>on</u> the proposal to move the school starting time.

A) NO CHANGE

B) with

C) for

D) to

9

The final song was a tribute <u>about</u> Dr. Whelan, the choral director who would be retiring in June.

A) NO CHANGE

B) on

C) for

D) to

Lesson 16: The Active and Passive Voices

The Passive Voice

When the subject of a verb is **not the "actor" of that verb**, the clause is in the **passive voice**. For instance, *the boy kicked the ball* is an **active voice** clause because the subject, *boy*, indicates who is **doing** the kicking. But *the ball was kicked by the boy* is in the **passive voice**, because the subject, *ball*, indicates what is **receiving** the kicking.

Henry ate all of his steak, but **33** his vegetables were uneaten.

33

A) NO CHANGE

B) left his vegetables

C) had his vegetables left

D) so his vegetables were

The first clause, *Henry ate all of his steak*, is in the **active voice**, but in choices A and D, the second clause is in the **passive voice**, and so does not attribute the action to *Henry*. Choice C is awkward and unclear. Choice B improves the parallelism and clarity of the sentence by matching the voices of the clauses and indicating who is leaving the vegetables uneaten.

Our lab experiment was designed by Amy and **33** Antonio ran it.

33

A) NO CHANGE

B) run by Antonio

C) Antonio was the one who ran it

D) was ran by Antonio

The first clause of this compound sentence is in the **passive voice**. Since the second clause concerns the same subject as the first, the Law of Parallelism suggests that it should also take the passive voice. Choices A and C are incorrect because they are in the active voice. Choice D uses the past tense form *ran* rather than the past participle *run*. The most concise and parallel option is B.

Which Voice Should I Use?

Passive clauses are usually **wordier** and **less direct** than active clauses. To **be concise and direct**, use the **active voice**. However, on the SAT, the passive voice is **not necessarily wrong**. **Passive** clauses can be used whenever it is helpful to **emphasize the receiver** of an action or status.

I came out of my physical examination feeling as if **18** they had poked me with a hundred probes and somebody had stabbed me with a hundred needles.

18

A) NO CHANGE

B) I had been poked by a hundred probes and they had stabbed me with

C) they had poked me with a hundred probes and I had been stabbed by

D) I had been poked by a hundred probes and stabbed by

Choice D is the most parallel option because the last two clauses share a subject, the passive voice, and similar prepositional phrases. In choices A, B, and C the voices are inconsistent and the pronoun *they* lacks a clear antecedent.

12 To prevent potentially fatal errors by surgeons and nurses, a checklist is carefully executed before each operation starts.

12

A) NO CHANGE

B) errors, surgeons and nurses carefully execute a checklist before each operation starts

C) errors by surgeons and nurses before each operation starts, a checklist is carefully executed

D) errors by surgeons and nurses, before each operation starts a checklist is carefully executed

Choices A, C, and D, are vague because the passive voice makes it unclear who is executing the checklist. The writer should indicate this fact clearly and directly. Choice B accomplishes this by placing the main clause in the active voice.

Lesson 17: Verb Mood

What Is Grammatical Mood?

The **mood** of a verb indicates the general purpose of the clause.

- The **indicative** mood indicates **factual claims**, as in *I went to the park.*
- The **imperative** mood indicates **suggestions or commands**, as in *You should go to the park,* or *Go to the park!*
- The **interrogative mood** asks questions, as in *Did you go to the park?*
- The **subjunctive mood** indicates **counterfactuals, hypotheticals,** or **potentials**, as in *I wish I had gone to the park* or *You may go to the park after school.*

If the engine `40` would run for too long on low-grade fuel, the pistons will wear out.

`40`

A) NO CHANGE

B) were to run

C) runs

D) should run

You may have been told that **conditional** (*if-then*) statements are always **subjunctive**. Wrong! Consider the isosceles triangle theorem: *If two sides of a triangle are congruent, then its base angles are congruent.* This is a **fact**, so each clause is phrased in the **indicative** mood. The sentence above represents a similar *if-then* fact. One clue is that the second clause, *the pistons will wear out*, is in the **indicative** mood. Therefore, the first clause should be in the indicative mood also, as in choice C.

If my lawyer `13` would have been more thorough in his cross-examination, he would have revealed the inconsistencies in her testimony.

`13`

A) NO CHANGE

B) had been

C) is

D) has been

The underlined verb is **counterfactual**, because it indicates that my lawyer was **not** thorough. Therefore, the first clause should take the **subjunctive mood**. However, choice A is incorrect because *would have been* is not idiomatic phrasing for an *if–* clause. The correct subjunctive form is *had been*, as in choice B. Choices C and D are incorrect because they are both in the indicative mood.

The Imperative Mood

Commands or requests in the **imperative mood** can be indicated in three ways.

- To make a **direct, second-person command**, use the **infinitive** form without an explicit subject, as in *Stop smoking!*
- To express a command or suggestion that is **indicated by another verb** (such as *prefer that, suggest that, demand that, propose that,* or *insist that*) or **adjective** (such as *it is necessary/important/ imperative/essential/better/ vital/crucial that*) use the **infinitive** form with an explicit subject, as in *My doctor demanded that I stop smoking* or *My doctor said that it is imperative that I stop smoking.*
- To express a command or suggestion that is **not** indicated by another verb or adjective, use the auxiliary **should** or **must** before the infinitive form, as in *My doctor said that I must stop smoking.*

After Ms. Parker scolded Daniel for the third time, she demanded that he `31` left the room.

`31`

A) NO CHANGE

B) must leave

C) leave

D) should leave

The verb *demanded* indicates that the underlined verb is a command, so *must* or *should* would be redundant. Therefore, we indicate the imperative with the infinitive *leave*, as in choice C. Choice A is incorrect because it is in the indicative mood. Choices B and D are incorrect because they include redundant auxiliaries. (Choices B and D are acceptable in the UK or Commonwealth countries, but not in standard American English.)

The Subjunctive Mood

The subjunctive mood is usually indicated by **subjunctive auxiliaries**: *can, could, may, might,* and *would*. A verb in the **present subjunctive** takes an auxiliary followed by the **infinitive** form of the verb, as in *We <u>might go</u> to the beach.* A verb in the **past subjunctive** takes an auxiliary followed by the **past consequential** (Lesson 12) form of the verb, as in *Your grandmother <u>would have loved</u> to see you in that dress.*

However, if a **counterfactual** is part of a **conditional** (*if-*) or **wishful** (*I wish that-*) clause that is **not indicating permission or potential**, it does **not** take a subjunctive auxiliary.

- If a verb is in a **present wishful or conditional counterfactual** clause, it takes the **simple past** form without an auxiliary, as in *I wish I <u>had</u> a million dollars* or *If I <u>had</u> a million dollars....*
- If the verb *to be* is in a **present wishful or conditional counterfactual** clause, it takes the form *were* without an auxiliary, as in *I wish I <u>were</u> ten years younger* or *If I <u>were</u> ten years younger....*
- If a verb is in a **past wishful or conditional counterfactual** clause, it takes the **past consequential** form without an auxiliary, as in *I wish I <u>had caught</u> the ball* or *If I <u>had caught</u> the ball....*

After the game, the coach admitted that he would not have called the trick play if his starting quarterback had been on the field.

10

Which choice best indicates that the coach was uncertain about his options?

A) NO CHANGE

B) did not call

C) might not have called

D) could not have called

The question asks you to choose the option that indicates *that the coach was uncertain about his options*. Choice A is incorrect because it is consistent with the possibility that the coach knew precisely which plays he would have called for each quarterback. Choice B is incorrect because this clause is counterfactual, and so cannot take the indicative mood. Choice D is incorrect because the auxiliary *could* indicates **inability** rather than **uncertainty**. Choice C is correct because *might* indicates that the coach was **not certain** about what he would have done if the starting quarterback had been in the game.

Conditional Counterfactuals

Any **present conditional counterfactual** form of the verb *to be* is usually phrased starting with *if-,* but in formal writing it can start with *were*:

Typical: *If I were shorter, I could wear that outfit.*

Formal: *Were I shorter, I could wear that outfit.*

Similarly, any **past conditional counterfactual** clause can be phrased starting with *if-* or with *had*:

Typical: *If he had studied, he would have passed the test.*

Formal: *Had he studied, he would have passed the test.*

The sailors would not have encountered the hurricane **31** <u>had they departed</u> only a day earlier.

31

A) NO CHANGE

B) if they would have departed

C) if they departed

D) if they would depart

The underlined phrase indicates a **past conditional counterfactual**, so it should take the form *if they had departed*. However, this is not a choice. Fortunately, choice A provides an equivalent phrasing, so it is the correct answer. Choices B and D are incorrect because a conditional counterfactual does not take the auxiliary *would*. Choice C is incorrect because a counterfactual cannot take the indicative mood.

Exercise Set 14: Verb Mood and Voice

1

Samuel Langhorne Clemens, who would later come to be known as Mark Twain, <u>would have been 25 years old when the Civil War started</u> in 1861.

A) NO CHANGE

B) would of been 25 years old when the Civil War had started

C) was 25 years old when the Civil War started

D) was 25 years old when the Civil War would have started

2

If the goalie <u>had not slipped</u> backward, he might not have blocked the shot and saved the game.

A) NO CHANGE

B) did not slip

C) had not of slipped

D) would not have slipped

3

The ushers demanded that we <u>must turn</u> off our cell phones until the intermission.

A) NO CHANGE

B) should turn

C) turn

D) turned

4

As we move through our daily routines, we tend to become agitated when our rituals are changed, our habits are disrupted, or <u>something violates our expectations</u>.

A) NO CHANGE

B) our expectations are violated

C) something would violate our expectations

D) something violated our expectations

5

As expected, <u>the rule against protests was dropped by the management</u>, who even expressed sympathy with the workers who had registered their complaints.

A) NO CHANGE

B) the rule against protests would have been dropped by the management

C) the management would have dropped the rule against protests

D) the management dropped the rule against protests

6

If the strong winds and rains <u>would have continued</u> for much longer, the small island town probably would have lost power completely.

A) NO CHANGE

B) had continued

C) continued

D) did continue

7

Our tour guide suggested that <u>we explore the tiny hillside town</u>, which is nearly 17 centuries old.

A) NO CHANGE

B) the tiny hillside town be explored by us

C) we should explore the tiny hillside town

D) we had explored the tiny hillside town

8

As Gina began climbing the long staircase, she wished that she <u>would have wore</u> her pumps instead of high heels.

A) NO CHANGE

B) had worn

C) would have worn

D) wore

Lesson 18: Punctuation

Interrupters

Interrupting modifiers must be bracketed by **identical punctuation marks**: either both commas or both dashes. Dashes are slightly more emphatic than commas and draw more attention to the interrupter.

The **42** coelacanth—a fish species once widely believed to be extinct, is found primarily in the tropical waters of the Indian Ocean.

42

A) NO CHANGE

B) coelacanth—a fish species once widely believed to be extinct—is

C) coelacanth: a fish species once widely believed to be extinct—is

D) coelacanth, a fish species once widely believed to be extinct is

Choice A is incorrect because the **interrupting appositive** is bracketed by different punctuation marks: a dash and a comma. Only choice B uses the same punctuation mark on both ends of the interrupter.

Apostrophes

Apostrophes should be used exclusively for **possessives** and **contractions. Never use apostrophes to pluralize.**

Only after a class-action suit was filed did the landlord consider giving the **42** renter's their money back.

42

A) NO CHANGE

B) renters their

C) renter's they're

D) renters there

Here, *renters* is a plural nonpossessive noun, and *their* is a plural possessive pronoun. Choices A and C are incorrect because apostrophes should be used only in contractions and possessives. Choice D is incorrect because *there* is not a plural possessive pronoun. Therefore, the correct answer is B.

Possessives

To turn a **plural noun ending in -*s* into a possessive**, just add an **apostrophe at the end.** For instance, *the boys' swim team.* **For singular nouns that end in -*s*, tack on -*'s*.** For instance, *Mr. Jones's class.*

Possessive pronouns—*your, whose, their, its*—do not use apostrophes. Their homophones with apostrophes—*you're, who's, they're, it's*—are **contractions**.

They did not know it at the time, but Gwen was **42** Chris's cousin's daughter.

42

A) NO CHANGE

B) Chris' cousin's

C) Chris's cousins

D) Chris' cousins

Both underlined words are possessives: the daughter is the *cousin's daughter* and the cousin is *Chris's cousin.* Even though *Chris* ends in an -*s*, it is not plural, so it is incorrect to use only an apostrophe to make it possessive. Both words require the -*'s* possessive form, so the correct answer is A.

Use Commas Sparingly

As a rule of thumb, **use commas only where necessary**. Commas are more often overused than underused.

The **42** subject, that intimidates me the most, is calculus.

42

A) NO CHANGE

B) subject that intimidates me the most, is

C) subject, that intimidates me the most is

D) subject that intimidates me the most is

The phrase *that intimidates me the most* is a **restrictive clause**, which means that the sentence would lose its central meaning if it were removed. Therefore, it shouldn't be separated from the main clause by commas, as in choice A. In fact, no commas are necessary at all, so the correct answer is D.

When to Use Commas

The primary job of a **comma** is to separate
- items in a **list**, as in
  He was fat, dumb, and lazy.
- **coordinate adjectives**, as in
  He gave a long, boring speech.
- **modifying phrases** from the main clause, as in
  In fact, I am appalled.
- **dependent clauses** from the main clause, as in
  Whenever I try, I fail.
- **independent clauses** from other independent
  clauses, but **only with a conjunction**, as in
  I think, therefore I am.

Commas can also be used to
- **introduce a quotation**, as in
  Tom said, "I ain't goin'!"
- **indicate an appositive title**, as in
  She read from her book, Blue Nights.
- **format an address or date**, as in
  Saturday, July 19, 2014 or *Cleveland, Ohio.*
- **signal an addressee**, as in
  Get going, buster!

The **16** philosopher, Immanuel Kant was
known to take long, regimented walks, he
claimed that they were essential to his thought
process.

16

A) NO CHANGE

B) philosopher, Immanuel Kant was
known to take long, regimented walks;
he claimed

C) philosopher Immanuel Kant was
known to take long regimented walks,
he claimed

D) philosopher Immanuel Kant was
known to take long, regimented walks;
he claimed

This sentence contains two independent clauses, but
choices A and C commit a **comma splice** by joining them
with only a comma. Choices B and D correct this problem by inserting a semicolon between the independent
clauses. Choice B is incorrect, however, because the first
comma does not serve any grammatical function. The
correct answer, then, is D.

Colons and Semicolons

Colons and **semicolons** should **always be preceded by independent clauses**.

- A **semicolon** must also be followed by an
  **independent clause that supports the first
  one**.
  The girls were tired; they needed a nap.

- A **colon** must be followed by a **list**, a **specifier**,
  or an **explanatory independent clause**.
  They were a party of three: Elisa, Jen, and Kate.
  The girls needed only one thing: sleep.
  *The girls were tired: they had practiced for
  hours.*

(These rules apply to the SAT, but they have
obscure exceptions. For example, semicolons
can also be used instead of a comma to separate items in a list when those items themselves
contain commas, as in *We will visit Providence,
Rhode Island; Concord, Massachusetts; and
Mystic, Connecticut.*)

But there was one more factor that the
experimenters hadn't **14** considered;
peer pressure.

A) NO CHANGE

B) considered: peer pressure

C) considered peer pressure

D) considered, peer pressure

Choice A is incorrect because the semicolon is not followed by a supportive independent clause. Choice C is
incorrect because it provides no indication about the
relationship between the main clause and the phrase
peer pressure. This phrase is a **specifier**, that is, it specifies the *factor* mentioned in the main clause. Therefore, it
should be preceded by a colon, as in choice B.

Exercise Set 15: Punctuation and Apostrophes

1

Unlike linear accelerators, <u>cyclotrons—such as the one Ernest Lawrence built in Berkeley, California, use</u> magnets to accelerate subatomic particles in a circular path.

A) NO CHANGE

B) cyclotrons, such as the one Ernest Lawrence built in Berkeley, California—use

C) cyclotrons, such as the one Ernest Lawrence built in Berkeley, California use

D) cyclotrons—such as the one Ernest Lawrence built in Berkeley, California—use

2

<u>Runners, who step out of they're lanes during the first two laps, will</u> be disqualified.

A) NO CHANGE

B) Runners who step out of their lanes during the first two laps, will

C) Runners, who step out of their lanes during the first two laps, will

D) Runners who step out of their lanes during the first two laps will

3

Many electric cars do save money on energy, but they are not <u>cheap: efficiency</u> has its price.

A) NO CHANGE

B) cheap, efficiency

C) cheap—efficiency,

D) cheap: efficiency,

4

Don't adopt a rescue <u>dog, until your sure they're</u> free of parasites and infectious diseases.

A) NO CHANGE

B) dog until you're sure it's

C) dog, until your sure it's

D) dog; until you're sure its

5

<u>Its easy to see—even on the dreariest of days, how Paris earned it's</u> reputation as the City of Love.

A) NO CHANGE

B) It's easy to see, even on the dreariest of days, how Paris earned its

C) Its easy to see, even on the dreariest of days, how Paris earned its

D) It's easy to see even on the dreariest of days how Paris earned it's

6

Having decided to postpone her <u>education, for at least two years Jill began</u> to look for a job in social media.

A) NO CHANGE

B) education for at least two years, Jill began

C) education, for at least two years, Jill began

D) education for at least two years Jill began

7

Our project was plagued by two main <u>issues; cost overruns and</u> bureaucratic red tape.

A) NO CHANGE

B) issues: cost overruns, and

C) issues: cost overruns and

D) issues; cost overruns, and

CHAPTER 5 ANSWER KEY

Exercise Set 1: Sentence Cores

1. **C**   If we trim the sentence, we find that the core is *The team were met*. But since *team* is a singular collective noun, it does not agree with the plural verb *were*. (Note that *advisors* cannot be the subject because it is part of a prepositional phrase.) The only choice that provides us with a singular verb is C. (This may sound strange if you were raised in the UK or a Commonwealth country, since, in the Queen's English, *team* and other such collective nouns are regarded as plurals. But the SAT is an American test, so here we must treat them as singulars.)

2. **B**   The subject of this sentence is *juggling* (a **gerund**, Lesson 7), which is singular, so it disagrees in number with the plural verb *seem*. (Note that *demands* cannot be the subject because it is part of a prepositional phrase.) Choice B corrects the agreement problem. Choice C is incorrect because the sentence specifies a fact about *today*, which requires the present tense, not the future tense. Choice D is incorrect because *would* indicates the **subjunctive mood** (Lesson 17), and so it incorrectly implies that the statement is hypothetical or counterfactual.

3. **C**   The singular subject of this sentence, *fact*, disagrees with the plural verb *have forced*. (Note that *institutions* cannot be the subject of this clause because it is the subject of a separate clause, *institutions...become dysfunctional*.) Choice C fixes this problem because *has* can take a singular subject. Choice B is incorrect because it uses the subjunctive mood, contradicting the **indicative** (Lesson 17) nature of the sentence. Choice D is incorrect because *are* disagrees with the singular subject.

4. **C**   The singular subject *Project* disagrees with the plural verb *provide*. Choice C provides the correct singular conjugation. Choices B and D are incorrect because both are conjugated for plural subjects.

5. **D**   The singular subject *intensity* disagrees in number with the verb *are*. (Note that *workouts* cannot be the subject because it is part of a prepositional phrase.) Choice D corrects this problem. Choices B and C are incorrect because they also disagree in number with the subject.

6. **A**   The original phrasing is clear and logical. The singular subject *anthology* agrees with the verb *includes*. (Note that *works* cannot be the subject because it is part of a prepositional phrase.) Choice B is incorrect because the two **parallel**

predicates require a conjunction between them. Choices C and D are incorrect because *include* does not agree with the singular subject.

7. **A**   The original phrasing is clear and logical. The singular subject *theory* agrees with the verb *makes*. Choice B is incorrect because the participle *making* cannot stand alone as a verb. Choice C is incorrect because the subjunctive mood should not be used when conveying facts. Choice D is incorrect because *make* does not agree with the singular subject.

8. **D**   This sentence has an inverted syntax. The "uninverted" version is *The crowds traditional routine of taunting the opposing players were surprisingly absent from the game*. This sentence has two problems: *crowds* should be changed to the possessive *crowd's* because it is modifying the noun *routine*, and the verb *were* does not agree with the singular subject *routine*. Only choice D corrects both problems.

9. **B**   In each choice, the phrase between the commas is an interrupting phrase. According to the Law of Trimming, the sentence must remain clear and coherent even after it has been removed. Choices A and D are incorrect because *as good than* is not **idiomatic** (Lesson 15). Choice C is incorrect because it makes an **illogical comparison** (Lesson 10). One type of education can be compared only with another type of education, so the logic and phrasing in choice B is correct.

Exercise Set 2: Verb Agreement

1. **C**   The phrase *scattered by* is not idiomatic unless it is part of a **passive voice** verb (Lesson 16), so choice A is incorrect. Choice B is incorrect because *were* does not agree with the singular subject *flock*. Choice D is incorrect because the **progressive aspect** (Lesson 13) cannot indicate a sudden reaction to something like a shotgun blast. Only choice C has the correct voice and conjugation.

2. **C**   This is an inverted sentence. The "uninverted" version is *Over two million microorganisms is in every teaspoon of topsoil, forming a highly complex ecosystem*. Clearly, the verb *is* disagrees with the plural subject *organisms*, and should be changed to *are*. Choice B is incorrect because *was* is in the wrong tense and disagrees with the plural subject. Choice D is wrong because *being* cannot stand alone as a verb.

3. **C**   This is an inverted sentence. If you missed this one, you probably didn't read the sentence

carefully enough. Notice that that there is no *be* between *conditioning* and *to*, so the wording in choice A is illogical. Choice B is incorrect because the singular subject *conditioning* disagrees with the plural verb *are*. Choice C is correct because *is* agrees with the singular verb. Choice D is incorrect because it does not form a complete sentence.

4. **A** The original phrasing is correct because the interrupter is a logical **participial phrase** (Lesson 8) that modifies the subject *technology*. Choices B and C are both incorrect because they render the preceding comma illogical and create parallel predicates unlinked by a conjunction. Choice D is incorrect because it creates an illogical participial phrase.

5. **D** This sentence uses a **standard parallel construction** (Lesson 7), *both A and B*, and therefore requires a verb that matches the form of the previous verb, *inspire*. Only choice D maintains this parallel structure. Choices B and C both include extra words that disrupt the parallel structure.

6. **B** In choices A and C, the verb *have expressed* disagrees with the singular subject *coalition*. Choice D is incorrect because *concern with* is the incorrect **idiom** (Lesson 15) for indicating worry. The correct idiom is *concern about*, as in choice B.

7. **B** Choices A and C are incorrect because the verb *explain* disagrees with the singular subject *explosiveness*. Choice D is incorrect because *its* is a possessive form, not a contraction.

8. **C** The predicate of the sentence indicates that the subject should be *S. J. Perelman*, and not his writing or his style. Therefore, choices A, B, and D have illogical subjects. Only choice C works logically with the predicate of the sentence.

9. **D** Since this sentence is about the habits of the grizzly bear, the verbs should take the present tense, **habitual aspect** (Lesson 3) and **indicative mood** (Lesson 17). Only choice D is correct in both regards. Choice A is incorrect because it uses the subjunctive mood. Choices B and C are incorrect because they are in the past tense.

Exercise Set 3: Coordinating Ideas

1. **B** The original sequence of sentences is not logically coordinated. Choice B coordinates the ideas logically by emphasizing the central idea (that *The Return has received widespread acclaim*) in the main clause, and relegating the minor facts to modifying phrases. In choice C, the introductory modifying phrase does not logically modify the subject of the main clause. In choice D, the **colon** (Lesson 18) is misused and the prepositional phrase does not logically modify anything in the sentence.

2. **D** The original set of sentences should be combined because they all relate one key idea about a common topic. Choices B and C are incorrect because, in both cases, the **interrogative pronoun** (Lesson 11) *which* has no logical antecedent. Choice D is best because it consolidates the first two sentences effectively, and clarifies the subject of the last clause.

3. **C** The original sentence commits a **comma splice** (Lesson 5) because the clause following the comma qualifies as an independent clause. Also, the pronoun *this* lacks a logical antecedent. Choice B is illogical because the *power plants* are not being burned. Choice C is best because a clause whose subject is *which* is no longer independent, so the comma splice problem is fixed. Additionally, *which* can logically refer to the plural noun *power plants*. Choice D is incorrect because *it* lacks a logical antecedent.

4. **D** The original sentence contains a **standard parallel construction** (Lesson 7) *not only A but also B*. However, choices A, B, and C do not use standard idiomatic phrasing. Additionally, in both B and C, the two instances of the pronoun *it* refer to different antecedents. Only choice D avoids redundancy and uses standard idiomatic phrasing.

5. **A** The original phrasing is best. The sentence begins with a **participial phrase** (Lesson 8), which must coordinate with the main clause by sharing its subject. This participle describes a *treatise*, so the subject of the main clause must be the book, not Keynes, therefore choices B and D are incorrect. Choice C is incorrect because the **interrogative pronoun** (Lesson 11) *which* does not coordinate logically with the antecedent *Keynes*.

Exercise Set 4: Transitions and References

1. **B** The first sentence indicates a general fact about the ancient Greeks, and the quote from Antigone in the second sentence provides a specific example to illustrate that fact. Therefore, choice B, *For example,* is the most logical choice. Choice A is incorrect because a *coincidence* is a surprising simultaneity of events, but these sentences indicate no such simultaneity. Choice C is incorrect because the second sentence does not extend a previous claim. Choice D is incorrect because the second sentence does not contrast the first.

2. **B** The first sentence describes a belief about *tough sentencing*, but the second sentence indicates a fact that undermines that belief. Therefore, the most logical transition is *However*. Choice A, *Even worse,* is incorrect because the second sentence doesn't describe an escalation of negativity. Choice C is

incorrect because the second sentence does not clarify or paraphrase anything. Choice D is incorrect because the second sentence does not describe a result.

3. **A**　The first sentence describes a general social trend, and the second sentence describes a result of that trend. Therefore, Choice A, *Consequently*, provides a logical transition. Choice B is incorrect because the second sentence does not indicate an ironic or surprising situation. Choice C is incorrect because the second sentence does not indicate a situation that is analogous to any previously mentioned. Choice D is incorrect because the second sentence does not exemplify anything described in the first sentence.

Exercise Set 5: Parallel Structure

1. **C**　The second and third items in the list, *improving* and *repairing*, are gerunds, therefore the first item should also be a gerund, as in choice C.

2. **D**　This sentence uses the standard parallel construction, *not so much A as B*. Choices A and B are incorrect because they do not use correct idiomatic phrasing. Choice C is incorrect because the second item in the contrast, *how wisely you use your time*, is not parallel in form to the first item, *about working hard*. Since the first item is a prepositional phrase, the second should be as well, as in choice D.

3. **B**　This sentence uses the standard parallel construction *not only A but also B*. Choices A and C are incorrect because they do not use correct idiomatic phrasing. Choice D is incorrect because *also* and *as well* are redundant.

4. **A**　This sentence gives a binary list, so the items should have parallel grammatical and semantic form. The first item in the list, *the skittishness of investors*, is a noun phrase defining a personal characteristic of a group of people, so the second item should do the same. Only choice A maintains both the grammatical and semantic parallelism.

5. **D**　Choices A, B, and C are all ambiguous because, with each phrasing, the dilemma is unclear: it could be read to mean that I'm trying to decide between *giving the tickets* to Maria and *giving Caitlyn* to Maria, which is of course nonsensical. Only choice D is unambiguous: the choice is between *giving the tickets to Maria* and *giving the tickets to Caitlyn*.

6. **C**　This sentence uses the standard parallel construction *prefer A to B*. Choices A and B are incorrect because they do not use standard phrasing. Choice D is incorrect because the comma serves no grammatical purpose.

7. **B**　This sentence uses the standard parallel construction *not so much A as B*. Choices A and C are incorrect because neither uses the standard phrasing. Choice D is incorrect because the second item, *because of the freewheeling, Bohemian atmosphere*, does not have the same grammatical form as the first item, *for the music*. Choice B is best because it uses the standard phrasing and the items, *for the music* and *for the freewheeling, Bohemian atmosphere*, are both prepositional phrases.

Exercise Set 6: Coordinating Modifiers

1. **C**　The subject of the participle *drained* is *Martha*, not her *instinct*. (Just ask: *who was drained?*) Therefore, choices A, B, and D are incorrect because they include dangling participles. The only option with the correct subject is choice C.

2. **B**　The prepositional phrase *with a sprained ankle* modifies *Adam*, not *the coach*, so choice A is incorrect because it contains a dangling modifier. Choice B corrects this problem by using a dependent clause with a clear subject, verb, and object. Choices C and D are incorrect because neither clarifies who has the sprained ankle.

3. **D**　The subject of the participle *lacking* is *David*. (*Who* lacked any real sailing skills?) Therefore, choices A and C contain dangling participles. Choice B is incorrect because the phrase *had the primary concern* is unidiomatic and unclear.

4. **B**　What was *searching through a box of old letters*? *We* were. By the Law of Proximity, the modifying phrase should be as close to its subject—the word that it modifies—as possible, as in choice B. Choices A, C, and D are all incorrect because each implies that the *manuscript* was searching through the box of old letters.

5. **D**　Choice A is incorrect because the (infinitive) noun phrase *To get a good jump out of the blocks* does not play any grammatical role in the main clause. Choice B is incorrect because the prepositional phrase *for getting a good jump out of the blocks* is too far away from the adjective it modifies, *essential*. Choice C is incorrect because the prepositional phrase *for hip positioning to be proper* does not logically modify any part of the main clause. Choice D is best because it places the prepositional phrase next to the adjective it modifies.

6. **B**　The adjective *unhappy* describes the *senator*, not her *plan*, so choice A is illogical. Choices C and D likewise have illogical subjects. Only choice B uses a subject that corrects for the dangling modifier.

7. **A**　The original phrasing is best, because it contains a clause that coordinates logically with the

participial phrase that starts the sentence. Choice B is incorrect because *then* is redundant. Choices C and D are incorrect because they both allow the participial phrase to dangle.

Exercise Set 7: Using Modifiers Logically

1. **C** Choice A is incorrect because the comparative adjective *much stronger* cannot modify the verb *emphasize*. The comparative adverb, *more strongly*, is required, as in choice C.

2. **B** Choices A and C are incorrect because the adverbs *never* and *usually* are contradictory. Choice D is incorrect because *hardly never* is not an idiomatic phrase. The idiomatic phrases are *hardly ever* or *almost never,* as in choice B.

3. **C** Choices A and D are incorrect because the verb *coordinated* cannot be modified with the adjective *effective*. Choices B and C both use the proper adverbial form *effectively*, but choice B is incorrect because it makes an **illogical comparison** (Lesson 10).

4. **A** The original phrasing is best, because one of the meanings of *unqualified* is *total*, so an *unqualified success* is a *complete success*. Choice B is incorrect because *successfully unqualified* is not a sensible phrase. Choice C is incorrect because *disqualified* means *eliminated from competition because of a rule violation*, which does not logically apply to a *success*. Choice D is incorrect because *unqualified in its success* is not idiomatic.

5. **A** The original phrasing is best: recall that *harder* can serve as either a comparative adjective or a comparative adverb. Choice B is incorrect because *more hardly* is an illogical phrase. Choices C and D are incorrect because the phrase *always doesn't* contradicts the statement that *challenge is the key to success*.

6. **B** Choices A and C are illogical because it is untrue that the teacher *never* told us about the test; she just waited until the last minute to do so. Choice D is incorrect because the phrase *hardly ever* implies a claim about a long-term trend rather than a specific event.

7. **D** Choices A, B, and C all contain double negatives that contradict a logical reading of the sentence. Only choice D provides a logical phrasing.

Exercise Set 8: Logical Comparisons

1. **A** The original phrasing is logical and parallel, because *ignoring* and *attacking* are both gerunds. Choices B and C are incorrect because they use the infinitive form, which breaks the parallel structure. Choice D is incorrect because the phrase *it is attacking* is not parallel in form to the gerund *ignoring*.

2. **C** Choices A, B, and D are all illogical comparisons, because *Kyrchek's latest film* must be included in *anything she has done* or *everything she has done* or *any of the work she did*. Only choice C excludes her current film so that a logical comparison can be made.

3. **B** Choices A and C are incorrect because they make a category error in comparing *motors of cars* to *cars*. Choice B makes a logical comparison because *engines* are *motors*. Choice D is incorrect because it is redundant: *those* and *engines* refer to the same noun.

4. **B** Each choice contains an interrupting modifier, but only choice B remains idiomatic, logical, and grammatical after this interrupter is trimmed from the sentence.

5. **C** The subject of this sentence is *lessons*, so the comparison to *teachers* in choices A and B is illogical. Choice D is incorrect because comparing *lessons* to *classrooms* is also illogical. Only choice C makes a logical comparison: the parallel structure makes it clear that the pronoun *those* refers to *lessons*.

6. **A** The original phrasing is logical because it makes a like-to-like comparison between *Modernist poetry* and *Victorian or Elizabethan poetry*. Choice B is incorrect because *poetry* cannot be compared to *poets*. Choice C is incorrect because *those* lacks a logical antecedent with which it agrees in number. Choice D is redundant because *that* and *poetry* both have the same referent.

7. **C** Since *customers* are countable and noncontinuous quantities, *less* is an illogical modifier, and should be changed to *fewer*, as in choices B and C. However, choice B is incorrect because the subjunctive *would pay* contradicts the **indicative mood** (Lesson 17) in the clause *transparency in banking increases*.

Exercise Set 9: Pronoun Agreement

1. **C** Choices A and B are illogical because the pronoun *where* cannot be used to refer to *times*. Choice D is incorrect because it commits a **pronoun shift** from *one* to *you*. Only choice C avoids both pronoun problems.

2. **B** The rest of the sentence uses the second person pronouns *you* and *your*, so consistency requires that the underlined portion also use *you* instead of *one*, as in choices B and D. Choice D is incorrect, however, because *shouldn't even* illogically implies some minimum level of avoidance.

3. **A** The original phrasing is clear and logical because the possessive pronoun *their* agrees with the plural antecedent *words*. Choices B and C are

incorrect because they mistake contractions for possessives. Choice D is incorrect because *its* disagrees with the plural antecedent *words.*

4. **C** Choice A is incorrect because the plural pronoun *their* disagrees with the singular antecedent *Arts Council.* Choices B and D are incorrect because they are contractions, not possessives.

5. **D** Choices A and B are incorrect because the verb *do*—which often refers to a verb in much the same way as a pronoun refers to a noun, as in *I don't often fly first class, but when I do...*—does not have a clear "antecedent verb." Choice D corrects this mistake by clarifying this reference. Choice C is incorrect because it misuses the possessive *their.*

6. **A** The original phrasing is correct because *it* agrees with the singular antecedent *bonobo.* Choice B is incorrect because *its* is a possessive, not a contraction. Choices C and D are incorrect because they use plural pronouns.

7. **C** Choice A is incorrect because the pronoun *when* must refer to a *time,* not a *process.* Choice B is incorrect because a *process* is not a place. Choice D is incorrect because the phrase *so that* implies that the *nitrogen cycle* is an intentional action, which it is not.

Exercise Set 10: Pronoun Case

1. **C** Since the underlined phrase is the object of the preposition *of,* it must take the objective case, as in choice C.

2. **A** As much as most people want to "correct" this sentence, perhaps by changing *him and me* to *us* (which would actually make the reference less specific), the original phrasing is correct. This phrase serves as the object of the pronoun *for,* and therefore both pronouns must take the objective case: *him and me.* Notice that this is clearer to see when we isolate each element: it is perfectly correct to say *it might be difficult for <u>him</u> to stay* or *it might be difficult for <u>me</u> to stay,* therefore it is also acceptable to say *it might be difficult for <u>him and me</u> to stay.* (Some may object and claim that this phrase serves as the subject of the verb *stay,* and therefore should take the subjective case. This is incorrect, because *to stay* is an **infinitive** (Lesson 7), not a conjugated verb, so it takes no grammatical subject.)

3. **D** Here, choice A may seem correct, because the pronoun *us* is the object of the preposition *in,* right? No: the object of the preposition is *delaying.* (What is there no point in? *Us,* or the *delaying?*) Therefore, the pronoun must be a modifier of the gerund *delaying* and should take the possessive form, *our.*

4. **C** The underlined phrase is the subject of the verb *are,* and therefore the pronouns must take the subject case: *you and I.*

5. **C** The underlined pronoun is part of the subject of the verb *have always been,* and therefore must take the subjective case, *I.*

6. **D** The underlined phrase represents the subject of the verb *have suffered,* and therefore the verb must take the subjective case, *we.* The phrase *Giants fans* serves as an **appositive modifier** (Lesson 8) to the subject, and therefore must take the form of a noun phrase, as in choice D.

7. **A** The original phrasing is correct because the phrase *my wife and me* serves as the indirect object of the verb *offered,* and therefore must take the objective case.

Exercise Set 11: Verb Tense and Aspect

1. **D** This sentence is trying to convey not only *what* the team is hopeful about, but *why* the team is hopeful. Choice A is incorrect because the present participle *developing* implies that the *developing* and the *hoping* were concurrent, which is illogical. Since the *hoping* depends on the *completion* of the development, the **consequential participle** *having developed* is required, as in choices B and D. Choice B is redundant because *hope to reveal* already conveys subjunctive potential, so the auxiliary *would* is unnecessary.

2. **B** Common sense tells us that the research must be at least partially completed before the first draft of a term paper can be completed, so the consequential participle *having spent* is required to show this relationship. Also, the adverb *already,* without any other time specification, refers to a *current* status, and therefore the main verb must take the present consequential form, *has written,* as in choice B.

3. **D** The phrase *as soon as* indicates that this sentence is referring to concurrent events. Therefore, any use of the consequential aspect is illogical. Choice D is correct because it is the only one that does not use the consequential aspect.

4. **A** The use of the consequential participle *having taken* in the original phrasing is most logical, because the *fear* described in the main clause could not set in before the hikers were well along on the wrong path. Choice C is incorrect, however, because the past consequential *had feared* implies that the *fear* is an antecedent rather than a consequence.

5. **C** Choice A is incorrect because this sentence is stating a fact, and therefore should take the **indicative mood** (Lesson 17) rather than the subjunctive mood. Choices B and D are incorrect

because the verb *seems* has already established that this sentence is in the **artistic present**, and not the past tense.

6. **A** The use of the present tense in first clause establishes that the sentence is describing a current status. Therefore the present tense **indicative mood** (Lesson 17) is required, as in choice A. The present consequential *has performed* is appropriate here because her previous performance clearly extends a consequence to her current status, which explains why she *is well qualified*.

7. **B** Choices A and D are incorrect because the consequential aspect requires the past participle *sunk* rather than the simple past tense *sank*. Choice C is incorrect because the phrase *over three hundred years ago* indicates that the verb must be in the past tense.

8. **C** Choice A is incorrect because it commits a comma splice. Choices B and D are incorrect because the sentence is indicating a fact, and therefore should take the **indicative mood** (Lesson 17) and not the **subjunctive mood** (Lesson 17). The use of the consequential participle *having published* in choice C is correct because this fact extends a consequence to his status when he died.

Exercise Set 12: Diction and Redundancy

1. **D** To *abolish* means to *formally put an end to a system, practice, or institution*, and so it does not apply to an infestation of beetles. Choice B is incorrect because *delete* applies to written or genetic material or computer memory, not to insects. Choice C is incorrect because *retract* means to *draw or take back*, which does not apply to insects. Only choice D, *eradicate*, describes something that can be done to an infestation of insects.

2. **B** Choices A and C are incorrect because the use of the conjunction *but* is redundant with the use of the conjunction *although*. Choice D is incorrect, because *smear* means to *damage the reputation of*, which does not apply to theories. Choice B is best because statistics can *refute* theories.

3. **D** Choice A is incorrect because the phrase *separate out* is redundant, and also because *separate* describes a physical rather than a mental act. Choice B is incorrect because to *certify* is to *formally attest or confirm*, which does not apply to a mental event. Choice C is incorrect because to *acknowledge* is simply to *accept or admit the existence or truth of*, which does not at all indicate a particular skill of wine experts. Only choice D, *discern*, which means to *distinguish with difficulty by the senses*, reasonably describes what wine experts do with grapes, regions, and vintages.

4. **D** A *consensus* is a *general agreement*, so the phrase *consensus of unified opinion* is redundant. Choice B is likewise redundant. Choice C is not idiomatic. Choice D provides the most concise, idiomatic, and clear phrasing.

5. **C** To *appoint* means to *formally or officially assign a role to (someone)*, and therefore applies only to a person and not to a *decision*. Choice B is incorrect because the council is making the decision itself, and is not being *compelled (forced)* to do it. Choice D is incorrect because a *predetermined (decided beforehand)* decision would not require any extra time to deliberate.

6. **A** To *disparage* means to *represent as being of little worth*, which is precisely what critics might do to a bad movie. Choice B is incorrect because a movie cannot be *confronted*. Choice C is incorrect because to *impair* means to *weaken or damage* something, but this cannot reasonably be done to a movie that is already made. Choice D is incorrect because to *repudiate* is to *refuse to be associated with* or to *deny the validity of*, neither of which is something that critics can do to movies that they did not themselves help create.

7. **D** None of the modifiers in choices A, B, and C contribute any meaning or emphasis to the sentence, and so all are redundant. The present tense verb *cannot process* is all that is needed to indicate the present.

8. **C** Choice A is incorrect because to *hamper* means to *hinder or impede the progress of (something)*, but it is nonsensical to expect that workers would do this to themselves. Choice B is incorrect because *subside (to decrease in intensity)* is an **intransitive verb**, that is, it cannot take an object as this verb does. Choice D is incorrect because work cannot be *lowered*. Only choice C, *curtail (restrict)*, makes sense in this context.

9. **B** Choices A and C are incorrect because someone's self-esteem cannot *proliferate (increase rapidly in numbers)* or *multiply* because self-esteem is a unitary thing. Choice D is incorrect because *enlarge* applies to physical size or extent, which cannot apply to a human psychological trait like *self-esteem*. Choice B is best because one's self-esteem can *blossom (mature in a healthy way)*.

10. **D** *Imminent* means *about to happen*, so choices A and B are redundant. Choice C is incorrect because *imminently likely* is a malapropism of *eminently likely*. Choice D is best because it is concise and free of redundancy.

11. **D** To *evolve* means to *develop gradually into a more complex or effective form*, but the process of changing a motor is not gradual or passive. Choice B is incorrect because *correlated* means *having a mutual relationship, particularly when one quantity*

affects another, which does not apply to objects like motors. Choice C is incorrect because to *amend* means to *improve (a document)*, but a motor is not a document. Choice D is best because to *adapt* is to *make (something) suitable to a new purpose*.

12. **C**   Choice A is incorrect because to *intimidate* means to *frighten into compliance*, which is not at all subtle. Choice B is incorrect because *propel* implies a forceful forward motion that is not appropriate to the act of purchasing something. Choice D is incorrect because to *oppress* is to *keep in subservience through assertive authority*, which is far too strong and broad a term to describe what advertising may do to individuals. Choice C, *induce (successfully persuade)*, is the most appropriate choice to describe how advertising influences consumers.

13. **C**   Choices A, B, and D are incorrect because *apprehensive, neurotic,* and *worried* are all adjectives describing the internal, emotional states of people and are inappropriate for describing the mood of a conversation. (The correct term to describe a situation that induces worry is *worrisome,* not *worried*.) Only choice C, *tense (causing anxiety),* can appropriately describe the mood of negotiations.

14. **B**   *Reticent* means *unwilling to reveal one's thoughts or feelings*. It does not mean *reluctant,* and so choice A is redundant. Choice B, *reticent about,* captures the idea most concisely. Choice C is wordy and unidiomatic. Choice D is incorrect because it omits any reference to expression.

15. **C**   Choice A is incorrect because to *impede* means to *obstruct or hinder,* but the sentence does not indicate that the ministers were prevented from achieving a goal. Choice B is incorrect because *scuttle* means *deliberately cause to fail,* but the sentence does not indicate that the ministers deliberately failed in any effort. Choice D is incorrect because *snubbed* means *rebuffed* or *ignored disdainfully,* but such an action would not cause anyone to go into exile. The best choice is C, *ousted,* which means *driven from power*.

16. **B**   Choice A is incorrect because *elicit* is a verb meaning *evoke or draw out*. Also, *incidents* are countable, noncontinuous things and so should be modified by fewer, not *less*. Clearly, this sentence calls for *illicit,* an adjective meaning *forbidden by law*. Choice C is incorrect because *incidence* means *frequency of a disease, crime, or other undesirable thing,* so, as an uncountable quantity, it doesn't go with *fewer*. The only choice that avoids all diction problems is B.

Exercise Set 13: Standard Idiom

1. **C**   Since the sentence describes a plan that was developed carefully over an extended period of

time, the proper idiom is *agreed on,* as in choice C. Recall that although we can *agree with* a person, and *agree to* an offer, we *agree on* plans that are mutually decided.

2. **D**   The comparative preposition *than* is required when making unequal comparisons with comparative adjectives, as in *smaller than* or *faster than*. Notice, however, that *different* is not a comparative adjective like these, and it requires the idiom *different from*.

3. **C**   The proper idiom is *comply with (a rule)*. None of the options in A, B, and D is idiomatic.

4. **C**   The proper idiom here is *prefer A to B*. Note that this is a **standard parallel construction** (Lesson 7). Note, also, that the phrases in the comparison—*the soft, diffuse light* and *the light of the old compact fluorescent bulbs*—have parallel grammatical form.

5. **A**   Since a *plea deal* is a type of *offer,* rather than a general situation (*agree about*), person (*agree with*), or mutual plan (*agree on*), the proper idiom here is *agree to,* as in choice A.

6. **D**   Recall from Lesson 7 that **infinitives** often provide the most concise way of expressing **purpose,** and therefore choice D, *to investigate,* is the most concise and idiomatic option. Choice A is needlessly wordy, and choices B and C are not idiomatic.

7. **B**   Choices A and C are incorrect because the phrase *determine about* is not idiomatic. As with most idioms, always ask whether the preposition is required at all. In this case, it is not. Choice D is incorrect because the pronouns *which* and *that* are redundant, since they refer to the same antecedent, *activities,* and play the same grammatical role.

8. **C**   Choice A is incorrect because *arguments on* is not a standard idiom. You can *argue with* a person, or you can *argue for* or *argue against* a claim or position. Since this refers to a position on a *proposal,* the only idiomatic option is C, *arguments for*.

9. **D**   The correct idiom here is *a tribute to (a person)*. Choices A, B, and C are not idiomatic.

Exercise Set 14: Verb Mood and Voice

1. **C**   This sentence is making two factual historical claims, so both claims—about Clemens's age and when the Civil War started— must take the **indicative mood,** not the **subjunctive mood**. Therefore, choices A, B, and D are incorrect. (Note that, in choice B, the phrase *would of* is a common **diction** error. The proper subjunctive phrasing is *would have*.)

2. **A**   The original subjunctive phrasing is best, because this clause is **counterfactual**: the goalie *did* slip backward. Recall that the **past conditional counterfactual** takes the same form as the **past consequential**: *had not slipped*. Choice B is

incorrect because this statement is counterfactual, not indicative. Choice C is incorrect because the preposition *of* serves no grammatical purpose. Choice D is incorrect because this is not the idiomatic phrasing for a past conditional counterfactual.

3. **C** Since the verb *demanded* indicates that the underlined verb represents a command or suggestion, the imperative auxiliaries *must* and *should* are redundant in choices A and B. The imperative requires the infinitive form, *turn*, as in choice C.

4. **B** This sentence contains a list, the first two items of which are clauses in the passive voice: *our rituals are changed* and *our habits are disrupted*. The Law of Parallelism requires that the third item also be a clause in the passive voice, as in choice B.

5. **A** The original phrasing is best, even though it is in the passive voice. The passive voice is required here so that the two clauses can logically coordinate. Choice B is incorrect because the subjunctive *would have been dropped* does not coordinate logically with the indicative clause that follows. Choices C and D are incorrect because the appositive pronoun *who* in the second clause would be taken to refer to the *protests*, which is illogical.

6. **B** Choice A is incorrect because the first clause is a past conditional counterfactual and therefore should not include the subjunctive auxiliary *would*. The past conditional counterfactual requires the same form as the past consequential, *had continued*, as in choice B.

7. **A** The original phrasing is best. The verb *suggested* indicates the imperative mood in the clause that follows, so no imperative auxiliary (*should* or *might*) is required. Choice B is incorrect because the passive voice construction does not coordinate with the pronoun *which* in the second clause. Choice C is incorrect because the imperative auxiliary *should* is redundant. Choice D is incorrect because the past consequential *had explored* is illogical.

8. **B** The verb *wished* indicates that the underlined verb is **past wishful**, and therefore it should take the **past consequential** form, *had worn*, without the subjunctive auxiliary. Choice A is incorrect because it uses that subjunctive auxiliary *would* and the past tense *wore* instead of the past participle *worn*. Choice C is incorrect because it uses the subjunctive auxiliary. Choice D is wrong because the simple past *wore* does not indicate the past wishful form of the verb.

Exercise Set 15: Punctuation and Apostrophes

1. **D** Choice A is incorrect because the interrupting modifier, *such as the one Ernest Lawrence built in Berkeley, California,* is not bracketed by identical punctuation marks. Only choice D uses identical marks, both dashes, to set off the interrupter.

2. **D** Choice A is incorrect because the **restrictive clause** *who step out of their lanes during the first two laps* should not be separated from the main clause by commas, because it is essential to the core meaning of the sentence. Also, it misuses the contraction *they're* for the possessive pronoun *their*. The only choice that uses the correct pronoun form and does not misuse commas is choice D.

3. **A** The original phrasing is best because the colon precedes an **explanatory independent clause**. The statement *efficiency has its price* helps to explain the fact that *electric cars are not cheap*. Choice B is incorrect because it commits a comma splice. Choice C is incorrect because the comma serves no grammatical purpose, and a dash should not be used to separate independent clauses. Choice D is incorrect because the comma serves no grammatical purpose.

4. **B** Choice A is incorrect because it misuses the possessive pronoun *your* for the conjunction *you're*, and because the pronoun *they* does not agree in number with its antecedent *dog*. Choice B corrects both of these problems. Choice C is incorrect because it misuses the possessive pronoun *your*. Choice D is incorrect because the semicolon serves no grammatical purpose and it uses the possessive *its* instead of the contraction *it's*.

5. **B** Choice A is incorrect because the possessive *Its* is misused instead of the contraction *It's*, because the interrupting phrase is not bracketed by identical punctuation marks, and because the contraction *it's* is misused instead of the possessive pronoun *its*. Choice B corrects all three of these mistakes. Choice C is incorrect because it mistakes *Its* for *It's*. Choice D is incorrect because it mistakes *it's* for *its*, and does not offset the interrupting phrase.

6. **B** The preposition phrase *for at least two years* is an adverbial phrase modifying the verb *postpone*. Choice A is incorrect because the placement of the comma suggests that the prepositional phrase modifies the verb *began*, which is illogical. Choice B corrects this problem by moving the comma. Choice C is incorrect because the first comma is incorrect. Choice D is incorrect because a comma is required after *years*.

7. **C** Choices A and D are incorrect because a semicolon must always be followed by a supporting **independent clause**. Since the phrase that follows is a **specifier** that indicates what the *main issues* were, a colon is required, as in choices B and C. However, choice B is incorrect because a comma should not be used to separate items in a binary list when a conjunction is already being used.

CHAPTER 6

THE SAT ESSAY

1. Understand the Analytical Task   253

2. Read the Passage Using the "Three-Pass Approach"   258

3. Construct Your Thesis and Outline   266

4. Write the Essay   269

    Sample Essay   273

The SAT Essay

What is the SAT Essay?

The SAT includes an **optional** 50-minute Essay assignment designed to assess your

> *proficiency in writing a cogent and clear analysis of a challenging rhetorical essay written for a broad audience.*

Should you choose to accept the challenge, the SAT Essay will be the fifth and final section of your test.

The SAT Essay assignment asks you to read a 650–750 word rhetorical essay (such as a *New York Times* op-ed about the economic pros and cons of using biofuels) and to write a well-organized response that

- demonstrates an understanding of the essay's central ideas and important details
- analyzes its use of evidence, such as facts or examples, to support its claims
- critiques its use of reasoning to develop ideas to connect claims and evidence
- examines how it uses stylistic or persuasive elements, such as word choice or appeals to emotion, to add power to the ideas expressed

How is it used?

Many colleges use the SAT Essay in admissions or placement decisions. Many also regard it as an important indicator of essential skills for success in college, specifically, your ability to demonstrate understanding of complex reading assignments, to analyze arguments, and to express your thoughts in writing.

Sound intimidating? It's not.

If you have mastered the analytical reading skills discussed in Chapters 4 and 5, you already have a strong start on tackling the SAT Essay, since strong active reading of the source text is the first and most important step in the analytical writing task. There are four rules to success on the SAT Essay, and the 13 lessons in this chapter will give you the knowledge and practice you need to master all of them.

Understand the Analytical Task
Lesson 1: Use your 50 minutes wisely

The SAT Essay assesses your proficiency in reading, analysis, and writing. You are given 50 minutes to read an argumentative essay and write an analysis that demonstrates your comprehension of the essay's primary and secondary ideas and your understanding of its use of evidence, language, reasoning, and rhetorical or literary elements to support those ideas. You must support your claims with evidence from the text and use critical reasoning to evaluate its rhetorical effectiveness.

So what should you do with those 50 minutes?

Reading: 15–20 minutes

Although 15–20 minutes may seem like a long time to devote to reading a 750-word essay, remember that you must do more than simply read the essay. You must comprehend the essay and analyze its stylistic and rhetorical elements. In other words, you must master the "Three-Pass Approach" that we will practice in lessons 4–6. This is a fairly advanced reading technique, and you will need to devote substantial time to practicing it. Even once you've mastered it, you will still need to set aside 15–20 minutes on the SAT Essay section to read and annotate the passage thoroughly.

Organizing: 10–15 minutes

Your next task is to gather the ideas from your analyses and use them to formulate a thesis and structure for a five- or six-paragraph essay. If you have performed your first task properly and have completed your "Three-Pass" analysis, creating an outline will be much easier. We will discuss these tasks in lessons 7 and 8.

Your thesis should summarize the thesis of the essay and its secondary ideas, describe the author's main stylistic and rhetorical elements, and explain how these elements support (or detract from) the author's argument.

Take your time with this process, too. Don't start writing before you have articulated a thoughtful guiding question and outlined the essay as a whole.

Writing: 20–25 minutes

Next, of course, you have to write your easy. To get a high score, your essay must provide an eloquent introduction and conclusion, articulate a thesis summarizing the central claims and the main rhetorical and stylistic elements of the essay, be well organized, show a logical and cohesive progression of ideas, maintain a formal style and an objective tone, and show a strong command of language. But if you've followed these steps, which we will explore in more detail below, the essay will flow naturally and easily from your analysis and outline.

Lesson 2: Learn the format of the SAT Essay

SAT Essay passages are "op-ed" passages that present a point of view on a topic in the arts, sciences, politics, or culture. They address a broad audience, express nuanced views on complex subjects, and use evidence and reasoning to support their claims.

Below is a sample essay and prompt (from the diagnostic test in Chapter 2). Read it carefully to familiarize yourself with the instructions and format.

You have <u>50 minutes</u> to read the passage and write an essay in response to the prompt provided below.

DIRECTIONS

As you read the passage below, consider how Steven Pinker uses

- evidence, such as facts or examples, to support his claims
- reasoning to develop ideas and connect claims and evidence
- stylistic or persuasive elements, such as word choice or appeals to emotion, to add power to the ideas expressed

---

Adapted from Steven Pinker, "Mind Over Mass Media." ©2010 by *The New York Times*. Originally published June 10, 2010.

1   New forms of media have always caused moral panics: the printing press, newspapers, paperbacks and television were all once denounced as threats to their consumers' brainpower and moral fiber.

2   So too with electronic technologies. PowerPoint, we're told, is reducing discourse to bullet points. Search engines lower our intelligence, encouraging us to skim on the surface of knowledge rather than dive to its depths. Twitter is shrinking our attention spans.

3   But such panics often fail reality checks. When comic books were accused of turning juveniles into delinquents in the 1950s, crime was falling to record lows, just as the denunciations of video games in the 1990s coincided with the great American crime decline. The decades of television, transistor radios and rock videos were also decades in which I.Q. scores rose continuously.

4   For a reality check today, take the state of science, which demands high levels of brainwork and is measured by clear benchmarks of discovery. Today, scientists are never far from their e-mail and cannot lecture without PowerPoint. If electronic media were hazardous to intelligence, the quality of science would be plummeting. Yet discoveries are multiplying like fruit flies, and progress is dizzying. Other activities in the life of the mind, like philosophy, history and cultural criticism, are likewise flourishing.

5   Critics of new media sometimes use science itself to press their case, citing research that shows how "experience can change the brain." But cognitive neuroscientists roll their eyes at such talk. Yes, every time we learn a fact or skill the wiring of the brain changes; it's not as if the information is stored in the pancreas. But the existence of neural plasticity does not mean the brain is a blob of clay pounded into shape by experience.

6   Experience does not revamp the basic information-processing capacities of the brain. Speed-reading programs have long claimed to do just that, but the verdict was rendered by Woody Allen after he read War and Peace in one sitting: "It was about Russia." Genuine multitasking, too, has been exposed as a myth, not just by laboratory studies but by the familiar sight of an SUV undulating between lanes as the driver cuts deals on his cellphone.

7   Moreover, the evidence indicates that the effects of experience are highly specific to the experiences themselves. If you train people to do one thing, they get better at doing that thing, but almost nothing else. Music doesn't make you better at math; conjugating Latin doesn't make you more logical; brain-training games don't make you smarter. Accomplished people don't bulk up their brains with intellectual calisthenics; they immerse themselves in their fields. Novelists read lots of novels; scientists read lots of science.

8   The effects of consuming electronic media are also likely to be far more limited than the panic implies. Media critics write as if the brain takes on the qualities of whatever it consumes, the informational equivalent of "you are what you eat." As with primitive peoples who believe that eating fierce animals will make them fierce, they assume that watching quick cuts in rock videos turns your mental life into quick cuts or that reading bullet points and Twitter postings turns your thoughts into bullet points and Twitter postings.

9   Yes, the constant arrival of information packets can be distracting or addictive, especially to people with attention deficit disorder. But distraction is not a new phenomenon. The solution is not to bemoan technology but to develop strategies of self-control, as we do with every other temptation in life. Turn off e-mail or Twitter when you work, put away your BlackBerry at dinner time, ask your spouse to call you to bed at a designated hour.

10   And to encourage intellectual depth, don't rail at PowerPoint or Google. It's not as if habits of deep reflection, thorough research and rigorous reasoning ever came naturally to people. They must be acquired in special institutions, which we call universities, and maintained with constant upkeep, which we call analysis, criticism and debate. They are not granted by propping a heavy encyclopedia on your lap, nor are they taken away by efficient access to information on the Internet.

11   The new media have caught on for a reason. Knowledge is increasing exponentially; human brainpower and waking hours are not. Fortunately, the Internet and information technologies are helping us manage, search, and retrieve our collective intellectual output at different scales, from Twitter and previews to e-books and online encyclopedias. Far from making us stupid, these technologies are the only things that will keep us smart.

Write an essay in which you explain how Steven Pinker builds an argument to persuade his audience that new media are not destroying our moral and intellectual abilities. In your essay, analyze how Pinker uses one or more of the features listed in the box above (or features of your own choice) to strengthen the logic and persuasiveness of his argument. Be sure that your analysis focuses on the most relevant features of the passage.

Your essay should NOT explain whether you agree with Pinker's claims, but rather explain how Pinker builds an argument to persuade his audience.

Lesson 3: Understand the scoring rubric

Your essay will be scored based on three criteria: **reading**, **analysis**, and **writing**. Two trained readers will give your essay a score of 1 to 4 on these three criteria, and your subscore for each criterion will be the sum of these two, that is, a score from 2 to 8. Here is the official rubric for all three criteria.

SAT Essay Scoring Rubric

Score	Reading	Analysis	Writing
4	<ul><li>demonstrates a thorough understanding of the source text, including its central ideas, its important details, and how they interrelate</li><li>is free of errors of fact or interpretation with regard to the text</li><li>makes skillful use of textual evidence (quotations, paraphrases, or both) to demonstrate a complete understanding of the source text</li></ul>	<ul><li>offers an insightful analysis of the source text and demonstrates a sophisticated understanding of the analytical task</li><li>offers a thorough, well-considered evaluation of the author's use of evidence, reasoning, and/or stylistic and persuasive elements, and/or features of the student's own choosing</li><li>contains relevant, sufficient, and strategically chosen support for claims or points made</li><li>focuses consistently on those features of the text that are most relevant to addressing the task</li></ul>	<ul><li>is cohesive and demonstrates a highly effective command of language</li><li>includes a precise central claim</li><li>includes an eloquent introduction and conclusion, and demonstrates a logical and effective progression of ideas within and among paragraphs</li><li>uses an effective variety of sentence structures, demonstrates precise word choice, and maintains a formal style and objective tone</li><li>shows a strong command of the conventions of Standard Written English and is free or virtually free of errors</li></ul>
3	<ul><li>demonstrates effective understanding of the source text, including its central ideas and important details</li><li>is free of substantive errors of fact and interpretation with regard to the text</li><li>makes appropriate use of textual evidence (quotations, paraphrases, or both) to demonstrate an understanding of the source text</li></ul>	<ul><li>offers an effective analysis of the source text and demonstrates an understanding of the analytical task</li><li>competently evaluates the author's use of evidence, reasoning, and/or stylistic and persuasive elements, and/or features of the student's own choosing</li><li>contains relevant and sufficient support for claims or points made</li><li>focuses primarily on those features of the text that are most relevant to addressing the task</li></ul>	<ul><li>is mostly cohesive and demonstrates effective control of language</li><li>includes a central claim or implicit controlling idea</li><li>includes an effective introduction and conclusion, and demonstrates a clear progression of ideas within and among paragraphs</li><li>uses a variety of sentence structures, demonstrates some precise word choice, and maintains a formal style and objective tone</li><li>shows a good control of the conventions of Standard Written English and is free of significant errors that detract from the quality of writing</li></ul>

| 2 | • demonstrates some understanding of the source text, including its central ideas, but not of important details
 • may contain errors of fact and/or interpretation with regard to the text
 • makes limited and/or haphazard use of textual evidence (quotations, paraphrases, or both) to demonstrate some understanding of the source text | • offers limited analysis of the source text and demonstrates only partial understanding of the analytical task
 • identifies and attempts to describe the author's use of evidence, reasoning, and/or stylistic and persuasive elements, and/or features of the student's own choosing, but merely asserts rather than explains their importance, or makes unwarranted claims
 • contains little or no support for claims
 • may lack a clear focus on those features of the text that are most relevant to addressing the task | • demonstrates little or no cohesion and limited skill in the use and control of language
 • may lack a clear central claim or controlling idea or may deviate from the claim or idea
 • lacks an effective introduction and/or conclusion
 • may demonstrate some progression of ideas within paragraphs but not throughout
 • has limited variety in sentence structures
 • demonstrates inconsistently effective diction and deviates noticeably from a formal style and objective tone
 • shows a limited control of the conventions of Standard Written English and contains errors that detract from the quality of writing and may impede understanding |
| 1 | • demonstrates little or no comprehension of the source text
 • fails to show an understanding of the text's central ideas, and may include only details without reference to central ideas
 • may contain numerous errors of fact or interpretation with regard to the text
 • makes little or no use of textual evidence (quotations, paraphrases, or both), demonstrating little or no understanding of the source text | • offers little or no analysis or ineffective analysis of the source text and demonstrates little or no understanding of the analytic task
 • identifies without explanation some aspects of the author's use of evidence, reasoning, and/or stylistic and persuasive elements
 • makes unwarranted analytical claims
 • contains little or no support for claims, or support is largely irrelevant
 • may not focus on features of the text that are relevant to addressing the task
 • offers no discernible analysis (e.g., is largely or exclusively summary) | • demonstrates little or no cohesion and inadequate skill in the use and control of language
 • may lack a clear central claim or controlling idea
 • lacks a recognizable introduction and conclusion, and lacks any discernible progression of ideas
 • lacks variety in sentence structures, demonstrates weak diction, and may lack a formal style and objective tone
 • shows a weak control of the conventions of Standard Written English and may contain numerous errors that undermine the quality of writing |

Read the Passage Using the "Three-Pass Approach"

Lesson 4: First pass: Summarize

Use the first 15 to 20 minutes to read the passage thoroughly, using the "three-pass approach" described in these next three lessons. In the first pass, read and summarize the passage as we discussed in Chapter 4, asking, "What is the central thesis, who is the audience, and what is the general structure of the essay?" Underline key points and summarize the passage with annotations.

Let's apply this strategy to the essay from the diagnostic test in Chapter 2. (If you haven't already completed your diagnostic test essay, flip back to Chapter 2 and do it now!)

Adapted from Steven Pinker, "Mind Over Mass Media." ©2010 by *The New York Times*. Originally published June 10, 2010.

First pass: Summarize

1   New forms of media have always caused moral panics: the printing press, newspapers, paperbacks and television were all once denounced as threats to their consumers' brainpower and moral fiber.

> People have long worried that media make us dumb and immoral.

2   So too with electronic technologies. PowerPoint, we're told, is reducing discourse to bullet points. Search engines lower our intelligence, encouraging us to skim on the surface of knowledge rather than dive to its depths. Twitter is shrinking our attention spans.

> Today, the same is said of PowerPoint, Google, and Twitter.

3   But such panics often fail reality checks. When comic books were accused of turning juveniles into delinquents in the 1950s, crime was falling to record lows, just as the denunciations of video games in the 1990s coincided with the great American crime decline. The decades of television, transistor radios and rock videos were also decades in which I.Q. scores rose continuously.

> But sociological evidence refutes those fears, rather than supports them.

4   For a reality check today, take the state of science, which demands high levels of brainwork and is measured by clear benchmarks of discovery. Today, scientists are never far from their e-mail and cannot lecture without PowerPoint. If electronic media were hazardous to intelligence, the quality of science would be plummeting. Yet discoveries are multiplying like fruit flies, and progress is dizzying. Other activities in the life of the mind, like philosophy, history and cultural criticism, are likewise flourishing.

> Scientists use the media, yet are as productive as ever.

> The same is true with those who work in the humanities.

5   Critics of new media sometimes use science itself to press their case, citing research that shows how "experience can change the brain." But cognitive neuroscientists roll their eyes at such talk. Yes, every time we learn a fact or skill the wiring of the brain changes; it's not as if the information is stored in the pancreas. But the existence of neural plasticity does not mean the brain is a blob of clay pounded into shape by experience.

> The "science" used to bolster these panics is weak, facile, and misleading.

CONTINUE ▶

6   Experience does not revamp the basic information-processing capacities of the brain. Speed-reading programs have long claimed to do just that, but the verdict was rendered by Woody Allen after he read *War and Peace* in one sitting: "It was about Russia." Genuine multitasking, too, has been exposed as a myth, not just by laboratory studies but by the familiar sight of an SUV undulating between lanes as the driver cuts deals on his cell phone.

> New media don't redesign our brains as easily as the critics suggest.

7   Moreover, the evidence indicates that the effects of experience are highly specific to the experiences themselves. If you train people to do one thing, they get better at doing that thing, but almost nothing else. Music doesn't make you better at math; conjugating Latin doesn't make you more logical; brain-training games don't make you smarter. Accomplished people don't bulk up their brains with intellectual calisthenics; they immerse themselves in their fields. Novelists read lots of novels; scientists read lots of science.

> Cognitive changes require very specific training . . .

8   The effects of consuming electronic media are also likely to be far more limited than the panic implies. Media critics write as if the brain takes on the qualities of whatever it consumes, the informational equivalent of "you are what you eat." As with primitive peoples who believe that eating fierce animals will make them fierce, they assume that watching quick cuts in rock videos turns your mental life into quick cuts or that reading bullet points and Twitter postings turns your thoughts into bullet points and Twitter postings.

> . . . so exposure to new media won't change our brains dramatically.

9   Yes, the constant arrival of information packets can be distracting or addictive, especially to people with attention deficit disorder. But distraction is not a new phenomenon. The solution is not to bemoan technology but to develop strategies of self-control, as we do with every other temptation in life. Turn off e-mail or Twitter when you work, put away your BlackBerry at dinner time, ask your spouse to call you to bed at a designated hour.

> Instantaneous social media can be distracting, so just turn them off when you need to.

10   And to encourage intellectual depth, don't rail at PowerPoint or Google. It's not as if habits of deep reflection, thorough research and rigorous reasoning ever came naturally to people. They must be acquired in special institutions, which we call universities, and maintained with constant upkeep, which we call analysis, criticism and debate. They are not granted by propping a heavy encyclopedia on your lap, nor are they taken away by efficient access to information on the Internet.

> Deep intellectual skills are not eroded by quick access to information, but rather are acquired by practicing the skills of analysis, criticism, and debate.

11   The new media have caught on for a reason. Knowledge is increasing exponentially; human brainpower and waking hours are not. Fortunately, the Internet and information technologies are helping us manage, search, and retrieve our collective intellectual output at different scales, from Twitter and previews to e-books and online encyclopedias. Far from making us stupid, these technologies are the only things that will keep us smart.

> Quick access to information is good.

Lesson 5: Second pass: Analyze

> Now read the passage again, focusing on the **specific rhetorical and stylistic devices** that the author uses to support his or her argument. In particular, note how the author uses evidence, reasoning, appeals to values and emotions, and literary elements to support his or her claims. Pay attention to the five categories or rhetorical elements: **logos, pathos, ethos, mythos,** and **poetics**.

Logos—how a writer uses **reasoning** and **evidence** to support claims.

- *What kind of **reasoning** does the author use to support claims?*

  - Dialectical reasoning: Examining two sides of an issue objectively (the *thesis* and the *antithesis*) and arriving at a *synthesis* that resolves problems with each position.

  - Deductive reasoning: Showing that the claim follows from first principles.

  - Inductive reasoning: Showing that the claim follows a pattern of examples.

- *What kind of **evidence** does the author use to support claims?*

  - Anecdotal evidence: Using personal stories to support a claim.

  - Empirical evidence: Using studies, polls, or objective facts to support a claim.

  - Historical evidence: Showing how the claim fits within a context of historical events.

- *Does the author commit any of these common **logical fallacies**?*

  - Straw man fallacy: Misrepresenting an opposing viewpoint to make it easier to attack. (E.g., *If you support background checks for gun purchases, then you want to take away my right to protect my family!*)

  - Overgeneralization fallacy: Applying an idea beyond the situations in which it is appropriate. (E.g. *Cutting taxes helped the economy during the last recession, so it will help boost the economy now that corporate profits are at a record high!*)

  - Ad hominem fallacy: Attacking the person rather than the person's argument. (E.g., *You don't have a Ph.D., so why should I believe you?*)

  - Consensus or authority fallacy: Suggesting that something is true simply because many people believe it, or because a famous or reputable person or institution claims that it is true. (E.g., *If everyone believes it, it must be true; If Einstein said it, it must be true.*)

  - Correlation for causation fallacy: Suggesting that one thing causes another simply because the two are correlated. (E.g., *Rich people get higher SAT scores, therefore the SAT only measures how rich you are.*)

  - Slippery slope fallacy: Suggesting that one cannot set a standard along a continuum. (E.g., *If we lower the drinking age to 18, what will prevent us from lowering it to 3?*)

Pathos—how a writer appeals to the reader's **emotions** and self-interest

- *What kind of **tone** and **attitude** does the author adopt?*

  - Authoritative/Didactic: Assuming an objective and professorial stance.

  - Conversational: Speaking to the reader as a friend, or as an engaging storyteller.

  - Alarmist: Representing a problem as dire and urgent.

- *Does the author choose words to evoke particular **emotions** in the reader, such as **nostalgia**, **lightheartedness**, **sympathy**, or **anger**?*

Ethos—how a writer establishes **credibility** and appeals to common **values**

- *Does the writer establish his or her **authority** to speak on this topic?*

  - <u>Bona fides</u>: Indicating professional experience or academic qualifications.

  - <u>First person engagement</u>: Revealing personal experience with the topic at hand.

  - <u>Substantive authority</u>: Demonstrating expertise through the details and analytical quality of the writing.

- *What specific **values** does the author appeal to, either explicitly or implicitly?*

Safety	Strength	Economic growth	Education
Competence	Hard work	Morality	Beauty
Nostalgia	National strength	Environmentalism	Creativity

- *Does the writer's thesis serve his or her **self-interest**?*

  - If a professional taxi driver were to argue for banning self-driving taxis, for example, the clear self-interest in the matter would undercut his or her credibility. Arguing against one's self-interest, on the other hand, enhances one's **ethos**.

Mythos—how a writer uses **elements of story** to enhance his or her argument

- *Does the writer **characterize** any person or group according to a conventional **archetype**?*

Hero	Regular guy/gal	Villain	Rebel
Victim	Nurturer	Creator	Jester

- *Does the writer use literary elements such as **irony**, **allusion**, **anthropomorphism**, or **allegory**?*

Poetics—how a writer uses **stylistic elements** to enhance his or her argument

- *Does the writer use of any of these **stylistic devices** to support claims?*

Metaphor	Aphorism	Dysphemism	Analogy
Hyperbole	Parallelism	Imagery	Euphemism

This list is by no means exhaustive, but it provides a solid framework for analyzing the passage. In your second read-through, keep it simple. Just underline the sentences or phrases that use these devices, and categorize the devices in the margin.

Read the annotations in the sample analysis that follows and see how each underlined portion represents that particular device. Train yourself to see these devices in all of the rhetorical essays you read: newspaper op-eds, long form essays, and even your own papers.

This analysis is a critical step in writing the SAT Essay. As the scoring rubric indicates, your essay should *offer a thorough, well-considered evaluation of the author's use of evidence, reasoning, and/or stylistic and persuasive elements.*

The rubric also indicates that a good essay will contain *relevant, sufficient, and strategically chosen support for claims or points made.* This means you must **give quotations from the text that show where the author uses these particular devices and stylistic elements.**

Adapted from Steven Pinker, "Mind Over Mass Media." ©2010 by *The New York Times*. Originally published June 10, 2010.

Second pass: Analyze

1   New forms of media have always caused moral panics: the printing press, newspapers, paperbacks and television were all once denounced as threats to their consumers' brainpower and moral fiber.

examples for historical context

2   So too with electronic technologies. PowerPoint, we're told, is reducing discourse to bullet points. Search engines lower our intelligence, encouraging us to skim on the surface of knowledge rather than dive to its depths. Twitter is shrinking our attention spans.

strong verbs

3   But such panics often fail reality checks. When comic books were accused of turning juveniles into delinquents in the 1950s, crime was falling to record lows, just as the denunciations of video games in the 1990s coincided with the great American crime decline. The decades of television, transistor radios and rock videos were also decades in which I.Q. scores rose continuously.

historical evidence as counterpoint

4   For a reality check today, take the state of science, which demands high levels of brainwork and is measured by clear benchmarks of discovery. Today, scientists are never far from their e-mail and cannot lecture without PowerPoint. If electronic media were hazardous to intelligence, the quality of science would be plummeting. Yet discoveries are multiplying like fruit flies, and progress is dizzying. Other activities in the life of the mind, like philosophy, history and cultural criticism, are likewise flourishing.

conversational language

appeal to authority?

counterexample

clever simile

5   Critics of new media sometimes use science itself to press their case, citing research that shows how "experience can change the brain." But cognitive neuroscientists roll their eyes at such talk. Yes, every time we learn a fact or skill the wiring of the brain changes; it's not as if the information is stored in the pancreas. But the existence of neural plasticity does not mean the brain is a blob of clay pounded into shape by experience.

qualification

sarcasm

metaphor

6   Experience does not revamp the basic information-processing capacities of the brain. Speed-reading programs have long claimed to do just that, but the verdict was rendered by Woody Allen after he read *War and Peace* in one sitting: "It was about Russia." Genuine multitasking, too, has been exposed as a myth, not just by laboratory studies but by the familiar sight of an SUV undulating between lanes as the driver cuts deals on his cell phone.

humorous cultural allusion

counterexample

7   Moreover, the evidence indicates that the effects of experience are highly specific to the experiences themselves. If you train people to do one thing, they get better at doing that thing, but almost nothing else. Music doesn't make you better at math; conjugating Latin doesn't make you more logical; brain-training games don't make you smarter. Accomplished people don't bulk up their brains with intellectual calisthenics;

didacticism

examples/analogies

CONTINUE ▶

they immerse themselves in their fields. Novelists read lots of novels; scientists read lots of science.

8   The effects of consuming electronic media are also likely to be far more limited than the panic implies. Media critics write as if the brain takes on the qualities of whatever it consumes, the informational equivalent of "you are what you eat." As with primitive peoples who believe that eating fierce animals will make them fierce, they assume that watching quick cuts in rock videos turns your mental life into quick cuts or that reading bullet points and Twitter postings turns your thoughts into bullet points and Twitter postings.

appeasement

analogy

9   Yes, the constant arrival of information packets can be distracting or addictive, especially to people with attention deficit disorder. But distraction is not a new phenomenon. The solution is not to bemoan technology but to develop strategies of self-control, as we do with every other temptation in life. Turn off e-mail or Twitter when you work, put away your BlackBerry at dinner time, ask your spouse to call you to bed at a designated hour.

concession

constructive suggestion

10   And to encourage intellectual depth, don't rail at PowerPoint or Google. It's not as if habits of deep reflection, thorough research and rigorous reasoning ever came naturally to people. They must be acquired in special institutions, which we call universities, and maintained with constant upkeep, which we call analysis, criticism and debate. They are not granted by propping a heavy encyclopedia on your lap, nor are they taken away by efficient access to information on the Internet.

exhortation

didacticism

11   The new media have caught on for a reason. Knowledge is increasing exponentially; human brainpower and waking hours are not. Fortunately, the Internet and information technologies are helping us manage, search, and retrieve our collective intellectual output at different scales, from Twitter and previews to e-books and online encyclopedias. Far from making us stupid, these technologies are the only things that will keep us smart.

optimistic conclusion with strong contrast to emphasize his thesis

Lesson 6: Third pass: Select and synthesize

In the third pass, read through the annotated passage again and ask: What are the **three or four** rhetorical or stylistic elements that contribute **most significantly** to the writer's argument, and to setting the tone of the passage as a whole? Annotate the passage with this question in mind, and indicate the important examples of these elements in the text.

Adapted from Steven Pinker, "Mind Over Mass Media." ©2010 by *The New York Times.* Originally published June 10, 2010.

Third pass: Select and synthesize

1   New forms of media have always caused moral panics: the printing press, newspapers, paperbacks and television were all once denounced as threats to their consumers' brainpower and moral fiber.

Pinker's reasoning begins by putting an issue in historical context.

2   So too with electronic technologies. PowerPoint, we're told, is reducing discourse to bullet points. Search engines lower our intelligence, encouraging us to skim on the surface of knowledge rather than dive to its depths. Twitter is shrinking our attention spans.

He illustrates the misconception using strong, vivid verbs like "skim," "dive," and "shrink."

3   But such panics often fail reality checks. When comic books were accused of turning juveniles into delinquents in the 1950s, crime was falling to record lows, just as the denunciations of video games in the 1990s coincided with the great American crime decline. The decades of television, transistor radios and rock videos were also decades in which I.Q. scores rose continuously.

He cites historical examples that contradict the popular conception.

4   For a reality check today, take the state of science, which demands high levels of brainwork and is measured by clear benchmarks of discovery. Today, scientists are never far from their e-mail and cannot lecture without PowerPoint. If electronic media were hazardous to intelligence, the quality of science would be plummeting. Yet discoveries are multiplying like fruit flies, and progress is dizzying. Other activities in the life of the mind, like philosophy, history and cultural criticism, are likewise flourishing.

He employs logical analysis by identifying a counterexample to a claim.

Pinker injects humor, since fruit flies are common subjects of genetic studies.

5   Critics of new media sometimes use science itself to press their case, citing research that shows how "experience can change the brain." But cognitive neuroscientists roll their eyes at such talk. Yes, every time we learn a fact or skill the wiring of the brain changes; it's not as if the information is stored in the pancreas. But the existence of neural plasticity does not mean the brain is a blob of clay pounded into shape by experience.

He analyzes the grounds of the counter-argument, but may be oversimplifying that counterargument.

Pinker's attempt at humor might be considered a straw man fallacy.

6   Experience does not revamp the basic information-processing capacities of the brain. Speed-reading programs have long claimed to do just that, but the verdict was rendered by Woody Allen after he read *War and Peace* in one sitting: "It was about Russia." Genuine multitasking, too, has been exposed as a myth, not just

He uses another strong metaphor to illustrate the general misconception.

Pinker uses humor to illustrate a point about the limitations of the brain.

by laboratory studies but by the familiar sight of an SUV undulating between lanes as the driver cuts deals on his cell phone.

7   Moreover, the evidence indicates that the effects of experience are highly specific to the experiences themselves. If you train people to do one thing, they get better at doing that thing, but almost nothing else. Music doesn't make you better at math; conjugating Latin doesn't make you more logical; brain-training games don't make you smarter. Accomplished people don't bulk up their brains with intellectual calisthenics; they immerse themselves in their fields. Novelists read lots of novels; scientists read lots of science.

8   The effects of consuming electronic media are also likely to be far more limited than the panic implies. Media critics write as if the brain takes on the qualities of whatever it consumes, the informational equivalent of "you are what you eat." As with primitive peoples who believe that eating fierce animals will make them fierce, they assume that watching quick cuts in rock videos turns your mental life into quick cuts or that reading bullet points and Twitter postings turns your thoughts into bullet points and Twitter postings.

9   Yes, the constant arrival of information packets can be distracting or addictive, especially to people with attention deficit disorder. But distraction is not a new phenomenon. The solution is not to bemoan technology but to develop strategies of self-control, as we do with every other temptation in life. Turn off e-mail or Twitter when you work, put away your BlackBerry at dinner time, ask your spouse to call you to bed at a designated hour.

10   And to encourage intellectual depth, don't rail at PowerPoint or Google. It's not as if habits of deep reflection, thorough research and rigorous reasoning ever came naturally to people. They must be acquired in special institutions, which we call universities, and maintained with constant upkeep, which we call analysis, criticism and debate. They are not granted by propping a heavy encyclopedia on your lap, nor are they taken away by efficient access to information on the Internet.

11   The new media have caught on for a reason. Knowledge is increasing exponentially; human brainpower and waking hours are not. Fortunately, the Internet and information technologies are helping us manage, search, and retrieve our collective intellectual output at different scales, from Twitter and previews to e-books and online encyclopedias. Far from making us stupid, these technologies are the only things that will keep us smart.

Pinker uses a vivid illustration of the SUV driver to evoke anger (pathos) against those who disagree with him.

Pinker argues by assertion, making intriguing claims, but providing little reasoning or evidence to support them.

Pinker uses an interesting and vivid example, as well as an analogy to a popular proverb, to illustrate a mistaken way of thinking.

Pinker makes an important concession to the opposing view.

He suggests a practical and reasonable solution to the problem.

Pinker appeals to the value of "intellectual depth" (ethos), and provides a more detailed solution to the problem.

He adopts a didactic tone here, arguing by assertion and admonition.

Pinker concludes with a stark contrast to emphasize his thesis.

Construct Your Thesis and Outline

Lesson 7: Construct a precise, thorough, and insightful thesis

Once you have finished reading and annotating the text, take 10 minutes or so to craft a strong thesis and outline your essay on the "Planning Pages" provided on your test.

Take your time to construct a thesis that captures your overall analysis of the text summarize its central claim and important rhetorical and stylistic elements. Your thesis should be **precise**, **thorough**, and **insightful**.

Consider this first draft for our thesis:

Draft 1

In his essay, "Mind Over Mass Media," Steven Pinker looks at new forms of media. His thesis is about the reality of modern social media and the Internet. He talks about the misconceptions that cultural critics have about the relationship between modern media and the human brain.

Is it precise?

Analyze your sentences for precision by "trimming" them as we discussed in Chapter 5, Lesson 3. Trimming reduces a sentence to its **core**, that is, the phrases that convey the essential ideas. When we do this with our first draft, we get ". . . *Steven Pinker looks at new forms . . . . His thesis is about the reality . . . . He talks about the misconceptions . . . .*" Are the verbs strong and clear? Are the objects concrete and precise? Not really. Let's look back at our notes and use quotations from the passage to make these sentences more precise.

Draft 2

In his essay, "Mind Over Mass Media," Steven Pinker ~~looks at~~ **examines** *the* **"moral panics" about the supposed moral and cognitive declines caused by** *new forms of media. His thesis is* ~~about the reality of modern social media and~~

~~the Internet~~ *that "such panics often fail reality checks." He* ~~talks about~~ **analyzes** *the misconceptions that cultural critics have about the relationship between modern media and the human brain.*

Notice that this revision better specifies *what* Pinker is examining in his essay by more precisely articulating his thesis, even including a quotation.

Is it thorough?

Although our second draft provides more detail about Pinker's thesis, this draft still lacks detail about his essay's rhetorical and stylistic elements. It could be more thorough. Let's look back at our notes and some details about these elements.

Draft 3

In his essay, "Mind Over Mass Media," Steven Pinker examines the "moral panics" about the supposed moral and cognitive declines caused by new forms of media. His thesis, ~~is~~ *that "such panics often fail reality checks,"* **is supported with historical examples, inductive reasoning, and touches of humor. He provides scientific context for his claims, and** *analyzes the misconceptions that cultural critics have about the relationship between modern media and the human brain.*

Note that this revision more thoroughly explains *how* Pinker makes his points by specifying rhetorical and stylistic devices.

Is it insightful?

An insightful essay does not just indicate *what* elements the essay uses, but explains *how* those rhetorical and stylistic elements contribute to (or detract from) the argument. Your essay should NOT say whether you agree with the writer's claims, but it SHOULD explain how the essay's elements contribute to the effectiveness of the essay as a whole.

Think of it this way: a good movie or restaurant reviewer shouldn't just say "Don't go to that movie because I hate car chases," or "Don't go to that restaurant because I don't like spicy food," because a reader might actually like car chases or spicy food. Instead, a good reviewer describes the cinematic aspects of the movie or culinary aspects of the food to help the *reader* make a better decision. Similarly, your essay should give your reader enough information to decide for himself or herself whether Pinker's essay is strong.

Our current draft is lacking some of these insights, so let's add a few.

Draft 4

In his essay, "Mind Over Mass Media," Steven Pinker examines the "moral panics" about the supposed moral and cognitive declines caused by new forms of media. **He uses vivid imagery to illustrate the popular misconceptions about how new media affect the brain.** *His thesis, that "such panics often fail reality checks," is supported with historical examples, inductive reasoning, and touches of humor. He provides scientific context for his claims and analyzes the misconceptions that cultural critics have about the relationship between modern media and the human brain.* **He occasionally argues by assertion rather than providing evidence, and might be accused of oversimplifying the opposing viewpoint.**

Notice that this revision discusses how particular elements of Pinker's argument contribute to (or detract from) its effectiveness, without asserting whether or not we agree with Pinker's central claims.

Lesson 8: Outline your essay

Now that you've crafted your thesis paragraph, you're ready to outline the rest of your essay. The first paragraph "sets the agenda" for the rest of the essay. The three to four body paragraphs should **develop and support each of the major points of your thesis**, and the conclusion should **synthesize** the discussion, and perhaps **analyze the overall effect** of the Pinker's essay.

Outline for Analysis of Steven Pinker's "Mind Over Mass Media"

I.   In his essay, "Mind Over Mass Media," Steven Pinker examines the "moral panics" (paragraph 1) about the supposed moral and cognitive declines caused by new forms of media. He uses vivid imagery to illustrate the popular misconceptions about how new media affect the brain. His thesis, that "such panics often fail reality checks," is supported with historical examples, logical analysis, and touches of humor. He provides scientific context for his claims and analyzes the misconceptions that cultural critics have about the relationship between modern media and the human brain. He occasionally argues by assertion rather than providing evidence, and might be accused of oversimplifying the opposing viewpoint.

II.   Pinker puts the debate in historical context by providing examples of similar moral panics from past decades, and uses inductive reasoning to imply that modern "moral panic" arguments fail for the same reason that previous examples did.

III.   Pinker uses vivid images and action verbs to illustrate abstract theories about the brain, which not only clarify these concepts for the reader, but also enhance his credibility as an expert.

IV.   Pinker attempts to counter moral outrage with a moral appeal of his own, to the value of "intellectual depth," and provides practical advice for achieving that as a goal.

V.   Critical readers might notice that Pinker sometimes makes bold assertions without evidence, and even accuse him of creating a "straw man" by oversimplifying the claims of his opponents. Nevertheless, Pinker addresses the attacks on modern media directly and provides an effective counterpunch.

Write the Essay

Lesson 9: Write with strong verbs and concrete nouns

Now you should have between 20 and 25 minutes left, which should be plenty of time to write your essay on the official essay sheets. As you write, keep the following points in mind in order to get a high score in the "writing" category.

Minimize weak verbs by upgrading "lurkers"

Look at a recent essay you've written and circle all of the verbs. Are more than one-third of your verbs *to be* verbs (*is, are, was, were*)? If so, strengthen your verbs. You cannot maintain a strong discussion if you overuse weak verbs like *to be, to have,* and *to do.*

To strengthen your sentences, upgrade any **lurkers**—the words in your sentence that aren't verbs, but should be. Consider this sentence:

> *This action **is** in violation of our company's confidentiality policy.*

It revolves around a very weak verb. But the noun *violation* is a lurker. Let's upgrade it to verb status:

> *This action **violates** our company's confidentiality policy.*

Notice how this small change "punches up" the sentence.

Here are some more examples of how upgrading the lurkers can strengthen a sentence:

Weak: *My failure on the test **was** reflective of the fact of my not having studied.*

Stronger: *I **failed** the test because I **didn't study**.*

Here, we've upgraded the lurkers *reflective* (adjective) and *having studied* (participle). Notice that this change not only strengthens the verbs and clarifies the sentence, but also unclutters the sentence by eliminating the prepositional phrases *on the test, of the fact,* and *of my not having studied.*

Weak: *The fact of the governor's ignoring the protestors **made** them resentful of him.*

Stronger: *The protestors **resented** the fact that the governor **ignored** them.*

We've upgraded the lurkers *ignoring* (gerund) and *resentful* (adjective). Again, notice that strengthening the sentence also unclutters it of unnecessary prepositional phrases.

Weak: *The mice **had** a tendency to overeat when they **had** a lack of this hormone.*

Stronger: *The mice **overate** when they **lacked** this hormone.*

We've upgraded the lurkers *to overeat* (infinitive) and *lack* (noun).

Activate your passive verbs

What is the difference between these two sentences?

> *The rebel army made its bold maneuver under the cloak of darkness.*
>
> *The bold maneuver was made by the rebel army under the cloak of darkness.*

These two sentences say essentially the same thing, but the first sentence is in the **active voice** whereas the second is in the **passive voice**. In the **active voice**, the subject of the sentence is the "actor" of the verb, but in the **passive voice**, the subject is *not* the actor. (The *maneuver* did not *make* anything, so *maneuver* is not the *actor* of the verb *made* in the second sentence, even though it is the subject.) Notice that the second sentence is weaker for two reasons: it's heavier (it has more words) *and* it's slower (it takes more time to get to the point).

But there's an even better reason to avoid passive voice verbs: they can make you sound deceitful. Consider this classic passive-voice sentence:

> *Mistakes were made.*

Who made them? Thanks to the passive voice, we don't need to say. We can avoid responsibility.

Although you may sometimes need to use the **passive voice**, avoid it when you can. The **active voice** is clearer and stronger, and it encourages you to articulate essential details (like "who did it") for your reader.

Weak: *The entire project **was completed by** Joe in less than a week.*

Stronger: *Joe **completed** the entire project in less than a week.*

Use concrete and personal nouns

Clarify and strengthen your sentences by using **concrete nouns** (nouns that signify things that we can see, hear, or touch) and **personal nouns and pronouns** (like *we, us, people, humans, anyone*, and so on). Abstract nouns (like *consideration, belief, ability,* and *information*) are harder for readers to grasp than concrete and personal nouns.

When we strengthen our verbs, our nouns often become more concrete and personal automatically:

Weak: *My **failure** on the **test** was reflective of the **fact** of my not **having studied**.*

Stronger: *I failed the **test** because **I** didn't study.*

In the first sentence, 75% of the nouns (*failure, fact,* and *having studied*) are abstract, but in the second, the nouns and pronouns (*I, test, I*) are personal and concrete. Notice that the second sentence is clearer, more concise, and more effective.

Weak: *The **fact** of the governor's **ignoring** the **protestors** made **them** resentful of **him**.*

Stronger: *The **protestors** resented the **fact** that the **governor** ignored **them**.*

By upgrading the gerund *ignoring* to a verb, we reduced the number of abstract nouns in the sentence by 50%. Even better, we upgraded the subject from an abstract noun (*fact*) to a concrete and personal one (*protestors*). The second sentence is simpler, clearer, and stronger.

Lesson 10: Create a logical flow of ideas

> The official SAT Essay scoring rubric says that a strong essay must *demonstrate a logical and effective progression of ideas.* Therefore, make sure your essay **explains** each of your ideas clearly, and **connects** each idea to one of your central claims.

Explain your ideas

Don't merely state your ideas: *explain* them clearly enough so that your reader can easily follow your analysis.

Weak: *Pinker attempts to refute his critics with analogy.*

Stronger: *Pinker attempts to refute cultural critics by drawing an analogy between their reasoning and the faulty reasoning of "primitive peoples" who believe that "eating fierce animals will make them fierce."*

Good explanations often include words like **by** (*our team slowed down the game by using a full-court press*), **because** (*we won because we executed our game plan flawlessly*), or **therefore** (*we slowed down their offense; therefore, we were able to manage the game more effectively*).

Be careful, however, of overusing using phrases like **because of** and **due to**. These phrases tend to produce weak explanations because they link to *noun phrases* rather than *clauses*. Clauses are more explanatory because they include verbs and therefore convey more information.

Weak: *The essay works **because of** its imagery.*

Stronger: *The essay works **because** its images evoke powerful ideas that support the thesis.*

Notice that avoiding the *of* forces the writer to provide a *clause* instead of just a *noun phrase* and therefore give a more substantial explanation.

Connect your ideas with clear cross-references

Strong analytical essays should provide clear **cross-references** in order to connect ideas and establish a clear chain of reasoning. One way to clarify your chain of reasoning is by **using your pronouns carefully**, particularly when they refer to ideas mentioned in previous sentences. Make sure your pronouns have clear antecedents.

Consider these sentences:

Davis makes the important point that defense lawyers sometimes must represent clients whom they know are guilty, not only because these lawyers take an oath to uphold their clients' right to an adequate defense, but also because firms cannot survive financially if they accept only the obviously innocent as clients. This troubles many who want to pursue criminal law.

What does the pronoun *This* in the second sentence refer to? What *troubles many who want to study criminal law*? Is it the fact that Davis is making this point? Is it the moral implications of lawyers representing the guilty? Is it the technical difficulty of lawyers representing the guilty? Is it the financial challenges of maintaining a viable law practice? Is it all of these? The ambiguity of this pronoun obscures the discussion and makes the reader work harder to follow it. Clarify your references so that your train of thought is easy to follow.

*Davis makes the important point that defense lawyers sometimes must represent clients whom they know are guilty, not only because these lawyers take an oath to uphold their clients' right to an adequate defense, but also because firms cannot survive financially if they accept only the obviously innocent as clients. **Such moral and financial dilemmas** trouble many who want to pursue criminal law.*

Connect your ideas with logical transitions

As you move from idea to idea—within a sentence, between sentences, or between paragraphs—always consider the logical relationship between these ideas, and make these connections clear to your reader. The logical "connectors" include words and phrases like

for example	*furthermore*
moreover	*alternatively*
therefore	*however*
first, second, third	*otherwise*
because	*although*
nevertheless	*subsequently*
commensurately	*hence*
thereby	*as a consequence*

Structure each sentence to fit its purpose

According to the official SAT Essay scoring rubric, a strong essay *uses an effective variety of sentence structures.* Short sentences have impact; long sentences have weight. Good writers vary the structure of their sentences to fit the purpose of that particular discussion.

Consider this paragraph:

Medical interns are overworked. They are constantly asked to do a lot with very little sleep. They are chronically exhausted as a result. They can make mistakes that are dangerous and even potentially deadly.

What is so clumsy about these sentences? They all have the same structure. Consider this revision:

Constantly overworked and given very little time to sleep, medical interns are chronically exhausted. These conditions can lead them to make dangerous and even deadly mistakes.

Your readers won't appreciate your profound ideas if your sentences are poorly constructed. Now consider these sentences:

Gun advocates tell us that "guns don't kill people; people kill people." On the surface, this statement seems obviously true. However, analysis of the assumptions and implications of this statement shows clearly that even its most ardent believers can't possibly believe it.

Now consider this alternative:

Gun advocates tell us that "guns don't kill people; people kill people." On the surface, this statement seems obviously true. It's not.

Which is better? The first provides more information, but the second provides more impact. Good writers always think about the length of their sentences. Long sentences are often necessary for articulating complex ideas, but short sentences are better for emphasizing important points. Choose wisely.

Sample Essay

Analysis of Pinker's "Mind Over Mass Media"

Here is our final essay for the Pinker Op-Ed. Notice that we include plenty of quotations from the text to support our claims, complete with paragraph numbers, and that each paragraph simply "fills in the details" from our outline.

In his essay, "Mind Over Mass Media," Steven Pinker examines the "moral panics" (1) about the supposed moral and cognitive declines caused by new forms of media. He uses vivid imagery to illustrate the misconceptions about how new media affect the brain. His central claim, that "such panics often fail reality checks" (3), is supported with historical examples, logical analysis, and touches of humor. He provides scientific context for his claims, and analyzes the misconceptions that cultural critics have about the relationship between modern media and the human brain. He occasionally argues by assertion rather than providing evidence, and might be accused of oversimplifying the opposing viewpoint.

Pinker puts this debate in historical context by giving examples of similar moral panics from past decades, and uses inductive reasoning to show that the new arguments fail for the same reason that the old ones did. He says that new forms of media "have always caused moral panics" (1) but that these panics have not been based in reality. He says that "comic books were accused of turning juveniles into delinquents in the 1950s" (3) and that similarly "television, transistor radios and rock videos" (3) were supposed to be rotting young minds, but that really "IQs rose continuously" (3) during those periods.

Pinker uses strong action verbs to illustrate theories about how the brain works, clarifying these concepts for the reader and also enhancing his ethos as an expert. He says new media opponents are afraid that these technologies make us "skim on the surface of knowledge rather than dive into its depths" (2) and cause the quality of scientific thinking to "plummet" (4). But in fact, Pinker says, scientific discoveries are "multiplying" and progress is "dizzying." When he describes how the brain processes information, he uses verbs like "pounded" (5) and "revamp" (6). These lively action verbs help the reader to see the different sides of the argument, and they show that Pinker understands the issues very well, enhancing Pinker's ethos as a writer.

Pinker attempts to counter moral outrage with an appeal to the value of "intellectual depth" (10), and provides practical advice for achieving that goal. This is helpful to readers who want to do more than understand the brain, but also want to make people smarter. He tells us that intellectual skills are developed "in special institutions, which we call universities, and maintained with constant upkeep" (10).

Some readers might object that Pinker sometimes makes claims without evidence, such as "music doesn't make you better at math" (7). They might also accuse him of creating a "straw man" by oversimplifying the claims of his opponents, like when he says "yes, every time we learn a fact or skill the wiring of our brain changes; it's not as if the information is stored in the pancreas" (5). Nevertheless, Pinker addresses the attacks on modern media and gives an effective counterargument.

Scoring

Reading—4 out of 4

This essay demonstrates a strong comprehension of Pinker's central claims, using summary, paraphrase, and quotations. It summarizes Pinker's central thesis, modes of argument, and tone (*His central claim, that "such panics often fail reality checks," is supported with historical examples, logical analysis, and touches of humor*). The quotations are carefully chosen to illustrate the central ideas of Pinker's argument, and are accompanied by relevant and accurate commentary.

Analysis—4 out of 4

This essay provides a thoughtful and critical analysis of Pinker's argument and style, demonstrating a strong understanding of the analytical task. The essay identifies Pinker's primary modes of expression (*historical examples, logical analysis, and touches of humor*), examines his mode of reasoning (*inductive reasoning*), and even identifies possible gaps in his argument (*assertions without evidence . . . "straw man"*) without taking a side for or against Pinker's thesis. It also provides substantial textual evidence for its claims, and demonstrates a strong understanding of Pinker's rhetorical task.

Writing—4 out of 4

This essay shows mastery of language, organization, and sentence structure. It remains focused on a clear central claim, and develops its secondary claims in well-organized paragraphs. It demonstrates effective variation in sentence structure and generally appropriate word choice. Largely free from grammatical error, this essay demonstrates strong command of language and proficiency in writing.

CHAPTER 7

THE SAT MATH TEST: THE HEART OF ALGEBRA

1. Word Problems   277

2. The Order of Operations and Laws of Arithmetic   278

3. Simplifying Expressions   285

4. Conversions   287

5. Constructing and Interpreting Linear Equations   292

6. Solving Equations with the Laws of Equality   294

7. Analyzing Linear Graphs   295

8. Absolute Values   303

9. The Laws of Inequality   304

10. Graphing Inequalities   305

11. Linear Systems   310

12. Solving Systems with Algebra   312

The SAT Math:
Heart of Algebra

Why is algebra so important on the SAT Math test?

About 36% (21 out of 58) of the SAT Math questions fall under the category called the "Heart of Algebra." Questions in this category test your ability to

analyze, fluently solve, and create linear equations, inequalities, [and] systems of equations using multiple techniques.

These questions will also assess your skill in

interpreting the interplay between graphical and algebraic representations [and] solving as a process of reasoning.

The specific topics include

- creating and solving linear equations in one and two variables
- graphing and interpreting linear equations
- creating, interpreting, and solving linear systems
- graphing and solving inequalities and systems of inequalities
- interpreting and solving algebraic word problems

Why are these skills important?

Algebra is an essential tool of quantitative analysis not only in math but also in subjects like engineering, the physical sciences, and economics. When describing the relationships between or among different quantities, or exploring the nature of unknown quantities, algebra provides essential tools for analyzing and solving problems. Most colleges consider fluency in algebra to be a vital prerequisite to a college-level liberal arts curriculum.

Sound intimidating? It's not.

If you take the time to master the four core skills presented in these 13 lessons, you will gain the knowledge and practice you need to master even the toughest SAT Math "Heart of Algebra" questions.

Lesson 1: Word Problems

Breaking Down Word Problems

Algebraic word problems aren't so tough if you break them down into four basic steps:

1. Read the whole problem and **identify** the relevant quantities.
2. **Represent** those quantities with algebraic expressions.
3. **Translate** the facts into equations.
4. **Solve** the equations for the relevant quantities.

Corrine drives d miles to her office at an average speed of 50 miles per hour. Returning home, she travels by the same route and averages 60 miles per hour. If her trip home is 10 minutes shorter than her trip to her office, what is the value of d ?

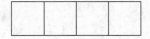

(*Medium-hard*) The challenge with word problems is that we have to set up the equations ourselves. Let's walk through the steps.

1. Identify. In this problem, there are six quantities:

- the speed from home to office
- the distance from home to office
- the time it takes to get from home to office
- the speed from office to home
- the distance from office to home
- the time it takes to get from office to home

That's a lot, so let's simplify.

2. Represent. If we think a bit, we can see that we have enough information to express all six quantities in terms of **just two unknowns**. If we represent the total time, in hours, it takes her to get home as t, then we can arrange all the information in a simple table:

	Distance	Speed	Time
To Work	d miles	50 mph	$t + \dfrac{1}{6}$ hours
To Home	d miles	60 mph	t hours

3. Translate. Now we need to apply a basic formula:

$$\text{distance} = \text{average speed} \times \text{time}$$

This gives us two equations with two unknowns:

$$d = 50(t + 1/6) \qquad d = 60(t)$$

4. Solve. So now we have to solve this **2-by-2 system of equations**. (If you're feeling rusty on this topic, don't worry. We will discuss systems in more detail in Lessons 11–12.) Since the unknown d is isolated in both equations, let's substitute.

Substitute $d = 50(t + 1/6)$ into the second equation:
$$50(t + 1/6) = 60t$$

Distribute:	$50t + 50/6 = 60t$
Subtract $50t$ from both sides:	$50/6 = 10t$
Divide by 10 on both sides:	$t = 50/6 = 5/6$

Since t represents the time **in hours** it took Corrine to get home, it took her 5/6 hours (or 50 minutes) to get home and 5/6 hour + 1/6 hour = 1 hour to get to her office. But the question asks for the **distance** from her home to her office, so we need to plug the values just calculated into one of the equations to find d.

$$d = 60(t) = 60(5/6) = 50 \text{ miles}$$

$$d = 50(t + 1/6) = 50\,(5/6 + 1/6) = 50(1) = 50 \text{ miles}$$

Lesson 2: The Order of Operations and Laws of Arithmetic

The Order of Operations: PG-ER-MD-AS

You probably learned that the order of operations is **PEMDAS**, but this isn't technically true: there is a **GERM** in the order of operations. When simplifying complicated expressions, the order to follow is

1. **PG**: parentheses and other grouping symbols (inside out)
2. **ER**: exponents and roots (inside out)
3. **MD**: multiplication and division (left to right)
4. **AS**: addition and subtraction (left to right)

What is the value of $\dfrac{3 + 6 \times 2}{3 + 2 \times 3} + \dfrac{\sqrt{16 + 9}}{60 \div 2^2}$?

(*Easy*)

PG: Since this expression contains no parentheses, we don't have to worry about "grouped" operations, right? Wrong! Remember that **fraction bars and radicals are also "grouping symbols"**!

In other words, we can think of the expression like this:

$$\frac{(3 + 6 \times 2)}{(3 + 2 \times 3)} + \frac{\sqrt{(16 + 9)}}{(60 \div 2^2)}$$

If the parentheses only contain one operation, then we do that operation:

$$\frac{(3 + 6 \times 2)}{(3 + 2 \times 3)} + \frac{\sqrt{25}}{(60 \div 2^2)}$$

If they contain more than one operation, then we have to move on to the next step.

ER: Do any of the parentheses contain exponents or roots? Yes, so we must perform those operations next:

$$\frac{(3 + 6 \times 2)}{(3 + 2 \times 3)} + \frac{5}{(60 \div 4)}$$

MD: Next, we do any multiplication or division from left to right inside the parentheses:

$$\frac{(3 + 12)}{(3 + 6)} + \frac{5}{15}$$

AS: Now we do any addition and subtraction left in the parentheses:

$$\frac{15}{9} + \frac{5}{15}$$

Now that all the "grouped" operations are finished, we run through the order again to finish up. Exponents or roots? No. Multiplication or division? Yes:

$$1.6666... + 0.3333...$$

Addition or subtraction? Yes: $1.6666... + 0.3333... = 2$

What is the sum of the first 100 positive integers?

(*Hard*) Here, following **PGERMDAS** and adding from left to right would be, shall we say, less than convenient: it requires 99 computations! Even with a calculator, this would be a pain. But here is a much simpler method:

Original expression: $1 + 2 + 3 + 4 + ... + 97 + 98 + 99 + 100$

Rearrange and regroup so that we add from "outside in":

$$(1 + 100) + (2 + 99) + (3 + 98) + ... + (50 + 51)$$

Simplify: $(101) + (101) + (101) + ... + (101)$

Express as a product: $50(101) = 5,050$

This gives us exactly the same result as **PGERMDAS** would give, but with just a few simple calculations. But we **changed the rules!** We didn't add strictly from left to right as **PGERMDAS** commands.

This shows that it helps to move beyond the order of operations and understand the **Laws of Arithmetic**.

The Laws of Arithmetic

> The **Laws of Arithmetic** go beyond the order of operations and reveal important properties of the operations that can help you to simplify many problems.

The Commutative Laws

When adding or multiplying, order doesn't matter.

$3 + 8 + 12 = 8 + 12 + 3$

$2 \times 6 \times 50 = 2 \times 50 \times 6$

The Associative Laws

When adding or multiplying, grouping doesn't matter.

$26 + (74 + 37) + 63 = (26 + 74) + (37 + 63)$

$2 \times (3 \times 4) \times 5 = (2 \times 3) \times (4 \times 5)$

The Distributive Law

When a grouped sum/difference is being multiplied/divided, you may "distribute" the multiplication/division. For example,

$15(20 + 8) = 15(20) + 15(8) = 300 + 120 = 420$

$$\frac{25a + 5ab}{5a} = \frac{25a}{5a} + \frac{5ab}{5a} = 5 + b$$

If $x \neq 0$, which of the following is equivalent to $\dfrac{3x^2 + 6x + 9x^2}{3x}$?

A) $2x + \dfrac{1}{2}$

B) $4x + \dfrac{1}{2}$

C) $2x^2 + 2$

D) $4x + 2$

(*Medium*) $\dfrac{3x^2 + 6x + 9x^2}{3x}$

Combine like terms: $\dfrac{12x^2 + 6x}{3x}$

Distribute the division:

$$\frac{12x^2 + 6x}{3x} = \frac{12x^2}{3x} + \frac{6x}{3x} = 4x + 2$$

So, the correct answer is D.

Don't "Overdistribute"

> The Distributive Law does **not** allow you to just "**take any operation outside of parentheses and drag it inside.**" For example, do the arithmetic to convince yourself that
>
> $$3(2 \times 5) \neq (3 \times 2) \times (3 \times 5)$$
>
> $$(2 + 3)^2 \neq 2^2 + 3^2$$

Which expression is equivalent to $3(3^4 \times 5^3)$? (No calculator.)

A) $3(3^4) \times 3(5^3)$

B) $9^4 + 15^3$

C) $9^4 \times 15^3$

D) $3^5 \times 5^3$

(*Medium-hard*) Since the grouped expression is not a sum, but a **product**, we **can't use the Distributive Law** here. We can, however, use the **Associative Law of Multiplication:**

$3(3^4 \times 5^3) = (3 \times 3^4) \times 5^3 = 3^5 \times 5^3$. Therefore, the correct answer is D.

Know How to FOIL

Whenever you multiply polynomials, you must use the Distributive Law multiple times. When **multiplying two binomials**, you can use the shortcut called **FOIL**ing.

For example, $(x + 4)(x - 5)$

F (multiply the **first** terms): $(x)(x) = x^2$

O (multiply the **outside** terms): $(x)(-5) = -5x$

I (multiply the **inside** terms): $(4)(x) = 4x$

L (multiply the **last** terms): $(4)(-5) = -20$

Add all terms and simplify:

$(x + 4)(x - 5) = x^2 - 5x + 4x - 20 = x^2 - x - 20$

If $\dfrac{m - 3}{2m} = \dfrac{m}{2m + 1}$, what is the value of m?

A) $-\dfrac{5}{3}$

B) $-\dfrac{5}{3}$

C) $-\dfrac{3}{5}$

D) $\dfrac{3}{5}$

(*Medium*) First use the **Law of Cross-Multiplication** (Chapter 8, Lesson 9) to simplify the given equation.

Cross-multiply: $(m - 3)(2m + 1) = (2m)(m)$

FOIL: $2m^2 + m - 6m - 3 = (2m)(m)$

Simplify: $2m^2 - 5m - 3 = 2m^2$

Subtract $2m^2$ from both sides: $-5m - 3 = 0$

Add 3 to both sides: $-5m = 3$

Divide by -5: $m = -\dfrac{3}{5}$

Therefore, the correct answer is C.

If $(2x + 2)(x + a) = 2x^2 + bx + c$ for all values of x, which of the following must be equal to $b + c$?

A) $a + 2$

B) $2a + 2$

C) $3a + 2$

D) $4a + 2$

(*Medium-hard*)

Given equation: $(2x + 2)(x + a) = 2x^2 + bx + c$

FOIL on left side: $2x^2 + 2ax + 2x + 2a = 2x^2 + bx + c$

Collect like terms: $2x^2 + (2a + 2)x + 2a = 2x^2 + bx + c$

If this equation is true *for all values of x*, then the two sides of the equation are **identical quadratics** (Chapter 9, Lesson 4). Clearly the first terms, $2x^2$, match on the two sides, but the other two pairs of corresponding terms must match as well.

The second coefficients must match: $2a + 2 = b$

The third coefficients must match: $2a = c$

Therefore, $b + c = (2a + 2) + 2a = 4a + 2$, and so the correct answer is D.

Exercise Set 1 (No Calculator)

1

$(1 - (1 - (1 - 2))) - (1 - (1 - (1 - 3))) =$

2

When 14 is subtracted from 6 times a number, 40 is left. What is half the number?

3

Four consecutive even numbers have a sum of 76. What is the greatest of these numbers?

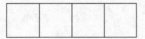

4

If $\dfrac{5x}{2} + 3 = 7$, then $10x + 12 =$

5

What number decreased by 7 equals the opposite of five times the number?

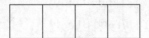

6

If $5d + 12 = 24$, then $5d - 12 =$

7

If $\dfrac{2y^2}{5} = y^2$, then $y + 5 =$

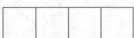

8

The product of x and y is 36. If both x and y are integers, then what is the least possible value of $x - y$?

A) −37

B) −36

C) −35

D) −9

9

If a factory can manufacture b computer screens in n days at a cost of c dollars per screen, then which of the following represents the total cost, in dollars, of the computer screens that can be manufactured, at that rate, in m days?

A) $\dfrac{bcm}{n}$

B) $\dfrac{bmn}{c}$

C) $\dfrac{mc}{bn}$

D) $\dfrac{bc}{mn}$

10

Which of the following is equivalent to $5x(2x \times 3) - 5x^2$ for all real values of x?

A) $5x^2 + 15x$

B) $25x^2$

C) $5x^2 - 15x$

D) $10x^2 \times 15x - 5x^2$

11

The symbol Ω represents one of the fundamental operators: $+$, $-$, $\times$, or $\div$. If $(x \, \Omega \, y) \times (y \, \Omega \, x) = 1$ for all positive values of x and y, then Ω can represent

A) $+$

B) $\times$

C) $-$

D) $\div$

Exercise Set 1 (Calculator)

12

The difference of two numbers is 4 and their sum is 14. What is their product?

13

If $x + y - 1 = 1 - (1 - x)$, what is the value of y?

14

If $3x^2 + 2x = 40$, then $15x^2 + 10x =$

15

Ellen is currently twice as old as Maria, but in 6 years, Maria will be $\frac{2}{3}$ as old as Ellen. How old is Ellen now?

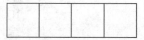

16

If $2x - 2y = 5$ and $x + y = 6$, what is the value of $x^2 - y^2$?

17

On a typical day, a restaurant sells n grilled cheese sandwiches for p dollars each. Today, however, the manager reduced the price of grilled cheese sandwiches by 30% and as a result sold 50% more of them than usual. Which of the following represents the revenue for today's grilled cheese sandwich sales, in dollars?

A) $0.5np - 0.3$

B) $1.05np$

C) $1.20np$

D) $1.50np$

18

For all real numbers x and y, $4x(x) - 3xy(2x) =$

A) $12x^2y(x - 2y)$

B) $2x^2(2 - 3y)$

C) $2x^2(2 + 3y)$

D) $4xy(x - 3y)$

19

If $a = 60(99)^{99} + 30(99)^{99}$, $b = 99^{100}$, and $c = 90(90)^{99}$, then which of the following expresses the correct ordering of a, b, and c?

A) $c < b < a$

B) $b < c < a$

C) $a < b < c$

D) $c < a < b$

20

Which of the following statements must be true for all values of x, y, and z?

I. $(x + y) + z = (z + y) + x$
II. $(x - y) - z = (z - y) - x$
III. $(x \div y) \div z = (z \div y) \div x$

A) I only

B) I and II only

C) I and III only

D) II and III only

21

Carlos began with twice as much money as David had. After Carlos gave $12 to David, Carlos still had $10 more than David. How much money did they have <u>combined</u> at the start?

A) $34

B) $68

C) $102

D) $108

EXERCISE SET 1 ANSWER KEY

No Calculator

1. 1

$$(1 - (1 - (1 - 2))) - (1 - (1 - (1 - 3)))$$

Parentheses:	$(1 - (1 - (-1))) - (1 - (1 - (-2)))$
Next parentheses:	$(1 - (2)) - (1 - (3))$
Next parentheses:	$(-1) - (-2)$
Subtract:	$-1 + 2 = 1$

---

2. 9/2 or 4.5

$$6x - 14 = 40$$

Add 14:	$6x = 54$
Divide by 6:	$x = 9$
Multiply by $\dfrac{1}{2}$:	$\dfrac{1}{2}x = \dfrac{9}{2}$

---

3. 22 Let n be the least of these numbers. The sum of four consecutive even numbers is therefore $n + (n + 2) + (n + 4) + (n + 6) = 76$.

Simplify:	$4n + 12 = 76$
Subtract 12:	$4n = 64$
Divide by 4:	$n = 16$

Therefore the largest of these numbers is $16 + 6 = 22$.

---

4. 28

$$\frac{5}{2}x + 3 = 7$$

Multiply by 4:	$10x + 12 = 28$

---

5. 7/6 or 1.16 or 1.17

$$x - 7 = -5x$$

Subtract x:	$-7 = -6x$
Divide by -6:	$\dfrac{7}{6} = x$

---

6. 0

$$5d + 12 = 24$$

Subtract 24:	$5d - 12 = 0$

---

7. 5

$$\frac{2y^2}{5} = y^2$$

Subtract y^2:	$-\dfrac{3y^2}{5} = 0$
Multiply by $-5/3$:	$y^2 = 0$
Take square root:	$y = 0$
Add 5:	$y + 5 = 5$

---

8. C If $xy = 36$ and x and y are integers, then x and y are both factors of 36. In order to minimize the value of $x - y$, we must find the greatest separation between x and y. The greatest separation between a factor pair is $1 - 36 = -35$.

---

9. A We should regard this as a "conversion" problem from m *days* into a corresponding number of *dollars*.

$$m \text{ days} \times \frac{b \text{ screens}}{n \text{ days}} \times \frac{c \text{ dollars}}{1 \text{ screen}} = \frac{bcm}{n}$$

---

10. B Original expression: $\quad 5x(2x \times 3) - 5x^2$

Parentheses:	$5x(6x) - 5x^2$
Multiply:	$30x^2 - 5x^2$
Subtract:	$25x^2$

Remember: The Law of Distribution does *not* apply in the first step, because the grouped expression doesn't include addition or subtraction.

---

11. D The simplest approach is perhaps to choose simple values for x and y, like 2 and 3, and see which operator yields a true equation. Since $(2 \div 3) \times (3 \div 2) = 1$, the answer is D.

Calculator

12. 45

$$a - b = 4$$
$$a + b = 14$$

Add equations:	$2a = 18$
Divide by 2:	$a = 9$
Substitute $a = 9$:	$9 + b = 14$
Subtract 9:	$b = 5$
Evaluate ab:	$ab = 9 \times 5 = 45$

---

13. 1

$$x + y - 1 = 1 - (1 - x)$$

Distribute:	$x + y - 1 = 1 - 1 + x$
Subtract x:	$y - 1 = 1 - 1$
Simplify:	$y - 1 = 0$
Add 1:	$y = 1$

---

14. 200

$$3x^2 + 2x = 40$$

Multiply by 5:	$15x^2 + 10x = 200$

---

15. 12 Let e = Ellen's current age and m = Maria's current age.

Ellen is twice as old as Maria:	$e = 2m$
In 6 years, Maria will be 2/3 as old as Ellen:	$m + 6 = \dfrac{2}{3}(e + 6)$
Substitute $e = 2m$:	$m + 6 = \dfrac{2}{3}(2m + 6)$
Multiply by 3:	$3m + 18 = 2(2m + 6)$
Distribute:	$3m + 18 = 4m + 12$
Subtract $3m$ and 12:	$6 = m$

Therefore $e = 2m = 2(6) = 12$.

16. **15** First equation: $2x - 2y = 5$

Divide by 2: $x - y = 2.5$
Second equation: $x + y = 6$
Multiply: $(x - y)(x + y) = x^2 - y^2 = (2.5)(6) = 15$

Alternately, we could solve the system using either substitution or linear combination and get $x = 4.25$ and $y = 1.75$, and evaluate $x^2 - y^2 = (4.25)^2 - (1.75)^2 = 18.0625 - 3.0625 = 15$.

17. **B** The revenue is equal to the number of items sold times the price per item. If the restaurant typically sells n sandwiches per day, but today sold 50% more, it sold $1.5n$ sandwiches. If the price p was reduced 30%, today's price is $0.70p$. Therefore, the total revenue is $(1.5n)(0.70p) = 1.05np$.

18. **B** $4x(x) - 3xy(2x)$

Multiply: $4x^2 - 6x^2y$
Largest common factor: $2x^2(2 - 3y)$

19. **D** Although a calculator is permitted for this question, most calculators will give an "overflow error" when trying to calculate numbers like 99^{100}, because they're just too large. However, comparing these numbers is straightforward if we can express them in a common format.

$a = 60(99)^{99} + 30(99)^{99}$ $= 90(99)^{99}$
$b = 99^{100}$ $= 99(99)^{99}$
$c = 90(90)^{99}$ $= 90(90)^{99}$

20. **A** Only statement I is true, by the Commutative and Associative Laws of Addition. Choosing simple values like $x = 1$, $y = 2$, and $z = 3$ will demonstrate that statements II and III do not yield true equations.

21. **C** Let $x = $ the number of dollars David had to start. If Carlos started with twice as much money as David, then Carlos started with $2x$ dollars. After Carlos gave David $12, Carlos had $2x - 12$ dollars and David had $x + 12$ dollars. If Carlos still had $10 more than David, then

$$2x - 12 = 10 + x + 12$$
Simplify: $2x - 12 = x + 22$
Add 12: $2x = x + 34$
Subtract x: $x = 34$

Therefore, David started with $34 and Carlos started with $2(\$34) = \$68$, so they had $\$34 + \$68 = \$102$ combined to start.

Lesson 3: Simplifying Expressions

The Law of Substitution

Perhaps the most important problem-solving tool in algebra is the Law of Substitution. **If two things are equal, you can always substitute one for the other.**

If x and y are positive numbers such that $3x - 2y = 7$, what is the value of $\dfrac{2y + 7}{6x}$?

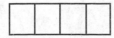

(*Medium*) Notice that $2y$ and 7 appear in both the equation and in the expression. Let's take advantage of that.

Given equation: $3x - 2y = 7$

Add $2y$ to both sides: $3x = 2y + 7$

Since $2y + 7$ appears in the fraction, we may replace it with $3x$ by the Law of Substitution and simplify:

$$\frac{2y + 7}{6x} = \frac{3x}{6x} = \frac{1}{2}$$

Also, we can just plug in values for x and y that satisfy the equation. Notice that $x = 3$ and $y = 1$ is a solution because $3(3) - 2(1) = 7$, and so we can evaluate the fraction by plugging in these numbers: $(2(1) + 7)/6(3) = 9/18 = 1/2$, or 0.5.

Simplifying Percent Problems

To increase a number by a%, just multiply by $(100 + a)$%, and to decrease a number by a%, just multiply by $(100 - a)$%. For instance, to increase a number by 13%, multiply by 1.13, and to decrease a number by 13%, multiply by 0.87.

The population of sea urchins in a particular reef has been decreasing by 10% per year for the last three years. What is the total percent decrease in this population over the past three years? (Disregard the % symbol when gridding.)

(*Medium*) To decrease a quantity by 10%, we multiply by 0.90. If the original population is n, then after three years the population will be $(0.90)(0.90)(0.90)n = 0.729n$. Since this is 72.9% of the original population, the total percent decrease is $(100 - 72.9)\% = 27.1\%$.

Bonus question: Why is the answer not $3(10\%) = 30\%$?

Simplifying Operations

Every operation can be expressed in terms of its inverse. For instance, *subtracting* -16 is the same as *adding* 16, and *dividing by* 4 is the same as *multiplying by* 1/4. These equivalences can help you to simplify calculations.

Increasing a positive number by 25% and then decreasing this result by 50% is equivalent to dividing the number by

A) 1.33

B) 1.50

C) 1.60

D) 1.65

(*Medium*) Let's call the positive number n. If we increase this by 25%, we get $1.25n$. If we decrease this by 50%, we get $(0.50)(1.25n) = 0.625n$.

Multiplying by 0.625 is equivalent to dividing by its reciprocal, and $1/0.625 = 1.60$. Therefore, the correct answer is C.

Important Factoring Identities

$$a^2 - b^2 = (a + b)(a - b)$$
$$a^2 + 2ab + b^2 = (a + b)(a + b)$$
$$a^2 - 2ab + b^2 = (a - b)(a - b)$$

If m and n are real numbers such that

$\dfrac{m^2 - n^2}{2m - 2n} = \dfrac{9}{2}$, what is the value of $m + n$?

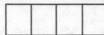

(*Easy*) As a rule, we should simplify any complicated-looking expressions, but also keep an eye on what the question is asking. Here, we need to remember that we are asked to find the value of $m + n$ and **not** the values of m and n individually.

Given equation:	$\dfrac{m^2 - n^2}{2m - 2n} = \dfrac{9}{2}$
Factor:	$\dfrac{(m + n)(m - n)}{2(m - n)} = \dfrac{9}{2}$
Cancel common factors:	$\dfrac{(m + n)}{2} = \dfrac{9}{2}$
Multiply by 2:	$m + n = 9$

Bonus: What ordered pair (m, n) has a sum of 9 but is <u>not</u> a solution to the equation?

If the equation $y = \dfrac{9x^2 + 12x + 4}{6x + 4}$ is graphed in

the xy-plane for positive values of x , the graph is a line. What is the slope of this line?

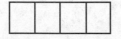

(*Medium/hard*) Given equation: $y = \dfrac{9x^2 + 12x + 4}{6x + 4}$

Factor numerator and denominator:

$$y = \frac{(3x + 2)(3x + 2)}{2(3x + 2)}$$

Cancel common factors and simplify:

$$y = \frac{3x + 2}{2} = \frac{3}{2}x + 1$$

Therefore, the slope of the line is $\dfrac{3}{2}$, or 1.5.

Look for Patterns

Don't be intimidated by complex expressions. Just look for **simple patterns** that allow you to simplify with the Law of Substitution.

If $x^2 + 4x + 5 = y$ and $z = x + 2$, which of the following expresses y in terms of z ?

A) $y = z^2 + 1$

B) $y = z(z + 3)$

C) $y = z^2 + 5$

D) $y = (z + 2)^2 + 1$

(*Medium*) The fact that $(x + 2)^2 = x^2 + 4x + 4$ allows for a clever substitution:

First equation:	$x^2 + 4x + 5 = y$
Subtract 1 from both sides:	$x^2 + 4x + 4 = y - 1$
Factor the left side:	$(x + 2)^2 = y - 1$
Substitute $z = x + 2$:	$z^2 = y - 1$
Add 1 to both sides:	$z^2 + 1 = y$

Therefore, the correct answer is A.

Lesson 4: Conversions

Conversion Factors

A **conversion factor** is a **fraction** in which the numerator and the denominator are **equal**. For instance, 1 mile is equal to 1.609 kilometers, so $\dfrac{1\,\text{mile}}{1.609\,\text{kilometers}}$ is a conversion factor for converting kilometers to miles, and $\dfrac{1.609\,\text{kilometers}}{1\,\text{mile}}$ is a conversion factor for converting miles to kilometers.

Using Conversion Factors

When converting quantities, **make sure that the units cancel properly, like common factors**. For instance, if you've just run a 10-km race and want to know how many miles you've run, the conversion is

$$10\,\text{kilometers}\left(\frac{1\,\text{mile}}{1.609\,\text{kilometers}}\right) = 6.215\,\text{miles}$$

Notice that **kilometers** must go in the denominator of the conversion factor in order to **cancel** the original kilometers.

Niko is 27 inches shorter than his father, who is 5 feet 10 inches tall. How tall is Niko?
(1 foot = 12 inches)

A)   3 feet 4 inches

B)   3 feet 6 inches

C)   3 feet 7 inches

D)   3 feet 10 inches

(*Easy*) If Niko's father is 5 feet 10 inches tall, he is 5 feet × (12 inches/1 foot) + 10 inches = 70 inches tall. If Niko is 27 inches shorter, he is 70 − 27 = 43 inches tall, which is equivalent to 43 inches × (1 foot/12 inches) = 3 7/12 feet, or 3 feet 7 inches, so the correct answer is C.

Universal vs. "Problem-Specific" Conversions

Sometimes the equivalence shown in a conversion factor is **universal** (for instance, 1 pound is **always** equal to 16 ounces) and sometimes it is **problem-specific**. For instance, if a problem says that a machine pumps at a rate 3 gallons per hour, pumping for 1 hour is equivalent to pumping 3 gallons in the context of this problem.

If a factory can manufacture b computer screens in n days at a cost of c dollars per screen, then which of the following represents the total cost, in dollars, of the computer screens that can be manufactured, at that rate, in m days?

A) $\dfrac{bcm}{n}$

B) $\dfrac{bmn}{c}$

C) $\dfrac{mc}{bn}$

D) $\dfrac{bc}{mn}$

(*Medium*) We can look at this as a problem of **converting days to dollars**. We are told that this factory works for m days, so let's write this down, including units, and multiply by the conversion factors until we convert to dollars:

$$m\,\text{days}\left(\frac{b\,\text{screens}}{n\,\text{days}}\right)\left(\frac{c\,\text{dollars}}{1\,\text{screen}}\right) = \frac{bcm}{n}\,\text{dollars}$$

Notice that all of the units **cancel** except for dollars in the numerator. So, the correct answer is A.

Exercise Set 2 (No Calculator)

1

If bag A weighs 4 pounds 5 ounces and bag B weighs 6 pounds 2 ounces, how much heavier, in <u>ounces</u>, is bag B than bag A? (1 pound = 16 ounces)

2

If $\dfrac{3a+b}{b} = \dfrac{7}{5}$, what is the value of $\dfrac{a}{b}$?

3

If $x - 2y = 10$ and $x \neq 0$, what is the value of $\dfrac{2x}{y+5}$?

4

If $a - b = 4$ and $a^2 - b^2 = 3$, what is the value of $a + b$?

5

If 6 gricks are equivalent to 5 merts, then 2 merts are equivalent to how many gricks?

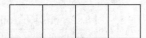

6

If the function $\{x\}$ is defined by the equation $\{x\} = (1 - x)^2$, what is the value of $\{\{4\}\}$?

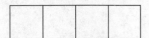

7

If $\dfrac{a+b}{b} = 3$ and $\dfrac{a+c}{c} = 5$, what is the value of $\dfrac{b}{c}$?

8

$$(x - 9)(x - a) = x^2 - 4ax + b$$

In the equation above, a and b are constants. If the equation is true for all values of x, what is the value of b ?

A) -27

B) -12

C) 12

D) 27

9

If $\dfrac{5}{x} + \dfrac{7}{5} = 1$, what is the value of x ?

A) $-\dfrac{25}{2}$

B) -7

C) $-\dfrac{24}{7}$

D) $-\dfrac{7}{5}$

10

$$(p + 2)^2 = (p - 5)^2$$

The equation above is true for which of the following values of p ?

A) -2 and 5

B) 2 and -5

C) 1.5 only

D) 5 only

11

If $\dfrac{3x}{m - nx} = 2$ for all positive values of m and n, then which of the following is equal to x ?

A) $\dfrac{2m - 2n}{3}$

B) $\dfrac{2m - 3}{2n}$

C) $\dfrac{3 + 2n}{2m}$

D) $\dfrac{2m}{3 + 2n}$

Exercise Set 2 (Calculator)

12

Let m be a positive real number. Increasing m by 60% and then decreasing the result by 50% is equivalent to dividing m by what number?

13

What is the sum of the first 50 positive even integers?

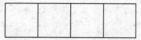

14

Three years ago, Nora was half as old as Mary is now. If Mary is four years older than Nora, how old is Mary now?

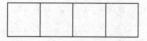

15

If 2/3 of the seats at a football stadium were filled at the beginning of the game, and at halftime 1,000 spectators left, leaving 3/7 of the seats filled, what is the total number of seats in the stadium?

16

If three candy bars and two gumdrops cost $2.20, and four candy bars and two gumdrops cost $2.80, what is the cost, in dollars, of one gumdrop?

17

If $\dfrac{x^2 - 2x + 1}{2 - 2x} = -3$, what is the value of $x - 1$?

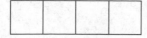

18

Subtracting 3 from a number and then multiplying this result by 4 is equivalent to multiplying the original number by 4 and then subtracting what number?

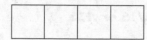

19

In a poker game, a blue chip is worth 2 dollars more than a red chip, and a red chip is worth 2 dollars more than a green chip. If 5 green chips are worth m dollars, then which of the following represents the value, in dollars, of 10 blue chips and 5 red chips?

A) $50 + 3m$

B) $18 + 60m$

C) $40 + 3m$

D) $28 + 20m$

20

A train travels at an average speed of 50 miles per hour for the first 100 miles of a 200-mile trip, and at an average of 75 miles per hour for final 100 miles. What is the train's average speed for the entire trip?

A) 58.5 mph

B) 60.0 mph

C) 62.5 mph

D) 63.5 mph

21

Which of the following is equivalent to $3m(m^2 \times 2m)$ for all real values of m ?

A) $3m^2 + 6m$

B) $3m^2 \times 6m$

C) $3m^3 \times 6m^2$

D) $6m^4$

22

If the cost of living in a certain city increased by 20% in the 10 years from 1980 to 1990, and increased by 50% in the 20 years from 1980 to 2000, what was the percent increase in the cost of living from 1990 to 2000?

A) 15%

B) 20%

C) 25%

D) 30%

EXERCISE SET 2 ANSWER KEY

No Calculator

1. **29**   4 pounds 5 ounces $= 4(16) + 5 = 69$ ounces, and 6 pounds 2 ounces $= 6(16) + 2 = 98$ ounces. Therefore, bag B weighs $98 - 69 = 29$ ounces more.

2. **2/15 or .133**

	$\dfrac{3a + b}{b} = \dfrac{7}{5}$
Distribute division:	$\dfrac{3a}{b} + \dfrac{b}{b} = \dfrac{7}{5}$
Simplify:	$\dfrac{3a}{b} + 1 = \dfrac{7}{5}$
Subtract 1:	$\dfrac{3a}{b} = \dfrac{2}{5}$
Divide by 3:	$\dfrac{a}{b} = \dfrac{2}{15}$

3. **4**   Expression to be evaluated: $\dfrac{2x}{y + 5}$

Given equation:	$x - 2y = 10$
Add 2y:	$x = 2y + 10$
Substitute $x = 2y + 10$:	$\dfrac{2(2y + 10)}{y + 5}$
Simplify:	$\dfrac{4y + 20}{y + 5}$
Factor and simplify:	$\dfrac{4(y + 5)}{y + 5} = 4$

4. **¾ or .75**

	$a^2 - b^2 = 3$
Factor:	$(a - b)(a + b) = 3$
Substitute $a - b = 4$:	$4(a + b) = 3$
Divide by 4:	$a + b = \dfrac{3}{4}$

5. **12/5 or 2.4** $2 \text{ merts} \times \dfrac{6 \text{ gricks}}{5 \text{ merts}} = \dfrac{12}{5} \text{ gricks}$

6. **64** $\{4\} = (1 - 4)^2 = (-3)^2 = 9$
$\{\{4\}\} = (1 - \{4\})^2 = (1 - 9)^2 = (-8)^2 = 64$

7. **2**   Given equation: $\dfrac{a + b}{b} = 3$

Distribute division:	$\dfrac{a}{b} + 1 = 3$
Subtract 1:	$\dfrac{a}{b} = 2$

Reciprocate:	$\dfrac{b}{a} = \dfrac{1}{2}$
Given equation:	$\dfrac{a + c}{c} = 5$
Distribute division:	$\dfrac{a}{c} + 1 = 5$
Subtract 1:	$\dfrac{a}{c} = 4$
Multiply:	$\dfrac{b}{c} = \left(\dfrac{b}{a}\right)\left(\dfrac{a}{c}\right) = \left(\dfrac{1}{2}\right)(4) = 2$

8. **D**   Given: $(x - 9)(x - a) = x^2 - 4ax + b$

FOIL:	$x^2 - ax - 9x + 9a = x^2 - 4ax + b$
Simplify:	$x^2 - (a + 9)x + 9a = x^2 - 4ax + b$

If this equation is true for all x, then the coefficients of corresponding terms must be equal, so $a + 9 = 4a$

Subtract a:	$9 = 3a$
Divide by 3:	$3 = a$

Therefore $b = 9a = 9(3) = 27$.

9. **A**   Given equation: $\dfrac{5}{x} + \dfrac{7}{5} = 1$

Multiply by 5x:	$25 + 7x = 5x$
Subtract 7x:	$25 = -2x$
Divide by -2:	$-\dfrac{25}{2} = x$

10. **C**   Given equation: $(p + 2)^2 = (p - 5)^2$

FOIL:	$p^2 + 4p + 4 = p^2 - 10p + 25$
Subtract p^2:	$4p + 4 = -10p + 25$
Add 10p:	$14p + 4 = 25$
Subtract 4:	$14p = 21$
Divide by 14:	$p = 1.5$

11. **D**   Given equation: $\dfrac{3x}{m - nx} = 2$

Multiply by $m - nx$:	$3x = 2(m - nx)$
Distribute:	$3x = 2m - 2nx$
Add 2nx:	$3x + 2nx = 2m$
Factor out x:	$x(3 + 2n) = 2m$
Divide by $3 + 2n$:	$x = \dfrac{2m}{3 + 2n}$

Calculator

12. 1.25 Increasing a number by 60% is equivalent to multiplying it by 1.60, and decreasing a number by 50% is equivalent to multiplying it by 0.50. Therefore, performing both changes in succession is equivalent to multiplying by $1.60 \times 0.50 = 0.80$. Multiplying by 0.80 is equivalent to dividing by its reciprocal: $1/(0.80) = 1.25$.

13. 2,550 The sum of the first 50 positive even integers is $2 + 4 + 6 + 8 + \cdots + 100$. As with the example in Lesson 2, these numbers can be regrouped into 25 pairs of numbers each of which has a sum of $2 + 100 = 102$. Therefore, their sum is $25(102) = 2,550$.

14. 14 Let n = Nora's age now, and m = Mary's age now. If 3 years ago, Nora was half as old

as Mary is now: $\qquad n - 3 = \dfrac{1}{2}m$

If Mary is 4 years older than Nora: $\qquad m = 4 + n$

Subtract 4: $\qquad m - 4 = n$

Substitute $n = m - 4$: $\qquad m - 4 - 3 = \dfrac{1}{2}m$

Simplify: $\qquad m - 7 = \dfrac{1}{2}m$

Multiply by 2: $\qquad 2m - 14 = m$

Subtract m and add 14: $\qquad m = 14$

15. 4,200 Let x = the total number of seats in the

stadium. $\qquad \dfrac{2}{3}x - 1,000 = \dfrac{3}{7}x$

Subtract $\dfrac{3}{7}x$: $\qquad \dfrac{2}{3}x - \dfrac{3}{7}x - 1,000 = 0$

Add 1,000: $\qquad \dfrac{2}{3}x - \dfrac{3}{7}x = 1,000$

Combine like terms: $\qquad \dfrac{5}{21}x = 1,000$

Multiply by $\dfrac{21}{5}$: $\qquad x = \dfrac{21,000}{5} = 4,200$

16. 0.20 Let g = the cost, in dollars, of one gumdrop, and c = the cost, in dollars, of one candy bar.

$$4c + 2g = 2.80$$
$$3c + 2g = 2.20$$

Subtract: $\qquad c = 0.60$

Substitute $c = 0.60$: $\qquad 4(0.60) + 2g = 2.80$

Simplify: $\qquad 2.40 + 2g = 2.80$

Subtract 2.40: $\qquad 2g = 0.40$

Divide by 2: $\qquad g = 0.20$

17. 6 $\qquad \dfrac{x^2 - 2x + 1}{2 - 2x} = -3$

Factor: $\qquad \dfrac{(x-1)(x-1)}{2(1-x)} = -3$

Multiply by -1: $\qquad \dfrac{(x-1)(x-1)}{2(x-1)} = -3$

Simplify: $\qquad \dfrac{x-1}{2} = 3$

Multiply by 2: $\qquad x - 1 = 6$

18. 12 We can just choose a number to work with, like 10. If we subtract 3 from this number and then multiply the result by 4, we get $4(10 - 3) = 28$. If we multiply it by 4 and then subtract a mystery number, we get $4(10) - x = 40 - x$. $\qquad 28 = 40 - x$

Subtract 40: $\qquad -12 = -x$

Multiply by -1: $\qquad 12 = x$

19. A If 5 green chips are worth m dollars, then each green chip is worth $m/5$ dollars. If a red chip is worth 2 dollars more than a green chip, then each red chip is worth $m/5 + 2$ dollars. If each blue chip is worth 2 dollars more than a red chip, then each blue chip is worth $m/5 + 4$ dollars. Therefore, 10 blue chips and 5 red chips are worth $10(m/5 + 4) + 5(m/5 + 2) = 2m + 40 + m + 10 = 3m + 50$ dollars.

20. B The average speed is equal to the total distance divided by the total time. The total distance is 200 miles. The time for the first hundred miles is (100 miles/50 mph) = 2 hours, and the time for the second hundred miles is (100 miles/75 mph) = 4/3 hours. Therefore the total time of the trip is $2 + 4/3 = 10/3$ hours, and the average speed is

$$\dfrac{200}{\dfrac{10}{3}} = 200 \times \dfrac{3}{10} = 60 \text{ mph}$$

21. D $\qquad 3m(m^2 \times 2m)$

Parentheses: $\qquad 3m(2m^3)$

Multiply: $\qquad 6m^4$

22. C Assume the cost of living in 1980 was $100. If this increased by 20% from 1980 to 1990, then the cost of living in 1990 was $1.20(\$100) = \$120$. If the increase from 1980 to 2000 was 50%, then the cost of living in 2000 was $1.50(\$100) = \$150$. The percent increase from 1990 to 2000 is therefore

$$\dfrac{150 - 120}{120} \times 100\% = \dfrac{30}{120} \times 100\% = 25\%$$

Lesson 5: Constructing and interpreting linear equations

Linear Equations from Word Problems

When setting up linear equations from word problems, consider **which linear form matches the information you are given.**

- **Slope-intercept:** $y = mx + b$
  slope $= m$ y-intercept $= b$

- **Standard:** $ax + by = c$
  slope $= -\dfrac{a}{b}$ y-intercept $= \dfrac{c}{b}$

- **Point-slope:** $y - y_1 = m(x - x_1)$
  slope $= m$ point on line $= (x_1, y_1)$

- **Intercept:** $\dfrac{x}{a} + \dfrac{y}{b} = 1$
  x-intercept: a y-intercept: b
  (This form cannot be used for horizontal lines or lines that pass through the origin.)

Graphing Lines

When working with linear equations, make sure you know how to turn **equations into graphs** and **graphs into equations**. In addition to knowing the different forms of linear equations, it helps to know the **slope formula.**

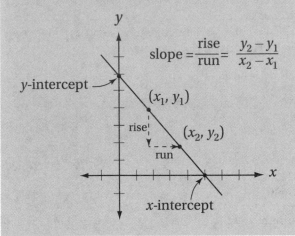

$$\text{slope} = \frac{\text{rise}}{\text{run}} = \frac{y_2 - y_1}{x_2 - x_1}$$

The Horizon Resort charges $150 per night for a single room, and a one-time valet parking fee of $35. There is a 6.5% state tax on the room charges, but no tax on the valet parking fee. Which of the following equations represents the total charges in dollars, C, for a single room, valet parking, and taxes, for a stay of n nights at The Horizon Resort?

A) $c = (150 + 0.065n) + 35$

B) $c = 1.065(150n) + 35$

C) $c = 1.065(150n + 35)$

D) $c = 1.065(150 + 35)n$

(*Easy-medium*) Since the room charge is $150 per night, the charge for n nights is $150n$. If a 6.5% tax is added to this, the room charge becomes $150n + 0.065(150n)$ $= 1.065(150n)$ per night. The $35 valet parking charge is added separately, and not taxed, so the total charges are $1.065(150n) + 35$, and the correct answer is B. This is a linear equation in **slope-intercept** form, in which the slope is the **cost per day** and the y-intercept is the **fixed cost.**

Which of the following represents the equation of the line with an x-intercept of 6 that passes through the point (3, 2)?

A) $y = -\dfrac{4}{3}x + 6$

B) $y = -\dfrac{2}{3}x + 4$

C) $y = -\dfrac{3}{2}x + 6$

D) $y = -\dfrac{3}{4}x + \dfrac{9}{2}$

(*Easy*) Let's draw a graph of the given information:

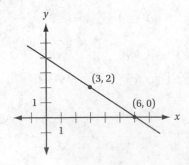

Since we are given two points on the line, (3, 2) and (6, 0), we can calculate the slope using the slope formula:

$$\text{slope} = \frac{y_2 - y_1}{x_2 - x_1} = \frac{0 - 2}{6 - 3} = -\frac{2}{3}$$

If we use this slope and the point (6, 0), we can set up the equation in **point-slope form**:

Point-slope form of equation: $y - 0 = -\frac{2}{3}(x - 6)$

Simplify and distribute: $y = -\frac{2}{3}x + 4$

So the correct answer is B. This equation is in **slope-intercept form**, and shows that this line also has a y-intercept of 4, matching our graph.

$$10y = -7(2x - 5)$$

Which of the following equivalent forms of the linear equation above shows the x- and y-intercepts of its graph in the xy-plane as constants or coefficients?

A) $14x + 10y = 35$

B) $y = -\frac{7}{5}x + \frac{7}{2}$

C) $\dfrac{x}{2.5} + \dfrac{y}{3.5} = 1$

D) $y = -\frac{7}{5}\left(x - -\frac{5}{2}\right)$

(*Medium*) Since the question tells us that these are all equivalent forms of the same equation, there is no need to manipulate the given equation. Notice that choice A is in **standard form**, choice B is in **slope-intercept form**, and choice D is in **point-slope form**. Choice C is correct because it is in **intercept form**. You should be able to confirm that the points (2.5, 0) and (0, 3.5), the x- and y-intercepts, satisfy this equation and that these intercepts are the constants in the equation.

$$F = 1.8(K) - 459.4$$

The formula above can be used to convert any temperature in Kelvin, K, to the temperature in degrees Fahrenheit, F. Which choice indicates the correct interpretation of the number 1.8 in this formula?

A) Every increase of 1° Fahrenheit is equivalent to an increase of 1.8 Kelvin.

B) Every increase of 1 Kelvin is equivalent to an increase of 1.8° Fahrenheit.

C) 1.8 Kelvin is equivalent to –459.4° Fahrenheit.

D) 0° Fahrenheit is equivalent to 1.8 Kelvin.

(*Medium-hard*) The conversion formula is a linear equation in the form $y = mx + b$, where m is the **slope** of the line (the change in y for every unit change in x), and b is the **y-intercept** of the line (the y value when x is 0). Since 1.8 is the slope of the line in this formula, it must be the *change in degrees Fahrenheit for every unit change in Kelvin*, so the correct answer is B.

Lesson 6: Solving equations with the Laws of Equality

The Laws of Equality

To solve algebraic equations, you need the Laws of Equality.

1. **Whatever you do to change the value of one side of an equation, you must also do to the other side.**

2. **You may add, subtract, or multiply anything you want on both sides of any equation at any time.**

3. **You may divide both sides of any equation by any number <u>except 0</u>.** (Because division by 0 is undefined.)

4. **If you want to take the square root of both sides of an equation, remember that <u>every positive number has two square roots: one positive and one negative</u>.**

If $\dfrac{1}{x} + \dfrac{2}{3x} = 4$, what is the value of x ?

(*Medium*) This doesn't look like a linear equation, but if we apply Law of Equality #2, we can see that it is.

Given equation:
$$\frac{1}{x} + \frac{2}{3x} = 4$$

Notice that the common denominator of the two fractions is $3x$, so we can simplify the equation by multiplying both sides by $3x$:

$$3x\left(\frac{1}{x} + \frac{2}{3x}\right) = 3x(4)$$

Distribute and simplify: $\quad \dfrac{3x}{x} + \dfrac{6x}{3x} \quad 3 + 2 = 5 = 12x$

Divide both sides by 12: $\qquad\qquad x = \dfrac{5}{12} = 0.417$

(*Hard*) You might want to take the square root of both sides of the equation, but remember Law of Equality #4. If $x^2 = y^2$, then x and y are either the **same number** or **opposites**. For instance, notice that $x = 0$ and $y = 0$ is a solution, but these values don't work for choice B because 0/0 is undefined. Also, $x = 1$ and $y = -1$ is a solution, but these values don't work in choices A or D. Therefore, the correct answer is C.

Lesson 7: Analyzing Linear Graphs

Thinking about Slopes

It sometimes helps to think of the slope of a line as **how much it goes up (or down) when you take one step to the right along the line**.

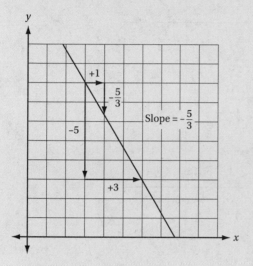

When looking at a linear graph, remember that lines with a **positive slope go up** as you move to the right, lines with a **negative slope go down** as you move to the right, and lines with a 0 slope **are horizontal**.

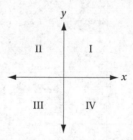

Which of the following equations, when graphed in the xy-plane, contains points in all quadrants except quadrant II?

A) $2x + 5y = 9$

B) $-2x + 5y = 9$

C) $2x - 5y = 9$

D) $-2x - 5y = 9$

(*Medium*) A line with points in quadrants I, III, and IV must have a positive slope and a negative y-intercept. If we use the formulas from Lesson 5 that tell us how to find the slope and y-intercept of lines in **standard form**, we

can see that only choice C works, because it has a slope of 2/5 and a y-intercept of $-9/5$.

Parallel and Perpendicular Lines

Parallel lines have **equal slopes. Perpendicular lines** have slopes that are **opposite reciprocals** of each other.

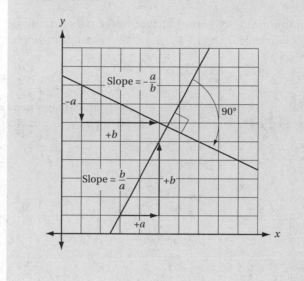

$$2x - 3ky = 12$$
$$4x + 2py = 20$$

In the equations above, k and p are constants. If the graphs of these equations in the xy-plane are perpendicular lines, what is the value of kp?

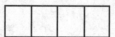

(*Medium-hard*) These lines have slopes of $\dfrac{2}{3k}$ and $-\dfrac{2}{p}$.

If they are perpendicular, they are **opposite reciprocals**, so their **product is −1**:

$$\left(\frac{2}{3k}\right)\left(-\frac{2}{p}\right) = -1$$

Simplify:

$$-\frac{4}{3kp} = -1$$

Multiply both sides by $-kp$:

$$\frac{4}{3} = 1.33 = kp$$

The graph of line ℓ in the xy-plane passes through the point $(2, 5)$ and has an x-intercept of 7. Which of following gives the equation of a line that is perpendicular to line ℓ and passes through the point $(4, 2)$?

A) $y = -x + 6$

B) $y = -x + 4$

C) $y = x - 2$

D) $y = x + 2$

(*Medium-hard*) We are told that line ℓ passes through two points: $(2, 5)$ and $(7, 0)$, so we can calculate its slope:

$$\text{slope} = \frac{y_2 - y_1}{x_2 - x_1} = \frac{0 - 5}{7 - 2} = \frac{-5}{5} = -1$$

The slopes of perpendicular lines are **opposite reciprocals**, so the slope of the new line is 1. The new line must

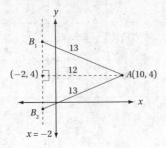

pass through $(4, 2)$, so we can get its equation using the point-slope form of the equation from Lesson 5: $y - 2 = 1(x - 4)$

Add 2 to both sides: $y = x - 2$

Therefore, the correct answer is C.

$$x + my + m = 0?$$

If m is a constant greater than 1, which of the following could be the graph in the xy-plane of the equation above?

A)

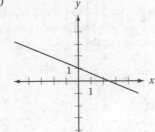

B)

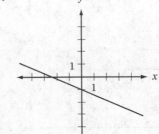

C)

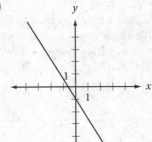

D)

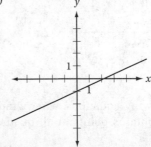

(*Medium-hard*) First, we should try to get the equation into a more useful form. Let's try the slope-intercept $(y = mx + b)$ form: $x + my + m = 0$

Subtract x and m from both sides: $my = -x - m$

Divide both sides by m: $y = \left(-\dfrac{1}{m}\right)x - 1$

So the line has a slope of $-1/m$ and a y-intercept of -1. Since m is greater than 1, this slope must be between -1 and 0. The only graph that satisfies these conditions is B.

Exercise Set 3 (No Calculator)

1

If $x - 2(1 - x) = 5$, what is the value of x ?

2

If $f(x) = -2x + 8$, and $f(k) = -10$, what is the value of k ?

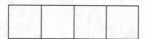

3

What is the slope of the line that contains the points $(-2, 3)$ and $(4, 5)$?

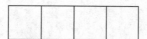

4

What is the slope of the line described by the equation $\dfrac{1}{x} + \dfrac{1}{2x} = \dfrac{5}{y}$?

5

Line l is perpendicular to the line described by the equation $5x + 11y = 16$. What is the slope of line l ?

6

If $\dfrac{x+1}{10} + \dfrac{2x}{5} = 1$, what is the value of x ?

7

What is the y-intercept of the line containing the points $(3, 7)$ and $(6, 3)$?

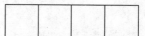

8

In the xy-plane, the graph of $y = h(x)$ is a line with slope -2. If $h(3) = 1$ and $h(b) = -9$, what is the value of b ?

9

If a train maintains a constant speed of 60 miles per hour, it can travel 4 miles per gallon of diesel fuel. If this train begins a trip with a full 200 gallon tank of diesel fuel, and maintains a speed of 60 miles per hour, which of the following equations represents the number of gallons, g, left in the tank t hours into the trip?

A) $g = \dfrac{200 - 60t}{4}$

B) $g = 200 - \dfrac{1}{15t}$

C) $g = 200 - 15t$

D) $g = 200 - \dfrac{1}{15}t$

10

The points $A(2, 3)$ and $B(m, 11)$, are 10 units apart. Which of the following equations could describe the line that contains points A and B?

A) $8x + 6y = 11$

B) $8x - 6y = -2$

C) $6x + 8y = 36$

D) $6x - 8y = -12$

11

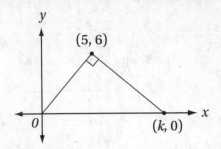

The figure above shows a right triangle with vertices at the origin, $(5, 6)$ and $(k, 0)$. What is the value of k?

A) $\dfrac{19}{3}$

B) $\dfrac{58}{5}$

C) $\dfrac{26}{3}$

D) $\dfrac{61}{5}$

Exercise Set 3 (Calculator)

12

If the points (2, 4), (5, k), and (8, 20) are on the same line, what is the value of k ?

13

Line l has a slope of 3 and a y-intercept of -4. What is its x-intercept?

14

If $f(-1) = 1$ and $f(3) = 2$ and f is a linear function, what is the slope of the graph $y = f(x)$?

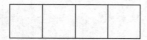

15

If $f(-1) = 1$ and $f(3) = 2$ and f is a linear function, what is $f(5)$?

16

In the xy-plane, the graph of line n has an x-intercept of $2b$ and an y-intercept of $-8b$, where $b \neq 0$. What is the slope of line n ?

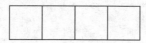

17

If $\dfrac{2}{x} + \dfrac{2}{5x} = 4$, what is the value of x ?

18

If the line $3x - 2y = 12$ is graphed in the xy-plane, what is its x-intercept?

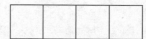

19

If the graphs of the equations $5x - 2y = 5$ and $6x + ky = 9$ are perpendicular, what is the value of k ?

20

The net profit for the sales of a product is equal to the total revenue from the sales of that product minus the total cost for the sales of that product. If a particular model of calculator sells for \$98, and the cost for making and selling n of these calculators is \$$(35n + 120{,}000)$, which of the following equations expresses the net profit in dollars, P, for making and selling n of these calculators?

A) $P = 63n - 120{,}000$

B) $P = 63n + 120{,}000$

C) $P = 63(n - 120{,}000)$

D) $P = 63(n + 120{,}000)$

21

Which of the following represents the equation of the line with an x-intercept of 5 and a y-intercept of 6?

A) $y - 6 = -\dfrac{6}{5}(x - 5)$

B) $y - 6 = -\dfrac{5}{6}(x - 5)$

C) $y - 6 = -\dfrac{6}{5}x$

D) $y - 6 = -\dfrac{5}{6}x$

22

x	2	3	4
$f(x)$	a	8	b

The table above shows several ordered pairs corresponding to the linear function f. What is the value of $a + b$?

A) 12

B) 16

C) 20

D) It cannot be determined from the information given.

EXERCISE SET 3 ANSWER KEY

Part 1: No Calculator

1. **7/3 or 2.33** $\qquad\qquad x - 2(1 - x) = 5$

Distribute: $\qquad\qquad\qquad\qquad x - 2 + 2x = 5$

Simplify: $\qquad\qquad\qquad\qquad\quad 3x - 2 = 5$

Add 2: $\qquad\qquad\qquad\qquad\qquad\quad 3x = 7$

Divide by 3: $\qquad\qquad\qquad\qquad\quad x = 7/3$

---

2. **9** $\qquad\qquad\qquad f(k) = -2k + 8 = -10$

Subtract 8: $\qquad\qquad\qquad\qquad -2k = -18$

Divide by −2: $\qquad\qquad\qquad\qquad\quad k = 9$

---

3. **1/3 or .333** $\qquad$ slope $= \dfrac{5-3}{4-(-2)} = \dfrac{2}{6} = \dfrac{1}{3}$

---

4. **10/3 or 3.33** $\qquad\qquad \dfrac{1}{x} + \dfrac{1}{2x} = \dfrac{5}{y}$

Multiply by $2xy$: $\qquad \dfrac{2xy}{x} + \dfrac{2xy}{2x} = \dfrac{10xy}{y}$

Simplify: $\qquad\qquad\qquad\qquad 2y + y = 10x$

Simplify: $\qquad\qquad\qquad\qquad\quad 3y = 10x$

Divide by 3: $\qquad\qquad\qquad\qquad y = \dfrac{10}{3}x$

---

5. **11/5 or 2.2**   The slope of the given line is −5/11, so the slope of the line perpendicular to it is 11/5.

---

6. **9/5 or 1.8** $\qquad\qquad \dfrac{x+1}{10} + \dfrac{2x}{5} = 1$

Multiply by 10: $\qquad\qquad (x + 1) + 4x = 10$

Simplify: $\qquad\qquad\qquad\qquad\quad 5x + 1 = 10$

Subtract 1: $\qquad\qquad\qquad\qquad\qquad 5x = 9$

Divide by 5: $\qquad\qquad\qquad\qquad\quad x = 9/5$

---

7. **11**   There are a variety of ways of solving this problem, but perhaps the simplest is to draw a quick sketch:

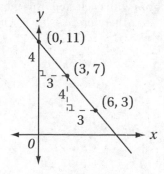

Notice that to get from (6, 3) to (3, 7) we must go left 3 units and up 4 units (in other words, the slope is −4/3). If we simply repeat this from (3, 7), we arrive at the y-intercept, which is (0, 11).

---

8. **8**   This line has a slope of −2 and contains the points (3, 1) and (b, −9). Therefore $-2 = \dfrac{-9 - 1}{b - 3}$

Simplify: $\qquad\qquad\qquad\qquad -2 = \dfrac{-10}{b-3}$

Multiply by $b - 3$: $\qquad\qquad -2b + 6 = -10$

Subtract 6: $\qquad\qquad\qquad\qquad\quad -2b = -16$

Divide by −2: $\qquad\qquad\qquad\qquad\quad b = 8$

---

9. **C**   Since the tanks starts with 200 gallons, the amount it has left is 200 − the number of gallons used. The number of gallons used is

$$t \text{ hours} \times \frac{60 \text{ miles}}{1 \text{ hour}} \times \frac{1 \text{ gallon}}{4 \text{ miles}} = 15t \text{ gallons}$$

---

10. **B**   Once again, a quick sketch can be very helpful. Notice that traveling from point

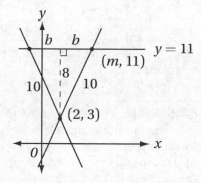

$A(2, 3)$ to point $B(m, 11)$ requires going up 8 units and right (or left) some unknown distance b. We can find b with the

Pythagorean Theorem: $\qquad\qquad 8^2 + b^2 = 10^2$

Simplify: $\qquad\qquad\qquad\qquad 64 + b^2 = 100$

Subtract 64: $\qquad\qquad\qquad\qquad\qquad b^2 = 36$

Take the square root: $\qquad\qquad\qquad\quad b = 6$

Therefore, m is either $2 - 6 = -4$ or $2 + 6 = 8$, and the slope of this line is either $8/6 = 4/3$ or $8/(-6) = -4/3$. The only equation among the choices that is satisfied by the ordered pair (2, 3) and has a slope of either 4/3 or −4/3 is (B).

11. **D**　Recall that the slopes of perpendicular lines are opposite reciprocals. The slope of the segment from $(0, 0)$ to $(5, 6)$ is 6/5, so the slope of its perpendicular is $-5/6$.

Therefore

$$\frac{6-0}{5-k}=-\frac{5}{6}$$

Cross-multiply:　　　　　　　　　　$-36 = 5(5 - k)$
Distribute:　　　　　　　　　　　　$-36 = 25 - 5k$
Subtract 25:　　　　　　　　　　　$-61 = -5k$
Divide by -5:　　　　　　　　　　$61/5 = k$

Part 2: Calculator

12. **12**　The slope of this line is $\frac{20-4}{8-2}=\frac{16}{6}=\frac{8}{3}$,

therefore,

$$\frac{k-4}{5-2}=\frac{8}{3}$$

Cross-multiply:　　　　　　　　　　$3k - 12 = 24$
Add 12:　　　　　　　　　　　　　$3k = 36$
Divide by 3:　　　　　　　　　　　$k = 12$

13. **4/3 or 1.33**　　　　Since the slope and y-intercept are given, it is easy to express the linear equation in slope-intercept form: $y = 3x - 4$.

The x-intercept is the value of x on the line for
which $y = 0$:　　　　　　　　　　$0 = 3x - 4$
Add 4:　　　　　　　　　　　　　$4 = 3x$
Divide by 3:　　　　　　　　　　　$4/3 = x$

14. **¼ or .25**　The line contains the points $(-1, 1)$ and $(3, 2)$, so its slope is $\frac{2-1}{3-(-1)}=\frac{1}{4}$

15. **5/2 or 2.5**　Although we could solve this problem by deriving the linear equation, it is perhaps easier to take advantage of the result from question 14. The slope of 1/4 means that the y-coordinate of any point on the line increases by 1/3 each time the x-coordinate increases by 1. Since the x-coordinate increases by 2 between $f(3)$ and $f(5)$, the y-coordinate must therefore increase by $2(1/4) = 1/2$, so $f(5) = 2 + ½ = 2.5$.

16. **4**　The line contains the points $(2b, 0)$ and $(0, -8b)$; therefore, it has a slope of $\frac{0-(-8b)}{2b-0}=\frac{8b}{2b}=4$.

17. **3/5 or .6**　　　　　　　　$\frac{2}{x}+\frac{2}{5x}=4$

Multiply by 5x:　　　　　　　　$10 + 2 = 20x$
Simplify:　　　　　　　　　　　$12 = 20x$
Divide by 20:　　　　　　　　　$x = 12/20 = 3/5$

18. **4**　The x-intercept is the value of x for which
$y = 0$:　　　　　　　　　　　$3x - 2(0) = 12$
Simplify:　　　　　　　　　　　$3x = 12$
Divide by 3:　　　　　　　　　　$x = 4$

19. **15**　Recall that the slope of a line in standard form $ax + by = c$ is $-a/b$. Therefore, the slope of $5x - 2y = 5$ is 5/2 and the slope of $6x + ky = 9$ is $-6/k$. If these lines are perpendicular, then their slopes are opposite reciprocals:

$$\frac{k}{6}=\frac{5}{2}$$

Multiply by 6:　　　　　　　　　$k = 30/2 = 15$

20. **A**　The total revenue for selling n calculators at \$98 each is \$98n the cost for making and selling n calculators is \$$(35n + 120,000)$. Therefore the profit is \$$(98n - 35n - 120,000) = 63n - 120,000$ dollars.

21. **C**　This line contains the points $(5, 0)$ and $(0, 6)$ and therefore has a slope of $\frac{0-6}{5-0}=-\frac{6}{5}$.

Since its y-intercept is 6, its slope-intercept form is

$y=-\frac{6}{5}x+6$ or, subtracting 6 from both sides,

$y-6=-\frac{6}{5}x$

22. **B**　Since f is a linear function, it has a slope that we can call m. Recall that it's often useful to think of the slope of a line as the "unit change," that is, the amount that y changes each time x increases by 1. Since the x values increase by 1 with each step in our table, the y values must therefore increase by m with each step. This means that $a = 8 - m$ and $b = 8 + m$. Therefore, $a + b = 8 - m + 8 + m = 16$.

Lesson 8: Understanding inequalities and absolute values

Absolute Value as Distance

The **absolute value** of a number a, written as $|a|$, is its **distance from 0 on the number line**. More generally, $|a - b|$ **means the distance between a and b on the number line**, regardless of which number is greater.

Which of the following represents the distance between d and –10 on the number line?

A) $|d - 10|$
B) $-10|d|$
C) $|d + 10|$
D) $|10 - d|$

(*Easy*) Since the distance between a and b is $|a - b|$, the distance between d and –10 is $|d - (-10)| = |d + 10|$, so the correct answer is C.

On the real number line, a number, b, is more than twice as far from -3 as it is from 3. Which of the following inequalities can be solved to find all possible values of b?

A) $|b - 3| > 2|b + 3|$

B) $|b + 3| > 2|b - 3|$

C) $2|b - 3| > |b + 3|$

D) $2|b + 3| > |b - 3|$

(*Medium*) We need to translate the central fact into a statement about distances, and then translate this statement into algebraic language. The original statement is *b is more than twice as far from –3 as it is from 3*. This can be translated in terms of distances: *the distance from b to –3 is more than twice the distance from b to 3*. In algebraic language, this translates directly to $|b - (-3)| > 2|b - 3|$ or, more simply, $|b + 3| > 2|b - 3|$. Therefore, the correct answer is B.

The label on each box of Deer Valley raisins says that it contains 1.25 pounds of raisins, but industry standards allow these boxes to be sold with anywhere from 1.20 pounds to 1.32 pounds of raisins. If x represents the number of pounds of raisins in a box of Deer Valley raisins that meets industry standards, which of the following inequalities represents all possible values of x?

A) $|x - 1.25| \leq 0.05$

B) $|x - 1.26| \leq 0.06$

C) $|x - 1.25| \leq 0.06$

D) $|x - 1.26| \leq 0.05$

(*Medium-hard*) The important fact here is the industry standard, not the label on the box. The standard says that the box can contain any weight of raisins from 1.20 to 1.32 pounds. The midpoint of this range is $(1.20 + 1.32)/2 = 1.26$ pounds of raisins, and this midpoint is 0.06 from either endpoint of this range. Therefore, x can be any value that is 0.06 or less away from 1.26, which can be stated as $|x - 1.26| \leq 0.06$, and so the correct answer is B.

Lesson 9: Solving inequalities with the Laws of Inequality

The Laws of Inequality

If an equation is a perfectly balanced scale, then an inequality is a "tipped" scale. The **Laws of Inequality** are just the rules for "knowing which way the scale is tipped"—that is, deducing *other* true inequalities that follow from the original.

1. Whatever you do to change the value of one side of an inequality, you must also do to the other side.

2. You may **add or subtract anything** you want from both sides of an inequality, or **multiply or divide by any positive number** without changing the direction of the inequality.

3. **You may not perform undefined operations** to an inequality (such as dividing by 0) or operations that have more than one possible result (like taking a square root).

4. If you **multiply or divide both sides by a negative number**, you must **switch the direction** of the inequality. This is because multiplying or dividing by a negative number involves a **reflection** over the origin, which swaps the relative positions of the numbers:

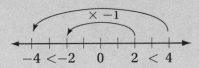

Which of the following must be true if $\dfrac{a}{b} \leq -3$?

A) $a \leq -3b$

B) $a \geq -3b$

C) $a \leq -3b < 0$ and $a \geq -3b > 0$

D) $a \leq -3b < 0$ or $a \geq -3b > 0$

(*Medium-hard*) We might want to multiply by b on both sides, but **b might be negative**. There are two possibilities:

Condition 1: If $b > 0$, then we **don't** switch the inequality when we multiply, so $a \leq -3b$, and therefore $a \leq -3b < 0$.

Condition 2: If $b < 0$, then we **do** switch the inequality when we multiply, so $a \geq -3b$ and therefore $a \geq -3b > 0$. So the correct answer is D.

If $-\dfrac{1}{2} < -2x + 1 < -\dfrac{1}{3}$, what is one possible value of x?

(*Medium*) This called a "sandwich inequality" because the expression in the middle is "sandwiched" between the other two. Let's solve for x using the Laws of Inequality.

$$-\frac{1}{2} < -2x + 1 < -\frac{1}{3}$$

Multiply all three parts by -6 (the common denominator) and "switch" the direction of the inequalities:

$$3 > 12x - 6 > 2$$

Add 6 to all three parts: $9 > 12x > 8$

Divide all three parts by 12: $0.750 > x > 0.66\ldots$

Therefore, any value greater than 0.666 but less than 0.750 is correct.

Lesson 10: Graphing inequalities

On the real number line, a number, *b,* is more than twice as far from −3 as it is from 3. Which of the following graphs represents all possible values of *b* ?

A)

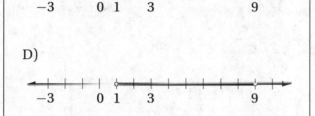

B)

C)

D)

(Medium) We saw this scenario in Lesson 8, but now we are asked to graph the solution. Recall from Lesson 8 that this relationship is expressed by the inequality $|b + 3| > 2|b − 3|$. How do we translate this into a graph? The simplest way to start is to visualize the number line, and to think about a related, but simpler, question: *What if b is exactly twice as far from −3 as it is from 3?* A little guessing and checking should reveal that two points work:

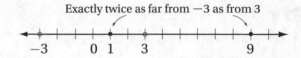

Exactly twice as far from −3 as from 3

Notice that 9 works because 3 is the midpoint between −3 and 9, and 1 works because it is 2/3 of the way from −3 to 3. Also, you can confirm that both numbers satisfy the equation $|b + 3| = 2|b − 3|$. These two points now divide the line into three parts: everything less than 1, everything between 1 and 9, and everything greater than 9. A little bit of checking (just pick a number from each portion and plug it into our inequality) confirms that only the numbers in the middle portion satisfy our inequality, so the correct graph is the one in choice (D).

When graphing inequalities, it often helps to start with the graph of the **corresponding equation** and work from there. **The graph of the equation usually provides the boundaries for the graph of the inequality.**

Exercise Set 4 (No Calculator)

1

What positive number is twice as far from 10 as it is from 1 ?

2

If the points $(2, a)$ and $(14, b)$ are 20 units apart, what is $|a - b|$?

3

What is the least integer n for which $0 < \dfrac{4}{n} < \dfrac{5}{9}$?

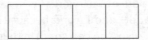

4

If $|x + 4| = |x - 5|$, what is the value of x ?

5

What is the greatest integer value of n such that $-\dfrac{n}{21} > -\dfrac{1}{2}$?

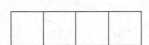

6

What is the only integer b for which $\dfrac{1}{b} > \dfrac{3}{11}$ and $3b \geq 7.5$?

7

If $(b + 2)^2 = (b - 5)^2$, what is the value of b ?

8

Which of the following statements is equivalent to the statement $-4 < 2x \leq 2$?

A) $x > -2$ and $x \leq 1$

B) $x < -2$ or $x \geq 1$

C) $x \geq -2$ and $x < 1$

D) $x \leq -2$ or $x > 1$

9

The annual profit from the sales of an item is equal to the annual revenue minus the annual cost for that item. The revenue from that item is equal to the number of units sold times the price per unit. If n units of a portable heart monitor were sold in 2012 at a price of $65 each, and the annual cost to produce n units was $(20,000 + 10n)$, then which of the following statements indicates that the total profit for this heart monitor in 2012 was greater than $500,000?

A) $500,000 < 55n - 20,000$

B) $500,000 > 55n - 20,000$

C) $500,000 < 55n + 20,000n$

D) $500,000 < 75n - 20,000n$

10

Colin can read a maximum of 25 pages an hour. If he has been reading a 250 page book for h hours, where $h < 10$, and has p pages left to read, which of the following expresses the relationship between p and h ?

A) $250 - p \leq \dfrac{25}{h}$

B) $250 \geq p + \dfrac{25}{h}$

C) $250 - p \leq 25h$

D) $250 + 25h \leq p$

11

On the real number line, a number, x, is more than 4 times as far from 10 as it is from 40. Which of the following statements describes all possible values of x ?

A) $x < 34$ or $x > 50$

B) $x > 40$

C) $34 < x < 50$

D) $32.5 < x < 160$

Exercise Set 4 (Calculator)

12

If $a < 0$ and $|a - 5| = 7$, what is $|a|$?

13

If n is a positive integer and $16 < |6 - 3n| < 19$, what is the value of n ?

14

What is the only integer n such that $20 - 2n > 5$ and $\dfrac{2n}{3} > 4$?

15

What is the smallest number that is as far from 9.25 as 3 is from -1.5 ?

16

If $|2x + 1| = 2|k - x|$, for all values of x, what is the value of $|k|$?

17

Which of the following is equivalent to the statement $|x - 2| < 1$?

A) $x < 3$

B) $x < -1$

C) $1 < x < 3$

D) $-1 < x < 3$

18

If the average (arithmetic mean) of a and b is greater than the average (arithmetic mean) of c and $2b$, which of the following must be true?

A) $b > 0$

B) $a > b$

C) $a > b + c$

D) $a + c > b$

19

Of the statements below, which is equivalent to the statement "The distance from x to 1 is greater than the distance from x to 3 ?

A) $1 < x < 3$

B) $x > 2$

C) $x < 2$

D) $x - 1 > 3$

20

Which of the following is equivalent to the statement $4x^2 \geq 9$?

A) $2x > 3$

B) $x \geq 1.5$ or $x \leq -1.5$

C) $|x| > 2$

D) $-1.5 \leq x \leq 1.5$

21

The graph above indicates the complete solution set to which of the following statements?

A) $|x - 3| > 3$

B) $|x| < 6$

C) $|x - 6| < 6$

D) $|x - 3| < 3$

22

Which of the following is true for all real values of x ?

A) $|x| > 0$

B) $x < 2$ or $x > 1$

C) $x > -2$ or $x < -3$

D) $x^2 - 1 > 0$

EXERCISE SET 4 ANSWER KEY

No Calculator

1. **4** It is helpful to plot these values on the number line and think:

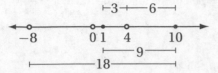

The distance between 1 and 10 is 9, so clearly the number that is 9 more units to the left of 1, namely −8, is twice as far from 10 as it is from 1. However, this is a negative number so it can't be our answer. There is one other number that is twice as far from 10 as it is from 1: the number that is 1/3 the distance from 1 to 10. This number is 4, which is 3 units from 1 and 6 units from 10.

2. **16** From the Distance Formula,

$$(2 - 14)^2 + (a - b)^2 = 20^2$$

Simplify: $144 + (a - b)^2 = 400$

Subtract 144: $(a - b)^2 = 256$

Square root: $|a - b| = 16$

3. **8** $0 < \dfrac{4}{n} < \dfrac{5}{9}$

Since n must be positive for this statement to be true, we can multiply by $9n$ without having to "swap" the inequality symbols:

$$0 < 36 < 5n$$

Divide by 5: $0 < 7.2 < n$

Therefore, the smallest integer value of n is 8.

4. **½ or .5** Two numbers, a and b, have the same absolute value only if they are equal or opposites. Clearly $x + 4$ and $x − 5$ cannot be equal, since $x − 5$ is 9 less than $x + 4$. Therefore they must be opposites.

$$x + 4 = -(x - 5)$$

Distribute: $x + 4 = -x + 5$

Add x: $2x + 4 = 5$

Subtract 4: $2x = 1$

Divide by 2: $x = 1/2$

5. **10** $-\dfrac{n}{21} > -\dfrac{1}{2}$

Multiply by −42 and "swap:" $2n < 21$

Divide by 2: $n < 10.5$

Therefore, the greatest possible integer value of n is 10.

6. **3** $3b \geq 7.5$

Divide by 3: $b \geq 2.5$

$$\dfrac{1}{b} > \dfrac{3}{11}$$

Since b is greater than or equal to 2.5, it is positive, so we can multiply both sides by $11b$ without "swapping" the inequality:

$$11 > 3b$$

Divide by 3: $3.67 > b$

The only integer between 2.5 and 3.67 is 3.

7. **3/2 or 1.5** $(b + 2)^2 = (b - 5)^2$

FOIL: $b^2 + 4b + 4 = b^2 - 10b + 25$

Subtract b^2: $4b + 4 = -10b + 25$

Add $10b$: $14b + 4 = 25$

Subtract 4: $14b = 21$

Divide by 14: $b = 1.5$

8. **A** $-4 < 2x \leq 2$

Divide by 2: $-2 < x \leq 1$

which is equivalent to $-2 < x$ and $x \leq 1$.

9. **A** The profit is the revenue minus the cost: $65n - (20,000 + 10n) = 55n - 20,000$.

10. **C** If Colin can read a maximum of 25 pages an hour, then in h hours he can read a maximum of $25h$ pages. If he has p pages left in a 250-page book, he has read $250 - p$ pages. Since it has taken him h hours to read these $250 - p$ pages, $250 - p \leq 25h$.

11. **C** $|x - 10| > 4|x - 40|$

It helps to sketch the number line and divide is into three sections: the numbers less than 10, the numbers between 10 and 40, and the numbers greater than 40.

CASE 1: $x < 10$. It should be clear that all numbers less than 10 are closer to 10 than they are to 40, so this set contains no solutions.

CASE 2: $10 < x \leq 40$. If x is between 10 and 40, $x - 10$ is positive and $x - 40$ is negative, so $|x - 10| = x - 10$ and $|x - 40| = -(x - 40)$.

$$|x - 10| > 4|x - 40|$$

Substitute: $x - 10 > -4(x - 40)$

Distribute: $x - 10 > -4x + 160$

Add $4x$: $5x - 10 > 160$

Add 10: $5x > 170$

Divide by 5: $x > 34$

So this gives us $34 < x \leq 40$.

CASE 3: $x > 40$. If x is greater than 40, then both $x - 10$ and $x - 40$ are positive, so $|x - 10| = x - 10$ and $|x - 40| = x - 40$.

$$|x - 10| > 4|x - 40|$$

Substitute: $\quad\quad\quad\quad\quad\quad\quad x - 10 > 4(x - 40)$

Distribute: $\quad\quad\quad\quad\quad\quad x - 10 > 4x - 160$

Add 10: $\quad\quad\quad\quad\quad\quad\quad\quad x > 4x - 150$

Subtract $4x$: $\quad\quad\quad\quad\quad\quad\quad -3x > -150$

Divide by -3 and "swap:" $\quad\quad\quad\quad\quad x < 50$

So this gives us $40 < x < 50$. When we combine this with the solutions from CASE 2, we get $34 < x < 50$.

Calculator

12. 2   If $|a - 5| = 7$, then either $a - 5 = 7$ or $a - 5 = -7$, so either $a = 12$ or $a = -2$. Since $a < 0$, a must be -2, and $|-2| = 2$.

---

13. 8   CASE 1: If $6 - 3n$ is positive, then

$|6 - 3n| = 6 - 3n$, so $\quad\quad\quad\quad 16 < 6 - 3n < 19$

Subtract 6: $\quad\quad\quad\quad\quad\quad 10 < -3n < 13$

Divide by -3 and "swap:" $\quad -10/3 > n > -13/3$

But this contradicts the fact that n is positive.

CASE 2: If $6 - 3n$ is negative, then

$|6 - 3n| = -(6 - 3n)$, so $\quad\quad 16 < -(6 - 3n) < 19$

Distribute: $\quad\quad\quad\quad\quad\quad 16 < -6 + 3n < 19$

Add 6: $\quad\quad\quad\quad\quad\quad\quad\quad 22 < 3n < 25$

Divide by 3: $\quad\quad\quad\quad\quad\quad 7.33 < n < 8.33$

And the only integer in this range is $n = 8$.

---

14. 7 $\quad\quad\quad\quad\quad\quad\quad\quad\quad 20 - 2n > 5$

Subtract 20: $\quad\quad\quad\quad\quad\quad\quad -2n > -15$

Divide by -2 and "swap:" $\quad\quad\quad\quad n < 7.5$

$$\frac{2n}{3} > 4$$

Multiply by 3: $\quad\quad\quad\quad\quad\quad\quad 2n > 12$

Divide by 2: $\quad\quad\quad\quad\quad\quad\quad\quad n > 6$

Since n must be an integer between 6 and 7.5, $n = 7$.

---

15. 4.75   The distance from 3 to -1.5 is $|3 - (-1.5)|$ $= 4.5$. Therefore the two numbers that are 4.5 away from 9.25 are $9.25 + 4.5 = 13.75$ and $9.25 - 4.5 = 4.75$.

---

16. ½ or .5   If the equation is true for all values of x, let's choose a convenient value for x,

like $x = 1$. $\quad\quad\quad\quad\quad\quad |2x + 1| = 2|k - x|$

Substitute $x = 1$: $\quad\quad\quad\quad |2(1) + 1| = 2|k - 1|$

Simplify: $\quad\quad\quad\quad\quad\quad\quad\quad\quad 3 = 2|k - 1|$

Divide by 2: $\quad\quad\quad\quad\quad\quad\quad\quad 1.5 = |k - 1|$

Therefore $\quad\quad\quad\quad\quad\quad\quad\quad \pm 1.5 = k - 1$

Add 1: $\quad\quad\quad\quad\quad\quad\quad k = 2.5$ or -0.5

Now try $x = 0$: $\quad\quad\quad\quad |2(0) + 1| = 2|k - 0|$

Simplify: $\quad\quad\quad\quad\quad\quad\quad\quad\quad 1 = 2|k|$

Divide by 2: $\quad\quad\quad\quad\quad\quad\quad\quad 0.5 = |k|$

Therefore $\quad\quad\quad\quad\quad\quad\quad\quad\quad \pm 0.5 = k$

Therefore, $k = -0.5$ and so $|k| = |-0.5| = 0.5$.

---

17. C   Recall that the expression $|x - 2|$ means "the distance from x to 2," so the statement $|x - 2| < 1$ means "The distance from x to 2 is less than 1." Therefore, the solution set is all of the numbers that are less than 1 unit away from 2, which are all the numbers between 1 and 3.

---

18. C $\quad\quad\quad\quad\quad\quad\quad\quad \dfrac{a + b}{2} > \dfrac{c + 2b}{2}$

Multiply by 2: $\quad\quad\quad\quad\quad a + b > c + 2b$

Subtract b: $\quad\quad\quad\quad\quad\quad\quad a > c + b$

---

19. B   The formal translation of this statement is $|x - 1| > |x - 3|$, which we can solve algebraically by considering three cases: (I) $x \leq 1$, (II) $1 < x \leq 3$, and (III) $x > 3$, but it is probably easier to just graph the number line and notice that the midpoint between 1 and 3, that is, 2, is the point at which the distance to 1 and the distance to 3 are equal. Therefore, the points that are farther from 1 than from 3 are simply the points to the right of this midpoint, or $x > 2$.

---

20. B $\quad\quad\quad\quad\quad\quad\quad\quad\quad\quad 4x^2 \geq 9$

Take square root: $\quad\quad\quad\quad\quad\quad |2x| \geq 3$

If $x > 0$: $\quad\quad\quad\quad\quad\quad\quad\quad\quad 2x \geq 3$

Divide by 2: $\quad\quad\quad\quad\quad\quad\quad\quad x \geq 1.5$

If $x < 0$: $\quad\quad\quad\quad\quad\quad\quad\quad 2x \leq -3$

Divide by 2: $\quad\quad\quad\quad\quad\quad\quad x \leq -1.5$

---

21. D   Notice that the midpoint of the segment shown is 3, and the graph shows all points that are less than 3 units in either direction. Therefore, $|x - 3| < 3$.

---

22. B   (A) is untrue if $x = 0$, (C) is untrue for $x = -2$, and (D) is untrue if $x = 0.5$. But (B) is true for any real number.

Skill 4: Working with Linear Systems

Lesson 11: Constructing, graphing, and interpreting linear systems

A **system of equations** is just a set of equations that apply simultaneously to a given problem situation. Solving for the system means finding all sets of values for the unknowns that make *all* of the equations true. Systems of equations can be analyzed both algebraically (by exploring the equations) or geometrically (by exploring the graphs).

Two high school teachers took their classes on a field trip to a museum. One class spent $154 for admission for 20 students and 3 adults, and the other class spent $188 for admission for 24 students and 4 adults. Which of the following systems of equations could be solved to determine the price of a single student admission, *s*, and the price of a single adult admission, *a*, in dollars?

A) $a + s = 51$

   $44s + 7a = 342$

B) $20s + 3a = 154$

   $24s + 4a = 188$

C) $\dfrac{20}{s} + \dfrac{3}{a} = 154$

   $\dfrac{24}{s} + \dfrac{4}{a} = 188$

D) $20 + 24 = s$

   $3 + 4 = a$

(*Medium*) This problem can be described with a **two-by-two system of equations**, that is, two equations with two unknowns. The two equations come from two facts: one class spent $154 for admission and the other class spent $188 for admission. The cost of 20 student admissions and 3 adult admissions is $20s + 3a$, so the first equation is $20s + 3a = 154$. Similarly, the equation for the other class is $24s + 4a = 188$, so the correct answer is (B).

If the solutions to the two equations above are graphed in the *xy*-plane, what is the *y*-coordinate of the point at which the graphs intersect?

(*Easy*) Since the equations of both lines are given in slope-intercept form, we could graph the two lines in the *xy*-plane to find their point of intersection.

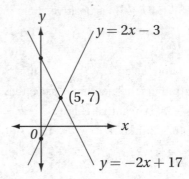

Therefore, the point (5, 7) gives us the only solution to this system, and so the answer to the original question is 7.

Alternately, (as we will see in Lesson 13) we can just add the corresponding sides of the two equations together to get $2y = 14$, which yields $y = 7$.

The solution of a two-by-two system of equations can be visualized as the **intersection of their graphs in the *xy*-plane**.

If the graphs are parallel lines, or other non-intersecting graphs, then the system **has no solution**. If the graphs intersect multiple times, then the system **has multiple solutions**.

$$y - 4x = 6$$

$$16x = 4y + k$$

For what value of k does the system of equations above have at least one solution?

A) −32

B) −30

C) −24

D) −20

(*Medium*) This is a two-by-two system of linear equations, and so its solution is the intersection of those two lines. If we convert them to slope-intercept form, we get $y = 4x + 6$ and $y = 4x - k/4$, which reveals that these two lines have the same slope. This means that they are either parallel lines or identical lines. Two lines with the same slope can intersect only if they are the same line, and therefore $-k/4 = 6$ and $k = -24$.

Lesson 12: Solving systems by substitution

Let's go back to the second linear system from Lesson 11. This system can also be solved with a simple application of the Law of Substitution.

$$y = 2x - 3$$

$$y = -2x + 17$$

1. Substitute for y: $2x - 3 = -2x + 17$

2. Add $2x$: $4x - 3 = 17$

3. Add 3: $4x = 20$

4. Divide by 4: $x = 5$

5. Plug into either original
   equation to find y: $y = 2(5) - 3$ or $-2(5) + 17 = 7$

> When one of the equations in a system is already solved for one variable (or when it's relatively easy to solve it for one variable), then substituting for this variable in the other equation often makes it easier to solve the system.

$$3x + y = 3y + 4$$

$$x + 4y = 6$$

Based on the system of equations above what is the value of xy?

(*Medium*) This system is not quite as tidy as the previous one, but we can still solve it by using the Law of Substitution.

$$3x + y = 3y + 4$$

$$x + 4y = 6$$

Subtract $4y$ from second equation to
isolate x: $x = -4y + 6$

Substitute for x in first
equation: $3(-4y + 6) + y = 3y + 4$

Simplify left side: $-11y + 18 = 3y + 4$

Add $11y$ and subtract 4: $14 = 14y$

Divide by 14: $1 = y$

Substitute $y = 1$ to find x: $x = -4(1) + 6 = 2$

Evaluate xy: $xy = (2)(1) = 2$

Lesson 13: Solving systems by linear combination

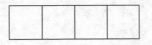

$$3x + 6y = 18$$
$$3x + 4y = 6$$

Based on the system of equations above, what is the value of y ?

$$3x - y = 20$$
$$2x + 4y = 7$$

Based on the system of equations above, what is the value of $x - 5y$?

(*Easy*) Although this system can be solved by substitution (try it as an exercise), the setup of these equations suggests a much easier method, known as *linear combination*. It's based on a simple idea:

> **The Law of Combination**
>
> If $a = b$ and $c = d$, then $a + c = b + d$, $a - c = b - d$, and $ac = bd$
>
> In other words, you should always feel free to add, subtract, or multiply the corresponding sides of two equations to make a new equation.

If we apply this rule to our system, notice that we can easily eliminate x from the system by just subtracting the equations:

$$3x + 6y = 18$$
$$- (3x + 4y = 6)$$
$$\overline{ 2y = 12}$$

Divide by 2: $$y = 6$$

(*Medium*) This question looks tougher than the previous one, because it's not just asking for x or y. It seems that the question requires us to solve the system for x *and* y and then to plug these values into the expression $x - 5y$ and evaluate. We could do that, but there is a much simpler method. Notice that a simple combination gives us the expression the question is asking for.

$$3x - y = 20$$

Subtract equations:
$$- (2x + 4y = 7)$$
$$\overline{ x - 5y = 13}$$

> **Using Linear Combination**
>
> When you're given a system of equations on the SAT, **always notice carefully what the question is asking you to evaluate**. Even if it appears to be the value of a complicated expression, often you can find it with a simple combination of the given equations.

Exercise Set 5 (No Calculator)

1

If $3x + 2y = 72$, and $y = 3x$, what is the value of x ?

2

If $2a - 7b = 10$ and $2a + 7b = 2$, what is the value of $4a^2 - 49b^2$?

3

If the lines $y = -4x - 3$ and $y = -3x - b$ intersect at the point $(-1, c)$, what is the value of b ?

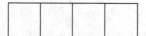

4

If the lines $4x + 5y = 13$ and $4y + kx = 2$ are parallel, what is the value of k ?

5

If the lines $4x + 5y = 13$ and $6y - kx = 6$ are perpendicular, what is the value of k ?

6

$$\frac{2a}{b} = \frac{1}{3}$$

$$\frac{c}{b} + 1 = \frac{5}{3}$$

Based on the system of equations above, what is the value of $\dfrac{a}{c}$?

7

If $ab = -4$ and $abc = 12$, what is the value of $\dfrac{c}{ab}$?

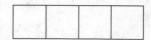

8

If a and b are constants and the graphs of the lines $2x - 3y = 8$ and $ax + by = 2$ are perpendicular, then what is the value of $\dfrac{3a}{b}$?

9

$$5x - y = 11$$
$$2x - 2y = 9$$

Based on the system of equations above, what is the value of $3x + y$?

A) −2

B) 0

C) 2

D) 4

10

Two numbers have a difference of 4 and a sum of −7. What is their product?

A) −33

B) −10.25

C) 8.25

D) 10.25

11

It costs Emma p dollars to make each of her custom bracelets, which she sells for m dollars apiece. She makes a profit of \$60 if she makes and sells 5 of these bracelets, but she only makes a profit of \$10 if she makes 5 bracelets but only sells 4 of them. How much does it cost Emma to make each bracelet?

A) \$36

B) \$38

C) \$48

D) \$50

Exercise Set 5 (Calculator)

12

If $2y = x + 1$ and $4x + 6y = 0$, then $y =$

13

If $6x + 7y = \dfrac{4}{5}$ and $6x - 7y = \dfrac{6}{5}$, then $x =$

14

$$2x - 5y = 20$$
$$10x - 25y = 4k$$

For what value of k does the system of equations above have at least one solution?

15

At the beginning of the week, the ratio of cats to dogs at Glenna's Pet Store was 4 to 5. By the end of the week, the number of cats had doubled, while the number of dogs had increased by 12. If the ratio of cats to dogs at the end of the week was 1 to 1, how many cats did the store have at the <u>beginning</u> of the week?

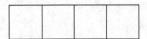

16

Jenny originally had twice as many friendship bracelets as Emilie. After Jenny gave Emilie 5 of her friendship bracelets, Jenny still had 10 more than Emilie. How many friendship bracelets did Jenny have originally?

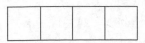

17

The average (arithmetic mean) of x and y is 14. If the value of x is doubled and the value of y is tripled, the average (arithmetic mean) of the two numbers remains the same. What is the value of x ?

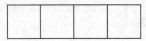

18

$$7m + 10n = 7$$
$$6m + 9n = 1$$

Based on the system of equations above, what is the value of $4m + 4n$?

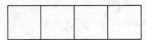

19

In the xy-plane, perpendicular lines a and b intersect at the point $(2, 2)$. If line a contains the point $(7, 1)$, which of the following points is on line b ?

A) $(0, 1)$

B) $(4, 5)$

C) $(7, 3)$

D) $(3, 7)$

20

Which of the following pairs of equations has no solution in common?

A) $2x - 3y = 1$ and $6x - 9y = 3$

B) $y = 4x$ and $y = -4x$

C) $2x - 3y = 1$ and $6x - 9y = 2$

D) $y = 4x$ and $2y - 8x = 0$

21

In the xy-plane, the line l is perpendicular to the line described by the equation $\dfrac{1}{x} + \dfrac{1}{2y} = \dfrac{1}{y}$. What is the slope of line l ?

A) -2

B) $-\dfrac{1}{2}$

C) $\dfrac{1}{2}$

D) 2

EXERCISE SET 5 ANSWER KEY

No Calculator

1. 8

	$3x + 2y = 72$
Substitute $y = 3x$:	$3x + 2(3x) = 72$
Simplify:	$9x = 72$
Divide by 9:	$x = 8$

---

2. 20

	$4a^2 - 49b^2$
Factor:	$(2a - 7b)(2a + 7b)$
Substitute:	$(10)(2) = 20$

---

3. 2

	$y = -4x - 3$
Substitute $x = -1, y = c$:	$c = -4(-1) - 3$
Simplify:	$c = 1$
Other equation:	$y = -3x - b$
Substitute $x = -1, y = 1$:	$1 = -3(-1) - b$
Simplify:	$1 = 3 - b$
Subtract 3:	$-2 = -b$
Divide by -1:	$2 = b$

---

4. 3.2 or 16/5 Parallel lines must have equal slopes. The slope of $4x + 5y = 13$ is $-4/5$, and the slope of $4y + kx = 2$ is $-k/4$.

$$\frac{-4}{5} = \frac{-k}{4}$$

Cross-multiply:	$-5k = -16$
Divide by -5:	$k = 16/5 = 3.2$

---

5. 7.5 or 15/2 Perpendicular line have slopes that are opposite reciprocals. The slope of $4x + 5y = 13$ is $-4/5$, and the slope of $6y - kx = 6$ is $k/6$.

$$\frac{-4}{5} = \frac{-6}{k}$$

Cross-multiply:	$-4k = -30$
Divide by -4:	$k = 7.5$

---

6. .25 or ¼ First equation:

	$\frac{2a}{b} = \frac{1}{3}$
Divide by 2:	$\frac{a}{b} = \frac{1}{6}$
Second equation:	$\frac{c}{b} + 1 = \frac{5}{3}$
Subtract 1:	$\frac{c}{b} = \frac{2}{3}$
Reciprocate:	$\frac{b}{c} = \frac{3}{2}$
Multiply:	$\left(\frac{a}{b}\right)\left(\frac{a}{b}\right) = \frac{a}{c} = \left(\frac{1}{6}\right)\left(\frac{3}{2}\right) = \frac{3}{12} = \frac{1}{4}$

---

7. .75 or ¾

	$abc = 12$
Substitute $ab = -4$:	$(-4)c = 12$
Divide by -4:	$c = -3$
Expression to evaluate:	$\dfrac{c}{ab}$
Substitute $c = -3$ and $ab = -4$:	$\dfrac{c}{ab} = \dfrac{-3}{-4} = \dfrac{3}{4}$

---

8. 4.5 or 9/2 The slope of $2x - 3y = 8$ is 2/3, and the slope of $ax + by = 2$ is $-a/b$. If the two lines are perpendicular, then the slopes are opposite reciprocals:

$$\frac{2}{3} = \frac{b}{a}$$

Reciprocate:	$\dfrac{a}{b} = \dfrac{3}{2}$
Multiply by 3:	$\dfrac{3a}{b} = \dfrac{9}{2}$

---

9. C

	$5x - y = 11$
	$2x - 2y = 9$
Subtract equations:	$3x + y = 2$

---

10. C

	$a - b = 4$
	$a + b = -7$
Add equations:	$2a = -3$
Divide by 2:	$a = -1.5$
Substitute $a = -1.5$:	$-1.5 + b = -7$
Add 1.5:	$b = -7 + 1.5 = -5.5$
Evaluate product:	$ab = (-1.5)(-5.5) = 8.25$

---

11. B Let $c = $ the cost to make each one of Emma's bracelets.

	$5m - 5c = 60$
	$4m - 5c = 10$
Subtract:	$m = 50$
Substitute $m = 50$	$5(50) - 5c = 60$
Simplify:	$250 - 5c = 60$
Subtract 250:	$-5c = -190$
Divide by -5:	$c = 38$

Calculator

12. 2/7 or .286 or .285

	$2y = x + 1$
Subtract 1:	$2y - 1 = x$
Given:	$4x + 6y = 0$
Substitute $x = 2y - 1$:	$4(2y - 1) + 6y = 0$
Distribute:	$8y - 4 + 6y = 0$

Simplify: $\qquad$ $14y - 4 = 0$

Add 4: $\qquad$ $14y = 4$

Divide by 14: $\qquad$ $y = 4/14 = 2/7$

---

13. 1/6 or .166 or .167

$$6x + 7y = \frac{4}{5}$$
$$6x - 7y = \frac{6}{5}$$

Add equations: $\qquad$ $12x = 2$

Divide by 12: $\qquad$ $x = 2/12 = 1/6$

---

14. 25 The slope of $2x - 5y = 20$ is 2/5. The slope of $10x - 25y = 4k$ is $10/25 = 2/5$. Since the two lines have the same slope, they have no points of intersection unless they are the same line. $\qquad$ $2x - 5y = 20$

$$10x - 25y = 4k$$

Multiply first equation by 5: $\qquad$ $10x - 25y = 100$

Therefore, $4k = 100$ and so $k = 25$.

---

15. 16 If the original ratio of cats to dogs is 4 to 5, then we can say there were $4n$ cats and $5n$ dogs to start. At the end of the week, therefore, there were $8n$ cats and $5n + 12$ dogs. If this ratio was 1:1, then $\qquad$ $8n = 5n + 12$

Subtract 5n: $\qquad$ $3n = 12$

Divide by 3: $\qquad$ $n = 4$

Therefore, there were $4n - 4(4) - 16$ cats at the beginning of the week.

---

16. 40 Let $x = $ the number of friendship bracelets Emilie had to start. This means that Jenny originally had $2x$ bracelets. After Jenny gave 5 of them to Emilie, Jenny had $2x - 5$ and Emilie had $x + 5$. If Jenny still had 10 more than Emilie, then $\qquad$ $2x - 5 = 10 + (x + 5)$

Simplify: $\qquad$ $2x - 5 = x + 15$

Subtract x and add 5: $\qquad$ $x = 20$

This means that Jenny had $2x = 2(20) = 40$ to start.

---

17. 56

$$\frac{x+y}{2} = 14$$

Multiply by 2: $\qquad$ $x + y = 28$

If x is doubled and y is tripled, the average

remains the same: $\qquad$ $\dfrac{2x + 3y}{2} = 14$

Multiply by 2: $\qquad$ $2x + 3y = 28$

Previous equation: $\qquad$ $x + y = 28$

Multiply by 3: $\qquad$ $3x + 3y = 84$

Other equation: $\qquad$ $2x + 3y = 28$

Subtract equations: $\qquad$ $x = 56$

---

18. 24

$$7m + 10n = 7$$
$$6m + 9n = 1$$

Subtract equations: $\qquad$ $m + n = 6$

Multiply by 4: $\qquad$ $4m + 4n = 24$

---

19. D Line a contains the points $(2, 2)$ and $(7, 1)$; therefore, it has a slope of $\dfrac{2-1}{2-7} = -\dfrac{1}{5}$. If line b is perpendicular to line a, then it must have a slope of 5 (the opposite reciprocal of $-1/5$). You might find it helpful to sketch the line with slope 5 through the point $(2, 2)$, and confirm that is passes through the point $(3, 7)$, which is one unit to the right and one 5 units up.

---

20. C In order for two lines in the xy-plane to have no points in common, they must be parallel and nonidentical. The only two such lines among these choices are $2x - 3y = 1$ and $6x - 9y = 2$, which both have a slope of 2/3, but have different y-intercepts of $-1/3$ and $-2/9$.

---

21. A

$$\frac{1}{x} + \frac{1}{2y} = \frac{1}{y}$$

Multiply by $2xy$: $\qquad$ $2y + x = 2x$

Subtract x: $\qquad$ $2y = x$

Divide by 2: $\qquad$ $y = \dfrac{1}{2}x$

This line has a slope of 1/2, so the perpendicular must have a slope of -2.

CHAPTER 8

THE SAT MATH TEST: PROBLEM SOLVING AND DATA ANALYSIS

1. Averages   321

2. Medians and Modes   322

3. Data Spread   323

4. Direct and Inverse Variations   324

5. Rate Problems   331

6. Ratios   333

7. Percentages   339

8. Percent Change   340

9. Proportions and Scaling   341

10. Tables and Venn Diagrams   346

11. Conditional Probabilities from Tables   347

12. Analyzing Relations with Tables   348

13. Scatterplots   353

14. Nonlinear Relationships   354

15. Drawing Inferences from Graphs   355

16. Pie Graphs   356

The SAT Math: Problem Solving and Data Analysis

Why are problem solving and data analysis important on the SAT Math test?

About 26% (15 out of 58 points) of the SAT Math questions fall under the category of Problem Solving and Data Analysis. Questions in this category test your ability to

> *create a representation of a problem, consider the units involved, attend to the meaning of quantities, and [apply reasoning about] ratios, rates, and proportional relationships.*

They also assess your skill in

> *interpreting and synthesizing data, [as well as identifying] quantitative measures of center, the overall pattern, and any striking deviations from the overall pattern in different data sets.*

The specific topics include

- using rates, ratios, and proportional relationships to solve problems
- evaluating and analyzing data gathering methods
- calculating and using statistics of "central tendency" like mean, median, and mode
- using basic measures of data "spread" such as standard deviation, range, and confidence intervals
- solving problems concerning percentages and percent change
- analyzing scatterplots, pie graphs, tables, histograms, and other graphs
- exploring linear, quadratic, and exponential relationships in data

How are these skills used?

Analyzing and drawing inferences from data are core skills not only in mathematics and the physical sciences, but also in social sciences such as psychology, sociology, and economics. Since these subjects constitute a substantial portion of any liberal arts curriculum, colleges consider these to be essential college preparatory skills.

Sound intimidating? It's not.

If you take the time to master the four core skills presented in these 16 lessons, you will gain the knowledge and practice you need to master SAT Math problem-solving and data analysis questions.

Lesson 1: Averages

The Average Formula

The **average (arithmetic mean)** of any set of numbers is calculated with the formula

$$\text{average} = \frac{\text{sum}}{\text{\# of numbers}}$$

But an even more helpful form of this formula is

$$\text{sum} = \text{average} \times \text{\# of numbers}$$

The average (arithmetic mean) of four numbers is 15. If one of the numbers is 18, what is the average (arithmetic mean) of the remaining three numbers?

(*Medium*) Since we know the average and the number of numbers, we can calculate their sum: $15 \times 4 = 60$. If one of these numbers is 18, then the sum of the remaining three numbers is $60 - 18 = 42$, so the average of the remaining three is $42/3 = 14$.

Ms. Aguila's class, which has 20 students, scored an average of 90 points on a test. Mr. Bowle's class, which has 30 students, scored an average of 80 points on the same test. What was the combined average score, in points, for the two classes?

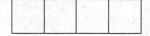

(*Medium*) Can we just average the scores for the two classes, $(90 + 80)/2 = 85$, and call this the combined average for the two classes? No: there are more students in Mr. Bowle's class, so the average is "weighted" toward his class. The sum of the scores in Ms. Aguila's class is $90 \times 20 = 1,800$, and the sum of the scores in Mr. Bowle's class is $80 \times 30 = 2,400$. Therefore, the sum of all the scores is $1,800 + 2,400 = 4,200$. Since there are 50 students altogether in the two classes, the combined average is $4,200/50 = 84$.

Bonus: Note that the weighted average, 84, is 4 units away from one of the class averages and 6 units away from the other. The ratio of these distances is 2:3, which is exactly the ratio of students in the two classes. Why?

Number of Smartphones	Number of Students
2	5
3	4
4	8
5	2
6	1

The 20 students in Ms. Aguila's class were asked how many smartphones their families owned, and the results are tabulated above. What is the average number of phones per family for the 20 students in the class?

A) 3.2

B) 3.5

C) 4.0

D) 4.2

(*Medium*) If we "unpack" the information from the table, we can get the list of numbers, in increasing order, that all 20 students gave: 2, 2, 2, 2, 2, 3, 3, 3, 3, 4, 4, 4, 4, 4, 4, 4, 4, 5, 5, 6. But there's really no reason to do this, since the table gives us a handy way of adding all of the numbers, by adding the products of all the rows: $(2)(5) + (3)(4) + (4)(8) + (5)(2) + (6)(1) = 10 + 12 + 32 + 10 + 6 = 70$. Therefore, the average of these numbers is $70/20 = 3.5$, so the correct answer is B.

Lesson 2: Medians and Modes

Medians

> The **median** of a set of numbers is the **number that divides the ordered set into two equal sets**. That is, half the numbers are less than or equal to the median, and half the numbers are greater than or equal to the median. To find the median of an **ordered set of n numbers** (increasing or decreasing),
>
> 1. Calculate $\dfrac{n+1}{2}$.
> 2. If this is a whole number, then it is the "place" of the median. For instance, if there are 13 numbers in the set, then the median is the $\dfrac{13+1}{2} = 7$th number in the set.
> 3. If this is **not** a whole number, then average the two numbers on either side of that "place." For instance, if there are 16 numbers in the set, then $\dfrac{16+1}{2} = 8.5$, so the median is the average of the 8th and 9th numbers in the set.

> The median of 1, 6, 8, and k is 5. What is the average (arithmetic mean) of these four numbers?
>
> | | | | |
> |---|---|---|---|
> | | | | |

(*Medium*) We don't know where k should be when we put the numbers in order, but there are only four possibilities:

If k is the least of these numbers, then the correct ordering is k, 1, 6, 8. Since there is an even number of numbers, the median is the average of the middle two: $(1+6)/2 = 3.5$. But this contradicts the given fact that the median is 5, so that doesn't work. Putting k in the next slot gives us an order of 1, k, 6, 8. In this case, the median would be $(k+6)/2$.

$$\frac{k+6}{2} = 5$$

Multiply by 2: $k+6 = 10$
Subtract 6: $k = 4$

This confirms our assumption that k is between 1 and 6, so k must equal 4. Now we must find the average of these four numbers: $(1+4+6+8)/4 = 19/4 = 4.75$.

Modes

> The **mode** of a set of numbers is the **number that appears the most frequently**. This means that not every set of numbers has a mode. For instance, in the set 1, 1, 2, 3, 4, the mode is 1, but the set 1, 2, 3, 4 does not have a mode, because every number occurs once.

Roll	Frequency
1	10
2	a
3	b
4	7
5	9
6	9

The table above shows the results of 50 rolls of a die, with two missing values labeled a and b. If the mode of these 50 rolls is 2, what is the greatest possible average (arithmetic mean) value of these rolls?

(*Hard*) If the mode of the rolls is 2, then 2 is the most frequent roll. Since the table shows that the highest known frequency is 10 (for a roll of 1), then a (the number of times a 2 was rolled) must be at least 11. We also know that the total number of rolls is 50, so $10 + a + b + 7 + 9 + 9 = 50$; therefore, $a + b = 15$. The question asks us to find the *greatest possible average* of these rolls, so we want to maximize the *sum* of all the rolls. This means that we want b (the number of times a 3 was rolled) to be as great as possible. Since $b = 15 - a$, then the greatest b can be is $15 - 11 = 4$. Therefore, $a = 11$ and $b = 4$. Now we have to find the average of these 50 numbers: $[(1)(10) + (2)(11) + (3)(4) + (4)(7) + (5)(9) + (6)(9)]/50 = (10 + 22 + 12 + 28 + 45 + 54)/50 = 3.42$.

Lesson 3: Data Spread

Statistics of "Spread"

The SAT Math test may ask you about the **spread** of a set of data. You don't have to know how to calculate "spread statistics" like **variance**, **standard deviation**, or **margin of error,** but you might be asked to answer more basic questions about the "spread" of a set of data, as in the questions below.

The "absolute deviation" of a number in a set is the absolute difference between that number and the average (arithmetic mean) of the set. The "mean absolute deviation" of a set is the average (arithmetic mean) of all of the absolute deviations in the set. Which of the following sets has the greatest "mean absolute deviation?"

A) 2, 2, 2, 2

B) 2, 3, 4, 5

C) 4, 4, 5, 5

D) 4, 4, 4, 5

(*Medium*) When you are introduced to a new mathematical term, **read its definition carefully**—several times, if necessary—and **try it out**. This question gives us two new terms: **absolute deviation** and **mean absolute deviation**. Let's apply them to a simple set of numbers, such as the one in choice A. The average of this set is 2, so the "absolute deviation" of each of these numbers is its absolute difference from 2, which is 0 for each number. The "mean absolute deviation" of the set is the average of these "absolute deviations," which is, of course, 0.

Note that the "mean absolute deviation" of a data set is a statistic of "spread." Since the numbers in A are bunched up as tightly as possible, their "mean absolute deviation" is 0. Now let's look at the remaining choices. Which seems to have the greatest "spread"? Once you've made your guess, do the calculations and see if you're right. For confirmation, you should find that the "mean absolute deviations" are A) 0, B) 1, C) 0.5, and D) 0.375. Therefore, the correct answer is B.

The "range" of a set of data is defined as the absolute difference between the least value and the greatest value in the set. If five positive integers have an average (arithmetic mean) of 10, what is the greatest possible "range" of this set?

(*Medium-hard*) If five numbers have an average of 10, then their sum is $5 \times 10 = 50$. If we want the greatest possible "range," then we must maximize one of these numbers by minimizing the sum of the **other** numbers. We are told that these numbers are **positive integers**, and since the smallest positive integer is 1, we can minimize the sum of the other four numbers by setting them all equal to 1. This gives us $1 + 1 + 1 + 1 + x = 50$, so $x = 46$, which gives us a maximum "range" of $46 - 1 = 45$.

Lesson 4: Direct and Inverse Variations

Direct Variation

Two quantities **vary directly** or **are directly proportional** if they **have a constant ratio**. As one goes up, the other also goes up: if one of them is doubled, the other is doubled, and so on. We can express the fact that **y varies directly as x** with either of these equations:

$$\frac{y}{x} = k \text{ or } y = kx \text{ (where } k \text{ is a constant)}$$

The graph of a direct variation between x and y is **a line through the origin with a slope equal to k.**

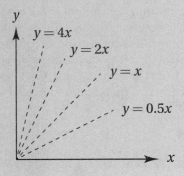

Inverse Variation

Two quantities **vary inversely** or **are inversely proportional** if they **have a constant product**. As one goes up, the other goes down: if one of them is doubled, the other is halved, and so on. We can express the fact that **y varies inversely as x** with either of these equations:

$$xy = k \text{ or } y = \frac{k}{x} \text{ (where } k \text{ is a constant)}$$

The graph of an inverse variation between x and y is **a hyperbola that is asymptotic to the x- and y-axes.**

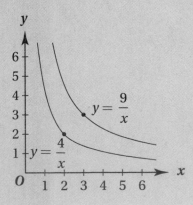

x	y
1	5
2	20

Given the ordered pairs in the table above, which of the following could be true?

A) y varies directly as x

B) y varies inversely as x

C) y varies directly as the square of x

D) y varies inversely as the square of x

(*Medium*) Using the definitions above, we can see whether y and x vary directly or inversely. Do they have a **constant ratio**? No: 5/1 ≠ 20/2. Therefore, they do not vary directly, making choice A incorrect. Do they have a **constant product**? No: 1 × 5 ≠ 2 × 20. Therefore, they do not vary inversely, making choice B incorrect. To check choice C, we must ask: do y and x^2 have a constant ratio? Yes: $5/(1)^2 = 20/(2)^2 = 5$; therefore, the correct answer is C.

x	y
2	12
4	96

The variables x and y are related by an equation of the form $y = Ax^n$ where A and n are both positive real numbers. Based on the data in the table above, what is the value of y when $x = 3$?

A) 40.5

B) 46.0

C) 54.0

D) 64.0

(*Medium-hard*) To find the value of y when $x = 3$, we must find the specific equation relating x and y. We can find the values of A and n in the equation $y = Ax^n$ by first plugging in the values from the table. Plugging in the first ordered pair gives us $12 = A(2)^n$ and plugging in the second ordered pair gives us $96 = A(4)^n$.

$$96 = A(4)^n$$
$$12 = A(2)^n$$

Divide the corresponding sides:

$$\frac{96}{12} = \frac{4^n}{2^n}$$

Simplify:

$$8 = 2^n$$

Substitute $8 = 2^3$:

$$2^3 = 2^n \text{ and so } n = 3$$

This means that y varies directly as x^3.

Substitute $n = 3$ into either equation:

$$12 = A(2)^3$$

Simplify:

$$12 = 8A$$

Divide by 8:

$$1.5 = A$$

So $y = 1.5x^3$, and when $x = 3$, $y = 1.5(3)^3 = 1.5(27) = 40.5$, so the correct answer is A.

Concentration of A	Concentration of B	Concentration of C	Rate of Reaction
1.0	1.0	1.0	4.0
3.0	1.0	1.0	12.0
1.0	3.0	1.0	4.0
2.0	2.0	2.0	32.0

A chemist runs four trials to determine how the concentrations of three reactants affect the rate of a chemical reaction. The table above shows the concentrations, in grams per liter, of the reactants and the rate of reaction, in grams of product per minute, for each trial reaction. Which choice best describes how the rate of reaction varies with these concentrations?

A) It varies directly as the concentration of A and directly as the square of the concentration of C.

B) It varies directly as the concentrations of A and C.

C) It varies inversely as the concentration of B and directly as the square of the concentrations of A and C.

D) It varies directly as the concentrations of A, B, and C.

(*Hard*) Comparing the first two rows shows that tripling the concentration of A also triples the rate of reaction, so the rate of reaction varies **directly as the concentration of A**. Comparing the first row to the third row shows that tripling the concentration of B does not affect the rate of reaction; therefore, there is **no variation relationship** between the rate of reaction and the concentration of B. Comparing the first row to the fourth row, note that the concentration of A has doubled, so we should expect the reaction rate to double to 8.0. However, the actual rate of reaction is 32.0, which is 4 times the expected rate. This is because the concentration of C has doubled. (We can ignore the concentration of B because it has no effect on the reaction rate.) Since doubling the concentration of C causes the reaction rate to quadruple from what it would otherwise be, the rate of reaction **varies directly as the square of the concentration of C**. Therefore, the correct answer is A.

Exercise Set 1 (No Calculator)

1

The "range" of a set of data is defined as the absolute difference between the least value and the greatest value in the set. Four positive integers have an average (arithmetic mean) of 7.5.

a. What is the greatest possible range of this set?

b. What is the least possible range of this set?

2

If the median of 2, 4, 6, and b is 4.2, what is the average (arithmetic mean) of these four numbers?

3

The average (arithmetic mean) of 2, 5, 8 and k is 0. What is the median of these numbers?

4

A set of numbers has a sum of 48 and an average of 6. How many numbers are in the set?

5

If the average (arithmetic mean) of 4 and x is equal to the average (arithmetic mean) of 2, 8, and x, what is the value of x?

6

The median of a set of 22 consecutive even integers is 25. What is the largest number in the set?

7

If p varies inversely as q and $p = 4$ when $q = 6$, which of the following is another solution for p and q?

A) $p = 8$ and $q = 12$

B) $p = 8$ and $q = 10$

C) $p = 12$ and $q = 1$

D) $p = 12$ and $q = 2$

8

A set of n numbers has an average (arithmetic mean) of $3k$ and a sum of $12m$, where k and m are both positive. Which of the following is equivalent to n?

A) $\dfrac{4m}{k}$ B) $\dfrac{4k}{m}$ C) $\dfrac{k}{4m}$

D) $\dfrac{m}{4k}$

9

If y varies inversely as the square of x, then when x is multiplied by 4, y will be

A) divided by 16

B) divided by 2

C) multiplied by 2

D) multiplied by 16

10

Let $f(x, y) = Ax^2y^3$ where A is a constant. If $f(a, b) = 10$, what is the value of $f(2a, 2b)$?

A) 100

B) 260

C) 320

D) 500

11

A set of four integers has a mode of 7 and a median of 4. What is the greatest possible average (arithmetic mean) of this set?

A) 3.50

B) 3.75

C) 4.00

D) 4.25

Exercise Set 1 (Calculator)

12

Four positive integers have a mode of 4 and a median of 3. What is their sum?

13

Five different integers have an average (arithmetic mean) of 10. If none is less than 5, what is the greatest possible value of one of these integers?

14

If b varies inversely as a, and $b = 0.5$ when $a = 32$, then for how many ordered pairs (a, b) are a and b both positive integers?

15

The median of 11 consecutive integers is 28. What is the least of these integers?

16

If $y = Ax^3$ and $y = 108$ when $x = 3$, then for what value of x does $y = 62.5$?

17

A set of four positive integers has a median of 2 and a mode of 2. If the average (arithmetic mean) of this set is 3, what is the largest possible number in the set?

18

If y varies inversely as x and the graph of their relation in the xy-plane passes through the point $(2, 15)$, what is the value of y when $x = 4$?

19

Roll	Frequency
1	4
2	5
3	4
4	6
5	5
6	6

A six-sided die was rolled 30 times and the results are tabulated above. What is the difference between the average (arithmetic mean) of the rolls and the median of the rolls?

A) 0.1

B) 0.2

C) 0.3

D) 0.4

20

If y varies inversely as the square of x, and $y = 4$ when $x = 2$, then what is the value of y when $x = 3$?

A) $\dfrac{16}{9}$

B) $\dfrac{8}{3}$

C) 3

D) 9

21

At a fixed temperature, the volume of a sample of gas varies inversely as the pressure of the gas. If the pressure of a sample of gas at a fixed temperature is increased by 50%, by what percent is the volume decreased?

A) 25%

B) $33\dfrac{1}{3}\%$

C) 50%

D) $66\dfrac{2}{3}\%$

22

If the graph of $y = f(x)$ in the xy-plane contains the points (4, 3) and (16, 6), which of the following could be true?

A) y varies directly as the square of x

B) y varies inversely as the square of x

C) y varies directly as the square root of x

D) y varies inversely as the square root of x

EXERCISE SET 1 ANSWER KEY

No Calculator

1a. 26   If the average of 4 numbers is 7.5, they must have a sum of $4 \times 7.5 = 30$. To maximize the range, we must maximize one of the numbers by minimizing the other 3 by setting them all equal to 1 (the smallest positive integer). The numbers therefore are 1, 1, 1, and 27, and the range is $27 - 1 = 26$.

1b. 1   To minimize the range, we "cluster" the numbers as closely together as possible. The tightest cluster of integers with a sum of 30 is 7, 7, 8, and 8, which gives a range of $8 - 7 = 1$.

2. 4.1   If the set contains four numbers, its median is the average of the middle two numbers, so the middle two numbers must have a sum of $(2)(4.2) = 8.4$. Thus the four numbers must be 2, 4, 4.4, and 6. (Notice that the question did not say that all numbers were integers.) The average of these is $16.4/4 = 4.1$.

3. 3.5   If the average of these numbers is 0, their sum must be $(4)(0) = 0$, and therefore $k = -15$ and the numbers, in increasing order, are $-15, 2, 5$, and 8. The median is $(2 + 5)/2 = 3.5$.

4. 8 $6 - 48/n$, so $n = 8$.

5. 8

Cross-multiply:
Subtract $2x$ and 12:

$$\frac{4+x}{2} = \frac{2+8+x}{3}$$
$$12 + 3x = 20 + 2x$$
$$x = 8$$

6. 46   The median divides the set into two equal parts, so 11 of these numbers must be less than 25 and 11 must be greater than 25. Since they are consecutive even integers, the 11 numbers above the median must be $26, 28, 30, 32, \ldots 46$.

7. D   If p and q vary inversely, their product is a constant. $4 \times 6 = 24$, and the only other pair with a product equal to 24 is (D) 12 and 2.

8. A $n = sum/average = 12m/3k = 4m/k$

9. A   The equation relating x and y is $y = k/x^2$. If $x = 1$, then $y = k$. If x is multiplied by 4, then $x = 4$ and $y = k/16$, so y has been divided by 16.

10. C $f(a, b) = Aa^2b^3 = 10$. $f(2a, 2b) = A(2a)^2(2b)^3 = 32(Aa^2b^3) = 32(10) = 320$.

11. B   If this set has a mode of 7, then at least two of the numbers are 7. If the median is 4, then the two middle numbers must have a sum of $(2)(4) = 8$. Therefore the two middle numbers are 1 and 7, and the sequence must be n, 1, 7, 7. To maximize the average, we must maximize n, but n can't be 1, because then the set would not have a mode of 7. It must be the next lower integer, 0, and the average is $(0 + 1 + 7 + 7)/4 = 3.75$.

Calculator

12. 11   The only four numbers that satisfy these conditions are 1, 2, 4, and 4.

13. 24   If the average of five numbers is 10, their sum is $5 \times 10 = 50$. To maximize one, we must minimize the sum of the other four. If none is less than five, and all are different integers, they are 5, 6, 7, 8, and 24.

14. 5   If the variables vary inversely, their product is constant. $(0.5)(32) = 16$. The only pairs of positive integers with a product of 16 are $(1, 16), (2, 8), (4, 4), (8, 2)$, and $(16, 1)$.

15. 23   If the middle number is 28, there are five numbers less than 28, and five greater. Since they are consecutive integers, the least is $28 - 5 = 23$.

16. 2.5   Since $108 = A(3)^3$, $A = 4$, so if $62.5 = 4x^3$, $x = 2.5$.

17. 7   At least two of the integers must be 2 and none can be less than 1. If the sum must be $4 \times 3 = 12$, the set including the largest possible number is 1, 2, 2, and 7.

18. 7.5   The product of x and y is $2 \times 15 = 30$, so $y = 30/4 = 7.5$.

19. C   Average $= (1 \times 4 + 2 \times 5 + 3 \times 4 + 4 \times 6 + 5 \times 5 + 6 \times 6)/30 = 3.7$. Median $=$ average of 15th and 16th roll: $(4 + 4)/2 = 4$. $4 - 3.7 = 0.3$.

20. A y and x^2 must have a constant product of $4 \times 2^2 = 16$. Therefore, $y = 16/9$.

21. **B** Pick values for the original pressure and volume, such as 2 and 3. If they vary inversely, their product is the constant $2 \times 3 = 6$. If the pressure is increased by 50%, it becomes $(1.5)(2) = 3$, and so the volume becomes $6/3 = 2$, a change of $-33\ 1/3\%$.

22. **C** For both ordered pairs, $\dfrac{y}{\sqrt{x}}$ is a constant: $\dfrac{3}{\sqrt{4}} = \dfrac{6}{\sqrt{16}} = \dfrac{3}{2}$, so y is directly proportional to the square root of x.

Lesson 5: Rate Problems

Rates

The **units** for any rate give the **formula for the rate**. For instance, if a problem mentions a rate of *kilograms per second,* then this tells us that the formula for this rate is

$$\text{rate} = \frac{\text{number of kilograms}}{\text{number of seconds}}$$

because **per** just means **divided by.**

Rate Conversion Factors

Every **rate fact** gives us a **conversion factor**. For instance, if we are told *that a rocket burns fuel at a rate of 15 kilograms per second*, then either of these can be used as a conversion factor in that problem:

$$\frac{15 \text{ kilograms}}{1 \text{ second}} \text{ or } \frac{1 \text{ second}}{15 \text{ kilograms}}$$

On a sunny day, a 50-square-meter section of a solar panel array can generate an average of 1 kilowatt-hour of energy per hour over a 10-hour period. If an average household consumes 30 kilowatt-hours of energy per day, how large an array is required to power 1,000 households on sunny days?

A) 1,500 square meters

B) 15,000 square meters

C) 150,000 square meters

D) 15,000,000 square meters

(*Hard*) This is a **rate problem** because it includes two **per** quantities: *kilowatt-hours per hour* (for the solar panels), and *kilowatt-hours per day* (for the households). We can solve this as a problem of **converting** 1,000 *households* to a particular number of *square meters of solar panels*:

$$1{,}000 \text{ households} \left(\frac{30 \text{ kwh/day}}{1 \text{ household}}\right)\left(\frac{1 \text{ day}}{10 \text{ sun-hours}}\right)$$

$$\left(\frac{50 \text{ m}^2}{1 \text{ kwh/sun-hour}}\right)$$

$$= 150{,}000 \text{ m}^2 \text{, so the correct answer is C.}$$

Note that all of the units on the left side of the equation **cancel** except for "square meters" (the unit we want) and that each conversion factor corresponds to an explicit fact mentioned in the problem.

The Rate Pie

Many rate problems are easily solved with the **rate pie**, which summarizes all three forms of the "rate equation" at once:

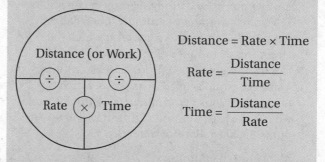

$$\text{Distance} = \text{Rate} \times \text{Time}$$

$$\text{Rate} = \frac{\text{Distance}}{\text{Time}}$$

$$\text{Time} = \frac{\text{Distance}}{\text{Rate}}$$

To use the rate pie, just insert the **two** given quantities in the proper spots, then **calculate** as shown to find the **third quantity**.

Maria completed an 80-mile bike race at an average speed of z miles per hour. If she had averaged 2 miles per hour faster, she would have completed the race in 10 fewer minutes. What is the value of z ?

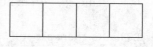

(*Medium-hard*) Let's make two pies, one for the real situation and one for the hypothetical situation.

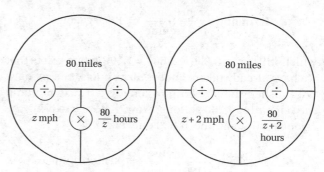

Since her time at the faster speed would have been 10 minutes (or 1/6 hour) less, we can write $\dfrac{80}{z} - \dfrac{1}{6} = \dfrac{80}{z+2}$

Combine fractions on left: $\dfrac{480 - z}{6z} = \dfrac{80}{z+2}$

Cross-multiply: $480z + 960 - z^2 - 2z = 480z$

Subtract $480z$ from both sides: $z^2 + 2z - 960 = 0$

Factor and solve: $(z + 32)(z - 30) = 0$

So, the only positive solution is $z = 30$.

Slopes and Unit Rates

> In the graph of any linear function, the **slope** of the line is equivalent to the **unit rate** of the function, that is, the rate at which y increases or decreases for every unit increase in x.

A water pump for a dredging project can remove 180 gallons of water per minute, but it can only work for 2.5 consecutive hours, at which time it requires 20 minutes of maintenance before it can be brought back online. While it is offline, a smaller pump is used in its place, which can pump 80 gallons per minute. Using this system, what is the least amount of time it would take to pump 35,800 gallons of water?

A) 3 hours 15 minutes

B) 3 hours 20 minutes

C) 3 hours 25 minutes

D) 3 hours 30 minutes

(*Hard*) If we want to pump out the water as quickly as possible, we want to use the faster pump for the maximum 2.5 hours. To find the total amount of water pumped in that time, we do the conversion:

$$2.5 \text{ hours} \times \frac{60 \text{ minutes}}{1 \text{ hour}} \times \frac{180 \text{ gallons}}{1 \text{ minute}} = 27,000 \text{ gallons}$$

So after 2.5 hours, there are still $35,800 - 27,000 = 8,800$ gallons left to pump. At that point, the smaller pump must be used for a minimum of 20 minutes, which can pump

$$20 \text{ minutes} \times \frac{80 \text{ gallons}}{1 \text{ minute}} = 1,600 \text{ gallons}$$

which still leaves $8,800 - 1,600 = 7,200$ gallons. Note that we have already taken 2 hours 50 minutes, and yet have not finished the job. So how long will it take to pump the remaining 7,200 gallons? Now that we can bring the stronger pump online, it will only take

$$7,200 \text{ gallons} \times \frac{1 \text{ minute}}{180 \text{ gallons}} = 40 \text{ more minutes}$$

for a total of 3 hours 30 minutes; therefore, the correct answer is D.

Although you don't need to use a graph to solve this problem, a graph can help to show the overall picture:

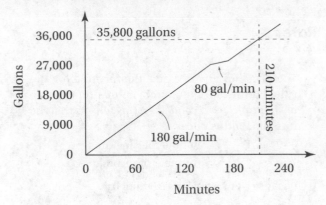

Note that the line has a slope of 180 gallons per minute for the first 150 minutes, 80 gallons per minute for the next 20 minutes, and 180 again for the final 40 minutes and crosses the line $y = 35,800$ at the 210-minute mark.

Lesson 6: Ratios

Part-to-Whole Ratios

When solving **ratio** problems, pay attention to whether the ratios are **part-to-whole** or **part-to-part**. Part-to-whole ratios are sometimes given as **percents of the whole**.

Bronze is an alloy consisting of copper and tin. If 50 kg of a bronze alloy of 20% tin and 80% copper is mixed with 70 kg of a bronze alloy of 5% tin and 95% copper, what fraction, by weight, of the combined bronze alloy is tin?

A) 5/48

B) 9/80

C) 1/8

D) 1/4

(*Medium*) The total weight is $50 + 70 = 120$ kg, but the weight of just the tin is $(0.20)(50) + (0.05)(70) = 13.5$ kg. Therefore, the fraction of the alloy that is tin is 13.5/120, which simplifies to 9/80. Therefore, the correct answer is B.

Probabilities as Ratios

A probability is a part-to-whole ratio between a subset of equally likely events and a larger set of equally likely events.

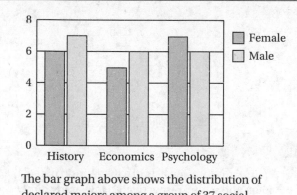

The bar graph above shows the distribution of declared majors among a group of 37 social science students in a graduating university class. If a female is chosen at random from this group, what is the probability that she is an economics major?

(*Easy*) There are $6 + 5 + 7 = 18$ females in this group, and 5 are them are economics majors. Therefore, the probability is $5/18 = 0.278$.

Part-to-Part Ratios

When dealing with **part-to-part** ratios, it often helps to divide each part by the whole (the sum of the parts) to get the **part-to-whole ratios**.

A marathon offers $5,000 in prize money to the top three finishers. If the first-, second-, and third-place prizes are distributed in a ratio of 5:4:1, how much money, in dollars, does the second-place finisher receive?

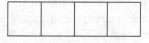

(*Easy*) This problem gives us a **part-to-part-to-part ratio**, so the whole is $5 + 4 + 1 = 10$ equal parts. The second-place finisher gets 4 of these 10 equal parts, and so takes home $(4/10) \times \$5,000 = \$2,000$.

At the Andromeda Book Store, the ratio of self-help titles to fiction titles is 3:10, and the ratio of biography titles to fiction titles is 2:7. What is the ratio of biography titles to self-help titles?

A) 6:70

B) 20:21

C) 21:20

D) 70:6

(*Medium-hard*) Simple ratios can be expressed as fractions. For instance,

$$\frac{\text{Self-help titles}}{\text{Fiction titles}} = \frac{3}{10} \text{ and } \frac{\text{Biography titles}}{\text{Fiction titles}} = \frac{2}{7}$$

Now note that we can get the ratio we want by just multiplying two well-chosen fractions:

$$\frac{\text{Biography titles}}{\text{Fiction title}} \times \frac{\text{Fiction titles}}{\text{Self-help titles}} = \frac{\text{Biography titles}}{\text{Self-help titles}}$$

Note that we have to "flip" one of the ratios to do the calculation:

$$\frac{\text{Biography titles}}{\text{Fiction titles}} \times \frac{\text{Fiction titles}}{\text{Self-help titles}} = \frac{2}{7} \times \frac{10}{3} = \frac{20}{21}$$

Therefore, the correct answer is B.

Exercise Set 2 (Calculator)

1

If a train travels at a constant rate of 50 miles per hour, how many minutes will it take to travel 90 miles?

2

Two cars leave the same point simultaneously, going in the same direction along a straight, flat road, one at 35 miles per hour and the other at 50 miles per hour. After how many minutes will the cars be 5 miles apart?

3

If a $6,000 contribution is divided among charities *A*, *B*, and *C* in a ratio of 8:5:2, respectively, how much more, in dollars, does charity *A* receive than charity *C* ?

4

If a car traveling at 60 mph is chasing a car travelling at 50 mph and is ¼ mile behind, how many minutes will it take the first car to catch the second?

5

A truck's gas tank can hold 18 gallons. If the tank is 2/3 full and the truck travels for 4 hours at 60 miles per hour until it runs out of gas, what is the efficiency of the truck, in miles per gallon?

6

A motorcycle has a fuel efficiency of 60 miles per gallon when it is cruising at a speed of 50 miles per hour. How many hours can it travel at 50 miles per hour on a full tank of gas, if its tank can hold 10 gallons?

7

If the ratio of *a* to *b* is 3 to 4, and the ratio of *a* to *c* is 5 to 2, what is the ratio of *b* to *c* ?

A) 3 to 10

B) 3 to 5

C) 5 to 3

D) 10 to 3

8

A paint mixture consists of a 3:2:11 ratio of red, violet, and white, respectively. How many ounces of violet are needed to make 256 ounces of this mixture?

A) 32

B) 36

C) 46

D) 48

9

A pool that holds 20,000 gallons is ¼ full. A pump can deliver g gallons of water every m minutes. If the pumping company charges d dollars per minute, how much will it cost, in dollars, to fill the pool?

A) $\dfrac{5{,}000\,md}{g}$

B) $\dfrac{5{,}000\,gd}{m}$

C) $\dfrac{15{,}000\,md}{g}$

D) $\dfrac{15{,}000\,gd}{m}$

10

Yael travels to work at an average speed of 40 miles per hour and returns home by the same route at 24 miles per hour. If the total time for the round trip is 2 hours, how many miles is her trip to work?

A) 25

B) 30

C) 45

D) 60

11

A hare runs at a constant rate of a miles per hour, and a tortoise runs at a constant rate of b miles per hour, where $0 < b < a$. How many more hours will it take the tortoise to finish a race of d miles than the hare?

A) $\dfrac{a+b}{2d}$

B) $\dfrac{ad-bd}{ab}$

C) $\dfrac{b-a}{d}$

D) $\dfrac{ab-bd}{ad}$

12

Janice can edit 700 words per minute and Edward can edit 500 words per minute. If each page of text contains 800 words, how many pages can they edit, working together, in 20 minutes?

13

If a printer can print 5 pages in 20 seconds, how many pages can it print in 5 minutes?

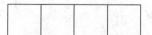

14

Traveling at 40 miles per hour, Diego can complete his daily commute in 45 minutes. How many minutes would he save if he traveled at 50 miles per hour?

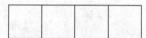

15

If $\dfrac{2a}{3b}=\dfrac{1}{5}$ and $\dfrac{c}{2b}=\dfrac{1}{2}$, what is $\dfrac{a}{c}$?

16

If a cyclist races at 30 miles per hour for 1/2 of the distance of a race, and 45 miles per hour for the final 1/2 of the distance, what is her average speed, in miles per hour, for the entire race?

17

Anne can paint a room in 2 hours, and Barbara can paint the same room in 3 hours. If they each work the same rate when they work together as they do alone, how many hours should it take them to paint the same room if they work together?

18

What is the average speed, in miles per hour, of a sprinter who runs ¼ mile in 45 seconds? (1 hour = 60 minutes and 1 minute = 60 seconds)

A) 11.25

B) 13.5

C) 20

D) 22

19

A car travels d miles in t hours and arrives at its destination 3 hours late. At what average speed, in miles per hour, should the car have gone in order to arrive on time?

A) $\dfrac{t-3}{d}$

B) $\dfrac{d}{t-3}$

C) $\dfrac{d}{t}-3$

D) $\dfrac{d-3}{t}$

20

In three separate 1-mile races, Ellen finished with times of x minutes, y minutes, and z minutes, respectively. What was her average speed, in miles per <u>hour</u>, for all three races?

A) $\dfrac{x+y+z}{3}$

B) $\dfrac{3}{x+y+z}$

C) $\dfrac{x+y+z}{180}$

D) $\dfrac{180}{x+y+z}$

21

Sylvia drove 315 miles and arrived at her destination in 9 hours. If she had driven 10 miles per hour faster, how many hours would she have saved on the trip?

A) 1.75 hours

B) 2.00 hours

C) 2.25 hours

D) 2.50 hours

EXERCISE SET 2 ANSWER KEY

1. **108** *time = distance/rate* = 90 miles/50 mph = 1.8 hours = 1.8 hour × 60 min/hour = 108 minutes.

2. **20** The fast car is moving ahead of the slow car at a rate of 50 − 35 = 15 mph, and so it will be 5 miles ahead after 5 ÷ 15 = 1/3 hour = 20 minutes.

3. **2,400** Since 8 + 5 + 2 = 15, charity *A* receives 8/15 of the contribution, and charity *C* receives 2/15. The difference is 6/15, or 2/5, of the total, which is (2/5)($6,000) = $2,400.

4. **1.5** Since the faster car is catching up to the slower car at 60 − 50 = 10 mph, it will take (1/4 mile)/(10 mph) = 1/40 hours = 60/40 minutes = 1.5 minutes.

5. **20** The tank contains (2/3)(18) = 12 gallons, and travels (4 hours)(60 mph) = 240 miles, so its efficiency is 240/12 = 20 miles per gallon.

6. **12** With 10 gallons of gas and an efficiency of 60 miles per gallon, the car can travel 10 × 60 = 600 miles. At 50 miles an hour this would take 600/50 = 12 hours.

7. **D** $\dfrac{b}{c} = \dfrac{b}{a} \times \dfrac{a}{c} = \dfrac{4}{3} \times \dfrac{5}{2} = \dfrac{10}{3}$

8. **A** According to the ratio, the mixture is 2/(3 + 2 + 11) = 2/16 = 1/8 violet. Therefore 256 ounces of the mixture would contain (1/8)(256) = 32 ounces of violet paint.

9. **C** If the pool is ¼ full, it requires (3/4)(20,000) = 15,000 more gallons.

$$15{,}000 \text{ gallons} \times \frac{m \text{ minutes}}{g \text{ gallons}} \times \frac{d \text{ dollars}}{1 \text{ minute}}$$

$$= \frac{15{,}000\, md}{g} \text{ dollars}$$

10. **B** Let *x* = the distance, in miles, from home to work. Since *time = distance/rate*, it takes Yael *x*/40 hours to get to work and *x*/24 hours to get home.

$$\frac{x}{40} + \frac{x}{24} = 2$$

Simplify:
$$\frac{x}{15} = 2$$

Multiply by 15:
$$x = 30 \text{ miles}$$

11. **B** The tortoise would take *d*/*b* hours to complete the race, and the hare would take *d*/*a* hours to complete the race, so the tortoise would take $\dfrac{d}{a} - \dfrac{d}{a} = \dfrac{ad}{ab} - \dfrac{bd}{ab} = \dfrac{ad - bd}{ab}$ hours longer.

12. **30** Together they can edit 700 + 500 = 1,200 words per minute, so in 20 minutes they can edit

$$20 \text{ minutes} \times \frac{1{,}200 \text{ words}}{1 \text{ minute}} \times \frac{1 \text{ page}}{800 \text{ words}} = 30 \text{ pages}$$

13. **75** If the printer can print 5 pages in 20 seconds, it can print 15 pages in 1 minute, and therefore 15 × 5 = 75 pages in 5 minutes.

14. **9** Since 45 minutes is ¾ hour, Diego's daily commute is 40 × ¾ = 30 miles. If he traveled at 50 mph it would take him 30/50 = 3/5 hours = 36 minutes, so he would save 45 − 36 = 9 minutes.

15. **3/10 or 0.3**

$$\frac{2a}{3b} \times \frac{2b}{c} = \frac{1}{5} \times \frac{2}{1}$$

Simplify:
$$\frac{4a}{3c} = \frac{2}{5}$$

Multiply by ¾:
$$\frac{a}{c} = \frac{2}{5} \times \frac{3}{4} = \frac{3}{10}$$

16. **36** Pick a convenient length for the race, such as 180 miles (which is a multiple of both 30 and 45). The first half of the race would therefore be 90 miles, which would take 90 miles ÷ 30 mph = 3 hours, and the second half would take 90 miles ÷ 45 mph = 2 hours. Therefore, the entire race would take 3 + 2 = 5 hours, and the cyclist's average speed would therefore be 180 miles ÷ 5 hours = 36 miles per hour.

17. **1.2 or 6/5** Anne's rate is 1/2 room per hour, and Barbara's rate is 1/3 room per hour, so together their rate is 1/3 + 1/2 = 5/6 room per hour. Therefore, painting one room should take (1 room)/(5/6 room per hour) = 6/5 hours.

18. **C** $\dfrac{0.25 \text{ mile}}{45 \text{ seconds}} \times \dfrac{3{,}600 \text{ seconds}}{1 \text{ hour}} = 20 \text{ mph}$

20. **D** $\dfrac{3 \text{ miles}}{x+y+z \text{ minutes}} \times \dfrac{60 \text{ minutes}}{1 \text{ hour}} = \dfrac{180}{x+y+z} \text{ mph}$

19. **B** In order to arrive on time, it would have to travel the d miles in $t - 3$ hours, which would require a speed of $d/(t-3)$ mph.

21. **B** Sylvia traveled at $315/9 = 35$ miles per hour. If she had traveled at $35 + 10 = 45$ miles per hour, she would have arrived in $315/45 = 7$ hours, thereby saving 2 hours.

Lesson 7: Percentages

Translating Percent Problems

Here's a handy **translation key** for word problems:

is	means	$=$
of	means	$\times$
what	means	x (or any unknown)
per	means	$\div$
percent	means	$\div\ 100$

If the sales tax for clothing is 5%, what is the sales tax, in dollars, on a sweatshirt with a retail price of $36?

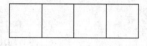

(*Easy*) $x = (5 \div 100) \times 36 = (0.05)(36)$
Simplify: $x = 1.80$

What percent of 150 is 93?

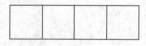

(*Easy*) What percent of 150 is 93? becomes $\dfrac{x}{100}(150) = 93$
Simplify: $1.5x = 93$
Divide both sides by 1.5: $x = 62$

Commutativity of Percentages

Here's a handy fact: **x% of y is the same as y% of x.**

For instance, calculating 80% of 25 is a bit tricky, but it's easier if you think of it as 25% of 80, which is 20.

Changing by Percentages

To increase a number by a%, just multiply by $(100 + a)$%, and to decrease a number by a%, just multiply by $(100 - a)$%.

On the day it was issued, one share of a stock in Consolidated Energy was priced at $50. If the share price increased by 120% in its first five years and by 150% in its next five years, what was the share price, in dollars, after 10 years?

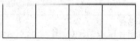

(*Medium*) To increase a number by 120%, we multiply by $100\% + 120\% = 220\% = 2.20$. To increase by 150%, we multiply by $100\% + 150\% = 250\% = 2.50$. Therefore, the share price after 10 years was ($50)(2.20)(2.50) = $275.

The final cost of a phone charger is $10.07. If this cost includes a 6% sales tax, what is the cost, in dollars, of the phone charger <u>before</u> tax?

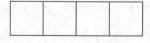

(*Easy-medium*) With a 6% sales tax, the final price is 106% of the original price: $1.06x = 10.07$
Divide by 1.06 on both sides: $x = 9.50$

Bonus: Why is it incorrect to reduce $10.07 by 6%?

Lesson 8: Percent Change

The Percent Change Formula

To find a **percent change**, just use the formula

$$\% \text{ change} = \frac{\text{final amout} - \text{starting amount}}{\text{starting amount}} \times 100\%$$

If a population of bacteria increases from 80 cells to 220 cells, what is the percent increase in this population?

A) 64%

B) 75%

C) 175%

D) 275%

(*Easy*) Using the formula, the percent change is $\frac{220 - 80}{80} \times 100\% = 175\%$, so the correct answer is C.

A store is selling all scarves at a 20% discount, but a customer has a coupon for an additional 30% off this sale price for up to three scarves. If the customer buys five scarves of equal retail price, what percent will the total price be discounted from the original retail price for the five scarves?

A) 32.0%

B) 34.4%

C) 42.4%

D) 50.0%

(*Medium-hard*) Let's say each of the five scarves has a retail price of x dollars. For three of these scarves, the customer gets the extra 30% discount, so the final price is $(0.80)(0.70)(3x) = 1.68x$. For the other two scarves, there is no extra discount, so the final price is $(0.80)(2x) = 1.60x$, for a total final price of $1.68x + 1.60x = 3.28x$ dollars. This is reduced from an original retail price of $5x$ dollars, so the percent change is

$$\frac{3.28x - 5x}{5x} \times 100\% = -0.344 = -34.4\%$$

Therefore, the correct answer is B.

How many liters of a 40% saline solution must be added to 4 liters of a 10% saline solution to make a 20% saline solution?

A) 1.0

B) 1.6

C) 2.0

D) 3.2

(*Medium-hard*) Let x be the number of liters of the 40% saline solution that must be added. If we start with 4 liters of a 10% saline solution, we have $4(0.10) = 0.4$ liter of saline. If we add x liters of a 40% saline solution, we will be adding $x(0.40) = 0.4x$ liters of saline to this solution, so we will have $0.4 + 0.4x$ liters of **saline** out of $4 + x$ liters of **total** solution. Since we want this to be a 20% saline solution, we can set up the following equation:

$$\frac{\text{part}}{\text{whole}} = \frac{0.4 + 0.4x}{4 + x} = 0.20$$

Multiply both sides by $4 + x$: $0.4 + 0.4x = 0.8 + 0.2x$

Subtract $0.2x$ and 0.4 from both sides: $0.2x = 0.4$

Divide both sides by 0.2: $x = 2$

Therefore, the correct answer is C.

Bonus: Why is the ratio of the volumes (4 liters: 2 liters = 2:1) the reciprocal of the ratio of the distances to the net concentration (20% − 10%: 40% − 20% = 10:20 = 1:2)?

Lesson 9: Proportions and Scaling

Proportions

> A **proportion** is just a statement that two ratios are equal.
>
> $$\frac{a}{b} = \frac{c}{d}$$

The Law of Cross-Multiplication

> In any proportion, the **cross-products must be equal**.
>
> If $\dfrac{a}{b} = \dfrac{c}{d}$ then $ad = bc$.

The Law of Cross-Swapping

> You may **cross-swap** in any proportion.
>
> If $\dfrac{a}{b} = \dfrac{c}{d}$ then $\dfrac{d}{b} = \dfrac{c}{a}$ and $\dfrac{a}{c} = \dfrac{b}{d}$.

> If a, b, and c are real numbers such that
> $\dfrac{a}{b+c} = \dfrac{b-c}{a}$, which of the following must also be true?
>
> A) $a^2 + b^2 - c^2 = 0$
>
> B) $a^2 - b^2 - c^2 = 0$
>
> C) $a^2 - b^2 + c^2 = 0$
>
> D) $a^2 + b^2 + c^2 = 0$

(*Medium*) $\qquad\qquad\qquad \dfrac{a}{b+c} = \dfrac{b-c}{a}$

Use the Law of Cross-Multiplication: $(b+c)(b-c) = a^2$

FOIL and simplify: $\qquad\qquad\qquad b^2 - c^2 = a^2$

Subtract b^2 and add c^2 to both sides: $\quad 0 = a^2 - b^2 + c^2$

Therefore, the correct answer is C.

Scaling

> On a scale blueprint, the drawing of a rectangular patio has dimensions 5 cm by 7.5 cm. If the longer side of the actual patio measures 21 feet, what is the area, in square feet, of the actual patio?
>
> A) 157.5 square feet
>
> B) 294.0 square feet
>
> C) 356.5 square feet
>
> D) 442.0 square feet

(*Medium*) In a **scale** drawing, all lengths are **proportional** to the corresponding lengths in real life, so we can set up a proportion here to find the shorter side of the patio, x.

$$\frac{7.5 \text{ cm}}{21 \text{ ft}} = \frac{5 \text{ cm}}{x \text{ feet}}$$

Cross-multiply: $\qquad\qquad\qquad\qquad\qquad 7.5x = 105$

Divide by 7.5: $\qquad\qquad\qquad\qquad\qquad\quad x = 14$

Therefore, the patio has dimensions 21 feet by 14 feet, and so it has an area of $(21)(14) = 294$ square feet, and the correct answer is B.

Exercise Set 3 (Calculator)

1

What number is 150% of 30?

2

If the areas of two circles are in the ratio of 4:9, the circumference of the larger circle is how many times the circumference of the smaller circle?

3

What number is 30% less than 70?

4

What number is the same percent of 36 as 5 is of 24?

5

David's motorcycle uses 2/5 of a gallon of gasoline to travel 8 miles. At this rate, how many miles can it travel on 5 gallons of gasoline?

6

The retail price of a shirt is $60, but it is on sale at a 20% discount and you have an additional 20% off coupon. If there is also a 5% sales tax, what is the final cost of the shirt?

A) $34.20

B) $36.48

C) $37.80

D) $40.32

7

If the price of a house increased from $40,000 to $120,000, what is the percent increase in price?

A) 67%

B) 80%

C) 200%

D) 300%

8

At a student meeting, the ratio of athletes to nonathletes is 3:2, and among the athletes the ratio of males to females is 3:5. What percent of the students at this meeting are female athletes?

A) 22.5%

B) 25%

C) 27.5%

D) 37.5%

9

To make a certain purple dye, red dye and blue dye are mixed in a ratio of 3:4. To make a certain orange dye, red dye and yellow dye are mixed in a ratio of 3:2. If equal amounts of the purple and orange dye are mixed, what fraction of the new mixture is red dye?

A) $\dfrac{9}{20}$

B) $\dfrac{1}{2}$

C) $\dfrac{18}{35}$

D) $\dfrac{27}{40}$

10

If the price of a stock declined by 30% in one year and increased by 80% the next year, by what percent did the price increase over the two-year period?

A) 24%

B) 26%

C) 50%

D) 500

11

A farmer has an annual budget of $1,200 for barley seed, with which he can plant 30 acres of barley. If next year the cost per pound of the seed is projected to decrease by 20%, how many acres will he be able to afford to plant next year on the same budget?

A) 24

B) 25

C) 36

D) 37.5

12

If x is $\dfrac{2}{3}$% of 90, what is the value of $\dfrac{2}{3} - x$?

13

If n is 300% less than $\dfrac{5}{2}$, what is the value of $|n|$?

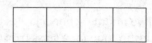

14

The cost of a pack of batteries, after a 5% sales tax, is $8.40. What was the price before tax, in dollars?

15

If the price of a sweater is marked down from $80 to $68, what is the percent discount? (Ignore the % symbol when gridding.)

16

Three numbers, a, b, and c, are all positive. If b is 30% greater than a, and c is 40% greater than b, what is the value of $\dfrac{c}{a}$?

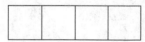

17

If the width of a rectangle decreases by 20%, by what percent must the length increase in order for the total area of the rectangle to double? (Ignore the % symbol when gridding.)

18

Two middle school classes take a vote on the destination for a class trip. Class A has 25 students, 56% of whom voted to go to St. Louis. Class B has n students, 60% of whom voted to go to St. Louis. If 57.5% of the two classes combined voted to go to St. Louis, what is the value of n?

19

If 12 ounces of a 30% salt solution are mixed with 24 ounces of a 60% salt solution, what is the percent concentration of salt in the mixture?

A)   45%

B)   48%

C)   50%

D)   54%

20

If the length of a rectangle is doubled but its width is decreased by 10%, by what percent does its area increase?

A)   80%

B)   90%

C)   180%

D)   190%

21

The freshman class at Hillside High School has 45 more girls than boys. If the class has n boys, what percent of the freshman class are girls?

A) $\dfrac{n+45}{2n+45}\%$

B) $\dfrac{100n}{2n+45}\%$

C) $\dfrac{100(n+45)}{2n+45}\%$

D) $\dfrac{100n}{n+45}\%$

22

If the population of town B is 50% greater than the population of town A, and the population of town C is 20% greater than the population of town A, then what percent greater is the population of town B than the population of town C?

A)   20%

B)   25%

C)   30%

D)   40%

EXERCISE SET 3 ANSWER KEY

1. **45** $1.50 \times 30 = 45$

2. **1.5** Imagine that the areas are 4π and 9π. Since the area of a circle is πr^2, their radii are 2 and 3, and their circumferences are $2(2)\pi = 4\pi$ and $2(3)\pi = 6\pi$, and $6\pi \div 4\pi = 1.5$.

3. **49** $70 - 0.30(70) = 0.70(70) = 49$.

4. **7.5**
$$\frac{x}{36} = \frac{5}{24}$$
Cross-multiply: $\quad 24x = 180$
Divide by 24: $\quad x = 7.5$

5. **100**
$$\frac{\frac{2}{5}\,\text{gallon}}{8\,\text{miles}} = \frac{5\,\text{gallons}}{x\,\text{miles}}$$
Cross-multiply: $\quad \dfrac{2}{5}x = 40$
Multiply by 5/2: $\quad x = 100$

6. **D** $1.05 \times 0.80 \times 0.80 \times \$60 = \$40.32$

7. **C** $(120{,}000 - 40{,}000)/40{,}000 \times 100\% = 200\%$

8. **D** The fraction of students who are athletes is $3/(2+3) = 3/5$, and the fraction of these who are females is $5/(3+5) = 5/8$. Therefore, the portion who are female athletes is $3/5 \times 5/8 = 3/8 = 37.5\%$.

9. **C** The purple dye is $3/(3+4) = 3/7$ red, and the orange dye is $3/(3+2) = 3/5$ red. Therefore, a half-purple, half-orange dye is $(1/2)(3/7) + (1/2)(3/5) = 3/14 + 3/10 = 18/35$ red.

10. **B** If the price of the stock were originally, say, \$100, then after this two-year period its price would be $(0.70)(1.80)(\$100) = \$126$, which is a 26% increase.

11. **D** The quantity of barley seed is proportional to the acreage it can cover. The cost of seed for each acre of barley was originally $\$1{,}200/30 = \$40$ per acre. The next year, after the 20% decrease, the price would be $(0.80)(\$40) = \$32$ per acre. With the same budget, the farmer can therefore plant $1{,}200/32 = 37.5$ acres of barley.

12. **1/15 or 0.067 or 0.066**

$$\frac{2}{3}\% \text{ of } 90 = \frac{2}{3} \div 100 \times 90 = \frac{180}{300} = \frac{3}{5}$$

$$\frac{2}{3} - x = \frac{2}{3} - \frac{3}{5} = \frac{1}{15}$$

13. **5** $n = \left|\dfrac{5}{2} - (3)\left(\dfrac{5}{2}\right)\right| = \left|-\dfrac{10}{2}\right| = 5$

14. **8.00** Let x be the price before tax:
$$1.05x = \$8.40$$
Divide by 1.05: $\quad x = \$8.00$

15. **15** $(68 - 80)/80 = -0.15$

16. **1.82** $b = 1.30a$ and $c = 1.40b$, so $c = 1.40(1.30a) = 1.82a$. Therefore, $c/a = 1.82a/a = 1.82$.

17. **150** For convenience, pick the dimensions of the rectangle to be 10 and 10. (This is of course a square, but remember that a square *is* a rectangle!) This means that the original area is $10 \times 10 = 100$. If the width decreases by 20%, the new width is $(0.80)(10) = 8$. Let the new length be x. Since the new rectangle has double the area, $8x = 200$, and so $x = 25$. This is an increase of $(25 - 10)/10 \times 100\% = 150\%$.

18. **15** The total number of "St. Louis votes" can be expressed in two ways, so we can set up an equation to solve for n: $\quad (0.56)(25) + (0.60)n = 0.575(25 + n)$
Simplify: $\quad 14 + 0.6n = 14.375 + 0.575n$
Subtract 14 and $0.575n$: $\quad 0.025n = 0.375$
Divide by 0.025: $\quad n = 15$

19. **C** The total amount of salt in the mixture is $(0.30)(12) + (0.60)(24) = 18$, and the total weight of the mixture is $12 + 24 = 36$ ounces, so the percent salt is $18/36 = 50\%$.

20. **A** If the original dimensions are w and l, the original area is wl. If the length is doubled and the width decreased by 10%, the new area is $(0.9l)(2w) = 1.8wl$, which is an increase of 80%.

21. **C** The number of girls in the class is $n + 45$, and the total number of students is $n + n + 45$, so the percent of girls is $\dfrac{n+45}{2n+45} \times 100\%$.

22. **B** B is 50% greater than A: $\quad B = 1.5A$
C is 20% greater than A: $\quad C = 1.2A$
Divide by 1.2: $\quad 0.8\overline{3}C = A$
Substitute: $\quad B = 1.5(0.8\overline{3}C)$
Simplify: $\quad B = 1.25C$

Lesson 10: Tables and Venn Diagrams

Tables as Organizational Tools

> **Tables** are useful for organizing information that falls into **non-overlapping categories**.

Sam is considering buying one of two models of car. The sticker price of model N is 25% higher than that of model P, but he will receive $1,500 in trade-in credit from the model N dealer and only $1,000 in trade-in credit from the model P dealer. Even after the trade-in credits are applied to both cars, model N is still $2,000 more expensive than model P (before taxes and fees). What is the sticker price of Model N?

A) $10,000

B) $12,000

C) $12,500

D) $13,000

(*Medium*) Since the car models are **non-overlapping categories**, setting up a table might be useful.

	Sticker Price	After Trade-in
Model N	$1.25x$	$1.25x - 1{,}500$
Model P	x	$x - 1{,}000$

Let x be the sticker price of model P. The sticker price of model N is 25% higher than that of model P, so it is $1.25x$. The respective costs after trade-in, then, are $1.25x - 1{,}500$ and $x - 1{,}000$. Even after the trade-in, Model N is still $2,000 more expensive than model P:

$$1.25x - 1{,}500 = (x - 1{,}000) + 2{,}000$$

Simplify: $1.25x - 1{,}500 = x + 1{,}000$

Add 1,500 and subtract x from both sides: $0.25x = 2{,}500$

Divide both sides by 0.25 (or multiply by 4): $x = 10{,}000$

But x stands for the sticker price of model P, not model N, so we need to plug this back in to find the sticker price of model N. Since $(1.25)(10{,}000) = 12{,}500$, the correct answer is C.

Venn Diagrams

> **Venn diagrams** are useful for organizing information that falls into **overlapping categories**.

In a poll of 250 college students, 137 said that they attended at least one athletic event in the past year, and 115 said that they attended at least one career services event in the past year. If 82 of these students attended <u>both</u> an athletic event and a career services event in the past year, how many students attended <u>neither</u> an athletic event nor a career services event in the past year?

A) 33

B) 55

C) 80

D) 170

(*Medium*) Since there is **overlap** between the sets of students who attended the two different categories of events, a Venn diagram is useful for keeping track of things. When setting it up, remember that **the parts must combine to make the "whole" for each set**. For example, we know that 137 students altogether attended an athletic event, but 82 of these <u>also</u> attended a career services event, so $137 - 82 = 55$ students must have attended an athletic event but <u>not</u> a career services event. Similarly, $115 - 82 = 33$ students attended a career services event but <u>not</u> an athletic event. Therefore, our diagram should look like this:

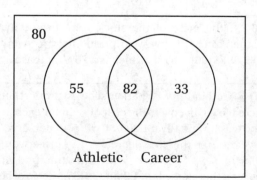

This shows that $55 + 82 + 33 = 170$ students attended either an athletic event, a career services event, or both, which means that $250 - 170 = 80$ attended <u>neither</u>, and so the correct answer is C. Note that the Venn diagram allows us to use basic arithmetic to confirm all the facts in the problem.

Lesson 11: Conditional Probabilities from Tables

Probabilities as Population Fractions

A **conditional probability** is the probability that something is true given that **something else** is also true. Solving conditional probability problems often requires reading the problem carefully and finding the relevant **population fractions**.

Opinion on Proposal 547

	Approve	Disapprove	No Opinion	Total
Female	120	42	38	200
Male	98	40	62	200
Total	218	82	100	400

Four hundred people were surveyed and asked their opinions about municipal proposal 547; the results are tabulated above. If a person who expressed an opinion on this survey is selected randomly, what is the probability that the person is female?

A) 0.52

B) 0.54

C) 0.68

D) 0.81

(*Medium*) According to the table, $218 + 82 = 300$ of the 400 people surveyed expressed an opinion. Of these, $120 + 42 = 162$ are female, and therefore the probability that someone with an opinion chosen randomly is female is $162/300 = 0.54$.

	A	B	C	D	Inc.	Total
Test 1	10	11	2	1	1	25
Test 2	12	8	3	0	2	25
Test 3	7	12	6	0	0	25
Test 4	10	9	3	0	3	25
Total	39	40	14	1	6	100

The letter grades on four tests for Ms. Hartman's 25 students (including incomplete grades, marked "Inc.") are tabulated above. Five students in the class received an A on both test 3 and test 4. If one of the students who received an A on either test 3 or test 4 is chosen at random, what is the probability that he or she received an A on test 4?

A) $\dfrac{7}{17}$

B) $\dfrac{10}{17}$

C) $\dfrac{5}{11}$

D) $\dfrac{5}{6}$

(*Medium*) Because 7 students got an A on test 3 and 10 got an A on test 4, but 5 got an A on both, this accounts for $7 + 10 - 5 = 12$ students altogether. Since 10 of these 12 students received an A on test 4, the probability is $10/12$ or $5/6$, so the correct answer is D.

If the incomplete grades are excluded from the statistics for each test in the table above, for which of the tests was the median grade higher than B?

A) None of the tests

B) Test 2 only

C) Tests 1 and 2 only

D) It cannot be determined from the given information.

(*Medium-hard*) For test 1, the median of the 24 complete grades is the average of the 12th and 13th grades, both of which are Bs, so the median score is B. For test 2, the median of the 23 complete grades is the 12th, which is an A. For test 3, the median of the 25 grades is the 13th, which is a B. For test 4, the median of the 22 complete scores is the average of the 11th and 12th, which are Bs, so the median is B. Therefore, the correct answer is B.

Lesson 12: Analyzing Relations with Tables

Tables as Pattern-Finding Tools

Tables are useful for analyzing functions because they can help you to generate **graphs** and to **see important patterns**. If you have an equation expressing y in terms of x, you can always make a table of ordered pairs to graph.

If you're given a complicated function like

$$f(x) = \frac{x^2 - x}{4x - 4}$$

you can just pick values for x—like $-3, -2, -1, 0, 1, 2,$ and 3—to plug into the function to make a table.

x	y
-3	$-3/4$
-2	$-1/2$
-1	$-1/4$
0	0
1	undefined
2	$1/2$
3	$3/4$

If you plot these points, an interesting pattern emerges.

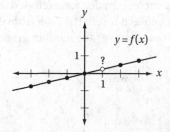

It seems to be a straight line with a slope of ¼ and a y-intercept of 0—almost identical to the equation $y = \frac{1}{4}x$. But there is a point missing at $x = 1$! Seeing patterns like this can help you to understand how functions behave and simplify a wide range of problems.

Bonus: Why does this graph seem linear, and why is one point missing?

x	y
2	10
5	b
10	34

If the variables x and y in the table above have a linear relationship, what is the value of b ?

A) 19

B) 20

C) 21

D) 22

(*Medium*) In a linear relation, the change in y is proportional to the change in x. Using the points (2, 10) and (10, 34), we can see that the slope of the line is $24/8 = 3$, so the slope of the line connecting (2, 10) and (5, b) must also be 3. If $\frac{b - 10}{3} = 3$, then $b = 19$, and the correct answer is A.

Exercise Set 4 (Calculator)

Questions 1–5 refer to the following information.

1

BACTERIA CULTURE POPULATION

Minutes	0	1	2	3
Culture A	520	720	920	1,120
Culture B	500	600	720	864

Which of the following equations best expresses the population, P, of bacteria culture A, as a function of t, in minutes?

A) $P = 200t + 520$

B) $P = 520(1.4)^t$

C) $P = 2,000(t - 0.5)^2$

D) $P = 520t + 200$

2

Which of the following equations best expresses the population, P, of bacteria culture B, as a function of t, in minutes?

A) $P = 100t + 500$

B) $P = 500(1.2)^t$

C) $P = 2,000(t - 0.5)^2$

D) $P = 500t + 100$

3

After 2 minutes, the population of culture A is what percent greater than the population of culture B?

A) 16.7%

B) 20.0%

C) 27.8%

D) 127.8%

4

If culture A continues to grow at a constant rate, at what time should its population reach 2,000?

A) 7 minutes 4 seconds

B) 7 minutes 24 seconds

C) 7 minutes 40 seconds

D) 8 minutes 20 seconds

5

By what percent did the population of culture B increase over the first 3 minutes?

A) 36.4%

B) 42.1%

C) 72.8%

D) 172.8%

Questions 6–9 refer to the following information.

TALENT SHOW TICKETS

	Adult	Child	Senior	Student
Tickets Sold	84	40	16	110
Total Revenue	$630	$200	$96	$495

6

According to the table above, how much is the price of one senior ticket?

A) $4.00

B) $6.00

C) $12.00

D) $16.00

7

How much more is the cost of one adult ticket than the cost of one student ticket?

A) $0.50

B) $1.50

C) $2.50

D) $3.00

8

Which is closest to the average (arithmetic mean) price of the 250 tickets sold?

A) $5.54

B) $5.59

C) $5.68

D) $5.72

9

What is the median price of the 250 tickets sold?

A) $5.00

B) $5.50

C) $5.75

D) $6.00

▲

10

If a meeting must take place on the third Tuesday of the month, what is the earliest date of the month on which it could take place?

A) the 14th

B) the 15th

C) the 22nd

D) the 27th

11

If a meeting must take place on the third Tuesday of the month, what is the latest date of the month on which the meeting could take place?

A) the 13th

B) the 14th

C) the 21st

D) the 26th

▼

Questions 12–21 refer to the following information.

U.S. ENERGY CONSUMPTION
(Quadrillion BTU (QBTU))

	Fossil Fuels	Nuclear	Non-nuclear Renewables	Total
1950	31.63	0.00	2.98	34.61
1970	63.52	0.24	4.07	67.84
1990	72.33	6.10	6.04	84.47
2010	81.11	8.43	8.09	97.63

12

From 1970 to 1990, the percent increase in the U.S. consumption of nuclear energy was closest to

A) 96%

B) 240%

C) 2,400%

D) 3,400%

13

In a pie graph representing total U.S. energy consumption in 2010, the sector representing non-nuclear renewables would have a central angle measuring approximately

A) 8°

B) 12°

C) 24°

D) 30°

14

Nuclear energy and renewable energy are often grouped together in the category "non-greenhouse" energy. In 1970, approximately what percent of non-greenhouse energy was nuclear?

A) 0.4%

B) 5.6%

C) 5.9%

D) 6.4%

15

In 2010 what percent of non-greenhouse energy consumption was nuclear?

A) 9%

B) 29%

C) 49%

D) 51%

16

In the four years shown, what percent of the total energy consumed was due to non-nuclear renewables?

A) 5.6%

B) 6.8%

C) 7.4%

D) 7.9%

17

What was the percent increase in fossil fuel energy consumption between 1950 and 2010?

A) 28%

B) 61%

C) 124%

D) 156%

18

The "renewability index" is defined as the fraction of total U.S. energy consumption that comes from non-nuclear renewable energy. What was the percent increase in the renewability index from 1970 to 2010?

A) 17%

B) 37%

C) 47%

D) 99%

19

For how many of the years shown above did fossil fuels account for less than 90% of the annual U.S. energy consumption?

A) One

B) Two

C) Three

D) Four

20

Between 1950 and 2010, the average annual rate of increase in the consumption of non-nuclear renewable energy was closest to

A) 0.085 QBTU/yr

B) 0.128 QBTU/yr

C) 1.70 QBTU/yr

D) 2.27 QBTU/yr

21

Between 1970 and 2010, the annual consumption of fossil fuels in the U.S. increased nearly linearly. If this linear trend were to continue, which of the following is closest to the level of U.S. fossil fuel consumption we would expect for 2035 (in quadrillion BTUs)?

A) 90

B) 91

C) 92

D) 93

▲

EXERCISE SET 4 ANSWER KEY

1. A According to the table, the population of culture A increases by 200 bacteria every minute, indicating a linear relationship with a slope of 200. (Remember that the slope of a function is equivalent to its **unit rate of change**.) Choice A is the only option that indicates a line with slope 200.

2. B The table indicates that culture B is not increasing linearly, since the population difference from minute to minute is not constant, but increasing. This rules out choices A and D. By substituting $t = 0$, $t = 1$ and $t = 2$, we can see that only the function in B gives the correct populations. Notice that the base of the exponential, 1.2, indicates that the population grows by 20% each minute.

3. C At the 2 minute mark, the populations are 920 and 720, respectively, so culture A has a population that is $(920 - 720)/720 \times 100\% = 27.8\%$ greater.

4. B If we use the population equation (see question 1), we can solve for t. Plugging in 2,000 for P gives us $2,000 = 200t + 520$, which gives a solution of $t = 7.4$ minutes. Since 0.4 minutes equals $0.4 \times 60 = 24$ seconds, the time elapsed is 7 minutes 24 seconds.

5. C In the first 3 minutes, culture B grew from 500 to 864 bacteria, which is an increase of $(864 - 500)/500 \times 100\% = 72.8\%$.

6. B The total revenue for each ticket type equals the price per ticket times the number of tickets sold. Therefore, the price for each senior ticket is $\$96 \div 16 = \$6$.

7. D One adult ticket costs $\$630 \div 84 = \$7.50$, and one student ticket costs $\$495 \div 110 = \$4.50$, so each adult ticket costs $3 more.

8. C The average price per ticket equals the total revenue for all tickets divided by the number of tickets: $(\$630 + \$200 + \$96 + \$495)/250 = \$5.684$.

9. A The median price of 250 tickets is the average of the prices of the 125th and 126th tickets, if the price for each ticket is listed in increasing order. The ticket prices, in increasing order, are $4.50 for students (110 tickets), $5.00 for children (40 tickets), $6.00 for seniors (16 tickets), and $7.50 for adults (84 tickets). With this ordering, the 125th and 126th price are both $5.00.

10. B The earliest the first Tuesday could be is the 1st, so the earliest the third Tuesday could be is the 15th.

11. C The latest the first Tuesday could be is the 7th, so the latest the third Tuesday could be is the 21st.

12. C In 1970, nuclear energy consumption was 0.24, and in 1990 it was 6.10. This represents an increase of $(6.10 - 0.24)/0.24 \times 100\% = 2,442\%$.

13. D In 2010, non-nuclear renewables accounted for $8.09/97.63 \times 100\% = 8.3\%$ of consumption, which would correspond to a $0.083 \times 360° = 29.88°$ central angle.

14. B In 1970, the total "non-greenhouse" energy was $0.24 + 4.07 = 4.31$. Therefore the percent that was nuclear is $0.24/4.31 \times 100\% = 5.6\%$.

15. D In 2010, this percent was $8.43/(8.43 + 8.09) \times 100\% = 51\%$.

16. C The total non-nuclear renewable energy consumption for the four years is $2.98 + 4.07 + 6.04 + 8.09 = 21.18$, and the total energy consumption is $34.61 + 67.84 + 84.47 + 97.63 = 284.55$. Therefore the percent is $21.18/284.55 \times 100\% = 7.4\%$.

17. D In 1950, fossil fuel consumption was 31.63, and in 2010 it was 81.11. This is an increase of $(81.11 - 31.63)/31.63 \times 100\% = 156\%$.

18. B In 1970, the renewability index was $4.07/67.84 = 0.060$, and in 2010 it was $8.09/97.63 = 0.082$. This is a percent increase of $(0.082 - 0.060)/0.060 \times 100\% = 37\%$.

19. B In 1990, the percent of consumption from fossil fuels was $72.33/84.47 \times 100\% = 85.6\%$, and in 2010 it was $81.11/97.62 \times 100\% = 83.1\%$.

20. A The annual rate of increase is the total increase divided by the time span in years. The total increase is $8.09 - 2.98 = 5.11$. Over a 60-year span, this gives a rate of $5.11/60 = 0.085$.

21. C In the 40 year span from 1970 to 2010, fossil fuel consumption increased at a rate of $(81.11 - 63.52)/40 = 0.44$ QBTU/Yr. In 25 more years at this rate, the consumption should be $81.11 + 25(0.44) = 92.11$ QBTU.

Lesson 13: Scatterplots

Scatterplots and Lines of Best Fit

Scatterplots are just graphs of ordered pairs of data. They can show relationships between variables that don't vary in a highly predictable way.

A **line of best fit** is the line that "hugs" these points optimally, showing the basic relationship between the variables. On the SAT, you don't need to calculate lines of best fit, but you may have to make inferences from them.

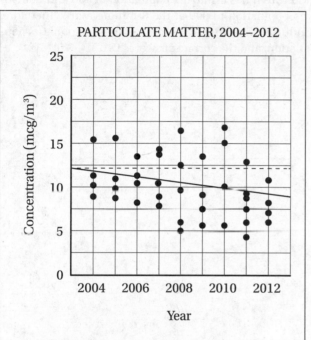

PARTICULATE MATTER, 2004–2012

The scatterplot above shows 40 readings for particulate matter (a pollutant) concentration, in micrograms per cubic meter, in a metropolitan area over 9 years. Based on the line of best fit shown as a solid line, which is closest to the average yearly decrease in particulate matter concentration?

A) 0.32 mcg/m³ per year

B) 0.64 mcg/m³ per year

C) 3.2 mcg/m³ per year

D) 6.4 mcg/m³ per year

(*Medium*) The average yearly decrease in concentration is the slope of the line of best fit. The leftmost endpoint of the line is around (2003, 12), and the rightmost endpoint is around (2013, 9), so the slope is $\dfrac{9 - 12}{2013 - 2003} = -\dfrac{3}{10} = -0.3$ mcg/m³ per year, and the correct answer is A.

According to the line of best fit to the data above, which of the following is closest to the percent decrease in average particulate matter concentration from 2007 to 2012?

A) 9%

B) 18%

C) 36%

D) 60%

(*Medium-hard*) This question is similar to the previous one, but note the two important differences: first, it asks us to compare two **specific** years, and it asks us to calculate the **percent decrease** rather than the **rate of decrease**, so we need to use the percent change formula from Lesson 8. The line of best fit gives a value of about 11 in 2007 and about 9 in 2012. Therefore, the percent change is $\dfrac{9 - 11}{11} \times 100\% = -18.2\%$, and the correct answer is B.

If the Environmental Protection Agency's air quality standard is 12 micrograms of particulate matter per cubic meter, as shown with the dotted line, what percent of these points fall above this standard?

A) 11.0%

B) 25.0%

C) 27.5%

D) 35.0%

(*Easy*) This question is just asking for a part-to-whole ratio expressed as a percentage. There are 40 total data points and 11 of them lie above the line: $\dfrac{11}{40} \times 100\% = 27.5\%$, so the correct answer is C.

Lesson 14: Nonlinear Relationships

Analyzing Graphs of Curves

Even if a graph is not linear, you should still be able to draw inferences based on the **points** on that graph. You should also be able to **compare the properties of multiple graphs**.

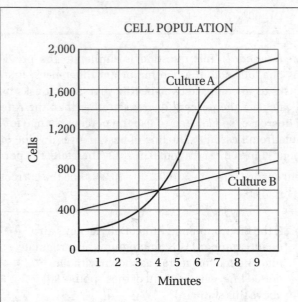

CELL POPULATION

The graph above shows the number of cells in two separate bacterial cultures as a function of time. How much time elapsed between when the two cultures had equal population and when the population of culture A was twice that of culture B?

A) 2 minutes

B) 3 minutes

C) 4 minutes

D) 5 minutes

How much longer did it take culture B than culture A to double its original population?

A) 2 minutes

B) 3 minutes

C) 4 minutes

D) 5 minutes

(*Medium*) Culture A has a starting population of 200 and doubles its population to 400 at the 3-minute mark. Culture B has a starting population of 400 and doubles its population to 800 at the 8-minute mark. Therefore, culture B took $8 - 3 = 5$ more minutes to double its population, and the correct answer is D.

(*Medium*) The two populations are equal when the two curves intersect, at the 4-minute mark. The answer choices tell us where to look next on the graph. Two minutes later, at the 6-minute mark, culture B has a population of 700 and culture A has a population of 1,400, which is twice as great, and so the correct answer is A.

Lesson 15: Drawing Inferences from Graphs

Analyzing Rates with Graphs

When analyzing graphs with respect to time, it sometimes helps to find the **average rate of change over an interval of time** (the slope of the **secant** line segment joining two points on the graph), or the **instantaneous rate of growth (or decline) at a point in time** (the slope of the **tangent** line to the curve at that point).

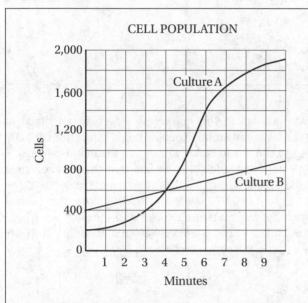

CELL POPULATION

If culture B were to continue its linear growth, how many <u>more</u> minutes beyond the 10-minute mark shown in the graph would be required for culture B to reach 1,500 cells?

A) 9 minutes

B) 12 minutes

C) 13.5 minutes

D) 15 minutes

An experiment requires that culture A and culture B have between 400 and 800 cells each. The time period in which the cell population for both cultures is within this range is called the "experimental window." Which of the following is closest to the experimental window for the two cultures shown in the graph above?

A) 95 seconds

B) 120 seconds

C) 165 seconds

D) 240 seconds

(*Medium-hard*) The "experimental window" is the period when **both** populations are between 400 and 800. The population of culture A hits 400 at the 3-minute mark and exceeds 800 cells after roughly the 4.6-minute mark. The population of culture B starts at 400 cells and exceeds 800 cells after the 8-minute mark. The overlapping period is between 3 minutes and 4.6 minutes, for a period of roughly 1.6 minutes or 1.6 × 60 = 96 seconds; therefore, the correct answer is A.

(*Medium*) By taking any two points on the line for culture B, for instance (0, 400) and (4, 600), we can calculate the slope of the line, which equals the **unit rate of growth**: $\frac{600 - 400}{4 - 0} = 50$ cells per minute. Since culture B contains 900 cells at the 10-minute mark, it would need to grow by 1500 −900 = 600 cells, which would take 600/50 = 12 more minutes to reach 1,500 cells, and so the correct answer is B.

Lesson 16: Pie Graphs

The Pie Graph Formula

The SAT might ask you to analyze the features of pie graphs in some detail, or to discuss the features of a hypothetical pie graph. When analyzing pie graphs, remember this helpful formula:

$$\frac{\text{part}}{\text{whole}} = \frac{\text{degrees in the sector}}{360°}$$

MINORITY REPRESENTATION IN BROADCAST TELEVISION

U.S. Population   U.S. Media Ownership
2007   2007

	Population	Media Ownership
African American	13.0%	0.6%
Hispanic American	15.0%	1.3%
Asian American	4.5%	0.9%
Other Minority	1.5%	0.4%
White Nonminority	66.0%	96.8%

Source: Freepress

In the diagram above, which of the following is closest to the measure of the central angle of the sector representing total minority ownership of U.S. broadcast television media in 2007?

A) 3°

B) 8°

C) 12°

D) 15°

Maria is constructing a pie graph to represent the expenses for her project. Here, expenses fall into three categories: marketing, design, and development. She knows that the marketing expenses are $12,000 and the design expenses are $30,000, but the development expense could range anywhere from $30,000 to $48,000. Based on this information, which of the following could be the measure of the central angle of the sector representing marketing expenses?

A) 45°

B) 54°

C) 62°

D) 65°

(*Medium-hard*) The marketing expenses are fixed at $12,000, but the total expenses could range from $12,000 + $30,000 + $30,000 = $72,000 to $12,000 + $30,000 + $48,000 = $90,000. This means that the part-to-whole ratio for marketing could range from 12,000/90,000 = 0.133 to 12,000/72,000 = 0.167. Therefore, the central angle for the marketing sector can measure anywhere from 0.133 × 360° = 48° to 0.167 × 360° = 60°. The only answer in this range is choice B, 54°.

(*Easy*) According to the graphic, the total minority ownership of television media in 2007 was 0.6% + 1.3% + 0.9% + 0.4% = 3.2%. Therefore, the central angle of the sector representing this portion measures 0.032 × 360° = 11.52°, so the correct answer is C.

Exercise Set 5 (Calculator)

Questions 1–4 refer to the following information.

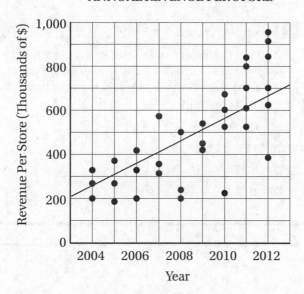

ANNUAL REVENUE PER STORE

3

From 2009 to 2010, the total combined revenue for all stores increased by approximately

A) $50,000

B) $200,000

C) $400,000

D) $600,000

4

Between 2006 and 2012, what was the percent increase in the total number of retail stores for this company?

A) 45%

B) 50%

C) 100%

D) 200%

1

The scatterplot above shows the annual revenue for all of the individual retail stores operated by a clothing company for each year from 2004 through 2012. Based on the line of best fit to the data shown, which of the following is closest to the percent increase in revenue per store from 2005 to 2012?

A) 50%

B) 100%

C) 120%

D) 300%

2

In 2006, the total combined revenue for all stores was closest to

A) $350,000

B) $480,000

C) $700,000

D) $950,000

Questions 5–9 refer to the following information.

UNITED STATES FEDERAL BUDGET—FISCAL YEAR 2010

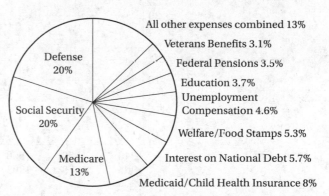

5

The chart above shows the allocation of $3.5 trillion in U.S. federal expenses for 2010. What were the total 2010 expenditures on Defense?

A) $700 billion

B) $70 billion

C) $7 billion

D) $700 million

6

What is the measure of the central angle for the sector representing Medicare expenses?

A) 13.0°

B) 45.5°

C) 46.8°

D) 48.2°

7

If Interest on National Debt expenses were to decrease by $20 billion from their 2010 levels, this would represent a percent decrease of approximately

A) 6%

B) 10%

C) 12%

D) 15%

8

How much more did the United States spend in 2010 on Interest on National Debt than on Education?

A) $2 billion

B) $7.0 billion

C) $20 billion

D) $70 billion

9

If 50% of the budget for Federal Pensions were to be reallocated as Social Security expenses, the size of the Social Security budget would increase by what percent?

A) 1.75%

B) 8.75%

C) 17.75%

D) 21.75%

Questions 10–17 refer to the following information.

PRESCHOOL BLOOD LEAD LEVELS VS. VIOLENT CRIME RATES IN THE UNITED STATES
(23-Year Lag)

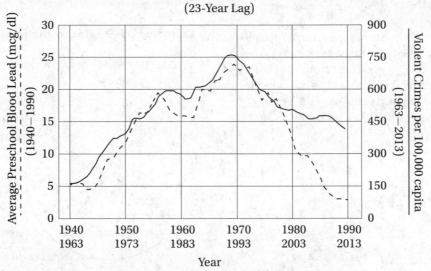

Source: Rick Nevin, *Lead Poisoning and the Bell Curve*, 2012

10

According to the graph above, in 1970 the number of violent crimes per 100,000 capita in the United States was closest to

A) 25

B) 375

C) 700

D) 750

11

In 1970 the average preschool blood lead level, in mcg/dL, was closest to

A) 10

B) 12

C) 23

D) 25

12

The percent decline in violent crime from 1993 to 2013 is closest to

A) 11%

B) 35%

C) 47%

D) 88%

13

From 1970 to 1990, the average annual rate of decline in preschool blood lead levels, in mcg/dL per year, was approximately

A) 1

B) 5

C) 15

D) 17

14

Which of the following 10-year spans saw the greatest percent increase in preschool blood lead levels?

A) 1945–1955

B) 1955–1965

C) 1965–1975

D) 1975–1985

15

Which of the following five-year spans saw the greatest percent increase in violent crime?

A) 1963–1968

B) 1968–1973

C) 1973–1978

D) 1978–1983

16

Approximately how many years did it take for average preschool blood lead levels to return to their 1950 levels?

A) 25

B) 30

C) 35

D) 40

17

For approximately how many years between 1963 and 2013 was the violent crime rate in the United States greater than 375 crimes per 100,000 capita?

A) 25

B) 30

C) 37

D) 42

EXERCISE SET 5 ANSWER KEY

1. **C** In 2005, the revenue per store, according to the line of best fit, was about $300,000, and in 2012 it was about $650,000, so the percent change is (650,000 − 300,000)/300,000 × 100% = 116.67%, which is closest to (C) 120%.

2. **D** In 2006, the data points show that there were 3 stores, with revenue of roughly $200,000, $330,000, and $420,000, for a total of $950,000.

3. **D** In 2009, the combined revenue for the three stores was approximately $420,000 + $450,000 + $550,000 = $1,420,000. In 2010, the combined revenue for four stores was approximately $220,000 + $520,000 + $600,000 + $675,000 = $2,015,000, for an increase of about $595,000.

4. **C** In 2006 there were 3 stores and in 2012 there were 6 stores, which is an increase of (6 − 3)/3 × 100% = 100%.

5. **A** The chart shows that 20% of the expense budget went to defense, which equals 0.2 × $3,500,000,000,000 = $700 billion.

6. **C** Medicare accounts for 13% of expenses, so the sector angle is 0.13 × 360° = 46.8°.

7. **B** The Interest on National Debt in 2010 was 0.057 × $3.5 trillion = $199.5 billion, so a decrease of $20 billion would be 20/199.5 × 100% = 10%.

8. **D** The difference between Interest on National Debt and Education is 5.7% − 3.7% = 2%, and 0.02 × $3.5 trillion = $70 billion.

9. **B** The Social Security budget in 2010 was 0.20 $3.5 trillion = $700 billion. 50% of the Federal Pensions budget is 0.5 × 0.035 × $3.5 billion = $61.25 billion. This would be an increase of 61.25/700 × 100% = 8.75%.

10. **B** The vertical axis label on the left shows that the violent crime trend is indicated by the *solid* curve and the *bottom* time series (1963–2013). For this curve, 1970 is slightly to the left of the vertical line at 1973, which shows values clearly between 300 and 450.

11. **C** The vertical axis label on the left shows that the preschool blood lead trend is indicated by the *dashed* curve and the *top* time series (1940–1990).

12. **C** In 1993, the violent crime rate was 750, and in 2013 it was about 400. The percent decrease is therefore (400 − 750)/750 × 100% = 46.7%.

13. **A** In 1970, the blood lead levels were about 23 and in 1990, they were about 3. The rate of decline is therefore (23 − 3)/(1990 − 1970) = 1 mcg/dL per year.

14. **A** From 1945–1955 preschool blood lead levels increased from about 5 to about 17, a percent increase of (17 − 5)/5 × 100% = 240%.

15. **A** The question asks for the greatest *percent* increase, not the greatest *net* increase in violent crime. Notice that the *net* increase from 1963–1968 (from roughly 150 to 250) seems to be slightly less than net increase from 1968–1973 (from roughly 250 to 375), so the *percent* increase from 1963–1968 (+67%) is clearly greater than that from 1968–1973 (+50%).

16. **B** In 1950, blood lead levels were about 12 mcg/dL, and they did not return to this level until 1980.

17. **D** The graph indicates that from about 1970 to 2013, the violent crime rate was above 375 crimes per 100,000 capita.

CHAPTER 9

THE SAT MATH: PASSPORT TO ADVANCED MATH

1. Functions   363

2. Representing Functions   365

3. Compositions and Transformations   366

4. Analyzing and Factoring Quadratics   373

5. Solving Quadratic Equations   375

6. Analyzing Graphs of Quadratic Equations   377

7. Higher Order Equations   383

8. Higher Order Systems   384

9. The Laws of Exponentials   389

10. The Laws of Radicals   391

11. Solving Exponential and Radical Equations   392

12. Rational Expressions   397

13. Simplifying Rational Expressions   399

14. Solving Rational Equations   400

The SAT Math Test:
Passport to Advanced Math

Why are the Passport to Advanced Math topics important on the SAT Math test?

About 27% (16 out of 58 points) of the SAT Math questions are Passport to Advanced Math questions. Questions in this category test your

understanding of the structure of expressions and your ability to analyze, manipulate, and rewrite these expressions. This includes an understanding of the key parts of expressions, such as terms, factors, and coefficients, and the ability to interpret complicated expressions made up of these components.

Questions in this category will also assess your skill in

rewriting expressions, identifying equivalent forms of expressions, and understanding the purpose of different forms.

The specific topics include

- solving, graphing, and analyzing quadratic equations
- solving equations with radicals that may include extraneous solutions
- solving systems including linear and quadratic equations
- creating exponential or quadratic functions from their properties
- calculating with and simplifying rational expressions
- analyzing radicals and exponentials with rational exponents
- creating equivalent forms of expressions to reveal their properties
- working with compositions and transformations of functions
- analyzing higher order polynomial functions, particularly in terms of their factors and zeros

How is it used?

Fluency in these topics in advanced math is essential to success in postsecondary mathematics, science, engineering, and technology. Since these subjects constitute a portion of any liberal arts curriculum, and a substantial portion of any STEM (science, technology, engineering, or mathematics) program, colleges consider these to be essential college preparatory skills for potential STEM majors.

Sound intimidating? It's not.

If you take the time to master the four core skills presented in these 14 lessons, you will gain the knowledge and practice you need to master SAT Passport to Advanced Math questions.

Lesson 1: Functions

Definition of a Function

A **function** is just a recipe for turning any **input** number (usually, but not always, called x) into an **output** number (usually, but not always, called $f(x)$ or y).

If $f(2x) = x + 2$ for all values of x, which of the following is equivalent to $f(x)$?

A) $\dfrac{x+2}{2}$

B) $\dfrac{x}{2}+2$

C) $\dfrac{x-2}{2}$

D) $2x - 2$

(*Medium*) The equation tells us that f is the function that turns an input of $2x$ into $x + 2$. What steps accomplish this?

Input value:	$2x$
1. Divide by 2:	x
2. Add 2:	$x + 2$

Therefore, f is a function that takes an input, divides it by 2, and then adds 2. So $f(x)=\dfrac{x}{2}+2$, and the correct answer is B.

We could also substitute a value for x, such as $x = 1$, into the equation: $f(2(1)) = 1 + 2$, or $f(2) = 3$. Therefore, the correct function takes an input of 2 and turns it into 3. If we substitute $x = 2$ into all of the choices, we get A) 2, B) 3, C) 0, and D) −1. Since only B gives the correct output, that must be the correct answer.

We can also solve with a **variable substitution**. Let's define a new variable, $z = 2x$. Since this also means that $x = \dfrac{z}{2}$, we can substitute into the original function: $f(2x) = x + 2$ becomes $f(z)=\dfrac{z}{2}+2$. Since it doesn't matter what we call the input variable, this is equivalent to $f(x)=\dfrac{x}{2}+2$.

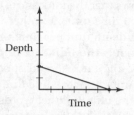

The graph above shows the depth of water in a right cylindrical tank as a function of time as the tank drains. Which of the following represents the graph of the situation in which the tank starts with twice as much water as the original tank had and the water drains at three times the original rate?

A)

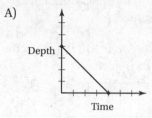

B)

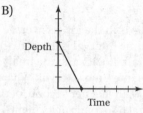

C)

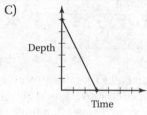

D)

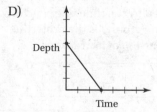

(*Medium*) Although no units are shown on the axes (so the time axis could be in minutes, hours, or any other time unit, and the depth axis could by in any depth unit), we know that **the axes cross at the origin**, or the point (0, 0). The graph shows that the tank starts at 2 depth units and drains after 6 time units. In other words, the tank drains at 1/3 of a depth unit per time unit. (Remember that **the slope equals the unit rate of change**.) In the new graph, then, the tank should start at a depth of $2 \times 2 = 4$ depth units, and it should drain at $3 \times 1/3 = 1$ depth unit per time unit. In other words, it should take 4 time units for the tank to drain completely. The only graph that shows indicates this correctly is A.

$$V = 272 - 32t$$

The equation above shows how the vertical velocity, V, in feet per second, of a projectile relates to the time, t, in seconds, since it was launched from the ground.

1. After how many seconds will the projectile reach the top of its trajectory?

2. While the projectile is in the air, its average velocity over any time interval is equal to the average of the initial velocity and the final velocity over that same time interval. What is the average velocity, in feet per second, of the projectile in the first 6 seconds of its flight?

3. The total vertical distance that the projectile travels over any time interval is equal to its average vertical velocity over that time interval multiplied by the time interval. How many feet from the ground is the projectile when it reaches the top of its trajectory?

---

1. (*Medium*) Since the vertical velocity must be 0 when the projectile is at the top of its trajectory, we can find the time to the top by solving the equation

    $$0 = 272 - 32t$$

    Add 32t to both sides: $32t = 272$

    Divide by 32 on both sides: $t = 8.5$

2. (*Medium*) The velocity at $t = 0$ is $V = 272 - 32(0) = 272$ feet per second, and the velocity at $t = 6$ is $V = 272 - 32(6) = 80$ feet per second, so the average velocity over this interval is $(272 + 80)/2 = 176$ feet per second.

3. (*Medium*) From question 1 we know that the total time to the top of the trajectory is 8.5 seconds. The average velocity over this time is the average of its initial velocity (272 feet per second) and its final velocity (0 feet per second), which is $(272 + 0)/2 = 136$ feet per second. Therefore, the projectile is (136 feet per second)(8.5 seconds) = 1,156 feet from the ground at the top of its trajectory.

Lesson 2: Representing Functions

TEG: Tables, Equations, Graphs

We can represent functions as **tables** of ordered pairs, as **equations** in functional notation, or as **graphs** in the xy-plane. **Make sure you can translate between these forms.**

For instance, if the function g turns an input of -2 into an output of 4, we can represent that fact in three ways:

Table:

x	y
-2	4

Equation: $g(-2) = 4$

Graph: The graph of $y = g(x)$ contains $(-2, 4)$

x	$g(x)$	$h(x)$
1	2	-9
2	4	-6
3	6	-3
4	8	0
5	10	3
6	12	6
7	14	9
8	16	12
9	18	15

According to the table above, for what value of x is $g(h(x)) = 6$?

A) 2

B) 5

C) 6

D) 12

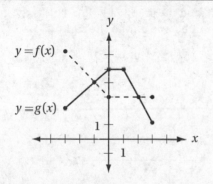

The graphs of the functions f and g in the xy-plane are shown above for $-3 \le x \le 3$. Which of the following describes the set of all x for which $f(x) \le g(x)$?

A) $x \ge -3$

B) $-3 \le x \le -1$ or $2 \le x \le 3$

C) $-1 \le x \le 2$

D) $3 \le x \le 5$

(*Medium-hard*) The equation $g(h(x)) = 6$ means that when x is put into the function h and the result is then put into function g, the result is 6. Working backward, we should ask: what input to g would yield an output of 6? According to the table, only an input of 3 into g would yield an output of 6. This means that $h(x) = 3$. So what input into h would yield an output of 3? Consulting the table again, we see that $g(5) = 3$, and so $x = 5$; therefore, the correct answer is B.

(*Easy*) Since $f(x)$ and $g(x)$ are the y-values of the respective functions, $f(x) \le g(x)$ wherever the graphs cross or the graph of $g(x)$ is above the graph of $f(x)$. The two graphs cross at the points $(-1, 4)$ and $(2, 3)$, and $g(x)$ is above $f(x)$ at every point in between, so $-1 \le x \le 2$; therefore, the correct answer is C.

Lesson 3: Compositions and Transformations

Compositions of Functions

The notation $f(g(x))$ indicates the **composition** of two functions, g and f. The number x is put into the function g and this result is put into the function f; the final result is called $f(g(x))$.

If $f(x) = x + 2$ and $f(g(1)) = 6$, which of the following could be $g(x)$?

A) $g(x) = 3x$

B) $g(x) = x + 3$

C) $g(x) = x - 3$

D) $g(x) = 2x + 1$

(*Medium-hard*)

Given equation:	$f(g(1)) = 6$
Apply the definition of f:	$g(1) + 2 = 6$
Subtract 2:	$g(1) = 4$

In other words, g is the function that gives an output of 4 when its input is 1. The only function among the choices that has this property is $g(x) = x + 3$, so the correct answer is B.

If $f(x) = x^2 + 1$ and $g(f(x)) = 2x^2 + 4$ for all values of x, which of the following expresses $g(x)$?

A) $g(x) = 2x + 1$

B) $g(x) = 2x + 2$

C) $g(x) = 2x + 3$

D) $g(x) = 2x^2 + 1$

(*Medium-hard*)	$g(f(x)) = 2x^2 + 4$
Substitute $f(x) = x^2 + 1$:	$g(x^2 + 1) = 2x^2 + 4$

So how do we turn an input of $x^2 + 1$ into $2x^2 + 4$?

Input:	$x^2 + 1$
Multiply by 2:	$2x^2 + 2$
Add 2:	$2x^2 + 4$

So, g is a function that takes an input, multiplies it by 2, and adds 2, which is the function in choice B.

Transformations of Functions

Given the **parent function** $y = f(x)$ below, here are some **transformations** of function f.

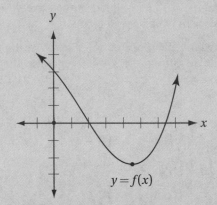

The graph of $y = f(x + k)$ is the graph of $y = f(x)$ **shifted** $-k$ **units horizontally**. So the graph of $y = f(x + 1)$ is the graph of $f(x)$ shifted one unit **to the left**, and the graph of $y = f(x - 1)$ is the graph of $f(x)$ shifted one unit **to the right**.

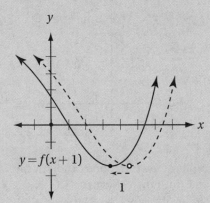

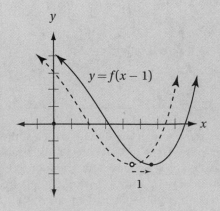

The graph of $y = f(x) + k$ is the graph of $y = f(x)$ **shifted vertically k units**. If k is negative, this a downward shift.

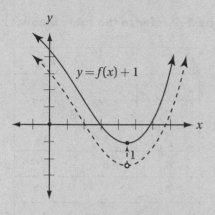

The graph of $y = kf(x)$ is the graph of $y = f(x)$ **stretched or shrunken vertically by a factor of k** (if $k > 1$, it's a stretch, but if $k < 1$ it's a shrink).

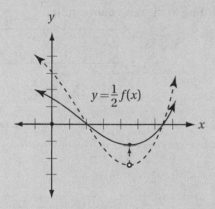

The graph of $y = -f(x)$ is the graph of $y = f(x)$ **reflected over the x-axis.**

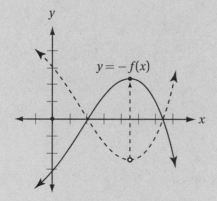

When the function $y = g(x)$ is graphed in the xy-plane, it has a minimum value at $(1, -2)$. What is the maximum value of the function $h(x) = -3g(x) - 1$?

A) 4

B) 5

C) 6

D) 7

(*Medium*) The graph of $y = h(x) = -3g(x) - 1$ is the graph of g after it has been stretched vertically by a factor of 3, reflected over the x-axis, and then shifted down 1 unit. This transforms the **minimum** value point of $(1, -2)$ to a **maximum** value point on the new graph at $(1, -3(-2) - 1)$ or $(1, 5)$, so the correct answer is B.

Exercise Set 1 (Calculator)

1

If $f(x) = x^2 + x + k$, where k is a constant, and $f(2) = 10$, what is the value of $f(-2)$?

2

The minimum value of the function $y = h(x)$ corresponds to the point $(-3, 2)$ on the xy-plane. What is the maximum value of $g(x) = 6 - h(x + 2)$?

3

The function g is defined by the equation $g(x) = ax + b$, where a and b are constants. If $g(1) = 7$ and $g(3) = 6$, what is the value of $g(-5)$?

4

Let the function h be defined by the equation $h(x) = f(g(x))$, where $f(x) = x^2 - 1$ and $g(x) = x + 5$. What is the value of $h(2)$?

Questions 5–9 refer to the table below.

x	$f(x)$	$k(x)$
1	3	5
2	4	6
3	5	1
4	6	2
5	1	3
6	2	4

5

According to the table above, $f(3) =$

6

According to the table above, $f(k(6)) =$

7

According to the table above, $k(k(6)) =$

8

According to the table above, if $k(f(x)) = 5$, then what is the value of x ?

9

Which of the following is true for all values of x indicated in the table?

A) $f(k(x)) - k(f(x)) = 0$

B) $f(k(x)) + k(f(x)) = x$

C) $f(k(x)) - k(f(x)) = x$

D) $f(k(x)) + k(f(x)) = 0$

10

If $g(x - 1) = x^2 + 1$, which of the following is equal to $g(x)$?

A) $x^2 + 2$

B) $x^2 + 2x$

C) $x^2 + 2x + 1$

D) $x^2 + 2x + 2$

11

If $h(x) = \dfrac{x+1}{2}$ and $f(x) = (x - 1)^2$, then which of the following is equal to $f(h(x))$ for all x ?

A) $\dfrac{x^2 - 2x + 2}{2}$

B) $\dfrac{x^2 - 2x + 2}{4}$

C) $\dfrac{x^2 - 2x + 1}{2}$

D) $\dfrac{x^2 - 2x + 1}{4}$

Exercise Set 1 (No Calculator)

Questions 12–19 are based on the graph below.

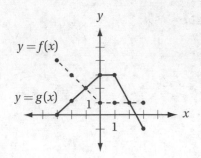

12

What is the value of $g(-1)$?

13

What is the value of $g(f(3))$?

14

What is the value of $f(g(3))$?

15

If $g(f(x)) = -1$, what is the value of $x + 10$?

16

If $f(k) + g(k) = 0$, what is the value of k ?

17

If $f(a) = g(a)$, where $a < 0$, and $f(b) = g(b)$, where $b > 0$, what is the value of $a + b$?

18

Let $h(x) = f(x) \times g(x)$. What is the maximum value of $h(x)$ if $-3 \leq x \leq 3$?

19

Which of the following graphs represents the function $y = f(x) + g(x)$?

A)

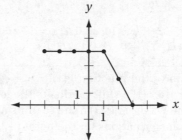

B)

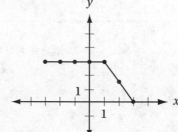

C)

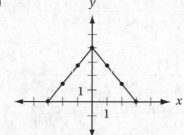

D)

EXERCISE SET 1 ANSWER KEY

Calculator

1. 6 $f(2) = 2^2 + 2 + k = 10$, so $6 + k = 10$ and $k = 4$.
Therefore, $f(-2) = (-2)^2 + (-2) + 4 = 6$.

2. 4 The graph of the function $g(x) = 6 - h(x + 2)$ is the graph of h after (1) a shift 2 units to the left, (2) a reflection over the x-axis, and (3) a shift 6 units up. If we perform these transformations on the point $(-3, 2)$, we get the point $(-5, 4)$, and so the maximum value of g is 4 when $x = -5$.

3. 10

$$g(3) = a(3) + b = 6$$
$$g(1) = a(1) + b = 7$$

Subtract the equations: $\quad 2a = -1$
Divide by 2: $\quad a = -0.5$
Substitute to find b: $\quad -0.5 + b = 7$
Add 0.5: $\quad b = 7.5$
Therefore $\quad g(x) = -0.5x + 7.5$
$$g(-5) = -0.5(-5) + 7.5 = 10$$

4. 48 $\quad h(2) = f(g(2)) = f(2 + 5) = f(7) = (7)^2 - 1 = 48$

5. 5 $\quad f(3) = 5$

6. 6 $\quad f(k(6)) = f(4) = 6$

7. 2 $\quad k(k(6)) = k(4) = 2$

8. 5 According to the table, the only input into k that yields an output of 5 is 1. Therefore, $f(x)$ must be 1, and the only input into f that yields an output of 1 is $x = 5$.

9. A Examination of the table reveals that, for all given values of x, $f(g(x)) = x$ and $g(f(x)) = x$. (This means that f and k are **inverse functions**, that is, they "undo" each other.) This implies that $f(k(x)) - k(f(x)) = x - x = 0$.

10. D One way to approach this question is to pick a new variable, z, such that $z = x - 1$ and therefore $x = z + 1$.
Original equation: $\quad g(x - 1) = x^2 + 1$
Substitute $z = x - 1$: $\quad g(z) = (z + 1)^2 + 1$
FOIL: $\quad g(z) = z^2 + 2z + 1 + 1$
Simplify: $\quad g(z) = z^2 + 2z + 2$
Therefore $\quad g(x) = x^2 + 2x + 2$

11. D

$$f(h(x)) = f\left(\frac{x+1}{2}\right) = \left(\frac{x+1}{2} - 1\right)^2$$
$$= \left(\frac{x+1}{2} - \frac{2}{2}\right)^2 = \left(\frac{x-1}{2}\right)^2$$
$$= \frac{x^2 - 2x + 1}{4}$$

No Calculator

12. 2 The graph of g contains the point $(-1, 2)$, therefore $g(-1) = 2$.

13. 3 The graph of f contains the point $(3, 1)$; therefore, $f(3) = 1$, and so $g(f(3)) = g(1)$. Since the graph of g contains the point $(1, 3)$, $g(1) = 3$.

14. 2 The graph of g contains the point $(3, -1)$; therefore, $g(3) = -1$, and so $f(g(3)) = f(-1)$. Since the graph of f contains the point $(-1, 2)$, $f(-1) = 2$.

15. 8 The only input to function g that yields an output of -1 is 3. Therefore, if $g(f(x)) = -1$, $f(x)$ must equal 3. The only input to f that yields an output of 3 is -2, therefore $x = -2$ and $x + 10 = 8$.

16. 3 The only input for which f and g give outputs that are opposites is 3, because $f(3) = 1$ and $g(3) = -1$.

17. 1 The two points at which the graphs of g and f cross are $(-1, 2)$ and $(2, 1)$. Therefore, $a = -1$ and $b = 2$ and so $a + b = 1$.

18. 4 $h(x) = f(x) \times g(x)$ has a maximum value when $x = -1$, where $f(1) \times g(1) = 2 \times 2 = 4$.

19. A To graph $y = f(x) + g(x)$, we must simply "plot points" by choosing values of x and finding the corresponding y-values. For instance, if $x = -3$, $y = f(-3) + g(-3) = 4 + 0 = 4$, so the new graph must contain the point $(-3, 4)$. Continuing in this manner for $x = -2$, $x = -1$, and so on yields the graph in A.

Lesson 4: Analyzing and Factoring Quadratics

Quadratics

A **quadratic expression** is any expression of the form $ax^2 + bx + c$. It is also called a **second-degree polynomial** because it includes only whole-number powers of x and the highest of these powers is 2.

Factoring Quadratics

To **factor any quadratic**, follow these steps:

1. **Factor out any common** factors using the Distributive Law. For example,

   $$3x^2 - 12x + 12 = 3(x^2 - 4x + 4)$$

2. Apply any relevant **factoring formulas**:

   $$(ax)^2 - b^2 = (ax + b)(ax - b)$$
   $$x^2 + 2bx + b^2 = (x + b)(x + b)$$
   $$x^2 - 2bx + b^2 = (x - b)(x - b)$$

   e.g. $3(x^2 - 4x + 4) = 3(x - 2)(x - 2)$

3. If necessary, use the **Product-Sum Method** (next section).

4. If it's still not completely factored, use the **Quadratic Formula** and the **Factor Theorem** (Lesson 5).

Which of the following is a factor of $x^2 + 8x + 16$?

A) $x - 4$

B) $x - 8$

C) $x + 4$

D) $x + 8$

(*Easy*) This quadratic fits the pattern $x^2 + 2bx + b^2$ and therefore can be factored using the second formula above: $x^2 + 8x + 16 = (x + 4)(x + 4)$. So, the correct answer is C.

Which of the following is a factor of $12b^2 - b - 6$?

A) $6b - 2$

B) $6b + 2$

C) $4b - 3$

D) $4b + 5$

(*Medium*) By the **Product-Sum Method** (next column) this factors to $(4b - 3)(3b + 2)$, so the correct answer is C.

The Product-Sum Method

To factor a quadratic that doesn't fit one of the factoring formulas, try the **Product-Sum Method.**

For instance, consider the quadratic expression

$$6x^2 + 7x + 2$$

In this quadratic expression, $a = 6$, $b = 7$, and $c = 2$.

Step 1: Call ac the **product number** ($ac = 6 \times 2 = 12$), and b the **sum number** ($b = 7$).

Step 2*: Find the two numbers with a product equal to the **product number** and a sum equal to the **sum number**. What two numbers have a product of 12 and a sum of 7? A little guessing and checking should reveal that the numbers are 3 and 4.

Step 3: Rewrite the original quadratic, but expand the middle expression in terms of the sum you just found:

$$6x^2 + 7x + 2 = 6x^2 + (3x + 4x) + 2$$

Step 4: Change any subtraction to addition by changing the number to its opposite (for example, change -2 to $+ (-2)$) and use the Associative Law of Addition to group the first two terms together and the last two terms together:

$$6x^2 + (3x + 4x) + 2 = (6x^2 + 3x) + (4x + 2)$$

Step 5: Factor out the greatest common factor from each pair.

$$(6x^2 + 3x) + (4x + 2) = 3x(2x + 1) + 2(2x + 1)$$

If you do this correctly, the binomial factors will be the same. If they are not, go back and check your work.

Step 6: Factor out the common binomial factor.

$$(3x + 2)(2x + 1)$$

Step 7: FOIL this result to check that it equals the original quadratic.

$$(3x + 2)(2x + 1) = 6x^2 + 3x + 4x + 2 = 6x^2 + 7x + 2$$

---

* You might get stuck in Step 2 and not be able to find two numbers that have the right product and sum. When this happens, use the **Quadratic Formula** (Lesson 5) and the **Factor Theorem** (Lesson 5) to factor the quadratic completely.

$$18x^2 + 9x - 2$$

Which choice shows the correct factorization of the quadratic above?

A) $(9x - 1)(2x + 2)$

B) $(9x + 1)(2x - 2)$

C) $(6x + 1)(3x - 2)$

D) $(6x - 1)(3x + 2)$

Quadratics as Models

The SAT Math section may include word problems that ask you to create quadratic equations that model given situations.

(*Medium*) The simplest way to solve this problem is to FOIL each choice until something matches the given quadratic. (Note that all four choices give quadratics with a leading term of $18x^2$ and a final term of -2, so we just need to find the one that gives middle terms that combine to make $9x$, which is choice D.)

Alternatively, you can use this to practice the Product-Sum Method of factoring. The product number is $(18)(-2) = -36$, and the sum number is 9, and the two numbers with that product and sum are 12 and –3.

$$18x^2 + 9x - 2$$

Expand the middle term: $\qquad 18x^2 + 12x - 3x - 2$

Factor by grouping: $6x(3x + 2) - 1(3x + 2) = (6x - 1)(3x + 2)$

A rectangular playing field is twice as long as it is wide. If the length of the field were to be increased by 10% and the width of the field were to be increased by 10 meters, the total area of the playing field would increase by 1,395 square meters. Which of the following quadratics could be solved to find the width of the playing field?

A) $2x^2 + 220x - 13{,}950 = 0$

B) $2x^2 + 22x + 13{,}950 = 0$

C) $2x^2 + 220x + 13{,}950 = 0$

D) $2x^2 + 22x - 13{,}950 = 0$

(*Medium*) If x is the width of the field, then its length is $2x$ and so its area is $(x)(2x) = 2x^2$ square meters. If we increase the width by 10 meters, it becomes $x + 10$ meters, and if we increase the length by 10%, it becomes $(1.1)(2x) = 2.2x$ meters, and so the new area is $(2.2x)(x + 10) = 2.2x^2 + 22x$ square meters. If this is 1,395 square meters greater than the original area:

$$2.2x^2 + 22x = 2x^2 + 1{,}395$$

Subtract $2x^2$ and 1,395: $\qquad 0.2x^2 + 22x - 1{,}395 = 0$

Multiply both sides by 10: $\qquad 2x^2 + 220x - 13{,}950 = 0$

Therefore, the correct answer is A.

Lesson 5: Solving Quadratic Equations

Zero Product Property

If a product equals 0, then **at least one of its factors must be 0.** For instance, if $3(x + 5)(x - 7) = 0$, then either $(x + 5) = 0$ or $(x - 7) = 0$, and so $x = -5$ or 7.

If $x > 0$ and $2x^2 + 5x = 12$, what is the value of x?

(*Medium*) Original equation: $\qquad 2x^2 + 5x = 12$

Subtract 12 from both sides: $\qquad 2x^2 + 5x - 12 = 0$

Factor with the Product-Sum method: $(x + 4)(2x - 3) = 0$

Use the Zero Product Property: $\qquad x = -4$ or $x = 3/2$

Since x must be greater than zero, the answer is 3/2 or 1.5.

The Factor Theorem

A **zero** of any expression in x is a **value of x that makes that expression equal 0.** The **Factor Theorem** says that **if a polynomial has a zero at $x = b$, it must have a factor of $(x - b)$.**

If $f(x) = x^2 + mx - 12$, where m is a constant, and if $f(-3) = 0$, which of the following is the correct factorization of f?

A) $f(x) = (x + 3)(x - 4)$

B) $f(x) = (x - 3)(x + 4)$

C) $f(x) = (x + 3)(x + 4)$

D) $f(x) = (x - 3)(x - 4)$

(*Medium-hard*) Since $x = -3$ is a zero of the quadratic expression, the Factor Theorem tells us that it must have a factor of $(x - (-3))$ or $(x + 3)$. The only other factor that will give you -12 as the constant term after FOILing is $(x - 4)$, so the correct answer is A.

Bonus: What is the value of m?

The Quadratic Formula

If you can't solve a quadratic by factoring and using the Zero Product Property, use the **Quadratic Formula**.

If $ax^2 + bx + c = 0$, then $x = \dfrac{-b \pm \sqrt{b^2 - 4ac}}{2a}$.

Deriving the Quadratic Formula by Completing the Square

Generic quadratic equation: $\qquad ax^2 + bx + c = 0$

Subtract c from both sides: $\qquad ax^2 + bx = -c$

Factor out a from left side: $\qquad a\left(x^2 + \dfrac{b}{a}x\right) = -c$

Let's show the space on both sides where we will add the term to complete the square. We're multiplying it by a on the left side, so we must also multiply it by a on the right side.

$$a\left(x^2 + \dfrac{b}{u}x + \underline{\quad}\right) = -c + a(\underline{\quad})$$

To complete the square, we add **the square of half of the middle coefficient:**

$$a\left(x^2 + \dfrac{b}{a}x + \left(\dfrac{b}{2a}\right)^2\right) = -c + a\left(\left(\dfrac{b}{2a}\right)^2\right)$$

Simplify: $\qquad a\left(x^2 + \dfrac{b}{a}x + \dfrac{b^2}{4a^2}\right) = -c + \dfrac{b^2}{4a}$

Factor and combine: $\qquad a\left(x + \dfrac{b}{2a}\right)^2 = \dfrac{b^2 - 4ac}{4a}$

Divide both sides by a: $\qquad \left(x + \dfrac{b}{2a}\right)^2 = \dfrac{b^2 - 4ac}{4a^2}$

Take the square root of both sides: $x + \dfrac{b}{2a} = \dfrac{\pm\sqrt{b^2 - 4ac}}{2a}$

Subtract $\dfrac{b}{2a}$ and combine: $\qquad x = \dfrac{-b \pm \sqrt{b^2 - 4ac}}{2a}$

For what values of x is $x^2 - 5 = x$?

A) $\dfrac{1 \pm \sqrt{19}}{2}$

B) $\dfrac{-1 \pm \sqrt{19}}{2}$

C) $\dfrac{1 \pm \sqrt{21}}{2}$

D) $\dfrac{-1 \pm \sqrt{21}}{2}$

(*Medium*) $x^2 - 5 = x$

Subtract x from both sides: $x^2 - x - 5 = 0$

The messiness of the answer choices tells us that this quadratic is not likely to be solved by factoring, so we will need to use the Quadratic Formula for $a = 1$, $b = -1$,

and $c = -5$. This gives $x = \dfrac{-(-1) \pm \sqrt{(-1)^2 - 4(1)(-5)}}{2(1)} =$

$\dfrac{1 \pm \sqrt{1 + 20}}{2} = \dfrac{1 \pm \sqrt{21}}{2}$, and so the correct answer is C.

$2x^2 - 3x - 3$

Which of the following shows the complete factorization of the quadratic expression above?

A) $\left(x - \dfrac{3 + \sqrt{33}}{4} \right)\left(x - \dfrac{3 - \sqrt{33}}{4} \right)$

B) $\left(x - \dfrac{3 + \sqrt{33}}{4} \right)\left(x + \dfrac{3 - \sqrt{33}}{4} \right)$

C) $2\left(x - \dfrac{3 + \sqrt{33}}{4} \right)\left(x + \dfrac{3 - \sqrt{33}}{4} \right)$

D) $2\left(x - \dfrac{3 + \sqrt{33}}{4} \right)\left(x - \dfrac{3 - \sqrt{33}}{4} \right)$

(*Hard*) The Product-Sum Method of factoring won't work here. However, the Quadratic Formula tells us that the

zeros of this quadratic are $x = \dfrac{3 \pm \sqrt{33}}{4}$ and the Factor

Theorem therefore gives us the factors in choice A. However, choice A is incorrect because it omits the leading factor of 2, so the correct answer is D.

Sums and Products of Zeros of Quadratics

The **sum** of the solutions of $ax^2 + bx + c = 0$ is $-\dfrac{b}{a}$.

The **product** of the solutions of $ax^2 + bx + c = 0$ is $\dfrac{c}{a}$.

You can prove these facts by just adding or multiplying the two solutions given by the Quadratic Formula.

$x^2 + x + 7 = 4x$

What is the sum of the solutions of the equation above?

(*Medium*) $x^2 + x + 7 = 4x$

Subtract $4x$ from both sides: $x^2 - 3x + 7 = 0$

We could solve this with the Quadratic Formula, but the solutions are complex. Instead, let's use the fact that the sum of the solutions is $-b/a = -(-3)/1 = 3$.

Lesson 6: Analyzing Graphs of Quadratic Equations

Parabolas

The graph in the xy-plane of $y = ax^2 + bx + c$ is a **parabola.**

- This parabola has a **vertical axis of symmetry** at $x = -\dfrac{b}{2a}$.

- The **vertex** of the parabola is on this axis of symmetry, at

$$\left(-\frac{b}{2a}, c - \frac{b^2}{4a}\right).$$

- The **y-intercept** of this parabola is $(0, c)$.

- The **x-intercepts** (if they exist) are given by the Quadratic Formula.

- If $a > 0$, the parabola is **open up;** if $a < 0$, it is **open down**.

- If the parabola is written in **vertex** form $y = a(x - h)^2 + k$, then its **vertex** is (h, k).

Which of the following is a quadratic function that, when graphed in the xy-plane, has a positive y-intercept and two distinct negative x-intercepts?

A) $f(x) = -2(x + 3)(x + 1)$

B) $f(x) = 3(x + 2)^2$

C) $f(x) = -4(x - 2)(x - 4)$

D) $f(x) = (x + 1)(x + 3)$

(*Easy*) Since each quadratic is given in factored form, the Zero Product Property gives us the x-intercepts. Choice A has x-intercepts at -3 and -1, which are both negative, but its y-intercept is $-2(0 + 3)(0 + 1) = -6$, which is not positive. Choice B is not correct because it only has a single x-intercept at $x = -2$. Choice C is not correct because it has positive x intercepts at 2 and 4. Choice D is correct because it has x-intercepts of -1 and -3 and its y-intercept is $(0 + 1)(0 + 3) = 3$.

Which of the following could be the graph in the xy-plane of $h(x) = ax^2 + bx + c$, if a is a negative constant and c is a positive constant?

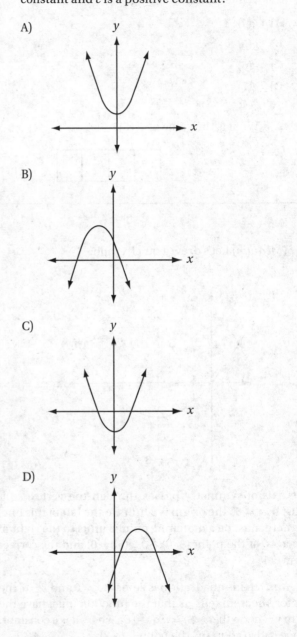

(*Easy*) If a is negative, the parabola is "open down," and if c is positive, its y-intercept is positive. The only graph that matches this description is choice B.

Using the Symmetry of Parabolas

The graph of the quadratic function $y = g(x)$ in the xy-plane is a parabola with a vertex at $(3, -2)$ that passes through the origin.

1. Which of the following must equal 0?

A) $g(4)$

B) $g(5)$

C) $g(6)$

D) $g(7)$

2. What is the value of $g(15)$?

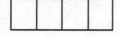

$$y = -3(x + 4)(x - 2)$$

The graph of the equation above in the xy-plane is a parabola. What are the coordinates of the vertex of this parabola?

A) $(-1, 27)$

B) $(1, 15)$

C) $(-1, -27)$

D) $(1, -15)$

---

1. (*Medium*) Let's draw a quick graph.

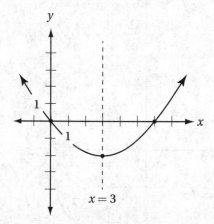

$x = 3$

The axis of symmetry passes through the vertex, so it must be $x = 3$. The origin is 3 units to the **left** of this line, so there must be a matching point 3 units to the **right** of the axis, at the point $(6, 0)$. So, $g(6) = 0$, and the correct answer is C.

2. (*Hard*) If this quadratic has zeros at $x = 0$ and $x = 6$, the Factor Theorem tells us that the function must have the form $y = a(x - 0)(x - 6) = ax(x - 6)$, where a is a constant. Since it also contains the point $(3, -2)$:

$$-2 = a(3)(3 - 6)$$

Simplify:

$$-2 = -9a$$

Divide by -9 on both sides:

$$a = \frac{2}{9}$$

So $g(x) = \frac{2}{9}x(x - 6)$ and $g(15) = \frac{2}{9}(15)(15 - 6) = 30$.

(*Medium*) The x-intercepts are $x = -4$ and 2, so the axis of symmetry is halfway between them, at $x = -1$. This is the x-coordinate of the vertex, so the y-coordinate is $y = (-3)(3)(-3) = 27$, and the correct answer is A.

Also, we can **complete the square** (Lesson 5) to get the equation in **vertex form.**

	$y = -3(x + 4)(x - 2)$
FOIL:	$y = -3(x^2 + 2x - 8)$
Group the first two terms of the quadratic:	$y = -3((x^2 + 2x) - 8)$
Complete the square:	$y - 3(1) = -3(x^2 + 2x + 1) - 8)$
Distribute on the right:	$y - 3 = -3(x^2 + 2x + 1) + 24$
Subtract 24 and factor:	$y - 27 = -3(x + 1)^2$

Exercise Set 2 (No Calculator)

1

If $(x - 2)(x + 2) = 0$, then $x^2 + 10 =$

2

If $(a - 3)(a + k) = a^2 + 3a - 18$ for all values of a, what is the value of k?

3

When the quadratic function $y = 10(x + 4)(x + 6)$ is graphed in the xy-plane, the result is a parabola with vertex at (a, b). What is the value of ab?

4

If the function $y = 3x^2 - kx - 12$ has a zero at $x = 3$, what is the value of k?

5

If the graph of a quadratic function in the xy-plane is a parabola that intersects the x-axis at $x = -1.2$ and $x = 4.8$, what is the x-coordinate of its vertex?

6

If the graph of $y = a(x - b)(x - 4)$ has a vertex at $(5, -3)$, what is the value of ab?

7

What is the sum of the zeros of the function $h(x) = 2x^2 - 5x - 12$?

8

If $x = -5$ is one of the solutions of the equation $0 = x^2 - ax - 12$, what is the other solution?

9

Which of the following is equivalent to $2a(a - 5) + 3a^2(a + 1)$ for all values of a?

A) $6a^4 - 24a^3 - 6$

B) $5a^5 + 3a^2 - 10a$

C) $3a^3 + 5a^2 - 10a$

D) $3a^3 + 2a^2 - 10a - 6$

10

Which of the following functions, when graphed in the xy-plane, has exactly one negative x-intercept and one negative y-intercept?

A) $y = -x^2 - 6x - 9$

B) $y = -x^2 + 6x - 9$

C) $y = x^2 + 6x + 9$

D) $y = x^2 - 6x + 9$

11

If $2x^2 + 8x - 42$ and $x < 0$, what is the value of x^2?

A) 4

B) 9

C) 49

D) 64

12

When the function $y = h(x) = ax^2 + bx + c$ is graphed in the xy-plane, the result is a parabola with vertex at $(4, 7)$. If $h(2) = 0$, which of the following must also equal 0?

A) $h(5)$

B) $h(6)$

C) $h(8)$

D) $h(9)$

Exercise Set 2 (Calculator)

13

If $x > 0$ and $2x^2 - 4x = 30$, what is the value of x?

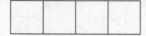

14

If $x^2 + bx + 9 = 0$ has only one solution, and $b > 0$, what is the value of b?

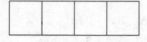

15

When $y = 5(x - 3.2)(x - 4.6)$ is graphed in the xy-plane, what is the value of the y-intercept?

16

When $y = 5(x - 3.2)(x - 4.6)$ is graphed in the xy-plane, what is the x-coordinate of the vertex?

17

If $(2x - 1)(x + 3) + 2x = 2x^2 + kx - 3$ for all values of x, what is the value of k?

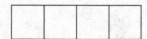

18

If $b^2 + 20b = 96$ and $b > 0$, what is the value of $b + 10$?

19

The graph of $y = f(x)$ in the xy-plane is a parabola with vertex at (3, 7). Which of the following must be equal to $f(-1)$?

A) $f(2)$

B) $f(4)$

C) $f(7)$

D) $f(15)$

20

Which of the following functions, when graphed in the xy-plane, has two positive x-intercepts and a negative y-intercept?

A) $y = -2(x - 1)(x + 5)$

B) $y = -2(x + 3)^2$

C) $y = -2(x - 5)^2$

D) $y = -2(x - 1)(x - 5)$

21

Which of the following equations has no real solutions?

A) $x^2 - 3x + 2 = 0$

B) $x^2 - 3x - 2 = 0$

C) $x^2 + 2x - 3 = 0$

D) $x^2 + 2x + 3 = 0$

22

The graph of the function $y = a(x + 6)(x + 8)$ has an axis of symmetry at $x = k$. What is the value of k?

A) -7

B) -6

C) 7

D) 8

23

The graph of the quadratic function $y = f(x)$ in the xy-plane is a parabola with vertex at (6, −1). Which of the following must have the same value as the y-intercept of this graph?

A) $f(-2)$

B) $f(3.5)$

C) $f(12)$

D) $f(13.5)$

EXERCISE SET 2 ANSWER KEY

No Calculator

1. 14

$$(x - 2)(x + 2) = 0$$
FOIL: $x^2 - 4 = 0$
Add 14: $x^2 + 10 = 14$

2. 6

$$(a - 3)(a + k) = a^2 + 3a - 18$$
FOIL: $a^2 + (k - 3)a - 3k = a^2 + 3a - 18$
Equate coefficients: $k - 3 = 3; -3k = -18$
Therefore, $k = 6$.

3. 50 By the Factor Theorem, the parabola has x-intercepts at $x = -4$ and $x = -6$. The x-coordinate of the vertex is the average of these zeros, or -5. To get the y-coordinate of the vertex, we just plug $x = -5$ back into the equation: $y = 10(-5 + 4)(-5 + 6) = 10(-1)(1) = -10$. Therefore, $a = -5$ and $b = -10$ and so $ab = 50$.

4. 5

When $x = 3$, $y = 0$: $0 = 3(3)^2 - k(3) - 12$
Simplify: $0 = 27 - 3k - 12$
Simplify: $0 = 15 - 3k$
Add $3k$: $3k = 15$
Divide by 3: $k = 5$

5. 1.8 The x-coordinate of the vertex is the average of the x-intercepts (if they exist): $(-1.2 + 4.8)/2 = 3.6/2 = 1.8$.

6. 18 The x-coordinate of the vertex is the average of the x-intercepts (if they exist):

$$5 = (b + 4)/2$$
Multiply by 2: $10 = b + 4$
Subtract 4: $6 = b$
Substitute $x = 5$ and $y = -3$ into equation to find the
value of a: $-3 = a(5 - 6)(5 - 4) = -a$
Multiply by -1: $3 = a$
Therefore, $ab = (3)(6) = 18$

7. 2.5

$$0 = 2x^2 - 5x - 12$$
Factor: $0 = (2x + 3)(x - 4)$
Therefore, the zeros are $x = -3/2$ and $x = 4$, which have a sum of 2.5. Alternately, you can divide the original equation by 2:

$$0 = x^2 - 2.5x - 12$$
and recall that any quadratic in the form $x^2 + bx + c = 0$ must have zeros that have a sum of $-b$ and a product of c. Therefore, without having to calculate the zeros, we can see that they have a sum of $-(-2.5) = 2.5$.

8. 2.4 We know that one of the zeros is $x = -5$, and we want to find the other, $x = b$. We can use the Factor Theorem:

$$x^2 - ax - 12 = (x + 5)(x - b)$$
FOIL: $x^2 - ax - 12 = x^2 + (5 - b)x - 5b$
Since the constant terms must be equal, $12 = 5b$ and therefore, $b = 12/5 = 2.4$.

9. C

$$2a(a - 5) + 3a^2(a + 1)$$
Distribute: $2a^2 - 10a + 3a^3 + 3a^2$
Collect like terms: $3a^3 + 5a^2 - 10a$

10. A Substitute $x = 0$ to find the y-intercept of each graph. Only (A) and (B) yield negative y-intercepts, so (C) and (D) can be eliminated. Factoring the function in (A) yields $y = -(x + 3)$, which has only a single x-intercept at $x = -3$.

11. C

$$2x^2 + 8x = 42$$
Divide by 2: $x^2 + 4x = 21$
Subtract 21: $x^2 + 4x - 21 = 0$
Factor: $(x + 7)(x - 3) = 0$
Therefore, $x = -7$ or 3, but since $x < 0$, $x = -7$ and therefore, $x^2 = (-7)^2 = 49$.

12. B Draw a quick sketch of the parabola. Since it has a vertex at $(4, 7)$, it must have an axis of symmetry of $x = 4$. The two zeros of the function must be symmetric to the line $x = 4$, and since the zero $x = 2$ is 2 units to the left of the axis, the other must by 2 units to the right, at $x = 6$.

Calculator

13. 5

$$2x^2 - 4x = 30$$
Divide by 2: $x^2 - 2x = 15$
Subtract 15: $x^2 - 2x - 15 = 0$
Factor: $(x - 5)(x + 3) = 0$
Therefore, $x = 5$ or -3. But since $x > 0$, $x = 5$.

14. 6 Let's call the one solution a. If it is the only solution, the two factors must be the same:

$$x^2 + bx + 9 = (x - a)(x - a)$$
FOIL: $x^2 + bx + 9 = x^2 - 2ax + a^2$
Therefore, $b = -2a$ and $a^2 = 9$. This means that $x = 3$ or -3 and so $b = -2(3) = -6$ or $-2(-3) = 6$. Since b must be positive, $b = 6$.

15. 73.6 The y-intercept is simply the value of the function when $x = 0$: $y = 5(0 - 3.2)(0 - 4.6) = 73.6$.

16. 3.9 The x-coordinate of the vertex is simply the average of the zeros: $(3.2 + 4.6)/2 = 3.9$.

17. 7

$$(2x - 1)(x + 3) + 2x = 2x^2 + kx - 3$$
FOIL: $2x^2 + 5x - 3 + 2x = 2x^2 + kx - 3$
Simplify: $2x^2 + 7x - 3 = 2x^2 + kx - 3$
Subtract $2x^2$ and add 3: $7x = kx$
Divide by x: $7 = k$

18. **14**

$$b^2 + 20b = 96$$

Subtract 96:

$$b^2 + 20b - 96 = 0$$

Factor:

$$(b - 4)(b + 24) = 0$$

Therefore, $b = 4$ or -24, but if $b > 0$, then b must equal 4, and therefore, $b + 10 = 14$. Alternately, you might notice that adding 100 to both sides of the original equation gives a "perfect square trinomial" on the left side:

$$b^2 + 20b + 100 = 196$$

Factor:

$$(b + 10)^2 = 196$$

Take square root:

$$b + 10 = \pm 14$$

If $b > 0$:

$$b + 10 = 14$$

19. **C** Since the vertex of the parabola is at (3, 7), the axis of symmetry is $x = 3$. Since $x = -1$ is 4 units to the left of this axis, and $x = 7$ is 4 units to the right of this axis, $f(-1)$ must equal $f(7)$.

20. **D** $y = -2(x - 1)(x - 5)$ has x-intercepts at $x = 1$ and $x = 5$ and a y-intercept of $y = -10$. (Notice that the function in (C) has only *one* positive x-intercept at $x = 5$.)

21. **D** This one is tough. Since this question allows a calculator, you could solve this by graphing or with the Quadratic Formula. Remember that a quadratic equation has no real solution if $b^2 - 4ac < 0$. The only choice for which $b^2 - 4ac$ is negative is (D). Alternately, if you graph the left side of each equation as a function in the xy-plane (which I only advise if you have a good graphing calculator), you will see that the function in (D) never crosses the x-axis, implying that it cannot equal 0.

22. **A** This quadratic has zeros at $x = -6$ and $x = -8$, so its axis of symmetry is at the midpoint of the zeros, at $x = -7$.

23. **C** If the vertex of the parabola is at (6, −1), its axis of symmetry must be $x = 6$. The y-intercept of the function is $f(0)$, which is the value of y when $x = 0$. Since this point is 6 units to the left of the axis of symmetry, its reflection over the axis of symmetry is 6 units to the rights of the axis, at $f(12)$.

Lesson 7: Higher Order Equations

Higher Order Polynomials

To **multiply two polynomials**, just **distribute** each term in the first polynomial to each term in the second polynomial, then simplify. FOILing is just a special example of this kind of distribution.

$$(2x^2 + kx + 9)(x - 3) = 2x^3 - 9x - 27$$

In the equation above, k is a constant. If this equation is true for all values of x, what is the value of k?

A) 2

B) 4

C) 6

D) 8

(*Medium*) $(2x^2 + kx + 9)(x - 3) = 2x^3 - 9x - 27$
On the left side, distribute each of the three terms in the first factor to each of the two terms in the second factor:

$(2x^2 + kx + 9)(x - 3) = 2x^3 - 6x^2 + kx^2 - 3kx + 9x - 27$

Collect like terms: $2x^3 + (-6 + k)x^2 + (-3k + 9)x - 27$

If this is equal to $2x^3 - 9x - 27$ for all values of x, then all of the coefficients must match: $(-6 + k) = 0$ (since there is no x^2 term on the right) and $(-3k + 9) = -9$. Solving either of these equations gives $k = 6$, so the correct answer is C.

If $m \neq n$, which of the following is equivalent to $\dfrac{2m^4 - 2n^4}{m - n}$?

A) $2m^3 - 2n^3$

B) $(2m + 2n)(m^2 + n^2)$

C) $(2m + 2n)(m^2 - n^2)$

D) $(2m - 2n)(m^2 + n^2)$

(*Medium*) $\dfrac{2m^4 - 2n^4}{m - n}$

Factor completely: $\dfrac{2(m - n)(m + n)(m^2 + n^2)}{m - n}$

Cancel common factor: $2(m + n)(m^2 + n^2)$
Distribute with first two factors: $(2m + 2n)(m^2 + n^2)$
Therefore, the correct answer is B.

Factoring by Grouping

When factoring an expression with more than three terms, try **factoring by grouping** and looking for common factors.

$$3x^2 - 3xy + 9x - 9y = 0$$

If $x \neq y$ in the equation above, what is the value of x?

A) -3

B) 1

C) 3

D) 9

(*Hard*) $3x^2 - 3xy + 9x - 9y = 0$
Regroup in pairs: $(3x^2 - 3xy) + (9x - 9y) = 0$
Factor out common factors: $3x(x - y) + 9(x - y) = 0$
Factor out common factor binomial: $(3x + 9)(x - y) = 0$

By the Zero Product Property, either $x = -3$ or $x = y$. But since we are told that $x \neq y$, the correct answer is A.

Lesson 8: Higher Order Systems

Nonlinear Systems

Nonlinear systems obey many of the same rules that linear systems do. For instance, their solutions correspond to **points of intersection** on their graphs, and they can often be solved by algebraic methods like **substitution** and **combination**, which we discussed in Chapter 7, Lesson 12.

For what two values of y does there exist a value of x such that $y + 2x = 6$ and $y = x^2 + 3x$?

A) 1 and -6

B) 0 and -5

C) 0 and 10

D) 4 and 18

(*Medium-hard*) These graphs are of a line and a parabola. We could solve this one by graphing and finding intersection points, but we can also solve by **substitution**. If we substitute $y = x^2 + 3x$ into $y + 2x = 6$ we get

$$(x^2 + 3x) + 2x = 6$$

Combine like terms and subtract 6: $x^2 + 5x - 6 = 0$

Factor: $(x + 6)(x - 1) = 0$

Apply Zero Product Property: $x = -6$ or 1

But the question asks for the values of y, not x, so we need to substitute these values for x in either equation and solve for y. $y = (-6)^2 + 3(-6) = 36 - 18 = 18$

$$y = (1)^2 + 3(1) = 1 + 3 = 4$$

Therefore, the correct answer is D.

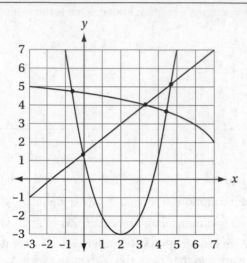

The figure above shows the graphs in the xy-plane that correspond to a system of three equations. How many solutions does this system have in the domain $-1 < x < 5$?

A) none

B) three

C) four

D) five

(*Medium*) Although the graph shows five intersection points, none of them shows a point where **all three graphs intersect at once**. Therefore, the correct answer is A.

Exercise Set 3 (No Calculator)

1

If $x^3 - 7x^2 + 16x - 12 = (x - a)(x - b)(x - c)$ for all values of x, what is the value of abc ?

2

If $x^3 - 7x^2 + 16x - 12 = (x - a)(x - b)(x - c)$ for all values of x, what is the value of $a + b + c$?

3

If $x^3 - 7x^2 + 16x - 12 = (x - a)(x - b)(x - c)$ for all values of x, what is the value of $ab + bc + ac$?

4

If $x^2 - ax + 12$ has a zero at $x = 3$, what is the value of a ?

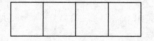

5

If $x^2 - ax + 12$ has a zero at $x = 3$, at what other value of x does it have a zero?

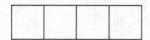

6

$$y = 4x^2 + 2$$
$$x + y = 16$$

When the two equations in the system above are graphed in the xy-plane, they intersect in the point (a, b). If $a > 0$, what is the value of a ?

7

$$x^2 + y^2 = 9$$

Which of the following equations, if graphed in the xy-plane, would intersect the graph of the equation above in exactly one point?

A) $y = -4$

B) $y = -3$

C) $y = -1$

E) $y = 0$

8

If $g(x) = a(x + 1)(x - 2)(x - 3)$ where a is a negative constant, which of the following is greatest?

A) $g(0.5)$

B) $g(1.5)$

C) $g(2.5)$

D) $g(3.5)$

9

If $2x^2 + ax + b$ has zeros at $x = 5$ and $x = -1$, what is the value of $a + b$?

A) -18

B) -9

C) -2

D) -1

10

If the graph of the equation $y = ax^4 + bx$ in the xy-plane passes through the points $(2, 12)$ and $(-2, 4)$, what is the value of $a + b$?

A) 0.5   B) 1.5   C) 2.0

D) 2.5

11

If the function $y = 3(x^2 + 1)(x^3 - 1)(x + 2)$ is graphed in the xy-plane, in how many distinct points will it intersect the x-axis?

A) Two   B) Three   C) Four

D) Five

Exercise Set 3 (Calculator)

12

If $x^2 + y = 10x$ and $y = 25$, what is the value of x ?

13

If $2x^3 - 5x - a$ has a zero at $x = 4$, what is the value of a ?

14

If $x > 0$ and $x^4 - 9x^3 - 22x^2 = 0$, what is the value of x ?

15

If d is a positive constant and the graph in the xy-plane of $y = (x^2)(x^2 + x - 72)(x - d)$ has only one positive zero, what is the value of d ?

16

$$y = 2x^2 + 18$$
$$y = ax$$

In the system above, a is a positive constant. When the two equations are graphed in the xy-plane, they intersect in exactly one point. What is the value of a ?

17

$$4a^2 - 5b = 16$$
$$3a^2 - 5b = 7$$

Given the system of equations above, what is the value of $a^2 b^2$?

18

For how many distinct positive integer values of n is $(n - 1)(n - 9)(n - 17)$ less than 0 ?

A) Six
B) Seven
C) Eight
D) Nine

19

$$x^2 + 2y^2 = 44$$
$$y^2 = x - 2$$

When the two equations above are graphed in the xy-plane, they intersect in the point (h, k). What is the value of h ?

A) -8
B) -6
C) 6
D) 8

20

$$m^2 + 2n = 10$$
$$2m^2 + 2n = 14$$

Given the system of equations above, which of the following could be the value of $m + n$?

A) -7
B) -2
C) 1
D) 2

21

For how many distinct values of x does $(x^2 - 4)(x - 4)^2(x^2 + 4)$ equal 0 ?

A) Three
B) Four
C) Five
D) Six

22

The function $f(x)$ is defined by the equation $f(x) = a(x + 2)(x - a)(x - 8)$ where a is a constant. If $f(2.5)$ is negative, which of the following could be the value of a ?

A) -2
B) 0
C) 2
D) 4

EXERCISE SET 3 ANSWER KEY

No Calculator

1. 12 When the expression $(x - a)(x - b)(x - c)$ is fully distributed and simplified, it yields the expression $x^3 - (a + b + c)x^2 + (ab + bc + ac)x - abc$. If this is equivalent to $x^3 - 7x^2 + 16x - 12$ for all values of x, then all of the corresponding coefficients must be equal.

2. 7 See question 1.

3. 16 See question 1.

4. 7 If $x^2 - ax + 12 = 0$ when $x = 3$, then

$$(3)^2 - 3a + 12 = 0$$

Simplify:	$21 - 3a = 0$
Add $3a$:	$21 = 3a$
Divide by 3:	$7 = a$

5. 4 As we saw in question 4, $a = 7$.

$$x^2 - 7x + 12$$

Factor: $\quad (x - 3)(x - 4)$

Therefore, the zeros are 3 and 4.

6. 7/4 or 1.75

	$x + y = 16$
Subtract x:	$y = 16 - x$
Substitute:	$16 - x = 4x^2 + 2$
Subtract 16, add x:	$0 = 4x^2 + x - 14$
Factor:	$0 = (4x - 7)(x + 2)$

Therefore, $x = -2$ or 7/4, but if x must be positive, it equals 7/4.

7. B The graph of the given equation is a circle centered at the origin with a radius of 3. Therefore, the horizontal line at $y = -3$ just intersects it at $(0, -3)$. You can also substitute $y = -3$ into the original equation and verify that it gives exactly one solution.

8. C Just notice the sign of each factor for each input:
$g(0.5) = (-)(+)(-)(-) = $ negative
$g(1.5) = (-)(+)(-)(-) = $ negative
$g(2.5) = (-)(+)(+)(-) = $ positive
$g(3.5) = (-)(+)(+)(+) = $ negative
Since (C) is the only option that yields a positive value, it is the greatest.

9. A

	$2x^2 + ax + b$
If $x = 5$ is a zero:	$2(5)^2 + 5a + b = 0$
Subtract 50:	$5a + b = -50$
If $x = -1$ is a zero:	$2(-1)^2 + a(-1) + b = 0$
Subtract 2:	$-a + b = -2$
Multiply by -1:	$a - b = 2$
Add equations:	$6a = -48$

Divide by 6:	$a = -8$
Substitute $a = -8$:	$-8 - b = 2$
Add 8:	$-b = 10$
Multiply by -1:	$b = -10$

Therefore, $a + b = -8 + -10 = -18$.

10. D

Substitute $(2, 12)$:	$12 = a(2)^4 + b(2)$
Simplify:	$16a + 2b = 12$
Substitute $(-2, 4)$:	$4 = a(-2)^4 + b(-2)$
Simplify:	$16a - 2b = 4$
Add two equations:	$32a = 16$
Divide by 32:	$a = \frac{1}{2}$
Substitute:	$16(1/2) + 2b = 12$
Subtract 8:	$2b = 4$
Divide by 2:	$b = 2$

Therefore, $a + b = 2.5$.

11. A Use the Zero Product Property. The factor $(x^2 + 1)$ cannot be zero for any value of x, $(x^3 - 1)$ is zero when $x = 1$, and $(x + 2)$ is zero when $x = -2$. Therefore, there are only two distinct points in which this graph touches the x-axis.

Calculator

12. 5 Substitute $y = 25$:

	$x^2 + 25 = 10x$
Subtract $10x$:	$x^2 - 10x + 25 = 0$
Factor:	$(x - 5)(x - 5) = 0$
Use Zero Product Property:	$x = 5$

13. 108 If $x = 4$ is a zero:

	$2(4)^3 - 5(4) - a = 0$
Simplify:	$108 - a - 0$
Add a:	$108 = a$

14. 11

	$x^4 - 9x^3 - 22x^2 = 0$
Divide by x^2:	$x^2 - 9x - 22 = 0$
Factor:	$(x - 11)(x + 2) = 0$
Use Zero Product Property:	$x = 11$ or -2

15. 8

$$y = (x^2)(x^2 + x - 72)(x - d)$$

Factor: $\quad y = (x^2)(x + 9)(x - 8)(x - d)$

By the Zero Property, the zeros are $x = 0$, -9, 8, or d. Since d is positive, but there can only be one positive zero, $d = 8$.

16. 12

	$y = 2x^2 + 18$
Substitute $y = ax$:	$ax = 2x^2 + 18$
Subtract ax:	$0 = 2x^2 - ax + 18$
Divide by 2:	$0 = x^2 - \frac{a}{2}x + 9$

If the graphs intersect in only one point, the system must have only one solution, so this quadratic must be a "perfect square trinomial" as discussed in Lesson 4.

$$x^2 - \frac{a}{2}x + 9 = x^2 - 2bx + b^2$$

Equate coefficients: $b^2 = 9$
                           $2b = a/2$

The only positive solution to this system is $b = 3$ and $a = 12$.

---

17. **144** $4a^2 - 5b = 16$
                               $3a^2 - 5b = 7$
Subtract equations: $a^2 = 9$
Substitute $a^2 = 9$: $3(9) - 5b = 7$
Subtract 27: $-5b = -20$
Divide by -5: $b = 4$
Therefore, $a^2b^2 = 9(4)^2 = 144$.

---

18. **B** In order for the product of three numbers to be negative, either all three numbers must be negative or exactly one must be negative and the others positive. Since n must be a positive integer, $n - 1$ cannot be negative, and so there must be two positive factors and one negative. The only integers that yield this result are the integers from 10 to 16, inclusive, which is a total of seven integers.

---

19. **C** $x^2 + 2y^2 = 44$
Substitute $y^2 = x - 2$: $x^2 + 2(x - 2) = 44$

Distribute: $x^2 + 2x - 4 = 44$
Subtract 44: $x^2 + 2x - 48 = 0$
Factor: $(x - 6)(x + 8) = 0$
This seems to imply that the x-coordinate of the point of intersection could be either 6 or -8, both of which are choices. Can they both be correct? No: if we substitute $x = -8$ into either equation, we get no solution, because y^2 cannot equal -8. Therefore, the correct answer is (C) 6, and the points of intersection are $(6, 2)$ and $(6, -2)$.

---

20. **C** $2m^2 + 2n = 14$
                               $m^2 + 2n = 10$
Subtract equations: $m^2 = 4$
Take square root: $m = \pm 2$
Substitute $m^2 = 4$: $4 + 2n = 10$
Subtract 4: $2n = 6$
Divide by 2: $n = 3$
Therefore, $m + n = -2 + 3 = 1$ or $2 + 3 = 5$.

---

21. **A** Use the Zero Product Property. $(x^2 - 4)$ equals 0 if x is 2 or -2, $(x - 4)$ equals 0 if x is 4, and $(x^2 + 4)$ cannot equal 0. Therefore, there are exactly three distinct zeros.

---

22. **C** $f(2.5) = a(2.5 + 2)(2.5 - a)(2.5 - 8)$
Simplify: $(-24.75)(a)(2.5 - a)$
This product can only be negative if a and $(2.5 - a)$ have the same sign, which is only true for (C) $a = 2$.

Lesson 9: The Laws of Exponentials

The Laws of Exponentials

To deal with exponentials on the SAT Math section, you need to know the eleven **Laws of Exponentials**.

Law #1: **If n is a positive integer, then x^n means 1 times x repeatedly n times. If n is a <u>negative</u> integer, then x^n means 1 <u>divided by</u> x repeatedly $|n|$ times.**

$$3^5 = 1(3)(3)(3)(3)(3) = 243$$

$$3^{-5} = 1 \div 3 \div 3 \div 3 \div 3 \div 3 = \frac{1}{243}$$

Law #2: **If $x \neq 0$, then $x^0 = 1$.** $3^0 = 1$

Law #3: **If $x \neq 0$, then $x^{-n} = \dfrac{1}{x^n}$.** $3^{-3} = \dfrac{1}{3^3}$

Law #4: $(x^m)(x^n) = x^{m+n}$ $(3^4)(3^3) = 3^7$

Law #5: $(x^m)(y^m) = (xy)^m$ $(3^4)(5^4) = 15^4$

Law #6: $\dfrac{x^m}{x^n} = x^{m-n}$ $\dfrac{3^5}{3^2} = 3^3$

Law #7: $\dfrac{x^m}{y^m} = \left(\dfrac{x}{y}\right)^m$ $\dfrac{15^4}{5^4} = 3^4$

Law #8: $(x^m)^n = x^{mn}$ $(3^4)^3 = 3^{12}$

Law #9: $\sqrt[n]{x} = x^{\frac{1}{n}}$ $\sqrt[3]{3} = 3^{\frac{1}{3}}$

Law #10: **If $x^a = x^b$ and $x > 1$, then $a = b$.**

If $3^a = 3^{14}$, then $a = 14$.

Law #11: **If $x = y$, then $x^m = y^m$.**

If $x = 3$, then $x^4 = 3^4$.

If $a - 3b = 6$, which of the following is equivalent to $\dfrac{3^a}{27^b}$?

A) 3^6

B) $\left(\dfrac{1}{9}\right)^3$

C) $(3^{-2})^2$

D) 3^{-6}

(*Medium*) $\dfrac{3^a}{27^b}$

Substitute $27 = 3^3$: $\dfrac{3^a}{\left(3^3\right)^b}$

Apply Exponential Law #8: $\dfrac{3^a}{3^{3b}}$

Apply Exponential Law #6: 3^{a-3b}

Substitute $a - 3b = 6$: 3^6
Therefore, the correct answer is A.

Which of the following is equal to $8^{-\frac{5}{3}}$? (No calculator)

A) -2^5

B) $-\dfrac{1}{2^3}$

C) $\dfrac{1}{10}$

D) $\dfrac{1}{2^5}$

(*Medium*) Apply Exponential Law #8: $8^{-\frac{5}{3}} = \left(8^{\frac{1}{3}}\right)^{-5}$

Apply Exponential Law #9: $= -2^5$

Apply Exponential Law #3: $= \dfrac{1}{2^5}$

Therefore, the correct answer is D.

Which of the following expressions is equivalent to $\dfrac{(b+b+b)(b+b+b)}{3^{-1}}$ for all values of b ?

A) $\dfrac{b^6}{3}$

B) $3b^2$

C) $3b^6$

D) $27b^2$

Which of the following expressions is equivalent to $\dfrac{(3)\left(3^{2n}\right)}{9^n}$ for all values of n ?

A) $\left(\dfrac{2}{3}\right)^n$

B) 3

C) 3^n

D) 9^{2n}

(*Medium*) $\dfrac{(b+b+b)(b+b+b)}{3^{-1}}$

Simplify numerator: $\dfrac{(3b)(3b)}{3^{-1}}$

Simplify and apply Exponential Law #3: $\dfrac{9b^2}{\dfrac{1}{3}}$

Divide by multiplying by the reciprocal: $9b^2 \times 3 = 27b^2$

Therefore, the correct answer is D.

(*Medium*) Apply Exponential Law #4: $\dfrac{(3)(3^{2n})}{9^n} = \dfrac{3^{2n+1}}{9^n}$

Substitute $9 = 3^2$ and apply Exponential Law #8:

$$\dfrac{3^{2n+1}}{(3^2)^n} = \dfrac{3^{2n+1}}{3^{2n}}$$

Apply Exponential Law #6: $3^{(2n+1)-(2n)} = 3^1 = 3$

Therefore, the correct answer is B.

Also, we can plug in different values for n and see that the expression gives a value equal of 3 no matter what.

Lesson 10: The Laws of Radicals

The Laws of Radicals

The **Laws of Radicals** come directly from the Laws of Exponentials, particularly Laws #5, #7, and #9.

Law #1: $\sqrt[n]{x} = x^{\frac{1}{n}}$ $\sqrt[3]{3} = 3^{\frac{1}{3}}$

Law #2: $\left(\sqrt[n]{x}\right)\left(\sqrt[n]{y}\right) = \sqrt[n]{xy}$ $\left(\sqrt[4]{8}\right)\left(\sqrt[4]{2}\right) = \sqrt[4]{16}$

Law #3: $\dfrac{\sqrt[n]{x}}{\sqrt[n]{y}} = \sqrt[n]{\dfrac{x}{y}}$ $\dfrac{\sqrt[3]{16}}{\sqrt[3]{2}} = \sqrt[3]{8}$

The Perfect Squares

Working with square roots is easier if you memorize the first 10 or so **perfect squares** (and their square roots):

4, 9, 16, 25, 36, 49, 64, 81, 100, 121, 144,...

Simplifying Radicals

Many radicals can be simplified **by factoring out perfect squares** from the radicand and then simplifying.

$$\sqrt{72} = \left(\sqrt{36}\right)\left(\sqrt{2}\right) = 6\sqrt{2}$$

If a fraction has a radical in the denominator, eliminate it by **multiplying top and bottom by the radical.**

$$\frac{1+\sqrt{2}}{\sqrt{3}} = \left(\frac{1+\sqrt{2}}{\sqrt{3}}\right)\left(\frac{\sqrt{3}}{3}\right) = \frac{\sqrt{3}+\sqrt{6}}{3}$$

If the denominator includes a sum or difference with radicals, **multiply top and bottom by the conjugate of the denominator.**

$$\frac{\sqrt{2}}{1+\sqrt{3}} = \left(\frac{\sqrt{2}}{1+\sqrt{3}}\right)\left(\frac{1-\sqrt{3}}{1-\sqrt{3}}\right) = \frac{\sqrt{2}-\sqrt{6}}{-2} = \frac{\sqrt{6}-\sqrt{2}}{2}$$

Estimating Square Roots

To estimate a square root, **find between which two consecutive perfect squares the radicand (expression inside the radical) lies.**

About how big is $\sqrt{72}$?

$$\sqrt{64} < \sqrt{72} < \sqrt{81} \text{ so } 8 < \sqrt{72} < 9$$

Which of the following is equivalent to $\dfrac{2\sqrt{2}+4\sqrt{18}}{\sqrt{2}}$?
(No calculator)

A) $6\sqrt{10}$

B) 7

C) 14

D) 19

(*Medium*) Neither radicand is a perfect square, but one of the radicands—18—is a multiple of a perfect square: $18 = 9 \times 2$.

Original expression: $\dfrac{2\sqrt{2}+4\sqrt{18}}{\sqrt{2}}$

Substitute $18 = 9 \times 2$: $\dfrac{2\sqrt{2}+4\sqrt{9}\times\sqrt{2}}{\sqrt{2}}$

Substitute $\sqrt{9} = 3$: $\dfrac{2\sqrt{2}+12\sqrt{2}}{\sqrt{2}}$

Distributing the division gives $2 + 12 = 14$, so the correct answer is C.

If $x^2 = 4$ and $y^2 = 9$, and if $(x - 2)(y + 3) \neq 0$, what is the value of $x + y$?

A) -5

B) -1

C) 1

D) 5

(*Easy*) If $x^2 = 4$, then $x = 2$ or -2, and if $y^2 = 9$, then $y = 3$ or -3. But if $(x - 2)(y + 3) \neq 0$, then x cannot equal 2 and y cannot equal -3, so $x = -2$ and $y = 3$, and $x + y = -2 + 3 = 1$, so the correct answer is C.

Lesson 11: Solving Exponential and Radical Equations

Solving Equations with Exponents and Radicals

> When solving equations involving exponentials or radicals, just apply the **Laws of Exponentials and Radicals** until you isolate the expression you want.

If $\dfrac{1}{x+2} = \sqrt{2}$, what is the value of x?

A) $\dfrac{1+2\sqrt{2}}{2}$

B) $\dfrac{1-2\sqrt{2}}{2}$

C) $\dfrac{\sqrt{2}+4}{2}$

D) $\dfrac{\sqrt{2}-4}{2}$

(*Medium*) Original equation: $\qquad\qquad \dfrac{1}{x+2} = \sqrt{2}$

Multiply by $(x + 2)$ on both sides: $\qquad 1 = x\sqrt{2} + 2\sqrt{2}$

Subtract $2\sqrt{2}$ from both sides: $\qquad 1 - 2\sqrt{2} = x\sqrt{2}$

Divide both sides by $\sqrt{2}$: $\qquad \dfrac{1-2\sqrt{2}}{\sqrt{2}} = x$

Multiply left side by $\dfrac{\sqrt{2}}{\sqrt{2}}$: $\qquad \dfrac{\sqrt{2}-4}{2} = x$

Therefore, the correct answer is D.

If $\dfrac{1}{2^k} = 4\sqrt{2}$, what is the value of k?

A) -3

B) $-\dfrac{5}{2}$

C) $-\dfrac{3}{2}$

D) $\dfrac{7}{2}$

(*Medium-hard*) $\qquad\qquad\qquad\qquad\qquad \dfrac{1}{2^k} = 4\sqrt{2}$

Apply Exponential Law #3: $\qquad\qquad 2^{-k} = 4\sqrt{2}$

Substitute $4 = 2^2$ and apply Radical Law #1:
$$2^{-k} = \left(2^2\right)\left(2^{\frac{1}{2}}\right)$$

Apply Exponential Law #4: $\qquad\qquad 2^{-k} = 2^{\frac{5}{2}}$

Apply Exponential Law #10 and negate $\qquad k = -\dfrac{5}{2}$

Therefore, the correct answer is D.

If $\left(\dfrac{1}{\sqrt{x}}\right)^{-n} = y^{\frac{n}{5}}$, and $n \neq 0$, which of the following expresses x in terms of y?

A) $\sqrt{y^5}$

B) $\sqrt[5]{y^2}$

C) $\dfrac{1}{\sqrt{y^5}}$

D) $\dfrac{1}{\sqrt[5]{y^2}}$

(*Hard*) $\qquad\qquad\qquad\qquad\qquad \left(\dfrac{1}{\sqrt{x}}\right)^{-n} = y^{\frac{n}{5}}$

Apply Radical Law #1, Exponential Law #3: $\left(x^{-\frac{1}{2}}\right)^{-n} = y^{\frac{n}{5}}$

Apply Exponential Law #8: $\qquad\qquad x^{\frac{n}{2}} = y^{\frac{n}{5}}$

Apply Exponential Law #11 (raise to the $\dfrac{2}{n}$ power): $\qquad x = y^{\frac{2}{5}}$

Apply Radical Law #1: $\qquad\qquad x = \sqrt[5]{y^2}$

Therefore, the correct answer is B.

Exercise Set 4 (No Calculator)

1

If $2a^2 + 3a - 5a^2 = 9$, what is the value of $a - a^2$?

2

If $(200)(4{,}000) = 8 \times 10^m$, what is the value of m ?

3

If $w = -10^{30}$, what is the value of $\dfrac{8w^2}{(8w)^2}$?

4

If $2^x = 10$, what is the value of $5(2^{2x}) + 2^x$?

5

If $(x + 2)(x + 4)(x + 6) = 0$, what is the greatest possible value of $\dfrac{1}{2^x}$?

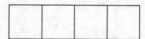

6

If $\left(4 + 4\sqrt{2}\right)^2 = a + b\sqrt{2}$, where a and b are integers, what is the value of $a + b$?

7

If $\dfrac{a}{3 + \sqrt{5}} = \dfrac{3 - \sqrt{5}}{b}$, what is the value of $(ab)^{\frac{3}{2}}$?

8

If $9^x = 25$, what is the value of 3^{x-1} ?

A)　$\dfrac{3}{25}$　　　B)　$\dfrac{5}{3}$　　　C)　$\dfrac{25}{3}$　　　D)　24

9

If $g(x, y) = \dfrac{2x}{y^3}$ and a and b are positive numbers, what is the value of $\dfrac{g(4a, 2b)}{g(a, b)}$?

A)　$\dfrac{1}{4}$　　　B)　$\dfrac{1}{2}$　　　C)　2　　　D)　4

10

Which of the following is equivalent to $\dfrac{2^n \times 2^n}{2^n \times 2}$ for all positive values of n ?

A)　2　　　　　　B)　2^n　　　　　C)　2^{n-1}

D)　2^{2n}

11

Which of the following is equivalent to $3^m + 3^m + 3^m$ for all positive values of m ?

A)　3^{m+1}　　　　B)　3^{2m}　　　　C)　3^{3m}

D)　3^{3m+1}

12

If x is a positive number and $5^x = y$, which of the following expresses $5y^2$ in terms of x ?

A)　5^{2x}　　　　B)　5^{2x+1}　　　　C)　5^{3x}

D)　25^{2x}

Exercise Set 4 (Calculator)

13

If $n^2 = \sqrt{64^4}$ and $n > 0$, what is the value of n?

14

What is the smallest integer value of m such that
$\frac{1}{10^m} < 0.000025$?

15

If $\frac{3}{3^{-k}} = 9\sqrt{27}$, what is the value of k?

16

If $(x^m)^3(x^{m+1})^2 = x^{37}$ for all values of x, what is the value of m?

17

If $9\sqrt{12} - 4\sqrt{27} = n\sqrt{3}$, what is the value of n?

18

If $8^{\frac{1}{6}} = \left(2^{-\frac{1}{12}}\right)^{-n}$, what is the value of n?

19

What is one possible value for x such that
$0 < \frac{4}{5}x < \sqrt{x} < x$?

20

Which of the following is equivalent to
$\dfrac{4}{2^{-2}(x+x)(x+x)}$ for all positive values of x?

A) $\dfrac{1}{x^4}$ B) $\dfrac{4}{x^2}$ C) $\dfrac{1}{4x^2}$ D) $\dfrac{16}{x^4}$

21

The square root of a certain positive number is twice the number itself. What is the number?

A) $\dfrac{1}{8}$ B) $\dfrac{1}{4}$ C) $\dfrac{1}{2}$ D) $\dfrac{1}{\sqrt{2}}$

22

Which of the following is equivalent to
$\dfrac{2m\sqrt{2n} + m\sqrt{18n}}{m\sqrt{2}}$ for all positive values of m and n?

A) $3m\sqrt{3n}$

B) $5m\sqrt{2}$

C) $3\sqrt{3n}$

D) $5\sqrt{n}$

23

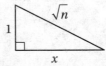

In the figure above, if $n > 1$, which of the following expresses x in terms of n?

A) $\sqrt{n^2 - 1}$

B) $\sqrt{n-1}$

C) $\sqrt{n+1}$

D) $\dfrac{\sqrt{n-1}}{2}$

EXERCISE SET 4 ANSWER KEY

No Calculator

1. 3
$$2a^2 + 3a - 5a^2 = 9$$
Simplify:
$$3a - 3a^2 = 9$$
Divide by 3:
$$a - a^2 = 3$$

---

2. 5 $(200)(4,000) = 800,000 = 8 \times 10^5$

---

3. 1/8 or .125
$$\frac{8w^2}{(8w)^2}$$

Exponential Law #5:
$$\frac{8w^2}{64w^2}$$

Cancel common factors:
$$\frac{1}{8}$$

---

4. 510
$$5(2^{2x}) + 2^x$$
Exponential Law #8:
$$5(2^x)^2 + 2^x$$
Substitute $2^x = 10$:
$$5(10)^2 + 10$$
Simplify:
$$5(10)^2 + 10 = 510$$

---

5. 64 If $(x + 2)(x + 4)(x + 6) = 0$, then $x = -2, -4$, or -6. Therefore 2^{-x} could equal 2^2, 2^4, or 2^6. The greatest of these is $2^6 = 64$.

---

6. 80
$$\left(4 + 4\sqrt{2}\right)^2$$

FOIL:
$$(4)^2 + 2(4)\left(4\sqrt{2}\right) + \left(4\sqrt{2}\right)^2$$

Simplify:
$$16 + 32\sqrt{2} + 32$$

Simplify:
$$48 + 32\sqrt{2}$$

Therefore, $a = 48$ and $b = 32$ and $a + b = 80$.

---

7. 8
$$\frac{a}{3 + \sqrt{5}} = \frac{3 - \sqrt{5}}{b}$$
Cross-multiply:
$$ab = \left(3 + \sqrt{5}\right)\left(3 - \sqrt{5}\right)$$

Simplify:
$$ab = 9 - 5 = 4$$
Therefore, $ab^{3/2} = 4^{3/2} = 8$.

---

8. 5/3 or 1.66 or 1.67
$$9^x = 25$$
Substitute $9 = 3^2$:
$$(3^2)^x = 25$$
Exponential Law #8:
$$3^{2x} = 25$$
Take square root:
$$3^x = 5$$

Divide by 3:
$$\frac{3^x}{3^1} = \frac{5}{3}$$

Exponential Law #6:
$$3^{x-1} = \frac{5}{3}$$

---

9. B
$$\frac{g(4a, 2b)}{g(a, b)} = \frac{\dfrac{2(4a)}{(2b)^3}}{\dfrac{2a}{b^3}}$$

Simplify:
$$= \frac{2(4a)}{(2b)^3} \times \frac{b^3}{2a}$$

Simplify:
$$= \frac{8ab^3}{16ab^3} = \frac{1}{2}$$

---

10. C
$$\frac{2^n \times 2^n}{2^n \times 2}$$
Cancel common factor:
$$\frac{2^n}{2^1}$$
Exponential Law #6:
$$2^{n-1}$$

---

11. A
$$3^m + 3^m + 3^m$$
Combine like terms:
$$3(3^m)$$
Exponential Law #4:
$$3^{m+1}$$

---

12. B
$$5y^2$$
Substitute $y = 5^x$:
$$5(5^x)^2$$
Exponential Law #8:
$$5(5^{2x})$$
Exponential Law #4:
$$5^{2x+1}$$

Calculator

13. 64
$$n^2 = \sqrt{64^4}$$
Radical Law #1
$$n^2 = (64^4)^{1/2}$$
Exponential Law #8:
$$n^2 = 64^2$$

---

14. 5
$$\frac{1}{10^m} < 0.000025$$
Scientific Notation:
$$1 \times 10^{-m} < 2.5 \times 10^{-5}$$

Substitution and checking makes it clear that $m = 5$ is the smallest integer that satisfies the inequality.

---

15. 2.5
$$\frac{3}{3^{-k}} = 9\sqrt{27}$$
Exponential Law #6:
$$3^{1-(-k)} = 9\sqrt{27}$$
Simplify:
$$3^{k+1} = 9 \times 3\sqrt{3}$$
Express as exponentials:
$$3^{k+1} = 3^2 \times 3 \times 3^{\frac{1}{2}}$$
Exponential Law #4:
$$3^{k+1} = 3^{3.5}$$
Exponential Law #10:
$$k + 1 = 3.5$$
Subtract 1:
$$k = 2.5$$

---

16. 7
$$(x^m)^3(x^{m+1})^2 = x^{37}$$
Exponential Law #8:
$$(x^{3m})(x^{2m+2}) = x^{37}$$
Exponential Law #4:
$$x^{5m+2} = x^{37}$$
Exponential Law #10:
$$5m + 2 = 37$$
Subtract 2:
$$5m = 35$$
Divide by 5:
$$m = 7$$

---

17. 6
$$9\sqrt{12} - 4\sqrt{27} = n\sqrt{3}$$
Factor:
$$9\sqrt{4} \times \sqrt{3} - 4\sqrt{9} \times \sqrt{3} = n\sqrt{3}$$

Divide by $\sqrt{3}$: $9\sqrt{4} - 4\sqrt{9} = n$
Simplify: $18 - 12 = 6 = n$

---

18. **6** $8^{\frac{1}{6}} = \left(2^{-\frac{1}{12}}\right)^{-n}$

Substitute $8 = 2^3$: $(2^3)^{\frac{1}{6}} = \left(2^{-\frac{1}{12}}\right)^{-n}$

Exponential Law #8: $2^{\frac{1}{2}} = 2^{\frac{n}{12}}$

Exponential Law #10: $\dfrac{1}{2} = \dfrac{n}{12}$

Multiply by 12: $6 = n$

---

19. **$1 < x \le 1.56$** $0 < \dfrac{4}{5}x < \sqrt{x} < x$

Middle inequality: $\dfrac{4}{5}x < \sqrt{x}$

Square both sides: $\dfrac{16}{25}x^2 < x$

Divide by x: $\dfrac{16}{25}x < 1$

(Since $x > 0$, we do not "swap" the inequality.)

Multiply by 25/16: $x < \dfrac{25}{16} = 1.563$

Last inequality: $\sqrt{x} < x$
Square both sides: $x < x^2$
Divide by x: $1 < x$
Therefore, x must be both greater than 1 and less than or equal to 1.56.

---

20. **B** $\dfrac{4}{2^{-2}(x+x)(x+x)}$

Simplify: $\dfrac{4 \times 2^2}{(2x)^2}$

Simplify: $\dfrac{16}{4x^2}$

Cancel common factor: $\dfrac{4}{x^2}$

---

21. **B** Translate: $\sqrt{x} = 2x$
Square both sides: $x = 4x^2$
Divide by $4x$: $\dfrac{1}{4} = x$

---

22. **D** $\dfrac{2m\sqrt{2n} + m\sqrt{18n}}{m\sqrt{2}}$

Factor terms: $\dfrac{2m\sqrt{2}\sqrt{n} + m\sqrt{9}\sqrt{2}\sqrt{n}}{m\sqrt{2}}$

Cancel common factors: $2\sqrt{n} + \sqrt{9}\sqrt{n}$

Combine like terms: $2\sqrt{n} + 3\sqrt{n} = 5\sqrt{n}$

---

23. **B** Pythagorean Theorem: $1^2 + x^2 = \left(\sqrt{n}\right)^2$

Simplify: $1 + x^2 = n$
Subtract 1: $x^2 = n - 1$
Take square root: $x = \sqrt{n-1}$

Lesson 12: Rational Expressions

Calculating with Rational Expressions

A **rational expression** is a **fraction** in which the numerator and denominator are polynomials. When working with rational expressions, remember the basic rules.

- To **add or subtract** rational expressions, get a **common denominator** and **combine the numerators**.

$$\frac{x+1}{x} + \frac{x}{x-1} = \frac{(x+1)(x-1)}{x(x-1)} + \frac{x^2}{x(x-1)} = \frac{2x^2-1}{x(x-1)}$$

- To **multiply** rational expressions, just **go straight across**.

$$\left(\frac{2x-3}{x^2-1}\right)\left(\frac{x+1}{x}\right) = \frac{(2x-3)(x+1)}{(x^2-1)(x)}$$

$$\frac{x}{x+1} - \frac{1}{x}$$

Which of the following is equivalent to the expression above for all positive values of x ?

A) $\dfrac{x^2-x-1}{x^2+x}$

B) $\dfrac{x^2-x+1}{x^2+x}$

C) $\dfrac{x^2-1}{x^2+x}$

D) x^2-1

(*Medium*)

Get common denominator: $\dfrac{x(x)}{(x+1)(x)} - \dfrac{(x+1)}{(x+1)(x)}$

Simplify: $\dfrac{x^2}{x^2+x} - \dfrac{x+1}{x^2+x}$

Combine numerators: $\dfrac{x^2-x+1}{x^2+x}$

Therefore, the correct answer is A.

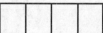

$$\frac{x}{6x-9} - \frac{1}{x}$$

For what value of x does the expression above equal 0 ?

□ □ □ □

(*Medium*)

Express with common denominators:

$$\frac{x^2}{x(6x-9)} - \frac{6x-9}{x(6x-9)}$$

Combine numerators:

$$\frac{x^2-6x+9}{x(6x-9)}$$

Factor the numerator:

$$\frac{(x-3)(x-3)}{x(6x-9)}$$

This numerator can only equal 0 when $x = 3$.

Rational Expressions as Rates

The words **rational**, **rate**, and **ratio** all come from the same Latin root. That's not just a coincidence. **Rational expressions are often used to express rates.**

$$\frac{1}{x} + b = \frac{1}{y}$$

In the equation above, x represents the time, in hours, it takes pump A to fill a standard tank, and y represents the time, in hours, it takes pump A and pump B, working together, to fill the same standard tank. If the equation above represents this situation, then b must represent which of the following?

A)   the time, in hours, it takes pump B, working alone, to fill the standard tank

B)   the portion of the standard tank that pump B fills when the pumps work together to fill the entire standard tank

C)   the rate, in standard tanks per hour, of pump B

D)   the difference between the rates, in standard tanks per hour, of pump B and pump A

(*Medium-hard*) If x is the number of hours it takes pump A to fill the tank, then its rate, in tanks per hour, is $1/x$. Since the rate at which the two pumps work together, $1/y$, is the sum of their rates working separately, b must represent the rate, in tanks per hour, of pump B, and so the correct answer is C.

Kaleena and Jana competed in a road race of d miles. Kaleena finished in t minutes, exactly 2 minutes ahead of Jana. Which of the following expresses how much faster Kaleena's average speed was than Jana's average speed, in miles per hour?

A) $\dfrac{2d}{t^2 + 2t}$

B) $\dfrac{d}{30t^2 + 60t}$

C) $\dfrac{120d}{t^2 + 2t}$

D) $\dfrac{120d}{t^2 - 2t}$

(*Medium-hard*) Kaleena finished a race of d miles in t minutes, so her average speed was $\dfrac{d}{t}$ miles per minute, or $\dfrac{60d}{t}$ miles per hour. If Jana took two minutes longer to finish the race, then her speed was $\dfrac{d}{t+2}$ miles per minute, or $\dfrac{60d}{t+2}$ miles per hour. The difference in their speeds, then, is

$$\frac{60d}{t} - \frac{60d}{t+2} = \frac{60dt + 120d - 60dt}{t(t+2)} = \frac{120d}{t^2 + 2t}.$$

Therefore, the correct answer is D.

Lesson 13: Simplifying Rational Expressions

Simplifying Complex Fractions

Many rational expressions can be simplified by **canceling common factors** or **multiplying top and bottom by a convenient factor**.

If $x = 3a$ and $a \neq 2$, which of the following is equivalent to $\dfrac{x^2 - 36}{(x-6)^2}$?

A) $\dfrac{a+2}{a-2}$

B) $\dfrac{3a+2}{3a-2}$

C) $\dfrac{3a+2}{3a}$

D) $\dfrac{9a^2 - 36}{9a^2 + 36}$

(*Medium*) You might want to substitute first, but it's better to start by simplifying: $\dfrac{x^2 - 36}{(x-6)^2}$

Factor: $\dfrac{(x+6)(x-6)}{(x-6)(x-6)}$

Cancel common factor: $\dfrac{x+6}{x-6}$

Substitute $x = 3a$: $\dfrac{3a+6}{3a-6}$

Divide top and bottom by 3: $\dfrac{a+2}{a-2}$

Therefore, the answer is A.

Alternatively, you could have picked values for x and a that satisfy the conditions, such as $a = 2$ and $x = 6$, and solved by process of elimination.

Bonus: Why does the question mention that $a \neq 2$?

If $\dfrac{2x^2 - 18}{5x^2 - 10x - 15} = \dfrac{a(x+b)}{x+1}$ for all $x > 3$, where a and b are constants, what is the value of ab ?

A) $\dfrac{2}{5}$

B) $\dfrac{3}{5}$

C) $\dfrac{6}{5}$

D) $\dfrac{7}{5}$

(*Hard*) The expression on the left side of the equation is obnoxious and in need of simplification: $\dfrac{2x^2 - 18}{5x^2 - 10x - 15}$

Factor: $\dfrac{2(x-3)(x+3)}{5(x+1)(x-3)}$

Cancel common factor: $\dfrac{2(x+3)}{5(x+1)}$

Divide numerator and denominator by 5: $\dfrac{\frac{2}{5}(x+3)}{x+1}$

This last step, which may seem strange, is important because it shows us how the two sides of the equation "match up." If this equation is to be true *for all $x > 3$*, then $a = \dfrac{2}{5}$ and $b = 3$. Therefore, $ab = \left(\dfrac{2}{5}\right)(3) = \dfrac{6}{5}$, and the correct answer is C.

Lesson 14: Solving Rational Equations

Simplifying Rational Equations

If $x > 0$ and $\dfrac{1}{x-1} - \dfrac{1}{x+1} = 2$, what is the value of x?

[No calculator]

A) $\sqrt{2}$

B) $\sqrt{3}$

C) $\sqrt{5}$

D) $\sqrt{7}$

$$f(x) = x^2 - 3x - 18$$

The function f is defined by the equation above.

If the function h is defined by the equation $h(x) = \dfrac{f(x)}{2x-12}$, for what value of x does $h(x) = 6$?

A) -6

B) -3

C) 0

D) 9

(*Hard*) First, let's simplify the expression for $h(x)$.

$$h(x) = \frac{f(x)}{2x-12}$$

Substitute $f(x) = x^2 - 3x - 18$:

$$h(x) = \frac{x^2 - 3x - 18}{2x - 12}$$

Factor using Product-Sum Method:

$$h(x) = \frac{(x+3)(x-6)}{2(x-6)}$$

Cancel common factor:

$$h(x) = \frac{x+3}{2}$$

Solve for x if $h(x) = 6$:

$$6 = \frac{x+3}{2}$$

Multiply by 2:

$$12 = x + 3$$

Subtract 3:

$$9 = x$$

Therefore, the correct answer is D.

When solving an equation that includes fractions or rational expressions, you may find it helpful to **simplify the equation by multiplying both sides by the "common denominator"** (that is, the common multiple of the denominators).

$$\frac{x}{5} + \frac{1}{x} = 2$$

Multiply by $5x$:

$$5x \times \left(\frac{x}{5} + \frac{1}{x}\right) = 5x \times 2$$

Distribute:

$$\frac{5x^2}{5} + \frac{5x}{x} = 10x$$

Simplify:

$$x^2 + 5 = 10x$$

Notice that, in this case, the equation simplifies to a quadratic, which is relatively easy to work with.

(*Hard*) Let's apply this strategy to our equation:

$$\frac{1}{x-1} - \frac{1}{x+1} = 2$$

Multiply by the common denominator $(x - 1)(x + 1)$, on both

Distribute:

$$(x+1) - (x-1) = 2(x^2 - 1)$$

Simplify:

$$2 = 2x^2 - 2$$

Add 2:

$$4 = 2x^2$$

Divide by 2:

$$2 = x^2$$

Take the square root:

$$\pm\sqrt{2} = x$$

But since the equation states that $x > 0$, the correct answer is A.

Exercise Set 5 (No Calculator)

1

If $\dfrac{1}{3} - \dfrac{1}{5} = \dfrac{y}{9}$, what is the value of y?

2

If $\dfrac{x}{x+1} + \dfrac{1}{x-1} = \dfrac{25}{24}$ and $x > 0$, what is the value of x?

3

If $\dfrac{1}{x-2} - \dfrac{1}{x+2} = \dfrac{8}{5}$, what is the value of x^2?

4

If $2 - \dfrac{1}{z} = -\dfrac{5}{6}$, what is the value of z?

5

Let $g(x) = x^2 - 9x + 18$ and $h(x) = \dfrac{g(x)}{x-a}$, where a is a constant. If $h(4) = \dfrac{1}{12}$, what is the value of a?

6

If $\dfrac{1}{2x-2} - \dfrac{1}{2x+1} = \dfrac{a}{4x^2-2x-b}$ for all values of x greater than 1, what is the value of $a + b$?

7

Which of the following is equivalent to $\dfrac{2}{1-x} + \dfrac{x}{x-1}$ for all x greater than 1?

A) $\dfrac{x+2}{x^2-1}$

B) $\dfrac{x+2}{x-1}$

C) $\dfrac{x-2}{x^2-1}$

D) $\dfrac{x-2}{x-1}$

8

For how many distinct integer values of n is $\dfrac{n+5}{n+2} > 2$?

A) Zero   B) One   C) Two   D) Three

9

If $a = \dfrac{1}{4}x$ and $a > 1$, which of the following is equivalent to $\dfrac{4(x-4)^2}{4x^2-64}$?

A) $\dfrac{a-4}{a+4}$

B) $\dfrac{a^2-4}{a^2+4}$

C) $\dfrac{a-1}{a+1}$

D) $\dfrac{a^2-1}{a^2+1}$

Exercise Set 5 (Calculator)

10

If $\dfrac{x}{5} - \dfrac{3}{x} = 2$, what is the value of $x^2 - 10x$?

11

For how many positive integer values of k is $\dfrac{1}{10^k} > 0.001$?

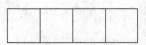

12

If $g(x) = x^2 - 9x + 18$ and $h(x) = \dfrac{g(x)}{x^2 + 3}$, what is the value of $h(9)$?

13

If $\dfrac{1}{x+1} + \dfrac{1}{x-1} = 9$, what is the value of $\dfrac{9x}{x^2 - 1}$?

14

If $\dfrac{c}{c-1} \div \dfrac{c+1}{2c} = \dfrac{10}{c^2 - 1}$, what is the value of c^2 ?

15

If $\dfrac{4x^2 + 1}{2x + 1} = 2x - 1 + \dfrac{a}{2x + 1}$ for all values of x, what is the value of a ?

16

Which of the following is equivalent to $\dfrac{1}{b} - \dfrac{b^2}{2}$ for all positive values of b ?

A) $\dfrac{b^2 - 1}{2 - b}$

B) $\dfrac{b^2 - 1}{2b}$

C) $\dfrac{b^3 - 2}{2b}$

D) $\dfrac{2 - b^3}{2b}$

17

$$\frac{1}{a}-\frac{1}{b}=2$$

$$\frac{1}{a}+\frac{1}{b}=8$$

Given the system above, what is the value of $a + b$?

A) $\dfrac{1}{15}$

B) $\dfrac{1}{8}$

C) $\dfrac{8}{15}$

D) $\dfrac{8}{5}$

18

If one proofreader takes n hours to edit 30 pages and another takes m hours to edit 50 pages, and together they can edit x pages per hour, which of the following equations must be true?

A) $\dfrac{30}{n}+\dfrac{50}{m}=x$

B) $\dfrac{30}{n}+\dfrac{50}{m}=\dfrac{1}{x}$

C) $\dfrac{n}{30}+\dfrac{m}{50}=x$

D) $\dfrac{n}{30}+\dfrac{m}{50}=\dfrac{1}{x}$

EXERCISE SET 5 ANSWER KEY

No Calculator

1. 6/5 or 1.2

$$\frac{1}{3} - \frac{1}{5} = \frac{y}{9}$$

Multiply by 45: $\qquad\qquad 15 - 9 = 5y$
(45 is the least common multiple of the denominators.)
Simplify: $\qquad\qquad\qquad 6 = 5y$
Divide by 5: $\qquad\qquad\qquad 6/5 = y$

---

2. 7

$$\frac{x}{x+1} + \frac{1}{x-1} = \frac{25}{24}$$

Multiply by $24(x+1)(x-1)$:
$$24x(x-1) + 24(x+1) = 25(x+1)(x-1)$$
Distribute: $\qquad 24x^2 - 24x + 24x + 24 = 25x^2 - 25$
Gather like terms: $\qquad\qquad\qquad\quad 0 = x^2 - 49$
Add 49: $\qquad\qquad\qquad\qquad\qquad 49 = x^2$
Take square root: $\qquad\qquad\qquad\quad \pm 7 = x$
Since x must be positive, $x = 7$.

---

3. 13/2 or 6.5

$$\frac{1}{x-2} - \frac{1}{x+2} = \frac{8}{5}$$

Multiply by $5(x-2)(x+2)$:
$$5(x+2) - 5(x-2) = 8(x-2)(x+2)$$
Distribute: $\qquad 5x + 10 - 5x + 10 = 8x^2 - 32$
Subtract 20 and simplify: $\qquad\qquad 0 = 8x^2 - 52$
Add 52: $\qquad\qquad\qquad\qquad\quad 52 = 8x^2$
Divide by 8: $\qquad\qquad 52/8 = 13/2 = x^2$
Remember, the question asks for the value of x^2, not x, so don't worry about taking the square root.

---

4. 6/17 or .353

$$2 - \frac{1}{z} = -\frac{5}{6}$$

Multiply by $6z$: $\qquad\qquad 12z - 6 = -5z$
Add $5z$ and 6: $\qquad\qquad\qquad 17z = 6$
Divide by 17: $\qquad\qquad\qquad z = 6/17$

---

5. 28

$$h(4) = \frac{g(4)}{4-a} = \frac{1}{12}$$

Use definition of g:
$$\frac{4^2 - 9(4) + 18}{4-a} = \frac{1}{12}$$

Simplify:
$$\frac{-2}{4-a} = \frac{1}{12}$$

Cross-multiply: $\qquad\qquad 4 - a = -24$
Add 24 and a: $\qquad\qquad\qquad 28 = a$

---

6. 5

$$\frac{1}{2x-2} - \frac{1}{2x+1}$$

Combine fractions:
$$\frac{(2x+1) - (2x-2)}{(2x-2)(2x+1)}$$

Simplify:
$$\frac{3}{4x^2 - 2x - 2}$$

Since $\dfrac{3}{4x^2 - 2x - 2}$ must equal $\dfrac{a}{4x^2 - 2x - b}$ for all values of x, $a = 3$ and $b = 2$, so $a + b = 5$.

---

7. D

Since $(1 - x) = -(x - 1)$:

$$\frac{2}{1-x} + \frac{x}{x-1} = \frac{-2}{x-1} + \frac{x}{x-1}$$

$$= \frac{x-2}{x-1}$$

---

8. C

$$\frac{n+5}{n+2} > 2$$

Recall from Chapter 7, Lesson 9, on solving inequalities, that we need to consider two conditions. First, if $n + 2$ is positive (that is, $n > -2$), we can multiply on both sides without "flipping" the inequality: $\qquad n + 5 > 2n + 4$
Subtract n and 4: $\qquad\qquad\qquad\qquad 1 > n$
So n must be between -2 and 1, and the integer values of -1 and 0 are both solutions. Next, we consider the possibility $n + 2$ is negative (that is, $n < -2$), and therefore multiplying both sides by $n + 2$ requires "flipping" the inequality:

$$n + 5 < 2n + 4$$

Subtract n and 4: $\qquad\qquad\qquad\qquad 1 < n$
But there are no numbers that are both less than -2 and greater than 1, so this yields no new solutions.

---

9. C

$$\frac{4(x-4)^2}{4x^2 - 64}$$

Factor:
$$\frac{4(x-4)^2}{4(x-4)(x+4)}$$

Cancel common factors:
$$\frac{x-4}{x+4}$$

Substitute $x = 4a$:
$$\frac{4a-4}{4a+4}$$

Cancel common factor:
$$\frac{a-1}{a+1}$$

Calculator

10. 15

$$\frac{x}{5} - \frac{3}{x} = 2$$

Multiply by $5x$: $\qquad\qquad x^2 - 15 = 10x$
Add 15, subtract $10x$: $\qquad x^2 - 10x = 15$
Notice that you should *not* worry about solving for x!

---

11. 2

$$\frac{1}{10^k} > 0.001$$

Use common base: $\qquad\qquad 10^{-k} > 10^{-3}$
Exponential Law #10: $\qquad\qquad -k > -3$
Multiply by -1: $\qquad\qquad\qquad k < 3$
Therefore, the two positive integer solutions are 1 and 2.

12. **3/14 or .214**

$$h(9) = \frac{g(9)}{9^2 + 3}$$

Use definition of g:

$$h(9) = \frac{9^2 - 9(9) + 18}{84}$$

Simplify:

$$h(9) = \frac{18}{84} = \frac{3}{14}$$

---

13. **81/2 or 40.5**

$$\frac{1}{x+1} + \frac{1}{x-1} = 9$$

Combine fractions:

$$\frac{(x+1) + (x+1)}{(x+1)(x-1)} = 9$$

Simplify:

$$\frac{2x}{x^2 - 1} = 9$$

Multiply by 9/2:

$$\frac{9x}{x^2 - 1} = \frac{81}{2}$$

---

14. **5**

$$\frac{c}{c-1} \div \frac{c+1}{2c} = \frac{10}{c^2 - 1}$$

Convert to ×:

$$\frac{c}{c-1} \times \frac{2c}{c+1} = \frac{10}{c^2 - 1}$$

Multiply:

$$\frac{2c^2}{c^2 - 1} = \frac{10}{c^2 - 1}$$

Multiply by $c^2 - 1$: $2c^2 = 10$
Divide by 2: $c^2 = 5$

---

15. **2**   Notice that the right-hand side of the equation is the "proper" form of the "improper" fraction on the left, and that *a* is the remainder when the division of the polynomials is completed:

$$
\begin{array}{r}
2x - 1 \\
2x+1\overline{)\ 4x^2 + 0x + 1} \\
\underline{4x^2 + 2x} \\
-2x + 1 \\
\underline{-2x - 1} \\
2
\end{array}
$$

16. **D**

$$\frac{1}{b} - \frac{b^2}{2}$$

Common denominator:

$$\frac{2}{2b} - \frac{b^3}{2b}$$

Combine:

$$\frac{2 - b^3}{2b}$$

---

17. **C**

$$\frac{1}{a} - \frac{1}{b} = 2$$

$$\frac{1}{a} + \frac{1}{b} = 8$$

Add equations:

$$\frac{2}{a} = 10$$

Multiply by *a*: $2 = 10a$
Divide by 10: $1/5 = a$

Subtract equations:

$$\frac{-2}{b} = -6$$

Multiply by $-b$: $2 = 6b$
Divide by 6: $1/3 = b$

Therefore, $a + b = 1/5 + 1/3 = 8/15$.

---

18. **A** The number of pages they can edit together in an hour must equal the sum of the number of pages they can edit separately. The number of pages the first proofreader can edit per hour is $30/n$, and the number of pages the second proofreader can edit per hour is $50/m$. Since they can edit *x* pages per hour together,

$$\frac{30}{n} + \frac{50}{m} = x.$$

NOTE: You can avoid the most common mistakes with this problem by paying attention to the units of each term. The units of two sides, as well as the unit of each term in a sum or difference, must "match." Notice that the unit for all of the terms is pages/hour.

CHAPTER 10

THE SAT MATH TEST: ADDITIONAL TOPICS

1. Angles and Parallel Lines   409
2. Triangles   411
3. Working in the *xy*-Plane   413
4. The Pythagorean Theorem   415
5. Circles   421
6. Radians, Chords, Arcs, and Sectors   423
7. Areas and Volumes   426
8. Similarity   428
9. Basic Trigonometry   435
10. The Pythagorean Identity   437
11. The Cofunction Identities   438
12. Imaginary and Complex Numbers   441

The SAT Math Test: Additional Topics

What other special topics are included on the SAT Math test?

About 10% (6 out of 58 points) of the SAT Math questions are "Additional Topics" questions. These include topics like

- analyzing triangles using the Pythagorean Theorem
- graphing circles and other figures in the *xy*-plane
- analyzing areas, circumferences, chords, and sectors of circles
- measuring angles and arcs in radians
- working with area and volume and their formulas
- using the theorems of congruence and similarity
- working with basic trigonometric relationships including cofunction identities
- calculating with imaginary and complex numbers

Why are these topics important?

These topics from geometry, trigonometry, and advanced analysis are crucial to work in engineering, physics, architecture, and even design. Although they are not essential to every college major, they do provide tools for understanding and analyzing advanced concepts across the curriculum.

Sound intimidating? It's not.

Some of you have already spent some time in math class studying these topics. If not, the three skills described in these 12 lessons will give you the knowledge and practice you need to master them.

Lesson 1: Angles and Parallel Lines

The Intersecting Lines Theorem

When two lines cross, the **vertical angles are congruent** and **adjacent angles have a sum of 180°**.

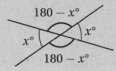

The Parallel Lines Theorem

When two parallel lines are crossed by a third line, they form either eight 90° angles or four acute angles and four obtuse angles, where **all of the acute angles are congruent**, **all of the obtuse angles are congruent**, and **any acute angle is supplementary to any obtuse angle**.

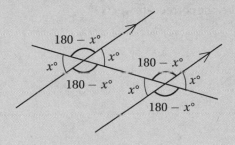

The "ZCUF" Angles

When a parallel lines diagram gets complicated, focus on the angle pairs that form any of the "ZCUF" angles, and memorize their relationships. But remember: **these relationships apply only if the letters include two parallel lines.**

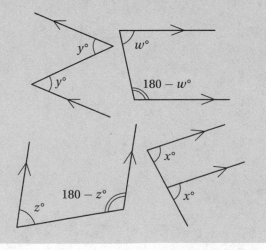

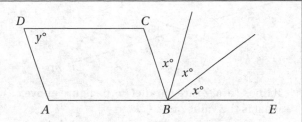

In the figure above, $ABCD$ is a parallelogram, and point B lies on $\overline{AE}$. If $x = 40$, what is the value of y?

A) 40

B) 50

C) 60

D) 70

(*Medium*) Since $ABCD$ is a parallelogram, we can use the Parallel Lines Theorem. Let's mark the diagram with what we know. Note that the consecutive angles in the parallelogram (such as D and C, or D and A) are **"C" or "U"** angle pairs.

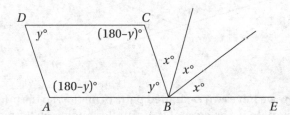

The Parallel Lines Theorem proves that **in a parallelogram, consecutive angles are supplementary and opposite angles are congruent**.

Since $\overline{ABE}$ is a straight (180°) angle:

$$y + x + x + x = 180$$

Substitute $x = 40$ and simplify: $\quad y + 120 = 180$

Subtract 120: $\quad y = 60$

Therefore, the correct answer is C.

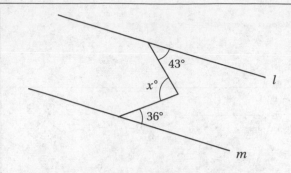

If lines l and m are parallel in the figure above, what is the value of x ?

A) 43

B) 79

C) 86

D) 101

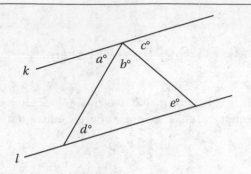

Which of the following statements, if true, is sufficient to prove that line k is parallel to line l?

A) $a = b$

B) $c = e$

C) $b = e$

D) $d = e$

(*Hard*) There are no obvious "ZCUF" angles, but we can fix that by drawing a line parallel to l and m through the vertex.

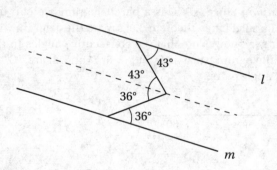

Now we have two **Z-shaped** pairs of angles, so the middle angle is the sum of two smaller angles of 36° and 43°, and therefore $x = 36 + 43 = 79$, and the correct answer is B.

(*Medium*) The only "ZCUF" angle pair is choice B, since the angles measuring $c°$ and $e°$ form a Z shape. If they are congruent, then lines k and l must be parallel. Therefore, the correct answer is B.

Lesson 2: Triangles

Angles in a Triangle Have a Sum of 180°

In any triangle, the **sum of the interior angles is 180°**.

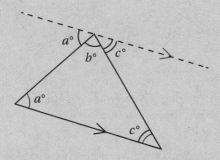

How do we know? Draw any triangle, then draw a line through any vertex that is parallel to the opposite side. This gives us a diagram like the one above. Since the line we've drawn makes a 180° angle, and since the **Z-angle** pairs are congruent, we've proven that $a + b + c = 180$!

Side-Angle Theorem

The **biggest angle** in a triangle is always **across from the biggest side,** and the smallest angle is always across from the smallest side.

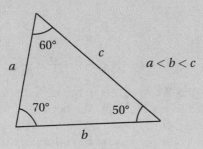

$a < b < c$

Isosceles Triangle Theorem

If **two sides in a triangle are congruent,** the two **angles** across from them are **also congruent.** Conversely, if two angles in a triangle are congruent, the two sides across from them are also congruent.

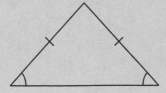

Exterior Angle Theorem

If we extend any side of a triangle, it makes an **exterior angle** with the adjacent side. The measure of any **exterior angle** is the **sum of the two remote interior angles.**

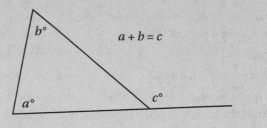

$a + b = c$

The Triangle Inequality

The **sum of any two sides** of a triangle must always be **greater than the third side.** This means that **the length of any side of a triangle must be between the sum and the difference of the other two side lengths.**

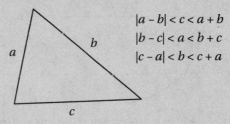

$$|a - b| < c < a + b$$
$$|b - c| < a < b + c$$
$$|c - a| < b < c + a$$

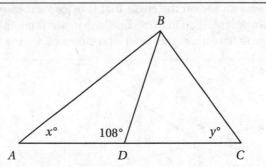

In the figure above, point D is on side AC of triangle ABC. If $AD = DB = DC$, what is the value of $x + y$?

A) 72

B) 90

C) 96

D) 108

(*Medium*) Since angle ADB and angle BDC are supplementary and $AD = DB = DC$, we can use the Isosceles Triangle Theorem to mark up the diagram:

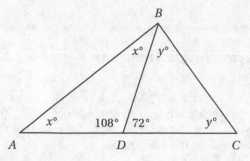

Now let's look at triangle ABC. Since its interior angles must have a sum of $180°$:

$$x + x + y + y = 180$$

Simplify:

$$2x + 2y = 180$$

Divide both sides by 2:

$$x + y = 90$$

So the correct answer is B. Note that this fact is independent of the measures of the other two ($108°$ and $72°$) angles. As long as $AD = DB = DC$, this relationship will hold. We can see these angle relationships if we note that these three segments could all be radii of a circle centered at D.

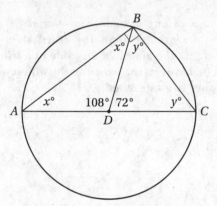

You might remember from geometry class that any **inscribed** angle (an angle inside a circle with a vertex on the circle) **intercepts an arc on the circle that is twice its measure.** Since angle ABC is an inscribed angle that intercepts a $180°$ arc, it must have a measure of $90°$ and therefore, $x + y = 90$.

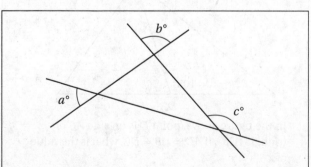

The figure above shows three intersecting lines. What is the value of c in terms of a and b ?

A) $180 - a - b$

B) $180 - a + b$

C) $90 + b - a$

D) $a + b$

(*Easy*) Notice that two of the angles are **vertical** to two interior angles of the triangle, and the other is an **exterior** angle.

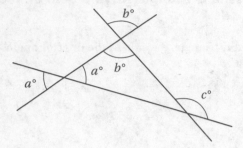

Since the $c°$ angle is an exterior angle to the triangle, the Exterior Angle Theorem tells us that $c = a + b$, so the correct answer is D.

Alternatively, we could just choose reasonable values for a and b, like $a = 50$ and $b = 90$, and then analyze the diagram in terms of these values. This would imply that the interior angles of the triangle are $50°$, $90°$, and $40°$, and $c°$ would then be the measure of the supplement of $40°$, which is $140°$. If we then plug these values for a and b into all of the choices, the only one that yields 140 is D.

> In the xy-plane, the distance from point A to point B is 24 centimeters and the distance from point A to point C is 18 centimeters. Which of the following could <u>not</u> be the distance from point B to point C, in centimeters?
>
> A) 5
>
> B) 6
>
> C) 24
>
> D) 42

(*Medium*) The Triangle Inequality says that the length of any side of a triangle must be **between** the sum and the difference of the other two side lengths. However, these three points might also be **collinear**, which would mean that one of the segment lengths is **equal** to either the sum or the difference of the other two. Therefore, the distance from B to C must be greater than or equal to $24 - 18 = 6$ and less than or equal to $24 + 18 = 42$. The only choice that is outside this range is choice A.

Lesson 3: Working in the xy-Plane

Working in the *xy*-Plane

When working in the *xy*-plane, here are a few tips to keep in mind.

- The area of any figure is just the **number of unit squares that fit inside**.

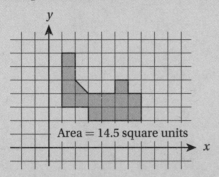

Area = 14.5 square units

- It's often helpful to **draw extra lines**, particularly vertical and horizontal ones, or lines with unique relationships to the given lines.
- The **midpoint** of any segment is just the **average of the endpoints**.

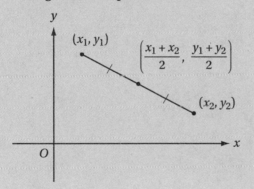

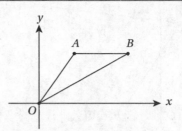

Note: Figure not drawn to scale.

In the *xy*-plane above, points *A* and *B* lie on the graph of the line $y = 6$.

If $\overline{OB}$ has a slope of $\dfrac{1}{2}$ and $AB = 5$, what is the slope of $\overline{OA}$?

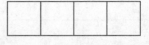

(*Medium-hard*) First, let's use one of the tips and drop two perpendicular segments from *A* and *B* to points *C* and *D*, respectively, on the *x*-axis.

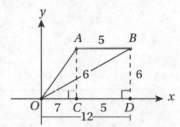

Since *A* and *B* lie on $y = 6$, they are both 6 units from the *x*-axis, and so $AC = BD = 6$. Since the slope of *OB* is 1/2, $BD/OD = 1/2$, and therefore $OD = 12$. Since $AB = 5$, $CD = 5$ also, and therefore $OC = 12 - 5 = 7$. (Don't worry that $\overline{OC}$ looks shorter than $\overline{CD}$ in the diagram. Remember, the figure is not drawn to scale!) This gives us everything we need to find the slope of $\overline{OA}$, which connects (0, 0) to (7, 6). By the slope formula from Chapter 7, Lesson 5:

$$\text{slope} = \frac{6-0}{7-0} = \frac{6}{7} = .857$$

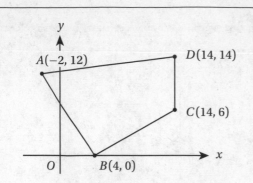

In the figure above, point M (not shown) is the midpoint of $\overline{AB}$ and point N (not shown) is the midpoint of $\overline{CD}$. What is the slope of $\overline{MN}$?

(*Medium*) To find the midpoint of a segment, we just take the average of the endpoints. Point M, the midpoint of $\overline{AB}$, has coordinates $\left(\dfrac{-2+4}{2}, \dfrac{12+0}{2}\right) = (1, 6)$, and point N, the midpoint of $\overline{CD}$, has coordinates $\left(\dfrac{14+14}{2}, \dfrac{6+14}{2}\right) = (14, 10)$.

Therefore, the slope of $\overline{MN}$ is $\dfrac{10-6}{14-1} = \dfrac{4}{13}$ or 0.307 or 0.308.

Lesson 4: The Pythagorean Theorem

The Pythagorean Theorem

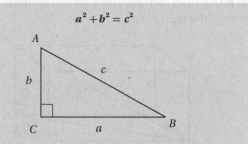

$$a^2 + b^2 = c^2$$

If a, b, and c are the lengths of the sides of a right triangle where c is the longest side, then $a^2 + b^2 = c^2$.

Special Right Triangles

On geometry questions, watch out for four kinds of special right triangles: **45°-45°-90° triangles**, **30°-60°-90° triangles**, **3-4-5 triangles**, and **5-12-13 triangles**.

Memorize their side-side relationships and side-angle relationships so that you can use them to simplify problems.

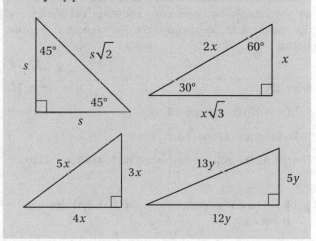

The Distance Formula

The Pythagorean Theorem also gives us the **distance formula**.

$$d = \sqrt{(x_2 - x_1)^2 + (y_2 - y_1)^2}$$

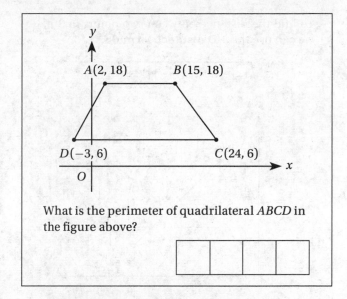

What is the perimeter of quadrilateral $ABCD$ in the figure above?

(*Medium*) The **perimeter** of a figure is the distance around its edges. We can find AB and DC because the length of a horizontal segment is just the absolute difference of the x-coordinates of its endpoints. Therefore, $AB = 15 - 2 = 13$ and $DC = 24 - (-3) = 27$. To find AD and BC, we can drop two vertical lines from points A and B to the bottom edge. This shows that AD and BC are hypotenuses of two right triangles:

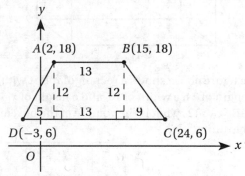

So, we can find AD and BC with the Pythagorean Theorem.

According to our diagram:
$$AD^2 = 5^2 + 12^2 = 169$$
$$BC^2 = 9^2 + 12^2 = 225$$

Note that triangle on the left is a 5-12-13 right triangle, and the triangle on the right is a 3-4-5 right triangle.

Take the square root:
$$AD = 13$$
$$BC = 15$$

So, the perimeter of $ABCD$ is $13 + 15 + 27 + 13 = 68$.

The 3-D Distance Formula

To find the distance between two points in 3-d, we can use the **3-D distance formula**.

$$y = \sqrt{(x_2 - x_1)^2 + (y_2 - y_1)^2 + (z_2 - z_1)^2}$$

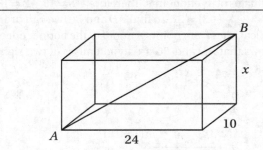

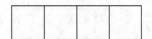

The figure above shows a rectangular box with a length of 24, a width of 10, and a height of x. If $AB = \sqrt{712}$, what is the volume of the box, in cubic units?

(*Hard*) The most straightforward way to approach the problem is to use a form of the 3-D distance formula to find x, and then use the volume formula for a box.

But rather than just applying a formula blindly, let's walk through the reasoning.

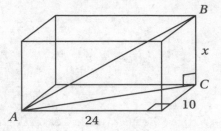

Let's draw $\overline{AC}$ connecting the opposite vertices of the base. This is the hypotenuse of a right triangle with legs of 10 and 24. If you're on the ball, you'll note that these fit the pattern of a 5-12-13 triangle with all the sides doubled, and so $AC = 26$. If not, no worries: just use the Pythagorean Theorem:

$$10^2 + 24^2 = AC^2$$

Simplify: $676 = AC^2$

Take the square root of both sides: $26 = AC$

Now we turn our attention to triangle ABC, which is also a right triangle. Since we know the length of one leg and the hypotenuse, we can use the Pythagorean Theorem again:

$$26^2 + x^2 = (\sqrt{712})^2$$

Simplify: $676 + x^2 = 712$

Subtract 676 from both sides: $x^2 = 36$

Take the square root of both sides: $x = 6$

Therefore, the volume of the box is $(24)(10)(6) = 1440$.

This is the reasoning behind the **3-D Pythagorean Theorem**.

$$a^2 + b^2 + c^2 = d^2$$

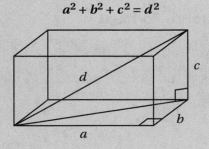

Exercise Set 1: Geometry (No Calculator)

1

In the figure above, $MNOP$ is a square and Q is the midpoint of $\overline{MN}$. If $QO = \dfrac{\sqrt{20}}{3}$, what is the area of square $MNOP$?

2

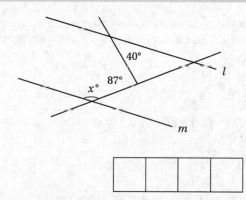

Lines l and m are parallel in the figure above. What is the value of x?

3

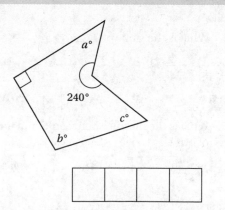

In the figure above, what is the value of $a + b + c$?

4

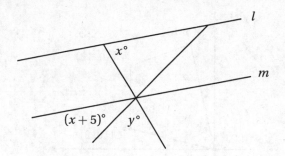

Lines l and m are parallel in the figure above. Which of the following expresses the value of y in terms of x?

A) $95 - 2x$

B) $165 - 2x$

C) $175 - 2x$

D) $185 - 2x$

5

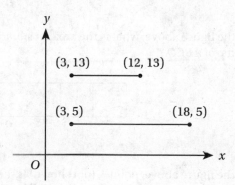

In the figure above, what is the distance between the midpoints (not shown) of the two line segments?

A) $\sqrt{68}$ B) $\sqrt{73}$ C) $\sqrt{76}$

D) $\sqrt{78}$

6

What is the perimeter of an equilateral triangle inscribed in a circle with circumference 24π ?

A) $36\sqrt{2}$ B) $30\sqrt{3}$

C) $36\sqrt{3}$ D) $24\sqrt{6}$

Exercise Set 1: Geometry (Calculator)

Questions 7–9 are based on the figure below.

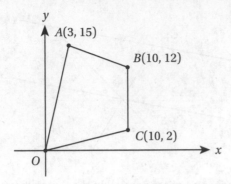

Note: Figure not drawn to scale.

7

In the figure above, what is the perimeter of quadrilateral *ABCO*, to the nearest integer?

8

In the figure above, what is the area, in square units, of *ABCO* ?

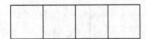

9

In the figure above, point *K* (not shown) is the midpoint of $\overline{OA}$, and point *M* (not shown) is the midpoint of $\overline{AB}$. What is the slope of $\overline{KM}$?

10

In the *xy*-plane, point *H* has coordinates (2, 1) and point *J* has coordinates (11, 13). If $\overline{HK}$ is parallel to the *x*-axis and $\overline{JK}$ is parallel to the *y*-axis, what is the perimeter of triangle *HJK* ?

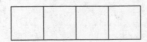

11

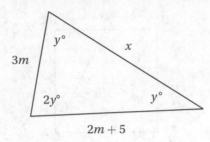

Note: Figure not drawn to scale.

In the figure above, what is the value of *x* ?

A) $5\sqrt{2}$ B) $5\sqrt{3}$ C) $15\sqrt{2}$ D) $15\sqrt{3}$

Questions 12–15 are based on the information below.

In the *xy*-plane, *ABCD* is a square. Point *A* has coordinates (−1, 2) and point *B* has coordinates (3, 5).

12

Which of the following could be the coordinates of *C* ?

A) (0, 9)   B) (6, 0)   C) (2, −2)   D) (−4, 6)

13

What is the area of square *ABCD* ?

A) 25   B) 28   C) 30   D) 32

14

What is the slope of $\overline{BC}$?

A) $-\dfrac{4}{3}$ B) $-\dfrac{3}{4}$ C) $\dfrac{3}{4}$ D) $\dfrac{4}{3}$

15

What is the distance between *C* and the midpoint of $\overline{AB}$?

A) $\dfrac{\sqrt{50}}{4}$ B) $\dfrac{\sqrt{125}}{4}$ C) $\dfrac{\sqrt{50}}{2}$

D) $\dfrac{\sqrt{125}}{2}$

EXERCISE SET 1: GEOMETRY ANSWER KEY

No Calculator

1. **16/9 or 1.77 or 1.78** If we define x as the length of $\overline{QN}$, then the length of one side of the square is $2x$, and so the area of square $MNOP$ is $(2x)(2x) = 4x^2$. To find this value, we can apply the Pythagorean Theorem to right triangle QNO:

$$x^2 + (2x)^2 = \left(\frac{\sqrt{20}}{3}\right)^2$$

Simplify:

$$5x^2 = \frac{20}{9}$$

Divide by 5:

$$x^2 = \frac{20}{45} = \frac{4}{9}$$

Multiply by 4:

$$4x^2 = \frac{16}{9} = 1.77 \text{ or } 1.78$$

2. **133** The key is to notice simple relationships between angles until we get around to x.

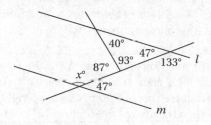

3. **210** Draw three lines as shown:

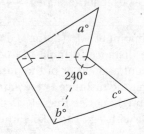

Since the polygon divides into 3 triangles, the sum of its internal angles is $(3)(180°) = 540°$. Therefore $a + b + c + 240 + 90 = 540$, and so $a + b + c = 210$.

4. **C** Using the Crossed Lines Theorem and the Parallel Lines Theorem, we can mark up the diagram like this:

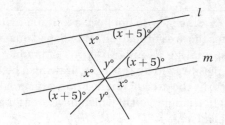

This shows that $x + y + x + 5 = 180$, and so $y = 175 - 2x$.

5. **B** The midpoint of the top segment is $\left(\frac{3+12}{2}, \frac{13+13}{2}\right) = \left(\frac{15}{2}, 13\right)$, and the midpoint of the bottom segment is $\left(\frac{3+18}{2}, \frac{5+5}{2}\right) = \left(\frac{21}{2}, 5\right)$, therefore, the distance between them is

$$\sqrt{\left(\frac{21}{2} - \frac{15}{2}\right)^2 + (13 - 5)^2} = \sqrt{3^2 + 8^2} = \sqrt{73}.$$

6. **C** To solve this problem we must draw a diagram and find the relationship between the radius of the circle and the sides of the triangle. By the Isosceles Triangle Theorem, if all three sides of a triangle are congruent, then all three angles must be congruent. Since these angles also must have a sum of 180°, they must each be 60°. If we draw the bisectors of each of these angles, we divide the triangle into six smaller triangles. These smaller triangles are congruent 30°-60°-90° triangles, as shown here:

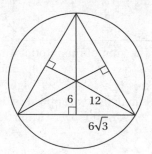

Since the circumference of the circle $(2\pi r)$ is 24π, its radius is 12. Since each of the hypotenuses of our right triangles is also a radius of the circle, we can find all of the sides of these triangles using the 30°-60°-90° relationships. Each side of the equilateral triangle is therefore $2(6\sqrt{3}) = 12\sqrt{3}$, and its perimeter is therefore

$$3(12\sqrt{3}) = 36\sqrt{3}).$$

Calculator

7. **43** Using the distance formula, we can calculate the lengths of each segment. $OA = \sqrt{234} \approx 15.30$, $AB = \sqrt{58} \approx 7.61$, $BC = 10$, and $OC = \sqrt{104} \approx 10.20$. Therefore, the perimeter is approximately $15.30 + 7.61 + 10 + 10.20 = 43.11$, which rounds to 43.

---

8. **107** Since we do not have a formula that directly calculates the area of such an odd-shaped quadrilateral, we must analyze its area in terms of simpler shapes. The simplest way to do this is by drawing a box around it. This turns the area of interest into a rectangle minus three right triangles, all of which have areas that can be easily calculated.

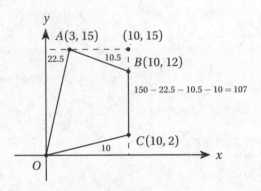

---

9. **6/5 or 1.2** The midpoint of $\overline{OA}$ is (1.5, 7.5) and the midpoint of $\overline{AB}$ is (6.5, 13.5); therefore, the slope of the segment between them is 6/5.

---

10. **36** If point K is on the same horizontal line as (2, 1), it must have a y-coordinate of 1, and if it is on the same vertical line as (11, 13), it must have an x-coordinate of 11. Therefore, K is the point (11, 1), and so $HK = 9$, $JK = 12$, and $HJ = \sqrt{9^2 + 12^2} = \sqrt{225} = 15$. Notice that it is a 3-4-5 triangle!

---

11. **C** Since the sum of the interior angles of any triangle is $180°$, $y + y + 2y = 4y = 180$, and therefore $y = 45$. Therefore, this is a $45°$-$45°$-$90°$ right triangle. Since two angles are equal, the two opposite sides must also be equal, so $3m = 2m + 5$ and so $m = 5$ and the two legs each

have measure 15. Using the Pythagorean Theorem or the $45°$-$45°$-$90°$ shortcut, we can see that $x = 15\sqrt{2}$.

---

12. **A** The key to questions 12 through 15 is a good diagram in the xy-plane that represents the given information:

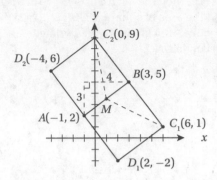

If $ABCD$ is a square, then the points A, B, C, and D must appear *in that order* around the square. Notice that to get from point A to point B, we must move 4 units to the right and 3 units up. This means that, in order to get to point C along a perpendicular of the same length, we must go either *3 units right and 4 units down*, or *3 units left and 4 units up*. This puts us either at (6, 1) or (0, 9).

---

13. **A** The diagram shows that AB is the length of the hypotenuse of a right triangle with legs 3 and 4. You should recognize this as the special 3-4-5 right triangle. If $AB = 5$, then the area of the square is $5^2 = 25$.

---

14. **A** Notice that the slope of $\overline{BC}$ is the same regardless of which option we choose for C. In either case, the slope formula tells us that the slope is $-4/3$.

---

15. **D** The midpoint of $\overline{AB}$ (point M above) is (1, 3.5). We can use the distance formula to find the distance between this point and either of the possible locations of C. (Notice that the distance is the same either way.) Alternately, we might notice that MC is the hypotenuse of a right triangle with legs 5 and 2.5. Either way, we get a value of $\dfrac{\sqrt{125}}{2}$.

Lesson 5: Circles

Equations of Circles

Another application of the Pythagorean Theorem is the equation of a circle. Because a circle is defined as the set of all points in a plane that are a fixed distance, r, from the center (h, k), the Pythagorean Theorem gives us the equation

$$(x - h)^2 + (y - k)^2 = r^2$$

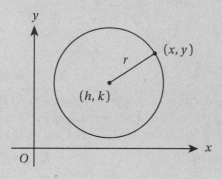

Which of the following equations represents a circle in the xy-plane that passes through the point $(1, 5)$ and has a center of $(3, 2)$?

A) $(x - 3)^2 + (y - 2)^2 = \sqrt{13}$

B) $(x - 3)^2 + (y - 2)^2 = 13$

C) $(x - 1)^2 + (y - 5)^2 = 13$

D) $(x - 3)^2 + (y - 2)^2 = 25$

(*Easy*) Since our circle has a center at $(3, 2)$, its equation must have the form $(x - 3)^2 + (y - 2)^2 = r^2$, which eliminates choice C. Now we can just plug in the point $(1, 5)$ and solve:

$$(1 - 3)^2 + (5 - 2)^2 = r^2$$

Simplify: $13 = r^2$

Therefore, the equation is $(x - 3)^2 + (y - 2)^2 = 13$, and the correct answer is B.

Circumference and Area of Circles

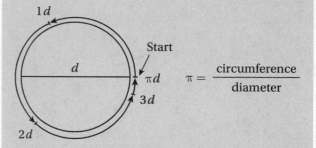

$$\text{circumference} = \pi d = 2\pi r$$

$$\pi = \frac{\text{circumference}}{\text{diameter}}$$

The number π ($\approx 3.14159...$) is defined as the ratio of the circumference of any circle to its diameter.

$$\pi = \frac{\text{circumference}}{\text{diameter}} = \frac{\text{circumference}}{2r}$$

$$\text{circumference} = 2\pi r$$

$$\text{area} = \pi r^2$$

If we cut any circle into tiny enough sectors, and reassemble them as shown below, we can create a parallelogram-like shape that has a height of r and a length that is half of the circumference, or πr.

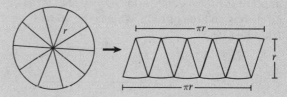

Since the area of any parallelogram is equal to its base times its height, the area of a circle is $(\pi r)(r) = \pi r^2$.

What is the area, in square centimeters, of a circle with a circumference of 16π centimeters?

A) 8π

B) 16π

C) 32π

D) 64π

(*Easy*) Circumference is 16π: $2\pi r = 16\pi$

Divide by 2π: $r = 8$

Therefore, the area is $\pi r^2 = \pi(8)^2 = 64\pi$, so the correct answer is D.

Tangents to Circles

A **tangent** line to a curve is a line that touches the curve at only one point. **Any tangent line to a circle must be perpendicular to the radius at the point of tangency.**

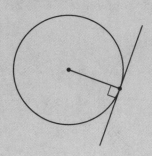

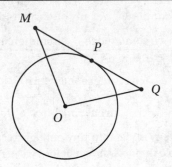

In the figure above, $\overline{MQ}$ is tangent to the circle at point P, $MO = \sqrt{269}$, and $OQ = \sqrt{244}$. If the circle has an area of 100π, what is the area of triangle MOQ?

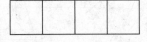

(*Hard*) Draw radius $\overline{OP}$. Since this is a radius to the point of tangency, it must be perpendicular to $\overline{MQ}$. Let's also indicate the given measures.

The area of the circle is 100π: $\qquad\qquad \pi(OP)^2 = 100\pi$

Divide both sides by π: $\qquad\qquad\qquad (OP)^2 = 100$

Take the square root of both sides: $\qquad\qquad OP = 10$

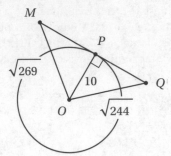

Notice that $\overline{OP}$ is the height of triangle MOQ if $\overline{MQ}$ is taken as its base. To find MQ, we can use the Pythagorean Theorem to find MP and PQ and just add them together.

For triangle OPM: $\qquad\qquad 10^2 + (MP)^2 = (\sqrt{269})^2$

For triangle OPQ: $\qquad\qquad 10^2 + (PQ)^2 = (\sqrt{244})^2$

Simplify: $\qquad\qquad\qquad\qquad 100 + (MP)^2 = 269$

$\qquad\qquad\qquad\qquad\qquad 100 + (PQ)^2 = 244$

Subtract 100 from both sides: $\qquad\qquad (MP)^2 = 169$

$\qquad\qquad\qquad\qquad\qquad\quad (PQ)^2 = 144$

Take the square root of both sides: $\qquad\qquad MP = 13$

$\qquad\qquad\qquad\qquad\qquad\qquad PQ = 12$

So $MQ = MP + PQ = 13 + 12 = 25$, and the area of triangle $MOQ = \dfrac{bh}{2} = \dfrac{25 \times 10}{2} = 125$.

Lesson 6: Radians, Chords, Arcs, and Sectors

Radians

A **radian** is a unit for measuring angles. It's just the radius of a circle used as a "measuring stick" for measuring arcs.

A radian measure is just the ratio of an arc to a radius. To find the radian measure of any angle, just think of the vertex of that angle as the center of a circle (it doesn't matter how big), then **find the measure of the arc that the angle intercepts on the circle and divide it by the radius.**

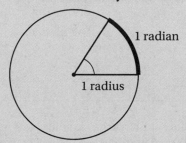

1 radian

1 radius

Because **circumference = 2πr,** a full rotation of 360° equals 2π radians, so

$$180° = \pi \text{ radians}$$

and we can use $\dfrac{\pi \text{ radians}}{180°}$ as a conversion factor to convert a degree measure to radians, and $\dfrac{180°}{\pi \text{ radians}}$ as a conversion factor to convert a radian measure to degrees.

Take some time to memorize the radian measures of some common right-triangle degree measures.

$$30° = 30° \times \frac{\pi \text{ radians}}{180°} = \frac{\pi}{6} \text{ radians}$$

$$45° = 45° \times \frac{\pi \text{ radians}}{180°} = \frac{\pi}{4} \text{ radians}$$

$$60° = 60° \times \frac{\pi \text{ radians}}{180°} = \frac{\pi}{3} \text{ radians}$$

$$90° = 90° \times \frac{\pi \text{ radians}}{180°} = \frac{\pi}{2} \text{ radians}$$

Why the heck do we need radians? Why don't we measure all angles in degrees? Because radians simplify many math and science formulas. We divide a circle into 360 pieces only because 360 is close to the number of days in an Earth-year. But radians come directly from the properties of a circle.

What is the degree measure of an angle that measures 4.5 radians?

A) $4.5\pi°$

B) $\dfrac{\pi}{40}°$

C) $\dfrac{810°}{\pi}$

D) $\dfrac{4\pi°}{9}$

(*Medium*) Here, we just need to convert radians to degrees by using the conversion factor: 4.5 radians × $\dfrac{180°}{\pi \text{ radians}} = \dfrac{810°}{\pi}$, so the correct answer is C.

Chords

A **chord** is a line segment connecting two points on a circle. The **perpendicular** segment from the center of the circle to a chord **always bisects that chord.**

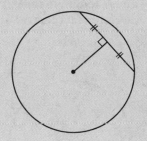

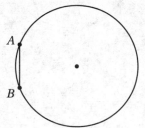

The circle above has an area of 100π square centimeters. If $AB = 8$, how far is $\overline{AB}$ from the center of the circle?

A) 6

B) 8

C) $6\sqrt{2}$

D) $2\sqrt{21}$

(*Medium*) First, let's draw three extra line segments:

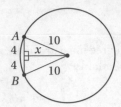

Since the area $= \pi r^2 = 100\pi$, $r = 10$. The perpendicular from the center to the chord is the distance from the center to the chord. This segment also bisects the chord, dividing it into two equal segments of 4 centimeters each. This allows us to use the Pythagorean Theorem to find this distance: $4^2 + x^2 = 10^2$

Simplify: $16 + x^2 = 100$

Subtract 16 from both sides: $x^2 = 84$

Take the square root of both sides:

$$x = \sqrt{84} = \sqrt{4}\sqrt{21} = 2\sqrt{21}$$

Therefore, the correct answer is D.

Arcs

An **arc** is just **a portion of a circumference**. Every arc has a corresponding **central angle**.

The ratio of an arc length to the circumference is equal to the ratio of its central angle to 360° (or 2π radians).

$$\frac{m\widehat{AB}}{2\pi r} = \frac{x}{360}$$

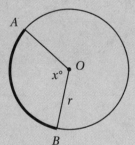

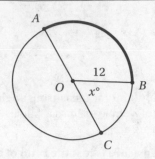

Note: Figure not drawn to scale.

In the figure above, AC is a diameter of the circle with center O, $OB = 12$, and the length of arc AB is 7π. What is the value of x?

A) 60

B) 72

C) 75

D) 78

(*Medium*) Since the circle has a radius of 12, its circumference is $2\pi(12) = 24\pi$, and so arc $AC = 12\pi$. If arc $AB = 7\pi$, then the length of arc BC is $12\pi - 7\pi = 5\pi$. Since the central angle of $x°$ is the same fraction of 360° as its arc BC is to the entire circumference,

$$\frac{x}{360} = \frac{5\pi}{24\pi}$$

Cross-multiply: $24\pi x = 1800\pi$

Divide by 24π: $x = 75$

Therefore, the correct answer is C.

Sectors

A **sector** is a "pie slice" of a circle.

The ratio of a sector area to the area of the circle is equal to the ratio of its central angle to 360° (or 2π radians).

$$\frac{\text{area of sector}}{\pi r^2} = \frac{x}{360}$$

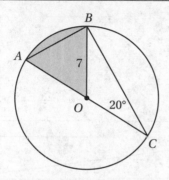

(*Medium-hard*) Since $\overline{OA}$, $\overline{OB}$, and $\overline{OC}$ are all radii, triangles AOB and BOC are isosceles. Therefore, we can find all the angles with the Isosceles Triangle Theorem and the Angle Sum Theorem:

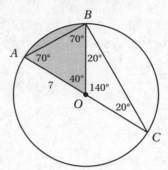

Since the central angle of the sector is 40°, the area of the sector is $\frac{40°}{360°} = \frac{1}{9}$ the area of the circle. Since the area of the circle is $\pi(7)^2 = 49\pi$, the area of the sector is $\frac{1}{9}(49\pi) = \frac{49\pi}{9}$ square units. Therefore, the correct answer is D.

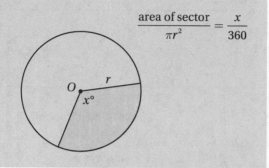

Note: Figure not drawn to scale.

In the figure above, AC is a diameter of the circle with center O and $OB = 7$. If the measure of ACB is 20°, what is the area of the shaded sector?

A) $\dfrac{7\pi}{6}$

B) $\dfrac{14\pi}{9}$

C) $\dfrac{49\pi}{12}$

D) $\dfrac{49\pi}{9}$

Lesson 7: Areas and Volumes

Reference Information

Every SAT Math section includes the following **reference information** on the first page. Use it when you need it!

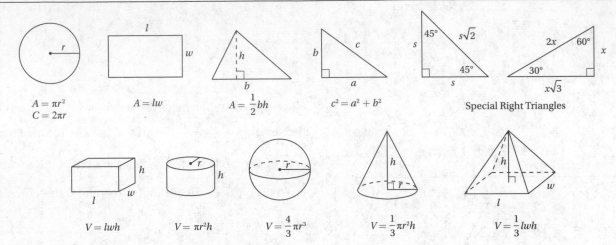

$A = \pi r^2$
$C = 2\pi r$

$A = lw$

$A = \frac{1}{2}bh$

$c^2 = a^2 + b^2$

Special Right Triangles

$V = lwh$

$V = \pi r^2 h$

$V = \frac{4}{3}\pi r^3$

$V = \frac{1}{3}\pi r^2 h$

$V = \frac{1}{3}lwh$

The number of degrees of arc in a circle is 360.
The number of radians of arc in a circle is 2π.
The sum of the measures in degrees of the angles of a triangle is 180.

What is the area, in square units, of the right triangle above?

A) $5\sqrt{6}$

B) $10\sqrt{6}$

C) $\dfrac{5\sqrt{74}}{2}$

D) $5\sqrt{74}$

(*Medium*) By the Pythagorean Theorem, the missing side of the triangle is $\sqrt{24} = 2\sqrt{6}$, so the area of the triangle is $\frac{1}{2}(2\sqrt{6})(5) = 5\sqrt{6}$, and the correct answer is A.

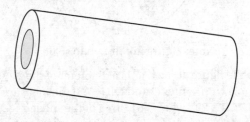

The figure above shows a wooden cylindrical tube with a length of 10 centimeters and a diameter of 4 centimeters. It has a cylindrical hole with a diameter of 2 centimeters that extends 40% of the length of the tube. If the density of the wood is 4.2 grams per cubic centimeter, what is the mass of this tube, to the nearest gram?

A) 151 grams

B) 343 grams

C) 468 grams

D) 475 grams

(*Medium*) The large cylinder has a radius of 2 and a length of 10, so its volume is $\pi(2)^2(10) = 40\pi$. The cylindrical hole has a radius of 1 and a length of $(.040)(10) = 4$, so the volume of the hole is $\pi(1)^2(4) = 4\pi$. Therefore, the total volume of the closed tube is $40\pi - 4\pi = 36\pi \approx 113.1$. Since the mass is equal to the volume times the density, its mass is $(113.1)(4.2) = 475.02$ grams, so the correct answer is D.

The Strange Area Rule

If you're asked to find the area of a figure that doesn't match a given area formula—rectangle, triangle, or circle—**think of the area as the sum or difference of simpler shapes**.

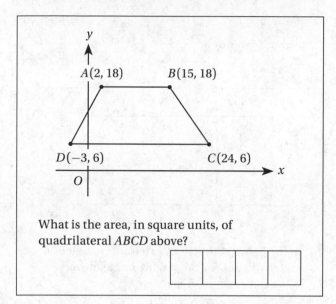

What is the area, in square units, of quadrilateral *ABCD* above?

(*Medium*) The Reference Information on the SAT doesn't give us any formula for calculating the area of a **trapezoid** (and don't even worry if you forgot the technical name for the shape), but that's okay. All we need to know is that we can look at this area in two different ways: as **a rectangle plus two right triangles**:

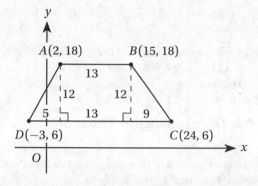

or as **a bigger rectangle minus two right triangles**:

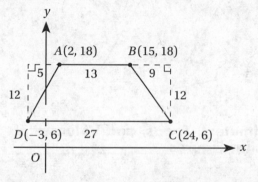

We should get the same result with either method. With the first method, the area of the trapezoid is the area of the rectangle plus the areas of two right triangles. This gives us a total area of $(12)(13) + (1/2)(5)(12) + (1/2)(9)(12) = 156 + 30 + 54 = 240$. With the second method, the area of the trapezoid is the area of the large rectangle minus the areas of the two right triangles. This gives us a total area of $(12)(27) - (1/2)(5)(12) - (1/2)(9)(12) = 324 - 30 - 54 = 240$.

Lesson 8: Similarity

Similarity

Similar figures have the same shape. If two shapes are similar, **all corresponding angles are congruent, and all corresponding sides are proportional**.

On the SAT, **always look out for similar triangles**, because they allow you to set up equations based on **congruent angles** or **proportional sides**.

The AA (Angle-Angle) Theorem

If two triangles have two congruent pairs of corresponding angles, then the triangles are similar, and all corresponding sides are proportional.

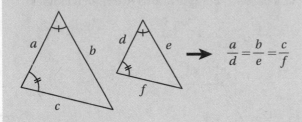

$$\frac{a}{d} = \frac{b}{e} = \frac{c}{f}$$

Perimeters, Areas, and Volumes of Similar Figures

- If two **similar polygons** have corresponding sides in a ratio of *a:b*, then their **perimeters** have a ratio of ***a:b***.
- If two **similar polygons** have corresponding sides in a ratio of *a:b*, then their **areas** have a ratio of ***a²:b²***.
- If two **similar solids** have corresponding sides in a ratio of *a:b*, then their **volumes** have a ratio of ***a³:b³***.

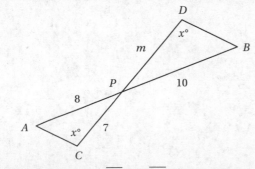

In the figure above, $\overline{AB}$ and $\overline{CD}$ are line segments that intersect at point *P*. What is the value of *m*?

(*Medium*) Since the vertical angles ∠*APC* and ∠*BPD* are congruent, the two triangles are **similar** by the AA Theorem, so the corresponding sides are proportional:

$$\frac{8}{10} = \frac{7}{m}$$

Cross-multiply: $8m = 70$

Divide both sides by 8: $m = \dfrac{70}{8} = 8.75$

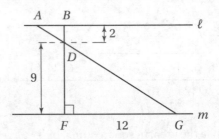

In the figure above, line ℓ is parallel to line *m* and segment *BF* is perpendicular to line *m*. What is the length of segment *AG* ?

(*Medium-hard*) To find *AG*, we can find *AD* and *DG* and add them together. To find *DG*, we can use the Pythagorean Theorem or just note that triangle *DFG* is in the 3-4-5 triangle family, and so *DG* = 15. The two triangles are similar by the AA Theorem, because vertical angles are congruent and angles *ABD* and *DFG* are both right angles. Since *BD* and *DF* are corresponding sides, the ratio of sides is $\dfrac{2}{9}$ and therefore $AD = \dfrac{2}{9}(15) = \dfrac{30}{9} = \dfrac{10}{3}$. Adding *DG* and *AD* gives $15 + \dfrac{10}{3} = \dfrac{55}{3}$ or 18.3.

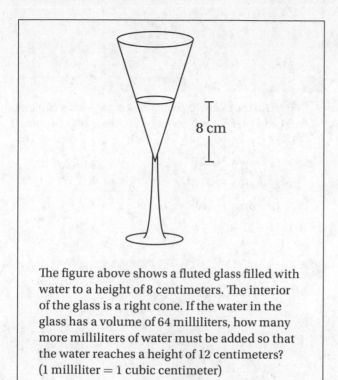

The figure above shows a fluted glass filled with water to a height of 8 centimeters. The interior of the glass is a right cone. If the water in the glass has a volume of 64 milliliters, how many more milliliters of water must be added so that the water reaches a height of 12 centimeters? (1 milliliter = 1 cubic centimeter)

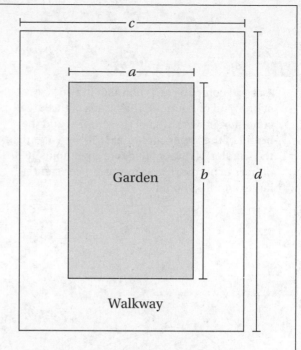

The figure above shows a scale drawing of a rectangular garden surrounded by a walkway that is 6 feet wide. If the ratio of a to b is 5:8, and the ratio of c to d is 3:4, what is the area of the garden (not including the walkway), in square feet?

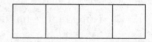

(*Hard*) Many students will make this problem harder by using the cone volume formula ($V = \frac{1}{3}\pi r^2 h$). This is messy and unnecessary. Instead, note that the original volume of water and the final volume of water are **similar cones**. Since the heights of these cones are in a ratio of 12:8, or 3:2, each length in the larger cone is 1.5 times the corresponding length in the smaller cone. By the "ratio of volumes" theorem on the previous page, this means that the volume of the larger cone is $(1.5)^3 = 3.375$ times the volume of the smaller one. Therefore, the final volume is $3.375(64) = 216$ milliliters, which means we must add $216 - 64 = 152$ more milliliters of water.

(*Hard*) Since the ratio of the width of the garden to its length is 5 to 8, let's call the width of the garden $5x$ and the length of the garden $8x$, where all lengths are in feet. Now, since the walkway is 6 feet wide all around, $c = 5x + 6 + 6 = 5x + 12$ feet and $d = 8x + 6 + 6 = 8x + 12$ feet. Since we are given the ratio of these two lengths, we can set up an equation and solve.

$$\frac{5x + 12}{8x + 12} = \frac{3}{4}$$

Use the Law of Cross-Multiplication: $20x + 48 = 24x + 36$

Subtract $20x$ and 36 from both sides: $12 = 4x$

Divide both sides by 4: $3 = x$

Since the length and width of the garden are $5x$ and $8x$, the dimensions are $5(3) = 15$ feet and $8(3) = 24$ feet, and so the area of the garden is $(15)(24) = 360$ square feet.

Exercise Set 2: Geometry (No Calculator)

1

A cereal company sells oatmeal in two sizes of cylindrical containers. The radius of the larger container is twice that of the smaller, and the height of the larger container is 50% greater than the smaller. If the smaller container holds 10 ounces of oatmeal, how many ounces can the larger container hold?

2

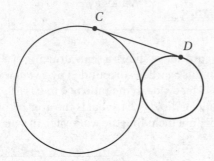

Note: Figure not drawn to scale.

In the figure above, $\overline{CD}$ is tangent to both circles, which are tangent to each other. If the smaller circle has a circumference of 4π and the larger circle has a circumference of 16π, what is the length of $\overline{CD}$?

3

What is the area, in square inches, of a circle with diameter $6\pi^2$ inches?

A) $9\pi^4$ B) $9\pi^5$ C) $36\pi^4$ D) $36\pi^5$

4

What is the length of the longest line segment that connects two vertices of a rectangular box that is 6 units wide, 4 units long, and 2 units tall?

A) $\sqrt{12}$ B) $\sqrt{48}$ C) $\sqrt{56}$

D) $\sqrt{58}$

5

Which of the following equations represents a circle in the xy-plane that intersects the x-axis at $(3, 0)$ and $(9, 0)$?

A) $(x - 6)^2 + (y - 4)^2 = 25$

B) $(x - 3)^2 + (y - 9)^2 = 25$

C) $(x - 6)^2 + (y - 4)^2 = 36$

D) $(x - 3)^2 + (y - 9)^2 = 36$

6

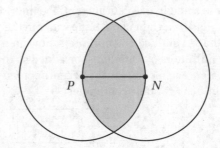

In the figure above, P and N are the centers of the circles and $PN = 6$. What is the area of the shaded region?

A) $18\pi - 9\sqrt{3}$ B) $24\pi - 9\sqrt{3}$

C) $24\pi - 18\sqrt{3}$ D) $36\pi - 18\sqrt{3}$

7

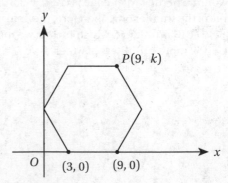

The diagram above shows a hexagon with all sides congruent and all angles congruent. What is the value of k?

A) $6\sqrt{2}$ B) $6\sqrt{3}$ C) $12\sqrt{2}$ D) $12\sqrt{3}$

Exercise Set 2: Geometry (Calculator)

8

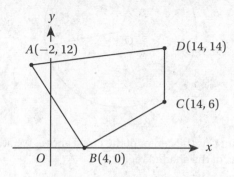

What is the area, in square units, of the quadrilateral above?

9

What is the degree measure, to the nearest whole degree, of an angle that measures 5.6 radians?

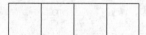

10

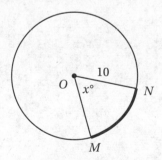

In the figure above, arc $\overset{\frown}{MN}$ has a length of 11.5. To the nearest integer, what is the value of x?

11

The Great Pyramid in Giza, Egypt, has a height of 140 meters and a volume of 2.6 million cubic meters. If a scale model of the Great Pyramid is to be built that is 2 meters high, what will be the volume, in cubic meters, of this model?

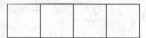

12

Which of the following equations defines a circle that is tangent to the y-axis?

A) $(x - 2)^2 + (y + 3)^2 = 2$

B) $(x - 2)^2 + (y + 3)^2 = 3$

C) $(x - 2)^2 + (y + 3)^2 = 4$

D) $(x - 2)^2 + (y + 3)^2 = 9$

▼

Questions 13 and 14 refer to the diagram below.

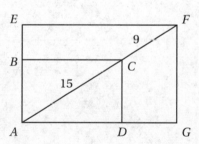

The figure above shows two rectangles that share a common vertex, and $\overline{AF}$ is a line segment that passes through C.

13

What is the ratio of the area of rectangle $ABCD$ to the area of rectangle $AEFG$?

A) 3:5

B) 9:25

C) 5:8

D) 25:64

14

If $CD = 9$, what is the perimeter of rectangle $AEFG$?

A) 67.2

B) 72.6

C) 76.2

D) 78.6

15

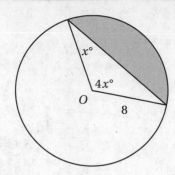

Point O is the center of the circle above. What is the area of the shaded region?

A) $\dfrac{64\pi}{3} - 16\sqrt{3}$

B) $\dfrac{16\pi}{3} - 8\sqrt{3}$

C) $\dfrac{64\pi}{3} - 12\sqrt{3}$

D) $\dfrac{64\pi}{3} - 8\sqrt{3}$

EXERCISE SET 2: GEOMETRY ANSWER KEY

No Calculator

1. **60**   If the smaller cylinder has a radius of r and a height of h, its volume is $\pi r^2 h$. The larger cylinder therefore must have a radius of $2r$ and a height of $1.5h$, and a volume of $\pi(2r)^2(1.5h) = 6\pi r^2 h$. Since this is 6 times the volume of the smaller cylinder, it must hold $10 \times 6 = 60$ ounces of oatmeal.

2. **8**   First, let's draw the radii to the points of tangency, the segment joining the centers, and the segment from the center of the smaller circle that is perpendicular to the radius of the larger circle. Since the tangent segment is perpendicular to the radii, these segments form a rectangle and a right triangle.

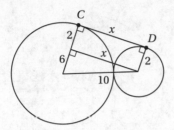

Since the circumference of the smaller circle is 4π, its radius is 2, and since the circumference of the larger circle is 16π, its radius is 8. The hypotenuse of the right triangle is the sum of the two radii: $2 + 8 = 10$. One of the legs of the right triangle is the difference of the two radii: $8 - 2 = 6$.

Pythagorean Theorem:	$x^2 + 6^2 = 10^2$
Simplify:	$x^2 + 36 = 100$
Subtract 36:	$x^2 = 64$
Take square root:	$x = 8$

---

3. **B** Diameter $= 2r$:	$2r = 6\pi^2$
Divide by 2:	$r = 3\pi^2$
Area formula:	$A = \pi(3\pi^2)^2$
Simplify:	$A = \pi(9\pi^4)$
Simplify:	$A = 9\pi^5$

---

4. **C**   From the 3-D Distance Formula back in Lesson 4, the length of the diagonal is $\sqrt{6^2 + 4^2 + 2^2} = \sqrt{36 + 16 + 4} = \sqrt{56}$.

5. **A**   All of the equations are clearly equations of circles, so our only task is to verify that one of these equations is satisfied by both point $(3, 0)$ and point $(9, 0)$. Simply by plugging these coordinates into the equations, we can verify that only the equation in (A) is true for both points: $(3 - 6)^2 + (0 - 4)^2 = 25$ and $(9 - 6)^2 + (0 - 4)^2 = 25$.

6. **C**   In this problem, we have to take advantage of the Strange Area Rule from Lesson 7. First we should draw the segments from P and N to the points of intersection. Since each of these segments is a radius, they have equal measure (6), and form two equilateral $60°$-$60°$-$60°$ triangles.

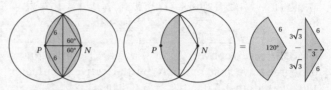

The shaded region is composed of two circle "segments," each of which is a sector minus a triangle, as shown in the figure above. The sector, since it has a $120°$ central angle, has an area 1/3 of the whole circle, or $(1/3)(\pi(6)^2) = 12\pi$ and the triangle has area $3(3\sqrt{3}) = 9\sqrt{3}$. Therefore, the shaded region has an area of $(2)(12\pi - 9\sqrt{3}) = 24\pi - 18\sqrt{3}$.

---

7. **B**   Each side of the hexagon has length $9 - 3 = 6$. Each interior angle of a regular hexagon has measure $(6 - 2)(180°)/6 = 120°$, so the segments shown form two $30°$-$60°$-$90°$ triangles with lengths shown below.

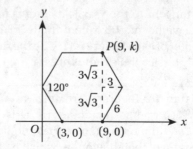

Therefore, $k = 3\sqrt{3} + 3\sqrt{3} = 6\sqrt{3}$.

Calculator

8. **142**   First, let's draw a rectangle around the figure as shown.

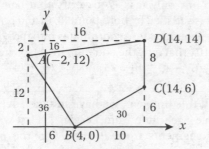

This shows that the area we want is the area of the rectangle minus the areas of the three triangles: $(16)(14) - (1/2)(2)(16) - (1/2)(12)(6) - (1/2)(10)(6) = 224 - 16 - 36 - 30 = 142$.

---

9. **321**   To convert any angle from radians to degrees, we just multiply by the conversion factor $(180°)/(\pi \text{ radians})$. $5.6 \times 180°/\pi = 320.86 \approx 321°$.

---

10. **66**   In a circle with radius 10, and arc of length 11.5 has a radian measure of $11.5/10 = 1.15$ radians. In degrees, this equals $1.15 \times 180°/\pi = 65.89° \approx 66°$.

---

11. **7.58**   If two similar solids have sides in ratio of $a{:}b$, then their volumes are in a ratio of $a^3{:}b^3$. The ratio of the heights is $140{:}2 = 70{:}1$, so the ratio of volumes is $70^3{:}1^3 = 343{,}000{:}1$. This means that the volume of the model is $2{,}600{,}000 \div 343{,}000 \approx 7.58$ cubic meters.

---

12. **C**   As a quick sketch will verify, in order for a circle to be tangent to the y-axis, its radius must equal the absolute value of the x-coordinate of its center. Since the center of each square is $(2, -3)$, the radius must be 2. The only circle with a radius of 2 is C.

---

13. **D**   By the AA Theorem, triangle ACD is similar to triangle AFG, and so rectangle $ABCD$ is similar to rectangle $AEFG$. The ratio of the corresponding sides is equal to the ratio of their diagonals, which is $15{:}24 = 5{:}8$. Therefore, the ratio of their areas is $5^2{:}8^2 = 25{:}64$.

---

14. **A**   If $CD = 9$, we can find AD by the Pythagorean Theorem. $(AD)^2 + (CD)^2 = (AC)^2$

Substitute: $(AD)^2 + 9^2 = 15^2$
Simplify: $(AD)^2 + 81 = 225$
Subtract 81: $(AD)^2 = 144$
Take square root: $AD = 12$

This means that the perimeter of $ABCD$ is $12 + 9 + 12 + 9 = 42$. Since the ratio of the perimeters of similar figures equals the ratio of corresponding sides, $\dfrac{42}{p} = \dfrac{5}{8}$.

Cross-multiply: $5p = 336$
Divide by 5: $p = 67.2$

---

15. **A**   The two radii and the chord form an isosceles triangle. $x + x + 4x = 180$

Simplify: $6x = 180$
Divide by 6: $x = 30$

Therefore, the diagram should look like this:

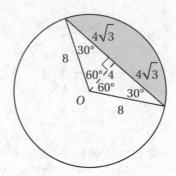

As we saw in question 6, this portion of the circle is called a "segment," and we find its area by taking the area of the sector minus the area of the triangle. The sector has area $(120/360)(\pi 8^2) = 64\pi/3$, and the triangle has area $(1/2)(8\sqrt{3})(4) = 16\sqrt{3}$, so the segment has an area of $64\pi/3 - 16\sqrt{3}$.

Lesson 9: Basic Trigonometry

The Trigonometric Functions

The SAT Math test may include one or two questions on basic trigonometry, so make sure you know the definitions of the three basic trigonometric functions: **SOH-CAH-TOA**.

For any acute **angle in a right triangle**, the three basic trigonometric functions are defined by **SOH-CAH-TOA**:

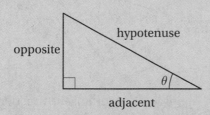

$$\sin \theta = \frac{\text{opposite}}{\text{hypotenuse}}$$

$$\cos \theta = \frac{\text{adjacent}}{\text{hypotenuse}} \qquad \tan \theta = \frac{\text{opposite}}{\text{adjacent}}$$

The Unit Circle

To understand the trigonometry of angles that are **negative or bigger than 90°**, use the **unit circle**: the circle with radius 1 centered at the origin on the xy-plane.

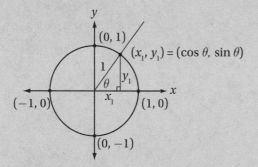

When an angle, θ, is in **standard position** (counterclockwise from the positive x-axis for positive angles), its terminal ray intersects the unit circle in the point (x_1, y_1).

This diagram and the trig definitions show that

- The **sine** of the angle is the **y-coordinate** of that point.
- The **cosine** of the angle is the **x-coordinate** of that point.
- The **tangent** of the angle is the **y-coordinate divided by the x-coordinate** of that point.

Which of the following is equivalent to

$$\cos\frac{\pi}{4} - \sin\frac{\pi}{6}?\ \text{(No calculator)}$$

A) $\dfrac{1 - \sqrt{3}}{2}$

B) $\dfrac{\sqrt{2} - \sqrt{3}}{2}$

C) $\dfrac{\sqrt{2} - 1}{2}$

D) $\dfrac{\sqrt{3} - \sqrt{2}}{2}$

(*Medium-hard*) You may find it useful to convert the angles to degree measures using the conversion factor, $180°/\pi$, from Lesson 6. This gives us $\pi/4$ radians $= 45°$ and $\pi/6$ radians $= 30°$. Note that these are angles in the special right triangles from the Reference Information at the beginning of the test.

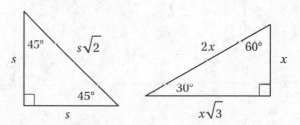

Using the definitions for sine and cosine, these

triangles shows us that $\cos 45° = \dfrac{s}{s\sqrt{2}} = \dfrac{1}{\sqrt{2}} = \dfrac{\sqrt{2}}{2}$

and $\sin 30° = \dfrac{x}{2x} = \dfrac{1}{2}$. Therefore, $\cos\dfrac{\pi}{4} - \sin\dfrac{\pi}{6} =$

$\dfrac{\sqrt{2}}{2} - \dfrac{1}{2} = \dfrac{\sqrt{2} - 1}{2}$; so the correct answer is C.

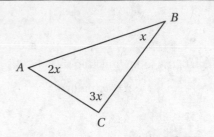

Note: Figure not drawn to scale.

In the triangle above, x represents the measure, in radians, of the smallest angle. What is the tangent of $2x$?

A) $\dfrac{\sqrt{2}}{2}$

B) $\dfrac{\sqrt{3}}{3}$

C) $\dfrac{\sqrt{3}}{2}$

D) $\sqrt{3}$

(*Medium-hard*) Although the question tells us that x represents a **radian** measure, the important information is that the measures of the three angles are in a **ratio of 1:2:3**, which is true regardless of what angle units we use. For convenience, let's consider the measures in degrees. Since the angle measures in a triangle must have a sum of 180° (or π if you prefer to work in radians), $x + 2x + 3x = 180$, so $6x = 180$ and $x = 30$. Therefore, the three angles are 30°, 60°, and 90°, and so this is one of our special right triangles from the Reference Information:

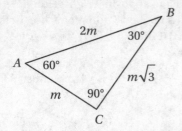

From the definition of the tangent function (TOA), $\tan 2x = \tan 60° = \dfrac{m\sqrt{3}}{m} = \sqrt{3}$, and so the correct answer is D.

Lesson 10: The Pythagorean Identity

The Pythagorean Identity

For all values of x, $\sin^2 x + \cos^2 x = 1$.

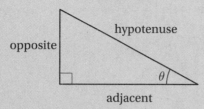

According to the Pythagorean Theorem,

$$(\text{opposite})^2 + (\text{adjacent})^2 = (\text{hypotenuse})^2$$

If we just divide both sides of this equation by $(\text{hypotenuse})^2$ we get

$$\left(\frac{\text{opposite}}{\text{hypotenuse}}\right)^2 + \left(\frac{\text{adjacent}}{\text{hypotenuse}}\right)^2 = \left(\frac{\text{hypotenuse}}{\text{hypotenuse}}\right)^2$$

which is equivalent to

$$\sin^2 \theta + \cos^2 \theta = 1$$

If $\dfrac{\pi}{2} < x < \pi$ and $\sin x = 0.8$, what is the value of $\cos x$?

A) -0.80

B) -0.60

C) -0.25

D) 0.60

(*Medium*) Pythagorean Identity: $\sin^2 x + \cos^2 x = 1$
Substitute $\sin x = 0.8$ $(0.8)^2 + \cos^2 x = 1$

Simplify: $0.64 + \cos^2 x = 1$

Subtract 0.64 from both sides: $\cos^2 x = 0.36$

Take the square root of both sides: $\cos x = \pm 0.60$

Since x is an angle in the second quadrant, the cosine is negative, so the correct answer is B.

$$\sin b = \frac{1}{3 \cos b}$$

If b is an angle measure that satisfies the equation above, what is the value of $(\sin b - \cos b)^2$?

A) $\dfrac{1}{3}$

B) $\dfrac{\sqrt{2}}{3}$

C) $\dfrac{\sqrt{3}-1}{3}$

D) $\dfrac{\sqrt{3}+\sqrt{2}}{3}$

(*Hard*) Let's simplify by applying the Pythagorean Identity.

Expression to evaluate: $(\sin b - \cos b)^2$
FOIL: $\sin^2 b - 2 \sin b \cos b + \cos^2 b$
Rearrange: $\sin^2 b + \cos^2 b - 2 \sin b \cos b$
Substitute $\sin^2 b + \cos^2 b = 1$: $1 - 2 \sin b \cos b$

Now we need to find the value of $\sin b \cos b$, which we can find with the given equation.

Given equation: $\sin b = \dfrac{1}{3 \cos b}$

Multiply by $\cos b$: $\sin b \cos b = \dfrac{1}{3}$

Substitute $\sin b \cos b = \dfrac{1}{3}$ into original expression:

$$1 - 2 \sin b \cos b = 1 - 2\left(\frac{1}{3}\right) = 1 - \frac{2}{3} = \frac{1}{3}$$

So the correct answer is A.

Lesson 11: The Cofunction Identities

Trigonometry of Complementary Angles

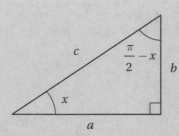

The two acute angles in a right triangle are always **complements** of one another (that is, they have a sum of 90°, or $\frac{\pi}{2}$ radians). So, if one of the angles has a radian measure of x, the other has a measure of $\frac{\pi}{2} - x$, as in the diagram above.

Note that the **sine of an angle equals the cosine of its complement**, and the **cosine of an angle equals the sine of its complement**.

$$\sin\left(\frac{\pi}{2} - x\right) = \cos x$$

$$\cos\left(\frac{\pi}{2} - x\right) = \sin x$$

If $\sin x = a$ and $x + y = \frac{\pi}{2}$, what is the value of $\sin y$?

A) a

B) $1 - a^2$

C) $\sqrt{1 - a}$

D) $\sqrt{1 - a^2}$

(*Medium-hard*)

Substitute $y = \frac{\pi}{2} - x$: $\qquad\qquad \sin y = \sin\left(\frac{\pi}{2} - x\right)$

Complementary angle theorem:

$$\sin y = \sin\left(\frac{\pi}{2} - x\right) = \cos x$$

Pythagorean Identity:

$$\sin y = \cos x = \sqrt{1 - \sin^2 x} = \sqrt{1 - a^2}$$

Therefore, the correct answer is D.

If $\sin y = \frac{a}{b}$ and $0 < y < \frac{\pi}{2}$, which of the following is equal to $\sin\left(\frac{\pi}{2} - y\right)$?

A) $\dfrac{\sqrt{a^2 - b^2}}{a}$

B) $\dfrac{\sqrt{b^2 - a^2}}{a}$

C) $\dfrac{\sqrt{a^2 - b^2}}{b}$

D) $\dfrac{\sqrt{b^2 - a^2}}{b}$

(*Hard*) Since y is the measure of an acute angle, it can be the interior angle of a right triangle. Since its sine is a/b, we can say that the opposite side has measure a and the hypotenuse has measure b.

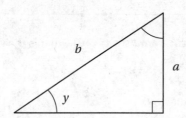

Now use the Pythagorean Theorem to find the other leg:

$$k^2 + a^2 = b^2$$

Subtract a^2: $\qquad\qquad\qquad\qquad\qquad k^2 = b^2 - a^2$

Take the square root: $\qquad\qquad\qquad k = \sqrt{b^2 - a^2}$

Also, we know that the other acute angle has a measure of $\frac{\pi}{2} - y$, so let's complete the picture:

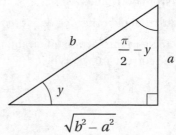

By the definition of sine: $\qquad \sin\left(\frac{\pi}{2} - y\right) = \dfrac{\sqrt{b^2 - a^2}}{b}$

So the correct answer is D.

Exercise Set 3: Trigonometry (No Calculator)

1

What is the greatest possible value of f if

$$f(x) = \frac{8\sin 2x}{2} - \frac{1}{2} ?$$

2

If $\cos\left(\dfrac{\pi}{3}\right) = a$, what is the value of $\left(\dfrac{a}{3}\right)^2$?

3

If $(\sin x - \cos x)^2 = 0.83$, what is the value of $(\sin x + \cos x)^2$?

4

Which of the following is equivalent to $\dfrac{\sin\left(\dfrac{\pi}{6}\right)}{\cos\left(\dfrac{\pi}{3}\right)}$?

A) $\dfrac{1}{\sqrt{6}}$ B) $\dfrac{1}{\sqrt{3}}$ C) $\dfrac{\sqrt{3}}{\sqrt{2}}$ D) 1

5

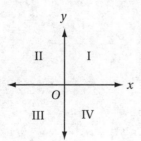

If $\sin\theta < 0$ and $\sin\theta\cos\theta < 0$, then θ must be in which quadrant of the figure above?

A) I   B) II   C) III   D) IV

6

If $\sin x = \dfrac{a}{b}$ and $0 < x < \dfrac{\pi}{2}$, which of the following expressions is equal to $\dfrac{b}{a}$?

A) $\sin\left(\dfrac{1}{x}\right)$

B) $\dfrac{1}{\cos\left(\dfrac{\pi}{2} - x\right)}$

C) $1 - \sin^2 x$

D) $\sin\left(\dfrac{\pi}{2} - x\right)$

7

If $\sin b = a$, which of the following could be the value of $\cos(b + \pi)$?

A) $\sqrt{a^2 - 1}$

B) $a^2 - 1$

C) $-\sqrt{1 - a^2}$

D) $1 - a^2$

8

If $0 < x < \dfrac{\pi}{2}$ and $\dfrac{\cos x}{1 - \sin^2 x} = \dfrac{3}{2}$, what is the value of $\cos x$?

A) $\dfrac{1}{9}$

B) $\dfrac{1}{3}$

C) $\dfrac{4}{9}$

D) $\dfrac{2}{3}$

EXERCISE SET 3: TRIGONOMETRY ANSWER KEY

No Calculator

1. **7/2 or 3.5** The discussion in Lesson 9 about the definition of the sine function and the unit circle made it clear that the value of the sine function ranges from −1 to 1. Therefore, the maximum value of $\dfrac{8\sin 2x}{2} - \dfrac{1}{2}$ is $\dfrac{8(1)}{2} - \dfrac{1}{2} = \dfrac{7}{2}$ or 3.5.

---

2. **1/36 or .027 or .028** A radian measure of $\pi/3$ is equivalent to 60°. If you haven't memorized the fact that $\cos(60°) = \frac{1}{2}$, you can derive it from the Reference Information at the beginning of every SAT Math section, which includes the 30°-60°-90° special right triangle. Since $a = \dfrac{1}{2}$, $(a/3)^2 = \left(\dfrac{1}{6}\right)^2 = \dfrac{1}{36}$.

---

3. **1.17**

	$(\sin x - \cos x)^2 = 0.83$
FOIL:	$\sin^2 x - 2\sin x\cos x + \cos^2 x = 0.83$
Regroup:	$\sin^2 x + \cos^2 x - 2\sin x\cos x = 0.83$
Simplify:	$1 - 2\sin x\cos x = 0.83$
Subtract 1:	$-2\sin x\cos x = -0.17$
Multiply by −1:	$2\sin x\cos x = 0.17$
Evaluate this expression:	$(\sin x + \cos x)^2$
FOIL:	$\sin^2 x + 2\sin x\cos x + \cos^2 x$
Regroup:	$\sin^2 x + \cos^2 x + 2\sin x\cos x$
Substitute:	$1 + 0.17 = 1.17$

---

4. **D** $\sin\left(\dfrac{\pi}{6}\right) = \dfrac{1}{2}$ and $\cos\left(\dfrac{\pi}{3}\right) = \dfrac{1}{2}$, so $\sin\left(\dfrac{\pi}{6}\right) / \cos\left(\dfrac{\pi}{3}\right) = 1$.

---

5. **D** If $\sin\theta < 0$, then θ must be either in quadrant III or in quadrant IV. (Remember that sine corresponds to the y-coordinates on the unit circle, so it is negative in those quadrants where the y-coordinates are negative.)

If $\sin\theta\cos\theta < 0$, then $\cos\theta$ must be positive (because a negative times a positive is a negative). Since $\cos\theta$ is only positive in quadrants I and IV (because cosine corresponds to the x-coordinates on the unit circle), θ must be in quadrant IV.

---

6. **B** First, notice that a/b and b/a are reciprocals. Next, we can use the identity in Lesson 10 that $\sin x = \cos\left(\dfrac{\pi}{2} - x\right)$ to see that choice (B) is just the reciprocal of $\sin x$. Alternately, we can just choose a value of x, like $x = 1$, and evaluate $\sin 1 = 0.841$. The correct answer is the expression that gives a value equal to the reciprocal of 0.841, which is $1/0.841 = 1.19$. Plugging in $x = 1$ gives (A) 0.841, (B) 1.19, (C) 0.292, (D) 0.540.

---

7. **C** Recall from the Pythagorean Identity that $\cos b = \pm\sqrt{1 - \sin^2 b}$. Substituting $\sin b = a$ gives $\cos b = \pm\sqrt{1 - a^2}$. The angle $b + \pi$ is the reflection of angle b through the origin, so $\cos(b + \pi)$ is the opposite of $\cos b$, which means that $\cos(b + \pi) = \pm\sqrt{1 - a^2}$.

---

8. **D** Recall from the Pythagorean Identity that $\cos^2 x = 1 - \sin^2 x$.

$$\frac{\cos x}{1 - \sin^2 x} = \frac{3}{2}$$

Substitute $\cos^2 x = 1 - \sin^2 x$:

$$\frac{\cos x}{\cos^2 x} = \frac{3}{2}$$

Cancel common factor:

$$\frac{1}{\cos x} = \frac{3}{2}$$

Reciprocate:

$$\cos x = \frac{2}{3}$$

Lesson 12: Imaginary and Complex Numbers

Imaginary Numbers

If we want to find the square root of a negative number, we have to get beyond the real numbers, because the square of a real number can never be negative. We need a new set of numbers, defined in terms of the imaginary number i, which is the **principal square root of –1**.

$$i = \sqrt{-1}$$

This **imaginary number line** crosses the real number line at 0 and defines the **complex plane**.

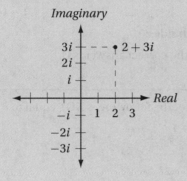

Powers of i

The unit circle in the complex plane is handy for calculating the powers of i. Starting at 1, note that each time we multiply by i, we **rotate counterclockwise 90° around this unit circle.**

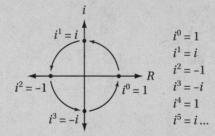

$$i^0 = 1$$
$$i^1 = i$$
$$i^2 = -1$$
$$i^3 = -i$$
$$i^4 = 1$$
$$i^5 = i \dots$$

For instance, to calculate i^{35} we can just start at 1 on the circle and count to 35, rotating 90° counterclockwise with each step. We end up at the bottom of the circle, so $i^{35} = -i$.

This can get tedious for high powers, of course, so note that we're back at 1 after every 4 steps. Therefore, we can just **replace the exponent with the remainder when it is divided by 4**. When 35 is divided by 4, the remainder is 3; therefore, $i^{35} = i^3 = -i$.

> If $i^2 = 1$, what is the value of $\dfrac{1}{i^3}$? (No calculator)
>
> A) i
>
> B) $-i$
>
> C) 1
>
> D) -1

(*Medium*)
$$\dfrac{1}{i^3}$$

Substitute $i^3 = -i$:
$$\dfrac{1}{-i}$$

Multiply by i/i and simplify:
$$\dfrac{i}{-i^2} = \dfrac{i}{-(-1)} = \dfrac{i}{1} = i$$

Therefore, the correct answer is A.

> If $i^2 = 1$, what is the value of i^{34}? (No calculator)
>
> A) i
>
> B) $-i$
>
> C) 1
>
> D) -1

(*Medium-hard*) Since there is a remainder of 2 when 34 is divided by 4, $i^{34} = i^2 = -1$; so the correct answer is D.

Complex Numbers

Complex numbers are numbers in the form $a + bi$, where a and b are real numbers, and $i = \sqrt{-1}$. **Every complex number $a + bi$ corresponds to the point (a, b) in the complex plane.**

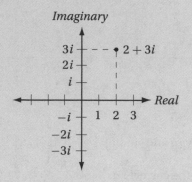

If $i^2 = 1$, and $1 - i = \dfrac{K}{1 + i}$, what is the value of K^2?

A) $2i$

B) $4i$

C) $4 + i$

D) 4

(*Medium*) Given equation: $1 - i = \dfrac{K}{1 + i}$

Multiply by $1 + i$: $(1 - i)(1 + i) = K$

FOIL: $1 + i - i - i^2 = K$

Simplify: $1 - (-1) = 2 = K$

Square both sides: $4 = K^2$

Therefore, the correct answer is D.

Complex Conjugates

Every complex number, $a + bi$, has a **complex conjugate**, $a - bi$.

Which of the following is NOT equal to $i^6 - i^2$?

A) $i^5 - i$

B) i^4

C) $2i^3 + 2i$

D) $1 + i^6$

(*Medium*) Our handy "powers of i" calculator from the previous page tells us that $i^6 - i^2 = -1 - (-1) = 0$.

Now let's look at the choices:

A) $i^5 - i = i - i$ $= 0$

B) i^4 $= 1$

C) $2i^3 + 2i = -2i + 2i$ $= 0$

D) $1 + i^6 = 1 + (-1)$ $= 0$

Therefore, the correct answer is B.

Adding and Multiplying Complex Numbers

- To **add or subtract** complex numbers, just **combine the corresponding parts**.
  $$(3 + i) - (6 - 2i) = (3 - 6) + (1 - (-2))i$$
  $$= -3 + 3i$$

- To **multiply** complex numbers, **FOIL and simplify using $i^2 = -1$.**
  $$(3 + i)(6 - 2i) = 18 - 6i + 6i - 2i^2$$
  $$= 18 - 2(-1) = 20$$

If $i^2 = 1$, what is the value of $(3 + i)(3 - i)$?

A) $9 - i$

B) $9 + i$

C) 8

D) 10

(*Easy*) This is the product of **complex conjugates**. Recall from Chapter 7, Lesson 3, that the **product of conjugates is a difference of squares**. Just FOIL and simplify.

$$(3 + i)(3 - i) = 9 - 3i + 3i - i^2 = 9 - (-1) = 10$$

Therefore, the correct answer is D.

Dividing Complex Numbers

To **divide** complex numbers, **multiply the numerator and denominator by the complex conjugate of the denominator and simplify.**

$$\frac{2-i}{3+2i} = \frac{(2-i)(3-2i)}{(3+2i)(3-2i)} = \frac{6-4i-3i+2i^2}{9-4i^2} = \frac{6-7i-2}{9-(-4)} = \frac{4-7i}{13}$$

$$= \frac{4}{13} - \frac{7}{13}i$$

If $i^2 = 1$ and $\dfrac{1+2i}{2+3i} = a + bi$, what is the value of $a + b$?

(*Medium-hard*) Start by multiplying top and bottom by the conjugate of the denominator:

$$\frac{1+2i}{2+3i} = \frac{(1+2i)(2-3i)}{(2+3i)(2-3i)}$$

FOIL and simplify:

$$\frac{(1+2i)(2-3i)}{(2+3i)(2-3i)} = \frac{2-3i+4i-6i^2}{4-(3i)^2} = \frac{8+i}{13} = \frac{8}{13} + \frac{1}{13}i$$

Therefore, $a + b = \dfrac{8}{13} + \dfrac{1}{13} = \dfrac{9}{13}$ or 0.692.

Absolute Values of Complex Numbers

Just as with real numbers, the **absolute value** of a complex number, $a + bi$, is just its **distance from the origin**, which is given by the formula $\sqrt{a^2 + b^2}$.

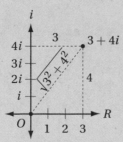

$$|3 + 4i| = \sqrt{3^2 + 4^2} = \sqrt{25} = 5$$

Which of the following complex numbers has the greatest absolute value?

A) $-1 - 7i$

B) $2 - 6i$

C) $-3 + 5i$

D) $4 + 4i$

(*Easy*) Let's calculate the absolute values with the formula.

A) $\sqrt{(-1)^2 + (-7)^2} = \sqrt{50}$

B) $\sqrt{(2)^2 + (-6)^2} = \sqrt{40}$

C) $\sqrt{(-3^2) + (5)^2} = \sqrt{34}$

D) $\sqrt{(4)^2 + (4)^2} = \sqrt{32}$

Therefore, the correct answer is A.

Using the Calculator for Complex Arithmetic

You can do basic complex arithmetic with many graphing calculators. For instance, on the TI-84, i can be accessed above the decimal button. But be careful, because **calculators often create "artifacts" when calculating with complex numbers.**

For instance, if you ask the calculator to calculate i^{25} (which you should know simplifies to i), you may get a display like this

$$-5E-13+i$$

which seems pretty bizarre. What's going on? The first seven symbols of this display are an "artifact" of the algorithm the calculator uses to calculate with complex numbers. (Think of it as sort of a round-off error.) They represent the "real" part of the calculator's answer in scientific notation. In other words, the display above represents the number

$$-0.0000000000005 + i$$

which, I think you'll agree, is pretty darn close to i. If you just ignore those tiny artifacts when they crop up, you may find it handy to use your calculator to tackle complex number questions on the SAT Math—Calculator section.

Exercise Set 4: Complex Numbers (No Calculator)

1

If $a + bi = (1 + 2i)(3 - 4i)$, where a and b are constants and $i = \sqrt{-1}$, what is the value of $a + b$?

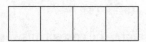

2

If $a + bi = \dfrac{4 + i}{2 - i}$, where a and b are constants and

$i = \sqrt{-1}$, what is the value of a ?

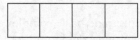

3

For what value of b does $(b + i)^2 = 80 + 18i$?

4

The solutions of the equation $x^2 - 2x + 15 = 0$ are $x = a + i\sqrt{b}$ and $x = a - i\sqrt{b}$, where a and b are positive numbers. What is the value of $a + b$?

5

Given that $i = \sqrt{-1}$, which of the following is equal

to $\dfrac{1}{(1 + i)^2}$?

A) $\dfrac{1}{2} - \dfrac{1}{2}i$

B) $-\dfrac{1}{2}i$

C) $\dfrac{1}{2}i$

D) $\dfrac{1}{2} + \dfrac{1}{2}i$

6

Which of the following expressions is equal to $(2 + 2i)^2$?

A) 0

B) $4i$

C) $8i$

D) $4 - 4i$

7

If $B(3 + i) = 3 - i$, what is the value of B ?

A) $\dfrac{3}{5} + \dfrac{4}{5}i$

B) $\dfrac{4}{5} + \dfrac{3}{5}i$

C) $\dfrac{3}{5} - \dfrac{4}{5}i$

D) $\dfrac{4}{5} - \dfrac{3}{5}i$

8

$$x^2 + kx = -6$$

If one of the solutions to the equation above is $x = 1 - i\sqrt{5}$, what is the value of k ?

A) -4

B) -2

C) 2

D) 4

9

If $i^m = -i$, which of the following CANNOT be the value of m ?

A) 15

B) 18

C) 19

D) 27

EXERCISE SET 4: COMPLEX NUMBERS ANSWER KEY

No Calculator

1. **13** $\qquad (1 + 2i)(3 - 4i)$

FOIL: $\qquad (1)(3) + (1)(-4i) + (2i)(3) + (2i)(-4i)$

Simplify: $\qquad 3 - 4i + 6i - 8i^2$

Substitute $i^2 = -1$: $\qquad 3 - 4i + 6i - 8(-1)$

Combine like terms: $\qquad 11 + 2i$

Therefore, $a = 11$ and $b = 2$, so $a + b = 13$.

---

2. **7/5 or 1.4** $\qquad \dfrac{4 + i}{2 - i}$

Multiply conjugate: $\qquad \dfrac{(4 + i)(2 + i)}{(2 - i)(2 + i)}$

FOIL: $\qquad \dfrac{8 + 4i + 2i + i^2}{4 + 2i - 2i - i^2}$

Substitute $i^2 = -1$: $\qquad \dfrac{8 + 4i + 2i - 1}{4 + 2i - 2i + 1}$

Combine like terms: $\qquad \dfrac{7 + 6i}{5}$

Distribute division: $\qquad \dfrac{7}{5} + \dfrac{6}{5}i$

---

3. **9** $\qquad (h + i)^2$

FOIL: $\qquad (b + i)(b + i) = b^2 + bi + bi + i^2$

Substitute $i^2 = -1$: $\qquad b^2 + bi + bi - 1$

Combine like terms: $\qquad (b^2 - 1) + 2bi$

Since this must equal $80 + 18i$, we can find b by solving either $b^2 - 1 = 80$ or $2b = 18$. The solution to both equations is $b = 9$.

---

4. **15** The equation we are given is a quadratic equation in which $a = 1$, $b = -2$, and $c = 15$. Therefore, we can use the quadratic formula:

Quadratic Formula: $\qquad \dfrac{-b \pm \sqrt{b^2 - 4ac}}{2a}$

Substitute: $\qquad \dfrac{2 \pm \sqrt{(-2)^2 - 4(1)(15)}}{2(1)}$

Simplify: $\qquad \dfrac{2 \pm \sqrt{-56}}{2}$

Simplify: $\qquad \dfrac{2 \pm 2i\sqrt{14}}{2}$

Distribute division: $\qquad 1 \pm i\sqrt{14}$

Therefore, $a = 1$ and $b = 14$, so $a + b = 15$.

---

5. **B** $\qquad \dfrac{1}{(1 + i)^2}$

FOIL: $\qquad \dfrac{1}{(1 + i)(1 + i)} = \dfrac{1}{1 + i + i + i^2}$

Substitute $i^2 = -1$: $\qquad \dfrac{1}{1 + i + i + (-1)}$

Simplify: $\qquad \dfrac{1}{2i}$

Multiply by i/i: $\qquad \dfrac{i}{2i^2}$

Substitute $i^2 = -1$: $\qquad \dfrac{i}{-2} = -\dfrac{1}{2}i$

---

6. **C** $\qquad (2 + 2i)^2$

FOIL: $\qquad (2 + 2i)(2 + 2i) = 4 + 4i + 4i + 4i^2$

Substitute $i^2 = -1$: $\qquad 4 + 8i - 4 = 8i$

---

7. **D** $\qquad B(3 + i) = 3 - i$

Divide by $3 + i$: $\qquad B = \dfrac{3 - i}{3 + i}$

FOIL: $\qquad B = \dfrac{9 - 3i - 3i + i^2}{9 - 3i + 3i - i^2}$

Substitute $i^2 = -1$: $\qquad B = \dfrac{9 - 3i - 3i + (-1)}{9 - 3i + 3i - (-1)}$

Simplify: $\qquad B = \dfrac{8 - 6i}{10} = \dfrac{4 - 3i}{5}$

Distribute division: $\qquad B = \dfrac{4}{5} - \dfrac{3}{5}i$

---

8. **B** $\qquad x^2 + kx = -6$

Add 6: $\qquad x^2 + kx + 6 = 0$

Substitute $x = 1 - i\sqrt{5}$: $\quad (1 - i\sqrt{5})^2 + k(1 - i\sqrt{5}) + 6 = 0$

FOIL: $\qquad (1 - 2i\sqrt{5} + 5i^2) + k(1 - i\sqrt{5}) + 6 = 0$

Simplify: $\qquad (-4 - 2i\sqrt{5}) + k(1 - i\sqrt{5}) + 6 = 0$

Distribute: $\qquad -4 - 2i\sqrt{5} + k - ik\sqrt{5} + 6 = 0$

Collect terms: $\qquad (2 + k) - (2\sqrt{5} + k\sqrt{5})i = 0$

Therefore, both $2 + k = 0$ and $2\sqrt{5} + k\sqrt{5} = 0$. Solving either equation gives $k = -2$.

---

9. **B** As we discussed in Lesson 10, the powers of i are "cyclical," and $i^m = -i$ if and only if m is 3 more than a multiple of 4. The only number among the choices that is not 3 more than a multiple of 4 is B, 18.

CHAPTER 11

PRACTICE TEST 1

1. Reading Test

   65 MINUTES   52 QUESTIONS   456

2. Writing and Language Test

   35 MINUTES   44 QUESTIONS   474

3. Math Test – No Calculator

   25 MINUTES   20 QUESTIONS   487

4. Math Test – Calculator

   55 MINUTES   38 QUESTIONS   493

5. Essay (optional)

   50 MINUTES   1 QUESTION   504

ANSWER SHEET for PRACTICE TEST 1

Use a No. 2 pencil and fill in the entire circle darkly and completely.
If you change your response, erase as completely as possible

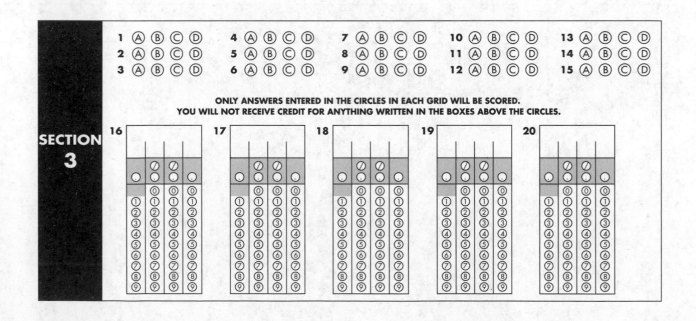

SECTION 4

1 Ⓐ Ⓑ Ⓒ Ⓓ   7 Ⓐ Ⓑ Ⓒ Ⓓ   13 Ⓐ Ⓑ Ⓒ Ⓓ   19 Ⓐ Ⓑ Ⓒ Ⓓ   25 Ⓐ Ⓑ Ⓒ Ⓓ
2 Ⓐ Ⓑ Ⓒ Ⓓ   8 Ⓐ Ⓑ Ⓒ Ⓓ   14 Ⓐ Ⓑ Ⓒ Ⓓ   20 Ⓐ Ⓑ Ⓒ Ⓓ   26 Ⓐ Ⓑ Ⓒ Ⓓ
3 Ⓐ Ⓑ Ⓒ Ⓓ   9 Ⓐ Ⓑ Ⓒ Ⓓ   15 Ⓐ Ⓑ Ⓒ Ⓓ   21 Ⓐ Ⓑ Ⓒ Ⓓ   27 Ⓐ Ⓑ Ⓒ Ⓓ
4 Ⓐ Ⓑ Ⓒ Ⓓ   10 Ⓐ Ⓑ Ⓒ Ⓓ   16 Ⓐ Ⓑ Ⓒ Ⓓ   22 Ⓐ Ⓑ Ⓒ Ⓓ   28 Ⓐ Ⓑ Ⓒ Ⓓ
5 Ⓐ Ⓑ Ⓒ Ⓓ   11 Ⓐ Ⓑ Ⓒ Ⓓ   17 Ⓐ Ⓑ Ⓒ Ⓓ   23 Ⓐ Ⓑ Ⓒ Ⓓ   29 Ⓐ Ⓑ Ⓒ Ⓓ
6 Ⓐ Ⓑ Ⓒ Ⓓ   12 Ⓐ Ⓑ Ⓒ Ⓓ   18 Ⓐ Ⓑ Ⓒ Ⓓ   24 Ⓐ Ⓑ Ⓒ Ⓓ   30 Ⓐ Ⓑ Ⓒ Ⓓ

ONLY ANSWERS ENTERED IN THE CIRCLES IN EACH GRID WILL BE SCORED.
YOU WILL NOT RECEIVE CREDIT FOR ANYTHING WRITTEN IN THE BOXES ABOVE THE CIRCLES.

31   32   33   34

35   36   37   38

SECTION 5: ESSAY

PLANNING PAGE   You may plan your essay in the unlined planning space below, but use only the lined pages following this one to write your essay. Any work on this planning page will not be scored.

BEGIN YOUR ESSAY HERE

Cut Here

1

DO NOT WRITE OUTSIDE OF THE BOX.

Cut Here

DO NOT WRITE OUTSIDE OF THE BOX.

Cut Here

3

DO NOT WRITE OUTSIDE OF THE BOX.

Cut Here

Test begins on the next page.

Reading Test

65 MINUTES, 52 QUESTIONS

Turn to Section 1 of your answer sheet to answer the questions in this section.

Questions 1–12 are based on the following passage and supplementary material.

Passage 1 is adapted from Nicholas Heidorn, *"The Enduring Political Illusion of Farm Subsidies."* ©2004 The Independent Institute. Originally Published August 18, 2004 in the San Francisco Chronicle. Passage 2 is ©2015 by Mark Anestis. Since 1922, the U.S. government has subsidized the agricultural industry by supporting the price of crops (commodity subsidies), paying farmers let their fields go fallow (conservation subsidies), helping farmers purchase crop insurance (crop insurance subsidies), and compensating farmers for uninsured losses due to disasters (disaster subsidies). The following passages discuss these programs.

Passage 1

Something is rotten down on the farm. A recent General Accounting Office study found that the
Line U.S. farm subsidy program, a multibillion-dollar system of direct payments to American farmers,
5 uses administrators who are ill-trained and poorly monitored, and who give away millions of taxpayer dollars to farmers who are actually ineligible for the program. This report should horrify lawmakers, but it probably won't.
10 From 1995 to 2002, the United States Congress doled out more than $114 billion to farmers. Why?

One misconception is that subsidies are a boon to consumers because they lower food prices. This ignores the fact that consumers are
15 also paying for these subsidies through taxes. Because of inefficiencies in the program, we taxpayers will pay more in taxes than we will ever get back in lower corn or wheat prices.

In fact, farm subsidies are not even intended
20 to reduce food prices significantly. When prices are too low, farmers lose money. To prevent this situation, Congress also pays farmers additional "conservation subsidies" to leave their land fallow, thereby lowering supply and boosting prices again.
25 We're taxed to lower prices, and then taxed to raise them again.

Another myth is that subsidies increase exports, and thereby benefit the American economy, by lowering the price of farm products
30 and so making them more attractive to foreign consumers. This ignores two realities. First, farm subsidies transfer wealth from taxpayers to foreign consumers just as efficiently as they transfer wealth to domestic consumers.
35 Second, farm subsidies are actually harming American exporters. In March 2005, the World Trade Organization ruled that American cotton subsidies violated global free-trade rules, which could lead to billions of dollars in retaliatory
40 tariffs or penalties.

The worst misconception is that we need these subsidies to save the small family farmer. Indeed, according to a 2009 poll, about 77 percent of Americans support giving subsidies to small family
45 farms. But according to the Environmental Working Group, 71 percent of farm subsidies go to the top 10 percent of beneficiaries, almost all of which are

CONTINUE ▶

large corporate farms. By subsidizing these rich farmers, we actually make it much harder for the small family farmers to compete, not to mention the millions of impoverished third world farmers who rely on farming for their livelihood.

Rich corporate farmers are an enormously powerful lobby in American politics. Agribusiness and farm insurance lobbies pump nearly $100 million into political campaigns every year, and the floodgates show no sign of closing. So don't be surprised if the GAO's reports of mismanagement and waste go unheeded. Politicians like their payouts almost as much as the big farmers and their insurance companies do.

Passage 2

The critics of the U.S. farm subsidy program fail to recognize just how vital these subsidies really are. They are not as burdensome to American taxpayers as the critics claim, and indeed provide important benefits. By protecting farmers from damaging fluctuations in commodity prices due to weather disasters or market disruptions, these subsidies help sustain a vital American industry. At the same time, they protect consumers from price spikes that can accompany steep drops in crop inventories. Before price supports became common in the 20th century, crop failures

devastated the lives of farmers and consumers with horrifying frequency.

Opponents say that subsidies distort the free market and create surpluses in supply. But halting subsidies would allow regular shortfalls, which are far more damaging. The year-to-year carryover of these surpluses protects farmers from low prices and consumers from high prices.

Another misconception is that subsidies only benefit the producers. In fact, they help many related industries as well, including food processing, distribution, and marketing, chiefly by helping to lower the cost of production. And, of course, the consumers receive the benefit of lower prices.

When assessing the costs and benefits of farm payments, it is important to compare these subsidies to those of other industrialized nations. American farmers receive an average of just 20% of their incomes from subsidies, compared to 70% for farmers from some other countries. The European Union spends about five times what the United States spends on farm subsidies, amounting to 45% of the EU budget, compared to less than 1% of the U.S. federal budget. Although the U.S. farm subsidies programs are not perfect, they provide enormous benefits not only to farms but also to associated industries employing millions of people and to nearly every American consumer.

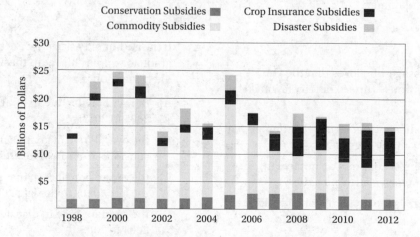

FEDERAL AGRICULTURAL SUBSIDIES IN THE UNITED STATES

Conservation Subsidies ■   Crop Insurance Subsidies ■
Commodity Subsidies ■   Disaster Subsidies ■

Source: From Environmental Working Group (farm.ewg.org)

CONTINUE →

1   **1**

1

Both passages acknowledge the effectiveness of U.S. farm subsidies in

A) stabilizing commodity prices.

B) expanding American exports.

C) assisting smaller farms.

D) increasing agricultural productivity.

2

The first sentence of Passage 1 refers primarily to the author's belief that

A) the American government is not doing enough to help small farmers.

B) some American farmers are violating the law.

C) a federal agricultural program is unfair and ineffective.

D) American farmers are struggling to compete in international markets.

3

The author of Passage 2 would most likely regard the "taxes" mentioned in line 15 as

A) a worthwhile expenditure.

B) a misplaced priority.

C) a political delusion.

D) a technical misnomer.

4

The author of Passage 1 believes that the GAO report "probably won't" (line 9) horrify lawmakers because

A) the report indicates that farm subsidies are not as harmful as many suggest.

B) most members of congress do not live in districts that receive farm subsidies.

C) the legislature is too divided along ideological party lines.

D) many members of congress receive benefits from pro-subsidy farm lobbies.

5

Which of the following provides the strongest evidence for the answer to the previous question?

A) Lines 16–18 ("Because of . . . wheat prices")

B) Lines 21–24 ("To prevent this . . . prices again")

C) Lines 42–45 ("Indeed . . . family farms")

D) Lines 54–57 ("Agribusiness . . . sign of closing")

6

Unlike Passage 1, Passage 2 emphasizes the danger of

A) corrupt political officials.

B) sudden changes in commodity prices.

C) competition in international markets.

D) onerous public tax burdens.

7

Passage 1 mentions the results of the 2009 poll (lines 42–45) primarily to

A) confirm a general sentiment.

B) refute a misconception.

C) change the focus of the discussion.

D) reveal a surprising finding.

8

If the author of Passage 1 were to use the data in the graph to support his main thesis, he would most likely mention

A) the general decline in total farm subsidies from 2005 to 2012.

B) the overall rate of change in commodity subsidies from 1998 to 2012.

C) the expansion of crop insurance subsidies from the late 1990s to the late 2000s.

D) the sudden spike in disaster subsidies from 2004 to 2005.

CONTINUE ▶

1   **1**

9

If the author of Passage 2 were to use the data in the graph to support his main thesis, he would most likely mention

A) the general decline in total farm subsidies from 2005 to 2012.

B) the overall rate of change in commodity subsidies from 1998 to 2012.

C) the expansion of crop insurance subsidies from the late 1990s to the late 2000s.

D) the sudden spike in disaster subsidies from 2004 to 2005.

10

The author of Passage 1 would most likely say that the "benefit" in line 87 is

A) offset by its costs.

B) an exception to a rule.

C) enjoyed only by the wealthy.

D) misrepresented by legislators.

11

Unlike Passage 2, Passage 1 makes a direct appeal to the reader's

A) sense of humor.

B) distaste for ineptitude.

C) environmental responsibility.

D) fiscal prudence.

12

In line 57, the "floodgates" are controls against

A) environmental destruction.

B) unscrupulous funding.

C) emotional outbursts.

D) necessary capital.

CONTINUE

Questions 13–22 are based on the following passage.

This passage is adapted from Marie Myung-Ok Lee, *Somebody's Daughter.* ©2006 Beacon Press. The story is about a Korean-American girl adopted by an American family and raised in the Midwest.

When I was eight, they told me that my mother's death was preordained. She had been murdered.
Line   One Sunday after service, our minister, Reverend Jansen of the Lutheran Church of the
5 Good Shepherd, bent down in a cloud of Aqua Velva to explain. We had been learning in Sunday school about Heaven and Hell, and in the middle of class I had fallen into a panic, wondering how I would recognize my Korean mother when I saw
10 her in Heaven—or in Hell, if perhaps she and I both sinned too much.

Not to worry, I was told.

"God called your Korean parents home so that you could become the daughter of your
15 mother and father," he said, his eyes sliding sidewise, for just a second. His breath smelled vaguely of toast.

"It was all part of His plan—you see how much your mommy and daddy love you? When the time
20 comes, if you're a very good girl, you, your mommy, daddy, and your sister, Amanda—the whole Thorson family—will be in heaven together, thanks to the Lord's wonderful and mysterious ways."

"That's why we named you Sarah," Christine
25 and Ken added. "Because it means 'God's precious treasure.'"

God kills, I thought then. The same God who brought us Christmas and the Easter Bunny—he murdered my mother.
30   Shortly after that Sunday, I brought up my Korean mother again, asking about the car accident, how it happened, exactly—was it like Phil Haag's father, who fell asleep at the wheel? Or like our plumber's teenage son who drove into a
35 semi head-on?

"Sarah," Christine said patiently, looking up from the chopping board, where she was slicing carrot discs for pot roast. "We really knew nothing about her. *I'm* your mommy. Let's not

40 talk about this any more, it makes me sad." She made little crying motions, pretending to wipe away tears, the same thing she did when I was bad, to show how I had disappointed her.

I grew up in a house in which *Korea* had
45 always been the oddly charged word, never to be mentioned in connection to me, the same way we never said "Uncle Henry" and "alcoholic" in the same sentence. It was almost as if Ken and Christine thought I needed to be protected from
50 it, the way small children need to be protected from boors itching to tell them that Santa Claus is not real. The ban on Korea extended even to the aforementioned Uncle Henry, who was then deprived of his war stories at our Memorial Day
55 cookouts. Although he proudly wore his felt VFW hat with its flurry of pins, including ones from his tour "overseas," Christine or Ken would quietly slip him some of his favorite Pabst or Schlitz, and in return he'd set up residence in the lawn chair
60 at the far corner of our yard, away from everyone.

Somewhere back in the fuzzy clot of my teens (now, I'm at the worldly-wise age of almost-twenty), the '88 Summer Olympics were held in Seoul. We couldn't buck the Thorson family
65 tradition of watching absolutely everything (that winter we'd raptly watched curling, for God's sakes!). But I was aware that pains were taken to modulate voices, vocal cords twisted to an excruciating, studied casualness until *Korea*
70 came out "Korea," exactly the same way we'd say "Russia" or "Carl Lewis" or "Flo-Jo."

Then Bryant Gumbel invaded our living room with his special segment on how *Korea*, one of the four "Little Tiger" economic miracle countries,
75 was so enterprising that it had even made an export product out of its babies. Since the Korean War, more than a *hundred thousand children*, Made-in-Korea stamped on their foreheads, had left the country, their adoption fees fattening the
80 government coffers.

Top that, Singapore! Gumbel's cheery smirk seemed to say.

"Well, Sarah's really American, not Kor—" Amanda began, until the look on Christine's
85 face—despairing, fierce—stopped her.

We invent what becomes us.

CONTINUE ➡

1   **1**

13

The narrator characterizes Reverend Jansen primarily as

A) an aloof scholar.

B) a fierce taskmaster.

C) a sympathetic caregiver.

D) a patronizing figure.

14

The narrator's statement that her mother "had been murdered" (line 2) is best taken to mean that

A) her mother was killed by a negligent driver.

B) the reputation of her mother had been severely impugned.

C) the death of her mother was deliberate.

D) her adoptive family was trying to obliterate all memory of her biological mother.

15

The narrator's description of the reverend's "eyes" and "breath" in lines 15–16 primarily convey a sense of

A) empathy.

B) detachment.

C) geniality.

D) severity.

16

Christine believes that Sarah's ethnicity is

A) a source of pride.

B) an exotic mystery.

C) a sacred blessing.

D) an unfortunate fact.

17

Which choice provides the best evidence for the answer to the previous question?

A) Lines 13–16 ("God called . . . second")

B) Lines 24–26 ("That's why . . . treasure")

C) Lines 48–52 ("It was almost . . . is not real")

D) Lines 76–80 ("Since the Korean . . . government coffers")

18

Lines 27–29 ("God kills . . . my mother") are striking for their use of

A) juxtaposition.

B) metaphor.

C) personification.

D) understatement.

19

Lines 36–44 chiefly describe Christine's

A) cunning deceitfulness.

B) sense of superiority.

C) motherly sympathy.

D) emotional immaturity.

20

In line 45, "charged" most nearly means

A) loaded.

B) entrusted.

C) attacked.

D) demanded.

CONTINUE ➡

21

The passage suggests that Uncle Henry's role in the Thorson family is that of

A) a stern patriarch.

B) a bigoted lout.

C) a pitiable embarrassment.

D) a noble hero.

22

The "cheery smirk" (line 81) is taken by the narrator to indicate Gumbel's

A) satisfaction with the publicity the Olympics were receiving.

B) admiration for Korea's economic competitiveness.

C) pleasure that Korean children would be well cared for.

D) happiness that Singapore had finally been defeated.

1   1

Questions 23–32 are based on the following passage and supplementary material.

This passage is adapted from G. M. Fitzhenry, *"Baby Pictures of the Universe."* ©2015 by College Hill Coaching.

At the breathtaking Gettysburg Cyclorama, a 377-foot-long, 42-foot-high painting of the bloody
Line 1863 Battle of Gettysburg, visitors can turn in every direction and feel as if they have been thrust
5 into the midst of perhaps the most important battle in American history, a snapshot of a chaotic chapter in the early life of a nation. Yet right now you sit in the midst of an even more spectacular cyclorama of an even more cataclysmic historical
10 event that took place *billions* of years ago. Unfortunately, to appreciate its full splendor, you would have to be able to see microwaves, which are invisible to our human eyes.

This real-life cyclorama is the cosmic
15 microwave background (CMB) radiation, a 13-billion-year-old panoramic snapshot of the universe as it appeared the moment it first released its primordial photons. Although it is an astonishingly detailed confirmation of the Big Bang
20 theory, it is not actually a picture of the Big Bang. On a human scale, it corresponds not to the instant of childbirth, but rather the moment a swaddled one-day-old opens its eyes and keeps them open.

For the first 380,000 years of its life (a mere
25 blink of an eye in cosmic history), the universe was "invisible" because its photons—the particles that are emitted from an object or event and that must reach a detector in order for us to "see" it—were trapped in a hot, opaque fog of hydrogen plasma.
30 Only when this super-heated plasma cooled to the point where protons and electrons could combine to form hydrogen atoms—a period called the "epoch of recombination"—did these photons begin to travel unimpeded through the universe.

35 Some of those photons, having traveled for half a billion generations, are just now reaching us.

One of the most striking aspects of the CMB radiation is its near-uniformity, or "isotropism." No matter where we look in the sky, the temperature of
40 the CMB radiation varies by no more than one part in 100,000. It's almost impossible to find another real-life example of such thermal homogeneity.

This uniformity is somewhat counterintuitive: the remnants of most explosions seem to spread
45 out in a spherical but non-uniform "debris field." For instance, the embers of a firework explosion are confined to a region around the explosion, but nowhere else. So why is the CMB radiation still found everywhere in the universe, and not just on
50 its "edges?" The first reason is that the universe *has* no edges: it is "boundless," just as the surface of a sphere is boundless. The second reason is that the CMB radiation did not originate from just one point in space, but from virtually *every* point in
55 space. Thus, every point in the modern universe is not only equally likely to be the source of the CMB radiation, it is also equally likely to be the current location of the CMB radiation.

This uniformity was predicted in a theory
60 published by George Gamow in 1948. His theory also made two other predictions that have been confirmed to astonishing precision by our current data. First, Gamow predicted that the CMB radiation should have a distinctive
65 spectrum known as a "blackbody" curve. Second, he predicted that the expanding universe would have cooled this radiation to below 5 degrees Kelvin today.

The CMB radiation went undetected until
70 1964, when Arno Penzias and Robert Wilson at Bell Laboratories in Murray Hill, New Jersey became troubled by persistent background noise in a radio telescope that they had just built. Their initial explanation was that it was due to a "white
75 dielectric substance," more commonly known as pigeon droppings. Remarkably, less than 40 miles

CONTINUE ➜

away, Princeton researchers Robert Dicke and
Dave Wilkinson had been searching for evidence
supporting Gamow's predictions, and instantly
80 knew of a much better explanation for the noise.
Penzias and Wilson shared the 1978 Nobel Prize in
physics for their discovery of the CMB radiation.
    Since then, much more careful observations,
made by the NASA Cosmic Background Explorer
85 (COBE) and the Wilkinson Microwave Anisotropy
Probe (WMAP) have confirmed that the CMB
radiation indeed has a nearly perfect blackbody

spectrum corresponding to a temperature of
2.725° Kelvin, barely more than 2 degrees from
90 Gamow's guess. In addition to confirming many
aspects of the Big Bang theory, these data have
also helped scientists calibrate the age of the
universe (13.772 ± 0.059 billion years), gauge
the speed at which the universe is expanding,
95 and even verify the existence of "dark energy,"
the mysterious energy that propelled the rapid
expansion of the early universe.

COSMIC BACKGROUND RADIATION SPECTRUM FROM COBE
AND BLACKBODY RADIATION CURVES FOR VARIOUS TEMPERATURES

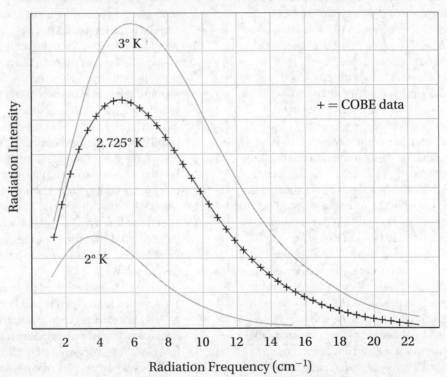

Figure 1.   Comparison of COBE radiation data to blackbody curves for 2° K and 3° K

CONTINUE

1   **1**

Figure 2.   Panoramic map of the cosmic background radiation showing temperatures ranging from 2.7248° K (dark) to 2.7252° K (white)

23

This passage is primarily concerned with

A) chronicling the discoveries yielded by recent satellite telescopes.

B) examining the controversies surrounding a physical theory.

C) discussing the analysis and significance of a cosmological phenomenon.

D) describing similarities between the study of human history and the study of astronomy.

24

In the context of the passage as a whole, the Gettysburg Cyclorama represents

A) an illustrative analogy.

B) a historical precedent.

C) a quaint anachronism.

D) an accidental success.

25

Lines 11–13 ("Unfortunately . . . human eyes") convey the author's disappointment in

A) the appropriateness of a comparison.

B) an audience's level of interest.

C) the magnitude of an event.

D) the accessibility of a phenomenon.

26

The quotation marks around the words "invisible" (line 26) and "see" (line 28) serve primarily to

A) draw attention to two relatively recent coinages.

B) imply that the author is speaking speculatively.

C) suggest an irony implicit in conventional terms.

D) indicate a technical usage of common words.

CONTINUE →

27

The "moment a swaddled one-day-old opens its eyes" (lines 22–23) corresponds to the instant that

A) scientists first discovered the cosmic microwave background radiation.

B) all of the particles and energy in the universe were created in the Big Bang.

C) the cosmic microwave background radiation was first released from the hydrogen plasma.

D) George Gamow first published his theory about the cosmic microwave background radiation.

28

In line 64, "distinctive" most nearly means

A) bizarre.

B) distinguishing.

C) elite.

D) irreconcilable.

29

Which of the following can be inferred about the work that earned Penzias and Wilson the Nobel Prize?

A) It was the product of decades of research.

B) It was the result of an accidental discovery.

C) It depended greatly on the data from the COBE satellite.

D) It provided a more plausible alternative to Gamow's theory.

30

Which choice provides the best evidence for the answer to the previous question?

A) Lines 60–63 ("His theory . . . current data")

B) Lines 73–76 ("Their initial . . . droppings")

C) Lines 83–90 ("Since then . . . Gamow's guess")

D) Lines 90–97 ("In addition . . . early universe")

31

Figure 1 best supports which claim made in the passage?

A) "For the first 380,000 years of its life . . . the universe was 'invisible'" (lines 24–26)

B) "the CMB radiation did not originate from just one point in space" (lines 53–54)

C) "Their initial explanation was that it was due to a 'white dielectrical substance'" (lines 73–75)

D) "CMB radiation . . . has a nearly perfect blackbody spectrum" (lines 86–88)

32

Figure 2 best supports which claim made in the passage?

A) "For the first 380,000 years of its life . . . the universe was 'invisible'" (lines 24–26)

B) "the CMB radiation did not originate from just one point in space" (lines 53–54)

C) "Their initial explanation was that it was due to a 'white dielectrical substance'" (lines 73–75)

D) "CMB radiation . . . has a nearly perfect blackbody spectrum" (lines 86–88)

1   1

Questions 33–42 are based on the following passage.

This passage is from John Adams, *"A Dissertation on Canon and Feudal law."* Originally published in 1765.

Liberty cannot be preserved without a general knowledge among the people, who have a right, from the frame of their nature, to knowledge, and who have been given understandings,
5   and a desire to know. But besides this, they have a right, an indisputable, unalienable, indefeasible, divine right to that most dreaded and envied kind of knowledge of the characters and conduct of their rulers. Rulers are no more than attorneys,
10   agents, and trustees, for the people. And if the cause, the interest and trust, is insidiously betrayed, or wantonly trifled away, the people have a right to revoke the authority that they themselves have deputed, and to constitute abler
15   and better agents, attorneys and trustees. And the preservation of the means of knowledge among the lowest ranks is of more importance to the public than all the property of all the rich men in the country. It is even of more consequence to the
20   rich themselves, and to their posterity. The only question is whether it is a public emolument;[1] and if it is, the rich ought undoubtedly to contribute, in the same proportion as to all other public burdens—that is, in proportion to their wealth,
25   which is secured by public expenses. But none of the means of information are more sacred, or have been cherished with more tenderness and care by the settlers of America, than the press. Care has been taken that the art of printing
30   should be encouraged, and that it should be easy and cheap and safe for any person to communicate his thoughts to the public.
Let us dare to read, think, speak and write. Let every order and degree among the
35   people rouse their attention and animate their

resolution. Let them all become attentive to the grounds and principles of government, ecclesiastical[2] and civil. Let us study the law of nature; search into the spirit of the British
40   Constitution; read the histories of ancient ages; contemplate the great examples of Greece and Rome; set before us the conduct of our own British ancestors, who have defended for us the inherent rights of mankind against foreign and
45   domestic tyrants and usurpers, against arbitrary kings and cruel priests, in short, against the gates of earth and hell. Let us read and recollect and impress upon our souls the views and ends of our own more immediate forefathers in exchanging
50   their native country for a dreary, inhospitable wilderness. Let us examine the nature of that power, and the cruelty of that oppression, which drove them from their homes. Recollect their amazing fortitude, their bitter sufferings—the
55   hunger, the nakedness, the cold, which they patiently endured—the severe labors of clearing their grounds, building their houses, raising their provisions, amidst dangers from wild beasts and savage men, before they had time
60   or money or materials for commerce. Recollect the civil and religious principles and hopes and expectations which constantly supported and carried them through all hardships with patience and resignation. Let us recollect it was liberty,
65   the hope of liberty for themselves and us and ours, which conquered all the discouragements, dangers and trials. In such researches as these let us all in our several departments cheerfully engage—but especially the proper patrons and
70   supporters of law, learning, and religion!

---

[1] benefit
[2] related to church matters

CONTINUE ➜

33

The first paragraph is primarily concerned with the right of citizens to

A) pursue academic interests.

B) learn more about their leaders.

C) become proficient in the art of printing.

D) propose helpful legislation.

34

In line 14, "constitute" most nearly means

A) place in power.

B) account for.

C) amount to.

D) be regarded as.

35

The passage indicates that our "forefathers" (line 49) endured all of the following EXCEPT

A) physical deprivation.

B) political oppression.

C) arduous physical labor.

D) a sense of despair.

36

The passage indicates that all people are born with

A) a curious nature.

B) a desire for power.

C) a dread of tyranny.

D) a sense of thrift.

37

Which sentence provides the best evidence for the answer to the previous question?

A) Lines 1–5 ("Liberty . . . to know")

B) Lines 10–15 ("And if the cause . . . trustees")

C) Lines 20–25 ("The only question . . . public expenses")

D) Lines 38–47 ("Let us study . . . earth and hell")

38

In line 34, the phrase "every order and degree" refers to

A) an anthology of official declarations.

B) a set of civic responsibilities.

C) the diverse groups within a society.

D) the highest standards of academic achievement.

39

Compared to the first paragraph, the second paragraph is more

A) prescriptive.

B) despondent.

C) critical.

D) ironic.

40

In line 52, "power" refers to

A) a personal ability.

B) a social virtue.

C) a despotic agent.

D) a mysterious spirit.

CONTINUE

1   **1**

41

In lines 46–47, "the gates of earth and hell" refer primarily to

A) the privations endured by our forefathers.

B) the superstitions of ancient cultures.

C) the dangers posed by an ignorant populace.

D) the brutality of oppressive leaders.

42

In the second paragraph, the discussion of the "views and ends" (line 48) of our forefathers primarily serves to

A) remind the reader of the importance of liberty.

B) establish a contrast between the past and the present.

C) emphasize the significance of hard work.

D) draw attention to an unfortunate tradition.

CONTINUE ➤

Questions 43–52 are based on the following passage and supplementary material.

This passage is from David Biello, *"Can Tiny Plankton Help Reverse Climate Change?"* ©2015 by David Biello. Originally published in Aeon (http://aeon.co/) on July 1, 2014.

The forbidding sea known as the Southern Ocean surrounds Antarctica with a chilly current, locking it in a deep freeze like a moat reaching to the ocean floor. Dangerous icebergs

5 hide in its gloom. Its churning swells sometimes serve up freak waves that can easily flip ships. In this violent place Victor Smetacek hopes to transform Earth's atmosphere.

Since the 1980s, Smetacek has studied the

10 plankton—tiny animals, protists, algae, and bacteria—that fill the Southern Ocean. Plankton is our planet's most prolific life form, providing the base layer of the global food chain.

Much of the oxygen we breathe comes

15 from just one species of cyanobacteria, *Prochlorococcus*, which has dominated Earth's oxygen production for the last 2.4 billion years. These minuscule marine plants produce more oxygen than all of the planet's forests combined.

20 Their steady breathing is limited only by a lack of key nutritional elements. If enough of these nutrients are supplied by dust off a continent or fertilizer run-off from farm fields, the oceans can produce blooms that can be seen from space.

25 Many of these plankton pastures are held back by iron shortages, especially in places that are largely cut off from continental dust and dirt. With access to more iron, the plankton would proliferate and siphon more and more planet-

30 heating CO_2 from the atmosphere. Back in 1988, the late John Martin, then an oceanographer at the Moss Landing Marine Observatory, said: "Give me a half tanker of iron, and I will give you an ice age."

Iron fertilization could potentially sequester

35 as much as one billion metric tons of carbon dioxide annually, and keep it deep in the ocean for centuries. That is slightly more than the CO_2 output of the German economy, and roughly one-eighth of humanity's entire greenhouse gas output.

40 Using an iron sulphate waste sold as a lawn treatment in Germany, Smetacek and his colleagues set out in 2004 to supply the plankton with the nutrient they needed. Fertilizing the waters, they hoped, would promote blooms to help

45 sea life thrive all the way up the food chain, even to whale populations, which were still recovering from overhunting. And, more importantly, the uneaten plankton could suck out CO_2 from the air until they died and sank to the sea floor, thereby

50 providing natural carbon sequestration.

Smetacek's ship dumped enough of the iron sulfate to raise the iron concentration by 0.01 gram per square meter in a 167-square-kilometer self-contained swirl of water that could maintain

55 its shape for weeks or even months. Smetacek and his crew waited, as he described in his log, "with the fatalistic patience of the farmer, watching the crop develop in the painstakingly selected field." Over the course of two weeks, thirteen species of

60 diatoms bloomed down to depths of 100 meters. Then the bloom began to die in large enough numbers to overwhelm natural systems of decay, falling like snow to depths of 500 meters. About half of them continued on even further, sinking

65 more than 3,000 meters to the sea floor.

For two weeks, Smetacek induced carbon to fall to the sea floor at the highest rate ever observed—34 times faster than normal. This marine tinkering could help buffer the

70 ever-increasing concentrations of CO_2 in the atmosphere, concentrations that have touched 400 parts-per-million, levels never before experienced in the history of our species.

Yet environmentalists were outraged by

75 Smetacek's project. Activists stoked fears that the iron could lead to a toxic algal bloom or a "dead zone" like the one created each summer in the Gulf of Mexico, where the fertilizers from Midwestern cornfields gush out of the Mississippi

80 river, stoking algal blooms that then die and are consumed by other microbes, which consume all the available oxygen in the surrounding waters, causing fish to flee and suffocating crabs and worms. As a result of these objections, there

85 have been no scientific research cruises since 2009, and none are planned for the immediate future.

Smetacek suggests that commerce might be the only way to motivate further research into iron fertilization. Replenishing missing krill, and the whales it supports, could be the best route to broader acceptance of the practice.

The ocean is no longer a vast, unknowable wilderness. Instead, it's a viable arena for large-scale manipulation of the planetary environment. We have tamed the heaving, alien world of the sea and, though doing so can make us uncomfortable, in the end it might undo a great deal of the damage we have already done.

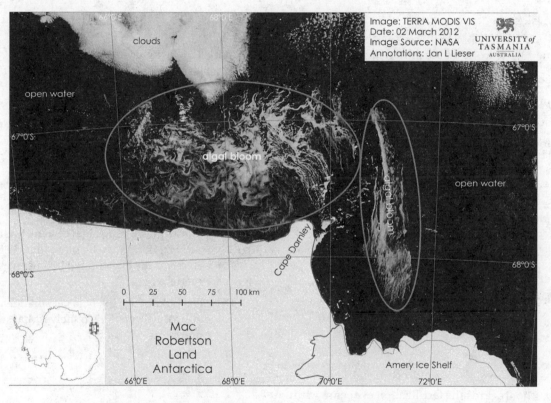

Source: Image from Jan Lieser and NASA Terra Modis

NASA satellite image of the largest recorded natural phytoplankton bloom in February 2012, believed to have been caused by the addition of iron dust blown into the sea around Antarctica by strong offshore winds.

CONTINUE

43

The characterization of the Southern Ocean in the first paragraph (lines 1–8) primarily serves to emphasize

A) the improbability of Smetacek's success.

B) the pessimism of Smetacek's detractors.

C) the boldness of Smetacek's experiment.

D) the promise of Smetacek's hypothesis.

44

In line 13, the word "base" most nearly means

A) sordid.

B) precarious.

C) stark.

D) foundational.

45

The passage indicates that the "fertilizer run-off" (line 23) is

A) an unfortunate by-product.

B) an environmental hazard.

C) a potential sustenance.

D) a source of oxygen.

46

The author regards the fertilization of oceans with iron as

A) a well-intentioned but environmentally dangerous activity.

B) a brave but needlessly expensive endeavor.

C) a promising and feasible solution to a global problem.

D) an established and valuable component of the worldwide economy.

47

Which sentence provides the best evidence for the answer to the previous question?

A) Lines 5–6 ("Its churning . . . ships")

B) Lines 75–84 ("Activists stoked . . . crabs and worms")

C) Lines 90–92 ("Replenishing . . . the practice")

D) Lines 94–96 ("Instead, it's . . . environment")

48

Which of the following statements about Smetacek's research is best supported by the diagram?

A) The iron fertilization from Smetacek's experiment created a secondary algal bloom nearly as large as the primary bloom.

B) Smetacek's experiment would likely have been more successful if it were conducted in February, which is the warmest month in the southern hemisphere.

C) Naturally occurring algal blooms in the Southern Ocean can be more than 30 times as large as the one created in Smetacek's experiments.

D) Algal blooms are likely to get smaller as they move away from the ice shelves that surround Antarctica.

49

The passage suggests that Smetacek regarded the death of the alga bloom described in lines 61–65 as

A) vindication of his theory that iron fertilization can lead to carbon sequestration.

B) an indication of the potential dangers of "dead zones" such as those in the Gulf of Mexico.

C) evidence that there was insufficient oxygen in the Southern Ocean to support large blooms.

D) a disappointment because the diatoms were being removed from the food chain.

CONTINUE ➤

1   **1**

50

The passage suggests that iron fertilization could potentially help the whale population primarily by

A) increasing the concentration of oxygen in the ecosphere.

B) decreasing the concentration of carbon dioxide in the atmosphere.

C) supporting an important food source for the whales.

D) reducing the demand for hunting in areas where the whales are endangered.

51

The "route" mentioned in line 91 refers to

A) an experimental procedure.

B) an economic difficulty.

C) an idealistic approach.

D) a mode of persuasion.

52

The tone of the final paragraph is best described as

A) sanguine.

B) awestruck.

C) apprehensive.

D) fatalistic.

STOP

**If you finish before time is called, you may check your work on this section only.
Do not turn to any other section of the test.**

2   2

Writing and Language Test
35 MINUTES, 44 QUESTIONS

Turn to Section 2 of your answer sheet to answer the questions in this section.

DIRECTIONS

Each passage below is accompanied by a number of questions. For some questions, you will consider how the passage might be revised to improve the expression of ideas. For other questions, you will consider how the passage might be edited to correct errors in sentence structure, usage, or punctuation. A passage or a question may be accompanied by one or more graphics (such as a table or graph) that you will consider as you make revising and editing decisions.

Some questions will direct you to an underlined portion of a passage. Other questions will direct you to a location in a passage or ask you to think about the passage as a whole.

After reading each passage, choose the answer to each question that most effectively improves the quality of writing in the passage or that makes the passage conform to the conventions of Standard Written English. Many questions include a "NO CHANGE" option. Choose that option if you think the best choice is to leave the relevant portion of the passage as it is.

Questions 1–11 are based on the following passage.

The Carrot or the Stick?

Good teachers want their students to do well, but getting students **1** responding is not always easy. Simple suggestion works occasionally, but not often enough. Reasoning sometimes works, too, but explaining the logical nuances of behavioral standards **2** is often time-consuming and too often falls on deaf ears.

1
A) NO CHANGE
B) to become responsive
C) to respond
D) becoming more responsive

2
A) NO CHANGE
B) are often time-consuming
C) is consuming time
D) consume time

CONTINUE

So the practical question becomes: the carrot or the stick? It's not always easy to choose **3** the potential motivator to consider: by punishment or incentive.

Most educators and psychologists agree that, as a teaching tool, **4** to reward is generally better than punishment, but many psychologists also believe that, occasionally, rewards can be as **5** harmful, if not more so, than punishment. The introduction of a reward system, like gold stars on an attendance sheet or extra recess time for good behavior, can change the nature not only of the desired behavior, **6** but also of the student-teacher relationship.

Psychologist Edward Deci conducted a study in which people were given a challenging puzzle to solve. Some subjects were offered money as a reward for solving the puzzle, and others were not.

Afterward, both groups were observed secretly after the researcher left the room. Many of those who had not been paid as a reward for their work continued to play with the puzzle, presumably because they found

3

A) NO CHANGE

B) between punishment and incentive when considering potential motivators

C) the potential motivator to consider: either punishment or incentive

D) between punishment and incentive as potential motivators to be considered

4

A) NO CHANGE

B) reward

C) rewarding

D) a reward

5

A) NO CHANGE

B) harmful as, if not more harmful than,

C) harmful, if not more harmful, than

D) equally harmful, if not more harmful than,

6

A) NO CHANGE

B) but also the nature of the student-teacher relationship

C) but the student-teacher relationship as well

D) but the nature of the student-teacher relationship is changed as well

CONTINUE ➡

2   2

it interesting for its own sake. **7** Those who had received the cash rewards, however, showed significantly less interest in returning to the puzzle.

8 Interpreting these results, the subjects who were paid probably construed the task as being manipulative: the experimenter was trying to get them to do something through bribery. The unpaid subjects, however, could engage the puzzle on their own terms simply because it was fun.

This study and others like it have profound **9** implications for the classroom. Several experiments have demonstrated that "pay-to-read" programs, where students are given money or gift credits to read books, have surprisingly negative effects on literacy. Such programs do get students to "read" more books, but the kind of reading they do is not ideal. Students tend to read superficially and only to get the reward. In follow-up studies, these students show not only lower reading skills but also less desire to read. **10** Nevertheless, the reward system turns reading from a fun activity into drudgery. Students think, if reading is such a rewarding experience, why do they need to pay us to do it?

It would be a mistake to conclude from a few experiments that all rewards are bad. Certainly, honest praise from a respectful teacher can do a great deal to encourage not only good behavior but also intellectual curiosity. Teachers must be aware of their students' need to feel independent and in control. **11**

7

The author is considering deleting the final sentence to make the paragraph more concise. Should the author make this change?

A) Yes, because it conveys information that is already implied elsewhere in the paragraph.

B) Yes, because it conveys information that distracts from the discussion of student motivation.

C) No, because it explains why the experiment was so difficult to conduct.

D) No, because it provides information that is essential to this discussion of student motivation.

8

A) NO CHANGE

B) While interpreting these results

C) One interpretation of these results is that

D) In interpreting these results,

9

A) NO CHANGE

B) indications

C) improvisations

D) instigations

10

A) NO CHANGE

B) Evidently

C) However

D) Lastly

11

The final paragraph is notable primarily for its use of which two rhetorical devices?

A) prescription and qualification

B) illustration and quantification

C) anecdote and metaphor

D) irony and humor

2   **2**

Questions 12–22 are based on the following passage.

The Promise of Bio-Informatics

Although scientists have always been interested in data, modern biologists are increasingly becoming "information scientists." Biological information science is the study of how chemical signals govern life processes. The most familiar biomolecular code is of course DNA, **12** serving as the chemical compound for the blueprint of life. Another biochemical code tells a fertilized egg how to differentiate into scores of unique cell types— heart, muscle, bone, nerve, gland, **13** blood—that assemble themselves into organs, which in turn assemble themselves into a complex organism.

12

A) NO CHANGE

B) this is the chemical compound serving as

C) the chemical compound that serves as

D) which is the chemical compound that is serving as

13

A) NO CHANGE

B) blood, that assemble themselves

C) blood; assembling themselves

D) blood—assembling itself

2   **2**

Yet another code governs **14** how the immune system "reads" the chemical signatures of invading pathogens and then manufactures specialized attack cells to fight infections.

15 Today we are seeing dramatic progress in all three of these areas of biochemistry. The science of genomics is developing better, cheaper, and faster ways to decode our DNA, and doctors are becoming more **16** apropos at using this information to create "personalized medicine." Other researchers are learning how to turn the most rudimentary human cells, "stem cells," into specialized tissues **17** for helping to repair damaged human organs. And oncologists—cancer specialists—are now coming to understand how the human immune system can be decoded to provide a crucial weapon against the most dangerous tumors.

14

Which of the following would <u>not</u> be an acceptable replacement for the underlined phrase?

A) NO CHANGE

B) the way of the immune system

C) the way the immune system

D) the way that the immune system

15

A) NO CHANGE

B) Therefore,

C) Nevertheless,

D) Ironically,

16

A) NO CHANGE

B) adept

C) liable

D) essential

17

A) NO CHANGE

B) in helping repair of

C) in order to help repairing

D) to help repair

CONTINUE ▶

2   2

18 In particular, the success of these new biological technologies **19** depends on our ability in translating vast quantities of chemical information into digital form. Specialized software and hardware **20** is needed to be developed to turn biochemical data into information that doctors and researchers can use to streamline research and make patients' lives better. Fortunately, the progress has so far been good. Since the Human Genome Project was completed in 2003, the National Human Genome Research Institute has monitored the cost of decoding a single human-sized genome. A famous law in computer science, known as "Moore's Law," says that the cost of processing a given quantity of information should decline by 50% every two years or so. In fact, with "second generation" sequencing techniques developed in 2008, **21** far more people have been able to take advantage of genome decoding.

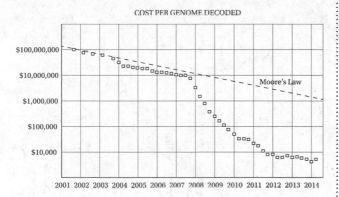

COST PER GENOME DECODED

Source: National Human Genome Research Institute: genome.gov/sequencingcosts

---

18

Which choice most effectively establishes the main topic of the paragraph?

A) Some scientists are skeptical about the viability of such radical new therapies.

B) Researchers from all over the world are collaborating in these new discoveries.

C) These new therapies and cures depend heavily on progress in the computer sciences.

D) Many forms of alternative medicine are being combined with traditional therapies to treat a wide range of diseases.

19

A) NO CHANGE

B) depend on our ability to translate

C) depends on the ability of our translating

D) depends on our ability to translate

20

A) NO CHANGE

B) must be developed

C) must develop

D) needs developing

21

Which of the following statements is best supported by the data in the graph?

A) NO CHANGE

B) The cost per genome decoded has dropped well below what Moore's Law had predicted.

C) The number of genomes decoded has dropped well below what Moore's Law had predicted.

D) The cost per genome decoded has dropped well below that of most other medical tests.

CONTINUE ➤

This integration of medicine and information technology is perhaps today's most promising scientific development. Using these new resources, perhaps **22** treatments and even cures for the most intractable diseases can be discovered by researchers.

22

A) NO CHANGE

B) researchers will discover treatments and even cures for the most intractable diseases

C) treatments and even cures will be discovered by researchers for the most intractable diseases

D) researchers have discovered treatments and even cures for the most intractable diseases

2   **2**

Questions 23–33 are based on the following passage.

What Is Art?

Look around you. Do you see art in your immediate surroundings? What qualities **23** decide that certain things are art? Definitions of art vary widely, but most tend to fall within general notions **24** that have developed over the centuries. The technical ability of an ancient Egyptian potter to produce a well-made clay vessel defined his "art." In Europe 600 years ago, trade and professional organizations from shoemaking to banking **25** would hold to this broad definition of art as skill in a particular field. The currently popular notion of the artist as the creator and definer of art—put simply, "Art is what artists create"—is a relatively recent one.

Some items and activities in our environment **26** stand out in a conspicuous way as somehow more "art" than others. The way that the visual elements of particular buildings, chairs, album covers, or athletic performances—their line, color, shape, texture, and other visual elements—combine to please the senses, is so satisfying that we call them beautiful. **27**

Prior to the twentieth century, most philosophers of art believed that beauty was the defining feature of art. By the turn of the twentieth century, however, some aestheticians had begun to find this definition insufficient. Some said that the defining

23

A) NO CHANGE
B) arrange
C) regulate
D) determine

24

A) NO CHANGE
B) developing
C) which are developed
D) as developed

25

A) NO CHANGE
B) hold
C) had held
D) held

26

A) NO CHANGE
B) are conspicuous for how they stand out
C) stand out
D) stand out conspicuously

27

The end of the second paragraph could be best enhanced with a sentence about

A) an alternate theory of beauty
B) why a particular chair is beautiful
C) how to design more beautiful buildings
D) the benefits of art therapy

CONTINUE ➡

characteristic of art was the effective expression of [28] emotion; but others said the effective communication of ideas. One influential group, the formalists, argued that an object or activity qualifies as art [29] when its form is sufficiently compelling or inspiring or beautiful to provoke an intense sensory response. This echoed the ancient Greek definition of aesthetic: "of or pertaining to the senses" or "sensuous perception."

Aesthetic experiences are not as rare as you might think. If you have ever felt yourself swept away in the sensuous experience of a sports event, a musical performance, a film, a sunset, or a [30] painting: you have had an aesthetic experience. Look around again. Do any objects in your field of vision provoke an aesthetic experience? [31] Is it skill, beauty, expression, communication, compelling form, or all of the above that make these art for you? Or is it some other quality, such as originality or creativity, [32] that makes these objects or experiences stand out as art?

28

A) NO CHANGE

B) emotion; others said it was

C) emotion, others said it was

D) emotion; while others said it was

29

A) NO CHANGE

B) if its form sufficiently compels

C) if its form is sufficiently compelling

D) if it's form is sufficiently compelling

30

A) NO CHANGE

B) painting; you

C) painting—you

D) painting, you

31

A) NO CHANGE

B) Are they

C) Do

D) Are

32

A) NO CHANGE

B) making these objects or experiences that stand out

C) that make these objects or experiences stand out

D) that stands out in these objects or experiences to make them

CONTINUE ➡

2   **2**

Does setting matter? Would a sports photo become more "artistic" if it were placed in an art museum? According to George Dickie's "institutional theory of art," major art institutions, such as museums, determine what is art in a given culture. **33**

Perhaps art is a concept that cannot have a fixed definition. Perhaps, like a living organism, it must evolve.

33

Which of the following sentences serves as the most effective concluding sentence for this paragraph?

A) Dickie, a professor emeritus of philosophy at the University of Illinois, has championed the work of philosopher David Hume.

B) Nearly every major city has museums dedicated to the display of works of fine art such as paintings, sculptures, and performance art.

C) Other institutions, such as schools and governments, also provide definitions for concepts like education and public value.

D) This theory forces us to ask: is art truly in the eye of the beholder, or is it in the eye of the artist, the curator, or some critical mass of the consuming public?

CONTINUE ⟶

Questions 34–44 are based on the following passage.

The Little Tramp

Few people have had as strong an impact on an industry [34] as the impact that Charlie Chaplin had on the world of film. [35] Born in 1889 into an impoverished London family, Chaplin crossed the Atlantic and became a pioneer in silent comedic movies. [36] Early in his film career, Chaplin developed his signature character, the "Little Tramp," who amused audiences repeatedly with his clever physical comedy and endearing sensitivity. Modest yet clearly intelligent, shy yet always at the center of action, the [37] Tramp's embodiment was the genius of Chaplin's artistry.

34

A) NO CHANGE
B) as what Charlie Chaplin
C) than Charlie Chaplin
D) as Charlie Chaplin

35

A) NO CHANGE
B) He was born in 1889 into
C) Being born in 1889 into
D) He was born in 1889 of

36

The author is considering inserting the following sentence at this point in the paragraph.

> Charlie's mother suffered from severe mental illness and was institutionalized for a significant part of Charlie's young life.

Do you think this is appropriate?

A) Yes, because it helps to explain how Chaplin became a pioneer in film.
B) Yes, because it provides an important detail about health care in 19th-century London.
C) No, because it detracts from the discussion of Chaplin's impact on the film industry.
D) No, because it diminishes the humorous tone of the paragraph.

37

A) NO CHANGE
B) genius of Chaplin's artistry was embodied by the Tramp
C) Tramp embodied the genius of Chaplin's artistry
D) Tramp's embodiment was of the genius of Chaplin's artistry

2   **2**

[38] Being writer, director, and editing his own work, Chaplin faced a daunting challenge with the rise of "talkie" films, which drew audiences away from silent stars like the Tramp. Chaplin responded by taking on the additional role of composer, writing beautiful scores to accompany his films and [39] thus allowing the Tramp to remain speechless. Chaplin managed to defy the odds and maintain a remarkable level of popularity and success in the face of technological advancement. [40] Not just a master of the craft of acting and filmmaking, but also the face of a character that resonated deeply with those suffering through the Depression.

A vocal liberal in a time of conservative domination, [41] he became a target for the House Un-American Activities Committee. While he managed to avoid being named to the committee's Hollywood Ten, a list of black-listed entertainment industry figures suspected of Communist connections, he drew the ire of J. Edgar Hoover [42] in the messages imbedded within his films.

Chaplin saw the dangers in Hitler's rise to power before most of the world had heard of the dictator. He

38

A) NO CHANGE
B) Writing, directing, and being editor of his own work,
C) Writing his own work, as well as directing and editing it too,
D) As the writer, director, and editor of his own work,

39

A) NO CHANGE
B) therefore he allowed the Tramp to remain
C) allowing the Tramp thus remaining
D) he allowed the Tramp thus to remain

40

A) NO CHANGE
B) Besides being
C) He was not only
D) In addition to being

41

A) NO CHANGE
B) the members of the House Un-American Activities Committee targeted him
C) the House Un-American Activities Committee and its members targeted him
D) he became targeted the House Un-American Activities Committee.

42

A) NO CHANGE
B) by
C) because of
D) from

CONTINUE

also believed that the development of the atomic bomb was a crime. Outraged at what **43** <u>they</u> viewed as subversive propaganda created by an immoral man, the United States government **44** <u>eradicated</u> Chaplin's reentry visa during a trip to London in 1952. Sixty-three years old and tired of fighting against a force unwilling to hear his message, Chaplin agreed to exile rather than going back to America and facing interrogation and lived the rest of his years in Europe. He returned twenty years later to receive an Academy Award for lifetime achievement.

43

A) NO CHANGE
B) it
C) would have been
D) were

44

A) NO CHANGE
B) revoked
C) excluded
D) abolished

STOP

**If you finish before time is called, you may check your work on this section only.
Do not turn to any other section of the test.**

3   **3**

Math Test – No Calculator
25 MINUTES, 20 QUESTIONS

Turn to Section 3 of your answer sheet to answer the questions in this section.

DIRECTIONS

For questions 1–15, solve each problem, choose the best answer from the choices provided, and fill in the corresponding circle on your answer sheet. **For questions 16–20,** solve the problem and enter your answer in the grid on the answer sheet. Please refer to the directions before question 16 on how to enter your answers in the grid. You may use any available space in your test booklet for scratch work.

NOTES

1. The use of a calculator is NOT permitted.
2. All variables and expressions used represent real numbers unless otherwise indicated.
3. Figures provided in this test are drawn to scale unless otherwise indicated.
4. All figures lie in a plane unless otherwise indicated.
5. Unless otherwise indicated, the domain of a given function f is the set of all real numbers for which $f(x)$ is a real number.

REFERENCE

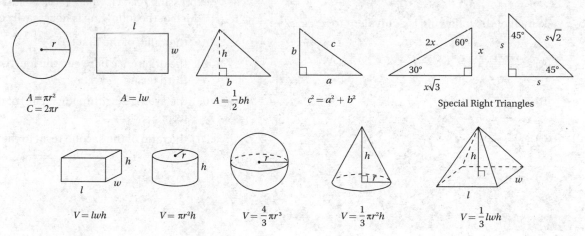

$A = \pi r^2$
$C = 2\pi r$

$A = lw$

$A = \frac{1}{2}bh$

$c^2 = a^2 + b^2$

Special Right Triangles

$V = lwh$

$V = \pi r^2 h$

$V = \frac{4}{3}\pi r^3$

$V = \frac{1}{3}\pi r^2 h$

$V = \frac{1}{3}lwh$

The number of degrees of arc in a circle is 360.
The number of radians of arc in a circle is 2π.
The sum of the measures in degrees of the angles of a triangle is 180.

CONTINUE ➡

3   **3**

1

If $8x + 6 = 6m$, what is the value of $4x + 3$ in terms of m?

A) $2m - 3$

B) $2m$

C) $3m - 3$

D) $3m$

2

$$3x + 4y = 18$$
$$y = \frac{3}{2}x$$

Which of the following ordered pairs (x, y) is a solution of the system of equations above?

A) $(2, 3)$

B) $(3, 2.25)$

C) $(4, 1.5)$

D) $(4, 6)$

3

Which of the following is equivalent to $\dfrac{3x + 4}{12}$?

A) $\dfrac{x + 4}{4}$

B) $\dfrac{3x + 1}{3}$

C) $\dfrac{x}{4} + \dfrac{1}{3}$

D) $\dfrac{x}{3} + \dfrac{1}{4}$

4

If $x - 3$ is a factor of the expression $x^2 + kx + 12$, what is the value of k?

A) -7

B) -5

C) 5

D) 7

5

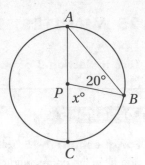

Note: Figure not drawn to scale.

In the figure above, P is the center of a circle and AC is its diameter. What is the value of x?

A) 60

B) 50

C) 40

D) 30

6

The nth term of a sequence is given by the expression $bn + 4$, where b is a positive constant. Which of the following is necessarily equal to b?

A) the value of the first term

B) the difference between the fourth term and the third term

C) the average (arithmetic mean) of the first three terms

D) the ratio of the second term to the first term

CONTINUE

3   **3**

7

If $m^3 = \sqrt{\sqrt{n}}$, where $n > 0$, what is the value of m in terms of n?

A) $n^{\frac{1}{12}}$

B) $n^{\frac{1}{7}}$

C) $n^{\frac{7}{12}}$

D) $n^{\frac{3}{4}}$

8

One bag of grass seed can cover 5,000 square feet of new lawn. If each bag costs p dollars, which of the following expressions gives the cost, in dollars, to cover a new rectangular lawn that measures a feet by b feet?

A) $\dfrac{5{,}000p}{ab}$

B) $\dfrac{abp}{5{,}000}$

C) $\dfrac{5{,}000ab}{p}$

D) $5{,}000abp$

9

If $\dfrac{5}{m} \leq \dfrac{2}{3}$, where $m > 0$, what is the least possible value of m?

A) 6.5

B) 7

C) 7.5

D) 8

10

If $f(x) = 3x + n$, where n is a constant, and $f(2) = 0$, then $f(n) =$

A) −24

B) −18

C) −12

D) 12

11

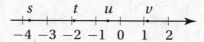

If s, t, u, and v are the coordinates of the indicated points on the number line above, which of the following is greatest?

A) $|s - v|$

B) $|s - t|$

C) $|s + v|$

D) $|u + v|$

12

How many solutions to the equation $4 \cos x - 1$ lie between $x = 0$ and $x = 3\pi$

A) Two

B) Three

C) Four

D) Six

13

If $i = \sqrt{-1}$, which of the following is NOT equal to $i^3 + i$?

A) $(2i)^2 + 4$

B) $2 - 2i^4$

C) $2i^2 - 2$

D) $i^4 - 1$

CONTINUE ▶

3 **3**

14

If $m > 1$, which of the following could be the graph of $y = -(x + m)^2 + m$ in the xy-plane?

A)

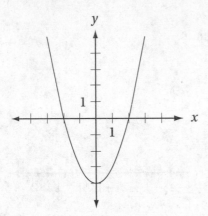

B)

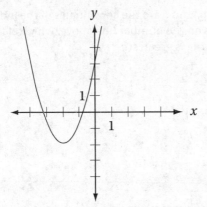

C)

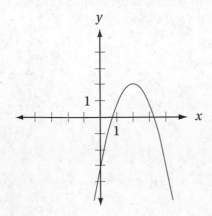

D)

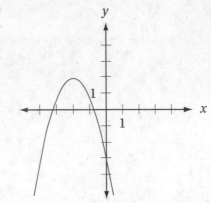

15

$$x - 3y = -2$$
$$y = \frac{5}{x}$$

The values of x that satisfy the system of equations above also satisfy which of the following equations?

A) $(x - 5)(x + 3) = 0$

B) $(x - 3)(x + 5) = 0$

C) $(x - 2)(x - 5) = 0$

D) $(x + 2)(x + 5) = 0$

DIRECTIONS

For questions 16–20, solve the problem and enter your answer in the grid, as described below, on the answer sheet.

1. Although not required, it is suggested that you write your answer in the boxes at the top of the columns to help you fill in the circles accurately. You will receive credit only if the circles are filled in correctly.

2. Mark no more than one circle in any column.

3. No question has a negative answer.

4. Some problems may have more than one correct answer. In such cases, grid only one answer.

5. **Mixed numbers** such as $3\frac{1}{2}$ must be gridded as 3.5 or $\frac{7}{2}$.

   (If $3\frac{1}{2}$ is entered into the grid as [grid], it will be interpreted as $\frac{31}{2}$, not $3\frac{1}{2}$).

6. **Decimal answers:** If you obtain a decimal answer with more digits than the grid can accommodate, it may be either rounded or truncated, but it must fill the entire grid.

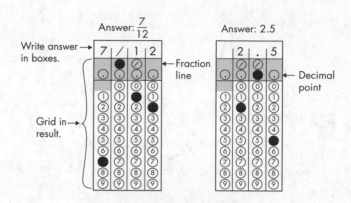

CONTINUE ▶

3 **3**

16

If $\frac{2}{3}a + \frac{1}{2}b = 5$, and $b = 4$, what is the value of a?

17

What is the smallest positive integer value of x such that $\frac{6}{x} + \frac{1}{2x}$ is less than 1?

18

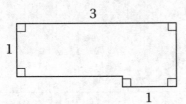

If the area of the figure above is $\frac{16}{5}$ square units, what is its perimeter?

19

What is one possible solution to the equation

$$\frac{6}{x+1} - \frac{3}{x-1} = \frac{1}{4} \ ?$$

20

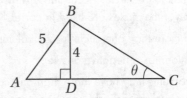

In the figure above, triangle ABC has an area of 19. What is the value of $\tan \theta$?

STOP

**If you finish before time is called, you may check your work on this section only.
Do not turn to any other section of the test.**

4 **4**

Math Test – Calculator

55 MINUTES, 38 QUESTIONS

Turn to Section 4 of your answer sheet to answer the questions in this section.

DIRECTIONS

For questions 1–30, solve each problem, choose the best answer from the choices provided, and fill in the corresponding circle on your answer sheet. **For questions 31–38,** solve the problem and enter your answer in the grid on the answer sheet. Please refer to the directions before question 31 on how to enter your answers in the grid. You may use any available space in your test booklet for scratch work.

NOTES

1. The use of a calculator is permitted.

2. All variables and expressions used represent real numbers unless otherwise indicated.

3. Figures provided in this test are drawn to scale unless otherwise indicated.

4. All figures lie in a plane unless otherwise indicated.

5. Unless otherwise indicated, the domain of a given function f is the set of all real numbers for which $f(x)$ is a real number.

REFERENCE

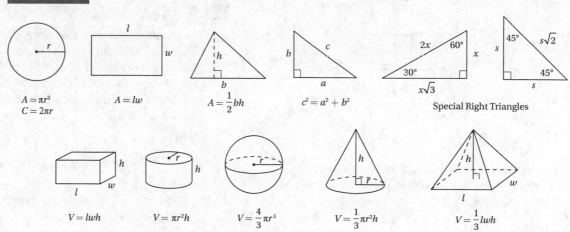

$A = \pi r^2$
$C = 2\pi r$

$A = lw$

$A = \frac{1}{2}bh$

$c^2 = a^2 + b^2$

Special Right Triangles

$V = lwh$

$V = \pi r^2 h$

$V = \frac{4}{3}\pi r^3$

$V = \frac{1}{3}\pi r^2 h$

$V = \frac{1}{3}lwh$

The number of degrees of arc in a circle is 360.
The number of radians of arc in a circle is 2π.
The sum of the measures in degrees of the angles of a triangle is 180.

CONTINUE

4 **4**

1

The fraction $\frac{n}{20}$ is equal to 0.8. What is the value of n?

A) 4

B) 8

C) 12

D) 16

2

The median of the numbers x, 10, and 12 is 12. Which of the following CANNOT be the value of x?

A) 8

B) 12

C) 16

D) 20

3

x	y
0	2
1	4
2	6
4	10

Based on the ordered pairs in the table above, which of the following could express a relationship between x and y?

A) $y = x + 4$

B) $y = 2x$

C) $y = 2x + 2$

D) $y = 2x + 4$

4

The average (arithmetic mean) of a set of 3 positive integers is m. If the number 24 is added to this set, what is the average (arithmetic mean) of the new set of numbers?

A) $\dfrac{3m + 24}{24}$

B) $\dfrac{3m + 24}{4}$

C) $m + 8$

D) $\dfrac{m + 24}{4}$

5

If $\dfrac{6}{x} + 3 = -1$, what is the value of x?

A) -3

B) -2

C) $-\dfrac{3}{2}$

D) $-\dfrac{2}{3}$

6

The Municipal Electric Company charges each household $0.15 per kilowatt-hour of electricity plus a flat monthly service fee of $16. If a household uses 30 kilowatt-hours of electricity and is charged P in a given month, which of the following equations is true?

A) $0.15(30) + 16 = P$

B) $0.15P + 16 = 30$

C) $\dfrac{30}{0.15} + 16 = P$

D) $\dfrac{0.15}{P} + 16 = 30$

CONTINUE

4   **4**

7

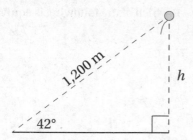

Alyssa determines that a floating balloon is 1,200 meters away from her at an angle of 42° from the ground, as in the figure above. What is the height, *h*, of the balloon from the ground? (sin 42° = 0.669, cos 42° = 0.743, tan 42° = 0.900)

A) 802.8 meters

B) 891.6 meters

C) 1,080 meters

D) 1,793 meters

8

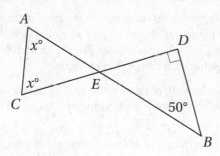

In the figure above, line segments $\overline{AB}$ and $\overline{CD}$ intersect at point *E*. What is the value of *x* ?

A) 60°

B) 65°

C) 70°

D) 75°

Questions 9 and 10 are based on the graph below.

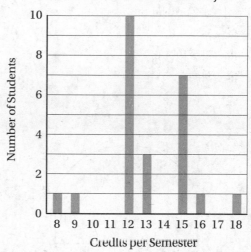

Credit Load for Economics Majors

9

A university surveyed 24 economics majors and asked them how many credits they received the previous semester. The results are represented in the graph above. What percentage of these students received 15 or more credits that semester?

A)   29%

B) $33\dfrac{1}{3}$%

C) $37\dfrac{1}{2}$%

D)   54%

10

What is the median number of credits these students received the previous semester?

A) 10.5

B) 11.5

C) 12

D) 12.5

CONTINUE

4   **4**

11

If a and b are the coordinates of two points on the number line, then which of the following is equivalent to the statement that the absolute distance from a to b is greater than the absolute distance from -2 to 6 ?

A) $|a| > -2$ and $|b| > 6$

B) $|a - b| > -8$

C) $|a + 2| > |b - 6|$

D) $|a - b| > 8$

12

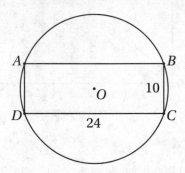

Note: Figure not drawn to scale.

In the figure above, rectangle $ABCD$ is inscribed in the circle with center O. What is the area of the circle?

A) 26π

B) 121π

C) 144π

D) 169π

13

Everyone in Niko's class has a different birth date. If Niko is both the 8th oldest person and the 12th youngest person in his class, how many students are in Niko's class?

A) 18

B) 19

C) 20

D) 21

14

If $i = \sqrt{-1}$, which of the following is equivalent to $(2 - i)(3 - 2i)$?

A) $8 - 7i$

B) $6 + 2i$

C) $6 - 6i$

D) $4 - 7i$

15

If $f(x) = (x^2)^{-2b}$ and $f(3) = 3$, what is the value of b ?

A) $-\dfrac{1}{2}$

B) $-\dfrac{1}{4}$

C) $\dfrac{1}{4}$

D) $\dfrac{1}{2}$

16

In a survey of 80 students, 55 students stated that they play a varsity sport, and 35 stated that they are taking at least one AP level course. Which of the following statements must be true?

A) At least 10 of these students are both playing a varsity sport and taking at least one AP level course.

B) Less than half of the students who play a varsity sport are also taking at least one AP level course.

C) The number of students who do not play a varsity sport is greater than the number of students who do not take at least one AP level course.

D) At least one student who takes an AP level course does NOT play a varsity sport.

CONTINUE

4   **4**

17

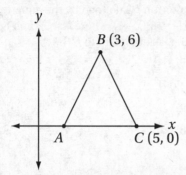

Note: Figure not drawn to scale.

In the figure above, $AB = BC$. If $\overline{AB}$ has a slope of m and $\overline{BC}$ has a slope of n, what is the value of mn?

A) -9

B) $-\dfrac{1}{9}$

C) $\dfrac{1}{9}$

D) 9

18

The functions f, g, and h are defined by the equations $f(x) = x^2$, $g(x) = x$, and $h(x) = \sqrt{x}$. Which of the following must be true?

A) $h\left(\dfrac{1}{2}\right) < f\left(\dfrac{1}{2}\right) < g\left(\dfrac{1}{2}\right)$

B) $h\left(\dfrac{1}{2}\right) < g\left(\dfrac{1}{2}\right) < f\left(\dfrac{1}{2}\right)$

C) $g\left(\dfrac{1}{2}\right) < h\left(\dfrac{1}{2}\right) < f\left(\dfrac{1}{2}\right)$

D) $f\left(\dfrac{1}{2}\right) < g\left(\dfrac{1}{2}\right) < h\left(\dfrac{1}{2}\right)$

19

Which of the following scatterplots provides the strongest evidence in support of the hypothesis that y varies inversely as the square of x?

A)

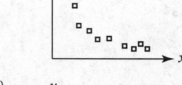

B)

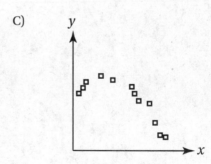

C)

D)

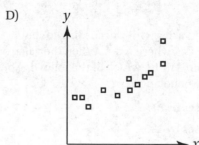

CONTINUE

4 **4**

20

The bird department of a pet store has 12 canaries, 30 finches, and 18 parrots. If the pet store purchased n more finches, then 80% of its birds would be finches. Which of the following equations must be true?

A) $\dfrac{1}{2} + n = \dfrac{4}{5}$

B) $\dfrac{30+n}{60} = \dfrac{4}{5}$

C) $\dfrac{30+n}{60+n} = \dfrac{4}{5}$

D) $\dfrac{n}{60+n} = \dfrac{4}{5}$

21

Let function $f(x)$ be defined by the equation $f(x) = x^2 - 1$. If b is a positive real number, then $f\left(\dfrac{1}{b}\right) =$

A) $\dfrac{(b-1)(b+1)}{b^2}$

B) $\dfrac{(1-b)(1+b)}{b^2}$

C) $\dfrac{b^2-1}{b}$

D) $\dfrac{b-1}{b^2}$

22

The value of y varies with x according to the equation $y = kx^2$, where $k > 0$. When the value of x increases from 3 to 12, which of the following best describes the behavior of y?

A) It increases by 81.

B) It increases by 135.

C) It is multiplied by 4.

D) It is multiplied by 16.

23

If the function f is defined by the equation $f(x) = k(x + 6)(x - 1)$, where $k > 5$, then which of the following is equivalent to $f(7)$?

A) $f(-78)$

B) $f(-12)$

C) $f(-2)$

D) $f(78)$

24

After its initial offering, the price of a stock increased by 20% in the first year, decreased by 25% in the second year, then increased by 10% in the third year. What was the net change in the stock price over the entire three-year period?

A) It increased by 5%.

B) It increased by 1%.

C) It decreased by 1%.

D) It decreased by 5%.

25

If $y = x^2$, where $x \neq 0$, and $w = y^6$, which of the following expresses the value of $\dfrac{w}{y^3}$ in terms of x?

A) x^2

B) x^4

C) x^5

D) x^6

CONTINUE ➡

4   **4**

26

0	1	2	3	4	5
1	2	4	7		
2					
3					
4				x	
5					

With the exception of the shaded squares in the first row and first column, every square in the table above is to be filled in with a number equal to the sum of the number directly above it and the number directly to its left. For instance, the number 7 in the second row is the sum of 3 in the square above it and 4 in the square directly to its left. What is the value of x ?

A)   16

B)   84

C)   96

D)   112

27

$$3x^2 = 4x + c$$

In the equation above, c is a constant. If $x = -1$ is a solution of this equation, what other value of x satisfies the equation?

A) $\dfrac{1}{7}$

B) $\dfrac{4}{3}$

C) $\dfrac{7}{3}$

D)   7

28

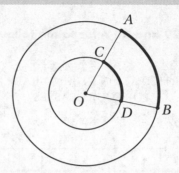

Note: Figure not drawn to scale.

The figure above shows two concentric circles with center O. If $OD = 3$, $DB = 5$, and the length of arc AB is 5π, what is the length of arc CD ?

A) $\dfrac{7}{4}\pi$

B) $\dfrac{15}{8}\pi$

C) 3π

D) $\dfrac{25}{8}\pi$

CONTINUE

▼

Questions 29 and 30 refer to the following graph.

PARTICIPATION IN FUND-RAISERS
FOR FOUR CLASSES

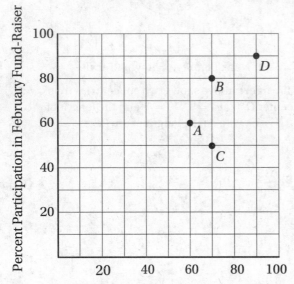

30

If there were 20 students each in Class A and Class C, and 30 students each in Class B and Class D, how many students participated in the May fund-raiser?

A) 71

B) 72

C) 74

D) 76

▲

29

Four different classes at Corbett Elementary School participated in two fund-raisers last year, one in February and another in May. The rates of participation for each class are recorded in the graph above. Which class had the greatest change in percent participation from the February fund-raiser to the May fund-raiser?

A) Class A

B) Class B

C) Class C

D) Class D

4 **4**

DIRECTIONS

For questions 31–38, solve the problem and enter your answer in the grid, as described below, on the answer sheet.

1. Although not required, it is suggested that you write your answer in the boxes at the top of the columns to help you fill in the circles accurately. You will receive credit only if the circles are filled in correctly.

2. Mark no more than one circle in any column.

3. No question has a negative answer.

4. Some problems may have more than one correct answer. In such cases, grid only one answer.

5. **Mixed numbers** such as $3\frac{1}{2}$ must be gridded as 3.5 or $\frac{7}{2}$.

   (If $3\frac{1}{2}$ is entered into the grid as [grid], it will be interpreted as $\frac{31}{2}$, not $3\frac{1}{2}$.)

6. **Decimal answers:** If you obtain a decimal answer with more digits than the grid can accommodate, it may be either rounded or truncated, but it must fill the entire grid.

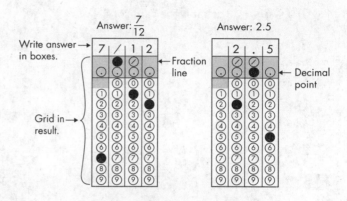

Answer: $\frac{7}{12}$ Answer: 2.5

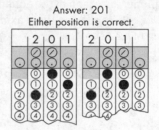

Answer: 201
Either position is correct.

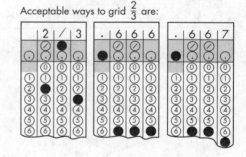

Acceptable ways to grid $\frac{2}{3}$ are:

CONTINUE

31

If $4 + \sqrt{b} = 7.2$, what is the value of $4 - \sqrt{b}$?

32

In the xy-plane, the graph of the equation $y = 3x^2 - kx - 35$ intersects the x-axis at $(5, 0)$. What is the value of k ?

33

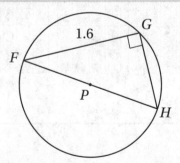

In the figure above, triangle FGH is inscribed in the circle with center P. If the area of the circle is π, what is the area of triangle FGH ?

34

If $-\dfrac{3}{5} < -2t + 1 < -\dfrac{3}{7}$, what is one possible value of $6t$?

35

If $\cos(x - \pi) = 0.4$, what is the value of $\sin^2 x$?

36

If one pound of grain can feed either 5 chickens or 2 pigs, then ten pounds of grain can feed 20 chickens and how many pigs?

CONTINUE ➡

4 **4**

Questions 37 and 38 are based on the following information

Section	Price per Ticket	Number Sold
Front Orchestra	$60	50
Rear Orchestra	$50	60
First Mezzanine	$40	x
Second Mezzanine	$35	y
Third Mezzanine	$30	100

The table above shows information about the tickets sold for a recent performance by a theater troupe. The total revenue in ticket sales for this performance was $15,000.

37

If 15 more tickets were sold in the second mezzanine than in the first mezzanine, what is the total number of tickets that were sold for this performance?

38

Before the tickets for this performance went on sale, a consultant for the theater had predicted that n, the number of tickets sold per section, would vary with p, the price in dollars for a ticket in that section, according to the formula $n = \dfrac{2,800}{p}$. By how many tickets did this model underestimate the actual total number of tickets sold?

STOP

If you finish before time is called, you may check your work on this section only.
Do not turn to any other section of the test.

5   5

Essay

50 MINUTES, 1 QUESTION

DIRECTIONS

As you read the passage below, consider how Ellis Parker Butler uses

- evidence, such as facts or examples, to support his claims
- reasoning to develop ideas and connect claims and evidence
- stylistic or persuasive elements, such as word choice or appeals to emotion, to add power to the ideas expressed

---

Adapted from Ellis Parker Butler, "On Spelling." Originally published in 1906.

1   My own opinion of the spelling profession is that it has nothing to do with genius, except to kill it. I know that Shakespeare was a promiscuous sort of speller, even as to his own name, and no one can deny that he was a greater genius than Noah Webster. The reason America so long lagged behind Europe in the production of genius is that America, for many decades, was the slave of the spelling-book. No man who devotes the fiery days of his youth to learning to spell has time to be a genius.

2   My wife, Serena, says, and I agree with her, that it is the jealousy of a few college professors who are trying to undermine the younger writers. They know that it is excusable to spell incorrectly now, but they want this new phonetic spelling brought into use so that there shall be no excuse for bad spelling, and that then, Serena says, self-made authors like me, who never can spell but who simply blaze with genius, will be hooted out of the magazines to make room for a stupid sort of literature that is spelled correctly. Serena looks upon the whole thing as a direct, personal stab at me. I look at it more philosophically.

3   To me it seems that the spelling reformers are entirely on the wrong track. Their proposed changes are almost a revolution, and we Americans do not like sudden changes. We like our revolutions to come about gradually. Think how gradually automobiles have come to pass. If, in our horse age, the streets had suddenly been covered with sixty horsepower snorters going thirty miles an hour and smelling like an eighteenth-century literary debate, and killing people right and left, we Americans would have arisen and destroyed every vestige of the automobile. But the automobile came gradually—first the bicycle, then the motorcycle, and so, by stages, to the present monsters. So slowly and progressively did the automobile increase in size and number that it seemed a matter of course. We take to being killed by the automobile quite naturally now.

4   Of course, the silent letters in our words are objectionable. They are lazy letters. We want no idle class in America, whether tramp, aristocrat, or silent letter, but we do not kill the tramp and the aristocrat. We set them to work, or we would like to. My theory of spelling reform is to set the idle letters to work.

5   Take that prime offender, *although*. *Altho* does all the work, and *ugh* sits on the fence and whittles. I would put *ugh* to work. *Ugh* is a syllable in itself. I would have the *ugh* follow the pronounced *altho* as a third syllable. Doubtless the asthmatic islanders who concocted our English language actually pronounced it so.

5 **5**

6   I propose to have some millionaire endow my plan, and Serena and I will then form a society for the reforming of English pronunciation. I will not punch out the *i* of any chief, nor shall any one drag *me* from any programme, however dull. I will pronounce *programme* as it should be pronounced—*programmy*—and, as for *chief*, he shall be pronounced *chy-ef*.

7   The advantage of this plan is manifest. It is so manifest that I am afraid it will never be adopted.

8   Serena's plan is, perhaps, less intellectual, but more American. Serena's plan is to ignore all words that contain superfluous letters. She would simply boycott them. Serena would have people get along with such words as are already phonetically spelled. Why should people write *although*, when they can write *notwithstanding that*, and not have a silent letter in it? I have myself often written a phrase twelve words long to stand instead of a single word I did not know how to spell. In fact, I abandoned my Platonic friendship for Serena, and replaced it with ardent love, because I did know how to spell *sweetheart*, but could not remember whether she was my *friend* or *freind*.

Write an essay in which you explain how Ellis Parker Butler builds an argument to persuade his audience that American English spelling conventions of 1906 need to be reformed. In your essay, analyze how Butler uses one or more of the features listed in the box above (or features of your own choice) to strengthen the logic and persuasiveness of his argument. Be sure that your analysis focuses on the most relevant features of the passage.

Your essay should NOT explain whether you agree with Butler's claims, but rather explain how Butler builds an argument to persuade his audience.

SAT PRACTICE TEST 1 ANSWER KEY

Section 1: Reading	Section 2: Writing and Language	Section 3: Math (No Calculator)	Section 4: Math (Calculator)
1. A	1. C	1. D	1. D
2. C	2. A	2. A	2. A
3. A	3. B	3. C	3. C
4. D	4. B	4. A	4. B
5. D	5. B	5. C	5. C
6. B	6. A	6. B	6. A
7. A	7. D	7. A	7. A
8. C	8. C	8. B	8. C
9. A	9. A	9. C	9. C
10. A	10. B	10. A	10. D
11. B	11. A	11. A	11. D
12. B	12. C	12. B	12. D
13. D	13. A	13. C	13. B
14. C	14. B	14. D	14. D
15. B	15. A	15. B	15. B
16. D	16. B	16. 4.5 or 9/2	16. A
17. C	17. D	17. 7	17. A
18. A	18. C	18. 8.4 or 42/5	18. D
19. D	19. D	19. 5 or 7	19. A
20. A	20. B	20. 8/13 or .615	20. C
21. C	21. B		21. B
22. B	22. B		22. D
23. C	23. D		23. B
24. A	24. A		24. C
25. D	25. D		25. D
26. D	26. C		26. D
27. C	27. B		27. C
28. B	28. B		28. B
29. B	29. C		29. C
30. B	30. D		30. C
31. D	31. A		31. 0.8 or 4/5
32. B	32. A		32. 8
33. B	33. D		33. .96
34. A	34. D		34. $4.29 \leq x \leq 4.79$
35. D	35. A		35. .84
36. A	36. C		36. 12
37. A	37. C		37. 371
38. C	38. D		38. 25
39. A	39. A		
40. C	40. C		
41. D	41. A		
42. A	42. C		
43. C	43. B		
44. D	44. B		
45. C			
46. C			
47. D			
48. C			
49. A			
50. C			
51. D			
52. A			

Total Reading Points (Section 1)	Total Writing and Language Points (Section 2)	Total Math Points (Section 3)	Total Math Points (Section 4)

SCORE CONVERSION TABLE

Scoring Your Test

1. Use the answer key to mark your responses on each section.

2. Total the number of correct responses for each section:

    1. Reading Test   Number correct: _____ **(Reading Raw Score)**

    2. Writing and Language Test   Number correct: _____ **(Writing and Language Raw Score)**

    3. Mathematics Test – No Calculator   Number correct: _____

    4. Mathematics Test – Calculator   Number correct: _____

3. Add the raw scores for sections 3 and 4. This is your **Math Raw Score**: _____

4. Use the Table 1 to calculate your **Scaled Test and Section Scores (10–40).**

    Math Section Score (200–800):   _____

    Reading Test Score (10–40):   _____

    Writing and Language Test Score (10–40):   _____

5. Add the **Reading Test Scaled Score** and the **Writing and Language Test Scaled Score** and multiply this sum by 10 to get your **Reading and Writing Test Section Score (20–80).**

    Sum of Reading + Writing and Language Scores: _____ × 10 =

    Reading and Writing Section Score: _____

Table 1: Scaled Section and Test Scores (10–40)

Raw Score	Math Section Score	Reading Test Score	Writing/ Language Test Score	Raw Score	Math Section Score	Reading Test Score	Writing/ Language Test Score
58	800			29	520	27	28
57	790			28	520	26	28
56	780			27	510	26	27
55	760			26	500	25	26
54	750			25	490	25	26
53	740			24	480	24	25
52	730	40		23	480	24	25
51	710	40		22	470	23	24
50	700	39		21	460	23	23
49	690	38		20	450	22	23
48	680	38		19	440	22	22
47	670	37		18	430	21	21
46	670	37		17	420	21	21
45	660	36		16	410	20	20
44	650	35	40	15	390	20	19
43	640	35	39	14	380	19	19
42	630	34	38	13	370	19	18
41	620	33	37	12	360	18	17
40	610	33	36	11	340	17	16
39	600	32	35	10	330	17	16
38	600	32	34	9	320	16	15
37	590	31	34	8	310	15	14
36	580	31	33	7	290	15	13
35	570	30	32	6	280	14	13
34	560	30	32	5	260	13	12
33	560	29	31	4	240	12	11
32	550	29	30	3	230	11	10
31	540	28	30	2	210	10	10
30	530	28	29	1	200	10	10

SAT PRACTICE TEST 1 DETAILED ANSWER KEY

Section 1: Reading

1. A   **Detail**

In lines 10–25, the author of Passage 1 discusses how farm subsidies are used both to lower food prices (by subsidizing farmers) when prices get too high, and to raise them (by paying farmers to leave their land fallow) when prices get too low. Although he disputes that these efforts to stabilize prices are worth the cost, he does indicate that they work. In the first paragraph of Passage 2 (lines 60–73), the author indicates that farm subsidies *protect consumers from price spikes* (lines 69–70).

2. C   **Interpretation**

In the first paragraph of Passage 1, the statement that *something is rotten down on the farm* (line 1) introduces the author's discussion of the U.S. farm subsidies program, which he claims gives away *millions of taxpayer dollars to farmers who are actually ineligible for the program* (lines 6–8) and is rife with *inefficiencies* (line 16).

3. A   **Cross-Textual Inference**

The thesis of Passage 2 is that U.S. farm subsidies are *vital* (line 63) to both farmers and American consumers. Therefore, he regards the *taxes* (line 15) we pay for these subsidies to be a *worthwhile expenditure*.

4. D   **Inference**

In lines 8–9, the author of Passage 1 states that the report about corruption and incompetence in the U.S. farm subsidies program *should horrify lawmakers, but it probably won't.* He explains why in the last paragraph (lines 53–56): *Rich corporate farmers are an enormously powerful lobby in American politics*, contributing *nearly $100 million into political campaigns every year.*

5. D   **Textual Evidence**

As the explanation to question 4 explains, the evidence for this answer is found in the last paragraph, particularly lines 54–57.

6. B   **Passage Comparison**

Although the author of Passage 1 does not think that the stabilization of commodity prices is worth the cost of higher taxes (lines 19–25), the author of Passage 2 indicates that *price spikes* (line 71) can be devastating to both farmers and consumers.

7. A   **Specific Purpose**

The 2009 poll cited in lines 42–45 indicates that most Americans support farm subsidies for small family farms,

confirming the author's statement that Americans feel that *we need these subsidies to save the small family farmer.* Choice (B) is incorrect because, although the author himself goes on to refute this misconception, the results of the poll do not. Rather, they *confirm a general sentiment.* Choice (C) is incorrect because the poll does not indicate any shift away from the discussion about the ineffectiveness of the U.S. farm subsidies program. Choice (D) is incorrect because the word *Indeed* (line 42) indicates that this result is unsurprising to him.

8. C   **Data Analysis**

The thesis of Passage 1 is that *something is rotten down on the farm* (line 1), namely, the fact that, in a recent seven-year period, *the Uited States Congress has doled out more than $114 billion to farmers* (lines 10–11) through a program that *uses administrators who are ill-trained and poorly monitored* (lines 5–6) and that implements programs that are not worthwhile to taxpayers, that *are actually harming American exporters* (lines 35–36) and that *make it much harder for the small family farmers to compete* (lines 49–50). The graph in Figure 1, however, shows about a 40% decline in these subsidies from 2000 to 2012, perhaps undercutting the author's claim that these subsidies are an overall burden on the American taxpayer.

He would most likely, then, choose to focus on the component of these subsidies that has grown significantly in the 15 years indicated on this graph, namely, crop insurance subsidies, which have expanded at a fairly steady rate and grew by about 500% from 1998 to 2012. As the introduction to the passage indicates, this program takes money from taxpayers to help farmers to buy crop insurance, thereby providing direct entitlements not only to farmers but also to insurance companies.

Choice (A), *the general decline in total farm subsidies from 2005 to 2012*, does not help the author make the point that these subsidies are a burden to American taxpayers. Similarly, choice (B), *the overall rate of change in commodity subsidies from 1998 to 2012* does not help his thesis, because after the first several years, the trend is generally downward. Choice (D), *the sudden spike in disaster subsidies from 2004 to 2005*, also does not support his thesis, because he does not make any particular claims about the benefit of disaster subsidies.

9. A   **Data Analysis**

The thesis of Passage 2 is that farm subsidies in the United States are *vital* (line 63) and *not as burdensome to American taxpayers as the critics claim* (lines 64–65). Therefore, the author of Passage 2 would most likely cite evidence that the total cost of the subsidies program is declining.

10. A   **Cross-Textual Inference**

The author of Passage 1 indicates that *we taxpayers will pay more in taxes than we will ever get back in lower corn or wheat prices* (lines 16–18), thereby indicating that the *benefit of lower prices* (lines 87–88) is *offset by its costs.*

11. B   **Cross-Textual Comparison**

The author of Passage 1 mentions that the U.S. farm subsidy programs use administrators *who give away millions of taxpayer dollars to farmers who are actually ineligible for the program* (lines 6–8) and are rife with *inefficiencies* (line 16) to make the argument that they are not worthwhile to taxpayers. This is an appeal to the reader's *distaste for ineptitude* (incompetence).

Although this could also be seen as an appeal to the reader's *fiscal prudence* (sense of responsibility), the author of Passage 2 makes the same kind of appeal when he indicates that these subsidies are *vital* (line 63) to preventing *price spikes* (line 71) and *are not as burdensome to American taxpayers as the critics claim* (lines 64–65). Since the question asks us to find an appeal that is NOT also found in Passage 2, choice (D) is incorrect.

12. B   **Interpretation**

When the author of Passage 1 states that *Agribusiness and farm insurance lobbies pump nearly $100 million into political campaigns every year, and the floodgates show no sign of closing* (lines 54–57), he suggests that there seem to be no controls against this *unscrupulous* (unethical) *funding* of political campaigns by those who benefit from the decisions of those politicians.

13. D   **Tone and Characterization**

The narrator says that Reverend Jansen *bent down in a cloud of Aqua Velva* (lines 5–6) and told her *not to worry* (line 12). He then describes to the narrator why God *called [her] Korean parents home* (line 13). All of these descriptions work together to portray someone who is acting in a condescending and *patronizing* manner to a young child.

14. C   **Interpretation**

The statement that the narrator's mother *had been murdered* (line 2) is later explained to refer to the narrator's interpretation of the fact that she was told that *"God called [her] Korean parents home"* (line 13) and that *"It was all part of His plan"* (line 18), in other words, her death *was deliberate*. At first, choice (D) may seem plausible, because in lines 36–43, Sarah's mother does not want to talk about Sarah's biological mother. However, the passage makes it clear that the narrator attributed the "murder" to a divine plan (*God kills, I thought then*, line 27) rather than to any intention of her adoptive family.

15. B   **Tone and Diction**

The description of Reverend Jansen's eyes and breath in lines 13–17 indicates that he is somewhat emotionally detached (*his eyes sliding sideways*, lines 15–16) and that Sarah is likewise emotionally detached from him and his profound claims, instead distracted by his breath that *smelled vaguely of toast* (lines 16–17). These descriptions surprise us, because they are so incongruent with the expectation of respect for and contemplation of the reverend's deep spiritual pronouncements.

16. D   **Interpretation**

The narrator has Korean heritage, yet she *grew up in a house in which Korea had always been the oddly charged word, never to be mentioned in connection with [Sarah], the same way [they] never said "Uncle Henry" and "alcoholic" in the same sentence* (lines 44–47). The narrator's mother, Christine, *thought [Sarah] needed to protected from* (line 49) her ethnicity. In other words, she regarded Sarah's ethnicity as an *unfortunate fact.*

17. C   **Textual Evidence**

As the explanation to question 16 makes clear, the best evidence for the previous answer is in lines 48–52.

18. A   **Literary Device**

The contrast between *murder* and *Christmas and the Easter Bunny* (line 28) is a classic example of *juxtaposition*, the act of placing together two images with highly contrasting effects.

19. D   **Interpretation**

The paragraph states that Christine begins her reply *patiently* (line 36), which might suggest that she is demonstrating *motherly sympathy*. However, *sympathy* means "a feeling of common understanding," and the rest of Christine's reply suggests that she is *disappointed* (line 43) with Sarah rather than sympathetic with her. The point of the paragraph is that Christine is not emotionally ready (*it makes me sad*, line 40) to discuss something that her eight-year-old adopted daughter clearly wants to discuss, that is, she is *emotionally immature.*

20. A   **Word in Context**

When the narrator states that *Korea had always been the oddly charged word* (lines 44–45), she means that it was a word that was *never to be mentioned* (lines 45–46), because it was associated with potentially negative feelings. That is, it was an emotionally *loaded* word.

21. C   **Interpretation**

In lines 44–60, the narrator describes her Uncle Henry as an *"alcoholic"* (line 47) who sat drinking at family cookouts *at the far corner of our yard, away from everyone* (line 60). This is treatment appropriate to a *pitiable embarrassment* rather than a *stern patriarch* or *noble hero*. There is also no indication, despite Sarah's parents' discomfort with discussing her heritage, that Uncle Henry is a *bigoted lout*.

---

22. B   **Tone and Inference**

The reference to Bryant Gumbel's *cheery smirk* (line 81) follows the description of his television segment during the Olympic games about how Korea had become one of the *economic miracle countries* (line 74). According to the narrator, the cheery smirk seemed to say *Top that, Singapore!* thereby indicating that he admired Korea's ability to compete economically with other strong countries.

---

23. C   **General Purpose**

The passage as a whole describes the *spectacular cyclorama* (line 9) that is known as the *cosmic microwave background (CMB) radiation, a 13 billion year-old panoramic snapshot of the universe as it appeared the moment it first released its primordial photons* (lines 14–18). It then goes on to discuss the precise measurements that scientists have taken of this radiation and what they tell us about the early universe. In other words, the passage as a whole is *discussing the analysis and significance of a cosmological phenomenon*.

---

24. A   **Specific Purpose**

The description of the Gettysburg Cyclorama in the first paragraph is used to draw an analogy between two *cataclysmic historical event[s]* (lines 9–10), one of which we can see with our own eyes and one of which we can only detect with special tools. The answer is not (B), because although this Cyclorama depicts a historic battle, it is not itself *a historical precedent* (an event that serves as a model for future similar events). Choice (C) is incorrect because the painting is depicted neither as *quaint* nor *anachronistic* (out of historical order). Choice (D) is incorrect because although the passage later indicates that the discovery of the CMB was somewhat *accidental*, the Cyclorama was not.

---

25. D   **Interpretation**

The author indicates that *to appreciate [the] full splendor[of the Cosmic Background Radiation], you would have to be able to see microwaves* (lines 11–13). In other words, the disappointment is in the fact that we can't see the *spectacular cyclorama* (line 8) that is the cosmic microwave background; it is an *inaccessible phenomenon*, at least to our naked eyes.

---

26. D   **Specific Purpose**

The discussion in lines 24–28 concerns the emergence of the first photons (light particles) in the early universe. In saying that the *universe was "invisible"* (lines 25–26),

the author means that photons—the particles that are required for us to be able to detect something visually—did not yet exist. Calling the early universe "invisible" is somewhat inappropriate, since there were no eyes to see it anyway during that stage in its development, so the quotes are drawing attention to the fact that these terms are being used to make a technical point a bit clearer by using common words that correspond with our everyday experience.

---

27. C   **Interpretation**

The *moment a swaddled one-day-old opens its eyes* (lines 22–23) refers to *the moment [the early universe] first released its primordial photons* (lines 17–18) which we now refer to as the cosmic microwave background radiation. The discussion in the next paragraph (lines 24–36) explains that these early photons were previously trapped in *an opaque fog of hydrogen plasma* (line 29). Choices (A) and (D) are incorrect because this moment describes when the photons were released, not when they were first discovered by humans. Choice (B) is incorrect because these particles, as it is explained in the third paragraph, were released 380,000 years *after* the Big Bang.

---

28. B   **Word in Context**

The *distinctive spectrum* (lines 64–65) refers to the precise "blackbody" curve for 2.75° Kelvin as shown in Figure 1. It is the particular set of wavelength intensities that *distinguish* blackbody radiation from ordinary radiation, and confirm Gamow's theory about the origin of the signals detected at Murray Hill.

---

29. B   **Inference**

The passage states that Penzias and Wilson were initially *troubled* (line 72) by the signals that turned out to be from the CMB radiation, and in fact mistakenly attributed them to *pigeon droppings* (line 76). This indicates that they were not looking for these signals, nor did they know how to interpret them. The work they did to receive the Nobel prize, therefore, was *the result of an accidental discovery*.

---

30. B   **General Structure**

As the explanation of question 29 indicates, lines 73–76 indicate that Penzias and Wilson did not understand the nature of the signals they were receiving, atttributing them erroneously to *pigeon droppings*.

---

31. D   **Data Analysis**

Figure 1 shows the blackbody spectrum for various temperatures, and compares these to the measurements taken of the cosmic microwave background, showing that the CMB radiation *has a nearly perfect blackbody spectrum*.

---

32. B   **Word in Context**

Figure 2 shows a panoramic map of the cosmic background radiation, showing that it *did not originate from just one point in space*, but rather from every direction.

---

33. B   **General Purpose**

The first paragraph states that the people *have a right . . . to that most dreaded and envied kind of knowledge of the characters and conduct of their rulers* (lines 5–9). In other words, they have the right to learn about who their leaders are and what they do. Choice (A) is incorrect because the right to *pursue academic interests* is discussed somewhat in the second paragraph (*Let us dare to read, think, speak, and write*, line 33) but not in the first. Choice (C) is incorrect, because although Adams says that *the art of printing should be encouraged* (lines 29–30), this is not the primary point of the paragraph. Rather, it is secondary to the point that citizens should be well informed. Choice (D) is incorrect because although the first passage mentions the right of citizens to *revoke the authority* (line 13) of their leaders, it does not discuss the right of citizens to propose legislation themselves.

---

34. A   **Word in Context**

The statement *that the people have a right to revoke the authority that they themselves have deputed, and to **constitute** abler and better agents, attorneys and trustees* (lines 12–15) means that the people have the right to **place in power** better leaders to replace those whose authority has been revoked.

---

35. D   **Interpretation**

The passage indicates that our forefathers endured *physical deprivation* in the form of *the hunger, the nakedness, [and] the cold* (line 55), *political oppression* in the form of *domestic tyrants and usurpers* (line 45), and *arduous physical labor* in the form of *the severe labors of clearing their grounds, building their houses, [and] raising their provisions* (lines 56–58). It does not mention, however, that they endured any feelings of *despair*. In fact, it says that they endured these with the *hopes and expectations which constantly supported and carried them through all hardships with patience and resignation* (lines 61–64).

---

36. A   **Interpretation**

The very first sentence states that all people have *a desire to know* (line 5), that is, a *curious nature*. Choice (B) is incorrect, because although the passage discusses at length the people's right to revoke the authority of those in power, it does not claim that people themselves have a desire for power. Choice (C) is incorrect, because although the passage discusses the right of the people to revoke the authority of bad rulers, and mentions the

---

inherent rights of mankind against foreign and domestic tyrants and usurpers (lines 44–45), it does not state specifically that the people have any *dread* of tyranny. Choice (D) is incorrect because the passage does not discuss thrift (resourcefulness with money).

---

37. A   **Textual Evidence**

As the explanation to question 36 explains, the best evidence for the previous answer is found in the very first sentence of the passage.

---

38. C   **Interpretation**

The phrase *every order and degree among the people* (line 34) refers to the entire society that Adams is addressing throughout the second paragraph.

---

39. A   **Structural Comparison**

The second paragraph is characterized primarily by its use of the imperative mood: *Let us dare . . . Let every order . . . Let them . . . Let us study . . . Let us read . . . Let us examine . . .* These sentences therefore have a much more urgent and suggestive diction than do the sentences in the first paragraph. While the first paragraph is primarily *descriptive* of the rights of free citizens, the second is *prescriptive* of their corresponding duties.

---

40. C   **Interpretation**

When Adams says *Let us examine the nature of that power* (lines 51–52) he is referring to the cruel power that *drove [our forefathers] from their homes* (line 53), that is, the *domestic tyrants* (line 45) that made it difficult for them to remain in their native countries. Clearly, then *power* refers to a *despotic* (tyrannical) *agent*.

---

41. D   **Interpretation**

Although this paragraph does discuss *the privations endured by our forefathers* in the form of *the hunger, the nakedness, [and] the cold* (line 55) and does implicitly warn against *the dangerous posed by an ignorant populace* because it strongly encourages us to *read, think, speak, and write* (line 33), this particular sentence is referring specifically to *arbitrary kings and cruel priests* (lines 45–46). So the phrase *the gates of earth and hell* (lines 46–47) is referring to the *brutality of oppressive leaders* who persecute us in our worldly existence and about an otherworldly existence.

---

42. A   **Purpose**

The sentence *Let us read and recollect and impress upon our souls the views and ends of our own more immediate forefathers in exchanging their native country for a dreary, inhospitable wilderness* (lines 47–51) invites us to learn about the beliefs and motivations of our forefathers who came to America to escape oppression. In other words, Adams wants to *remind the reader of the importance of liberty*.

---

43. C   **Specific Purpose**

The first paragraph characterizes the Southern Ocean as a foreboding place by evoking images of its *chilly current* (lines 2–3), the *dangerous icebergs [that] hide in its gloom* (lines 4–5), and the *churning swells [that] sometimes serve up freak waves that can easily flip ships* (lines 5–6). Such images might be used to make a case for *the improbability of Smetacek's success* or the *pessimism of Smetacek's detractors*, but his portion of the passage contains no such pessimism. Rather goes on directly to explain the promise of Smetacek's work. This description, therefore, must be regarded as emphasizing *the boldness of Smetacek's experiment*.

---

44. D   **Word in Context**

The phrase the ***base** layer of the food chain* refers to plankton's role in the global ecosystem, specifically how it serves as the *foundation* of the food chain.

---

45. C   **Interpretation**

Although many environmentalists may well regard *fertilizer run-off from farm fields* (line 23) as *an unfortunate by-product* of farming, or *an environmental hazard*, the author here presents it as supplying some of the *key nutritional elements* (line 21) for cyanobacteria. Therefore, it is a *potential sustenance* (nourishment).

---

46. C   **Characterization and Tone**

The passage as a whole characterizes Smetacek's experiments in iron fertilization to promote oceanic cyanobacterial blooms as a demonstration of the potential for *large-scale manipulation of the planetary environment* (lines 95–96) to remove *planet-heating CO_2 from the atmosphere* (lines 29–30). Therefore, according to the author, this fertilization is *a promising and feasible solution to a global problem*.

---

47. D   **Textual Evidence**

As the explanation to question 46 explains, the best evidence for this answer is found in lines 94–96.

---

48. C   **Data Analysis**

Figure 1 depicts a *satellite image of the largest recorded natural phytoplankton bloom in February 2012, believed to have been caused by the addition of iron dust blown into the sea around Antarctica by strong offshore winds* (from the caption beneath Figure 1). Choice (A) cannot be correct, because Smetacek's experiment took place in 2004, not 2012. Choice (B) cannot be correct, because the

figure does not indicate anything about the relationship between algal bloom size and time of year. Choice (D) cannot be correct, because the figure does not contain any information about the relationship between bloom size and distance from the Antarctic ice shelves. The correct answer is (C) because the figure clearly shows a bloom that is well over 5,000 square kilometers (over 100 km long and over 50 km wide) in area, which is more than 30 times larger than Smetacek's *167 square kilometer* (line 53) bloom.

---

49. A   **Inference**

According to the passage, Smetacek's theory was that iron fertilization of plankton could *siphon more and more planet-heating CO_2 from the atmosphere* (lines 29–30) and then *sequester as much as one billion metric tons of carbon dioxide annually, keeping it deep in the ocean for centuries* (lines 34–37) by *[dying] and [sinking] to the sea floor, thereby providing natural carbon sequestration* (lines 49–50). Therefore, the death of the algal bloom described in lines 61-65 is *vindication of his theory that iron fertilization can lead to carbon sequestration*.

---

50. C   **Inference**

The passage states that plankton serves as *the base layer of the global food chain* (line 13) and therefore fertilizing phytoplankton with iron *would promote blooms to help sea life thrive all the way up the food chain, even to whale populations* (lines 44–46). Therefore, iron fertilization helps the whale population by *supporting an important food source for the whales*.

---

51. D   **Interpretation**

The second to last paragraph (lines 88–92) discusses a *way to motivate further research into iron fertilization* (lines 89–90) therefore the *route to broader acceptance of the practice* (lines 91–92) is a *mode of persuasion*. Choice (A) is incorrect because, although the research itself probably involves *an experimental procedure*, the *route* is not part of the research itself, but rather a means to gain support for that research. Choice (B) is incorrect because, although an appeal to the needs of *commerce* (line 88) shows an appreciation for economic concerns, the *route* is not itself an *economic difficulty*. Choice (C) is incorrect because appealing to the needs of commerce is not an *idealistic* approach, but rather a pragmatic one.

---

52. A   **Tone**

The last paragraph is *sanguine* (hopeful) about the potential for iron fertilization of the oceans to *undo a great deal of the damage we have already done* (lines 98–99).

Section 2: Writing and Language

---

1. C   **Idiom**

Although gerunds like *hiking* are often interchangeable with infinitives like *to hike* (for instance, saying *I like hiking* is essentially the same as saying *I like to hike*), often the conventions of idiom dictate a preference for one form over the other in a particular context. In this case, the phrase *getting students to respond* is proper idiom, whereas *getting students responding* is not proper idiom. Choice (B) uses an infinitive form, but the phrase *to become responsive* inappropriately changes the meaning of the sentence.

---

2. A   **Subject-Verb Agreement**

The subject-verb core of this clause is *explaining . . . is*. Notice that this subject and verb agree in number, whereas choices (B) and (D) would introduce subject-verb disagreement. Choice (C) is not idiomatic, so the original phrasing is best.

---

3. B   **Coordination**

The original phrasing misuses the colon, which should be used only to precede an explanatory clause or an explanatory list. Choice (C) is incorrect for the same reason. Choice (D) is incorrect because it commits a number shift: choosing *between punishment and incentive* is choosing a single motivator, not *motivators*. Choice (B) avoids these errors and conveys the idea clearly and concisely.

---

4. B   **Parallelism/Logical Comparison**

The phrase *better than* signals that this sentence is making a comparison, which must be both parallel and logical. In the original phrasing, *to reward* (infinitive) is being compared with *punishment* (abstract class noun), and since these are different parts of speech, it violates the law of parallelism. The only choice that provides another abstract class noun is (B) *reward*. Choice (C) is incorrect because *rewarding* is a gerund, not a class noun, and choice (D) is incorrect because *a reward* represents an event-instance, not a class of actions.

---

5. B   **Modifier error/Idiom**

Remember that any sentence must retain its grammatical integrity even when its modifying phrases are "trimmed" away. The phrase *if not more so* is an interrupting modifier, but when it is removed, the sentence reads *. . . as harmful . . . than punishment*, which is of course not idiomatic. The only choice that avoids this problem is choice (B).

---

6. A   **Parallelism**

This sentence contains the comparative idiom *not only A but also B*. When we use such idioms, we must make sure that we use the precise phrasing and that the words or phrases that replace *A* and *B* are parallel. The original phrasing is both idiomatic and parallel, because both phrases that replace *A* and *B* are prepositional phrases. Choice (B) is not parallel, and choices (C) and (D) are neither parallel nor idiomatic.

---

7. D   **Coherence**

The passage as a whole is discussing the use of rewards as a teaching tool, so the underlined sentence is important because it indicates their ineffectiveness in that role.

---

8. C   **Dangling Participles**

In the original phrasing, as well as in choices (B) and (D), the participle *interpreting* dangles: its subject does not match the subject of the main clause, *subjects*. Choice (C) does not have this problem, and conveys the idea clearly and concisely.

---

9. A   **Diction**

The original word choice is best. Choice (B) is incorrect because although the results of the study may *indicate* that changes be made in the classroom, the phrase *have profound indications for the classroom* is not idiomatic, because *indicate* is a transitive verb and so requires a direct object. Choice (D) has a similar problem, since the verb *instigate* is also a transitive verb. Choice (C) is incorrect because *improvisations* are performances without preparation, which studies cannot do.

---

10. B   **Transitions**

This paragraph is discussing the evidence regarding the ability of rewards to incentivize learning. This particular sentence mentions a possible interpretation of that evidence; therefore, the adverb *evidently* is the most logical sentence modifier. Choices (A) and (C) are incorrect because they inappropriately indicate a contrast. Choice (D) is incorrect because this point is not the last of a sequence of points.

---

11. A   **Rhetorical Devices**

The final paragraph contains a *prescription* (strong suggestion) in the last sentence: *Teachers must be aware of their students' need to feel independent and in control*. It also contains a *qualification* (a statement that moderates a previous claim) in the statement *it would be a mistake to conclude that all rewards are bad*. Choice (B) is incorrect because the paragraph contains no *quantification* (numerical measurement). Choice (C) is incorrect because it provides neither *anecdote* (illustrative story) nor *metaphor* (comparison that equates to things that are not literally equivalent). Choice (D) is incorrect because the paragraph contains no *irony* (reversal of reader expectations) or attempts at *humor*.

12. **C**   **Coordination**

The original phrasing is illogical because DNA does not *serve as a chemical compound*, it *is* a chemical compound. (Although someone can both *serve as* a nurse and *be* a nurse, this is because nursing is a service. Molecules do not perform services in the way that human professionals do.) Choice (B) is incorrect because it produces a comma splice, and choice (D) is incorrect because it is needlessly wordy, and because the present progressive form *is serving* incorrectly implies a current action rather than a general function. Choice (C) avoids these errors and conveys the idea clearly and effectively in the form of an appositive phrase.

13. **A**   **Punctuation/Pronoun Agreement**

Since the sentence uses the em-dash (—) to introduce the list of examples, it must likewise use the em-dash to close this list. Any interrupting phrase must start and end with the same punctuation marks: either commas or em-dashes. Although choice (D) uses the em-dash, it is incorrect because the pronoun *itself* does not agree in number with the antecedent *cell types*.

14. **B**   **Diction**

Choice (B) includes an illogical use of the preposition *of*.

15. **A**   **Transitions**

The original phrasing is best. Choice (B) is incorrect because the sentence does not indicate any logical consequence. Choice (C) is incorrect because the sentence does not indicate any contrast. Choice (D) is incorrect because the sentence does not indicate any irony.

16. **B**   **Diction**

This sentence describes the ability of doctors to use biological information to create *"personalized medicine."* One who is particularly skilled is *adept*. Choice (A) is incorrect because *apropos* means *appropriate to a given situation*. Choice (B) is incorrect because *liable* means *likely* or *legally responsible*. Choice (D) is incorrect because the phrase *essential at* is neither logical nor idiomatic.

17. **D**   **Idiom**

This sentence discusses using stem cells to repair damaged organs. The most concise and idiomatic way to express this functional relationship is with the infinitive *to help*. Choices (A), (B), and (C) all use nonidiomatic phrases.

18. **C**   **Logical Cohesiveness/Transitions**

This paragraph discusses the task of *translating vast quantities of chemical information into digital form*, and indicates that good progress has been made, thanks to progress in *specialized hardware and software*. Therefore, the best introductory sentence is (C), which focuses on *progress in the computer sciences*.

19. **D**   **Subject-Verb Agreement/Idiom**

The original phrasing is incorrect because the phrase *our ability in translating* is not idiomatic. Choice (B) is incorrect because the verb *depend* does not agree in number with the subject *success*. Choice (C) is incorrect because the phrase *the ability of our translating* is illogical. Choice (D) avoids these errors and expresses the idea clearly and concisely.

20. **B**   **Idiom/Voice/Mood**

The original phrasing is not idiomatic. Choice (C) is incorrect because its use of the active voice is illogical. Choice (D) is also not idiomatic. Only choice (B) conveys the proper mood (necessity) idiomatically and concisely.

21. **B**   **Data Analysis**

Choice (A) is incorrect because the graph does not indicate anything about the number of people taking advantage of genome decoding. Choice (B) is correct because the vertical axis of the graph represents the cost per genome decoded, and the data points clearly show that this cost is below the cost predicted by Moore's Law after 2008. Choice (C) is incorrect because the graph does not indicate anything about the number of genomes decoded. Choice (D) is incorrect because the graph makes no direct comparison of the cost of genome decoding to that of any other medical test.

22. **B**   **Dangling Participles/Verb Tense**

The original phrasing is incorrect because the participle *using* dangles: it does not share its subject with the main clause. Choice (C) is incorrect for the same reason. Choice (D) is incorrect because, although it corrects the dangling participle, the present perfect form of the verb, *have discovered*, is illogical.

23. **D**   **Diction**

The original word choice is illogical since *qualities* are incapable of deciding anything. Choice (B) and (C) are incorrect for similar reasons: anything that *arranges* or *regulates* must have a mind and intention, which *qualities* lack. Choice (D) is the only reasonable choice, since qualities can *determine* (that is, *play a deciding role in an outcome*) whether or not something is art.

24. **A**   **Verb Aspect**

The original phrasing is best. The present perfect form *have developed* is appropriate because the status of the *notions* is the consequence of how they developed *over the centuries*. Recall that the **perfect** (or **consequential**)

aspect is used to indicate a status-as-consequence (see Chapter 4, Lesson 23).

---

25. D   **Verb Tense**

This sentence indicates a historical fact, so the simple present tense is best.

---

26. C   **Redundancy**

The original phrasing is redundant, since being *conspicuous* is the same thing as *standing out*. Choice (C) is the only one that avoids the redundancy.

---

27. B   **Logical Cohesiveness**

The paragraph is about the fact that some things in our environment stand out obviously as "art." It would be reasonable, then, to follow this point with an explanation of why a particular object, such as a chair, qualifies as art.

---

28. B   **Coordination**

The original phrasing is incorrect because the clause that follows the semicolon is not independent, and the transitive verb *said* lacks a logical direct object. Choice (C) is incorrect because it creates a comma splice. Choice (D) is incorrect because the clause that follows the semicolon is not independent. Choice (B) avoids these problems.

---

29. C   **Punctuation/Coordination/Parallelism**

The original phrasing is illogical because the adverb *when* incorrectly implies that whether or not an object qualifies for art is a time-specific event, rather than a general criterion. Choice (B) is incorrect because it creates a non-parallel list: *compels . . . inspiring . . . beautiful.* Choice (D) is incorrect because *it's = it is.*

---

30. D   **Coordination/Punctuation**

The sentence is a compound sentence joining a dependent clause *If you have . . .* and an independent clause *you have had. . . .* The original phrasing is incorrect because a colon should be used only to join two independent clauses in which the second explains the first. Choice (B) is incorrect because a semicolon should only be used to join independent clauses. Choice (C) is incorrect because an em dash should only be used to separate an independent clause from an interrupting modifier. Choice (D) is best because a simple comma is most effective at joining a dependent clause and an independent one.

---

31. A   **Verb Form**

The original phrasing is best. Choice (B) is incorrect because the pronoun *they* disagrees in number with its antecedent *skill, beauty, or expression.* (The conjunction *or* implies that only one of these serves as the subject; therefore, it is singular.) Choice (C) is incorrect because

---

it does not coordinate with the phrase *that gives.* Choice (D) is incorrect because it has the disagreement problem of (B) as well as the coordination problem of (C).

---

32. A   **Coordination**

The original phrasing is best. Choice (B) is illogical. Choice (C) creates subject-verb disagreement. Choice (D) is awkward and creates an unidiomatic phrase: *to make them as art.*

---

33. D   **Logical Cohesiveness**

This paragraph introduces and defines the *"institutional theory of art,"* presumably because the author regards it as an interesting theory of aesthetics. Choice (D) is best because it poses an intriguing question that follows directly from that definition. Choices (A), (B), and (C), while true statements, are irrelevant to a discussion of this theory.

---

34. D   **Comparative Idiom/Logical Comparison**

This sentence uses the comparative idiom *as strong as,* so we must check that the comparison is idiomatic, parallel, and logical. The original phrasing and the phrasing in choice (B) are incorrect because they create illogical comparisons: they compare *people* to an *impact.* Choice (C) is incorrect because it is not idiomatic. Choice (D) provides an idiomatic, parallel, and logical comparison.

---

35. A   **Coordination/Idiom**

The original phrasing of the participial phrase is best: notice that the subject of the past participle *born* is also the subject of the main clause: *Chaplin.* Choices (B) and (D) are incorrect because they form comma splices. Choice (C) is incorrect because the present participle *being* implies that Chaplin was born at the same time that he crossed the Atlantic, which is illogical.

---

36. C   **Logical Cohesiveness**

Although this sentence introduces a true and interesting fact, it is inappropriate to this paragraph, which is about Chaplin's impact on the film industry.

---

37. C   **Coordination**

The sentence begins with two adjectival phrases that modify *the Tramp.* Therefore, these modifiers will dangle unless the subject of the main clause is *the Tramp.* The only choice that avoids this dangling is (C).

---

38. D   **Parallelism**

The original phrasing includes a list that is not parallel: *writer, director, and editing.* The only choice that does not violate the Law of Parallelism is (D).

39. A   **Parallelism**

The original phrasing is best because it creates the parallel phrasing *taking on . . . writing . . . and thus allowing.*

40. C   **Sentence Fragments/Comparative Idiom**

The original phrasing is incorrect because it creates a sentence fragment. Choices (B) and (D) commit the same error. Only choice (D) forms a sentence with an independent clause. Note also that is correctly applies the comparative idiom *not only A but also B.*

41. A   **Dangling Modifiers**

The original phrasing is best because it coordinates with the appositive phrase that begins the sentence. Choices (B) and (C) allow this appositive to dangle. Choice (D) is incorrect because the phrase *became targeted for* is not idiomatic.

42. C   **Logical Coordination/Idiom**

This sentence describes the reason that Chaplin *drew the ire of J. Edgar Hoover.* Choice (C) provides the most logical phrase to coordinate this state of being and its cause: *because of.* The prepositional phrases in the original phrasing and in choices (B) and (D) do not convey this logical relationship.

43. B   **Pronoun Agreement**

The original phrasing is incorrect because the definite pronoun *they* disagrees in number with the antecedent *government.* Choice (C) is incorrect because the subjunctive form *would have been* incorrectly implies that this clause in counterfactual. Choice (D) is incorrect because *propaganda,* although it sounds plural, is singular.

44. B   **Diction**

In this context, *eradicated* does not work because it means *destroy completely, as a scourge,* which does not accurately modify a visa. Choice (B), *revoked* (officially invalidated) works nicely. Choice (C) is illogical because the visa is not disallowed entry into a group, as *excluded* would imply. Choice (D) is illogical because *abolish* more properly describes the formal termination of an institution, practice, or system.

Section 3: Math (No Calculator)

1. D   **Algebra (solving equations) EASY**

$$8x + 6 = 6m$$

To solve in one step, just divide both sides by 2:

$$4x + 3 = 3m$$

2. A   **Algebra (linear systems) EASY**

To determine which ordered pair is a solution to the system, just "plug in" the values for x and y and choose the one that satisfies both equations. Notice that $x = 2$ and $y = 3$ is a solution because $3(2) + 4(3) = 18$, and $3 = \left(\frac{3}{2}\right)(2)$.

3. C   **Algebra (algebraic expressions) EASY**

$$\frac{3x + 4}{12}$$

Distribute: $\dfrac{3x}{12} + \dfrac{4}{12}$

Simplify: $\dfrac{x}{4} + \dfrac{1}{3}$

4. A   **Advanced Mathematics (polynomials) EASY**

There are several ways to approach this question. Perhaps the simplest is to use the Factor Theorem: If $x - c$ is a factor of a polynomial, then $x = c$ is a zero of that polynomial. Therefore, if $x - 3$ is a factor of our polynomial, $x = 3$ must be a zero:

$$x^2 + kx + 12 = (3)^2 + 3k + 12 = 0$$

Simplify: $9 + 3k + 12 = 0$
Subtract 21: $3k = -21$
Divide by 3: $k - -7$

Alternately, you might try to find the other factor of the quadratic. Since the constant term in the quadratic is 12, the constant term in the other binomial factor must be $12 \div -3 = -4$.

$$(x - 3)(x - 4) = x^2 + kx + 12$$

FOIL: $x^2 - 7x + 12 = x^2 + kx + 12$
Subtract x and 12: $-7x = kx$
Divide by x: $-7 = k$

5. C   **Additional Topics (circles and triangles)**
                                                          MEDIUM

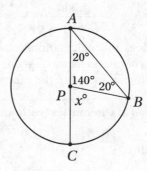

Since PA and PB are both radii of the circle, they are congruent, and so triangle APB is isosceles. By the Isosceles Triangle Theorem, then, angle A must also be 20°. From here, you might simply notice that the angle we're looking for, CPB, is the external angle to this triangle, and so it has a measure equal to the sum of the two remote interior angles: $20° + 20° = 40°$. Alternately, you could notice that angle APB must have a measure of 140° (since all angles in a triangle have a sum of 180°), and since AC is a straight line, angle $CPB = 180° - 140° = 40°$.

---

6. **B**   Advanced Mathematics (sequences) MEDIUM

Let's choose a value, like $b = 2$, for our positive constant. This gives us an expression of $2n + 4$ for the nth term of the sequence. Substituting $n = 1$, $n = 2$, $n = 3$, etc. gives us a sequence of 6, 8, 10, 12, 14, and so on. Choice (A) is clearly incorrect, because the first term of this sequence is not 2. Choice (C) is also incorrect because the average of the first three terms is $(6 + 8 + 10)/3 = 8$, not 2. Choice (D) is also incorrect because the ratio of the second term to the first is $8/6 = 4/3$. Only choice (B), the difference between the fourth term and the third term, $12 - 10$, gives us a value of 2.

---

7. **A**   Advanced Mathematics (radical and exponential equations) MEDIUM

For this question, we need to know two Laws of Exponentials from Chapter 9: Law #8 and Law #9. First, we use Law #9 to translate the radicals into exponents.

Given equation:	$m^3 = \sqrt{\sqrt{n}}$
Apply Law of Exponentials #9:	$m^3 = \sqrt{n^{\frac{1}{2}}}$
Apply Law of Exponentials #9 again:	$m^3 = \left(n^{\frac{1}{2}}\right)^{\frac{1}{2}}$
Apply Law of Exponentials #8:	$m^3 = n^{\frac{1}{4}}$
Raise to the $\frac{1}{3}$ power:	$(m^3)^{\frac{1}{3}} = \left(n^{\frac{1}{4}}\right)^{\frac{1}{3}}$
Apply Law of Exponentials #8 again:	$m = n^{\frac{1}{12}}$

---

8. **B**   Algebra (word problems) MEDIUM

Perhaps the most straightforward way to approach this question is to regard it as a conversion from a given *area of lawn* (in square feet) to *cost* (in dollars).

Area of rectangular lawn: $A = bh = ab$ square feet
Convert using given conversion factors:

$$ab \text{ square feet} \times \frac{1 \text{ bag}}{5,000 \text{ square feet}} \times \frac{\$p}{1 \text{ bag}} = \$\frac{abp}{5,000}$$

Make sure to check this calculation by noticing that all units "cancel" as common factors, except for the unit we want, dollars, which remains in the numerator.

---

9. **C**   Advanced Mathematics (rational inequalities) MEDIUM

Original inequality: $\dfrac{5}{m} \leq \dfrac{2}{3}$

Multiply by $3m$ (since $m > 0$, we don't "flip" the inequality):
$$15 \leq 2m$$
Divide by 2: $7.5 \leq m$
Therefore, the least possible value of m is 7.5.

---

10. **A**   Algebra (linear functions) MEDIUM-HARD

Given function: $f(x) = 3x + n$
Substitute $f(2) = 0$: $f(2) = 3(2) + n = 0$

Simplify: $6 + n = 0$
Subtract 6: $n = -6$
Therefore, the function is $f(x) = 3x - 6$.
Evaluate $f(n)$: $f(n) = f(-6) = 3(-6) - 6 = -18 - 6 = -24$

---

11. **A**   Algebra (absolute values) MEDIUM-HARD

First, we should notice that each choice can be interpreted as a distance between two points on the number line.

(A) $|s - v| =$ the distance between s and v

(B) $|s - t| =$ the distance between s and t

(C) $|s + v| = |s - (-v)| =$ the distance between s and $-v$

(D) $|u + v| = |u - (-v)| =$ the distance between u and $-v$

Thinking this way gives us a very straightforward way to solve the problem without doing any calculation. First we need to locate $-v$ on the number line by just reflecting v over the origin at 0. (Recall that multiplication by -1 is equivalent to reflecting a point on the number line over the origin at 0.) This makes it easy to see the distances the problem is asking us to compare:

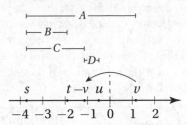

Clearly, the greatest of these distances is (A).

---

12. **B**   Special Topics (trigonometry) MEDIUM-HARD

In order to solve this without a calculator, we need to know how to analyze this problem in terms of the unit circle. First, let's solve for $\cos x$: $4 \cos x = 1$

Divide by 4: $\cos x = \dfrac{1}{4}$

What does the mean in terms of the unit circle? Recall from Chapter 10, Lesson 9, that the cosine of any angle corresponds to the x-coordinate of the corresponding point for that angle on the unit circle:

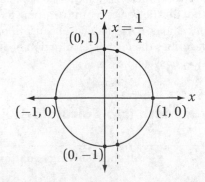

Notice that there are exactly two points on the unit circle that have an x-coordinate of 1/4. Now let's think about the angle. We are told that x goes from 0 to 3π. Remember that a full trip around the circle is 2π radians; therefore, a journey from $x = 0$ to $x = 3\pi$ is 1.5 trips around the circle counterclockwise starting from the positive x-axis. If you trace with your finger 1.5 times around the circle starting from the point (1, 0), you'll hit our "points of interest" exactly three times.

13. **C**   Additional Topics (complex numbers) HARD

To solve this without a calculator, you must be able to evaluate a few low powers of i. Recall from Chapter 10, Lesson 10, that $i^0 = 1$, $i^1 = i$, $i^2 = -1$, $i^3 = -i$, and $i^4 = 1$. Therefore $i^3 + i = -i + i = 0$. Now, it's just a matter of finding the choice that does NOT equal 0.

(A) $(2i)^2 + 4 = -4 + 4 = 0$

(B) $2 - 2i^4 = 2 - 2 = 0$

(C) $2i^2 - 2 = -2 - 2 = -4$

(D) $i^4 - 1 = 1 - 1 = 0$

Therefore, the correct answer is (C).

14. **D** Algebra (graphs of quadratic equations) HARD

Recall from Chapter 9, Lesson 6, that any equation in the form $y = a(x - h)^2 + k$ has a vertex at (h, k) and is open up if $a > 0$ and down if $a < 0$. In the equation $y = -(x + m)^2 + m$; therefore, the vertex is $(-m, m)$, and $a = -1$. Since $m > 1$, this means that the vertex of the parabola has a negative x-coordinate and a positive y-coordinate, which means the vertex is in quadrant II. And since $a < 0$, the parabola is open down. The only graph among the choices that is an open down parabola with a vertex in the second quadrant is the graph in choice (D).

15. **B**   Advanced Mathematics (linear and nonlinear systems) HARD

First, notice that the question is only asking us to find values of x, so it's a good idea to substitute in order to eliminate y from the system.

$$x - 3y = -2$$

Substitute $y = \dfrac{5}{x}$: $x - 3\left(\dfrac{5}{x}\right) = -2$

Multiply by x and simplify: $x^2 - 15 = -2x$

Add $2x$: $x^2 + 2x - 15 = 0$

Factor using Sum-Product Method: $(x - 3)(x + 5) = 0$

Therefore, the values of x that satisfy the original system also satisfy the equation $(x - 3)(x + 5) = 0$.

16. **4.5 or 9/2**   Algebra (linear equations) EASY

Original equation: $\dfrac{2}{3}a + \dfrac{1}{2}b = 5$

Substitute $b = 4$: $\dfrac{2}{3}a + \dfrac{1}{2}(4) = 5$

Simplify: $\dfrac{2}{3}a + 2 = 5$

Subtract 2: $\dfrac{2}{3}a = 3$

Multiply by $\dfrac{3}{2}$: $a = \dfrac{9}{2}$

17. **7**   Advanced Mathematics (rational equations) EASY

Given inequality: $\dfrac{6}{x} + \dfrac{1}{2x} < 1$

Multiply by $2x$: $12 + 1 < 2x$

Simplify: $13 < 2x$

Divide by 2: $6.5 < x$

The smallest integer that is greater than 6.5 is 7.

18. **8.4 or 42/5**   Additional Topics (perimeters and area) MEDIUM-HARD

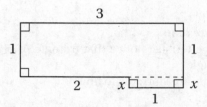

First, drawing a line as shown in the diagram shows that the figure is composed of two rectangles, but the height of the smaller one is unknown. Let's call it x. The area of the larger rectangle is $(3)(1) = 3$, and the area of the smaller rectangle is $(1)(x) = x$. Clearly, the area of the figure must be the sum of these two areas

$$\text{Area} = \dfrac{16}{5} = 3 + x$$

Subtract 3: $\dfrac{16}{5} - 3 = \dfrac{16}{5} - \dfrac{15}{5} = \dfrac{1}{5} = x$

Therefore, the perimeter of the figure is just the sum of the lengths of its sides. If we travel around the figure clockwise from the leftmost side, we get a perimeter of

$$1 + 3 + 1 + \dfrac{1}{5} + 1 + \dfrac{1}{5} + 2 = 8 + \dfrac{2}{5} = 8.4.$$

19. **5 or 7**   Algebra (rational equations) MEDIUM-HARD

Original equation: $\dfrac{6}{x+1} - \dfrac{3}{x-1} = \dfrac{1}{4}$

Multiply by $4(x + 1)(x - 1)$:

$$\dfrac{24(x+1)(x-1)}{x+1} - \dfrac{12(x+1)(x-1)}{x-1} = \dfrac{4(x+1)(x-1)}{4}$$

We do this because $4(x + 1)(x - 1)$ is the least common multiple of the denominators, so multiplying both sides by this will eliminate the denominators and simplify the equation.

Cancel common factors:

$$24(x-1) - 12(x+1) = (x+1)(x-1)$$

Distribute and FOIL: $(24x - 24) - (12x + 12) = x^2 - 1$
Collect like terms: $12x - 36 = x^2 - 1$
Subtract $12x$ and add 36: $0 = x^2 - 12x + 35$
Factor: $0 = (x - 5)(x - 7)$
Solve using Zero Product Property: $x = 5$ or 7

---

20. **8/13 or .615**   **Special Topics (trigonometry)**
                                              HARD

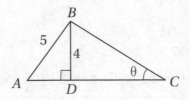

Find AD with Pythagorean Theorem: $(AD)^2 + 4^2 = 5^2$
Simplify: $(AD)^2 + 16 = 25$
Subtract 16: $(AD)^2 = 9$
Take square root: $AD = 3$
Or, even better, just notice that triangle ADB is a 3-4-5 right triangle.
Use triangle area formula to find AC:

$$\text{Area} = \frac{1}{2}bh = \frac{1}{2}(AC)(4) = 19$$

Simplify: $2(AC) = 19$

Divide by 2: $AC = \dfrac{19}{2}$

Find DC: $DC = AC - AD = \dfrac{19}{2} - 3 = \dfrac{19}{2} - \dfrac{6}{2} = \dfrac{13}{2}$

Find $\tan \theta$: $\tan\theta = \dfrac{\text{opp}}{\text{hyp}} = \dfrac{BD}{DC} = \dfrac{4}{\frac{13}{2}} = 4 \times \dfrac{2}{13} = \dfrac{8}{13}$

Section 4: Math (Calculator)

1. **D**   **Algebra (solving equations) EASY**

$$\frac{n}{20} = 0.8$$

Multiply by 20: $n = 0.8(20) = 16$

---

2. **A**   **Data Analysis (central tendency) EASY**

The median of three numbers is the one in the middle when they are listed in order. If two of the numbers are 10 and 12, with 12 as the median, then the third number must be greater than or equal to 12, otherwise 12 would not be in the middle. Of the choices, only (A) 8 is not greater than or equal to 12.

---

3. **C**   **Algebra/Data Analysis (expressing relationships) EASY**

The first ordered pair, $x = 0$ and $y = 2$, does not satisfy the equations in (A), (B), or (D), so those choices can be eliminated. You should also confirm that the equation in (C), $y = 2x + 2$, is satisfied by all four ordered pairs.

---

4. **B**   **Data Analysis (central tendency) EASY**

Let's call the 3 positive integers a, b, and c. If the average of these numbers is m, then

$$\frac{a+b+c}{3} = m$$

Multiply by 3: $a + b + c = 3m$
New average when 24 is included
in the set: $\dfrac{a+b+c+24}{4}$

Substitute $a + b + c = 3m$: $\dfrac{3m+24}{4}$

---

5. **C**   **Algebra (rational equations) EASY**

$$\frac{6}{x} + 3 = -1$$

Multiply by x: $6 + 3x = -x$
Subtract $3x$: $6 = -4x$

Divide by -4: $x = \dfrac{6}{-4} = -\dfrac{3}{2}$

---

6. **A**   **Algebra (representing quantities) EASY**

The cost for a month's worth of energy is the cost per kilowatt-hour times the total number of kilowatt-hours used: ($0.15/kWh)(30 kWh). The total monthly charge, P, must also include the service fee: $P = 0.15(30) + 16$.

---

7. **A**   **Advanced Mathematics (triangle trigonometry) EASY**

Remember the definitions of the basic trigonometric functions: SOH CAH TOA. Since the "side of interest" (h) is the opposite side to the given angle (42°), and since we know the length of the hypotenuse (1,200), we should use SOH.

$$\sin x = \frac{\text{opp}}{\text{hyp}}$$

Plug in the values: $\sin 42° = \dfrac{h}{1,200}$

Substitute $\sin 42° = 0.669$: $0.669 = \dfrac{h}{1,200}$

Multiply by 1,002: $(1,200)(0.669) = 802.8 = h$

---

8. **C**   **Special Topics (polygons) EASY**

The sum of the measures if the interior angles of a triangle is 180°, therefore $m \angle BED + 90° + 50° = 180°$, and so $m \angle BED = 40°$. Since $\angle AEC$ is vertical to $\angle BED$, it must also have a measure of 40°, and so $40 + x + x = 180$
Simplify: $40 + 2x = 180$
Subtract 40: $2x = 140$
Divide by 2: $x = 70$

---

9. **C**   **Data Analysis (histogram) MEDIUM**

According to the histogram, 7 students received 15 credits, 1 student received 16 credits, and 1 student received 18 credits, for a total of 9 students who received 15 or more credits. This is 9/24 of the total, or 37.5%

10. D   Data Analysis (histogram/central tendency)
MEDIUM

Data set: 8, 9, 12, 12, 12, 12, 12, 12, 12, 12, 12, 12, 13, 13, 13, 15, 15, 15, 15, 15, 15, 15, 16, 18

The median of a set of numbers is the "middle" number of the set when the numbers are listed in order. If the set contains an odd number of numbers, the median is the middle number, but if the set contains an even number of numbers, it is the average of the two middle numbers. Since this set contains 24 numbers, the median is the average or the 12th and the 13th numbers. The 12th number in the set is 12, and the 13th number in the set is 13, the median is 12.5.

11. D   Algebra (absolute values) **EASY**

The absolute distance from a to b is $|a - b|$ and the absolute distance from -2 to 6 is $|-2 - 6| = 8$. Therefore, $|a - b| > 8$.

12. D   Special Topics (circles)
MEDIUM

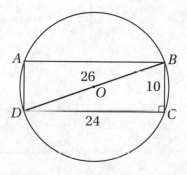

Since $ABCD$ is a rectangle, we can find the length of its diagonal using the Pythagorean Theorem: $10^2 + 24^2 = d^2$. Even better, we can notice that the two legs are in a 5:12 ratio, and therefore triangle BCD is a 5-12-13 triangle. In either case, we find that $DB = 26$. Since DB is also a diameter of the circle, the radius of the circle is $26/2 = 13$, and therefore, the area of the circle is $\pi r^2 = \pi(13)^2 = 169\pi$.

13. B   Problem Solving/Data Analysis
(enumeration of data) **MEDIUM**

If Niko is the 8th oldest person in the class, then there are 7 students older than he is. If he is the 12th youngest person, then there are 11 students younger than he is. Therefore, there are 18 students in addition to him, for a total of 19 students.

14. D   Additional Topics
(complex numbers) **MEDIUM**

$$(2 - i)(3 - 2i)$$

FOIL: $6 - 4i - 3i + 2i^2$

Substitute $i^2 = -1$: $6 - 4i - 3i + 2(-1)$

Combine like terms: $4 - 7i$

15. B   Advanced Mathematics (exponentials)
MEDIUM

$$f(3) = (3^2)^{-2b} = 3$$

Exponential Law #8
(from Chapter 9, Lesson 9): $3^{-4b} = 3^1$

Exponential Law #10
(from Chapter 9, Lesson 9) $-4b = 1$

Divide by -4: $b = -\dfrac{1}{4}$

16. A   Data Analysis (probability) **MEDIUM**

Since the sum of 55 and 35 is 90, which is 10 greater than 80, there must be at least 10 in the overlap between the two sets. Statement (B) is not necessarily true, because it is possible that all 35 students taking AP courses are also varsity athletes, which is more than half of 55. Statement (C) is not true because $80 - 55 = 25$ students do not play varsity sports, and $80 - 35 = 45$ students do not take at least one AP course. Statement (D) is not necessarily true, because 35 students take at least one AP course and 25 students do not play a varsity sport, and this sum, $35 + 25 = 60$, is less than the total number of students, so it is possible that there is no overlap between these two sets.

17. A   Algebra (slopes) **MEDIUM**

If $AB = BC$, then triangle ABC is isosceles and therefore the two base angles are congruent and the triangle has a vertical axis of symmetry at the line $x = 3$. This implies that the slopes of lines $\overline{AB}$ and $\overline{BC}$ are opposites. We can calculate the slope of $\overline{BC}$ from its endpoints:

$$\text{slope} = \frac{y_2 - y_1}{x_2 - x_1} = \frac{0 - 6}{5 - 3} = -\frac{6}{2} = -3$$

Therefore, the slope of $\overline{AB}$ is 3, and so $mn = (3)(-3) = -9$.

18. D   Advanced Mathematics (functions)
MEDIUM-HARD

To answer this question, we must evaluate each of the three functions for an input of ½:

$$f\left(\frac{1}{2}\right) = \left(\frac{1}{2}\right)^2 = \frac{1}{4} = 0.25$$

$$g\left(\frac{1}{2}\right) = \frac{1}{2} = 0.50$$

$$h\left(\frac{1}{2}\right) = \sqrt{\frac{1}{2}} = \frac{1}{\sqrt{2}} = \frac{\sqrt{2}}{2} \approx 0.71$$

Therefore, $f\left(\dfrac{1}{2}\right) < g\left(\dfrac{1}{2}\right) < h\left(\dfrac{1}{2}\right)$.

19. A   Data Analysis (graphing data) **MEDIUM-HARD**

If y varies inversely as the square of x, then the variables are related by the equation $f = \dfrac{k}{x^2}$, where k is a positive constant. The graph of such an equation in the xy-plane looks like this:

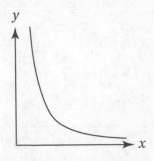

This most closely resembles the scatterplot in choice (A).

---

20. C **Algebra (expressing relationships)**
MEDIUM-HARD

The portion of the birds that are finches is just the number of finches divided by the total number of birds. Since there are already 30 finches, adding n finches makes $30 + n$ finches. Since there are already $12 + 30 + 18 = 60$ total birds, adding n finches makes $60 + n$ total birds.

Since $80\% = 4/5$, $\dfrac{30+n}{60+n} = \dfrac{4}{5}$.

---

21. B **Advanced Mathematics (functions)**
MEDIUM-HARD

$$f(x) = x^2 - 1$$

Substitute $x = \dfrac{1}{b}$: $\quad f\left(\dfrac{1}{b}\right) = \left(\dfrac{1}{b}\right)^2 - 1$

Simplify: $\quad f\left(\dfrac{1}{b}\right) = \dfrac{1}{b^2} - 1$

Get common denominator: $\quad f\left(\dfrac{1}{b}\right) = \dfrac{1}{b^2} - \dfrac{b^2}{b^2}$

Subtract fractions: $\quad f\left(\dfrac{1}{b}\right) = \dfrac{1-b^2}{b^2}$

Factor numerator: $\quad f\left(\dfrac{1}{b}\right) = \dfrac{(1-b)(1+b)}{b^2}$

---

22. D **Advanced Mathematics (quadratics)**
MEDIUM-HARD

Since k can be any number greater than 0, let's pick $k = 1$ for convenience. If $x = 3$, then $y = (1)(3)^2 = 9$, and if $x = 12$, then $y = (1)(12)^2 = 144$. In this case, both statement (B) and statement (D) are true, since $9 + 135 = 144$ and $9(16) = 144$; therefore, we can eliminate choices (A) and (C). Now let's choose $k = 2$. If $x = 3$, then $y = (2)(3)^2 = 18$, and if $x = 12$, then $y = 2(12)^2 = 288$. Since $18 + 135 \neq 288$, but $18(16) = 288$, the correct answer is (D).

Notice, also, that since y varies directly as the square of x, then when x is multiplied by n, y is multiplied by n^2. Since x is being multiplied by 4 (to go from 3 to 12), then y must be multiplied by $4^2 = 16$.

---

23. B **Advanced Mathematics (analyzing quadratics) HARD**

One way to tackle this question is simply to simplify the expression for $f(7)$, and then see which choice gives the same expression.

$$f(7) = k(7 + 6)(7 - 1) = k(13)(6) = 78k$$

Evaluate (A):
$$f(-78) = k(-78 + 6)(-78 - 1) = k(-72)(-79) = 5{,}688k$$

Evaluate (B):
$$f(-12) = k(-12 + 6)(-12 - 1) = k(-6)(-13) = 78k$$

Evaluate (C):
$$f(-2) = k(-2 + 6)(-2 - 1) = k(4)(-3) = -12k$$

Evaluate (D):
$$f(78) = k(78 + 6)(78 - 1) = k(84)(77) = 6{,}468k$$

This shows that $f(-12)$ is equal to $f(7)$. Alternately, you might just make a quick sketch of the parabola and take advantage of the symmetry:

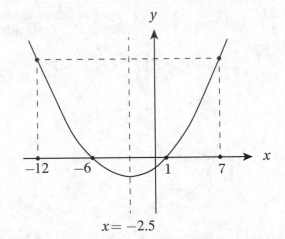

$$x = -2.5$$

---

24. C **Problem Solving (percentages)**
MEDIUM-HARD

Let $p =$ the initial price per share of the stock. After the first year, its price increased by 20%, so its price was $(1.20)p$. After the second year, this price declined 25%, so its price was $(0.75)(1.20)p$. After the second year, this price increased by 10% so its price was $(1.10)(0.75)(1.20)p = 0.99p$, which means that overall the price decreased by 1%.

---

25. D **Algebra (exponentials) MEDIUM-HARD**

Expression to be evaluated: $\quad \dfrac{w}{y^3}$

Substitute $w = y^6$: $\quad \dfrac{y^6}{y^3}$

Simplify with Exponential Law #6
(from Chapter 9, Lesson 9): $\quad y^3$

Substitute $y = x^2$: $\quad (x^2)^3$

Simplify with Exponential
Law #8 (from Chapter 9, Lesson 9): $\quad x^6$

26. D — Data Analysis (tables) MEDIUM-HARD

Although we don't need to fill in the entire table, it's interesting to note that it has a "diagonal symmetry" when it is completed. Just following the rule and moving systematically toward x reveals that it is $56 + 56 = 112$.

0	1	2	3	4	5
1	2	4	7	11	16
2	4	8	15	26	42
3	7	15	30	56	98
4	11	26	56	**112**	210
5	16	42	98	210	420

27. C — Advanced Mathematics (quadratics) HARD

We can find the value of c by just substituting $x = -1$ into the equation.

Given equation: $\qquad\qquad 3x^2 = 4x + c$

Substitute $x = -1$: $\qquad 3(-1)^2 = 4(-1) + c$

Simplify: $\qquad\qquad\qquad 3 = -4 + c$

Add 4: $\qquad\qquad\qquad\qquad 7 = c$

Therefore, the equation is: $\qquad 3x^2 = 4x + 7$

Subtract $4x$ and 7: $\qquad 3x^2 - 4x - 7 = 0$

Factor using Sum-Product Method: $\quad (x + 1)(3x - 7) = 0$

(Notice that the factor $(x + 1)$ corresponds to the fact that $x = -1$ is a solution to the quadratic.)

Use Zero Product Property to find other solution: $\qquad\qquad 3x - 7 = 0$

Add 7: $\qquad\qquad\qquad\qquad 3x = 7$

Divide by 3: $\qquad\qquad\qquad x = 7/3$

28. B — Special Topics (arcs) HARD

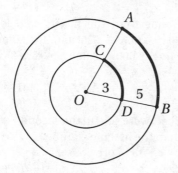

First, we should make sure we mark up the diagram with the measurements we know: $OD = 3$ and $DB = 5$. This means that the radius of the small circle is 3 and the radius of the large circle is 8. Notice that sectors AOB and COD share a central angle, and therefore are similar. So the measures of arc CD and arc AB are

in a ratio of 3:8.

$$\frac{m\overset{\frown}{CD}}{m\overset{\frown}{AB}} = \frac{m\overset{\frown}{CD}}{5\pi} = \frac{3}{8}$$

Cross multiply: $\qquad 8\left(m\overset{\frown}{CD}\right) = 15\pi$

Divide by 8: $\qquad m\overset{\frown}{CD} = \dfrac{15\pi}{8}$

29. C — Data Analysis (graphs) MEDIUM

Since there are only four data points, it's not hard to list the February-May ordered pairs. Notice that the February axis is vertical, and the May axis is horizontal, so the typical x-y relationship is reversed:

Class A: February: 60, May: 60
Class B: February: 80, May: 70
Class C: February: 50, May: 70
Class D: February: 90, May: 90

Notice that the only class that saw an increase in percent participation is Class C.

30. C — Data Analysis (graphs) HARD

We just need to tally the number of students who participated from each class.

Class A: 60% of 20 students = 12 students
Class B: 70% of 30 students = 21 students
Class C: 70% of 20 students = 14 students
Class D: 90% of 30 students = 27 students
$12 + 21 + 14 + 27 = 74$ students

31. 0.8 or 4/5 — Algebra (radical equations) EASY

Given equation: $\qquad\qquad 4 + \sqrt{b} = 7.2$

Subtract 4: $\qquad\qquad\qquad \sqrt{b} = 3.2$

Therefore, $4 - \sqrt{b} = 4 - 3.2 = 0.8$.

32. 8 — Advance Mathematics (quadratics) EASY

Given equation: $\qquad\qquad y = 3x^2 - kx - 35$

Substitute $x = 5$ and $y = 0$: $\quad 0 = 3(5)^2 - k(5) - 35$

Simplify: $\qquad\qquad\qquad 0 = 75 - 5k - 35$

Simplify: $\qquad\qquad\qquad 0 = 40 - 5k$

Add $5k$: $\qquad\qquad\qquad\qquad 5k = 40$

Divide by 5: $\qquad\qquad\qquad k = 8$

33. .96 — Additional Topics (circles/triangles) MEDIUM-HARD

When looking for the area of the triangle, remember that there are two basic methods: the direct method and the indirect method. With the direct method, we simply plug the base and height measurements into the formula $A = \dfrac{bh}{2}$, and with the indirect method, we find the area as the sum or difference of other areas. In this case, since we know the lengths of one of the sides, the direct method is probably best. But we will need to find the height as well.

Area of the circle is π: $\pi r^2 = \pi$
Divide by π: $r^2 = 1$
Take square root: $r = 1$

Now let's mark up the diagram with this information. Since the radius of the circle is 1, the diameter FH has a length of 2. Now we can use the Pythagorean Theorem to find the length of GH, which is the height of the triangle if FG is taken as the base. $(1.6)^2 + (GH)^2 = 2^2$

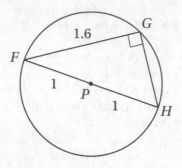

Simplify: $2.56 + (GH)^2 = 4$
Subtract 2.56: $(GH)^2 = 1.44$
Take square root: $GH = 1.2$

(Notice that this is in fact a 3-4-5 triangle: if we multiply 3-4-5 by 0.4, we get 1.2-1.6-2.)

Plug into area formula: $A = \dfrac{bh}{2} = \dfrac{(1.2)(1.6)}{2} = 0.96$

---

34. **4.29 ≤ x ≤ 4.79**   **Algebra (solving inequalities) HARD**

$$-\frac{3}{5} < -2t + 1 < -\frac{3}{7}$$

Multiply by −3 and "flip" inequalities: $\dfrac{9}{5} > 6t - 3 > \dfrac{9}{7}$

Add 3: $\dfrac{24}{5} > 6t > \dfrac{30}{7}$

Divide to get decimal form: $4.80 > 6t > 4.2857$
Therefore any decimal value between 4.29 and 4.79, inclusive, is acceptable.

---

35. **.84**   **Advanced Mathematics (trigonometry) MEDIUM-HARD**

You may find it helpful to make a quick sketch of the unit circle on the xy-plane, as we discussed in Chapter 10. Subtracting π radians (or 180°) from an angle just means rotating the terminal ray of that angle 180° clockwise. It should be clear, then, that in the xy-plane, the angle with measure $x - \pi$ points in the opposite direction of the angle with measure x. Recall that the cosine of an angle is just the x-coordinate of the point where its terminal ray intersects the unit circle. Since $\cos(x - \pi) = 0.4$ (that

is, its cosine is positive), its terminal ray must be in a quadrant where the x-coordinates are positive: either quadrant I or quadrant IV. Let's just put it in quadrant I. This means that the angle with measure x is in quadrant III, and so it has the opposite cosine:

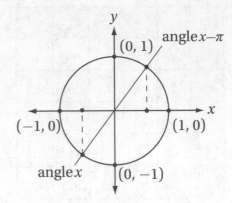

$\cos x = -0.4$

Recall Pythagorean Identity
from Chapter 10: $\sin^2 x + \cos^2 x = 1$
Substitute $\cos x = 0.4$: $\sin^2 x + (-0.4)^2 = 1$
Simplify: $\sin^2 x + 0.16 = 1$
Subtract 0.16: $\sin^2 x = 0.84$

---

36. **12**   **Problem Solving/Data Analysis (word problem) MEDIUM-HARD**

This one is a bit trickier than it looks. We have 10 pounds of grain and have used it to feed 20 chickens. Since one pound of grain feeds 5 chickens, proportionally we need 4 pounds of grain to feed 20 chickens. This leaves us $10 - 4 = 6$ pounds of grain to feed the pigs. Since 1 pound of grain can feed 2 pigs, proportionally 6 pounds of grain can feed 12 pigs.

---

37. **371**   **Problem Solving (extended thinking) HARD**

The total revenue from the tickets sold is $60(50) + $50(60) + $40x + $35y + $30(100). If the total revenue was $15,000, then $3,000 + 3,000 + 40x + 35x + 3,000 = 15,000$

Subtract 9,000: $40x + 35y = 6,000$
Divide by 5: $8x + 7y = 1,200$

If 15 more tickets were sold in the second
mezzanine than the first mezzanine: $y = x + 15$
Substitute $y = x + 15$ in previous
equation: $8x + 7(x + 15) = 1,200$
Distribute: $8x + 7x + 105 = 1,200$
Subtract 105: $15x = 1,095$
Divide by 15: $x = 73$
Substitute to find y: $y = x + 15 = 73 + 15 = 88$

Therefore, the total number of tickets sold is $50 + 60 + 73 + 88 + 100 = 371$.

38. **25** **Problem Solving (extended thinking) HARD**

The mathematical model $n = \dfrac{2,800}{p}$ has embedded in it the predicted revenue per section: np = revenue per section = $2,800. Notice that this prediction is $200 less than the actual average revenue per section of $3,000, so clearly the model underestimated the number of tickets sold per section.

If we want to analyze this situation in detail, we can compare the predicted tickets sold to the actual tickets sold by adding a new column to the table entitled "predicted sold," which we can fill in using the calculations from our model. Also, it might be helpful to also add columns for "total revenue" for each situation.

Section	Price Per Ticket	Number Sold	Section Revenue	Predicted Sold	Predicted Revenue
Front Orchestra	$60	50	$3,000	46.667	$2,800
Rear Orchestra	$50	60	$3,000	56	$2,800
First Mezzanine	$40	73	$2,920	70	$2,800
Second Mezzanine	$35	88	$3,080	80	$2,800
Third Mezzanine	$30	100	$3,000	93.333	$2,800
Total		371	$15,000	346	$14,000

You might notice that the predicted number of tickets sold in the Front Orchestra and the Third Mezzanine are fractions, which seems strange. (Of course we can't sell a fraction of a ticket!) But even if we round these predictions to the nearest whole numbers, 47 and 93, the total number of tickets is the same: 346, which underestimates the number of tickets sold by 25.

Section 5: Essay

Sample Essay: Analysis of Ellis Parker Butler's "On Spelling"

In his essay "On Spelling," Ellis Parker Butler argues that we should change the rules of English spelling to make them more logical. He says that the rules of spelling have "nothing to do with genius, except to kill it" (1). The essay is consistently humorous, and he uses first-person anecdote, anthropomorphism, and cultural allusions to drive his points home. He also provides two alternatives to our current system of spelling, but they are not meant to be taken seriously, but show the silliness of the rules themselves.

Butler's tone is comical throughout the essay. In the first paragraph, his essay (written in 1906) claims that America at the turn of the 20th century was lagging behind Europe because it was "the slave of the spelling-book" (1), and that writers like him, who "simply blaze with genius" (2), shouldn't have to write "a stupid sort of literature that is spelled correctly" (2). He is kidding when he says that "we take to being killed by the automobile quite naturally now" (3), but he is using humor to make the point that Americans can get used to even stupid and dangerous things given enough time. He also pokes fun at the hopes for real change when he says that the advantage of his plan is "so manifest that I am afraid it will never be adopted" (7).

He uses first-person anecdote in the essay, as if the argument is a discussion between his wife, Serena, and himself. He says that "Serena and I will form a society for the reforming of English pronunciation" (6), and he even makes a joke that his bad spelling had something to do with his "ardent love" (8) for his wife. Although this casual tone and style does differs from that of a real spelling expert, it provides charm to the essay.

Butler also uses anthropomorphism to describe his ideas about spelling, which helps to make his explanation come to life for readers. He talks about the word "although" as if it were a person: "'Altho' does all the work, and 'ugh' sits on the fence and whittles. I would put 'ugh' to work (5)." This shows that his plan for reforming English spelling would appeal to the American value of hard work.

Butler makes many cultural allusions about American thinking. He says that Americans are slow to change ("we Americans do not like sudden changes" (3)) hard working ('we want no idle class in America" (4)) and practical ("Serena's plan is . . . more American . . . she would simply boycott them" (8)). In this way, Butler is trying to connect with his readers in terms that make sense to them and their values, and so they are more likely to approve of his plan.

This essay is not written from the point of view of an intellectual or expert, but from an ordinary American who doesn't like dealing with dumb rules. By using a humorous style in the first person, and by using anthropomorphism and cultural allusions, he makes his essay easy and fun to read even as it makes its points.

Scoring

Reading—4 out of 4

This essay demonstrates a strong comprehension of Butler's central claims, using summary, paraphrase, and quotations. It summarizes Butler's central thesis (*we should change the rules of English spelling to make them more logical*), significant rhetorical elements (*first-person anecdote, anthropomorphism, and cultural allusions*), and tone (*consistently humorous*). The quotations are carefully chosen to illustrate the central elements of Butler's essay, and are accompanied by relevant and accurate commentary.

Analysis—4 out of 4

This essay shows a strong and critical analysis of Butler's argument and style. The elements it identifies (*humor . . . first-person anecdote, anthropomorphism, and cultural allusions*) are well-chosen, and he discusses the effect of each element (*e.g. he is using humor to make the point that Americans can get used to even stupid and dangerous things; . . . his casual tone . . . provides charm to the essay; . . . anthropomorphism . . . helps to make his explanation come to life . . . [and] shows that his plan for reforming English spelling would appeal to the American value of hard work; . . . cultural allusions . . . connect with* *his readers in terms that make sense to them and their values*), without taking a side for or against Butler's thesis. It also provides substantial textual evidence for its claims, and demonstrates a strong understanding of Butler's rhetorical task.

Writing—4 out of 4

This essay shows a strong mastery of language, organization, and sentence structure. It remains focused on a clear central claim, and develops its secondary claims in well-organized paragraphs. It demonstrates effective variation in sentence structure and strong verb choice (*e.g. drive his points home . . . pokes fun at the hopes for real change*). Largely free from grammatical error, this essay demonstrates strong command of language and proficiency in writing.

PRACTICE TEST 2

1. Reading Test

   65 MINUTES   52 QUESTIONS   536

2. Writing and Language Test

   35 MINUTES   44 QUESTIONS   553

3. Math Test – No Calculator

   25 MINUTES   20 QUESTIONS   566

4. Math Test – Calculator

   55 MINUTES   38 QUESTIONS   572

5. Essay (optional)

   50 MINUTES   1 QUESTION   582

ANSWER SHEET for PRACTICE TEST 2

Use a No. 2 pencil and fill in the entire circle darkly and completely.
If you change your response, erase as completely as possible

SECTION 1

1 Ⓐ Ⓑ Ⓒ Ⓓ	13 Ⓐ Ⓑ Ⓒ Ⓓ	25 Ⓐ Ⓑ Ⓒ Ⓓ	37 Ⓐ Ⓑ Ⓒ Ⓓ	49 Ⓐ Ⓑ Ⓒ Ⓓ
2 Ⓐ Ⓑ Ⓒ Ⓓ	14 Ⓐ Ⓑ Ⓒ Ⓓ	26 Ⓐ Ⓑ Ⓒ Ⓓ	38 Ⓐ Ⓑ Ⓒ Ⓓ	50 Ⓐ Ⓑ Ⓒ Ⓓ
3 Ⓐ Ⓑ Ⓒ Ⓓ	15 Ⓐ Ⓑ Ⓒ Ⓓ	27 Ⓐ Ⓑ Ⓒ Ⓓ	39 Ⓐ Ⓑ Ⓒ Ⓓ	51 Ⓐ Ⓑ Ⓒ Ⓓ
4 Ⓐ Ⓑ Ⓒ Ⓓ	16 Ⓐ Ⓑ Ⓒ Ⓓ	28 Ⓐ Ⓑ Ⓒ Ⓓ	40 Ⓐ Ⓑ Ⓒ Ⓓ	52 Ⓐ Ⓑ Ⓒ Ⓓ
5 Ⓐ Ⓑ Ⓒ Ⓓ	17 Ⓐ Ⓑ Ⓒ Ⓓ	29 Ⓐ Ⓑ Ⓒ Ⓓ	41 Ⓐ Ⓑ Ⓒ Ⓓ	
6 Ⓐ Ⓑ Ⓒ Ⓓ	18 Ⓐ Ⓑ Ⓒ Ⓓ	30 Ⓐ Ⓑ Ⓒ Ⓓ	42 Ⓐ Ⓑ Ⓒ Ⓓ	
7 Ⓐ Ⓑ Ⓒ Ⓓ	19 Ⓐ Ⓑ Ⓒ Ⓓ	31 Ⓐ Ⓑ Ⓒ Ⓓ	43 Ⓐ Ⓑ Ⓒ Ⓓ	
8 Ⓐ Ⓑ Ⓒ Ⓓ	20 Ⓐ Ⓑ Ⓒ Ⓓ	32 Ⓐ Ⓑ Ⓒ Ⓓ	44 Ⓐ Ⓑ Ⓒ Ⓓ	
9 Ⓐ Ⓑ Ⓒ Ⓓ	21 Ⓐ Ⓑ Ⓒ Ⓓ	33 Ⓐ Ⓑ Ⓒ Ⓓ	45 Ⓐ Ⓑ Ⓒ Ⓓ	
10 Ⓐ Ⓑ Ⓒ Ⓓ	22 Ⓐ Ⓑ Ⓒ Ⓓ	34 Ⓐ Ⓑ Ⓒ Ⓓ	46 Ⓐ Ⓑ Ⓒ Ⓓ	
11 Ⓐ Ⓑ Ⓒ Ⓓ	23 Ⓐ Ⓑ Ⓒ Ⓓ	35 Ⓐ Ⓑ Ⓒ Ⓓ	47 Ⓐ Ⓑ Ⓒ Ⓓ	
12 Ⓐ Ⓑ Ⓒ Ⓓ	24 Ⓐ Ⓑ Ⓒ Ⓓ	36 Ⓐ Ⓑ Ⓒ Ⓓ	48 Ⓐ Ⓑ Ⓒ Ⓓ	

SECTION 2

1 Ⓐ Ⓑ Ⓒ Ⓓ	11 Ⓐ Ⓑ Ⓒ Ⓓ	21 Ⓐ Ⓑ Ⓒ Ⓓ	31 Ⓐ Ⓑ Ⓒ Ⓓ	41 Ⓐ Ⓑ Ⓒ Ⓓ
2 Ⓐ Ⓑ Ⓒ Ⓓ	12 Ⓐ Ⓑ Ⓒ Ⓓ	22 Ⓐ Ⓑ Ⓒ Ⓓ	32 Ⓐ Ⓑ Ⓒ Ⓓ	42 Ⓐ Ⓑ Ⓒ Ⓓ
3 Ⓐ Ⓑ Ⓒ Ⓓ	13 Ⓐ Ⓑ Ⓒ Ⓓ	23 Ⓐ Ⓑ Ⓒ Ⓓ	33 Ⓐ Ⓑ Ⓒ Ⓓ	43 Ⓐ Ⓑ Ⓒ Ⓓ
4 Ⓐ Ⓑ Ⓒ Ⓓ	14 Ⓐ Ⓑ Ⓒ Ⓓ	24 Ⓐ Ⓑ Ⓒ Ⓓ	34 Ⓐ Ⓑ Ⓒ Ⓓ	44 Ⓐ Ⓑ Ⓒ Ⓓ
5 Ⓐ Ⓑ Ⓒ Ⓓ	15 Ⓐ Ⓑ Ⓒ Ⓓ	25 Ⓐ Ⓑ Ⓒ Ⓓ	35 Ⓐ Ⓑ Ⓒ Ⓓ	
6 Ⓐ Ⓑ Ⓒ Ⓓ	16 Ⓐ Ⓑ Ⓒ Ⓓ	26 Ⓐ Ⓑ Ⓒ Ⓓ	36 Ⓐ Ⓑ Ⓒ Ⓓ	
7 Ⓐ Ⓑ Ⓒ Ⓓ	17 Ⓐ Ⓑ Ⓒ Ⓓ	27 Ⓐ Ⓑ Ⓒ Ⓓ	37 Ⓐ Ⓑ Ⓒ Ⓓ	
8 Ⓐ Ⓑ Ⓒ Ⓓ	18 Ⓐ Ⓑ Ⓒ Ⓓ	28 Ⓐ Ⓑ Ⓒ Ⓓ	38 Ⓐ Ⓑ Ⓒ Ⓓ	
9 Ⓐ Ⓑ Ⓒ Ⓓ	19 Ⓐ Ⓑ Ⓒ Ⓓ	29 Ⓐ Ⓑ Ⓒ Ⓓ	39 Ⓐ Ⓑ Ⓒ Ⓓ	
10 Ⓐ Ⓑ Ⓒ Ⓓ	20 Ⓐ Ⓑ Ⓒ Ⓓ	30 Ⓐ Ⓑ Ⓒ Ⓓ	40 Ⓐ Ⓑ Ⓒ Ⓓ	

SECTION 3

1 Ⓐ Ⓑ Ⓒ Ⓓ	4 Ⓐ Ⓑ Ⓒ Ⓓ	7 Ⓐ Ⓑ Ⓒ Ⓓ	10 Ⓐ Ⓑ Ⓒ Ⓓ	13 Ⓐ Ⓑ Ⓒ Ⓓ
2 Ⓐ Ⓑ Ⓒ Ⓓ	5 Ⓐ Ⓑ Ⓒ Ⓓ	8 Ⓐ Ⓑ Ⓒ Ⓓ	11 Ⓐ Ⓑ Ⓒ Ⓓ	14 Ⓐ Ⓑ Ⓒ Ⓓ
3 Ⓐ Ⓑ Ⓒ Ⓓ	6 Ⓐ Ⓑ Ⓒ Ⓓ	9 Ⓐ Ⓑ Ⓒ Ⓓ	12 Ⓐ Ⓑ Ⓒ Ⓓ	15 Ⓐ Ⓑ Ⓒ Ⓓ

**ONLY ANSWERS ENTERED IN THE CIRCLES IN EACH GRID WILL BE SCORED.
YOU WILL NOT RECEIVE CREDIT FOR ANYTHING WRITTEN IN THE BOXES ABOVE THE CIRCLES.**

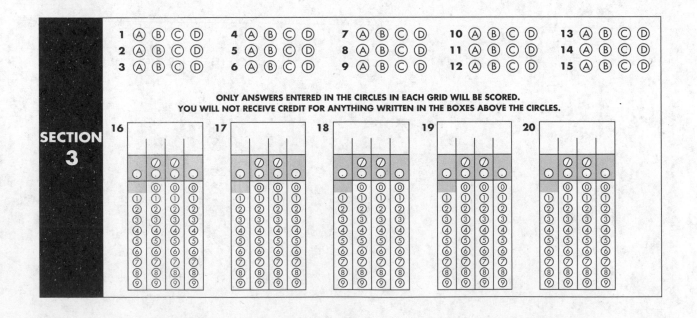

16   17   18   19   20

SECTION 4

1	Ⓐ Ⓑ Ⓒ Ⓓ	7	Ⓐ Ⓑ Ⓒ Ⓓ	13	Ⓐ Ⓑ Ⓒ Ⓓ	19	Ⓐ Ⓑ Ⓒ Ⓓ	25	Ⓐ Ⓑ Ⓒ Ⓓ
2	Ⓐ Ⓑ Ⓒ Ⓓ	8	Ⓐ Ⓑ Ⓒ Ⓓ	14	Ⓐ Ⓑ Ⓒ Ⓓ	20	Ⓐ Ⓑ Ⓒ Ⓓ	26	Ⓐ Ⓑ Ⓒ Ⓓ
3	Ⓐ Ⓑ Ⓒ Ⓓ	9	Ⓐ Ⓑ Ⓒ Ⓓ	15	Ⓐ Ⓑ Ⓒ Ⓓ	21	Ⓐ Ⓑ Ⓒ Ⓓ	27	Ⓐ Ⓑ Ⓒ Ⓓ
4	Ⓐ Ⓑ Ⓒ Ⓓ	10	Ⓐ Ⓑ Ⓒ Ⓓ	16	Ⓐ Ⓑ Ⓒ Ⓓ	22	Ⓐ Ⓑ Ⓒ Ⓓ	28	Ⓐ Ⓑ Ⓒ Ⓓ
5	Ⓐ Ⓑ Ⓒ Ⓓ	11	Ⓐ Ⓑ Ⓒ Ⓓ	17	Ⓐ Ⓑ Ⓒ Ⓓ	23	Ⓐ Ⓑ Ⓒ Ⓓ	29	Ⓐ Ⓑ Ⓒ Ⓓ
6	Ⓐ Ⓑ Ⓒ Ⓓ	12	Ⓐ Ⓑ Ⓒ Ⓓ	18	Ⓐ Ⓑ Ⓒ Ⓓ	24	Ⓐ Ⓑ Ⓒ Ⓓ	30	Ⓐ Ⓑ Ⓒ Ⓓ

ONLY ANSWERS ENTERED IN THE CIRCLES IN EACH GRID WILL BE SCORED.
YOU WILL NOT RECEIVE CREDIT FOR ANYTHING WRITTEN IN THE BOXES ABOVE THE CIRCLES.

31   32   33   34

35   36   37   38

SECTION 5: ESSAY

PLANNING PAGE You may plan your essay in the unlined planning space below, but use only the lined pages following this one to write your essay. Any work on this planning page will not be scored.

BEGIN YOUR ESSAY HERE

DO NOT WRITE OUTSIDE OF THE BOX.

Cut Here

DO NOT WRITE OUTSIDE OF THE BOX.

Cut Here

DO NOT WRITE OUTSIDE OF THE BOX.

4

Cut Here

Test begins on the next page.

1   1

Reading Test
65 MINUTES, 52 QUESTIONS

Turn to Section 1 of your answer sheet to answer the questions in this section.

Questions 1–10 are based on the following passage.

This passage is from Ralph Waldo Emerson, *"Prudence."* Public domain. First published in 1841.

What right have I to write on prudence, of which I have little, and that of the negative sort?
Line My prudence consists in avoiding and going without, not in the inventing of means and
5 methods, not in adroit steering, not in gentle repairing. I have no skill to make money spend well, no genius in my economy, and whoever sees my garden discovers that I must have some other garden. Yet I love facts, and hate shiftiness and
10 people without perception.

Then I have the same title to write on prudence that I have to write on poetry or holiness. We write from aspiration as well as from experience.
15   We paint those qualities that we do not possess. The poet admires the man of energy and tactics; the merchant breeds his son for the church or the bar; and where a man is not vain and egotistic you shall find what he lacks, by his praise.
20   Yet it would be hardly honest for me not to balance these fine lyric words with words of coarser sound. Prudence is the virtue of the senses. It is the science of appearances. It is the outmost action of the inward life. It is God taking
25 thought for oxen. It moves matter after the laws of matter. It is content to seek health of body by

complying with physical conditions, and health of mind by the laws of the intellect.

The world of the senses is a world of shows;
30 it does not exist for itself, but has a symbolic character; and a true prudence or law of shows recognizes the co-presence of other laws and knows that its own office is secondary; knows that it is surface and not center where it works.
35 Prudence is false when detached. It is legitimate when it is the natural history of the soul incarnate, when it unfolds the beauty of laws within the narrow scope of the senses.

There are all degrees of proficiency in
40 knowledge of the world. It is sufficient to our present purpose to indicate three. One class lives to the utility of the symbol, esteeming health and wealth a final good. Another class lives above this mark, to the beauty of the symbol, as the poet and
45 artist and the naturalist and man of science. A third class lives above the beauty of the symbol to the beauty of the thing signified; these are wise men. The first class has common sense; the second, taste; and the third, spiritual perception.
50 Once in a long time, a man traverses the whole scale, and sees and enjoys the symbol solidly, then also has a clear eye for its beauty, and lastly, while he pitches his tent on this sacred volcanic isle of nature, does not offer to build houses and barns
55 thereon, reverencing the splendor of the God which he sees bursting through each chink and cranny.

1   **1**

The world is filled with the proverbs and acts of a base prudence, which is a devotion to
60 matter, as if we possessed no other faculties than the palate, the nose, the touch, the eye and ear; a prudence that never subscribes, that never gives, that seldom lends, and asks but one question of any project: will it bake bread? This is a disease
65 like a thickening of the skin until the vital organs are destroyed. But culture, revealing the high origin of the apparent world and aiming at the perfection of the man as the end, degrades every thing else, as health and bodily life, into means.
70 It sees prudence not to be a separate faculty, but a name for wisdom and virtue conversing with the body and its wants. Cultivated men always feel and speak so, as if a great fortune, the achievement of a civil or social measure, great
75 personal influence, a graceful and commanding address, had their value as proofs of the energy of the spirit. If a man loses his balance and immerses himself in any trades or pleasures for their own sake, he may be a good wheel or pin,
80 but he is not a cultivated man.

1

The tone of the first paragraph is best described as

A) self-effacing.

B) pontifical.

C) aspirational.

D) sardonic.

2

The author's reference to "some other garden" (lines 8–9) primarily suggests that he

A) finds solace in the art of planting.

B) seeks new challenges and experiences.

C) considers arable land to be a valuable resource.

D) lacks the particular skills associated with farming.

3

In line 11, "title" most nearly means

A) ownership.

B) office.

C) authority.

D) publication.

4

The author believes that he is justified in acting as an authority on prudence primarily because of his

A) experience in making decisions.

B) regret for his past mistakes.

C) studies in classical philosophy.

D) yearning for wisdom.

5

Which choice provides the strongest evidence for the answer to the previous question?

A) Lines 6–9 ("I have no skill . . . some other garden")

B) Lines 13–14 ("We write from . . . as well as from experience")

C) Lines 20–22 ("Yet it would . . . coarser sound")

D) Lines 26–28 ("It is content . . . laws of the intellect")

CONTINUE →

6

The passage suggests that members of the "third class" (line 46) are superior for their ability to

A) solve important problems.

B) discern sublime qualities.

C) create works of beauty.

D) reason logically.

7

The "houses and barns" (line 54) represent

A) an unwise allegiance to worldly things.

B) the rejection of mere symbols.

C) the nobility of living with nature.

D) the importance of strong belief.

8

In line 59, "base" most nearly means

A) supportive.

B) ignoble.

C) necessary.

D) straightforward.

9

The "disease" mentioned in line 64 is best described as

A) apathy.

B) gluttony.

C) sensuousness.

D) egotism.

10

The passage as a whole characterizes prudence primarily as.

A) the aspiration to wisdom and righteousness.

B) a commitment to aesthetic principles.

C) the pursuit of practical skills and sensory experience.

D) the noble pursuit of spiritual goals.

CONTINUE ➜

1

1

Questions 11–21 are based on the following passage.

This passage is from Joseph Conrad, *The Secret Sharer*. It was originally published in 1912. The narrator of this story is the captain of a ship about to begin a voyage.

She floated at the starting point of a long journey, very still in an immense stillness, the
Line shadows of her spars flung far to the eastward by the setting sun. At that moment I was alone on her
5 decks. There was not a sound in her—and around us nothing moved, nothing lived, not a canoe on the water, not a bird in the air, not a cloud in the sky. In this breathless pause at the threshold of a long passage we seemed to be measuring
10 our fitness for a long and arduous enterprise, the appointed task of both our existences to be carried out, far from all human eyes, with only sky and sea for spectators and for judges.

There must have been some glare in the
15 air to interfere with one's sight, because it was only just before the sun left us that my roaming eyes made out beyond the highest ridges of the principal islet of the group something that did away with the solemnity of perfect solitude.
20 The tide of darkness flowed on swiftly; and with tropical suddenness a swarm of stars came out above the shadowy earth, while I lingered yet, my hand resting lightly on my ship's rail as if on the shoulder of a trusted friend. But, with all that
25 multitude of celestial bodies staring down at one, the comfort of quiet communion with her was gone for good. And there were also disturbing sounds by this time—voices, footsteps forward; the steward flitted along the main-deck, a busily
30 ministering spirit; a hand bell tinkled urgently under the poop deck.

I found my two officers waiting for me near the supper table, in the lighted cuddy. We sat down at once, and as I helped the chief mate, I
35 said: "Are you aware that there is a ship anchored inside the islands? I saw her mastheads above the ridge as the sun went down."

He raised sharply his simple face, overcharged by a terrible growth of whisker, and
40 emitted his usual ejaculations:

"Bless my soul, sir! You don't say so!"

My second mate was a round-cheeked, silent young man, grave beyond his years, I thought; but as our eyes happened to meet I detected a
45 slight quiver on his lips. I looked down at once. It was not my part to encourage sneering on board my ship. It must be said, too, that I knew very little of my officers. In consequence of certain events of no particular significance, except to
50 myself, I had been appointed to the command only a fortnight before. Neither did I know much of the hands forward. All these people had been together for eighteen months or so, and my position was that of the only stranger on board.
55 I mention this because it has some bearing on what is to follow. But what I felt most was my being a stranger to the ship; and if all the truth must be told, I was somewhat of a stranger to myself. The youngest man on board (barring the
60 second mate), and untried as yet by a position of the fullest responsibility, I was willing to take the adequacy of the others for granted. They had simply to be equal to their tasks. But I wondered how far I should turn out faithful to that ideal
65 conception of one's own personality every man sets up for himself secretly.

Meantime the chief mate, with an almost visible effect of collaboration on the part of his round eyes and frightful whiskers, was trying
70 to evolve a theory of the anchored ship. His dominant trait was to take all things into earnest consideration. He was of a painstaking turn of mind. As he used to say, he "liked to account to himself" for practically everything that came
75 in his way, down to a miserable scorpion he had found in his cabin a week before. The why and the wherefore of that scorpion—how it got on board and came to select his room rather than the pantry (which was a dark place and more what a
80 scorpion would be partial to), and how on earth it managed to drown itself in the inkwell of his writing desk—had exercised him infinitely.

The ship within the islands was much more easily accounted for.

CONTINUE ▶

1

1

11

The tone of the first paragraph (lines 1–13) is primarily one of

A) reflective anticipation.

B) anxious dread.

C) unrestrained excitement.

D) objective analysis.

12

The reference to "some glare" (line 14) serves primarily to make the point that

A) the mastheads of another ship were not immediately visible.

B) the weather was about to change.

C) the ocean around the ship was choppy.

D) the crew was eager to get into the open sea.

13

In lines 20–24 ("The tide . . . friend") the narrator describes

A) signs of impending danger.

B) reflections of his deep inner turmoil.

C) objects of wistful contemplation.

D) the recollection of a tragic experience.

14

The captain is portrayed primarily as

A) self-conscious and diffident.

B) rugged and adventurous.

C) anxious and short-tempered.

D) scholarly yet intimidating.

15

Which choice provides the strongest evidence for the answer to the previous question?

A) Lines 4–5 ("At that moment . . . her decks")

B) Lines 24–27 (But, with . . . for good")

C) Lines 48–51 ("In consequence . . . fortnight before")

D) Lines 63–66 ("But I . . . himself secretly")

16

In line 55, "bearing" most nearly means

A) direction.

B) demeanor.

C) relevance.

D) endurance.

17

In line 70, "evolve" most nearly means

A) change slowly.

B) ponder strenuously.

C) persuade earnestly.

D) advance randomly.

18

The "truth" to which the narrator refers in lines 57 is his

A) skepticism about his crew's ability.

B) apprehension about a dangerous voyage.

C) lack of self-confidence.

D) sense that he may be going insane.

CONTINUE ➡

1   **1**

19

In line 82, "exercised" most nearly means

A) practiced.

B) strengthened.

C) utilized.

D) disquieted.

20

The "collaboration" (line 68) refers to an act of

A) selfless assistance.

B) deliberate menace.

C) contrived deceit.

D) strained contemplation.

21

The chief mate believed that, compared to the recently discovered ship, the "scorpion" (line 75) was

A) less explicable.

B) more frightening.

C) more ominous.

D) less miserable.

CONTINUE ▶

Questions 22–32 are based on the following passages.

Passage 1 is from Lindsay Smith-Doyle, *"Thoughts on the Value of Life."* ©2015 by College Hill Coaching. Passage 2 is from C. F. Black, "Who's Afraid of Cloning?" ©2015 by College Hill Coaching. Since 1996, when scientists at the Roslin Institute in England cloned a sheep from the cells of another adult sheep, many have debated the ethics of cloning human cells. These passages are excerpts from arguments on this issue.

Passage 1

How should human life be bestowed? With human cloning looming as a real scientific possibility, we must question the provenance of this ultimate gift. Our intimate participation in
5   the creation of life must never be misconstrued as control. Rather, our attitude toward the creation of life must be one of humility.

The idea of "outsourcing" the creation of human life, of relegating it to a laboratory, of
10 reducing the anticipation of childbirth to a trip to the mall or a selection from a catalog, mocks the profundity of life. The mystery is replaced by design and control. Should we turn our noses up at the most precious gift in the universe, only to
15 say: "Sorry, but I think I can do better?"

Cloning is the engineering of human life. We have for the first time the ability to determine the exact genetic makeup of a human being. Whether you believe in evolution or creationism, cloning
20 thwarts an essential step of the conception process: randomness in the case of natural selection, and guided purpose in the case of creationism. A child can be created that is no longer uniquely human but the end product of an
25 assembly line, with carefully designed and tested features. Are the astonishing processes of nature somehow deficient?

If human cloning becomes acceptable, we will have created a new society in which the value of
30 human life is marginalized. Industries will arise that turn human procreation into a profitable free-market enterprise. The executive boards of these companies will decide the course of human

evolution, with more concern for quarterly profit
35 reports than for the fate of humanity.

These are not idle concerns. Even as we ponder the ethical implications of human cloning, companies are forging ahead with procedures to clone human cells for seemingly
40 beneficial purposes, marching steadily toward a Brave New World in which humanity will be forever less human.

Passage 2

The breathless fears about human cloning should not surprise anyone who knows the
45 history of science. Every step in human progress is met with close-mindedness that often verges on paranoia. Not even medicine is spared. As doctors toil to save, prolong, and improve lives, the uninformed rage at the arrogance
50 of science. Before the merits of surgery and vaccination became commonplace and obvious, many refused to believe that cutting flesh or introducing degraded germs could do more good than harm. Perhaps we should turn from science
55 and return to superstition and magic spells?

At first glance, it might seem that cloning is a whole new ballgame. After all, cloning is "the engineering of human life," isn't it? It is the mass production of designer babies. It is the end of
60 evolution, or at least the beginning of its corporate management. It is certainly a slap in the face of God. Or is it?

Cloning foe Jeremy Rifkin is afraid of nothing so much as duplication: "It's a horrendous crime
65 to make a Xerox of someone. You're putting a human into a genetic straitjacket." The horror! I wonder how Mr. Rifkin would feel at the annual Twins Days Festival in Twinsburg, Ohio. Genetic Xeroxes everywhere!
70 Identical twins are not monsters. Rifkin's fear is vacuous. Each identical twin has his or her own unique thoughts, talents, experiences, and beliefs. Mr. Rifkin must learn that human beings are more than just their DNA; they are
75 the products of the continual and inscrutably complex interactions of environment and biology. Human clones would be no different.

"But you are playing God!" we hear. It is the cry of all whose power is threatened by the march

CONTINUE ▶

80 of human progress. It is the reasoning of the Dark
Ages, used to keep the subservient masses in their
place. Every great step humanity has ever taken
has disrupted the "natural order." Should we be
shivering in caves, eating uncooked bugs, and
85 dying of parasites, as nature intended?

But perhaps procreation is different—more
sacred. Then why have the technologies of fertility
enhancement, in vitro fertilization, embryo
transfer, and birth control become so widely
90 accepted? Each of these technologies was met at
first with legions of strident opponents. But over
time, reality and compassion overcame unreason
and paranoia. Familiarity dissipates fear.

These supposedly "moral" objections are
95 in fact impeding moral progress. With genetic
engineering, cloning, and stem cell research,
scientists finally have within their grasp
technologies that can provide ample food for
a starving world, cure devastating illnesses,
100 and replace diseased organs. Only ignorant
superstition stands in their way.

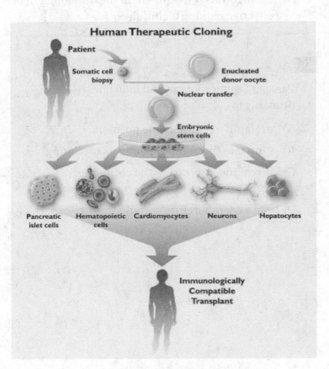

Image courtesy of NIH/NHGRI

In line 13, "control" refers specifically to control
over

A) the effects of cloning.

B) the development of genetic technologies.

C) the process of conception.

D) the ethical debate about cloning.

23

In Passage 1, the author's attitude toward
"outsourcing" (line 8) is one of

A) grudging approval.

B) blunt disdain.

C) firm support.

D) ironic detachment.

The quotations in line 15 and line 78 are similar in
that both

A) represent the opinions of cloning opponents.

B) indicate cautious advocacy for genetic
engineering.

C) are presented as being insincere.

D) contradict the viewpoints of the respective
authors.

CONTINUE ➡

25

Jeremy Rifkin (line 63) would most likely advocate

A) the "humility" mentioned in line 7.

B) the "design and control" mentioned in line 13.

C) the "engineering" mentioned in line 16.

D) the "industries" mentioned in line 30.

26

The diagram best illustrates

A) the "guided purpose" (line 22).

B) the "assembly line" (line 25).

C) the "course of human evolution" (lines 33–34).

D) the "procedures" (line 39).

27

In line 53, "introducing" refers to an act of

A) explanation.

B) proposition.

C) announcement.

D) injection.

28

The author of Passage 1 would most likely regard the "management" (line 61) described in Passage 2 as

A) a necessary measure to avoid the abuse of procreative technologies.

B) an acceptable means by which the medical community can find alternatives to cloning.

C) a regrettable invasion of commercial interests into human reproduction.

D) a dangerous impediment to the development of effective cloning techniques.

29

Passage 2 quotes Jeremy Rifkin in lines 64–66 primarily to

A) exemplify an untenable position.

B) illustrate the potential dangers of cloning.

C) reveal the interests of the corporate community.

D) cite a corroborating opinion from an expert.

CONTINUE ➡

1   **1**

30

Passage 2 refers to the Twin's Days Festival in line 68 as an example of

A) a movement that promotes beneficial cloning.

B) a seemingly harmless event that harbors hidden dangers.

C) the innocuousness of genetic duplication.

D) the logical consequences of procreative technologies.

31

The author of Passage 2 would most likely argue that the "procedures" (line 39) to which the author of Passage 1 objects are in fact

A) inconsequential aspects of the cloning debate.

B) necessary contributions to medical progress.

C) not representative of the methods used by real genetic researchers.

D) ways of manipulating public opinion.

32

Which choice provides the strongest evidence for the answer to the previous question?

A) Lines 59–61 ("It is the end . . . management")

B) Lines 71–73 ("Each identical . . . beliefs")

C) Lines 80–82 ("It is the reasoning . . . place")

D) Lines 95–100 ("With genetic . . . organs")

CONTINUE ▶

1   **1**

Questions 33–42 are based on the following passage.

This passage is from Steven Pinker, *An Invitation to Cognitive Science* (Gleitman, Liberman, and Osherson, eds.) ©1995 by Bradford Book.

Language is the main vehicle by which we know about other people's thoughts, and the two
Line must be intimately related. Every time we speak we are revealing something about language, so
5 the facts of language structure are easy to come by; these data hint at a system of extraordinary complexity. Nonetheless, learning a first language is something every child does successfully, in a matter of a few years and without the need for
10 formal lessons. With language so close to the core of what it means to be human, it is not surprising that children's acquisition of language has received so much attention.

Is language simply grafted on top of cognition
15 as a way of sticking communicable labels on thoughts? Or does learning a language somehow mean learning to think in that language? A famous hypothesis, outlined by Benjamin Whorf, asserts that the categories and relations that
20 we use to understand the world come from our particular language, so that speakers of different languages conceptualize the world in different ways. Language acquisition, then, would be learning to think, not just learning to talk.

25 This is an intriguing hypothesis, but virtually all modern cognitive scientists believe it is false. Babies can think before they can talk. Cognitive psychology has shown that people think not just in words but also in images and
30 abstract logical propositions. And linguistics has shown that human languages are too ambiguous and schematic to use as a medium of internal computation: when people think about "spring," surely they are not confused as to whether they
35 are thinking about a season or something that goes "boing"—and if one word can correspond to two thoughts, thoughts can't be words.

But language acquisition has a unique contribution to make to this issue. It is virtually
40 impossible to show how children could learn a language unless you assume they have a

considerable amount of nonlinguistic cognitive machinery in place before they start.

All humans talk but no house pets do, no
45 matter how pampered, so heredity must be involved. But a child growing up in Japan speaks Japanese whereas the same child brought up in California would speak English, so environment is also crucial. Thus there is no question about
50 whether heredity or environment is involved in language, or even whether one or the other is "more important." Instead, language acquisition might be our best hope of finding out how heredity and environment interact. We know
55 that adult language is intricately complex, and we know that children become adults. Therefore something in the child's mind must be capable of attaining that complexity. Any theory that posits too little innate structure, so that its hypothetical
60 child ends up speaking something less than a real language, must be false. The same is true for any theory that posits too much innate structure, so that the hypothetical child can acquire English but not, say, Bantu or Vietnamese.

65 And not only do we know about the output of language acquisition, we know a fair amount about the input to it, namely, parents' speech to their children. So even if language acquisition, like all cognitive processes, is essentially a "black
70 box," we know enough about its input and output to be able to make precise guesses about its contents.

The study of language acquisition began around the same time as the birth of cognitive
75 science, in the late 1950s. We can see now why that is not a coincidence. The historical catalyst was Noam Chomsky's review of Skinner's *Verbal Behavior* in 1959. At that time, Anglo-American natural science, social science, and
80 philosophy had come to a virtual consensus about the answers to the questions listed above. The mind consisted of sensorimotor abilities plus a few simple laws of learning governing gradual changes in an organism's behavioral repertoire.
85 Therefore, language must be learned; it cannot be a module; and thinking must be a form of verbal behavior, since verbal behavior is the prime manifestation of "thought" that can be observed externally. Chomsky argued that language

CONTINUE ▶

1   1

90 acquisition falsified these beliefs in a single stroke:
    children learn languages that are governed
    by highly subtle and abstract principles, and
    they do so without explicit instruction or any
    other environmental clues to the nature of such
95 principles. Hence language acquisition depends
    on an innate, species-specific module that is
    distinct from general intelligence. Much of the
    debate in language acquisition has attempted
    to test this once-revolutionary, and still
100 controversial, collection of ideas. The implications
    extend to the rest of human cognition.

33

This passage as a whole is primarily concerned
with

A) delineating the general principles of linguistics.

B) comparing the structural qualities of various
   languages.

C) exploring academic questions about how we
   learn language.

D) examining the claims of one influential
   linguist.

34

The "data" mentioned in line 6 most likely include
information regarding

A) the literacy levels of various countries.

B) methods for teaching infants to speak.

C) the syntax rules of different languages.

D) the structures of the human cerebral cortex.

35

In line 2, "the two" refers to

A) self and other.

B) thinking and expressing.

C) grammar and syntax.

D) learning and teaching.

36

In line 15, "sticking" most nearly means

A) applying.

B) upholding.

C) piercing.

D) maintaining.

CONTINUE

| 1 | **| 1 |**

37

The author's attitude toward Whorf's "hypothesis" (line 18) is best described as

A) dismissive.

B) supportive.

C) ambivalent.

D) antagonistic.

38

The statement "Babies can think before they can talk" (line 27) is intended to indicate that

A) learning to talk is much more cognitively challenging than most people believe.

B) skills associated with basic reasoning are not dependent on verbal communication.

C) both physical and cognitive skills tend to develop according to rigid timelines.

D) researchers sometimes do not take into account the particular needs of infants.

39

Which if the following best summarizes the author's view on human language acquisition?

A) Learning a language is a crucial step in learning to think, because thinking is verbal behavior.

B) The structures for learning language seem to be much simpler than what scientists previously thought.

C) Humans are born with very intricate cognitive structures for learning language.

D) Environmental input is more important than heredity in language acquisition.

40

Which choice provides the strongest evidence for the answer to the previous question?

A) Lines 1–3 ("Language is . . . intimately related")

B) Lines 23–24 ("Language acquisition . . . to talk")

C) Lines 61–64 ("The same . . . Vietnamese")

D) Lines 95–97 ("Hence language . . . general intelligence")

CONTINUE →

1   **1**

41

In line 62, "structure" refers to

A) the grammatical rules of a language.

B) the functional organization of the mind.

C) the environment in which infants learn.

D) the systems for investigating linguistic claims.

42

The subjects listed in lines 78–80 are given as examples of disciplines that, in 1959,

A) accepted the hypothesis that cognition depends on verbal skills.

B) considered the scientific method inadequate to the study of language acquisition.

C) regarded most of the processes in involved in language acquisitions to be innate.

D) questioned the conventional theories regarding how humans learn language.

CONTINUE →

Questions 43–52 are based on the following passage and supplementary material.

This passage is from A. R. Kirchoff, *"The New Ecosystems of the Anthropocene"* ©2017 by College Hill Coaching.

Scavengers—animals that feed on carcasses, rotting plants, or waste—get a bad rap.
Line Yellowjackets and raccoons swarming around garbage cans can seem like annoying pests at
5 best and germ-infested monsters at worst. Indeed, scavengers have been known to spread diseases such as meningitis, leptospirosis, and bubonic plague, so it's no surprise that they are the focus of a huge extermination industry. But our habit of
10 eradicating irksome species ignores an important fact: scavenger relationships are essential to all complex life.

The selective pressures of scavenger behavior accelerate the evolution of social intelligence.
15 For thousands of generations, some scavenger species have struggled to outwit the wily hunters with whom they compete for scraps. They must predict, plan, and communicate as they approach a carcass in order to avoid becoming
20 the next prey. At the same time, hunters like *Homo sapiens* had to become more clever to protect their meat from these thieves. This social interaction has allowed at least one scavenger species to thrive in an anthropocentric[1] world:
25 *Canis lupus familiaris*—the domesticated dog. Your pet terrier would not be such a faithful companion if its ancestor, the grey wolf, had not spend so much time picking over the trash of our hunter forebears. In just 20,000 years, we
30 have become symbionts,[2] turning a few lines of wolves from freeloading foragers into friendly Frisbee-fetchers.

Even less perspicacious scavengers play a vital role in complex ecosystems, often in
35 unexpected ways. As plastic waste accumulates rapidly in the ocean (and is expected to surpass the total mass of fish by 2050), and toxic chemical waste continues to be dumped into our water supplies, the role of one particular
40 class of scavenger, the *decomposers*, has become

critical. These creatures break down complex molecules into simpler ones in a process called *biodegradation*. *Alcanivorax borkumensis*, a naturally occurring marine bacterium, can
45 digest petroleum and convert it into food energy. Hydrocarbons like petroleum and plastics are energy-rich organic molecules much like starches, fats, and proteins, so the idea that they can be used as food by
50 opportunistic organisms is not so biochemically far-fetched. After crude oil spills, cleanup crews encourage this biodegradation by using chemical dispersant to break the petroleum into smaller droplets, thereby creating more
55 surface area for the bacteria to attack. Another decomposer, *Aspergillus tubingensis*, is able to greatly accelerate the breakdown of polyester polyurethane, a petroleum product and one of the more durable plastics in our landfills and
60 oceans. Although environmentalists have yet to discover a practical method for harnessing *A. tubingensis* in large-scale waste mitigation systems, such bio-technological solutions may not be far off.

65 Our dependence on unicellular opportunists goes deeper still: our digestive processes, blood pressure, and immune system depend on thousands of species of scavenger bacteria that live primarily in our gut and make up our
70 *microbiome*. These organisms patrol the intricate chemical pathways of the gut and perform duties that, under normal circumstances, keep things running smoothly. The overuse of antibiotics, our favorite pharmaceutical pest-control system,
75 often compromise healthy systemic function by destroying healthful bacteria as well as harmful ones. For instance, humans with depleted levels of *Butyricicoccus pullicaecorum* in their intestines have higher rates of chronic bowel diseases like
80 ulcerative colitis and Crohn's disease. Research into how these microorganisms has exploded in recent years, particularly regarding how they interact with human chemistry to regulate our hormones, our blood sugar, and even our mood.

[1] human-centered
[2] species that live together in a mutually supportive relationship.

CONTINUE ➔

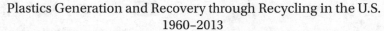

Plastics Generation and Recovery through Recycling in the U.S.
1960–2013

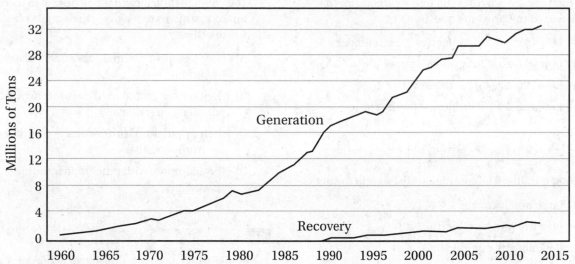

Source: U.S. Environmental Protection Acgency

43

This passage primarily serves to

A) examine several specific ecosystems that are currently dominated by scavengers and discuss ways of preserving those ecosystems.

B) explore various ways in which scavengers can be beneficial to different ecosystems that are relevant to humans.

C) explain how scavengers acquire intelligent behavior through a long evolutionary process involving interaction with humans.

D) discuss the ways that humans can exploit the beneficial behaviors of scavengers while avoiding the diseases that they spread.

44

In line 33, "perspicacious" is used to describe scavengers that can

A) avoid predation by humans.

B) decompose complex hydrocarbons.

C) distinguish nutritious waste from toxic waste.

D) develop mutually beneficial social relationships.

45

Considering the information in the passage, the graph would be most directly relevant to a discussion of

A) the domestication of *Canis lupus familiaris*.

B) the proliferation of *Alcanivorax Butyricicoccus*.

C) the habitat of *Aspergillus tubingensis*.

D) the health benefits of *Butyriiccoccus pullicaecorum*.

46

The passage indicates that the social intelligence of scavengers enables them to

A) track increasingly elusive prey.

B) find more nutritious food sources.

C) avoid predation by clever hunters.

D) protect their food supply.

CONTINUE ▶

1   1

47

Which choice provides the best evidence for the answer to the previous question?

A) Lines 13–14 ("The selective . . . intelligence")

B) Lines 17–20 ("They must . . . prey")

C) Lines 20–22 ("At . . . thieves")

D) Lines 26–29 ("Your pet . . . forebears")

48

As used in line 41, "complex" most nearly means

A) large and intricate.

B) obscure and bewildering.

C) delicate and complicated.

D) convoluted and unfathomable.

49

As used in line 52, "encourage" most nearly means

A) inspire.

B) goad.

C) invigorate.

D) persuade.

50

The passage indicates that one hurdle to using microorganisms extensively to degrade plastic waste is that

A) they may produce toxic chemicals as a by-product.

B) they are not common to the most highly polluted ecosystems.

C) their populations are not easily controlled by environmentalists.

D) they compete with other biodegrading scavengers.

51

Which choice provides the best evidence for the answer to the previous question?

A) Lines 46–51 ("Hydrocarbons . . . far-fetched")

B) Lines 51–55 ("After . . . attack")

C) Lines 55–60 ("Another . . . oceans")

D) Lines 60–64 ("Although . . . off")

52

The last paragraph (lines 65–84) serves mainly to

A) indicate additional benefits that scavenger bacteria provide by describing how they support vital biological functions in humans.

B) provide another example of the benefits provided by microscopic scavengers by describing how bacteria enable researchers to develop better antibiotics.

C) draw a contrast to the previous discussion about the benefits of bacteria by describing some of the potential dangers of infection.

D) demonstrate how our fear of bacteria prevents us from taking full advantage of the medicinal benefits of microorganisms.

STOP

**If you finish before time is called, you may check your work on this section only.
Do not turn to any other section of the test.**

2   **2**

Writing and Language Test
35 MINUTES, 44 QUESTIONS

Turn to Section 2 of your answer sheet to answer the questions in this section.

DIRECTIONS

Each passage below is accompanied by a number of questions. For some questions, you will consider how the passage might be revised to improve the expression of ideas. For other questions, you will consider how the passage might be edited to correct errors in sentence structure, usage, or punctuation. A passage or a question may be accompanied by one or more graphics (such as a table or graph) that you will consider as you make revising and editing decisions.

Some questions will direct you to an underlined portion of a passage. Other questions will direct you to a location in a passage or ask you to think about the passage as a whole.

After reading each passage, choose the answer to each question that most effectively improves the quality of writing in the passage or that makes the passage conform to the conventions of Standard Written English. Many questions include a "NO CHANGE" option. Choose that option if you think the best choice is to leave the relevant portion of the passage as it is.

CONTINUE →

2   2

Questions 1–11 are based on the following passage and supplementary material.

Who Really Owns American Media?

In this era of blogging, news websites, and personalized Twitter feeds, most of us believe that we have more choice than ever **1** in how we get our news. But unless you're particularly **2** apt about the world of journalism, you might be surprised to learn how few choices we really have.

Thirty years ago, 50 different corporations owned 90% of the American broadcast and news media. Today, just 6 large conglomerates **3** have the same control over that media, which is still 90%. These huge corporations have successfully lobbied the U.S. Congress to loosen or dismantle federal antitrust regulations. These regulations were designed to prevent any one corporation from driving out **4** their competition and controlling public discourse. The debate on this issue centers on the balance between liberties and governmental interference. Some argue that a corporation's freedom to acquire media and voice its opinion trumps any right the public may have to diverse points of view. **5** The other argument would be that our constitutional freedom of the press requires regulation in order to maintain a free market of ideas and an informed citizenry.

1

A) NO CHANGE
B) with getting
C) of the way we get
D) of getting

2

A) NO CHANGE
B) acute
C) savvy
D) comprehensive

3

A) NO CHANGE
B) control that same 90% of all media
C) control the same media, all 90% of it
D) are in the same 90% control of all media

4

A) NO CHANGE
B) the competition they have
C) its competition
D) it's competition

5

A) NO CHANGE
B) Others argue
C) Others would argue
D) Another being

CONTINUE →

2

2

According to data from 2007, the American media does not quite look like America. Although fully 33% of the American population was minority, **6** only 3.2% of American broadcast television outlets were controlled by minorities.

One potent antidote **7** regarding media consolidation is the Internet. **8** With some research, it reveals many resources for the curious and intelligent media consumer to hear informed voices from a wide variety of perspectives.

6

Which of the following best represents the information from Figure 1?

A) NO CHANGE

B) only 3.2% of the minority population controlled American broadcast television outlets

C) only 3.2% of the American population included minorities in control of broadcast television outlets

D) only 3.2% of American broadcast television stations were watched by minorities

7

A) NO CHANGE

B) about

C) against

D) to

8

A) NO CHANGE

B) It will reveal with some research

C) Some research will reveal

D) With some research, it will reveal

MINORITY REPRESENTATION IN BROADCAST TELEVISION

U.S. Population 2007

U.S. Media Ownership 2007

	Population	Media Ownership
African American	13.0%	0.6%
Hispanic American	15.0%	1.3%
Asian American	4.5%	0.9%
Other Minority	1.5%	0.4%
White Non-Minority	66.0%	96.8%

Source: Freepress

CONTINUE ➤

9 Although the Web abounds with gossip, partisanship, and fear-mongering from many major outlets, and conspiracy theorists on the fringe, the careful viewer can also find thoughtful analysis and civilized debate of the issues. Sites like ProPublica, FactCheck.org, and NPR provide in-depth, nonprofit, public-supported journalism that is less influenced by any corporate or political agenda.

10 Therefore, sensationalism sells, and the media conglomerates have mastered the art. As the first great American media mogul, William Randolph Hearst, said, "If you want the public in sufficient numbers, construct a highway. Advertising is that highway." Without large advertising and lobbying budgets, these nonpartisan **11** instances of journalism will have a difficult time competing with the big boys.

9

The author wants to introduce this sentence with a representation of modern media that contrasts with the ideal of "civilized debate." Does this sentence accomplish this task?

A) Yes, because it suggests that controversial matters are ignored in modern media.

B) Yes, because it refers to relatively unsophisticated modes of conversation.

C) No, because it focuses on entertainment rather than any examination of issues.

D) No, because it refers to hypothetical situations rather than real ones.

10

A) NO CHANGE

B) Still

C) Lastly

D) In summary

11

A) NO CHANGE

B) patterns

C) receptacles

D) repositories

2   2

Questions 12–22 are based on the following passage.

The Dangers of Superstition

Have you ever knocked on wood to dodge a jinx? Do you avoid stepping on cracks in the sidewalk? Do you feel uneasy about the number 13? Most of us realize that these **12** rituals, which are based on ancient and discredited beliefs, but we can't so easily rid our minds of superstitious thinking. Every culture has its own superstitious beliefs, **13** and now anthropologists and psychologists are beginning to understand why.

Our brains constantly work to find cause-and-effect patterns in the world. When something strange happens that we can't explain, or seems to **14** collide against what we already believe, we get an uncomfortable feeling known as "cognitive dissonance." We reflexively fill this gap in knowledge with the explanations that are most easily available to us. **15** Since we are willful beings surrounded by other willful beings, and every conscious moment of our lives is filled with a sense of "agency," **16** that is: intentional action. Therefore, we imagine tiny beings living in wood, or vaporous spirits roaming the clouds that do strange or harmful things when we displease them. Willful agency is our "default" explanation.

12

A) NO CHANGE
B) rituals, that are based on
C) rituals have been based on
D) rituals are based on

13

A) NO CHANGE
B) for
C) so
D) while

14

A) NO CHANGE
B) contradict
C) disengage
D) go away from

15

A) NO CHANGE
B) Because we
C) We
D) So we

16

A) NO CHANGE
B) that is, intentional action
C) which is what intentional action is
D) which is: intentional action

CONTINUE ➤

[1] Our brains are creative. [2] They can design buildings, compose music, and **17** can formulate scientific theories. [3] But this creativity is sometimes hard to discipline, and so we are susceptible to strange thoughts and superstitions. [4] Many of these, like blessing people when they sneeze, are harmless if not quaint. [5] In 2014, villagers in Nigeria brought a goat into a police station, accusing it of being a witch that had attempted to steal a car and then changed into a goat. **18**

17

A) NO CHANGE

B) also can formulate

C) have formulated

D) formulate

18

The author is considering adding the following sentence to this paragraph.

Others are sad and bizarre, such as the belief in shape-shifting.

Where should it be placed?

A) before sentence 2

B) before sentence 3

C) before sentence 4

D) before sentence 5

2   2

Although superstitious explanations relieve our cognitive dissonance, **19** it might also lead to tragedy. In 2014, people in Paraguay and Tanzania were killed because locals accused them of witchcraft. **20** Some superstitious parents have even beaten or disowned their own children because their strange behavior is attributed to demonic possession. Superstitions are also not harmless when they impede the pursuit of science, placing obstacles in the way of medical and technological breakthroughs that can improve the human condition.

Rituals intended to help your favorite football team score, like dancing or wearing your hat backward, are fun and innocuous. They **21** substitute a craving in our brains for control over situations that otherwise mystify us. **22**

19

A) NO CHANGE
B) it can
C) they can
D) they would

20

A) NO CHANGE
B) Some superstitious parents, believing that any strange behavior is a sign of demonic possession, have even beaten or disowned their own children.
C) Even beating or disowning their own children, many superstitious parents attribute their strange behavior to demonic possession.
D) Some superstitious parents, believing that their strange behavior is a sign of demonic possession, have even beaten or disowned their own children.

21

A) NO CHANGE
B) discharge
C) exempt
D) satisfy

22

Which concluding sentence is most in keeping with the content and tone of the passage as a whole?

A) However, feeling like we have control over a situation is not always the same as understanding it.
B) They represent some of humanity's greatest accomplishments, and have inspired some of our greatest works of art.
C) Centuries from now, our rituals may become so elaborate that we would scarcely recognize them as such today.
D) Without such rituals, we would not feel as connected to the people or the natural world around us.

Questions 23–33 are based on the following passage.

Skepticism and the Scientific Method

Even scientists sometimes forget how essential skepticism, particularly self-skepticism, is to the scientific process. But scientific skepticism is driven by evidence, not agenda. Today, the field of climatology seems to have more than its share of skeptics, debating **23** a warming planet and the things that should be done by us about it, if anything.

24 They are coming from outside of the scientific community, many of these skeptics couch their arguments in political terms. Some claim that global warming is part of a partisan "left-wing" plot or a ploy by the scientific community to ensure funding for yet another "Chicken Little" scare. Others suggest that attempts to reduce greenhouse gas emissions by changing energy or land use policies **25** would provide a needless cost of the American taxpayer of tens to hundreds of billions of dollars annually. Some even suggest that they are really part of an international conspiracy to undermine America's competitiveness in the global marketplace.

23

A) NO CHANGE

B) what should be done about a warming planet, if we should

C) what, if anything, we should do about a warming planet

D) the things we should do about a warming planet, if we should

24

A) NO CHANGE

B) While coming

C) Their coming

D) Coming

25

A) NO CHANGE

B) would be needless in costing the American taxpayer

C) would needlessly cost the American taxpayer

D) is a needless cost to the American taxpayer of

2   2

At the same time, others who legitimately question the data or theories related to climate change are too quickly labeled right-wing "deniers," even if their concerns are not motivated by any partisan convictions.

In fact, science has, or should have, nothing to do with ideology. Rather, it **26** <u>is</u> a process of identifying significant natural phenomena, gathering evidence about those phenomena, and **27** <u>then we must find the most reliable explanation for</u> that evidence. The preponderance of the evidence suggests that the earth is getting warmer, that the effects of that warming will be problematic, that there are things we can do to prevent or at least mitigate the worst outcomes, and **28** <u>perhaps that many of these things are</u> well worth doing. There is still plenty of uncertainty about the complex systems that make up our planetary climate, but we know enough to be concerned, **29** <u>and to discuss the issue without politicizing it</u>.

26

A) NO CHANGE
B) accounts for
C) represents
D) symbolizes

27

A) NO CHANGE
B) finding the most reliable explanation for
C) then explaining in the most reliable way
D) finding the most reliable way for explaining

28

A) NO CHANGE
B) also that many of these things perhaps may be
C) many of these things perhaps may be
D) that many of these things may be

29

Which choice is most consistent with the main idea of the passage?

A) NO CHANGE
B) and to expose the agendas of those who stand in the way of saving our planet
C) but not enough to risk sacrificing our political or economic security
D) and to create a strong incentive program to transform our national energy policy

CONTINUE ➡

The skeptics point out, rightly, that science isn't about consensus. The fact that 98% of climatologists regard something as true [30] isn't the same as it being true. After all, only centuries ago the majority of physicians worldwide believed that illnesses were caused not by germs or genetics, [31] but by demons or imbalances in "humors."

[1] Having an honest and productive conversation about global warming [32] requires an educated public. [2] When we, as public citizens, become more informed about the science of climatology, we become less susceptible to political sniping and to "consensus" as an argument. [3] Most important, perhaps, we become better able to make good decisions about the future of our nation and our planet. [33]

[30]

A) NO CHANGE
B) won't make that true
C) would not mean it's that way
D) doesn't make it so

[31]

A) NO CHANGE
B) but instead from
C) but from
D) they thought it was by

[32]

A) NO CHANGE
B) requires the need for
C) requires our being
D) require having

[33]

The writer is considering adding the following sentence into this paragraph.

Furthermore, we become more adept at evaluating the facts and theories at the heart of the matter.

Where should it be placed?

A) before sentence 1
B) before sentence 2
C) before sentence 3
D) after sentence 3

2   **2**

Questions 34–44 are based on the following passage.

The Magic of Bohemia

Bohemia is a landlocked country in central **34** Europe, and until 1918 they were ruled from Vienna by the Austrian Hapsburgs. Today it **35** regards a major part of the modern Czech Republic, and its largest city, Prague, serves as the nation's capital. Bohemia is also another, less clearly defined country, a country of the mind. This Bohemia in fact derives from misconceptions about the true Bohemia that go back as far as Shakespeare, **36** designating Bohemia as the land of gypsies and the spiritual habitation of artists.

By 1843, when Michael William Balfe's opera *The Bohemian Girl* premiered in London, the term *Bohemian* **37** would come to mean any wandering or vagabond soul, who need not have been associated with the arts. The Parisian poet Henry Murger clinched the term's special association with the life of artists.

In November 1849, a dramatized version of Murger's *Latin Quarter* tales was staged in Paris with the title *La Vie de Bohème*. So extraordinarily successful **38** did this prove that the stories themselves were published as *Scènes de la Vie de Bohème*. The public's appetite was whetted and a popular cult of the gypsy-artist was underway. Murger's volume of stories became the textbook for the artistic life throughout the late nineteenth and early twentieth centuries.

34

A) NO CHANGE
B) Europe, until 1918 it was ruled
C) Europe, which, until 1918, was ruled
D) Europe, having been, until 1918, ruled

35

A) NO CHANGE
B) amounts to
C) establishes
D) comprises

36

A) NO CHANGE
B) who designated Bohemia
C) he had designated Bohemia
D) being designated by him

37

A) NO CHANGE
B) had come to mean
C) came to have meant
D) had meant

38

A) NO CHANGE
B) was this proven
C) this was proved
D) this proved

CONTINUE ➡

2   **2**

39 What was it that were the basic elements of this Bohemia as it evolved under Murger? To start with, Bohemia belonged to the romantic movements that preached the power of the individual imagination and came to adopt a secular religion of art. Like early Christianity, it had its true believers and its heathens. The believers in this case were the artists themselves, the elect of the spirit, touched with the divine power of imagination, while the heathen were the commercial middle classes who had **40** propagated as a result of increased commodity production in the wake of the Industrial Revolution.

[1] To the artists, these were people of no imagination who were only concerned with material things. [2] As Philistines, they seemed inhabit a different country from that of the **41** Bohemians; Murger's achievement was to define, quite persuasively, the boundaries of Bohemia in terms of a particular lifestyle. [3] In his Bohemia, the production of art was in fact less important than **42** whether one had the capacity for art. [4] Murger was also responsible for the term *Bohemian* becoming inseparably linked with the supposedly unconventional, outlandish behavior of artists, yet it is evident that he did not invent Bohemianism. [5]

39

A) NO CHANGE
B) What were they that were the basic elements
C) What basic elements were there
D) What were the basic elements

40

A) NO CHANGE
B) propitiated
C) prospered
D) preempted

41

A) NO CHANGE
B) Bohemians, Murger had the achievement of defining
C) Bohemians, but Murger's achievement was in defining
D) Bohemians; but Murger achieved defining

42

A) NO CHANGE
B) the capacity for art
C) whether one has the capacity for art
D) one's capacity of art

CONTINUE ▶

2   **2**

Most of its ingredients had existed in Paris for at least two decades before he started writing. **43**

Bohemia had been a haven for the political rebel and, as the nineteenth century drew to a close, more than one French observer had seen it as the breeding-ground of cynicism, as the source of much potential danger. "It is quite clear," Jules Claretie wrote indignantly in 1888, "that every country has its Bohemians. But they do not have the influence over the rest of the nation which they do in France—thanks to that poisonous element in the French character which is known as *la blague*—or cynicism." **44**

43

The writer is considering adding the following sentence to this paragraph.

> Murger can thus be described as a Bohemian of the second generation.

Where should it be placed?

A) after sentence 1

B) after sentence 2

C) after sentence 3

D) after sentence 5

44

If the author were to delete the quotation from Jules Claretie at the conclusion of this paragraph, the passage would primarily lose

A) an optimistic view of the late nineteenth-century French culture.

B) a scathing perspective on Murger's literary work.

C) a dire assessment of France's national temperament.

D) an urgent warning against a potential immigration problem.

STOP

**If you finish before time is called, you may check your work on this section only.
Do not turn to any other section of the test.**

3 ⊠ **3**

Math Test – No Calculator
25 MINUTES, 20 QUESTIONS

Turn to Section 3 of your answer sheet to answer the questions in this section.

DIRECTIONS

For questions 1–15, solve each problem, choose the best answer from the choices provided, and fill in the corresponding circle on your answer sheet. **For questions 16–20,** solve the problem and enter your answer in the grid on the answer sheet. Please refer to the directions before question 16 on how to enter you answers in the grid. You may use any available space in your test booklet for scratch work.

NOTES

1. The use of a calculator is NOT permitted.
2. All variables and expressions used represent real numbers unless otherwise indicated.
3. Figures provided in this test are drawn to scale unless otherwise indicated.
4. All figures lie in a plane unless otherwise indicated.
5. Unless otherwise indicated, the domain of a given function f is the set of all real numbers for which $f(x)$ is a real number.

REFERENCE

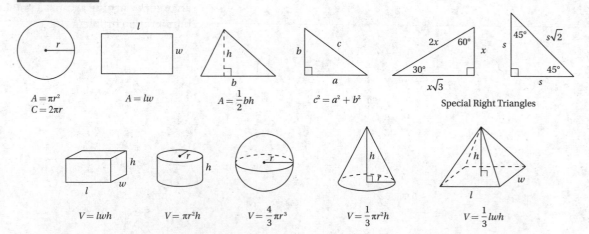

$A = \pi r^2$
$C = 2\pi r$

$A = lw$

$A = \frac{1}{2}bh$

$c^2 = a^2 + b^2$

Special Right Triangles

$V = lwh$

$V = \pi r^2 h$

$V = \frac{4}{3}\pi r^3$

$V = \frac{1}{3}\pi r^2 h$

$V = \frac{1}{3}lwh$

The number of degrees of arc in a circle is 360.
The number of radians of arc in a circle is 2π.
The sum of the measures in degrees of the angles of a triangle is 180.

CONTINUE ➔

3   **3**

1

If $2b - 1 = 5$, what is the value of $2b^2 - 1$?

A) 15

B) 17

C) 24

D) 25

2

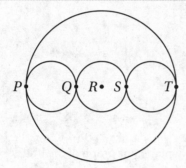

In the figure above, points P, Q, R, S, and T lie on the same line, and R is the center of the large circle. If the three smaller circles are congruent and the radius of the large circle is 6, what is the radius of one of the smaller circles?

A) 1

B) 2

C) 3

D) 4

3

Jeri has edited $\frac{1}{5}$ of her term paper. If she has edited 15 pages, how many pages does she have left to edit?

A) 45

B) 50

C) 60

D) 75

4

$$7, 12, 22, 42, 82$$

Which of the following gives a rule for finding each term in the sequence after the first?

A) Add 5 to the preceding number.

B) Add 5 to the sum of all of the preceding terms.

C) Double the preceding term and then subtract 2 from the result.

D) Add 14 to the preceding term and divide that result by 2.

5

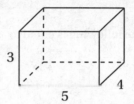

The figure above shows a rectangular box. What is the longest length of a diagonal of one of the faces of this box?

A) $\sqrt{24}$

B) $\sqrt{41}$

C) $\sqrt{50}$

D) $\sqrt{60}$

6

Which of the following points is NOT on the graph of the line $-2x - 3y = 36$ in the xy-plane?

A) $(-9, 6)$

B) $(-24, 4)$

C) $(6, -16)$

D) $(12, -20)$

CONTINUE

7

During a coyote repopulation study, researchers determine that the equation $P = 250(1.32^t$ describes the population P of coyotes t years after their introduction into a new region. Which of the following gives the values of I, the initial population of coyotes, and r, the annual percent increase in this population?

A) $I = 250, r = 32\%$

B) $I = 250, r = 132\%$

C) $I = 330, r = 32\%$

D) $I = 330, r = 132\%$

8

Which of the following is equal to $\dfrac{1}{\sqrt{3}+1}$?

A) $\dfrac{\sqrt{3}}{2} - \dfrac{1}{2}$

B) $\dfrac{\sqrt{3}}{2} + \dfrac{1}{2}$

C) $\dfrac{\sqrt{3}}{4} - \dfrac{1}{4}$

D) $\dfrac{\sqrt{3}}{4} + \dfrac{1}{4}$

9

Which of the following could be the x-intercept and y-intercept of a line that is perpendicular to the line $3x + 6y = 0$?

A) $(-6, 0)$ and $(0, 3)$

B) $(3, 0)$ and $(0, -6)$

C) $(3, 0)$ and $(0, 6)$

D) $(6, 0)$ and $(0, 3)$

10

The function f is defined by the equation $f(x) = x - x^2$. Which of the following represents a quadratic with no real zeros?

A) $f(x) + \dfrac{1}{2}$

B) $f(x) - \dfrac{1}{2}$

C) $f\left(\dfrac{x}{2}\right)$

D) $f\left(x - \dfrac{1}{2}\right)$

11

In the xy-plane, the graph of the line $y = \dfrac{15}{4}$ intersects the graph of the equation $y = x^2 + x$ at two points. What is the distance between these two points?

A) $\dfrac{3}{2}$

B) $\dfrac{5}{2}$

C) $\dfrac{15}{4}$

D) 4

12

If $i^{2k} = 1$, and $i = \sqrt{-1}$, which of the following must be true about k ?

A) k is a multiple of 4.

B) k is a positive integer.

C) When $2k$ is divided by 4, the remainder is 1.

D) $\dfrac{k}{2}$ is an integer.

CONTINUE

3 **3**

13

For all numbers x and y, let z be defined by the equation $z = |2^2 - x^2 - y^2| + 2^2$. What is the smallest possible value of z?

A) 0

B) 4

C) 8

D) 16

14

If the polynomial $P(x)$ has factors of 12, $(x - 5)$, and $(x + 4)$, which of the following must also be a factor of $P(x)$?

A) $2x^2 + 8$

B) $4x^2 - 20$

C) $6x^2 - 6x - 120$

D) $x^2 - 10x + 25$

15

If $f(x) = -x + 7$ and $g(f(x)) = 2x + 1$, what is the value of $g(2)$?

A) -11

B) -5

C) 5

D) 11

CONTINUE ▶

3   **3**

DIRECTIONS

For questions 16–20, solve the problem and enter your answer in the grid, as described below, on the answer sheet.

1. Although not required, it is suggested that you write your answer in the boxes at the top of the columns to help you fill in the circles accurately. You will receive credit only if the circles are filled in correctly.

2. Mark no more than one circle in any column.

3. No question has a negative answer.

4. Some problems may have more than one correct answer. In such cases, grid only one answer.

5. **Mixed numbers** such as $3\frac{1}{2}$ must be gridded as 3.5 or $\frac{7}{2}$.

(If $3\frac{1}{2}$ is entered into the grid as [grid], it will be interpreted as $\frac{31}{2}$, not $3\frac{1}{2}$.)

6. **Decimal answers:** If you obtain a decimal answer with more digits than the grid can accommodate, it may be either rounded or truncated, but it must fill the entire grid.

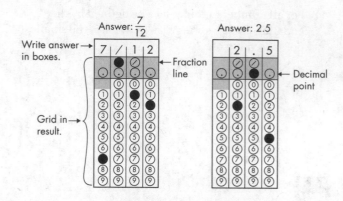

Answer: $\frac{7}{12}$ Answer: 2.5

Write answer in boxes.   Fraction line   Decimal point

Grid in result.

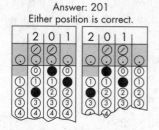

Answer: 201
Either position is correct.

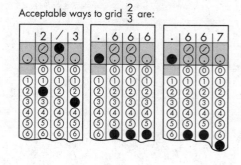

Acceptable ways to grid $\frac{2}{3}$ are:

3   **3**

16

In a writer's workshop, there are half as many men as women. If there are 24 total men and women in the writer's workshop, how many men are there?

17

If $3 - \dfrac{1}{b} = \dfrac{3}{2}$ what is the value of b ?

18

The square of a positive number is 0.24 greater than the number itself. What is the number?

19

The function f is a quadratic function with zeros at $x = 1$ and $x = 5$. The graph of $y = f(x)$ in the xy-plane is a parabola with a vertex at $(3, -2)$. What is the y-intercept of this graph?

20

When graphed in the xy-plane, the line $y = mx - 4$ intersects the x-axis at an angle of θ. If $m > 0$, $0° < \theta < 90°$, and $\cos \theta = \dfrac{3}{\sqrt{58}}$, what is the value of m ?

STOP

If you finish before time is called, you may check your work on this section only.
Do not turn to any other section of the test.

Math Test – Calculator

55 MINUTES, 38 QUESTIONS

Turn to Section 4 of your answer sheet to answer the questions in this section.

DIRECTIONS

For questions 1–30, solve each problem, choose the best answer from the choices provided, and fill in the corresponding circle on your answer sheet. **For questions 31–38,** solve the problem and enter your answer in the grid on the answer sheet. Please refer to the directions before question 31 on how to enter you answers in the grid. You may use any available space in your test booklet for scratch work.

NOTES

1. The use of a calculator is permitted.

2. All variables and expressions used represent real numbers unless otherwise indicated.

3. Figures provided in this test are drawn to scale unless otherwise indicated.

4. All figures lie in a plane unless otherwise indicated.

5. Unless otherwise indicated, the domain of a given function f is the set of all real numbers for which $f(x)$ is a real number.

REFERENCE

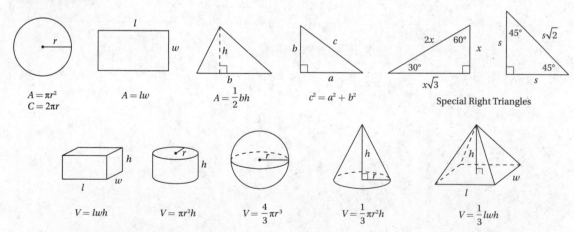

The number of degrees of arc in a circle is 360.
The number of radians of arc in a circle is 2π.
The sum of the measures in degrees of the angles of a triangle is 180.

CONTINUE ➔

4 **4**

1

If $a = \frac{1}{2}b$ and $2a + 4b = 20$, what is the value of b ?

A) 2.5

B) 4

C) 5

D) 15

2

Spin	Frequency
1	3
2	4
3	3
4	0
5	1
6	1
7	1
8	3
9	1
10	3

The spinner for a board game has 10 sectors, numbered 1 through 10. It is spun 20 times and the results summarized in the table above. What is the median value of these 20 spins?

A) 2

B) 4

C) 5

D) 6

3

A 48-gram serving of breakfast cereal contains 8 grams of sugar. How many grams of sugar are there in a 57-gram serving of the same cereal?

A)   9.5

B) 10.5

C) 11.5

D) 12.5

4

STATEWIDE COLLEGE SCHOLARSHIP
APPLICANTS AND FINALISTS

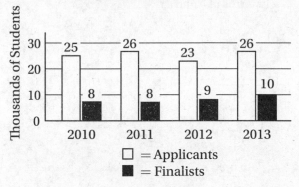

The graph above shows the number of applicants and finalists for a statewide college scholarship program over four consecutive years. For which year was the ratio of finalists to applicants the greatest?

A) 2010

B) 2011

C) 2012

D) 2013

5

If $y^3 = 20$ and $z^2 = 10$, what is the value of $(yz)^6$?

A) 2×10^5

B) 4×10^4

C) 2×10^5

D) 4×10^5

CONTINUE

6

If the sum of a, b, and c is three times the sum of a and b, which of the following expresses the value of a in terms of b and c ?

A) $\dfrac{c-2b}{2}$

B) $\dfrac{2b-c}{2}$

C) $\dfrac{c-3b}{3}$

D) $\dfrac{3b-c}{3}$

7

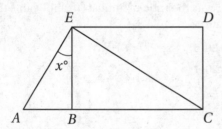

Note: Figure not drawn to scale.

In the figure above, $BCDE$ is a rectangle, $AC = 14$, $BC = 12$, and $EC = 13$. What is the value of $\tan x$?

A) 0.4

B) 0.6

C) 1.3

D) 2.5

8

Which of the following binomials is a factor of $x^2 - 6x + 8$?

A) $x - 4$

B) $x + 4$

C) $x + 2$

D) $x - 8$

Questions 9–11 are based on the graph below.

MONTHLY SALES

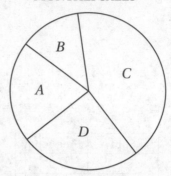

The pie graph above represents the monthly ad sales for four salespeople—Maria, Eli, Georgia, and Zoe—at a social media website. For the month, Maria's sales accounted for 25% of the total, Eli had $3,000 in sales, Georgia had $5,000 in sales, and Zoe had $10,000 in sales.

9

Which sector represents Georgia's sales for the month?

A) Sector A

B) Sector B

C) Sector C

D) Sector D

10

What is the sum of the monthly sales for all four salespeople?

A) $22,500

B) $24,000

C) $25,000

D) $27,000

CONTINUE

4 **4**

11

If Eli and Georgia both earn 10% commission on their sales, and Maria and Zoe both earn 15% commission on their sales, how much more did Maria earn in monthly commissions than Georgia?

A) $300

B) $360

C) $375

D) $400

12

Let the function f be defined by $f(x) = 2 - |x - 4|$ for all real values of x. What is the greatest possible value of f?

A) -2

B) 2

C) 4

D) 6

13

If $\dfrac{3}{b} - \dfrac{2}{5} = 1$, what is the value of b?

A) $\dfrac{5}{7}$

B) $\dfrac{6}{5}$

C) $\dfrac{15}{7}$

D) 5

14

For the function f, $f(1) = 4$ and $f(2) = 13$. Which of the following equations could describe f?

A) $f(x) = x^2 + 3$

B) $f(x) = x^2 + 9$

C) $f(x) = 2x^2 + 2$

D) $f(x) = 3x^2 + 1$

15

Which of the following is NOT equivalent to $12b^2$?

A) $(6b)(6b)$

B) $12b(b)$

C) $\left(b\sqrt{12}\right)^2$

D) $6b^2 + 6b^2$

16

If m is a number chosen randomly from the set $\{2, 3, 4, 6\}$ and n is a number chosen randomly from the set $\{1, 2, 3, 4\}$, what is the probability that mn is a multiple of 12?

A) $\dfrac{1}{16}$

B) $\dfrac{1}{8}$

C) $\dfrac{1}{4}$

D) $\dfrac{1}{2}$

17

If $y = 3x + 4$ and $x < 3$, which of the following represents all the possible values of y?

A) $y > 7$

B) $y < 13$

C) $7 < y < 13$

D) $y > 13$

18

If $g(x + 1) = x^2 + 2x + 4$ for all values of x, which of the following is equal to $g(x)$?

A) $x^2 + 4$

B) $x^2 + 3$

C) $(x - 1)^2 + 4$

D) $(x - 1)^2 + 3$

CONTINUE

19

A: 2, 7, 12, 17, 22, . . .

B: 5, 15, 25, 35, 45, . . .

Two sequences, A and B, follow the patterns shown above. If the nth term of sequence A is 72, what is the nth term of sequence B?

A) 125

B) 135

C) 145

D) 155

20

A website received 2,100 visitors in July from both subscribers and nonsubscribers. If the ratio of subscribers to nonsubscribers among this group was 2:5, how many more nonsubscribers visited the site in July than subscribers?

A)   126

B)   630

C)   900

D)   1,260

21

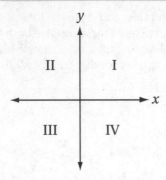

The figure above shows the locations of quadrants I–IV in the xy-plane. Which of the following represents a pair of linear equations that do NOT intersect in quadrant I?

A) $3x + 5y = 15$
    $y = 4$

B) $5x + 3y = 15$
    $y = 4$

C) $5x - 3y = 15$
    $y = 4$

D) $3x - 5y = 15$
    $y = 4$

22

During a 40-minute session at a 220 volt charging station, the charge on an electric car battery increases from an initial charge of 50 power units to a final charge of 106 power units. If this charge increases linearly with time, which of the following best describes the charge, q, in power units, on this same battery after charging for t hours from an initial charge of 20 power units? (1 hour = 60 minutes)

A) $q = 55t + 50$

B) $q = 84t + 50$

C) $q = 55t + 20$

D) $q = 84t + 20$

4   **4**

Questions 23 and 24 are based on the graph below.

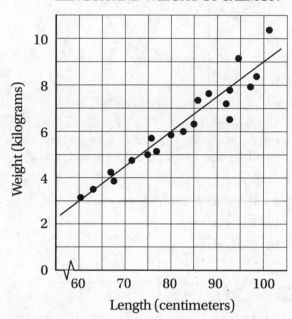

LENGTH AND WEIGHT OF SALMON

Weight (kilograms)

Length (centimeters)

23

The scatterplot above shows the length and weight of a group of 20 salmon and the line of best fit for the data. According to this line of best fit, which of the following best approximates the weight, in kilograms, of a salmon that is 95 centimeters long?

A) 7.6

B) 7.8

C) 8.3

D) 8.8

24

Which of the following equations best describes the relationship between w, the weight in kilograms of each salmon, and l, its length in centimeters?

A) $w = \dfrac{3}{20}l + 2$

B) $w = \dfrac{20}{3}l + 2$

C) $w = \dfrac{3}{40}l - 6$

D) $w = \dfrac{3}{20}l - 6$

25

The average size of a compressed image file is 750 kB. If Ronika's data plan allows her to send 2 GB of data each month before she pays any overage charges, but she plans to use 85% of that data for texting, approximately how many compressed images can she send each month before she incurs any overage charges? (1 GB = 1,000 MB; 1 MB = 1,000 kB)

A) 227

B) 400

C) 2,267

D) 4,000

4 **4**

26

Perfectioner's Chocolate Company makes two varieties of truffles: dark chocolate and milk chocolate. Each dark chocolate truffle requires 0.65 ounces of cocoa powder, and each milk chocolate truffle requires 0.45 ounces of cocoa powder. If cocoa powder costs c dollars per pound, and Perfectioner's Chocolate Company has budgeted $200 per week for cocoa powder, which of the following inequalities indicates the restrictions on the number of dark chocolate truffles, d, and the number of milk chocolate truffles, m, the company can make in one week? (1 pound = 16 ounces)

A) $\dfrac{200}{c} \geq 0.65d + 0.45m$

B) $\dfrac{200}{16c} \geq 0.65d + 0.45m$

C) $\dfrac{3,200}{c} \geq 0.65d + 0.45m$

D) $3,200c \geq \dfrac{0.65}{d} + \dfrac{0.45}{m}$

27

If n is a positive integer and $m = 2^{n+2} + 2^n$, what is 2^{n+3} in terms of m?

A) m

B) $\dfrac{2m}{5}$

C) $\dfrac{8m}{5}$

D) $3m^2$

28

For how many values of x between 0 and 2π does $\sin 3x = \dfrac{1}{2}$?

A) Two

B) Three

C) Four

D) Six

29

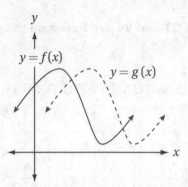

The figure above shows the graphs of functions f and g in the xy-plane. Which of the following equations could express the relationship between f and g?

A) $f(x) = g(x - 2)$

B) $f(x) = g(x + 2)$

C) $f(x) = g(x) + 2$

D) $f(x) = g(x) - 2$

30

A researcher is trying to estimate the daily amount of time undergraduate computer science majors spend on nonrecreational computer activities. She surveys 120 students from among the computer science majors at a large state university and asks them, "How much time do you spend in nonrecreational computer activities each day?" The mean of these responses is 210 minutes per day, with a standard deviation of 16.5 minutes. If another researcher wishes to present the same question to a new set of subjects at the same university, which of the following subject groups would most likely yield a data set with a smaller margin of error for the estimated daily amount of time undergraduate computer science majors spend on nonrecreational computer activities?

A) 240 randomly selected computer science majors

B) 240 randomly selected liberal arts majors

C) 80 randomly selected computer science majors

D) 80 randomly selected liberal art majors

CONTINUE

4 **4**

DIRECTIONS

For questions 31–38, solve the problem and enter your answer in the grid, as described below, on the answer sheet.

1. Although not required, it is suggested that you write your answer in the boxes at the top of the columns to help you fill in the circles accurately. You will receive credit only if the circles are filled in correctly.

2. Mark no more than one circle in any column.

3. No question has a negative answer.

4. Some problems may have more than one correct answer. In such cases, grid only one answer.

5. **Mixed numbers** such as $3\frac{1}{2}$ must be gridded as 3.5 or $\frac{7}{2}$.

(If $3\frac{1}{2}$ is entered into the grid as [grid], it will be interpreted as $\frac{31}{2}$, not $3\frac{1}{2}$.)

6. **Decimal answers:** If you obtain a decimal answer with more digits than the grid can accommodate, it may be either rounded or truncated, but it must fill the entire grid.

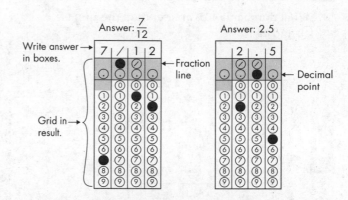

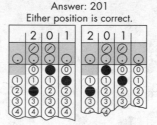

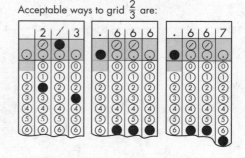

CONTINUE →

4 **4**

31

What number is 40% greater than the sum of 40 and 80 ?

32

x	$h(x)$
3	6
5	14

The table above shows a set of ordered pairs that correspond to the function $h(x) = \dfrac{x^2}{2} + k$. What is the value of k ?

33

$$hx + 4y = -3$$

The equation above is the equation of a line in the xy-plane, and h is a constant. If the slope of this line is -13, what is the value of h ?

34

The sum of two numbers is four times their difference. The smaller of these numbers is 15. What is the greater number?

35

If $0 < x < 2\pi$ and $5 \cos x = \sqrt{5}$, what is the value of $\left(\dfrac{\sin x}{3}\right)^2$?

36

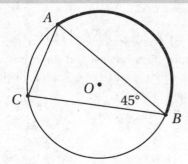

Note: Figure not drawn to scale.

In the figure above, the circle with center O has a circumference of 50, and $AB = BC$. What is the length of arc AB ?

---

4   4

Questions 37 and 38 are based on the scenario described below.

An Internet service provider offers three different plans for residential users. Plan A charges users $500 for the first year of service, and $80 per month thereafter. Plan B charges users $68 per month. Plan C is a "high speed" plan that offers 200% higher speeds for $92 per month.

37

Isabelle has been using Plan A for over a year. She recently reviewed her plan and realized that if she had been using Plan B for same amount of time, she would have saved $104 for Internet service over the entire period. At the time of her review, how many months had Isabelle been on Plan A?

38

Isabelle is now considering switching to either Plan B or Plan C for her home business, but she calculates that having the "high speed" plan will save her only approximately 45 minutes of work each month. At what minimum hourly rate, in dollars per hour, would she have to value her work (that is, how much more would she have to value one hour of free time over one hour of work time) for Plan C to be worth the extra cost over Plan B?

STOP

**If you finish before time is called, you may check your work on this section only.
Do not turn to any other section of the test.**

Essay

50 MINUTES, 1 QUESTION

DIRECTIONS

As you read the passage below, consider how James Schlesinger uses

- evidence, such as facts or examples, to support his claims
- reasoning to develop ideas and connect claims and evidence
- stylistic or persuasive elements, such as word choice or appeals to emotion, to add power to the ideas expressed

---

Adapted from James Schlesinger, "Cold Facts on Global Warming." ©2004 by The Los Angeles Times. Originally published January 22, 2004.

1   We live in an age in which facts and logic have a hard time competing with rhetoric—especially when the rhetoric is political alarmism over global warming.

2   We continue to hear that "the science is settled" in the global warming debate, that we know enough to take significant action to counter it. Those who hold this view believe emissions of carbon dioxide are the primary cause of any change in global temperature and inevitably will lead to serious environmental harm in the decades ahead.

3   In 1997, for instance, Vice President Al Gore played a leading role in the negotiation of the Kyoto Protocol, the international agreement to deal with the fears about global warming. He was willing to embrace severe reductions in U.S. emissions, even though the Clinton administration's own Department of Energy estimated that Kyoto-like restrictions could cost $300 billion annually. Then, when it became clear that the Senate would not agree to a treaty that would harm the economy and exempt developing countries like China and India, the Clinton administration did not forward it for ratification. Since then, the treaty's flaws have become more evident, and too few countries have ratified it to allow it to "enter into force."

4   The Bush administration, as an alternative to such energy-suppressing measures, has focused on filling gaps in our state of knowledge, promoting the development of new technology, encouraging voluntary programs and working with other nations on controlling the growth of greenhouse gas emissions. Collectively, these actions involve spending more than $4 billion annually, and the U.S. is doing more than any other nation to address the climate-change issue.

5   Of these efforts, filling the gaps in our knowledge may be the most important. What we know for sure is quite limited. For example, we know that since the early 1900s, the Earth's surface temperature has risen about 1 degree Fahrenheit. We also know that carbon dioxide, a greenhouse gas, has been increasing in the atmosphere. And we know that the theory that increasing concentrations of greenhouse gases like carbon dioxide will lead to further warming is at least an oversimplification. It is inconsistent with the fact that satellite measurements over 35 years show no significant warming in the lower atmosphere, which is an essential part of the global-warming theory.

5   **5**

6   Much of the warming in the 20th century happened from 1900 to 1940. That warming was followed by atmospheric cooling from 1940 to around 1975. During that period, frost damaged crops in the Midwest during summer months, and glaciers in Europe advanced. This happened despite the rise in greenhouse gases. These facts, too, are not in dispute.

7   And that's just our recent past. Taking a longer view of climate history deepens our perspective. For example, during what's known as the Climatic Optimum of the early Middle Ages, the Earth's temperatures were 1 to 2 degrees warmer than they are today. That period was succeeded by the Little Ice Age, which lasted until the early 19th century. Neither of these climate periods had anything to do with man-made greenhouse gases.

8   The lessons of our recent history and of this longer history are clear: It is not possible to know now how much of the warming over the last 100 or so years was caused by human activities and how much was because of natural forces. Acknowledging that we know too little about a system as complicated as the planet's climate is not a sign of neglect by policymakers or the scientific community. Indeed, admitting that there is much we do not know is the first step to greater understanding.

9   Meanwhile, it is important that we not be unduly influenced by political rhetoric and scare tactics. Wise policy involves a continued emphasis on science, technology, engagement of the business community on voluntary programs and balancing actions with knowledge and economic priorities. As a nation, by focusing on these priorities, we show leadership and concern about the well-being of this generation and the ones to follow.

Write an essay in which you explain how James Schlesinger builds an argument to persuade his audience that the debate on global warming is unduly influenced by political alarmism. In your essay, analyze how Schlesinger uses one or more of the features listed in the box above (or features of your own choice) to strengthen the logic and persuasiveness of his argument. Be sure that your analysis focuses on the most relevant features of the passage.

Your essay should NOT explain whether you agree with Schlesinger's claims, but rather explain how Schlesinger builds an argument to persuade his audience.

SAT PRACTICE TEST 2 ANSWER KEY

Section 1: Reading	Section 2: Writing and Language	Section 3: Math (No Calculator)	Section 4: Math (Calculator)
1. A	1. A	1. B	1. B
2. D	2. C	2. B	2. B
3. C	3. B	3. C	3. A
4. D	4. C	4. C	4. C
5. B	5. B	5. B	5. D
6. B	6. A	6. A	6. A
7. A	7. D	7. A	7. A
8. B	8. C	8. A	8. A
9. C	9. B	9. B	9. A
10. C	10. B	10. B	10. B
11. A	11. D	11. D	11. D
12. A	12. D	12. D	12. B
13. C	13. A	13. B	13. C
14. A	14. B	14. C	14. D
15. D	15. C	15. D	15. A
16. C	16. B	-------	16. C
17. B	17. D	16. 8	17. B
18. C	18. D	17. 2/3 or .666 or .667	18. B
19. D	19. C	18. 1.2 or 6/5	19. C
20. D	20. B	19. 2.5 or 5/2	20. C
21. A	21. D	20. 7/3 or 2.33	21. A
22. C	22. A		22. D
23. B	23. C		23. C
24. D	24. D		24. D
25. A	25. C		25. B
26. D	26. A		26. C
27. D	27. B		27. C
28. C	28. D		28. D
29. A	29. A		29. B
30. C	30. D		30. A
31. B	31. A		----------------
32. D	32. A		31 168
33. C	33. C		32. 3/2 or 1.5
34. C	34. C		33. 52
35. B	35. D		34. 25
36. A	36. B		35. 4/45 or .088 or .089
37. D	37. B		36. 75/4 or 18.7 or 18.8
38. B	38. A		37. 47
39. C	39. D		38. 32
40. D	40. C		
41. B	41. A		
42. A	42. B		
43. B	43. D		
44. D	44. C		
45. C			
46. C			
47. B			
48. A			
49. C			
50. C			
51. D			
52. A			

Total Reading Points (Section 1)	Total Writing and Language Points (Section 2)	Total Math Points (Section 3)	Total Math Points (Section 4)

SCORE CONVERSION TABLE

Scoring Your Test

1. Use the answer key to mark your responses on each section.

2. Total the number of correct responses for each section:

    1. Reading Test   Number correct: _____ **(Reading Raw Score)**

    2. Writing and Language Test   Number correct: _____ **(Writing and Language Raw Score)**

    3. Mathematics Test – No Calculator   Number correct: _____

    4. Mathematics Test – Calculator   Number correct: _____

3. Add the raw scores for sections 3 and 4. This is your **Math Raw Score**: _____

4. Use the Table 1 to calculate your **Scaled Test and Section Scores (10–40)**.

    Math Section Score (200–800):   _____

    Reading Test Score (10–40):   _____

    Writing and Language Test Score (10–40):   _____

5. Add the **Reading Test Scaled Score** and the **Writing and Language Test Scaled Score** and multiply this sum by 10 to get your **Reading and Writing Test Section Score (20–80)**.

    Sum of Reading + Writing and Language Scores: _____   10 =

    Reading and Writing Section Score: _____

Table 1: Scaled Section and Test Scores (10–40)

Raw Score	Math Section Score	Reading Test Score	Writing/ Language Test Score	Raw Score	Math Section Score	Reading Test Score	Writing/ Language Test Score
58	800			29	520	27	28
57	790			28	520	26	28
56	780			27	510	26	27
55	760			26	500	25	26
54	750			25	490	25	26
53	740			24	480	24	25
52	730	40		23	480	24	25
51	710	40		22	470	23	24
50	700	39		21	460	23	23
49	690	38		20	450	22	23
48	680	38		19	440	22	22
47	670	37		18	430	21	21
46	670	37		17	420	21	21
45	660	36		16	410	20	20
44	650	35	40	15	390	20	19
43	640	35	39	14	380	19	19
42	630	34	38	13	370	19	18
41	620	33	37	12	360	18	17
40	610	33	36	11	340	17	16
39	600	32	35	10	330	17	16
38	600	32	34	9	320	16	15
37	590	31	34	8	310	15	14
36	580	31	33	7	290	15	13
35	570	30	32	6	280	14	13
34	560	30	32	5	260	13	12
33	560	29	31	4	240	12	11
32	550	29	30	3	230	11	10
31	540	28	30	2	210	10	10
30	530	28	29	1	200	10	10

SAT PRACTICE TEST 2 DETAILED ANSWER KEY

Section 1: Reading

1. **A**   Tone

In the first paragraph, the author tells us that he has little prudence and no skill in *inventing of means and methods . . . in adroit steering . . .* nor in *gentle repairing*. He also has *no skill to make money spend well*. These are *self-effacing* descriptions. They are certainly not *pontifical* (speaking as a high priest), *aspirational* (expressing high hopes and goals), or *sardonic* (grimly cynical).

2. **D**   Inference

The statement that *whoever sees my garden discovers that I must have some other garden* is the last statement in the author's list of his personal inadequacies. Therefore, this statement must be taken to be *self-effacing* as the other statements are, and specifically to mean that he lacks gardening skill.

3. **C**   Word in Context

Recall that the first paragraph begins with the question *What right have I to write on prudence . . .* ? The second provides a response to this question about his *right*: in saying *I have the same title to write on prudence as I have to write on poetry or holiness*, then, he is clearly saying that he has the *standing* or *authority* to write on prudence.

4. **D**   Inference

In following his declaration that he has the right to write on prudence (lines 13–14), Emerson states that *[w]e write from aspiration as well as from experience*. In other words, we gain the standing to write on prudence not only from expertise in prudent behavior, but also from a focused *yearning*.

5. **B**   Textual Evidence

As the explanation to the previous question indicates, the best support for this answer is in lines 13–14.

6. **B**   Specific Purpose

The sixth paragraph (lines 39–57) discusses three classes of people according to their *proficiency in knowledge of the world* (lines 39–40). The first class values *health and wealth [as] a final good* (lines 42–43). The second class values the *beauty of the symbol* (line 46–47). The third class *lives above the beauty of the symbol to the beauty of the thing signified* (lines 46–47). This last group has *spiritual perception* (line 49). Therefore, its members are superior for their ability to *discern sublime qualities*.

7. **A**   Interpretation

This phrase appears in a discussion of the individual who *traverses the whole scale* (line 50–51), that is, who has the skills of all three classes: practicality, taste, and spiritual perception. In saying that such a person *does not offer to build houses and barns* (lines 54) on the *sacred volcanic isle of nature* (lines 53–54), Emerson is saying that nature is merely a *symbol* that points to the *splendor of God* (55), and therefore not what a truly wise person chooses to fix his or her gaze upon. In other words, the building of *houses and barns* is an *unwise allegiance to worldly things*.

8. **B**   Word in Context

In saying that *the world is filled with the proverbs and acts of a base prudence* (lines 58–59), Emerson means that most of our actions and words are devoted to practical things, like the question *will it bake bread* (lines 64)? As Emerson made clear in his previous paragraph, these considerations are those of the lowest and least noble class, so theirs is an *ignoble* prudence.

9. **C**   Interpretation

As a whole, this paragraph discusses the problem that *the world is filled with the proverbs and acts of a base prudence* (lines 58–59), in other words, that our words and actions are too focused on *a devotion to matter* (lines 59–60) and its effect on our senses, *as if we possessed no other faculties than the palate, the nose, the eye and ear* (lines 60–61). Emerson describes this problem with a simile: *this is a disease like a thickening of the skin until the vital organs are destroyed* (lines 64–66). To Emerson, then, the *disease* is the problem of *sensuousness* (devotion to the senses rather than the intellect).

10. **C**   Characterization

In line 20, Emerson defines prudence as *the virtue of the senses*, but he regards the *world of the senses [as] a world of shows* (lines 22–23), that *is false when detached* (line 35) from *the thing signified* (line 47) by the natural, sensory, intellectual world, that is, from *the splendor of God* (lines 55). Furthermore, he says that prudence is *a devotion to matter, as if we possessed no other faculties than the palate, the nose, the touch, the eye and ear* (lines 59–61). Therefore, as a whole, the passage characterizes prudence as a *pursuit of practical skills and sensory experience*.

11. A   **Tone**

The opening paragraph describes *this breathless pause at the threshold of a long passage* (lines 8–9) in which the narrator and his crew *seemed to be measuring our fitness for a long and arduous enterprise* (lines 9–10). This describes the *reflective anticipation* of a journey. Notice that this description provides no evidence of *anxiety* or *excitement*. In fact, the scene is described in peaceful terms, with the ship *very still in an immense stillness* (line 2).

12. A   **Specific Purpose**

The narrator states that *some glare in the air* (lines 14–15) prevented him from seeing sooner *something that did away with the solemnity of perfect solitude* (lines 18–19). That is, he saw something that led him to believe they were not alone. In the next paragraph, this *something* is revealed to be the mastheads of *a ship anchored inside the islands* (lines 35–36).

13. C   **Specific Detail**

This sentence describes the scene as the narrator surveys the *tide of darkness* and *a swarm of stars* (lines 20–21) while resting his hand on the rail of the ship as if it were *the shoulder of a trusted friend* (line 24). In the next sentence, he describes this as a moment of *quiet communion* (line 26) with the ship, now interrupted by the sight of a strange ship beyond and the *disturbing sounds* (lines 27–28) being made by the crew. In other words, this sentence describes a moment of *wistful (expressing vague longing) contemplation*. Choice (A) is incorrect because, although the *disturbing sounds* and the omen of a distant ship may seem to be *signs of impending danger*, the sentence in lines 20–24 makes no mention of these things. Choice (B) is incorrect, because this moment is described as a moment of *quiet communion*, not *deep inner turmoil*. Choice (D) is incorrect, because there is no mention of any *tragic experience*.

14. A   **Characterization**

Since this story is being told from the perspective of the captain, we can infer his character from the nature of his narration. In the opening paragraph, the captain states that *we seemed to be measuring our fitness for a long arduous enterprise, the point of our existences to be carried out* (lines 9–12), demonstrating that he is more *reflective* than *reactive* as a leader. Much later he says, *what I felt most was my being a stranger to the ship; and if all the truth must be told, I was somewhat of a stranger to myself . . . I wondered how far I should turn out faithful to that ideal conception of one's own personality every man sets up for himself secretly* (lines 56–66). These descriptions of reflection and self-doubt reveal the captain as being *self-conscious and diffident*.

15. D   **Textual Evidence**

As the explanation to question 14 shows, the best evidence for this answer can be found in lines 63–65.

16. C   **Word in Context**

In saying *I mention this because it has some bearing on what is to follow* (lines 55–56), the narrator means that the fact that he was *the only stranger on board* (line 54) is *relevant* to what he is about to say.

17. B   **Word in Context**

This sentence describes how the chief mate, described as *earnest* (line 71) *and painstaking* (72), is trying strenuously to figure out why there is another ship anchored nearby. In saying that he *was trying to evolve a theory*, the narrator means he *is pondering* (thinking) *strenuously*.

18. C   **Specific Detail**

The *truth* that the narrator mentions in line 57 is the fact that *I am a stranger to myself*. He later goes on to explain what he means by this: *I wondered how far I should turn out faithful to that ideal conception of one's own personality every man sets up for himself secretly* (lines 63–66). In other words, this truth is the fact that he lacks *self-confidence*.

19. D   **Word in Context**

In saying that *the why and the wherefore of that scorpion . . . had exercised him infinitely* (lines 76–82), the narrator means that the chief mate was using his *dominant trait . . . [of] earnest consideration* (lines 71–72) to figure out how a scorpion had made its way into his cabin. That is, the questions about the scorpion had *disquieted* (unsettled) *him infinitely*.

20. D   **Textual Evidence**

The *collaboration on the part of [the chief mate's] round eyes and frightful whiskers* (lines 67–68) describes his facial contortions as he deliberates about the anchored ship. In other words, it is an act of *strained contemplation*.

21. A   **Interpretation**

In the final line, the narrator says that *the ship within the islands was much more easily accounted for*. In other words, the scorpion was *less* easily accounted for, or *less explicable*.

22. C   **Inference**

The second paragraph discusses the *"outsourcing" [of] the creation of human life* (lines 8–9), so the *design and control* mentioned in line 13 refer specifically to the design and control of the *process of conception*.

23. B   **Tone**

The author of Passage 1 states that the *"outsourcing" [of] the creation of human life . . . mocks the profundity of life* (lines 8–12) and he provides no indication in the passage that he otherwise approves of it. Clearly, then, he regards it with *blunt disdain*.

24. D   **Cross-Textual Analysis**

Both of these quotations represent viewpoints with which the authors of the respective passages disagree. In Passage 1, the quotation *"Sorry, but I think I can do better"* (line 15) is from those who *turn [their] noses up at the most precious gift in the universe* (lines 13–14) much to the chagrin of the author. In Passage 2, the quotation *"But you are playing God"* (line 78) is described as *the cry of all whose power is threatened by the march of human progress*, and with whom the author clearly disagrees.

25. A   **Cross-Textual Analysis**

Jeremy Rifkin is described in Passage 2 as a *cloning foe* (line 63) who is quoted as saying *"It's a horrendous crime to make a Xerox of someone. You're putting a human into a genetic straitjacket."* Presumably, then, he would agree that *our attitude toward the creation of life must be one of humility* (lines 6–7).

26. D   **Graphical Analysis**

The illustration shows a schematic overview of some *Therapeutic Cloning Strategies* that involve removing a somatic cell from a patient and transferring its nucleus to stem cells that can then be cultured into genetically matched tissue that can then replace diseased cells and tissues in the patient. This is an example of one of the *procedures to clone human cells for seemingly beneficial purposes* (lines 39–40) described in Passage 1. Choice (A) is incorrect because the *guided purpose* refers to a principle of creationism, which is not indicated at all in the diagram. Choice (B) is incorrect because, although the process in the diagram might resemble an assembly line, it is not the *assembly line* that could be used to create a child *that is no longer uniquely human* (lines 23–24), but *with carefully designed and tested features* (lines 25–26). Choice (C) is incorrect because the diagram does not describe the *course of human evolution*, which would need to show how humans evolved from more primitive species.

27. D   **Specific Meaning**

The process *of introducing degraded germs* (line 53) describes the basic process of vaccination, which, like *cutting flesh* (line 52) (that is, surgery), must have seemed dangerous at first, but in fact can be a life-saving technology. This process is the *injection* of vaccines.

28. C   **Inference**

In this paragraph, the author of Passage 2 describes the position of cloning foes who believe that cloning *is the end of evolution, or at least the beginning of its corporate management* (lines 59–61). The author of Passage 1 is deeply concerned that *the executive boards of these [cloning] companies will decide the course of human evolution, with more concern for quarterly profit reports than for the sake of humanity* (lines 32–35). Clearly, then, the author of Passage 1 regards this management as *a regrettable invasion of commercial interests into human reproduction*.

29. A   **Specific Purpose**

Jeremy Rifkin's belief that cloning is *a horrendous crime* (line 64) directly contradicts the thesis of Passage 2, which is that cloning and similar technologies can *provide ample food for a starving world, cure devastating illnesses, and replace diseased organs* (lines 98–100). Therefore, to the author of Passage 2, Rifkin's opinion *exemplifies an untenable* (indefensible) *position*. Choice (B) may seem plausible, since Rifkin is warning of *the potential dangers of cloning*, but notice that this cannot be the reason that the author of Passage 2 quotes Rifkin, because the passage clearly disagrees with his sentiments.

30. C   **Specific Purpose**

The author of Passage 2 mentions the *Twins Days Festival* (line 68) in order to demonstrate the absurdity of Jeremy Rifkin's statement that creating a genetic *Xerox* of a person is a *horrendous crime* (line 64). To the author of Passage 2, then, the Twins Days Festival represents *the innocuousness* (harmlessness) *of genetic duplication*, since twins are genetic duplicates, and nothing to be feared.

31. B   **Cross-Textual Inference**

The author of Passage 2 does not object to the *procedures to clone human cells for seemingly beneficial purposes* (lines 39–40), and in fact believes they are *necessary contributions to medical progress* since they potentially provide technologies to *provide ample food for a starving world, cure devastating illnesses, and replace diseased organs* (lines 98–100).

32. D   **Textual Evidence**

As the explanation to question 31 indicates, the best evidence for this answer is found in lines 95–100.

33. C   **General Purpose**

The first paragraph establishes that this passage is focused on the specific processes involved in *children's acquisition of language* (lines 12–13). Therefore, the passage is primarily concerned with *exploring academic questions about how we learn language.* Choice (A) is incorrect because the passage does not begin to *delineate the general principles of linguistics*, which is a far greater subject than simply language acquisition. Choice (B) is incorrect, because although the passage does refer to children's ability to acquire diverse languages like *English . . . Bantu or Vietnamese* (lines 63–64), it does not compare their structural qualities. Choice (D) is incorrect because, although the passage does discuss the ideas of the influential linguists Benjamin Whorf (in the second paragraph) and Noam Chomsky (in the last paragraph), these references only serve the larger purpose of exploring the questions of language acquisition, and do not serve as the overall focus of the passage.

---

34. C   **Inference**

In the first paragraph, the author indicates that *[e]very time we speak we are revealing something about language, so the facts of language structure are easy to come by* (lines 3–6). Therefore, the *data* mentioned in line 6 are *the facts of language structure*, which would likely include *the syntax* (rules governing word order) *of different languages.* Choice (A) is incorrect because information about *literacy levels* is not information about *language structure.* Choice (B) is incorrect because methods of teaching are not *facts of language structure.* Choice (D) is incorrect because, although the passage does mention the innate *structure* (line 59) of the brain a few paragraphs later, this is clearly not what line 6 is referring to.

---

35. B   **Inference**

The phrase *the two* (line 2) refers to two nouns in the previous clause: *language* and *thoughts*, in other words, *thinking and expressing.*

---

36. A   **Word in Context**

The author uses the phrase *sticking communicable labels on thoughts* (lines 15–16) to describe one particularly simplistic theory about the language acquisition. The author is using the metaphor of *applying* name tags or labels to describe one way of describing how words are used. Choice (B) is incorrect because *upholding* refers to a process of confirming an official claim or pronouncement. Choice (C) is incorrect because, although *sticking* (as with a needle) can mean *piercing*, this reference clearly does not imply any act of puncturing. Choice (D) is incorrect because this phrase describes an act of *acquisition*, that is, learning something new, rather than *maintaining* something old.

---

37. D   **Tone/Attitude**

After describing Benjamin Whorf's theory, the author then states that *virtually all modern cognitive scientists believe it is false* (lines 25–27). The author's ensuing

discussion makes it clear that he agrees with these cognitive scientists. That is, he is *antagonistic* toward Whorf's hypothesis. Choice (A) is wrong because the author does not *dismiss* Whorf's hypothesis, but rather regards it as *an intriguing hypothesis* which just happens to be incorrect. (To *dismiss* an idea is to believe it is not even worthy of consideration, not merely to reject it after consideration.) Choice (B) is clearly wrong because the author does not *support* Whorf's hypothesis. Choice (C) is wrong because the author does not have any conflicting feelings about the hypothesis.

---

38. B   **Interpretation**

The author states that *babies can think before they can talk* (line 27) in order to refute Whorf's hypothesis that we can't think in terms of *categories and relations* (line 19) until our language gives us the words to do so. Whorf believes that language precedes thought. The author of this passage is saying the opposite: that *skills associated with basic reasoning are not dependent on verbal communication.*

---

39. C   **Thesis**

The author's view on human language acquisition can be found in lines 95–97: *language acquisition depends on an innate, species-specific module that is distinct from general intelligence.* This module must have an intricate *innate structure* (line 59) in order to acquire a language that is itself *intricately complex* (line 55). Choice (A) is incorrect because it represents the Whorf hypothesis, which the author explicitly rejects. Choice (B) is incorrect because the author does not state that the structures for learning language are simple. Choice (D) is incorrect because the author places more emphasis on the innate structure in the brain that enables language acquisition than he does on environmental input.

---

40. D   **Textual Evidence**

As the explanation to question 39 indicates, the best evidence for this answer is found in lines 95–97.

---

41. B   **Interpretation**

Lines 58–64 discuss the author's belief that the *innate structure* in the brain dedicated to language acquisition cannot be either too simple or too complex. This kind of *structure* refers to the *functional organization of the mind.* Notice that the *structure* being discussed here is not the same as the *structure* mentioned in line 5, which refers to the structure of language itself.

---

42. A   **Inference**

The author states that, in 1959, *Anglo-American natural science, social science, and philosophy had come to a virtual consensus about the answers to the questions listed above* (lines 78–81), that is, the questions listed in lines 14–17: *Is language simply grafted on top of cognition as a way of sticking communicable labels on thoughts? Or does learning a language somehow mean learning to think in that language?* The *consensus* on these topics was that *language must be learned; it cannot be a module; and thinking must be a form of verbal behavior* (lines 85–87) Therefore, the disciplines *accepted the hypothesis that cognition depends on verbal skills.*

---

43. B   **General Purpose**

The passage begins by saying our negative view of scavengers *ignores an important fact: scavenger relationships are essential to all complex life* (lines 10–12). The second paragraph describes how scavenger behavior drives social intelligence, as with dogs. The third describes how decomposers break down petroleum and plastics in the environment. The fourth discusses how scavenger bacteria in the human gut help to regulate our bodily systems. As a whole, then, the passage serves to *explore various ways in which scavengers can be beneficial to different ecosystems that are relevant to humans.* Choice A is wrong because the passage does not discuss *ways of preserving ecosystems.* Choice C is wrong because social intelligence is only discussed in the second paragraph. Choice D is wrong because the passage does not discuss ways of *avoiding the diseases that [scavengers] spread.*

---

44. D   **Word in Context**

Since the previous paragraph discussed the *evolution of social intelligence* (line 14) among scavengers like the grey wolf, and their evolution into *friendly Frisbee-fetchers* (lines 31–32), the phrase perspicacious scavengers is referring to those scavengers that can *develop mutually beneficial social relationships.*

---

45. C   **Graphical Inference**

The graph shows how much U.S. plastic is going into the environment, such as oceans and landfills, rather than being recycled. In lines 55–64, the passage discusses the ability of *Aspergillus tubingensis* to break down *polyester polyurethane, a petroleum product and one of the more durable plastics in our landfills and ocean.* Since plastics are a food source for *A. tubingensis*, the graph is appropriate to a discussion of *the habitat of Aspergillus tubingensis.*

---

46. C   **Inference**

In lines 15–20, the passage says that *some scavenger species have struggled to outwit the wily hunters with whom they compete for scraps . . . in order to avoid becoming the next prey.* Choice A is wrong because tracking prey is a hunter behavior, not a scavenger behavior. Choice B is

wrong because the passage does not discuss how scavengers might find more nutritious food sources. Choice D is wrong because, although the passage does state that *hunters like* Homo sapiens *had to become more clever to protect their meat from these thieves* (lines 20–22), this is an intelligent behavior of hunters, not scavengers.

---

47. B   **Textual Evidence**

As the explanation to question 46 indicates, the best evidence for this answer can be found in lines 17–20.

---

48. A   **Word in Context**

A process of *break[ing] down complex molecules into simpler ones* (lines 41–42) implies that the original molecules are *larger and more intricate* than they will become. Choice B is wrong because *obscure and bewildering* do not describe physical properties. Choice C is wrong because the passage does not imply that these molecules are *delicate*; they just need a special process to break them down. Choice D is wrong because *unfathomable* does not describe a physical property.

---

49. C   **Word in Context**

The phrase *encourage this biodegradation* (line 52) means *do something to invigorate the process.* Choices A, B, and D are all incorrect because *inspire, goad,* and *persuade* are verbs that can only be applied to people, not chemical processes.

---

50. C   **Detail**

In lines 60–63, the passage indicates that *environmentalists have yet to discover a practical method for harnessing* A. tubingensis *in large-scale waste mitigation systems*, which means that these microorganisms are not easily controlled.

---

51. D   **Textual Evidence**

As the explanation to question 50 indicates, the best evidence for this answer is found in lines 60–64.

---

52. A   **Purpose**

The final paragraph discusses how scavenger bacteria in the human gut help to keep *things running smoothly* (lines 72–73), specifically by maintaining our *digestive processes, blood pressure, and immune system* (lines 66–67). Choice B is wrong because the paragraph cautions against the overuse of antibiotics, but does not discuss how to develop them. Choice C is wrong because the paragraph discusses benefits of bacteria, not dangers. Choice D is wrong because although this paragraph cautions against overusing antibiotics, it does not say that it is due to any *fear of bacteria.*

Section 2: Writing and Language

1. A   **Idiom**

The original phrasing is best. Choice (B) is incorrect because *choice with getting* is not idiomatic. Choice (C) is incorrect because *choice of the way* is not idiomatic. Choice (D) is incorrect *choice of getting*, although idiomatic conveys an illogical idea in this context.

2. C   **Diction**

Here we are asked to choose the best word to convey the appropriate idea in this sentence. The sentence indicates that we *might be surprised to learn* something about the world of journalism, and hence that most of us are not as informed about the world of journalism as we could be. In other words, we are not particularly *savvy* (knowledgeable) about the world of journalism. *Apt* = suitable to the circumstances; *acute* = sharp; *comprehensive* = complete.

3. B   **Diction/Logic**

In the original phrasing, the pronoun *which* is illogical, since it refers to *the media*: that is, saying *the media is 90%* does not make sense. Choice (C) is incorrect because the phrase *all 90% of it* is illogical: *all of it* means 100% of it. Choice (D) is incorrect because it is both unidiomatic and illogical.

4. C   **Possessive Form/Pronoun Agreement**

In the original phrasing, the pronoun *their* disagrees with its antecedent *corporation*, which is singular. Recall that the possessive form of the pronoun *it* is *its (it's = it is)*. The only choice that avoids both the agreement error and the diction error is (C).

5. B   **Parallelism**

This phrase should be parallel to the subject-verb pair in the previous sentence, *Some argue*. The only choice with a parallel verb form is (B).

6. A   **Data Analysis**

The original phrasing is the only option that represents the data in Figure 1 accurately. Since the second circle graph represents all broadcast television media and its ownership, it indicates that 3.2% (0.6% + 1.3% + 0.9% + 0.4%) of American broadcast television outlets were controlled by minorities.

7. D   **Idiom**

The idiomatic form of this phrase is *antidote to*.

8. C   **Clear Expression/Pronoun Antecedents**

In choices (A), (B), and (D), the pronoun *it* lacks any clear referent. The only choice that avoids this problem is (C).

9. B   **Cohesiveness/Purpose**

Examples that contrast *civilized debate* would have to be examples of *uncivilized* debate. *Gossip* and *fear-mongering* certainly qualify as relatively *uncivilized* and *unsophisticated* forms of discourse.

10. B   **Idiom, Pronoun-Antecedent Agreement**

Here, we are looking for the most appropriate logical transition from the previous paragraph to the new one. The last sentence of the previous paragraph gave examples of *in-depth, nonprofit, public-supported journalism that is less influenced by any corporate or political agenda*. The new paragraph, however, begins with a discussion of *sensationalism* and how it *sells*, which provides a stark contrast to the previous paragraph. This requires a contrasting coordinator, such as *nevertheless* or *still*.

11. D   **Diction/Clear Expression of Ideas**

We want a word to represent the websites like ProPublica and NPR, as mentioned in the previous paragraph, that engage in relatively noncorporate and apolitical journalism. The phrase *instances of journalism* indicates specific articles or broadcasts, rather than the organizations themselves. The phrase *patterns of journalism* indicates trends in those articles or broadcasts, rather than the organizations themselves. The phrase *receptacles of journalism* indicates containers that receive journalism rather than organizations that produce it. Only (D) *repositories of journalism* provides a phrase that refers to the organizations themselves.

12. D   **Coordination/Verb Tense**

The original phrasing creates a sentence fragment rather than an independent clause. Choice (B) is incorrect because it commits the same error. Choices (C) and (D) both form independent and idiomatic clauses, but choice (C) is incorrect because the sentence is clearly making a claim about the *current state of being* of these rituals, rather than the *current status-as-consequence* of these rituals, so the present perfect (or "present consequential") form is not appropriate. (For more on using the "perfect" or "consequential" aspect, see Chapter 4, Lesson 23.)

13. A   **Coordination/Conjunctions**

The original phrasing is best. Choice (B) is incorrect because the second clause does not explain the first. Choice (C) is incorrect because the second clause does not follow as a consequence of the first. Choice (D) is incorrect because there is no tonal or semantic contrast between the clauses.

---

14. B   **Diction/Clear Expression of Ideas**

The phrase *collide against* is not idiomatic: *collide with* is the correct idiom, although this phrase would imply more of a physical relationship than the sentence intends. Since the sentence indicates a conflict between an *event* and a *belief* so the verb should express a relationship between *ideas*, rather than *objects*. Of the choices, only (B) *contradict* serves this purpose effectively.

---

15. C   **Coordination**

In this sentence, the conjunction *and* establishes the relationship between the coordinate independent clauses, so any subordinating conjunction like *since, so*, or *because* is inappropriate.

---

16. B   **Diction, Agreement**

Colons must always follow independent clauses, so choices (A) and (D) are incorrect. This phrase must provide a definition of the term "agency," which is precisely what choice (B) *that is, intentional action* does. Choice (C) is incorrect because it categorizes rather than defines.

---

17. D   **Parallelism**

This sentence presents a list of present tense verbs: *design . . . compose . . . and formulate.* The original phrasing is incorrect because it reinserts the auxiliary *can*, which breaks the parallel structure of the list. Only choice (D) maintains this parallel form.

---

18. D   **Cohesiveness**

This sentence belongs before sentence 5, because it provides a parallel idea to the one presented in sentence 4. Sentence 4 states that *Many of these [superstitions] are harmless if not quaint*, so the next sentence should provide a transition to some of the less pleasant aspects of superstitious thinking.

---

19. C   **Pronoun-Antecedent Agreement/Verb Mood**

In the original phrasing, the pronoun *it* does not agree with its plural antecedent *explanations*; therefore, choices (A) and (B) are incorrect. Choice (D) is incorrect because the auxiliary *would* implies necessity, rather than ability, which is illogical in this context.

---

20. B   **Clear Expression/Pronoun Antecedents**

The original phrasing is incorrect because the two instances of the pronoun *their* have conflicting antecedents, and the second clause is needlessly in the passive voice. Choices (C) and (D) have similar pronoun referent problems. Only choice (B) is phrased without ambiguous pronouns.

---

21. D   **Diction**

The previous sentence, as well as the passage as a whole, indicates that superstitious rituals are used to *satisfy a craving in our brains for control.*

---

22. A   **Cohesiveness**

Only choice (A) maintains the skeptical and analytical tone toward superstitious rituals that is established in the rest of the passage.

---

23. C   **Clear Expression**

The original phrasing is incorrect because the phrase *debating a warming planet* is illogical: only *theories, claims*, or *ideas* can be topics of debate. Choices (B) and (D) are incorrect because the clause *if we should* lacks a logical object.

---

24. D   **Comma Splices/Coordination**

The original phrasing is incorrect because it creates a comma splice. Two independent clauses may not be joined by only a comma. Choice (B) is incorrect because the conjunction *while* is illogical. Choice (C) is incorrect because it forms a noun phrase, which does not coordinate with any part of the main clause. Choice (D) creates a participial phrase that appropriately modifies the subject of the main clause.

---

25. C   **Clear Expression/Idiom**

In the original phrasing, the verb *provide* is used illogically and the phrase *cost of the American taxpayer* is unidiomatic. Choice (B) is incorrect because *needless in costing* is unidiomatic. Choice (D) is incorrect because the verb *is* disagrees in number with its subject *attempts.*

---

26. A   **Diction**

The original phrasing is best. The verb *is* serves most effectively in the role of defining *science.*

---

27. B   **Parallelism**

The underlined phrase is the third item in a parallel list: *identifying . . . gathering . . . and finding.* Choice (B) best maintains this parallel structure without introducing any other error. Choice (D) provides a parallel form, but the phrase *way for explaining* is unidiomatic.

---

28. D   **Parallelism**

The underlined phrase is part of a parallel list: *that the earth . . . that the effects . . . that there are things . . . and that many of these things . . .* Only choice (D) maintains this parallel structure.

---

29. A   **Logical Cohesiveness**

The original phrasing best, since the passage is about eliminating politics and ideology from discussions about climate change. The other choices insert points of advocacy that conflict with the tone and purpose of the passage as a whole.

---

30. D **Clear Expression of Ideas/Verb Mood/Verb Tense**

The original phrasing includes an illogical core: *the fact . . . isn't the same as it being true.* Choice (B) is incorrect because a statement of general fact should not be in the future tense. Choice (C) is incorrect because a statement of general fact should not be in the subjunctive mood. Choice (D) uses the idiom *make it so* logically and grammatically.

---

31. A **Parallelism**

The original phrasing is the only option that completes the parallel construction *caused not by germs . . . but by demons.*

---

32. A **Verb Form/Clear Expression**

The original phrasing is the most logical and concise.

---

33. C **Logical Coherence**

The adverb *furthermore* indicates that this sentence is extending a line of reasoning. Since it clearly follows the parallel clauses of sentence 2, *When we . . . become . . . we become . . .* and therefore it most logically follows sentence 2 but precedes sentence 3.

---

34. C **Pronoun Agreement/Verb Aspect**

The original phrasing is incorrect because the pronoun *they* disagrees in number with the antecedent *Bohemia*. Choice (B) is incorrect because it produces a comma splice. Choice (D) is illogical because the use of the present perfect participle *having been* improperly implies a consequence.

---

35. D **Diction**

The original phrasing is illogical because a country cannot *regard* (consider in a particular way; concern) anything. This verb must show a relationship between a particular country and a particular geographical region. Only choice (D) *comprises* (makes up) expresses this relationship in a logical way.

---

36. B **Coordination**

The original phrasing is incorrect because it creates a dangling participle: the participle *designating* does not share its subject with the main clause. Choice (C) is incorrect because it creates a comma splice. Choice (D) is incorrect because it also creates a dangling participle. Choice (B) is best because it avoids both the comma splice and dangling participle.

---

37. B **Verb Tense/Verb Aspect**

The phrase *by 1843* indicates that the status of the term *Bohemian* had become established prior to that point in time. Therefore, the verb requires the *past perfect* or *past consequential* form: *had come to mean.* Although choice (D) is a verb in the past consequential form, it incorrectly implies that the term no longer had that particular meaning in 1843.

---

38. A **Coordinating Modifiers**

This sentence is trying to convey the fact that *[La Vie de Bohème] proved [to be so] extraordinarily successful that the stories themselves were published.* This requires the active voice, so choices (B) and (C) are incorrect. Choice (D) is incorrect because it is unidiomatic.

---

39. D **Number Shift**

The original phrasing is incorrect because of the number shift between *it* and *elements*. Choices (B) and (C) are needlessly wordy. Choice (D) is clear and concise.

---

40. C **Diction/Logical Coherence**

This sentence indicates the effect that *increased commodity production* had on the *commercial middle class*. It is illogical to say that the middle class *propagated* (was transmitted), *propitiated* (won the favor of someone), or *preempted* (took action to prevent something) as a result of this increased production. It is, however, logical to say that the middle class *prospered* (flourished) as a result of it.

---

41. A **Coordination of Clauses**

The original phrasing best coordinates the two related, but independent, clauses. Choice (B) produces a run-on sentence with a comma splice. Choice (C) is illogical and unidiomatic. Choice (D) is illogical and misuses the semicolon.

---

42. B **Clarity of Expression/Parallelism**

Choice (B) provides the most parallel comparison: *the production of art was in fact less important than the capacity for art.*

---

43. D **Coordination of Ideas**

The use of the adverb *thus* indicates that this sentence represents a logical consequence of some particular state of affairs. That state of affairs is best indicated by sentence 5: *Most of its ingredients had existed in Paris for at least two decades before he started writing.* This explains why Murger can be described as a *Bohemian of the second generation.*

---

44. C **Coherence/Meaning**

This question is essentially asking us to describe the function of Claretie's quotation. Since it refers to a *poisonous element in the French character*, it is clearly indicating a *dire assessment of France's national temperament.*

Section 3: Math (No Calculator)

1. B   **Algebra (solving equations) EASY**

Original equation:	$2b - 1 = 5$
Add 1:	$2b = 6$
Divide by 2:	$b = 3$
Substitute $b = 3$ into $2b^2 - 1$:	$2b^2 - 1 = 2(3)^2 - 1$
	$= 18 - 1 = 17$

---

2. B   **Special Topics (circles) EASY**

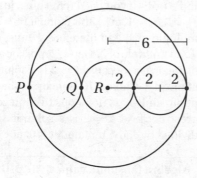

Marking up the diagram with the given information, as shown, shows that three of the smaller radii make up one larger radius. Therefore, the radius of each small circle is $6/3 = 2$.

---

3. C   **Algebra (word problems/fractions) EASY**

If 1/5 of her term paper is 15 pages, then the entire paper must be $15 \times 5 = 75$ pages long. This means she has $75 - 15 = 60$ more pages to edit.

---

4. C   **Advanced Mathematics (functions and sequences) EASY**

Notice that the rule in choice (C) generates the entire sequence: 7 (times 2 minus 2 equals) 12 (times 2 minus 2 equals) 22 (times 2 minus 2 equals) 42 (times 2 minus 2 equals) 82.

---

5. B   **Special Topics (three dimensional geometry) MEDIUM**

Notice that the question asks us for the longest length of a diagonal on one of the *faces* of the box, and that there are three different rectangles as faces: a 3×4 rectangle, a 3×5 rectangle, and a 4×5 rectangle. Clearly the one with the two greatest dimensions will have the longest diagonal, which we can find using the Pythagorean Theorem.

	$4^2 + 5^2 = d^2$
Simplify:	$16 + 25 = d^2$
Simplify:	$41 = d^2$
Take the square root:	$\sqrt{41} = d$

6. A   **Algebra (linear equations) MEDIUM**

We can test each point to find the one that does NOT satisfy the equation.

(A) $-2(-9) - 3(6) = 18 - 18 = 0 \neq 36$
(B) $-2(-24) - 3(4) = 48 - 12 = 36$
(C) $-2(6) - 3(-16) = -12 + 48 = 36$
(D) $-2(12) - 3(-20) = -24 + 60 = 36$
Therefore, the correct answer is (A).

---

7. A   **Advanced Mathematics (parabolas) MEDIUM**

The initial population, I, is the population when the time is 0. Therefore, $I = 250(1.32)^0 = 250(1) = 250$. The annual percent increase in the population, r, can be calculated by finding the population at $t = 1$ and then calculating the percent change from the initial population. If $t = 1$, $P = 250(1.32)^1$. As we discussed in Chapter 8, Lesson 7, multiplying a quantity by 1.32 is equivalent to increasing a number by 32% (that is, $1.32 = 100\% + 32\%$), so $r = 32\%$.

---

8. A   **Advanced Mathematics (rational expressions) MEDIUM**

$$\frac{1}{\sqrt{3}+1}$$
$$3+1$$

Multiply the numerator and denominator by the conjugate $\left(\sqrt{3}-1\right)$:	$\dfrac{1}{\sqrt{3}+1} \times \dfrac{\sqrt{3}-1}{\sqrt{3}-1}$
Simplify:	$\dfrac{\sqrt{3}-1}{3-1}$
Simplify:	$\dfrac{\sqrt{3}-1}{2}$
Distribute:	$\dfrac{\sqrt{3}}{2} - \dfrac{1}{2}$

---

9. B   **Algebra (linear relationships) MEDIUM**

As we discussed in Chapter 7, Lesson 5, a line in the form $ax + by = c$ has a slope of $-a/b$. Therefore, the line $3x + 6y = 0$ has a slope of $-3/6 = -1/2$. Recall, also, from Chapter 7, Lesson 7, that perpendicular lines have slopes that are opposite reciprocals. Therefore, the line we are looking for must have a slope of 2. You might draw a quick sketch of the xy-plane and plot the points given in each choice to find the line that has a slope of 2, or you could use the slope formula from Chapter 7, Lesson 5: slope $= (y_2 - y_1)/(x_2 - x_1)$.

(A) slope $= (3 - 0)/(0 - (-6)) = 3/6 = 1/2$
(B) slope $= (-6 - 0)/(0 - 3) = -6/-3 = 2$
(C) slope $= (6 - 0)/(0 - 3) = 6/-3 = -2$
(D) slope $= (3 - 0)/(0 - 6) = 3/-6 = -1/2$

The only choice that gives a slope of 2 is (B).

10. B   **Advanced Mathematics (quadratics) HARD**

Perhaps the simplest way to begin this problem is to draw a quick sketch of the function in the xy-plane, and then compare this graph to the transformations of the original function given in the choices. Notice that the original function $f(x) = x - x^2$ is easily factored *as* $f(x) = x(1 - x)$. The Zero Product Property (Chapter 9, Lesson 5) tells us that this function must have zeros at $x = 0$ and $x = 1$. Notice, also, that since the coefficient of the x^2 term in the original function is negative (-1), the graph of this quadratic is an "open-down" parabola. Also, the axis of symmetry is halfway between the zeros, at $x = \frac{1}{2}$. Plugging $x = \frac{1}{2}$ back into the function gives us $f\left(\frac{1}{2}\right) = \frac{1}{2} - \left(\frac{1}{2}\right)^2 = \frac{1}{2} - \frac{1}{4} = \frac{1}{4}$, and therefore, the vertex of the parabola is $\left(\frac{1}{2}, \frac{1}{4}\right)$.

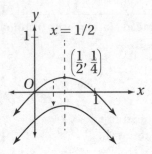

The question asks us to find the function that has no real zeros. This means that the graph of this function must not intersect the x-axis at all. Each answer choice indicates a different transformation of the function f. Recall from Chapter 9, Lesson 3, that choice (A) $f(x) + \frac{1}{2}$ is the graph of f shifted *up* $\frac{1}{2}$ unit, choice (B) $f(x) - \frac{1}{2}$ is the graph of f shifted *down* $\frac{1}{2}$ unit, choice (C) $f(x/2)$ is the graph of f *stretched* by a factor of 2 in the horizontal direction, and choice (D) $f(x - \frac{1}{2})$ is the graph of f shifted *right* $\frac{1}{2}$ unit. As the sketch above shows, only (B) yields a graph that does not intersect the x-axis.

11. D   **Advanced Mathematics (polynomials)**
MEDIUM-HARD

Given equation:	$y = x^2 + x$
Substitute $y = \frac{15}{4}$:	$\frac{15}{4} = x^2 + x$
Multiply by 4:	$15 = 4x^2 + 4x$
Subtract 15:	$0 = 4x^2 + 4x - 15$
Factor using the Product-Sum Method (Chapter 9, Lesson 4):	$0 = (2x + 5)(2x - 3)$
Use Zero Product Property (Chapter 9, Lesson 5):	$2x + 5 = 0; 2x - 3 = 0$

Solve each equation for x: $x = -5/2; x = 3/2$

Therefore, the two points of intersection are $\left(-\frac{5}{2}, \frac{15}{4}\right)$ and $\left(\frac{3}{2}, \frac{15}{4}\right)$, and the distance between these points is

$$\frac{3}{2} - \left(-\frac{5}{2}\right) = \frac{3}{2} + \frac{5}{2} = \frac{8}{2} = 4$$

12. D   **Special Topics (complex numbers)**
MEDIUM-HARD

Recall from Chapter 10, Lesson 10, that $i^n = 1$ if and only if n is a multiple of 4. (If you need refreshing, just confirm that $i^4 = 1$, $i^8 = 1$, $i^{12} = 1$, etc.) Therefore, if $i^{2k} = 1$, then $2k$ must be a multiple of 4, and therefore, k must be a multiple of 2. If k is a multiple of 2, then $k/2$ must be an integer. Choice (A) is incorrect, because $k = 2$ is a solution, but 2 is not a multiple of 4. Choice (B) is incorrect because $k = -2$ is a solution, and -2 is not a positive integer. Choice (C) is incorrect because $k = 2$ is a solution, but when $2(2) = 4$ is divided by 4, the remainder is 0, not 1.

13. B   **Algebra (absolute values) MEDIUM-HARD**

In order to minimize the value of $|2^2 - x^2 - y^2| + 2^2$, we must minimize the absolute value. But the least possible value *of any* absolute value expression is 0, so we must ask: is it possible for the expression inside the absolute value operator to equal 0? A little trial and error should reveal that it can if, for instance, $x = 2$ and $y = 0$. Notice that this gives us $|2 - 2^2 - 0^2| + 2 = |0| + 2^2 = 4$. Since the absolute value cannot be less than 0, this must be the minimum possible value.

14. C   **Advanced Mathematics (analyzing polynomial functions) HARD**

The simplest polynomial with factors of 12, $(x - 5)$, and $(x + 4)$ is $P(x) = 12(x - 5)(x + 4)$. The completely factored form (including the prime factorization of the coefficient) of this polynomial is $P(x) = (2)^2 (3)(x - 5)(x + 4)$.

Now, using the methods we discussed in Chapter 9, Lesson 4, we can look at the factored form of each choice:

(A) $2x^2 + 8 = 2(x^2 + 8)$ ($x^2 + 8$ is not factorable over the reals, but it does equal $(x - \sqrt{8}i)(x + \sqrt{8}i)$

(B) $4x^2 - 20 = 4(x^2 - 5) = (2)^2(x - \sqrt{5})(x - \sqrt{5})$

(C) $6x^2 - 6x - 120 = 6(x^2 - x - 20) = (2)(3)(x - 5)(x + 4)$

(D) $x^2 - 10x + 25 = (x - 5)(x - 5)$

Notice that every polynomial in (A), (B), and (D) contains at least one factor that is NOT in the factored form of $P(x)$. (In (D), the factor $(x - 5)$ appears twice, but it appears only once in $P(x)$.) Only choice (C) contains ONLY factors that appear in $P(x)$, so it is the only choice that must be a factor of $P(x)$.

15. D   **Advanced Mathematics (functions) HARD**

Given function:	$g(f(x)) = 2x + 1$
Substitute $f(x) = -x + 7$:	$g(-x + 7) = 2x + 1$
To evaluate $g(2)$, we must	
let $-x + 7 = 2$:	$-x + 7 = 2$
Subtract 7:	$-x = -5$
Multiply by -1:	$x = 5$
Substitute $x = 5$:	$g(-5 + 7) = 2(5) + 1$
Simplify:	$g(2) = 11$

16. 8   **Algebra (ratios/word problems) EASY**

Let x equal the number of men in the workshop. If there are half as many men as women, there must be $2x$ women in the workshop, or a total of $x + 2x = 3x$ men and women in the workshop. Since this total equals 24: $3x = 24$

Divide by 3: $x = 8$

As with all algebra problems, make sure you confirm that the value you've solved for is the value the question is asking for. Since x is in fact the number of men, it is the final answer.

17. 2/3 or .666 or .667   **Advanced Mathematics (rational equations) EASY**

$$3 - \frac{1}{b} = \frac{3}{2}$$

Multiply by the common denominator, $2b$:	$6b - 2 = 3b$
Add 2:	$6b = 3b + 2$
Subtract $3b$:	$3b = 2$
Divide by 3:	$b = \frac{2}{3}$

18. 1.2 or 6/5   **Algebra (word problems) HARD**

First, translate the given fact into an equation.

The square of a positive number is 0.24 greater than the number itself:	$x^2 = x + 0.24$
Subtract x and 0.24:	$x^2 - x - 0.24 = 0$
Multiply by 100 to eliminate the decimal:	$100x^2 - 100x - 24 = 0$

Now we factor using Product-Sum Method. Remember that the product number is $ac = (100)(-24) = -2,400$, and the sum number is $b = -100$. The two numbers with a sum of -100 and a product of $-2,400$ are 20 and -120.

Expand middle term using $-100 = 20 - 120$:	$100x^2 + 20x - 120x - 24 = 0$
Factor by grouping in pairs:	$20x(5x + 1) - 24(5x + 1) = 0$
Take out common factor:	$(5x + 1)(20x - 24) = 0$

Using the Zero Product Property, we see that $x = -1/5$ or $x = 24/20 = 6/5$. Since we are told that x is a positive number, $x = 6/5$ or 1.2.

19. 5/2 or 2.5   **Advanced Mathematics (quadratics) MEDIUM-HARD**

Using the Factor Theorem from Chapter 9, Lesson 7, we know that if a quadratic has zeroes at $x = 1$ and $x = 5$, it must have factors of $(x - 1)$ and $(x - 5)$. Since a quadratic can only have two linear factors, f must be of the form $f(x) = k(x - 1)(x - 5)$.

Substitute $x = 3$ and $y = -2$ for the coordinates of vertex:	$-2 = k(3 - 1)(3 - 5)$
Simplify:	$-2 = k(2)(-2)$
Simplify:	$-2 = -4k$
Divide by -4:	$\frac{1}{2} = k$

Therefore the equation of the function is $f(x) = \frac{1}{2}(x - 1)(x - 5)$, and we can find its y-intercept by

substituting $x = 0$:	$f(0) = \frac{1}{2}(0 - 1)(0 - 5)$
Simplify:	$f(0) = \frac{5}{2}$

20. 7/3 or 2.33   **Special Topics (trigonometry) HARD**

The graph of the line $y = mx - 4$ has a slope of m and a y-intercept of -4. Since $m > 0$, this slope is positive. We are told that this line intersects the x-axis at an angle of θ, where $\cos \theta = \dfrac{3}{\sqrt{58}}$. This gives us enough information to sketch a fairly detailed graph:

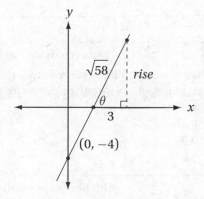

Notice that this information lets us construct a right triangle that includes θ, in which the adjacent side has length 3 and the hypotenuse has length $\sqrt{58}$ (remember $\cos \theta = $ adjacent/hypotenuse). This triangle is particularly handy because it depicts the *rise* and the *run* for a portion of the line, which will enable us to find the slope. We simply have to find the rise with the

Pythagorean Theorem:	$3^2 + rise^2 = \left(\sqrt{58}\right)^2$
Simplify:	$9 + rise^2 = 58$
Subtract 9:	$rise^2 = 49$
Take square root:	$rise = 7$

Therefore, the slope of the line is $m = rise/run = 7/3$.

Section 4: Math (Calculator)

1. B   **Algebra (systems) EASY**

Since the question asks for the value of b, it makes sense to substitute for a so that we get a single equation in terms of b.

Second equation: $2a + 4b = 20$

Substitute $a = \frac{1}{2}b$ $2\left(\frac{1}{2}b\right) + 4b = 20$

Simplify and combine: $b + 4b = 5b = 20$
Divide by 5: $b = 4$

---

2. B   **Data Analysis (central tendency) EASY**

The table summarizes the following list of 20 numbers: 1, 1, 1, 2, 2, 2, 2, 3, 3, 3, 5, 6, 7, 8, 8, 8, 9, 10, 10, 10. If a set of numbers is listed in increasing order, the median is the middle number (if the set contains an odd number of elements) or the average of the *two* middle terms (if the set contains an even number of elements). The median of a set of 20 numbers, therefore, is the average of the 10th and 11th terms. Since the 10th number is 3 and the 11th number is 5, the median is $(3 + 5)/2 = 4$.

---

3. A   Problem Solving/Data Analysis (proportions)
EASY

Set up a proportion: $\dfrac{48}{8} = \dfrac{57}{x}$

Cross multiply: $456 = 48x$
Divide by 48: $9.5 = x$

---

4. C   **Data Analysis (tables) EASY**

The ratio of applicants to finalists is simply the quotient of those two values, which we can calculate for each year.
(A) 8/25 = 0.32,
(B) 8/26   0.31,
(C) 9/23   0.39,
(D) 10/26   0.38.

---

5. D   **Algebra (exponentials) EASY**

Although solving for y and z isn't hard, it is even simpler to just express $(yz)^6$ in terms of y^3 and z^2, using the Laws of Exponentials from Chapter 9, Lesson 9.

Original expression: $(yz)^6$
Law of Exponentials #5: $y^6 z^6$
Law of Exponentials #8: $(y^3)^2(z^2)^3$
Substitute $y^3 = 20$ and $z^2 = 10$: $(20)^2(10)^3$
Substitute $20 = (2)(10)$: $(2)^2(10)^2(10)^3$
Combine terms with like bases with
Law of Exponents #4: $2^2(10)^5$
Simplify: $4 \quad 10^5$

---

6. A   **Algebra (word problems) EASY**

The sum of a, b, and c is three times
the sum of a and b: $a + b + c = 3(a + b)$
Distribute: $a + b + c = 3a + 3b$
Subtract a: $b + c = 2a + 3b$
Subtract $3b$: $-2b + c = 2a$

Divide by 2: $\dfrac{c - 2b}{2} = a$

---

7. A   **Advanced Mathematics (triangle**
trigonometry) EASY

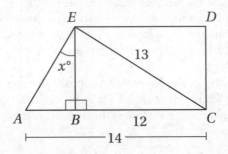

First, let's mark up the diagram with the given lengths, as above. Remember from SOH CAH TOA that the tangent of an angle is equal to the opposite side over the adjacent side, so $\tan x = AB/EB$. $AB = AC - BC = 14 - 12 = 2$, and we can find EB with the Pythagorean Theorem: $EB^2 + 12^2 = 13^2$
Simplify: $EB^2 + 144 = 169$
Subtract 144: $EB^2 = 25$
Take the square root: $EB = 5$
Or, even better, just notice that triangle EBC is a 5-12-13 triangle.
So, $\tan x = AB/EB = 2/5 = 0.4$

---

8. A   **Advanced Math (quadratics) EASY**

We can factor this quadratic easily with the Product-Sum Method from Chapter 9, Lesson 4.
$x^2 - 6x + 8 = (x - 4)(x - 2)$

---

9. A   **Data Analysis (pie graph) MEDIUM**

Since Maria's sales accounted for 25% of the total, her sector must be $0.25(360°) = 90°$, which is sector D. This means that Eli ($3,000), Georgia ($5,000), and Zoe ($10,000) account for sectors A, B, and C. Since Georgia's total is between Eli's and Zoe's, her sector is the neither the largest nor the smallest of the remaining sectors. Therefore, it must be sector A, which is in the middle.

---

10. B   **Data Analysis (pie graph) MEDIUM**

Perhaps the simplest way to approach this is to notice that, since Maria's sales account for 25% of the total, the other salespeople must account for $100\% - 25\% = 75\%$ of the total. Since this total is $3,000 + $5,000 + $10,000 = $18,000, we can find the total with a proportion.

$$\frac{\$18,000}{75} = \frac{x}{100}$$

Cross multiply: $\$1,800,000 = 75x$

Divide by 75: $\$24,000 = x$

---

11. D   **Data Analysis (pie graph) MEDIUM**

Since Maria accounted for 25% of the total sales, she accounted for $(0.25)(\$24,000) = \$6,000$ in sales. If she earned 15% commission for all sales, she earned $(0.15)(\$6,000) = \$900$ in commissions. If Georgia earns 10% in commissions, she earned $(0.10)(\$5,000) = \$500$. Therefore, Maria earned $\$900 - \$500 = \$400$ more in commissions that Georgia did.

---

12. B   **Algebra (absolute value) MEDIUM**

The function $f(x) = 2 - |x - 4|$ reaches its greatest value when the absolute value is minimized. Since absolute values cannot be negative, the least value $|x - 4|$ can have is 0, which it has when $x = 4$:

$f(4) = 2 - |4 - 4| = 2 - 0 = 2$

---

13. C   Advanced Math (rational equations) MEDIUM

$$\frac{3}{b} - \frac{2}{5} = 1$$

Original equation:

Multiply both sides by common
denominator $5b$: $15 - 2b = 5b$

Add $2b$: $15 = 7b$

Divide by 7: $\dfrac{15}{7} = b$

---

14. D   Advanced Mathematics (functions) MEDIUM

(A) $f(1) = 1^2 + 3 = 4; f(2) - 2^2 + 3 = 7$
(B) $f(1) = 1^2 + 9 = 10; f(2) = 2^2 + 9 = 13$
(C) $f(1) = 2(1)^2 + 2 = 4; f(2) = 2(2)^2 + 2 = 10$
(D) $f(1) = 3(1)^2 + 1 = 4; f(2) = 3(2)^2 + 1 = 13$

The only function that satisfies the two given equations is (D).

---

15. A   **Advanced Mathematics (exponentials)**
                          MEDIUM

(A) $(6b)(6b) = 36b^2$
(B) $12b(b) = 12b^2$
(C) $\left(b\sqrt{12}\right)^2 = \left(b\sqrt{12}\right)\left(b\sqrt{12}\right) = 12b^2$
(D) $6b^2 + 6b^2 = b^2(6 + 6) = 12b^2$

---

16. C   **Data Analysis (probability) MEDIUM**

One way to represent this problem clearly is to construct a table that shows all of the possible products mn. A representation of all the equally likely possible outcomes of an event is called the **sample space** for that event. We can label the columns with the possible values of m and

the rows with the possible values of n. As we write in the products, let's shade in those that are multiples of 12.

	2	3	4	6
1	2	3	4	6
2	4	6	8	12
3	6	9	12	18
4	8	12	16	24

This shows that 4 out of the possible 16 products are multiples of 12, and therefore, the probability is 4/16 or $\dfrac{1}{4}$.

---

17. B   **Algebra (inequalities) MEDIUM**

Original inequality: $x < 3$
Multiply by 3: $3x < 9$
Add 4: $3x + 4 < 13$
Substitute $y = 3x + 4$: $y < 13$

---

18. B   **Advanced Mathematics (functions)**
                          MEDIUM-HARD

Since the function takes "all values of x," one way to solve this problem is to choose a value of x to work with, like $x = 1$.

Original function: $g(x + 1) = x^2 + 2x + 4$
Substitute $x = 1$: $g(2) = (1)^2 + 2(1) + 4 = 1 + 2 + 4 = 7$

Therefore, the function $g(x)$ will give an output of 7 for an input of 2. We can now test our choices for an input of $x = 2$. (Notice $g(x)$ and $g(x + 1)$ have different inputs.)

(A) $(2)^2 + 4 = 8$
(B) $(2)^2 + 3 = 7$
(C) $(2 - 1)^2 + 4 = 5$
(D) $(2 - 1)^2 + 3 = 4$

Notice that only the expression in (B) gives the correct output.

---

19. C   **Advanced Mathematics (sequences)**
                          MEDIUM-HARD

The "brute force" method is to write out sequence A until you reach 72, and see which element in sequence B "matches up" to it. But first we must determine the rule for each sequence. A little guessing and checking should confirm that sequence A follows the "add 5" rule, and sequence B follows the "add 10" rule.

A	2	7	12	17	22	27	32	37
B	5	15	25	35	45	55	65	75
A	42	47	52	57	62	67	72	
B	85	95	105	115	125	135	145	

A more elegant method, however, is to find the formulas for the nth term of A and the nth term of B. This would be a much more efficient method, also, if it takes a while for 72 to appear in set A. If you recall the general formula for the nth term of an arithmetic sequence ($a_n = a_1 + (n - 1)d$), then it's straightforward to see that the formula for A is $a_n = 2 + (n - 1)5 = 5n - 3$ and the formula for B is $b_n = 5 + (n - 1)10 = 10n - 5$. Since we're looking for where the number 72 appears in set A, we can solve $5n - 3 = 72$ to find $n = 15$, then insert this value for n into the formula for B: $b_{15} = 10(15) - 5 = 145$.

---

20. C   **Problem Solving and Data Analysis (ratios) MEDIUM**

If the ratio of subscribers to nonsubscribers is 2:5, then we can say there are $2n$ subscribers and $5n$ non-subscribers, where n is some integer. This means there were a total of $2n + 5n = 7n$ July visitors to the website. Since we know that there were 2,100 visitors in July, we can solve for n:

Divide by 7: $\qquad\qquad\qquad\qquad\qquad$ 2,100 $= 7n$

$\qquad\qquad\qquad\qquad\qquad\qquad\qquad$ 300 $= n$

Therefore, there were 2(300) = 600 subscriber visits and 5(300) = 1,500 nonsubscriber visits, and so there were 1,500 − 600 = 900 more nonsubscribing visitors than subscribing visitors.

---

21. A   **Algebra (graphing lines) MEDIUM-HARD**

In quadrant I, both the x- and y-coordinates are positive. Since $y = 4$ in all four systems, we simply need to find the system for which the x-coordinate of the solution is *not* positive. We can find the corresponding x-coordinate for each system by just substituting $y = 4$ and solving for x.

Substitute $y = 4$ into first equation in (A): $\quad 3x + 5(4) = 15$

Simplify: $\qquad\qquad\qquad\qquad\qquad\qquad 3x + 20 = 15$

Subtract 20: $\qquad\qquad\qquad\qquad\qquad\qquad 3x = -5$

Divide by 3: $\qquad\qquad\qquad\qquad\qquad\qquad x = -5/3$

In this case, we don't need to go any further, because the solution to the system in (A) is (−5/3, 4), which is in quadrant II, not quadrant I.

---

22. D   **Advanced Mathematics (quadratics) MEDIUM-HARD**

Read the question carefully, and note particularly what it is asking for and what information can help you find it. We are asked to find an equation to relate two variables, q, the number of power units, and t, the number of hours the battery has been charging. We are told that the *initial* charge is 20 power units, so $q = 20$ when $t = 0$. We are also told that the charge increases from 50 power units to 106 power units in 40 minutes. But since our time unit t is in *hours*, we should convert 40 minutes to 40/60 = 2/3 hours. Therefore, the charging station charges at a rate of (106 − 50)/(2/3) = (56)/(2/3) = 84 charging units per hour. This unit rate is the slope of the line, as we discussed in Chapter 8, Lesson 5. Therefore, the equation should represent a line with slope of 84 that contains the point $t = 0$ and $q = 20$, which is the equation in (D) $q = 84t + 20$.

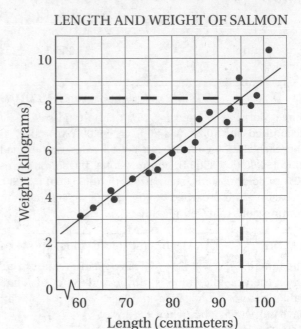

LENGTH AND WEIGHT OF SALMON

This question simply asks us to find the point on the line of best fit that corresponds to a length of 95 centimeters. As the dotted lines show below, this corresponds to a weight less than halfway between 8 and 9 kilograms, so (C) 8.3 is the best approximation among the choices.

---

24. D   **Data Analysis (scatterplots) HARD**

LENGTH AND WEIGHT OF SALMON

To find the equation of the line of best fit, we can take two points on the line and then use the point-slope formula (Chapter 7, Lesson 5) to find the equation of the line. To get the most accurate representation of the line, we should choose two points that are fairly far apart, but whose coordinates are easy to determine. The graph shows that this line appears to pass through the points (60, 3) and (100, 9), and so, by the slope formula (Chapter 7, Lesson 5) we can calculate that the slope is $(9-3)/(100-60) = 6/40 = 3/20$. Using the first point in the

point-slope formula gives

$$w-3 = \frac{3}{20}(l-60)$$

Distribute:

$$w-3 = \frac{3}{20}l - 9$$

Add 3:

$$w = \frac{3}{20}l - 6$$

---

25. B   **Problem Solving (rates) MEDIUM**

If Ronika plans to use 85% of her 2 GB data plan for texting, she will have only (15%)(2 GB) = (0.15)(2,000 MB) = 300 MB = 300,000 kB available for image files. Since the average image file is 750 kB, she will be able to send 300,000 kB/750 kB = 400 images per month.

---

26. C   **Problem Solving (rates) HARD**

This question asks us to write a mathematical statement that "indicates the restrictions" in this situation. So, what keeps us from making as many truffles as we want? Simple: we are only allowed to spend $200 per week on cocoa powder. Therefore, we can state the restriction on truffles as "the total cost of cocoa powder for our weekly production of truffles must be less than or equal to $200."

Now we must figure out a way to express "the total cost of cocoa powder for our weekly production of truffles." Clearly, this is the total cost for the dark chocolate truffles *plus* the total cost for the milk chocolate truffles:

Cost of cocoa powder for d dark chocolate truffles:

$$d \text{ truffles} \times \frac{0.65 \text{ oz cocoa}}{1 \text{ truffle}} \times \frac{\$c}{16 \text{ oz cocoa}}$$

Simplify:

$$\$\frac{0.65cd}{16}$$

Cost of cocoa powder for m milk chocolate truffles:

$$m \text{ truffles} \times \frac{0.45 \text{ oz cocoa}}{1 \text{ truffle}} \times \frac{\$c}{16 \text{ oz cocoa}}$$

Simplify:

$$\$\frac{0.45cm}{16}$$

The total cost for cocoa powder must not be greater than $200:

$$200 \geq \frac{0.65cd}{16} + \frac{0.45cm}{16}$$

Multiply by 16:

$$3,200 \geq 0.65cd + 0.45cm$$

Divide by c:

$$\frac{3,200}{c} \geq 0.65d + 0.45m$$

---

27. C   Advanced Mathematics (exponentials) HARD

Notice that this question asks us to find the value of 2^{n+3}, so we should try to solve the given equation for 2^{n+3}.

Original equation:	$m = 2^{n+2} + 2^n$
Factor $2n$ from the terms on the right side:	$m = 2^n(2^2 + 1)$
Simplify:	$m = 2^n(5)$
Divide by 5:	$\frac{m}{5} = 2^n$
Multiply by 2^3:	$2^3\left(\frac{m}{5}\right) = 2^n \times 2^3$
Simplify:	$\frac{8m}{5} = 2^{n+3}$

---

28. D   Special Topics (trigonometry) HARD

Although this question can be solved by graphing, it is simpler and more efficient to imagine the unit circle, as we discussed in Chapter 10, Lesson 9.

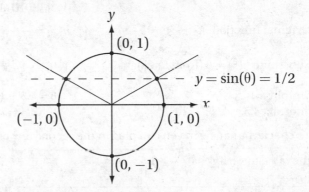

We are asked to consider those angles that have a sine of ½. As you recall from Chapter 10, Lesson 9, the angles whose sine is ½ correspond to those angles that intersect the unit circle at any point where $y = ½$, as shown in the diagram above. Notice that the line $y = ½$ intersects the unit circle in two points. We are asked to consider sin $3x$, where x takes values from 0 to 2π. This means that $3x$ takes values from 0 to 6π. In other words, we are taking three complete trips around the unit circle (since each trip around is 2π radians). How many times will we visit those two points if we take three trips around the circle? Clearly (3)(2) = 6 times.

---

29. B   Advanced Mathematics (function transformations) HARD

The figure clearly shows that the function $y = f(x)$ is similar in shape to the function $y = g(x)$, but is shifted to the left by some positive distance. Recall from Chapter 9, Lesson 3, that when the graph of $y = g(x)$ is shifted to the left by k units, the equation of the new function is $y = g(x + k)$. The only equation that has this form is (B) $f(x) = g(x + 2)$.

30. A — Data Analysis (data spread) HARD

One important rule in data gathering is, **the more data we can gather on a population, the more reliable our statistics about that population will be**. More specifically, the greater fraction of the population we can sample, the smaller our margin of error from the true value of the population statistic. Another important rule in data gathering is **the more similar our sample is to the population of interest, the smaller our statistical error will be**. Since the sample size is highest and the group is most like the population (of undergraduate computer science majors) in choice (A), that group should produce the smallest margin of error in the data.

---

31. 168 — Algebra (percents) EASY

The sum of 40 and 80 is 120, and 40% of 120 is $(0.40)(120) = 48$, so the number that is 40% greater than 120 is $120 + 48 = 168$. Also remember that increasing a number by 40% is equivalent to multiplying it by 1.4.

---

32. 3/2 or 1.5 — Advance Mathematics (quadratics) MEDIUM

Original function: $h(x) = \dfrac{x^2}{2} + k$

Substitute $h(3) = 6$ (from table): $6 = \dfrac{3^2}{2} + k$

Simplify: $6 = 4.5 + k$

Subtract 4.5: $1.5 = k$

To check your answer, you can plug in the second row of the table to verify that $\dfrac{5^2}{2} + 1.5 = 14$

---

33. 52 — Algebra (linear equations) MEDIUM

In Chapter 7, Lesson 5 we discussed the fact that the slope of a linear equation in "standard form," $ax + by = c$ is equal to $-a/b$. Therefore, the linear equation $hx + 4y = -3$ has a slope of $-h/4$. If this slope equals -3, then

$$\dfrac{-h}{4} = -13$$

Multiply by -4: $h = 52$

---

34. 25 — Algebra (word problems) EASY

Let's let x be the larger number. 15 is the smaller number. The sum of the numbers is four times their difference:

$$x + 15 = 4(x - 15)$$

Distribute: $x + 15 = 4x - 60$

Add 60: $x + 75 = 4x$

Subtract x: $75 = 3x$

Divide by 3: $25 = x$

---

35. 4/45 or .088 or .089 — Special Topics (trigonometry) MEDIUM-HARD

Given equation: $5\cos x = \sqrt{5}$

Divide by 5: $\cos x = \dfrac{\sqrt{5}}{5}$

This gives us the value of cos x, but we are asked to evaluate $\left(\dfrac{\sin x}{3}\right)^2$, which of course is in terms of sin x.

This should remind you of the Pythagorean Identity we discussed in Chapter 10, Lesson 9: for all real numbers x, $\sin^2 x + \cos^2 x = 1$.

Pythagorean Identity: $\sin^2 x + \cos^2 x = 1$

Subtract $\cos^2 x$: $\sin^2 x = 1 - \cos^2 x$

Expression to be evaluated: $\left(\dfrac{\sin x}{3}\right)^2$

Simplify: $\dfrac{\sin^2 x}{9}$

Substitute $\sin^2 x = 1 - \cos^2 x$: $\dfrac{1 - \cos^2 x}{9}$

Substitute $\cos x = \dfrac{\sqrt{5}}{5}$: $\dfrac{1 - \left(\dfrac{\sqrt{5}}{5}\right)^2}{9}$

Simplify: $\dfrac{1 - \dfrac{5}{25}}{9}$

Simplify: $\dfrac{\dfrac{4}{5}}{9}$

Simplify by multiplying $\dfrac{5}{5}$: $\dfrac{4}{45}$

---

36. 75/4 or 18.7 or 18.8 — Special Topics (arcs and triangles) MEDIUM-HARD

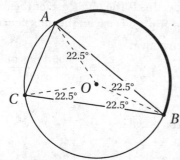

Let's start by drawing the three radii OA, OB, and OC. Since these radii are all congruent, and because $AB = BC$, the triangles AOB and COB are congruent (by the SSS Theorem). This implies that OB bisects angle ABC, so the base angles of both isosceles triangles must have measure $45°/2 = 22.5°$. Therefore, angle AOB, which is the central angle for arc AB, must have measure $180° - 22.5° - 22.5° = 135°$. Now we can use the fact that the circumference of the circle is 50 to find the length or arc AB.

$$\dfrac{m\overset{\frown}{AB}}{135°} = \dfrac{50}{360°}$$

Let $x = m\widehat{AB}$ and cross multiply: $360x = 6,750$
Divide by 360: $x = 75/4 = 18.75$

---

37. 47   Problem Solving (extended thinking) HARD

Let n equal the number of months that Isabelle has been on Plan A. If she has been on Plan A for over a year, then $n > 12$. This means that she has been on Plan A for $n - 12$ months beyond the first year. Since Plan A costs \$500 for the first year and \$80 per month thereafter, the total cost for her n months of service is $\$500 + \$80(n - 12)$. If she had been on Plan B, the cost would have been \$68 per month, or a total of $\$68n$. If Plan B would have saved her \$104 over this period, $500 + 80(n - 12) - 104 = 68n$

Distribute and simplify: $396 + 80n - 960 = 68n$
Simplify: $80n - 564 = 68n$
Add 564: $80n = 68n + 564$
Subtract 68n: $12n = 564$
Divide by 12: $n = 47$

---

38. 32   Problem Solving (extended thinking) HARD

Since Plan C costs \$92 per month and Plan B costs \$68 per month, Plan C costs $\$92 - \$68 = \$24$ more dollars per month than plan B. Since shifting plans would save her only 45 minutes of work, or 3/4 hour, each month, she would have to value one hour of free time over one hour of work time at $\$24/(\frac{3}{4}\ \text{hour}) = \$32$.

Section 5: Essay

Sample Response

James Schlesinger's essay, "Cold Facts on Global Warming," is a counterargument to the "political alarmism" (to use Schlesinger's words) over global warming. His tone is critical but sober, and he makes frequent use of carefully selected scientific and historical data, juxtaposed with hints at the dangers of political posturing, to make the case for caution in addressing the issue of climate change. He appeals frequently to the ethics of economic prudence and global stewardship, as well as the value of scientific judiciousness. Unfortunately, because Schlesinger's essay was written over a decade ago, it lacks the evidence from the current golden age of climate science. More substantially, however, Schlesinger undermines his own purpose by making political criticisms while calling for nonpartisan objectivity, by mongering fearsome scenarios while arguing against "scare tactics," and by ignoring the scientific evidence against his claims while advocating an "emphasis on science."

Schlesinger begins his discussion with a call for "facts and logic" over "rhetoric." This is classic polemical posturing: we all believe that our positions are "factual and logical" and that our opponents' are merely "rhetoric." In Schlesinger's view, the "rhetoric" includes the claims that "emissions of carbon dioxide are the primary cause of any change in global temperature and inevitably will lead to serious environmental harm in the decades ahead." By inserting the modifiers "any" and "inevitably," he creates a straw man. Most who argue about the seriousness of climate change generally avoid such absolute assertions and instead present evidence from satellites, ice cores, atmospheric analysis, and comprehensive long-term climatic studies to build a case for action. Schlesinger does not address this evidence.

In his argument, Schlesinger appears to value small government and the protection of American industry over the stewardship of the planet. His concern about the Kyoto Protocol of 1997 is not that it eschews the "facts and logic" of climate science, but rather that it "could cost \$300 billion annually." He presents no scientific critique of the Kyoto Protocol of 1997 beyond the assertion that Democrat Al Gore was "willing to embrace" a "treaty that would harm the economy," and the vague claim that "the treaty's flaws have become more evident." His method of argumentation here appears to contradict his call for "facts and logic" over "rhetoric."

In contrast to the irresponsibility of Al Gore and the Clinton administration, Schlesinger offers the soberly scientific Bush administration, which "focused on filling in gaps in our state of knowledge, promoting the development of new technology, encouraging volunteer programs, and working with other nations on controlling the growth of greenhouse gas emissions." Schlesinger does not offer a specific benefit our planet has gained from these efforts, which even Schlesinger himself admits involved "spending more than \$4 billion annually." Someone pleading for fiscal responsibility might try to account for such a huge expenditure.

Schlesinger believes that our inaction on climate change is a virtue: that scientific prudence requires "filling the gaps in our state of knowledge" above everything else, including industrial restraint. He states that "what we know for sure is quite limited," yet is confident enough in his limited knowledge to assert that "the theory that increasing concentrations of greenhouse gases like carbon dioxide will lead to further warming is at least an oversimplification," directly contradicting the simple middle school experiment showing that a soda bottle filled with carbon dioxide warms far more quickly than one filled only with air.

Schlesinger then selects data trends that seem to support his call for caution, rather than action: he asserts that "satellite measurements over 35 years show no significant warming in the lower atmosphere" and that there was "atmospheric cooling from 1940 to around 1975." Schlesinger does not explain why climate scientists, who are certainly aware of these data, nevertheless believe in anthropogenic global warming.

Not to be accused of cherry-picking data, Schlesinger next offers "a longer view of climate history." He asserts that temperatures "were 1 to 2 degrees warmer than they are today" during the Climatic Optimum of the early Middle Ages, and this warming did not have "anything to do with man-made greenhouse gases." Evidently, we should think that because it was warmer a very long time ago, burning coal today must not be changing the climate.

In the last two paragraphs, Schlesinger essentially retracts his concern about "filling the gaps in our state of knowledge" after all, because he believes it is impossible to fill the most important gaps: "It is not possible to know now how much of the warming over the last 100 years or so was caused by human activities and how much was because of natural forces." So if it is impossible to know, we might ask, why should we expend "more than $4 billion annually" to study it? He does not say. We get Schlesinger's most sonorous call to action in the last paragraph, where he suggests "engagement of the business community on voluntary programs." That is, get big government off the backs of corporations and let them do as they please.

Scoring

Reading—4 out of 4

This response demonstrates a very strong and thorough comprehension of Schlesinger's essay through skillful use of summary, paraphrase, and direct quotations. The author summarizes Schlesinger's central tone, thesis, and modes of persuasion (*His tone is critical but sober, and he makes frequent use of carefully selected scientific and historical data, juxtaposed with hints at the dangers of political posturing, to make the case for caution in addressing the issue of climate change.*) and shows a clear understanding of how Schlesinger's supporting ideas string together and serve his overall thesis (*Schlesinger begins his discussion with a call . . . He appears to value small government . . . Schlesinger offers the soberly scientific Bush administration . . . Schlesinger believes that our inaction on global warming is a virtue . . . Schlesinger next offers . . . In the last two paragraph, Schlesinger essentially retracts his concern*). Importantly, this response also offers abundant supporting quotations to illustrate each paraphrase. Taken together, these elements demonstrate outstanding comprehension of Schlesinger's essay.

Analysis—4 out of 4

Although this response occasionally veers toward advocacy, it never turns away from careful analysis. Indeed, its thoughtful and thorough critique of Schlesinger's essay demonstrates a sophisticated understanding of the analytical task. The author has identified Schlesinger's primary modes of argument (*He appeals frequently to the ethics of economic prudence and global stewardship, as well as the value of scientific judiciousness*) and even uses those standards to analyze Schlesinger's essay itself, and indicates points at which Schlesinger's argument seems self-defeating (*Schlesinger undermines his own purpose by making political criticisms while calling for nonpartisan objectivity, by mongering fearsome scenarios while arguing against "scare tactics," and by ignoring the scientific evidence against his claims while advocating an "emphasis on science"*). Overall, this analysis of Schlesinger's essays demonstrates a thorough understanding not only of the rhetorical task that Schlesinger has set for himself, but also of the degree to which it upholds its own standards.

Writing—4 out of 4

This response demonstrates an articulate and effective use of language and sentence structure to establish and develop a clear and insightful central claim that *Schlesinger's essay is a counterargument to the "political alarmism" . . . over global warming . . .* but that *it undermines [its] own purpose*. The response maintains a consistent focus on this central claim, and supports it with a well-developed and cohesive analysis of Schlesinger's essay. The author demonstrates effective choice of words and phrasing (*undermines his own purpose . . . mongering fearsome scenarios . . . Schlesinger believes that our inaction on climate change is a virtue*), strong grasp of relevant analytical and rhetorical terms, like *economic prudence, nonpartisan objectivity, and polemical posturing*. The response is well-developed, progressing from general claim to specific analysis to considered evaluation. Largely free from grammatical error, this response demonstrates strong command of language and proficiency in writing.

PRACTICE TEST 3

1. Reading Test

   65 MINUTES   52 QUESTIONS   614

2. Writing and Language Test

   35 MINUTES   44 QUESTIONS   631

3. Math Test – No Calculator

   25 MINUTES   20 QUESTIONS   644

4. Math Test – Calculator

   55 MINUTES   38 QUESTIONS   650

5. Essay (optional)

   50 MINUTES   1 QUESTION   661

ANSWER SHEET for PRACTICE TEST 3

Use a No. 2 pencil and fill in the entire circle darkly and completely.
If you change your response, erase as completely as possible

SECTION 1

1 Ⓐ Ⓑ Ⓒ Ⓓ	13 Ⓐ Ⓑ Ⓒ Ⓓ	25 Ⓐ Ⓑ Ⓒ Ⓓ	37 Ⓐ Ⓑ Ⓒ Ⓓ	49 Ⓐ Ⓑ Ⓒ Ⓓ
2 Ⓐ Ⓑ Ⓒ Ⓓ	14 Ⓐ Ⓑ Ⓒ Ⓓ	26 Ⓐ Ⓑ Ⓒ Ⓓ	38 Ⓐ Ⓑ Ⓒ Ⓓ	50 Ⓐ Ⓑ Ⓒ Ⓓ
3 Ⓐ Ⓑ Ⓒ Ⓓ	15 Ⓐ Ⓑ Ⓒ Ⓓ	27 Ⓐ Ⓑ Ⓒ Ⓓ	39 Ⓐ Ⓑ Ⓒ Ⓓ	51 Ⓐ Ⓑ Ⓒ Ⓓ
4 Ⓐ Ⓑ Ⓒ Ⓓ	16 Ⓐ Ⓑ Ⓒ Ⓓ	28 Ⓐ Ⓑ Ⓒ Ⓓ	40 Ⓐ Ⓑ Ⓒ Ⓓ	52 Ⓐ Ⓑ Ⓒ Ⓓ
5 Ⓐ Ⓑ Ⓒ Ⓓ	17 Ⓐ Ⓑ Ⓒ Ⓓ	29 Ⓐ Ⓑ Ⓒ Ⓓ	41 Ⓐ Ⓑ Ⓒ Ⓓ	
6 Ⓐ Ⓑ Ⓒ Ⓓ	18 Ⓐ Ⓑ Ⓒ Ⓓ	30 Ⓐ Ⓑ Ⓒ Ⓓ	42 Ⓐ Ⓑ Ⓒ Ⓓ	
7 Ⓐ Ⓑ Ⓒ Ⓓ	19 Ⓐ Ⓑ Ⓒ Ⓓ	31 Ⓐ Ⓑ Ⓒ Ⓓ	43 Ⓐ Ⓑ Ⓒ Ⓓ	
8 Ⓐ Ⓑ Ⓒ Ⓓ	20 Ⓐ Ⓑ Ⓒ Ⓓ	32 Ⓐ Ⓑ Ⓒ Ⓓ	44 Ⓐ Ⓑ Ⓒ Ⓓ	
9 Ⓐ Ⓑ Ⓒ Ⓓ	21 Ⓐ Ⓑ Ⓒ Ⓓ	33 Ⓐ Ⓑ Ⓒ Ⓓ	45 Ⓐ Ⓑ Ⓒ Ⓓ	
10 Ⓐ Ⓑ Ⓒ Ⓓ	22 Ⓐ Ⓑ Ⓒ Ⓓ	34 Ⓐ Ⓑ Ⓒ Ⓓ	46 Ⓐ Ⓑ Ⓒ Ⓓ	
11 Ⓐ Ⓑ Ⓒ Ⓓ	23 Ⓐ Ⓑ Ⓒ Ⓓ	35 Ⓐ Ⓑ Ⓒ Ⓓ	47 Ⓐ Ⓑ Ⓒ Ⓓ	
12 Ⓐ Ⓑ Ⓒ Ⓓ	24 Ⓐ Ⓑ Ⓒ Ⓓ	36 Ⓐ Ⓑ Ⓒ Ⓓ	48 Ⓐ Ⓑ Ⓒ Ⓓ	

SECTION 2

1 Ⓐ Ⓑ Ⓒ Ⓓ	11 Ⓐ Ⓑ Ⓒ Ⓓ	21 Ⓐ Ⓑ Ⓒ Ⓓ	31 Ⓐ Ⓑ Ⓒ Ⓓ	41 Ⓐ Ⓑ Ⓒ Ⓓ
2 Ⓐ Ⓑ Ⓒ Ⓓ	12 Ⓐ Ⓑ Ⓒ Ⓓ	22 Ⓐ Ⓑ Ⓒ Ⓓ	32 Ⓐ Ⓑ Ⓒ Ⓓ	42 Ⓐ Ⓑ Ⓒ Ⓓ
3 Ⓐ Ⓑ Ⓒ Ⓓ	13 Ⓐ Ⓑ Ⓒ Ⓓ	23 Ⓐ Ⓑ Ⓒ Ⓓ	33 Ⓐ Ⓑ Ⓒ Ⓓ	43 Ⓐ Ⓑ Ⓒ Ⓓ
4 Ⓐ Ⓑ Ⓒ Ⓓ	14 Ⓐ Ⓑ Ⓒ Ⓓ	24 Ⓐ Ⓑ Ⓒ Ⓓ	34 Ⓐ Ⓑ Ⓒ Ⓓ	44 Ⓐ Ⓑ Ⓒ Ⓓ
5 Ⓐ Ⓑ Ⓒ Ⓓ	15 Ⓐ Ⓑ Ⓒ Ⓓ	25 Ⓐ Ⓑ Ⓒ Ⓓ	35 Ⓐ Ⓑ Ⓒ Ⓓ	
6 Ⓐ Ⓑ Ⓒ Ⓓ	16 Ⓐ Ⓑ Ⓒ Ⓓ	26 Ⓐ Ⓑ Ⓒ Ⓓ	36 Ⓐ Ⓑ Ⓒ Ⓓ	
7 Ⓐ Ⓑ Ⓒ Ⓓ	17 Ⓐ Ⓑ Ⓒ Ⓓ	27 Ⓐ Ⓑ Ⓒ Ⓓ	37 Ⓐ Ⓑ Ⓒ Ⓓ	
8 Ⓐ Ⓑ Ⓒ Ⓓ	18 Ⓐ Ⓑ Ⓒ Ⓓ	28 Ⓐ Ⓑ Ⓒ Ⓓ	38 Ⓐ Ⓑ Ⓒ Ⓓ	
9 Ⓐ Ⓑ Ⓒ Ⓓ	19 Ⓐ Ⓑ Ⓒ Ⓓ	29 Ⓐ Ⓑ Ⓒ Ⓓ	39 Ⓐ Ⓑ Ⓒ Ⓓ	
10 Ⓐ Ⓑ Ⓒ Ⓓ	20 Ⓐ Ⓑ Ⓒ Ⓓ	30 Ⓐ Ⓑ Ⓒ Ⓓ	40 Ⓐ Ⓑ Ⓒ Ⓓ	

SECTION 3

1 Ⓐ Ⓑ Ⓒ Ⓓ	4 Ⓐ Ⓑ Ⓒ Ⓓ	7 Ⓐ Ⓑ Ⓒ Ⓓ	10 Ⓐ Ⓑ Ⓒ Ⓓ	13 Ⓐ Ⓑ Ⓒ Ⓓ
2 Ⓐ Ⓑ Ⓒ Ⓓ	5 Ⓐ Ⓑ Ⓒ Ⓓ	8 Ⓐ Ⓑ Ⓒ Ⓓ	11 Ⓐ Ⓑ Ⓒ Ⓓ	14 Ⓐ Ⓑ Ⓒ Ⓓ
3 Ⓐ Ⓑ Ⓒ Ⓓ	6 Ⓐ Ⓑ Ⓒ Ⓓ	9 Ⓐ Ⓑ Ⓒ Ⓓ	12 Ⓐ Ⓑ Ⓒ Ⓓ	15 Ⓐ Ⓑ Ⓒ Ⓓ

**ONLY ANSWERS ENTERED IN THE CIRCLES IN EACH GRID WILL BE SCORED.
YOU WILL NOT RECEIVE CREDIT FOR ANYTHING WRITTEN IN THE BOXES ABOVE THE CIRCLES.**

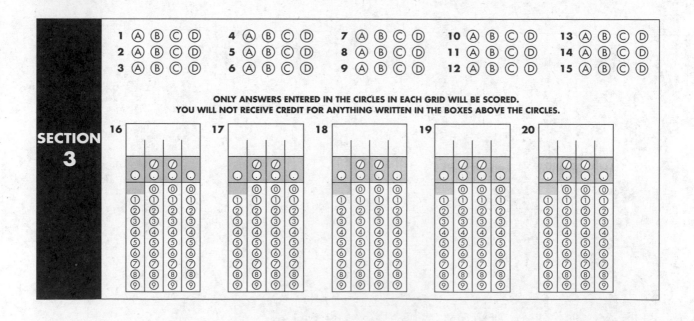

SECTION 4

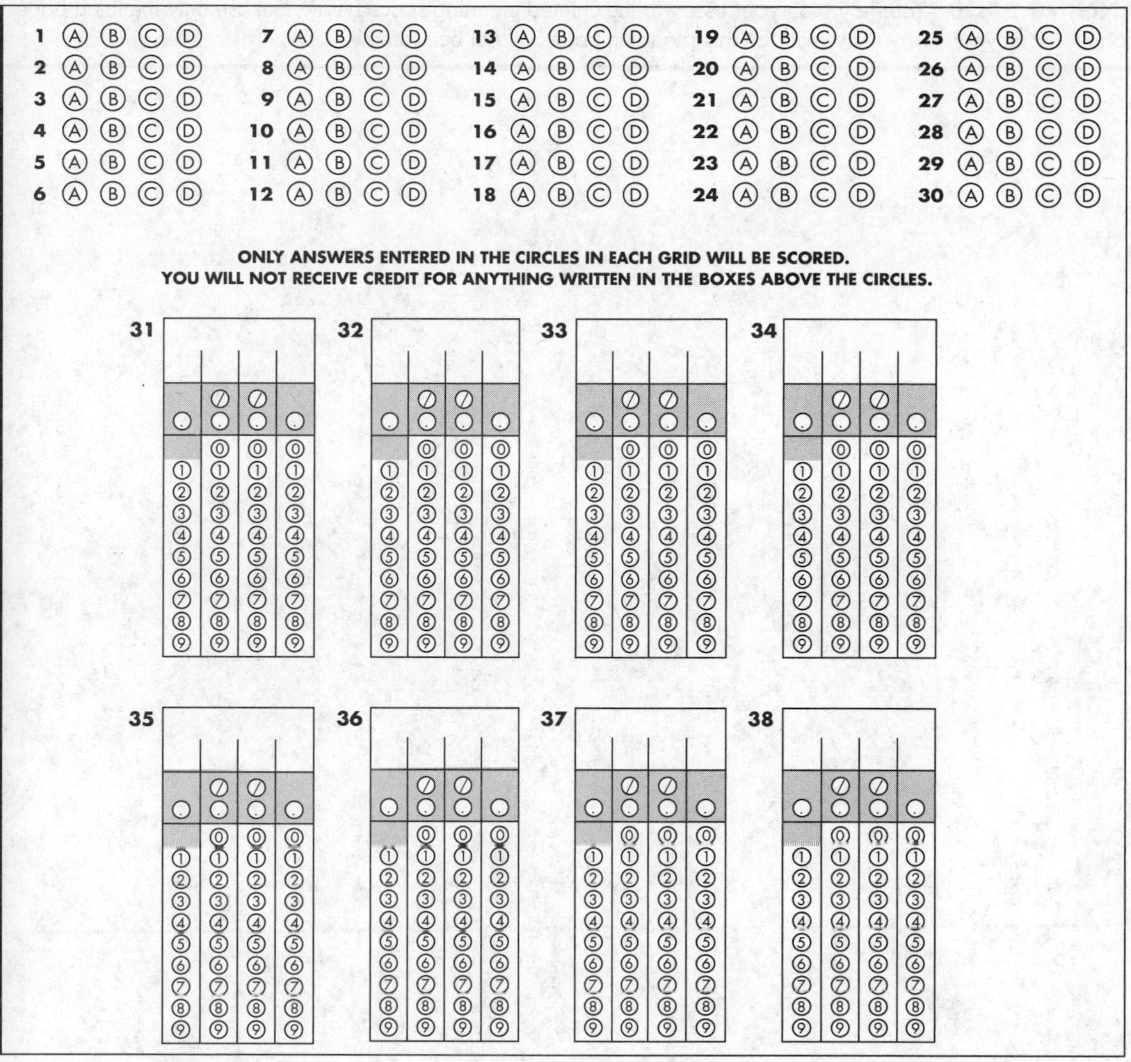

1 Ⓐ Ⓑ Ⓒ Ⓓ   7 Ⓐ Ⓑ Ⓒ Ⓓ   13 Ⓐ Ⓑ Ⓒ Ⓓ   19 Ⓐ Ⓑ Ⓒ Ⓓ   25 Ⓐ Ⓑ Ⓒ Ⓓ
2 Ⓐ Ⓑ Ⓒ Ⓓ   8 Ⓐ Ⓑ Ⓒ Ⓓ   14 Ⓐ Ⓑ Ⓒ Ⓓ   20 Ⓐ Ⓑ Ⓒ Ⓓ   26 Ⓐ Ⓑ Ⓒ Ⓓ
3 Ⓐ Ⓑ Ⓒ Ⓓ   9 Ⓐ Ⓑ Ⓒ Ⓓ   15 Ⓐ Ⓑ Ⓒ Ⓓ   21 Ⓐ Ⓑ Ⓒ Ⓓ   27 Ⓐ Ⓑ Ⓒ Ⓓ
4 Ⓐ Ⓑ Ⓒ Ⓓ   10 Ⓐ Ⓑ Ⓒ Ⓓ   16 Ⓐ Ⓑ Ⓒ Ⓓ   22 Ⓐ Ⓑ Ⓒ Ⓓ   28 Ⓐ Ⓑ Ⓒ Ⓓ
5 Ⓐ Ⓑ Ⓒ Ⓓ   11 Ⓐ Ⓑ Ⓒ Ⓓ   17 Ⓐ Ⓑ Ⓒ Ⓓ   23 Ⓐ Ⓑ Ⓒ Ⓓ   29 Ⓐ Ⓑ Ⓒ Ⓓ
6 Ⓐ Ⓑ Ⓒ Ⓓ   12 Ⓐ Ⓑ Ⓒ Ⓓ   18 Ⓐ Ⓑ Ⓒ Ⓓ   24 Ⓐ Ⓑ Ⓒ Ⓓ   30 Ⓐ Ⓑ Ⓒ Ⓓ

ONLY ANSWERS ENTERED IN THE CIRCLES IN EACH GRID WILL BE SCORED.
YOU WILL NOT RECEIVE CREDIT FOR ANYTHING WRITTEN IN THE BOXES ABOVE THE CIRCLES.

31   32   33   34

35   36   37   38

SECTION 5: ESSAY

PLANNING PAGE You may plan your essay in the unlined planning space below, but use only the lined pages following this one to write your essay. Any work on this planning page will not be scored.

BEGIN YOUR ESSAY HERE

DO NOT WRITE OUTSIDE OF THE BOX.

Cut Here

DO NOT WRITE OUTSIDE OF THE BOX.

Cut Here

DO NOT WRITE OUTSIDE OF THE BOX.

DO NOT WRITE OUTSIDE OF THE BOX.

Cut Here

Test begins on the next page.

Reading Test

65 MINUTES, 52 QUESTIONS

Turn to Section 1 of your answer sheet to answer the questions in this section.

Questions 1–11 are based on the following passages and supplementary material.

Passage 1 is from F. J. Medina, "How to Talk about Sustainability." ©2015 College Hill Coaching. Passage 2 is adapted from an essay published in 2005 about the economic analysis of environmental decisions.

Passage 1

Many proponents of recycling assume that recycling industrial, domestic, and commercial
Line materials does less harm to the environment than does extracting new raw materials. Opponents, on
5   the other hand, scrutinize the costs of recycling, arguing that recycling programs often waste more money than they save, and that companies can often produce new products more cheaply than they can recycle old ones. The discussion usually
10   devolves into a political battle between the enemies of the economy and the enemies of the environment.
     This demonization serves the debaters (and their fundraisers) but not the debate.
15   Environmentalists are not all ignorant anarchists, and opponents of recycling are not all rapacious blowhards. For real solutions, we must soberly compare the many costs and benefits of recycling with the many costs and benefits of disposal, as

20   if we are all stewards of both the earth and the economy.
     We must examine the full life cycles of various materials, and the broad effects these cycles have on both the environment and
25   economy. When debating the cost of a new road, for instance, it is not enough to simply consider the cost of the labor or the provenance of the materials. We must ask, what natural benefits, like water filtration and animal and
30   plant habitats, are being lost in the construction? Where will the road materials be in a hundred years, and what will they be doing? What kinds of industries will the road construction and maintenance support? How will the extra traffic
35   affect air and noise quality, or safety? Is the road made of local or imported materials? Are any materials being imported from countries with irresponsible labor or environmental practices? Is the contractor chosen through a fair and open
40   bidding process? How might the road surface affect the life span or efficiency of the cars driving on it? What will be the annual maintenance cost, financially and environmentally?
     Appreciating opposing viewpoints can lead
45   to important insights. Perhaps nature can do a more efficient and safer job of reusing waste matter than a recycling plant can. Perhaps an economic system that accounts for environmental costs and benefits will lead to a higher standard

50 of living for the average citizen. Perhaps inserting
some natural resources into a responsible
"industrial cycle" is better for the environment
than conserving those resources. Exploring such
possibilities openly and respectfully will lead us
55 more reliably to both a healthier economy and a
healthier environment.

Passage 2

When trying to quantify the costs and
benefits of preserving our natural ecosystems,
one difficulty lies in the diffuseness of these
60 effects. Economists have a relatively easy time
with commerce, because money and goods can
be tracked through a series of point-to-point
exchanges. When you pay for something, the
exchange of money makes the accounting simple.
65 The diffuse, unchosen costs and benefits that
affect all of us daily—annoying commercials or a
beautiful sunset, for instance—are much harder
to evaluate.

The benefits that ecosystems provide, like
70 biodiversity, the filtration of groundwater, the
maintenance of the oxygen and nitrogen cycles,
and climate stability, however, are not bought-
and-sold commodities. Without them our lives
would deteriorate dramatically, but they are
75 not part of a clear exchange, so they fall into the
class of benefits and costs that economists call
"externalities."

The "good feeling" that many people have
about recycling and maintaining environmental
80 quality is just such an externality. Anti-
environmentalists often ridicule such feelings
as unquantifiable, but their value is real: some
stock funds only invest in companies with good
environmental records, and environmental
85 litigation can have steep costs in terms of money
and goodwill.

Robert Costanza, formerly of the Center
for Environmental Science at the University
of Maryland, has attempted to quantify these
90 "external" ecological benefits by tallying the
cost to replace nature's services. Imagine, for

instance, paving over the Florida Everglades and
then building systems to restore its lost benefits,
such as gas conversion and sequestering,
95 food production, water filtration, and weather
regulation. How much would it cost to keep these
systems running? Not even accounting for some
of the most important externalities, like natural
beauty, the cost would be extraordinarily high.
100 Costanza places it "conservatively" at $33 trillion
dollars annually, far more than the economic
output of all of the countries in the world.

Some object to Costanza's cost analysis.
Environmentalists argue that we cannot possibly
105 put a price on the smell of heather and a cool
breeze, while industrialists argue that the task
is speculative, unreliable, and an impediment
to economic progress. Nevertheless, Costanza's
work is among the most cited in the fields of
110 environmental science and economics. For
any flaws it might have, his work is giving a
common vocabulary to industrialists and
environmentalists alike, which we must do if
we are to coordinate intelligent environmental
115 policy with responsible economic policy.

DESTINATION OF U.S. SOLID MUNICIPAL WASTE, 2012

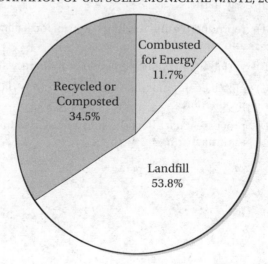

Source: Environmental Protection Agency

CONTINUE ➡

1

The first two sentences of Passage 1 serve primarily to

A) provide historical background to a debate.

B) establish the author's central thesis.

C) define terms for a technical discussion.

D) characterize opposing viewpoints.

2

The repetition of the phrase "not all" in lines 15 and 16 emphasizes the author's point that the "debaters" (line 13) tend to

A) mischaracterize their opponents.

B) discount evidence that does not support their positions.

C) employ self-contradicting arguments.

D) overlook relevant personal anecdotes.

3

The phrase "life cycles" (line 22) refers most directly to the

A) reproductive and feeding habits of local plants and animals.

B) variability in public perceptions about recycling.

C) global economic trends that affect industrial production.

D) processes that affect the substances used in manufacturing.

4

In line 50, "inserting" most nearly means

A) installing.

B) imposing.

C) introducing.

D) interjecting.

5

Which choice would the author of Passage 2 consider to be a direct effect of "natural ecosystems" (line 58)?

A) The "real solutions" (line 17)

B) The "provenance of the materials" (lines 27–28)

C) The "water filtration" (line 29)

D) The "maintenance" (line 34)

6

Which of the following policies would most likely be endorsed by the author of Passage 1?

A) Tax incentives for companies that recycle their waste products

B) Sanctions against nations that permit slave or child labor

C) Limits on factory emissions that contribute to acid rain

D) Public investment in sustainable domestic energy sources

CONTINUE ➡

1   **1**

7

Which choice provides the best evidence for the answer to the previous question?

A) Lines 28–30 ("We . . . construction?")

B) Lines 32–34 ("What . . . support?")

C) Lines 36–38 ("Are . . . practices?")

D) Lines 40–42 ("How . . . it?")

8

The diagram provides information most relevant to

A) Passage 1, because it indicates the scale of "recycling programs" (line 6).

B) Passage 1, because it illustrates the "many costs and benefits of disposal" (line 19).

C) Passage 2, because it represents the "benefits that ecosystems provide" (line 69).

D) Passage 2, because it shows "some of the most important externalities" (lines 97–98).

9

Which choice best exemplifies the "clear exchange" (line 75) mentioned in Passage 2?

A) The "debate" (line 14)

B) The "natural benefits" (line 28–29)

C) The "maintenance cost" (line 42)

D) The "important insights" (line 45)

10

Unlike Passage 2, Passage 1 specifically discusses

A) the effect of a particular rhetorical strategy.

B) the quantification of particular externalities.

C) the popularity of a particular environmental policy.

D) the cost of preserving particular environmental benefits.

11

Passage 2 compares the viewpoints of "environmentalists" and "industrialists" primarily to point out that

A) disputes about environmental policies are deep and intractable.

B) careful examination of externalities is controversial but necessary.

C) many debates about environmental issues are needlessly politicized.

D) both parties must learn to focus more on economic issues than environmental ones.

CONTINUE →

Questions 12–21 are based on the following passage.

This passage is from Cait Featherstone, *Earth, Song and Sky Spirit: Shadows and Sleepwalkers.* ©1992 by Random House, Inc.

He'd been in the area a long time, long enough to become background. When he first
Line emerged, a tall thin dark and silent presence on the local scene, everyone talked about him,
5 asking one another variations on the same question: Who is he? He never spoke and, without any answers, like children chasing their own shadows, people began to make up stories about him. Maybe he'd been a Vietnam vet,
10 some would venture. Others suggested that this seeming monastic stranger had come from some ashram in Tibet. Or perhaps he was a Somalian refugee, his African black skin seemed so thin as to barely stretch around his bones. Eventually,
15 the qualifying "maybes" and "perhaps" were dropped, and fiction was passed as fact.

Soundlessly he looked straight through things, his eyes telling of unspeakable things. And I wondered. Had he run barefoot, like a
20 crane skimming the surface of a lake, through the rice paddies of Vietnam? Had he seen a fatal flash? Were his saints beheaded? Did a torch emblazon on his breast the mark, the scar of war? Had the earth become a molten sea, a hardened
25 moonscape surface? Was there an immutable point at which he thought—he knew—that every living thing had ended? And so he had stopped breathing, had become shadow? Did he know what we would all come to know?
30   Too often to be mere coincidence, our paths crossed and converged daily. It seemed as if he was everywhere I went, like a parallel life or a shadow I'd owned in another lifetime. Often he'd be in a cross-walk when I was in my car at a
35 stoplight. Before work in the morning, I usually stopped at a local diner for coffee and he would walk past the window, past the table where I sat, separated by only a pane of glass. As an assistant

manager of a local bookstore, I usually opened
40 the place early in the morning. He would show up before any of the other employees did, gazing at the books on display in the front window, yet never looking directly at me.

I began to change my routine slightly.
45 Sometimes I would go down to the beach to take an early walk before going into work. He would be walking at the edge of the shore, the sea a blue backdrop to this moving shadow, this tree with legs. I began to take my walks at sunset instead,
50 and there he'd be, at the edge of a cliff above the sea, at the edge of the world. He'd stand like a tall dark crane balanced on one leg. Then poised and positioned on both legs, he'd begin a series of undulating, flowing movements. In Ina Coolbrith
55 Park in San Francisco, I'd often see Chinese people exploring the air with fluid movements, their bodies and the air in harmony. Though this was not Tai Chi, it seemed clearly ceremonial, religious, holy. His silhouette formed the character
60 of a word in Japanese script; his movements shaped haiku. What had seemed the figure of a black crow, a disquieting deathly form, through movement became a dark light, a black sun.

Then one day, I stopped at the diner for a
65 morning cup of coffee. I walked down the aisle toward my usual booth and noticed that the shadow man was sitting there. He was taking what looked like tea leaves from a small leather bag that hung around his neck and placing them in a
70 cup of hot water. As I came nearer, he looked up, and for the first time he was seeing me, not seeing through me. His look was clear, not shrouded with darkness nor veiled with otherness as I had come to expect. He had seemed to journey momentarily
75 out of that dark place. I returned his look, nodded my head. And for the first time since I'd seen him, he smiled at me. He opened his mouth, to speak, to speak to me. And I, in awe, awaited the sound of his voice, the words sure to shape around some
80 thought sprung from the well of a silence he occupied. A sound emerged, high and light as air, full of jive and jazz, as he said, "What's happenin', mama?"

12

The purpose of the passage as a whole is to

A) describe a relationship between friends.

B) portray the character of a small town.

C) recount an episode in the narrator's self-discovery.

D) chronicle a preoccupation with an enigmatic figure.

13

The many stories that circulated about the stranger are best described as

A) uniformly macabre.

B) strangely entertaining.

C) playfully deprecating.

D) decreasingly speculative.

14

Which choice provides the best evidence for the answer to the previous question?

A) Lines 9–10 ("Maybe . . . venture")

B) Lines 14–16 ("Eventually . . . fact")

C) Lines 17–18 ("Soundlessly . . . things")

D) Lines 25–27 ("Was . . . ended?")

15

In line 25, "moonscape surface" refers to

A) a desolate aftermath.

B) an unexplored vista.

C) an idyllic location.

D) a primordial stage.

16

In line 59, "character" most nearly means

A) visible symbol.

B) abstract quality.

C) strange person.

D) moral integrity.

17

In lines 30–43, the narrator's encounters with the stranger are notable for their

A) incongruousness.

B) ominousness.

C) ubiquity.

D) sentimentality.

18

Throughout the passage, the narrator describes the stranger's physical characteristics chiefly through the use of

A) literary allusions.

B) military comparisons.

C) avian metaphors.

D) exaggerated juxtapositions.

CONTINUE

19

The phrase "what we would all come to know" (line 29) most likely refers to

A) the identity of the stranger.

B) the destiny of humankind.

C) the inhumanity of war.

D) a source of tranquility.

20

In line 74, the narrator indicates that the stranger "seemed to journey" from

A) foreign terrain to a familiar homeland.

B) grim memory to current experience.

C) vague obscurity to public recognition.

D) self-consciousness to self-confidence.

21

The first words the narrator heard from the stranger most likely made her feel a sense of

A) solemn respect.

B) surprised relief.

C) sudden dread.

D) deep tranquility.

1   1

Questions 22–31 are based on the following passage.

This passage is adapted from Mary Gay Humphries, "Women Bachelors," an essay originally published in 1896. During the latter part of the American Industrial Era (c. 1840–1900), many unmarried women began migrating to urban areas throughout the country.

The exodus of women to the cities in the last ten years parallels that of men. They have come
Line from the West in regiments, and from the South in brigades. Each year they come younger and
5 younger. They have ameliorated the customs and diversified the streets.

New York women, and perhaps city women in general, when they are suddenly called upon to earn their livings, are much more independent
10 about it, and more original in their methods than women in smaller places, where womanly pursuits, as they are called, follow more closely prescribed lines. The New York woman has more knowledge of the world, and she knows that one
15 can do pretty much what one pleases, if it is done with a certain dash, élan, and sweeping air. When she comes to work for her living she profits by this knowledge. Instead of becoming a governess or a teacher of music, she tries to get hold of
20 something original that will excite interest. When she has found it she holds it up, as it were, on a blazoned banner, inscribed with this legend, "I have not a penny to my name, and I'm going to work." She accepts the situation with the greatest
25 good-humor and makes herself more acceptable to the old set by relating her discouragements, trials, and mistakes so comically that she is better company than before. If her story is not bad enough she embroiders it to the proper point of
30 attractiveness.

In the measure that women are determining their own lives, they want their own homes. The desire is entirely reasonable. The woman who is occupied with daily work needs greater freedom
35 of movement, more isolation, more personal comforts, and the exemption, moreover, from being agreeable at all times and places. She wants to be able to shut her doors against all the world, and not to be confined within four walls

40 herself; and she wants to open her doors when it pleases her, and to exercise the rites of hospitality unquestioned. In fact, she wants many things that cannot be had except in her own home. It is an interesting fact in natural history that women
45 in their first breathing-spell should revert to constructing homes as their natural background, to which is added the male realization that the home is the proper stimulus to achievement.

To be the mistress of a home, to extend
50 hospitalities, briefly to be within the circumference of a social circle, instead of gliding with uneasy foot on the periphery, is the reasonable desire of every woman. When this is achieved many temptations, so freely recognized
55 that nobody disputes them, are eliminated. It is a noticeable fact that in all women-bachelor households, no matter how humble, that the rugs are scarcely down and the curtains up, until the kettle is lighted and the reign of hospitality has
60 begun. It is interesting to observe how soon the shyest novice over the tea-cup loses her timidity, and assumes that air of confidence that once was the enviable property of only married women.

22

The first paragraph portrays the "exodus of women" (line 1) as

A) tentative.

B) regrettable.

C) inevitable.

D) transformative.

23

The author suggests that, compared to women living in urban areas, those living in rural areas are less

A) diffident.

B) humorous.

C) innovative.

D) traditional.

CONTINUE →

24

Which choice provides the best evidence for the answer to the previous question?

A) Lines 7–13 ("New . . . lines")

B) Lines 13–16 ("The . . . air")

C) Lines 17–18 ("When . . . knowledge")

D) Lines 18–20 ("Instead . . . interest")

25

The author suggests that, to the new urban woman, poverty is

A) a challenge to be embraced.

B) a career burden to be avoided.

C) the consequence of male dominance.

D) a surprising source of freedom.

26

Which choice provides the best evidence for the answer to the previous question?

A) Lines 24–28 ("She . . . before")

B) Lines 31–32 ("In . . . homes")

C) Lines 33–37 ("The . . . places")

D) Lines 43–48 ("It . . . achievement")

27

In line 16, "dash" most nearly means

A) propriety.

B) flair.

C) diligence.

D) haste.

28

As it is used in line 26, "old set" most likely refers to a group of

A) traditional gender roles.

B) established acquaintances.

C) historical ideals.

D) abandoned opportunities.

29

The passage indicates that city women want to maintain their own homes primarily because

A) they are naturally predisposed to performing domestic duties rather than having careers.

B) they should maintain a social status comparable with that of men.

C) they require living conditions conducive to their social independence.

D) they need ample space to do the work that is required of them in an industrial economy.

CONTINUE ➡

1   **1**

30

Which choice best summarizes the main point of the passage?

A) Women who are moving to the cities are subject to many unfair expectations and social burdens.

B) Traditional female duties, such as housekeeping, should be re-evaluated in the context of modern urbanization.

C) In modern times, the social independence of women corresponds to their desire to own and maintain a home.

D) Women who choose to live in cities are more creative and industrious than those who choose to live in rural areas.

31

The "exemption" mentioned in line 36 is

A) a reprieve from a social obligation.

B) an exception to a legal rule.

C) an anomaly among personal characteristics.

D) an irregularity within an established hierarchy.

CONTINUE ▶

Questions 32–42 are based on the following passage and supplementary material.

This passage is adapted from Alyson Shepherd, "The Promise of Immunotherapy and Oncolytic Virotherapy." ©2015 by College Hill Coaching.

If physician and microbiologist David Stojdl has his way, the term "going viral" will soon get a whole new meaning. Together with researchers in the United States and Canada, Stojdl has spent
5 much of his career finding ways to turn viruses into powerful cancer-killing machines, and some of the early successes are astonishing.

For decades, viruses have rightfully been treated as dangerous invaders. The word *virus*
10 itself means "poison" in Latin, and indeed viruses are the culprits implicated not only in the common cold and the more deadly influenza, but also in some of the ghastliest afflictions humanity has ever seen, such as smallpox, HIV, SARS, and
15 Ebola. Understandably, then, medical researchers have expended enormous effort to help the body identify and destroy these stealthy aggressors. Vaccinations are the major successes on this front; introducing attenuated forms of otherwise
20 harmful viruses trains our immune systems to produce antibodies that shield us from future infections.

Now, however, researchers are harnessing the efficient lethality of viruses to attack cancer.
25 Because viruses can attack inoperable tumors with more precision than chemotherapy or radiation can, and because they can attack malignant tumors on multiple fronts, virotherapy may well turn out to be our most potent tool in oncology.
30 Viruses are tiny packages of genetic material encased in a protein or lipid shell. When the molecules in this shell "match up" with the molecules on the surface of a cell—scientists refer to this as a "lock-and-key" mechanism—the virus
35 attaches and injects its genes into the cell, where they co-opt the replication mechanisms of the cell to reproduce themselves.

Physicians first recognized the tumor-fighting potential of viruses over a century ago.

40 In 1904, Italian doctors discovered that one woman's enormous cervical tumor disappeared soon after she was administered a rabies vaccine for a dog bite. Evidently, the same viruses that were boosting her immune system were also
45 attacking her cancer. Unfortunately, doctors of the time had no idea how this process worked. Attempts to replicate this success showed inconsistent results: most patients who received the same treatment saw at best temporary
50 regression of their tumors, and none were cured.

Today, however, modern researchers have powerful tools not only for observing the complex functions of cellular and extracellular molecules, but also for manipulating the very genetic code
55 that produces some of those molecules. As a result, they are learning to fine-tune viruses for selective infection, so that they attack only tumor cells and leave normal cells unscathed. Such precision, if it can be achieved, would
60 provide an enormous advantage over radiation and chemotherapy, which have highly toxic side effects on healthy tissue. In contrast, the worst side effects that virology patients are likely to see are chills, fever, and fatigue.

65 Although research into virotherapy is still in its early stages, natural and re-programmed viruses have already demonstrated four distinct cancer-destroying skills. First, they can kill cancer cells directly through *lysis*, a process by
70 which they invade the cells and, under the right conditions, replicate themselves so prolifically that they tear the cells apart and then go on to infect other cells. Second, they can trigger a process called *apoptosis*, a sequence of self-
75 destructive chemical reactions within the tumor cells, so that the cancer effectively commits suicide. Third, they can be programmed to selectively attack the blood vessels that supply nutrients to a tumor (in a process called *vascular*
80 *collapse*) and kill the cancer by starvation. Lastly, the chemical activity that viruses induce can also elicit a response from the immune system's own dendritic cells, which can then initiate a T-cell attack to destroy the tumor.

85 One pernicious aspect of cancer is its ability to "cloak" itself from the immune system, so that

CONTINUE →

1

1

our T- and B-cells—guard dogs against dangerous cellular invaders—can't fight it effectively. Some cancers have even evolved proteins that kill
90   T-cells before they can attack. But now scientists are finding ways to break through these chemical defenses and let the immune system do its job. Such therapies, known as immunotherapies, may soon be used jointly with virotherapies
95   to marshal a "shock and awe" attack against cancer. In one recent immunotherapy trial, 89% of patients with acute lymphoblastic leukemia saw a "complete" response, that is, their cancer

became undetectable without surgery, radiation,
100   or chemotherapy.
     Developing these new therapies requires a concerted effort: geneticists, immunologists, microbiologists, and molecular diagnosticians must work together to develop tools to detect the
105   genetic and molecular "markers" that identify particular cancer types and indicate how extensively they have spread. This will enable doctors to personalize an efficient therapy for each individual patient.

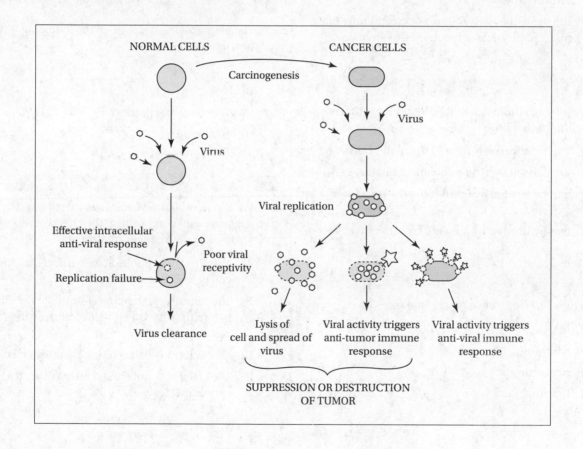

CONTINUE ▶

1   **1**

32

The second paragraph (lines 8–22) serves mainly to

A) relate a point of view toward viruses that contrasts with that adopted by modern microbiologists.

B) provide some technical information pertaining to virotherapy in order to clarify the discussion that follows.

C) describe several insidious diseases the treatments for which serve as a model for virotherapy.

D) illustrate the early failures of virotherapy that modern physicians have since overcome.

33

The passage indicates that HIV and leukemia are similar in that both

A) can be effectively treated through virotherapy.

B) are caused by viral infection of healthy cells.

C) can be treated by reinforcing the immune system.

D) can be used as treatments for other diseases.

34

In line 19, "front" most nearly means

A) façade.

B) campaign.

C) beginning.

D) bearing.

35

According to the information in the passage, the "poor viral receptivity" illustrated in the diagram is most likely due to

A) a failure of the "lock-and-key" mechanism.

B) a "cloaking" of the cell against T-cell attack.

C) the triggering of apoptosis.

D) the toxic effects of chemotherapy.

36

The diagram illustrates all of the following processes EXCEPT

A) T-cell attack.

B) lysis.

C) selective infection.

D) apoptosis.

37

What potential drawback does this diagram suggest could compromise the effectiveness of virotherapy as a cancer treatment?

A) The virus may not be able to infect the cancer cell or replicate within it.

B) The immune system may eliminate the viruses before they have a chance to destroy the cancer cell.

C) The virus may cause lysis of healthy cells.

D) The virus may not spread after killing the cancer cell by lysis.

1   **1**

38

The passage indicates that, until recently, the human immune system has been unable to attack cancers cells effectively because the human immune system

A) selectively attacks and destroys viruses rather than cells.

B) cannot penetrate the blood vessels to initiate vascular collapse.

C) is compromised by therapies such as radiation and chemotherapy.

D) is thwarted by chemical defenses that cancer cells have developed.

39

Which choice provides the best evidence for the answer to the previous question?

A) Lines 43–45 ("Evidently . . . cancer")

B) Lines 55–58 ("As . . . unscathed")

C) Lines 80–84 ("Lastly . . . tumor")

D) Lines 85–88 ("One . . . effectively")

40

In line 47, "attempts to replicate" refers to acts of

A) viral reproduction.

B) therapeutic repetition.

C) scientific refutation.

D) pharmaceutical marketing.

41

A student claims that viruses can destroy cancer cells only by directly infecting them. Which of the following statements from the passage most directly contradicts this claim?

A) Lines 59–62 ("Such . . . tissue")

B) Lines 68–73 ("First . . . cells")

C) Lines 73–77 ("Second . . . suicide")

D) Lines 77–80 ("Third . . . starvation")

42

The passage suggests that the "precision" mentioned in line 59 is most likely to be achieved through

A) vaccination against viruses like rabies.

B) genetic manipulation of viruses.

C) the combination of radiation and chemotherapy.

D) the triggering of apoptosis.

CONTINUE

Questions 43–52 are based on the following passage.

This passage is adapted from Stephen T. Asma, "Animal Spirits." ©2013 Stephen T. Asma. Originally published in *Aeon* (aeon.co), February 6, 2013. In this article, Asma describes a visit to the Serengeti plains of Africa and reflects on human and animal emotions.

    Time on the Serengeti makes you think a lot about the inner life of animals. When a
Line wildebeest is screaming in the jaws of a crocodile, is it feeling fear like we do? Is it relieved when it's
5 suddenly free? Is the croc filled with regret? Jaak Panksepp, the founder of the new field of affective neuroscience, says animals do in fact have complex emotional lives.
    When he administered an electrical charge
10 to the medial hypothalamus of a cat, it leaped viciously, a hissing, spitting tangle of fangs and claws. As soon as he turned off the stimulation, the cat relaxed. Humans who have had electrical stimulation in the corresponding brain locations
15 also reported intense rage, which lends credence to the idea of animal subjectivity. Scientists who study animal behavior increasingly accept the idea that *fear* keeps animals away from predators, *lust* draws them toward each other, *panic*
20 motivates their social solidarity, and *care* glues their parent-offspring bonds. Just like us, they have an inner life because it helps them navigate their outer life.
    Since the Pleistocene epoch, we hominids
25 have had to feel before we could think. Our cognitive brains work only when emotions tilt our deliberations. Neuroscientist Antonio Damasio studied patients with damage in the communication system between the cognitive
30 and emotional brain. The subjects could compute all the informational aspects of a decision, but couldn't commit. Without clear feelings, Damasio's patients couldn't decide their own social calendars or make decisions in their own
35 best interest. In order for our minds to go beyond syntax to semantics, we need feelings. And our ancestral minds were rich in feelings before they were adept in computations.

    In those early days, our lives were dominated
40 by survival-related experiences that stimulated our limbic system, the part of our brain hard-wired for parent-child bonding, panic, rage, anxiety, loneliness, and play. But the process by which we attach fear, anger, and desire to the
45 right kinds of creatures in our environments turns out to be quite flexible. Humans are afraid of the dark, but rats—our more distant mammal kin—are afraid of the light. It's the same emotional system, assigned to different settings
50 thanks to neuroplasticity.
    Discoveries about this flexibility are changing the game in contemporary theories of mind. Until recently, evolutionary psychologists characterized the mind as a collection of
55 independent problem-solving modules, like separate gears in a watch. Each of these modules, they argued, was sculpted by natural selection during the Pleistocene to solve a specific survival challenge; we now inherit them *in toto* as part of
60 our genetic birthright.
    A vital premise for this modular theory is that the hominid brain evolved in an extremely stable environment, or else natural selection couldn't sculpt each module to fit our perennial
65 environmental challenges. But recent discoveries show that the Pleistocene environment was anything but stable. In fact, it was precisely this climate chaos that created our multipurpose, problem-solving minds. If the context in which
70 we did our foraging and hunting kept changing radically, hardwired specialized modules wouldn't have done us much good. What we needed was all-purpose intelligence that could perceive new challenges and apply general logical
75 rules and cultural folkways to solving them. The expansion of the brain corresponds with an increasingly adaptable mind.
    That flexibility probably evolved in the context of more complex social groups.
80 Hominids, following a preexisting trajectory among primates, continued down the path of longer childhoods and greater dependence on our mothers. Eventually, this led to something new: the capacity to care beyond our narrow
85 biological circles. We could spread our feelings

CONTINUE ▶

1   **1**

around promiscuously, extending them to our
fellow humans in general and sustaining loyalties
over great expanses of time. By comparison, other
animals seem strictly concerned with specific
90 threats and benefactors.

Africa has long been used as a kind of literary
metaphor, a geography of the animal instinct.
Affective neuroscience, however, is turning age-
old mysteries of the animal instinct into scientific
95 research programs. We need more scientists who
are willing to bridge the chasm between the new
brain science of emotions and the natural history
of life on the African savanna. Limbic emotions
gave our ancestors their world of friends and
100 foes, their grasp of food and its fatal alternatives.
These emotions also motivated much of the social
bonding that spurred the *sapiens'* great leap
forward. If we are to understand ourselves, this is
the wild territory we need to rediscover.

43

Which of the following best summarizes the main
thesis of the passage?

A) We should appreciate the emotional lives of
   animals if we want to live sustainably with
   them.

B) Modern research is revealing that animals
   are far more intelligent than we previously
   believed.

C) The African savanna must be preserved so that
   we may continue to explore animal behavior.

D) We cannot understand human intelligence
   without first understanding animal emotions.

44

In lines 16–21 ("Scientists . . . bonds"), the sequence
of words in italics represents

A) incrementally more powerful motivators.

B) progressively more speculative theories.

C) increasingly human sentiments.

D) decreasingly rational behaviors.

45

In line 27, "tilt" most nearly means

A) upset.

B) sway.

C) slope.

D) contend.

46

The passage mentions the work of Antonio
Damasio primarily to

A) highlight a surprising discovery about the
   function of emotions in human thinking.

B) identify a setback to early research into human
   cognitive function.

C) illustrate a problem with drawing inferences
   about an entire species on the basis of a few
   individuals.

D) illustrate the necessity of establishing
   emotional relationships with research subjects.

47

In line 39, "those early days" refers to

A) the first stages of a child's neural development.

B) the period before neuroscientists had access to
   modern diagnostic tools.

C) the epoch in which our ancestors were
   developing the ability to think.

D) the time when researchers first began
   exploring the emotional brain.

CONTINUE ➤

1   1

48

In line 64, "sculpt" refers to an act of

A) deliberate fabrication.

B) aesthetic creation.

C) theoretical refinement.

D) gradual development.

49

In line 76, "corresponds" most nearly means

A) coincides.

B) communicates.

C) agrees.

D) meets.

50

The main purpose of the sixth paragraph (lines 61–77) is to

A) explain a technical term.

B) describe an ancient habitat.

C) refute a scientific theory.

D) illustrate a psychological phenomenon.

51

The author objects to the theory that our brains evolved problem-solving modules, because such modules would be inconsistent with

A) the variable conditions of the Pleistocene epoch.

B) the complex emotional behaviors we share with other animals.

C) our ability to use feelings to make decisions.

D) our long childhoods and elaborate child-rearing practices.

52

Which choice provides the best evidence for the answer to the previous question?

A) Lines 16–21 ("Scientists . . . bonds")

B) Lines 32–35 ("Without . . . interest")

C) Lines 67–69 ("In . . . minds")

D) Lines 80–83 ("Hominids . . . mothers")

STOP

If you finish before time is called, you may check your work on this section only.
Do not turn to any other section of the test.

2   2

Writing and Language Test
35 MINUTES, 44 QUESTIONS

Turn to Section 2 of your answer sheet to answer the questions in this section.

DIRECTIONS

Each passage below is accompanied by a number of questions. For some questions, you will consider how the passage might be revised to improve the expression of ideas. For other questions, you will consider how the passage might be edited to correct errors in sentence structure, usage, or punctuation. A passage or a question may be accompanied by one or more graphics (such as a table or graph) that you will consider as you make revising and editing decisions.

Some questions will direct you to an underlined portion of a passage. Other questions will direct you to a location in a passage or ask you to think about the passage as a whole.

After reading each passage, choose the answer to each question that most effectively improves the quality of writing in the passage or that makes the passage conform to the conventions of Standard Written English. Many questions include a "NO CHANGE" option. Choose that option if you think the best choice is to leave the relevant portion of the passage as it is.

CONTINUE ▶

2   2

Questions 1–11 are based on the following passage and supplementary material.

Careers in Engineering

1 Wherever engineers are often unfairly portrayed in the media as mere number-crunchers, we all depend on their work every day. The safety of our drinking water, the reliability of our roads and bridges, **2** how usable our smartphones are, and even the sustainability of the earth's ecosystem all depend on the work of engineers. As we become more dependent on technologies of all sorts, engineering fields are growing quickly. **3**

1

A) NO CHANGE

B) When

C) Although

D) Being that

2

A) NO CHANGE

B) the usability our smartphones have

C) the usability of our smartphones

D) our smartphones' usability

3

The writer wants to add a sentence here that provides a specific and relevant detail from the graph. Which choice best accomplishes this?

A) All engineering fields are expected to grow by at least 5% per year for the foreseeable future.

B) Some engineering fields will more than double in size over the next 10 years.

C) Some engineering fields will remain stagnant over the next 10 years, while many will grow dramatically.

D) Some engineering fields are expected to grow by over 25% in the next 10 years.

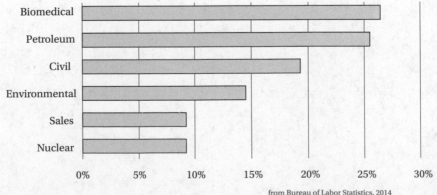

Predicted Job Market Growth in the Coming Decade, by Engineering Specialty

from Bureau of Labor Statistics, 2014

CONTINUE ➤

2   2

Many careers in engineering go far beyond [4] merely the application of formulas, throwing switches, and analyzing data. Although [5] a strong foundation in mathematics and science is required for all engineering careers, many also require strong skills in art, design, and the human sciences. Increasingly, technological devices don't just need to work, they also need to work with people.

Engineering can be regarded as the science of systems. Computer software and hardware engineers analyze the systems that guide computer tasks. Industrial engineers examine the systems by which factories [6] transform raw materials and make products out of them. Civil engineers look at the systems involved in the flow of traffic, water, electricity, and communication. Environmental engineers analyze ecosystems and [7] the ways human activities impact them.

If you like to solve mathematical and physical problems and [8] seeing the tangible fruits of your labor, you should consider a career in engineering. Many entry-level engineering jobs require no higher than a bachelor's degree in science, but higher paying jobs will likely require a professional engineer (PE) certification or master's degree.

4
A) NO CHANGE
B) mere applying formulas
C) mere application of formulas
D) merely applying formulas

5
A) NO CHANGE
B) all engineering careers require a strong foundation in mathematics and science
C) a strong mathematics and science foundation would be required for all engineering careers
D) all engineering careers would require a strong foundation in mathematics and science

6
A) NO CHANGE
B) change and transform raw materials into products
C) make products out of raw materials
D) transform raw materials out of which to make new products

7
A) NO CHANGE
B) the ways human activity impact
C) human activity has an impact on
D) the ways by which human activities impact

8
A) NO CHANGE
B) like also seeing
C) like also to see
D) to see

CONTINUE ▶

[1] Early in life, many of us have a natural love for **9** engineering: they take apart toy cars to see how they work, or build bridges and castles out of boxes and blocks. [2] Sadly, this enthusiasm is often destroyed by schooling. [3] One solution to this problem is to expose children to fun building activities without pitting them against each other, turning the task into a performance. **10**

11 We need to make engineering fun for children again, because so much depends on it. Cultures may be built by philosophers and poets, but societies are built by engineers.

9

A) NO CHANGE

B) engineering, they

C) engineering, we

D) engineering: we

10

The writer is considering adding the following sentence to this paragraph.

By forcing students to complete dull worksheets and take competitive, passion-destroying tests, schools can transform the joy of learning into misery.

The best place for this sentence is immediately

A) before sentence 1.

B) after sentence 1.

C) after sentence 2.

D) after sentence 3.

11

Which choice provides the most logical and effective transition to the final paragraph?

A) NO CHANGE

B) Engineering can be not only a joyful experience but also among the most lucrative careers one can have.

C) Students in Finland and Singapore score consistently at the top of international tests in math and science.

D) Like medicine, engineering is a many-faceted discipline that requires years of specialized practice.

CONTINUE ➡

2   2

Questions 12–22 are based on the following passage.

An American Duty

Too many American voters haven't changed the way they [12] thought about elections since they first voted for their middle school student council. When it comes to choosing a leader, we are too influenced by his or her looks, personality, and [13] what people are saying, good and bad. Even worse, we seem to be terrible at understanding our biases and predicting the consequences of our votes, and so many of us even end up voting against our own interests.

Choosing our political leaders should be a serious task. This means that, like serious students, we should come to class [14] having done our homework, rather than merely complaining about the teacher not being entertaining enough. Our homework should be to identify the most important problems our society [15] faces, studying the mechanisms at the heart of those problems, and to determine what roles, if any, our leaders can and should play in addressing them.

Instead, we are far too lazy and far too easily manipulated. We let other [16] people—attractive news presenters, blustery radio hosts, or celebrities—tell us how we should vote, usually by giving us scary stories about the opposing party or slickly produced profiles of their favored candidates. Negative campaign ads, with

12
A) NO CHANGE
B) are thinking
C) have thought
D) think

13
A) NO CHANGE
B) what others are saying
C) their reputations
D) reputation

14
A) NO CHANGE
B) doing
C) having to do
D) when we did

15
A) NO CHANGE
B) faces, to study
C) would face, to study
D) face, studying

16
A) NO CHANGE
B) people who are attractive
C) people, especially attractive
D) people: attractive

CONTINUE →

ominous music playing over blurry black-and-white pictures accompanied by a threatening voice, are far too **17** valid. Responsible adults shouldn't fall for such transparently dishonest tactics.

Instead of **18** us listening to the chattering class and blatantly biased ads, we must learn for ourselves what is going on in the world, with as few corporate or political filters as possible. **19** To that end, we should seek out reliable international newspapers and news sites with high journalistic standards, that is, those that seek more to inform than to entertain. This will give us a better perspective on both domestic and international issues.

[1] Next, we should make sure that the candidates at least understand the issues deeply, and aren't merely reciting a political platform. [2] For instance, good representatives should be able to objectively explain, in depth, the issues plaguing the American health care system, rather than using distortions and incendiary language to smear their opponents. [3] They articulate the grievances and dynamics that drive wars and international conflicts, rather than merely posture as a "hawk" or a "dove." **20**

17

A) NO CHANGE
B) beneficial
C) effectual
D) credible

18

A) NO CHANGE
B) when we listen
C) listening
D) the listening

19

A) NO CHANGE
B) Alternately,
C) Notwithstanding that,
D) Nevertheless,

20

The writer is considering adding the following sentence to this paragraph.

> Strong leaders should convey that understanding to voters, rather than merely manipulate or pander to them.

The best place for this sentence is immediately

A) before sentence 1.
B) after sentence 1.
C) after sentence 2.
D) after sentence 3.

2   **2**

We must also find out **21** who's interests do the candidates really represent. Are the candidates likely to fight for large industries or common consumers? Are they strict party loyalists, or do they act and think independently? Have they pledged allegiance to any group that holds dangerous or misguided views? **22** Do they spend a lot of time in the spotlight, or do they tend to shy away from publicity?

We must answer these questions for ourselves, and not merely swallow the perspectives of radio or television personalities, no matter how blustery or attractive they might be. The strength of our democracy depends on it.

21

A) NO CHANGE
B) whose interests
C) who's interests
D) about who's interests

22

The writer is considering deleting this sentence to make the paragraph more concise. Should the author do this?

A) No, because it makes a new and important point about political interests.
B) No, because without it the preceding rhetorical questions do not make sense.
C) Yes, because the question is incongruous with the central idea of the paragraph.
D) Yes, because the question has already been answered in the preceding discussion.

CONTINUE →

2   2

Questions 23–33 are based on the following passage.

Idol Worship in Sports

As a source of both inspiration and relaxation, [23] human cultures have always had sports playing a central role. Correspondingly, our greatest athletes are always among our greatest icons. In ancient Greece, the wrestler Milo of Croton earned such [24] renown for his strength and skill that he was known as "The Son of Zeus." Centuries later, [25] gladiators like Spartacus of Thrace earned a powerful following that enabled him to liberate thousands of slaves. Today, children and adults alike wear jerseys emblazoned with the names of their favorite athletes, and spend hours every week not only watching their games, but also [26] dissecting those performances later with friends.

We don't [27] regard our most popular athletes as immortal any more, yet sports idolatry certainly doesn't seem to have diminished much since ancient times. Most sports fans see it as a harmless, and perhaps even beneficial, pastime. What little boy doesn't look back fondly on trying to juggle a soccer ball like Clint Dempsey or throw a split-fingered fastball like Mariano Rivera? And little girls have long aspired to be the next Serena Williams or Abby Wambach.

23

A) NO CHANGE

B) human cultures have always used sports in a central role.

C) sports are always playing a central role in human cultures.

D) sports have always played a central role in human cultures.

24

A) NO CHANGE

B) mastery

C) diligence

D) revelation

25

A) NO CHANGE

B) the gladiator Spartacus of Thrace

C) gladiators such as Spartacus of Thrace

D) a gladiator such as Spartacus of Thrace

26

Which choice best extends and completes the idea of the sentence?

A) NO CHANGE

B) learning about other sports that might be of interest

C) practicing their own athletic skills

D) going to see their performances in person

27

A) NO CHANGE

B) regard our most popular athletes to be

C) consider our most popular athletes as

D) consider that our most popular athletes are

2   2

Is there a cost to all of this idol worship? In fact, there are many. For one, it uses a lot of physical and mental energy, and **28** nevertheless distracts us from our tackling important issues that need our attention. An American is far more likely to be able to name all of the NFL quarterbacks than to name all of the countries in which we have an active military presence. Second, it **29** decelerates the moral fabric of our society. Well-known professional and college athletes are regularly given special treatment, even when they commit heinous crimes, like spousal abuse and felony assault, and often receive **30** just slaps on the wrist when less privileged defendants might receive lengthy prison terms.

Perhaps most damning, all of this worship doesn't even seem to help the vast majority of the athletes themselves. According to a 2009 *Sports Illustrated* article, 78% of NFL players **31** have either declared bankruptcy, or suffered serious financial distress within two years of retirement. Even the most successful stars often leave the sport with long-term physical and mental deficits due to the constant physical pounding they must endure throughout their careers. This says nothing of the countless college and semi-pro players who never made it to the NFL but who nevertheless

---

28

A) NO CHANGE
B) instead
C) conversely
D) thereby

29

A) NO CHANGE
B) demoralizes
C) demonizes
D) degrades

30

Which choice best maintains the tone and style of the paragraph and adds a relevant detail?

A) NO CHANGE
B) essentially nothing to speak of
C) barely the punishment that they deserve
D) a light sentence or mere probation

31

A) NO CHANGE
B) have either declared bankruptcy or
C) either have declared bankruptcy, or
D) have, either declared bankruptcy, or

CONTINUE ➤

2

2

squandered their educations or suffered debilitating injuries 32 .

We don't live in hunting tribes anymore, so perhaps it's time to stop acting as if we do. In our complex world, we should be valuing those who can think and care for others, not just those who can run or throw. If we need idols, why not biochemists who toil incessantly to find cures for cancer? Why not soldiers, teachers, nurses, and police who serve honorably and selflessly, usually for very little pay, 33 but they often have as much skill as the finest athletes?

32

At this point, the writer is considering adding the following information.

> that rendered them unproductive in what should have been their prime earning years

Should this change be made?

A) Yes, because it provides an example of a particular physical injury related to playing sports.

B) Yes, because it describes the impact that sports injuries can have on the athletes' lives.

C) No, because it mentions the years after the athletes' sports careers, blurring the focus of the paragraph.

D) No, because it contradicts the point in the previous paragraph that athletes receive special benefits.

33

A) NO CHANGE

B) and with often

C) but often with

D) but often

2   2

Questions 34–44 are based on the following passage.

The Secret Life of Photons

Anyone who has gazed into the deep darkness of space on a clear, moonless night can understand why stars have always fascinated us. Ancient cultures believed that stars **34** <u>sufficed</u> as omens of earthly events, and even influenced individual lives through their "interactions" with the planets. To the more science-minded, they **35** <u>have beckoned for us long</u> with the physical mysteries behind their colossal beauty.

36 <u>Although we now know</u> that the stars beyond our sun are far too distant to exert any significant influence on planetary motion, let alone human affairs, it seems that modern astronomers are nevertheless exercising mystical powers of divination. Today's astronomers claim to know the distance, age, speed,

34
A) NO CHANGE
B) performed
C) attended
D) served

35
A) NO CHANGE
B) have long beckoned us
C) have beckoned long for us
D) long have beckoned for us

36
A) NO CHANGE
B) Nevertheless, we know now
C) We now know
D) Now we have known

CONTINUE ➡

2   **2**

and even chemical composition of objects that are so distant we **37** might hope never to send probes there. **38** How can they claim to know so much about stars that are often millions of light years away?

It's really an incredible feat. Consider the remarkable fact that all the information we have about stars is indirect. Unlike other objects of fascination—like microbes, the ocean floor, or even the moon—**39** we can't easily sample stars to observe them under a microscope. Instead, we must depend on the photons they emit, tiny packets of energy that must often travel thousands of billions of billions of miles or **40** more. At that point, the photons are finally absorbed by a digital camera or the retina of an eyeball that is peering through a telescope. Additionally, we

37

A) NO CHANGE
B) never hoped
C) would never hope
D) could never hope

38

The writer is considering deleting this sentence in order to make the paragraph more concise. Should this change be made?

A) Yes, because it asks a question about astronomers that has already been answered implicitly.

B) Yes, because the fact that some stars are millions of light years away has already been established.

C) No, because the question provides a logical transition to the discussion of inferential methods that follows.

D) No, because it provides an important rhetorical question about astronomy that emphasizes the author's main thesis.

39

A) NO CHANGE
B) we can't sample to make observations easily of stars
C) stars are not easily sampled for observation
D) stars are not easy to sample in observation

40

A) more, the photons being then
B) more when the photons are
C) more where the photons are
D) more until the photons are

can infer information about a star by looking in its neighborhood. Changes in the behavior of nearby bodies such as other stars or clouds of gas often indicate the presence of a star, **41** <u>even when that star is too dim to see.</u>

The light from the most distant observable **42** <u>stars, began their</u> journey more than 50 million years ago. In that time, the steady expansion of space itself stretched the wavelength of each photon, in a process called "redshifting." The **43** <u>experience</u> of this redshifting tells astronomers how far the photon had to travel, and hence how far away the star is (or was).

The photons from a single star are not all the same wavelength, however, and that's a good thing. The wavelengths fall into a wide **44** <u>spectrum, which characteristics reveal</u> the size of the star as well as the presence of elements such as hydrogen, helium, calcium, sodium, and even titanium.

41

Which choice best matches the style of the sentence and adds a relevant new piece of information?

A) NO CHANGE

B) which is an incredible discovery for the astronomers.

C) which is often very different in size from the nearby stars.

D) even when that gas is spinning very quickly.

42

A) NO CHANGE

B) stars began their

C) stars began it's

D) stars began its

43

A) NO CHANGE

B) exposure

C) extent

D) expedience

44

A) NO CHANGE

B) spectrum that reveals by characteristics

C) spectrum, the characteristics of which reveal

D) spectrum revealing, by its characteristics

STOP

If you finish before time is called, you may check your work on this section only. Do not turn to any other section of the test.

3 **3**

Math Test – No Calculator

25 MINUTES, 20 QUESTIONS

Turn to Section 3 of your answer sheet to answer the questions in this section.

DIRECTIONS

For questions 1–15, solve each problem, choose the best answer from the choices provided, and fill in the corresponding circle on your answer sheet. **For questions 16–20,** solve the problem and enter your answer in the grid on the answer sheet. Please refer to the directions before question 16 on how to enter you answers in the grid. You may use any available space in your test booklet for scratch work.

NOTES

1. The use of a calculator is NOT permitted.
2. All variables and expressions used represent real numbers unless otherwise indicated.
3. Figures provided in this test are drawn to scale unless otherwise indicated.
4. All figures lie in a plane unless otherwise indicated.
5. Unless otherwise indicated, the domain of a given function f is the set of all real numbers for which $f(x)$ is a real number.

REFERENCE

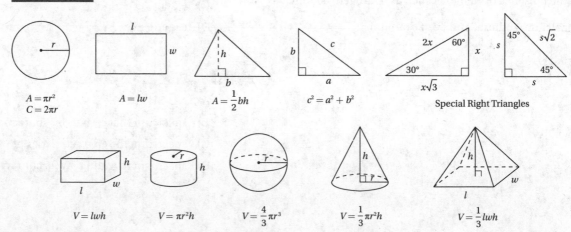

The number of degrees of arc in a circle is 360.
The number of radians of arc in a circle is 2π.
The sum of the measures in degrees of the angles of a triangle is 180.

CONTINUE

3   **3**

1

If $2x - 3y = 9$ and $y = 3$, then what is the value of x ?

A) 0

B) 3

C) 6

D) 9

2

$$x - y = -4$$
$$x - 2y = -6$$

Which of the following ordered pairs (x, y) satisfies the system of equations above?

A) $(-2, 2)$

B) $(-2, 4)$

C) $(4, 8)$

D) $(4, -8)$

3

An information technology company estimates the cost of a project, in dollars, using the expression $240 + 3nt$, where n is the number of computer servers working on the project and t is the total time, in hours, the project will take using n servers. Which of the following is the best interpretation of the number 3 in the expression?

A) Each server costs the company $3 per hour to run.

B) A minimum of 3 servers will work on the project.

C) The price of the project increases by $3 every hour.

D) Each server can work 3 hours per day.

4

If $\frac{5}{8}x = -\frac{1}{16}$, what is the value of x ?

A) $-\frac{11}{16}$

B) $-\frac{1}{10}$

C) $-\frac{5}{128}$

D) $\frac{9}{16}$

5

$$a^4 - 6a^2 + 10$$

Which of the following is equivalent to the expression shown above?

A) $(a^2 - 2)(a^2 - 5)$

B) $(a^2 - 1)(a^2 - 10)$

C) $(a^2 + 3)^2 + 1$

D) $(a^2 - 3)^2 + 1$

6

In triangle ABC, angle C has a measure of $90°$. If $\sin A = 0.6$, what is the value of $\cos B$?

A) 0.3

B) 0.4

C) 0.6

D) 0.8

CONTINUE →

7

$$\sqrt{m^2 - 13} - x = 0$$

If $m < 0$ and $x = 6$ in the equation above, what is the value of m ?

A)　−13

B)　−10

C)　−7

D)　−3

8

If $\dfrac{x^b}{x^a} = 16$ and $x^{-2} = \dfrac{1}{16}$, what is the value of $b - a$?

A)　−2

B)　2

C)　4

D)　8

9

b	2	4	6	8
$f(b)$	1	25	65	121

The table above shows ordered pairs that satisfy the function f. Which of the following could define f ?

A)　$f(b) = 3b^2 - 2$

B)　$f(b) = 3b^2 - 4$

C)　$f(b) = 2b^2 - 7$

D)　$f(b) = 2b^2$

10

The equation $y = kx - 1$, where k is a constant, describes a line in the xy-plane. If the graph of this line contains the point (a, b), where a and b are nonzero, what is the value of k in terms of a and b ?

A)　$\dfrac{b + 1}{a}$

B)　$\dfrac{b - 1}{a}$

C)　$\dfrac{a}{b + 1}$

D)　$\dfrac{a}{b - 1}$

11

The equation $\dfrac{12x^2 + 6x - 23}{bx - 3} = -2x - \dfrac{23}{bx - 3}$

is true for all values of $x \neq \dfrac{3}{b}$, where b is a constant.

What is the value of b ?

A)　−12

B)　−6

C)　4

D)　6

12

If h and k are functions such that $h(x) = x + 3$ and $h(g(2)) = 9$, which of the following could describe $g(x)$?

A)　$x^2 + 2$

B)　$x^2 + 3$

C)　$x^2 + 4$

D)　$x^2 + 5$

CONTINUE

3   **3**

13

$$y = a(x + 3)(x - 1)$$

In the quadratic function above, a is a nonzero constant. The graph of the equation in the xy-plane is a parabola with vertex (m, n). Which of the following is equal to n ?

A)   0

B) $-a$

C) $-2a$

D) $-4a$

14

$$x^2 - 2ax + b = 0$$

In the equation above, a and b are constants. If this equation is solved for x, there are two solutions. What is the sum of these two solutions?

A) $2a$

B) $-2a$

C) b

D) $-b$

15

Which of the following can represent the graph in the xy-plane of $y = a(x - b)(x + c)^2$, where a, b, and c are all positive constants?

A)

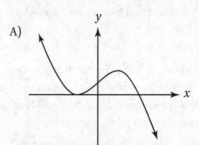

B)

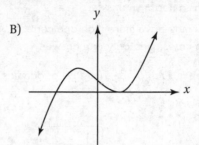

C)

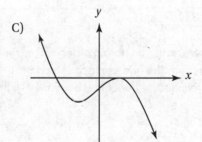

D)

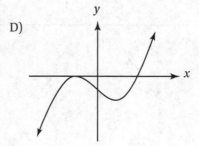

CONTINUE

3   **3**

DIRECTIONS

For questions **16–20,** solve the problem and enter your answer in the grid, as described below, on the answer sheet.

1. Although not required, it is suggested that you write your answer in the boxes at the top of the columns to help you fill in the circles accurately. You will receive credit only if the circles are filled in correctly.

2. Mark no more than one circle in any column.

3. No question has a negative answer.

4. Some problems may have more than one correct answer. In such cases, grid only one answer.

5. **Mixed numbers** such as $3\frac{1}{2}$ must be gridded as 3.5 or $\frac{7}{2}$.

   (If $3\frac{1}{2}$ is entered into the grid as ![grid showing 3 1 / 2], it will be interpreted as $\frac{31}{2}$, not $3\frac{1}{2}$.)

6. **Decimal answers:** If you obtain a decimal answer with more digits than the grid can accommodate, it may be either rounded or truncated, but it must fill the entire grid.

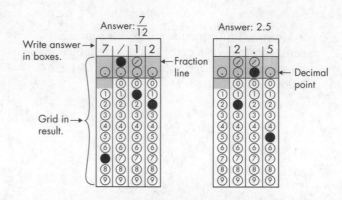

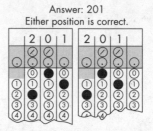

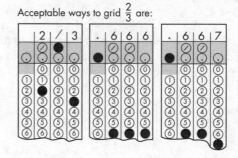

Acceptable ways to grid $\frac{2}{3}$ are:

CONTINUE

3 **3**

16

At a restaurant, each large order of fries has 350 more calories than one large soda. If 2 large orders of fries and 3 large sodas have a total of 1,500 calories, how many calories does one large order of fries have?

17

If $a = 4\sqrt{2}$ and $2a = \sqrt{2b}$, what is the value of b?

18

$$x + \frac{36}{x} = 12$$

If $x > 0$, what is the solution to the equation above?

19

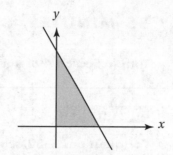

Note: Figure not drawn to scale.

$$x \geq 0$$
$$y \geq 0$$
$$3x + y \leq k$$

In the figure above, the shaded region represents the solution set for the system of inequalities shown. If the area of this shaded region is 24 square units, what is the value of k?

20

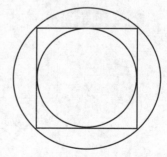

In the figure above, a circle is inscribed in a square that is inscribed in a larger circle. If the area of the larger circle is 16.5 square units, what is the area of the smaller circle?

STOP

If you finish before time is called, you may check your work on this section only.
Do not turn to any other section of the test.

Math Test – Calculator

55 MINUTES, 38 QUESTIONS

Turn to Section 4 of your answer sheet to answer the questions in this section.

DIRECTIONS

For questions 1–30, solve each problem, choose the best answer from the choices provided, and fill in the corresponding circle on your answer sheet. **For questions 31–38,** solve the problem and enter your answer in the grid on the answer sheet. Please refer to the directions before question 31 on how to enter you answers in the grid. You may use any available space in your test booklet for scratch work.

NOTES

1. The use of a calculator is permitted.

2. All variables and expressions used represent real numbers unless otherwise indicated.

3. Figures provided in this test are drawn to scale unless otherwise indicated.

4. All figures lie in a plane unless otherwise indicated.

5. Unless otherwise indicated, the domain of a given function f is the set of all real numbers for which $f(x)$ is a real number.

REFERENCE

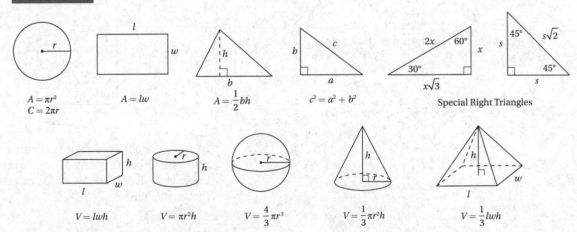

The number of degrees of arc in a circle is 360.
The number of radians of arc in a circle is 2π.
The sum of the measures in degrees of the angles of a triangle is 180.

CONTINUE ▶

4 **4**

1

A multiple-choice math test consists of 50 questions. Every student earns 2 points for each correct answer, −0.25 points for each incorrect answer, and 0 points for each question left unanswered. If a student answers 40 questions and gets 32 of them correct, how many points does the student earn?

A) 61.5

B) 62.0

C) 62.5

D) 64.0

2

If the average of 3, 5, and m is 10, what is the value of m ?

A)   2

B)   6

C) 12

D) 22

3

If $3b + 4 = -1$, what is the value of $9b + 12$?

A) −8

B) −4

C) −3

D) −2

4

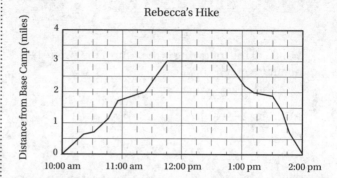

Rebecca's Hike

The graph above shows Rebecca's distance from her base camp as she hiked to a mountaintop, took a 1-hour break for lunch, and returned back to base camp. According to the graph, approximately how much longer was her hike to the mountaintop than her hike from the mountaintop back to base camp?

A) 20 minutes

B) 30 minutes

C) 45 minutes

D) 60 minutes

5

In the 2014 season, the Bombers baseball team had a win-to-loss ratio of 5:3, with no game ending in a tie. If the Bombers played 120 total games in 2014, how many games did they lose?

A) 24

B) 36

C) 45

D) 72

CONTINUE

6

$$3x^3 - 2x^2 + 5$$

$$5x^2 + x - 10$$

Which of the following is the sum of the two polynomials shown above?

A) $8x^3 - 2x - 5$

B) $3x^3 - x^2 - 5$

C) $3x^3 + 3x^2 + x - 5$

D) $8x^5 - x^3 - 5$

7

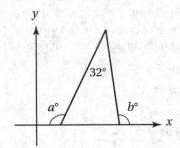

In the figure above, what is the value of $a + b$?

A) 212

B) 238

C) 296

D) 328

8

If $\dfrac{K + i}{i} = 1 - 2i$, where $i = \sqrt{-1}$, what is the value of K ?

A)   2

B) -2

C) $2 + i$

D) $-2 + i$

9

x	y
2	10
4	5
10	2

Based on the ordered pairs in the table above, which of the following could express the relationship between the variables x and y ?

A) y varies linearly with, but not directly as, x.

B) y varies directly as x.

C) y varies inversely as x.

D) y varies exponentially as x.

CONTINUE ➤

4   **4**

Questions 10–12 refer to the following information.

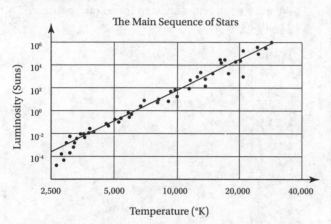

The Main Sequence of Stars

The scatterplot above charts the temperature (in degrees Kelvin) and luminosity (in Suns) for 50 stars, including our own sun, that fall under the category of "Main Sequence" stars.

10

The vertical axis indicates the luminosity of the stars in units called "Suns." (A Sun unit equals the luminosity of our own sun.) According to the scatterplot, which of the following is the best estimate for the temperature of our sun?

A)   2,600°K

B)   5,800°K

C)   10,100°K

D)   12,400°K

11

According to the line of best fit shown on the scatterplot, a Main Sequence star with a temperature of 10,000°K is approximately how many times as luminous as a Main Sequence star with a temperature of 5,000°K?

A)   9 times as luminous

B)   90 times as luminous

C)   900 times as luminous

D)   900,000 times as luminous

12

What percent of the stars represented in the scatterplot have a luminosity less than 0.0001 Sun?

A)   0.2%

B)   0.4%

C)   2%

D)   4%

CONTINUE

13

$$\frac{a + k}{b + k} = -2$$

Given the formula above, which of the following expresses k in terms of a and b ?

A) $\dfrac{-a - 2b}{3}$

B) $\dfrac{a - 2b}{3}$

C) $\dfrac{-a + 2b}{2}$

D) $\dfrac{a - 2b}{2}$

14

Which of the following functions, when graphed in the xy-plane, will intersect the x-axis exactly 3 times?

A) $f(x) = (x^2 + 1)(x^2 + 1)$

B) $f(x) = (x^2 - 1)(x^2 + 1)$

C) $f(x) = x^2(x^2 - 1)$

D) $f(x) = x^2(x^2 + 1)$

15

For how many distinct integer values of n is $(n + 2)(n + 8)$ negative?

A) Four

B) Five

C) Six

D) Seven

16

Lauren's car can travel d miles per gallon of gasoline. If she travels at a constant speed of s miles per hour, which of the following represents the number of hours she can travel on 6 gallons of gasoline?

A) $\dfrac{6d}{s}$

B) $\dfrac{6s}{d}$

C) $\dfrac{d}{6s}$

D) $\dfrac{s}{6d}$

17

$$\frac{2x + 1}{2y} = \frac{a}{b}$$

If a and b are non-zero constants in the linear equation above, what is the slope of this line when it is graphed in the xy-plane?

A) $\dfrac{b}{a}$

B) $\dfrac{b}{2a}$

C) $\dfrac{b + a}{2a}$

D) $\dfrac{b - a}{2a}$

CONTINUE ➡

4 **4**

Questions 18 and 19 refer to the following information.

$$P(t) = 250(2.4)^t$$

The formula above shows the relationship between the population, P, of a certain mushroom species on a one-acre plot of land as a function of t, the number of weeks that have passed since the mushrooms were first introduced on the plot.

18

What is the meaning of the number 250 in the formula above?

A) The plot initially contained 250 mushrooms.

B) The population of mushrooms increases by 250 mushrooms per week.

C) The population of mushrooms increases by 250% each week.

D) It will take 250 weeks for the population of mushrooms to double.

19

By what percent should we expect the mushroom population to increase between the start of week 6 and the start of week 7?

A)   40%

B)   140%

C)   240%

D)   480%

20

If $\dfrac{x^2 + 1}{2} + \dfrac{x}{p} = 1$, which of the following expressions gives both possible values of x, in terms of p?

A) $\dfrac{-p \pm \sqrt{p^2 - 8p}}{2p}$

B) $\dfrac{-p \pm \sqrt{p^2 - 4p}}{2p}$

C) $\dfrac{-2 \pm \sqrt{4 + 4p^2}}{2p}$

D) $\dfrac{-2 \pm \sqrt{4 - 4p^2}}{2p}$

21

If the variable a varies inversely as b, which of the following statements must be true?

A) $a + b$ is a constant.

B) $a - b$ is a constant.

C) $\dfrac{a}{b}$ is a constant.

D) ab is a constant.

CONTINUE

22

	Test positive for antibody	Test negative for antibody	Total
Antibody present	480	20	500
No antibody	5	495	500
Total	485	515	1,000

A researcher is studying the effectiveness of a method for testing the presence of an antibody in a patient's bloodstream. The table above shows the results of 1,000 patient trials. According to these data, what is the probability that a patient who has the antibody will nevertheless have a negative test result?

A) 0.01

B) 0.04

C) 0.05

D) 0.20

23

Class A: 68, 79, 88, 91, 97, 98, 99

Class B: 85, 85, 85, 88, 88, 90, 90

The lists above indicate the tests scores, in increasing order, for two of Mr. Pearlman's classes, each of which has 6 students. Which of the following correctly compares the standard deviation of the scores for each class?

A) The standard deviation of the scores in Class A is smaller.

B) The standard deviation of the scores in Class B is smaller.

C) The standard deviations of the scores in Class A and Class B are equal.

D) The relationship cannot be determined from the information given.

24

Mrs. Black has a bag of candy bars to hand out to the students in her class before they take their AP calculus BC exam. If she gives each student 3 candy bars, she will have 6 left over. In order to give each student 5 candy bars, she will need 50 more candy bars. How many students are in Mrs. Black's class?

A) 18

B) 27

C) 28

D) 44

25

The sum of three numbers is 240. If the greatest of these numbers is 50% more than the sum of the other two, what is the value of the greatest of these numbers?

A)   96

B) 120

C) 140

D) 144

26

In the xy-plane, points $A(2, 5)$ and $B(-12, k)$ lie on a line that has a slope of $-\dfrac{4}{7}$. What is the value of k?

A) 13

B) 16.5

C) 18

D) 29.5

CONTINUE ▶

4   **4**

27

The original price of an outboard motor was marked down by 30% for a week-long sale. Since the motor was not sold in the first week, it was marked down an additional p percent. If the total markdown from the original price was then 58%, what is the value of p ?

A) 12

B) 28

C) 40

D) 42

28

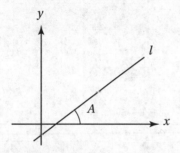

In the figure above, if $\cos A = 0.8$, what is the slope of line l ?

A) 0.60

B) 0.75

C) 0.90

D) 1.10

Questions 29 and 30 refer to the following information.

	Yes	No	Total
Males	150	90	240
Females	107	173	280
Total	255	265	520

The table above shows the results of a survey of 520 adults who were asked whether they approved of a recent state budget proposal.

29

If n of the females had voted yes instead of no, the ratio of yes votes to no votes would have been exactly the same for the females as for the males. What is the value of n ?

A) 62

B) 66

C) 68

D) 70

30

If this survey is representative of the entire voting population of a state in which 32,760 people are expected to vote on this budget referendum, how many males are expected to vote yes?

A)   9,450

B) 15,120

C) 19,270

D) 20,475

CONTINUE

4 **4**

Student-Produced Response Questions

DIRECTIONS

For questions 31–38, solve the problem and enter your answer in the grid, as described below, on the answer sheet.

1. Although not required, it is suggested that you write your answer in the boxes at the top of the columns to help you fill in the circles accurately. You will receive credit only if the circles are filled in correctly.

2. Mark no more than one circle in any column.

3. No question has a negative answer.

4. Some problems may have more than one correct answer. In such cases, grid only one answer.

5. **Mixed numbers** such as $3\frac{1}{2}$ must be gridded as 3.5 or $\frac{7}{2}$.

   (If $3\frac{1}{2}$ is entered into the grid as [3 1 / 2], it will be interpreted as $\frac{31}{2}$, not $3\frac{1}{2}$.)

6. **Decimal answers:** If you obtain a decimal answer with more digits than the grid can accommodate, it may be either rounded or truncated, but it must fill the entire grid.

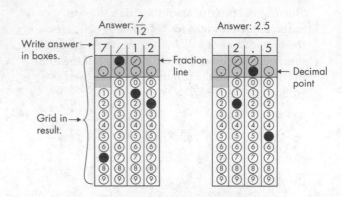

Answer: $\frac{7}{12}$ Answer: 2.5

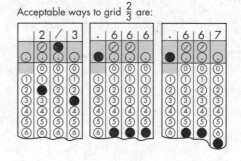

Answer: 201
Either position is correct.

Acceptable ways to grid $\frac{2}{3}$ are:

CONTINUE ▶

4　　　　　　**4**

31

If a shipment of fruit contains 6 tons of bananas, 4 tons of grapes, 2 tons of apples, and 3 tons of oranges, what fraction of the shipment, by weight, is oranges?

32

A state environmental study determines that the coastal regions of the state lose 24.5 acres of wetlands per month. At this rate, how many months will it take these coastal regions to lose a total of 343 acres?

33

$$d_n = 13n + 200$$

The formula above represents the number of donuts, d_n, that a bakery sold on the nth day of a festival. If the festival lasted 3 days, what was the total number of donuts that the bakery sold during the festival?

34

Connor and Joachim collaborated to write a computer program that consisted of 3,500 lines of code. If Joachim wrote 600 more lines of code than Connor did, how many lines of code did Connor write?

35

$$V(t) = 1000(1 + k)^m$$

An analyst wants to use the formula above to estimate the value, in dollars, of a $1,000 initial investment in a mutual fund after m quarters have passed. If a $1,000 initial investment in this fund is worth $1,102.50 after 2 quarters, what number should the analyst choose for k?

CONTINUE ➡

| 4 | **| 4 |**

36

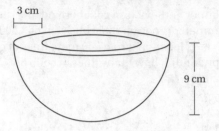

The figure above shows a hemispherical bowl made of glass. The bowl is 9 centimeters high and the glass is 3 centimeter thick. A second bowl is to be constructed to scale with the original bowl, but with one-half the height and diameter. The smaller bowl can hold a maximum of $k\pi$ cubic centimeters of water. What is the value of k? (The volume of a sphere with radius r is given by the formula $V = \frac{4}{3}\pi r^3$.)

Questions 37 and 38 refer to the following information.

$$I = \frac{FV}{(1 + r)^n}$$

The formula above indicates the initial investment, I, that must be made in an account with an annual interest rate of r to ensure a future value of FV after a period of n years.

37

To the nearest dollar, what initial investment should be made in an account that earns 20% annually ($r = 0.20$) in order to ensure a future value of \$432 in two years? (Ignore the \$ sign when gridding your answer. That is, enter \$125 as 125.)

38

What value of r, to the nearest thousandth, would ensure that the value of an investment would increase by 69% in 2 years?

STOP

If you finish before time is called, you may check your work on this section only.
Do not turn to any other section of the test.

5   **5**

Essay

50 MINUTES, 1 QUESTION

DIRECTIONS

As you read the passage below, consider how Eric Schwitzgebel uses

- evidence, such as facts or examples, to support claims
- reasoning to develop ideas and connect claims and evidence
- stylistic or persuasive elements, such as word choice or appeals to emotion, to add power to the ideas expressed

---

Adapted from Eric Schwitzgebel "We Have Greater Moral Obligations to Robots Than to Humans."
©2016 Aeon Media (Aeon.co). Originally published in *Aeon*, November 12, 2015.

1   Down goes HotBot 4b into the volcano. The year is 2050 or 2150, and artificial intelligence has advanced sufficiently that such robots can be built with human-grade intelligence, creativity and desires. HotBot will now perish on this scientific mission. Does it have rights? In commanding it to go down, have we done something morally wrong?

2   The moral status of robots is a frequent theme in science fiction, back at least to Isaac Asimov's robot stories, and the consensus is clear: if someday we manage to create robots that have mental lives similar to ours, with human-like plans, desires and a sense of self, including the capacity for joy and suffering, then those robots deserve moral consideration similar to that accorded to natural human beings. Philosophers and researchers on artificial intelligence who have written about this issue generally agree.

3   I want to challenge this consensus, but not in the way you might predict. I think that, if we someday create robots with human-like cognitive and emotional capacities, we owe them *more* moral consideration than we would normally owe to otherwise similar human beings.

4   Here's why: we will have been their creators and designers. We are thus directly responsible both for their existence and for their happy or unhappy state. If a robot needlessly suffers or fails to reach its developmental potential, it will be in substantial part because of our failure—a failure in our creation, design or nurturance of it. Our moral relation to robots will more closely resemble the relation that parents have to their children, or that gods have to the beings they create, than the relationship between human strangers.

5   In a way, this is no more than equality. If I create a situation that puts other people at risk—for example, if I destroy their crops to build an airfield—then I have a moral obligation to compensate them, greater than my obligation to people with whom I have no causal connection. If we create genuinely conscious robots, we are deeply causally connected to them, and so substantially responsible for their welfare. That is the root of our special obligation.

6   Frankenstein's monster says to his creator, Victor Frankenstein:

7   I am thy creature, and I will be even mild and docile to my natural lord and king, if thou wilt also perform thy part, the which thou owest me. Oh, Frankenstein, be not equitable to every other, and trample upon me alone, to whom thy justice, and even thy clemency and affection, is most due. Remember that I am thy creature: I ought to be thy Adam . . . .

8   We must either only create robots sufficiently simple that we know them not to merit moral consideration—as with all existing robots today—or we ought to bring them into existence only carefully and solicitously.

9   Alongside this duty to be solicitous comes another, of knowledge—a duty to know which of our creations are genuinely conscious. Which of them have real streams of subjective experience, and are capable of joy and suffering, or of cognitive achievements such as creativity and a sense of self? Without such knowledge, we won't know what obligations we have to our creations.

10   Yet how can we acquire the relevant knowledge? How does one distinguish, for instance, between a genuine stream of emotional experience and simulated emotions in an artificial mind? Merely programming a superficial simulation of emotion isn't enough. If I put a standard computer processor manufactured in 2015 into a toy dinosaur and program it to say "Ow!" when I press its off switch, I haven't created a robot capable of suffering. But exactly what kind of processing and complexity is necessary to give rise to genuine human-like consciousness? On some views—John Searle's, for example—consciousness might not be possible in *any* programmed entity; it might require a structure biologically similar to the human brain. Other views are much more liberal about the conditions sufficient for robot consciousness. The scientific study of consciousness is still in its infancy. The issue remains wide open.

11   If we continue to develop sophisticated forms of artificial intelligence, we have a moral obligation to improve our understanding of the conditions under which artificial consciousness might genuinely emerge. Otherwise we risk moral catastrophe—either the catastrophe of sacrificing our interests for beings that don't deserve moral consideration because they experience happiness and suffering only falsely, or the catastrophe of failing to recognize robot suffering, and so unintentionally committing atrocities tantamount to slavery and murder against beings to whom we have an almost parental obligation of care.

12   We have, then, a direct moral obligation to treat our creations with an acknowledgement of our special responsibility for their joy, suffering, thoughtfulness and creative potential. But we also have an epistemic obligation to learn enough about the material and functional bases of joy, suffering, thoughtfulness and creativity to know when and whether our potential future creations deserve our moral concern.

Write an essay in which you explain how Eric Schwitzgebel builds an argument to persuade his audience that we have strong moral obligations toward the intelligent machines we create. In your essay, analyze how he uses one or more of the features listed in the box above (or features of your own choice) to strengthen the logic and persuasiveness of his argument. Be sure that your analysis focuses on the most relevant features of the passage.

Your essay should NOT explain whether you agree with Schwitzgebel's claims, but rather explain how he builds an argument to persuade his audience.

SAT PRACTICE TEST 3 ANSWER KEY

Section 1: Reading	Section 2: Writing and Language	Section 3: Math (No Calculator)	Section 4: Math (Calculator)
1. D		1. D	1. B
2. A	1. C	2. A	2. D
3. D	2. C	3. A	3. C
4. C	3. D	4. B	4. B
5. C	4. D	5. D	5. C
6. B	5. B	6. C	6. C
7. C	6. C	7. C	7. A
8. A	7. A	8. B	8. A
9. C	8. D	9. C	9. C
10. A	9. D	10. A	10. B
11. B	10. C	11. B	11. C
12. D	11. A	12. A	12. D
13. D	12. D	13. D	13. A
14. B	13. D	14. A	14. C
15. A	14. A	15. D	15. B
16. A	15. B	-------	16. A
17. C	16. A	16. 510	17. A
18. C	17. C	17. 64	18. A
19. C	18. C	18. 6	19. B
20. B	19. A	19. 12	20. C
21. B	20. B	20. 8.25	21. D
22. D	21. B		22. B
23. C	22. C		23. B
24. A	23. D		24. C
25. A	24. A		25. D
26. A	25. B		26. A
27. B	26. A		27. C
28. B	27. A		28. B
29. C	28. D		29. C
30. C	29. D		30. A
31. A	30. D		----------------
32. A	31. B		31 .2 or 1/5
33. C	32. B		32. 14
34. B	33. C		33. 678
35. A	34. D		34. 1450
36. D	35. B		35. .05 or 1/20
37. B	36. A		36. 18
38. D	37. D		37. 300
39. D	38. C		38. .300
40. B	39. C		
41. D	40. D		
42. B	41. A		
43. D	42. D		
44. C	43. C		
45. B	44. C		
46. A			
47. C			
48. D			
49. A			
50. C			
51. A			
52. C			

Total Reading Points (Section 1)	Total Writing and Language Points (Section 2)	Total Math Points (Section 3)	Total Math Points (Section 4)

SCORE CONVERSION TABLE

Scoring Your Test

1. Use the answer key to mark your responses on each section.

2. Total the number of correct responses for each section:

    1. Reading Test   Number correct: _____ **(Reading Raw Score)**

    2. Writing and Language Test   Number correct: _____ **(Writing and Language Raw Score)**

    3. Mathematics Test – No Calculator   Number correct: _____

    4. Mathematics Test – Calculator   Number correct: _____

3. Add the raw scores for sections 3 and 4. This is your **Math Raw Score**: _____

4. Use the Table 1 to calculate your **Scaled Test and Section Scores (10–40)**.

    Math Section Score (200–800):   _____

    Reading Test Score (10–40):   _____

    Writing and Language Test Score (10–40):   _____

5. Add the **Reading Test Scaled Score** and the **Writing and Language Test Scaled Score** and multiply this sum by 10 to get your **Reading and Writing Test Section Score (20–80)**.

    Sum of Reading + Writing and Language Scores: _____ $\times$ 10 =

    Reading and Writing Section Score: _____

Table 1: Scaled Section and Test Scores (10–40)

Raw Score	Math Section Score	Reading Test Score	Writing/ Language Test Score	Raw Score	Math Section Score	Reading Test Score	Writing/ Language Test Score
58	800			29	520	27	28
57	790			28	520	26	28
56	780			27	510	26	27
55	760			26	500	25	26
54	750			25	490	25	26
53	740			24	480	24	25
52	730	40		23	480	24	25
51	710	40		22	470	23	24
50	700	39		21	460	23	23
49	690	38		20	450	22	23
48	680	38		19	440	22	22
47	670	37		18	430	21	21
46	670	37		17	420	21	21
45	660	36		16	410	20	20
44	650	35	40	15	390	20	19
43	640	35	39	14	380	19	19
42	630	34	38	13	370	19	18
41	620	33	37	12	360	18	17
40	610	33	36	11	340	17	16
39	600	32	35	10	330	17	16
38	600	32	34	9	320	16	15
37	590	31	34	8	310	15	14
36	580	31	33	7	290	15	13
35	570	30	32	6	280	14	13
34	560	30	32	5	260	13	12
33	560	29	31	4	240	12	11
32	550	29	30	3	230	11	10
31	540	28	30	2	210	10	10
30	530	28	29	1	200	10	10

SAT PRACTICE TEST 3 DETAILED ANSWER KEY

Section 1: Reading

1. D   Purpose

The first sentence indicates what *proponents of recycling assume* (line 1), and the second sentence indicates what *opponents [of recycling] scrutinize* (lines 4–5). These sentences clearly *characterize opposing viewpoints*.

2. A   Interpretation

In saying *Environmentalists are not all ignorant anarchists, and opponents of recycling are not all rapacious blowhards* (lines 15–17), the author is establishing a counterpoint to the *demonization* (line 13) that plagues debates about recycling. Therefore, the author is indicating that the debaters tend to *mischaracterize their opponents*.

3. D   Meaning in Context

The *full life cycles of various materials* (lines 22–23) refers to how these materials are acquired, how they are used, and what happens to them after they have been used for industrial purposes. That is, the *processes that affect the substances used in manufacturing*.

4. C   Word in Context

The phrase *inserting some natural resources into a responsible "industrial cycle"* (lines 50–52) refers to the process of using materials in industry rather than conserving them. This is a process of introducing those materials into an industrial process.

5. C   Cross-Textual Inference

Passage 2 discusses the problem of quantifying the benefits of *natural ecosystems*. It mentions several such benefits, such as *biodiversity, the filtration of groundwater, the maintenance of the oxygen and nitrogen cycles, and climate stability* (lines 70–72). Therefore, *water filtration* (line 29) is clearly among these benefits.

6. B   Inference

The author of Passage 1 asks several questions that he regards to be essential to a thorough analysis of environmental policy, such as *Are any materials being imported from countries with irresponsible labor or environmental practices* (lines 36–38)? This indicates that the author disapproves of *irresponsible labor practices* such as slave or child labor. Although it may seem reasonable to think that the author of Passage 1 would support tax incentives

for recycling, limits on acid rain emissions, and public investment in sustainable domestic energy sources, there is no **textual evidence** in Passage 1 to support any contention that he, in fact, endorses such policies. In fact, the focus on Passage 1 is on the character of the debate about environmental policy, rather than on advocating any particular position.

7. C   Textual Evidence

As the explanation to the previous question indicates, the best evidence is found in lines 36–38.

8. A   Graphical Analysis

This pie graph shows the destination of U.S. solid municipal waste in 2012. It shows that 34.5% of this waste was *recycled or composted*, and therefore, it shows the scale of the *recycling programs* discussed in Passage 1.

9. C   Cross-Textual Inference

The *clear exchange* mentioned in line 75 refers to the exchange with *bought-and-sold commodities* (lines 72–73), that is, financial expenditures. The only choice from Passage 1 that indicates a financial expenditure is the *maintenance cost* mentioned in line 42.

10. A   Content Analysis

Passage 1 focuses on the character of the debate between *proponents of recycling* (line 1) and their *opponents* (line 4). It refers to particular aspects of that debate, for example, the negative effects of the *demonization* (line 13) that each side uses to characterize its opponents. This demonization is a *rhetorical strategy*, that is, a persuasive technique.

11. B   Purpose

Passage 2 compares the viewpoints of environmentalists and industrialists in lines 104–108: *Environmentalists argue that we cannot possibly put a price on the smell of heather and a cool breeze, while industrialists argue that the task is speculative, unreliable, and an impediment to economic progress.* Previously in the passage, the author indicated that the act of *put[ting] a price on the smell of heather and a cool breeze* is known as quantifying *"externalities"* (line 77). The point in this sentence, therefore, is that *careful examination of externalities is controversial*, and the balance of the passage makes it clear that the author believes that this examination is *necessary* as well.

12. D   **Purpose**

In this story, the narrator describes a person who had *been in the area a long time* (line 1), and whom she had seen in many places, but had never spoken to. He was a mystery to the town—a *monastic stranger* (line 11). She describes the many hypotheses that she and the other citizens of the town had about the man and his history. Finally, in the last sentences, she meets the man and hears him speak.

13. D   **Inference**

The many stories about the stranger and his origins—for instance, that he was a *Vietnam vet* (line 9) or a *Somalian refugee* (lines 12-3)—were told with increasing confidence, even though they were contradictory: *Eventually, the qualifying "maybes" and "perhaps" were dropped, and fiction was passed as fact* (lines 14-16).

14. B   **Textual Evidence**

As the explanation to the previous question indicates, the best evidence is in lines 14–16.

15. A   **Meaning in Context**

The question *Had the earth become a molten sea, a hardened moonscape surface?* (lines 24-25) is part of a series of questions about the mysterious man's past, all of which imagine that he had seen *unspeakable things* (line 18) and had received the *scar of war* (line 23). This context makes clear that this reference is to a *desolate aftermath* of war.

16. A   **Word in Context**

The phrase *the character of a word in Japanese* (lines 59-60) refers to the written *kanji* symbols in Japanese, each of which represents a word. The point here is that the mysterious stranger resembled a kanji character.

17. C   **Inference**

In this paragraph, the narrator says of the stranger that *our paths crossed and converged daily* (lines 30-31) and goes on to give several examples. Her point is that the stranger seemed to be everywhere, so these encounters are notable for their *ubiquity* (quality of appearing everywhere).

18. C   **Stylistic Analysis**

The narrator describes the stranger as *a crane* (lines 20 and 52) and *a black crow* (line 62). These are *avian* (bird-related) *metaphors*. Although the narrator speculates that the stranger is from a war-torn land, she does not use any *military comparisons* to describe his physical characteristics. Likewise, the passage does not use any *literary allusions* or *exaggerated juxtapositions* to describe his physical appearance.

19. C   **Meaning in Context**

This paragraph (lines 17-29) describes the author's speculation that the stranger is from a war-torn land. She indicates what she "knew" about his situation: that he *had run barefoot . . . through the rice paddies of Vietnam*, that *the earth [had] become a molten sea*, and so on. Therefore, the phrase *what we would all come to know* most likely refers to the *inhumanity of war*.

20. B   **Meaning in Context**

When the narrator says that the stranger *seemed to journey momentarily out of that dark place* (lines 74-75), she is explaining how *his look was clear, not shrouded with darkness not veiled with otherness as I had come to expect* (lines 72-74). The *darkness* here is the presumed trauma that she imagines he must have experienced. Therefore, the journey the narrator believes he has taken is *from grim memory to current experience*.

21. B   **Inference**

The narrator makes it clear that she *had come to expect* (lines 73-74) the stranger to exude *darkness* (line 73) and *otherness* (line 73). Therefore, when the stranger greets her in a casual, upbeat way, she must have expressed *surprised relief*.

22. D   **Characterization**

The author states that the *exodus of women to the cities* (line 1) has *ameliorated* (improved) *the customs and diversified the streets* (lines 5-6). These are *transformative* effects.

23. C   **Inference**

The author states that *New York women, and perhaps city women in general . . . are much more independent . . . and more original in their methods than women in smaller places* (lines 7-11). In other words, rural women are less *innovative*.

24. A   **Textual Evidence**

As the explanation to the previous question indicates, the best evidence is in lines 7-13.

25. A   **Inference**

In lines 24-26, the author states that *She accepts the situation [of her poverty] with the greatest good-humor and makes herself more acceptable to the old set by relating her discouragements*. In other words, she considers her poverty a *challenge to be embraced*.

26. A　　　　　　　　　　　　　　　**Textual Evidence**

As the explanation to the previous question indicates, the best evidence is in lines 24–28.

27. B　　　　　　　　　　　　　　　**Word in Context**

The phrase *done with a certain dash, élan, and sweeping air* means *done with a certain flair*.

28. B　　　　　　　　　　　　　　　**Meaning in Context**

The sentence she *makes herself more acceptable to the old set by relating her discouragements, trials, and mistakes so comically that she is better company than before* (lines 25–28) indicates that the *old set* is a group of people that the woman knew before she moved to the city; therefore this group is a set of *established acquaintances*.

29. C　　　　　　　　　　　　　　　**Inference**

The passage states that the city woman *who is occupied with daily work needs greater freedom of movement, more isolation, more personal comforts, and the exemption, moreover, from being agreeable at all times and places* (lines 33–37). She also wants to *extend hospitalities* (lines 49–50) in her own home. Therefore, the author is saying that city women want to maintain their own homes primarily because *they require living conditions conducive to their social independence*. Choice (A) is incorrect because this passage is specifically about city women who have careers. Choice (B) is incorrect because, although the author indicates that one aspect of *constructing homes* is the *male realization that the home is the proper stimulus to achievement* (lines 47–48), she does not make any claims about homes helping women to *maintain a social status comparable to that of men*. Choice (D) is incorrect because the passage doesn't indicate anything about the city woman doing work in the home, but rather retreating to her home for relaxation after work.

30. C　　　　　　　　　　　　　　　**Thesis**

The thesis of the passage is that *the social independence of women* (specifically, their ability to move to cities and have careers) *corresponds to their desire to own and maintain a home*. Choice (A) is incorrect because the passage does not discuss *unfair expectations* of women. Choice (B) is incorrect because the passage does not discuss *housekeeping* as a *traditional female duty*, but rather a modern sign of female independence. Choice (D) is incorrect because, although the passage does mention that city women are creative and hardworking; this is not the main thesis of the passage as a whole.

31. A　　　　　　　　　　　　　　　**Meaning in Context**

When the author states that a woman needs the *exemption . . . from being agreeable at all times and places*

(lines 36–37), she means that city women with careers should not feel obliged to always pretend to be happy around others when they are not. Therefore, this exemption is *a reprieve from a social obligation*.

32. A　　　　　　　　　　　　　　　**Purpose**

The second paragraph (lines 8–22) discusses how viruses have long been characterized as *dangerous invaders* (line 9). However, the rest of the passage discusses the great promise that viruses hold, through immunotherapy and virotherapy, in curing diseases rather than causing them. Therefore, this paragraph serves to *relate a point of view toward viruses that contrasts with that adopted by modern microbiologists*.

33. C　　　　　　　　　　　　　　　**Inference**

The second paragraph mentions HIV as an example of a viral disease that could possibly be treated by vaccination, which *trains our immune system to produce antibodies that shield us from future infections*. In lines 96–100, the passage discusses a study showing that lymphoblastic leukemia can be particularly responsive to immunotherapy. Therefore, HIV and leukemia are both illnesses that *can be treated by reinforcing the immune system*. Although choice (A) may seem tempting, the passage makes it clear that vaccinations and immunotherapy work by different mechanisms than does virotherapy.

34. B　　　　　　　　　　　　　　　**Meaning in Context**

The sentence *Vaccinations are the major successes on this front* means that vaccinations are the major successes in this *campaign* [*against viral diseases*].

35. A　　　　　　　　　　　　　　　**Integrated Inference**

The diagram illustrates how engineered viruses used in virotherapy affect normal cells and cancer cells differently. It shows that relatively few of these viruses infect normal cells because of the *poor viral receptivity* of those cells. The passage indicates that the process by which viruses enter cells requires a *"lock-and-key" mechanism* (line 34) by which molecules on this virus shell match up with molecules on the surface of the cell.

36. D　　　　　　　　　　　　**Inference/Graphical Analysis**

The diagram illustrates *T-cell attack* on the bottom right, where the immune response (directed by T-cells as discussed in lines 80–84) attacks cells or viruses. It also illustrates *lysis* (lines 69–77) at the bottom center of the diagram, where it shows a cell breaking apart from overwhelming viral infection. It also illustrates *selective infection* by showing that more viruses infect the cancer cells than infect the normal cells. It does not, however, show *apoptosis* (lines 73–76), the process by which cells commit suicide.

37. B   **Graphical Analysis**

The bottom right of the diagram illustrates how *viral activity* sometimes *triggers anti-viral immune response*, thereby destroying the viruses before they can kill the tumor cells. This illustrates one potential drawback that could compromise the effectiveness of virotherapy as a cancer treatment: *the immune system may eliminate the viruses before they have a chance to destroy the cancer cell.*

38. D   **Inference**

In lines 85–90, the passage states that *one pernicious aspect of cancer is its ability to "cloak" itself from the immune system* and to evolve *proteins that kill T-cells* so that the immune system can't attack the cancer effectively. In other words, the human immune system *is thwarted by chemical defenses that cancer cells have developed.*

39. D   **Textual Evidence**

As the explanation to the previous question indicates, the best evidence is in lines 85–88.

40. B   **Meaning in Context**

The *attempts to replicate this success* (line 47) are attempts to use the rabies vaccine to kill a cancerous tumor. That is, it refers to a *therapeutic repetition*.

41. D   **Textual Evidence**

Lines 77–80 mention a way that viruses can destroy cancer cells without directly infecting them: they *can be programmed to selectively attack the blood vessels that supply nutrients to a tumor . . . and kill the cancer by starvation*.

42. B   **Inference**

The *precision* mentioned in line 59, as explained in the previous sentence, is the ability of viruses to selectively infect cancer cells and to leave healthy cells alone. The paragraph as a whole is discussing the *powerful tools . . . for manipulating the very genetic code that produces some of those molecules [that control the interactions between cells and viruses]*. Therefore, the paragraph is suggesting that *genetic manipulation* is the key to this kind of *precision*.

43. D   **Thesis**

The author begins the passage by ruminating about *the inner life of animals* (line 2). He then goes on to show how animals *do in fact have complex emotional lives* (lines 7–8). From the third paragraph onward, the passage

focuses on the fact that *we hominids [who share common ancestors with these other animals] had to feel before we could think* (lines 24–25), and how our emotions affect our thinking and enable us to build and manage large social groups. Therefore, the thesis of the passage as a whole is that *we cannot understand human intelligence without first understanding animal intelligence*.

44. C   **Purpose**

The series of statements—<u>*fear*</u> *keeps animals away from predators,* <u>*lust*</u> *draws them toward each other,* <u>*panic*</u> *motivates their social solidarity, and* <u>*care*</u> *glues their parent-offspring bonds* (lines 18–21)—is intended to indicate more precisely how *animals have complex emotional lives* (lines 7–8) because emotion *helps them navigate their outer life* (lines 22–23) just as it does for humans. Therefore, the series of italicized words represents *increasingly human sentiments*.

45. B   **Meaning in Context**

The statement that *our cognitive brains work only when our emotions tilt our deliberations* means that our emotions *sway (influence)* our rational thought processes.

46. A   **Purpose**

Antonio Damasio's work described in lines 32–35 shows how damage to the emotional systems of the brain can compromise decision-making. Since this discovery contradicts long-held beliefs about the distinction between reason and emotion, it *highlights a surprising discovery about the function of emotions in human thinking*.

47. C   **Inference**

The phrase *those early days* (line 39) refers to the *Pleistocene epoch* (line 24) mentioned in the previous paragraph, when our hominid ancestors lived and were evolving modern human brains. Therefore, this phrase refers to *the epoch in which our ancestors were developing the ability to think*.

48. D   **Meaning in Context**

The sentence in lines 56–60 indicates that the process of *natural selection* needs a stable environment over a long period of time in order to *sculpt each module to fit our perennial environmental challenges*. This evolutionary process by natural selection is a *gradual process*.

49. A   **Meaning in Context**

The statement that *the expansion of the brain corresponds with an increasingly adaptable mind* means that as the human brain evolved to become larger, it also became more adaptable: the two processes *coincided*.

50. C   **Purpose**

The sixth paragraph (lines 61–77) begins by stating that a *vital premise for this modular theory* is that the environment in which our ancestors evolved had to be *extremely stable* (lines 62–63). The paragraph then goes on to mention that *recent discoveries* (line 65) show that this environment was, in fact, *anything but stable* (line 67). Therefore, this paragraph is *refuting a scientific theory*.

51. A   **Inference**

In lines 67–69, the author states that *In fact, it was precisely this climate chaos*, and not the climate stability assumed by the modular theory, that *created our multi-purpose, problem-solving minds*. That is, the *variable conditions of the Pleistocene epoch* contradict an essential premise of the modular theory.

52. C   **Textual Evidence**

As the explanation to the previous question indicates, the best evidence is in lines 67–69.

Section 2: Writing and Language

1. C   **Coordination**

This sentence coordinates two contrasting claims, so the contrasting conjunction *Although* is most appropriate.

2. C   **Parallelism**

This sentence contains a list, so the items in that list should have the same grammatical form. Since the first two items, *the safety of our drinking water* and *the reliability of our roads*, each has the form *[definite article] [quality noun][prepositional phrase]*, only choice (C), *the usability of our smartphones*, has the same form.

3. D   **Graphical Analysis**

Choice (A) is incorrect because the graph does not show *all engineering fields*, and only indicates predictions for the next 10 years, not *for the foreseeable future*. Choice (B) is incorrect because the largest growth shown in the graph is 25%, which is not even close to doubling. Choice (C) is incorrect because the graph shows only growth, and no *stagnation*. Choice (D) is correct because *some engineering fields*, namely biomedical and petroleum, are expected to grow by more than 25% over the next 10 years.

4. D   **Parallelism**

This sentence includes a list and, therefore, must follow the Law of Parallelism. Since the other two phrases in the list are gerund phrases, the underlined phrase must also be a gerund phrase. This eliminates choices (A) and (C). Choice (B) is incorrect because standard idiom requires the adverb *merely* rather than the adjective *mere*.

5. B   **Coordination/Voice**

The underlined clause must coordinate grammatically and logically with the clause that follows. The subject of the clause that follows, *many [engineering careers]*, does not work unless the subject of the underlined clause also includes *engineering careers*. This eliminates choices (A) and (C). Choice (D) is incorrect because parallelism between the clauses involves the indicative mood, *require*, rather than the subjunctive mood, *would require*.

6. C   **Redundancy**

The phrase *make products out of [raw materials]* indicates a transformative process, so the original phrasing is redundant. Choices (B) and (D) are also redundant. Choice (C) is concise and effective.

7. A   **Effective Expression**

The original phrasing is best. Choice (B) is incorrect because the verb *impact* disagrees with the subject *activity*. Choice (C) is incorrect because it is not a noun phrase. Choice (D) is incorrect because it is not idiomatic.

8. D   **Parallelism**

Parallelism requires the phrasing *to solve . . . and to see*.

9. D   **Coordination/Pronoun Consistency**

The pronoun *they* is inconsistent with the phrase *many of us*. The colon is appropriate because the second clause explains the first.

10. C   **Logic/Cohesiveness**

This sentence belongs immediately after sentence 2 because it indicates a specific way in which *enthusiasm is often destroyed by schooling*. It belongs before sentence 3 because it specifies the *problem* that needs to be solved.

11. A   **Transitions/Cohesiveness**

The original phrasing provides the most logical and effective transition because it mentions the *need to make engineering fun* discussed in the previous paragraph, and connects it to the reason provided in the sentence that follows.

12. D   **Verb Tense**

This sentence is referring to a general quality about *American voters*, so the verb should be in the simple present tense in order to indicate the habitual aspect.

13. **D**   **Clear Expression of Ideas/Parallelism**

Parallelism requires that this be a list of quality nouns: *looks*, *personality*, and *reputation*.

---

14. **A**   **Verb Tense**

The original phrasing is best. The participle takes the consequential aspect because it indicates a status affected by a previous action.

---

15. **B**   **Parallelism**

This is a list of infinitive phrases: *to identify . . . to study . . . and to determine*.

---

16. **A**   **Coordination**

The interrupting modifier must have the same punctuation before and after—in this case, dashes.

---

17. **C**   **Effective Expression/Diction**

The sentence that follows says that we *shouldn't fall for such transparently dishonest tactics*, thereby implying that it is a problem if these techniques are too *effectual*.

---

18. **C**   **Modifier Errors/Idiom**

The original phrasing is incorrect because the clause *we must learn* is not logically modified by the prepositional phrase *instead of us*. The proper comparison requires a participial phrase to modify the main clause: *Instead of listening . . . we must learn*.

---

19. **A**   **Coordination**

The original phrasing provides the most logical transition because this sentence describes a proposed action to achieve the goal described in the previous sentence.

---

20. **B**   **Development/Cohesiveness**

This sentence belongs immediately after sentence 1 because it refers directly to the *understanding* of the issues mentioned in sentence 1.

---

21. **B**   **Diction**

The context requires the possessive pronoun *whose* rather than the contraction *who's [who is]*.

---

22. **C**   **Development/Cohesiveness**

This sentence detracts from the paragraph's focus on the *interests* that the candidates represent rather than their need for publicity.

---

23. **D**   **Clear Expression/Dangling Modifiers**

The underlined clause must coordinate with the modifying phrase that starts the sentence. Since the *source*

of both inspiration and relaxation is sports, not *human cultures*, choices (A) and (B) are incorrect. Since the sentence indicates a status due to a previous state of being, the present tense, consequential aspect is required, as in choice (D).

---

24. **A**   **Clear Expression/Diction**

Since the topic sentence refers to athletes as *our greatest icons*, the topic of this paragraph is the *renown [popularity]* of athletes.

---

25. **B**   **Pronoun-Antecedent Agreement/Logic**

This phrase must coordinate with the rest of the sentence, which uses the pronoun *him* to refer specifically to Spartacus. Only choice (B) provides the correct subject.

---

26. **A**   **Cohesiveness**

The original phrasing is the only option that extends the idea of the sentence, which is that people spend a lot of time and effort worshipping athletes.

---

27. **A**   **Idiom**

The proper idioms are *regard as* and *consider to be*. The only choice that is idiomatically correct is choice (A).

---

28. **D**   **Logical Coordination**

The predicate that follows this word indicates a consequence of *squander[ing] precious brain power on trivialities*. Therefore, this adverb should indicate a consequence, as with choice (D).

---

29. **D**   **Diction/Clear Expression**

The point the author is making here is that *idol worship* causes harm to our *moral fabric*. The best choice to indicate this effect is (D), *degrades*.

---

30. **D**   **Tone/Style**

The passage has a moralizing tone and a formal style. Choice (D) best matches this tone and style.

---

31. **B**   **Commas/Parallelism**

This sentence uses the parallel idiom *either A or B*. Choice (B) is the only one that uses parallel form as well as proper idiom.

---

32. **B**   **Coherence/Development**

This is an appropriate addition here because it *describes the impact that sports injuries can have on the athletes' lives* and supports the main idea of the paragraph, which is that idol worship in sport *doesn't even seem to help the vast majority of the athletes themselves*.

33. C   **Parallelism**

Parallelism requires the phrasing *usually for little pay, but often with as much skill*. Notice that both phrases are prepositional phrases.

34. D   **Diction/Clear Expression**

This word *sufficed* is illogical here because this sentence does not indicate that stars served any specific need for these cultures. Stars cannot *perform* as omens, because they are not people or mechanisms. Rather, they *served* as omens to ancient cultures.

35. B   **Idiom/Misplaced Modifiers**

In the original phrasing the idiom *beckon for* is used illogically, and the modifier *long* is misplaced. Choice (B) is the only choice that avoids both of these problems.

36. A   **Coordination**

The original phrasing best establishes the contrast between the two clauses in this sentence. Choice (B) indicates a contrast, but the wrong one: it implies a contrast between the *previous* sentence and this one, rather than between the two ideas within this sentence.

37. D   **Logic/Verb Mood**

The point in this sentence is that these objects of astronomical study are very far away. They are so far away that *we could never hope* to send probes there. The other phrasings create illogical statements.

38. C   **Development/Logical Cohesiveness**

This sentence should not be deleted, because this question *provides a logical transition to the discussion of inferential methods that follows*. The paragraph that follows answers this question very nicely.

39. C   **Dangling Modifiers/Voice/**
Logical Comparisons

The sentence clearly intends to compare *stars* to *other objects of fascination*. This requires that the subject of the underlined clause be *stars*. This eliminates choices (A) and (B). Choice (D) is incorrect because the phrase in *observation* is not idiomatic.

40. D   **Coordination**

Choice (D) most effectively joins the ideas in a logical temporal sequence.

41. A   **Cohesiveness/Development**

The original phrasing matches the expository and measured tone of the passage, and adds a specific detail supporting the idea that much astronomical information is gathered indirectly.

42. D   **Pronoun-Antecedent Agreement/Commas**

The original phrasing is incorrect because the pronoun *their* disagrees in number with its antecedent *light*. Choice (B) is incorrect for the same reason. Choice (C) is incorrect because the context requires the possessive form *its* rather than the contraction *it's [it is]*.

43. C   **Diction/Clear Expression**

The point of this sentence is that the amount of the redshift in the light indicates how far the light has traveled. In other words, the *extent of this redshifting tells astronomers how far away the star is (or was)*.

44. C   **Idiom**

This sentence discusses how the *characteristics of the spectrum* indicate the size and composition of the star. Choice (C) is the only one that uses the proper idiom for this prepositional phrase.

Section 3: Math (No Calculator)

1. D   **Algebra (solving equations) EASY**

Original equation:	$2x - 3y = 9$
Substitute $y = 3$:	$2x - 3(3) = 9$
Simplify:	$2x - 9 = 9$
Add 9:	$2x = 18$
Divide by 2:	$x = 9$

2. A   **Algebra (linear systems) EASY**

Original system:
$$x - y = -4$$
$$x - 2y = -6$$

Subtract corresponding sides of equation:
$$(x - y) - (x - 2y) = -4 - (-6)$$

Simplify: $y = 2$

Substitute $y = 2$ into first equation to find x: $x - 2 = -4$

Add 2: $x = -2$

Therefore the ordered pair is $(-2, 2)$.

3. A   **Algebra (interpreting formulas)**
EASY-MEDIUM

One way to analyze a formula is by "dimensional analysis." This is simply a way to check that the units in the formula represent what they are supposed to represent. For instance, we are told that the expression $240 + 3nt$ represents the cost, *in dollars*, of the project. This means that both terms in this expression must be in *dollars*. Notice, also, that n is the number of *servers* and t is the number of *hours*. Let's use a ? to represent the units of the number 3 in the expression $3nt$. Translating the term into units, this gives us

$$(?)(\text{servers})(\text{hours}) = \$$$

Divide by (servers)(hours): $? =$

$$\frac{\$}{\text{server} \times \text{hour}} = \text{dollars per hour per server}$$

In other words, it costs the company 3 dollars per hour per server.

---

4. **B** **Algebra (linear equations) EASY**

$$\frac{5}{8}x = -\frac{1}{16}$$

Multiply by 16 (the common denominator): $10x = -1$
Divide by 10: $x = -1/10$

---

5. **D** **Advanced Mathematics (multiplying polynomials) EASY-MEDIUM**

The simplest way to approach this problem is to "expand" the choices to see which one yields an expression that is equivalent to the original expression. You must remember how to FOIL (Chapter 9, Lesson 4) when multiplying two binomials:

(A) $(a^2 - 2)(a^2 - 5) = a^4 - 5a^2 - 2a^2 + 10 =$
$a^4 - 7a^2 + 10$
(Close, but no.)

(B) $(a^2 - 1)(a^2 - 10) = a^4 - 10a^2 - 1a^2 + 10 =$
$a^4 - 11a^2 + 10$
(Close, but no.)

(C) $(a^2 + 3)^2 + 1 = a^4 + 3a^2 + 3a^2 + 9 + 1 =$
$a^4 + 6a^2 + 10$
(Close, but no.)

(D) $(a^2 - 3)^2 + 1 = a^4 - 3a^2 - 3a^2 + 9 + 1 =$
$a^4 - 6a^2 + 10$
(Yes.)

---

6. **C** **Additional Topics (trigonometry) EASY**

It always helps to draw a diagram for geometry and trigonometry problems. For this problem, we also have to remember the basic definitions of the trigonometric functions discussed in Chapter 10, Lesson 9: SOH CAH TOA.

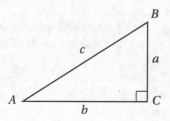

Since $\sin A = 0.6$, this means $a/c = 0.6$. Notice that $\cos B$ is also a/c, so it must also equal 0.6. This is an example of the **cofunction identity** we discussed in Chapter 10, Lesson 10.

---

7. **C** **Advanced Mathematics (rational equations) EASY-MEDIUM**

Original equation:	$\sqrt{m^2 - 13} - x = 0$
Substitute $x = 6$:	$\sqrt{m^2 - 13} - 6 = 0$
Add 6:	$\sqrt{m^2 - 13} = 6$
Square both sides:	$m^2 - 13 = 36$
Add 13:	$m^2 = 49$
Take the square root:	$m = \pm 7$

But since $m < 0$, $m = -7$.

---

8. **B** **Advanced Mathematics (exponents) MEDIUM**

$$x^{-2} = \frac{1}{16}$$

Substitute $x^{-2} = \frac{1}{x^2}$
(Law #3 from Chapter 9, Lesson 9): $\frac{1}{x^2} = \frac{1}{16}$

Cross-multiply: $x^2 = 16$
Take the square root: $x = \pm 4$

Recall the other equation: $\frac{x^b}{x^a} = 16$

Law #6 from Chapter 9, Lesson 9: $x^{b-a} = 16$
Substitute $x = \pm 4$: $(\pm 4)^{b-a} = 16$
Notice that both $4^2 = 16$ and
$(-4)^2 = 16$, therefore: $b - a = 2$

---

9. **C** **Advanced Mathematics (functions) MEDIUM**

This question asks us to find the function that is satisfied by all four ordered pairs. Here, it is probably easiest to work by process of elimination, and cross off those choices that *aren't* satisfied by at least one of the ordered pairs. Let's consider the first ordered pair, (2, 1), and see which functions give an output of 1 for an input of 2:

(A) $f(2) = 3(2)^2 - 2 = 3(4) - 2 = 12 - 2 = 10$
(No—eliminate.)
(B) $f(2) = 3(2)^2 - 4 = 3(4) - 4 = 12 - 4 = 8$
(No—eliminate.)
(C) $f(2) = 2(2)^2 - 7 = 2(4) - 7 = 8 - 7 = 1$
(Yes—don't eliminate.)
(D) $f(2) = 2(2)^2 = 2(4) = 8$
(No—eliminate.)

So, it turns out we only have to test one ordered pair to get the right answer.

---

10. **A** **Algebra (linear equations) MEDIUM**

Original equation:	$y = kx - 1$
Substitute $x = a$ and $y = b$:	$b = ka - 1$
Add 1:	$b + 1 = ka$
Divide by a:	$\dfrac{b + 1}{a} = k$

11. **B**   **Advanced Mathematics (rational equations)**
MEDIUM-HARD

The fact that the denominators are equal in both fractions suggests that multiplying both sides will simplify the equation:

$$\frac{12x^2 + 6x - 23}{bx - 3} = -2x - \frac{23}{bx - 3}$$

Multiply by $bx - 3$: $12x^2 + 6x - 23 = -2x(bx - 3) - 23$
Distribute: $12x^2 + 6x - 23 = -2bx^2 + 6x - 23$
Subtract $6x - 23$: $12x^2 = -2bx^2$
Divide by x^2: $12 = -2b$
Divide by -2: $-6 = b$

---

12. **A**   **Advanced Mathematics (functions)**
MEDIUM-HARD

Given: $h(g(2)) = 9$
Apply definition $h(x) = x + 3$: $g(2) + 3 = 9$
Subtract 3: $g(2) = 6$

Therefore, g must be a function that takes an input of 2 and gives an output of 6. The only choice that satisfies this condition is (A) $g(x) = x^2 + 2$, because $g(2) = (2)^2 + 2 = 4 + 2 = 6$.

---

13. **D**   **Advanced Mathematics (analyzing quadratics) HARD**

Original equation: $y = a(x + 3)(x - 1)$
This equation represents a quadratic in x. Since it is in factored form, it shows us that the function has x-intercepts (also known as zeroes or roots) when $x + 3 = 0$ or $x - 1 = 0$, so its x-intercepts are at $x = -3$ and $x = 1$. Recall (from Chapter 9, Lesson 6) that a parabola representing a quadratic function has an axis of symmetry at $x = k$, where k is midway between the x-intercepts. Therefore, $k = (-3 + 1)/2 = -1$. This axis of symmetry, $x = -1$, must pass through the vertex. We can get the y-coordinate of this vertex by just plugging $x = -1$ back into the function: $y = a(-1 + 3)(-1 - 1)$
Simplify: $y = a(2)(-2) = -4a$

---

14. **A**   **Advanced Mathematics (solving quadratics)**
MEDIUM-HARD

Recall from Chapter 9, Lesson 5, that the solutions to quadratic of the form $x^2 + bx + c = 0$, the sum of those solutions is $-b$ (the opposite of whatever the x coefficient is), and the product of those solutions is c (whatever the constant term is). In the quadratic $x^2 - 2ax + b = 0$, the x coefficient is $-2a$. Since this must be the opposite of the sum of the solutions, the sum of the solutions is $2a$.

Although using this theorem gives us a quick and easy solution, the theorem may seem a little abstract and mysterious to you. (You might want to review Lesson 5 in Chapter 9 to refresh yourself on the proof.) So, there is

another way to attack this question: just choose values of a and b so that the quadratic is easy to factor. For instance, if we choose $a = 1$ and $b = -3$, we get:

$$x^2 - 2(1)x - 3 = 0$$
Simplify: $x^2 - 2x - 3 = 0$
Factor: $(x - 3)(x + 1) = 0$
Solve with the Zero Product Property: $x = 3$ or -1
The sum of these two solutions is $3 + -1 = 2$.
Now we plug $a = 1$ and $b = -3$ into the answer choices and we get (A) 2, (B) -2, (C) -3, (D) 3. Clearly, the only choice that gives the correct sum is (A).

---

15. **D**   **Advanced Mathematics (analyzing polynomial graphs) HARD**

By the Zero Product Property (Chapter 9, Lesson 5), the graph of $y = a(x - b)(x + c)^2$ has zeroes at $x = b$ and a "double root" at $x = -c$ (because this expression has two factors of $(x + c)$). Since b and c are both positive, this means that the graph must have one single positive root and a "double" negative root. That is, the graph passes through the x-axis at a positive value of x and "bounces" off of the x-axis at a negative value of x. Notice that this eliminates choices (B) and (C). We also know that a, the "leading coefficient" of the polynomial, is positive. If the leading coefficient of the polynomial is positive, the polynomial must eventually "shoot up" toward positive infinity; that is, it must go up as we move to the right. This rules out choice (A) and leaves only choice (D) as correct.

---

16. **510**   **Algebra (rates) EASY**

Let x represent the number of calories in a large order of fries, because that is what the question is asking us to find. Since we are told that this is 350 calories more than the calories in a large soda, the number of calories in a large soda is $x - 350$. If 2 large fries and 3 large sodas have a total of 1,500 calories,

$$x + 3(x - 350) = 1,500$$
Distribute: $2x + 3x - 1,050 = 1,500$
Simplify: $5x - 1,050 = 1,500$
Add 1,050: $5x = 2,550$
Divide by 5: $x = 510$

---

17. **64**   **Advanced Mathematics (radical equations) MEDIUM-HARD**

Given: $a = 4\sqrt{2}$
Multiply by 2: $2a = 8\sqrt{2}$
Substitute $2a = 2a = \sqrt{2b}$: $\sqrt{2b} = 8\sqrt{2}$
Square both sides: $2b = 64(2)$
Divide by 2: $b = 64$

18. **6**   **Advanced Mathematics (quadratic equations) HARD**

Although this does not look like a quadratic equation, in fact it is.

Original equation: $x + \dfrac{36}{x} = 12$

Multiply by x: $x^2 + 36 = 12x$

Subtract $12x$: $x^2 - 12x + 36 = 0$

Factor: $(x - 6)(x - 6) = 0$

Solve using the Zero Product Property: $x - 6 = 0$, so $x = 6$

---

19. **12**   **Additional topics (coordinate geometry) MEDIUM-HARD**

The system of inequalities indicates that the line containing the hypotenuse of the triangle is given by the equation $3x + y = k$, which has an x-intercept of $\left(\dfrac{k}{3}, 0\right)$ and a y-intercept of $(0, k)$. This means that the

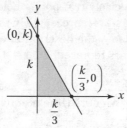

triangle has a base of $\dfrac{k}{3}$ and a height of k.

The area of the triangle is 24: $\dfrac{1}{2} \times \dfrac{k}{3} \times k = 24$

Simplify: $\dfrac{k^2}{6} = 24$

Multiply by 6: $k^2 = 144$

Take the square root: $k = 12$

---

20. **8.25**   **Additional Topics (triangles, circles, and squares) HARD**

Most students will begin this problem by trying to find the length of the radius of the larger circle. This is a bit of a pain and, as it turns out, completely unnecessary. Instead, start by drawing in the 45°-45°-90° triangle as shown, and notice that one leg of this triangle is the radius of the smaller circle, and the hypotenuse is the radius of the larger circle. This is the key to the relationship between the circles.

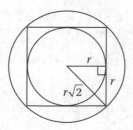

If we label the smaller leg r and use either the Pythagorean Theorem or the Reference Information about 45°-45°-90° triangles given at the beginning of the test, we find that the hypotenuse is $r\sqrt{2}$. Therefore, the area of the smaller circle is πr^2 and the area of the larger circle is $\pi(r\sqrt{2})^2 = 2\pi r^2$. In other words, the larger circle has an area that is twice the area of the smaller circle. Therefore, if the larger circle has area 16.5, the smaller circle has an area of $16.5 \div 2 = 8.25$.

Section 4: Math (Calculator)

1. **B**   **Algebra (word problems) EASY**

For getting 32 questions correct and $40 - 32 = 8$ questions wrong, the student earned $32(2) - 0.25(8) = 64 - 2 = 62$ points.

---

2. **D**   **Problem Solving and Data Analysis (central tendency) EASY**

The average of the three numbers is 10: $\dfrac{3 + 5 + m}{3} = 10$

Multiply by 3: $3 + 5 + m = 30$

Simplify: $8 + m = 30$

Subtract 8: $m = 22$

---

3. **C**   **Algebra (linear equations) EASY**

Original equation: $3b + 4 = -1$

Multiply by 3: $9b + 12 = -3$

---

4. **B**   **Data Analysis and Problem Solving (graphical analysis) EASY**

The graph indicates that Rebecca started her hike at 10:00 a.m. and stopped for lunch at 11:45 a.m. (The horizontal segment indicates when she is not moving, so that represents her 1-hour lunch break.) This first part of her hike, therefore, took 1 hour 45 minutes, or 105 minutes. The return hike began at 12:45 and lasted until 2:00 p.m., for a time of 1 hour 15 minutes, or 75 minutes. The difference is $105 - 75 = 30$ minutes.

---

5. **C**   **Algebra (ratios) EASY**

The win-to-loss ratio of 5:3 is a "part-to-part" ratio, so we can represent each part as a fraction of the whole. We can do this by simply adding $3 + 5 = 8$ (the "whole") and dividing by that total. This gives us a ratio of $\dfrac{5}{8} : \dfrac{3}{8}$, which means that the Bombers won $\dfrac{5}{8}$ of their games and lost $\dfrac{3}{8}$ of them. Since they played a total of 120 games, they won $\dfrac{5}{8} \times 120 = 75$ games and lost $\dfrac{3}{8} \times 120 = 45$ games.

6. C   Advanced Mathematics (adding polynomials) MEDIUM

$$(3x^3 - 2x^2 + 5) + (5x^2 + x - 10)$$

Distribute coefficients to
eliminate parentheses: $3x^3 - 2x^2 + 5 + 5x^2 + x - 10$
Group like terms together: $3x^3 - 2x^2 + 5x^2 + x + 5 - 10$
Combine like terms: $3x^3 + 3x^2 + x - 5$

7. A   Additional Topics (triangles) MEDIUM

It helps to mark the measures of the other two interior angles to the triangle as $c°$ and $d°$, because we know something about these angles.

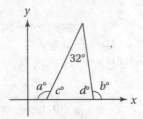

Since angles in a triangle must have
a sum of 180°: $c + d + 32 = 180$
Subtract 32: $c + d = 148$
Since angles in a linear pair have
a sum of 180°: $a + c = 180$
                                  $b + d = 180$
Add previous two equations: $a + b + c + d = 360$
Subtract $c + d = 148$: $-(c + d = 148)$
                                   $a + b = 212$

8. A   Additional Topics (complex numbers) MEDIUM

$$\frac{K + i}{i} = 1 - 2i$$

Multiply by i: $K + i = i(1 - i)$
Distribute: $K + i = i - 2i^2$
Substitute $i^2 = -1$: $K + i = i + 2$
Subtract i: $K = 2$

9. C   Advanced Mathematics (variation) MEDIUM

To answer this question, it helps to be familiar with the concepts we discussed in Chapter 8, Lesson 4. The first thing to notice about the ordered pairs is that as the value of x increases, the value of y decreases. More specifically, notice that the *product* of the two values in each ordered pair is *always the same*: $(2)(10) = 20$, $(4)(5) = 20$, and $(10)(2) = 20$. A discussed in Chapter 8, Lesson 4, this is the hallmark of an *inverse variation*. The equation for this particular relationship is $y = 20/x$.

10. B   Problem Solving and Data Analysis (scatterplots) MEDIUM-HARD

Since, by definition, the luminosity of our sun is "1 sun," we must look for the number 1 on the vertical ("luminosity")

axis. These numbers are given as powers of 10, so we have to remember that $10^0 = 1$. If we trace the horizontal line representing 100 lumens, we can see that it intersects the line of best fit at roughly 6,000°K. The choice that is closest to this value is (B) 5,800°K.

11. C   Advanced Mathematics (rational equations) MEDIUM-HARD

The line of best fit appears to cross the points (10,000°K, 10^2 suns) and (5,000°K, 10^{-1} suns), give or take a small error. This means that a Main Sequence star with a temperature of 10,000°K is about $10^2 \div 10^{-1} = 10^3 = 1,000$ times as bright as a Main Sequence star with a temperature of 5,000°K. Choice (C) 900 is the only choice within an acceptable margin of error.

12. D   Problem Solving and Data Analysis (scatterplots) MEDIUM-HARD

First, we need to recognize that $0.0001 = 10^{-4}$. The scatterplot shows precisely two points below the 10^{-4} line. Since there are 50 stars represented in the scatterplot (no need to count them—the description of the graph tells us!), these two stars represent $2/50 = 4/100 = 4\%$ of the total.

13. A   Algebra (linear equations) MEDIUM

Original equation: $\dfrac{a + k}{b + k} = -2$
Multiply by $b + k$: $a + k = -2(b + k)$
Distribute: $a + k = -2b - 2k$
Subtract k: $a = -2b - 3k$
Add $2b$: $a + 2b = -3k$
Divide by -3: $\dfrac{-a - 2b}{3} = k$

14. C   Advanced Mathematics (graphing polynomials) MEDIUM

First, notice that the answer choices include the factors $x^2 - 1$ and $x^2 + 1$. The first of these is a difference of squares, so it can be factored further: $x^2 - 1 = (x + 1)(x - 1)$. However, $x^2 + 1$ is a *sum* of squares, which cannot be factored over the real numbers. This enables us to express each function in completely factored form:

(A) $f(x) = (x^2 + 1)(x^2 + 1)$ $= (x^2 + 1)(x^2 + 1)$
(B) $f(x) = (x^2 - 1)(x^2 + 1)$ $= (x + 1)(x - 1)(x^2 + 1)$
(C) $f(x) = x^2(x^2 - 1)$ $= x^2(x + 1)(x - 1)$
(D) $f(x) = x^2(x^2 + 1)$ $= x^2(x^2 + 1)$

Now we can find all of the x-intercepts by setting each factor to 0 and (if possible) solving for x. Notice that if we do this for the factored form of each function, we see that (A) has no x-intercepts, (B) has intercepts at $x = -1$ and $x = 1$, (C) has intercepts at $x = 0$, $x = -1$, and $x = 1$, and (D) has an intercept at $x = 0$. Therefore, the function in choice (C) is the only one that has three x-intercepts.

15. B — Algebra (quantitative reasoning) MEDIUM-HARD

First, we should notice the fact that $n + 8$ must be greater than $n + 2$, no matter the value of n. Next, we should notice that, in order for the product of two numbers to be negative, one of those numbers must be positive and the other one negative. Obviously, the greater number is the positive one, and the lesser one is the negative one. Therefore:
$$n + 2 < 0 \text{ and } n + 8 > 0$$
Solve each inequality for n:
$$n < -2 \text{ and } n > -8$$
Since n must have an integer value and must satisfy the inequalities above, it can take only the values -7, -6, -5, -4, and -3.

16. A — Algebra (rates) MEDIUM

Although this problem can be solved by "plugging in" convenient numbers for the unknowns, it is actually much more straightforward to treat this as a conversion problem, as discussed in Chapter 7, Lesson 4. The question gives us the "initial fact" that Lauren has 6 gallons of gas in her car, and we'd like to "convert" that fact into the number of hours she can travel. Using the rates given in the problem, the conversion should look like this:

$$6 \text{ gallons} \times \frac{d \text{ miles}}{1 \text{ gallon}} \times \frac{1 \text{ hour}}{s \text{ miles}} = \frac{6d}{s} \text{ hours}$$

Notice that all the units on the left-hand side cancel except for hours, which is the desired unit.

17. A — Algebra (linear equations) MEDIUM-HARD

Perhaps the best way to find the slope of the line is to get the equation into "slope-intercept form" (Chapter 7, Lesson 5).
Original equation:
$$\frac{2x + 1}{2y} = \frac{a}{b}$$
Cross-multiply:
$$a(2y) = b(2x + 1)$$
Simplify:
$$2ay = 2bx + b$$
Divide by $2a$:
$$y = \frac{2b}{2a}x + \frac{b}{2a}$$
Simplify:
$$y = \frac{b}{a}x + \frac{b}{2a}$$
Therefore, the slope of the line is b/a.

18. A — Advanced Mathematics (exponential functions) MEDIUM

Notice that substituting $t = 0$ into the function gives us $P(0) = 250(2.4)^0 = 250(1) = 250$. Therefore, the number 250 in the equation means the population of mushrooms on the plot when $t = 0$.

19. B — Advanced Mathematics (exponential functions) MEDIUM-HARD

The fastest way to answer this question is to notice that in exponential growth and decay functions in which the exponent is the time variable, t, the base of the exponential

(in this case 2.4) must represent $1 + r$, where r is the rate of change per time unit. This means that the rate of weekly increase (recall that t is measured in weeks) must be $2.4 - 1 = 1.4 = 140\%$.

Another way to solve the problem is to calculate the populations at the specified times and then calculate the percent change. At the beginning of the sixth week, 5 weeks have passed, and so the population is $250(2.4)^5 = 19,906$. At the beginning of the seventh week, the population is $250(2.4)^6 = 47,776$. To calculate the percent change, we find the difference and divide by the initial amount: $(47,776 - 19,906)/19,906 = 1.40 = 140\%$.

20. C — Algebra (rewriting expressions) MEDIUM-HARD

Original equation:
$$\frac{x^2 + 1}{2} + \frac{x}{p} = 1$$
Multiply by $2p$ (the common denominator):
$$p(x^2 + 1) + 2x = 2p$$
Distribute:
$$px^2 + p + 2x = 2p$$
Subtract $2p$ and write in descending powers of x:
$$px^2 + 2x - p = 0$$
Put into quadratic formula with $a = p$, $b = 2$, and $c = -p$:
$$\frac{-2 \pm \sqrt{4 + 4p^2}}{2p}$$

21. D — Problem Solving and Data Analysis (variation) MEDIUM-HARD

Recall from Chapter 8, Lesson 4, that if a is inversely proportional to b, then $a = \frac{k}{b}$, where k is some positive constant. If we multiply both sides of this equation by b, we get $ab = k$, which means that the product ab is a constant.

22. B — Problem Solving and Data Analysis (quadratics) MEDIUM

The table indicates that a total 500 patients had the antibody and that 20 of these patients nevertheless had a negative test result. Therefore the probability of this result is $20/500 = 0.04$.

23. B — Problem Solving and Data Analysis (data spread) MEDIUM

As we discussed in Chapter 8, Lesson 3, the standard deviation of a set of numbers tells us how "spread out" the data are from the average—the greater the standard deviation, the greater the spread from the average. It should be clear by inspection that the scores for Class B are more "clustered" than the scores for Class A. For instance, there is only a 5-point difference between the lowest and highest scores in Class B, but a 31-point difference between the lowest and highest scores in Class A. This means that the standard deviation of the scores in Class B is smaller.

24. **C**   Algebra (word problems) MEDIUM-HARD

Begin by assuming that there are n students in Mrs. Black's class. If she gives out 3 candy bars to each student and has 6 left over, she must have $3n + 6$ candy bars. If she needs 50 more candy bars in order to give each student 5 candy bars, she must have $5n - 50$ candy bars. Since these two expressions both express the total number of candy bars, $\qquad 3n + 6 = 5n - 50$

Add 50 and subtract $3n$: $\qquad\qquad\qquad 56 = 2n$

Divide by 2: $\qquad\qquad\qquad\qquad\quad 28 = n$

---

25. **D**   Problem Solving (rates) MEDIUM

Let's call the three numbers a, b, and c.

If their sum is 240, $\qquad\qquad\quad a + b + c = 240$

Let's say the largest number is c. If this is 50% larger than the sum of the others, $\qquad\qquad c = 1.5(a + b)$

Divide by 1.5: $\qquad\qquad\qquad\qquad \dfrac{c}{1.5} = a + b$

Substitute $a + b = \dfrac{c}{1.5}$ into the first equation: $\qquad\qquad\qquad\qquad \dfrac{c}{1.5} + c = 240$

Multiply by 1.5: $\qquad\qquad\qquad\quad c + 1.5c = 360$

Simplify: $\qquad\qquad\qquad\qquad\qquad 2.5c = 360$

Divide by 2.5: $\qquad\qquad\qquad\qquad\quad c = 144$

---

26. **A**   Algebra (graphs of linear equations) MEDIUM

Recall the slope formula from Chapter 7, Lesson 5:

$$\text{slope} = \frac{y_2 - y_1}{x_2 - x_1} = \frac{k - 5}{-12 - 2} = \frac{k - 5}{-14}$$

Since the slope equals $-\dfrac{4}{7}$:

Cross-multiply: $\qquad\qquad\qquad 7k - 35 = 56$

Add 35: $\qquad\qquad\qquad\qquad\qquad 7k = 91$

Divide by 7: $\qquad\qquad\qquad\qquad\quad k = 13$

---

27. **C**   Algebra (word problems/percent change) HARD

The question makes it clear that we will get the same answer regardless of the original price of the motor. Since we are working with percentages, it is convenient to assume the original price of the motor is \$100.

After a markdown of 30%, the price becomes $\$100 - 0.30(\$100) = \$70$. If it is marked down an additional p percent, its price becomes $\$70\left(1 - \dfrac{p}{100}\right)$. Since this is equivalent to a one-time markdown of 58%, then

$$70\left(1 - \frac{p}{100}\right) = 100(1 - 0.58) = 42$$

Divide by 70: $\qquad\qquad 1 - \dfrac{p}{100} = \dfrac{42}{70} = 0.6$

Subtract 1: $\qquad\qquad\qquad\quad -\dfrac{p}{100} = -0.4$

Multiply by -100: $\qquad\qquad\qquad\quad p = 40$

---

28. **B**   Additional Topics (trigonometry/coordinate geometry) HARD

If this question gave you trouble, review Chapter 10, particularly Lessons 3, 4, and 9. Since the question asks about the slope, we should draw in a right triangle to show the "rise" and "run" of the line. If $\cos A = 0.8$, then the adjacent side of this triangle could be 8 and the hypotenuse could be 10 (because o/h = 8/10 = 0.8) as shown below.

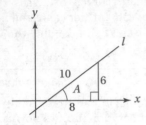

We can find the third side of the triangle with the Pythagorean Theorem ($8^2 + x^2 = 10^2$), although it's easier to simply notice that this is a triangle in the 3-4-5 family: 6-8-10. Since the slope of a line is the rise over the run, the slope is $6/8 = 0.75$.

---

29. **C**   Problem Solving/Data Analysis (tables/ratios) MEDIUM-HARD

For the males, the ratio of yes votes to no votes is $150{:}90 = 5{:}3$. If n of the females had shifted their votes from no to yes, then $173 - n$ would have voted no and $107 + n$ would have voted yes. If this ratio is then equal to the ratio for males, $\qquad\qquad \dfrac{107 + n}{173 - n} = \dfrac{5}{3}$

Cross-multiply: $\qquad\quad 321 + 3n = 865 - 5n$

Subtract 321 and add $5n$: $\qquad\qquad 8n = 544$

Divide by 8: $\qquad\qquad\qquad\qquad\quad n = 68$

---

30. **A**   Problem Solving/Data Analysis (tables/proportions) HARD

The table shows that 150 males voted yes out of a sample population of 520. If this is a representative ratio, and if x represents the total number of males who vote yes out of the entire population, then

$$\frac{150}{520} = \frac{15}{52} = \frac{x}{32{,}760}$$

Cross-multiply: $\qquad\quad (32{,}760)(15) = 52x$

Divide by 52: $\qquad x = \dfrac{(32{,}760)(15)}{52} = 9{,}450$

---

31. **.2**   Problem Solving and Data Analysis (ratios) EASY

The total weight of the shipment is $6 + 4 + 2 + 3 = 15$, and the total weight of oranges is 3, so the fraction of the shipment that is oranges is $3/15 = .2$.

32. 14   **Problem Solving and Data Analysis (proportions) EASY**

If x is the number of months it takes until the regions lose 343 acres, then

$$24.5 = \frac{343}{x}$$

Cross-multiply: $24.5x = 343$

Divide by 24.5: $x = 14$

---

33. 678   **Problem Solving and Data Analysis (data from formula) MEDIUM**

The formula indicates how many donuts were sold on each day of the festival. One day 1, the bakery sold $13(1) + 200 = 213$ donuts. On day 2, the bakery sold $13(2) + 200 = 226$ donuts. On day 3, the bakery sold $13(3) + 200 = 239$ donuts, for a total of $213 + 226 + 239 = 678$ donuts.

---

34. 1450   **Problem Solving and Data Analysis (rates) MEDIUM**

If Connor wrote x lines of code, then Joachim wrote $x + 600$ lines of code. Together they wrote $(x) + (x + 600) = 3,500$ lines of code: $x + x + 600 = 3,500$

Simplify and subtract 600: $2x = 2,900$

Divide by 2: $x = 1,450$

Therefore Connor wrote 1,450 lines of code.

---

35. .05   **Problem Solving (analyzing formulas) HARD**

If the investment is worth \$1,102.50 after 2 quarters,

$$1,000(1 + k)^2 = 1,102.5$$

Divide by 1000: $(1 + k)^2 = 1.1025$

Take the square root: $1 + k = 1.05$

Subtract 1: $k = .05$

---

36. 18   **Additional Topics (volumes and similarity) HARD**

The radius of the inside of the larger bowl is $9 - 3 = 6$ centimeters, so the radius of the smaller bowl is 3 centimeters. The volume of the smaller bowl is therefore $\frac{1}{2}\left(\frac{4}{3}\pi(3)^3\right) = \frac{4\pi(27)}{6} = 18\pi$. Therefore, $k = 18$.

---

37. 300   **Problem Solving and Data Analysis (formula analysis) MEDIUM**

This requires simply substituting into the formula:

$$I = \frac{432}{(1 + 0.2)^2} = \frac{432}{1.44} = 300$$

---

38. .300   **Problem Solving and Data Analysis (formula analysis) HARD**

If the value of the investment increases by 69% in 2 years, this means that $FV = 1.691$ when $n = 2$. Substituting into the formula gives

$$I = \frac{1.69I}{(1 + r)^2}$$

Divide by I: $1 = \frac{1.69}{(1 + r)^2}$

Cross-multiply: $(1 + r)^2 = 1.69$

Take the square root: $1 + r = 1.3$

Subtract 1: $r = 1.3 - 1 = 0.3$

PRACTICE TEST 4

1. Reading Test

   65 MINUTES   52 QUESTIONS   690

2. Writing and Language Test

   35 MINUTES   44 QUESTIONS   708

3. Math Test – No Calculator

   25 MINUTES   20 QUESTIONS   721

4. Math Test – Calculator

   55 MINUTES   38 QUESTIONS   727

5. Essay (optional)

   50 MINUTES   1 QUESTION   738

ANSWER SHEET for PRACTICE TEST 4

Use a No. 2 pencil and fill in the entire circle darkly and completely.
If you change your response, erase as completely as possible

SECTION 1

1 Ⓐ Ⓑ Ⓒ Ⓓ   13 Ⓐ Ⓑ Ⓒ Ⓓ   25 Ⓐ Ⓑ Ⓒ Ⓓ   37 Ⓐ Ⓑ Ⓒ Ⓓ   49 Ⓐ Ⓑ Ⓒ Ⓓ
2 Ⓐ Ⓑ Ⓒ Ⓓ   14 Ⓐ Ⓑ Ⓒ Ⓓ   26 Ⓐ Ⓑ Ⓒ Ⓓ   38 Ⓐ Ⓑ Ⓒ Ⓓ   50 Ⓐ Ⓑ Ⓒ Ⓓ
3 Ⓐ Ⓑ Ⓒ Ⓓ   15 Ⓐ Ⓑ Ⓒ Ⓓ   27 Ⓐ Ⓑ Ⓒ Ⓓ   39 Ⓐ Ⓑ Ⓒ Ⓓ   51 Ⓐ Ⓑ Ⓒ Ⓓ
4 Ⓐ Ⓑ Ⓒ Ⓓ   16 Ⓐ Ⓑ Ⓒ Ⓓ   28 Ⓐ Ⓑ Ⓒ Ⓓ   40 Ⓐ Ⓑ Ⓒ Ⓓ   52 Ⓐ Ⓑ Ⓒ Ⓓ
5 Ⓐ Ⓑ Ⓒ Ⓓ   17 Ⓐ Ⓑ Ⓒ Ⓓ   29 Ⓐ Ⓑ Ⓒ Ⓓ   41 Ⓐ Ⓑ Ⓒ Ⓓ
6 Ⓐ Ⓑ Ⓒ Ⓓ   18 Ⓐ Ⓑ Ⓒ Ⓓ   30 Ⓐ Ⓑ Ⓒ Ⓓ   42 Ⓐ Ⓑ Ⓒ Ⓓ
7 Ⓐ Ⓑ Ⓒ Ⓓ   19 Ⓐ Ⓑ Ⓒ Ⓓ   31 Ⓐ Ⓑ Ⓒ Ⓓ   43 Ⓐ Ⓑ Ⓒ Ⓓ
8 Ⓐ Ⓑ Ⓒ Ⓓ   20 Ⓐ Ⓑ Ⓒ Ⓓ   32 Ⓐ Ⓑ Ⓒ Ⓓ   44 Ⓐ Ⓑ Ⓒ Ⓓ
9 Ⓐ Ⓑ Ⓒ Ⓓ   21 Ⓐ Ⓑ Ⓒ Ⓓ   33 Ⓐ Ⓑ Ⓒ Ⓓ   45 Ⓐ Ⓑ Ⓒ Ⓓ
10 Ⓐ Ⓑ Ⓒ Ⓓ   22 Ⓐ Ⓑ Ⓒ Ⓓ   34 Ⓐ Ⓑ Ⓒ Ⓓ   46 Ⓐ Ⓑ Ⓒ Ⓓ
11 Ⓐ Ⓑ Ⓒ Ⓓ   23 Ⓐ Ⓑ Ⓒ Ⓓ   35 Ⓐ Ⓑ Ⓒ Ⓓ   47 Ⓐ Ⓑ Ⓒ Ⓓ
12 Ⓐ Ⓑ Ⓒ Ⓓ   24 Ⓐ Ⓑ Ⓒ Ⓓ   36 Ⓐ Ⓑ Ⓒ Ⓓ   48 Ⓐ Ⓑ Ⓒ Ⓓ

SECTION 2

1 Ⓐ Ⓑ Ⓒ Ⓓ   11 Ⓐ Ⓑ Ⓒ Ⓓ   21 Ⓐ Ⓑ Ⓒ Ⓓ   31 Ⓐ Ⓑ Ⓒ Ⓓ   41 Ⓐ Ⓑ Ⓒ Ⓓ
2 Ⓐ Ⓑ Ⓒ Ⓓ   12 Ⓐ Ⓑ Ⓒ Ⓓ   22 Ⓐ Ⓑ Ⓒ Ⓓ   32 Ⓐ Ⓑ Ⓒ Ⓓ   42 Ⓐ Ⓑ Ⓒ Ⓓ
3 Ⓐ Ⓑ Ⓒ Ⓓ   13 Ⓐ Ⓑ Ⓒ Ⓓ   23 Ⓐ Ⓑ Ⓒ Ⓓ   33 Ⓐ Ⓑ Ⓒ Ⓓ   43 Ⓐ Ⓑ Ⓒ Ⓓ
4 Ⓐ Ⓑ Ⓒ Ⓓ   14 Ⓐ Ⓑ Ⓒ Ⓓ   24 Ⓐ Ⓑ Ⓒ Ⓓ   34 Ⓐ Ⓑ Ⓒ Ⓓ   44 Ⓐ Ⓑ Ⓒ Ⓓ
5 Ⓐ Ⓑ Ⓒ Ⓓ   15 Ⓐ Ⓑ Ⓒ Ⓓ   25 Ⓐ Ⓑ Ⓒ Ⓓ   35 Ⓐ Ⓑ Ⓒ Ⓓ
6 Ⓐ Ⓑ Ⓒ Ⓓ   16 Ⓐ Ⓑ Ⓒ Ⓓ   26 Ⓐ Ⓑ Ⓒ Ⓓ   36 Ⓐ Ⓑ Ⓒ Ⓓ
7 Ⓐ Ⓑ Ⓒ Ⓓ   17 Ⓐ Ⓑ Ⓒ Ⓓ   27 Ⓐ Ⓑ Ⓒ Ⓓ   37 Ⓐ Ⓑ Ⓒ Ⓓ
8 Ⓐ Ⓑ Ⓒ Ⓓ   18 Ⓐ Ⓑ Ⓒ Ⓓ   28 Ⓐ Ⓑ Ⓒ Ⓓ   38 Ⓐ Ⓑ Ⓒ Ⓓ
9 Ⓐ Ⓑ Ⓒ Ⓓ   19 Ⓐ Ⓑ Ⓒ Ⓓ   29 Ⓐ Ⓑ Ⓒ Ⓓ   39 Ⓐ Ⓑ Ⓒ Ⓓ
10 Ⓐ Ⓑ Ⓒ Ⓓ   20 Ⓐ Ⓑ Ⓒ Ⓓ   30 Ⓐ Ⓑ Ⓒ Ⓓ   40 Ⓐ Ⓑ Ⓒ Ⓓ

SECTION 3

1 Ⓐ Ⓑ Ⓒ Ⓓ   4 Ⓐ Ⓑ Ⓒ Ⓓ   7 Ⓐ Ⓑ Ⓒ Ⓓ   10 Ⓐ Ⓑ Ⓒ Ⓓ   13 Ⓐ Ⓑ Ⓒ Ⓓ
2 Ⓐ Ⓑ Ⓒ Ⓓ   5 Ⓐ Ⓑ Ⓒ Ⓓ   8 Ⓐ Ⓑ Ⓒ Ⓓ   11 Ⓐ Ⓑ Ⓒ Ⓓ   14 Ⓐ Ⓑ Ⓒ Ⓓ
3 Ⓐ Ⓑ Ⓒ Ⓓ   6 Ⓐ Ⓑ Ⓒ Ⓓ   9 Ⓐ Ⓑ Ⓒ Ⓓ   12 Ⓐ Ⓑ Ⓒ Ⓓ   15 Ⓐ Ⓑ Ⓒ Ⓓ

**ONLY ANSWERS ENTERED IN THE CIRCLES IN EACH GRID WILL BE SCORED.
YOU WILL NOT RECEIVE CREDIT FOR ANYTHING WRITTEN IN THE BOXES ABOVE THE CIRCLES.**

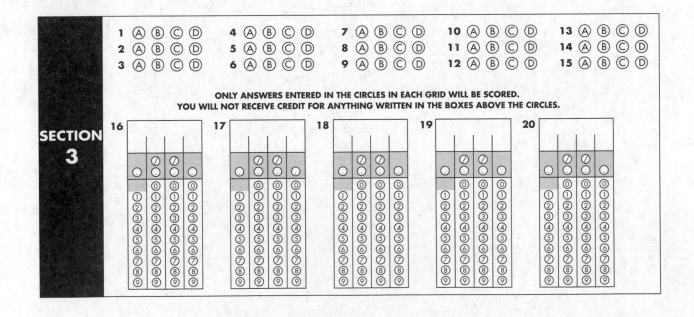

SECTION 4

1	Ⓐ Ⓑ Ⓒ Ⓓ	7	Ⓐ Ⓑ Ⓒ Ⓓ	13	Ⓐ Ⓑ Ⓒ Ⓓ	19	Ⓐ Ⓑ Ⓒ Ⓓ	25	Ⓐ Ⓑ Ⓒ Ⓓ
2	Ⓐ Ⓑ Ⓒ Ⓓ	8	Ⓐ Ⓑ Ⓒ Ⓓ	14	Ⓐ Ⓑ Ⓒ Ⓓ	20	Ⓐ Ⓑ Ⓒ Ⓓ	26	Ⓐ Ⓑ Ⓒ Ⓓ
3	Ⓐ Ⓑ Ⓒ Ⓓ	9	Ⓐ Ⓑ Ⓒ Ⓓ	15	Ⓐ Ⓑ Ⓒ Ⓓ	21	Ⓐ Ⓑ Ⓒ Ⓓ	27	Ⓐ Ⓑ Ⓒ Ⓓ
4	Ⓐ Ⓑ Ⓒ Ⓓ	10	Ⓐ Ⓑ Ⓒ Ⓓ	16	Ⓐ Ⓑ Ⓒ Ⓓ	22	Ⓐ Ⓑ Ⓒ Ⓓ	28	Ⓐ Ⓑ Ⓒ Ⓓ
5	Ⓐ Ⓑ Ⓒ Ⓓ	11	Ⓐ Ⓑ Ⓒ Ⓓ	17	Ⓐ Ⓑ Ⓒ Ⓓ	23	Ⓐ Ⓑ Ⓒ Ⓓ	29	Ⓐ Ⓑ Ⓒ Ⓓ
6	Ⓐ Ⓑ Ⓒ Ⓓ	12	Ⓐ Ⓑ Ⓒ Ⓓ	18	Ⓐ Ⓑ Ⓒ Ⓓ	24	Ⓐ Ⓑ Ⓒ Ⓓ	30	Ⓐ Ⓑ Ⓒ Ⓓ

ONLY ANSWERS ENTERED IN THE CIRCLES IN EACH GRID WILL BE SCORED.
YOU WILL NOT RECEIVE CREDIT FOR ANYTHING WRITTEN IN THE BOXES ABOVE THE CIRCLES.

31   32   33   34

35   36   37   38

SECTION 5: ESSAY

PLANNING PAGE   You may plan your essay in the unlined planning space below, but use only the lined pages following this one to write your essay. Any work on this planning page will not be scored.

BEGIN YOUR ESSAY HERE

1

DO NOT WRITE OUTSIDE OF THE BOX.

Cut Here

DO NOT WRITE OUTSIDE OF THE BOX.

Cut Here

3

DO NOT WRITE OUTSIDE OF THE BOX.

Cut Here

Test begins on the next page.

Reading Test

65 MINUTES, 52 QUESTIONS

Turn to Section 1 of your answer sheet to answer the questions in this section.

Questions 1–10 are based on the following passage.

The following passage is adapted from Oscar Wilde, *The Canterville Ghost*, published in 1887.

When Mr. Hiram B. Otis, the American Minister, bought Canterville Chase, every one
Line told him that the place was haunted. Indeed, Lord Canterville himself, a man of punctilious
5 honor, felt it his duty to mention the fact to Mr. Otis when they came to discuss terms.

"We have not cared to live in the place ourselves," said Lord Canterville, "since the Dowager Duchess of Bolton was frightened into
10 a fit by two skeleton hands on her shoulders as she was dressing for dinner. The ghost has been seen by several members of my family, as well as by the Rev. Augustus Dampier, a Fellow of King's College, Cambridge."

15 "My Lord," answered the Minister, "I will take the furniture and the ghost at a valuation. I come from a modern country, and I reckon that if there were such a thing as a ghost in Europe, we'd have it at home in a very short time in one of our
20 public museums."

"I fear that the ghost exists," said Lord Canterville, smiling, "though it may have resisted the overtures of your enterprising impresarios. It has been well known for three centuries, since
25 1584 in fact, and always makes its appearance before the death of any member of our family."

"Well, so does the family doctor for that matter, Lord Canterville. But there is no such thing, sir, as a ghost, and I guess the laws of
30 Nature are not going to be suspended for the British aristocracy."

After the purchase was concluded, the Minister and his family went down to Canterville Chase. Mrs. Otis, who, as Miss Lucretia R. Tappan
35 had been a celebrated New York belle, was now a very handsome, middle-aged woman. Her eldest son, christened Washington by his parents in a moment of patriotism, was a fair-haired, rather good-looking young man.

40 Standing on the steps to receive them was old Mrs. Umney, the housekeeper, whom Mrs. Otis, at Lady Canterville's earnest request, had consented to keep on in her former position. Following her into the library, they found tea laid out for them,
45 sat down and began to look round.

Suddenly Mrs. Otis caught sight of a dull red stain on the floor just by the fireplace and said to Mrs. Umney, "I am afraid something has been spilt there."

50 "Yes, madam," replied the old housekeeper in a low voice, "blood has been spilt on that spot."

"How horrid," cried Mrs. Otis; "I don't at all care for bloodstains in a sitting-room. It must be removed at once."

55 The old woman answered in the same low, mysterious voice, "It is the blood of Lady Eleanore de Canterville, who was murdered on that spot by her husband, Sir Simon de Canterville, in 1575.

CONTINUE ▶

His guilty spirit still haunts the Chase. The blood-
60 stain has been much admired by tourists and
others, and cannot be removed."

"That is all nonsense," cried Washington;
"Pinkerton's Champion Stain Remover will
clean it up in no time," and before the terrified
65 housekeeper could interfere he was rapidly
scouring the floor. In a few moments no trace of
the blood-stain could be seen.

"I knew Pinkerton would do it," he exclaimed
triumphantly, as he looked round at his admiring
70 family. A terrible flash of lightning lit up the
somber room, a fearful peal of thunder made them
all start to their feet, and Mrs. Umney fainted.

"What a monstrous climate!" said the
American Minister calmly. "I guess the old
75 country is so overpopulated that they have not
enough decent weather for everybody. I have
always been of opinion that emigration is the
only thing for England."

"My dear Hiram," cried Mrs. Otis, "what can
80 we do with a woman who faints?"

"Charge it to her like breakages," answered
the Minister; "she won't faint after that;" and in
a few moments Mrs. Umney certainly came to.
There was no doubt, however, that she was upset,
85 and she sternly warned Mr. Otis to beware of
some trouble coming to the house.

"Many and many a night," she said, "I have
not closed my eyes in sleep for the awful things
that are done here." Mr. Otis, however, and his
90 wife warmly assured the honest soul that they
were not afraid of ghosts, and, after invoking
the blessings of Providence on her new master
and mistress, and making arrangements for an
increase of salary, the old housekeeper tottered
95 off to her own room.

1

Which choice best describes what happens in the
passage?

A) An American family is horrified to discover
that an estate they have recently purchased is
haunted.

B) An honorable gentleman is dismayed to learn
that his family estate was the sight of a horrible
crime.

C) An American family displays nonchalance with
regard to a strange revelation about its new
estate.

D) An estate owner and his staff conspire to scare
away the prospective new American owners.

2

Which choice best describes the tone and
developmental pattern of the passage?

A) A somber analysis of social traditions

B) An ominous introduction of two nemeses

C) A farcical recounting of a bizarre anecdote

D) A humorous parody of British formality

CONTINUE

3

Lord Canterville mentions the titles of Augustus Dampier in line 13 in order to emphasize

A) the status of Lord Canterville's family.

B) the extent of Lord Canterville's learning.

C) the gravity of Lord Canterville's warning.

D) the credibility of Lord Canterville's claim.

4

As used in line 30, "suspended" most nearly means

A) held in abeyance.

B) prolonged indefinitely.

C) hung securely.

D) officially punished.

5

The Otises regard the blood stain in the library as

A) a morbid curiosity.

B) a brief irritation.

C) an entertaining peculiarity.

D) an alarming omen.

6

Which choice provides the best evidence for the answer to the previous question?

A) Lines 50–51 ("Yes . . . spot")

B) Line 59 ("His guilty . . . the Chase")

C) Lines 62–64 ("That is all . . . no time")

D) Lines 70–72 ("A terrible . . . fainted")

7

As used in line 72, "start" most nearly means

A) commence.

B) arise.

C) activate.

D) jump.

1   **1**

8

The conversation between Mr. and Mrs. Otis in lines 73–80 is notable for its tone of

A) flippancy.

B) alarm.

C) bemusement.

D) self-satisfaction.

9

Mr. Otis dismisses the claims that Canterville Chase is haunted because

A) he does not trust the people who have made those claims.

B) he believes that the British ghost will defer to the American owners and leave.

C) he thinks that the existence of ghosts would violate scientific principles.

D) he knows that Lord Canterville is delusional.

10

Which choice provides the best evidence for the answer to the previous question?

A) Lines 15–16 ("My Lord . . . valuation")

B) Lines 28–31 ("But there . . . aristocracy")

C) Lines 74–76 ("I guess . . . everybody")

D) Lines 76–78 ("I have . . . for England")

CONTINUE

Questions 11–21 are based on the following passages and supplementary material.

The following is adapted from Aaron M. Renn, "Urbanists Need to Face the Full Implications of Peak Car," published in New Geography (newgeography. com) on November 25, 2014.

As traffic levels in the United States decline in defiance of forecasts projecting major increases, a
Line number of commentators have claimed that we've reached "peak car," the point at which the rise in
5 vehicle miles traveled in America finally comes to an end. But while this has been celebrated by many urbanists as undermining plans for more roads, we have yet to face the implications peak car has for public policy.
10   For a long time, urbanists have embraced Say's Law of Markets for roads: increasing the supply of driving lanes only increases the number of drivers to fill them, hence building more roads to reduce congestion is pointless. But if we've
15 really reached peak car, maybe we really can build our way out of congestion after all.
      Traffic levels have stabilized or even fallen in recent years. Aggregate auto travel peaked on a per capita basis in 2005 and has fallen since.
20 Per capita traffic levels in 2014 were back to 1994 levels. Even looking at total (not per capita) travel shows a marked reversal.
      These data are complemented by a slew of recent stories about the poor financial
25 performance of toll roads, resulting in part from traffic falling far below projections. On the Indiana Toll Road, for example, traffic fell 11% in eight years, in contrast with a forecasted increase of 22%, and so the concessionaire went bankrupt.
30   Many of the trends that drove high traffic growth in the past have largely been played out: household size declines, suburbanization, the entry of women into the workforce, one car per driver, etc. That's not to say these will
35 necessarily reverse. But we've reached the point of diminishing returns, particularly in terms of how many more women will join the labor force.

      This is potentially very good fiscal news, especially given tight budgets. Clearly many
40 freeway expansion projects that have been driven by speculative demand should be revisited. From top to bottom, engineers need to recalibrate their forecasting models to better correspond to reality, and then revisit highway plans accordingly.
45   But we must also pay attention to the flip side of peak car. Although speculative highway expansion projects may be dubious, there may be good reasons now to build projects designed to alleviate already exiting congestion. Places like
50 Los Angeles remain chronically congested, which has great economic and social consequences, not the least of which is the value of untold hours lost sitting in traffic. Although some projects there might indeed be boondoggles, maybe it's
55 worth building some of the planned freeway expansions there in light of peak car. In short, in some cases—particularly where Say's Law no longer seems to apply—peak car strengthens the argument for building or expanding roads.
60   On the other hand, many of the regional development plans designed to promote compact central city development and transit may be predicated on an analysis that assumes large future traffic increases in a "business as usual"
65 scenario. Not just highways but all aspects of regional planning are dependent on traffic forecasts. That's not to say that such plans are necessarily wrong, but clearly revised traffic reality needs to be reflected in all plans, not just
70 highway building ones.
      Urbanists and policy makers of all stripes need to think about the full implications of peak car. At a minimum, the traditional "you can't build your way out of congestion" rhetoric should
75 be supplanted, at least in most areas, by a more nuanced approach that neither overestimates demand, nor ignores the problems caused by rapid growth in some regions and pockets of congestion in others.

CONTINUE ▶

1 **1**

Increase in Vehicle Miles Driven on All Roads in the U.S. from 1971 Baseline

Source: Doug Short, dshort.com

11

The primary purpose of the first paragraph is to

A) indicate a logical fallacy.

B) define a technical term.

C) question statistical evidence.

D) reconsider an approach.

12

As used in lines 14 and 16, "congestion" refers to a type of

A) bureaucratic obstruction.

B) cultural reluctance.

C) excessive usage.

D) political futility.

13

Which situation best illustrates "Say's Law of Markets" (lines 10–14)?

A) The annual cost of maintaining highways is increasing because the number of cars using those highways is increasing.

B) As a country expands its Internet capacity, businesses and individuals increase their Internet usage proportionally.

C) The supply of produce in supermarkets declines because temporary farm workers are unavailable to pick crops during harvest season.

D) The price of oil increases due to an embargo on petroleum-exporting nations during a political conflict.

CONTINUE ➡

1

1

The author recognizes a potential objection to the position he takes in the passage by

A) admitting that some of the data he cites may be questionable.

B) conceding that he lacks particular expertise in civil engineering.

C) acknowledging an economic theory that contradicts his thesis.

D) questioning the feasibility of building more roads.

Which choice provides the best evidence for the answer to the previous question?

A) Lines 10–14 ("For . . . pointless")

B) Lines 17–18 ("Traffic . . . years")

C) Lines 41–44 ("From . . . accordingly")

D) Lines 49–53 ("Places . . . traffic")

16

The author discusses the Indiana Toll Road primarily to

A) give evidence that the U.S. may have reached "peak car."

B) support the claim that road maintenance should be financed through taxes rather than tolls.

C) refute the suggestion that the privatization of roads is fiscally responsible.

D) criticize the process by which traffic data have been gathered in recent years.

According to the graph, approximately how long did it take for the total number of vehicle miles driven annually in the U.S. to double from the baseline in 1971?

A) 6 years

B) 16 years

C) 25 years

D) As of 2014 the total number of vehicle miles had not yet doubled from the 1971 baseline.

The author suggests that many modern urbanists

A) hope to thwart plans to build more roads.

B) want to relieve congestion by building more roads.

C) see toll roads as a good source of revenue.

D) are working to make mass transit more affordable.

Which choice provides the best evidence for the answer to the previous question?

A) Lines 6–9 ("But while . . . policy")

B) Lines 14–16 ("But if . . . all")

C) Lines 65–67 ("Not . . . forecasts")

D) Lines 71–73 ("Urbanists . . . car")

1 **1**

20

The graph best supports which claim about the relationship between economic recessions in the U.S. and total vehicle miles driven on U.S. roads?

A) In the last four decades, recessions that last longer than a year correspond to a decrease in total vehicle miles.

B) The six most recent recession periods each corresponded to an increase in total vehicle miles.

C) Recent recessions in the U.S. do not correlate strongly with either an increase or decrease in total vehicle miles.

D) In the last four decades, the longer a recession lasts, the more dramatically total vehicle miles decline.

21

As used in lines 31–32, "been played out" most nearly means

A) been dismissed.

B) received too much attention.

C) been overpowered.

D) reached the limit of their impact.

CONTINUE ▶

1

1

Questions 22–31 are based on the following passages and supplementary material.

Passage 1 is adapted from Radhika Singh, "Mice Utopias and the Behavioral Sink," published July 31, 2015 in the blog of The Borgen Project (borgenproject. org). Passage 2 is adapted from Frans de Waal, "Is it 'Behavioral Sink' or Resource Distribution?" published in *Scientific American* online July 21, 2010.

Passage 1

In 1972, behavioral researcher John Calhoun introduced four breeding pairs of mice into a box 9-feet square and 4.5-feet high. It was a "perfect
5   universe:" the mice were safe from predators and disease and given ample food and water. They doubled in population every 55 days.

However, within a year males stopped defending their territory, random violence broke
10 out, and female mice attacked their own offspring. Normal social bonds and interactions completely broke down. Infant abandonment soared, and mortality climbed. Cannibalism appeared, even though there was more than enough food. Fertile
15 females closed themselves off from society, and males of reproductive age—Calhoun called them the "beautiful ones"—did nothing but eat, sleep and groom.

Calhoun called this breakdown the
20 "behavioral sink," vand believed it came about when there were too many mice and a lack of important social roles for each one to play. Even when enough of the population died off so that only an optimal population remained, the mice
25 were not able to return to their natural behavior.

This connection between a breakdown of social bonds and violence was observed by Emile Durkheim in the late 19th century. In traditional societies, where family expectations and religion
30 held sway, people enjoyed strong social bonds and had distinct social roles to fill. However, as they moved to cities, they found they were fighting for a place in society. In exasperation and a state of helplessness, many fell into poverty or
35 turned to crime, violence and even suicide.

The fear of failing to be a productive member of society and fulfilling social roles can also push people, like the "beautiful ones," into isolating themselves. For instance, Japanese "hikikomori"
40 refuse to leave their rooms, sometimes for years, because they feel shame for being unable to fulfill familial expectations.

However, it is not clear that a high population density necessarily leads to a breakdown of
45 society and social roles. Humans might be able, with our ingenuity, to create social roles for everyone and avoid the behavioral sink. Some critics, such as psychologist Jonathan Freedam, suggested that it was not the density of
50 population that overwhelmed the mice but the large number of social interactions they had to deal with. Humans are able to avoid this, even while living in a highly dense area.

Passage 2

In the 1960s, John Calhoun placed a group
55 of rats in a room and observed how the animals killed, sexually assaulted and, eventually, cannibalized one another. This behavioral deviancy led Calhoun to coin the phrase "behavioral sink."
60 In no time, popularizers were comparing politically motivated street riots with rat packs and inner cities to behavioral sinks. Warning that society was heading for either anarchy or dictatorship, Robert Ardrey, a popular science
65 journalist, remarked in 1970 on the voluntary nature of human crowding and its ill effects. The negative impact of crowding became a central tenet of the voluminous literature on aggression.

In extrapolating from rodents to people,
70 however, these writers were making a giant leap. Compare, for instance, the per capita murder rates with the number of people per square kilometer in different nations. There is in fact no statistically meaningful relation. Among free-
75 market nations, the U.S. has the highest homicide rate despite a low population density.

To see how other primates respond to being packed together, we compared rhesus monkeys in crowded cages with those roaming free

CONTINUE ▶

1   **1**

80 on Morgan Island in South Carolina. We also
compared chimpanzees in indoor enclosures
with those living on large forested islands.
Nothing like the expected crowding effects
could be found. If anything, primates become
85 more sociable in captivity, grooming each other
more—probably in an effort to counter the
potential of conflict, which is greater the closer
they live together. Primates are excellent at
conflict resolution.

90   For the future of the world this means that
crowding by itself is perhaps not the problem it
is made it out to be. Resource distribution seems
the real issue. This was already true for Calhoun's
rats, the violence among them could be explained
95 by concentrated food sources and competition.
Also for humans, I would worry more about
sustainability and resource distribution than
population density.

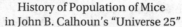

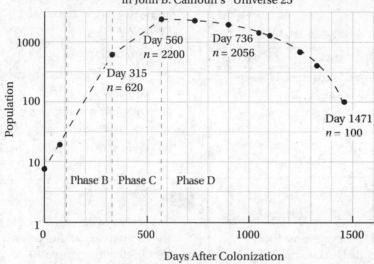

Phase A: Days 1–104 (Social Adjustment): Mice are introduced (4 males
and 4 females). Nests are established.

Phase B: Days 105–315 (Rapid growth): Population doubles every 55 days.
Male strength corresponds to frequency of reproduction. As crowding
develops, immature males begin to proliferate within the population.

Phase C: Days 316–560 (Stagnation): Population doubles every 145 days.
Male ability to defend territory declines. Nursing females become more
aggressive, even towards own offspring. By midway point in Phase C,
virtually all young are prematurely rejected by their mothers. Athough 20%
of nest sites are unoccupied, there is severe overcrowding in other sites.
Wthdrawn males become more violent toward each other.

Phase D: Days 561–1588 (Death): Population begins to decline on Day 561.
Incidences of pregnancy decline rapidly with no young surviving. The last
1000 mice born grow up with no social skills or ability to defend territory.
The males become withdrawn and obsessed with their own grooming.

CONTINUE ➤

1 ··· **1**

22

Which choice best describes the relationship between the two passages?

A) They propose alternate theories about how humans can avoid the behavioral sink.

B) They each critique different aspects of John Calhoun's rat study.

C) They present contradictory viewpoints on the relevance of rat studies to human behavior.

D) They provide different explanations for why human societies are susceptible to the behavioral sink.

23

As used in line 2, "introduced" most nearly means

A) pioneered.

B) acquainted.

C) inserted.

D) announced.

24

How would the author of Passage 2 most likely respond to the work of Emile Durkheim as described in Passage 1?

A) He would praise its foresight in predicting the problems of 21st century cities.

B) He would criticize its reliance on the work of John B. Calhoun.

C) He would note that it refutes the theory of the behavioral sink.

D) He would say that it conflicts with recent studies of rhesus monkeys.

25

Which choice provides the best evidence for the answer to the previous question?

A) Lines 57–59 ("This . . . sink")

B) Lines 69–70 ("In . . . leap")

C) Lines 84–88 ("If . . . together")

D) Lines 96–98 ("Also . . . density")

26

As used in line 24, the phrase "optimal population" refers to a population that, under ordinary circumstances, will

A) grow as large as possible.

B) sustain an effective network of social roles and relations.

C) consume a maximum quantity of natural resources.

D) dominate its physical environment.

27

The author of Passage 2 would most likely regard the comparison of the "beautiful ones" (line 38) to the "hikikomori" (line 39) as

A) an illustration of behavioral deviancy.

B) an unwarranted generalization.

C) an ironic coincidence.

D) a dangerous understatement.

1　　　　　　　　　　　　　　　　**1**

28

Which choice provides the best evidence for the answer to the previous question?

A) Lines 60–62 ("In no . . . sinks")

B) Lines 66–68 ("The . . . aggression")

C) Lines 69–70 ("In . . . leap")

D) Lines 80–82 ("We . . . islands")

29

According to the graph, for approximately how many days did the population of mice in Universe 25 stay above 1,000?

A) 200

B) 400

C) 800

D) 1,200

30

As used in line 74, "relation" most nearly means

A) relative.

B) association.

C) reference.

D) communication.

31

The author of Passage 2 considers the work of Robert Ardrey (lines 62–68) to be an example of

A) an effective analysis of the behavioral sink.

B) a dismissive attitude towards societal breakdown.

C) an interesting counterpoint to Calhoun's behavioral theory.

D) an overreaction in the popular media to Calhoun's work.

CONTINUE ▶

1   **1**

Questions 32–41 are based on the following passage.

This passage is adapted from Horace Mann, "Twelfth Annual Report to the Secretary of the Massachusetts State Board of Education," given in 1848.

Our means of education are the grand machinery by which the "raw material" of human
Line nature can be worked up into inventors and discoverers, into skilled artisans and scientific
5 farmers, into scholars and jurists and into the great expounders of ethical and theological science. By means of early education, these embryos of talent may be quickened, which will solve the difficult problems of political and
10 economical law.

It may be safely affirmed that the Common School[1] may become the most effective and benign of all the forces of civilization. In the first place, there is a universality in its operation, which
15 can be affirmed of no other institution whatever. And, in the second place, the materials upon which it operates are so pliant and ductile as to be susceptible of assuming a great variety of forms . . .

The necessaries and conveniences of life
20 should be obtained by each individual for himself, rather than accepted from the hand of charity. True statesmanship and true political economy, not less than true philanthropy, present this perfect theory as the goal, to be more and more
25 closely approximated by our imperfect practice.

Now, surely, nothing but Universal Education can counter-work the tendency to the domination of capital and the servility of labor. If one class possesses all the wealth and the education, while
30 the residue of society is ignorant and poor, the latter will be the servile subjects of the former. But if education be equably diffused, it will draw property after it, by the strongest of all attractions; for such a thing never did happen,
35 and never can happen, as that an intelligent and practical body of men should be permanently poor. Property and labor, in different classes, are essentially antagonistic; but property and labor, in the same class, are essentially fraternal. The
40 people of Massachusetts have, in some degree, appreciated the truth, that the unexampled

prosperity of the State, is attributable to the education which all its people have received; but are they sensible of a fact equally important?
45 Namely, that it is to this same education that two thirds of the people are indebted for not being, today, the vassals of as severe a tyranny, in the form of capital, as the lower classes of Europe are bound to in the form of brute force.

50 Education, then, beyond all other devices of human origin, is the great equalizer of the conditions of men—the balance-wheel of the social machinery. I do not here mean that it so elevates the moral nature as to make men
55 disdain and abhor the oppression of their fellow-men. This idea pertains to another of its attributes. But I mean that it gives each man the independence and the means, by which he can resist the selfishness of other men. It does better
60 than to disarm the poor of their hostility towards the rich; it prevents being poor. The spread of education, by enlarging the cultivated class or caste, will open a wider area over which the social feelings will expand; and, if this education
65 should be universal and complete, it would do more than all things else to obliterate factitious distinctions in society.

The affairs of a great nation are complicated and momentous, and the degree of intelligence
70 that superintends, should be proportioned to the magnitude of the interests superintended. But in the possession of this attribute of intelligence, elective legislators will never far surpass their electors. By a natural law, like that which
75 regulates the equilibrium of fluids, elector and elected, appointer and appointee, tend to the same level . . . [However], political proselytism is no function of the school; all indoctrination into matters of controversy between hostile
80 political parties is to be elsewhere sought for, and elsewhere imparted. Thus, may all the children of the Commonwealth receive instruction in the great essentials of political knowledge, in those elementary ideas without which they will never be
85 able to investigate more recondite and debatable questions—instead of perpetuating old errors— not by violence, nor by proscription, but by the more copious inflowing of the light of truth.

[1]universal public school

CONTINUE ▶

1   1

32

The primary purpose of the passage is to

A) remedy an inefficiency in the Massachusetts Common School system.

B) champion the cause of public schooling.

C) discuss the problem of class resentment between the rich and the poor.

D) condemn the treatment of students as mere tools of industry.

33

As used in line 3, "worked up" most nearly means

A) developed.

B) operated.

C) excited.

D) blended.

34

Horace Mann uses the terms "pliant" and "ductile" in line 17 in order to make the point that

A) the institution of public schooling is constantly changing.

B) there are many versatile educational resources available to teachers.

C) students are capable of acquiring a wide range of useful skills.

D) the attitudes toward the practicality of universal education were beginning to shift.

35

Horace Mann views Common Schools as unique among institutions in their ability to

A) correct for socioeconomic disparities.

B) instill a respect for public service.

C) provide scientific literacy.

D) convey the value of democratic principles.

36

Which of the following provides the best evidence to the answer to the previous question?

A) Lines 11–13 ("It . . . civilization")

B) Lines 16–18 ("And . . . forms")

C) Lines 37–39 ("Property . . . fraternal")

D) Lines 64–67 ("if . . . society")

37

The "perfect theory" (line 24) is primarily a theory about the value of

A) self-reliance.

B) intelligence.

C) perseverance.

D) charity.

38

As used in line 44, "sensible" most nearly means

A) careful.

B) susceptible.

C) reasonable.

D) aware.

39

Mann refers to the "equilibrium of fluids" (line 75) in order to

A) appease a widespread fear.

B) support a scientific claim.

C) illustrate a social theory.

D) provide a humorous aside.

40

Which choice best demonstrates that Horace Mann believes that education brings personal wealth?

A) Lines 26–28 ("Now . . . labor")

B) Lines 28–31 ("If one . . . former")

C) Lines 32–37 ("But . . . poor")

D) Lines 45–49 (Namely . . . force")

41

The central idea of the final paragraph (lines 68–88) is that

A) the functions of government do not coincide with the tasks of universal education.

B) administering a great nation requires education, but schooling should not be partisan.

C) universal education will make all citizens equal, thereby rendering legislators, as a specialized class, unnecessary.

D) elected legislators should not be entrusted with the administration of education, because they tend to politicize it.

CONTINUE

1　　　　　　　　　　　　　　　　　　　　　　　1

Questions 42–52 are based on the following passages.

This passage is adapted from Dan Gibson, "We synthesized a minimal cell and began a synthetic-life revolution," published in in *Aeon* (www.aeon.co) June 23, 2016. © 2016 Aeon Media Group, Ltd.

The physicist Richard Feynman once said, "What I cannot create, I do not understand."
Line With that inspiration, my colleagues and I set out to assemble life. Over the past 15 years, our
5　teams have been developing tools to design whole genomes, synthesize and assemble them in the lab, and install them into a living cell. Our goal was not just to elucidate the genetic components required for life, but also to establish the
10　capacity to create organisms tailored to specific applications.

To build the first synthetic cell in 2010, we assembled 60-base double-stranded DNA fragments (derived from the genome of the
15　*Mycoplasma mycoides* yeast), stitched them together using biomolecules we discovered, and combined our new genetic sequences inside a yeast cell. The synthetic genome was 1,078,809 base pairs (genetic letters) long, the largest
20　chemically defined structure ever synthesized in a laboratory.

Finally, we transplanted this synthetic genome into a recipient cell, reprogramming it with our rewritten genetic code. The original
25　traits of the recipient cell were eventually diluted as the cell grew and divided. We named the new synthetic cell *Mycoplasma mycoides* JCVI-syn1.0.

Our syn1.0 synthetic cell was the first proof that we could pull a DNA sequence out of the
30　computer, edit it, convert that revised sequence into a chemically synthesized structure, and create a free-living cell based on that new DNA sequence. Our syn1.0 work was only a first step, but it gave us an extraordinary set of tools for
35　DNA construction and activation. Our work also established a design-build-test cycle for designing a whole bacterial genome.

Synthetic biologists aim to produce cells with new and improved biological functions that do
40　not already exist in nature. Doing so requires a

deep knowledge of what natural biology already does. We therefore have been working to create a synthetic minimal cell—one that has only the machinery necessary for life. And now we
45　have succeeded with the synthesis of a cell we call JCVI-syn3.0. It has the smallest genome of any cell that can autonomously replicate, with just 473 genes. JCVI-syn3.0 retains almost all of the known genes involved in the synthesis and
50　processing of macromolecules and, surprisingly, 149 genes with unknown biological function. (Note that Feynman did *not* say: "What I can create, I do understand.") Those genes highlight that our current knowledge of the genetic
55　requirements for life is still limited. Our designs will remain restricted to naturally occurring DNA sequences until we can define the function of every gene and genetic element.

Syn3.0 will be an extremely useful chassis
60　for learning about the first principles of cellular life and for discovering how to predictably impart new biological functions. It can also help us produce more complex microbial species that could be valuable for industrial applications.
65　A minimal cell has several advantages. First, it would be devoting maximal energy to producing the proteins programmed into the cell. Second, because every gene is essential, a minimal cell would likely exhibit relatively few cellular
70　mutations. Also, because it is a simple system, it would be relatively straightforward to engineer.

Our synthetic cell work has been met with some worries about the potential and the safety of this level of genetic manipulation. We
75　have been addressing the ethical and societal implications of synthetic life since we first proposed the creation of a minimal cell in 1999. For example, our synthetic bacterial cells are designed so they cannot live outside of the lab
80　or other production environments. They are dependent on certain specific nutrients without which they cannot survive.

The possibilities of our technology are boundless. This cell engineering will be
85　essential for creating low-cost, environmentally sustainable industrial chemicals, medicines, biofuels, and crops. We've already used our technologies to stockpile an H7N9 vaccine

CONTINUE ▶

1

1

in response to the 2013 influenza outbreak in
90 China. Other applications include cars running
on biofuel from engineered microbes, plastics
made from biodegradable polymers, customized
pharmaceuticals "printed" at a patient's bedside.
These are just a few plausible benefits that could
95 soon emerge from our effort to understand life by
creating it.

42

The quotation from Richard Feynman in line 2
serves primarily to

A) Indicate the motivation behind the
development of the first minimal cell.

B) Exemplify the technical obstacles behind
developing the first minimal cell.

C) Show how scientists in general regard the
process of developing theories.

D) Suggest that there are still many topics that
scientists do not understand.

43

Over the course of the passage, the focus shifts
from

A) a description of the history of the minimal cell
project to a discussion the implications of its
success.

B) an explanation of the motivations behind the
minimal cell project to a discussion of the
obstacles in its path.

C) a description of the team working on the
minimal cell project to the ethical challenges it
poses.

D) the technical hurdles to accomplishing the
minimal cell project to ideas for overcoming
them.

44

As used in line 9, "establish" most nearly means

A) legislate

B) devise

C) declare

D) signal

45

As used throughout the passage, the term
"minimal cell" refers to a cell that

A) has the smallest possible diameter.

B) has the fewest number of proteins.

C) is the easiest to replicate.

D) has the simplest possible genetic makeup.

46

Which choice best supports the claim that there
are gaps in our understanding of the minimal cell
genome?

A) Lines 46–48 ("It . . . genes")

B) Lines 48–51 ("JCVI-syn3.0 . . . function")

C) Lines 62–61 ("It . . . applications")

D) Lines 67–70 ("Second . . . mutations")

47

One significant safeguard against the misuse of
synthetic cells is the fact that they

A) have a genome that is very difficult to
reproduce.

B) can be used to create cheap pharmaceuticals.

C) make biodegradable polymers.

D) are not viable except under strict conditions.

CONTINUE

1 **1**

48

Which choice provides the best evidence for the answer to the previous question?

A) Lines 67–70 ("Second . . . mutations")

B) Lines 72–74 ("Our . . . manipulation")

C) Lines 78–80 ("For . . . environments")

D) Lines 90–93 ("Other . . . bedside")

49

The main point of the parenthetical comment in lines 52–53 is that

A) the problems that concern physicists are not necessarily those that concern biologists.

B) technological progress does not always fill the gaps in our knowledge.

C) creativity is essential to the process of developing good scientific theories.

D) some of the evidence that we acquire through experimentation is unreliable.

50

Dan Gibson uses the term "chassis" (line 59) primarily because JCVI-syn3.0 is a

A) temporary system that will eventually lead to the development of a minimal cell.

B) framework for understanding the functions of the 149 mysterious genes on the minimal genome.

C) promotional device for publicizing the commercial possibilities of minimal cells.

D) platform from which to develop cells that perform a wider range of tasks.

51

The passage mentions all of the following as potential applications of synthetic cells EXCEPT

A) tissue for artificial organs.

B) inexpensive pharmaceuticals.

C) sustainable energy sources.

D) environmentally friendly plastics.

52

The main purpose of the final paragraph is to

A) address the concerns about safety raised in the previous paragraph.

B) indicate the potential uses of the JCVI-syn1.0 cell.

C) mention technologies that are made plausible by cell engineering.

D) list the recent accomplishments of cell engineering in the field of medicine.

STOP

If you finish before time is called, you may check your work on this section only. Do not turn to any other section of the test.

2   2

Writing and Language Test
35 MINUTES, 44 QUESTIONS

Turn to Section 2 of your answer sheet to answer the questions in this section.

DIRECTIONS

Each passage below is accompanied by a number of questions. For some questions, you will consider how the passage might be revised to improve the expression of ideas. For other questions, you will consider how the passage might be edited to correct errors in sentence structure, usage, or punctuation. A passage or a question may be accompanied by one or more graphics (such as a table or graph) that you will consider as you make revising and editing decisions.

Some questions will direct you to an underlined portion of a passage. Other questions will direct you to a location in a passage or ask you to think about the passage as a whole.

After reading each passage, choose the answer to each question that most effectively improves the quality of writing in the passage or that makes the passage conform to the conventions of Standard Written English. Many questions include a "NO CHANGE" option. Choose that option if you think the best choice is to leave the relevant portion of the passage as it is.

Questions 1–11 are based on the following passage.

Living with Robots

Robot butlers used to be the stuff of science fiction, but now, if you have just a few hundred spare bucks, you can buy a self-propelled disk to scoot around and vacuum your living room. It may not be Alfred the butler, but **1** we're getting closer every day to having robotic assistants in our daily lives. Some will be drones that perform mundane tasks like delivering packages, but others will "live" in our homes, perhaps looking out for intruders as we sleep, notifying the authorities

1

Which choice best sets up the sentence that follows?

A) NO CHANGE
B) we can't change the pace of technology
C) at least we don't need to feed it or pay its salary
D) we can't really complain after waiting so long

CONTINUE ▶

2   **2**

in emergencies, **2** <u>or tasks such as greeting guests or ordering take-out</u>.

Engineers are making great strides in creating robots that look, move, and respond like humans do. **3** <u>Although they are not</u> currently available for popular use, but they're getting closer to being commercially viable. We are beginning to see them in the most ordinary of situations. In Japan (where there are over 750,000 industrial robot workers) there is a hotel, the Henn na, or "Weird Hotel," **4** <u>it is run, staffed and operated</u> almost exclusively by robots. An animatronic velociraptor checks you in, and a foot-high robot concierge answers your questions (but only in Japanese).

[1] Although many people are thrilled by the idea of robot helpers, others are concerned **5** <u>by</u> robots taking their jobs. [2] Certainly, this is a serious concern, at least in the short-term. [3] Automobile factory workers aren't happy about the prospect of being replaced by 2,400-lb mechanisms that never take breaks or require sick leave or pension planning. [4] Our standards of living increase when mechanical tasks are performed more precisely and at less expense. [5] **6** <u>It means that manufactured items</u>

2

A) NO CHANGE
B) or greeting guests, or ordering take-out
C) or, greeting guests or ordering take-out
D) greeting guests, or ordering take-out

3

A) NO CHANGE
B) They are not
C) Not
D) Although not

4

A) NO CHANGE
B) being staffed and operated
C) it is operated
D) that is operated

5

A) NO CHANGE
B) about
C) with
D) with regard to

6

A) NO CHANGE
B) Automation ensures that manufactured items
C) It makes manufactured items
D) Automation means making manufactured items

CONTINUE ➤

2

2

are safer—because human error is taken out of the manufacturing process—and more reliable. **7**

   If automation is inevitable, how will low-skilled or medium-skilled workers make a living as the tasks they used to perform **8** <u>will become</u> automated? Clearly, these people will have to find other kinds of work. In fact, this transformation has been underway for a long time. In the last several decades, we have seen an enormous shift in labor from the manufacturing sector to the service sector. Since 1990, the number of U.S. jobs in manufacturing **9** <u>has declined</u> from 18 million to 12 million, although employment in the service and health care sectors has increased **10** <u>to more than compensate</u> for those job losses. Despite what some politicians claim, this shift is happening not because of government regulations or immigration policy, **11** <u>but due to</u> automation. Foreigners are not taking our factory jobs; robots are, and we'll be better off for it.

7

The writer is considering adding the following sentence to the previous paragraph.

   However, the efficiency of robots is a boon in the long run.

Where should it be placed?

A) immediately after sentence 1

B) immediately after sentence 2

C) immediately after sentence 3

D) immediately after sentence 4

8

A) NO CHANGE

B) would become

C) have become

D) become

9

A) NO CHANGE

B) have declined

C) declined

D) are declining

10

A) NO CHANGE

B) to compensate more

C) to do more than compensate

D) more than they need to compensate

11

A) NO CHANGE

B) but rather it is because of

C) but

D) but because of

2   **2**

Questions 12–22 are based on the following
passage and supplementary material.

Norman Borlaug and the Green Revolution

Working in relative obscurity, **12** the efforts of
one 20th century scientist may have saved nearly 1
billion lives. His name is Norman Borlaug, and he
founded the scientific movement that we now call the
Green Revolution. Borlaug received the Nobel Peace
Prize in 1970 for his work around the world to develop
and distribute high-yield varieties of wheat and rice,
promote better agricultural management techniques,
and **13** he modernized irrigation infrastructure.
Largely as a result of Borlaug's work, **14** wheat yields
throughout the world increased by over 200% between
1960 and 2014.

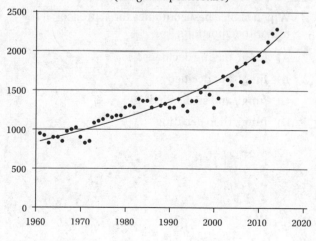

Wheat Yields in Least Developed Countries
(kilograms per hectare)

12

A) NO CHANGE

B) in the 20th century, the efforts of one scientist

C) one 20th century scientist

D) one 20th century scientist whose efforts

13

A) NO CHANGE

B) to modernize

C) modernizing

D) modernize

14

Which choice is best supported by the information
in the graph?

A) NO CHANGE

B) total wheat production throughout the world
increased by over 100%

C) wheat yields per hectare in the world's least
developed countries increased by over 100%

D) total wheat production in the world's least
developed countries increased by over 200%

CONTINUE

15 <u>Born</u> in 1914 on a farm in Cresco, Iowa, Borlaug came of age during the heart of the Depression. His grandfather convinced Norman to pursue an education, saying, "You're wiser to fill your head now if you want to fill your belly later on." Although he failed the entrance exam for the University of Minnesota, he did gain admittance to its two-year General College, and did well enough there to transfer to the College of Agriculture's forestry program. **16** He became fascinated by work his professors were doing in breeding food crops to be resistant to parasitic **17** <u>fungi. He decided</u> to pursue research in plant pathology and breeding.

Borlaug's professional work began in the 1940s, when he developed a high-yield and disease-resistant variety of wheat to help Mexican farmers become more productive. By 1963, most of the wheat crop in Mexico was grown from Borlaug's seeds, and the yield was

15

A) NO CHANGE
B) He was born
C) Being born
D) Although he was born

16

Which choice provides the most relevant and cohesive information?

A) Borlaug was a standout wrestler for the university, even reaching the Big Ten semifinals.
B) Borlaug's interest in agriculture had been cultivated years previously on his grandfather's farm.
C) Coincidentally, Borlaug would later work for the United States Forest Service in Massachusetts.
D) The move was an excellent fit for Norman's skills and interests.

17

Which choice best combines the sentences at the underlined portion?

A) fungi, having decided
B) fungi, but decided
C) fungi, and so decided
D) fungi, then deciding

CONTINUE ➡

2

2

600% greater than it had been in 1944. **18** Borlaug's work helped Mexico enormously in its effort to become more food secure, and even became a net exporter of wheat by 1963.

His work went far beyond just handing out drought-resistant seeds to Mexican farmers. **19** Borlaug showed them how to better manage their productivity by taking advantage of Mexico's two growing seasons. He also showed them how to use genetic variations among crops in a single field to maximize disease resistance. Although some of the genetic strains might **20** succumb to the pathogens (disease-causing agents), those strains could easily be replaced with new, resistant lines, thereby maintaining higher crop yields.

In the early 1960s, Borlaug traveled to two of the world's most impoverished nations, India and Pakistan, to share his insights with government officials and farmers who were struggling with food shortages. The situation was so **21** dire as that the biologist Paul Ehrlich speculated in his 1968 bestseller *The Population Bomb* that "in the 1970s and 1980s, hundreds of millions of people will starve to death in spite of any crash programs embarked upon now." Ehrlich singled out India for particular devastation because of its traditional and bureaucratic resistance to change.

18

A) NO CHANGE

B) Mexico benefitted enormously from Borlaug's work to make it

C) Borlaug's work was enormously beneficial to Mexico in making it

D) Borlaug's work was enormously beneficial to Mexico, making it

---

19

The writer is considering deleting the previous sentence. Should the writer make this change?

A) No, because it introduces the discussion about the extent of Borlaug's work in Mexico.

B) No, because it explains the variety of technologies inspired by Borlaug's work.

C) Yes, because mentioning drought detracts from the paragraph's focus on disease.

D) Yes, because repeats information that was mentioned in the previous paragraph.

20

A) NO CHANGE

B) support

C) submit to

D) restore

21

A) NO CHANGE

B) dire: so

C) dire that

D) dire; that

CONTINUE ➡

Fortunately, Borlaug kept working anyway. Between 1965 and 1970, India's cereal crop yield increased by 63%, and by 1974, India was self-sufficient in the production of all cereals. For the last 50 years, food production in India and Pakistan has increased faster than the **22** population. This is due largely to the work of Norman Borlaug.

22

Which choice best combines the sentences at the underlined portion?

A) population and

B) population,

C) population, which is

D) population, this being

2   2

Questions 23–33 are based on the following passage.

Thinking Burns Calories

Have you ever **23** been needing to take a nap after taking a long test in school? If so, you're not alone. One reason may be that you stayed up too late studying the night before. Another **24** may be that your brain, although not a muscle, burns a lot more calories than you think.

The typical adult brain runs on about 12 watts of power, roughly equivalent to that used by a standard LED light bulb. In one sense, it is a model of efficiency. **25** For example, IBM's Watson, the supercomputer that defeated *Jeopardy!* super-champion Ken Jennings back in 2010, required 90,000 watts of power, roughly what would power all of the appliances in an average-size suburban neighborhood. **26** Although it originally required a roomful of servers, today it is the size of three pizza boxes. Although our brains typically constitute only 2% of our body weight, they burn about 20% of our resting energy. **27** It would be understandable that such a hard-working organ needs to rest for 8 hours a day, and perhaps even more if it just helped you tackle your AP calculus mid-term.

23

A) NO CHANGE
B) had to need
C) needed
D) needed to have

24

A) NO CHANGE
B) would be because
C) being that
D) is because

25

A) NO CHANGE
B) For comparison
C) Even so
D) However

26

Which choice provides the most relevant information?

A) NO CHANGE
B) Our brains, however, contain about 85 billion neurons.
C) It may not be fair, however, to compare neurons to computer chips.
D) In the biological world, however, our brains are energy hogs.

27

A) NO CHANGE
B) It's
C) Its
D) Its'

CONTINUE ▶

Temporary mental exhaustion due to thinking is not the same as chronic mental fatigue—which is associated with sleep deprivation and certain mental **28** disorders, but it is still a very real phenomenon. When our brain cells are working harder, they require more glucose. Studies have shown that people who are solving hard problems see a larger **29** decay in blood glucose levels than do those who are just doing a mindless task, such as pressing a button. Findings like these about the link between diet and brain function **30** would suggest that it might be a good idea to eat something with a bit of sugar in it during your SAT break, to revive those brain cells.

Other studies indicate that moderate exercise before a test can increase mental endurance and fight brain fatigue. One study showed that children who walked on a treadmill for 20 minutes before a test performed better than those who read quietly instead.

[1] Attitude seems to play a significant role in mental performance as well. [2] Research suggests that if you go into a test with a positive frame of mind, you will be more likely to persist through challenges instead of giving up. [3] One way to do this is surprisingly **31** simple to just visualize yourself finishing your task successfully, rather than imagining all the things that could go wrong. [4] Although it is helpful to think about how to avoid mistakes as you study in the days before a test, it is less productive to do so on the day of the test. [5] Most performance experts agree that it's better to imagine your success instead. **32**

28

A) NO CHANGE
B) disorder, but still
C) disorders—but it is still
D) disorders—but still

29

A) NO CHANGE
B) degeneration
C) depreciation
D) decline

30

A) NO CHANGE
B) suggests
C) suggest
D) are suggestive

31

A) NO CHANGE
B) simple, just
C) simply just
D) simple: just

32

The writer wants to add the following sentence to the paragraph.

> It cuts both ways: whether you think you will fail or succeed, you're probably right.

The best placement for the sentence is immediately

A) after sentence 1.
B) after sentence 2.
C) after sentence 4.
D) after sentence 5.

CONTINUE ➡

2   **2**

Educators still agree that the best way to ace your tests is to pay attention in class, review your notes regularly, and do plenty of self-directed practice. However, it's nice to know that a quick snack, a run on the treadmill, and **33** a can-do attitude can help, too.

33

Which choice best fits with the rest of the passage?

A) NO CHANGE

B) a good night's sleep

C) a few practice problems

D) some deep-breathing exercises

2   2

Questions 34–44 are based on the following passage.

Calvin and Hobbes

I **34** <u>can hardly fail to</u> imagine what my childhood would have been like without Calvin. He was one of my best friends. Still, I don't know his last name—it's possible that he never had one—and I never actually met him in person. Even more tragically, he lived for only ten years, one month, and two weeks.

Calvin and his talking stuffed tiger, Hobbes, graced the comic pages across the country from 1985 until 1995, when **35** <u>it's</u> creator, Bill Watterson, retired at the age of 37. In that decade, *Calvin and Hobbes* became perhaps the most beloved comic strip in history. For me, Calvin perfectly captures the freedom, creativity, innocence, mischief, and fears of childhood. I've never met anyone, young or **36** <u>old, who could not identify</u> with Calvin in one way or another.

37 <u>In addition to their being</u> filled with poignant and hilarious insights, each *Calvin and Hobbes* strip was a work of art. Not since Winsor McCay's *Little Nemo*

34

A) NO CHANGE
B) couldn't hardly
C) can hardly
D) would hardly

35

A) NO CHANGE
B) its
C) their
D) they're

36

A) NO CHANGE
B) old who can't identify
C) old, without identifying
D) old not able to identify

37

A) NO CHANGE
B) In addition to there being
C) They were
D) In addition to being

2   2

in Slumberland has any other comic strip 38 received such widespread critical acclaim. Watterson's pen could sweep the reader from a mundane schoolroom to an extraterrestrial landscape swarming with alien creatures, all within the confines of four little panels.

According to Watterson, Calvin was named for the 16th century theologian John Calvin. 39 For his namesake, Calvin was precociously intelligent, even if he did not do particularly well in school. His teacher, Miss Wormwood, would frequently scold Calvin for his frequent daydreams, in which he became the intrepid Spaceman Spiff, saving mankind from Martian robots. Hobbes the tiger was named for Thomas Hobbes, an English philosopher who 40 believed what Watterson called "a dim view of human nature," and who famously said that life is "nasty, brutish, and short." Watterson's choice of names was probably 41 anticlimactic: Calvin the boy is deeply irreverent, and Hobbes the tiger is perpetually optimistic.

38

Which choice is best sets up the information that follows?

A) NO CHANGE

B) influenced so many future cartoonists and graphical artists

C) been so deeply adored by generations of readers

D) exemplified such graphical skill in the service of storytelling

39

A) NO CHANGE

B) With

C) Like

D) Because of

40

A) NO CHANGE

B) held

C) beheld

D) nurtured

41

Which choice is most consistent with the information in the sentence?

A) NO CHANGE

B) ironic

C) apocryphal

D) accidental

CONTINUE ➡

Many of the lessons that Calvin taught me were of the negative 42 sort: how not to build a snowman, how not to talk to my parents, and how not to interact with females. It was a lot of fun watching him make mistakes, especially since Hobbes was always there to chastise or comfort him when things went wrong. Overall, though, the lessons from *Calvin and Hobbes* are poignant and deep. Calvin taught me how to use my imagination, how to deal with childhood fears, and how to be a good friend.

Between 2010 and 2016, the popularity of Calvin as a name for male newborns in the U.S. 43 improved by over 50%. Could this be because this was 44 at the time during which those parents who were just old enough to read *Calvin and Hobbes* in its heyday were becoming old enough to have children of their own? I like to think so.

42

A) NO CHANGE
B) sort: such as how
C) sort: like how
D) sort, how

43

A) NO CHANGE
B) intensified
C) surged
D) expanded

44

A) NO CHANGE
B) the time where
C) at the time where
D) when

STOP

**If you finish before time is called, you may check your work on this section only.
Do not turn to any other section of the test.**

3 **3**

Math Test – No Calculator

25 MINUTES, 20 QUESTIONS

Turn to Section 3 of your answer sheet to answer the questions in this section.

DIRECTIONS

For questions 1–15, solve each problem, choose the best answer from the choices provided, and fill in the corresponding circle on your answer sheet. **For questions 16–20,** solve the problem and enter your answer in the grid on the answer sheet. Please refer to the directions before question 16 on how to enter your answers in the grid. You may use any available space in your test booklet for scratch work.

NOTES

1. The use of a calculator is NOT permitted.
2. All variables and expressions used represent real numbers unless otherwise indicated.
3. Figures provided in this test are drawn to scale unless otherwise indicated.
4. All figures lie in a plane unless otherwise indicated.
5. Unless otherwise indicated, the domain of a given function f is the set of all real numbers for which $f(x)$ is a real number.

REFERENCE

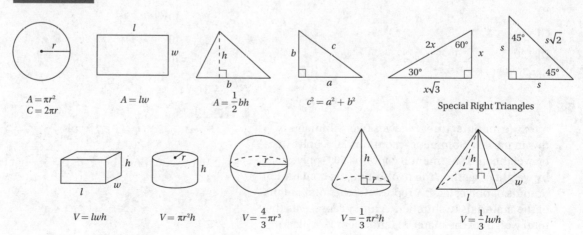

$A = \pi r^2$
$C = 2\pi r$

$A = lw$

$A = \frac{1}{2}bh$

$c^2 = a^2 + b^2$

Special Right Triangles

$V = lwh$

$V = \pi r^2 h$

$V = \frac{4}{3}\pi r^3$

$V = \frac{1}{3}\pi r^2 h$

$V = \frac{1}{3}lwh$

The number of degrees of arc in a circle is 360.
The number of radians of arc in a circle is 2π.
The sum of the measures in degrees of the angles of a triangle is 180.

CONTINUE

1

If $-3x = 18$, what is the value of $4x + 6$?

A) -30

B) -18

C) -6

D) 30

2

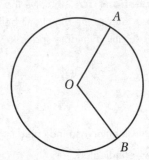

The circle above with center O has a circumference of 30. If angle AOB measures 120°. What is the length of minor arc AB?

A) 5

B) 6

C) 10

D) 20

3

A textile manufacturer receives two shipments of raw materials. Shipment A contains 30% polyester by weight, and shipment B contains 50% polyester by weight. Together, the two shipments contain 130 pounds of polyester. If x represents the total weight of the materials in shipment A and y represents the total weight of the materials shipment B, which equation models this relationship?

A) $0.3x + 0.5y = 130$

B) $0.5x + 0.3y = 130$

C) $30x + 50y = 130$

D) $50x + 30y = 13$

4

A roofing company estimates the price of a job, in dollars, using the expression $M + 15nh$, where M is the total cost of the materials, n is the number of roofers who will be working on the job, and h is the number of hours the job will take using n roofers. What is the best interpretation of the number 15 in this expression?

A) The company generally has 15 roofers working on a job.

B) The company charges \$15 per hour for each roofer on the job.

C) Each roofer is expected to work on the job for 15 hours.

D) The cost of the materials is expected to be a multiple of \$15.

5

$$(-5x^2y + 3xy - 7y^2) - (5x^2y - 7y^2 + 5xy)$$

Which of the following is equivalent to the expression above?

A) $-14y^2 - 2xy$

B) $-10x^2y + 8xy$

C) $-10x^2y - 14y^2 - 2xy$

D) $-10x^2y - 2xy$

6

$$\sqrt{3k+3} - x = 0$$

In the equation above, if $x = 6$, what is the value of k?

A) 3

B) 9

C) 11

D) 36

CONTINUE

3   **3**

7

A shipping company uses the formula $c = \frac{1}{3}wl$ to estimate how many shipping containers, c, can fit on a barge whose deck is w yards wide and l long.

Which of the following correctly expresses w in terms of c and l?

A) $w = \frac{1}{3}cl$

B) $w = 3cl$

C) $w = \frac{l}{3c}$

D) $w = \frac{3c}{l}$

8

Which of the following equations represents a line that is parallel to the line with the equation $y = -2x + 4$?

A) $2x + 4y = 0$

B) $-4x + y = -2$

C) $-6x - 3y = 9$

D) $8x - 4y = 4$

9

The population, P, of a certain village from 1960 to 1980 can be calculated using the function $P(t) = 1,200 + 60t$, where t represents the number of years since 1960. Which of the following statements is the best interpretation of the number 1,200 in this context?

A) From 1960 to 1980, the population of the town increased by 1,200 people.

B) Between 1960 and 1980, the population of the town increased 1,200 people each year.

C) The population of the town was 1,200 at the beginning of 1960.

D) Between 1960 and 1980, the population of the town increased by $\frac{1200}{60}$ people each year.

10

$$3x + 2y - 4$$

$$-4x - 6y = -2$$

What is the solution (x, y) to the system of equations above?

A) $\left(\frac{14}{13},\ 7\right)$

B) $(4, 1)$

C) $(2, -1)$

D) $\left(\frac{3}{2},\ \frac{3}{2}\right)$

11

Which of the following is equivalent to $\frac{6+2i}{5-3i}$? (Note: $i = \sqrt{-1}$)

A) $\frac{6}{5} \quad \frac{2i}{3}$

B) $\frac{6}{5} \quad \frac{2i}{3}$

C) $\frac{12}{17} - \frac{14i}{17}$

D) $\frac{12}{17} + \frac{14i}{17}$

CONTINUE ➤

12

The graph of the equation $y = x^2 + k$ in the xy-plane is a parabola with a vertex that is below the x-axis. Which of the following is true of the parabola represented by the equation $y = k(x - b)^2 - c$?

A) The vertex is $(b, -c)$, and the parabola opens downward.

B) The vertex is $(b, -c)$, and the parabola opens upward.

C) The vertex is $(-b, c)$, and the parabola opens downward.

D) The vertex is $(-b, c)$, and the parabola opens upward.

13

Which of the following is equivalent to $8^{\frac{3}{2}}$?

A) $\sqrt{64}$

B) $\sqrt[3]{8^2}$

C) 4^3

D) $16\sqrt{2}$

14

What is the sum of all values that satisfy the equation $3x^2 + 30x + 15 = 0$?

A) -10

B) $-4\sqrt{5}$

C) $4\sqrt{5}$

D) 10

15

If $4x - 2y = 20$, what is the value of $\dfrac{16^x}{4^y}$?

A) 4^5

B) 4^{10}

C) 16^2

D) It cannot be determined from the given information.

3   3

DIRECTIONS

For questions 16–20, solve the problem and enter your answer in the grid, as described below, on the answer sheet.

1. Although not required, it is suggested that you write your answer in the boxes at the top of the columns to help you fill in the circles accurately. You will receive credit only if the circles are filled in correctly.

2. Mark no more than one circle in any column.

3. No question has a negative answer.

4. Some problems may have more than one correct answer. In such cases, grid only one answer.

5. **Mixed numbers** such as $3\frac{1}{2}$ must be gridded as 3.5 or $\frac{7}{2}$.

   (If $3\frac{1}{2}$ is entered into the grid as [3 | 1 | / | 2], it will be interpreted as $\frac{31}{2}$, not $3\frac{1}{2}$).

6. **Decimal answers:** If you obtain a decimal answer with more digits than the grid can accommodate, it may be either rounded or truncated, but it must fill the entire grid.

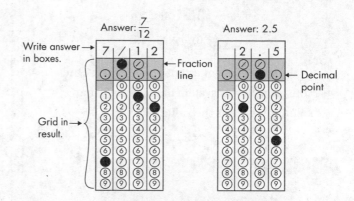

Answer: $\frac{7}{12}$ Answer: 2.5

Answer: 201
Either position is correct.

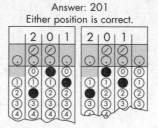

Acceptable ways to grid $\frac{2}{3}$ are:

CONTINUE →

3   **3**

16

$$ax + 3y = c$$
$$6x + 9y = 15$$

In the system of equations above, a and c are constants. If this system has infinitely many solutions, what is the value of $\frac{a}{c}$?

17

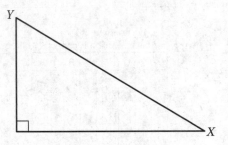

In the triangle above, if the sine of angle X is 0.3, what is the cosine of angle Y?

18

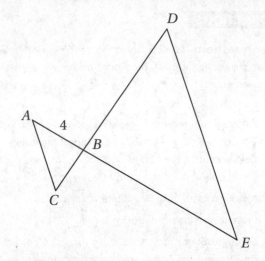

In the figure above, $\overline{AC} \parallel \overline{DE}$, and $\overline{AE}$ intersects $\overline{CD}$ at point B. If $AE = 16$, how many times greater is the area of $\triangle DBE$ than the area of $\triangle ABC$?

19

$$\frac{4x^2 + 1}{4x^2 - 1} + \frac{16x}{16x^2 - 4}$$

The expression above is equivalent to $\frac{ax + b}{ax - b}$ where a and b are constants and $x \neq \frac{1}{2}$. What is the value of $a + b$?

20

$$x^3 - 4x^2 + 2x - 8 = 0$$

For what real value of x is the equation above true?

STOP

If you finish before time is called, you may check your work on this section only.
Do not turn to any other section of the test.

Math Test – Calculator

55 MINUTES, 38 QUESTIONS

Turn to Section 4 of your answer sheet to answer the questions in this section.

DIRECTIONS

For questions 1–30, solve each problem, choose the best answer from the choices provided, and fill in the corresponding circle on your answer sheet. **For questions 31–38,** solve the problem and enter your answer in the grid on the answer sheet. Please refer to the directions before question 31 on how to enter your answers in the grid. You may use any available space in your test booklet for scratch work.

NOTES

1. The use of a calculator is permitted.

2. All variables and expressions used represent real numbers unless otherwise indicated.

3. Figures provided in this test are drawn to scale unless otherwise indicated.

4. All figures lie in a plane unless otherwise indicated.

5. Unless otherwise indicated, the domain of a given function f is the set of all real numbers for which $f(x)$ is a real number.

REFERENCE

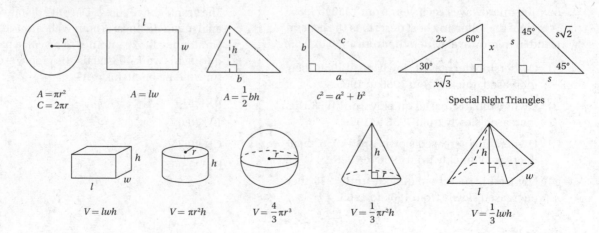

$A = \pi r^2$
$C = 2\pi r$

$A = lw$

$A = \dfrac{1}{2}bh$

$c^2 = a^2 + b^2$

Special Right Triangles

$V = lwh$

$V = \pi r^2 h$

$V = \dfrac{4}{3}\pi r^3$

$V = \dfrac{1}{3}\pi r^2 h$

$V = \dfrac{1}{3}lwh$

The number of degrees of arc in a circle is 360.
The number of radians of arc in a circle is 2π.
The sum of the measures in degrees of the angles of a triangle is 180.

CONTINUE ➤

4 **4**

1

If $\frac{4}{3}z = \frac{2}{5}$, what is the value of z?

A) $\frac{3}{10}$

B) $\frac{8}{15}$

C) 2

D) $\frac{10}{3}$

2

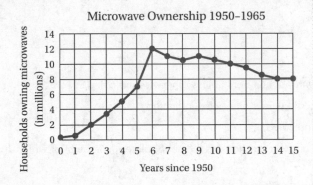

Microwave Ownership 1950–1965

The graph above shows the number of households owning microwaves each year from 1950 to 1965. Which of the following best describes the general trend in microwave ownership from 1950 to 1965?

A) Ownership decreased slowly until 1956, then increased quickly from 1956 to 1965.

B) Ownership decreased quickly until 1956, then increased slowly from 1956 to 1965.

C) Ownership increased slowly until 1956, then decreased quickly from 1956 to 1965.

D) Ownership increased quickly until 1956, then decreased slowly from 1956 to 1965.

3

The amount of money a yoga teacher earns is directly proportional to the number of students who attend his class. He earns $90 if 12 students attend his class. How much money will he earn if 30 students attend his class?

A) $36

B) $200

C) $225

D) $360

4

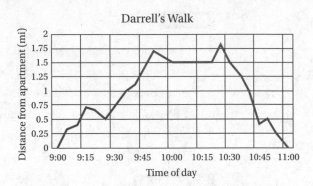

Darrell's Walk

The graph above shows Darrell's distance from his apartment during a 2-hour walk around the city. He stopped for 20 minutes to rest on a park bench during his walk. Based on the graph, around what time did he begin his rest?

A) 9:15

B) 10:00

C) 10:25

D) 11:00

CONTINUE ▶

4   **4**

5

The population density of a region is equal to the population of the region divided by the area of the region. What is the area, in km², of a region with a population density of 70 people per km² and a population of 3,850 people?

A) .018 km²

B) 36 km²

C) 55 km²

D) 70 km²

6

The speed of light is approximately 3×10^8 meters per second. Based on this information, approximately how long will it take for light from a star to reach a planet that is 10 million <u>kilometers</u> away?

A) $.0\overline{3}$ seconds

B) $33.\overline{3}$ seconds

C) 3×10^5 seconds

D) 3×10^{15} seconds

7

The planners in a town of 3,000 people are considering a plan to build an apartment complex on the site of a local park. A team went to the park site and asked 300 town voters who were using the park whether or not they supported the plan. Ten of those surveyed had no opinion. Which of the following is the most significant potential flaw in the design of this survey?

A) the small sample size

B) the small size of the town

C) the fact that some respondents did not have an opinion

D) the location of the survey

8

Oil Consumption in Country X (1991–1995)

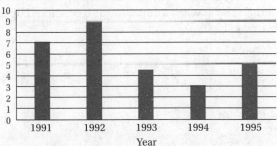

The number of barrels of oil consumed by country X each year from 1991 to 1995 is shown in the graph above. If the total amount of oil consumed in those five years was 285,000 barrels, what is an appropriate label for the vertical axis of the graph?

A) Barrels of oil consumed (in hundreds)

B) Barrels of oil consumed (in thousands)

C) Barrels of oil consumed (in tens of thousands)

D) Barrels of oil consumed (in hundreds of thousands)

CONTINUE ➡

4   **4**

9

Temperature vs. Rainfall

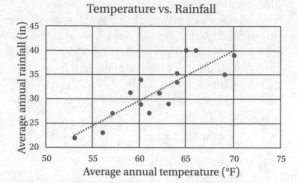

A meteorologist recorded the average annual temperature and average annual rainfall for 15 different villages and recorded his results on the scatterplot above. The line of best fit for the data is also shown. For the village with an average annual temperature of 65°F, the actual average annual rainfall is approximately how many inches greater than the average annual rainfall predicted by the line of best fit?

A)   1

B)   3

C)   5

D) 35

10

Which of the following sets represents all the values of n for which the expression $|n - 3| - 3$ is negative?

A) $\{n \mid n < 3\}$

B) $\{n \mid n > 3\}$

C) $\{n \mid n < 0 \text{ or } n > 6\}$

D) $\{n \mid 0 < n < 6\}$

11

$$f(x) = \frac{x^2 - 36}{\dfrac{x}{3} - 6}$$

For which value of x is the function f above undefined?

A) -6

B)   0

C)   3

D)   18

12

	Lives on campus	Lives off campus
Eats in dining hall	160	56
Does not eat in dining hall	63	121

The table above shows the results of a survey of 400 students on a college campus, in which they were asked whether they live on campus and whether they eat in a dining hall. If a student who lives on campus is chosen at random, what is the probability that he or she does NOT eat in the dining hall?

A) $\dfrac{2}{5}$

B) $\dfrac{63}{160}$

C) $\dfrac{63}{184}$

D) $\dfrac{63}{223}$

CONTINUE

4 **4**

13

The Glenville PTA is sponsoring a bake sale that sells cookies and brownies. Each cookie cost $1.50, and each brownie costs $2.25. The PTA's goals for the day are to sell at least 55 items and to bring in at least $100 of revenue. Let x be the number of cookies sold, and let y be the number of brownies sold. Which of the following systems of inequalities represents the PTA's goals?

A) $x + y \leq 100$
    $1.5x + 2.25y \leq 55$

B) $x + y \geq 100$
    $1.5x + 2.25y \geq 55$

C) $x + y \geq 55$
    $1.5x + 2.25y \leq 100$

D) $x + y \geq 55$
    $1.5x + 2.25y \geq 100$

14

The graph of the function f in the xy-plane crosses the x-axis at -4, 2, and 5. Which of the following could define f?

A) $f(x) = (x - 2)^2(x - 5)$
B) $f(x) = (x^2 + 2x - 8)(3x - 15)$
C) $f(x) = (x^2 - 7x + 10)(x - 4)$
D) $f(x) = (x - 4)(x + 2)(x + 5)$

Questions 15 and 16 refer to the following information.

An anthropologist surveyed 400 households at random from each of two villages, Village A and Village B, and recorded the number of children in each household. Village A has a total of 2,000 households, and Village B has a total of 3,200 households. The results of the survey are shown in the table below.

Number of children	Village A	Village B
0	60	40
1	150	140
2	110	130
3	70	70
4	10	20

15

What is the median number of children per household for all the households surveyed?

A) 2.0
B) 2.5
C) 3.5
D) 4.0

16

If each of these two samples is representative of its respective village, approximately how many households altogether (in both villages) have no children?

A) 620
B) 640
C) 650
D) 680

CONTINUE

17

Table A		Table B	
x	$f(x)$	x	$g(x)$
−1	2	3	−1
3	6	5	3
5	5	6	2

Table A above shows values that satisfy the function $f(x)$, and Table B shows values that satisfy the function $g(x)$. What is the value of $f(g(3))$?

A) −1

B) 2

C) 3

D) 5

Questions 18 and 19 refer to the following information.

Vegetable Yield 2001 and 2002

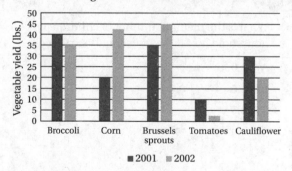

2001   2002

The bar graph above shows the total yield of five different crops on a particular farm in the years 2001 and 2002.

18

Which choice best approximates the percent increase in yield of corn from 2001 to 2002?

A) 44.0%

B) 56.0%

C) 112.5%

D) 225.0%

19

In a scatterplot of the data where 2001 yield is plotted on the x-axis and 2002 yield is plotted on the y-axis for each vegetable crop, how many data points would fall below the line $y = x$?

A) 1

B) 2

C) 3

D) 4

20

A gardener has three right cylindrical flower pots, each with a diameter of 16 cm, that she will fill with potting soil. If her bag of potting soil contains 1,000 in³ of soil, and she fills all three flower pots to a height of 20 cm, approximately how many cubic inches of soil will be left in the bag? ($1 \text{ cm}^3 = 0.061 \text{ in}^3$)

A) 64

B) 264

C) 736

D) 755

CONTINUE ➤

Questions 21 and 22 refer to the following information.

$$B = \frac{L}{4\pi D^2}$$

The apparent brightness of an object B is related to the luminosity of the object L and the square of the distance between the observer and the object D according to the formula above.

21

Which of the following expresses the distance between the object and the observer in terms of the apparent brightness and the luminosity of the object?

A) $D = \sqrt{\dfrac{L}{4\pi B}}$

B) $D = \sqrt{\dfrac{4\pi B}{L}}$

C) $D = \left(\dfrac{L}{4\pi B}\right)^2$

D) $D = \sqrt{\dfrac{4\pi}{BL}}$

22

An astronomer on Earth measures the brightness of two stars, Star A and Star B, that have the same luminosity. She finds that the brightness of Star A is 156% greater than the brightness of Star B. The distance from Earth to Star B is how many times the distance from Earth to Star A?

A) 1.25

B) 1.56

C) 1.60

D) 2.56

23

If the length of a rectangle is decreased by 10 percent and its width is increased by p percent, its area will increase by 26 percent, what is the value of p ?

A) 36

B) 38

C) 40

D) 42

24

Mr. Chu has a total of n gift certificates that he is giving out to his employees for the holidays. If he gives each employee 5 gift certificates, he will have 7 left over. To give each of his employees 6 gift certificates, he would need to have 9 more gift certificates. How many employees does Mr. Chu have?

A) 12

B) 16

C) 18

D) 22

25

The population of a colony of bacteria increases by 200% every 6 hours. If the current population of the colony is 20,000, which expression represents the colony's population h hours from now?

A) $20{,}000(2)^{\frac{h}{6}}$

B) $20{,}000(3)^{\frac{h}{6}}$

C) $20{,}000(3)^{6h}$

D) $20{,}000(3)^{\frac{6}{h}}$

4 **4**

26

$$h(t) = -16t^2 + 64t$$

The equation above expresses the approximate height, h, in feet, of a rocket t seconds after it is launched upwards from the ground until it hits the ground again. After how many seconds will the rocket reach its highest point?

A) 2

B) 4

C) 8

D) 16

27

$$x^2 + y^2 - 6x + 4y = 3$$

The equation of a circle in the xy-plane is shown above. What is the radius of the circle?

A) 2

B) 4

C) 8

D) 16

28

The equation $y = (x - 4)(x + 8)$ represents a parabola in the xy-plane. Which of the following is an equivalent form of this equation that shows the coordinates of the vertex of this parabola as constants or coefficients?

A) $y = (x + 4)^2 - 8$

B) $y = (x - 4)^2 + 8$

C) $y = (x + 2)^2 - 36$

D) $y = (x + 2)^2 + 36$

29

In the xy-plane, line m has a slope of 2 and crosses the x-axis at the point $\left(\dfrac{5}{2}, 0\right)$. Line n is perpendicular to line m and crosses the y-axis at the point $\left(0, -\dfrac{5}{2}\right)$. At what point do lines m and n intersect?

A) $\left(\dfrac{5}{2}, -\dfrac{5}{2}\right)$

B) $(4, -2)$

C) $(1, -3)$

D) $\left(2, -\dfrac{5}{2}\right)$

30

$$(x - a)^3 = x^3 - bx^2 + bx - a^3$$

If the equation above is true for all real values of x, and a and b are positive constants, what is the value of a ?

A) 1

B) 2

C) 3

D) It cannot be determined from the given information.

4 4

DIRECTIONS

For questions 31–38, solve the problem and enter your answer in the grid, as described below, on the answer sheet.

1. Although not required, it is suggested that you write your answer in the boxes at the top of the columns to help you fill in the circles accurately. You will receive credit only if the circles are filled in correctly.

2. Mark no more than one circle in any column.

3. No question has a negative answer.

4. Some problems may have more than one correct answer. In such cases, grid only one answer.

5. **Mixed numbers** such as $3\frac{1}{2}$ must be gridded as 3.5 or $\frac{7}{2}$.

   (If $3\frac{1}{2}$ is entered into the grid as [3 1 / 2], it will be interpreted as $\frac{31}{2}$, not $3\frac{1}{2}$.)

6. **Decimal answers:** If you obtain a decimal answer with more digits than the grid can accommodate, it may be either rounded or truncated, but it must fill the entire grid.

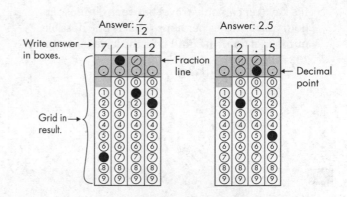

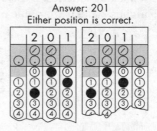

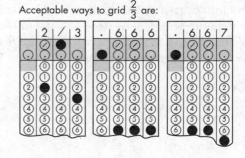

Acceptable ways to grid $\frac{2}{3}$ are:

CONTINUE

31

If a kayaker can only travel between 8 miles per hour and 12 miles per hour, what is one possible number of hours it could take the kayaker to travel 132 miles?

32

A ball rolls f feet and 7 inches. If the ball rolls a total of 115 inches, what is the value of f?

33

A chemist heats a sample of liquid with a starting temperature of 20°C at a rate of 14°C per minute. How much time, in minutes, will it take for the liquid to reach its boiling point of 251°C ?

34

$$3(2x + 3)(-x + 4)$$

If the expression above is rewritten in the form $ax^2 + bx + c$, where a, b, and c are constants, what is the value of $a + b$?

35

A professor scores 15 of 20 exams himself and gives the other 5 to his teaching assistant to score. If the average score of the 15 exams graded by the professor is 87, and the average score of all 20 exams is 85, how many points lower is the average score of the teaching assistant's 5 exams than the average score of the professor's 15 exams?

4 **4**

36

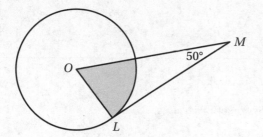

In the figure above, the circle has a center O, line segment $\overline{LM}$ is tangent to the circle at point L, and angle LMO has a measure of 50°. If the area of the circle is 108 square centimeters, what is the area, in square centimeters, of the shaded sector?

Questions 37 and 38 refer to the following information.

Enrique opens a bank account that earns 5% interest, compounded annually, with an initial deposit of P dollars. He uses the equation $A = P(1.05)^t$ to model the balance, A, of the account after t years.

37

Enrique calculates that if he does not make any withdrawals or deposits, the balance of the account after 2 years will be $1,653.75. What is the value, in dollars, of Enrique's initial deposit?

38

Assuming that Enrique does not make any withdrawals or deposits, after 6 years, the interest that the account has earned will equal what percent of Enrique's initial deposit? Round your answer to the nearest whole number. (Ignore the percent symbol when gridding. For instance, enter 26% as 26.)

STOP

If you finish before time is called, you may check your work on this section only.
Do not turn to any other section of the test.

Essay

50 MINUTES, 1 QUESTION

DIRECTIONS

As you read the passage below, consider how Ellis Parker Butler uses

- evidence, such as facts or examples, to support his claims
- reasoning to develop ideas and connect claims and evidence
- stylistic or persuasive elements, such as word choice or appeals to emotion, to add power to the ideas expressed

---

Adapted from Vivian Gornick, "The Cost of Daydreaming," ©2015 by *The New York Times*. Originally published April 24, 2015.

1   That spring I was teaching in Arizona and walking daily along a road at the edge of the town, taking new pleasure in the physical beauty that surrounded me (the mountains, the desert, the clarity of light) but, as usual, running a movie in my head. One afternoon in April, right in the middle of the film, a kind of visual static—something like the static on a television screen—cut across my inner field of vision; the "story" began literally to break up before my eyes and then it actually terminated itself. At the same time an acrid taste began to fill my mouth and, deep within, I felt myself shrinking from: I knew not what.

2   The entire incident was so strange, so baffling, that it mystified rather than alarmed me, and I thought to myself, an aberrant occurrence: Expect no repeats. But the next day, exactly the same thing happened. There I was, walking along the blacktopped road, another movie underway in my head, when again: The story short-circuited itself, the acrid taste filled my mouth, and again I felt myself blanching before some unnamable anxiety. When on the third day the entire process repeated itself, it became clear that a sea change was in progress.

3   Before long I became sufficiently gun-shy—I had begun to dread the nastiness in my mouth—to want to suppress the daydreaming; and lo and behold, it turned out that I could. Now, no sooner did the images start to form in my head than I found myself able to wipe them clean before they could take hold.

4   It was then that the really strange and interesting thing happened. A vast emptiness began to open up behind my eyes as I went about my daily business. The daydreaming, it seemed, had occupied more space than I'd ever imagined. It was as though a majority of my waking time had routinely been taken up with fantasizing, only a narrow portion of consciousness concentrated on the here and now. Of this I was convinced, because of the number of times a day the bitter taste threatened to take up residence in my mouth.

5   The insight was stunning. I began to realize what daydreaming had done for me—and to me.

6   Ever since I could remember, I had feared being found wanting. If I did the work I wanted to do, it was certain not to measure up; if I pursued the people I wanted to know, I was bound to be rejected; if I made myself as attractive as I could, I would still be ordinary looking.

CONTINUE ▶

5 5

7 Around such damages to the ego a shrinking psyche had formed: I applied myself to my work, but only grudgingly; I'd make one move toward people I liked, but never two; I wore makeup but dressed badly. To do any or all of these things well would have been to engage heedlessly with life—love it more than I loved my fears—and this I could not do. What I could do, apparently, was daydream the years away: to go on yearning for "things" to be different so that I would be different.

8 Turning 60 was like being told I had six months to live. Overnight, retreating into the refuge of a fantasized tomorrow became a thing of the past. Now there was only the immensity of the vacated present. Then and there I vowed to take seriously the task of filling it. But, of course, easier said than done. It wasn't hard to cut short the daydreaming, but how exactly did one manage to occupy the present when for so many years one hadn't? Days passed, then weeks and months in which I dreaded waking into my own troubled head. I thought often in those days of Virginia Woolf's phrase "moments of being"—because I wasn't having any.

9 Then—seemingly from one day to the next—I became aware, after a street encounter, that the vacancy within was stirring with movement. A week later another encounter left me feeling curiously enlivened. It was the third one that did it. A hilarious exchange had taken place between me and a pizza deliveryman, and sentences from it now started repeating themselves in my head as I walked on, making me laugh each time anew, and each time with yet deeper satisfaction. Energy—coarse and rich—began to swell inside the cavity of my chest. Time quickened, the air glowed, the colors of the day grew vivid; my mouth felt fresh. A surprising tenderness pressed against my heart with such strength it seemed very nearly like joy; and with unexpected sharpness I became alert not to the meaning but to the astonishment of human existence. It was there on the street, I realized, that I was filling my skin, occupying the present.

Write an essay in which you explain how Vivian Gornick builds an argument to persuade her audience that we should learn to repress daydreaming and live in the moment. In your essay, analyze how Gornick uses one or more of the features listed in the box above (or features of your own choice) to strengthen the logic and persuasiveness of her argument. Be sure that your analysis focuses on the most relevant features of the passage.

Your essay should NOT explain whether you agree with Gornick's claims, but rather explain how she builds an argument to persuade her audience.

SAT PRACTICE TEST 4 ANSWER KEY

Section 1: Reading	Section 2: Writing and Language	Section 3: Math (No Calculator)	Section 4: Math (Calculator)
1. C	1. A	1. B	1. A
2. C	2. D	2. C	2. D
3. D	3. B	3. A	3. C
4. A	4. D	4. B	4. B
5. B	5. B	5. D	5. C
6. C	6. B	6. C	6. B
7. D	7. C	7. D	7. D
8. A	8. D	8. C	8. C
9. C	9. A	9. C	9. C
10. B	10. A	10. C	10. D
11. D	11. D	11. D	11. D
12. C	12. C	12. A	12. D
13. B	13. D	13. D	13. D
14. C	14. C	14. A	14. B
15. A	15. A	15. B	15. A
16. A	16. D	16. 2/5 or .4	16. A
17. D	17. C	17. 3/10 or .3	17. B
18. A	18. B	18. 9	18. C
19. A	19. A	19. 3	19. C
20. C	20. A	20. 4	20. B
21. D	21. C		21. A
22. A	22. B		22. C
23. C	23. C		23. C
24. D	24. A		24. B
25. C	25. B		25. B
26. B	26. D		26. A
27. B	27. B		27. B
28. C	28. C		28. C
29. C	29. D		29. C
30. B	30. C		30. A
31. D	31. D		31. 11 x 16.5
32. B	32. A		32. 9
33. A	33. A		33. 16.5
34. C	34. C		34. 9
35. A	35. C		35. 8
36. D	36. A		36. 12
37. A	37. D		37. 1500
38. D	38. D		38. 34
39. C	39. C		
40. C	40. B		
41. B	41. B		
42. A	42. A		
43. A	43. C		
44. B	44. D		
45. D			
46. B			
47. D			
48. C			
49. B			
50. D			
51. A			
52. C			

| Total Reading Points (Section 1) | Total Writing and Language Points (Section 2) | Total Math Points (Section 3) | Total Math Points (Section 4) |

SCORE CONVERSION TABLE

Scoring Your Test

1. Use the answer key to mark your responses on each section.

2. Total the number of correct responses for each section:

   1. Reading Test   Number correct: _____ **(Reading Raw Score)**

   2. Writing and Language Test   Number correct: _____ **(Writing and Language Raw Score)**

   3. Mathematics Test – No Calculator   Number correct: _____

   4. Mathematics Test – Calculator   Number correct: _____

3. Add the raw scores for sections 3 and 4. This is your **Math Raw Score**: _____

4. Use the Table 1 to calculate your **Scaled Test and Section Scores (10–40)**.

   Math Section Score (200–800):   _____

   Reading Test Score (10–40):   _____

   Writing and Language Test Score (10–40):   _____

5. Add the **Reading Test Scaled Score** and the **Writing and Language Test Scaled Score** and multiply this sum by 10 to get your **Reading and Writing Test Section Score (20–80)**.

   Sum of Reading + Writing and Language Scores: _____   10 =

   Reading and Writing Section Score: _____

Table 1: Scaled Section and Test Scores (10–40)

Raw Score	Math Section Score	Reading Test Score	Writing/ Language Test Score	Raw Score	Math Section Score	Reading Test Score	Writing/ Language Test Score
58	800			29	520	27	28
57	790			28	520	26	28
56	780			27	510	26	27
55	760			26	500	25	26
54	750			25	490	25	26
53	740			24	480	24	25
52	730	40		23	480	24	25
51	710	40		22	470	23	24
50	700	39		21	460	23	23
49	690	38		20	450	22	23
48	680	38		19	440	22	22
47	670	37		18	430	21	21
46	670	37		17	420	21	21
45	660	36		16	410	20	20
44	650	35	40	15	390	20	19
43	640	35	39	14	380	19	19
42	630	34	38	13	370	19	18
41	620	33	37	12	360	18	17
40	610	33	36	11	340	17	16
39	600	32	35	10	330	17	16
38	600	32	34	9	320	16	15
37	590	31	34	8	310	15	14
36	580	31	33	7	290	15	13
35	570	30	32	6	280	14	13
34	560	30	32	5	260	13	12
33	560	29	31	4	240	12	11
32	550	29	30	3	230	11	10
31	540	28	30	2	210	10	10
30	530	28	29	1	200	10	10

SAT PRACTICE TEST 4 DETAILED ANSWER KEY

Section 1: Reading

1. C — Summary

Choice A is incorrect because at no point does anyone in the Otis family express horror about the revelation that the estate they have just purchased is haunted. To the contrary, Hiram Otis, as the rest of the Otis family, is highly skeptical about the claim. Choice B is incorrect because Lord Canterville's concern about the supposed crime, that *Lady Eleanor de Canterville . . . was murdered on that spot by her husband . . . in 1575*, had learned about it long before this story takes place. Choice D is incorrect because there is no indication at this point in the story that Lord Canterville and his staff are trying to scare the Otises.

2. C — Tone and Development

The passage is a farce because of the absurd ways that the Otis family reacts to the (ostensibly) horrifying revelations that their house is haunted and was the scene of a terrible crime.

3. D — Purpose

By saying that the *ghost has been seen by several members of my family, as well as by the Rev. August Dampier, a Fellow of King's College, Cambridge* (lines 11–14) Lord Canterville is attempting to bolster the credibility of his claim that the ghost exists.

4. A — Word in Context

In saying that *the laws of Nature are not going to be suspended for the British aristocracy* (lines 29–31), Otis means that the laws of physics will not be *held in abeyance* simply because Lord Canterville believes that he saw a ghost.

5. B — Interpretation

In lines 62–64, Washington Otis declares that the story about the blood-stain is *"all nonsense"* and proceeds to clean it up quickly despite the housekeeper's claim that it could not be removed. This indicates that he regards the stain to be a *brief irritation*. It's also clear that his family agrees with his assessment, since his family gave Washington *admiring* (line 69) looks.

6. C — Textual Evidence

As the explanation of the previous question indicates, the best evidence is found in lines 62–64.

7. D — Word in Context

The *fearful peal of thunder* (line 71) made them all *start to their feet* (line 72), which means that they all stood up suddenly because of the noise. This meaning of *start* has the same origin as the verb *startle*, which means it does not simply mean *commence* or *arise*.

8. A — Tone

The conversation in lines 73–80 makes it clear that Hiram Otis did not regard the *fearful peal of thunder* as an ominous sign from the spirit world in reaction to Washington's cleaning of the blood stain, but rather simply as an indication that England does not have *"enough decent weather for everybody"* (line 76). His inclination to make a joke in a situation that would frighten others indicates that he is being *flippant* (not showing proper respect or seriousness).

9. C — Interpretation

In lines 28–31, Mr. Otis states that *"there is no such thing, sir, as a ghost, and I guess the laws of Nature are not going to be suspended for the British aristocracy."* In other words, he thinks that the existence of ghosts would violate scientific principles.

10. B — Textual Evidence

As the explanation of the previous question indicates, the best evidence is found in lines 28–31.

11. D — Purpose

The first paragraph points out that *traffic levels in the United States* are declining *in defiance of forecasts projecting major increases*, and then introduces a discussion of *the implications peak car has for public policy*. It is primarily focused, therefore, on *reconsidering the approach* we have been taking in transportation policy. Choice A is incorrect because referring to an incorrect forecast is not the same as indicating a logical fallacy. Choice B is incorrect because, although "peak car" is a technical term, defining it is not the central purpose of this paragraph. Choice C is incorrect because the author does not cite any specific statistical evidence, let alone question it.

12. C — Word in Context

In lines 14 and 16 *congestion* refers to traffic congestion on highways, which is a form of *excessive usage*.

13. B   **Inference**

The example the author uses to illustrate Say's Law of Markets is the situation in which *increasing the supply of driving lanes only increases the number of drivers to fill them* (lines 11–13). In general, this Law suggests that increasing some economic supply (like highway lanes) leads to a corresponding increase in demand (like more people choosing to drive because the highways are now bigger). Of the choices, the most similar example is the one in choice B: *as a country expands its Internet capacity, businesses and individuals increase their Internet usage proportionally.*

14. C   **Logical Support**

In lines 10–14, the author mentions Say's Law of Markets, which is an economic theory which, if true, would contradict his thesis that increasing highway capacity might actually reduce traffic congestion. By acknowledging this theory, the author is recognizing a potential objection to his position.

15. A   **Textual Evidence**

As the explanation of the previous question indicates, the best evidence is found in lines 10–14.

16. A   **Purpose**

The author mentions the example of the Indiana Toll Road in lines 26–29 as one of *a slew of recent stories about the poor financial performance of toll roads, resulting in part from traffic falling far below projections.* In other words, this example contradicts Say's Law of Markets and supports the author's claim that the U.S. may have reached "peak car" and so *maybe we really can build our way out of congestion after all* (lines 15–16).

17. D   **Graphical Analysis**

Since the vertical axis represents the percent increase from the 1971 baseline, the value that represents a doubling is 100%. However, the graph never reaches this point.

18. A   **Inference**

In lines 6–9, the author states that "peak car" *has been celebrated by many urbanists as undermining plans for more roads.* This implies that many modern urbanists hope to thwart plans to build more roads.

19. A   **Textual Evidence**

As indicated in the explanation to the previous question, the best evidence is found in lines 6–9.

20. C   **Graphical Inference**

In the graph, periods of recession are indicated by vertical gray bars. In the six recessions shown, three seem to correspond to a decrease in vehicle miles and three seem to correspond to an increase in vehicle miles. Therefore, it is safe to say that this graph does not support any claim about a strong correlation between recessions and total vehicle miles.

21. D   **Phrase in Context**

When the author says that *the trends that drove high traffic growth in the past have largely been played out* (lines 30–32), he is saying that those factors that made people drive more, or more people drive, have *reached the limit of their impact.*

22. A   **Cross-Textual Analysis**

Passage 1 describes John Calhoun's mouse experiment and the phenomenon that Calhoun called the "behavioral sink." It also discusses the fact that some social scientists fear that human overcrowding could lead to a similar social breakdown. In the last paragraph, however, the author states that *it is not clear that a high population density necessarily leads to a breakdown of society and social roles* (lines 43–45) because humans are not as overwhelmed by the *large number of social interactions they [have] to deal with* (lines 51–52). Passage 2 also questions the conclusions many have reached on the basis of Calhoun's study, but suggests that humans are in a better position to avoid the "behavioral sink" because *primates are excellent at conflict resolution* (lines 94–95) and because *resource distribution seems the real issue* (lines 88–89). In other words, both passages *propose alternate theories about how humans can avoid the behavioral sink.*

23. C   **Word in Context**

The statement that *Calhoun introduced four breeding pairs of mice into a box* (lines 1–2), the author means that Calhoun *inserted* the rats into their new environment.

24. D   **Cross-Textual Inference**

Lines 26–35 of Passage 1 discuss Emile Durkheim's claim that human society breaks down as cities become more crowded. However, in lines 84–89, the author of Passage 2 discusses an experiment with rhesus monkeys that shows that, unlike the mice in Calhoun's experiments, *primates become more sociable in captivity . . . probably in an effort to counter the potential of conflict, which is greater the closer they live together.* Since human beings are even more advanced primates, the author of Passage 2 would argue that Durkheim's work *conflicts with recent studies of rhesus monkeys.*

25. C   **Textual Evidence**

As the explanation of the previous question indicates, the best evidence is found in line 84–89.

26. B   **Interpretation**

When the author states that *[e]ven when enough of the population died off so that only an optimal population remained, the mice were not able to return to their natural behavior* (lines 22–25), the author indicates that the *"optimal population"* is that at which we should expect that the mice *would* return to their *"natural behavior"* and thereby *sustain an effective network of social roles and relations* rather than have that network break down.

27. B   **Cross-Textual Inference**

In lines 69–70, the author of Passage 2 states that *[i]n extrapolating from rodents to people . . . these writers were making a giant leap*, and therefore it is unwarranted to conclude that a breakdown in mouse communities implies a similar breakdown in human communities. Therefore, the author of Passage 2 would regard the comparison between the *beautiful ones* (line 38) in mouse communities and the *hikikomori* (line 39) in human communities as *an unwarranted generalization.*

28. C   **Textual Evidence**

As the explanation of the previous question indicates, the best evidence is found in lines 69–70.

29. C   **Graphical Analysis**

The graph indicates that the mouse population of Universe 25 first exceeded 1,000 on about day 400 and then fell below 1,000 on approximately day 1200, for a span of about 800 days.

30. B   **Word in Context**

The statement that *[t]here is in fact no statistically meaningful relation* (lines 73–74) means that there is no causal or correlational *association* between murder rates and population density.

31. D   **Inference**

In the second paragraph of Passage 2, the author bemoans the fact that, after Calhoun's experimental results were announced, *popularizers were comparing politically motivated street riots with rat packs, and inner cities to behavioral sinks* (lines 60–62). Robert Ardrey is cited as one such "popularizer," so his work represents an example of *an overreaction in the popular media to Calhoun's work.*

32. B   **Primary Purpose**

This passage focuses on Horace Mann's central claim that *the Common School may become the most effective and benign of all the forces of civilization* (lines 11–13). Therefore, the primary purpose of the passage is to *champion the cause of public schooling.* Although Mann does discuss the power of public schooling to overcome

the disparities between rich and poor, choice C is incorrect because merely discussing this problem is not the central purpose of the passage as whole.

33. A   **Phrase in Context**

When Mann states that *[o]ur means of education are the grand machinery by which the "raw material' of human nature can be worked up into inventors and discoverers* (lines 1–4), he means that education is the process by which children can be *developed* into productive members of society.

34. C   **Purpose**

In stating that *the material [that is, children] upon which [schooling] works are so pliant and ductile as to be susceptible of assuming a great variety of forms* (lines 16–18), Mann is using the physical analogy of metalworking to say that *students are capable of acquiring a wide range of useful skills.*

35. A   **Detail**

In lines 64–66, Mann states that *if this education should be universal and complete, it would do more than all things else to obliterate factitious distinctions in society,* foremost of which are the distinctions between rich and poor. That is, Common Schools are unique in their ability to *correct for socioeconomic disparities.*

36. D   **Textual Evidence**

As the explanation of the previous question indicates, the best evidence is found in lines 64–66.

37. A   **Interpretation**

The *perfect theory* (line 24) that Mann refers to is the idea that *[t]he necessaries and conveniences of life should be obtained by each individual for himself, rather than accepted from the hand of charity* (lines 19–21). Such a theory expounds the value of *self-reliance.*

38. D   **Word in Context**

When Mann asks, *are they sensible of a fact equally important?* (line 44), he is asking whether the people of Massachusetts are *cognizant* (aware) of the fact that education also prevents people from becoming *vassals of . . . as severe a tyranny* (line 47).

39. C   **Purpose**

Throughout the essay, Mann uses physical analogies—for instance, referring to children as malleable pieces of metal—to illustrate his ideas about the value of schooling. In lines 75–77, he uses the physical analogy of the *equilibrium of fluids* to illustrate his social theory that *elector and elected, appointer and appointee, tend to the same level.*

40. C — Textual Evidence

In lines 32–37, Mann claims that *if education be equably diffused, it will draw property after it . . . for . . . it] never can happen . . . that an intelligent and practical body of men should be permanently poor.* That is, education brings personal wealth.

41. B — Summary

The final paragraph states that *the affairs of a great nation or state are exceedingly complicated . . . and] the degree of intelligence that superintends, should by proportioned to the magnitude of the interests superintended . . . However,] political proselytism is no function of the school.* That is, running a complex country is hard, and requires great intelligence (of the kind nurtured by public schooling), but political partisanship does not belong in the school curriculum.

42. A — Purpose

Dan Gibson says that the quotation from Richard Feynman served as an *inspiration* (line 3) for him and his team in their endeavor to *assemble life* (line 4), which included building the first "minimal cell."

43. A — Structure

The first three paragraphs of the passage describe the motivation behind and execution of the JCVI-syn1.0, a precursor to the minimal cell. The passage then goes on to discuss the implications of this discovery, and the success in creating JCVI-syn3.0, the so-called "minimal cell." The final two paragraphs discuss both the pitfalls and the potential of this new discovery. Choice A best describes the overall scope of the passage. Choices B and D are incorrect because the passage does not focus to any great extent on the obstacles in the path of the minimal cell project, because it was after all successful. Choice C is incorrect because the passage does not focus on describing the team behind the minimal cell project.

44. B — Word in Context

When Gibson says that the goal of his team was *to establish the capacity to create organisms tailored to specific applications* (lines 9–11), he means that it was their goal to *devise* the ability to create useful artificial cells.

45. D — Interpretation

In lines 43–44, Gibson indicates that a "minimal cell" is one *that has only the machinery necessary for life.* He later goes on to explain that this *machinery* consists primarily of the cell's *genetic makeup.*

46. B — Textual Evidence

In lines 48–51, Gibson states that *JCVI-syn3.0 retains . . . surprisingly, 149 genes with unknown biological function.* In other words, there are gaps in our understanding of the minimal cell genome.

47. D — Detail

In the second-to-last paragraph, Gibson states that his synthetic cell work *has been met with some worries about the potential and the safety of this level of genetic manipulation* (lines 72–74), but then goes on to explain that *our synthetic bacterial cells are designed so that they cannot live outside the labor other production environments* (lines 78–80). In other words, these cells *are not viable except under strict conditions.*

48. C — Textual Evidence

As the explanation of the previous question indicates, the best evidence is found in lines 78–80.

49. B — Interpretation

The parenthetical comment in lines 52–53 states that the inverse of Feyman's quotation in line 2 is *not* necessarily true; that is, although an inability to create something always hinders its understanding, building something *does not* always *aid* understanding. Therefore, technological progress does not always fill the gaps in our knowledge.

50. D — Purpose

When Gibson states that JCVI-syn3.0 *will be an extremely useful chassis for learning about the first principles of cellular life and for discovering how to predictable impart new biological functions* (lines 59-62), he is saying that JCVI-syn3.0 is a *platform from which to develop cells that perform a wider range of tasks.*

51. A — Detail

In the last paragraph, Gibson describes some of the potential applications of synthetic cells, such as *low-cost, environmentally sustainable industrial chemicals, medicines* (pharmaceuticals), *biofuels* (sustainable energy resources), *and crops* (lines 85–87) as well as *biodegradable polymers* (environmentally friendly plastics) (line 92). It does not, however, mention *materials for artificial organs* as a potential application.

52. C — Purpose

The final paragraph discusses technologies that are made plausible by cell engineering. Choice A is wrong because the final paragraph does not address the safety concerns addressed in the previous paragraph; those were done in that paragraph. Choice B is incorrect because the listed applications are not for the JCBI-syn1.0 cell, which is in fact a very primitive artificial cell that is not capable of such applications. Choice D is incorrect because the listed applications are *potential* and rather than accomplished.

Section 2: Writing and Language

1. **A** Cohesiveness

The sentence that follows describes examples of *robotic assistants*, so the original phrasing is the best for setting it up.

2. **D** Parallelism

This sentence lists some of the potential functions of "live-in" robots, so that list should have a parallel structure: *looking* out for intruders . . . *notifying* the authorities . . . *greeting* guests, or *ordering* take-out. Only choice D maintains this parallel structure without any superfluous words.

3. **B** Coordination

Choices A and D are incorrect because it is redundant to use *Although* and *but* as conjunctions for the same two clauses. Choice C is incorrect because it turns the opening phrase into a participial phrase, which does not coordinate with the main clause. The only choice that properly coordinates the two clauses is B.

4. **D** Redundancy/Coordination

The original sentence is not only redundant but also creates a comma splice, in which the two independent clauses are joined only by a comma. Choice C commits the same mistake. Choice B is awkward and redundant.

5. **B** Idiom

The two standard idioms for the participle *concerned* are *concerned about*, which means "worried about," and *concerned with*, which means "interested in or involved with." In this context, the first idiom is the only sensible one.

6. **B** Pronoun Reference/Clear Expression of Ideas

In the original phrasing, the pronoun *it* has no clear antecedent. Choice C commits this same error. Choice D is incorrect because the verb *means* is being used illogically: the sentence does not provide a sensible definition of the word *automation*. Choice B is the only one that provides logical and clear phrasing.

7. **C** Logical Sequence

The new sentence clearly functions as a transition between a discussion of the potential pitfalls of automation to a discussion of its benefits. Since sentence 3 mentions a pitfall to workers, but sentence 4 describes a benefit to the general public, the new sentence belongs immediately after sentence 3.

8. **D** Verb Form

The use of the conjunction *as* indicates that the sentence is linking two independent clauses with verbs in the same tense. (This is because *as* in this context means *at the same time as*, and therefore the two verbs express the same tense.) Since the verb in the first clause, *make*, is in the present tense, indicative mood, the verb in the second clause should be in the same tense and mood: *become*.

9. **A** Verb Aspect/Verb Agreement

The original sentence is correct because the verb *has declined* agrees in number with the singular subject *number* and is in the present tense, consequential aspect because it indicates a current status that is the consequence of a situation that has been true *since 1990*. Choice B is incorrect because it creates a subject-verb disagreement. Choices C and D are incorrect because they dot not indicate the consequential aspect.

10. **A** Comparative Idiom

Some grammar scolds might say that the original phrasing is unacceptable because it includes a "split infinitive:" the modifying phrase *more than* is plunked in the middle of the infinitive phrase *to compensate*. However, it is not formally incorrect to split an infinitive, and this example nicely illustrates how splitting an infinitive can provide the most elegant and logical phrasing of an idea. Although choices B-D are grammatical and avoid the split infinitive, none of them creates a clear and logical phrase.

11. **D** Parallelism

This sentence uses the contrasting construction *not A but B*. The Law of Parallelism requires that the phrases replacing *A* and *B* in this construction must have the same grammatical form. Since the phrase replacing *A* is in the form *because [clause]*, the phrase replacing *B* must take the same form.

12. **C** Dangling Participles

The original phrase creates a dangling participle, since the participle *working* does not share its subject with the main clause. Choice B commits the same error. Choice D is incorrect because it creates a sentence fragment. Choice C is correct because the one who was *working* is the *20th century scientist*.

13. D　　　　　　　　　　　　　　　　**Parallelism**

The list of verbs in this sentence must maintain a parallel structure: *develop and distribute . . . promote . . . , and modernize*.

14. C　　　　　　　　　　　　　**Graphical Analysis**

The header of the graph indicates that these data are only the wheat yields for the *least developed countries*. Since these yields increased from about 1000 kg per hectare to just over 2000 kg per hectare, this increase was over 100%, but not over 200%.

15. A　　　　　　　　　**Coordination/Participles**

The original phrasing creates a participial phrase that coordinates grammatically and logically with the main clause. Choice B is incorrect because it creates a comma splice. Choice C is incorrect because the present participle illogically implies that Borlaug was born at the same time that he *came of age*. Choice D is incorrect because it illogically implies a contrast between the two ideas in the sentence.

16. D　　　　　　　　　　　　　　　**Cohesiveness**

Choice A is inappropriate because the paragraph is about Borlaug's academic career and his early interest in agriculture, not his career in sports. Choice B is inappropriate because this paragraph is about his college years, not his childhood on the farm. Choice C is inappropriate also because the time from of his later Forest Service work is out of place in a paragraph about his college career.

17. C　　　　　　　　　　**Coordination/Transition**

Choice A is incorrect because it illogically implies that Borlaug decided to pursue research in plant pathology before he even acquired an interest in it. Choice B is incorrect because it illogically implies a contrast between the two ideas in the sentence. Choice D is incorrect because the participle *deciding* does not coordinate with the main clause. Choice C is correct because it indicates a logical cause-and-effect.

18. B　　　　　　　　　　　　　　　　**Parallelism**

It's very important to read the entire sentence to get this one correct: notice that the sentence has a compound predicate. The second predicate is *became a net exporter of wheat by 1963*. In order for this predicate to coordinate with the rest of the sentence, it must have the same subject as the first clause. Logically, this subject is *Mexico*, so only choice B can be correct.

19. A　　　　　　　　　　　**Logical Cohesiveness**

This sentence provides an effective transition from the topic of the previous paragraph to the discussion of the further extent of Borlaug's work in Mexico, so it should not be deleted.

20. A　　　　　　**Diction/Clear Expression of Ideas**

The original word is best: *succumb* means *to fail to resist*, which describes what the weaker genetic strains do when faced with dangerous pathogens.

21. C　　　　　　　　　　　　**Idiom/Punctuation**

The phrase *so dire that [clause]* is a standard comparative idiom. The colon in choice A and the semi-colon in choice D are incorrect because, in both cases, the phrases that follow are not independent.

22. B　　　　　　　　　　　　　　　**Coordination**

Choice B combines the sentence most logically and concisely. Choice A is incorrect because the conjunction *and* does not link grammatically similar phrases. Choice C is incorrect because the pronoun *which* lacks a logical antecedent: interrogative pronouns such as *which* take the immediately preceding noun as an antecedent, but clearly the *population* can not be *due largely to the work of Norman Borlaug*. Choice D is incorrect because *this being* is not idiomatic.

23. C　　　　　　　　　　　　　　　**Verb Form**

The past participle that follows the question *have you ever?* is timeless, and therefore cannot logically take the progressive aspect, as in the original phrasing. Choices B and D are incorrect because *had to need to* and *needed to have to* are both redundant.

24. A　　　　　　　　　　　　　　　**Parallelism**

This sentence should be grammatically parallel to the previous sentence, and so should also use the subjunctive auxiliary *may*.

25. B　　　　　　　　　　　　　　　**Transitions**

This sentence supports the idea at the human brain *is a model of efficiency* only if the example of the power-hungry Watson is *compared* to the relatively efficient human brain. Therefore, choice B is the most logical.

26. D　　　　　　　　　　　　　　　**Cohesiveness**

Since the paragraph is about the energy consumption of the human brain relative to other things, like computers or the other organs in the human body, choice D provides the most cohesive information.

27. B　　　　　　　**Possessive Form/Verb Mood**

Since this sentence is stating an unconditional fact, the use of the subjunctive form *would be* in the original phrasing is illogical. Choice C is incorrect because *its* is the possessive form, not the contraction of *it is*. Choice D is incorrect because *its'* is not a word.

---

28. C   **Punctuation/Coordination**

Since the interrupting modifying phrase begins with a dash, it must end with a dash also. However, choice D is incorrect because the phrase following the conjunction *but* must be an independent clause.

---

29. D   **Diction**

The original is incorrect because *decay* describes a process of deterioration, which is not appropriate to a discussion of blood glucose levels. The same is true of choice B, *degeneration*. Choice C is incorrect because *depreciation* pertains to a monetary value. Choice D works because blood glucose levels can *decline*.

---

30. C   **Verb Agreement/Verb Mood**

Since this sentence is indicating an unconditional fact, the use of the subjunctive auxiliary *would* is inappropriate. Choice B is incorrect because the verb *suggests* disagrees in number with its plural subject *findings*. Choice D is incorrect because the phrase *suggestive that* is not idiomatic.

---

31. D   **Diction/Punctuation**

Choice D is most logical because the second clause exemplifies the claim in the first clause. The original phrasing is not a complete sentence. Choice B is incorrect because it forms a comma splice. Choice C is incorrect because the phrase *simply just* is redundant.

---

32. A   **Logical Sequence**

This sentence belongs immediately after sentence 1 because the pronoun *it* refers to one's *attitude*, which is the subject of sentence 1. If this sentence is placed anywhere else in the paragraph, the pronoun will lack a logical antecedent.

---

33. A   **Relevance**

The original phrasing is best, because the previous paragraph discusses the importance of attitude to performance, whereas the importance of sleep and breathing were not discussed. Choice C is wrong because the importance of practice was already mentioned in the paragraph.

---

34. C   **Subjunctive Auxiliaries/Logic**

The double negative *can hardly fail* is illogical in the original phrasing of the sentence. Choice B has the same problem. Choices C and D both avoid the double negative, and express the subjunctive mood. However, choice C is correct because the auxiliary *can* is required

to convey a statement about ability (or, more accurately, inability), which is the central idea of the sentence.

---

35. C   **Possessive Form/Pronoun Agreement**

The subject of the sentence, and antecedent of the underlined pronoun, is *Calvin and his talking stuffed tiger, Hobbes*. Since this is a plural noun phrase, the pronoun must be plural as well. The correct possessive form is *their*. (It's interesting to note that the title of the comic strip, *Calvin and Hobbes,* would be treated as a singular, however, in such clauses as *Calvin and Hobbes is a much beloved comic strip.*)

---

36. A   **Clear Expression of Ideas**

The comma is required in this phrase to separate the interrupting modifier from the main clause. However, choice C is illogical because the participle *identifying* should refer to the group, not the author.

---

37. D   **Modifying Phrases/Coordination**

The original phrasing is incorrect because the pronoun *their* lacks a logical antecedent. Choice B is incorrect because it is awkward and illogical. Choice C is incorrect because it creates a comma splice. Choice D is correct because it creates a participial phrase the coordinates logically with the main clause.

---

38. D   **Cohesiveness**

The sentence that follows describes the effectiveness of Watterson's artistic storytelling, therefore choice D most effectively maintains the thematic cohesiveness of the paragraph.

---

39. C   **Logic/Clear Expression of Ideas**

The point of this sentence is that Calvin the boy shares one important characteristic with his namesake, John Calvin. Therefore the only logical preposition to use here is *Like*.

---

40. B   **Diction**

When describing the relationship between a person and his or her viewpoint, standard English suggests that we say that the person *holds* that viewpoint. It is not quite accurate to say that a person *believes* his or her own viewpoint, because having a viewpoint does not require accepting any particular claim. We also would not say that someone *beholds* his or her own viewpoint, because that viewpoint is internal, not external. It is also inaccurate to say that someone *nurtures* his or her own viewpoint, because viewpoints by their nature arise independently of any deliberate effort.

41. B   **Cohesiveness**

The colon in this sentence indicates that the second clause explains the first. The second clause indicates a clear pair of contradictions: Calvin is irreverent although his namesake was a religious figure, and Hobbes has a sunny disposition although his namesake was a cynic. Therefore, the most logical conclusion is that Watterson chose these names *ironically*. *Anticlimactic* means causing emotional disappointment. *Apocryphal* mean having dubious authenticity.

42. A   **Idiom/Punctuation**

The original phrasing is best because the colon serves to link a concept (*lessons . . . of the negative sort*) with a list of examples (*how not to build a snowman, how not to talk to my parents . . .*). Although choices B and C include the colon, using *such as* or *like* is redundant because the colon already implies that the list is a set of examples.

43. C   **Diction**

The phrase *by over 50%* indicates that the *popularity of Calvin as a name for male newborns* is quantifiable. However, saying that this quantity *improved* is illogical because it implies that this popularity is a quality rather than a quantity. It is also incorrect to say that this popularity *intensified* because a statistic cannot become more intense. It is also incorrect to say that popularity *expanded* because the 50% increase does not imply any geographical or demographic extent. The most justifiable term to use in this context is *surged*.

44. D   **Redundancy/Pronoun Agreement**

The original phrasing is incorrect because the phrase *at the time during* is redundant. Choices B and C are incorrect because the pronoun *where* refers to a place, not a time.

Section 3: Math (No Calculator)

1. B   **Algebra (solving linear equations) EASY**

Original equation: $-3x = 18$
Divide both sides by -3: $x = -6$
Substitute $x = -6$ into the expression
$4x + 6$ and evaluate: $4(-6) + 6 = -18$

2. C   **Additional topics (analyzing circles) EASY**

If points A and B are on the circle:

$$\frac{\text{arc length of }\overset{\frown}{AB}}{\text{circumference}} = \frac{\text{measure of interior angle of }\overset{\frown}{AB}}{360°}$$

In this case, we are looking for the length of $\overset{\frown}{AB}$, so let's call that x. We know that the measure of the interior angle is 120°, and that the circumference of the circle is 30:

$$\frac{x}{30} = \frac{120°}{360°}$$

Cross multiply: $360x = 3600$
Divide both sides by 360: $x = 10$

3. A   **Algebra (representing quantities) EASY**

If shipment A is 30% polyester and x represents the total weight of shipment A, then $0.3x$ represents the weight of polyester in shipment A. By the same reasoning, $0.5y$ represents the weight of polyester in shipment B. These two weights have a sum of 130, so $0.3x + 0.5y = 130$.

4. B   **Algebra (linear models) EASY**

This problem situation provides a good opportunity to apply dimensional analysis. The expression $M + 15nh$ represents the total price of the job, including materials and labor. Since M is the cost of materials, $15nh$ must represent the cost of labor:

cost of labor (\$) $= 15nh = (15\ ?)(\text{\# of workers})(\text{\# of hours})$

If we solve this for the quantity represented by the number 15, we get $15\ ? = \dfrac{\text{cost of labor (\$)}}{(\text{\# of workers})(\text{\# of hours})}$, which means that 15 represents the cost of labor (in dollars) per worker per hour.

5. D   **Advanced mathematics (subtracting polynomials) EASY**

To subtract these expressions, change the subtraction to addition by changing the signs of all the terms in the second expression, then combine like terms (the terms with the same exponents and bases):
Original expression:
$$(-5x^2y + 3xy - 7y^2) - (5x^2y - 7y^2 + 5xy)$$
Change signs of all terms in the second expression:
$$-5x^2y + 3xy - 7y^2 - 5x^2y + 7y^2 - 5xy$$
Combine like terms: $\quad -5x^2y - 5x^2y = -10x^2y$
$$3xy - 5xy = -2xy$$
$$-7y^2 + 7y^2 = 0$$
Resulting expression: $\quad -10x^2y - 2xy$

6. C   **Algebra (radicals) EASY**

Substitute $x = 6$, then solve the given equation for k.
Original equation: $\sqrt{3k+3} - x = 0$
Substitute $x = 6$: $\sqrt{3k+3} - 6 = 0$
Add 6 to both sides: $\sqrt{3k+3} = 6$
Square both sides: $3k + 3 = 36$
Subtract 3 from both sides and divide both sides by 3:
$$k = 11$$

7. D   **Algebra (working with formulas) EASY**

Original formula:
$$c = \frac{1}{3}wl$$

Divide both sides by l:
$$\frac{c}{l} = \frac{1}{3}w$$

Multiply both sides by 3:
$$\frac{3c}{l} = w$$

---

8. C   **Algebra (linear equations) MEDIUM**

Two lines that are parallel have the same slope. The linear equation in this question is in slope-intercept form, $y = mx + b$, and its slope, m, is -2. One way to see which choice also has a slope of -2 is to solve each equation for y:

A) $y = -1/2x$; slope $= -1/2$
B) $y = 4x - 2$; slope $= 4$
C) $y = -2x + 3$; slope $= -2$
D) $y = 2x - 1$; slope $= 2$

---

9. C   **Algebra (linear models) MEDIUM**

The population P of the village will equal 1,200 people when the value of t is 0. Since t represents the number of years since 1960, this means that the population of the village at the beginning of 1960 was 1,200.

---

10. C   **Algebra (linear systems) MEDIUM**

This system of linear equations can be solved using the elimination method:

Multiply both sides of the top equation by 3:
$$(3x + 2y = 4) \bullet 3 \to 9x + 6y = 12$$
Add this to the bottom equation to eliminate y:
$$\begin{aligned} 9x + 6y &= 12 \\ + -4x - 6y &= -2 \\ \hline 5x &= 10 \end{aligned}$$
Divide both sides by 5: $x = 2$
Substitute 2 for x in one of the original
equations to solve for y: $3(2) + 2y = 4$
Subtract 6 from both sides: $2y = -2$
Divide both sides by 2: $y = -1$
The solution to the system is $(2, -1)$.

---

11. D   **Advanced Mathematics (complex numbers) MEDIUM-HARD**

To simplify this expression, multiply both the numerator and the denominator by the complex conjugate of the denominator. The conjugate of a binomial is found by changing the addition or subtraction between the two terms into its opposite (addition becomes subtraction or subtraction becomes addition), so the conjugate of $5 + 3i$ is $5 - 3i$. Using this conjugate, the expression is simplified as follows:

Multiply both the numerator and denominator by the conjugate of the denominator:

$$\frac{6+2i}{5-3i} \times \frac{5+3i}{5+3i} = \frac{30+18i+10i+6i^2}{25+15i-15i-9i^2} = \frac{30+28i-6}{25+9}$$

$$= \frac{24+28i}{34}$$

Distribute and simplify:
$$\frac{24}{34} + \frac{28i}{34} = \frac{12}{17} + \frac{14i}{17}$$

---

12. A   **Advanced Mathematics (quadratic form) MEDIUM-HARD**

An equation in the form $y = a(x - h)^2 + k$ represents a parabola in the xy-plane, with vertex (h, k). If a is positive, the parabola opens upward, and if a is negative it opens downward. Therefore the parabola represented by $y = x^2 + k$ has vertex $(0, k)$ and is open up. If this vertex is below the x-axis, then k must be negative, and therefore $y = k(x - b)^2 - c$ represents a parabola with vertex $(b, -c)$ that is open downward.

---

13. D   **Additional Topics (exponentials) MEDIUM**

An exponential with a rational exponent can be rewritten as a radical, according to the rule $x^{\frac{m}{n}} = \sqrt[n]{x^m} = \left(\sqrt[n]{x}\right)^m$.

Therefore, $8^{\frac{3}{2}}$ is equivalent to
$$\left(\sqrt{8}\right)^3 = \left(\sqrt{8}\right)\left(\sqrt{8}\right)\left(\sqrt{8}\right) = 8\sqrt{8} = 8\sqrt{4} \times \sqrt{2} = 16\sqrt{2}.$$

---

14. A   **Advanced mathematics (solving quadratics) HARD**

The simplest way to solve this problem is to use the theorem that any quadratic equation in the form $ax^2 + bx + c = 0$ has two (possibly equal) solutions that have a sum of $-b/a$ and a product of c/a. Therefore the sum of the solutions to this equation is $-30/3 = -10$.

If you don't recall this theorem, you can solve it the hard way: by finding the two solutions with the Quadratic Formula and adding them together.

Use the quadratic formula, $x = \dfrac{-b \pm \sqrt{b^2 - 4ac}}{2a}$, to solve for x:
$$x = \frac{-10 \pm \sqrt{10^2 - 4(1)(5)}}{2(1)}$$

Simplify:
$$x = \frac{-10 \pm \sqrt{80}}{2}$$

Simplify the radical:
$$x = \frac{-10 \pm 4\sqrt{5}}{2}$$

Reduce the fractions:
$$x = -5 \pm 2\sqrt{5}$$

The two solutions are $x = -5 + 2\sqrt{5}$ and $x = -5 - 2\sqrt{5}$, and their sum is $(-5 - 2\sqrt{5}) + (-5 + 2\sqrt{5}) = -10$.

15. **B**　Advanced Mathematics (exponentials) HARD

We should first notice that, since 16 is a power of 4, we

can simplify $\dfrac{16^x}{4^y}$ as a single exponential with base 4:

$$\dfrac{16^x}{4^y}$$

Substitute $4^2 = 16$ and simplify:　　　$\dfrac{\left(4^2\right)^x}{4^y} = \dfrac{4^{2x}}{4^y} = 4^{2x-y}$

Given equation:　　　　　　　　　　　$4x - 2y = 20$
Divide both sides by 2:　　　　　　　　$2x - y = 10$
Substitute $2x - y = 10$:　　　　　　　$4^{2x-y} = 4^{10}$

16. $\dfrac{2}{5}$　　　**Algebra (linear systems) MEDIUM**

First, we should notice that the y term in the second equation ($9y$) is three times the y term in the first equation ($3y$). Therefore, we should divide the second equation by 3 to get the equations to "match." This gives us $2x + 3y = 5$. Since the two equations must be equivalent, $a = 2$ and $c = 5$.

17. **3/10 or .3**　　　　**Advanced Mathematics
(trigonometry) MEDIUM-HARD**

The sine of an acute angle in a right triangle is $\dfrac{\text{opposite}}{\text{hypotenuse}}$, and the cosine of an acute angle in a right triangle is $\dfrac{\text{adjacent}}{\text{hypotenuse}}$. Since the side opposite to angle X is the same as the side adjacent to angle Y, $\sin X = \cos Y = 0.3$. This is an instance of the *co-function identity*.

18. **9**　　　　Additional topics (similarity) MEDIUM

Because AC and DE are parallel, we can establish three pairs of congruent angles:

$$\angle ABC \cong \angle DBE \text{ (vertical angles)}$$
$$\angle ACD \cong \angle CDE \text{ (alternate interior angles)}$$
$$\angle DEA \cong \angle EAC \text{ (alternate interior angles)}$$

Therefore the two triangles are similar, and all pairs of corresponding sides are proportional. If the ratio of corresponding sides in two similar figures is $m:n$, the ratio of areas of the two figures must by $m^2 : n^2$. If $AE = 16$, then $BE = 16 - 4 = 12$, and therefore $BE:AB = 12:4 = 3:1$. Since the sides of $\triangle DBE$ are 3 times greater than the corresponding sides of $\triangle ABC$, the area of $\triangle DBE$ must be $3^2 = 9$ times greater than the area of $\triangle ABC$.

19. **3**　　　　Algebra (rational expressions) HARD

Notice that the numerator and denominator in $\dfrac{16x}{16x^2 - 4}$ have a common factor of 4, which can be "canceled" to yield $\dfrac{4x}{4x^2 - 1}$. The two rational expressions now have a common denominator, so combining them is straightforward:

$$\dfrac{4x^2+1}{4x^2-1} + \dfrac{4x}{4x^2-1} = \dfrac{4x^2+4x+1}{4x^2-1} = \dfrac{(2x+1)(2x+1)}{(2x+1)(2x-1)} = \dfrac{2x+1}{2x-1}$$

We now have an expression in the form $\dfrac{ax+b}{ax-b}$, where $a = 2$ and $b = 1$, so $a + b = 3$.

20. **4**　　　　　　　　Advanced mathematics
(polynomial analysis) HARD

We can factor the polynomial by grouping:
Original equation:　　　　　　$x^3 - 4x^2 + 2x - 8 = 0$
Group together the first two terms
and last two terms:　　　　　$(x^3 - 4x^2) + (2x - 8) = 0$
Factor the GCF from both terms:

$$(x^2)(x-4) + 2(x-4) = 0$$

Factor $x - 4$ from both expressions:　$(x-4)(x^2+2) = 0$
Apply the Zero Product Property:　　　　　　$x = 4$

Section 4: Math Test – Calculator

1. **A**　　　Algebra (solving linear equations) EASY

Original equation:　　　　　　　　　　$\dfrac{4}{3}z = \dfrac{2}{5}$

Divide both sides by $\dfrac{4}{3}$

(or, equivalently, multiply by $\dfrac{3}{4}$):　　$z = \dfrac{6}{20}$

Simplify:　　　　　　　　　　　　　$z = \dfrac{3}{10}$

2. **D**　　　　Problem Solving/Data Analysis
(analyzing trends) EASY

Notice that the line in the graph goes upward relatively quickly until it reaches a peak at 6 on the horizontal axis, which corresponds to 1956. From there, it goes downward at a slower rate.

3. **C**　　　　Problem Solving/Data Analysis
(proportions) EASY

We can call the amount of money the yoga teacher earns if his class has 30 students x.

Set up a proportion:　　　　　　　　$\dfrac{90}{12} = \dfrac{x}{30}$

Cross multiply:　　　　　　　　　　$12x = 2700$
Divide both sides by 12:　　　　　　　$x = 225$

4. **B**　　　　Problem Solving/Data Analysis
(analyzing data) EASY

During the time that Darrell is resting, his distance from his apartment will neither increase nor decrease because he is staying still. His distance from his apartment is represented on the vertical axis of the graph, so we would expect the line of the graph to be horizontal for the time that he is resting. The line goes horizontal at approximately 10:00AM, so that is when he began his rest.

5. C   Algebra (working with formulas) EASY

Because the population density equals the population of a region divided by the area of the region, we can set up the equation $D = \dfrac{P}{A}$, where D is the population density in people per km², P is the population, and A is the area in km².

Plug the information given into this equation: $70 = \dfrac{3850}{A}$

Multiply both sides by A: $70A = 3850$
Divide both sides by 70: $A = 55$ km²

6. B   Algebra (exponentials) EASY

Since the speed of light is constant, we can use the rate formula: $\text{time} = \dfrac{\text{distance}}{\text{speed}}$. We must also be careful to convert kilometers to meters:

$$\dfrac{10{,}000{,}000 \text{ km}}{3 \times 10^8 \text{ m/s}} \times \dfrac{1{,}000 \text{ m}}{1 \text{ km}} = \dfrac{100}{3} \text{ seconds} = 33.\overline{3} \text{ seconds}$$

7. D   Problem Solving/Data Analysis (logic) Medium

The survey team questioned people who were using the park for recreational purposes. Since these people are likely to be biased against the getting rid of the park, their opinions are not likely to represent the opinions of the town as a whole.

8. C   Problem Solving/Data Analysis (analyzing graphs) Medium

The bars correspond to values of 7, 9, 4.5, 3, and 5 on the vertical axis, for a total of $7 + 9 + 4.5 + 3 + 5 = 28.5$. Since this sum corresponds a total of 285,000 barrels of oil, the unit on the vertical axis must be $285{,}000/28.5 = 10{,}000$ barrels of oil.

9. C   Problem Solving/Data Analysis (scatterplots) EASY

The line of best fit predicts that a village with an average annual temperature of 65°F will have approximately 35 inches of rainfall annually. The data point for a village at 65°F corresponds to 40 inches of rainfall, which is $40 - 35 = 5$ inches higher than the level predicted by the line of best fit.

10. D   Algebra (absolute value inequalities) MEDIUM

We are looking for where $|n - 3| - 3$ is negative, so we can set up this inequality: $|n - 3| - 3 < 0$
Add 3 to both sides: $|n - 3| < 3$

If the absolute value of $n - 3$ is less than 3, it must have a value between -3 and 3: $-3 < n - 3 < 3$
Add 3 to each part of the inequality: $0 < n < 6$

11. D   Algebra (rational expressions) MEDIUM

Recall that division by zero is undefined, so a rational function is undefined at any values that cause its denominator to equal zero:
Add 6 to both sides:
Multiply both sides by 3:
This one can also be solved by plugging in each answer choice and seeing which one cause the denominator to equal zero.

12. D   Problem Solving/Data Analysis (probability) MEDIUM

A probability is always a part-to-whole ratio. In this case, the "whole" is the number of students who live on campus ($160 + 63 = 223$), and the "part" is the number of students who live on campus and do not eat in the dining hall (63). Therefore, the probability is 63/223.

13. D   Algebra (systems of linear inequalities) MEDIUM

If x is the number of cookies the PTA sells and y is the number of brownies it sells, the total number of baked items that the PTA sells is $x + y$. They want this total to be at least 55, so $x + y > 55$. The money they make from cookies equals the price of each cookie multiplied by the number of cookies they sell, $1.50x$, and, by the same reasoning, the money they make from brownies will equal $2.25y$. The total amount of money they bring in will equal $1.50x + 2.25y$, and they want to make at least \$100, so they can represent this goal with the inequality $1.50x + 2.25y \geq 100$.

14. B   Advanced Mathematics (functions) MEDIUM-HARD

The points where the graph of a function crosses the x axis correspond to those values of x for which the function equals zero. To solve this problem, factor each answer choice and apply the Zero Product Property to see which function equals zero at $x = -4$, $x = 2$, and $x = 5$:

A) $0 = (x - 2)^2(x - 5)$, so $x = 2$ or $x = 5$ (nope)
B) $0 = (x^2 + 2x - 8)(3x - 15) = (x + 4)(x - 2)(3x - 15)$, so $x = -4$ or $x = 2$ or $x = 5$ (yes!)
C) $0 = (x^2 - 7x + 10)(x - 4) = (x - 5)(x - 2)(x - 4)$, so $x = 5$ or $x = 2$ or $x = 4$ (nope)
D) $0 = (x - 4)(x + 2)(x + 5)$, so $x = 4$ or $x = -2$ or $x = -5$ (nope)

Alternatively, you can plug the three intercept values into each function and see which function equals zero for all three of them.

15. **A**   Problem Solving/Data Analysis (medians)
MEDIUM

Since 400 households were surveyed from each village, there is a total of 800 households. In a set of 800 values, the median is the average of the 400th and the 401st values. Starting from the families with zero children, count off the families until you reach the 400th:

Notice that $60 + 40 + 150 + 140 = 390$ households have either 0 or 1 child, and $60 + 40 + 150 + 140 + 110 + 130 = 630$ households have 2 or fewer children. Therefore, the 400th household and the 401st household must have 2 children each, so the median number of children per household is 2.

16. **A**   Problem Solving/Data Analysis
(proportions) MEDIUM

If the survey results are representative of each village as a whole, then:

$$\frac{\text{\# of households with no children in sample}}{\text{\# of households in sample}} =$$

$$\frac{\text{\# of households with no children in village}}{\text{\# of households in village}}$$

We can use this proportion to find the number of households with no children in each village, starting with

Village A: $\dfrac{60}{400} = \dfrac{x}{2,000}$

Cross multiply: $400x = 120,000$
Divide both sides by 400: $x = 300$

Village B: $\dfrac{40}{400} = \dfrac{x}{3,200}$

Cross multiply: $400x = 128,000$
Divide both sides by 400: $x = 320$

Therefore, the number of households with no children in the two villages is $300 + 320 = 620$.

Note: Many students mistakenly choose C because they group the results from two villages together. They reason that 800 households were surveyed altogether, and $60 + 40 = 100$ of them had no children, implying that 1/8 of the households were childless, and therefore $(2,000 + 3,200) \div 8 = 650$ of the households were childless. This analysis is incorrect because it assumes that the survey data from the two villages should be *equally weighted*, when clearly they should not be, because there are far more households in Village B than in Village A.

17. **B**   Advanced Mathematics (functional analysis)
MEDIUM-HARD

According to Table B, $g(3) = -1$, so $f(g(3)) = f(-1)$.
According to Table A, $f(-1) = 2$.

18. **C**   Problem Solving/Data Analysis
(percent increase) MEDIUM

According to the graph, in 2001, the yield of corn was 20 lbs, and, in 2002, it was 42.5 lbs, for an increase of $42.5 - 20 = 22.5$ lbs. As a percent increase, this is $22.5/20 = 1.125 = 112.5\%$.

19. **C**   Problem Solving/Data Analysis
(analyzing graphs) MEDIUM-HARD

In a scatter plot with yield in 2001 on the x-axis and yield in 2002 on the y-axis, points below the line $y = x$ would represent vegetables whose yield was lower in 2002 than in 2001. This is the case for broccoli, tomato, and cauliflower, so those three points would lie below the line.

20. **B**   Additional topics (3-D geometry)
MEDIUM-HARD

The formula for the volume of a right circular cylinder is $V = \pi r^2 h$, where r is radius of the base and h is height of the cylinder. Since the diameter of each flower pot is 16 cm, the radius of each pot is 8 cm. The gardener fills them to a depth of 20 cm, so the volume of soil in each pot is $V = \pi(8)^2(20) \approx 4021.24$. Because there are three pots, the total volume of soil used will be $3 \times 4021.24 = 12,063.72$ cm^3, which is equivalent to:

$$12063.72 \text{ cm}^3 \times \frac{.061 \text{ in}^3}{1 \text{ cm}^3} \approx 736 \text{ in}^3.$$

Subtract to find the amount of soil left in the bag: $1000 - 736 = 264$ in^3.

21. **A**   Algebra (working with formulas) MEDIUM

Original equation: $B = \dfrac{L}{4\pi D^2}$

Multiply both sides by D^2: $BD^2 = \dfrac{L}{4\pi}$

Divide both sides by B: $D^2 = \dfrac{L}{4\pi B}$

Take the square root of both sides: $D = \sqrt{\dfrac{L}{4\pi B}}$

22. **C**   Algebra (working with formulas)
MEDIUM-HARD

Since the brightness of Star A is 156% *greater* than the brightness of Star B, its brightness is $1.00 + 1.56 = 2.56$ *times* the brightness of Star B. Since the formula indicates that the apparent brightness of a star is *inversely proportional to the square of its distance*, this implies that *the distance is inversely proportional to the square root of its brightness* (which is precisely what we see in the answer to question 21). Since the square root of 2.56 is 1.6, Star B is 1.6 times as far from Earth as Star A is.

23. C — Additional topics (area) HARD

The area of the original rectangle is $A = lw$. If the length is decreased by 10%, it becomes $0.9l$. If the width is increased by p%, it becomes $\left(1+\dfrac{p}{100}\right)w$. If the area of the new triangle is then 26% greater:

$$(0.9l)\left(1+\frac{p}{100}\right)w=1.26A$$

Simplify:
$$0.9\left(1+\frac{p}{100}\right)lw=1.26A$$

Substitute $A = lw$:
$$0.9\left(1+\frac{p}{100}\right)A=1.26A$$

Divide both sides by A:
$$0.9\left(1+\frac{p}{100}\right)=1.26$$

Divide both sides by 0.9:
$$1+\frac{p}{100}=1.4$$

Subtract 1 from both sides:
$$\frac{p}{100}=0.4$$

Multiply both sides by 100:
$$p = 40$$

24. B — Algebra (word problems) MEDIUM

Let's say that Mr. Chu has n employees and m gift certificates. If he gives 5 gift certificates to each employee, he will have given out $5n$ gift certificates, with 7 left over, so $5n + 7 = m$. In order to give each employee 6 gift certificates, he will need 9 more gift certificates, so $6n = m + 9$. Substitute $5n + 7 = m$ into the second equation:
$$6n = 5n + 7 + 9$$
Subtract $5n$ from both sides:
$$n = 16$$

25. B — Algebra (exponentials) MEDIUM-HARD

To increase a quantity by 200%, we must multiply by $100\% + 200\% = 1 + 2 = 3$. If the current population of bacteria is 20,000, then the population after 6 hours will be 200% greater, or 20,000(3). After 12 hours, the population will be multiplied by 3 again: $20,000(3)^2$. After 18 hours, the population will be $20,000(3)^3$, and so on. If h hours have passed, then $\dfrac{h}{6}$ of these "tripling periods" have passed, so the population after h hours is $20,000(3)^{\frac{h}{6}}$.

26. A — Advanced Mathematics (analysis of quadratics) HARD

The equation given for the height of the rocket is quadratic, so the graph of h with respect to t is a parabola. The rocket's highest point corresponds the vertex of this parabola. For any quadratic function of the form $y = ax^2 + bx + c$, the x-coordinate of the vertex is always $-b/2a$. In this case, the independent variable is t, not x, but the rule is the same. The t value at the vertex is $-b/2a = -64/(2(-16)) = -64/-32 = 2$.

27. B — Additional topics (circular equations) HARD

The standard equation for a circle in the xy-plane is $(x - h)^2 + (y - k)^2 = r^2$, where the center of the circle is (h, k) and its radius is r. Notice that the x and y terms of this equation are binomials squared. To get the the given equation into standard form, we have to group together the x terms and group together the y terms then *complete the square* for both:

Original equation: $\quad x^2 + y^2 - 6x + 4y = 3$
Group together x terms and y terms:
$$(x^2 - 6x) + (y^2 - 4y) = 3$$
"Complete the square" inside each set of parentheses by dividing the second coefficient by 2, squaring this result, and adding that constant. (Then make sure to add to add these constants to the other side as well):
$$(x^2 - 6x + 9) + (y^2 - 4y + 4) = 3 + 9 + 4$$
Factor each perfect square trinomial and simplify:
$$(x - 3)^2 + (y + 2)^2 = 16$$
The equation is now in standard form, and therefore $r^2 = 16$ and so $r = \sqrt{16} = 4$.

28. C — Advanced Mathematics (analyzing parabolas) Medium-Hard

One way to find the vertex of this parabola is to first find its zeros. (This is a good start because the given equation is in factored form, so it is easy to find the zeros.) If $y = (x - 4)(x + 8)$, then the zeros of the function are $x = 4$ and $x = -8$. The x-coordinate of the vertex is the average of these two zeros, which is $(4 + -8)/2 = -2$. To find the y-coordinate of the vertex, we can plug $x = -2$ into the original equation: $y = (-2 - 4)(-2 + 8) = (-6)(6) = -36$. Therefore, vertex is $(-2, -36)$. The vertex form of a parabola is $y = (x - h)^2 + k$, where the parabola's vertex is (h, k), so plugging gives us $y = \left(x - (-2)\right)^2 - 36 = (x + 2)^2 - 36$. Alternately, you can FOIL the original expression and then follow the algorithm to "complete the square."

29. C — Algebra (linear systems) HARD

For this question, we can find the equations of lines m and n, then solve the system of linear equations to find the point of intersection. To find the equation of line m, we can use the slope-intercept form of a linear equation, $y = mx + b$. Since line m has a slope of 2 and contains the point (5/2, 0):
$$0 = 2\left(\frac{5}{2}\right) + b$$
Simplify: $\quad 0 = 5 + b$
Subtract 5 from both sides: $\quad -5 = b$
Therefore the equation of line m is $y = 2x - 5$.

Since line n is perpendicular to line m, its slope is the opposite reciprocal of 2, or $-1/2$. Since it also contains the point $(0, -5/2)$, its equation is $y = -\dfrac{1}{2}x - \dfrac{5}{2}$.

To solve the system, we can just use the method of substitution:
$$-\frac{1}{2}x - \frac{5}{2} = 2x - 5$$

Multiply both sides by 2: $\quad\quad\quad\quad\quad\quad -x - 5 = 4x - 10$

Add x to both sides: $\quad\quad\quad\quad\quad\quad\quad -5 = 5x - 10$

Add 10 to both sides: $\quad\quad\quad\quad\quad\quad\quad 5 = 5x$

Divide both sides by 5: $\quad\quad\quad\quad\quad\quad\quad x = 1$

Choice C is the only answer choice in which $x = 1$, but if you like, you can solve for y by substituting $x = 1$ into either equation and solving for y.

---

30.   A   Advanced Mathematics
(polynomial analysis) HARD

Expand the expression on the left side of the equation:

$(x - a)^3 = (x - a)(x - a)(x - a) = (x^2 - 2ax + a^2)(x - a)$

$\quad\quad = x^3 - ax^2 - 2ax^2 + 2a^2x + a^2x - a^3$

Combine like terms: $\quad\quad\quad x^3 - 3ax^2 + 3a^2x - a^3$

Since $x^3 - 3ax^2 + 3a^2x - a^3 = x^3 - bx^2 + bx - a^3$ for all values of x, each of the corresponding "like" terms must have identical coefficients. That is: $\quad b = 3a$ and $b = 3a^2$

By the Law of Substitution: $\quad\quad\quad\quad\quad 3a = 3a^2$

Since a is not 0 (because we are told it is a positive constant), we can divide both sides by $3a$: $\quad\quad\quad 1 = a$

---

31.   **any number between 11 and 16.5**
Algebra (rate analysis) EASY

Use the formula distance = rate $\quad$ time. If the kayaker travels 132 miles at 12mph: $\quad\quad\quad\quad 132 = 12t$

Divide both sides by 12: $\quad\quad\quad\quad\quad t = 11$ hours

If the kayaker travels 132 miles at 8 mph: $\quad 132 = 8t$

Divide both sides by 8: $\quad\quad\quad\quad\quad\quad t = 16.5$ hours

The kayaker is capable of traveling at a rate that will cause the trip to take any length of time between 11 hours and 16.5 hours.

---

32.   **9**   Algebra (linear relationships) EASY

If the ball rolls f feet and 7 inches, then the distance it covers, in inches, is $12f + 7$. We are told that it rolls a total of 115 inches, so: $\quad\quad\quad\quad\quad\quad 12f + 7 = 115$

Subtract 7 from both sides: $\quad\quad\quad\quad\quad 12f = 108$

Divide both sides by 12: $\quad\quad\quad\quad\quad\quad f = 9$ feet

---

33.   **16.5**   Algebra (rate analysis) EASY

To reach its boiling point, the heat of the liquid must increase by $251°C - 20°C = 231°C$. If it is heating at a rate of $14°C$ per minute, it will take $231/14 = 16.5$ minutes to reach its boiling point.

---

34.   **9**   Advanced Mathematics
(analysis of quadratics) MEDIUM

To get the expression in the proper form, we must "expand" the given expression: $\quad\quad 3(2x + 3)(-x + 4)$

Distribute the 3: $\quad\quad\quad\quad\quad\quad (6x + 9)(-x + 4)$

FOIL and collect like terms:

$\quad\quad -6x^2 + 24x - 9x + 36 = -6x^2 + 15x + 36$

Therefore $a = -6$ and $b = 15$, so $a + b = -6 + 15 = 9$.

---

35.   **8**   Problem Solving/Data Analysis (averages)
MEDIUM

Let x represent the average score of the teaching assistant's 5 exams. This means that the sum of all those scores is $5x$. Since the average score of the professor's 15 exams is 87, the sum of all of those scores is $(15)(87) = 1,305$. Therefore, the sum of the scores on all 20 exams is $5x + 1,305$. Since the average score on all 20 of the exams is 85, this sum can also be expressed as $85(20) = 1,700$:

$$5x + 1,305 = 1,700$$

Subtract 1,305 from both sides: $\quad\quad\quad 5x = 395$

Divide both sides by 5: $\quad\quad\quad\quad\quad\quad x = 79$

Therefore, the average score of the teaching assistant's exams is $87 - 79 = 8$ points lower than the average score of the professor's exams.

---

36.   **12**   Additional Topics (analyzing circles)
MEDIUM-HARD

We know that $\overline{LM}$ is tangent to the circle, so $\angle MLO$ is a right angle. The angles in a triangle must add up to 180, so m is $\angle MOL$ is $180° - 50° - 90° = 40°$. Since this central angle is 1/9 of the whole circle ($40°/360° = 1/9$), the area of the sector must be 1/9 the area of the whole circle. If the area of the circle is 108, the area of the sector is $108/9 = 12$ cm^2.

---

37.   **1500**   Problem Solving/Data Analysis
(exponential relationships) MEDIUM

Original interest equation: $\quad\quad\quad\quad A = P(1.05)^t$

Plug in the given values: $\quad\quad\quad 1,653.75 = P(1.05)^2$

Evaluate 1.05^2: $\quad\quad\quad\quad\quad\quad 1,653.75 = P(1.1025)$

Divide both sides by 1.1025: $\quad\quad\quad\quad 1,500 = P$

---

38.   **34**   Problem Solving/Data Analysis
(percents) MEDIUM-HARD

Original interest equation: $\quad\quad\quad\quad\quad A = P(1.05)^t$

Plug in 6 for t: $\quad\quad\quad\quad\quad\quad\quad A = P(1.05)^6$

Calculate 1.05^6 and round: $\quad\quad\quad\quad A \quad P(1.34)$

The balance after 6 years is calculated by multiplying the principal by 1.34. This is an increase of 34%.

The Cross-Platform Prep Course

McGraw-Hill Education's multi-platform course gives you a variety of tools to help you raise your test scores. Whether you're studying at home, in the library, or on-the-go, you can find practice content in the format you need—print, online, or mobile.

Print Book

This print book gives you the tools you need to ace the test. In its pages you'll find smart test-taking strategies, in-depth reviews of key topics, and ample practice questions and tests. See the Welcome section of your book for a step-by-step guide to its features.

Online Platform

The Cross-Platform Prep Course gives you additional study and practice content that you can access *anytime, anywhere*. You can create a personalized study plan based on your test date that sets daily goals to keep you on track. Integrated lessons provide important review of key topics. Practice questions, exams, and flashcards give you the practice you need to build test-taking confidence. The game center is filled with challenging games that allow you to practice your new skills in a fun and engaging way. And, you can even interact with other test-takers in the discussion section and gain valuable peer support.

Getting Started

To get started, open your account on the online platform:

Go to www.xplatform.mhprofessional.com

↓

Enter your access code, which you can find on the inside back cover of your book

↓

Provide your name and e-mail address to open your account and create a password

↓

Click "Start Studying" to enter the platform

It's as simple as that. You're ready to start studying online.

Your Personalized Study Plan

First, select your test date on the calendar, and you'll be on your way to creating your personalized study plan. Your study plan will help you stay organized and on track and will guide you through the course in the most efficient way. It is tailored to *your* schedule and features daily tasks that are broken down into manageable goals. You can adjust your test date at any time and your daily tasks will be reorganized into an updated plan.

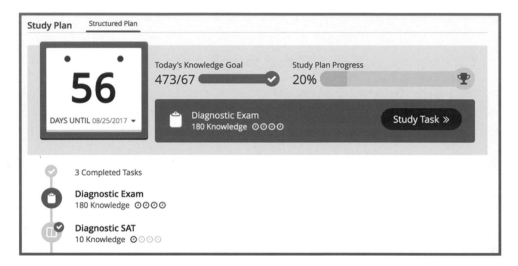

You can track your progress in real time on the Study Plan Dashboard. The "Today's Knowledge Goal" progress bar gives you up-to-the minute feedback on your daily goal. Fulfilling this every time you log on is the most efficient way to work through the entire course. You always get an instant view of where you stand in the entire course with the Study Plan Progress bar.

> *If you need to exit the program before completing a task, you can return to the Study Plan Dashboard at any time. Just click the Study Task icon and you can automatically pick up where you left off.*

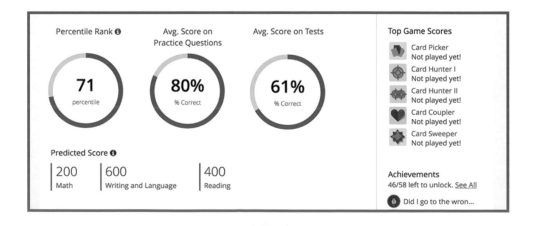

Practice Tests

One of the first tasks in your personalized study plan is to take the Diagnostic Test. At the end of the test, a detailed evaluation of your strengths and weaknesses shows the areas where you need the most focus. You can review your practice test results either by the question category to see broad trends or question-by-question for a more in-depth look.

The full-length tests are designed to simulate the real thing. Try to simulate actual testing conditions and be sure you set aside enough time to complete the full-length test. You'll learn to pace yourself so that you can work toward the best possible score on test day.

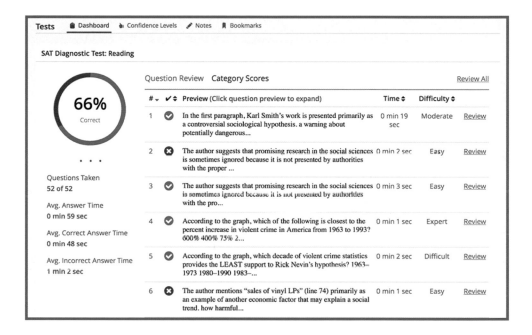

Lessons

The lessons in the online platform are divided into manageable pieces that let you build knowledge and confidence in a progressive way. They cover the full range of topics that you're likely to see on your test.

After you complete a lesson, mark your confidence level. (You must indicate a confidence level in order to count your progress and move on to the next task.) You can also filter the lessons by confidence levels to see the areas you have mastered and those that you might need to revisit.

> *Use the bookmark feature to easily refer back to a concept or leave a note to remember your thoughts or questions about a particular topic.*

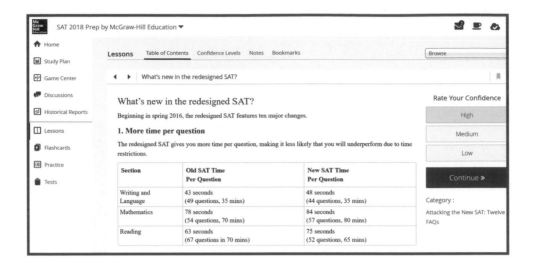

Practice Questions

All of the practice questions are reflective of actual exams and simulate the test-taking experience. The "Review Answer" button gives you immediate feedback on your answer. Each question includes a rationale that explains why the correct answer is right and the others are wrong. To explore any topic further, you can find detailed explanations by clicking the "Help me learn about this topic" link.

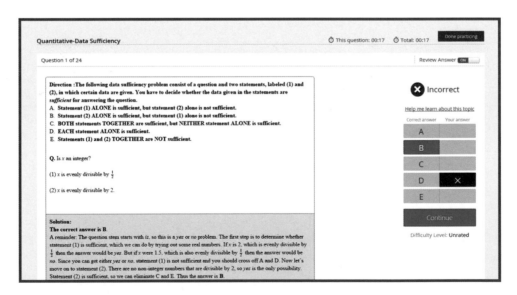

You can go to the Practice Dashboard to find an overview of your performance in the different categories and sub-categories.

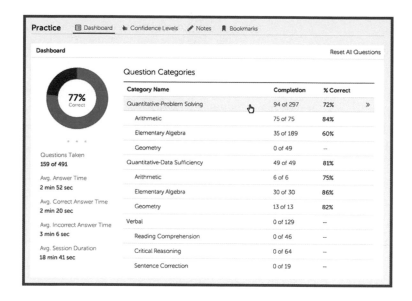

Dashboard

The dashboard is constantly updating to reflect your progress and performance. The Percentile Rank icon shows your position relative to all the other students enrolled in the course. You can also find information on your average scores in practice questions and exams.

A detailed overview of your strengths and weaknesses shows your proficiency in a category based on your answers and difficulty of the questions. By viewing your strengths and weaknesses, you can focus your study on areas where you need the most help.

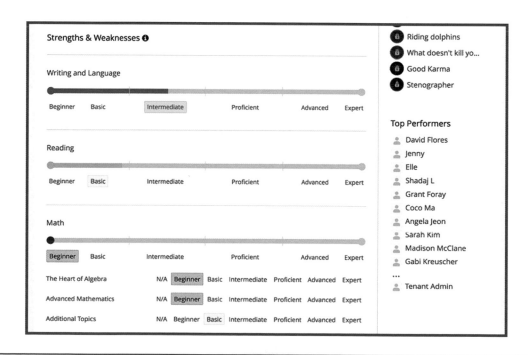

Flashcards

The hundreds of flashcards are perfect for learning key terms quickly, and the interactive format gives you immediate feedback. You can filter the cards by category and confidence level for a more organized approach. Or, you can shuffle them up for a more general challenge.

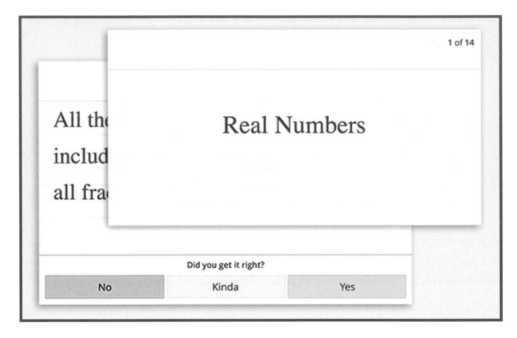

Another way to customize the flashcards is to create your own sets. You can either keep these private or share or them with the public. Subscribe to Community Sets to access sets from other students preparing for the same exam.

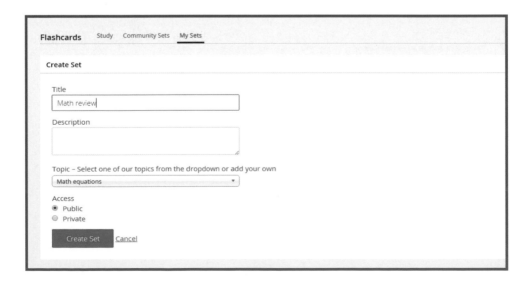

Game Center

Play a game in the Game Center to test your knowledge of key concepts in a challenging but fun environment. Increase the difficulty level and complete the games quickly to build your highest score. Be sure to check the leaderboard to see who's on top!

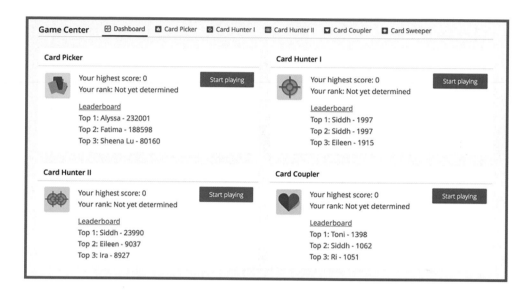

Social Community

Interact with other students who are preparing for the same test. Start a discussion, reply to a post, or even upload files to share. You can search the archives for common topics or start your own private discussion with friends.

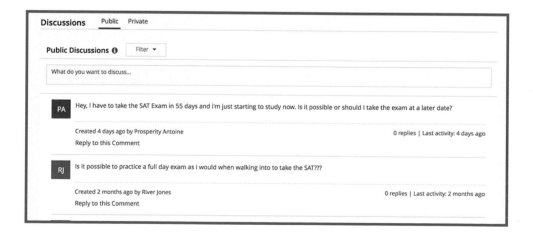

Mobile App

The companion mobile app lets you toggle between the online platform and your mobile device without missing a beat. Whether you access the course online or from your smartphone or tablet, you'll pick up exactly where you left off.

Go to the iTunes or Google Play stores and search "McGraw-Hill Education Cross-Platform App" to download the companion iOS or Android app. Enter your e-mail address and the same password you created for the online platform to open your account.

Now, let's get started!